P9-CQG-433

WORLD TOPICS YEAR BOOK 1997

A Review of the Events of 1996

TANGLEY OAKS EDUCATIONAL CENTER
THE UNITED EDUCATORS, INC.
Lake Bluff, Illinois, 60044

PUBLISHED BY THE UNITED EDUCATORS, INC. 1997

This year book is also published as *The Americana Annual.*

Library of Congress Catalog Card Number 48-171
ISBN 0-7172-0867-2

Printed and manufactured in the United States of America

Contents

Feature Articles of the Year

© Mark Peterson/Saba

© Alexander Zemlianichenko/AP/Wide World Photos

Used by permission of Security First Network Bank

© Richard Martin, Vandystadt/Allsport

© Globe Photos

The Alphabetical Section

Entries on the continents, major nations of the world, and chief cities will be found under their own alphabetical headings.

A Review of the Year 1996

© Charles Krupa/AP/Wide World Photos

On a summer night in July 1996, Flight 800 was bound for Paris, France, from New York's Kennedy International Airport. Moments later the plane crashed into the Atlantic Ocean off Long Island, NY, killing all 230 persons aboard. For days thereafter, experts searched the Atlantic for bodies of the victims and for the plane itself (*photo, above*) so that the cause of the crash—be it a terrorist bomb, a missile attack, or mechanical difficulty—could be determined. The reason remained a mystery as the year ended.

Many simply assumed that the crash was due to terrorism because terrorism again was a headliner in 1996. Renewed violence struck the Middle East, bringing into question the possibility of peace between the Israelis and the Palestinians. The chances of peace in Northern Ireland, which also had seemed so real in late 1995, were frustrated by bombing attacks in England. The festivities of the XXVI Summer Olympic Games in Atlanta were disrupted by a bomb blast, and 19 U.S. servicemen were killed when a truck bomb exploded at a housing complex in Saudi Arabia.

On the U.S. scene, Bill Clinton became the first Democrat since Franklin D. Roosevelt to win a second term, even though a cloud of ethical charges against him remained in the air. The GOP, meanwhile, retained control of both houses of Congress, but saw its House speaker, Newt Gingrich, facing the chamber's ethical committee as 1996 ended. Legislatively, welfare and immigration reform were enacted, but seemed to remain items of possible revision. It was a good year for the U.S. stock market, but job security was a worry for workers. A suspect in the Unabomber case was arrested in a remote Montana cabin, and sexual harassment in the military drew attention.

On the international scene, Russia's President Boris Yeltsin, whose health was questionable for much of the year, was elected to a new term, and the concept of democracy in Russia was strengthened. The election of Benjamin Netanyahu of the Likud party as prime minister of Israel led to uncertainty about his nation's intentions toward the peace process. In Europe eyes remained on the former Yugoslavia during the first year of a peace accord as elections in Bosnia and Herzegovina failed to consolidate the unity of the state. Forces from the North Atlantic Treaty Organization (NATO) monitored the peace and were ordered to remain in the region for an additional 18 months. Meanwhile, the enlargement of NATO and the European Union's move toward a single monetary system were debated. The travels of Turkey's pro-Islamic new prime minister to Iran and Libya made Turkey's NATO allies take notice.

© Vatican/Reuters/Archive Photos

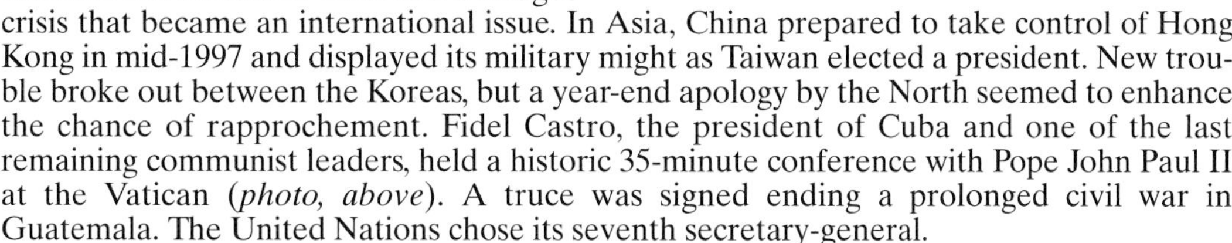
Africa witnessed continued conflict between the Hutu and Tutsi and a refugee crisis that became an international issue. In Asia, China prepared to take control of Hong Kong in mid-1997 and displayed its military might as Taiwan elected a president. New trouble broke out between the Koreas, but a year-end apology by the North seemed to enhance the chance of rapprochement. Fidel Castro, the president of Cuba and one of the last remaining communist leaders, held a historic 35-minute conference with Pope John Paul II at the Vatican (*photo, above*). A truce was signed ending a prolonged civil war in Guatemala. The United Nations chose its seventh secretary-general.

© Bebeto Matthews/AP/Wide World Photos

The musical *Rent* proved that a less expensive Broadway production could be the hit of the season; Madonna starred as Mrs. Perón in the movie version of *Evita*; labor difficulties hampered the classical-music season; and the macarena was the new dance craze. U.S. astronaut Shannon Lucid spent 188 days aboard the Russian space station, *Mir*; new debate broke out regarding the question of life on Mars; and the public enjoyed a greater familiarity with the Internet.

The New York Yankees again were baseball's world champions and a new contract was reached between major-league baseball owners and the players. Heavyweight boxer Evander Holyfield defeated Mike Tyson in a classic upset; track star Michael Johnson and the U.S. women gymnasts set the marks at the centennial Olympics; and Tiger Woods turned pro and dazzled the world of golf.

The year drew to a close with holiday shoppers paying almost any price to purchase the season's must-have toy—the Tickle Me Elmo doll (*photo, left*).

THE EDITORS

January

6 U.S. President Bill Clinton signs a stopgap spending measure ending a 21-day partial shutdown of the federal government.

7 In Guatemala, Alvaro Arzú Irigoyen of the center-right National Advancement Party is elected president in a runoff vote.

8 The northeastern United States is devastated by a powerful snowstorm, tagged the "Blizzard of '96."

11 The Japanese Diet (parliament) elects Ryutaro Hashimoto, the 58-year-old leader of the Liberal Democratic Party, to succeed Tomiichi Murayama as prime minister. Murayama, the leader of the Social Democratic Party of Japan, had resigned as prime minister on January 5.

Italy's Prime Minister Lamberto Dini resigns under pressure but will remain in office until elections are held or a new government is formed.

15 Russian troops launch an all-out attack against separatist guerrillas in the breakaway republic of Chechnya. The guerrillas had seized hundreds of hostages and occupied the village of Pervomayskoye in Russia's Dagestan region.

17 Sheikh Omar Abd al-Rahman is sentenced to life in prison following his October 1995 conviction on charges of plotting to bomb New York City landmarks and to assassinate Egypt's President Hosni Mubarak during a U.S. visit.

18 In Greece the ruling Panhellenic Socialist Movement (Pasok) selects former Industry Minister Costas Simitis as prime minister, succeeding the ailing Andreas Papandreou, who had resigned.

20 Palestinian voters in the Gaza Strip and the West Bank choose a new self-rule Palestinian National Authority government. Yasir Arafat of the Palestine Liberation Organization (PLO) is elected president of the Palestinians.

© Gifford/Gamma-Liaison

The year 1996 began with a devastating snowstorm striking the northeastern United States. The "Blizzard of '96" dropped a minimum of 18 inches (46 cm) of snow on New York City and made getting to such landmarks as Radio City Music Hall (below) *difficult.*

23 President Clinton delivers his State of the Union message, declaring that the "era of big government" has ended.

26 The U.S. Senate ratifies the second Strategic Arms Reduction Treaty (START), committing the United States and Russia to reducing their long-range nuclear arsenals to about one third of 1993 levels. To become effective, the agreement must be ratified by both houses of the Russian parliament.

President Clinton signs a measure to fund the federal government through March 15, 1996.

27 Mahamane Ousmane, the first democratically elected president of Niger, is overthrown in a military coup.

28 The Dallas Cowboys defeat the Pittsburgh Steelers, 27–17, to win the National Football League's Super Bowl XXX.

© Daniel Morel/Sygma

René Préval, 53-year-old former prime minister and defense minister of Haiti, was sworn in to succeed Jean-Bertrand Aristide as president of the Caribbean nation on February 7. He had been elected to the office on Dec. 17, 1995.

February

2 Entertainer Gene Kelly dies at the age of 83.

7 Wlodzimierz Cimoszewicz takes office as premier of Poland, succeeding Jozef Oleksy, who had resigned to defend himself against charges that he had spied for the former USSR.

René Préval is sworn in as president of Haiti, succeeding Jean-Bertrand Aristide.

Crown Prince Letsie David Mohato becomes king of Lesotho following the death of his father, King Moshoeshoe II, in a car accident on January 15.

8 President Clinton signs into law a major overhaul of the nation's communications laws.

10 The Provisional Irish Republican Army (IRA) takes responsibility for a February 9 bomb explosion near a London office complex. The blast killed two persons and ended an 18-month cease-fire.

16 An Amtrak passenger train and a Maryland Area Rail Commuter (MARC) system train collide in Silver Spring, MD, killing 11 persons.

18 At the conclusion of a two-day conference in Rome, President Alija Izetbegovic of Bosnia and Herzegovina, President Franjo Tudjman of Croatia, and President Slobodan Milosevic of Serbia issue a declaration pledging to resolve their differences over implementation of the 1995 treaty to end the civil war in Bosnia.

22 President Clinton nominates Alan Greenspan to a third four-year term as chairman of the Federal Reserve Board. The president also names Alice M. Rivlin, the current director of the Office of Management and Budget, as the board's vice-chairman, and Laurence H. Meyer, an economic consultant, to a vacant seat on the board.

Saudi Arabia's King Fahd announces that he has recovered from his illness and that he will resume ruling his nation. The king had ceded power temporarily to Crown Prince Abdullah on January 1.

23 The U.S. Department of Commerce announces that the U.S. economy grew at an annual rate of 2.1% in 1995.

24 Cuban MiG fighter jets shoot down two unarmed private planes belonging to Brothers to the Rescue, a Cuban exiles' organization, killing four airmen.

25 Twenty-seven persons, including two Americans, are killed and scores are injured in two apparently coordinated suicide-bombing attacks in Israel.

28 The U.S. Department of Commerce reports that the nation's 1995 deficit in trade in goods and services totaled $111.04 billion.

March

1 Barry R. McCaffrey takes office as director of the Office of National Drug Control Policy after resigning as a four-star general of the U.S. Army.

3 In Spain the center-right Popular Party, led by José María Aznar, receives the most votes in parliamentary elections but falls short of gaining an absolute parliamentary majority.

4 Fourteen persons are killed by a suicide-bombing attack in a busy intersection of Tel Aviv. On March 3, 19 persons lost their lives in a bombing on a bus in downtown West Jerusalem. The military wing of the Palestinian Islamic movement is believed to be responsible for the attacks, which threaten the Israeli-Palestinian peace process.

7 Three U.S. servicemen are convicted in a Japanese court of the rape of a 12-year-old Japanese girl in Okinawa in September 1995.

9 American comedian George Burns dies at his Beverly Hills, CA, home. He had marked his 100th birthday on January 20.

11 John Howard is sworn in as prime minister of Australia. The Liberal Party–National Party coalition headed by Howard had scored a decisive victory in national elections on March 2.

13 At the Egyptian resort of Sharm El-Sheik, leaders from 27 nations—including U.S. President Clinton, Israel's Prime Minister Shimon Peres, Jordan's King Hussein, and Russia's President Boris Yeltsin—demonstrate support for the Arab-Israeli peace process and the need to combat international terrorism.

A gunman opens fire on a kindergarten class in Dunblane, Scotland, killing 16 children, their teacher, and himself.

20 In Van Nuys, CA, a superior-court jury finds Erik Menendez and his brother Lyle Menendez guilty of the first-degree murders of their parents in Beverly Hills in 1989. In 1994 two separate juries had deadlocked in the brothers' murder case. Both brothers had admitted to the shotgun killings of their parents but claimed that they had killed them out of fear that they themselves would be killed by the couple for revealing years of sexual and emotional abuse.

23 President Lee Teng-hui wins a decisive 54% of the vote in Taiwan's first democratic presidential election. In anticipation of the voting, Communist China had fired four unarmed surface-to-surface missiles at targets in waters close to Taiwan on March 8 and March 13. The missile firings apparently were intended to intimidate the Taiwanese.

© Brooks Kraft/Sygma

With victories in several Republican presidential primaries on March 26, Robert Dole clinched the GOP's presidential nomination. On the eve of his victory, the U.S. Senate majority leader was greeted enthusiastically at a rally in his hometown of Russell, KS, right.

© Wally MacNamee/Sygma

U.S. President Bill Clinton led the mourners at the funeral of Ronald H. Brown at the National Cathedral in Washington, DC, on April 10. The secretary of commerce was among 35 persons killed in a plane crash near the airport at Dubrovnik, Croatia, on April 3.

26 Robert Dole captures the Republican presidential primaries in California, Nevada, and Washington. Together with the delegates the Kansas senator won in earlier primaries and caucuses, he now has a sufficient number of delegates to gain the Republican presidential nomination.

27 In Israel, Yigal Amir, 25, is sentenced to life imprisonment after being found guilty of the November 1995 murder of Prime Minister Yitzhak Rabin.

30 Russia's President Yeltsin and the leaders of Kazakhstan, Kyrgyzstan, and Belarus sign an agreement on economic integration. On March 23, Russia and Belarus agreed to establish a "union state" that would link the two nations economically, politically, and culturally.

April

1 The University of Kentucky wins the National Collegiate Athletic Association Division I men's basketball title.

3 U.S. Secretary of Commerce Ronald H. Brown is among 35 persons killed when a U.S. military plane slams into a mountainside near the airport at Dubrovnik, Croatia. Secretary Brown and a delegation of U.S. corporate executives were in Croatia on a trade mission.

4 Theodore J. Kaczynski, a 53-year-old former mathematics professor, is arraigned in Helena, MT, on a felony charge of possessing bomb components. He is suspected of being the Unabomber, the mail-bomb terrorist who has killed three persons and injured 23 others since May 1978.

6 Fighting between government soldiers and rebels loyal to a besieged military leader break out anew in Liberia. A peace plan had been accepted in the African nation in August 1995.

9 Dan Rostenkowski (D), former U.S. congressman from Illinois who served as chairman of the House Ways and Means Committee, pleads guilty to two charges of mail fraud. He is to serve a 17-month prison sentence and pay a fine of $100,000.

10 President Clinton vetoes a bill that would have outlawed a late-term-abortion procedure.

11 Jessica Dubroff, a 7-year-old girl from California; her father; and her flight instructor are killed as their single-engine plane crashes near Cheyenne, WY. The girl was attempting to become the youngest person to pilot a plane across the United States.

12 U.S. Trade Representative Mickey Kantor is designated to succeed the late Ronald Brown as commerce secretary; Charlene Barshefsky, the deputy trade representative, is appointed acting trade representative; and Franklin Raines, vice chairman of the Federal National Mortgage Association, is named director of the Office of Management and Budget.

17 In Tokyo, Japan's Prime Minister Ryutaro Hashimoto and President Clinton sign a declaration endorsing a U.S. military presence in the Asian region as "essential for preserving peace and stability."

18 During the eighth day of an Israeli offensive against Hezbollah (Party of God) guerrillas inside southern Lebanon, the Israeli army fires an artillery barrage into a UN peacekeeping camp in Qana, Lebanon, killing at least 75 Lebanese civilians and wounding more than 100. Prime Minister Shimon Peres claims that Israel did not know that the camp was packed with civilian refugees.

In Cairo, Egypt, gunmen open fire on a group of Greek tourists, killing 18 persons and injuring 17 others. Egyptian officials call the attack part of a four-year-old campaign by Islamic militant groups against the government.

20 Concluding a summit conference with Russia's President Yeltsin in Moscow, President Clinton and the leaders of the major industrialized nations (the G-7) call for the prompt enactment of a nuclear-test ban and announce steps to halt the smuggling of nuclear-bomb ingredients.

21 In parliamentary elections in Italy, the new Olive Tree center-left coalition wins control of the 315-seat Senate and captures 284 seats in the 630-member Chamber of Deputies.

24 President Clinton signs into law a counterterrorism bill, establishing new methods to fight terrorism.

The Palestine National Council votes to remove from the charter of the Palestine Liberation Organization (PLO) clauses that contradict the PLO's pledge to respect Israel's right to exist and to renounce "terrorism and other acts of violence."

26 Israel and Lebanon, "in consultation with Syria," agree to end 16 days of rocketing and shelling in northern Israel and southern Lebanon.

Following an April 24 agreement between negotiators for Congress and the White House on a permanent budget for fiscal year 1996, President Clinton signs a budget bill.

May

1 President Clinton meets with Yasir Arafat, chairman of the Palestine Liberation Organization, at the White House.

2 President Clinton vetoes legislation that would restrict the amount that people injured by faulty products could receive in punitive damages in lawsuits.

5 José María Aznar, the leader of Spain's Popular Party, is sworn in as the nation's prime minister.

The Federal Bureau of Investigation (FBI) issues preliminary figures indicating that serious crime dropped across the United States in 1995 for the fourth consecutive year. Meanwhile violent crime by young people continued to rise.

10 In Uganda, Yoweri Museveni, who came to power early in 1986, scores a landslide victory in the nation's first presidential elections. Opposition leader Paul Ssemogerere refuses to accept "the results as valid."

11 A ValuJet Airlines DC-9, en route from Miami, FL, to Atlanta, GA, crashes in the Florida Everglades. The 105 passengers and five crew members are presumed dead.

15 Robert Dole announces that he is resigning not only as majority leader of the U.S. Senate but from the Senate itself, effective on or before June 11. The Kansas Republican plans to concentrate his time on running for the presidency.

16 Adm. Jeremy M. Boorda, the chief of U.S. naval operations, commits suicide shortly after he learns that a newsmagazine article will question military decorations that he wore.

17 President Clinton signs legislation mandating the release of "relevant information" about child molesters and sexually violent offenders who are released from prison or placed on parole.

18 A new center-left government, with Romano Prodi as prime minister, takes office in Italy.

20 The United Nations and Iraq reach an agreement permitting Iraq to sell oil for the first time since its invasion of Kuwait in 1990.

The U.S. Supreme Court rules unconstitutional a provision of the constitution of the state of Colorado nullifying existing civil-rights protection for homosexuals and barring the passage of new antidiscrimination laws.

26 Buddy Lazier, a 28-year-old resident of Vail, CO, wins the 80th Indianapolis 500 auto race.

27 In Moscow, Russia's Prime Minister Viktor Chernomyrdin and Zelimkhan Yandarbiyev, the leader of the Chechnya rebels, sign a cease-fire agreement calling for an end to combat by June 1, the release of all prisoners, and the establishment of commissions to seek a permanent peace agreement.

28 In the first trial involving the Whitewater case in Arkansas, James McDougal—the owner of an Arkansas savings and loan association—is convicted of 18 felony charges, his former wife Susan is convicted of four felony charges, and Arkansas Gov. Jim Guy Tucker is convicted of one count of conspiracy and one count of mail fraud.

31 Final results of Israel's May 29 elections reveal that Benjamin Netanyahu of the Likud Party has defeated Prime Minister Shimon Peres by 29,457 votes.

© Heidi Levine/Sipa

Israelis show their support for Benjamin Netanyahu, the Likud Party candidate for the nation's prime ministership. In a close election on May 29, Netanyahu defeated the incumbent, Shimon Peres.

June

1 In India a new coalition government—led by H.D. Deve Gowda, the chief minister of Karnataka state, as prime minister—takes power. Facing a vote of no confidence, Atal Behari Vajpayee and his government of Hindu nationals had resigned on May 28 after less than two weeks in power.

3 A Japanese naval destroyer accidentally shoots down a U.S. bomber during joint military maneuvers in the central Pacific. Two U.S. crew members are forced to bail out of the bomber but escape serious injury.

7 White House officials announce that the White House improperly has obtained from the Federal Bureau of Investigation the confidential files of 330 persons, including prominent Republicans.

8 China announces that it has conducted an underground nuclear test.

Nineteen Americans were killed when a truck bomb exploded at an apartment complex housing U.S. military personnel near Dhahran, Saudi Arabia, on June 25. An investigation into the attack followed.

11 The Colorado Avalanche win the National Hockey League's Stanley Cup.

13 At a farm complex outside Jordan, MT, members of an antitax group known as the Freemen end an 81-day standoff with authorities.

15 Ella Fitzgerald, the "First Lady of Song," dies in her Beverly Hills, CA, home at the age of 79.

16 In Russia's presidential election, President Boris N. Yeltsin wins 35.28% of the vote; Communist Party leader Gennadi Zyuganov is second with 32.04%; and retired paratrooper Aleksandr Lebed finishes third with 14.52%. A runoff election between Yeltsin and Zyuganov is scheduled for early July.

The Chicago Bulls win the National Basketball Association (NBA) championship.

17 China and the United States agree on a plan to crack down on the piracy of music, motion pictures, and computer software in China. The agreement averts U.S. trade sanctions against China.

18 Benjamin Netanyahu takes the oath as prime minister of Israel.

19 The Irish Republican Army (IRA) claims responsibility for a June 15 bomb explosion in Manchester, England, that injured more than 200 persons.

23 Sheikh Hasina Wazed of the Awami League is sworn in as prime minister of Bangladesh. The Awami League, Bangladesh's principal opposition party, had won the nation's general elections of June 12—the nation's second balloting in four months.

25 Near Dhahran, Saudi Arabia, a truck bomb explodes at an apartment complex housing U.S. military personnel. Nineteen Americans are killed and more than 150 are injured.

26 The U.S. Supreme Court rules that women cannot be excluded from attending the Virginia Military Institute, the military college supported by the state of Virginia.

28 Meeting in Lyons, France, the leaders of the Group of Seven (G-7) nations and Russia endorse a 40-point program to increase cooperation in fighting crime.

In Turkey, Mecmettin Erbakan, the leader of the Welfare Party, forms a new coalition government. Tansu Ciller, the former prime minister, is appointed deputy prime minister and foreign minister.

30 Leonel Fernández Reyna, 42-year-old leader of the Dominican Liberation Party, emerges as the winner in runoff presidential elections in the Dominican Republic.

July

2 In Mongolia official results of parliamentary elections held on June 30 reveal that the Democratic Union Coalition won 50 seats, the former Communist Mongolian People's Revolutionary Party (MPRP) took 25, and the Mongolian Traditional Conservative Party captured the remaining seat.

3 Russia's President Boris N. Yeltsin is reelected in runoff elections.

5 The U.S. unemployment rate is reported at 5.3% for June 1996—the lowest rate in six years.

7 In Washington, Israeli Prime Minister Benjamin Netanyahu meets with President Clinton for the first time.

Abdalá Bucaram Ortiz of the center-left Roldosista Party is elected president of Ecuador in runoff balloting.

The U.S. space shuttle *Columbia* lands at the Kennedy Space Center in Cape Canaveral, FL, completing the longest shuttle flight in history—405 hours, 48 minutes.

At the Wimbledon tennis tournament, Richard Krajicek of the Netherlands is the second unseeded men's player to win the singles title. On July 6, Steffi Graf of Germany won the women's singles crown for a seventh time.

12 In Great Britain, Buckingham Palace announces that Prince Charles and Princess Diana have agreed on the terms for their divorce.

14 A bomb rips apart a luxury hotel in Enniskillen, Northern Ireland, causing minor injuries. It, however, is the first such attack in Northern Ireland since a peace initiative led to a cease-fire in late August 1994.

17 A Trans World Airlines (TWA) 747 jetliner, with 230 persons aboard, crashes into the Atlantic Ocean about one half hour after takeoff from New York City's Kennedy International Airport.

19 U.S. envoy Richard Holbrooke announces that Radovan Karadzic, the Bosnian Serb political chief who had been indicted for genocide and other war crimes, has agreed to give up his political power.

The XXVI Summer Olympic Games open in Atlanta, GA.

21 Myanmar is granted observer status in the Association of Southeast Asian Nations (ASEAN).

24 Japan's Prime Minister Ryutaro Hashimoto pledges government action to combat a serious outbreak of food poisoning that has affected some 8,000 Japanese.

25 In Burundi the Tutsi-dominated army announces it has staged a coup against the Hutu president and names a Tutsi as president of the nation, whose population is 85% Hutu. Renewed fighting between the Hutu and the Tutsi is feared.

© Ken Hawkins/Sygma

The explosion of a pipe bomb at Centennial Olympic Park during the 1996 Summer Games in Atlanta killed one person and injured more than 100. A Turkish television cameraman died of a heart attack during the bombing on July 27. Although the incident dampened the Olympic spirit, the Games continued without further disruption.

August

2 In Israel the Likud government lifts a four-year freeze on the expansion of settlements in the West Bank and Gaza.

4 Hussein Mohammed Aidid succeeds his father, Mohammed Farah Aidid, as leader of Somalia. The elder Aidid died on August 1 after being wounded in fighting in Mogadishu.

The XXVI Summer Olympic Games conclude.

5 President Clinton signs legislation that will impose sanctions on foreign companies that invest heavily in Iran or Libya.

6 Officials from the National Aeronautics and Space Administration (NASA) report that an ancient meteorite from Mars contains chemical, mineral, and structural signs representing the first direct evidence that life once existed beyond Earth.

9 Boris Yeltsin is inaugurated as the first democratically elected head of state of Russia.

15 Robert J. Dole accepts the Republican Party nomination for the presidency. Jack Kemp, former U.S. representative and secretary of housing and urban development, accepts the party's nomination for the vice-presidency.

20 President Clinton signs legislation increasing the minimum wage from $4.25 per hour to $5.15 per hour. The increase is to be effective in two steps—an increase of $0.50 per hour on Oct. 1, 1996, and one of $0.40 per hour on Sept. 1, 1997.

21 President Clinton signs legislation expanding access to health insurance. The new law allows workers to maintain their health-insurance coverage if they change or lose their jobs.

22 President Clinton signs a bill ending "welfare as we know it." The new legislation ends the federal guarantee of aid to the poor and allows the states to enact welfare programs that require recipients to work for time-limited benefits.

Gen. Aleksandr I. Lebed, Russia's security-council secretary, and Gen. Aslan Maskhadov, chief of staff of the secessionist rebels in Chechnya, sign an agreement to bring about a cease-fire in the breakaway republic.

29 Bill Clinton and Al Gore accept renomination by the Democratic Party for second terms as president and vice-president, respectively.

September

4 The United States launches a second missile attack against Iraq to counter Iraqi actions against Kurdish enclaves.

Israel's Prime Minister Netanyahu meets with Yasir Arafat, the Palestine National Authority leader, at the Erez checkpoint on the Israel–Gaza Strip border.

8 Pete Sampras and Steffi Graf win the men's and women's singles titles, respectively, at tennis' U.S. Open.

9 Susan McDougal, a former business partner of President Clinton and Mrs. Clinton in the Whitewater real-estate venture in Arkansas who in August 1996 had been sentenced to two years in prison after being convicted of accepting a fraudulent government-backed loan, is sent to jail for refusing to answer prosecutors' questions regarding President Clinton before a grand jury in Little Rock.

10 The United Nations General Assembly approves the Comprehensive Test Ban Treaty by a vote of 158–3. India, Bhutan, and Libya cast the three votes against the agreement.

Reform Party presidential nominee Ross Perot names Pat Choate, a 55-year-old economist, as his running mate.

13 Rap star Tupac Shakur dies in Las Vegas from wounds he suffered during a shooting on September 7.

14 Nationwide elections are held in Bosnia and Herzegovina in accordance with the 1995 peace agreement. Bosnia's President Alija Izetbegovic, a Muslim, is chosen as chairman of a three-man collective presidency. Momcilo Krajisnik, a Bosnian Serb, and Kresimir Zubak, a Bosnian Croat, also are elected to the panel.

The United States defeats Canada to win the first-ever World Cup of Hockey.

© Farnood/Sipa Press

Kurdish refugees, left, *fled after Iraqi forces seized the Kurdish city of Erbil in the northern no-flight zone. The Iraqis were assisting the Kurdish Democratic Party, which had been involved in a long-standing conflict with the Patriotic Union of Kurdistan—a rival Kurdish faction that had been dominant in Erbil. In response to Iraq's action, the United States launched two missile attacks against Iraq.*

15 Umberto Bossi, leader of the Northern League political party, declares "Padania," which includes many of Italy's northern provinces, "an independent and sovereign federal republic."

17 The 51st session of the UN General Assembly opens.

Spiro T. Agnew, who resigned as vice-president of the United States on Oct. 10, 1973, after pleading guilty to tax-evasion charges, dies at the age of 77.

18 An abandoned North Korean submarine is found run aground off the city of Kangnung, South Korea, increasing tensions between the two nations.

19 The government of Guatemala and leftist rebels in the Central American nation sign an agreement to end their prolonged war.

21 President Clinton signs into law the Defense of Marriage Act, a bill denying federal recognition of same-sex marriages.

22 Greece's ruling party, the Panhellenic Socialist Movement, remains in power after a narrow victory in parliamentary elections.

26 At least 40 Palestinians and 11 Israelis are killed during two days of violence between Israeli soldiers and Palestinian police and demonstrators in Palestine self-rule zones in the West Bank and Gaza Strip. Israel's opening of a second entrance to an archaeological tunnel at the Temple Mount in Jerusalem, a site sacred to Muslims and Jews, led to the unrest.

Shannon Lucid returns to Earth after spending 188 days in space—a record for a U.S. astronaut and for a woman.

27 Najibullah, the former communist president of Afghanistan, and Shahpur Ahmadzai, the nation's former security chief and Najibullah's brother, are hanged in Kabul, Afghanistan, as the Taliban—a rebel force led by militant Islamics—takes over the country.

October

2 A two-day emergency summit meeting between Israel's Prime Minister Netanyahu and Palestinian leader Arafat to quell recent violence in the West Bank and Gaza Strip ends inconclusively, but the two leaders agree to continue negotiations.

4 The second session of the 104th U.S. Congress adjourns.

October

2 A two-day emergency summit meeting between Israel's Prime Minister Netanyahu and Palestinian leader Arafat to quell recent violence in the West Bank and Gaza Strip ends inconclusively, but the two leaders agree to continue negotiations.

4 The second session of the 104th U.S. Congress adjourns.

6 U.S. presidential candidates Bill Clinton and Bob Dole engage in the first of two scheduled televised debates.

11 Bishop Carlos Filipe Ximenes Belo and José Ramos Horta are awarded the Nobel Peace Prize for their efforts toward "a just and peaceful solution to the conflict in East Timor," a former Portuguese colony annexed by Indonesia in 1976.

12 No clear winner emerges from general elections in New Zealand.

13 Leaders of the Republican Party, including House Speaker Newt Gingrich, call for an investigation into what they claim were illegal contributions to the Democratic National Committee by members and associates of a prominent Indonesian family.

14 The Dow Jones industrial average of U.S. blue-chip stocks exceeds the 6,000 mark for the first time.

17 Russia's President Boris Yeltsin fires Gen. Aleksandr Lebed as national security chief.

20 In general elections for the lower house of the Japanese Diet (parliament), Prime Minister Ryutaro Hashimoto's Liberal Democratic Party wins 239 of 500 seats.

21 José Arnoldo Alemán Lacayo of Liberal Alliance Party declares himself the winner of Nicaragua's presidential election of October 20.

23 During a state visit to Israel, France's President Jacques Chirac reiterates his support for the establishment of a Palestinian state.

A 21-day strike by Canadian Auto Workers against General Motors of Canada Ltd. ends.

25 Thorbjoern Jagland is sworn in as prime minister of Norway, succeeding Gro Harlem Brundtland, who resigned on October 23.

26 The U.S. Justice Department issues a statement saying that, "barring any newly discovered evidence," security guard Richard Jewell is no longer a "target" in the investigation of the pipe bombing at Atlanta's Centennial Olympic Park in July. Although Jewell was identified publicly as a suspect in the case, he was neither charged nor arrested.

The New York Yankees capture baseball's World Series, defeating the Atlanta Braves, four games to two.

November

3 In Bulgaria, Peter Stoyanov of the opposition Union of Democratic Forces is chosen president in runoff elections.

5 Elections are held throughout the United States. Bill Clinton becomes the first Democrat since Franklin D. Roosevelt to win a second term. The Republican Party retains control of both houses of the U.S. Congress.

In Pakistan, President Farooq Leghari dismisses Prime Minister Benazir Bhutto and dissolves the National Assembly. Bhutto's government had been under fire for corruption and economic mismanagement.

Bill Clinton, his wife Hillary, and their daughter Chelsea greeted supporters and enjoyed a lavish fireworks display as part of an election-victory celebration in Little Rock. The president had captured a second term by winning 49% of the popular vote and 379 electoral votes to 41% of the popular vote and 159 electoral votes for his GOP opponent, Robert Dole.

© Brooks Kraft/Sygma

© David Berkwitz/Sipa

Russia's President Yeltsin undergoes a multiple-bypass heart operation in Moscow.

6 A cyclone strikes southeastern India, killing as many as 2,000 persons and leaving hundreds of thousands homeless.

7 U.S. District Court Judge Norma Holloway Johnson sentences Joseph P. Waldholtz to 37 months in prison. The former husband of U.S. Rep. Enid Greene (R-UT) had pleaded guilty to charges of bank, election, and tax fraud in June.

The U.S. Army reveals that it is conducting a wide-ranging investigation into charges of sexual harassment and assault at the Army Ordnance Center and School at the Aberdeen Proving Ground in Maryland.

8 President Clinton names Erskine B. Bowles to succeed Leon E. Panetta as White House chief of staff.

12 A Saudi Arabian Airlines 747 and a Kazakhstan Airlines Ilyushin-76 collide in midair some 60 mi (96 km) west of the airport in New Delhi, India, killing all 349 persons aboard the two planes.

15 President Clinton announces that some 8,500 U.S. troops will remain in Bosnia and Herzegovina until June 1998.

An estimated 500,000 Hutu refugees begin returning to Rwanda voluntarily after spending more than two years in refugee camps in eastern Zaire.

Alger Hiss, a U.S. State Department diplomat who was convicted of perjury in a famous 1950 communist-espionage case, dies in New York City at the age of 92.

17 In Romania, Emil Constantinescu, the leader of the opposition coalition, the Democratic Convention, is elected president in runoff elections.

In Thailand the ruling Chart Thai Party is defeated in parliamentary elections as the New Aspiration Party, led by Defense Minister Chavalit Yongchaiyudh, wins a narrow plurality.

The six-ton Russian spaceship Mars 96, bound for Mars, crashes into the Pacific Ocean, one day after being launched.

The World Food Summit, hosted by the UN Food and Agricultural Organization (FAO), concludes in Rome, Italy. Some 10,000 delegates from 194 nations had attended the conference.

19 Pope John Paul II and Cuba's President Fidel Castro confer for 35 minutes at the Vatican.

20 During a four-day visit to Australia, President Clinton addresses a joint session of Parliament.

21 Harold James Nicholson, a career Central Intelligence Agency (CIA) officer, is indicted by a federal grand jury on one count of conspiracy to commit espionage for Russia.

23 An Ethiopian 767 passenger jet crashes into the Indian Ocean near the Comoros, resulting in the deaths of 125 people. The plane had been hijacked en route from Addis Ababa, Ethiopia, to Nairobi, Kenya, and then to Abidjan, Ivory Coast.

25 A two-day summit of leaders of the 18 members of the Asia-Pacific Economic Cooperation (APEC) forum concludes in Manila, the Philippines. During the conference, President Clinton and China's President Jiang Zemin had agreed to exchange state visits in 1997 and 1998.

Dr. David A. Kessler announces his resignation as director of the U.S. Food and Drug Administration (FDA).

26 Major-league-baseball-team owners ratify a new five-year collective-bargaining agreement.

28 Voters in Algeria approve a referendum on a new constitution, which extends presidential power and bans political parties "founded on a religious basis"—for example, by the Islamic fundamentalists.

29 A 12-day national strike by truck drivers concludes in France.

30 The government of Sierra Leone and rebel forces sign a peace agreement, ending a five-year civil war.

December

1 In Moldova, Petru Lucinschi, the speaker of parliament, is chosen president in runoff elections.

4 Mars Pathfinder, an unmanned U.S. space vessel that is designed to discover data about Mars, is launched from Cape Canaveral, FL.

5 President Clinton announces his national-security team for his second term: Madeleine K. Albright is designated as secretary of state; William S. Cohen is chosen as secretary of defense; Anthony Lake is picked as director of the Central Intelligence Agency; and Samuel R. Berger is slated to succeed Lake as head of the National Security Council.

7 Ghana's President Jerry Rawlings is reelected in voting that is judged free and fair by international observers.

9 UN Secretary-General Boutros Boutros-Ghali approves a plan to allow Iraq to export oil again. Iraq's oil revenue is to be used to alleviate the nation's food and medical-supply shortage.

10 South Africa's President Nelson Mandela signs into law a new national constitution.

In New Zealand the National Party and the New Zealand First party agree to form a coalition government, with Jim Bolger of the National Party remaining prime minister.

12 India's Prime Minister H.D. Deve Gowda and Bangladesh's Prime Minister Sheikh Hasina Wajed sign a 30-year treaty under which the two nations will share water from the Ganges River.

© Manuel Llanos/Reuters/Archive Photos

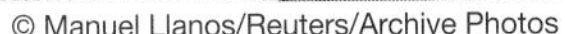

© Fernando Llano/AP/ Wide World Photos

On December 17 in Peru, some 25 members of the Túpac Amaru Revolutionary Movement (MRTA) attacked the Japanese ambassador's residence in Lima during a reception, taking some 400 hostages. The guerrilla group was demanding the release of imprisoned MRTA members. By year's end, the efforts of the Red Cross, the Peruvian government, and other nations had helped obtain the release of many of the hostages (left)*, but some 80 remained in captivity and the crisis continued into the new year.*

14 Ron Carey is reelected president of the International Brotherhood of Teamsters.

15 The Boeing Company announces that it plans to purchase McDonnell Douglas Corp. for $13.3 billion.

17 The UN General Assembly elects Kofi Annan of Ghana, a 58-year-old career diplomat who had served as UN undersecretary-general for peacekeeping, as secretary-general.

18 The local school board in Oakland, CA, decides that it will be the nation's first school district to recognize "black English"—a form of English spoken by some African-Americans and called "Ebonics" by its proponents—as a distinct language.

19 Earl Edwin Pitts, an agent for the Federal Bureau of Investigation (FBI), is indicted by a federal grand jury on 16 counts of conspiracy to commit espionage.

A panel of television-industry representatives unveils a planned system for rating television programs based on their level of violence and sexual content.

20 Astronomer Carl Sagan dies at the age of 62.

21 An ethics subcommittee of the U.S. House of Representatives concludes that Speaker Newt Gingrich had used tax-exempt donations for political purposes, in violation of House rules.

23 Russia's President Boris Yeltsin returns to work after heart surgery on November 5.

An agreement is reached to end a four-year civil war in Tajikistan.

25 In Belgrade, Serbia, clashes erupt between government supporters and opposition forces that since mid-November have been staging protests against the government's failure to recognize the result of municipal elections.

26 China's Prime Minister Li Peng begins a three-day visit to Russia.

29 In Guatemala the government and leftist guerrillas sign a peace agreement, ending a prolonged civil war that took some 100,000 lives.

North Korea expresses "deep regret" for sending a submarine full of armed commandos into South Korean waters in September.

Special Features

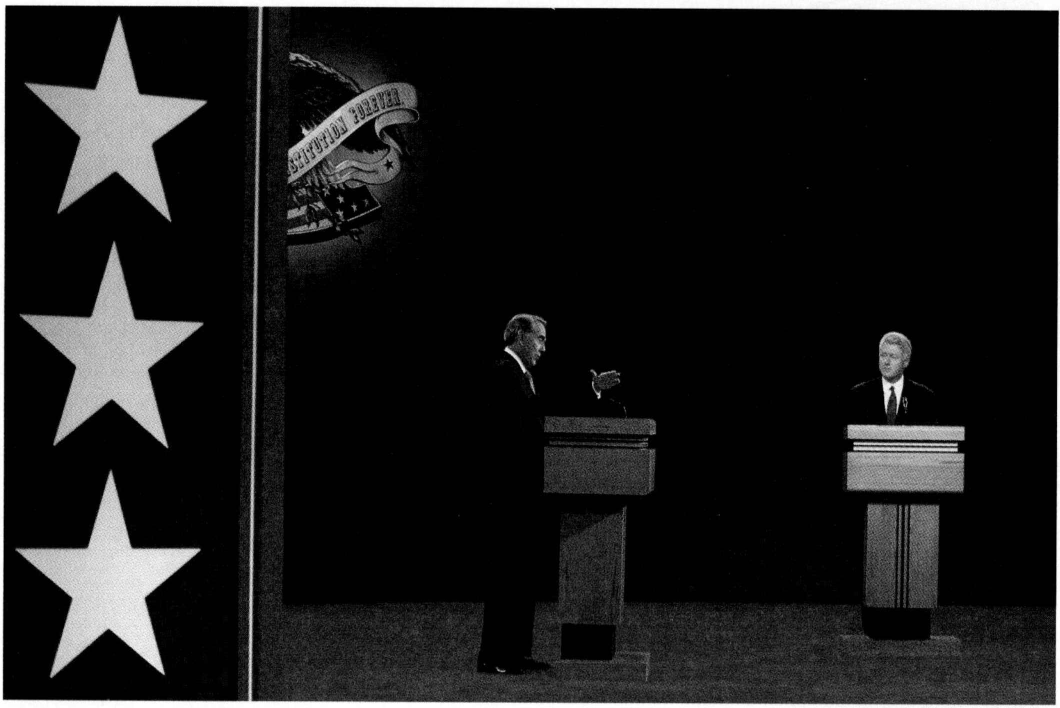

After a prolonged 1996 election campaign that featured two televised debates between the major candidates—former U.S. Sen. Bob Dole (*above left*) and President Bill Clinton—the incumbent Democrat was reelected. Russia, too, went to the polls in 1996 and put its young democracy to a successful test. President Boris Yeltsin (*photo bottom left, page 23*) was returned to office.

Also in 1996, Atlanta, GA, hosted the XXVI Summer Games (*photo top left, page 23*), marking the 100th anniversary of the revival of the Olympic movement; the British colony of Hong Kong (*center left, page 23*) prepared to revert to Chinese sovereignty at midnight on June 30, 1997; and the war against cancer—with the mammogram as the prime technique for detecting breast cancer (*photo bottom right, page 23*)—continued. The blockbuster movie *Independence Day* (*photo top right, page 23*) illustrated the popularity of the science-fiction genre; and the Smithsonian Institution, a U.S. jewel, became 150 years young. Meanwhile, more and more people were turning to computers and the Internet for the latest news (*photo right*), other reference information, help with their daily tasks, and just fun.

Accordingly, the editors selected the U.S. election, Russia as an emerging democracy, Hong Kong during a time of dramatic change, cancer, the Internet, the Olympics at 100, the science-fiction invasion, and the Smithsonian Institution at 150 for special feature discussion. An update on the nations of the former Yugoslavia follows.

© Vandystadt/Allsport

© Adrian Bradshaw/Saba

© Globe Photos, Inc.

© Laski Diffusion/Liaison

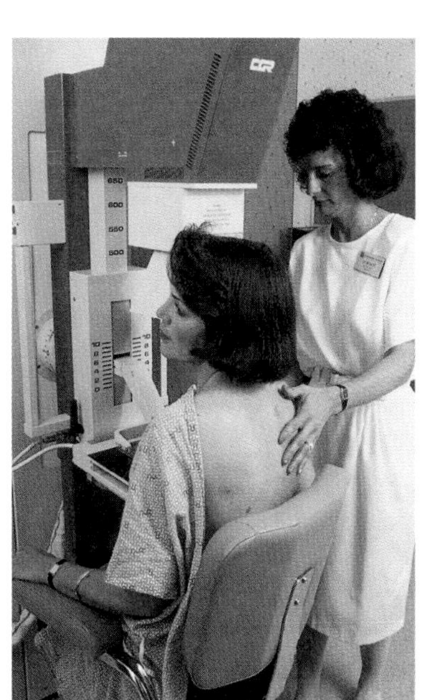
© Blair Seitz/Photo Researchers

THE 1996 U.S. ELECTION

© Ted Soqui/Sygma

A Vote for the Status Quo

By Robert Shogan

After being renominated at the Democratic National Convention in Chicago in August 1996, above, *President Bill Clinton and Vice-President Al Gore went on to win a second term in November. With the Republicans retaining control of both houses of the U.S. Congress, however, the election was considered "a vote for the status quo."*

The story of the struggle for the U.S. presidency in 1996 begins with the Republican conquest of both houses of Congress in November 1994. For it was the Republican Party's effort to exploit its historic election success in the months that followed that made it possible for Democrat incumbent Bill Clinton to retain the White House.

The 1994 "Republican Revolution" and Other Background. The dominant figure in what came to be called the "Republican revolution" was Newt Gingrich of Georgia, who was chosen as the new speaker of the House of Representatives. From the very first, Representative Gingrich acted not just as the leader of the GOP forces in the House but almost as if he had been chosen president. Two factors made this possible. More than most other national political figures, he actually had an agenda of his own—the Contract with America—that he had been developing and promoting for years. And while Gingrich set about amid much fanfare and hullabaloo promulgating the ambitious blueprints of cutbacks in government outlined in the contract, the real president in the White House seemed shocked into a passive silence by the magnitude of the election defeat suffered by his party.

Indeed, the dwindling of Clinton's role was so conspicuous that at a press conference in April 1995 he was asked point-blank about whether he was relevant to the great public debate raging around him. "The Constitution gives me relevance; the power of our ideas gives me relevance; the record we have built up over the last two years and the things we're doing to implement it give me relevance," he said. As it happened, it was not a product of political strategy but rather an accident of fate that allowed the president to thrust himself back into the center of the stage. In the wake of the April 19, 1995, bombing of the Oklahoma City federal building that took more than 160 lives, Clinton seemed suddenly to recover his tongue. He urged Americans to recognize the "duty to purge ourselves of the dark forces which give rise to this evil" and, as some GOP leaders spoke sympathetically of antigovernment militias, Clinton condemned the militias as extremist. His poll numbers soared to their highest level of his term. Clinton appeared to have captured the political center, and his Republican foes had been forced on the defensive.

"Let me be the bridge to a time of tranquility, faith, and confidence in action."

Bob Dole, Republican National Convention Aug. 15, 1996

But most of the damage suffered by the Gingrich-led Republicans was self-inflicted. Their fundamental problem was defined by harsh economic realities—in order to keep their 1994 campaign promises of tax cuts and a balanced budget in seven years, they would have to cut Medicare and Medicaid growth by nearly $300 billion. While Clinton came forward with his own plan for balancing the budget, the White House proposals for tightening spending on Medicare were on a much smaller scale than those advanced by the GOP. And the president issued a warning that he intended to veto legislation that contained the current Republican proposals for Medicare cuts and tax reductions—even if it meant shutting down the government.

"Let us resolve to build that bridge to the 21st century, to meet our challenges and protect our values."

Bill Clinton, Democratic National Convention Aug. 29, 1996

The Republicans took up his dare and tried to force their ideas into law. But Clinton, accusing the Republicans of blackmail, stood his ground and vetoed the Republican initiatives. In the eyes of most citizens, Clinton held the high ground. And Gingrich made matters worse for his party when, in the midst of budget negotiations, the speaker blurted out to reporters that the GOP had hardened its bargaining position because he and Senate Majority Leader Robert Dole of Kansas felt they were snubbed by the White House during their trip the previous week to Israel for the funeral of Israeli Prime Minister Yitzhak Rabin. The next day the *New York Daily News*, reflecting the judgment of many Americans, depicted Gingrich as a sobbing baby in diapers next to the headline: "Cry Baby. Newt's tantrum: He closed down the government because Clinton made him sit at back of plane."

The budget dispute finally was settled in the spring with a compromise agreement. But Clinton emerged as the clear political winner, as the polls demonstrated. And by the time the Republican race for president began late in 1995, Clinton had gained an advantage in the polls that he was never to lose.

About the author. Robert Shogan, the national political correspondent in the Washington Bureau of *The Los Angeles Times*, is the author of *The Riddle of Power: Presidential Leadership from Truman to Bush* (1991) and *None of the Above: Why Presidents Fail & What Can Be Done About It* (1982). A longtime observer of the Washington political scene, Mr. Shogan also has served as an assistant editor of *The Wall Street Journal* and as a correspondent with *Newsweek* magazine.

The GOP Contenders and the Primaries. Early on, the contest for the GOP presidential nomination had four principal contenders, each of whom represented one of the principal tributaries of belief that would compete for supremacy in defining the mainstream of Republicanism. Bob Dole would become the chief tribune for Midwestern Republicanism—the stolid but

© Bob Galbraith/AP/Wide World Photos

After winning the New Hampshire Republican presidential primary on February 20, journalist and television commentator Pat Buchanan posed the most serious challenge to Bob Dole's nomination as the GOP presidential standard-bearer.

enduring faith in a marriage of convenience between the rewards of the free market and the obligations of government. Sen. Phil Gramm of Texas, a former Democrat, was his new party's most aggressive apostle of the swaggering take-no-prisoners conservatism spawned by his Sunbelt base. Drawing on his experience as former governor of Tennessee, Lamar Alexander epitomized with his candidacy the old notion that the government closest to the people is the government most to be trusted, by rallying support behind a new cognomen—devolution. Journalist and former Nixon aide Pat Buchanan championed a populist brand of conservatism whose nationalist overtones not only outraged adversaries on the left but also antagonized former allies on the right.

Dole was the front-runner by virtue of his prestige as Senate leader, his far-flung alliances among party leaders, and his fund-raising resources. But his inability to offer a compelling message to the electorate stirred misgivings even among his supporters and left a vacuum in the race. Rushing in to fill it in the fall of 1995 was publishing magnate Steve Forbes, who—by pouring millions of dollars of his own money into television commercials to promote his flat-tax proposal and attack the other candidates—emerged as a top contender.

But as Dole and his allies trained their guns on Forbes in a counterattack, Dole was ambushed by Buchanan. The columnist knocked Gramm out of contention by upsetting him in the Louisiana caucus—the first contest of the nominating campaign—on February 6, finished right on Dole's heels in Iowa on February 12, and then captured the New Hampshire primary. This was a stunning blow to Dole's candidacy. But the saving grace was that the Kansan managed to finish ahead of Alexander, who wound up in third place. Alexander would have been more acceptable over the long run to party leaders, who viewed the prospect of Buchanan as the nominee as portending electoral disaster because of his hard-line views. Aided by this widespread opposition to Buchanan, and by his own formidable financial resources, Dole rallied. The majority leader won a key victory in the South Carolina primary and followed that up with a string of successes in contests in New York, the South, and the Midwest, which allowed him to nail down the nomination.

But even after he had established his supremacy in his own party, Dole still was handicapped by the lack of an effective message and faced an uphill fight against Clinton. For his part, the president benefited greatly from the seeming unity within his own party. This was due largely to the 1994 Republican victory in the midterm election—which initially made Democratic prospects in 1996 seem dim—and also to Clinton's success in building up a big campaign treasury in advance of the campaign, which discouraged potential challengers. No Democratic president since FDR had sailed through to renomination with so little opposition.

© Les Stone/Sygma

Former U.S. Sen. Bob Dole (extreme left) *and former U.S. Rep. and professional-football player Jack Kemp greeted the delegates after accepting the Republican Party's nominations for president and vice-president, respectively, in San Diego, on Aug. 15, 1996. Earlier, Elizabeth Dole, the candidate's wife, took to the convention floor and mingled with the delegates as she praised her husband.*

© Brooks Kraft/Sygma

The president also drew strength from the continued economic recovery, which he claimed reflected in good measure the spending cuts and tax hikes of his 1993 economic plan. Even those who questioned how much credit Clinton deserved for the better times could not quarrel with the favorable economic indicators. Unemployment had dropped and so had the budget deficit, by more than 60%. The Dow Jones average had more than doubled, and consumer confidence climbed to a level that in the past always had guaranteed an incumbent's reelection. And foreign policy, which had been one of the president's early weaknesses, now became a plus. When Clinton in 1995 shouldered the risks of a U.S. troop deployment in Bosnia, his action helped to foster the impression that this president would risk calamity and unpopularity if he believed the cause was just, and his standing in the polls rose correspondingly.

Summer Developments and the Conventions. With these factors aiding the incumbent, challenger Dole took several steps in the late spring and summer to bolster his chances in the general election. But none of these efforts achieved the significant change he sought. First, in June 1996 he startled the political world by resigning the Senate seat he had held for nearly 30 years to devote all his time and energy to his challenge to Clinton. "The very least a presidential candidate owes America is his full attention," Dole declared. To dramatize the change, Dole—on his first day on the campaign trail after he left the Senate—sported a light-blue blazer, an open-necked shirt, and chinos. But despite the fresh appearance, Dole had no new message to offer.

Then, trying to broaden his appeal by reaching voters who supported the right to abortion, Dole sought to soften the language of his party platform condemning abortion under any circumstances. "I will stand up for my beliefs with confidence, but I will not silence those who disagree," Dole declared. But when the GOP platform committee met in San Diego in August, in advance of the national convention's opening in that city, hard-line foes of abortion shredded Dole's proposal for change, strip-

The Democrats held their national convention in Chicago in late August. The Clinton-Gore ticket was renominated without opposition. Like the GOP convention, the Democrats' gathering was staged with the television audience in mind. In a prime-time address, First Lady Hillary Rodham Clinton (below) *focused on family issues.*

© Mark Peterson/Saba

© Reuters/Luc Novovitch/Archive Photos

ping even its hallmark phrase, "tolerance is a virtue," from the document.

In his most important move, Dole unveiled his plan for reviving the economy, built around a $500 billion tax reduction that he claimed would boost economic growth and make it easier for middle-class Americans to get ahead. The plan included a 15% cut in income-tax rates. Dole did not say exactly how he would pay for these tax cuts, claiming that any losses in government revenue would be offset by economic growth. Critics charged that this argument contradicted Dole's own past stress on fiscal responsibility, and many believed that, for this reason, the idea did not catch on with voters.

Dole's final step before the GOP convention once again surprised many in his party; he selected as his vice-presidential running mate former U.S. Rep. and Housing Secretary Jack Kemp, with whom he long had disagreed over economic issues. Dole's advisers hoped that Kemp's enthusiasm and strength with minority groups would give the ticket a fresh look. Still, as Dole himself realized, support for the Republican ticket would depend far more on the electorate's view of him than on his running mate's appeal. And in his acceptance speech in San Diego, Dole sought to cast his age, which many viewed as one of his biggest handicaps, in a more positive perspective. "Age has its advantages," the 73-year-old Republican nominee contended, pointing to the traditional values of the nation's past. "Let me be the bridge to a time of tranquility, faith, and confidence in action," Dole added. "And to those who say it was never so, that America has not been better, I say, you're wrong, and I know, because I was there."

But Democrats seized upon that metaphor at their convention in Chicago, two weeks after the Republican conclave, contrasting Dole's promise to build a bridge to the past with President Clinton's pledge in his acceptance speech to build "a bridge to the future." In that address, which served as a template for the campaign speech he would give countless times in the

© John Sommers/Sipa Press

© Dirck Halstead/Gamma-Liaison

On the campaign trail, Bob Dole (left) *put forward a plan for a 15% income-tax cut and, especially in the final days before the balloting, charged that President Clinton's character should stop people from voting for the incumbent. The president, meanwhile, spoke of the accomplishments of his administration and emphasized that Americans were better off in 1996 than they were four years earlier when a Republican was chief executive.*

next ten weeks, Clinton depicted himself as a forward-looking centrist, offering Americans a grab bag of ideas—from targeted tax credits for education to teenage curfews—to help deal with the problems of everyday life. At the same time the president defended popular government programs such as Medicare and environmental protection.

In general, the Democrats succeeded in maintaining the appearance of unity but could not suppress totally evidence of the continuing deep-rooted conflict in the party between Clinton's New Democrat thrust to the center and the commitment to government activism that has been the basis of the party's tradition. For example, when Clinton declared, "let us proclaim to the American people we will balance the budget," the convention delegates were silent; but they burst into applause when he added that "we will do it in a way that preserves Medicare, Medicaid, education, the environment...."

In between the two major party conventions, the Reform Party founded by Ross Perot—in a weeklong balloting procedure using the mail, phones, and computers—nominated the Texas billionaire as its presidential candidate over former Colorado Gov. Richard D. Lamm. Perot later chose economist and free-trade critic Pat Choate as his running mate. In a change from 1992, when Perot poured millions of his own money into financing his candidacy, he decided this time to accept federal funding. Another difference from 1992 was that Perot, who got 19% of the vote in that election, was unable to raise the level of his support above the single-digit level. For that reason he was

The Rise of Political Consultants

In the late summer of 1996, just as the presidential campaigns of the standard-bearers of the two major parties were toeing the mark for the race for the White House, each was shaken by the resignation of a political consultant.

The departure of Dick Morris, President Bill Clinton's chief strategist, on August 29—the climactic day of the Democratic convention—got more attention, because it was triggered by news reports linking Morris to a call girl, to whom he supposedly divulged confidential matters about the inner workings of the White House. By contrast, Don Sipple, who was Dole's chief media adviser and message formulator, and his colleague, consultant Michael Murphy, resigned on September 5 on more mundane grounds—a policy disagreement. But each of these episodes illustrated the dramatic and, to many analysts, disturbing rise of outside consultants to power and influence in the modern American political system.

Politicians always have had staff members to whom they turned for advice or help, usually when some special skill—such as speechwriting or advertising—was called for. But in the past, these assistants had been longtime retainers or, as in the case of Jim Farley—President Franklin Roosevelt's top political manager and Democratic national chairman during his first two terms—leaders of the politician's party. But political consultants are known with good reason as "hired guns," motivated not by personal loyalty or principled belief but by their own ambitions, rendering their services to whichever candidate offers the most in remuneration or in prestige. "Consultants' obligation to the campaign is only short term," Patrick Caddell—a consultant to George McGovern, Jimmy Carter, and other Democrats—told *The New York Times*. "Their obligation to their careers is long term."

Morris, for example, though he had helped Clinton during his time as Arkansas governor in the 1980s, was recalled to duty following the Republican midterm-election victory in 1994. And Sipple had worked for a Dole rival for the GOP nomination, California Gov. Pete Wilson, until Wilson dropped out of the race late in 1995. Murphy had been the chief strategist for another unsuccessful Dole rival, former Tennessee Gov. Lamar Alexander. None of these operatives ever had held any position in their respective parties, and Morris, the adviser to Democratic President Clinton, had been a consultant to numerous Republicans, including Mississippi Sen. Trent Lott, the GOP Senate leader.

Businessman Ross Perot again staged a third-party race for the White House. As the Reform Party candidate, Perot captured 8% of the popular vote, compared with 19% four years earlier.

© Stephen Rose/Gamma-Liaison

denied the chance to participate in the two nationally televised debates between Clinton and Dole, an action that he unsuccessfully challenged in the federal courts.

The Debates and the Final Days of the Campaign. By the time the debates took place in October it was clear that they represented Dole's sole chance for overtaking Clinton. But he was hindered by the same factors that accounted for Clinton's big lead—the favorable economic conditions and his own limited ability to communicate. Dole did show flashes of the wit for which he was famed. Asked in the first debate by moderator Jim Lehrer of the Public Broadcasting System about Clinton's opening-statement claim that Americans were better off in 1996 than in 1992, Dole nodded in Clinton's direction and retorted: "Well, he's better off than he was four years ago." That got Dole a big laugh, but it did not change the reality that most Americans agreed with Clinton's claim.

But Dole passed up an opportunity to pursue the so-called character issue, which many Republicans believed was Clinton's Achilles' heel because of past allegations about the president evading the draft and womanizing, as well as the continuing

Indeed, it has been the steady decline of political parties in the post–World War II era that has cleared the way for the advent of consultants. The parties, whatever their faults, at least served as institutional mechanisms for linking the promises of politics to the performance of government, a role the consultants, driven by their own personal agendas, are ill suited to fill. Another factor contributing to the rise of consultants has been the increasing importance of technology—notably in television and polling—in politics, which stimulated the market for operatives with expertise in these areas. The first consultants were specialists, such as Lou Harris, who polled for John Kennedy in the 1960 presidential campaign, and Tony Schwartz, who—as media adviser to Lyndon Johnson's 1964 presidential campaign—created one of the most controversial and most effective television commercials ever shown. Designed to underline anxiety about Johnson's challenger, Barry Goldwater, as an alleged warmonger, the ad depicted a little girl counting petals pulled from a flower, who when she reached the count of ten was blotted out by a nuclear mushroom cloud.

Dick Morris (left) *was forced to resign as Bill Clinton's political strategist just as the campaign neared its final stage.*

The ranks of consultants have multiplied steadily. The American Association of Political Consultants, founded in 1969 by fewer than 50 consultants, now has more than 600 members who work for candidates at every level of government. And in recent years, consultants have outgrown their initial limited role as specialists. More and more often they take overall charge of a campaign, as James Carville did with the 1992 Clinton campaign, providing it with the theme which carried it to victory—"It's the economy, stupid." By 1995, Carville had fallen out of favor and Clinton turned to Dick Morris to rescue his floundering presidency. Morris responded with a strategy he dubbed "triangulation." It called for Clinton to distance himself from both the GOP on one side and the Democratic members of Congress on the other, while taking a position on the issues that best would advance his own individual interests.

ROBERT SHOGAN

probes into the Whitewater affair and other matters (*see* UNITED STATES—*Domestic Affairs*). But when asked by moderator Lehrer whether there were "significant differences in the more personal areas that are relevant to this election," Dole said: "I don't like to get into personal matters. As far as I'm concerned, this is a campaign about issues." By the second debate, Dole had decided that Clinton's character indeed was an issue, but his points came across more as sniping than as a coherent argument that would demonstrate why Clinton was not fit to serve in the White House.

In the wake of the debates, most Republicans privately conceded that the race for the presidency was lost, and concentrated on trying to hold the party's majorities in the House and Senate. One tactic that some GOP candidates pursued was to try to turn the seeming inevitability of Clinton's victory to their own advantage by stressing to voters the importance of electing Republican lawmakers so that the reelected president would not have a "blank check." In a last-minute move that seemed to underline the desperateness of his plight, Dole sought to persuade Perot to abandon his own candidacy and support Dole, but Perot rejected the notion out of hand.

© Daniel Hulshizer/AP/Wide World Photos

© Scott Perry/AP/Wide World Photos

In U.S. Senate races that drew national attention, Democratic U.S. Rep. Robert G. Torricelli (above left) *defeated U.S. Rep. Dick Zimmer for the New Jersey seat being vacated by Bill Bradley, and Democrat Max Cleland* (below) *was chosen over Republican Guy Millner, an employment-agency owner, to take over the Georgia seat held by retiring Sam Nunn. The Torricelli-Zimmer race was considered particularly vicious. Meanwhile women scored big wins in two U.S. Senate races. Maine Republican Susan Collins* (above) *was elected to succeed her former boss, Sen. William S. Cohen, and Mary Landrieu* (left) *took a tight victory in Louisiana to leave the Bayou State as the only southern state with two Democratic senators.*

© Bill Haber/AP/Wide World Photos

© Erik S. Lesser/AP/Wide World Photos

The Republican cause may have been helped in the closing weeks of the campaign by disclosures that the Democratic National Committee had raised millions of dollars from sources apparently connected to business interests overseas, particularly in Indonesia and other Asian countries. While it is illegal for foreign governments, corporations, or citizens to contribute to U.S. political campaigns, exceptions are made for U.S. subsidiaries of foreign businesses and for foreign citizens who are legal residents in this country. Critics charged that the Democrats had used these loopholes to violate the spirit and in some cases the letter of the ban on foreign contributions. Dole accused the president and his campaign of abetting "the foreign corruption of America," adding: "We've finally got foreign aid coming to America and it's all going to the Democratic National Committee." But Dole's ability to exploit this issue was hampered because his own party had accepted huge sums in so called "soft money" from business interests at home. Nevertheless the controversy pushed the issue of campaign-finance reform to the forefront of the political agenda.

Rob Rogers, reprinted by permission of United Feature Syndicates, Inc.

The Results. On November 5, Clinton won handily with 49% of the popular vote and 379 electoral votes to 41% and 159 electoral votes for Dole, while holding Perot to 8% of the popular vote. But Clinton's failure to win a majority of the popular vote was a disappointment to himself and his fellow Democrats. For their part, Republicans congratulated themselves on retaining their majorities in both houses of Congress for two consecutive elections—the first time that had happened since 1928.

The bad news for both parties was that the voter-turnout rate of 48.8% was the lowest since Calvin Coolidge was elected in 1924 and the second lowest since 1824, according to Curtis Gans, head of the Committee for the Study of the American Electorate. Some Americans considered the political campaign too long.

The Republican forces in the House, which had spearheaded the Gingrich revolution, were weakened by the defeat of 13 of 70 of the 1994 freshmen who had sought reelection. All told, the Republicans lost nine seats in the House, leaving them with 227 to 207 for the Democrats and one independent. But in the Senate the GOP increased its majority by two seats—by winning what had been Democratic Senate seats in Alabama, Arkansas, and Nebraska, where retirements had left vacancies. In turn, the GOP lost only one of its own seats: In South Dakota incumbent Larry Pressler was defeated by Tim Johnson (D). That left the Senate with 55 Republicans to 45 Democrats.

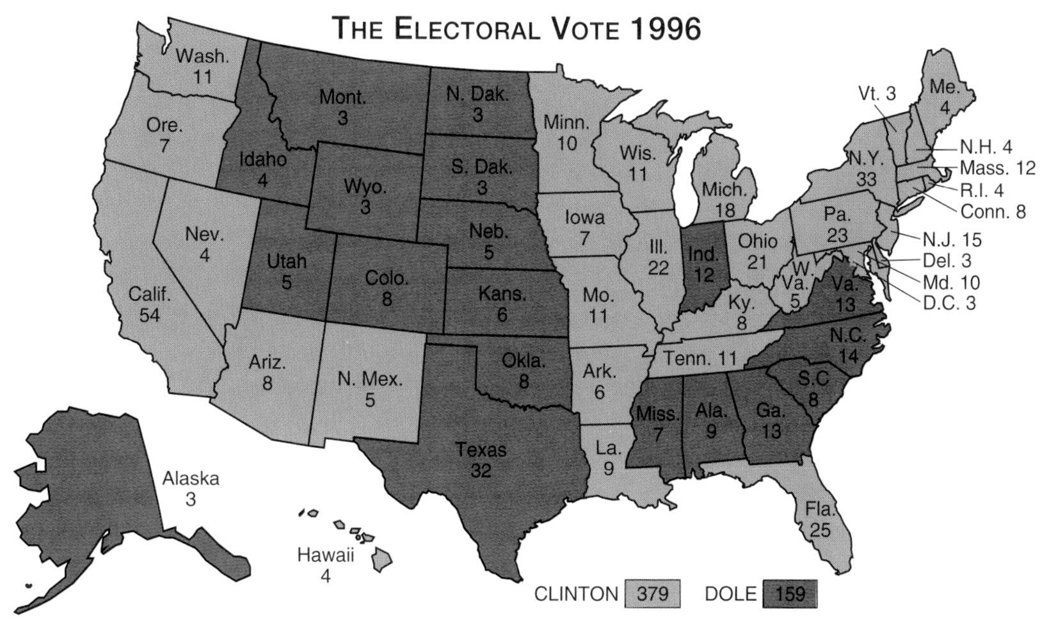

RUSSIA
AS AN EMERGING DEMOCRACY
FIVE YEARS AFTER THE FALL OF THE USSR

© Alexander Zemlianichenko/AP/Wide World Photos

By Robert Sharlet

The international spotlight fell on Russia during 1996 as it continued to move toward democracy. The Eurasian nation of 147.7 million people held a dramatic election in June and July.

As 1996 ended, five years had passed since the collapse of the USSR, an event of historic resonance that set in motion vast changes in the post-Soviet successor states. Although a mere half decade is but a moment in the life of a nation, Russia, in particular, has risen from the ashes of the former Soviet system and has begun to forge its future as a free society. Although Russia's progress from its authoritarian past still may be wanting by Western standards, it is quite striking when compared to that of most of the post-Soviet republics, the so-called Newly Independent States (NIS). While Russia's development may lag that of the Baltic states, it has been far more progressive than that of its other neighbors, including Ukraine, Georgia, Armenia, and the Central Asian states that had been part of the former Soviet Union.

Since the fall of the Soviet Union, Russia has outstripped the NIS in carrying out post-Soviet reforms, remaining on the cutting edge of change in politics, economics, law, and, to a lesser extent, social policy in the region. Under the rubric of political reform, state-building moves forward, while political-party development still is sluggish. In the area of economic reform, Russia is the undisputed leader in the privatization of formerly state-owned retail, wholesale, and industrial enterprises, as well as in the development of a market economy, although the question of landownership remains in limbo. Legal reform followed in the wake of significant political and economic change, although it still is only in its initial phase. Civil society in Russia is growing steadily based more on social initiative "from below" than public action from above, and thus its development will be a slower and more evolutionary process. In short, Russia has to go some distance to diminish further the influence of its past as a closed society, but the country's progress through 1996 has been impressive, warranting its designation as an emerging democracy.

Russia's journey toward democratic development has gone through three phases. The first phase was the twilight period of the late Soviet Union, the time when Mikhail Gorbachev tried to reform and humanize the Soviet system. With the demise of the USSR in December 1991, Russia gained its independence and entered phase two, the First Post-Soviet Russian Republic. The First Republic came to an abrupt end during the autumn of 1993, and was followed by a brief interregnum. Then on the eve of 1994, Russia began its present phase of democratic development with the inception of the current Second Republic.

About the author. Robert Sharlet is Chauncey Winters Professor of Political Science at Union College in Schenectady, NY, and an associate at the Harriman Institute of Columbia University in New York City. During the period 1994–96, Dr. Sharlet served as senior coordinator of the Rule of Law Consortium in Washington, DC, working on the issue of legal reform in the former Soviet Union. He has published six books, including *Soviet Constitutional Crisis* (1992), and has written numerous articles and essays on Russia and the former Soviet Union. Dr. Sharlet has appeared on the *MacNeil/Lehrer NewsHour*, has been interviewed on Soviet radio, and is consulted regularly by leading newspapers and magazines.

The Twilight of the Soviet Union. In the early 1990s, Russia—or the Russian Soviet Federated Socialist Republic (RSFSR), as it then was known—was more committed to reform than the Soviet Union itself, of which the RSFSR still was a constituent part. The gap reflected the different political personas and ambitions of Gorbachev, then president of the USSR, and his Russian counterpart and arch rival, Boris Yeltsin. Yeltsin had been part of the leadership of the Communist Party of the Soviet Union during the early years of *perestroika* until the more cautious Gorbachev, then party leader, forced him out for his overzealousness toward reform.

© Novosti/Sipa

As leader of the USSR (1985–91), Mikhail Gorbachev sought to bring about "perestroika" (restructuring) and "glasnost" (openness) throughout Soviet society. His tenure ended and the Soviet Union fell in December 1991, beginning a new era in Russian history.

The two men became political enemies, and with Yeltsin's subsequent rise to head the pro-reform RSFSR leadership, Gorbachev faced a major challenger in his erstwhile party colleague. When the coup attempt of August 1991 nearly toppled Gorbachev, it was Yeltsin who faced down the plotters and politically rescued his rival. The event, however, only served to strengthen Yeltsin further while weakening Gorbachev fatally. In the end, a number of factors contributed to the collapse of the Soviet system several months later, but, more than anyone else, Yeltsin played a key role in bringing about the Soviet Union's downfall and, with it, the effective end of the political career of Mikhail Gorbachev.

"The greater openness he [Mikhail Gorbachev] has brought about in the Soviet society has also helped promote international trust."

Norwegian Nobel Committee names Mikhail Gorbachev winner of Nobel Peace Prize Oct. 15, 1990

Independent Russia emerged from the debris of the USSR with a mixed legacy. New institutions were in place, but they coexisted uneasily. Following the Soviet reform model, Russia had introduced nearly free elections that had produced a more representative parliament. Not surprisingly, though, given its authoritarian pedigree, the Russian parliament was dominated by conservative deputies. The institution of the presidency was added in 1991, and—in the first direct, popular election for head of state—Yeltsin won. Parliament and president then collaborated to create a constitutional court—the first of its kind in Russian history. The new Russian institutions, however, were forced to operate under a constitution derived from the Soviet period and so heavily amended since 1990 that it had become a patchwork of contradictions and ambiguities. As a consequence, in the final years of the USSR, Russia's separation-of-powers doctrine still was only a work in progress.

The First Post-Soviet Russian Republic. On Christmas Day 1991, Gorbachev resigned the presidency of the then defunct USSR, bringing to a close the Soviet period of Russian history while simultaneously launching Russia as a sovereign, independent republic. Although efforts to draft a new constitution continued from the previous period, Russia began its new era under its much revised, old Soviet-style constitution of 1978—a document that incompatibly mixed parliamentary supremacy with a strong, executive presidency. Thus, from early 1992, legacies of the immediate past and imperatives of the near future were set on a collision course within the short-lived First Republic.

The main areas of contention between President Yeltsin and the Russian parliament were economic reform, as well as the politics of drafting a constitution. Russia already had begun a modest program of market reforms in the Soviet period, but beginning in January 1992 the pace and depth of change accelerated rapidly. Yeltsin had surrounded himself with a group of "Young Turk" economists who were determined to banish socialism and bring Russia to capitalism as quickly as possible. Armed with a presidential decree, Yegor Gaidar, Yeltsin's chief economist, led the way by initially decontrolling nearly all fixed prices with the stroke of a pen. Problematically, the Russian economy still was dominated by Soviet-type monopoly producers, who now were free to set prices arbitrarily for their captive consumers. By spring, inflation was surging as Yeltsin's economic policies began to affect millions of citizens whose wages and pensions could not keep pace with soaring prices for items of everyday consumption.

The conservative parliament reacted, passing protectionist social legislation and demanding that Yeltsin slow the pace of economic reform. The president, a shrewd reader of the public mood, took steps to pacify public anger by bringing into his cabinet several former Soviet industrial executives, including Victor Chernomyrdin, head of the natural-gas monopoly. Nonetheless, the president still backed Acting Prime Minister Gaidar and his privatization chief Anatoly Chubais as they continued their push toward the market by launching the process of divesting the state of its monopoly ownership of property. The privatization of retail and wholesale businesses, especially in the area of consumer goods and services, quickly made headway, creating a new social class of private owners. Divestiture of medium and large industrial enterprises was slower to get under way.

Prices climbed higher, hyperinflation raged, and social pain intensified. Complicating the situation, privatization fell prey to haste, rigged outcomes, political corruption, and even organized crime. By the end of 1992, parliament was in a rebellious state, discussing the possible impeachment of Yeltsin. To placate his foes, Yeltsin sacrificed Gaidar, replacing him with the stolid Chernomyrdin as prime minister. Chernomyrdin's ascension was expected to signal the end of market reforms, but, to general surprise, he continued support for Chubais' ambitious privatization program, which pushed ahead rapidly in 1993. As a result, relations between president and parliament progressively worsened.

The other major conflictual issue, which eventually led to the abrupt end of the First Republic, was constitutional reform. The Constitutional Commission created by the Russian *perestroika*-era parliament in 1990 continued working on a new constitution during the First Republic. The drafting process was riven over whether Russia should be a presidential polity or a parliamentary republic. By spring 1993, an increasingly frustrated Yeltsin impaneled his own executive Constitutional Commission, which

© Filip Horvat/Saba

In August 1991, Soviet hard-liners staged a coup against President Gorbachev. The efforts of Boris Yeltsin, the future president of Russia, helped to prevent the takeover and continue—but only for a short time—Gorbachev's rule. During the uprising, statues of such Communist stalwarts as Feliks Dzerzhinsky, the founder of the Soviet political police (the KGB), were toppled (left).

was followed by Russia's first Constitutional Convention. These were designed to produce a draft more to the president's liking.

However, neither initiative yielded a widely supported draft constitution, and, by late summer, legislative-executive relations were approaching their nadir. After the parliamentary opposition prepared constitutional amendments scaling back the presidency, Yeltsin struck back by dissolving parliament. In the ensuing stalemate, diehard anti-Yeltsin deputies barricaded themselves in the parliament building. The First Republic then came to its tragic conclusion on Oct. 4, 1993, when, after an exchange of violence, the president's forces prevailed. A brief interregnum followed during which President Yeltsin pushed through a friendly draft constitution and presided over a constitutional referendum and elections for a new, redesigned parliament.

The Second Russian Republic. Russia's post-Soviet constitution was ratified by public referendum, and with its official publication on Christmas Eve 1993, the current Second Republic came into existence. In spite of gloomy forecasts that the "Yeltsin Constitution" would reinvoke authoritarian aspects of Russia's traditional political culture, the country has continued its passage from a controlled economy to a market society, as well as staying the course toward democratic development. Indeed, there have been lapses that would be unacceptable in a Western democracy, but independent Russia—especially its Sec-

In 1993 a debate over proposed constitutional changes led to a crisis in the new Russian republic. On October 4, troops loyal to Boris Yeltsin seized the Russian parliament building from parliamentarians who earlier had barricaded themselves in the building after voting to impeach the Russian president (photo, page 39)*. Violence and demonstrations, including the pro-Yeltsin one* below, *marked the upheaval that saw the president prevail. More than 125 persons were killed in the disturbance.*

© Jon Jones/Sygma

ond Republic—still are young by any historic measure. On the credit side, two well-organized, free elections have taken place since 1993; an imbalanced but more credible separation and balance of powers appears to be working; inflation, while not eliminated, has been reduced sharply; and a viable, multiparty system is emerging slowly.

The Second Republic's restructured parliament, a bicameral institution initially written off as constitutionally weak vis-à-vis the presidency, gradually has been developing into a stable legislative body. By the end of the first parliament's initial term of two years, a legislative subculture had begun to form; the two legislative houses—the State Duma and the Federation Council—were learning to work together; and the Federal Assembly as a whole was building a constructive relationship with the president. Given the legislators' general lack of experience, the first parliament's legislative output was fairly impressive. The second parliament, elected in 1995, has a mandate to sit for a full constitutional term of four years. Although at first caught up in the presidential-election campaign of 1996, the Federal Assembly, no doubt, will strive to continue past trends, including trying to further strengthen its position vis-à-vis the executive branch.

The Constitutional Court of the Second Republic, a restructured institution, was designed to avoid the unhappy experience of its predecessor in the First Republic. Caught in the middle of the bitter legislative-executive struggle, the first Constitutional

© Haviv/Saba

After becoming president of the new Russian Federation on June 12, 1991, Boris Yeltsin met various times with Western leaders, including U.S. President Bill Clinton in Moscow in May 1995, right. *Yeltsin sought to take full advantage of his experience on the international scene during his 1996 bid for a second term.*

© Alexander Zemlianichenko/AP/Wide World Photos

Court became politicized, stumbled badly, and fell victim to politics during the death throes of the First Republic. The successor court is larger, better organized, and more professionally led. Aside from one instance—a 1995 case in which the second Constitutional Court succumbed to political considerations and backed Yeltsin's decrees that led to the fighting in Chechnya—its decisions generally have reflected improvement over past performance, both qualitatively and quantitatively.

Another area of the emerging new Russian political system—federal relations—has been slower to respond to change. Historically, the Russian Empire and the Soviet Union functioned as unitary states. Consistent with democratic development, Yeltsin recognized that some devolution of authority from the center to the periphery was necessary. Thus far, President Yeltsin has taken this step through a series of ad hoc bilateral power- and revenue-sharing treaties with individual republics and certain regions of the Russian Federation. The process goes on, with the gubernatorial elections of 1996 likely to increase its momentum.

The 1996 Presidential Election. In Russia's journey as an emerging democracy, the first post-Soviet presidential election of 1996 was a significant milestone. Among the large field of candidates, only two were given any chance of success—Gennadi Zyuganov, the communist-nationalist candidate, and the incumbent, Boris Yeltsin. At the start of the campaign in early 1996, Zyuganov led with Yeltsin far back in the pack. As president, candidate Yeltsin bore heavy burdens for policies both successful and failed. Although economic reform largely had succeeded in moving Russia toward a market economy, its success rested on the backs of the multitude left behind. Conversely, Yeltsin's policy of force against the rebellious Chechen Republic, launched in December 1994, had cost more than 30,000 lives in little more than a year (later estimates rose to 80,000), and generally was deemed a failure. Given these political liabilities, even some of Yeltsin's closest advisers believed he could not win reelection.

© Laski/Diffusion/Liaison

Campaigning Russian Style: *Running for a second term as president, Boris Yeltsin appealed for the youth vote by dancing the twist during a rock concert in Rostov. Continued national stability was the campaign theme of the 65-year-old incumbent. Gennadi Zyuganov,* right, *51-year-old leader of the Communist Party in Russia, promised to roll back the "mistakes of market reform and restore state control of the economy." He posed the greatest challenge to Yeltsin's reelection effort. Alexander Lebed,* bottom, *a 46-year-old retired general who had seen service in Afghanistan, ran as a patriot who would restore law and order throughout Russia. He threw his support to Yeltsin in the July runoff, ensuring the president a second term.*

© Wojtek Laski/Gamma-Liaison

© Peter Blakely/Saba

© Gleb Garanich/Reuters/Archive Photos

A total of 75,744,244 votes were cast by about 70% of the electorate in the first round of voting on June 16. Turnout was estimated at 67% in the July 3 runoff. International observers judged the voting to be fair and free.

Yeltsin himself, always a battler, was more sanguine about his chances. Setting in motion what was to become a remarkable comeback, Yeltsin's campaign strategy included focusing exclusively on the front-runner, Zyuganov; maximizing the advantages of his own incumbency; preempting criticism of issues on which his administration was vulnerable; and co-opting certain key communist-nationalist issues.

Relentlessly defining Yeltsin as the leader of Russia's anticommunist future, the president's campaign rhetoric consistently relegated Zyuganov to the discredited Soviet past. As the incumbent, Yeltsin the candidate made the most of the pomp and circumstance of office—including state visits—and, in the process, dominated the media. Preempting Zyuganov on the hot-button issue of arrearages, President Yeltsin publicly scapegoated—and, in some cases, dismissed—senior government officials for unpaid salaries, wages, and pensions. Going on the offensive, candidate Yeltsin in his presidential capacity co-opted a core communist-nationalist issue, political nostalgia or the "Back to the USSR" theme, by signing an "Integration Agreement" with three other newly independent states—Kazakhstan, Kyrgyzstan, and Belarus—and a largely symbolic but highly visible unification accord with Belarus.

The one liability Yeltsin could not overcome easily, however, was the Chechen crisis. At best, he was only able to mute the issue temporarily by theatrically signing a peace agreement with the Chechen rebel leader on election eve. Yeltsin's campaign strategy was working, and his poll numbers were rising as Zyuganov's plateaued. In the final drive up to the first round of voting on June 16, 1996, Yeltsin's superior campaign skills as

© Sygma

U.S. Vice-President Al Gore (center) *held a postelection meeting with President Yeltsin and Prime Minister Viktor Chernomyrdin* (extreme right) *in Russia. When the president abruptly canceled his first scheduled talks with the U.S. vice-president, new speculation arose concerning Yeltsin's health.*

© David Brauchli/AP/Wide World Photos

Boris Yeltsin was inaugurated for a second presidential term in a 16-minute ceremony before 3,000 invited guests in Moscow's State Kremlin Palace on August 9. It later was revealed that Yeltsin was suffering from serious heart disease.

well as his common touch were additional assets compared with Zyuganov's doctrinaire style and wooden manner. Yeltsin and Zyuganov finished first and second in the voting—35.28% to 32.04%—qualifying them for the runoff election. The surprise third-place finisher was retired Gen. Alexander Lebed, the law-and-order candidate, who had been supported surreptitiously by the Yeltsin campaign to draw votes away from Zyuganov. In the interval before the July 3 runoff, Yeltsin gained Lebed's endorsement and went on to beat Zyuganov by the ample margin of 53.7% to 40.4% for reelection as president of Russia.

Although aspects of the election fell short of Western standards, the process generally was judged fair by participants as well as international observers, lending further credibility to Russia's aspiration to become a democratic society. However, after the election, the Chechen crisis reignited, pushing the issue of war and peace, along with Yeltsin's failing health, to the fore of Russian politics for the near future.

For a summary of postelection and other developments of 1996 in Russia, *see* article in Alphabetical Section, beginning on page 441.

© Kasyan Bartlett/Woodfin Camp & Assoc.

HONG KONG

A Time of Dramatic Change

By David Chuenyan Lai

The British colony of Hong Kong, known for its deep port, dense population, and dynamic economy, would revert to Chinese sovereignty at midnight on June 30, 1997. The Chinese have promised to respect Hong Kong's existing economic and social systems.

The year 1997 will be a historically significant one for Hong Kong: The vestige of British colonialism on China's territory will be removed; the British rule of Hong Kong will end; and a Special Administrative Region (SAR) under Chinese sovereignty is to be born at midnight on June 30. Following China's "one country, two systems" policy, Hong Kong, as an SAR, will enjoy socioeconomic autonomy with some political control.

As the transfer of sovereignty neared, the world was watching to see if the handover would be smooth and peaceful, if China truly would be committed to the two systems, and if the SAR would work.

The British Colony. The Colony of Hong Kong is made up of Hong Kong Island, Kowloon Peninsula, and the New Territories. Hong Kong Island and Kowloon Peninsula were ceded to Britain in 1842 and 1860, respectively. The New Territories, which includes the mainland extending northward from Kowloon Peninsula to Shenzhen River and 235 adjacent islands, was leased to Britain in 1898 for 99 years. The colony is situated on the coast of South China, about 90 mi (145 km) from Guangzhou (Canton), the capital of Guangdong province. Hong Kong is hilly and rugged, with mountain slopes that run close to the coast. Its severely weathered and decomposed granitic rocks can be excavated easily for rock fill used in reclaiming land from the sea—an important factor in the territory's development. Hong Kong has a total land area of about 380 sq mi (990 km^2), which is increasing constantly as new land for housing and industry is reclaimed from the sea.

Hong Kong's excellent deep harbor, free-port status, and nodal position on the South China coast favored its development after the mid-19th century as a commercial center and transshipment seaport. Before World War II, more than 40% of its export trade and 30% of its import trade were with China. Most of its exports were reexports of entrepôt goods rather than locally manufactured products.

Hong Kong was occupied by the Japanese between 1941 and 1945 and its population dropped to about 600,000 by August 1945. Between the Japanese surrender in 1945 and the establishment of the People's Republic of China in 1949, more than 2 million people came to Hong Kong from Guangdong province, Shanghai, and other commercial centers. Since 1949, Hong Kong's population has continued to increase; it totaled 6.4 mil-

About the author. David Chuenyan Lai is a professor of geography at the University of Victoria, Victoria, BC. Since 1970 he has spent every summer in Hong Kong, doing research on the colony and on China in general. Dr. Lai has written extensively on Hong Kong and is coauthor of *The Small Industrial Unit in Hong Kong: Patterns and Policies*. Born in Canton (Guangzhou), China, he was educated at the University of Hong Kong and the London School of Economics and Political Science.

Map designed by Joe LeMonnier

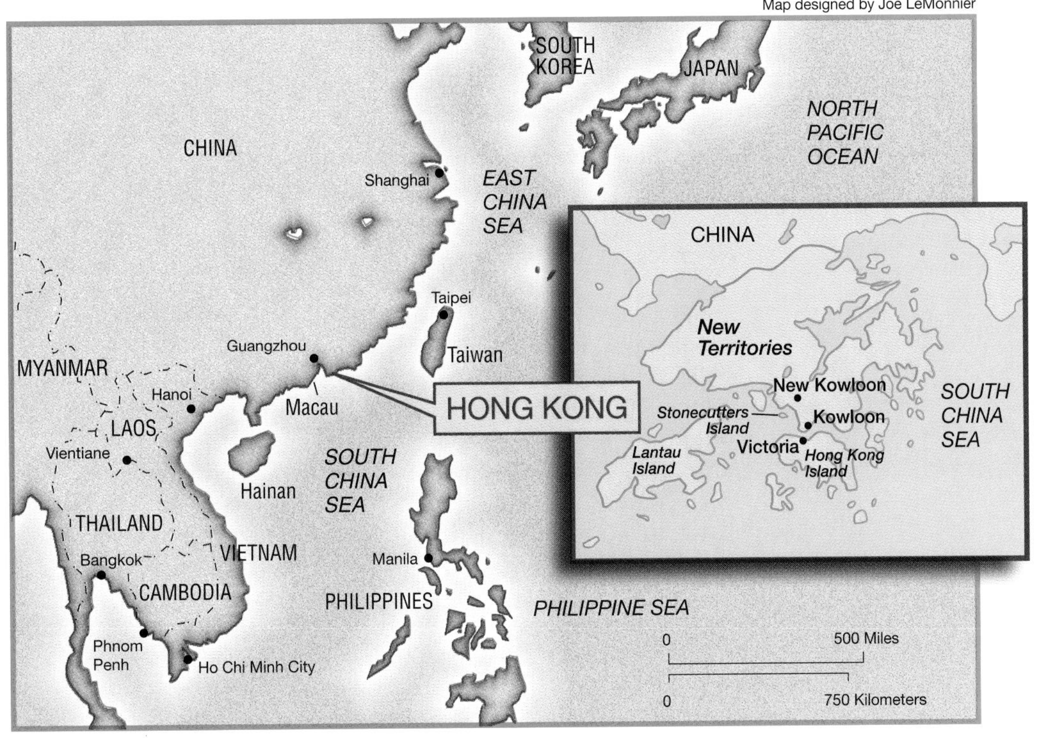

lion in mid-1996. Although Hong Kong had meager natural resources and few suitable sites for industry, the territory was developed into one of the fastest-growing industrial centers in Asia. Domestic manufactures dominated its export trade. Subsequently, as international banking and related services assumed increasing importance in the economy, Hong Kong became a leading world financial center.

"The world's largest communist country is setting out to maintain probably the most lively, dynamic, most successful capitalist community."

Sir Geoffrey Howe
Foreign Secretary of Great Britain
September 1984

Soon after China adopted an open-door economic policy in 1979, the colony's economic and transportation ties with China were restored. Direct passenger-train service between Hong Kong and Guangzhou, which ceased for 30 years, was resumed and regular air, hovercraft, and container transportation between the two locales was introduced in 1979. During the 1980s and early 1990s, many Sino–Hong Kong joint ventures were signed. Hong Kong manufacturers relocated their factories or set up branches in Guangdong province to take advantage of lower labor costs and cheaper factory sites. Hong Kong provided 80% of the total foreign investment in China between 1979 and 1985, and contributed half of China's $40 billion foreign investment in 1995.

The monetary system of Hong Kong also has been integrated increasingly with that of China. In 1993 about 30% of Hong Kong's banknotes were circulating in China, and the People's Republic's currency was accepted increasingly in Hong Kong. Throughout the 1990s several Chinese companies with links to various Chinese ministries and departments purchased Hong Kong firms and took over control of some public utilities. In April 1996, for example, the British-controlled Swire Pacific agreed to sell off its shares of two Hong Kong–based airlines—25% of Cathay Pacific and 36% of Dragonair—to Chinese companies for $936 million in order to ensure that Beijing would not seek to set up rival carriers in the SAR. A new railway, which runs through nine provinces and municipalities in China to provide an unbroken north-south link from Beijing to Kowloon, came into service in September 1996. The economic ties of Hong Kong with the Pearl River delta in South China have been increasingly stronger, and augur prosperity for both China and the SAR.

Political Changes. In October 1982, Britain and China began discussions on the return of the New Territories to Chinese sovereignty. After two years of difficult negotiations, the Sino-British Joint Declaration—by which Britain agreed to return all the ceded land and the New Territories to China—was signed on Dec. 19, 1984. In return, China promised that Hong Kong would be a self-governing SAR and that its lifestyle and socioeconomic system would remain unchanged for 50 years after 1997. Then the Basic Law, the constitution of the SAR, was written and approved by Britain and China in 1990.

In the past, Hong Kong had limited autonomy. Its highest lawmaking body, the Legislative Council (Legco), consisted of the governor and his appointed members and officials. In September 1985 an indirect election to the 57-member Legco was introduced for the first time; 24 Legco members were elected by "functional constituencies"—such as industrial, commercial,

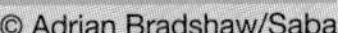
© Adrian Bradshaw/Saba

© Frank Fournier/Woodfin Camp & Assoc.

Manufacturing has accounted for about 17% of Hong Kong's gross domestic product. The colony has been a shopper's mecca for some time, above. *The Stock Exchange of Hong Kong Ltd.,* left, *formed from four existing exchanges, opened in April 1986. It has become one of the world's most active stock markets. Under British rule, Hong Kong has been a free port and one of the world's largest traders. Goods from China and elsewhere are reexported from Hong Kong,* bottom. *China and the United States have been Hong Kong's principal trading partners.*

© J. Greenberg/The Image Works

© Superstock

Tourism remains one of Hong Kong's major industries; more than 10 million visitors arrived in the colony in 1995. Repulse Bay, above, *is known for its picturesque beach, mild climate, and a variety of hotels, shops, and restaurants.*

educational, and labor—and by an "electoral college" that was made up of urban councils and district boards. In September 1991 the Legco was expanded from 57 to 60 seats; 18 seats were to be chosen by universal suffrage. Political groups were organized to run for these directly elected seats, marking the first direct election for Legco seats in the history of Hong Kong. The pro-democracy political groups won 15 of the 18 seats in the 1991 Legco election. In 1992, Gov. Christopher Patten proposed political reforms as a result of which the 1995 Legco would include 20 members elected by popular vote, 30 members by "functional constituencies," and ten members by an "electoral college." The Democratic Party and its allies dominated the 1995 Legco election, taking 24 of the 60 seats. China claimed that Patten's reforms did not conform with the Joint Declaration and that, therefore, the 1995 Legco would be replaced by a provisional legislature on July 1, 1997.

In December 1995, China approved the Preparatory Committee (PC) that would oversee Hong Kong's reversion to Chinese sovereignty. The PC's 150 members—94 from Hong Kong and 56 from China—were installed during a ceremony in China in January 1996. The PC was empowered to elect the SAR's first chief executive, form a provisional legislature, organize the reunification celebrations, and deal with other transitional issues. In April the Hong Kong government received from the PC ten requests regarding such issues as security and travel arrangements for PC members, information on government departments, and airtime on the government-owned Radio Television Hong Kong. The Hong Kong government acceded to all but two of the requests—rejecting the call for a venue for the provisional legislature and wanting "further clarification" regarding the request of airtime on radio and TV.

In August the PC announced that a 400-member Selection Committee would be set up on September 15 to choose the chief executive. The public was invited to make nominations; more than 4,000 nomination forms were issued. The chief executive was scheduled to be appointed by November.

Fears and Uncertainties. Between 1980 and 1989, some 260,000 Hong Kong residents emigrated to Canada, the United States, and other countries. After the suppression of the pro-democracy demonstrations in Beijing's Tiananmen Square by the Chinese military in 1989, more Hong Kongers decided to leave; within the following two years, some 130,000 people emigrated. Having lived abroad and obtained a foreign passport or established their "landed" immigrant status, many of these emigrants have returned to Hong Kong. A large number of so-called "astronauts" have left their families in a foreign country to ensure eventual citizenship while they maintain their jobs or businesses in Hong Kong. These people were worried that Hong Kong may not be free and stable after China's takeover. In case China does not live up to its promises, they will be able to depart Hong Kong and live elsewhere. Many concerned citizens also have deep-seated fears that there may be an influx of people from China to Hong Kong and that, in turn, China's corruption and other malpractices may spread to the region.

"It's understandable that senior Chinese officials, given their backgrounds, find it difficult understanding the nature of a free society, what makes Hong Kong tick. They require a bit of assistance in learning about Hong Kong. They haven't always gotten the assistance they deserve from their appointed advisers in Hong Kong, who have believed that they should go and tell Chinese officials what they think Chinese officials want to hear."

Christopher Patten
Governor of Hong Kong
June 1996

Although several important transitional issues had been resolved by late 1996, many uncertainties regarding Hong Kong's return to Chinese rule remained. It still was not certain whether former Hong Kong residents living abroad or returning emigrants holding foreign passports could retain the right of abode in Hong Kong. China—ever suspicious of British intentions—worried that large infrastructure projects might take away Hong Kong's reserve funds. It repeatedly declared that expensive contracts, extending beyond the handover date, required its prior approval—otherwise it might not honor them after the takeover. Hence, large projects, such as the $10 billion Western Corridor Railway, might not be implemented. There also was uncertainty on how China or the SAR government would deal with the consulates of countries that have diplomatic relationships with Taiwan.

The degree to which Beijing would tolerate political freedom also was unclear. For example, would the SAR government permit the annual Tiananmen commemoration march, or would the Hong Kong Alliance in Support of the Patriotic Democratic Movement in China, branded counterrevolutionary by Beijing, be outlawed after the handover? Chinese officials had said that although media criticism was permitted, anti-China activities—such as advocating independence for Taiwan or Tibet—would

© AP/Wide World Photos

not be tolerated. Freedom of the press would be regulated by new SAR laws, but most critics expressed concern regarding how these laws would be interpreted.

The Outlook. Hong Kong SAR will continue to prosper as a regional business hub in Asia because of its strategic location as the gateway to China. Such a confidence is shown in part by heavy purchases of commercial properties in Hong Kong by Singaporean and Indonesian developers throughout the first half of 1996. Many businesspeople who have invested heavily in Hong Kong and China are optimistic about the future of the SAR because they feel that China will try to maintain its prosperity and stability and use it as a model for the reunification of Macau in 1999 and Taiwan in the near future. China definitely will try to oversee a smooth transition from colonial to Communist rule. Its major concerns probably are the defiance of pro-democracy and human-right activists, and

During a March 1996 stop in Hong Kong, British Prime Minister John Major (above, center) *conferred with Gov. Christopher Patten* (left). *The British leader promised visa-free entry to Britain for Hong Kong passport holders after June 1997 and said that Britain would "pursue any legal challenge or other avenues available" if the Chinese reneged on the Sino-British Joint Declaration of December 1984. On June 30, 1996—exactly one year prior to Hong Kong's transfer to China—demonstrators marched in support of and against* (right) *the diplomatic action.*

© Vincent Yu/AP/Wide World Photos

foreign governments' support of their protests and demonstrations, which may cause instability in the SAR.

China will continue to assure the world that Hong Kong will remain unchanged for 50 years. Many Hong Kongers who have or have not secured foreign passports or right of abode in foreign countries will remain in Hong Kong and wait to see what changes occur before they make a move. Therefore, the SAR's prosperity and people's confidence depend very much on the efforts of Chinese leaders to make the "one country, two systems" policy work.

The Ongoing War Against Cancer

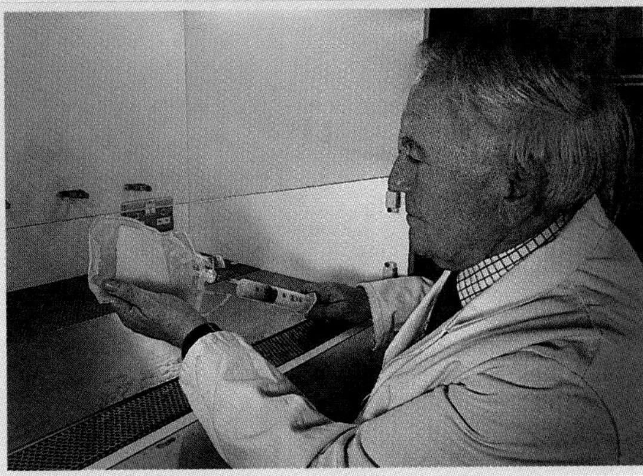

© Simon Fraser/Department of Hematology, RVI, Newcastle/Science Photo Library/ Photo Researchers

By Fran Pollner

"Cancer genes" are becoming household words. They strike fear and hope into the hearts of family members—fear that they might carry such genes; hope that if a genetic cause is identified, then a genetic cure can be achieved.

Cancer genetics is galvanizing the cancer-research community. The hereditary gene mutations that predispose family members to certain cancers are not different from the genetic mutations that occur as a result of environmental assaults and that underlie the development of cancer in the general population. Cancer genetics is a concept that applies to *all* cancer, and it has been making news in recent years. But cancer, perhaps more than most other diseases, always has been in the news.

Roads to Reality. Cancer is not one but a multitude of diseases of cells gone awry, cells whose growth patterns and behavior no longer are controlled by the body's normal regulatory mechanisms. These patterns are influenced by the location of the cancer, the environmental and genetic triggers of the deranged growth, and the physiologic and genetic makeup of the individual in whom the cancer is growing.

As a society, the public's response to cancer has been dramatic and emotional. Before the National Cancer Institute (NCI) was established in 1937—and even for decades afterward—cancer was a whispered word, a loathsome and frightening affliction that not only shortened human life but also tainted it with stigma.

A story told by a physician at a medical conference captures how some professionals used to approach cancer in what they believed to be an astute and compassionate manner. One of the first lessons this physician learned during his residency in the 1950s at a hospital for "cancer and allied diseases" was that every patient was there for an "allied disease." Common wisdom was that it was better for the patient not to know the truth. The public and medical community have come a long way since then. They still have a way to go; but the road is better illumi-

About the author. This article was written by Fran Pollner with the assistance of the Office of Cancer Communications of the National Cancer Institute. Ms. Pollner is a medical writer who has written extensively on cancer and other diseases. She currently is managing editor of *The NIH Catalyst*, a publication of the intramural research program of the National Institutes of Health.

Courtesy, National Cancer Institute

In a White House ceremony on Dec. 23, 1971, President Richard M. Nixon signed the National Cancer Act to expand the fight against cancer. The legislation's provisions included the appropriation of $1.6 billion, primarily for research, during a three-year period and the establishment of 15 cancer centers, where patients would be treated in conjunction with research.

nated now. Physicians and patients today have a lot more than denial to bring to bear against cancer.

The journey into the light well may have begun with the passage of the 1971 National Cancer Act. That act launched the United States' "war on cancer," marshaling more resources for cancer research, creating the National Cancer Program, and providing the director of the National Cancer Institute with a direct line for transporting the yearly cancer-research budget request to the president. What the National Cancer Act signified was not that science had identified the route to cancer eradication—in fact, there was a good deal of dissension among cancer clinicians and researchers at the time—but that the national response to cancer had evolved from simple dread to a collective will to face this enemy, dissect it, and overcome it. Since that time, cancer research has been carried out under the spotlight of national commitment and has made enormous strides.

Few medical questions have so challenged the scientific community—and been so popular a subject for newspaper headlines—as the question of what causes cancer. Throughout the decades of the second half of the 20th century, the emphasis has shifted among chemicals, viruses, and individual genetic legacy as the predominant cause of cancer. Each retains its position as a factor in cancer requiring research into prevention and treatment. But scientists recently have come to realize that changes in genes that regulate cell growth underlie the development of cancer, whether those changes are generated by inherited gene mutations that predispose one to cancer or are provoked by chemical or viral assault.

Carcinogens, or cancer-causing agents, have been found literally everywhere—in the soil that grows food, the air, sunlight, workplace chemicals, even in anticancer medications and radiation therapies. The body's own hormones have been implicated as factors in the growth of some cancers, such as estrogen and breast cancer. Some viruses have been found to cause not only the infectious diseases they are known for but cancers as well—such as hepatitis B virus and liver cancer or papilloma virus and cervical cancer. It sometimes has seemed that virtually everything can cause cancer, that there is no escape from it. But prevention is a marvelous thing, and some cancers are preventable. Modern methods of food refrigeration, a technological rather than medical advance, per se, can be thanked in good part for the decline in stomach-cancer incidence in the United States. That diet influences cancer risk is a hypothesis being tested now in many human diet studies focusing variously on fat and fiber content, the amount of fruits and vegetables, and the levels of particular nutrients in one's daily diet in relation to specific cancers or cancer in general.

In the public-health arena, the decline in cervical-cancer-death rates is largely attributable to cervical-cancer screening, which can detect cervical-cell changes before they fulfill their malignant potential. Hepatitis B–related liver cancer can be prevented by hepatitis B vaccine. And nearly all cases of lung cancer never would occur if people did not smoke. Yet lung-cancer-death rates tower above all others and have been soaring in women—a consequence of the phenomenon of women's securing the right to smoke cigarettes in public and to become addicted to what women's-health activists have designated an equal-opportunity killer.

In November 1996 the NCI announced that the overall cancer-death rate in the United States fell almost 3% between 1991 and 1995. The decline marked the first sustained decrease in the rate since national record-keeping began in the 1930s. Said NCI director Dr. Richard Klausner, "The 1990s will be remembered as the decade when we measurably turned the tide against cancer." Although the lung-cancer-death rate among women has risen, death rates for many other kinds of cancer have declined in people under the age of 65 and most especially in children, whose five-year survival rates for all childhood cancers have moved from less than 30% in the 1960s to nearly 70% in the mid-1990s. And dramatic drops in death rates among people of all ages have been achieved in Hodgkin's disease (a cancer of the lymphatic system) and cancers of the testis, cervix, uterus, stomach, bladder, colon, rectum, oral cavity, pharynx, and thyroid gland.

Dr. Richard Klausner, 45, became director of the National Cancer Institute in 1995. The cell biologist had served earlier as a researcher and medical official in the National Institutes of Health.

The sadder statistics are that older people continue to sustain rising cancer-death rates and that more than two in every five people will develop cancer at some point in their lives; half of those who do—or one fifth of the population—will die of that cancer. Even within these grim numbers, however, are points of progress. The quality and length of life following cancer treatment have improved for many patients, the result of earlier diagnosis, less drastic surgery, more effective chemotherapeutic regimens, the harnessing and enhancing of the body's immune defenses, and better pain control. Scientists and the medical profession are seeking ways of achieving earlier and more accurate cancer diagnosis. One is the use of more sophisticated imaging methods, such as magnetic resonance imaging (now being tested as a screening and diagnostic tool in many cancers, including breast cancer in younger women with denser breast tissue). Another is blood tests to detect proteins secreted by incipient cancers before they likely would be discovered otherwise, such as prostate-specific antigen in the case of prostate cancer.

Moreover, the discoveries of the early 1990s are revolutionizing the way the experts think about cancer. Scientists are at the threshold of fighting cancer on its own turf, at the cellular level, guided into this theater by sequential insights into the mechanisms of cancer genetics. They are learning how genetic abnormalities, either hereditary or acquired, can derail normal cellular growth and differentiation. These genetic mutations in essence throw a cellular switch, either turning on abnormal growth through mutant genes called oncogenes or turning off normal controls through the mutation of genes that normally function as tumor suppressors. In their normal, nonmutated versions, these genes ensure that cells divide and grow normally, repair genetic damage cells may sustain, and preside over necessary cell death. When these genes are mutant or missing, growth becomes deranged and cell structure and function diverge from the norm; cells that normally would be programmed to die persist, divide rapidly, and overtake normal cells.

This knowledge opens up research opportunities—inconceivable a few years ago—aimed at detecting and blocking these cellular genetic changes before the cancer has run amok. It offers the glimmering of a hope of engineering a means for the body to guard the switch against whatever force might throw it in reverse.

(Continued on page 60.)

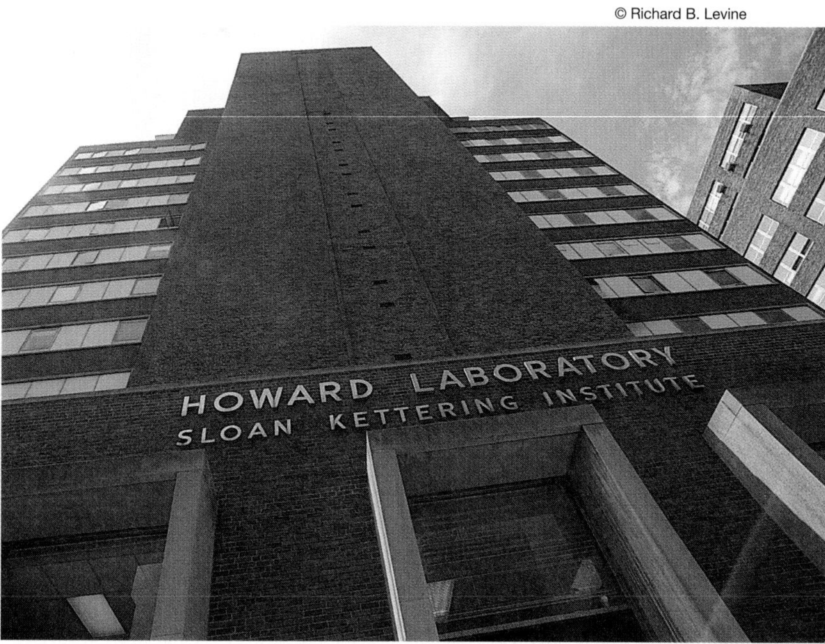

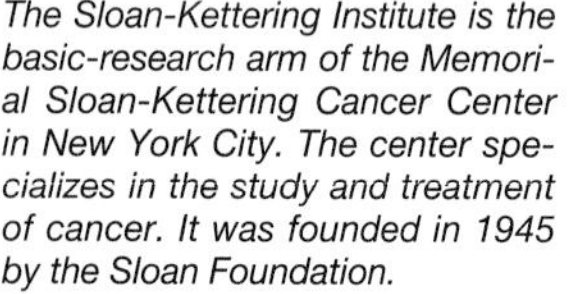
The Sloan-Kettering Institute is the basic-research arm of the Memorial Sloan-Kettering Cancer Center in New York City. The center specializes in the study and treatment of cancer. It was founded in 1945 by the Sloan Foundation.

Six Major Cancers

Breast Cancer

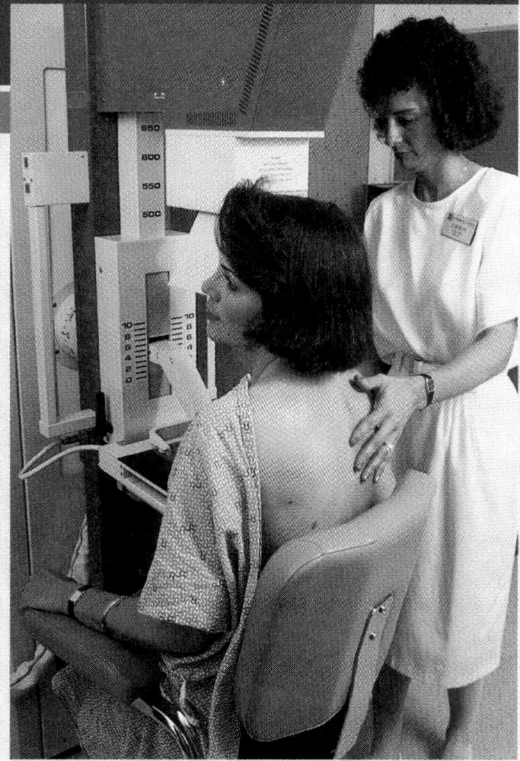

© Blair Seitz/Photo Researchers

A mammogram—a special type of X ray with very low levels of radiation—is the most prevalent technique for detecting breast cancer. It is not completely foolproof, however.

About one in eight women in the United States will develop breast cancer during her lifetime. In 1996 an estimated 184,300 new cases of the disease were diagnosed in women, and approximately 44,300 women died from the disease. Men, too, can get breast cancer; about 1,400 new cases and about 260 deaths were expected to occur in men in 1996.

Major risk factors include a personal or family history of breast cancer, a personal history of certain benign breast diseases, early onset of menstruation, late menopause, and never having children or giving birth for the first time after age 30. Other factors that may increase risk include estrogen-replacement therapy, the use of oral contraceptives, high dietary fat intake, smoking, alcohol consumption, physical inactivity, and exposure to certain chemicals in the environment.

Early detection is critical. All women should perform monthly self-screenings for lumps in their breasts. Because the risk of breast cancer increases with age, women age 50 and older should have a mammogram annually; some experts recommend that women ages 40 to 49 have a mammogram every one to two years. Mammograms can detect tumors when they still are tiny—that is, too small to feel—and thus less likely to have spread.

Suspicious lumps are biopsied for a definitive diagnosis. There are two surgical options: a lumpectomy—the removal of the tumor and some surrounding tissue; or a mastectomy—the removal of the entire breast. Survival rates are equivalent. In either case, surgery may be followed by radiation therapy, chemotherapy, or hormone-blocking therapy.

A variety of potential treatments, including the use of substances that boost the immune system's response to tumors, were being investigated in 1996. A ten-year study was testing the ability of the drug tamoxifen to prevent breast cancer in healthy women; studies of breast-cancer patients already have shown that tamoxifen significantly reduced the incidence of new tumors. The discovery that inherited mutations in the BRCA1 and BRCA2 genes increase breast-cancer risk has spurred the development of blood tests to identify these mutations in women with a family history of the disease. And a study of mice with human breast-cancer tumors found that injections of a normal version of the BRCA1 gene eliminated tumors in some of the mice and extended the lives of others.

Breast-cancer-mortality rates declined in the early 1990s, probably as a result of early detection plus improvements in treatment. The five-year survival rate for localized breast cancer is 96%. If the cancer has spread to adjacent lymph nodes, the rate is 75%. If it has spread to other parts of the body, the survival rate is only 20%.

Colorectal Cancer

The incidence of cancer of the colon (large intestine) and rectum varies widely throughout the world, with the highest rates seen in highly developed, urbanized countries of North America and Western Europe and the lowest rates seen in the poorer, rural nations of Africa and Asia. In 1996 colorectal cancer was diagnosed in an estimated 133,500 patients in the United States, and caused an estimated 54,900 deaths.

Flawed genes are believed to contribute to many cases of colorectal cancer. The failure of the p53 gene has been linked to cancer in the left part of the colon, whereas the RII gene has been associated with cancer in the right part of the colon. People with a history of ulcerative colitis or other inflammatory bowel diseases have a heightened risk of developing colorectal cancer. A growing body of evidence suggests that diet plays a significant role in colorectal cancer. Diets high in fat appear to increase risk, whereas high-fiber diets have been associated with reduced risk. Physical inactivity also may increase risk.

Research suggests that estrogen-replacement therapy after menopause may reduce women's risk of colorectal cancer significantly. Other research indicates that aspirin, ibuprofen, and other nonsteroidal anti-inflammatory drugs also may inhibit the development of colorectal cancer; one study concluded that taking an aspirin tablet every other day for 20 years could cut a person's risk nearly in half.

Symptoms that may indicate colorectal cancer include rectal bleeding, blood in the stool, and a change in bowel habits. One study found that people who had annual tests for blood in their stools had 33% fewer deaths from colorectal cancer than people who did not have such tests. Because many patients may be asymptomatic and because catching colorectal cancer in its earliest stages significantly reduces the risk of death, it is recommended that, starting at age 40, people should have an annual digital rectal exam. People over age 50 also should have a yearly fecal blood test; every three to five years they should have a sigmoidoscopy, in which the colon is examined with a flexible, lighted tube.

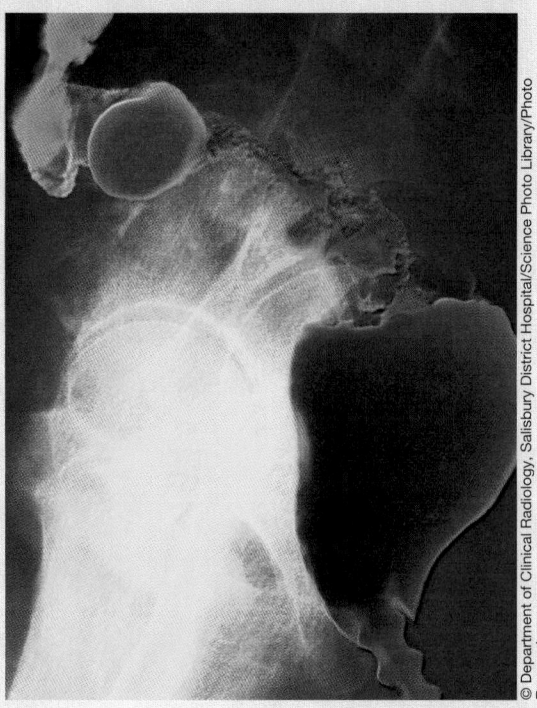

© Department of Clinical Radiology, Salisbury District Hospital/Science Photo Library/Photo Researchers

When medical exams indicate the possibility of colorectal cancer, more extensive studies—including detailed X rays—are required. The X ray of the human pelvis (above) *reveals cancer of the rectum* (green-colored area).

Surgery, sometimes combined with radiation or chemotherapy, is the treatment of choice for colorectal cancer. The five-year survival rate is 61%. However, if the cancer is detected in an early, localized stage, the five-year survival rate increases to 91%.

Leukemia

A malignant disease of the blood, leukemia claimed an estimated 21,000 lives in the United States in 1996. There are two major types of leukemia—acute and chronic—and these are subdivided further according to the cell type involved (lymphocytic, granulocytic, hairy-cell, and other). Cause, treatment, and prognosis vary depending on which cells are affected. There also are significant age variations. Acute leukemia can be seen at all ages; it accounts for almost all leukemia in children and young adults, and for less than half in older adults. Chronic leukemia is almost exclusively

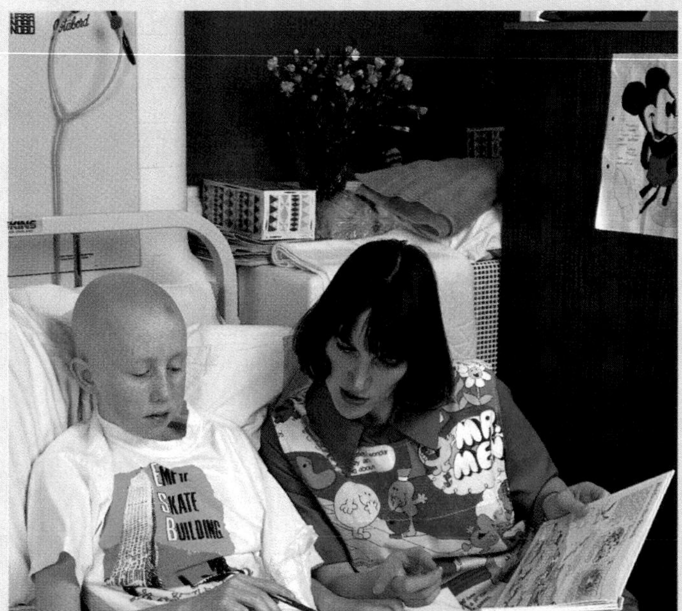

© Simon Fraser/Royal Victoria Infirmary, Newcastle/Science Photo LIbrary/Photo Researchers

Chemotherapy, which frequently results in a loss of hair, is the most common treatment for acute leukemia, which accounts for almost all leukemia in children and young adults.

a disease of adulthood, with the most common forms—chronic lymphocytic and chronic myelogenous leukemia—striking primarily in middle age or later.

Leukemia appears to be caused by a variety of factors that act alone or in combination. These factors include genetic traits, the retrovirus HTLV-1, and environmental factors such as exposure to ionizing radiation and certain chemicals.

Early symptoms resemble those of many other conditions: fatigue, weakness, pallor, weight loss, easy bruising, repeated or persistent infections, and pain in the joints or bones. Diagnosis involves blood tests and bone-marrow biopsy. Chemotherapy is the treatment of choice to counter the disease, with antibiotics, blood transfusions, and bone-marrow transplants used as supporting therapy.

The five-year survival rate for all types of leukemia is 40%, a significant increase since 1950, when it was 10%. The most dramatic improvement has occurred among patients with acute lymphocytic leukemia: The five-year survival rate jumped from 0% in 1950, when no treatment was available, to 56% by the late 1980s, after the variety of treatments mentioned above had been introduced and refined. The improvement in the survival rate was even more encouraging among children between the ages of 0 and 14 years.

Lung Cancer

Each year more than 170,000 people in the United States are diagnosed as having lung cancer. At one time, the disease was much more prevalent among men, but in recent years the incidence rate in women has increased markedly. Today, lung cancer is the leading cause of cancer deaths for both sexes. An estimated 158,700 Americans died from the disease in 1996.

Cigarette smoking and the use of other tobacco products are the primary causes of lung cancer, and are estimated to be responsible for 87% of lung cancers. In fact, the findings of a study published in October 1996 revealed the strongest direct link to date between smoking and lung cancer. A team of researchers reported that a chemical found in cigarette smoke has been discovered to lead to genetic damage in lung cells that is identical to the damage seen in malignant tumors of the lung. Other risk factors include exposure to environmental tobacco smoke, carcinogens such as asbestos, and high levels of radon.

Major symptoms include a constant cough, chest pain, shortness of breath, repeated bouts of pneumonia or bronchitis, and hoarseness. A diagnosis of lung cancer is confirmed with chest X rays, CAT scans, and a biopsy of lung cells. Symptoms of lung cancer often do not appear until the disease is well advanced and has moved beyond the lungs. Thus, the physician must determine the cancer's stage—that is, whether it has spread and, if so, which body parts are affected.

Treatment depends on the type of lung cancer, the size and location of tumors, and the stage of the disease. Surgery, radiation therapy, and chemotherapy are the usual options. Surgery is performed if the cancer is localized and the physician believes that all the cancer cells can be removed. Radiation therapy and chemotherapy often are used in combination to kill cancer cells.

A study reported in 1996 found that using this two-pronged therapy instead of only radiation increased the number of lung-cancer patients who lived at least five years following treatment from 6% to 17%.

New treatment methods being evaluated in 1996 included gene therapy, in which patients' tumors are injected with normal copies of the p53 gene, which is missing or defective in tumor cells. The first study on this method, published in 1996, showed that the procedure can shrink or stop the growth of some tumors.

If lung cancer is detected while still localized, the five-year survival rate is 47%. However, only 15% of lung cancers are discovered that early, and the five-year survival rate for all stages of the disease combined is only 13%.

Prostate Cancer

The incidence of prostate cancer has increased rapidly in recent years—from about 85,000 cases in 1985 to an estimated 317,000 in 1996. The number of deaths from the disease also has been on the rise—from some 30,000 in 1988 to an estimated 43,400 in 1996. Perhaps because of this "epidemic," prostate cancer no longer is a taboo subject. Various celebrities have acknowledged their battles with the disease, and it has received increasing publicity. Gen. Norman Schwarzkopf of Persian Gulf–war fame, a prostate-cancer patient, served as chairman of Prostate Cancer Awareness Week in 1996, and the publisher and novelist Michael Korda wrote *Man to Man: Surviving Prostate Cancer* to encourage discussion of the disease.

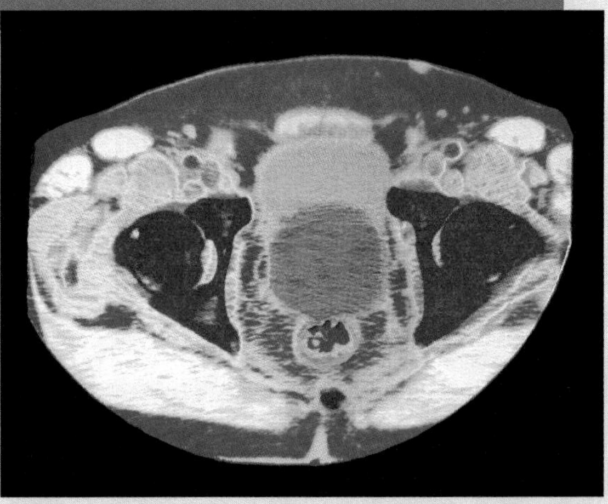

A colored computed tomography scan of an axial section through the human pelvis shows an enlarged prostate (green area) *with cancer. The incidence of prostate cancer has increased in recent years.*

The exact cause of prostate cancer, which primarily afflicts older men, is unknown. Heredity and a high-fat diet may be risk factors. Difficulty urinating is a symptom. Early detection—usually through a PSA (prostate-specific antigen) test or a digital rectal exam—and treatment may reduce the disease's mortality rate. The PSA test, approved by the Food and Drug Administration in August 1994, measures a man's PSA count. This antigen is produced only by the prostate and increases with age. Its level jumps significantly when cancer is present. Authorities warn that the test may miss some cancers and detect other small ones that can be left alone.

The various treatments include surgical removal of the entire prostate gland—prostatectomy. The operation involves several weeks of recovery, during which the patient must be connected to a catheter. There also is the risk of incontinence. Until recently the operation frequently led to impotency. External beam radiation is another approach to treatment. However, it has failed to kill all of the cancer cells at times. Another radiation treatment places dozens of small radioactive palladium or iodine seeds directly in the prostate. Since the radiation affects only the immediate area of the prostate, damage to nearby healthy tissue is lessened. The latter procedure can be performed in about one hour on an outpatient basis. Incontinence for weeks afterward may result. Impotence results less often in men under 70, but may occur more frequently in older men. Cryotherapy entails inserting metallic probes into the prostate and circulating liquid nitrogen at –195°F (–91°C) through the probes, forming an ice ball that freezes and kills the prostate cells. Some 60% of patients undergoing this treatment are left impotent; incontinence usually is not a problem. In addition, since the male hormone testosterone stimulates the growth of prostate-cancer cells, a hormone treatment that curtails testosterone's production may be beneficial.

The National Cancer Institute has established two large-scale prostate-cancer trials to curtail some of the guesswork about prevention and treatment. Former junk-bond dealer Michael Milken, who contracted prostate cancer at a relatively young age, has established CaP Cure, a public charity with the purpose of finding a cure for the disease. He pledged $25 million over a five-year period for basic and clinical research involving prostate cancer.

Six Major Cancers

	Estimated New Cases			*Estimated Deaths*		
	Both sexes	*Male*	*Female*	*Both sexes*	*Male*	*Female*
Breast	*185,700*	*1,400*	*184,300*	*44,560*	*260*	*44,300*
Colorectal: Large intestine (colon)	*94,500*	*45,500*	*49,000*	*46,400*	*22,700*	*23,700*
Colorectal: Rectum	*39,000*	*22,100*	*16,900*	*8,500*	*4,700*	*3,800*
Leukemia	*27,600*	*15,300*	*12,300*	*21,000*	*11,600*	*9,400*
Lung	*177,000*	*98,900*	*78,100*	*158,700*	*94,400*	*64,300*
Prostate	*317,100*	*317,100*	—	*43,400*	*43,400*	—
Skin (melanoma)	*38,300*	*21,800*	*16,500*	*7,300*	*4,600*	*2,700*

Skin Cancer

The most common of all cancers, skin cancers are diagnosed in more than 800,000 Americans annually. The great majority of these are basal-cell and squamous-cell cancers. Much more serious is malignant melanoma, which can spread rapidly to other parts of the body. The incidence of melanoma is increasing faster than that of any other type of cancer: In 1994 the American Academy of Dermatologists reported a 500% increase in incidence from 1950 to 1985, a trend that has continued to the present. Melanoma was diagnosed in approximately 38,300 people in 1996.

Chronic overexposure to ultraviolet radiation, such as that emitted by the Sun, is a primary risk factor in skin cancer. People with fair complexions who sunburn easily or are unable to tan are especially vulnerable to the harmful effects of ultraviolet radiation. People who have a family or personal history of skin cancer or who work in occupations where they are exposed to chemicals such as coal tar and radium also are at increased risk.

People are advised to examine their skin monthly to detect any changes in the color, border, or surface texture of moles and other growths or spots on the skin. Non-melanoma cancers are most common on visible parts of the body, particularly the face and arms. Melanomas, which tend to be asymmetrical and have uneven edges, tend to occur on the trunk and legs. All changes should be checked promptly by a physician.

Surgical removal is used in 90% of cases; in some cases, this surgery must be followed by a skin graft. For malignant melanoma, removal of lymph nodes near the cancerous skin also may be required.

Basal-cell and squamous-cell cancers are almost always curable if detected and treated early. If treated when localized, malignant melanoma has a five-year survival rate of 94%. If the melanoma has spread to regional or distant sites, survival rates drop to 60% and 16%, respectively. Of the estimated deaths from skin cancer in 1996, 7,300 were from malignant melanoma and 2,130 from other skin cancers.

Editor's Note. The section on the forms of cancer was written by freelance science and medical writer Jenny Tesar. Ms. Tesar and the editors of the Annual are most grateful to the members of the Office of Cancer Communications at the National Cancer Institute who carefully reviewed the material.

Although for many, a good vacation means a good tan, unprotected exposure to the sun can lead to skin cancer. People with fair skin that burns or freckles easily are especially susceptible to melanoma—the most serious form of the disease.

(Continued from page 54.)

Treatment Transitions. According to interpretations of hieroglyphics, the ancient Egyptians removed surface tumors surgically. They used concoctions of barley and pigs' ears for what appear to be tumors of the stomach and uterus. Ointments, enemas, castor oil, suppositories, and poultices rounded out their arsenal. Four thousand years later, surgery still was the primary weapon against cancer, both the surface variety and any reachable, operable cancer. Only decades ago, bone cancer in an extremity meant the limb was amputated; breast cancer meant the entire breast and underlying muscle were removed. While this approach certainly saved lives—and still is appropriate in some cases today—it also exacted a psychic and physical toll and by itself had no impact on the metastatic process that in so many cases had begun before the cancer even was diagnosed.

As the understanding of cancer biology deepened and the nature of cancer as a systemic, not a local, disease became clearer, scientists concentrated their efforts on designing systemic therapies. Since cancer cells could invade surrounding tissues and travel anywhere in the body via the blood and lymphatic systems, surgery was unthinkable as a cure for metastatic cancer. Cancer-killing drugs that could function on as global a basis as the cancer cells themselves were sought. Radiation therapy also was used to kill cancer cells unreachable by surgery as well as those lurking but as yet undetectable.

Chemotherapy and irradiation still are mainstays of cancer therapy, and are being used today not only after surgery but to shrink the tumor to enable surgery in some cases where the tumor otherwise would be deemed inoperable due to size or position. But the more potent these weapons are, the more damaging they can be to normal cells as well as to cancer cells. Precision has become a driving force of cancer research; the challenge for the doctor and specialist is to target therapies to exact locations so that they are tumor-specific instead of destructive to any rapidly growing cell.

Chemotherapy is the mainstay for cancer treatment. The portable drug pump, below, *allows the chemotherapy drug to be administered to a breast-cancer patient in measured dosage through a tube into a vein near the shoulder.*

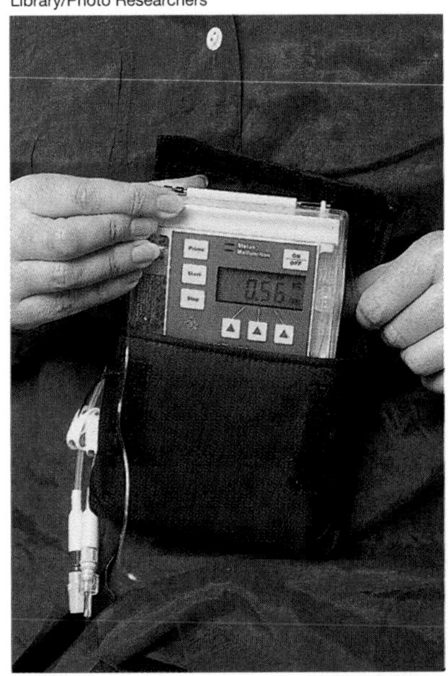

In the modern war on cancer, the arsenal of weapons to fight the disease includes oncolytic viruses—viruses that grow only in cancer cells, infecting and killing them without harming normal cells; immunotoxins—deadly toxins coupled to tumor-specific antibodies that deliver the poison directly to the target tumor; anti-sense constructs—genetically engineered blockers of cancer protein synthesis; and tumor-specific vaccines, which incorporate the purified antigen of the patient's own tumor into a vaccine to generate specific antibodies against the tumor. These and other novel approaches are in the early stages of human clinical trials.

Variations on these themes include infecting a cancer with a virus against which extremely effective drug therapy exists and then using that drug to kill the virus and by extension the cells it has invaded. Another is using material from a particular patient's tumor to build a vaccine based on purified tumor-specific antigen (which would elicit immunity against the antigen but would not itself be cancerous) to stimulate an immune response in a suitable bone-marrow donor, and then to transplant the responsive bone marrow into the cancer patient. The immunotoxin strategy has been tested in a few patients with metastatic breast and colon cancer, using an antibody to a protein found in many of the most common cancers—such as colon, breast, and lung cancer—coupled to a bacterial toxin (*Pseudomonas* exotoxin A). The results thus far are promising.

Between 1986 and 1996, scientists identified and cloned 18 familial cancer genes, 17 in the 1990s. Some confer a predisposition to rarer malignancies like Wilms' tumor, others to more common ones like breast and colon cancer and melanoma. Although only 5% to 10% of all cancers in the United States occur in individuals with such inherited genetic mutations, that translates to millions of people and, more to the point, the sporadic (or nonfamilial) mutations that underlie the other 90% or so of cancers are the same as their inherited counterparts except that they were acquired through other mechanisms.

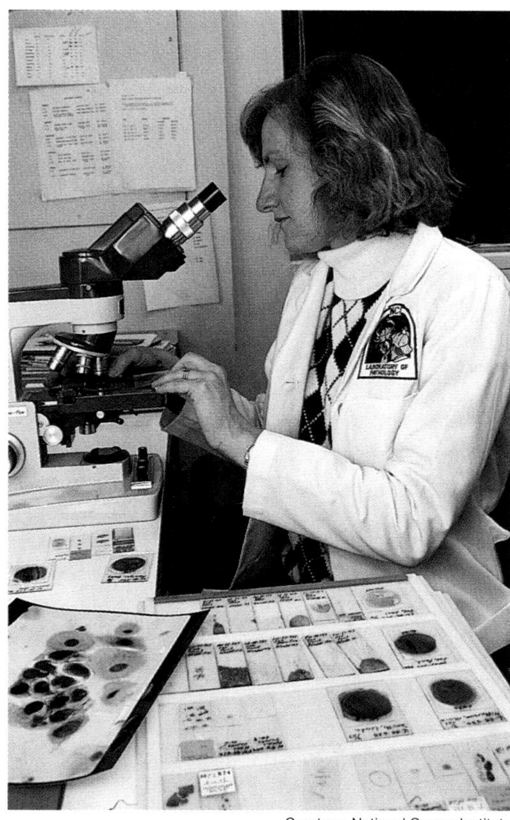

Courtesy, National Cancer Institute

Scientists and researchers at the National Cancer Institute (NCI) seek to acquire a greater understanding not only of the causes and prevention of cancer but also of its diagnosis and treatment. NCI, a division of the National Institutes of Health of the Department of Health and Human Services, was established in 1937.

Scientists suspect that there are hundreds of cancer genes, but not more than 1,000, and they expect to identify all of them. They know that it takes several mutations within a cell, not just one, to trigger cancer. And they anticipate expanding their knowledge tremendously through studying cancer genetics. Cancer specialists can study human-cancer-gene mutations in the laboratory and epidemiologically, and they can study these same mutations in specially bred mice. In these animal models, they can see which mutations are needed to spur the blood-vessel development, or angiogenesis, that enables the budding cancer to grow, as well as the mutations that underlie the metastatic process. And they can test therapies that interfere with these processes.

If scientists can prevent cancer from developing in animals born with genes that make them susceptible to specific cancers, then they may apply that strategy to humans with hereditary predispositions—and to everyone else at risk of exposure to environmental factors that induce these same mutations. A challenge that accompanies identifying cancer-susceptibility genes is safeguarding people found to harbor such genes against misuse of that information by employers, insurers, or others who might discriminate on the basis of genetic profile. It is also incumbent upon society to ensure that information about genetic makeup is accompanied by intelligent counseling and access to state-of-the-art health care. As the 20th century nears an end and as the U.S. government's war against cancer enters its second 25-year period, there are many working hard throughout society to ensure that each of these imperatives is fulfilled.

THE WORLD OF THE INTERNET

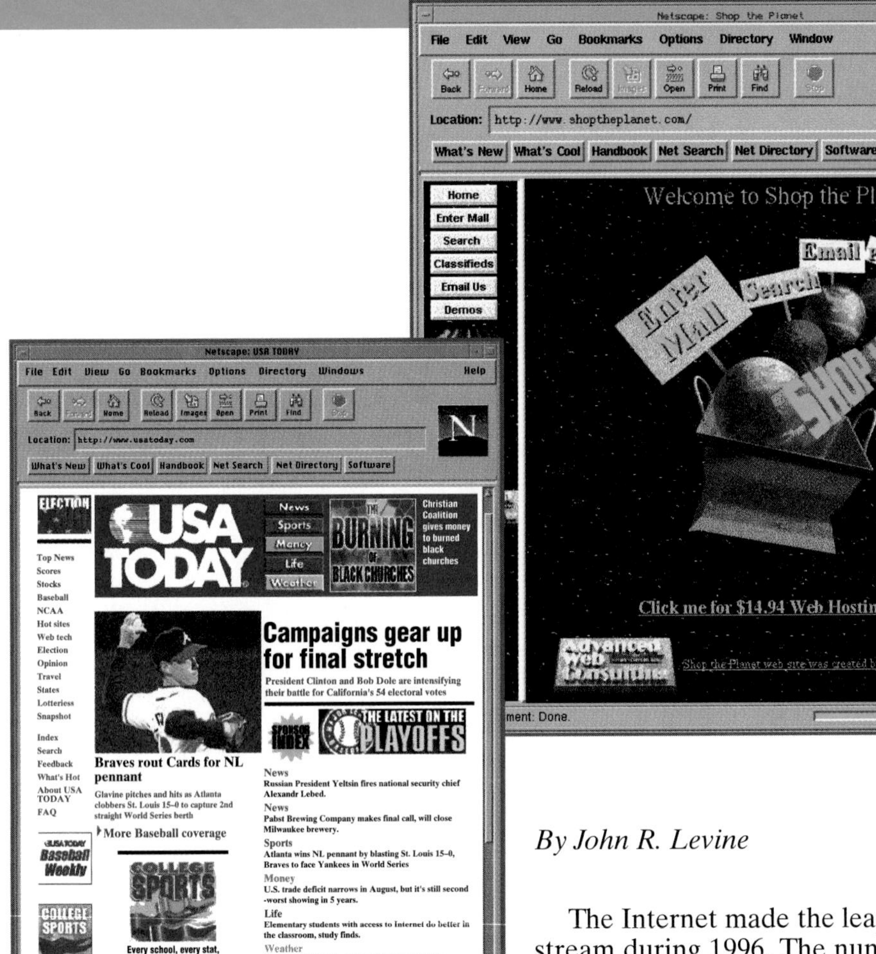

Among the mind-boggling array of services available in 1996 on the Internet's World Wide Web were access to the latest news (above) *and to electronic malls* (top right) *featuring a huge assortment of virtual merchandise. The user-friendly Web made it increasingly easy to keep in touch with world events—often updated every hour or two; to view and order merchandise; or to research and learn about virtually any subject without leaving the comfort of one's home.*

By John R. Levine

The Internet made the leap into the mainstream during 1996. The number of Internet users worldwide passed 30 million, and surveys estimated that one in ten U.S. households used the Internet at least occasionally. The World Wide Web, the Net's premier application, fueled this spectacular growth. The Web combines the visual appeal of combined text, graphics, sound, and animation with easy to use "point and click" controls.

Growth of the Internet. In 1996 the Internet's geometric growth continued as users continued to flock to the Net—principally to the World Wide Web—to take advantage of new information, entertainment, and business opportunities, and as companies rushed to provide new services. Network Wizards—which has been surveying the size of the Net for many years—estimated that in June 1996 there were 12.8 million hosts (com-

(Continued on page 64.)

What Is the Internet?

The Internet's technology has made it possible for users to access on-line banking services through easy-to-use interfaces. The popularity of such services has led to the creation of electronic banks like SFNB, above, that exist only on the Internet.

The Internet is, quite simply, the world's largest group of cooperating computer networks. All the computers on the more than 100,000 networks that comprise the Internet voluntarily use the same technical standards for their network data so that any of the computers on any of the networks can exchange messages with any other. Each message sent is broken up into small chunks of roughly uniform size, called packets; each packet is sent along to its destination. If a packet's destination is on a different network from its origin, the packet is switched from network to network until it reaches its destination, often traversing 15 or 20 networks along the way. The destination computer reassembles incoming packets into the desired message. This "packet switched" design has let the Internet grow from its original two networks to its current size and beyond without any fundamental changes in the way that it works.

The Internet's origins date from the late 1960s, when the U.S. Defense Department's Advanced Research Projects Agency (ARPA) funded computer network research to build an experimental packet-switched network called the Arpanet. The Arpanet project started in 1967, and by the end of 1969 a working network connected four computers in California and Utah. By the mid-1970s it was clear that the Arpanet was a success, so much so that it was becoming impractical to connect all of the computers that desired to communicate to a single network. As a result, a new Internet Protocol (known as IP) was devised that let computers on many networks exchange data packets, and a Transmission Control Protocol (TCP, the combination being TCP/IP), which managed conversations between computers using IP.

(Incidentally, the Internet is named after IP, not the other way around.) By 1983 all computers on the Arpanet were using TCP/IP, and the military's computers were split off onto a separate network known as Milnet, but still connected to the Arpanet.

During the 1980s, many new networks connected to the growing Internet—including both academic networks funded by the National Science Foundation and commercial networks—and in 1989 the original Arpanet was shut down, since all its functions were being done better by the new networks. The design of the Internet makes it possible to add new user-level facilities at any time on top of the existing TCP/IP framework. For the Net's first decade, the primary applications were Telnet (remote terminal access), File Transfer Protocol (FTP—copying data files from one computer to another), and electronic mail (E-mail).

In the late 1980s, as more academic institutions joined the Net, easier-to-use facilities appeared, notably Archie, from McGill University, which provides an index to the files available by FTP; Gopher, from the University of Minnesota, which provides a convenient menu system that makes it easier to find and use resources on the Net; and WAIS, a text-searching system from Thinking Machines, Inc. These three facilities pointed the way toward an easier-to-use Internet.

In 1991, English researcher Tim Berners-Lee, who was working at CERN, the international physics-research lab near Geneva, Switzerland, wrote the first version of the World Wide Web. The Web provides a unifying model of pages connected by links, based on hypertext work by Douglas Englebart and Ted Nelson as far back as the 1960s. The Web's first application was to present the masses of data from CERN's physics experiments, but its wide applicability was immediately apparent. Student programmers at the University of Illinois soon developed Mosaic, a Web "browser" that added pictures to the Web, which became extremely popular throughout the Net. Many corporations created Web browsers based directly or indirectly on Mosaic; the most notable of these was Netscape Communications, cofounded by Mosaic programmer Marc Andreesen. Netscape's

Navigator rapidly became the most popular program used for access to the Web.

In 1996, Microsoft's Explorer challenged Netscape's dominance as Microsoft aggressively released new versions at no charge. Most Internet growth since 1994 has been centered around the Web, which has subsumed or made obsolete most of the older services other than E-mail. The Web is far easier to use than previous Net services, since it combines graphics with text and requires little typing; most actions are clicks of the mouse. Remarkably, since the departure of the original military funders, the Internet has had no central administration other than some volunteer organizations that develop and maintain technical standards and address registries that assign names and numbers used to identify hosts (computers) on the Net.

How the World Wide Web Works

The World Wide Web organizes all of its information into "pages" of data. Each page consists of text intermixed with codes in Hypertext Markup Language (HTML). The HTML codes describe the structure of the page, with elements such as headings, colors, italics, tables, columns, and links to other pages. HTML codes also can call for pictures, sounds, and other media to be inserted into pages and combined on user screens. Every page on the Web has a Universal Resource Locator (URL) that uniquely identifies it, along with the type of page and the server on which it resides.

For example, the URL http://publishing.grolier.com/publishing.html refers to a page accessible via the Web's Hypertext Transfer Protocol (HTTP), on the server publishing.grolier.com, with the page name of publishing.html. User programs known as "browsers" send the URL to the appropriate server, which returns the page to be displayed. Each link on the page refers to a URL. When a user clicks on a link, the browser fetches that new URL. The Web is designed to handle any kind of information, not just HTML pages. Each page retrieved is identified with a "media type," such as text, image, or sound. If a page is not of a type that the browser can handle itself, the browser runs a separate program known as a helper or plug-in to display the page.

JOHN R. LEVINE

Visitors to the Web site of the U.S. White House can take a virtual guided tour of the president's home and be told its history.

(Continued from page 62.)

puters) on more than 130,000 networks connected to the Internet. This was an approximate doubling from the previous year.

The World Wide Web, the Net's popular multimedia hypertext system, grew even faster than did the Net as a whole. A November survey by Netcraft found more than 525,000 Web servers—a 13% increase over the 462,000 found just a month earlier, and greater by a factor of 16 than the 31,000 in November 1995.

Due to the Internet's prodigious growth, some observers predicted a major network collapse in 1996. A few localized failures did occur—including a 19-hour failure at America Online (AOL) and several mail failures at AT&T's Worldnet service—but the Net as a whole continued to work. On the evening of the November U.S. presidential election, millions of users turned to the Internet for early results. The most popular servers reported millions of "hits," or visits, and slowed down considerably, but no outages were reported.

About the author. John R. Levine is a writer, lecturer, and consultant in the computer field. His book *Internet for Dummies* was called a "good practical guide" by the *Times Literary Supplement* and has sold more than 1.3 million copies. Dr. Levine has served as a computer consultant, especially on language design, for numerous clients, has developed computer software, and has spoken in many countries about the Internet. He is the recipient of a B.A. and a doctorate in computer science from Yale University.

Business on the Internet. Businesses flocked to the Internet in record numbers in 1996. The number of names registered in ".com," the Internet naming domain for commercial entities, increased from 200,000 to more than 600,000 by the end of the year. Web pages became a mainstream communication medium rather than an exotic experiment, and businesses displayed their Net address on everything from business cards to billboards.

Many traditional mail-order catalog companies opened Web sites, including L.L. Bean, which displayed its catalog on its site; and Lands' End, which both put its catalog on the Net and accepted orders through its Web page. Holiday Inns created a Web site allowing prospective travelers to "visit" its hotels via virtual-reality technology; the site took $1 million in reservations during its first month.

New World Wide Web–based storefronts proliferated as well. Amazon.com Books offered a 1-million-title catalog—three times as many as the largest conventional store—from a small office near Seattle; two- to three-day delivery was available on most orders. PC Flowers and Gifts, which relaunched its Web site in December 1995, became one of the two largest FTD florists in the United States.

Financial institutions embraced the Net with a flood of investment-related material appearing on the Web. Many brokerages and mutual funds opened Web sites; some offered trading directly from Web pages, usually at rock-bottom prices as low as $10 per trade. A few banks moved onto the Web as well, including the Security First Network Bank of Pineville, KY, which signs up its customers and does practically all of its business via the Internet.

Web sites were opened by many newspapers, from national papers like *The New York Times*, *The Wall Street Journal*, and *USA Today* to tiny local papers such as *The Shetland Times* of the Shetland Isles, north of Great Britain. Typical newspaper sites contained many or all of the articles in the print edition,

cathy® **by Cathy Guisewite**

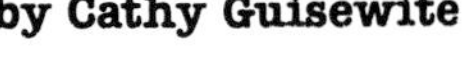

Many U.S. library patrons, including the New York City students at right, *gained access to the world of the Internet in 1996 when Microsoft's Bill Gates and the American Library Association joined to launch "Libraries Online!." The project provided millions of dollars to help several U.S. library systems connect to the Internet.*

along with advertisements, links to Net resources, and, frequently, large databases of information from the paper's files, news services, and financial sources. Some, but not all, offered free access, and nearly all displayed advertising.

Consumer reluctance to send credit-card payment over the Net remained a major stumbling block for Net-based commerce, although there was no evidence of credit-card fraud due to Internet communication. Digital cash, which would permit Net-based services to sell content for a few cents per page, moved forward slowly.

Inspired by the huge success of Netscape's public stock offering, many Internet-related stocks came to market in 1996, buoyed by the investing public's enthusiasm for the Internet. Yahoo!, Lycos, and Excite—three advertiser-supported Net search engines—all successfully came to market even though all had lost money consistently since they were founded.

Intranets. An intranet is a network within a single organization using Internet technology such as the Web. Intranets grew even faster than did the Internet during 1996, and it was estimated that intranet spending would grow from about $200 million in 1996 to more than $5 billion by the year 2000. Many companies used Internet technology to take information that had been locked up in older database systems and bring it quickly to employees, while others found that small informal groups using inexpensive PC servers quickly could build useful intranet services. The most popular intranet application was the Web, but E-mail, calendar scheduling, and project management were used widely as well.

Net Access and Usage. As the Net continued to grow, both the number and quality of network connections increased as well. In the United States the fastest "backbone" network connections in 1996 ran at 155 million bits per second. Typical consumer dial-up connections used modems that ran at 28,000 to 33,000 bits per second (bps)—double the 14,400 bps that was standard a year or two earlier. Late in the year, Rockwell International and Lucent Technologies (formerly part of AT&T) announced modems that would permit users to receive data at up to 56,000 bps. As regional phone companies lowered prices and streamlined installations, ISDN—a digital telephone system that permits connections at speeds of up to 128,000 bps—became more popular among individuals and small businesses.

Dial-up Internet use became popular enough that, late in the year, some phone companies claimed that large numbers of long calls to Internet providers were jamming their switches; the companies proposed that Internet providers be charged per-minute fees for incoming calls, or that all local calls be charged by the minute. Providers and members of the on-line community disputed these claims, noting that many phone companies vigorously had been selling second phone lines and encouraging customers to use them for the very on-line calls that allegedly had been the problem.

Cable-television companies, which had been promising Internet access via CATV for years, finally started to deliver in 1996. Adapting an existing cable system for two-way data turned out to be far more difficult than originally expected, and the cable modems required to connect a computer to the cable were more expensive and harder to obtain than anticipated, but both problems started to come under control. In suburban Boston, for example, Continental Cablevision started connecting Internet customers at rates of 500,000 bps and greater. Other small but successful installations in Michigan, New York, and elsewhere portended wide CATV Internet availability with speeds ten or more times greater than is available over telephone lines.

Outside the United States, Internet use also increased rapidly in 1996. The country with the highest per-capita Internet use was Finland, but use increased all over the world. Many countries connected to the Net for the first time. In many Third World countries—including Albania, Belize, Bolivia, the Cayman Islands, Guatemala, Jordan, Mauritius, Saudi Arabia, and

Compuserve's Wow! on-line service, launched in March 1996, endeavored to make navigating the Web easier and less intimidating for children or the computer-shy. Wow! featured bright graphics, left, *and easily understandable instructions. Due largely to increased competition, however, Compuserve planned to shut down Wow! early in 1997 and return to its concentration on more technically oriented computer users.*

Uganda—the Internet is the fastest and cheapest way of communicating with the outside world. An E-mail message can move around the world in a few seconds for a few pennies—far faster and cheaper than phone calls, faxes, or paper mail.

Internet service providers (ISPs)—that is, services that only provide Internet access without the proprietary additions of the on-line services—continued to grow. The three major long-distance telephone companies—AT&T, MCI, and Sprint—all offered consumer dial-up Internet access, jumping into competition with established providers ranging from large national and international companies to small "mom and pop" providers operating out of houses or apartments. Nearly all providers moved to a flat-fee scheme priced between $15 and $20 per month regardless of the number of hours used.

The major on-line services continued to garner a large share of Internet users, but profits remained elusive. America Online extended its lead as the largest on-line service, reporting more than 7 million users by year's end, but during 1996 it took accounting charges of more than $400 million, more than wiping out all profits reported since the company's founding. In December, AOL joined the other services in offering a flat-rate pricing plan, causing some defections among content providers that previously had received commissions based on the hours that users spent in their areas. Compuserve, with about 3.3 million users, also lost money and announced plans to close down its consumer-oriented Wow! service, returning to its traditional focus on business, technical, and professional users. Microsoft Network, with 1.6 million users, passed Prodigy for the Number 3 spot. Prodigy, with about 1 million users, was sold by former owners IBM and Sears, Roebuck to a management group after years of losses. Although the on-line-service business as a whole continued to grow somewhat, all of the major providers found that old customers left almost as fast as new ones signed up. The future of on-line services was very unclear, particularly as more and more previously proprietary content moved to the Internet, where anyone with access could use it.

There was spirited opposition to the 1996 Communications Decency Act—which restricted the transmission of "indecent material" over computer networks—among Internet users and others concerned with potential infringements on free speech. Students at the University of Pennsylvania, below, demonstrated during a February visit by Vice-President Al Gore. The protesters won at least a temporary victory when enforcement of the act was blocked by a panel of federal judges, which declared it unconstitutional.

Internet Technologies. Several new technologies became established on the Net during 1996. RealAudio, a system that plays radio-like sound through a network connection, became the de facto standard sound system. Many radio stations made their programs available via RealAudio to allow listeners outside their geographic area to listen to their programs. This was particularly popular with stations offering university sports.

Two-way phone-style voice communication became available as well. The various Internet telephone products were relatively difficult to use and had much worse voice quality than regular telephone calls, but had the great appeal of costing nothing beyond the users' basic Internet connection. Particularly for international calls, the cost savings made Internet calls increasingly popular. A group of small long-distance phone companies, fearing unfair competition, petitioned the Federal Communications Commission (FCC) to regulate or prohibit Internet telephony. Major long-distance companies all opposed the petition, and the FCC declined to take any action.

Three-dimensional graphics gained popularity as well. The two most popular 3-D systems, Virtual Reality Modelling Language (VRML) and Apple Computer's Quicktime VR, both were integrated into the Web, allowing users to move around a 3-D scene displayed on their monitor. High-quality graphics require extensive computing, so as consumer PCs became more powerful, the use and quality of 3-D graphics likely would increase.

In November, WebTV introduced an Internet access system that used existing televisions and phone lines, along with a set-top box costing about $200, to provide access to E-mail and the Web.

Legal and Political Developments. Despite vigorous opposition by on-line users, the Communication Decency Act (CDA) was added to the Telecommunications Act of 1996, signed into law on February 8. A coalition of on-line and civil-rights groups filed suit to block enforcement of the CDA and, on June 11, a three-judge panel ruled the CDA unconstitutional on broad free-speech grounds. (*See also* COMMUNICATION TECHNOLOGY; CONSUMER AFFAIRS.)

Many schools across the United States gained access to the Internet during 1996. NetDay projects, first in California and later in many other states, symbolically installed network wiring in a few classrooms in many schools, to encourage school systems, local businesses, and community members to help complete the task of installing computers in the schools and connecting them to the Internet. The Telecommunications Act of 1996 also provided for Internet-access subsidies to schools; and President Bill Clinton, during his reelection campaign, stated a goal of providing Internet access to every 12-year-old schoolchild in the United States.

Future Trends. Although the Internet appeared in far more businesses and homes than ever before, it remained far less common than telephones, televisions, or even cable TV. But as access becomes widely available through telephone, cable-TV, wireless, and other companies over the next few years, the Net likely will become as familiar as TV or phones, and a wide range of interactive consumer-oriented content will appear, including entertainment, shopping, information services, communications, and doubtless many others not yet invented.

© Richard Martin, Vandystadt/Allsport

THE OLYMPIC GAMES 1896–1996

By Mike Spence

Marking the 100th anniversary of the revival of the Olympic movement, a tribute to the ancient Greek games was part of the opening ceremonies of the XXVI Summer Games, above, *in Atlanta, GA, in July 1996.*

Like all previous Olympiads, the 1996 Summer Olympics in Atlanta will be remembered for its many triumphs. Like one other, it also will be remembered for tragedy.

A pipe bomb exploded in the heart of crowded Centennial Olympic Park in the early hours of July 27, 1996, killing one spectator and injuring 111. In addition, a Turkish cameraman suffered a fatal heart attack while rushing to cover the bombing. The incident brought back memories of the 1972 Olympics in Munich, when Black September, an Arab terrorist group, stormed the Athletes' Village. The attack resulted in the deaths of 11 Israeli athletes. The violence in Munich brought the Olympics to a halt for 24 hours. In Atlanta the Games stopped only for a moment of silence to honor the victims. Then the competitions resumed. By Games' end, the explosion was remembered as little more than a brief, terrifying interlude—a civil disturbance, perhaps, or, maybe, a prank gone horribly awry.

Comparisons to Munich soon were forgotten, washed away by the achievements of the athletes, who regained their rightful place on the 1996 Olympics' center stage. One of the foremost stars of 1996 was Canadian sprinter Donovan Bailey, who ran away from the field in the men's 100-m dash and set a world record of 9.84 seconds. In other Olympics, the winner of the men's 100-m was hailed as the world's fastest human. In Atlanta, Bailey had a challenger—U.S. sprinter Michael Johnson, who set a world record of 19.32 seconds in the men's 200-m dash en route to becoming the first man to win the 200-m and 400-m races in the same Olympics. While Bailey and Johnson were vying to be *the* top star of the 1996 Olympics, an Olympic legend, Carl Lewis, made his own plausible case for the honor. Lewis, arguably the greatest Olympian in the first 100 years of the Modern Games, leaped 27', 10 3/4" in the men's long jump. Although not even close to Lewis' personal best, it was good enough to win the gold medal and secure his place in Olympic history. Lewis became only the second man or woman to win the same event in four consecutive Olympics, equaling the mark set by U.S. discus thrower Al Oerter.

In regard to the Olympic Games, at least, 1996 was billed as the year of the woman. French sprinter Marie-José Pérec duplicated Johnson's feat, winning the women's 200-m and 400-m races. She was only the second woman to accomplish the double; American Valerie Brisco-Hooks had won both races at the 1984 Games in Los Angeles. Russia's Svetlana Masterkova was a surprise, sweeping the women's 800-m and 1,500-m track events. U.S. women's teams dominated their competition, winning gold medals in softball, soccer, gymnastics, and basketball. Women also made the most waves in the 1996 Olympic swimming competition. Ireland's Michelle Smith won three individual gold medals and a bronze, amid unsubstantiated charges that she used performance-enhancing drugs. Amy Van Dyken became the first U.S. woman to win four gold medals in one Olympics, capturing two individual races and swimming on two victorious U.S. relays. *See* SPORTS—*Olympic Games.*

Despite these accomplished performances, perhaps the greatest achievement of all may have been that the Olympic movement had survived for 100 years.

Early History and Challenges. The Modern Games were the idea of France's Baron Pierre de Coubertin, a part-time fencer who was convinced that physical culture and competition build moral fiber. He also hoped to use the Games as a way of promoting world peace. De Coubertin was enamored with the romance of the Ancient Olympics. Every four years, athletes had gathered to compete and rival factions in Greece had called a "sacred truce" to protect spectators at the competition from assault for as long as three months. De Coubertin first proposed the revival of the

About the author. Mike Spence, who has been a newspaper reporter for 22 years, has been covering the Olympic Games for the *Colorado Springs Gazette Telegraph* since the 1980s. In addition to the Olympics, his beats include basketball and football—especially Denver's pro teams. Mr. Spence is the coauthor of *Broncos: Three Decades of Football*, published by Foghorn Press in 1987.

Pierre de Coubertin (1863–1937), below, *was personally responsible for the revival of the Olympic Games in 1896. The French nobleman was fascinated with the way education and sports seemed to be intertwined. Twenty-four years after the Games' revival, the five interlocking rings—depicted on an ancient altar near the stadium at Delphi, Greece, in the photo* at bottom*—became the official Olympic symbol.*

© AP/Wide World Photos

Politics has intervened at various Olympics since their revival. Misha the Bear, the official mascot, was present throughout the 1980 Summer Games in Moscow, but some 55 nations, including the United States, boycotted the competition to protest the policy of the Soviet Union toward Afghanistan.

Games in 1892 and spent the next three and one half years building support for the idea. Athens, Greece, was selected as the site for the first Modern Olympics in 1896.

Yet, since the inaugural Olympics, the movement has faced challenges from within and without. World War I forced the cancellation of the 1916 Olympics. The 1940 and 1944 Olympics were called off because of World War II. Even in supposed peacetime, the Games often have been troubled. Terrorists broke the Olympic peace at the 1972 Games. The 1976 Olympics in Montreal were a financial disaster, costing nearly $1.1 billion more than the $310 million original estimate. Cold War adversaries the United States and the Soviet Union alternately boycotted the 1980 and 1984 Games. The boycotts, coming on the heels of two disastrous Olympics, nearly sounded the Olympic movement's death knell. Somehow, the Games managed to survive, although de Coubertin hardly would recognize them.

Costs and Security. The 1896 Games in Athens were financed by a gift of 1 million drachmas from Georgios Averoff and the sale of souvenir stamps and medals. The competition attracted 311 athletes from 13 countries. Every competitor was male and all of them were pure amateurs, as mandated by the Olympic Charter. By comparison, the 1996 Games in Atlanta cost $1.7 billion, funded mainly by television revenue and corporate sponsors who each paid $40 million for the right to associate their name with the Games. The Atlanta Olympics drew 10,750 athletes from 197 nations. Many of the athletes were professional—thanks to the International Olympic Committee's (IOC's) relaxation of the rules of eligibility. Nearly one third of the athletes were female.

Yet the Olympic movement continues to hold many of de Coubertin's ideals in high regard. The Games and the United Nations remain the only two places on earth where, in theory, all nations are welcome. At least for a few days every Olympic cycle, that may be true. Billions of people—from every walk of life, from every religious and political persuasion, from virtually every country on earth—watched the 1996 Games on television. Despite that impact, the Atlanta Olympics also underscored many of the problems now facing the Olympic movement. Security has been a growing concern since 1972. The bomb blast in downtown Atlanta resulted in the first deaths connected to the Olympics since 1972 and served as a painful reminder that the Games are not simply games anymore.

Planners of the Montreal Olympics originally sought to have an open, college-campus-type layout for their Athletes' Village in 1976. That was before the Munich Games. Now, athletes' villages look more like fortresses. Atlanta was no different. The main Athletes' Village was surrounded by 11 mi (18 km) of barbed wire and armed troops. Athletes used a new electronic-scanning system to gain entrance to the village. Security at venues also was tightened. Athletes, officials, and spectators alike had to pass through a gauntlet of X-ray machines, metal detectors, and security checks before being allowed entry. Atlanta's elaborate security system was enhanced even further following the bombing incident at Centennial Olympic Park.

Size and Eligibility. The Atlanta Games were the largest in history, a fact that did not please all factions of the IOC. Many IOC dignitaries feel there are too many sports, too many athletes, and too many team officials, putting an unnecessary burden on the organizing committee to provide housing, food, and transportation. After the 1992 Olympics, IOC officials decided to take steps to control the growth of the Games. They limited the number of entries in different sports. Yet the impact was minimal. IOC officials also said they planned to remove unpopular sports from the Olympic program. Instead, they added women's soccer and softball, as well as men's and women's beach volleyball. Men's and women's mountain biking became part of the cycling program.

Eligibility long has been an issue of controversy within the Olympic movement. The concept of amateurism developed in 19th-century England as a way of preventing the working classes from competing against the aristocracy. The wealthy could participate in sports without the worry of having to make money. The less well-off had to choose between training and earning a living. Adding to the confusion was the changing definition of amateurism from one decade to another, from one sport to another, and from one country to another.

The IOC finally put an end to the debate over amateurism after the 1988 Games when it voted to declare all professionals eligible for the Olympics, subject to the approval of the international federation of each sport. In Atlanta all but two federations—baseball and boxing—allowed at least some professionals to compete. Baseball and boxing continued to prohibit professionals from Olympic competition. Soccer partially complied, allowing each participating country to include three professionals on its Olympic roster. However, a strong sentiment against allowing professionals to compete in the Games remained among a faction of the IOC and the public.

(Continued on page 78.)

The fear of a terrorist attack has become another big concern for Olympic officials and organizers. Although Atlanta developed an elaborate security system for the 1996 Games, left, *a pipe bomb exploded at Centennial Olympic Park on July 27—killing a spectator and injuring 111. The Games continued, however, and the park, which was a gathering spot for Olympic fans, reopened under tighter security on July 30,* below.

© Hulton Deutch/Allsport

JIM THORPE, 1912

As athletes from around the world gathered in Atlanta, GA, in July 1996 to participate in the Games of the XXVI Olympiad, the 100th anniversary of the modern Olympics was commemorated. For it was on April 6, 1896, that King George I of Greece had proclaimed the Games of Olympiad I opened. The Olympic movement, which had begun in Greece in 776 B.C. and had been suspended by Rome's Emperor Theodosius I in A.D. 393, thereby was revived.

Although figure skating was part of the Olympic program in 1908 and 1920 and an ice-hockey tournament took place in 1920, the Olympic Winter Games were held first in Chamonix, France, in 1924. Except for the World War II years of 1940 and 1944, they were contested every four years through 1992.

After that, the timing of the Olympic Games was changed. The Winter Games still would be held at four-year intervals, but would be placed two years apart from the Summer Games. Accordingly, the XVII Winter Olympics were held in Lillehammer, Norway, in 1994—two years prior to the XXVI Summer Olympics in Atlanta.

1896

Athens, Greece. In the first modern Olympics, competitions were held in swimming, wrestling, weight lifting, cycling, fencing, gymnastics, shooting, and lawn tennis, as well as track and field. Spyridon Louis, a native of the small Greek town of Marousi, delighted the crowd by winning the marathon. Greece's King George I awarded the prizes—a diploma, silver medal, and crown of olive branches for a first-place finish and a diploma, bronze medal, and laurel crown to the runner-up—on April 15, the final day of the Games. *Participation:* 311 athletes from 13 countries.

1900

Paris, France. Archery and rowing were introduced as Olympic sports. Ray Ewry of the United States won gold medals in standing long jump, standing high jump, and standing triple jump. In all, Ewry would capture ten gold medals in four Olympics. *Participation:* 1,330 athletes from 22 countries.

1904

St. Louis, MO. It was the first competition to be designated an "Olympics." U.S. trackmen Archie Hahn, Harry Hillman, and Jim Lightbody each won three gold medals. The difficulty of traveling to St. Louis kept the number of competitors down. *Participation:* 625 participants from 12 nations.

1906

Athens, Greece. Since 1906 was not an official Olympic year, the International Olympic Committee (IOC) did not include the results of these games in their records. As Canada's William Sherring entered the stadium on his way to victory in the marathon, he was joined by Greece's Prince George in the run to the finish line. *Participation:* 884 competitors from 20 countries.

© UPI/Bettmann

SONJA HENIE
1928, 1932, 1936

1908

London, England. A swimming pool was built within a new 68,000-seat stadium at Shepherd's Bush in the western edge of Greater London. The schedule was expanded to include events in 22 sports. *Participation:* 2,035 athletes from 22 nations.

1912

Stockholm, Sweden. Hannes Kolehmainen, the first of the "Flying Finns," and Jim Thorpe, an Oklahoma-born Sauk and Fox Indian, dominated the Games. Kolehmainen won gold medals in the 5,000- and 10,000-m races—both new to the Olympic program—and in the individual cross-country race. He also took a silver medal in the team cross-country race. Thorpe, hailed as the world's greatest athlete, was victorious in the decathlon and pentathlon but was forced to return his medals because he had been paid for playing professional baseball. It took until January 1983 for the IOC to return the medals, posthumously, to Thorpe. *Participation:* 2,547 participants from 28 countries.

1916

Berlin, Germany. Canceled due to World War I.

1920

Antwerp, Belgium. The Olympic flag flew for the first time and the Olympic oath was introduced. The great Finnish runner Paavo Nurmi won gold medals in the

10,000-m race, the 10,000-m cross-country, and the team cross-country relay. *Participation:* 2,606 competitors from 29 nations.

© IOC/Allsport

MILDRED "BABE" DIDRIKSON, 1932

1924

Winter Games—Chamonix, France. Charles Jewtraw of Lake Placid, NY, scored a surprise victory in the 500-m speed-skating race to become the first gold-medal winner in the Winter Olympics. *Participation:* 293 athletes from 16 nations.

Summer Games—Paris, France. The 1924 Olympics provided collective housing for the athletes for the first time. U.S. swimmer Johnny Weissmuller—who would go on to gain fame as Tarzan—swam the 100-m freestyle and the 400-m freestyle in Olympic-record time, and anchored the U.S. 400-m freestyle team in world-record time, for three gold medals. *Participation:* 3,092 competitors from 44 countries.

1928

Winter Games—St. Moritz, Switzerland. Gillis Grafstrom of Sweden won his third consecutive men's figure-skating title. Sudden changes of temperature and rain hampered the Games. *Participation:* 491 athletes representing 25 nations.

Summer Games—Amsterdam, the Netherlands. Women's track and field competition was introduced, with five events being contested and five world records being set. *Participation:* 3,014 athletes from 46 nations.

1932

Winter Games—Lake Placid, NY. The United States swept the men's speed-skating competition as Irving Jaffe won the 5,000-m and 10,000-m races, and Jack Shea was first in the 500-m and 1,500-m. *Participation:* 17 nations entered 307 athletes.

Summer Games—Los Angeles, CA. Mildred Didrikson, who became known as "Babe" because she hit a baseball like Babe Ruth and who would be judged as the greatest woman athlete of the first half of the 20th century, took gold medals in the javelin and the 80-m hurdles. In the high jump, her style of diving headfirst over the bar was ruled out of order and she was awarded the silver medal. *Participation:* 1,408 athletes from 37 countries.

1936

Winter Games—Garmisch-Partenkirchen, Germany. Norway's Sonja Henie won the gold medal in women's figure skating for an unprecedented third time. Great Britain ended Canada's streak of four consecutive ice-hockey championships. Norway's Ivar Ballangrud earned gold medals in the men's 500-m, 5,000-m, and 10,000-m speed-skating events. *Participation:* 756 athletes from 28 nations.

Summer Games—Berlin, Germany. Adolf Hitler's Germany spared no expense in staging the 1936 Winter and Summer Olympics. At the Summer Olympics, for the first time, the Olympic flame was carried from Olympia, Greece, to burn for the duration of the Games. James Cleveland "Jesse" Owens, a black U.S. track star, captured four gold medals and personally disproved Hitler's claim of Aryan supremacy. *Participation:* 4,066 athletes from 49 countries.

1940

Helsinki, Finland. Canceled due to World War II.

1944

London, England. Canceled due to World War II.

1948

Winter Games—St. Moritz, Switzerland. France's Henri Oreiller took gold medals in the downhill and the combined as Alpine skiing became part of the Winter program. Gretchen Fraser of the United States was the star of women's Alpine skiing. *Participation:* 28 nations represented by a total of 713 athletes.

Summer Games—London, England. Dutch track star Fanny Blankers-Koen returned home with four gold medals. Bob Mathias, a future U.S. congressman, won the first of two gold medals in the decathlon. *Participation:* 4,099 competitors from 59 nations.

1952

Winter Games—Oslo, Norway. Finishing first in the woman's giant slalom and slalom, Andrea Mead Lawrence was the first American to win two gold medals in Olympic skiing. U.S. figure skater Dick Button repeated as a gold medalist. *Participation:* 30 nations sent 732 athletes.

© IOC/Allsport

JESSE OWENS, 1936

© Archives du CIO/Olympic Photo Association

FANNY BLANKERS-KOEN
1948

Summer Games—Helsinki, Finland. Czechoslovakia's Emil Zátopek set three Olympic records—in the 5,000-m and 10,000-m races and the marathon. His wife, Dana Zátopková, captured the women's javelin competition as the Zátopeks became the first husband and wife to win Olympic gold medals. *Participation:* 4,925 athletes from 69 countries.

1956

Winter Games—Cortina d'Ampezzo, Italy. Toni Sailer of Austria swept Alpine skiing, winning the slalom, giant slalom, and downhill. *Participation:* 924 athletes representing 32 nations.

Summer Games—Melbourne, Australia. In view of Australia's requirement of a six-month quarantine before horses could be admitted into the country, the IOC determined that the equestrian events would be held in Stockholm, Sweden, five months before the Australian Games. A total of 158 persons from 29 nations took part in the equestrian competition. Later, in Melbourne, American Al Oerter won the first of four consecutive gold medals in the discus and Pat McCormick of the United States became the first diver to capture gold in the springboard and high board in consecutive Olympics. *Participation:* 3,184 athletes from 67 nations.

1960

Winter Games—Squaw Valley, CA. The U.S. hockey team scored an upset and won the gold medal. David Jenkins of Colorado Springs succeeded his brother Hayes Alan Jenkins as the men's figure-skating champion. Carol Heiss of the United States captured the gold in women's figure skating. She later became Mrs. Hayes Alan Jenkins. *Participation:* 30 nations represented by 693 athletes.

Summer Games—Rome, Italy. Cassius Clay, the future Mohammed Ali, won gold in the light-heavyweight boxing division. Rafer Johnson finished first in an exciting decathlon. Abebe Bikila was the first Olympic champion from Ethiopia. Running barefoot, he took the gold medal in the marathon. Wilma Rudolph became the first U.S. woman to win the 100-m and 200-m dashes. She also anchored the gold-winning U.S. 400-m relay team. *Participation:* 5,348 athletes from 83 nations.

© Hulton Deutch/Allsport

PAT MCCORMICK
1952, 1956

1964

Winter Games—Innsbruck, Austria. Lidia Skoblikova, a 24-year-old Siberian schoolteacher, won all four of the women's speed-skating events. A lack of snow hampered the competition. *Participation:* 36 countries represented by 1,332 athletes.

Summer Games—Tokyo, Japan. Don Schollander of the United States became the first swimmer to win four gold medals in the same Games. Australian swimmer Dawn Fraser took an unprecedented third consecutive Olympic 100-m freestyle gold medal. Billy Mills was the first American to win the 10,000-m track race. Judo joined the program. *Participation:* 5,140 participants representing 93 countries.

1968

Winter Games—Grenoble, France. Peggy Fleming of the United States delighted the figure-skating audience with her gold-medal-winning endeavor. France's Jean-Claude Killy dominated men's Alpine skiing, with gold-medal performances in the slalom, giant slalom, and downhill. *Participation:* 1,272 athletes from 37 nations.

Summer Games—Mexico City. Bob Beamon soared 29' 2 $^1/_2$" in the long jump—a world record that was not broken until Aug. 30, 1991. Gymnast Vera Caslavska of Czechoslovakia was the first woman to win four gold medals in a Summer Games. Debbie Meyer of the United States became the first swimmer to win three individual gold medals in a single Olympics. *Participation:* 5,531 athletes from 112 nations.

1972

Winter Games—Sapporo, Japan. Ard Schenk of the Netherlands won gold medals in the 1,500-m, 5,000-m, and 10,000-m men's speed-skating competition. *Participation:* 35 nations represented by 1,125 athletes.

Summer Games—Munich, Germany. Swimmer Mark Spitz, a 22-year-old U.S. predental student, made Olympic history by winning seven gold medals. The United States suffered its first loss in Olympic men's basketball. The personality and performance of Olga Korbut, a 17-year-old gymnast from the USSR who won three gold medals and a silver medal, captivated world television audiences. Arab terrorists stormed the Israeli living quarters at the Olympic village, killing two Israeli athletes and taking nine others as hostages. *Participation:* 7,147 athletes from 122 countries.

© Hulton Deutch/Allsport

MARK SPITZ, 1972

1976

Winter Games—Innsbruck, Austria. In an exciting Alpine-skiing competition, Austria's Franz Klammer captured the men's downhill by .33 of a second; West Germany's Rosi Mittermaier took the gold in the women's downhill and slalom and

©Allsport

OLGA KORBUT, 1972

the silver in the giant slalom. *Participation:* 37 countries represented by 1,054 competitors.

Summer Games—Montreal, Quebec, Canada. Romania's Nadia Comaneci became the Olympics' new gymnastics queen, winning three gold medals, one silver, and one bronze. Finland's Lasse Viren finished first in the 5,000-m and 10,000-m runs, as he had in 1972. Bruce Jenner of the United States set a world record in winning the gold medal in the decathlon. Women's basketball became an Olympic sport. *Participation:* 7,356 athletes from 88 nations.

1980

Winter Games—Lake Placid, NY. The U.S. hockey team, nicknamed the "Boys of Winter," staged a surprise gold-medal-winning effort. U.S. speed skater Eric Heiden was the first athlete to win five individual gold medals in a single Games. *Participation:* 37 nations represented by 1,283 athletes.

Summer Games—Moscow, USSR. The United States, West Germany, and Japan were among some 55 nations that boycotted the 1980 Summer Games in response to the Soviet Union's invasion of Afghanistan. East Germans dominated the women's swimming competition. Aleksandr Dityatin, a 22-year-old Soviet, earned a medal in each of the men's gymnastic events. *Participation:* 5,687 competitors from 81 nations.

1984

Winter Games—Sarajevo, Bosnia, Yugoslavia. With a gold-medal-winning performance, the British team of Jayne Torvill and Christopher Dean gained new fans for the sport of ice dancing. Cross-country skier Marja-Liisa Hamalainen of Finland took three gold medals in individual competition. *Participation:* 49 nations represented by 1,437 athletes.

Summer Games—Los Angeles, CA. Following the U.S. boycott of the 1980 Games in Moscow, the USSR and 13 nations from the Warsaw Pact stayed away from the 1984 Games. On the field, Carl Lewis won gold medals in the 100-m and 200-m dashes, the long jump, and the 400-m relay. Joan Benoit, also of the United States, was first in the Olympics' first women's marathon. U.S. gymnast Mary Lou Retton, 16, took five medals. *Participation:* 7,575 athletes from 140 nations.

1988

Winter Games—Calgary, Alberta, Canada. Italy's flamboyant Alberto Tomba dominated men's Alpine skiing, taking gold medals in the slalom and giant slalom. Swiss skier Vreni Schneider shone among the women, with gold medals in the slalom and giant slalom. *Participation:* 1,793 athletes from 57 nations.

Summer Games—Seoul, South Korea. U.S. swimmer Matt Biondi took five gold medals, one silver, and one bronze. East German swimmer Kristin Otto captured six gold medals—the most by a woman athlete in a single Olympics. Greg Louganis of the United States dove for gold for a second consecutive time in the springboard and platform events. Florence Griffith Joyner of the United States won gold medals in the 100-m and 200-m dashes and the 400-m relay. Tennis, a former Olympic sport, rejoined the program. *Participation:* Some 9,700 athletes from 160 nations.

1992

Winter Games—Albertville, France. Finland's Toni Nieminen, 16, was the youngest male to win a gold medal in the Winter Games as he finished first in team ski jumping and the 120-m ski jump. *Participation:* 2,174 athletes from 63 nations.

Summer Games—Barcelona, Spain. Although Estonia, Latvia, and Lithuania competed as separate nations, most athletes from the former Soviet Union were members of the Unified Team. South Africa took part in its first Olympics since 1960. Players from the National Basketball Association (NBA) were allowed to take part in men's basketball for the first time. Jackie Joyner-Kersee won a second consecutive Olympic heptathlon. Gymnast Vitaly Scherbo of the Unified Team took the all-around and five other gold medals. Baseball, badminton, and women's judo joined the program. *Participation:* Some 10,000 athletes from 169 nations.

1994

Winter Games—Lillehammer, Norway. Speed skater Bonnie Blair won gold medals in the 500-m and 1,000-m races to become the United States' most decorated female Olympian of all time—five gold medals and one bronze in three Olympiads. *Participation:* 66 nations represented by 1,920 athletes.

1996

Summer Games—Atlanta, GA. *See* SPORTS—*Olympic Games.*

©Allsport

ERIC HEIDEN, 1980

(Continued from page 73.)

Drugs. Another problem pressing the Olympic movement is the use of performance-enhancing drugs. The use of drugs is not new. Thomas Hicks, winner of the 1904 Olympic marathon, was given several doses of strychnine and brandy during the race. In 1960, Danish cyclist Knut Jensen died during the Olympic road race after taking amphetamines and nicotinyl tartrate.

The IOC Medical Commission began outlawing drugs in 1967. Sweden's Hans-Gunnar Liljenvall, a modern pentathlete, was the first person disqualified. He was caught using alcohol. Full-scale testing began in 1972. Through 1992, there had been 46 positive tests at the Summer Games and five at the Winter Games. The most notable athlete caught was Canadian sprinter Ben Johnson, the 1988 Olympic champion in the 100-m race. Just days after his victory, he was stripped of his gold medal for using the steroid stanozolol.

Despite the number of cheaters caught, the use of performance-enhancing drugs continues to be a problem. Although many sports federations have called for or instituted unannounced out-of-competition testing, the IOC did not endorse or participate in those programs fully prior to the 1996 Olympics. Nevertheless, at the Atlanta Games the IOC announced that three Russian athletes and a Lithuanian cyclist had tested positive for drug use.

Politics and the Games. Finally, the use of the Olympics for political purposes remains a significant concern. Although politics never was supposed to play a part in the Games, it has loomed as an unwelcome influence from the very beginning. The Greek royal family was highly visible at the 1896 Games, sitting in box seats at the finish line and participating in key moments of the competition, such as victory celebrations and award ceremonies. The British royal family played a similar role in the 1908 Games. In 1912 awards were handed out by King Gustav V of Sweden and Czar Nicholas II of Russia.

At the 1936 Games in Berlin, Adolf Hitler and his Nazi government used the Games as a showcase for Nazi power and ideology. However, the four gold medals won by black U.S. track and field star Jesse Owens took much of the luster off Nazi claims of Aryan superiority. By 1972 it had become evident that the Olympics could be used for political purposes because the Games attracted significant international interest. That prompted the terrorist attack at Munich. It also encouraged Olympic boycotts, which had begun in 1956 but became an almost quadrennial occurrence by 1976, when black African governments boycotted the Montreal Games as a protest against apartheid in South Africa.

The U.S. boycott of the Moscow Games followed in 1980 as a way to protest Soviet aggression in Afghanistan. The Soviets retaliated at the 1984 Games in Los Angeles. Although many expected the Olympics to die after the Soviets announced their boycott, the Los Angeles Games were highly successful, producing a $150 million surplus. The notion that the Olympics could make money saved the movement.

© Vandystadt/Allsport

By permission of Mike Luckovich/Creators Syndicate

Excessive commercialism and the use of performance-enhancing drugs by athletes also are problems for the Olympic movement. Since private enterprise provided much of the funding for the 1996 Summer Games, logos for such corporate sponsors as Coca-Cola were seen on numerous Olympic venues in Atlanta.

Los Angeles was the only city to bid for the 1984 Games. After the 1984 Olympics, the IOC has had the luxury of choosing between several cities for each successive Games. The Olympic movement may have had its most profound impact in 1988. That year's Summer Olympics were awarded to Seoul, South Korea—a nation then ruled by a dictatorship. However, the government gave way to democratic elections to soothe international opinion prior to the Games. Even so, North Korea, Cuba, Ethiopia, Nicaragua, Seychelles, and Albania did not accept invitations. In addition, Madagascar accepted an invitation but did not send a team.

By 1992, however, the Olympics welcomed the 12 separate former Soviet republics as one team; Estonia, Latvia, and Lithuania participated as independent nations; and Cuba, North Korea, and Ethiopia ended their boycotts. In 1996 all 197 nations invited to the Games participated, setting a record and achieving for the first time one of de Coubertin's original goals for the Games—uniting the world through sport.

© Henryk Kaiser/Leo de Wys

Atlanta: An Olympic City

The city of Atlanta—the capital of the state of Georgia and of the South, generally, and perhaps best known as the setting for some of the antics of Scarlett O'Hara in Margaret Mitchell's *Gone With the Wind*—historically has marketed itself as a place that has enjoyed a successful business climate. It began in 1885 with a marketing scheme calculated to attract industries to a city left in ruins after the Civil War. During the devastating conflict, the city had been burned to the ground by Gen. William Sherman's troops. Unlike other southern cities, Atlanta welcomed carpetbaggers from the North following the war.

Economy and Civil Rights. During the 1920s, Atlanta launched the "Forward Atlanta" campaign to encourage major companies to open branch offices in Atlanta. Nabisco, Lay's Potato Chips, and Chevrolet decided to make Atlanta their southern base. Although lacking a port and an industrial base, the city emphasized its strategic location as a place to transport goods and transact business. Between 1940 and 1960, city leaders directed funds toward the building of a modern airport and efficiently used federal money for an interstate-transportation system. Atlanta, therefore, was positioned to become a nexus in the distribution and service economy. Today the headquarters of many Fortune 500 companies are located in Atlanta, and the city is home to Delta Air Lines, Coca-Cola, and United Parcel Service of America (UPS). These Atlanta-based companies formed the core of corporate sponsorship for the 1996 Summer Olympics, which, in true Atlanta style, was a privately financed spectacle.

When former Mayor Maynard Jackson, an African-American, addressed an organizational meeting dedicated to restoring the Atlanta home of Margaret Mitchell, he announced unequivocally, "this [restoration] is about money." In that setting, Jackson summed up Atlanta's perennial problem, as well as its innovative solution. The problem involved how to capitalize on an antebellum history that is both a romantic, alluring identity and a source of shame. As an answer to that problem, Atlanta decided to market itself as a place of the future where the entrepreneurial spirit thrives. This has forced attention away from the city's divisive past. With the slogan "a city too busy to hate," Atlanta supposedly is a locale where economic success overrides all other concerns. The implication is that "making it" in Atlanta is an attainable dream for everyone.

In making this claim, Atlanta can point to some remarkable success stories by its hometown folks: Jimmy Carter, a peanut farmer, was chosen as the 39th president of the United States; Ted Turner rose from being a billboard salesman to head of the largest news organization in the world; real-estate lawyer Billy Payne served as president of the Atlanta Committee for the Olympic Games (ACOG); Newt Gingrich, a former college professor, was elected by his Republican colleagues as speaker of the U.S. House of Representatives; and former barbershop owner Alonzo Herndon became a multimillionaire and founder of a life-insurance company.

Atlanta also can claim a noteworthy civil-rights legacy. The dream of native son Martin Luther King, Jr., is alive in the city's government. The city's last three mayors—Andrew Young, Maynard Jackson, and Bill Campbell; the U.S. congresswoman from the 11th District, Cynthia McKinney; and the police chief, Beverly Harvard, are African-Americans. With the largest concentration of black colleges in the United States, a record of black middle-class achievement, and a history of black leadership, Atlanta offers a picture of interracial unity and tolerance for differences. This also is reflected in the fact that Atlanta is home to the largest gay population in the United States.

In Atlanta economic progress always has moved in tandem with advances in race relations because of a recognition that the city as a whole would succeed when all Atlanta citizens had a chance to prosper. As ambassador to the United Nations and later mayor of Atlanta, Andrew Young traveled the world proclaiming his city as a place of open opportunities for economic success for all people.

The Atlanta economy has cooperated in making opportunities available. Based on service industries, Atlanta's economy has been relatively recession-proof, resulting in continued growth since the 1970s. A 1973 agreement between Mayor Maynard Jackson and white business leaders led to a sharing of federal dollars allocated for infrastructure development. Consequently, black businesses became involved in the design and building of the rapid-transit system and the expansion of Hartsfield Airport. This radically changed the composition of the business community as black firms emerged as major contractors.

Uninterrupted economic growth since the 1970s has given Atlanta a technologically advanced infrastructure that attracts new industries and major convention business. The 1996 Olympics, backed by tremendous public support, will extend the economic growth by increasing state-tax revenue by $176 million, creating 60,000 new jobs, and contributing $600 million in permanent construction projects.

Culture. Emphasis on pursuing economic growth and improving race relations has not been matched by an equal concern for developing the cultural climate of the city. The Atlanta arts community struggles, and the city is devoid of a cultural identity. While the city boasts of a nationally recognized orchestra, noted theater groups, and

The 21-acre (8.5-ha), $55 million Centennial Olympic Park—the largest urban park to be built in the United States in some 25 years—is located in the heart of downtown Atlanta.

© Lesser/Gamma-Liaison

a new art museum designed by Richard Meier, critics point to the lack of genuine, sustained support for the arts. Corporate contributions to the arts are made mainly because a grand cultural presence is good for Atlanta's image, rather than due to a passion for cultural causes. For example, a major frustration of arts organizations during the 1996 Cultural Olympiad was that corporate buyers purchased blocks of tickets to arts events but failed to attend. Some performances, although sold out, had few actual attendees. Sports events, on the other hand, were the main attraction for Atlanta citizens. While Olympic soccer fans marveled at the attendance of 80,000 spectators at soccer venues, Atlantans are accustomed to encountering even larger crowds at routine weekend college-football matches.

Although the cultural climate leaves much to be desired, Atlanta provides a comfortable, amiable lifestyle. Dense greenery, rolling hills, and picturesque streets create lovely neighborhoods where residents can own homes at relatively low prices and with easy access to mountains, waterfalls, and lakes. The well-planned transportation system makes suburban commuting tolerable, and world-class malls are common.

Problems and the Olympic Legacy. The availability of a comfortable, relatively inexpensive suburban lifestyle continues to draw business relocations to the metropolitan area, and simultaneously underlines the differences between the metro area and downtown Atlanta; the latter accounts for 400,000 of metro Atlanta's population of 3 million. Downtown Atlanta is predominantly black, poor, crime-ridden, and subject to white flight. In the mid-1990s most major law firms, banks, and white-owned businesses moved to the suburbs.

In bidding for the 1996 Games, the ACOG emphasized the fact that the city's downtown population is predominantly black, exaggerated the degree of racial harmony in the city, and promised to revitalize the downtown area. During the early years of preparation for the Games, black political leaders reminded the ACOG that Atlanta—not the suburbs—had won the Olympic bid. In the end, it is downtown Atlanta that is benefiting most from Olympic development projects, many of which were paid for with private funds raised by Olympic officials. Once again, Atlanta leaders focused on what is good for Atlanta—whether it be for whites or blacks—and poured

The Olympic Village, located on the campus of Atlanta's Georgia Tech, was built to house Olympic athletes. After the Games, it became dorms for students from Georgia State University, which had been a commuter college.

money and energy into revitalizing the city's epicenter.

As a result of the Olympic Games, Atlanta has the new 21-acre (8.5-ha) Centennial Olympic Park—the largest urban park to be built in the United States in some 25 years. Located in the heart of downtown, the park is the focal point of a massive rebuilding of the Westside. This area was formerly Techwood Homes, a sprawling public-housing project inhabited by the hard-core poor. Using the park as the centerpiece, city leaders envisioned blocks of residential development between the park and the Georgia Tech campus and a business park within a tax-favored empowerment zone north of the Georgia World Congress Center. Linking the park development and the old downtown business district will be a sports arena–retail corridor and an entertainment district.

In addition, the ACOG built student housing that was used by the athletes and then turned over to Georgia State University, which is located in downtown Atlanta. The Olympic Stadium will become the new home of the Atlanta Braves, guaranteeing that the baseball club will remain downtown rather than move to the suburbs as had been suggested. Permanent sport facilities, built with private finances and valued at $25 million, were being given to downtown educational institutions and public organizations. Furthermore, the city government used the Olympics to convince the electorate to approve a $150 million bond issue to repair streets, viaducts, and bridges and to maintain municipal art projects.

In 1997, the 85,000-seat Olympic Stadium (background), *designed by HOK Sport of Kansas City, is to replace Atlanta–Fulton County Stadium* (foreground) *as the home of baseball's Atlanta Braves of the National League.*

The magnitude of change and the cost of the improvements led some city officials to call the $2.5 million spent by Olympic visitors "a mere pittance." But businesses on side streets and in areas such as Auburn Avenue—the historic heart of Atlanta's black community—did not see what they considered to be their share of the $2.5 million. As a result, they threatened a legal battle with the city over alleged breach of contract.

While the plans for the city's future are exciting, city officials cannot overlook persistent problems of crime—the highest homicide rate in the nation; poverty—43% of Atlanta's children live in poverty; and homelessness. In late 1996, there was nevertheless an air of confidence due to the number of visitors and the momentum created by the Olympics. All the basic components for revitalization of an area—e.g., large-scale construction projects and infrastructure improvements—were in place. This factor, combined with strong business backing and public support, make the dream of a thriving downtown seem possible. During the Olympics, most Atlantans spoke of the indescribable joy and pride they felt watching 2 million people wander the streets of their city, feeling safe and enjoying themselves. This euphoric experience made Atlantans wonder if it would last. They, of course, hoped that it would!

KAY BECK, *Georgia State University*

THE SCIENCE FICTION INVASION

© Globe Photos

By Tom Maddox

The year's biggest movie hit was "Independence Day," in which hostile aliens annihilate much of Earth's civilization, above, *before they are destroyed by a group of human heroes. High-tech special effects, combined with a classic B-movie plot, created a blockbuster in a nation increasingly fascinated by science fiction.*

In 1996 the Earth was invaded repeatedly by space aliens and afflicted by many other paranormal occurrences. On film and television, in particular, flying saucers landed to enormous applause. Recent films featured a seemingly endless string of science-fiction-inspired themes and characters. On television there were sinister aliens in *The X-Files* and *Dark Skies*, assorted alien (and human) screwballs in *3rd Rock from the Sun*, the ubiquitous *Star Trek* programs, the humans and creatures on *Babylon 5*, and a host of assorted aliens, monsters, possessed humans, androids, robots, and flat-out evil forces strewn across the broadcast and cable channels.

And on grocery and convenience-store racks, on bookstore shelves and anywhere else the long arm of mass merchandising reached, there was more of the same: novels from which films and television series were made, or "novelizations" made from the films and series. In addition, there were increasing sales of more serious sci-fi literature and magazines, as well as out-and-out fan magazines.

Science fiction, in short, had spawned mightily, shape-shifting and proliferating like so many of the creatures in its tales. In many cases, however, its aliens were not driven by a lust for interstellar dominance or other sinister and inscrutable motives. They served very human interests—the needs of Hollywood producers to feed the insatiable appetites of popular culture. Once sci-fi was seized upon as the latest fad, there was a demand for more and more such products.

Development of the Resurgence. Even when science fiction was largely out of favor in films and on television, the continued survival of *Star Trek* in all its forms must be acknowledged. For close to 30 years, *Star Trek* lore has spread through films, new television series, books, fan conventions, and magazines; it seems that all possible media continue to serve as carriers of this phenomenon, which prospers long past any reasonable or even inspired estimate of its lifespan. Many of the original show's signature images and phrases ("Beam me up, Scotty" or "Live long and prosper" are two examples) have become common currency, instantly recognizable by millions. In many ways, however, the enduring popularity of the world of *Star Trek* is a different beast altogether than the more recent invasion of science fiction into pop culture, involving as it does a core of fanatical devotees and an optimistic view of an enlightened, fairly peaceful future that has little in common with the darker themes in most of today's science fiction.

Two recent notable—and very different—instances of the 1990s sci-fi trend are television's *The X-Files* (Fox) and the 1996 blockbuster film *Independence Day*. During the 1995–96 season, *The X-Files* improved on the steady success of its two earlier seasons, when it grew from a hip cult favorite into a mainstream commercial success. It became a major contributor to the current sci-fi resurgence when network television paid the series its highest compliment by copying its themes (NBC's *Dark Skies*) and style (any number of shows, including NBC's *Profiler*). The show's creator himself introduced a new series

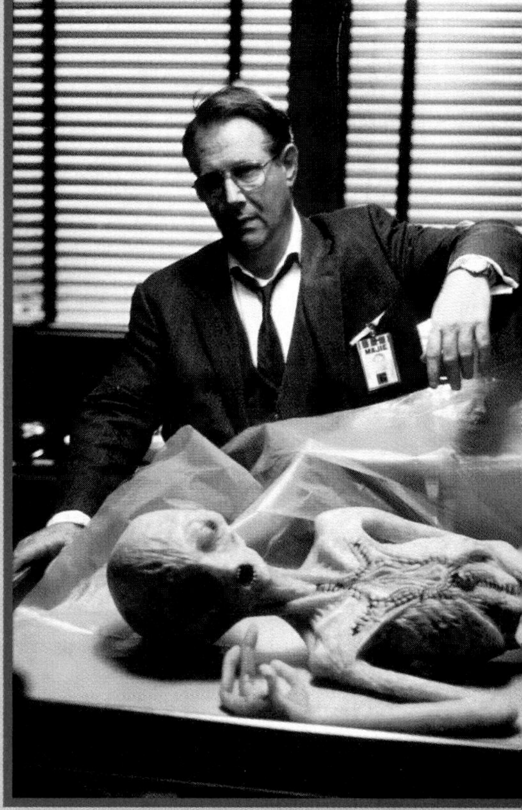

"Dark Skies," courtesy, Columbia Pictures Television

Sci-fi TV series featuring sinister alien plots and mysterious government conspiracies proliferated in 1996. Fox's "The X-Files," below, *successfully began the trend, and was followed by such shows as NBC's* "Dark Skies," above, *which posited a secret alien invasion of Earth and subsequent government cover-up.*

© Photofest

(*Millennium*) with an even darker tone to capitalize on his creation's success. *The X-Files*' vision is as murky and sinister as its sets and lighting, which have established what might be called the paranoid style of contemporary sci-fi. In this world, events are darkly lit, half-seen, monstrous, and bloody, and those who serve truth, justice, and goodness struggle—mostly ineffectually—against vast powers.

Nonetheless the *The X-Files* generates exhilarating rushes of creepiness. In it viewers see their most extreme fears blown up into grossly implausible plots. The melodramatic gloom often gets lightened by wit or by outlandish and grisly plot devices—for instance, an elephant necropsy in one episode, where special agent Dana Scully is seen standing in the disemboweled creature, attired in suitable protective clothing. Many scripts achieve a kind of popular sublime as they explore the narrative space of diverse monsters, paranormal phenomena, and science and technology gone awry. In short, the show ingeniously has worked the usual materials of sci-fi television into an original, entertaining, and often artful vision.

The film *Independence Day*, on the other hand, is a quintessential Hollywood B-movie of the 1950s, but done on a scale filmmakers of that era never could have imagined. *Independence Day* takes George Pal's *War of the Worlds* and splices it to *Star Wars*, the *Alien* films, and *Close Encounters of the Third Kind*, among others, adding the latest technological effects. Although *Independence Day* concerns invading aliens and includes government conspiracies that overlap some of those active in *The X-Files*, the film has an entirely different tone. Unlike the TV series, where characters suffer and bear the burden of their suffering, the film goes almost cheerfully about its bloody business. Although the president's wife dies of injuries resulting from the alien attack on Los Angeles and leaves behind a small, motherless child, her death seems not to impair anyone's enjoyment—the president's included—of the final victory over the aliens. And although almost every major world city has been annihilated, no one seems to grieve too much for

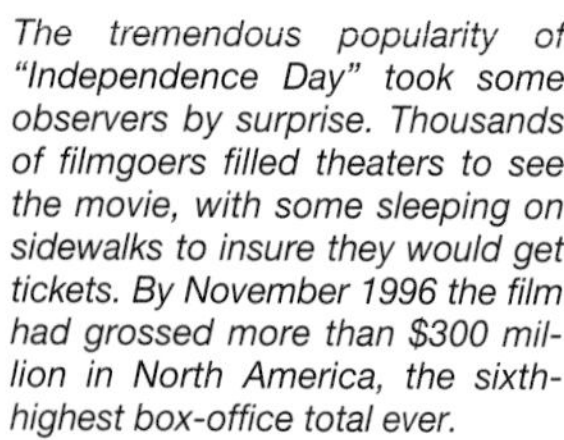
The tremendous popularity of "Independence Day" took some observers by surprise. Thousands of filmgoers filled theaters to see the movie, with some sleeping on sidewalks to insure they would get tickets. By November 1996 the film had grossed more than $300 million in North America, the sixth-highest box-office total ever.

© Andrew Lichtenstein/Sygma

these losses. Instead the film's heroes posture in the fighter-pilot mode popularized in World War II movies and taken to great lengths by the *Star Wars* films. It is an odd amalgam of patriotism, one-worldism, and bloodthirsty vengefulness, filled with absurd coincidences and miraculous escapes.

© NBC/Everett Collection

A lighter side of science fiction can be seen on the hit NBC comedy series "Third Rock from the Sun," above. *The show chronicles the often-humorous adjustment problems of four aliens who have taken on human form as they research what they consider to be the least important planet. Despite its improbable premise, the show consistently rated among the top 20 in viewership since its January 1996 premiere.*

Reasons Behind Sci-Fi's New Popularity. *The X-Files* and *Independence Day*, as well as most of the newly popular series and films, focus on a mythology of aliens and government cover-up. They also tend to regard science—at least as portrayed by their scientist characters—as dangerous, arrogant, and often loony. And in many, technology destroys as much as it nourishes. At the heart of these themes lie our fears.

What are we afraid of? Two different views prevail. As indicated in *The X-Files* and similar shows, our fears are of ourselves and our emerging capabilities. Hidden power elites send their agents—the "Men in Black"—out to steal and lie and kill and cover up. Thus the most menacing presences in the series are not the aliens after all, but the sinister human powers of those who bend the truth because they have determined that the people have no right to know it. They are politicians, bureaucrats, businessmen, scientists, even doctors, and they have set themselves above the rest of humanity. They are also producers or agents of scientific and technological change. As such, they are sometimes dupes of sinister powers, sometimes full-fledged members of one conspiracy or another. But they always bring trouble and are never to be trusted.

In contrast to this paranoid theme, *Independence Day* and its ilk offer murderous aliens who ask of humans only that they "Die!" One can neither negotiate with nor evade this vision of evil; it must simply be destroyed. This is a fantasy more typical of older science-fiction literature and earlier films, but one that is still being delivered with such compelling spectacle that millions are willing to join the lines waiting to see it.

Thus much of contemporary science fiction attempts to show us little, if anything, about aliens or interstellar life or life in the future. Instead it shows, as popular culture always does—perhaps too clearly—a portrait of ourselves: our fears and hopes and ways of imagining.

As the 21st century approaches, science and technology threaten to become overwhelming, the government reveals it has experimented on its citizens without their consent, and various covert governmental agencies have acquired rogue status.

About the author. Tom Maddox is currently writing coordinator at The Evergreen State College in Olympia, WA. He has published short science-fiction pieces in *Omni* and other magazines and in anthologies, as well as several critical articles. Mr. Maddox's science-fiction novel *Tor* was published in 1991; a second novel, *Mystified*, is forthcoming.

THE HISTORY OF SCIENCE FICTION

By 1996, science fiction had become associated in most people's minds with its hugely successful media manifestations. However, the genre developed as a literary form and from its beginnings until the present has found its most interesting ideas in stories and novels.

Brian Aldiss, in *Trillion Year Spree*, a history of science fiction, reads sci-fi as a response to the unprecedented social changes of the Industrial Revolution of the late 18th and early 19th centuries. He sees the genre as an escape from the rude and frightening complexities of the modern world and as a way of exploring those complexities. Thus he believes Mary Shelley's *Frankenstein*, published anonymously in 1818, to be the first sci-fi novel, with its archetypal story of forbidden scientific knowledge and a scientist's tragic pride combining to produce both catastrophe and pain.

However, science fiction in the modern mode developed most productively and influentially in the United States, beginning with the pulp magazines of the 1930s and continuing through John W. Campbell's *Astounding Stories* magazine and the so-called "Golden Age" of sci-fi—from 1939 through the 1950s—when writers such as Isaac Asimov, Robert Heinlein, and Arthur C. Clarke wrote their most influential and characteristic works. In later years the picture got both bigger and more complicated, as subgenres developed. For instance, in the 1960s the "New Wave" appeared, encompassing such accomplished writers as Samuel R. Delany, Jr., Thomas Disch, and Michael Moorcock. In addition, since the 1970s several phenomena have complicated the scene; among these are the influx of popular and esteemed women into the field (led by Ursula LeGuin and including, among many others, Pat Murphy, Connie Willis, and Karen Joy Fowler) and, beginning in the mid-1980s, the influence of a subgenre known as cyberpunk, with work typified most clearly by William Gibson, its best-known practitioner, and Bruce Sterling. Now, as the 21st century approaches, the field is more inclusive and less easily described than ever.

Although the literary branch of science fiction is considered by many purists to be the only "true" sci-fi, the newer and more widely popular television and film manifestations of the genre can be considered beneficial; they bring more people to science fiction as a whole, and many of the new fans' interest hopefully will turn to sci-fi literature as well.

TOM MADDOX

Originally conceived as a "'Wagon Train' to the stars," "Star Trek" undoubtedly is the best-known of all science-fiction TV series. Although not spectacularly successful during its three-season original run in 1966–69, left, *it later took on a life of its own, spawning innumerable books, seven hit films, and several new series, including "Deep Space Nine,"* above, *which premiered in 1993.*

© Ted Thai/"Time" Magazine

Sci-fi literature also was affected by renewed public interest in the genre. The biggest growth was in paperbacks based on films or TV shows; these were not considered true science fiction by purists. Other subgenres, however—such as "hard" sci-fi, fantasy, and cyberpunk—also surged in popularity.

As paranoids may have real enemies, *The X-Files* has real grounds for its fantasies. But, as *Independence Day* asserts, wouldn't it be nice if we could confront evil in its naked form and simply destroy it? Then all our fears could be allayed, at least for the moment. Today's world is one in which, increasingly, anything seems possible. Science fiction transforms necessary fears and hopes about this world into aliens, monsters, and mutants—all of them media masks for the dark spaces in the human heart.

The Future of the Sci-Fi Trend. Adding to the current science-fiction proliferation, television—when it is not producing new series or imitating existing ones—parades the history of sci-fi film and television before viewers: recent series, old but memorable series, forgettable series, popular films and unpopular films, made-for-TV films and films that never got theatrical distribution, all in an attempt to satisfy the current hunger.

The question, however, is: How long will it all last? How long before the fad fades and science fiction returns to being the hobby of a few enthusiasts rather than the latest pop-culture craze? On television, the Sci-Fi Channel continues to grow in popularity, and new series continue to be introduced while existing ones for the most part pull in decent ratings. Meanwhile, a line of science-fiction films is awaiting release and sci-fi literature continues its renaissance, with the number of titles published per year having more than doubled since the early 1970s. Growing preoccupation with the beginning of a new century—and millennium—seem to offer sufficient fodder for innumerable new twists on current sci-fi plots. If this preoccupation provides impetus as well for continued public fascination with the genre, the science-fiction invasion could be with us for quite some time to come.

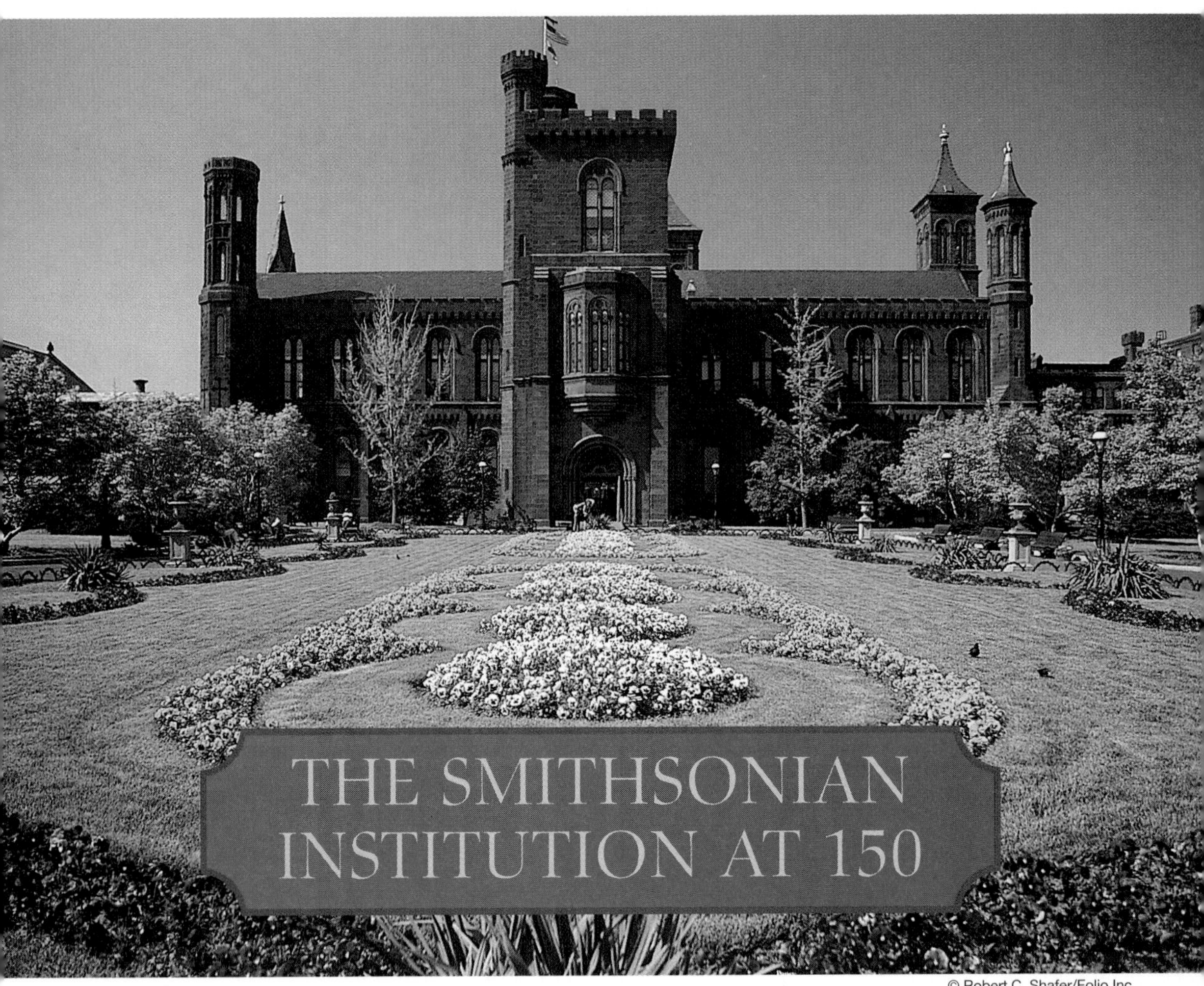

© Robert C. Shafer/Folio Inc.

The Smithsonian Institution, located in Washington, DC, celebrated its 150th anniversary in 1996. Its first building, known as the "Castle," was completed in 1855 and houses the institution's administration offices.

Editor's Note: This article was prepared by the editors of the Annual primarily from information supplied by the Smithsonian Institution. The editors are most grateful to Linda St. Thomas of the Office of Public Affairs of the Smithsonian for reviewing and checking the final draft.

The Smithsonian Institution is not a single museum. Rather it is a complex of 16 museums and galleries and a national zoo (*see* accompanying list). With all but two of its major facilities located in Washington, DC, the Smithsonian Institution is the leading tourist attraction in the United States. No visit to the U.S. capital is complete without a stop at the Smithsonian. Its museums and galleries attract more than 25 million people annually; some 3 million more people visit the National Zoo.

Smithsonian exhibits feature such valuable, interesting, and fun pieces of Americana as the Wright Brothers' plane the *Kitty Hawk* and Charles Lindbergh's plane the *Spirit of St. Louis*, inaugural gowns worn by the first ladies, Alexander Graham Bell's box telephone, tennis rackets belonging to Arthur Ashe and Chris Evert, priceless works of art by some of America's leading painters, the slippers worn by Judy Garland in the 1939 movie hit *The Wizard of Oz*, the Apollo 14 command module, the Hope diamond (the world's largest blue diamond), and television character Archie Bunker's chair. The Smithsonian Astrophysical Observatory at the Harvard-Smithsonian Center for

Astrophysics in Cambridge, MA, the Smithsonian Environmental Research Center in Edgewater, MD, and the Smithsonian Tropical Research Center in Panama are among the nation's foremost research centers. And one of the world's few remaining giant pandas resides at the National Zoo.

Throughout 1996 the spotlight shone on this national jewel in a special way: It turned 150 years old!

Birthday Celebrations. In honor of the Smithsonian's 150th anniversary, more than 300 treasures from its numerous collections—including the compass from the Lewis and Clark expedition, Abraham Lincoln's top hat, a turn-of-the-century-style carousel, a Samuel Morse telegraph key, Dizzy Gillespie's trumpet, and a Thomas Alva Edison lightbulb—were part of a traveling "America's Smithsonian" exhibition. The exhibit, called the "world's largest traveling museum show," was to visit 12 cities during a two-year period, appearing primarily in convention centers. It would give Americans who never have an opportunity to visit Washington a chance to enjoy a taste of the Smithsonian. I. Michael Heyman, who became the secretary (director) of the Smithsonian in 1994, noted that he could "think of no better way to celebrate the Smithsonian's birthday than to take the treasures of the Smithsonian home to as many regions as possible." An estimated 8 million to 10 million Americans were expected to view the exhibit, which took up more than 100,000 sq ft (9 290 m^2) of space. A team headed by J. Michael Carrigan of the National Museum of American History organized the exhibit. It was funded by Discover Card, Intel,

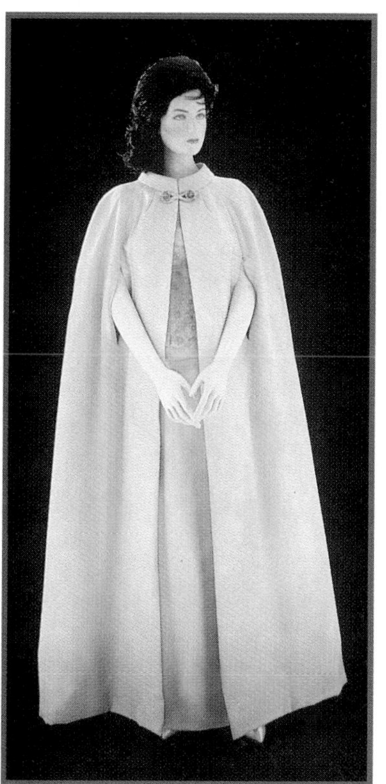

Courtesy, Smithsonian Institution

© Rene Macura/AP/Wide World Photos

Courtesy, Turner Entertainment

In honor of the Smithsonian's 150th birthday, a special exhibit, "America's Smithsonian," traveled throughout the United States. The gown Jacqueline Kennedy wore at her husband's inaugural ball, extreme left, *the Apollo 14 command module,* above, *and the slippers Judy Garland made famous in the movie hit "The Wizard of Oz" were among the more than 300 objects shown.*

THE SMITHSONIAN INSTITUTION

Museums, Galleries, and a National Zoo

© Tal McBride/Folio Inc.

Anacostia Museum, Fort Stanton section of southeast Washington. Founded in 1967, the museum serves as a resource for educational programs related to African-American history and culture.

Arts and Industries Building, Jefferson Drive and Independence Avenue at 9th Street, Washington. Completed in 1881 and restored in 1976, it focuses on Victorian-era Americana. A show of objects from the Philadelphia Centennial Exposition in 1876 is one of its features.

Cooper-Hewitt National Design Museum, 2 East 91st Street, New York City. Founded as the Cooper Union Museum in 1897 and part of the Smithsonian since 1968, the museum features more than 165,000 items and includes a reference library serving design professionals and students of design. A major renovation was completed in 1996.

Freer Gallery of Art, 12th Street and Jefferson Drive SW, Washington. Opened in 1923 and reopened in May 1993 after extensive renovation, the gallery houses a major collection of Asian art, the works of James McNeill Whistler, and other 19th- and early-20th-century American art. An underground exhibition gallery links it with the Sackler Gallery.

Hirshhorn Museum and Sculpture Garden, Eighth Street and Independence Avenue SW, Washington. Opened in 1974, the museum specializes in American and European painting and sculpture of the past 100 years, including more than 7,000 works of art presented to the American people by financier Joseph H. Hirshhorn (1899–1981).

National Air and Space Museum, Seventh Street and Independence Avenue SW, Washington. Founded in 1946 as the National Air Museum and located in its current building since 1976, it memorializes the development of aviation and spaceflight.

National Museum of African Art, 950 Independence Avenue SW, Washington. Established in 1964, incorporated as a bureau of the Smithsonian in 1979, and opened on Washington's National Mall in September 1987, the museum is the only art museum in the United States dedicated exclusively to the heritage of Africa.

National Museum of American Art, Eighth and G Streets NW, Washington. Originating in the mid-19th century and known by its present name since 1980, the museum emphasizes American painting, sculpture, folk art, photography, and

The popular National Zoological Park and the National Museum of Natural History are parts of the Smithsonian. After three years of planning and construction, at a cost of some $4 million, the zoo's Monkey House was converted into the Think Tank, above. *The Think Tank, which opened in the fall of 1995, explores animal thinking, especially regarding the orangutan. Since the Gem and Mineral Hall Gallery of the Natural History Museum has been closed for renovation—until late 1997—the Hope Diamond,* inset below, *has been on view on the second floor of the museum's Rotunda,* below.

© Fred J. Mason/Folio Inc. (inset); © Everett C. Johnson/Folio Inc.

graphic art from the 18th century to the present.

National Museum of American History, 12th Street and Constitution Avenue NW, Washington. Known as the National Museum of History and Technology from its foundation in 1846 until 1980, the museum offers a wide collection of exhibits covering U.S. history.

National Museum of the American Indian. Although some of the museum's collection now is located in the George Gustav Heye Center in the Alexander Hamilton U.S. Custom House in New York City, a permanent museum is to be built on the National Mall in Washington. The building is scheduled for completion early in the 21st century. Established on Nov. 28, 1989, the museum is dedicated to the collection, preservation, study, and exhibition of the living cultures, history, and arts of Native Americans.

© John Skowronski/Folio Inc.

National Museum of Natural History, Tenth Street and Constitution Avenue NW, Washington. Opened in 1910, the museum serves as a national and international center for the study of the natural sciences.

National Portrait Gallery, Eighth and F Streets NW, Washington. Established on April 27, 1962, the gallery is "for the exhibition and study of portraiture depicting men and women who have made significant contributions to the history, development, and culture of the people of the United States."

National Postal Museum, 2 Massachusetts Avenue NE, Washington. Opened on July 30, 1993, the Smithsonian's newest museum recalls the nation's postal history and houses a major philatelic collection.

National Zoological Park, Rock Creek, 2 mi (3.2 km) north of the center of Washington; a separate conservation and research center is located in Front Royal, VA. Established in 1889, the park features some 4,500 living mammals, birds, amphibians, and reptiles of 480 species.

Renwick Gallery, Pennsylvania Avenue and 17th Street NW, Washington. Designed by James Renwick as a public gallery for W.W. Corcoran's artworks and completed in 1874, it was acquired by the Smithsonian in 1965. The gallery exhibits contemporary American crafts as well as objects dating from 1900 from its permanent collection.

Arthur M. Sackler Gallery, National Mall, Washington. Opened to the public in September 1987, the gallery holds the collection of Asian and Near Eastern art donated by Dr. Arthur M. Sackler (1914–87), a medical researcher.

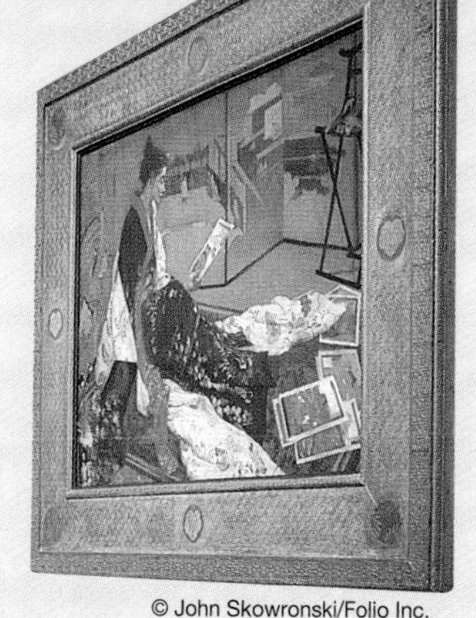

© John Skowronski/Folio Inc.

© Michael Ventura/Folio Inc.

The always-crowded National Air and Space Museum, top, *is home to the Wright Brothers' plane the "Kitty Hawk," Charles Lindbergh's craft the "Spirit of St. Louis," and various memorabilia from the space program. James McNeill Whistler's painting "The Golden Screen" (1864–65),* above, *hangs in the Smithsonian's Freer Gallery of Art. The National Postal Museum,* left, *opened in 1993 and tells the story of the U.S. postal service.*

and MCI Communications Corp.—the first three members of the anniversary's Corporate Partner Program.

On the Smithsonian's actual birthday, August 10, a full-day celebration of song, crafts, other entertainment, and fireworks was held on the National Mall in Washington. In addition, CBS television broadcast two prime-time specials devoted to the Smithsonian, and "Smithsonian Minutes" were aired by the network throughout the year. Such special anniversary exhibits as "Red, Hot, & Blue! American Musicals and the Rise of Popular Culture," "How Things Fly," and "Contemporary Printmaking in America: Collaborative Prints and Presses" opened at the National Portrait Gallery, the National Air and Space Museum, and the National Museum of American Art, respectively. Also, information about the Smithsonian was transmitted electronically on the Internet during the anniversary year. According to Secretary Heyman, the Smithsonian saw the 150th anniversary "as an opportunity to say 'thank you' to the American public" for its support for so many years.

"As we celebrate the sesquicentennial of the Smithsonian Institution, let us recognize the work done by its many museums, research facilities, and educational endeavors and rededicate ourselves to the 'increase and diffusion of knowledge' James Smithson sought to advance."

President Bill Clinton, Feb. 7, 1996

History and Administration. The British scientist James Smithson, who spent his career studying chemicals and minerals, died in 1829 at the age of 64. Although he named his nephew, Henry James Hungerford, as his heir, his will stipulated that if the nephew died without a child—as he did in 1835—the estate would go to the United States to found "at Washington, under the name of the Smithsonian Institution, an establishment for the increase and diffusion of knowledge among men." Smithson believed that knowledge allows learned people to "see a lot where others see nothing." He also wanted the Smithson name to "live in the memory of man." On July 1, 1836, the U.S. Congress accepted the legacy and pledged the faith of the United States to the charitable trust. In 1838 the United States received Smithson's estate, then the equivalent of $515,169.

Although arguments over the makeup of the future national gem ensued, legislation establishing the Smithsonian was signed by President James K. Polk on Aug. 10, 1846. Physicist Joseph Henry agreed to become the Smithsonian's first secretary "to prevent it from falling into worse hands, and with the hope of saving the noble bequest of Smithson from being squandered on chimerical or unworthy projects." Henry, who served as secretary until 1878, believed in the importance of "stimulating the talent of our country to original research" and of pouring new energy into science. He also believed in the importance of establishing collections and was an excellent guiding light for the institution during its initial years.

Architect James Renwick designed the Smithsonian's first building. Known as the "Castle," it took eight years (1847–55) to build. In 1904, Smithson's remains were transferred to Washington and were buried in a chapel at the entrance to the Castle. The Castle also houses the administrative offices, an information center, and the Woodrow Wilson International Center for Scholars. The Wilson Center, the nation's official memorial to the 28th president, is affiliated with the Smithsonian but has its own board of trustees and policies. Washington's National Gallery of Art, founded in 1937, and the John F. Kennedy Cen-

© John Skowronski/Folio Inc.

Thousands of visitors packed the National Mall in Washington, DC, Aug. 9–10, 1996, to mark the Smithsonian's actual birthday. Fireworks, an electronic card, 19 cakes, and a concert contributed to the festivities.

ter for the Performing Arts, which is located on the Potomac River in Washington and which opened in 1971, are two other Smithsonian affiliates that have their own boards of trustees.

The 1846 act establishing the Smithsonian provided that a board of regents, independent of the government itself, would administer the institution's trust. The board of regents includes the chief justice of the United States, the vice-president, three members of the U.S. Senate, three members of the U.S. House of Representatives, and nine citizen members appointed by joint resolution of Congress. The secretary of the Smithsonian, who is appointed by the board, is the institution's chief executive. I. Michael Heyman, the tenth secretary, is the first nonscientist to hold the post. Each museum has its own director and staff.

The Smithsonian employs a permanent staff of some 6,700 people. Nearly 5,000 people serve as volunteers. In fiscal year 1996 the Smithsonian's total net operating revenue was $495.7 million; some 76% of that amount was appropriated by Congress. The balance was received from trust funds; donations; monies raised from membership programs (including the organization's magazine, *Smithsonian*), a mail-order catalog, museum shops, food services, and a publishing program; and federal grants and contracts. The fact that federal appropriations for the Smithsonian increased by more than 3% in fiscal 1996—during a time of budget restraint and debate over budget balancing—illustrated the esteem that the Smithsonian enjoys as an American phenomenon. The enthusiastic public reception to the Smithsonian's 150th birthday attested to its expected increasing popularity during the decades ahead.

One Year After a Peace Agreement

During 1996 the former Yugoslav region remained preoccupied with the implementation of the Bosnian peace settlement—the Dayton Accords—that had been signed by the three Bosnian protagonists in December 1995. The fragile peace was enforced by North Atlantic Treaty Organization (NATO) troops, whose mission was extended in December for a further 18 months. Although general elections were held in Bosnia and Herzegovina, they failed to consolidate the unity of the state. In fact, they primarily strengthened the position of nationalist and authoritarian forces that favored partition of the country.

Meanwhile, both Serbia and Croatia remained racked by internal political turmoil, with growing public protests against the two autocratic regimes. The governments in both Belgrade and Zagreb continued clandestinely to support the partition of Bosnia into three ethnic states. Macedonia remained reasonably stable despite continuing political conflicts, interethnic problems, and tensions with neighbors. Meanwhile, Slovenia held its own general elections and the process of democratization and economic reform helped to move the country closer toward Europe's security and economic structures.

Bosnia and Herzegovina: Peace Without Unification. The Dayton Accords were enforced in Bosnia and Herzegovina during the course of the year. However, while the military aspects of the agreement were implemented fully and on schedule, the civil and political dimensions proved more problematic. NATO's IFOR (implementation force) mission was successful in enforcing the separation of rival armies, monitoring armaments, and deterring any hostile combat operations. However, neither NATO, the Organization for Security and Cooperation in Europe (OSCE), nor any other international agency was able to ensure nationwide freedom of movement, the return of refugees and displaced people to their homes, or the arrest of more than a handful of indicted war criminals.

The Dayton Accords promised peace with justice in Bosnia. But while peace was assured by the NATO presence, justice clearly was not secured in 1996 and only limited progress was made toward ethnic and political reintegration.

The presidents of Bosnia and Herzegovina, Croatia, and Serbia— (above, left to right) *Alija Izetbegovic, Franjo Tudjman, and Slobodan Milosevic—met in Rome, Italy, in February 1996 and pledged to resolve their differences over implementation of the 1995 Dayton Accords that ended Bosnia's civil war. Meanwhile, IFOR (implementation force) troops under the auspices of the North Atlantic Treaty Organization (NATO) sought to prevent the outbreak of new fighting. Their mission was extended for 18 months in December.*

© Haley/Sipa Press

Supporters of the Bosnian Party of Democratic Action (PDA) enjoyed the results of nationwide elections in Bosnia and Herzegovina in mid-September 1996. The PDA candidate, Alija Izetbegovic, a Muslim, was elected chairman of a three-man collective presidency. He was joined on the panel by Momcilo Krajisnik, a Bosnian Serb, and Kresimir Zubak, a Bosnian Croat.

IFOR's primary role was to prevent any new outbreak of fighting, but it was not mandated to engage in national reconstruction and state-building projects. The London Conference, organized by the international community in December, set new deadlines for the numerous civil and political reconstruction tasks that had not been completed. A lengthy list of objectives were specified in the realms of human rights, democracy building, and state construction.

Among the most-criticized features of the NATO operation was the failure to apprehend indicted war criminals. Only seven of the more than 70 indicted culprits were in custody at the International Criminal Tribunal for the former Yugoslavia (ICTY), based at The Hague in the Netherlands. All the detainees were low-level criminals and not the high-ranking officials—including the Bosnian Serb leader Radovan Karadzic—who planned and organized mass murders, rapes, expulsions, and the bombardment of civilian targets. Despite the public replacement of Karadzic by Biljana Plavsic as the Serb leader, Karadzic continued to exercise control from behind the scenes. There was little consensus among the leaders of the Western alliance to pursue war criminals actively because of fear of casualties and a resurgence of violence. (*See also* LAW—*International*.)

NATO also failed to ensure the return of refugees and freedom of movement for all Bosnian residents, a key ingredient of any democratization process. The United Nations estimated that only 250,000 of about 2 million refugees had returned to their original homes, and few families had ventured across the interentity line dividing the republic. All three sides hampered the free movement of people, and Muslims in particular continued to be expelled from Serb- and Croat-controlled areas.

The process of ethnic homogenization continued throughout the year in all three ethnic regions. Instead of cementing together the two halves of Bosnia, the general elections in September consolidated the power of the three ethnonationalist political forces—the Serb Democratic Party (SDP), the Croatian Democratic Union (CDU), and the Muslim Party of Democratic Action (PDA). For example, the PDA and the CDU obtained 23 of 28 seats in the Bosnian Federation parliament. The moderate democratic parties that favored a multiethnic society were elected only to a few seats in the cantonal, regional, and central governments.

After serious disputes, a three-man Bosnian presidency finally was formed, consisting of one Muslim (Alija Izetbegovic), one Serb (Momcilo Krajisnik), and one Croat (Kresimir Zubak). By December an executive cabinet finally was formed in which all three ethnic groups were represented. Nonetheless, the powers of the central government remained limited, while the local and regional authorities in the Muslim-Croat Federation (the Federation of Bosnia-Herzegovina) and the Serb Republic (Republika Srpska) retained greater control. The OSCE rescheduled the local elections for the spring of 1997 after blatant manipulation of refugee voting by the Serb Republic authorities, who were intent on consolidating an "ethnically pure" state.

In December, NATO leaders agreed to prolong their mission in Bosnia by 18 months. The new SFOR (stabilization force) was to consist of about 30,000 troops, approximately half the number of the IFOR operation. Washington agreed to station about 8,500 troops in the country, about half of the U.S. IFOR original total. The United States also launched an "arm and train" program for the Bosnian government army in order to bring it into parity with Serb forces. By the end of the year a $100 million arms shipment was delivered to Sarajevo as part of an overall $400 million program. Nonetheless, suspicions persisted that the Serbs maintained sizable arms stocks and were not complying with arms-reduction agreements.

Some fears remained that the unresolved territorial issue regarding the northern Bosnian town of Brcko could result in new hostilities. The city linked Serb-controlled territories in western and eastern Bosnia. The international arbitration commission postponed its decision on the region until February 1997. Observers believed that if the commission awarded the city to the Muslim-Croat Federation or placed it under an international protectorate, Serb resistance could result in new fighting. The 18-month limitation on the reduced NATO force also would leave insufficient time for political reconstruction and ethnic reconciliation.

The international community also remained concerned about the commitment of Serbian President Slobodan Milosevic and Croatian President Franjo Tudjman to the territorial integrity of

President Slobodan Milosevic (depicted in a prisoner outfit, below*) was the target as massive demonstrations protesting the government's failure to recognize the results of municipal elections in Serbia broke out in Belgrade in November.*

© Art Zamur/Gamma-Liaison

Information Highlights

Nation	Population (in millions)	Area (sq mi)		Capital (km²)	President(s)
Bosnia and Herzegovina	3.6	19,781	51 233	Sarajevo	Alija Izetbegovic (Muslim) Momcilo Krajisnik (Serb) Kresimir Zubak (Croat)
Croatia	4.4	21,829	56 538	Zagreb	Franjo Tudjman
Macedonia (The Former Yugoslav Republic of Macedonia)	2.1	9,781	25 333	Skopje	Kiro Gligorov
Slovenia	2.0	7,836	20 296	Ljubljana	Milan Kucan
Yugoslavia (Serbia and Montenegro)	10.2	39,517	102 350	Belgrade	Zoran Lilic

Bosnia and Herzegovina. Suspicions persisted that they continued to support the partition of the country and eventual annexation by Serbia and Croatia. Furthermore, neither Milosevic nor Tudjman proved cooperative in surrendering indicted war criminals who were residents of territories under their control.

International agencies warned the Bosnian protagonists that further reconstruction assistance would be dependent on full implementation of the Dayton Accords. It was hoped that such warnings would persuade the Serb leadership to be more cooperative, as the Serb Republic received only 2% of about $900 million of reconstruction aid earmarked for Bosnia during 1996. Failure to hand over war criminals or to permit refugees to return home could delay further reconstruction assistance. However, economic pressures alone are unlikely to foster political collaboration and state building. Moreover, Western governments have been divided on whether conditions should be attached to the granting of any future financial assistance.

Serbia-Montenegro: A New Revolt. While Serbia's President Milosevic was viewed as one of the guarantors of the Dayton Accords in Bosnia, he also increased pressures against the domestic opposition in Serbia. Early in the year, several independent media outlets were either closed down or taken over by the state. Official Serbian propaganda depicted Milosevic as a peacemaker who had weathered the storm of international sanctions. The economic sanctions imposed by the United Nations were removed. But the lifting of an "outer wall" of penalties, including access to international credits and financial institutions, remained contingent on definite progress in domestic political and economic reforms.

In November general elections were held to the Federal Republic of Yugoslav's Federal Assembly, consisting of deputies from Serbia and Montenegro; elections to the Montenegrin republican assembly also took place. Milosevic's Socialist Party, in coalition with the Communist Yugoslav United Left, captured the majority of seats in the Yugoslav federal legislature, but narrowly fell short of a two-thirds majority. In Montenegro the ruling Democratic Socialist Party (DSP) won 45 of 71 seats in the republican assembly. The remainder of seats in both parliaments was divided among Serb nationalists and an assortment of moderate parties, including the oppositionist *Zajedno* coalition.

To the surprise of observers, in the local election runoffs in Serbia, held in mid-November, *Zajedno* scored several major victories in Belgrade and a number of Socialist bastions, including Nis and Kragujevac. While *Zajedno* claimed success in 12 cities, the local election commissions overturned the results, claiming various irregularities in the voting. By the end of November, massive demonstrations shook Belgrade and several other towns as protesters claimed the government was defrauding the electorate.

As the protests gained momentum, tens of thousands of students and ordinary citizens joined in the rallies. The state-run media failed to report on the protests and the independent Radio B-92 was banned by the state. The ban later was overruled after a significant international outcry. *Zajedno* leaders initially demanded the reinstatement of the local-election results. But as the protests spread, some opposition spokesmen even demanded the resignation of President Milosevic. While the demonstrations remained peaceful, the security forces did not intervene. However, fears remained that the regime could mobilize its well-armed police forces, numbering about 80,000 troops, to stage a violent crackdown against demonstrators. Violence between government supporters and opponents broke out on December 24. Fifty-eight persons were wounded in the "worst violence in Serbia in five years." Subsequently, on Christmas night, Milosevic's Interior Ministry announced the banning of demonstrations throughout Serbia and warned that police would intervene to prevent protests. Despite a large number of police officers on the streets, tens of thousands of opposition demonstrators defied Milosevic's ban and protested in central Belgrade on December 26.

Milosevic came under growing pressure from the United States and several West European governments not to resort to violence. They threatened a reimposition of economic sanctions and other measures to isolate the Serbian regime. During the protests, Milosevic seemed willing to make some concessions to demonstrators by removing several Socialist officials and reassigning some local governments to the *Zajedno* opposition. The Serbian administration clearly feared that thousands of ordinary workers could join the protests and seriously undermine Socialist rule. The working class in Serbia was increasingly frustrated by falling living standards, unpaid wages, and rising unemployment in the country.

Milosevic proved less able to manipulate Serbian nationalism in order to stay in power as he had during the war in Croatia and Bosnia. With Serbian republican elections scheduled for 1997, Milosevic was concerned that opposition victories in the local elections could erode support for the Socialists in the national ballot. As he was unable under the constitution to stand as Serbian president for a third term, Milosevic probably would move to strengthen the Yugoslav or the federal presidency and maneuver himself into this position in order to maintain power. However, Serbia entered 1997 in a highly volatile state. In addition to mass domestic protests, the largely Albanian province of Kosovo remained extremely tense and, even in Montenegro, the movement for sovereignty grew as dissatisfaction with Belgrade's policies mounted.

Croatia: Political Stalemate. Croatia's President Franjo Tudjman also came under increasing public disaffection for his autocratic rule and the corruption that evidently was rampant in the ruling Croatian Democratic Union (CDU). Having benefited politically from the Croatian recapture of Serb-occupied territories in the Krajina region during the summer of 1995, the president's popularity slipped during the year, particularly in the larger cities.

On four occasions, President Tudjman blocked the Zagreb mayoral candidacy of the seven-party opposition coalition and eventually dissolved the Zagreb city council. The opposition had won control of the city council in October 1995. Despite public protests and charges of manipulation, the president appointed his own political loyalist as the mayor of Zagreb. The opposition subsequently boycotted Assembly sessions, leading to gridlock in the functioning of the city administration. They also staged walkouts from the national parliament, where the CDU maintained a governing majority.

In November, President Tudjman suddenly was rushed to the Walter Reed Hospital, outside Washington, DC; he evidently was suffering from a form of stomach cancer. While U.S. reports signaled that Tudjman had less than two years to live, the official Croatian media refused to report on the president's state of health. In order to thwart independent news, officials threatened to close down the major nongovernmental broadcast outlet, Radio 101, by revoking its license. This move outraged the citizens of Zagreb and, on November 21, about 100,000 demonstrators gathered in the capital to protest. The authorities quickly restored Radio 101's license in order to defuse public anger.

The radio incident indicated how much the authorities feared freedom of information. During the course of the year, pressures were applied on various independent newspapers and other media despite the protests of the international community. Croatia gained admittance to the Council of Europe under extreme reservations that democratization was threatened by Tudjman's autocratic policies. As the president's health likely would decline in the coming year, a major power struggle in the ruling party was expected. The opposition, meanwhile, geared itself for new presidential elections, scheduled for the fall of 1997.

Macedonia: Stability Maintained. Macedonia remained reasonably stable even though interethnic disputes continued with leaders of the large Albanian minority. In particular, the Albanian parties protested the government's refusal to allow for the opening of a separate Albanian university in the city of Tetovo. However, the Albanian parties themselves were split on whether to participate in the country's parliament and thereby support the postcommunist government.

Macedonia's first local elections since gaining independence were held in November. The ruling Social Democratic Alliance of Macedonia (SDAM), led by President Kiro Gligorov, won most of the local councils and mayoralties, ahead of the nationalist bloc as well as the Albanian and other ethnic-based parties. Despite allegations of fraud by some members of the opposition, the OSCE declared that the elections had few irregularities. The main opposition party, the Internal Macedonian Revolutionary Organization (IMRO), claimed that after its strong showing in the municipal ballot—gaining 28 out of 123 mayoralties—it would push for early parliamentary elections. The opposition had boycotted the second round of the general elections held during 1994, charging widespread fraud.

By the close of the year, Macedonia still had not resolved fully its disputes with neighboring Greece regarding the republic's name. Although the issue remained in arbitration, neither side seemed willing to compromise. Athens still claimed that Macedonian nationalists were laying claim to Greek territo-

© Laurent Van Der Stockt/Gamma-Liaison

Freedom of movement, including the return of refugees, remained an unresolved issue in Bosnia despite the Dayton Accords. In accordance with the agreement, however, Bosnian Muslims and Serbs freed some of the prisoners of war (above) *on Jan. 19, 1996.*

ry, while Skopje asserted that the Macedonian name was not a Greek copyright. Macedonia's relations with the Federal Republic of Yugoslavia (Serbia-Montenegro) gradually improved during the year after Belgrade formally agreed in April to recognize Macedonia's independence. UN troops with a small U.S. contingent also remained in the country as a potential deterrent to any hostile actions by the Milosevic regime.

Slovenia: Progress Toward Europe. Slovenia continued to make the fastest progress of all the former Yugoslav republics toward membership in Europe's economic and security institutions. The country remained politically stable with no domestic ethnic conflict or serious territorial disputes. Slovenia's differences with Croatia over access to the Adriatic Sea did not threaten to escalate, and Ljubljana largely settled its dispute with Rome regarding compensation for Italian residents who fled or were expelled from Slovenia at the close of World War II.

The country's general elections in November proved inconclusive. No party or coalition won a sufficient number of seats to form a governing majority quickly. The Liberal Democratic Party (LDP) of Prime Minister Janez Drnovsek obtained 25 seats to the National Assembly, the oppositionist Slovene People's Party (SPP) gained 19 seats, and the Social Democratic Party (SDP) won 16 seats. The former Communist United List lost most of its support base in the ballot. By the close of December, negotiations were continuing on forming a viable governing coalition. In early January 1997, Drnovsek looked set to form a new minority cabinet after a defector from a right-wing party broke the two-month standstill. His action apparently gave Drnovsek, a committed pro-European, a one-vote margin in parliament.

Slovenia's political progress and stability enhanced its international reputation as well as its bid for membership in the European Union (EU) and NATO. Although Ljubljana still needed to conduct a far-reaching privatization program and other economic reforms, its foreign trade increased and the country maintained the highest per-capita income of all the former communist states of Eastern Europe. In June, Slovenia signed an agreement to become an associate member of the EU.

Having developed military ties with several Western states, Slovenia also was being considered seriously for inclusion in NATO's enlargement, and was defined increasingly as a Central European state. The NATO summit, scheduled to be held in the spring of 1997, reportedly would specify the prime candidates for early membership in the alliance.

JANUSZ BUGAJSKI
Director of East European Studies
Center for Strategic and International Studies

The Alphabetical Section

As 1996 drew to a close, the United Nations General Assembly elected Kofi Annan (*below, left*), a 58-year-old career UN diplomat from Ghana, as the seventh secretary-general of the world body; and the public was flocking to purchase the best-selling *My Sergei: A Love Story*—Ekaterina Gordeeva's account of her life with her husband and ice-skating partner, Sergei Grinkov, who died of a heart attack at the age of 28 in November 1995. The Olympic and world-champion skater also delighted audiences by returning to the ice and performing solo (*below*). Broadway theatergoers, meanwhile, were captivated by the revival of *The King and I*, featuring Lou Diamond Phillips as the king of Siam and Donna Murphy as Anna (*top, page 103*). The show took a Tony for best musical revival and Donna Murphy captured one as best actress in a musical.

Economically, it was a good year for Wall Street as the Dow Jones industrial average celebrated its 100th birthday by breaking the 6,000 mark—then passing 6,500—before closing out the year at 6,448.27. Alan Greenspan, the chairman of the Federal Reserve Board, sent the market and economic analysts into a momentary tailspin when he suggested in December that stocks might be overvalued (*cartoon*). And politically, there was a record number of referenda and initiatives on November ballots across the United States. In California, Proposition 211, which would have made it easier for investors to sue corporations that forecast sales and profits that do not materialize, led to a heated exchange (*photo, bottom, page 103*). The proposition was defeated by a three-to-one margin.

© Sygma

© Jim McKnight/AP/Wide World Photos

© Joan Marcus

© Jeff Stahler/reprinted by permission of Newspaper Enterprise Association Inc.

© Andy Kuno/AP/Wide World Photos

ABORTION

Amid evidence that abortions are on the decline in the United States, a woman's right to obtain an abortion continued to be a volatile issue in 1996. The U.S. Supreme Court heard a case involving abortion opponents who prevent women from entering abortion clinics. A ruling was expected in 1997.

Trends. According to the Centers for Disease Control and Prevention (CDC), the rate at which U.S. women obtain legal abortions continued to fall after peaking in 1990. By 1994, the latest year for which statistics were available, the rate had fallen to 21 per 1,000—the lowest rate since 1976. It was unclear whether the decline in abortion rates was due to changing public attitudes, a reduction in availability of abortion services in recent years, or merely a decline in the number of fertile women resulting from the aging of the U.S. population.

Partial-Birth Abortions. Abortion opponents focused their efforts on a campaign to ban "partial-birth abortion," a late-term abortion technique in which a doctor removes the fetus feetfirst from the womb before crushing its skull to ease passage of the head through the birth canal. The procedure was banned by Congress on March 27 with a bill that would have made it a federal crime for a doctor to perform a partial-birth abortion unless it was needed to save the woman's life. Arguing that the procedure also should be allowed in order to protect the woman's ability to have children in the future, President Bill Clinton vetoed the measure (HR 1833) on April 10.

The drive to ban the procedure was mired in controversy stemming from graphic evidence presented in congressional hearings preceding the measure's passage. Pro-choice advocates, including the president, argued unsuccessfully that a partial-birth abortion was reserved for late-term abortions, when the decision to interrupt a pregnancy usually is dictated by evidence of grave birth defects that would result in the baby's death in any case. They maintained that such cases numbered no more than a few hundred per year and that alternative abortion techniques at that stage carried the risk of destroying the woman's ability to have children in the future. Pro-choice advocates also charged that the effort to ban the procedure was a ploy to establish a legal precedent aimed at overturning legalized abortion altogether.

The supporters of the ban claimed that doctors regularly elected to perform partial-birth abortions—and at earlier stages of pregnancy, when more humane techniques are available. On September 20 the House overrode the president's veto of the ban, but the veto stood after the Senate vote on September 26 fell nine votes short of the required two-thirds majority.

Despite the defeat of the ban, antiabortion advocates claimed a victory of sorts in the battle they are waging to obtain a reversal of the Supreme Court's landmark 1973 ruling in *Roe v. Wade*, which affirms a woman's right to obtain an abortion. Unlike previous campaigns, which focused on abortion in general, 1996's effort persuaded Congress to approve the first legislative ban of a specific abortion procedure. Both sides in the debate expected the newly elected Congress to take up the issue in 1997.

State Laws. Several tough antiabortion laws enacted by states in recent years were weakened or overturned in 1996. A 1991 Utah law banning abortions except in cases when the woman's life is in danger, when the child would be born with serious defects, or when the pregnancy resulted from rape or incest was ruled unconstitutional in December on grounds that it infringed on a woman's right to choose. Mississippi's abortion law, one of the toughest in the country, was weakened in September when a federal judge struck down provisions found to impose unconstitutional obstacles against abortion providers and their patients.

RU-486. Meanwhile, the Clinton administration made it easier for women to terminate unwanted pregnancies without resorting to surgical abortion—or facing harassment from antiabortion picket lines. The Food and Drug Administration (FDA) announced in September that it conditionally was approving the prescription sale of mifepristone, or RU-486, a drug that induces abortion. Additional information concerning labeling and manufacturing was needed before the FDA granted final approval of the drug. Although the "abortion pill" was introduced in 1988 in France, abortion opponents had succeeded in blocking the drug's availability in the United States by threatening to boycott its French manufacturer, Roussel Uclaf, and any American company that tried to market it in the United States. The Population Council, a family-planning research organization that acquired the drug's U.S. patent rights, said it would not reveal the name of the company that was expected to begin providing RU-486 in the United States sometime in 1997.

MARY H. COOPER
"The CQ [Congressional Quarterly] Researcher"

ACCIDENTS AND DISASTERS

AVIATION

Jan. 8—A cargo plane crashes into a busy market in Kinshasa, Zaire, killing at least 350 persons.

Feb. 6—A German jet carrying tourists home from the Dominican Republic crashes into the Atlantic Ocean about 13 mi (20 km) off the Dominican Republic's coast, killing all 189 aboard.

Feb. 26—A Sudanese military plane crashes and burns just before reaching the Khartoum airport; all 70 aboard are killed.

Feb. 29—All 123 persons aboard are killed when a Peruvian jet crashes in the Andes en route to Arequipa from Lima.

April 3—Thirty-five persons, including U.S. Commerce Secretary Ron Brown, are killed when a U.S. Air Force plane crashes near Dubrovnik, Croatia.

April 11—A single-engine plane crashes shortly after takeoff from Cheyenne, WY. The plane was piloted by 7-year-old Jessica Dubroff, who was attempting to become the youngest person to fly a plane across North America. Jessica, her flight instructor, and her father are killed.

May 10—During a joint U.S.-British training exercise in eastern North Carolina, two helicopters collide in midair, killing 14 U.S. Marines.

May 11—A passenger jet crashes into Florida's Everglades near Miami, killing all 110 persons aboard.

July 15—A Belgian-made military plane crashes and bursts into flames while trying to land at an airport in Eindhoven, the Netherlands; 32 persons are killed.

July 17—A TWA jetliner bound for Paris, France, explodes and crashes into the Atlantic shortly after takeoff from Kennedy International Airport in New York City, killing all 230 aboard.

Aug. 29—A Russian jet crashes into a mountain on the island of Spitsbergen, Norway, killing all 141 persons aboard.

Oct. 2—All 70 persons aboard are left dead when a Peruvian passenger jet crashes into the Pacific Ocean north of Lima, en route from Miami, FL, to Santiago, Chile.

Oct. 22—A cargo plane bound from Ecuador to Miami, FL, crashes into a crowded neighborhood in Manta, Ecuador, killing at least 30 persons.

Oct. 31—Shortly after takeoff, a Brazilian jet crashes into a residential section of São Paulo, killing at least 104 persons.

Nov. 7—A Nigerian jetliner crashes into a swampy area southeast of Lagos; all 141 on board are left dead.

Nov. 12—Two passenger airliners—a Saudi jumbo jet and a Kazakh plane—collide in midair north of New Delhi, India; 349 persons are killed.

Nov. 23—A hijacked Ethiopian passenger jet crash-lands in the Indian Ocean after running out of fuel; 125 persons are killed.

FIRES AND EXPLOSIONS

Jan. 31—Dynamite illegally stored in an apartment building in Shaoyang, China, explodes, killing more than 100 persons.

March 19—A fast-moving fire breaks out in a disco in a suburb of Manila, Philippines, killing more than 150 persons, most of them teenagers celebrating the end of the school year.

March 28—A shopping mall in Bogor, Indonesia, is swept by fire in the early-morning hours, killing at least 78 persons.

June 6—At least 72 persons are left dead when a fire sweeps through a ship traveling on the Red Sea between Eritrea and Saudi Arabia.

June 11—An explosion in a newly built shopping mall near São Paulo, Brazil, kills 39 persons.

June 29—An explosion at a fireworks factory in the village of Piya in southwestern China kills at least 36 persons.

July 17—Smoke from a restaurant fire spreads to an upstairs hotel in Shenzhen, China, killing 29 persons.

Nov. 19—Thirty-nine persons are killed when fire breaks out in a downtown high-rise building in Hong Kong.

Nov. 21—A violent explosion—apparently caused by a gas leak—at a store in San Juan, Puerto Rico, kills at least 27.

Nov. 27—A gas explosion in a coal mine in Henan province, north-central China, kills at least 91 miners. A similar accident in the same province killed 84 miners in May.

Dec. 22—An explosion tears through a metal-fabricating plant in Cypress, TX, killing eight employees.

LAND AND SEA TRANSPORTATION

Jan. 1—Twenty-six persons die near Sonoita, Mexico, when two buses collide on a highway.

Jan. 19—An overcrowded ferry sinks off the northern coast of Sumatra, Indonesia; at least 54 are left dead.

Feb. 10—A car and bus traveling through a road tunnel near Shakotan, Japan, are crushed when a 50,000-ton boulder falls on the mountain tunnel's roof; 20 persons are killed.

Feb. 16—An Amtrak passenger train headed for Chicago crashes into a local train in a snowstorm in Silver Spring, MD; 11 persons—all on the commuter train—are killed.

Feb. 18—An overloaded ferry capsizes at the entrance to the port at Cadiz, Philippines, killing at least 50 persons.

March 28—A ferry capsizes in a remote area off the southwestern coast of Haiti, killing more than 100 persons.

May 6—More than 140 persons are left dead or missing when an overloaded boat en route to Guinea capsizes off the coast of Sierra Leone.

May 21—A ferry traveling on Lake Victoria between two Tanzanian cities capsizes, killing more than 500 passengers.

STORMS, FLOODS, AND EARTHQUAKES

Feb. 3—A strong earthquake strikes a mountainous region of southwestern China, killing at least 240 persons.

Feb. 17—At least 100 are left dead when a powerful earthquake hits the remote islands of Biak and Yapen off Indonesia, setting off dangerous tsunamis.

April 22—Heavy floods hit Afghanistan, leaving at least 100 dead.

April 23—A series of major tornadoes tears through parts of Kentucky and Arkansas, killing 13 persons.

May 11—Eight mountain climbers are feared dead after a sudden severe storm hits Mount Everest; it is the worst single loss of life in the history of the mountain.

May 13—Central Bangladesh is hit by a tornado featuring 125-mph (200-km/hr) winds; some 600 persons are killed.

June 16—At least 125 are killed when a slow-moving cyclone hits coastal areas of southeastern India.

July 14—A landslide brought on by heavy monsoon rains causes a landslide in West Bengal state, India, killing 37 persons. At least 291 persons have been killed over two weeks by heavy monsoon-related flooding.

July 25—Prolonged flooding brought on by heavy seasonal rain hits much of China; more than 950 have been left dead by Yangtze River flooding since the year's start.

Aug. 7—Flash floods caused by a dam collapse after heavy rains hit a campground in the Spanish Pyrenees near the French border, killing at least 83 persons.

Aug. 22–23—Thousands of Hindu pilgrims are trapped—and at least 239 are left dead—when an unexpected snowstorm hits the Himalayan mountains in the Jammu and Kashmir section of India during a yearly pilgrimage to a mountain temple.

Sept. 1—Almost 400 persons have died since the beginning of July in northern Vietnam as the result of severe flooding caused by tropical storms and typhoons.

Sept. 5—At least 30 persons are left dead as Hurricane Fran devastates parts of the Carolinas with winds reaching 120 mph (193 km/h) and causes extensive flooding in Virginia, West Virginia, and Maryland.

Sept. 9—Guangdong province in southern China is struck by a powerful typhoon, killing at least 114 persons.

Nov. 6—A cyclone hits Andhra Pradesh province in southeastern India, killing more than 1,000 persons.

Nov. 21—At least 12 deaths result from severe storms that caused record rains, early snow, and an ice storm in the U.S. Pacific Northwest.

Nov. 25—Freezing rain and ice storms spread through the U.S. Plains states, killing 17 persons.

MISCELLANEOUS

March 16—An avalanche destroys several houses in the Neelum Valley of Pakistani-held Kashmir, killing at least 32 persons.

May 31–June 3—Heavy rains trigger landslides near a gold mine in southwestern China, killing at least 100 persons.

July 12—At least 20 persons in Texas and Oklahoma are killed by a heat wave featuring temperatures of more than 100° F (38° C) for eight consecutive days.

Aug. 31—A van containing five persons—including four children—rolls into a lake in Union, SC. The five in the car, as well as two other adults who attempt a rescue, drown. The group was visiting a memorial to two children whose mother intentionally drowned them in the lake in October 1994.

Oct. 16—Eighty fans are trampled to death at an overcrowded stadium in Guatemala City, Guatemala, just before a World Cup soccer qualifying match.

Oct. 27—A 12-story apartment building in a suburb of Cairo, Egypt, collapses, killing at least 15 persons.

ADVERTISING

The U.S. ad industry broke some long-standing taboos in 1996, but also exhibited self-regulatory restraint out of concern that freewheeling advertising practices could usher in regulatory or legislative action.

Children were the focus of the White House Conference on Children's Television in July, where children's marketers proposed initiatives to back quality TV programming for children. The standards of all media came into question, however, as the Federal Trade Commission launched a probe into the standards and practices used by various media to screen ads for truthfulness and consumer fraud.

Liquor and Tobacco Advertising. In perhaps the most controversial event of the year, the distilled-spirits industry lifted its self-imposed ban on broadcast advertising. Though the ban was never law, the move shocked consumer groups and regulators, who feared hard-liquor ads might encourage young people to drink. The decision inspired talk of legislation to ban broadcast liquor advertising; the Federal Communications Commission sought to bring the ads under its regulatory oversight.

Regulatory forces also had an impact on tobacco advertising. The Food and Drug Administration issued regulations, set to take effect in 1997, that would restrict tobacco ads in outdoor media near schools and playgrounds and in magazines with a significant percentage of young readers. The rules also barred tobacco sponsorship of certain types of sporting events. The tobacco industry and ad-trade groups went to court to challenge the regulations.

Some ad executives broke ranks to form the Initiative on Tobacco Marketing and Children, which sought an industry-imposed ban on tobacco advertising that could influence children. Meanwhile, outdoor advertising firm 3M Media ceased accepting tobacco ads. The National Advertising Review Council initiated, but then backed off from, an attempt to develop industry guidelines to self-regulate "age-restricted" forms of advertising for products such as alcohol and tobacco.

The Internet. On-line advertising was the rage in 1996, though it was still more talk than action. Internet and other on-line ad spending was estimated to have risen to as much as $300 million in 1996—a tiny fraction of the more than $100 billion spent on traditional media ads in the United States. Moreover, most of that spending was done by Internet-related companies. Few general consumer marketers were using the Internet in a meaningful way in 1996, though they were expected to step up their activity dramatically.

In an innovative advertising use of the Internet, CyberGold tested a method that paid cash to on-line users who devoted attention to ads. And "junk" E-mail became an issue as America Online went to court to stop CyberPromotions from sending unsolicited promotional offers to its members.

Ad Spending. Fueled by about $1.5 billion in incremental ad spending from the Atlanta Summer Olympics and the presidential-election campaign—as well as strong demand in most product categories—most major media saw significant gains. McCann-Erickson estimated that 1996 U.S. ad revenues rose 7.6%, to $173.2 billion, and forecast that U.S. ad spending would rise 5.6% in 1997, to $182.9 billion. The agency also predicted that worldwide ad spending would rise 5. 9%, to $413.8 billion. The robust growth belied a loss of confidence in the accountability of traditional ad media—particularly in the research systems used to measure audience exposure. Nielsen Media Research came under attack by TV networks and ad agencies, and major magazine publishers withdrew support for Mediamark Research Inc.'s readership reports.

Agencies. It was a record year in terms of industry consolidation, as major agency holding companies continued gobbling up independent ad agencies. The year began with Omnicom's acquisition of Ketchum Communications. Interpublic acquired direct-marketing agency Draft Direct; UK-based GGT Group purchased Paris-based BDDP; and Young & Rubicam bought Waring and LaRosa. True North acquired interactive-ad specialist Modem Media and merged it into its TN Technologies unit. In perhaps the year's most symbolic deal, MacManus Group acquired most of N.W. Ayer & Partners, Madison Avenue's oldest continuously operating full-service ad agency. European media-buying juggernaut Carat entered the U.S. marketplace with the acquisition of New York–based Media Buying Services.

Creativity. Creatively, 1996 was a relatively uncontroversial period. Computerized effects emerged as a major technique, with several campaigns "resurrecting" late pop-culture icons like John Wayne (Coors beer) and Jackie Gleason (Braun kitchen appliances). Madison Avenue reached out to an unusual crop of ad spokespersons, including defeated presidential candidate Bob Dole and anthropologist Jane Goodall.

JOE MANDESE, *"The Myers Reports"*

AFGHANISTAN

In 1996 the forces in Afghanistan's multisided civil war realigned themselves, with minority factions joining forces against the increasingly dominant Taliban. Narcotics trafficking financed much of the fighting. The economy declined as surrounding nations secretly supported warring groups, undercutting peacemaking efforts.

Civil War. The main conflict pitted the multiethnic government of Burhanuddin Rabbani, a Tajik, against Taliban, a Pashtun group of religious zealots under Mohammed Omar. On September 12, Taliban forces occupied the provincial capital of Jalalabad, and two weeks later marched into the capital, Kabul, virtually unopposed, as Rabbani and his forces fled north. Taliban immediately seized and executed former President Najib, the last Soviet-installed Afghan leader, who since 1992 had been secluded in a United Nations (UN) compound. By October, Taliban controlled two thirds of Afghanistan.

Taliban's successes drove other warring factions to ally themselves with Rabbani. In May, Gulbuddin Hekmatyar, formerly Rabbani's fiercest enemy, joined the government and in June became its prime minister. To the north, the Uzbek militia under Gen. Abdul Rashid Dostam signed a formal pact with the government, as did the United Party, a Shiite faction of the central highlands. The actual fighting, however, was between Taliban and government troops under Ahmad Shah Massoud, who retook key objectives north of Kabul in October.

Economy. With inflation running at 50% per month, the afghani fell in value from 5,000 to the dollar in 1995 to 15,500 to the dollar in July 1996. And with tens of millions of mines and other live explosives in the countryside, the reestablishment of agriculture was hindered. But poppy cultivation for heroin yielded such high and immediate profits that Afghanistan soon lagged behind only Myanmar (Burma) as an international supplier of narcotics. Taliban, which came to power vowing to establish law, order, and morality, did nothing to stop the traffic, financing its own movement and warfare with the profits that previously had gone to the drug lords it displaced.

Society. By 1996 the warfare that had started in 1978 had killed more than 1 million Afghans, displaced 8 million of the country's 15 million citizens, shredded its economy, and destroyed an age-old social fabric. As a result, many Afghans accepted Taliban as a necessary source of harsh discipline to restore stability. Although never before practiced in Afghanistan, such punishments as stoning to death of adulterers and amputation of hands or feet for thieves were imposed without objection.

AFGHANISTAN • Information Highlights

Official Name: Islamic State of Afghanistan.
Location: Central Asia.
Area: 250,000 sq mi (647 500 km²).
Population (mid-1996 est.): 21,500,000.
Chief Cities (1988 est.): Kabul, the capital, 1,424,400; Kandahar, 225,500; Herat, 177,300.
Government: *Head of state,* Burhanuddin Rabbani, president (took office January 2, 1993). *Head of government,* Gulbuddin Hekmatyar, prime minister (sworn in June 17, 1996). *Legislature*—unicameral Parliament (non-functioning).
Monetary Unit: Afghani (15,500 afghanis equal U.S.$1, July 1996).

Women were forbidden to work, to be educated, or to appear in public without an accompanying male relative, and they had to wear a head-to-toe tentlike *burka* whenever outside the home. Men were required to grow beards. Movies, soccer, kite flying, and even chess and marbles were outlawed. There were ritual "hangings" of television sets to show rejection of the modern age. Prayer was a five-times-daily obligation for all.

Eventually, however, reaction began to set in. Taliban was ethnically Pashtun, as were the areas it first took over. As Taliban moved into and beyond Herat and Kabul, its members confronted other ethnic groups, and reports of atrocities against minorities began to filter out. Tens of thousands of Kabul professionals and their families, including Pashtuns, fled the capital in fear of what Taliban rule would bring. At year's end, resistance to Taliban appeared to be growing as the traditional refusal of the Afghan populace to accept despotism reasserted itself.

Foreign Affairs. Covert foreign support of the government and its opponents undercut well-meaning but ineffective peacemaking efforts by special UN commissioners and U.S. officials. Russia and India continued to bolster the Rabbani government with money, arms, and munitions, as did Iran after its client United Party joined the anti-Taliban coalition. Uzbekistan and Russia supported General Dostam. Despite official denials, Pakistan probably still was sponsoring Taliban, both to thwart Russian and Indian influence in Afghanistan and to impose enough stability to permit construction of a railroad and pipeline into Central Asia.

ANTHONY ARNOLD
Freelance Writer on Afghanistan

AFRICA

Sub-Saharan Africa experienced both horror and hope in 1996. Burundi and Rwanda remained in perilous states of crisis (*see* SIDEBAR, page 112), while other conflicts remained unresolved in Liberia and Somalia. In Nigeria human rights and political freedom continued to be violated by the regime of Gen. Sani Abacha. On a more positive note, new attention was cast on the growth of democracy in Africa (*see* SPECIAL REPORT, page 110). Elections took place in 17 sub-Saharan African nations during the year. In such countries as Benin, Uganda, Zimbabwe, and Zambia, opposition parties and leaders faced restrictions or were intimidated, while in Ghana and Sierra Leone, international observers judged the elections to be free and fair. In December, President Nelson Mandela signed South Africa's new constitution, which guarantees an open and democratic political process and a wide range of human rights and freedoms.

In Somalia, Gen. Mohammed Farah Aidid, who had played a key role in the 1991 overthrow of former President Mohammed Siad Barre and who had defied the United Nations (UN) peacekeeping mission in 1993, died in July of wounds received in a battle with a rival clan group in the capital city of Mogadishu. Since the 1995 departure of UN troops, Aidid had taken over part of Somalia and had been fighting rivals for control of Mogadishu and the country. Early in August, he was succeeded by his 33-year-old son, Hussein Mohammed Aidid, a former U.S. Marine holding dual citizenship. At year's end the conflict between rival clans for the control of Mogadishu continued, with more than 100 killed and hundreds wounded in a December conflict that was said to have been organized by Aidid's major rival, Ali Mahdi Mohammed, whose clan controlled north Mogadishu. Aidid forces also were threatened by those of Osman Hassan Ali Atto, a former ally, who commanded the area east of the city. Aidid refused to participate in peace talks organized by Ethiopia that successfully had convened many of Somalia's leading warlords.

New attempts were made to implement a peace plan for war-torn Liberia. In April a cease-fire that had been established in September 1995 was broken when heavy fighting occurred in the capital city of Monrovia. However, at an August summit meeting in Abuja, Nigeria, Liberia's major warlords—Charles Taylor, Alhaji Kromah, George Boley, and Roosevelt Johnson—agreed that Ruth Perry, a former senator, would head a new interim government. The Economic Community of West African States (ECOWAS), which brought the groups together, had high hopes that a new cease-fire would end a conflict that had resulted in more than 150,000 deaths. Under the terms of the agreement, Taylor, Kromah, and Boley all would be part of a six-member interim Council of State. The new interim government was charged with preparing for national elections in May 1997 and for an elected administration to take power in June.

The Ghanian presidential and parliamentary elections, held in December, were in many ways a referendum on the rule of Jerry Rawlings, who first took over power in a coup in 1981. In 1991, under pressure from external sources, he opened up the political process,

At the presidential palace in Abidjan, Ivory Coast, on Nov. 30, 1996, Sierra Leone President Ahmad Tejan Kabbah (left) *and rebel leader Foday Sankoh* (right) *signed a peace agreement ending five years of civil war. The president of Ivory Coast, Henri Konan Bédié* (center), *hosted the ceremony.*

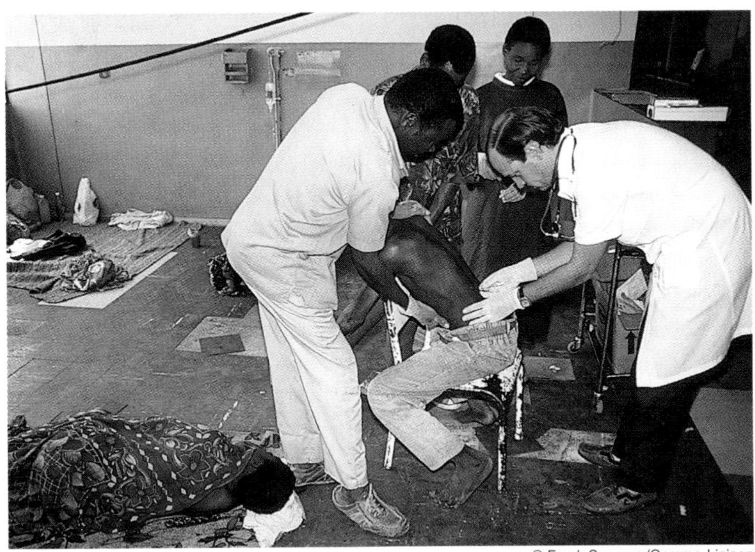

© Frank Spooner/Gamma-Liaison

An unusually severe outbreak of bacterial meningitis swept through West Africa in 1996, killing thousands of people. Children, in particular, were affected.

and a year later there was a return to multiparty electoral politics. In December 1996, Rawlings was reelected for a four-year term, with 57% of the votes cast. Opposition leader John Kufuor won 40% of the vote. In the parliamentary elections, Rawlings' party won 132 of 200 seats, while Kufuor's two-party coalition won 65 seats. Ghanaian and foreign observers agreed that the elections were fair.

In Zimbabwe a bitter strike that pitted the government against nurses and junior doctors ended in December. The strike all but closed down many urban hospitals and led to many deaths. The government, which refused to negotiate or to deliver on its promised pay increases, fired all the strikers but soon found that there were none ready to replace them. For many Zimbabweans this was seen as yet another example of the government's increasing insensitivity, especially during a year in which President Robert Mugabe was reelected to a third six-year term.

In December, President Mobutu Sese Seko of Zaire returned to the capital city of Kinshasa after recuperating from prostate-cancer surgery in France. On the day after his return, he named Lt. Gen. Mahele Bakungo Lieko as the chief of staff of the military, succeeding Gen. Eluki Monga, who was suspended in November after stating publicly that Zaire's army was demoralized and ill-equipped. The country faced major fighting in the eastern Kivu regions between the Zairian army and the Banyamulenge—Zairian Tutsi antigovernment forces led by Laurent Désiré Kabila that have resisted expulsion from the country.

PATRICK O'MEARA and N. BRIAN WINCHESTER
Indiana University

© Jean-Michel Turpin/Gamma-Liaison

At the request of the government of the Central African Republic, French troops intervened to quell an uprising by mutinous soldiers in the former French colony in the spring. The mutinous troops were demanding back pay.

Democracy in Africa

When the Berlin Wall fell in 1989, only five African states—Gambia, Senegal, Zimbabwe, Botswana, and Mauritius—could claim to be multiparty democracies. Little more than one year later, more than 20 African governments had been forced to initiate some semblance of democratic reform. Religious leaders, trade unionists, students, human-rights activists, and others challenged African autocrats to bring economic well-being and political stability after nearly three decades of mostly authoritarian rule. Within the space of four years (1990–94), half of sub-Saharan Africa's governments held multiparty elections and two thirds experienced some political liberalization in response to growing pressure for democratic change "from the streets" and from external donors. The spate of elections in 1996 and those scheduled for 1997 were the consequence of a pro-democracy "revolution" that began at the start of the 1990s.

Democracy and Change. Events in 1996 underscored the fragility of Africa's democratic successes. Coups overthrew the democratically elected government in Niger and replaced the military ruler of Sierra Leone with a supreme military council in January, although the military juntas in both countries made good on promises to hold presidential elections later in the year.

Africa was the world's most electorally active continent in 1996, with 17 contests that ranged from military-controlled elections (Chad, Equatorial Guinea, Gambia, Niger, Sudan, and Sierra Leone) to votes of confidence on governments formed during the multiparty, pro-democratic movement of the early 1990s (Benin, Cape Verde, São Tomé and Príncipe, and Zambia). There also were elections that essentially served as referenda on long-serving presidents in Zimbabwe, Uganda, and Ghana.

Jerry Rawlings, a former air-force pilot who had ruled Ghana since a 1981 coup, was reelected president with 57% of the vote in December balloting that was judged to be fair.

© Clement N'taye/AP/Wide World Photos

Perhaps the most surprising election occurred in Benin, which had been a model of democratic reform since 1991, when a national conference stripped Benin's dictator of his power and successfully organized the country's first democratic election in about 30 years. Five years later, Benin's voters reversed themselves by electing the former Marxist dictator, Mathieu Kérékou, to replace President Nicephore Soglo.

For the first time since independence in 1975, presidential succession in Comoros was decided by a free and fair election rather than by a coup or an assassination. Mohamed Taki Abdoulkarim, a veteran politician and leader of the Union for Democracy and Decentralization, became the new president in March, after receiving 64% of the vote. Two other island groups, Cape Verde and São Tomé and Príncipe, reinforced their commitment to democracy in their second multiparty presidential elections; incumbents were reelected.

Zambian President Frederick Chiluba won reelection and his ruling Movement for Multi-Party Democracy won an overwhelming majority of parliamentary seats, but the country's reputation as a champion of multiparty democracy was tarnished in the process. Certain opposition candidates, most notably former President Kenneth Kaunda, were excluded from competing because of a controversial law passed by the Chiluba government requiring both parents of candidates to have been born in Zambia. Opponents also charged the government with buying votes and omitting tens of thousands of names from the voters' roll. External donors, including the United States, considered the charges credible enough to threaten Zambia with a withdrawal of aid.

Military Regimes and the Struggle for Democracy. Most elections called by soldier-politicians were simple attempts to legitimize power seized by earlier coups. Not surprisingly, many were marred by irregularities. President Teodoro Obiang Nguema Mbasogo of Equatorial Guinea was reelected in February—with more than 98% of the votes cast—amid opposition charges of fraud and a call for an election boycott. (Three of the four opposition candidates eventually withdrew.) Foreign observers refused to participate.

Lt. Gen. Omar Hassan Ahmed al-Bashir, who came to power in Sudan in an Islamic military coup in 1989, was elected president in March with 76% of the vote in Sudan's first "national" election in a decade. Political parties had been banned and opponents alleged widespread coercion and fraud. Furthermore, the election hardly could be considered national in scope while the civil war in the south continued unabated.

So flawed was the July presidential election in Niger that some likened it to a coup. The national electoral commission was disbanded before polls had closed and government security forces "invaded" polling stations, ejected political-party delegates, and confiscated ballot boxes. Protests by the labor unions were ineffective and Col. Ibrahim Baré Maïnassara, who had seized power in a January 1996 coup, was declared president. Gambia's head of state, Capt. Yahya Jammeh, who overthrew former President Dawda Jawara in a coup in July 1994, was elected president in September with more than 60% of the vote. A ban on political activities had been lifted only weeks before the announced election date, but remained in effect on the three political parties that had dominated Gambian politics for the previous 20 years.

In Sierra Leone, despite a military coup in January and a civil war that had forced half of the country's inhabitants into exile, the military voluntarily relinquished power to civilian rule in a presidential election won by Ahmad Tejan Kabbah, a former civil servant and diplomat.

Incumbent Presidents Hold Onto Power. The results of Chad's first multiparty presidential election in history confirmed the reelection of President Idriss Déby but revealed serious differences between votes obtained by manual counting and computer results. Opposition candidates who had been defeated in the first round of voting alleged massive fraud.

In March, Zimbabweans reelected Robert Mugabe to a third six-year term as president. Curiously, while his two opponents posed no serious threat, Mugabe and his ruling Zimbabwean African National Union–Patriotic Front felt compelled to prevent any real opposition from emerging. The government-controlled media favored President Mugabe and ignored his opponents, who otherwise were harassed to such an extent that they both withdrew from the election. Only 31% of the electorate voted, raising concern about prospects for democracy in Zimbabwe.

Even though Yoweri Museveni had ruled Uganda for ten years, he was "elected" president for the first time in May with 74% of the vote. It widely was referred to as a "no party" election, since candidates were allowed to run only as individuals and could not hold rallies. International observers reported that the poll generally was fair even if the electoral process was restricted.

Long-Term Prospects for Democracy. On a continent more typically characterized by political instability and authoritarian rule, the widespread adoption of electoral politics in Africa represented significant progress. Notwithstanding the fact that many of these elections have not been fully free and fair in the Western democratic tradition, they nonetheless are replacing the coup d'état as the most reliable instrument of regime change. Of course, even free and fair elections are not in and of themselves sufficient to meet all of the requirements for democracy. If a culture of democracy is to develop, the principles that underlie constitutional democracy—such as a tolerance for opposition, adherence to the rule of law, and accountability—also must be encouraged to develop. For example, South Africa's attempts to sustain a transparent political process, a free press, an independent judiciary, respect for minorities, and free and fair elections have served as an important example for other African nations. Some entrenched leaders have shown open irritation at President Nelson Mandela's popularity and at the world attention that South Africa has received. However, for many opposition leaders and others in sub-Saharan Africa, such developments stand as a symbol for a more optimistic future.

N. Brian Winchester and Patrick O'Meara

On March 24, 1996, Benin's constitutional court declared Mathieu Kérékou, a former military ruler who lost at the polls in 1991, the winner of the nation's runoff presidential election.

Turmoil in Burundi and Rwanda

During 1996, Burundi and Rwanda remained plagued by violence and other problems. The strife—fueled by an ethnic conflict between Hutu majorities and powerful Tutsi minorities in both countries—seemed to defy resolution. The conflict was exacerbated by Hutu resentment of the "autocratic caste" status of the Tutsi, which had been reinforced by preferential treatment by Belgian colonialists.

Background. At independence in 1962, a hard-line Tutsi government took power in Burundi, while a coup d'état in Rwanda resulted in Hutu control. Ethnic animosity in both countries has led to occasional outbursts of extreme violence: An estimated 10,000 Tutsi were killed in Rwanda in 1963; hundreds of thousands of Hutu were killed in Burundi in 1972; interethnic violence in Burundi in 1993 claimed tens of thousands of lives following the assassination of the country's first Hutu president in a failed Tutsi coup attempt; and, in one of the worst cases of ethnic genocide in history, as many as half a million Tutsi and some moderate Hutu were killed in less than three months in Rwanda in 1994.

With each succeeding massacre, the intensity of the animosities between the feuding groups has escalated. Between the years 1994 and 1996, several million people were forced to flee into exile to the surrounding countries of Zaire, Tanzania, and Uganda. Both Tutsi and Hutu feared not only the other's revenge, but extremists within their own ethnic group targeting those in favor of reconciliation.

New Concerns. There was fear at the beginning of 1996 that Burundi's smoldering civil war, which was claiming an estimated 1,000 lives each month, might degenerate into the kind of widespread genocidal killing that occurred in Rwanda in 1994. The army, controlled by Tutsi, was in effect at war with the coalition government, and, indeed, staged a successful coup in July in which Hutu President Sylvestre Ntibantunganya was deposed and replaced by Maj. Pierre Buyoya, a Tutsi. The coup also forced Hutu government ministers to seek sanctuary in European embassies in the capital city of Bujumbura. Diplomats and human-rights organizations reported an increase in arbitrary arrests and killings by the army after the coup. African leaders from Kenya, Uganda, Zaire, Tanzania, and ultimately Rwanda—which had been attempting to mediate a settlement—agreed to impose economic sanctions on Burundi until constitutional rule was restored. Many foreign diplomats and humanitarian personnel were evacuated from the country as conditions worsened.

Charges and denials of regular massacres on a lesser scale continued to dominate politics in Rwanda. The April withdrawal of the last troops of the United Nations Mission to Rwanda (UNAMIR) was met with disappointment and fear by some and approval by others. The International Tribunal for Rwanda continued to meet in The Hague, but appealed to the international community to provide many more investigators to document the specifics of the 1994 genocide before memories faded. Meanwhile, an estimated 85,000 Hutu men who had been arrested on genocide charges over the previous two years in Rwanda continued to be incarcerated without going to trial.

The situation was confused further when local Zairian authorities, encouraged by Hutu extremists in refugee camps, unsuccessfully tried to expel Tutsi who had been living in eastern Zaire for generations. These Zairian Tutsi not only successfully resisted, but defeated the undisciplined Zairian army and captured a string of towns in eastern Zaire close to the border with Rwanda. This increasingly unsettled situation, combined with international pressure, forced more than 600,000 Hutu refugees to leave the refugee camps where they had been living for several years and return across the border to Rwanda. Some Hutu militants who presumably had been involved in killing Tutsi in 1994 feared revenge attacks or prosecution and disappeared into the Zairian countryside rather than return home. As Rwandan refugees began returning home from Zaire, Tanzania announced that the estimated 600,000 Rwandan refugees in camps within its borders also must prepare to be repatriated. Hundreds of thousands of these refugees fled the camps in December to avoid repatriation but eventually began returning to Rwanda.

Hutu refugees forced to return to Rwanda were terrified. For Rwandan Tutsi, the return of a million Hutu was equally frightening. In both Rwanda and Burundi, continued minority Tutsi domination did not seem viable in the long run; however, as a minority that has borne the brunt of a genocide, Tutsi were unlikely to give up power willingly to the majority that it feared. With no solutions at hand, many were wondering if the international community would be willing to come forward and impose a solution of its own.

See also LAW—*International*; REFUGEES AND IMMIGRATION; ZAIRE.

N. BRIAN WINCHESTER and PATRICK O'MEARA

AGRICULTURE

The year 1996 provided the world agricultural community challenges from adverse weather in several areas and declining food reserves. Even so, the agricultural community accommodated rising demand for higher-value food and industrial agricultural products. Policy changes and new technology helped the U.S. agricultural sector meet increasing environmental challenges and constraints that come with larger farming operations, suburban developments in rural areas, and increased public environmental awareness. New biotechnology products triggered consumer concerns about genetically engineered products.

The World Scene

Supply, Production, and Prices. Record-low world stocks of wheat, rice, and feed grains relative to annual use brought several concerns. The near absence of reserve supplies caused agricultural officials to review world food security and examine impacts on the food supplies of lower-income developing nations. Impacts were of special concern to sub-Saharan Africa, where food supplies have been chronically short. Record-high grain prices meant that the same number of dollars in financial assistance at times would purchase 50% less grain than a year earlier. With the European Union (EU) taxing grain exports to discourage shipments, Asia's Pacific Rim buyers worried that the United States might be forced to limit grain exports. An export embargo would have serious negative impacts on Pacific Rim livestock and poultry industries.

By late fall, the U.S. Department of Agriculture estimated that world feed-grain production would be one tenth larger than the previous year's short crop. Global wheat production rose 11%, with rice production 2% larger than in 1995. World production of oilseeds was up 1%. Crop estimates indicated global wheat and feed-grain stocks would increase modestly by midsummer of 1997, while oilseed stocks were expected to decline to historically low levels. Grain production increased in Western Europe, Canada, China, Russia, North Africa, Australia, and the United States, as well as in several smaller grain-producing nations. Canada, China, and Europe harvested smaller oilseed crops than in 1995. World cotton production was estimated to be down 5%.

Livestock and poultry production continued to expand in China, as the nation's economy and consumer incomes remained in a strong uptrend. China was a net feed-grain importer for the second consecutive year. Two years earlier, it was the world's second-largest exporter of feed grains. Despite areas of severe flooding in China, the nation's grain production increased modestly during the year, slightly reducing its need for imported grain. Economists projected that rapid growth of Chinese demand for meat and grains would

An Oklahoma wheat farmer sadly inspects one of his fields. A lack of rain in Oklahoma, Texas, and parts of Colorado and Kansas ruined the 1996 U.S. winter-wheat crop.

expand Chinese grain imports over the next decade. Cereal crops generally were favorable in neighboring parts of Asia.

Crops also were good in much of Western Europe and were at record highs in the EU and North Africa. With larger crops, the EU reinstated export subsidies for wheat and barley late in the year. Eastern European grain production was slightly less than in the previous year, but nearly adequate for domestic needs. Farmers in Russia and neighboring countries continued to adjust toward a market economy. Inadequate supplies of key inputs such as fertilizer and spare parts restricted production, as did adverse weather in some areas. Despite problems, the region had increased grain production modestly and was expected to reduce wheat imports. Australia's wheat and barley crops were large due to favorable weather. Sub-Saharan Africa continued its struggle to increase grain production, and per-capita supplies declined slightly for the year. Weather was more favorable for crop production in much of Latin America than in the previous year.

Trade Policies. Florida tomato growers protested imports of low-cost Mexican tomatoes resulting from the North American Free Trade Agreement (NAFTA). After a review of comparative costs, a minimum allowable price was set for imported Mexican tomatoes. Some trade analysts worried that these U.S. adjustments to free trade might lead to other restrictions. In Canada the dairy industry was able to maintain some protection against imports of U.S. dairy products after trade commissions reviewed NAFTA provisions and found a clause allowing such protection. With complaints from U.S. wheat growers, an upper limit was placed on imports of Canadian wheat into the United States. The EU reinstatement of grain-export subsidies late in the year created pressure for the United States to resume its Export Enhancement Program (EEP). In early spring, Russia temporarily halted imports of U.S. poultry because of concerns about alleged flaws in the U.S. meat-inspection system. Issues relating to China's violation of U.S. intellectual-property rights caused fear that China might retaliate with restrictions on purchases of U.S. agricultural products. Late in the year, China placed restrictions on imports of U.S. poultry because of potential poultry diseases.

Mad-Cow Disease. In Western Europe researchers found new evidence that a type of bovine spongiform encephalopathy (BSE)—"mad-cow disease"—may be passed from meat to humans. The new disease originated in British cattle and was believed to have come from by-product feeds produced from diseased sheep. As a result, feed regulations were tightened to prevent spread of the disease. Plans also were made to liquidate much of Britain's cattle herds to eradicate the disease. Other European nations placed restrictions on imports of British beef, and beef consumption in Europe fell sharply. British cattle imported into the United States more than a decade ago were located and examined to be sure they had no evidence of the disease.

United States

The Livestock Industry. The U.S. pork industry continued a shift to large-scale, capital-intensive production and scientifically developed genetics to provide consistent high-quality, low-fat pork. Record-high feed costs accelerated the shift toward this system because of its greater feed efficiency. Production continued to expand moderately in newer hog-producing areas such as Oklahoma, Utah, Colorado, and North Carolina. The trend toward fewer but larger hog producers also was accelerated as some smaller and medium-size producers chose to sell homegrown feed grains at high prices and exit from pork production, relying instead on grain income.

U.S. exports of beef, pork, and poultry continued to increase rapidly with less restrictive foreign-import policies and growing incomes of foreign consumers. U.S. pork and beef producers developed higher-quality animals and meat designed specifically for the Japanese market. Russia and China became major markets for U.S. poultry. Russians prefer dark meat, which provides a market for the type of poultry meat least preferred by U.S. consumers. China also was an important market for types of poultry not strongly preferred in the United States.

The U.S. cattle industry has three sectors—producers of beef feeder calves, feedlots that feed the calves to market weight, and the dairy industry. The first of these sectors experienced severe economic pressures. Large losses were due to extreme drought that destroyed pastures in the southern half of the Great Plains the first four months of the year, record-high feed costs that discouraged feedlots from buying feeder animals, and prices for feeder animals that were as much as 40% lower than just two years earlier. Federal farm programs were adjusted to help reduce financial losses and provide emergency pastures and credit for feed purchases. Purchases of beef for school-lunch programs were increased to take advantage of low beef prices and to help support the demand for beef in a time of financial crisis. In some cases, this assistance made the difference between survival or forced exit of ranchers from the industry after decades of successful ranching. By midyear the drought was broken but high feed costs continued to depress feeder-animal prices.

The feedlot sector experienced periods of large losses because of high feed costs. Ranchers and others continued to express concern over the concentrated ownership of slaughter plants among a relatively small number of firms. An extensive USDA study found that the industry remained competitive despite concentration. In contrast to serious and sometimes severe economic pressures in the beef industry, the dairy sector retained overall profitability due to a growing demand for processed dairy products such as cheese.

Grain Supplies, Corn, and Crops. Limited grain supplies and record-high corn prices during the first nine months of 1996 brought a sharp reduction in U.S. corn processing. This was the first actual decline in U.S. corn processing in more than 20 years. Processors converted less corn into ethanol for motor fuel and gasoline oxygen enhancers because of the high cost of corn and inability to compete with petroleum-based alternatives. Processing of corn into sweeteners for soft drinks and processed foods continued to expand. Domestic processing of wheat, mainly for flour and cereal production, changed very little despite the record-high wheat prices.

The nation's fruit and vegetable growers provided consumers with abundant supplies at moderate prices. Favorable weather contributed to good harvests of fresh and processed vegetables for freezing and canning in most areas. Citrus-fruit supplies were relatively large.

Legislation. The U.S. Congress passed and President Bill Clinton signed sweeping changes in U.S. farm policy. Long-standing production controls on major grain crops and cotton were removed, along with income-protection payments to farmers that increased when prices were low and declined with high prices. Farmers were provided with declining market-transition payments for seven years to help manage increased market risk. New crop insurance also was developed to let farmers insure income rather than production per acre. The long-standing grain-reserve program was eliminated. The program provided reserve supplies of feed and food grains for use in times of poor crops.

Environmental Concerns. Areas of environmental attention in U.S. agriculture included manure and odor problems from large livestock operations, a changing focus of the long-term land-idling program, definition and preservation of wetlands, and environmental impacts from grazing on federal lands. With several problem cases of manure runoff and groundwater contamination from hog production, some states tightened regulations related to large-scale livestock units. Researchers sought environmentally friendly ways to manage feedlot wastes and new methods for reducing feedlot odors. Emphasis in new entries or reentries of land into the ten-year Conservation Reserve Program shifted more toward protection of water quality and enhanced wildlife environments, in contrast to previous focus on agricultural-production control and reduced soil erosion. Efforts to reduce grazing on federal lands by increasing fees continued during the year. Higher fees would reduce grazing on public lands.

Biotech Products

The seed industry introduced genetically altered varieties of corn that are resistant to corn borers. Corn borers are insects that bore into stalks, weakening the plant, interfering with kernel development, and sometimes causing ears to fall to the ground before the crop is harvested. Entomology research indicated these pests are a major source of yield losses. The seed industry also introduced genetically altered soybean varieties that are resistant to herbicides, especially the broad-spectrum herbicide known as roundup. This development permits more effective control of weeds than in the past.

Seed companies also developed and promoted varieties of corn with higher oil and amino-acid content than traditional corn. The new corn was designed especially for nutritional needs of pork production. Arrangements were made to segregate the new corn from conventional varieties in commercial channels. Agriculturalists continued to develop technology for mapping yields in grain production and for adjusting input applications as soil types and fertility vary within areas of individual fields. This technology was intended to increase crop productivity, thus helping to meet growing global demand for grains without resorting to the use of more environmentally sensitive land.

See also FOOD.

ROBERT N. WISNER
Iowa State University

ALBANIA

During 1996, Albania's ruling Democratic Party consolidated its position through overwhelming victories in parliamentary and local elections. However, the government came under intense international criticism for its domination of the electoral process and alleged human-rights abuses. Albania also continued to make significant economic progress and improved its relations with various European nations and the North Atlantic Treaty Organization (NATO).

Political Consolidation. The governing Democratic Party strengthened its political position but came under increasing international attack for its antidemocratic tendencies. Human-rights organizations concluded that, five years after Albania's first free elections, the country still was plagued by serious human-rights violations, including restrictions on freedom of expression and association, manipulation of the legal system, and police violence. The government arrested several members of the former communist regime, including former President Ramiz Alia, on charges of political persecution and the repression of civilians. Tiranë also banned several dozen candidates from standing in the general elections on the basis of a law that prohibits former high-ranking communist officials from running for public office for ten years.

In April, Tritan Shehu, who was considered to be tied closely to President Sali Berisha, was elected as the new chairman of the Democratic Party. In the parliamentary elections in May, the Democrats won overwhelming majorities in most of the electoral districts, obtaining 122 seats in the 140-member People's Assembly. The Socialist Party gained ten seats, the Republicans three, the Greek-minority Party for Defense of Human Rights three, and the Nationalist Front Party two. International election monitors observed serious irregularities in the voting process and recommended the reholding of elections in a number of constituencies. The Democrats refused these requests and the Socialists announced they would boycott the new parliament until truly "free and fair" elections were held. Aleksander Meksi was reappointed prime minister, and the government established a new privatization ministry.

The Democratic Party further consolidated its position during the local elections in October. Democrats took 88% of the vote, gaining control of 37 districts and the vast majority of communes and town councils. The rest of the local seats were distributed among Socialists, Social Democrats, nationalists, and the Greek-minority party. Once again, the government was criticized for voting irregularities and for its monopoly over the mass media and the electoral commissions.

© Facelly/Sipa Press

Members of Albania's ruling Democratic Party showed their allegiance at a preelection rally. The party strengthened its position in 1996 parliamentary and local elections.

Economic Progress. Although Albania remained the poorest country in Europe, it continued to have one of the fastest-growing economies. The gross domestic product (GDP) again was projected to grow by some 10%, while the budget deficit only reached 7% of the GDP. The annual inflation rate fell to about 6% and foreign investment increased substantially. Although official unemployment was estimated to have fallen to about 14%, in the northern industrial parts of the country it reached nearly 50% of the economically active population.

Much of Albania's traditional industrial base is obsolete and uncompetitive and has failed to attract foreign investors. Some industrial unrest was evident during the year as a result of price hikes in bread, gas, and other products. The government invested more than $200 million on road reconstruction and several European governments pledged to assist in the reconstruction of Albania's dilapidated infrastructure. For example, Germany was providing funding for improving the country's archaic water-supply system.

International Relations. In March, President Berisha signed a friendship and cooperation treaty with Greece. After years of dispute and conflict with Athens, Tiranë pledged to respect the human rights of the Greek minority in Albania, while the Greek government agreed to regulate the status of the large number of illegal Albanian immigrants in Greece. The bilateral treaty also aimed to boost military and economic ties between the two states and increased the number of border crossings.

Tiranë signed military-cooperation agreements with members of NATO. France agreed to train Albanian soldiers, to engage in joint military maneuvers, and to supply military equipment. Germany also launched a number of military-cooperation projects with Albania, including military exercises and assistance in introducing modern command structures in the Albanian army. Meanwhile, the United States supplied more than $100 million to Tiranë in military hardware.

Although Albania was not considered a prime contender for early NATO membership, the government vigorously pursued closer contacts with the alliance in order to present itself as a viable future candidate. In July, Albania hosted multinational military exercises called "Peaceful Eagle 96," which included troops from the United States, Turkey, Greece, Italy, Macedonia, Romania, and Slovenia. The exercises took place within the framework of NATO's Partnership for Peace program. In August, Albanian and U.S. troops staged joint military exercises, called "Salvation Eagle 96." They focused on peacekeeping and search-and-rescue operations. The Albanian army also participated in the peacekeeping mission in Bosnia.

JANUSZ BUGAJSKI
Center for Strategic and International Studies

ALBANIA • Information Highlights

Official Name: Republic of Albania.
Location: Southern Europe, Balkan peninsula.
Area: 11,100 sq mi (28 750 km²).
Population (mid-1996 est.): 3,300,000.
Chief City (1990 est.): Tiranë, the capital, 244,200.
Government: *Head of state,* Sali Berisha, president (took office April 1992). *Head of government,* Aleksander Meksi, prime minister (took office April 1992). *Legislature* (unicameral)—People's Assembly.
Monetary Unit: New lek (111.710 leks equal U.S.$1, June 1996).
Gross Domestic Product (1994 est. U.S.$): $3,800,000,000 (purchasing power parity).
Economic Index (1995, 1992 = 100): *Consumer Prices,* all items, 244.4.

ALGERIA

President Lamine Zeroual, the victor in November 1995 elections, orchestrated a series of political consultations that led to a constitutional referendum in November 1996. Yet the country gained little respite from violence as radical Islamic militants continued their reign of terror.

Political Consultation. Initiating what he called a "national dialogue," Zeroual called in political and civic leaders in April to discuss the future of Algeria's institutions. The agenda included changes in the constitution and the electoral laws pending parliamentary elections. In May the president announced his preferred timetable for the reforms: a constitutional referendum in November; parliamentary elections before July 1997; and local elections in the second half of 1997. Several parties objected that legislative elections should take precedence and that changes in the constitution should be the prerogative of an elected assembly.

During further dialogue in July, the government declared that the majority of those consulted favored Zeroual's plan. It then organized a "Conference of National Understanding," attended by some 1,000 delegates on September 14–15. Although opposition parties—such as the Socialist Forces Front (FFS) and the Rally for Culture and Democracy (RCD)—boycotted this conclave, the conference gave its stamp of approval to the presidential proposal. A new constitutional text granting greater powers to the president was made public in October; major changes included a prohibition on the use of religion or language as the basis for formation of a political party and provision for a second chamber of parliament and a council of state. The government said that 85% of the voters approved the constitution on November 28, but opposition leaders charged electoral fraud.

No End to Violence. While President Zeroual directed this effort to reconstitute political legitimacy, Islamist terrorists continued to wreak havoc against the civilian population. On February 11 a car bomb blew up at the House of the Press in Algiers, killing 18 employees—including three journalists of the independent newspaper *Le Soir d'Algérie*. This raised to 58 the number of journalists murdered since May 1993. On the same day another bomb wounded 41 persons at the town hall in Algiers' Bab el Oued district.

In March the Armed Islamic Group (GIA) kidnapped seven Trappist monks from their monastery near Blida, an Islamist stronghold. In May they were executed brutally. The bishop of Oran, Pierre Claverie, well known for his work in interfaith dialogue, was assassinated in August, as was the popular singer Cheb Aziz in September. Thirty-four bus passengers were slaughtered at a roadblock in the south in October. Although the Islamic Salvation Front (FIS) condemned these acts of pure terrorism by the GIA and made gestures toward talks with the government, the latter refused to include the FIS in the dialogue or the national conference.

Government and Party Affairs. Zeroual appointed Ahmed Ouyahia prime minister on Dec. 31, 1995. A former diplomat and director of the presidential staff, Ouyahia was at age 43 the youngest person ever to occupy this office. His cabinet, while including many holdovers from the previous government, also included two representatives of the Hamas party and one from the Renewal Party (PRA) in minor ministries. In September, Zeroual offered positions in the government to other opposition parties, but shelved the offer after the FFS, RCD, and the Movement for Democracy (MDA) declined to participate.

A shake-up in the leadership of the National Liberation Front (FLN) occurred as well. In a January meeting, the central committee dismissed Abdelhamid Mehri, who had led the party into opposition after the 1992 annulment of parliamentary elections. In a close vote between the party's reformist and conservative wings, the central committee elected conservative Boualem Benhamouda to the post of secretary-general. Benhamouda promptly announced that the FLN would break ranks with the other opposition parties that had formed a coalition in January 1995, apparently intending to realign the party with the Zeroual regime. Conversely, at a March convention, Hocine Ait Ahmed retained leadership of the FFS, assuming a new title as president of the party, while naming Seddik Debaïli as its first secretary.

Foreign Policy. In a departure from past policy, Algeria attended the summit sponsored by the United States and Egypt and held in Charm el-Cheikh, Egypt, in March. Shortly thereafter, U.S. Assistant Secretary of State for Near Eastern Affairs Robert Pelletreau carried out the first visit by a high-level American to Algeria since 1992. He met with leaders of the opposition as well as with the government.

ALGERIA • Information Highlights

Official Name: Democratic and Popular Republic of Algeria.
Location: North Africa.
Area: 919,591 sq mi (2 381 740 km²).
Population (mid-1996 est.): 29,000,000.
Chief Cities (1987 census): Algiers, the capital, 1,507,241; Oran, 628,558; Constantine, 440,842.
Government: *Head of state,* Lamine Zeroual, president (took office January 1994). *Head of government,* Ahmed Ouyahia, prime minister (named Dec. 31, 1995). *Legislature*—unicameral National People's Assembly (suspended).
Monetary Unit: Dinar (55.095 dinars equal U.S.$1, June 1996).
Gross Domestic Product (1994 est. U.S.$): $97,100,000,000 (purchasing power parity).
Economic Indexes (1995, 1990 = 100): *Consumer Prices,* all items, 334.6; food, 347.1. *Industrial Production,* 86.
Foreign Trade (1994 est. U.S.$): *Imports,* $9,200,000,000; *exports,* $9,100,000,000.

Concerned by the United Nations' withdrawal of the bulk of the peacekeeping force in Western Sahara (MINURSO), Zeroual led the Algerian delegation to the July summit of the Organization of African Unity (OAU) in Yaoundé, Cameroon, in an effort to bolster the fortunes of the Algerian-backed Polisario Front in its dispute with Morocco over self-determination. He also visited Mauritania in order to maintain Algerian influence on the Western Sahara question there. Relations with Morocco remained tense, not only over the Saharan question but also following a rather large infiltration of Islamist rebels across the Moroccan border into Algeria in the spring. Despite a reduction in French economic aid, Algerians viewed the August visit by French Foreign Minister Hervé de Charette as a sign of improving relations. President Zeroual visited China, Southeast Asia, and the Gulf states in October.

Economy. Heavy debt and a 1995 trade deficit forced the government to impose austerity measures. The labor movement called a general strike for two days in February to protest government policies. Unemployment remained high, but population growth dipped below 2% for the first time since independence. The 1995–96 grain harvest was double that of the previous season, and new discoveries of oil and natural gas, coupled with a steady flow of foreign investment into the energy sector, augured well for the economy's future.

ROBERT MORTIMER, *Haverford College*

ANTHROPOLOGY

In 1996 researchers reported the discovery of fossils from two species of ancient apes; Chinese fossils of a direct human ancestor were assigned a markedly older age based on a new dating technique; and a fossil analysis found that limb proportion varied greatly among early members of the human evolutionary family.

Ancient Apes. Two separate fossil discoveries yielded new clues about apes that lived in Europe before the emergence of the human evolutionary family. An excavation in central Turkey produced the nearly complete jaws and face of a 9.8-million-year-old ape that its discoverers assigned to the species *Ankarapithecus meteai*. Previously, only fragments of the jaw and lower face had existed for this creature.

The new fossil possesses an arrangement of facial, jaw, and tooth features unlike that of any other fossil or living ape, contended a research team headed by Berna Alpagut of Ankara University in Turkey. Rather than serving as a direct ancestor of either modern apes or humans, *A. meteai* probably went extinct between 9 million and 8 million years ago, Alpagut's group argued. The unusual mosaic of anatomical parts observed on *A. meteai*'s skull is consistent with the theory that numerous now-extinct ape species evolved in Europe and Western Asia beginning about 18 million years ago, according to the scientists.

In Spain investigators unearthed the nearly complete, 9.5-million-year-old skeleton of an extinct ape known as *Dryopithecus*. The creature had long arms and relatively short legs, a large clavicle atop a broad chest, and large hands with long, curved fingers. Salvador Moyà-Solà and Meike Köhler of the Miquel Crusafont Institute of Paleontology in Sabadell, Spain, asserted that bone analyses suggest that *Dryopithecus* spawned a related extinct ape in Asia, *Sivapithecus*, and eventually led to modern orangutans. However, other investigators familiar with the find argued that *Dryopithecus* may have been a direct ancestor of African apes and the human evolutionary family, or perhaps an ancestor of all later apes and humans.

Peking Man. A scientific team concluded that a group of Chinese fossils known collectively as Peking Man dates to at least 400,000 years ago, much earlier than anthropologists had suspected previously. Most researchers place Peking Man in the species *Homo erectus*. If the revised age is confirmed in further studies, it would indicate that *H. erectus* lived in East Asia before modern humans appeared in that part of the world. The former age estimate of 200,000 to 300,000 years for the Chinese specimens had suggested that *H. erectus* and an early form of *H. sapiens* had existed at the same time in East Asia.

Richard Teh-Lung Ku, a geochronologist at the University of Southern California in Los Angeles, and his coworkers calculated Peking Man's age based on measurements of small amounts of radioactive thorium and uranium in soil located just above where the fossils first were found in 1921. Prior age estimates had relied on less precise analyses of fossilized bones.

Hominid Bodies. An analysis of fossil remains of ancient hominids, who belonged to the same evolutionary family as modern humans, suggested that these creatures traveled down an uneven path toward the upright stance observed in *H. sapiens*. Limb proportions of hominid species fluctuated a number of times before the appearance of direct human ancestors nearly 2 million years ago, asserted Henry M. McHenry of the University of California, Davis.

Recent fossil discoveries in a South African cave indicate that *Australopithecus africanus*, which lived between 2.8 million and 2.6 million years ago, had short legs and long arms relative to its size, much like chimpanzees and other apes. However, *A. afarensis*, which lived in East Africa more than 3 million years ago and includes the skeleton known as "Lucy," had relatively long legs and short arms, much like humans today.

BRUCE BOWER, *"Science News"*

ARCHAEOLOGY

New evidence of ancient wine, the discovery of the world's oldest rock art in Australia, and excavations in China that illuminate the roots of wool weaving were among 1996 highlights in archaeology.

Eastern Hemisphere

Old Wine and Egyptian Bread and Brew. Chemical analyses of splotches on a pottery fragment found at an Iranian site uncovered evidence of the oldest known wine, dating to between 7,000 and 7,400 years ago. The splotches contain remains of tartaric acid, a substance that occurs in large amounts only in grapes, and the resin of the terebinth tree. Researchers believe that the resin was used as a wine preservative and to mask offensive fla-

In 1996 archaeologists announced the excavation of the original fort at Jamestown, the first successful English settlement in North America. All traces of the structure had been lost for more than 200 years. Thousands of artifacts also were found.

vors in the wine. Prior to the new finding, the earliest instance of wine making had been dated to about 5,500 years ago.

The ancient Egyptians processed wheat for bread and beer production in more sophisticated ways than previously had been suspected, according to a study of stale bread loaves and beer-stained pottery fragments recovered at sites dating to between 3,200 and 4,000 years ago. Microscopic analyses of starch granules in the bread indicate that it was made of a prepared flour that had been kneaded slightly. The variety of starch granules in the beer suggests that Egyptian brewers used grain to make a malt, then combined cooked and uncooked malt, and finally strained fermentation out of the liquid.

Australian Settlers. Excavations at a rock shelter in northwestern Australia uncovered stone artifacts dating to between 176,000 and 116,000 years ago, at least doubling the estimated age of that continent's first human occupation. A fragment of stone at the same site contained engraved circular marks and was dated to between 78,000 and 56,000 years ago, making it the world's oldest rock art. Researchers theorize that people may have traveled by sea from Indonesia to Australia as early as 135,000 years ago, at a time when an ice age had lowered sea levels and shortened the distance between those landmasses.

Ancient Time Line. A team of scientists presented a revised chronology, based on a study of tree-ring sequences at several Turkish sites, for the early civilizations that rose and fell in regions bordering the eastern Mediterranean Sea. The proposed time line, which extends from 2220 B.C. to 718 B.C., may bring more precision to the study of early cultures in Mesopotamia, Egypt, Greece, and Rome.

Portuguese Rock Art. Controversy raged over the age of animal engravings found in northeastern Portugal. Radiocarbon dating of mineral layers that formed over the engravings, as well as microscopic analyses of their erosion, indicate that most were 3,000 years old or younger. But a stylistic comparison of the animal depictions to other prehistoric artworks in Western Europe places most of the engravings at about 20,000 years old. Construction of a dam in the vicinity of the engravings was halted during 1995; officials said the project would not be restarted until the controversy was resolved.

Roots of Weaving. Clothes worn by remarkably well-preserved 3,000-year-old mummies excavated at two sites in western China contain the oldest known cashmere threads and evidence of advanced wool-weaving techniques. The presence of cashmere—signified by the shape, fineness, and consistency of diameter of threads—indicates a high degree of skill in sorting and spinning fibers. Some mummies wore wool twills in a plaid design dating to 720 B.C. Chinese looms at that time were designed for silk, suggesting that the mummies belonged to a group that had originated in Eurasia and developed its own weaving technology.

Tools. A 600,000-year-old site in Israel yielded stone implements manufactured in a style thought to have been unique to human ancestors who lived in Africa at the time. A series of population movements may have resulted in the transfer of such African cultural traditions to the Middle East. Further evidence for this contention came from another Israeli site, dating to about 1 million years ago, where investigators found a simpler brand of stone tools previously known from several African sites of the same age.

Prehistoric inhabitants of Polynesia, a long chain of islands in the South Pacific, navigated vessels across vast ocean stretches to obtain rock suitable for tool production, a research team found. Chemical analyses of previously unearthed stone tools indicates that, as early as 3,000 years ago, people transported fine-grained basalt from a quarry on a western Polynesian isle to islands situated up to 1,000 miles (1 610 km) away.

Celtic Statue. Excavations at a Celtic grave near Frankfurt, Germany, uncovered a 2,500-year-old, life-size statue of an aristocrat that offers new insights into Celtic society. Most Celtic art portrays deities rather than real-life individuals. The sandstone figure, which once may have stood atop the aristocrat's burial, holds a shield and wears armor. Its head is crowned by a laurel wreath and two horn-shaped appendages. The grave also contained gold neck and arm rings, bronze clasps for clothing, and a bronze cup.

Western Hemisphere

Amazon Culture. A Brazilian cave yielded the remains of a distinctive tropical culture that arose about 11,000 years ago. Inhabitants of the site pursued a lifestyle that differed significantly from that of hunter-gatherers who lived in North America at about the same time. Finds at the cave include carbonized fruits and wood fragments from tropical trees, as well as fossils from fish, birds, reptiles, large forest animals, and shellfish. Lumps and drops of red pigment, probably used in paintings on the cave walls, also were uncovered.

Stone Points. Archaeologists reported finding a sharpened stone point in Siberia that was made in a style thought to have been unique to North America as many as 11,200 years ago. The Siberian artifact dates to at least 8,300 years ago. If further investigations confirm that its age exceeds 11,200 years, the find may represent a precursor of toolmaking techniques that later took root in North America after human groups crossed a land bridge that once connected Asia to Alaska. In contrast, a younger date for the stone implement would indicate that toolmaking knowledge coexisted in Siberia and North America, or perhaps moved across continents.

Maya Tomb. Researchers discovered the tomb of an adult male who they suspect was a Maya ruler more than 1,500 years ago. The tomb was found at the site of the ancient city of La Milpa in Belize. Along with the man's skeletal remains, excavators found a green jadeite pendant, ear spools inlaid with obsidian, and a large jadeite stone placed in the man's mouth. Although the identity of the man remains unknown, scientists believe that he may have been Bird Jaguar, who ruled in the 5th century A.D.

Oldest Mummy. New analyses indicated that a mummy excavated in 1940 and stored in a Nevada museum dates to about 9,420 years ago, making it the oldest mummy in North America. Researchers originally had thought that the well-preserved mummy was about 2,000 years old, but radiocarbon tests of hair, bone, and two mats covering the body yielded the much older age estimate. The mummy is that of an approximately 45-year-old man found in a Nevada cave.

Rock Art. Scientists reported that Native American rock shelters near the Texas-Mexico border contain painted scenes of shamans surrounded by powerful psychoactive plants. The shelters date to at least 4,000 years ago. Scenes show shaman figures holding staffs attached to oval, spiny shapes that resemble a regional plant known as jimsonweed, which causes disorientation and hallucinations when taken in low doses. Images also portray peyote, a cactus that causes hallucinations when dried and swallowed. Shamans apparently used these substances as aids in attempts to contact ancestors or mythical creatures in the spirit world.

BRUCE BOWER, *"Science News"*

ARCHITECTURE

A climate of modesty and financial constraint continued to influence architecture in 1996. The year's awards reflected trends toward simpler designs and the increased prominence of renovation, restoration, and addition projects.

Trend Toward Modesty. The 1996 Pritzker Prize, the top award in architecture, went to Spanish architect José Rafael Moneo. The jury praised him for regarding the practicality of "materials and construction to be just as important as the architect's vision and concept." Many observers felt that the selection reflected a growing pragmatism in architecture. In past years, many architects saw the coveted award as symbolic of creative aspirations placed out of reach by increasingly stringent construction-cost controls and other pragmatic considerations. Moneo's style was reflected in his 1993 U.S. debut, the Davis Museum and Cultural Center at Wellesley College in Wellesley, MA, an unextravagant rectilinear brick structure that was fitted carefully into the campus.

A trend toward modesty also was seen in the annual Honor Awards for 1996 given by the American Institute of Architects (AIA). Of the 26 projects cited by the AIA, only nine qualified as large (including four that were renovated older buildings).

Tight Constraints. While construction volume was growing steadily out of its slump of the early 1990s, architects' clients continued to exert cost controls and demand design and construction efficiencies. Many large architectural clients were hiring consultants to exercise many of the responsibilities for quality, contractor negotiations, and design-cost evaluations that traditionally had belonged to architectural firms. Such practices had a profound impact on the final buildings. Corporations that had displayed their muscle in the 1980s through ostentatious headquarters instead were displaying ostensible modesty. Government at every level, besieged by public pressures to cut expenditures, also reined in construction and allowable costs.

Architects in New York City took their case for municipal capital allotments to the public in an exhibit, "Civic Lessons: Recent New York Public Architecture," which displayed the improvements to citizens' quality

Spanish architect José Rafael Moneo, right, *was awarded the 1996 Pritzker Architectural Prize. His works include the Atocha Railway Station—which is noted for its impressive amount of public space—in Madrid,* aerial view below.

Photos, The Pritzker Architectural Prize/The Hyatt Foundation

of life provided by projects already built. After a local viewing, the show was moved to the National Building Museum in Washington, DC.

Renovation and Restoration. Renovation and restoration work represented a growing field for design firms. The AIA acknowledged this trend in its 1996 awards, although the program scarcely had noted the phenomenon two years earlier. Of the 26 projects receiving AIA honors, 11 were recycled or restored structures. Several awards honored noteworthy monuments and parks, such as Harry Weese Associates' faithful restoration of Chicago's baroque Buckingham Memorial Fountain and DLK Architecture's nearby Congress Viaduct and Plaza reconstruction, cited for resurrecting part of Daniel Burnham's sweeping turn-of-the-century city plan. Beyer Blinder Belle won honors for its plans for a 524-mi (943-km)-long park in upper New York state that would restore a 170-year-old canal system.

Honored large-scale building restorations included Richard C. Frank's work on the 1879 Michigan State Capitol in Lansing, which revealed the building's gilded-age decor. Architects Davis, Brody & Associates received an award for recycling an enormous 1894 industrial building into a library for Baruch College in New York City. At the other end of the scale, Skidmore, Owings & Merrill, a firm better known in the 1980s for major office buildings, gained honors in upgrading for chamber music the humble 92-year-old Murray Theater in Highland Park, IL. Hardy Holzman Pfeiffer Associates took honors for the David Saul Smith Union, a fanciful student center complete with stylized sunbursts and futuristic lights, inside a 1913 gymnasium at Bowdoin College in Brunswick, ME. The smallest renovated building honored was a modest 1930s cottage in Santa Monica, CA, altered and added onto by Koning Eizenberg Architecture.

Additions. Another growing category of architecture was that of adding onto existing buildings, which, like renovation, suited the conservation-minded times. The AIA award winners for additions ranged from the iridescent copper and glass Center for the Visual Arts (appended to the neoclassical Toledo Museum of Art) in Toledo, OH, designed by Frank O. Gehry & Associates, to R. M. Kliment & Francis Halsband Architects' straightforward rectilinear entrance pavilion for New York City's Pennsylvania Station, a glass tower executed with industrial sash and exposed steel trusses. A three-story, metal-panel and glass addition built atop the exposed poured-concrete Joslin Diabetes Center in Boston, MA, proved that Ellenzweig Associates could meld two different esthetics into one visually successful whole.

Small Projects. Among the AIA award winners was a day-care center at Warner Brothers' studio in Burbank, CA, designed by Rios Associates to remind children of a ranch-style house. A plan for the main street of Soldotna, AK, by M Mense Architects was not a building at all, but a proposal for signage, lights, and planting. William Rawn Associates' plan for West Main Street in Charlottesville, VA, was honored for proposing modest "infill" buildings between existing ones to help revive a struggling thoroughfare. A similar executed plan by Herbert S. Newman & Partners for the Ninth Square in New Haven, CT, placed small apartment buildings on vacant lots to restore the feeling of an urban street with styles sympathetic to the existing turn-of-the-century structures. A rectilinear glass-walled 20-unit building in Seattle, WA, was designed by Weinstein Copeland Architects as a building containing spaces for both living and working.

Return to Classicism. Although postmodern design had been declared dead by contemporary critics and did not show up in any awards programs, the year saw the opening of several major new buildings in true historic styles. For example, the Alabama Judicial Building in Montgomery was designed by Barganier Davis Sims Architects Associated to resemble the Jefferson Memorial in Washington, DC. Coors Field in Denver, CO, was designed by HOK Sports Facilities Group to resemble ballparks of old, complete with a sandstone and Flemish-bond brick facade. Architect Robert A. M. Stern, long a champion of using historic styles, showed how far the trend could be taken with two educational buildings. For the Colgate Darden School of Business at the University of Virginia in Charlottesville, Stern designed a modern complex clothed in the red brick and white trim of true Federal neoclassicism. For Stanford University in California, Stern produced a Richardsonian Romanesque exterior of heavy stone arches and characteristically broad proportions. Perhaps most spectacular of the new wave of historic designs was the Washington State History Museum in Tacoma. Moore/Andersson Architects took the vaulted-arch forms of the adjacent Beaux-Arts Union Station and produced a complimentary structure that appeared to have been built as part of a turn-of-the-century complex.

CHARLES KING HOYT, *"Architectural Record"*

ARGENTINA

Argentina's economic goals changed little during 1996, but the names of those ministers implementing them did.

Government and Politics. In a year of few triumphs for the Judicialist Peronist Party (PJ) administration of President Carlos Saúl Menem, one came in March, when Congress agreed at last to grant Menem emergency powers to raise taxes, introduce wage cuts, and otherwise trim expenditures. Menem was under intense pressure from the International Monetary Fund (IMF), the country's main creditor, to control growth in public outlays as a condition for obtaining additional credits needed to cover revenue shortfalls. Tax receipts had declined sharply because of the lingering recession.

In order to cover expenditures in 1996, the government would have to collect $4 billion per month. Crackdowns on tax evasion were renewed, with innovations such as requiring evidence of tax payment in order to travel abroad or make a major purchase. Economy Minister Domingo Cavallo assumed direct control over the internal revenue service in June and proceeded to cut overhead by merging several divisions and eliminating others.

Recovery was slow to come about, producing disagreements between the executive and legislative branches. The cabinet polarized over policies as well as personalities. Following Cavallo's allegations of corruption within the government, Menem began searching for an alternative to the once-indispensable and always politically ambitious minister. Cavallo was removed July 26. Observers credited the outgoing minister with eliminating hyperinflation and giving Argentina four years of record growth with economic stability.

The incoming economy minister was the more orthodox Roque Fernández, head of the central bank. Fernández did not make changes in the regime's dollar-convertibility plan, even though the fiscal deficit reached $3.3 billion for January–July 1996. In August, Fernández submitted new tax proposals to the executive and legislative branches amounting to $1.2 billion. The president preferred a crackdown on tax evasion over new taxes on fuels and a broader value-added tax. Congress approved only $600 million in new revenues at the end of September. The IMF granted a new waiver to Argentina in October, projecting the budget deficit for 1996 at $6 billion and setting new targets for 1997.

Other changes affected the composition of the cabinet. Interior Minister Gustavo Beliz resigned his post and party affiliation in January, blasting the pervasiveness of corruption in the PJ. He later ran as an independent for mayor of Buenos Aires. Carlos Corach replaced him. Eduardo Bauzá, Menem's cabinet chief and longtime friend, resigned in March for health reasons and was replaced by Education Minister Jorge Rodríguez. Justice Minister Rodolfo Barra stepped down in July after a past affiliation with an extreme right-wing youth group was revealed. He was replaced by Deputy Justice Minister Elías Jassan. Finally, Jorge Domínguez, recently defeated in his race for an elected term as mayor of Buenos Aires, replaced Oscar Camillón as defense minister in July. Camillón resigned due to controversy over allowing illegal arms sales to Ecuador during its border war with Peru in 1995.

Three-term Sen. Fernando de la Rúa of the Radical Civic Union (UCR) became the first elected mayor of Buenos Aires on June 30 with nearly 40% of the votes. Carrying the PJ's burden of record unemployment, increasing poverty, deep recession, and corruption, Domínguez, the incumbent, finished third. De la Rúa's victory made him an insider for the UCR presidential bid in 1999, while the UCR regained its political dominance in the capital.

Concerns about the nation's armed services were high. Budgetary support for the three military branches absorbed less than 8% of all expenditures and the number of generals and men in uniform had fallen steeply. The naval chief of staff complained in March that budget cuts had left only two of the navy's 49 warships in operation and only 15 of 68 airplanes in working order. Some military bases and factories were sold, while office space and land suitable for farming were rented. The chief of the joint general staff warned in July that while the nation was not in a state of defenselessness, no more cuts could be made.

ARGENTINA • Information Highlights

Official Name: Argentine Republic.
Location: Southern South America.
Area: 1,068,297 sq mi (2 766 890 km²).
Population (mid-1996 est.): 34,700,000.
Chief Cities (1991 census): Buenos Aires, the capital, 2,960,976; Cordoba, 1,148,305; San Justo, 1,111,811; Rosario, 894,645.
Government: *Head of state and government,* Carlos Saúl Menem, president (took office July 8, 1989). *Legislature*—National Congress: Senate and Chamber of Deputies.
Monetary Unit: Peso (.9988 peso equal U.S.$1, financial rate, Dec. 9, 1996).
Gross Domestic Product (1994 est. U.S.$): $270,800,000,-000 (purchasing power parity).
Economic Index (1995, 1988 = 100): *Consumer Prices,* all items, 321,465.3; food, 277,692.5.
Foreign Trade (1995 U.S.$): *Imports,* $20,123,000,000; *exports,* $20,967,000,000.

© C. Carrion/Sygma

In August 1996, Argentine workers jammed Plaza de Mayo in Buenos Aires to protest the economic policies of President Carlos Saúl Menem. Much of the nation was brought to a standstill again by another general strike in late September.

Economy. Exports and savings displaced consumer-driven growth in winding down the 18-month recession. Although unable to match the 33% rise in exports of a year earlier, export growth in 1996 was expected to top 8%, with sales abroad surpassing $22 billion. By May, bank deposits and loan activity had topped the best levels achieved in 1995.

Voluntary capital flows from abroad picked up after little interest was shown in 1995. A private survey of investors' intentions to the year 2000, released in August, found that about $24 billion would be spent on 254 projects, with the greatest activity in telecommunications, motor vehicles, and energy. Multinational companies in the auto industry announced investments in Argentina of $3.7 billion during the next five years. Under an agreement signed with Brazil in January, the two nations would exchange vehicles and auto parts duty-free. Three years in the drafting stage, new codes encouraged foreign investments in mining. Favorable terms were expected to attract $3 billion within five years to promising copper and gold deposits in the Andes Mountains.

Labor Unrest. The support that President Menem long had received from organized labor crumbled in August. A massive 24-hour general strike was held in Buenos Aires to protest official economic policy, based on free-market principles, that left at least 17% of the workforce without jobs and with a deteriorating standard of living and an increasingly regressive distribution of income. Menem and the IMF pushed ahead on measures that would "provide labor-market flexibility," dismantling 50 years of Peronist labor conquests, such as job security, severance pay, and social benefits. The nation's largest labor union staged the sixth general strike of the Menem tenure on September 26–27.

Foreign Affairs. Relations with Great Britain suffered in March when an Argentine-registered vessel fishing off South Georgia Island was forced to purchase a license. The British action was deplored in a Senate resolution that reiterated Argentine claims of sovereignty over British-held territories in the South Atlantic.

Israel and the United States pressed Argentina for progress in the investigation of a deadly 1994 explosion that destroyed the capital's Jewish community center and claimed 95 lives. In July additional arrests were made, as 14 current and former police officers were detained; at least three of the officers suspected of having a direct role in the disaster were indicted. The Supreme Court announced in August that the bomb that destroyed the Israel embassy in 1992 and left 29 dead had been placed inside the building. The finding was rejected by Israel.

LARRY L. PIPPIN, *University of the Pacific*

ART

Highlights of 1996 in the art world included a thought-provoking find of prehistoric art in Australia and a disputed discovery of a Renaissance master's work in New York City. Computers increasingly were employed in art making, marketing, exhibiting, and criticism, and more and more artists, museums, and magazines set up computerized shops on the World Wide Web. Several films directed by and featuring artists were released.

Meanwhile, commercial financing of big museum exhibitions became more prominent as government funding dwindled. Growing demand for greater knowledge of Asian cultures was reflected in the popularity of exhibitions of Asian art. Dadaism, the 20th-century art movement that broke down the barriers between traditional artistic media and challenged the separation of art and everyday life, was the subject of several major exhibitions. Significant staff changes, new contemporary-art facilities, and a varied slate of historical, modern, and contemporary exhibitions enlivened the museum landscape.

Exhibitions, Trends, and Events. Museum attendance for special exhibitions boomed in 1996, as did admission prices and commercial tie-ins. The Philadelphia Museum of Art was the sole U.S. venue for a spectacular retrospective of French Postimpressionist Paul Cézanne. More than half a million visitors paid the $12.50 fee to jostle through galleries displaying the artist's gorgeously colored and carefully structured landscapes, still lives, portraits, and bathers. Many visitors took advantage of hotel packages that included tickets to the show. Once home, they could tune in to the QVC home-shopping network to order items they had overlooked at the museum shop.

New York's Museum of Modern Art (MoMA) staged a more modest blockbluster. "Picasso and Portraiture," organized by curator emeritus William Rubin, included more than 200 images of the Spanish artist, his friends, and his lovers. The focus on Picasso's private life and its relation to his art was made even more public and commercial with Anthony Hopkins' portrayal of him as a bullying, womanizing genius in the feature film *Surviving Picasso*.

The 1996 Olympic Games in Atlanta also underscored the commercialized cult of personality and spectacle. "Rings: Five Passions in World Art"—organized by J. Carter Brown, former director of the National Gallery in Washington, DC—presented more than 125 works covering 7,500 years and linked to five themes suggestive of the five Olympic rings: anguish, awe, joy, love, and triumph.

The National Gallery presented a retrospective of Cézanne's—and Impressionism's—forbear, French landscape painter Camille Corot. The Corot exhibition traveled to New York's Metropolitan Museum, where it was shown concurrently with the Brooklyn Museum's broader "Corot and Early Open Air Painting." The National Gallery also hosted a large exhibition of Olmec art, the most ancient of recorded pre-Columbian American cultures, while the Brooklyn highlighted the post-Columbus era in an exhibition focusing on art in Peru and Mexico from the 16th through the 19th centuries. "Converging Cultures: Art and Identity in Spanish America" subsequently traveled to Phoenix, AZ.

Exhibitions presenting Asian cultures were much in evidence. New York's Metropolitan

Twenty-one paintings by 17th-century Dutch master Johannes Vermeer were on display at the National Gallery in Washington, DC, in late 1995 and early 1996. The show, shut down for a time due to the federal-budget debacle, drew thousands of art lovers a day to see the rare gathering, which encompassed two thirds of Vermeer's surviving works.

Among notable 1996 exhibitions at New York's Guggenheim Museum were "Africa: The Art of a Continent," which included such pieces as a 19th-century Fang reliquary guardian figure, above, *and "Abstraction in the Twentieth Century," displaying works such as Kandinsky's "Composition No. 8" (1923),* right.

Photo left: © John Bigelow Taylor/Courtesy, Guggenheim Museum; photo above: Courtesy, Guggenheim Museum

presented "Splendors of Imperial China: Treasures from the National Palace Museum, Taipei," organized with the National Palace Museum of Taiwan and traveling to the Art Institute of Chicago, Asian Art Museum of San Francisco, and National Gallery. "Imperial Tombs of China," presenting art from mainland China, was seen in Portland, OR; Denver; and Orlando. "New Art in China, Post-1989" was shown at the Fort Wayne (IN) Museum of Art, Kansas City's Kemper Museum, and elsewhere. "Traditions/Tensions: Contemporary Art in Asia" sprawled over three New York locations: the Asia Society, Queens Museum, and Grey Art Gallery. "Japan's Golden Age: Momoyama" at the Dallas Museum of Art included some 160 paintings, textiles, armor, and ceramics produced in Japan from 1573 to 1615.

Visitors to New York's Guggenheim Museum's Fifth Avenue rotunda saw such historical exhibitions as "Africa: The Art of a Continent," "Abstraction in the Twentieth Century: Total Risk, Freedom, Discipline," and a retrospective of contemporary U.S. abstract artist Ellsworth Kelly. "Media-scape," seen at the Guggenheim SoHo, highlighted that branch's focus on contemporary projects involving film, video, and computers.

Down Fifth Avenue from the Guggenheim, Kathleen Weil-Garris Brandt, a professor at New York University's Institute of Fine Arts, claimed to have found a forgotten sculpture by Michelangelo in the lobby of the neighboring French embassy's cultural center; the controversy was to be the basis of a future exhibition. Undisputed works by the Italian Renaissance master were on view in "Michelangelo and His Influence," a drawings show from the collection of Britain's Queen Elizabeth II seen at the National Gallery, Kimbell Art Museum, Fort Worth, and the Art Institute of Chicago. The Art Institute was the sole U.S. venue for a major show of the late work of French master Edgar Degas.

New York's MoMA organized a year-end retrospective of one of the most important contemporary U.S. artists, Jasper Johns. The city of Cleveland made itself the subject of contemporary art by commissioning 17 artists to make works on the theme "Urban Evidence: Cleveland." The pieces were shown at the Cleveland Museum of Art, Cleveland Center for Contemporary Art, and Spaces art center.

"Hall of Mirrors: Art and Film Since 1945" premiered at the Museum of Contemporary Art, Los Angeles, and also was seen at Ohio State University's Wexner Center for the Arts. This was a timely theme, as the distance between the artist's studio and the studio lot decreased noticeably during the year. Painter Julian Schnabel's debut as a feature-film director, *Basquiat*—based on the life and early death of another painter who rose to prominence in the 1980s—was one of several movies directed by contemporary artists, as well as one of several about art and artists.

The discovery of rock carvings in northern Australia that may be 75,000 years old suggested that the ancestors of modern *Homo sapiens* already were creating images (*see also* ARCHAEOLOGY). The discovery raises the question of whether art precedes reason (if

© Tass/Sovfoto/Eastfoto

In 1996, Moscow's Pushkin Museum displayed "The Gold of Troy," treasures discovered at the site of the lost city of Troy (in modern-day Turkey) in the 1870s. Among them were a bronze idol, above, *dating from 2600–2450 B.C.*

the ancient carvings are considered art). Modern art has been considering this question at least since the surrealists suggested in the 1920s that art could issue unplanned from the unconscious.

Dadaism, the movement that led to surrealism, questioned the idea that artworks must present the artist's own work. Marcel Duchamp took a urinal, turned it on its side, signed it "R. Mutt," titled it "Fountain," and presented it to a New York exhibiting society in 1917. They rejected it. In 1996, Duchamp and other New York dadaists had their first comprehensive exhibition, at the Whitney Museum of American Art. Earlier in the year, the Whitney showed the work of Edward and Nancy Reddin Kienholz, who from the 1950s through Edward's death in 1994 developed Dadaism's use of materials found in the everyday world into elaborate satirical and political tableaux. Berlin Dadaist Hannah Höch created one of the movement's most cutting works, the collage "Cut With the Kitchen Knife Dada: Through the Last Weimar Beer Belly Epoch," in 1919. Her 1996 U.S. retrospective was organized by the Walker Art Center in Minneapolis; it traveled to New York's MoMA and the Los Angeles County Museum of Art.

Painter Robert Colescott was chosen to represent the United States at the Venice Biennale in the summer of 1997—the first African-American artist so honored. Arts America, the U.S. Information Agency bureau that handled funding and logistics for such exhibitions, was cut from the federal budget.

Microsoft mogul Bill Gates showed one of his prizes, Leonardo da Vinci's Codex Leicester notebook, solely at New York's Museum of Natural History, as if to suggest that the Italian Renaissance genius' pen-on-parchment technique now belongs with the dinosaur bones.

Facilities. New facilities for contemporary art opened in Miami, San Diego, and Chicago. The Miami building is by Charles Gwathmey and the San Diego expansion by Venturi, Scott Brown and Associates, while German architect Josef Paul Kleihues completed his first U.S. commission in Chicago. At 220,000 sq ft (20 439 m^2) and occupying a 2-acre (0.8-ha) site, the Chicago building and sculpture garden increases the museum's space sevenfold. The museum displayed works by more than 150 artists in "Art in Chicago, 1945–1995" at year's end. The Miami museum closed the year with "Painting into Photography, Photography into Painting."

The renovated Barnes Foundation in Merion, PA, reopened amid legal battles with neighbors, who claimed that longer visiting hours at the treasure trove of modern masterpieces would endanger their suburban peace. Santa Fe announced the opening in fall 1997 of a museum dedicated to the work of U.S. modernist Georgia O'Keeffe.

Staffing. The Los Angeles County Museum of Art appointed a new director, Graham W.J. Beal, formerly of the Joslyn Art Museum in Omaha, NE. Peter C. Sutton went from Christie's in New York to a position as director of the Wadsworth Atheneum in Hartford. He replaced Patrick McCaughey, who became director of the Yale Center for British Art in New Haven. Emily Sano was named director of the Asian Art Museum of San Francisco. Thomas Sokolowski resigned as director of the Grey Art Gallery at New York University to take over as head of Pittsburgh's Andy Warhol Museum. Richard Armstrong was promoted to director of the Carnegie Museum of Art in Pittsburgh. Diane Waldman resigned as senior curator of the Guggenheim, to be replaced by art historian Robert Rosenblum and Mark Rosenthal, former head of the 20th-century department at the National Gallery. John Hanhardt, long the curator of film and video at the Whitney, now would head the Guggenheim's film program. The search for a new director was on at the Brooklyn, where director Robert Buck resigned.

PETER CHAMETZKY, *Adelphi University*

Art Market

Top-end collectors strained at the bit in 1996, hungering for great or very beautiful paintings. For example, there were the two paintings by Claude Monet that sold at auction. One, "Le Jardin de l'Artiste à Vetheuil," was a view of the artist's garden; the other was one of Monet's renderings of water lilies. Bidders waded in and dropped out at various stages on each painting. By the time the works had sold—for $13.2 million each—about ten people had made bids totaling more than $120 million.

All that money, but not enough great art to attach itself to—this was the story of the year. With the U.S. economy running at a good clip and European financial markets relatively strong, the money indeed was there. Yet, great pictures aside, the art market was restrained; many second-tier works elicited not one bid.

The Old Masters arena offered little of excitement until December, when a Raphael study for the head and hands of an apostle fetched $8.7 million.

The Monets fetched the top prices in the Impressionist and modern field for the year, followed closely by the $11.88 million notched by Edgar Degas' large bronze of a young ballerina, "Petite Danseuse de Quatorze Ans." The price was a record for a Degas sculpture. Two other works broke the $10 million barrier: a fine but far from brilliant Paul Cézanne landscape brought $11 million, and a rather cold and unmoving Vincent van Gogh interior fetched $10.34 million.

The surprise of the November season came when Mirage Resorts International chairman Steve Wynn bought two paintings for his company. The works were destined for a $1.3 billion resort and casino under construction in Las Vegas.

With one brilliant exception, the market for contemporary art continued to lag. The gem was Willem de Kooning's "Woman," from his first (and less famous) Women series. It brought $15.62 million, an astounding price; this marked the first time a contemporary painting had outpriced works in all other fields for the year. Other works crept past $2 million, but large chunks of auctions went unsold as buyers proved picky in this field.

American paintings continued to surge. In May, Mary Cassatt's "In the Box" brought $4 million, Maxfield Parrish's "Daybreak" notched an astonishing $4.29 million, and John Singer Sargent's "Capri Girl" fetched $4.8 million. Strong as these prices were, they were dwarfed in December, when Sargent's "Cashmere" sold for $11.1 million. It was the highest price ever paid for a U.S. painting, eclipsing the previous record by 35%.

A bronze sculpture by Edgar Degas, "Petite Danseuse de Quatorze Ans," above, *drew one of the year's highest prices when it sold in November for $11.88 million at Sotheby's New York.*

Although former first lady Jackie Kennedy Onassis had owned relatively little art, the highly publicized auction of property from her estate realized close to $34.5 million. Even Sotheby's, which handled the auction, did not expect the woods alone from President John F. Kennedy's golf bag to bring $772,500, or his humidor to fetch $574,500. (*See also* PEOPLE, PLACES, AND THINGS.)

Also in 1996, the Railway Pension Fund—one of England's largest pension funds—continued selling works of art it had acquired in the 1970s, when inflation made tangible goods like art seem like a good investment. By midyear, the fund had sold off most of its purchases and found that the rate of return, after inflation, came to a modest 5.33% a year. Art may be eternal, but apparently it does not keep up with inflation.

ANDREW DECKER, *Contributing Editor "ARTNews Magazine"*

ASIA

Asian regional political, economic, and security organizations grappled with a number of issues in 1996—some successfully, others less so.

ASEAN. The Association of Southeast Asian Nations (ASEAN) annual summit—held in Jakarta, Indonesia, in November—took another step toward the inclusion of all ten Southeast Asian states. Laos and Cambodia would be admitted to full membership in 1997; and Myanmar (Burma) was given observer status, the first step toward full membership. Controversy over the latter's admission sparked ASEAN's only significant disagreement. Because of Myanmar's abysmal human-rights situation, Thailand, the Philippines, and Singapore counseled delay on Myanmar's membership. Manila and Bangkok openly cited the Myanmar regime's lack of democracy and continued human-rights violations, while Singapore advocated delay on the grounds that Myanmar was not prepared yet to assume the economic obligations ASEAN required of its members. Either way, it appeared that Myanmar's accession to ASEAN would be put off.

With respect to the dispute over the Spratly Islands in the South China Sea—involving China, Vietnam, Malaysia, the Philippines, and Brunei—ASEAN, at its 29th ministerial meeting in Jakarta, endorsed the idea of a regional code of conduct that would lay the foundation for long-term stability. Although China did not accept this proposal formally, it expressed interest in the possibility of joint development in disputed areas. Meanwhile, both China and Vietnam continued unilaterally to engage in petroleum exploration in the portions of the South China Sea they claim.

Following ASEAN's annual ministerial meeting, the third ASEAN Regional Forum (ARF) also was held in Jakarta. Attending, along with the ASEAN states, were their dialogue partners from Northeast Asia (Japan, China, South Korea, and Russia), North America (the United States and Canada), and the European Union (EU). In 1996, India and Myanmar were added to the ARF. Reports were received from working groups on confidence-building measures, peacekeeping operations, and search-and-rescue cooperation—all prospectively the bases for collaborative activities by ARF members. For Northeast Asia, ARF noted the importance of the Korean Peninsula Energy Development Organization (KEDO), and urged ARF participants to provide financial support for activities designed to ensure that North Korea, in exchange for the construction of light-water nuclear reactors for electrical power in the North, does not develop nuclear weapons.

The Myanmar issue also surfaced in the ARF as Western delegations tried to convince the Forum to condemn the military government's treatment of political opponents. Because ASEAN was committed to a policy of constructive engagement, however, Myanmar was not mentioned in the ARF final communiqué—a sign that Yangon (Rangoon) already was being protected by its future ASEAN membership.

ASEM and APEC. The year 1996 also witnessed the first Asia-Europe Meeting (ASEM), which brought representatives from the EU and East Asia together on March 1 and 2 in Bangkok, Thailand. For Asia, the meeting served to balance its links to the United States. For Europe, the hope was to increase trade and investment opportunities in East Asia, which badly lagged behind the U.S. economic presence. Additionally, the Europeans, feeling outnumbered in the Asia Pacific Economic Cooperation (APEC) forum, saw the ASEM as a way of rectifying the balance. The agendas for each side at the ASEM differed. The Asians were interested in specific projects that the Europeans could fund, such as a trans-Asian railroad, while the Europeans stuck to general principles of trade liberalization.

Less-developed Asian members of APEC seemed bent on weakening U.S. efforts to further institutionalize trade liberalization at APEC's annual meeting in November in Manila, the Philippines. Greater flexibility was the order of the day. While the United States obtained an accelerated commitment to abolish tariffs on information technology by 2000, those states trying to protect fledgling information industries retained the right to keep their tariffs. Japan, South Korea, and the United States—all major information-technology exporters—favored the accord, which was to be formalized at the December 1996 World Trade Organization (WTO) meeting in Singapore.

The WTO did conclude an information-technology accord along the lines advocated by the industrial states—zero tariffs by the year 2000. However, of the ASEAN states, only Indonesia and Singapore acceded. Thailand, Malaysia, and the Philippines agreed to further discussion on liberalization, but Malaysia remained opposed to any change in tariff policy at this time.

SHELDON W. SIMON, *Arizona State University*

ASTRONOMY

The high-profile announcement in early August 1996 by the National Aeronautics and Space Administration that telltale signs of ancient life on Mars had been discovered captured world attention. Then, only days later, the U.S. space agency showcased another hint of life in the solar system from evidence gleaned by its Galileo space probe. Images returned to Earth suggest an ocean of water—the quintessential ingredient to foster life—might exist on Jupiter's moon Europa. In 1996 it also became clear that planetary-size bodies commonly circle nearby stars. Meanwhile the Great Comet Hyakutake visited Earth's doorstep (*see* SPECIAL REPORT, page 133).

Life on Mars? The jury still is out about whether ancient life existed on Mars, and skeptics abound. It may be years before scientists confirm or disprove the claim that a meteorite, a rock from space weighing 4.2 lb (1.9 kg), contains evidence of primitive life on Mars 3.6 billion years ago. That is about a billion years after our solar system formed, and it concides with a time when water probably was abundant on Mars and when life sprang forth on Earth. The greenish rock had been blasted off Mars by a cometary or asteroidal impact some 16 million years ago, wandered the solar system, and finally fell to Earth 13,000 years ago. The meteorite, called ALH84001, was discovered in 1984 on the Antarctic ice cap by a team sponsored by the National Science Foundation.

The evidence for life on Mars is collectively intriguing but separately fragile. There are three indicators:

1. *Polycyclic aromatic hydrocarbons (PAHs).* Polycyclic aromatic hydrocarbons (PAHs), organic molecules, can indicate life, but they also can be created by nonbiological processes. Ubiquitous in the universe, PAHS are found as decay or combustion products, and they pervade interstellar dust, clouds surrounding stars, and galaxies.

2. *Carbonate minerals.* No more than 0.01 inch (0.25 mm) in diameter, carbonate minerals or "globules" infiltrated fractures in the meteorite AHL84001 and contain particles of magnetite and iron sulfide, which are known to be produced by microorganisms on Earth. These compounds normally are not found together—except in the presence of anaerobic (oxygen-free) bacteria. Yet some scientists proposed that the carbonate in ALH84001 was deposited by a hot carbon dioxide fluid during the impact that launched the meteorite on its journey to Earth. Thus the presence of

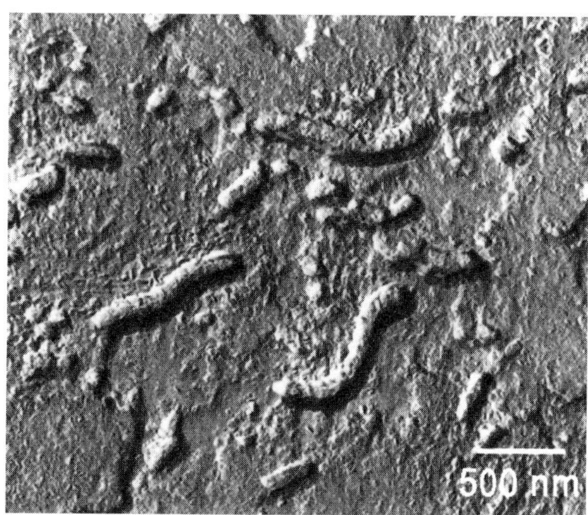

Photos, NASA

The high-resolution-transmission electron-microscope image (above) *of a cast from a chip of the meteorite ALH84001,* left, *shows what are believed to be microscopic fossils of bacteria-like organisms that may have lived on Mars. The meteorite fell to Earth 13,000 years ago and was discovered in 1984.*

carbonate would have nothing to do with the existence of life.

3. *Fossils.* Only some 4 millionths of an inch (100 nanometers) or less long, rice-shaped fossils strikingly resemble the earliest bacteria on Earth. Yet the structures in ALH-84001 are so tiny—roughly 100 times smaller than any fossil ever found on Earth—that they have volumes barely adequate to envelop all the enzymes and genetic material necessary for life as we know it. Another problem is that images reveal no cell walls, so mineral flecks might be masquerading as fossils.

All three indicators of life on Mars can be mimicked by inorganic processes. Yet it is the tight juxtaposition of this evidence within the Mars rock that provides the most compelling reason for believing that life once existed on Mars. A dedicated space mission probably will be needed to validate that life once existed on Mars. Although the two Viking spacecraft that landed on Mars in 1976 failed to find conclusive evidence of life, they may have set down in an inhospitable place. In addition, none of the probes that lifted off toward Mars in 1996 were designed to look for life.

Europa's Ocean? In 1996 another possible home for life in the solar system was investigated by the Galileo space probe studying Jupiter. Images of that planet's satellite Europa revealed an icy crust that once was fractured and then mended. This broken crust had been detected in 1979 by the Voyager 1 and 2 spacecraft, but Galileo's vastly clearer images permit a new interpretation of Europa's history.

Europa's crust—at a temperature of –229°F (–145°C) and possibly up to tens of miles thick—was shattered by Jupiter's gravity. After such cracking occurred, the ice floes refroze and reassembled themselves like pieces of a jigsaw puzzle to form the mosaic pattern seen today. Such movement suggests that the slabs are able to glide over a substrate some several miles deep that may be either warm, slushy ice or, more provocatively, liquid water.

The thousand-mile-long crisscrossing seams that mark the edges of Europa's ice floes have their own story to tell. Some 5 mi (8 km) wide, each seam looks like a tree-lined roadway seen from an airplane—a light center flanked by peripheral, fuzzy darkness. Planetary scientists interpret this "triple-band" pattern as indicating zones where dirty, silicate-rich water first spewed forth in geysers to cause the dark edging and then was followed by purer water, which froze to form the "road."

Whether Europa's ice glides on slush or water—heated by the squeezing and stretching tidal action of Jupiter—the slippery substrate is a promising place to harbor life. According to some scientists, if such a zone were infused with organic compounds, the development of life would be almost certain, perhaps mimicking biosystems that thrive in total darkness on Earth.

Planetary Finds. By the end of 1996, little more than one year after the first confirmed discovery of an extrasolar planet circling a Sunlike star, about a dozen other systems had been detected around such ordinary stars. Physically these planets range in mass from about 0.6 to 60 times that of Jupiter and orbit their parent stars in periods that range from three days to roughly 30 years.

Further refinements in detection techniques promise many more planetary discoveries in the years ahead. The new objective is to find a twin of the Earth, which has a mass only 0.003 that of Jupiter and circles the Sun in one year. That quest may be realized only when new space-based technologies become operational in the next decade or so.

Thanks to very detailed images from the Hubble Space Telescope, it has become known that many stars are surrounded by disks of dust and gas that are planetary systems in the making. For example, in the nearby Orion Nebula, which long has been known to be a stellar nursery, more than 150 such protoplanetary disks have been revealed. These disks appear very much as theorists imagine our Sun and solar system to have looked like 5 billion years ago.

Other studies have raised the possibility that newborn stars may spawn millions of planet-size objects. The evidence supporting such a vast number comes from tiny, rapid variations in the light of a quasar (probably the brilliant core of a distant galaxy) en route to Earth. When a quasar's light passes through an ordinary intervening galaxy, the gravity of any object in the galaxy that is aligned between the quasar and Earth causes the quasar's light to brighten briefly. From the duration and strength of such "flashes," the object's size and mass can be deduced. One astronomer has proposed a population of 1 quadrillion (10^{15}) Earth-size planets in one galaxy alone. More conservative estimates, based on the newly discovered planets in our galaxy, suggest that the Milky Way contains "only" millions of planetary bodies. In any event, the universe seems to hold an amazing number of potential biotic sites.

LEIF J. ROBINSON, *"Sky & Telescope"*

SPECIAL REPORT/ASTRONOMY

© "The Fayetteville Observer-Times"/Johnny Horne/AP/Wide World Photos

Great Comet Hyakutake

Within a mere four months of 1996, Comet Hyakutake burst on the scene from outer space, screamed past Earth, rounded the Sun, and retreated to oblivion. The comet that amateur astronomer Yuji Hyakutake discovered on Jan. 30, 1996, from Kagoshima, Japan, was the most spectacular visitor to cross Earth's doorstep in a generation. The comet, officially named C/1996 B2, was Hyakutake's second find; the first had come five weeks earlier.

Features. Experts still debate the definition of a "great" comet. But to those who saw Comet Hyakutake at its best—in late March when it passed only 9.3 million mi (15 million km) from Earth (40 times the separation between the Earth and the Moon)—it was great indeed. In the evening sky, Comet Hyakutake appeared as a huge turquoise fuzzball more than twice the diameter of the full Moon, a 162,000-mi (260 000-km)-wide blob of cotton candy floating in the heavens. The comet's head was visible even to sky gazers living in the most badly light-polluted metropolitan areas. Amazingly, some of these observers could glimpse a bit of Comet Hyakutake's tail. From dark, rural sites, the tail could be seen to stretch halfway across the sky. Adding to the spectacle was the comet's extreme speed relative to the background stars. At its peak, Comet Hyakutake raced past them so rapidly that, with only the unaided eye, its position could be seen to change in less than an hour.

Comet Hyakutake was extremely active. From its nucleus, gas was shed abundantly, then pushed away to form its tail by the "wind" of atoms and atomic fragments that blows endlessly from the Sun. Yet the nucleus of the comet was unexceptional in size—only 0.6–1.9 mi (1–3 km) in diameter.

Comet Hyakutake provided an ideal test bed for trying out state-of-the-art instruments and techniques that were not dreamed of when Comet West—the previous great one—appeared in 1976. All aspects of the 1996 visitor were observed, from low-energy radio waves to high-energy X rays. About a dozen molecular species—combinations of hydrogen, carbon, nitrogen, oxygen, and sulfur—were detected. In late March the strongest light emissions from the comet came from diatomic carbon (C_2), which also caused the turquoise color.

Jets of gas emanating from the comet's head were seen to rotate in a period of six to eight hours, probably reflecting the spin rate of the nucleus. The strangest observation, however, was by the Rosat satellite; it detected X rays, which never before had been recorded from a comet. How such energetic emission could occur in the tepid, Sunward-facing hemisphere of Comet Hyakutake remained unexplained late in 1996.

The Future. Comet Hyakutake will not return to Earth's neighborhood for some 14,000 years. Yet another cometary spectacle—the arrival of Comet Hale-Bopp—was anticipated by March–April 1997. By all expectations it would equal, and probably surpass, Comet Hyakutake.

LEIF J. ROBINSON

AUSTRALIA

In a clear redirection of national outlook, Australian voters on March 2, 1996, gave a landslide victory to a coalition of the Liberal and National parties led by John Howard (*see* BIOGRAPHY), a moderate conservative. The results brought to an end 13 years of Australian Labor Party (ALP) administration.

Politics. In elections for the House of Representatives, the Liberal-National coalition gained 94 seats (out of a total of 148); the ALP won only 49. However, in spite of gaining overwhelming numbers in the House, the coalition failed to secure a majority in the Senate, where the balance of power was held by minor parties (the Australian Democrats and the Greens) and two independents (both dissident Labor senators).

The result confirmed a drift from the ALP first apparent in the 1993 general election, when Prime Minister Paul Keating retained power with a slim majority, and came as a clear rejection of the philosophies Labor had come to represent. The women's vote favored the coalition, which endorsed high-profile women in a number of key seats. The socially conservative, blue-collar vote also drifted from the ALP to Howard. For Labor the March defeat ended the party's longest term in office federally. Following the loss, Keating resigned after 27 years in Parliament, including ten as treasurer and more than four as prime minister. Former Deputy Prime Minister Kim Beazley then was elected ALP leader.

At first Labor blamed its defeat on poor public understanding of the merit of its policies. However, the depth of the rejection was shown on March 30 in Victoria when Jeff Kennett, the high-profile and assertive Liberal premier of the state, retained power in spite of severe recovery measures he had carried through to reinstate Victoria's financial viability after a disaster-prone ten-year state Labor administration. Further humiliation came in October, when an ALP candidate performed very poorly in a federal by-election in Sydney. With close-knit community-group politics centered in the Liberal and National parties, the ALP found itself in search of core issues that were likely to appeal to an electorate with new aims.

The Budget. As prime minister, Howard drew his guidelines from a mixture of ideology and pragmatism. A Treasury Department report available to him immediately after the election revealed that snowballing budget deficits were in prospect. In August, Treasurer Peter Costello unveiled a new budget, which included A$8 billion in spending cuts over two years. The budget made expenditure reductions totaling A$3.7 billion for 1996–97. The heaviest cuts were in education funding and social-services outlays, while defense and employment programs were insulated.

Savings from staff cuts were relatively small; nevertheless, public-sector unions campaigned to protect their membership. Protest rallies were held in major cities, with sporadic office shutdowns. A large August rally in Can-

On April 28, 1996, a gunman opened fire on a crowd of people in and around the ruins of a colonial prison—a popular tourist spot—in Port Arthur, Tasmania, killing 35 persons. The incident was classified as the worst massacre in Australian history.

berra developed into a fracas with police after several hundred protesters stormed Parliament House.

Sales of public assets, including the government's remaining 51% of the Commonwealth Bank, were undertaken in order to retire debt. However, a plan to raise about A$8 billion by selling off one third of Telstra, the nation's dominant telecommunications operator, became stalled in the Senate in spite of the government's commitment to devote A$1 billion of the proceeds to new environmental programs.

Policy. Linked with fiscal rebalance was Howard's determination to carry through extensive industrial reform to free up the labor market and help reduce employers' reluctance to engage staff because of Labor's earlier "unfair dismissal" law. The House approved far-reaching legislation intended to cut back on the role of trade unions and reduce the power of the federal Industrial Relations Commission in favor of direct bargaining between employers and employees in workplace agreements. In the Senate, however, the legislation was modified considerably in negotiations with the Democrats.

Issues connected with immigration levels gained the media spotlight in September after an independent member of the House of Representatives, Pauline Hanson, voiced unbridled opposition to maintaining immigration from Asian sources. Vocal support for cuts to immigration developed, a sentiment running counter to the top priority given by the government to Asia in matters of trade and foreign affairs. In response, Parliament approved a bipartisan motion in late October opposing racial discrimination and reaffirming support for a nondiscriminating immigration policy. Specifically, Parliament reaffirmed its commitment to equal rights.

Economics. Australia's economic indicators were mixed. Gross-domestic-product (GDP) growth was 4.5% and inflation was 2.1%. The easing of interest rates (down to a 20-year low) improved housing affordability, but house sales remained sluggish. Disappointing retail sales were attributed to concerns arising from persistent unemployment, which rose to 8.7% in September.

Corporate Australia reported patchy trading and trimmed profit margins; total corporate earnings were down for the first time in five years. The poorest results were posted by some of the largest companies, including manufacturers, the building industry, and engineering and retailing companies. The stock market reached an all-time high in October, reflecting the easing in interest rates rather than profit performance. The incoming governor of the Reserve Bank of Australia, Ian Macfarlane, said the economy was in a period of sustained low inflation, with lower rates of return inevitable, and asserted that the business community needed to adjust its expectations on growth and profitability accordingly.

Profitability in the rural sector remained uncertain in spite of the return of good seasonal conditions in most areas. Grain growers had good crops but lowered prices; the price of wool remained low, while declines in beef prices hit cattlemen.

Foreign Affairs. Enhanced defense ties with the United States intended to support regional peace and security were formalized in high-level ministerial meetings in Sydney in July. Among the arrangements announced were a new series of joint military maneuvers for crisis planning and contingency response as well as an extension of the jointly operated Pine Gap spy-satellite station in central Australia to at least the year 2008. Against this background, Foreign Affairs Minister Alexander Downer subsequently explained the conceptual framework for the conduct of foreign policy by underscoring the point that engagement with Asia would remain Australia's highest foreign-policy priority.

A November visit by U.S. President Bill Clinton and Mrs. Clinton was received warmly. The president addressed Parliament.

Tragedy. Australia suffered the worst massacre in its modern history in late April, when a single gunman killed 35 persons in the Tasmanian town of Port Arthur. The incident helped prompt the passage of tougher gun-control measures throughout the nation.

R. M. YOUNGER
Author, "Australia and the Australians"

AUSTRALIA • Information Highlights

Official Name: Commonwealth of Australia.
Location: Southwestern Pacific Ocean.
Area: 2,967,896 sq mi (7 686 850 km²).
Population (mid-1996 est.): 18,300,000.
Chief Cities (mid-1993 est., metro. areas): Canberra, the capital, 325,400; Sydney, 3,719,000; Melbourne, 3,187,500; Brisbane, 1,421,700.
Government: *Head of state,* Elizabeth II, queen; represented by Sir William Deane, governor-general (took office February 1996). *Head of government,* John Howard, prime minister (took office March 1996). *Legislature*—Parliament: Senate and House of Representatives.
Monetary Unit: Australian dollar (1.2715 A$ equal U.S.$1, Nov. 11, 1996).
Gross Domestic Product (1994 U.S.$): $374,600,000,000 (purchasing power parity).
Economic Indexes (1995, 1990 = 100): *Consumer Prices,* all items, 113.2; food, 112.9. *Industrial Production,* 114.
Foreign Trade (1995 U.S.$): *Imports,* $60,317,000,000; *exports,* $53,097,000,000.

AUSTRIA

The year 1996 was a festive one for Austria, which commemorated the millennial anniversary of the first documented use of the term *Ostarrichi*—from Old German, *ostar* ("east") and *ricchi*, or *reich* in modern German ("realm" in this context). A medieval codex contains this term—the historical root word for *Osterreich* (Austria)—as a reference to a region situated in Neuhofen in the province of Lower Austria, the historical heartland of Austria. The commemoration of this event—with its various festivities, exhibitions, and publications—was not an attempt to construe 1,000 years of continuity in Austria's turbulent history. On the contrary, Austrians viewed it as an opportunity to reflect on how Austria as a territorial, cultural, and political entity has evolved throughout the ages and how it embodies diverse influences today.

Politics. A conflict over budgetary policy in the Social Democratic–Christian Democratic coalition government led to extraordinary general elections in December 1995 that were followed by the negotiation of a renewed coalition agreement between the two largest of the five parties represented in the Austrian parliament—the Austrian Social Democratic Party (SPÖ) and the Austrian People's Party (ÖVP). Federal Chancellor Franz Vranitzky, chairman of the SPÖ, was sworn into his fifth term of office since 1986 by Austrian President Thomas Klestil on March 12. Wolfgang Schüssel, the chairman of the ÖVP, assumed the positions of vice-chancellor and foreign minister in a "leaner" government cabinet of 14 ministers, instead of 16, and two state secretaries, instead of four.

The government coalition passed an "austerity package" for the 1996 federal budget that involved the curtailment of public expenditures, including the reduction of some social services and the progressive upward revision of income taxes. Although the populace as a whole accepted the necessity of these measures, items that affected benefits for university students and expenditures in higher education led to a wave of protests and strikes at universities in March and April. However, the government refused to make any major concessions.

On October 13 the results of national elections for the European Parliament and provincial elections in Vienna indicated a dramatic swing in voting patterns and the increasing popularity of the Austrian Freedom Party (FPÖ). In the past decade, under the leadership of its populist nationalist chairman Jörg Haider, the FPÖ has transformed itself into a formidable political force.

AUSTRIA • Information Highlights

Official Name: Republic of Austria.
Location: Central Europe.
Area: 32,375 sq mi (83 850 km^2).
Population (mid-1996 est.): 8,100,000.
Chief Cities (1991 census): Vienna, the capital, 1,539,848; Graz, 237,810; Linz, 203,044; Salzburg, 143,978; Innsbruck, 118,112.
Government: *Head of state,* Thomas Klestil, president (took office July 8, 1992). *Head of government,* Franz Vranitzky, chancellor (took office June 16, 1986). *Legislature*—Federal Assembly: Federal Council and National Council.
Monetary Unit: Schilling (10.543 schillings equal U.S. $1, Nov. 11, 1996).
Gross Domestic Product (1994 U.S.$): $139,300,000,000 (purchasing power parity).
Economic Indexes (1995, 1990 = 100): *Consumer Prices,* all items, 117.3; food, 112.8. *Industrial Production,* 108.
Foreign Trade (1994 U.S.$): *Imports,* $55,340,000,000; *exports,* $45,031,000,000.

In the Viennese elections, the SPÖ lost its absolute majority in the City Council for the first time since 1918—by dropping from 47.8% to 39.1% of the vote and from 52 to 42 seats. The FPÖ became the second-largest party in the city with an increase from 22.5% to 28.0% and from 23 to 30 seats, as many working-class voters—a traditional stronghold of the Social Democrats—vented their dissatisfaction with current policies by casting protest votes. The Christian Democratic ÖVP also lost ground (falling from 18.1% to 15.3% and from 18 to 15 seats), whereas the Greens remained stable (9.1% to 8.0% and seven seats). The Liberal Forum, an independent party established by a split in the FPÖ in 1993, ran for the first time in Vienna; it attracted 8.0% of the vote and received six seats.

European Parliament. Although observers tend to agree that elections for the European Parliament are not a very accurate indicator of voters' actual political preferences, and parties in power often perform poorly in them, the SPÖ managed to attract only 29% of the vote (minus 9.1% in comparison with the federal elections of 1995). The ÖVP received 29.6% (plus 1.3%) and the Liberal Forum 4.2% (minus 1.3%). The Freedom Party and the Greens—parties that ran anti–European Union campaigns—received 27.6% (plus 5.7%) and 6.8% (plus 1.8%), respectively. Austria's 21 seats in the European Parliament consequently were divided 14 to seven between pro–European Union parties of the SPÖ-ÖVP coalition government (six SPÖ, seven ÖVP, plus one Liberal Forum) and anti–European Union parties (six FPÖ and one Green).

LONNIE JOHNSON
Author, "Introducing Austria"

AUTOMOBILES

U.S. automakers enjoyed strong sales during 1996—a year that marked the industry's centennial (*see* SPECIAL REPORT). However, the year also ushered in developments that could impact traditional industry practices in the upcoming century.

With the Big Three automakers—General Motors (GM), Ford, and Chrysler—selling more trucks than cars for the first time, sales of all vehicles increased 3.4% in the first eight months of 1996 to 10,409,616 units, up from 10,063,455 in the comparable period of the previous year. Included in 1996 volume were a record-breaking 4,450,906 pickup trucks, vans, and sport-utility vehicles, exceeding the total from the comparable months of 1995 by more than 300,000 units.

Unabated consumer demand for trucks enabled the Big Three to post record or near-record results in the first half of 1996. Chrysler, for example, reported the highest net earnings in its history for the second quarter—$1.037 billion.

GM posted its best earnings per share in the second quarter, $2.65, on net profit of $2.095 billion. The Number 1 automaker was continuing to realign its production and sales operations throughout 1996, combining the Pontiac and GMC truck divisions and closing aging assembly plants in an effort to reduce operating costs.

Ford, producer of the world's top-selling truck model, the F-series pickup, earned $1.903 billion in the second quarter. Ford's earnings, however, were hurt by a slowdown in demand for luxury cars and for Ford's sharply restyled Taurus midsize model.

The Big Three maintained their share of the U.S. market at 73.2% in the first eight months of 1996, while vehicles made by Japanese automakers slipped to 22.5% from 22.8% in 1995. European manufacturers' share advanced from 3.1% to 3.4%.

Industry Developments. The year saw three landmark events carrying significant implications for the future of the U.S. auto industry. One was Ford's new contract with the United Automobile Workers (UAW), in which Ford agreed to maintain factory employment at 95% of late 1996 levels—a guarantee without precedent among major U.S. employers. Although the guarantee clause would allow further layoffs in the event of a sales slump, it rules out plant-closing or automated-equipment job reductions of the type that the Big Three had imposed in the late 1980s and early 1990s to reduce labor costs. Similar employment guarantees were won at Chrysler. Meanwhile, GM was hit by a strike by its Canadian workers in October.

Courtesy, Chevrolet

Courtesy, Dodge

Courtesy, Plymouth

New 1997-model cars and trucks included the Chevrolet Venture (top), *the Dodge Dakota Club Cab Sport* (middle), *and the Plymouth Prowler* (bottom). *The Venture features a four-speed automatic transmission, rear modular seats, dual air bags, and four or five passenger doors. The new-model Dodge truck has been restyled completely and offers a V6 or V8 engine. The Prowler is a factory-built hot rod, with a 214-hp V6 engine, leather interior, and a price tag of about $35,000.*

The century-old distribution system for new cars and trucks also was beginning to experience an upheaval. A wave of national chain-run "superstores" selling late-model used cars and new vehicles began to compete with the nation's 22,200 franchised new-car and -truck dealerships. The superstores were taking advantage of a rapidly growing demand for late-model used cars. New cars increasingly were running into an affordability problem among many consumers, as the average price of a new car neared the $20,000 mark.

The third watershed came with the sales launch by GM's Saturn division of the electric-powered EV1 subcompact car in southern California and Arizona. Saturn dealers at first were planning only to lease the car so that they could keep a close check on the vehicle's performance in field use. The EV1—to be followed in the spring of 1997 by the Honda EV car and later by battery-powered cars or trucks from Chrysler, Ford, Toyota, Nissan, and Mazda—was developed in response to California's approaching mandate for zero-emissions vehicles.

Early in the year, Chrysler chairman Robert J. Eaton orchestrated an agreement ending attempts by the company's leading shareholder, Kirk Kerkorian, to accumulate more stock than his 13.8% stake or to undertake a new takeover effort. Kerkorian had been allied with Eaton's predecessor, Lee A. Iacocca, who agreed to desist from further criticism of Chrysler management.

WORLD MOTOR VEHICLE DATA, 1995

Country	Passenger Car Production	Truck and Bus Production	Motor Vehicle Registrations
Argentina	226,504	58,768	5,666,331
Australia	314,142	29,709	10,517,796
Austria	43,466	3,217	4,240,195
Belgium	385,894	81,555	4,672,684
Brazil	1,296,586	327,555	15,340,000
Canada	1,339,474	1,077,702	17,439,600
China	320,578	1,114,210	9,450,000
Comm. of Ind. States	890,000	192,000	23,405,000
Czech Republic	189,434	26,589	4,430,233*
France	3,050,929	423,776	30,040,000
Germany	4,360,235	307,129	42,877,911
India	329,879	306,382	6,175,000
Italy	1,422,359	244,911	32,577,500
Japan	7,610,533	2,585,003	65,011,472
Korea, South	1,985,578	540,822	7,404,347
Malaysia	240,887	5,521	2,511,684
Mexico	699,312	235,705	12,300,000
The Netherlands	100,434	32,036	6,571,141
Poland	258,000	5,000	3,894,298
Spain	1,958,789	374,998	16,686,632
Sweden	387,659	102,483	3,912,033
Taiwan	282,006	124,474	4,658,772
Turkey	233,412	49,028	3,803,853
United Kingdom	1,532,084	233,001	27,436,878
United States	6,350,367	5,634,724	195,469,000**
Yugoslavia (former)	7,558	1,753	1,532,000
	35,816,099	14,118,051	629,077,117***

Source: American Automobile Manufacturers Association.

Other countries with more than one million registrations include Algeria, 1,205,000; Bulgaria, 1,536,300; Chile, 1,110,100; Colombia, 1,624,530; Denmark, 1,947,712; Egypt, 1,548,000; Finland, 2,150,950; Greece, 2,950,836; Hungary, 2,389,423; Indonesia, 3,585,597; Iran, 2,145,900; Iraq, 1,040,000; Ireland, 1,121,667; Israel, 1,314,775; Morocco, 1,278,033; New Zealand, 2,024,882; Nigeria, 1,379,000; Norway, 2,020,004; Pakistan, 1,010,000; Portugal, 3,242,500; Romania, 1,526,600; Saudi Arabia, 2,506,131; South Africa, 5,600,000; Switzerland, 3,457,085; Thailand, 2,847,939; and Venezuela, 1,929,985.

*Includes Slovakia.

**U.S. total does not include Puerto Rico, which has 1,685,000 vehicles.

***World total includes 479,532,564 cars and 149,544,553 trucks.

GM's struggles to reorganize itself after a traumatic period of vast financial and market-share losses in the early 1990s were highlighted by dramatic changes in its product philosophy. GM Chairman John F. Smith, Jr., stated that the company no longer would seek to serve every vehicle market or pursue sales dominance across the board. The automaker was stung in March by a 17-day strike of Ohio parts workers, losing considerable production over an issue hotly contested by the UAW—the outsourcing of supplier work to nonunion plants. Among other moves, GM launched a program to reduce its U.S. dealer count by at least 10% by the year 2000; the company also dropped its rear-wheel-drive cars, which had been popular with taxi drivers and police.

The Global Scene. Underscoring an aggressive expansion program by South Korea's five automakers, industry leader Hyundai introduced the Tiburon sports coupe in the United States. Meanwhile, GM affiliate Daewoo said it would enter the U.S. market in 1998 with a small-car line. Kia, in which Ford and Mazda have an equity, raised its dealer total in the United States to nearly 200 for sales of its Sephia compact car and Sportage utility vehicle.

Ford Chairman Alexander J. Trotman, facing product and fiscal problems at Mazda Motor, a foreign partner, took an unusual step by installing longtime Ford executive Henry Wallace as president of Mazda. Ford raised its Mazda equity from 25% to 33.4% in connection with the management change.

Many automakers were competing to open markets in developing countries with common vehicle platforms. GM's new minivan that entered production in the United States came in versions for Opel and Vauxhall. Ford was en route to "global" platforms on a worldwide basis as a part of a Ford 2000 project, which started in 1995 with the European Mondeo—sold in the United States as the Ford Contour and Mercury Mystique. Chrysler was finding increased acceptance overseas for such popular domestic vehicles as the Jeep Cherokee and Grand Cherokee, the all-wheel-drive minivan, and the Neon subcompact car.

GM approved Saturn's proposal to build an edition of the midsize European Opel Vectra model at a Delaware plant. This new upscale Saturn would join the 1997 Cadillac Catera compact as an Opel-created product adapted to the U.S. market (although Opel would be assembling the Catera for GM's luxury-car division in Germany).

MAYNARD M. GORDON, *Detroit Bureau Chief "Ward's Dealer Business Magazine"*

SPECIAL REPORT/AUTOMOBILES

The Centennial of Automobile Mass Production

Only 13 "motorized carriages" were built in 1896, but that was enough to establish it as the year when the newly invented "horseless carriage" gave birth to the automobile mass-production system that revolutionized transportation worldwide.

The founders of the concept of mass production of automobiles were brothers Charles and Frank Duryea of Peoria, IL. They located their fledgling factory in Springfield, MA. Unable to maintain quality standards, however, the Duryeas sold out in 1898 to the National Motor Carriage Company, which lasted only a few more years. By that time, competitors had emerged, and the automotive industry began in earnest.

Observance of the centennial of automobile mass production focused attention on the future of motor vehicles in the next century and on the nature of the ever-changing industry itself.

The Early Years of Auto Production. Ransom E. Olds formed the Olds Motor Vehicle Company, forerunner of the Oldsmobile division of the General Motors (GM) Corporation, in 1897 in Lansing, MI. He built his first factory in Detroit in 1899.

Also in 1899, a group of investors raised $15,000 to organize the Detroit Automobile Company with the idea of building the Quadricycle, which a 36-year-old inventor named Henry Ford had built in his spare time. The company closed in 1900 when shareholders concluded that "cars" never could become a mass-market commodity. By that time, though, excitement over the freshman crop of motorized carriages had spread across the land. The first auto show had been staged in New York City's Madison Square Garden, and a race—with a top prize of $2,000—was held in 1895 between downtown Chicago and Evanston, IL. The pioneering field of automaking was attracting entrepreneurs and visionaries like David D. Buick, John and Horace Dodge, William C. Durant, Henry Leland, James Packard, and Alexander Winton.

As automaking grew from a handful of units painstakingly built in back-alley machine shops to hundreds and then thousands per month among numerous start-up plants, the need for distribution agents unfolded quickly.

The first Duryea Motor Wagon had been sold in 1896 "factory direct" to George H. Horill, Jr., of Norwood, MA. The first auto dealer was William E. Metzger, who took on franchises in Detroit from 1896 to 1902. By 1903, when Ford Motor Company was formed, the Olds Curved Dash Runabout was dominating the field. Olds built 425 cars in 1901 and 4,696 in 1903 in locations in Detroit and Lansing. Olds outbuilt Ford's 1,708 cars in 1903,

Today's auto industry had its humble beginnings in 1896 with the production by Frank and Charles Duryea of 13 two-passenger runabouts. (Charles is shown below *with an early model.) Henry Ford's introduction of assembly-line production,* right, *revolutionized the young industry.*

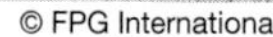
© FPG International

Courtesy, Ford Motor Company

but that was the last time it did so. Henry Ford's Model A Runabouts were selling like the proverbial hotcakes at a price of $850, and by 1905 he had built a Detroit plant ten times larger than his original factory.

The Contributions of Henry Ford. Although he was a relatively uneducated technical genius contending with hundreds of automaking entrepreneurs, Henry Ford turned out to be the "first among equals" in the business of forging a machine that truly did change the world. As bicycle maker/millionaire Billy Durant began building the General Motors empire by acquiring Buick in 1904 and Oldsmobile in 1908, Ford created three breakthroughs that transformed the auto industry from a provider of transportation for the affluent to a people mover for the masses.

Out of Ford's shop in 1908—the same year GM was formed—came the 20-horsepower Model T and, with it, a single-casting engine, simplified controls, and a price of $850. These features all were ingredients and benefits of Ford's streamlined system of mass production, which is still in use today. The system borrowed concepts from the production of sewing machines and small arms that never before had been applied to carriages or motor vehicles.

Due to the efficiencies of mass production, Ford was able to double the pay rate for unskilled labor to $5 a day on Jan. 5, 1914, following by a year the introduction of a moving assembly line at Ford's Highland Park, MI, plant. The company's cheapest runabout was priced at $440 in 1914, as its annual sales climbed to the $30 million mark.

Growth and Dominance of the "Big Three." Meanwhile, Durant's new GM organization had added the Oakland (Pontiac) and Cadillac divisions in 1909; it launched Chevrolet as a direct price competitor of Ford's in 1912. Ford remained the unchallenged Number 1 automaker until well into the 1920s, however. At that point a reorganized GM dethroned an unchanged Model T by introducing a modernized Chevrolet in the lowest-priced segment of the market.

Early independent automakers—including post–World War II survivors such as Hudson, Nash, Packard, Studebaker, and Willys—competed against GM and Ford throughout most of the century, but a major contender emerged in the mid-1920s when former GM manufacturing executive Walter P. Chrysler organized Chrysler Corporation and acquired the Dodge Brothers car and truck complex. Thus, the Big Three were in place by the onset of the Great Depression. During the 1930s the United Automobile Workers union was formed, and "necessity" inspired the invention of conveniences such as reclining seats and vent windows, and radical changes such as the automatic transmission. The concept that gears could be shifted automatically was just as startling at this time as Charles Kettering's self-starter had been in 1912 or GM design chief Harley Earl's annual model change had been in the 1920s.

During World War II, automakers produced tanks and airplanes for the armed forces. The inevitable postwar sales boom—as newly prosperous consumers rushed to buy the latest models—almost was missed by Ford Motor Company, however. Its new chief executive, Henry Ford II, grandson of the aging founder, had just resurrected the firm after a brush with near bankruptcy.

The eventual end of the postwar surge left independent automakers strapped and newcomers Kaiser-Frazer and Tucker unable to penetrate the Big Three's market dominance. Studebaker and Packard joined forces but eventually folded in the mid-1960s. George Romney—later to become governor of Michigan—led the American Motors combination of Nash and Hudson through a successful period featuring the 1950 introduction of the Rambler economy compact car.

Troubles in the U.S. Auto Industry. By the 1960s—with U.S. independents struggling and an estimated 25% to 30% of U.S. new-car buyers choosing cars other than the Big Three's often garish and look-alike products—the window of opportunity was open for invaders from abroad. Reaction against Big Three designs and business

Courtesy, General Motors

Three auto-industry milestones: The small, economical Volkswagen Beetle (far left), *popular in Germany since 1936, gained a foothold in the 1960s among U.S. consumers—thus opening the door for the large-scale sale of imports in the United States. The 1986 Ford Taurus* (center left) *represented a radical change in U.S. car design, from squared-off and boxy to sleek and aerodynamic. Perhaps the most revolutionary change, coming as the industry entered its second century, was the introduction of battery-powered cars, such as GM's 1997 EV1,* near left.

practices had escalated from the mid-1950s on. U.S. car designs had become bulbous. The failure of Ford's Edsel in 1958—when sharply finned fenders and shiny chrome striping marked most Detroit-built products—was an ominous sign.

The first of the foreign producers to reach high-volume sales in the United States was Volkswagen (VW), whose "bare bones" rear-engine Beetle, first introduced in Germany in 1936, found a receptive audience among postwar baby boomers in the 1960s and 1970s.

VW's success, which paved the way for the growth of imported-car and pickup-truck sales by nearly all European and most Japanese automakers, also coincided with the adoption of stringent federal safety, emissions, and fuel-economy regulations. The safety measures were a response to growing complaints about the neglect of safety, ignited by consumer advocate Ralph Nader and following well-publicized U.S. Senate investigations of new-car pricing practices and factory abuse of dealers. As for the fuel standards, they were triggered in large part by gasoline shortages in 1973–75 and 1980–81.

In 1978 the first of what was to become a wave of "transplant" auto-assembly facilities was opened by Volkswagen in Westmoreland, PA. The major Japanese automakers followed suit in the early 1980s, seeking to offset the imposition by the U.S. government of annual quotas on imports of new vehicles from Japan.

With foreign brands claiming steadily higher shares of the U.S. market, and the Big Three running into seemingly unsolvable quality problems, Chrysler and Ford faced top-level management crises by the late 1970s. Ford Chairman Henry Ford II in 1978 fired company President Lee Iacocca, who then became chairman of the nearly insolvent Chrysler Corporation. Iacocca engineered a turnaround for Chrysler, helped in large measure by an unprecedented $1 billion bailout loan from the U.S. government. By 1987, Chrysler was healthy enough to buy out the troubled American Motors.

The Changing Face of Today's U.S. Industry. The Big Three recouped from an early 1980s downturn and, with Japanese new-car sales also at record rates, chalked up an all-time-record sales year for new cars in 1986—11,459,518 units. A boom in minivans, pickups, and sport utility vehicles developed in the early 1990s, accounting for a 1994 all-time sales peak in the truck segment of 6,420,857 vehicles.

The Big Three had received a wake-up call with the impact of high-quality and efficiently produced cars from Japan, ranging from luxury models to fuel-efficient minicompacts. The responses of GM to the competition included both an unprecedented shake-up of its top management in 1992 and the creation of the "autonomous" Saturn division in the compact-car segment.

In 1996 battery-powered cars or trucks were on the way from Ford, Chrysler, Toyota, Honda, and Nissan. Though limited in quantity and carrying prices in the $25,000-to-$35,000 range, the new models herald the inception of a segment not dependent on gasoline. Saturn's 1997-model electric-powered car, the EV1, went on sale in California and Arizona. Safer and environmentally "cleaner" vehicles remain paramount concerns, with side-door air bags rapidly arriving on more vehicles and zero-emissions cars—either electric or gas-powered—likely to emerge in the near future.

The century-old system of selling new cars through franchised dealers also has begun yielding to changes as "superstores" take on sales of used and even new vehicles, especially in urban centers. The "no-haggle" policy touted by Saturn also has found imitators. Finally, with U.S. autoworker wages averaging $43 an hour, more production of new cars and trucks likely will move to Asian countries, particularly China and India, with input from automakers in the United States, Japan, and Europe. As the auto industry enters its second century, the only sure trend is continuing change.

MAYNARD M. GORDON

BALTIC REPUBLICS

The Baltic republics of Estonia, Latvia, and Lithuania continued to progress in their state-building efforts in 1996. In the five years since the collapse of the USSR, the Baltic states had gone further than other former Soviet republics in developing democratic polities, transforming their economies, and integrating their countries into the political and economic byways of international relations. During the year the three nations pursued normalized domestic political life, coped with problems of fledgling market economies, and broadened dialogue with the West. The main area of unresolved issues continued to be relations with Russia.

Politics. Campaigning and election outcomes drove politics in all three countries. Politically, Lithuania experienced the most dramatic year. A banking crisis late in 1995 helped bring about the downfall of Prime Minister Adolfas Slezevicius, who had withdrawn his sizable personal funds from a bank two days before his government ordered its closure. Additionally, it was revealed that he had earned double the normal interest on his funds. The scandal shook the governing Democratic Labor Party of Lithuania (LDDP). Early in February the parliament approved a decree from President Algirdas Brazauskas forcing Slezevicius' resignation. Laurynas Stankevicius was chosen as his successor. Subsequently, the fallen prime minister was arraigned on a charge of abuse of power. By mid-March, the new prime minister had gained parliamentary approval of his new government and its program.

Lithuania's first parliamentary elections since 1992 were held in October. The election campaign for the 141-seat Seimas kicked off in September with 28 parties contesting for the 71 party-list seats, and several hundred candidates running for the 70 single-mandate seats. The election, which required a second round of voting in November, resulted in a solid victory for the conservative Homeland Union that reduced the incumbent LDDP, a party led by former communists, to 12 seats in the Seimas. Consistent with the realignment, Vytautas Landsbergis, who had been the first president of post-Soviet Lithuania, was elected parliamentary speaker, while another conservative, Gediminas Vagnorius, was appointed prime minister.

In Latvia and Estonia, presidential elections were held that left the incumbents in place. In both countries, election was indirect by parliamentary deputies. In June, Latvian President Guntis Ulmanis gained reelection in a field of four, including Alfred Rubiks, the imprisoned former communist leader of Soviet Latvia. The contest in Estonia, however, was much closer. The election took place in August, with the winner required to gain a two-thirds majority of the 101 deputies in Estonia's parliament. President Lennart Meri faced a strong challenger in the deputy chairman of parliament, but neither candidate prevailed in two rounds of balloting. By law, the election was shifted to the electoral college composed of the deputies as well as 273 local government representatives chosen for the occasion. Meri finally won a second five-year term in a second round of electoral-college balloting in September.

The Baltic states continued to confront their troubled pasts. Lithuania opened a case against secret-police officers who served during the World War II Nazi occupation. Esto-

© Jamal Wilson/AFP/Corbis-Bettmann

The three Baltic nations—Estonia, Latvia, and Lithuania—were seeking to join the North Atlantic Treaty Organization (NATO) in 1996. The issue of such membership was high on the agenda when (left to right) *Latvia's President Guntis Ulmanis, U.S. President Bill Clinton, Estonia's President Lennart Meri, and Lithuania's President Algirdas Brazauskas conferred at the White House on June 25, 1996.*

BALTIC REPUBLICS • Information Highlights

Nation	Population (in millions)	Area (sq mi)	Area (km²)	Capital	Head of State and Government
Estonia	1.5	17,413	45 100	Tallinn	Lennart Meri, president Tiit Vahi, prime minister
Latvia	2.5	24,749	64 100	Riga	Guntis Ulmanis, president Andris Skele, prime minister
Lithuania	3.7	25,174	65 200	Vilnius	Algirdas Brazauskas, president Gediminas Vagnorius, prime minister

nia indicted the first Soviet-era secret policeman for responsibility in the executions of citizens, while Lithuania and Latvia initiated legal action against late-Soviet-period officials for official crimes in 1991.

Economy. Estonia continued to lead in economic reform and development, becoming the first Eastern European country to "graduate" from the U.S. foreign-aid program. In contrast, Lithuania and Latvia began to emerge slowly from their respective banking crises of 1995. In Lithuania by midyear, 18 of the country's 27 banks had resumed full or partial operations, but nine others faced bankruptcy. Lithuania also was beset by an energy crisis, forcing the government to consider raising domestic energy prices. Gazprom, the Russian natural-gas giant, had cut energy supplies to Lithuania the previous winter due to unpaid bills, and, by year's end, further cuts were being threatened if arrearages and penalties were not paid.

Economic policies increasingly were influenced by the three states' desire to comply with the criteria for full European Union (EU) membership, as well as the requirements for aid from the International Monetary Fund (IMF). For instance, Lithuania amended its constitution in order to permit foreigners to buy land, while Estonia passed a land-reform law—steps required of aspiring EU members. In turn, to satisfy the IMF, the Baltic governments signed an accord suspending agricultural tariffs. In other areas, Estonia resisted domestic pressure to raise the minimum wage, while Lithuania reduced its budget deficit by cutting back on social outlays. In the area of foreign private investment, Latvia signed an accord with the United States to insure prospective investments, but Estonia remained well ahead of its neighbors in attracting foreign investment.

Foreign Relations. Baltic foreign ministries continued their quest to join the EU and the North Atlantic Treaty Organization (NATO). All three Baltic states sought full EU membership, and to this end, lobbying was intense during 1996. The Nordic countries and Germany supported the EU aspirations of the Baltic states, offering such assistance as helping to revise legislation in conformity with EU standards. In January the presidents visited Germany together and received verbal support; during a summer meeting, their foreign ministers heard encouragement from their Nordic counterparts. In addition, both EU and NATO membership were on the agenda at the ninth meeting of the Baltic Assembly, which was held in October.

NATO membership was sought by the Baltic states in the interest of national security, given their geopolitical position next to Russia. NATO membership, however, found less vocal Western support, since Russia already was opposed to the possible inclusion of several Eastern European states in the organization. The Baltic countries, however, were included in the NATO Partnership for Peace program. Nevertheless, Baltic leaders pressed the NATO issue, especially with the United States. On a joint visit to Washington in June, the presidents of the three states raised the question with U.S. President Bill Clinton. As an interim response, the United States presented a proposal called the Baltic Action Plan, which included U.S. assistance for the Baltic states to integrate with the West on security issues, while stressing the necessity of good Baltic-Russian relations.

Relations with Russia continued to be nettlesome on a variety of issues, including disputed borders, citizenship and language rights for Russian minorities, and illegal immigrants transiting through Russia. In addition, each side seemed to provoke the other on symbolic issues such as the Russian parliamentary resolution in March nullifying the treaties that formally disbanded the USSR, and various public statements from Baltic officials supporting the Chechen rebels fighting Russia. The status of minority Russians as well as border disputes continued to complicate Estonia's and Latvia's relations with Russia. The Estonian-Russian border negotiations were the most contentious, but by year's end, an agreement had been reached.

ROBERT SHARLET
Union College

BANGLADESH

Two parliamentary elections and a peaceful transition in the nation's leadership dominated politics in Bangladesh in 1996.

Domestic Politics. Culminating a two-year standoff between the ruling Bangladesh National Party (BNP) and major opposition groups, Prime Minister Khaleda Zia called for parliamentary polls on February 15. Led by the Awami League (AL) and its leader Sheikh Hasina Wajed, virtually every major opposition party refused to participate, reiterating demands for Zia's resignation and the appointment of a caretaker government to oversee new elections. Zia refused, arguing that such a move would violate the constitution. Though the elections were held—with less than a 15% turnout—the BNP's victory was pyrrhic and short-lived.

Immediately, amid renewed charges of poll rigging and official corruption, fresh strikes and demonstrations virtually halted daily life. Late in March the civil service joined in forcing Zia to resign and agree to a constitutional amendment that would allow a caretaker administration. President Abdur Rahman Biswas named former Supreme Court Chief Justice Mohammad Habibur Rahman as head of the interim government until new elections were held on June 12.

Although more than 2,000 candidates—representing 81 parties and running as independents—fought for 300 seats, the major contest was between the BNP and AL. The BNP's campaign defended its economic-liberalization, education, and poverty-eradication programs. It attacked the AL for "ignoring proper democratic processes" and disrupting the economy. The AL concentrated on the BNP's performance, which it claimed was mainly talk with few results, and on corruption. Elections were held with minimum disruption and a record turnout of more than 73%. The AL won 146 seats and formed the new government, headed by Sheikh Hasina, with the support of former President H.M. Ershad's Jaitya Party (JP). The BNP won 116 seats despite the turmoil that brought down its government. Despite reports of growing Islamic fundamentalism, religious parties captured only three seats.

For observers and citizens concerned about Bangladesh's democratic future, the elections were especially heartening: The country came through a tumultuous period peacefully and without interference by the military. The major question asked was whether the BNP would resort to similar disruption to regain power. Although the new president, Shahabuddin Ahmed, appealed for cooperation among all parties, the BNP began a parliamentary boycott in November.

The Economy. Two years of instability affected the economic climate considerably. Small and medium businesses particularly felt the brunt of strikes and violence. While foreign businesses explored investment possibilities, few actually followed through, fearing potentially greater instability. By the end of 1995, it was almost impossible for the government to pursue its programs, even those utilizing international assistance. Donor agencies were also hesitant about future funding.

With potential stability at hand and promises by the AL government to continue economic liberalization, local and international investors seemed to regain confidence. A consortium of Western donors was ready to commit $2 billion, and Japanese interests were prepared to increase investments.

Foreign Relations. Two major issues dominated foreign affairs. First, the Friendship Treaty signed with India in 1972 was set to expire in March 1997. No major group supported the treaty's provisions, which from Bangladesh's viewpoint favored India's trade and market-access interests. Second was the continuing issue of sharing Ganges River water. Bangladesh maintained that India was using the Farakka Barrage, a dam on the upper Ganges, to divert water from Bangladesh in the dry season and to release too much water in seasons when flooding is a major problem. Some observers felt that India would be more accommodating to Bangladesh's interests in new negotiations in order to offer support to Sheikh Hasina's government and help maintain stability generally.

ARUNA NAYYAR MICHIE
Kansas State University

BANGLADESH • Information Highlights

Official Name: People's Republic of Bangladesh.
Location: South Asia.
Area: 55,598 sq mi (144 000 km²).
Population (mid-1996 est.): 119,800,000.
Chief Cities (1991 census): Dhaka, the capital, 3,637,892; Chittagong, 1,566,070; Khulna, 601,051.
Government: *Head of state,* Shahabuddin Ahmed, president (took office October 1996). *Head of government,* Sheikh Hasina Wajed, prime minister (sworn in June 1996). *Legislature*—unicameral Parliament.
Monetary Unit: Taka (41.75 takas equal U.S.$1, June 1996).
Gross Domestic Product (1994 est. U.S.$): $130,100,000,000 (purchasing power parity).
Economic Indexes: *Consumer Prices* (1995, 1990 = 100): all items, 122.5; food, 122.1. *Industrial Production* (1994, 1990 = 100): 154.
Foreign Trade (1995 U.S.$): *Imports,* $6,496,000,000; *exports,* $3,173,000,000.

BANKING AND FINANCE

The U.S. banking industry was impacted greatly by court decisions and new legislation in 1996. Courts affirmed banks' insurance powers, while Congress took steps to recapitalize the thrifts' deposit-insurance fund. Meanwhile, banks and thrifts continued to report near-record profits.

Court Decisions. In a landmark decision handed down in March, the U.S. Supreme Court confirmed the rights of national banks to sell insurance. In *Barnett Bank v. Nelson*, the high court ruled that the state of Florida could not restrict the sale of insurance by national banks with offices in small towns, despite state law written to prevent such sales.

In *Smiley v. Citibank*, the Supreme Court unanimously ruled in June that customers who carry credit cards issued by out-of-state banks must pay the late fees they are charged even if their own state does not allow these fees. In addition, the court ruled that national credit-card banks could charge other fees—such as membership or cash-advance fees—as long as they were permitted in the bank's home state.

In October a U.S. district court issued an order to implement an appeals-court ruling that federal regulators improperly had allowed credit unions to expand membership to individuals who do not share a "common bond" of occupation. At that time, federal credit unions were prohibited from adding any new members who did not meet the common occupational criteria. The case dealt with the AT&T Family Federal Credit Union having been authorized by the National Credit Union Administration—a federal agency that regulates and insures credit unions—to serve the employees of more than 150 other companies. It appeared likely that the decision, which would impact about 3,500 federally chartered credit unions, would be appealed to the Supreme Court or that legislative action would be pursued.

Legislation. The Small Business Job Protection Act, passed by Congress and signed into law by President Bill Clinton in August, removed a $3 billion tax liability of the thrift industry. Thrifts no longer would be responsible for paying taxes on bad debt reserves set aside before 1988. Without this financial impediment, thrifts were expected to convert to or merge with banks at a faster rate. In addition, the act would allow the tax-free conversion of common trust funds into mutual funds, and permit nonprofit groups to offer 401(k) plans. The act also contained provisions to raise the maximum annual contribution of nonworking spouses to individual retirement accounts (IRAs) to $2,000; and to create a new type of pension plan called a *s*avings *i*ncentive *m*atch *pl*an for *e*mployees, or SIMPLE. SIMPLE accounts resemble 401(k) plans, but require less paperwork for the small businesses expected to offer them to their employees.

The Health Insurance Portability and Accountability Act, which was signed into law in August, included provisions to create a four-year pilot program for medical savings accounts, which basically are IRAs for health care. Under the trial, people who work for companies with fewer than 50 employees, the self-employed, and the uninsured would be eligible to open these accounts. Participants would be allowed to contribute up to $2,250

© Michael Newman/Photo Edit

Although consumers continued to enjoy the convenience of more-sophisticated and more-widespread automatic-teller machines, debate over the levying of certain new surcharges for their use ensued.

for individuals and $4,500 for families to these tax-exempt accounts each year, and to make tax-free withdrawals for medical expenses. After age 65 (or after a participant dies or becomes disabled), withdrawals could be made for any purpose.

On September 30, Congress finally dealt with the issue of the recapitalization of the thrifts' deposit-insurance fund by passing the Deposit Insurance Funds Act as part of an omnibus appropriations bill. President Clinton signed the bill into law that same day. The initiative was necessary because the Savings Association Insurance Fund (SAIF), the thrifts' deposit-insurance fund, was undercapitalized, well below the required ratio of 1.25% of insured deposits. The Bank Insurance Fund (BIF), which insures commercial banks, on the other hand, was fully capitalized in 1995. Many officials feared that the resulting disparity in deposit-insurance premiums would lead to thrift-capitalization problems and possible failures.

The act ordered the thrifts to pay by Nov. 29, 1996, a onetime, $4.7 billion special assessment to recapitalize the SAIF. The act included a provision to make the thrifts' deposit-insurance premiums equal to those of commercial banks by the year 2000. The law also directed that commercial banks join savings institutions in making annual interest payments (estimated at $780 million) through 1999 only on so-called Financial Corporation (FICO) bonds, which financed the thrift bailout of the 1980s. The act paved the way for the eventual merger of the thrift and bank charters into one common charter and for the SAIF and BIF funds to be merged in 1999.

The omnibus spending bill also included regulatory-relief measures for banks in more than 40 areas, such as the simplification of disclosure requirements under the Truth in Lending Act and the Real Estate Settlement Procedures Act; the privatization of the Student Loan Marketing Association (Sallie Mae); the requirement that the Federal Reserve Board (Fed) study the issue of consumer protection as related to smart cards; and the clarification of lenders' and fiduciaries' liabilities in an environmental cleanup.

Failing to gain passage in 1996 was an effort to repeal the Glass-Steagall Act. The law, enacted in 1933 in the wake of the Depression, mandated a separation of banking from the securities business.

Consumer Issues. Two nationwide automated-teller-machine (ATM) networks—Visa's Plus and MasterCard's Cirrus—announced that, beginning April 1, 1996, they would allow their member banks to levy new surcharges on ATM customers. The surcharges meant that customers using ATMs that did not belong to their bank might face fees from both their own bank and the ATM owner. Legislation was introduced (but not passed) in Congress and state legislatures after consumers protested the new fees.

New reports on consumer debt renewed the discussion of the economic health of U.S. consumers. The American Bankers Association reported in June that delinquencies on credit-card payments had never been higher since the ABA started tracking them in 1974. Also, the Administrative Office of the U.S. Courts, which keeps statistics on personal bankruptcies, reported a soaring number of bankruptcy filings. Some experts estimated that there would be a record 1 million filings in 1996.

The Fed. Late in January the Fed cut the federal-funds rate, which applies to overnight loans between banks, to 5.25%. The following day a number of large banks cut their prime lending rates to 8.25%. In February, President Clinton reappointed Alan Greenspan as chairman of the Federal Reserve Board of Governors for a third four-year term. Clinton also appointed Alice Rivlin, director of the Office of Management and Budget, as Fed vice-chairman and economist Laurence Meyer as a Fed governor.

Bank and Thrift Profitability. Commercial banks continued to post near-record profits in 1996. During the second quarter, banks reported the second-highest quarterly level of profitability ever—$13.78 billion. This profit was attributed to increases in fee income, merger-related gains on sales of assets, and lower costs. By the end of the second quarter, the number of banks had declined to 9,689. During the first six months of 1996, 59 new banks were chartered, three banks failed, and 306 banks were absorbed by mergers, indicating a slowdown in bank mergers. The largest merger announced by November was NationsBank's purchase of Boatmen's Bancshares.

For the first time since 1937, the total number of thrifts fell to less than 2,000. The industry as a whole reported record earnings in the second quarter of 1996, with the thrifts regulated by the Office of Thrift Supervision reporting the highest return on assets in more than 30 years. During the first six months of the year, commercial banks absorbed 36 savings institutions, 43 institutions converted from mutual to stock ownership, and no thrifts failed.

ANN KESSLER, *American Bankers Association*

BELGIUM

Efforts for austerity and protest against malfeasance in the justice system highlighted 1996 in Belgium.

Economic Affairs. Reduction of the budget deficit to gain participation in the projected European Union (EU) single currency was the early and chief priority of Prime Minister Jean-Luc Dehaene. The prospect of success was dimmed by expectation of a wage explosion late in the year when the wage-freeze agreement with labor would expire.

Dehaene therefore devoted his efforts to the formation of a "Contract for the Future," tentatively agreed to by the government, employers, and trade unions in April. Its goals included cutting unemployment from 14% to 7% by early in the 21st century. Steps were to be taken to limit the black-market economy, encourage part-time work and thus redistribute employment, lessen high social-security payments of employers, institute a 39-hour workweek throughout the economy, and stimulate investment in small businesses. The core of the bargain was that wage growth would match that of neighboring countries.

The agreement fell apart, as one of the two largest trade unions failed to sign on, asserting that government plans for job creation were too vague. Layoffs of nearly 3,000 schoolteachers provoked a major demonstration in April. A motion of no confidence against the government in the Chamber of Representatives failed. Bolstered by that vote, Dehaene asked for and received emergency powers through 1997 to deal with specific economic matters. His budget preserved much of the defunct contract. As part of its austerity, it raised the retirement age for women and increased luxury taxes. It also proposed the sale of buildings currently rented to the EU for offices. Improved tax-collection measures were mooted; reports indicated Belgium's economy was 20% larger than shown by official figures, the difference concealed by semilegal actions and tax evasion.

Justice. In February the highest military court ruled that Irma Laplasse, a Belgian citizen executed in 1948 for collaborating with the occupying German forces, should have been imprisoned instead. The announcement stimulated calls by some Flemings for amnesty for all persons still under sentences for collaboration.

In April former Defense Minister Guy Coëme and seven others were found guilty of fraud and abuse of public office. Coëme received a suspended sentence but did resign from the legislature. In May a warrant was issued for the arrest of French businessman Serge Dassault on charges of bribing Belgian government officials in the late 1980s to deal with his aviation company. Though France refused to extradite him, the case further inflamed the long-running scandal involving Dassault Aviation and another military-aircraft manufacturer, Italy's Agusta S.p.A. In September former cabinet minister Alain Van der Biest was arrested for allegedly ordering the 1991 shooting of Socialist Party leader André Cools. That case in turn was linked to unsolved bank robberies and murders, in which the chief investigator was fired.

In August and September details emerged of a child-pornography ring that killed four girls and detained several others. Arrested was Marc Dutroux, a convicted child molester released after serving less than half of his sentence. The details of the imprisonment and deaths of the children stirred the population. Outrage mounted over the slowness of the investigation of the children's disappearance and news that police officers were arrested on charges of protecting the pornographers. Public opinion boiled when Belgium's highest court removed from the investigation the magistrate who cracked the case, on the grounds that his attendance at a benefit dinner for parents of missing children compromised his impartiality. Spontaneous demonstrations welled throughout the country, capped by a "White March" of 275,000 in Brussels on October 20.

Relations with Spain. Belgium's refusal to extradite Spaniards accused of terrorism led to a near collapse of judicial cooperation under the Schengen Convention—an open-border zone within the EU. The collapse was averted by an agreement to hold special talks.

JONATHAN E. HELMREICH, *Allegheny College*

BELGIUM • Information Highlights

Official Name: Kingdom of Belgium.
Location: Northwestern Europe.
Area: 11,780 sq mi (30 510 km²).
Population (mid-1996 est.): 10,200,000.
Chief Cities (Dec. 31, 1993): Brussels, the capital (incl. suburbs), 949,070; Antwerp (including suburbs), 462,880; Ghent, 228,490; Charleroi, 206,898; Liège, 195,389; Bruges, 116,724.
Government: *Head of state,* Albert II, king (acceded Aug. 9, 1993). *Head of government,* Jean-Luc Dehaene, prime minister (sworn in March 7, 1992). *Legislature*—Parliament: Senate and Chamber of Deputies.
Monetary Unit: Franc (31.72 francs equal U.S.$1, commercial rate, Dec. 31, 1996).
Gross Domestic Product (1994 est. U.S.$): $181,500,000,000 (purchasing power parity).
Economic Indexes (1995, 1990 = 100): *Consumer Prices,* all items, 112.7; food, 104.0. *Industrial Production,* 98.
Foreign Trade (1994 with Luxembourg, U.S.$): *Imports,* $125,617,000,000; *exports,* $137,272,000,000.

BIOCHEMISTRY

In 1995–96, biochemists solved mysteries involving acquired immune deficiency syndrome (AIDS), hemoglobin, obesity, and muscle contraction.

AIDS. Late in 1995 a team of scientists led by Robert Gallo and Paolo Lusso at the University of Maryland reported finding three proteins that stop the multiplication of human immunodeficiency virus (HIV) in laboratory cell cultures. The proteins—dubbed RANTES, MIP-1 alpha, and MIP-1 beta—were found to suppress the HIV strains that exist in the early stages of AIDS. The proteins are chemokines, molecules that immune cells use to communicate with each other.

Scientists have known for years that HIV attaches itself to immune cells possessing a receptor protein called CD4 prior to gaining entry and multiplying. Studies reported during 1996 indicated that HIV requires additional receptors to gain entry into its target cell. Two such "cofactors" were identified during the year. The first, fusin, was identified in May by Edward Berger and associates at the National Institute of Allergy and Infectious Diseases (NIAID). The researchers showed that HIV strains that infect T cells maintained in laboratory cultures—an experimental system that mimics the later stages of AIDS—do not infect the susceptible cells in the presence of the antibodies against fusin. One month later, the second receptor, CC-CKR-5, was identified independently by several research groups. This protein is used by the strains of HIV that exist in the early stages of infection to gain entry into target cells.

The existence of multiple cofactors acting in conjunction with CD4 may explain how HIV-infected individuals progress from early asymptomatic stages to full-blown AIDS. Scientists hypothesized that HIV may use CC-CKR-5 early in the course of infection and later switch to fusin, thereby avoiding the suppressive effect of chemokines. The discovery of two different receptors also may explain how some individuals—perhaps those with a genetic defect in their CC-CKR-5 receptor—avoid becoming infected with HIV despite repeated exposure to the virus. The possibility of developing drugs that would prevent HIV from binding to fusin and CC-CKR-5 was being investigated.

Hemoglobin and Nitric Oxide. Hemoglobin, a familiar constituent of red blood cells, transports oxygen and carbon dioxide between the lungs and the body's tissues. A scientific team led by Jonathan Stamler of Duke University reported in March 1996 the discovery of another component of hemoglobin's respiratory cycle—nitric oxide (NO). NO is synthesized in the lungs and blood-vessel walls. In the blood vessels, NO dilates capillaries, allowing oxygen-rich hemoglobin to pass through. Previously, oxygenated hemoglobin was thought to be a scavenger, binding NO at its iron-containing heme and then eliminating the NO from the blood. However, this discovery failed to explain how enough NO remains to dilate the blood vessels. The Duke researchers showed that nitric oxide binds not only at hemoglobin's heme but also to its amino acid cysteine. The researchers asserted that the cysteine enables NO to bind to hemoglobin without being degraded. The process thus would ensure that oxygenated hemoglobin could penetrate even the narrowest blood vessels.

Leptin and Obesity. Late in 1995, a team of researchers led by Louis Tartaglia and Robert Tepper of Millennium Pharmaceuticals reported finding two receptors for leptin—a protein hormone that controls body weight. The team's findings may help explain how leptin works. The researchers found the first receptor in mice, in a part of the brain known as the choroid plexus. The second receptor was located in human brain tissue. The scientists suggested that the first receptor transports leptin in the brain, while the second carries out leptin's physiological effects. The research was expected to lead to an antiobesity drug.

Muscle Contraction. One important component of the chain of molecular events that causes muscle contraction is troponin-C. This protein responds to a chemical signal—the release of calcium ions from within the cell—by changing its shape. Such a change alters its chemical interactions with neighboring proteins, and these interactions, in turn, eventually lead to cell contraction. But just how troponin-C undergoes the crucial shape change had remained a mystery.

Findings reported in December 1995 by biochemists led by Brian Sykes at the University of Alberta may have answered that question. The study indicated that a single amino acid—glutamic acid—controls the shape of troponin-C by dragging part of the protein toward a bound calcium ion. To confirm the result, researchers showed that mutant proteins without glutamic acid did not change shape. The scientists used a technique called nuclear magnetic resonance (NMR) to study the protein's structure.

PREM P. BATRA, *Wright State University*

Biography

A selection of profiles of persons prominent in the news in 1996 appears on pages 149–60. The affiliation of the contributor is listed on pages 591–94; biographies that do not include a contributor's name were prepared by the staff. Included are profiles of:

Amanpour, Christiane
Cage, Nicolas
Clinton, Hillary Rodham
Clinton, William Jefferson
Costas, Bob
Dole, Elizabeth
Dole, Robert Joseph
Gore, Albert, Jr.
Gowda, Haradanahalli Doddegowda Deve
Hashimoto, Ryutaro
Hilfiger, Tommy
Howard, John Winston
Johnson, Michael
Kemp, Jack French
Lott, Trent
Lucid, Shannon W.
Mfume, Kweisi
Murray, Eddie
Netanyahu, Benjamin
Sarandon, Susan
Woods, Eldrick (Tiger)

AMANPOUR, Christiane

Christiane Amanpour, a senior international correspondent for Cable News Network (CNN), found herself not just reporting the news in 1996, but being the subject of it as well. The foreign correspondent whom *The New York Times Magazine* featured as "the hottest property in American television" signed an unprecedented contract allowing her to work for two major networks simultaneously. Under the new contract, she would continue to cover world events for CNN but also would work on special assignments for the Columbia Broadcasting System's (CBS') highly-rated and prestigious *60 Minutes*.

Amanpour—who became known for her coverage in such global hot spots as Rwanda, Haiti, Somalia, and Bosnia—enjoys widespread respect and admiration from viewers and fellow reporters alike. "She's simply the best at what she does," said one colleague. Even U.S. President Bill Clinton, after a much-publicized 1994 on-air confrontation with Amanpour over U.S. policy in the former Yugoslavia, said of her reporting in the region, "She's done a great service to the whole world."

Amanpour is not without critics. Some reporters have complained that she oversteps the traditional bounds of objectivity, claiming she resorts to "advocacy journalism." Amanpour, however, denies the charge: "I never express my personal opinions. . . .I only report what I see."

Background. Christiane Amanpour was born in London on Jan. 12, 1958, the eldest daughter of an Iranian airline executive and his British wife. The family moved to Tehran, Iran, while Christiane was still an infant, but she was sent back to England at the age of 11 to attend Holy Cross Convent School, and later New Hall—the oldest Catholic girls' school in the United Kingdom. When the shah of Iran was overthrown in 1979, her newly impoverished father fled the fundamentalist Islamic regime, bringing the family back to London. The experience helped Amanpour know that she wanted to become a foreign correspondent. "If I was going to be affected by events, I wanted to be a part of them," she said as she recounted her decision to study journalism at the University of Rhode Island, in Providence.

Upon graduating summa cum laude in 1983, Amanpour took an entry-level job as a news assistant at CNN, then still a fledgling news organization. She was promoted to the position of reporter-producer in 1986 and took her first overseas posting—in Germany—in 1989. Her big break came during the Persian Gulf war in 1991, when her impassioned reports were seen by 140 million viewers in 200 countries around the world. Colleagues praised her special talent for unscripted live reports and her great news instincts. These qualities, combined with her exotic looks, British accent, and the rare ability to mix an air of authority with humanitarian zeal, have helped transform Amanpour from a news reporter into a full-fledged television personality with a distinct style.

Among her many awards (which include an Emmy), Amanpour counts three of the most respected honors in journalism—the George Foster Peabody Award, the George Polk Memorial Award, and the Alfred I. du Pont–Columbia University Silver Baton. When not on assignment—a rare circumstance—Amanpour resides in Paris.

BRUCE JACOBY

Christiane Amanpour

© Haley/Sipa Press

CAGE, Nicolas

With his role as a suicidal alcoholic in the 1996 film *Leaving Las Vegas*, actor Nicolas Cage found the type of role he was born to play: dark and bizarre—a character that easily could seem unlovable and turn viewers against him. Cage, however, managed to reveal the humanity of the character and get people to care about him. Surprising everyone, the low-budget independent film became a hit, both critically and at the box office, and earned Cage his first Oscar—for best actor.

Cage's choice of roles always has been daring. His complex, highly individualistic interpretations of truly odd characters have resulted in wildly varying reviews, with his performances being labeled as everything from "marvelous" to "truly awful"—with these divergent assessments sometimes being given for the same role. Earlier in his career, Cage was criticized for his peculiar mannerisms, overacting, and outrageously offbeat characterizations. He since has toned down his acting, and his giftedness shines through in disciplined, finely honed performances like the one in *Leaving Las Vegas*.

Background. Nicolas Coppola was born Jan. 7, 1964, in Long Beach, CA, the youngest of three sons of former dancer and choreographer Joy Vogelsang and comparative-literature professor August Coppola—the brother of director Francis Ford Coppola. His parents divorced when Nicolas was 12; his mother suffered from severe depres-

© Russ Einhorn/Gamma-Liaison

Nicolas Cage

sion, for which she was hospitalized for long periods when her children were young. The boys thus were raised mostly by their father, who instilled in them a love of art, films, and literature. Nicolas spent one summer during his teens studying character development at the American Conservatory Theatre in San Francisco. Never an inspired student, he dropped out of Beverly Hills High School at age 16 and received an equivalency diploma.

The future star's first substantial film role was given him by Francis Ford Coppola, in *Rumble Fish* (1983). (Cage changed his last name shortly afterward to distance himself professionally from his uncle.) His first screen appearance actually came in 1983's *Valley Girl*—which was released before *Rumble Fish*. His offbeat characterizations in these two films, followed by his "violently sincere" portrayal of a disfigured Vietnam vet in *Birdy* (1984), soon gained Cage a reputation as a highly daring, unique actor. He proceeded to take on a tremendous variety of roles, from a mobster in *The Cotton Club* (1984) to a well-meaning kidnapper in *Raising Arizona* (1987) to a baker in *Moonstruck* (1987). A role as romantic ex-con Sailor Ripley in David Lynch's *Wild at Heart* (1990) garnered Cage widespread recognition; the film won the Palme d'Or at Cannes. Cage then took on a few lighter roles in what he refers to as his "sunshine trilogy": *Honeymoon in Vegas* (1992), *Guarding Tess* (1994), and *It Could Happen to You* (1994). Although he was praised for his comedic instinct in these films, he chose to return to his darker leanings with *Kiss of Death* (1995), his Oscar-winning turn in *Leaving Las Vegas*, and a role in the 1996 action film *The Rock*.

Cage married the actress Patricia Arquette in April 1995. The two had dated briefly years earlier, and had not seen each other for several years. Cage has said he "was meant to be with her from long ago." Each of the two has a son from a previous relationship.

CLINTON, Hillary Rodham

From unabashed feminist to demure wife and mother, Hillary Rodham Clinton has tried on many roles during her tenure as first lady. And, as the wife of the U.S. president, she has been critiqued publicly for every one of those roles by one group or another.

During President Bill Clinton's first term, and during his successful 1996 campaign for reelection, Hillary Clinton proved to be both an asset to her husband due to her knowledge and insight on important issues—and a potential liability because of her outspoken views and alleged involvement in several scandals. Although she addressed the Democratic national convention in prime time and campaigned widely—including on her own—for the Clinton-Gore ticket and other Democrats, her role in the 1996 presidential campaign was more of a background one. This was a sharp change from the very visible role she played in the 1992 campaign and during the first few months of the new administration, when she was given influence and access unprecedented for a first lady.

Shortly after Bill Clinton became president, he named his wife to head one of his most important domestic initiatives—a task force on national health-care reform. The reform effort failed and, in the process, the controversy surrounding the first lady and her use of her considerable power grew. By the end of President Clinton's first term, his wife had been linked to the Arkansas land deal known as Whitewater (in connection with which she became the only first lady ever to be subpoenaed), had been involved in the sudden firing of the White House travel-office staff in 1993, and had had her financial profits from futures speculation questioned. As criticism grew, she retreated from the spotlight. Although not on the front lines anymore, the first lady was far from quiet. She wrote a best-selling book, *It Takes a Village*—which itself became a source of controversy—started a newspaper column, and made a number of public appearances.

Background. Hillary Diane Rodham was born on Oct. 26, 1947, the eldest of three children of business owner Hugh E. Rodham and Dorothy Howell Rodham. She grew up in Park Ridge, IL, a Chicago suburb. An excellent student and natural leader, she participated in student government and was a National Merit Scholarship finalist and member of the National Honor Society.

Raised as a Republican, she campaigned for Barry Goldwater in 1964 and headed the local chapter of the Young Republicans at Wellesley College. She embraced the Democratic Party following the assassinations of Malcolm X in 1965 and Martin Luther King, Jr., and Robert F. Kennedy in 1968, campaigning for Eugene McCarthy for president in 1968 and organizing Wellesley's first teach-ins on the Vietnam war.

The future first lady received a bachelor's degree in political science from Wellesley in 1969. At Yale Law School she met Bill Clinton, whom she married in 1975, and Marian Wright Edelman, a civil-rights lawyer and Yale alumna who inspired her later efforts in the area of children's rights. She worked for Edelman's Washington Research Project, which later became the Children's Defense Fund. Clinton was among the first female associates hired by Rose Law Firm in Little Rock, AR, and was made a partner there in 1980, the same year she gave birth to Chelsea Victoria Clinton.

Clinton has been a tireless campaign worker and adviser to her husband since he first ran for public office in 1974. While he was Arkansas' governor, she served in several official capacities, including as head of the Arkansas Education Standards Committee.

KRISTI VAUGHAN

CLINTON, William Jefferson

After Bill Clinton's candidacy for the Democratic Party's 1992 presidential nomination was battered by controversy over his past, the then Arkansas governor rallied in the crucial New Hampshire primary, finished a respectable second, pronounced himself "the comeback kid," and defeated President George Bush in the November 1992 election.

Clinton's success in transforming a ballot-box defeat into a moral victory was neither the first nor the last demonstration of the resiliency and tenacity that have shaped his personal life and defined his presidency. In fact, during the midpoint of his first term as president, many considered his chances of winning a second term doomed. Although he faced numerous charges against his character and severe criticism of his policies during the 1996 campaign, Clinton went on to become the first Democrat since Franklin D. Roosevelt to win a second four years in the White House. In fact, Clinton had won renomination from his own party without opposition, gained a substantial lead in the polls over his Republican challenger, Robert Dole, and captured reelection by a wide margin. (*See* U.S. ELECTIONS, page 24.)

Clinton had started off in the White House trying to redeem his campaign promise to revive the economy. To reduce the federal budget deficit and improve economic growth, he called for nearly $500 billion in taxes and spending cuts over four years. Though Republicans and some conservative Democrats complained that the president relied too much on raising taxes and not enough on cutting spending, the Democratic majorities in Congress saw to it that the new president got much of what he had sought. And in another major achievement, he won congressional approval for the North American Free Trade Agreement (NAFTA) with Canada and Mexico.

In his second year as president, Clinton ran into serious trouble. He was forced to abandon his proposal for health-care reform, which along with economic revival had dominated his domestic agenda. That setback was followed by a devastating defeat for the Democratic Party at the polls in the 1994 midterm election. It was the first time in 40 years that the Democrats had lost control of both houses of Congress. With many Democrats attributing the election results to dissatisfaction with Clinton's presidency, and with the Republicans proclaiming the start of a conservative revolution, Clinton's fortunes were at a low ebb. But he displayed flexibility, by offering his own plan for a balanced budget—the GOP's cherished goal—and by proclaiming that "the era of big government is over." Meanwhile, the congressional Republicans overplayed their hand by proposing deep cuts in projected spending for domestic programs—notably Medicare—which Clinton claimed would injure the middle class and the elderly. And when the GOP's differences with the White House led to a shutdown of government in the fall of 1995, the Republicans got most of the blame, while Clinton benefited greatly from the situation.

In dealing with foreign affairs, an area in which he had been criticized early in his presidency for temporizing, Clinton also bounced back. He was given credit for spurring efforts to reach a truce in the bloody fighting in Bosnia, where he agreed to send U.S. troops as part of a peacekeeping force. And he also helped to mediate the agreement under which Israel extended self-government to more than 1 million Palestinians who had been living under military occupation on the West Bank.

Background. Adversity sought out William Jefferson Clinton early in life; his father, William Blythe 3d, a traveling salesman, was killed in an auto accident three months before he was born on Aug. 19, 1946, in the little town of Hope, AR. His mother, Virginia Cassidy Blythe, left him with his grandparents while she went back to school for training as a nurse-anesthetist to support her son. The boy threw himself into his schoolwork in Hot Springs, where he was raised. His diligence paid off, launching an academic career that carried him from Georgetown University, where he took his bachelor's degree in 1968, to Oxford, where he was a Rhodes Scholar, to Yale University law school, from which he was graduated in 1973. It was at Yale that Clinton met a fellow student, Hillary Rodham, who became his wife and also in many ways his partner in politics.

His first try for elective office—a 1974 challenge to a well-established Republican congressman in his home state—ended in defeat. But Clinton bounced back, winning election as state attorney general in 1976. With that position as a launching pad, he gained the governorship in 1978, when he was only 32, becoming the youngest of the nation's state chief executives. After he was defeated for reelection in 1980—a bad year for Democrats—he put his energies into still another comeback, and succeeded in 1982.

This time, Clinton made sure to consolidate his support in the state and easily won reelection to another two-year term in 1984. And then, after Arkansas' constitution was amended to double the length of the governor's term, Clinton won two successive four-year terms in 1986 and 1990. Meanwhile, through his involvement in the National Governors' Association, Clinton was acquiring a national reputation as a forward-looking and practical reformer, particularly in the field of education. He also became chairman of the Democratic Leadership Council, which had been established to move the Democratic Party away from its liberal moorings. He used that position to aid his candidacy for the presidency in 1992.

The Clintons have one child, a daughter, Chelsea.

ROBERT SHOGAN

© Dirck Halstead/Gamma-Liaison

William Jefferson (Bill) Clinton

COSTAS, Bob

In the world of sports broadcasting, where specialization is the norm, finding a sportscaster who can cover almost any event with equal aplomb—and distinction—is almost unheard of. There are many who try, few who succeed, and one who stands preeminent in the field: Bob Costas. As the television host of the 1996 Summer Olympics, Costas became an inseparable part of the Atlanta Games for tens of millions of Americans, bringing viewers closer to the action with his trademark style and substance.

Whether hosting an Olympics or calling the World Series play-by-play, Costas is the consummate professional, earning enormous respect from colleagues and fans alike. In a profession dominated by clownish jocks and ham-fisted theatrics, Costas stands apart. He is bright and articulate, with a rare combination of expert journalism, encyclopedic memory, laid-back style, and irreverent sense of humor.

He also has an acute awareness of the way most sportscasters try to manipulate viewers' emotions, and often speaks out against that trend. In an interview conducted soon after he had hosted the Atlanta Games, Costas was asked to write his own Olympic epitaph. He replied that he hoped people would say, "he was well prepared, he enhanced my enjoyment and understanding of the Olympics without getting in the way....I didn't mind having him figuratively in my living room the last couple of weeks."

Background. Robert Quinlan Costas was born in New York City on March 22, 1952, and spent most of his childhood in the Long Island suburb of Commack, NY. His father was an electrical engineer who died when Bob was 18. The younger Costas credits his mother—who, although not a sports fan, was nevertheless "more indulgent of my whimsical nature and of my daydreaming." Costas fondly recalls a childhood of playing sandlot baseball and calling the play-by-play in his head. He has said that he knew he wanted to be a baseball announcer by the time he was 10 or 11.

After finishing high school in 1970, Costas matriculated as a communications major at Syracuse University in upstate New York. He quit college a few credits shy of his degree in 1974, however, after he was offered a job as a sportscaster at KMOX, an AM radio station in St. Louis. Two years later he began taking occasional freelance assignments for the Columbia Broadcasting System (CBS), and in 1980 he joined the National Broadcasting Company (NBC), mostly covering the National Football League (NFL).

His career soon took off. He returned to baseball—his favorite sport—on NBC's *Game of the Week* broadcasts, while still hosting the NFL pregame show. In 1990 he added the National Basketball Association (NBA) to his list of duties, hosting *NBA Showtime*. Two years later, Costas became the network's prime-time Olympics host, covering

© Kimberly Butler/NBC/AP/Wide World Photos

Bob Costas

the games in Barcelona, Spain, an assignment he repeated at the 1996 Atlanta Games. In addition to his sports broadcasting, he hosted a late-night interview show, *Later With Bob Costas*, which was broadcast for more than five years; he also contributes segments to a variety of NBC programs, including the prime-time newsmagazine *Dateline*.

Costas has won seven Emmy awards as outstanding sports personality/host, two more for writing, and another for his talk show. In addition, he has been honored as Sportscaster of the Year by the National Sportswriters and Sportscasters Association a record six times.

Bob and Randy Costas live in St. Louis with their two children, Keith and Taylor.

BRUCE JACOBY

DOLE, Elizabeth

Throughout the 1996 U.S. presidential campaign, comparisons between Elizabeth Dole—wife of Republican candidate Bob Dole—and President Bill Clinton's wife, Hillary Rodham Clinton, were inevitable. Both women are powerful leaders with their own careers and successes. Dole has been in public life for nearly three decades and is the only woman ever to hold cabinet positions in two presidential administrations, serving as secretary of transportation during the Ronald Reagan administration and as secretary of labor under President George Bush.

Like Clinton, Dole changed her political allegiance early in her public life. A registered Democrat during the Lyndon Johnson administration, she became an independent during the Nixon years, and, finally, joined the Republican Party when she married Bob Dole. And, like Hillary Clinton, Elizabeth Dole is a devout Methodist.

A subtle type of feminist, Dole is a Southern belle and perfectionist who publicly says her primary role is that of supportive spouse, but who has held a job throughout her 21-year marriage. She was one of only 24 women in her class of 550 at Harvard Law School and said that, had her husband been elected president, she still would have returned to her $200,000-per-year job as president of the American Red Cross.

Some wondered, however, whether Dole ever really wanted to be first lady. She clearly wanted her husband to be president and willingly, even enthusiastically, took the spotlight to help him achieve his goal; nevertheless, she is a woman who seems equally comfortable out of the public eye. In the end, the question was moot as Bob Dole did not win the presidency and Elizabeth Dole was free to return to her career unencumbered by the trappings of the position of first lady.

Background. Born on July 29, 1936, in Salisbury, NC, Elizabeth Hanford was the second of two children. Her father, John Van Hanford, was a successful flower wholesaler. Her mother, Mary Ella (Cathey) Hanford, was a member of the Daughters of the American Revolution.

After receiving a bachelor's degree in political science from Duke University, the future Mrs. Dole did postgraduate work at Oxford University, received a master's in education from Harvard University, and, in 1965, earned a law degree from Harvard. She then moved to Washington, DC, to pursue a career as a public servant, and worked in the Department of Health, Education and Welfare and the White House Office of Consumer Affairs, as well as in private law practice.

When she married Bob Dole in 1975 at the age of 39, she was in the middle of a seven-year term on the Federal Trade Commission (FTC). Taking on the role of supportive wife, Dole took a leave of absence from the FTC to work with her husband as he campaigned for vice-president under President Gerald Ford in 1976. Three years later she resigned from the FTC to assist her husband in his first bid for the Republican presidential nomination. She also resigned as transportation secretary when he tried for the 1988 nomination.

Among Dole's notable career accomplishments are laws requiring brake lights in the rear windows of cars and clear views of emergency exits in smoke-filled airline cabins. At the Red Cross, where she has been president since 1991, she has—at the insistence of the Food and Drug Administration (FDA)—led a restructuring of the organization.

Elizabeth and Bob Dole, who live in the Watergate apartments in Washington, DC, have no children.

KRISTI VAUGHAN

DOLE, Robert Joseph

The story of Robert J. Dole is in large part the chronicle of an authentic American hero. When he was a young man, wearing his country's uniform during World War II, an enemy artillery shell shattered his body. And he continued to demonstrate heroism of a less dramatic sort for the rest of his life, as he struggled against the damage done by his wartime wounds. The strength and determination he gained from this battle helped him immeasurably in his career in politics, where he became the chief spokesperson for Midwestern Republicanism—the stolid but enduring faith in a marriage of convenience between the rewards of the free market and the obligations of government.

In politics, Dole's sardonic wit and caustic retorts distinguished his style. But these traits also at times caused a negative impression among voters, as when—during the 1988 campaign for the GOP presidential nomination—he bluntly told his ultimately successful rival, George Bush, to "stop lying about my record."

Dole made the U.S. Senate his home for more than 27 years and rose to the summit of power there. Not content, he sought the highest office in the land, the presidency. Twice, in 1980 and 1988, he sought but failed to win the Republican Party presidential nomination. In 1996, at an age when most men have chosen to rest on their laurels, Dole again competed for that prize. This time he prevailed in becoming the GOP standard-bearer but lost the general election to the incumbent president, Democrat Bill Clinton. (*See* U.S. ELECTIONS, page 24.)

Elizabeth Dole

© Brooks Kraft/Sygma

© Robert Burroughs/Gamma-Liaison

Robert Joseph (Bob) Dole

Background. Robert Joseph Dole was born in Russell, KS, on July 22, 1923. He enrolled at the University of Kansas but in 1942 interrupted his sophomore year to enlist in the army. It was while serving as a platoon leader on the Italian front that he was wounded severely by a shell burst. Recovery took three years and left him with a withered and almost useless right arm. But he went back to college to get his bachelor's degree and then on to Washburn Municipal University in Topeka, where he earned a law degree.

Dole's political career began in 1950, when he won a seat in the Kansas legislature. After eight subsequent years as Russell county attorney, he was elected to the U.S. House of Representatives in 1960; he moved to the Senate after the election of 1968, while Richard Nixon was winning the first of two White House terms. Dole's militancy as a champion of the Nixon administration won him national attention and the approval of the president, who in 1971 recommended him for the chairmanship of the Republican National Committee.

In that post, Dole loyally sought to rebut attempts to link the Watergate scandal to the White House, but his independence and outspokenness offended some Nixon aides, who forced him out of the party post. This turned out to be a blessing in disguise, since it removed Dole from direct connection with the White House during the most damaging phase of the Watergate scandal. Nevertheless he still had to wage an uphill battle to retain his Senate seat in November 1974.

Dole ran unsuccessfully for the vice-presidency as Gerald Ford's running mate in 1976, and his first presidential bid in 1980 ended in defeat. Despite these setbacks, Dole won a third Senate term in 1980 and became chairman of the Senate Finance Committee. During Ronald Reagan's presidency, he emerged as a powerful force for fiscal discipline in the face of the freewheeling supply-side economic policy propounded by Reagan. In 1984 his Senate colleagues chose him as majority leader.

In his second try for the presidency in 1988, Dole raised the hopes of his supporters with his early victory in the Iowa caucuses. But he soon was driven out of the race by the better organized, better financed candidacy of then Vice-President Bush. Dole swallowed his resentment after his erstwhile rival won the White House, and served him loyally on Capitol Hill. But after President Bush's defeat by Clinton in 1992, the senator from Kansas moved quickly to establish himself as the prime candidate to challenge President Clinton in 1996.

The early front-runner in the 1996 battle for the Republican nomination, Dole once again suffered defeat in the New Hampshire primary—at the hands of Pat Buchanan. But this time he had the financial resources and backing of party leaders to help him recover and clinch the nomination. Finding himself far behind President Clinton in the public-opinion polls in June, he startled the political world by resigning his Senate seat to devote himself fully to his quest for the White House. But he continued to lag in the polls and, just before the Republican convention in San Diego, Dole staged another surprise—choosing former U.S. Rep. Jack Kemp, with whom he long had disagreed, as his running mate.

In 1948, Dole married Phyllis Holden, a physical therapist, who first met him at the hospital where he was recovering from his various war wounds. That marriage ended in divorce in 1972, and in 1975, Dole married Elizabeth Hanford. The former senator has one daughter, Robin, by his first marriage.

ROBERT SHOGAN

GORE, Albert, Jr.

When then Tennessee Sen. Albert Gore, Jr., was chosen as the Democratic vice-presidential running mate for Bill Clinton in 1992, critics labeled him as a "Clinton clone" who was selected to underline the main features of Clinton's own political appeal. Besides being a Southerner, like Clinton, Gore was another representative of the baby-boom generation and came from approximately the same sector of the national ideological spectrum as did Clinton—a point just slightly to the left of center.

But Gore contrasted with Clinton in ways that came to seem at least as significant, not only politically but also in terms of the substantive policy accomplishments of the Clinton administration. Unlike the Arkansas governor—whose entire career in government had been at the state level—Gore had served four terms in the U.S. House of Representatives, to which he first was elected in 1976, and nearly eight years in the Senate, where he took the seat once held by his father, Albert Gore, Sr. Apart from the broad grounding in the operations of the federal government he had acquired this way, Gore had used his time on Capitol Hill to build strengths in specific areas where Clinton's background was not particularly strong—notably national defense, foreign policy, and the environment.

Gore and Clinton both took advantage of the vice-president's experience during their first term in office. Gore's most important responsibility was to spearhead the administration's efforts to make the bureaucracy more efficient and responsive, labeled "reinventing government." Though progress often was hard to document, Gore's efforts persuaded many Americans that at least the administration had good intentions. In the field of the environment, Gore was active in helping shape administration positions on a range of issues—from climate change to forest management. And he used his expertise in nuclear-arms control to play a leading role with the National Science and Technology Council, advising Clinton on what role government should play in science, space, and technology issues. Gore also was influential in U.S.-Russian relations, through the special relationship he forged with Russian Prime Minister Viktor Chernomyrdin.

Apart from these positive accomplishments, Gore—in contrast with his predecessor, Dan Quayle—managed to avoid the sort of blunders and mishaps that cause political embarrassment. His overall performance drew praise even from Republicans. Bob Dole's Republican running mate, Jack Kemp, declared that Gore would be "my model" if he got the chance to fill Gore's shoes as vice-president. Moreover, by the time Gore was renominated at the Democratic convention, he clearly had established himself as the front-runner for the Democratic presidential nomination in the year 2000. That prospect was enhanced by the Clinton-Gore victory on election day 1996.

Previously criticized for his stiffness as an orator, Vice-President Gore showed in his speech before the 1996 Democratic convention that he could stir emotions to make a political point. He referred at length to the death of his older sister, Nancy, from lung cancer, which Gore attributed to the fact that she had begun smoking cigarettes as a teenager. Democrats had been striving to make President Clinton's efforts to regulate the tobacco industry a key issue against the Republicans.

Background. Born in Washington, DC, March 31, 1948, Albert Gore, Jr., was graduated from Harvard University in 1969. After service in the Vietnam war, he worked as a journalist for the Nashville *Tennessean* and studied law at Vanderbilt Law School before beginning his political career. He made an unsuccessful run for the Democratic presidential nomination in 1988.

His wife, the former Mary Elizabeth Aitcheson, called Tipper, was known widely even before her husband became vice-president for her battle against pornography in popular music. The Gores have four children.

ROBERT SHOGAN

GOWDA, Haradanahalli Doddegowda Deve

The surprising inauguration of H.D. Deve Gowda as India's prime minister on June 1, 1996, left many asking, "Deve who?" The leader of the centrist Janata Dal party from the southern state of Karnataka had little national name recognition, having served in Parliament for only three years prior to parliamentary elections in May 1996. The voting resulted in a "hung parliament," with the Hindu-nationalist Bharatiya Janata Party (BJP) holding a modest plurality. Although accorded with a chance to form a government and prove its majority under its leader Atal Behari Vajpayee, the BJP failed in the face of opposition from left and centrist parties.

Vajpayee's resignation opened the way for the 13-party United Front (UF) coalition government led by the Janata Dal. To curb BJP influence, the Marxists and the Congress Party offered tacit support without officially joining the UF. With this support, the UF gained a respectable but fragile majority. When Janata Dal leader V.P. Singh declined the premiership, Gowda emerged as the compromise choice of other leaders, most of whom had a strong regional rather than national base. Gowda and the new UF coalition government survived a key confidence vote on June 12.

Gowda's early months in office were dominated by a need to balance the diverse interests of his supporters. The composition of his cabinet reflected a diversity of castes, religions, regions, and ideologies. The Marxists, for example, wanted to slow economic liberalization, particularly the privatization of public enterprises. However, continued liberalization and fulfillment of antipoverty programs promised in 1995 by the Congress Party was critical to retaining that party's support. A compromise budget and economic plan promised continued commitment to liberalization and an antipoverty focus. The government also announced plans to decentralize many programs to the states to accommodate growing regional sentiments and lower the central government's growing fiscal burden.

Gowda is considered flexible but strong. He has resisted pressures from the Congress Party to stop anticorruption investigations against its members, including former Prime Minister P.V. Narasimha Rao and his sons. Early in his term, Gowda appeared to give his ministers considerable autonomy within the broad guidelines of his program.

H.D. Deve Gowda

© Reuters/Sunil Malhotra/Archive Photos

Background. Deve Gowda was born into a mid-level caste of farmers and landowners in the village of Haradanahalli on May 18, 1933. The son of a rice farmer, Gowda worked in his father's fields while pursuing a diploma in civil engineering, which he received in 1952. Active in local politics, especially farmers' issues, Gowda served in the Karnataka state assembly from 1962 to 1991, when he won election to the lower house of India's Parliament.

Proud of his humble origins, Gowda retained an open-door policy as prime minister, meeting the public without formal appointments. Since Gowda's native tongue is Kannada, his native regional language, he has spent much of his spare time since the election improving his knowledge of Hindi, India's dominant language. Reflective of his roots and his commitment to politics, Gowda has no hobbies and plays no sports. He and his wife Chennamma are the parents of four sons and two daughters.

ARUNA NAYYAR MICHIE

HASHIMOTO, Ryutaro

On Jan. 11, 1996, both houses of the Diet elected Ryutaro Hashimoto as Japan's prime minister. Hashimoto—president of the Liberal Democratic Party (LDP), the largest party in the Diet—was chosen six days after the abrupt resignation of Prime Minister Tomiichi Murayama.

Despite his party's strength, Hashimoto assembled a three-party coalition to govern. His cabinet reflected the tenuous nature of the peculiar coalition. Twelve portfolios went to LDP members, Murayama's Social Democrats took six, and the New Party (Sakigake) held two posts. The *Mainichi Shimbun*, noting that general elections would have to be held by July 1997, editorialized that Hashimoto should regard his cabinet as a "pre-election caretaker."

In a policy speech delivered to the Diet on January 22, the first LDP prime minister in more than two years set four priorities: rebuilding a resilient economy, creating a society in which the elderly are comfortable, enacting a "proactive foreign-policy position," and implementing administrative and fiscal reforms. In January various public-opinion polls showed a support level for the Hashimoto cabinet of between 50% and 60%.

Hashimoto's main opposition was represented not by the LDP's perennial foes, the Social Democrats (who had joined the governing coalition), but by the New Frontier Party (Shinshinto), led by Ichiro Ozawa. Japanese media dubbed the competition "the Ichi-Ryu war" (after the first units of their given names). Indeed, the coalition suffered a stalemate in the Diet. Major issues included negotiations concerning U.S. bases in Okinawa and the costly and unpopular liquidation of failed housing-loan firms. These issues also caused serious drops and fluctuations in the government's public-approval ratings throughout the spring and summer.

Hashimoto's government faced its most important referendum with national elections on October 20. From the premier's perspective, the results were mixed. On the positive side, the LDP won 239 seats in the lower house—a 28-seat improvement from the previous election and nearly enough for a majority in the 500-seat body—and Shinshinto failed to pick up new seats. On the other hand, the Social Democrats and Sakigake performed quite poorly in the election and then chose to withdraw from the LDP's governing coalition. In the end, Hashimoto and the LDP picked up enough allies to gain a fragile margin in the lower house, but were forced to govern Japan without a majority coalition.

Background. Ryutaro Hashimoto was born July 29, 1937, in Soja, Okayama prefecture. He was graduated from Keio University in 1960 and went to work for a textile firm. In 1963 he successfully ran as an LDP candidate for the House of Representatives from his late father's constituency in Okayama. He was elected for 11 successive terms, until 1993. During those years, he served several governments in various ministries. He became best known as Murayama's minister of international trade and industry (1994–January 1996), representing Japan in negotiations with the United States and gaining a reputation as a Japanese leader who could say "no" to the United States. With a greatly heightened political profile, Hashimoto was selected as LDP president in September 1995.

Some observers thought that Hashimoto's ascension represented the arrival of a new generation of Japanese leaders. He was known for being brusque and outspoken, but also as a shrewd negotiator. Long an aggressive nationalist, on assuming leadership he came to favor "a strong but humble Japan." He also is well-dressed, telegenic, and image-conscious.

Hashimoto and his wife, Kumiko, have five children.

ARDATH W. BURKS

HILFIGER, Tommy

From selling blue jeans to creating high fashion, Tommy Hilfiger—one of today's hottest names in fashion design—has done it all. After establishing a following in the early and mid-1990s in menswear and accessories, he moved into women's clothing in the summer of 1996 with the launch of a sportswear line and a women's fragrance, Tommy Girl. It was the first time a clothing line and fragrance had been introduced simultaneously. Hilfiger's push to become a top name in all areas of fashion—so far a resounding success—continued.

Unlike many designers, who create clothes and then expect customers' desires to follow, Hilfiger has earned his success by listening to his customers and designing what *they* want. His line of classic yet modern men's "all-American" sportswear, characterized by such design elements as bold nautical colors and stripes inside the lining of polo-shirt collars, is favored by a widely varied clientele, from those preferring the "preppy" look to those who consider themselves "rappers." Tommy Hilfiger clothes thus are worn by men as diverse as U.S. President Bill Clinton and the rap artist Snoop Doggy Dogg—as well as by legions of fashion-conscious teenagers. Given this broad-spectrum popularity, it is not surprising that, by the 1994–95 fiscal year, Tommy Hilfiger USA Inc. was the United States' second-largest manufacturer of menswear after Ralph Lauren; the company also has become the Number 1 apparel firm traded on the New York Stock Exchange. On a more artistic level, Hilfiger received the approval of his peers when he was named Menswear Designer of the Year for 1995 by the Council of Fashion Designers of America.

Background. Thomas Jacob Hilfiger was born in Elmira, NY, in 1952, the second of nine children. His father was a watchmaker with conservative tastes who did not agree with Hilfiger's choice of music or clothing or with his lack of desire to attend college. Hilfiger has said that his father's lack of faith in his ability has been a driving force in his push for success.

After graduating from high school in 1969, Hilfiger took his life savings of $150 and went to New York City, where he bought 20 pairs of bell-bottom jeans. He took the jeans back to Elmira, where such clothes were impossible to find, and sold them to friends at a profit. The young entrepreneur soon opened his own store, People's Place. By the time he turned 26, Hilfiger owned ten specialty shops in upstate New York.

His retail experiences led him toward design as he began creating clothes that his customers wanted but that were not available from suppliers. Hilfiger's career change was propelled further by the 1977 bankruptcy of People's Place. In 1979, he and his wife moved to New York City, where Hilfiger worked at Jordache and, later, as a freelance designer. He achieved his dream of starting his own line when, in 1984, he received the financial backing of Mohan Murjani. Hilfiger's popularity spread; in 1989 he ended the partnership and bought Murjani's stake in the business with a new partner, a Hong Kong apparel executive. In 1992 the company went public; it continued growing during the mid-1990s, in part through the licensing of the Tommy Hilfiger name for lines of jeans, eyewear, children's wear, shoes, and more.

Hilfiger lives on a converted farm in Greenwich, CT, with his wife and four children.

KRISTI VAUGHAN

© D. Fineman/Sygma

Tommy Hilfiger

HOWARD, John Winston

John Howard became Australia's prime minister after his coalition of the Liberal and National parties registered a resounding win in general elections on March 2, 1996, over the ruling Australian Labor Party led by incumbent Prime Minister Paul Keating. Howard's skilled campaign against his high-key opponent showed that 21 years in federal Parliament had made him the most politically adept Liberal leader to rise in recent years.

A firm, mild-mannered traditionalist, Howard sought a mandate to reduce immigration, safeguard family values, and care for the community's "forgotten people," while reining in welfare. Throughout the campaign, he hammered at the issues of unchecked budget deficits and worsening foreign debt and dismissed as irrelevant Keating's enthusiasm to move Australia to a federal republic by 2001.

After being sworn into office on March 11, Howard showed a willingness to face the wrath of vocal special-interest groups, including unionists. Adhering to a modified form of Thatcherism, Howard chose a cabinet of free-market proponents, supporting immediate expenditure cuts to reduce the deficit, the sale of publicly owned enterprises and assets, and extensive reform of labor-relations laws.

He also tackled immediate issues—most notably a tightening of gun laws following an April massacre in Tasmania, in which a gunman killed 35 people. On his initiative, all states and territories enacted uniform gun laws to ban automatic and semiautomatic weapons. His cuts to education and social-welfare spending ran into opposition from Labor and minor parties in the Senate.

Background. John Winston Howard was born on July 25, 1939, in Sydney and was raised in the city's suburbs. He attended Canterbury Boys' High School and went on to the University of Sydney, where he earned a degree in law.

After becoming a partner in a suburban law firm, he joined the local branch of the Liberal Party, where a fellow member (and his future wife), Janette Parker, encouraged him to pursue a career in politics. He entered national politics in 1974, winning a seat in the House of Representatives. Late in 1975, following a Liberal victory in the general election, he became minister for business and consumer affairs, and in 1977 was appointed federal treasurer, a post he held until the Liberal's defeat in 1983.

Two years later he successfully challenged Andrew Peacock for the party's leadership, beginning a period of discord between Peacock and Howard supporters. Howard's campaign in the 1987 elections failed, and subsequently he lost the party leadership to Peacock. However, Howard's

© Bill Frakes/"Sports Illustrated"/Time Inc.

Michael Johnson

tenacity and rare ability to survive parliamentary jousts with Keating led to his reinstatement as party leader in 1995.

The Howards, who were married in 1971, have two sons and a daughter, and remain based in Sydney. John Howard's interests include cricket, film, and reading.

R. M. YOUNGER

JOHNSON, Michael

U.S. sprinter Michael Johnson dashed into the record books at the 1996 Atlanta Summer Olympics with an awe-inspiring double triumph in the 200-m and 400-m dashes. The 28-year-old Texan came to Atlanta under a great deal of pressure—he had faced months of publicity surrounding his quest to become the first man to win the two events and had convinced Olympic officials to modify the timetable to make his attempt logistically possible. Although the updated schedule required him to run eight races in five days, many fans expected Johnson to win his events with ease.

Johnson responded to such expectations by exceeding them. In the 400-m final, he coasted to victory in 43.49, an Olympic record. Wearing his trademark gold shoes and sprinting with his unusual upright stance, Johnson defeated his nearest competitor by almost one second. He exhibited even greater domination in the 200-m finals, crossing the finish line several yards in front of silver medalist Frankie Fredericks of Namibia—who ran the third-fastest 200-m time in history. In an era in which sprint records improve by hundredths of a second at a time, Johnson's mark of 19.32 lopped an unbelievable .34 off his own standard. To some, the victory brought to mind Bob Beamon's long-jump heroics at the 1968 Olympics—another performance that seemed decades ahead of its time.

Background. Michael Johnson was born on Sept. 13, 1967, in Dallas, TX, the youngest of five children. He began sprinting at the age of 11, but throughout his adolescence, he was far more focused on his education than on athletics. In high school, he gained notice as one of the top prep sprinters in Texas. Yet few people felt that the studious teenager was destined for track-and-field stardom.

Such views quickly were revised during Johnson's freshman year at Baylor University, where the physically maturing sprinter posted much-improved times and defeated some of the nation's top 200-m runners. Johnson qualified for the 1988 U.S. Olympic Trials; however, a stress fracture in his leg forced him to abandon his attempt to run in the Seoul Olympics.

Back at Baylor, Johnson expanded his training to race at 400-m, an event thought to be too long for most pure sprinters. Within two years, he dispelled any doubts about the wisdom of the move. In 1990, Johnson became the first athlete ever to be ranked first in the world in the 200-m and 400-m. That year, he ended his career at Baylor with five National Collegiate Athletic Association (NCAA) titles—and a degree in business. In 1991, Johnson won his first world championship (at 200-m) and was installed as a favorite to win gold in the event at the 1992 Olympic Games in Barcelona. Unfortunately, Johnson was hit with a bout of food poisoning two weeks before the Games; he failed to qualify for the 200-m finals. (He, however, did win a gold medal in the 1,600-m relay.)

For the next three years, Johnson ran with a vengeance. He won his first 400-m world championship in 1993; the following year he was top ranked at both 200-m and 400-m for the third time. Buoyed by long winning streaks, he vowed to try the unprecedented—to win at 200-m and 400-m in a single major meet. Johnson notched such doubles twice during 1995: at the U.S. national championships and the world championships.

Johnson, a bachelor, splits his time between Dallas and Waco, TX, when he is not traveling. Known for his relentless workouts and obsessive neatness, Johnson likes to ride horses in his spare time.

KEMP, Jack French

Jack Kemp's once promising career in national politics seemed headed for permanent obscurity when he ruled himself out of the race for the 1996 Republican presidential nomination. He explained that he had deep misgivings that he could find enough support within his party for his philosophy, which, along with an abiding faith in supply-side economics, placed great stress on his conviction that the GOP badly needed to broaden its base by reaching out to minorities and urban residents.

Suddenly, though, on the eve of the August Republican convention in San Diego, Kemp was thrust back into the spotlight when the presumptive party standard-bearer Robert Dole chose him as his running mate. In so doing, Dole overlooked his long-standing differences with the former New York congressman on economic policy and other issues. Most Republicans rejoiced at the choice because Kemp was expected to bring much-needed exuberance and imagination to the ticket; others worried because of Kemp's past difficulty in focusing his campaign message, a lack of discipline that had undermined his own presidential candidacy in 1988. Although the Dole-Kemp ticket was defeated on November 5, Kemp had been given what few politicians get on the national scene—a second chance.

Background. Jack French Kemp was born in Los Angeles on July 13, 1935. After being graduated from Occidental College in Los Angeles in 1957, he began a 13-year pro-football career. The future politician was so dedicated to the game that when he broke a finger of his passing hand on a defender's helmet, he had it set bent, in a sideline procedure, to fit the shape of a football. His first stint in politics was as a special assistant to then California Gov. Ronald Reagan in 1967.

Jack French Kemp

© Brooks Kraft/Sygma

In 1970, Kemp ran successfully for a seat in the U.S. House of Representatives from a district in the suburbs of Buffalo, NY. When he first entered Congress, he had difficulty being taken seriously because of his background as a professional athlete. But the former Buffalo Bills quarterback soon solidified himself with his constituents and ultimately surprised his detractors with his forceful advocacy of an across-the-board cut in income-tax rates as a means of revitalizing the supply side of the economy and thus, Kemp argued, bringing prosperity to all. When Ronald Reagan made that theory the centerpiece of his economic policy as president, Kemp—a longtime Reagan booster—became an influential figure in the national Republican Party. His supporters viewed him as the logical heir to Reagan's mantle as conservative leader. But Kemp's efforts to fulfill these expectations failed along with his poorly organized presidential candidacy in 1988.

Having decided not to run for reelection to Congress in 1988, Kemp became George Bush's secretary of housing and urban development in 1989. As a cabinet member, he continued to champion schemes to expand the reach of his party beyond white middle-class voters. His role won him many admirers among minority groups, and even among liberal Democrats, but few adherents in his own party. After Bush's defeat in 1992, Kemp left public office and helped found a conservative think tank called Empower America. It gave him a forum to continue to promote his ideas on economic growth and party broadening, along with a substantial income.

Early in the 1996 contest for the Republican nomination, Kemp endorsed publisher Steve Forbes—one of Dole's principal rivals for the prize—because he agreed with Forbes' tax-cutting approach to economic policy. But once he became Dole's running mate, Kemp accepted the presidential nominee's view on issues on which they disagreed. Kemp thus gave his support to expelling the children of illegal immigrants from California public schools under the state's Proposition 187, which he had opposed. He also said that he favored repeal of California's affirmative-action programs, a move he previously had resisted.

In 1958, Kemp married Joanne Main. They are the parents of four children.

ROBERT SHOGAN

LOTT, Trent

For the better part of two centuries the U.S. Senate was legendary for its clubbiness, deference to seniority, and reverence for tradition. But in the third century of its existence, the Senate seems to be changing. That conclusion was buttressed by the rise in 1996 of Mississippi Republican Sen. Trent Lott to its leadership post—Senate majority leader.

In following the path that carried him to the top, Lott first shouldered aside a respected and well-liked colleague, Alan Simpson of Wyoming, to oust him from the job of Republican whip, the Number 2 post in the Senate hierarchy, on the heels of the big GOP midterm election victory in 1994. Then, 18 months later, when Senate Majority Leader Bob Dole decided to leave that job and resign from the Senate in order to devote himself full-time to his presidential candidacy, Lott had no compunctions about competing against his senior Mississippi colleague, Thad Cochran. Lott trounced him by a 44-to-8 vote.

The ascension of Lott, a hard-driving, hard-edged conservative, clearly demonstrated that what counts in today's Senate—more than the courtliness that ruled in the past—is ideology and ambition. And it also demonstrated the new dominance in GOP congressional ranks of Southerners like Lott and his House counterpart, Speaker Newt Gingrich of Georgia, a longtime ally. Indeed, Gingrich and Lott have been so close that some moderate Republican senators privately worried that their new leader might bring to their more sedate chamber the same zeal in the pursuit of conservative goals that characterized Gingrich's leadership in the House. Lott sought to relieve such a concern. Nevertheless, the careers of Lott and Gingrich illustrate the extent to which conservative Republicanism has come to dominate the South—a region that once was a stronghold of the Democratic Party.

Background. Born on Oct. 9, 1941, in Grenada, MS, and raised in the Gulf Coast town of Pascagoula, Trent Lott earned degrees in public administration and law from the University of Mississippi. After a brief stint in private law practice, he broke into politics as an aide to U.S. Rep. William Colmer, a conservative Mississippi Democrat, whose House seat he took in 1972 when Colmer retired. Symbolizing the shift in partisan power, though, Lott ran as a Republican and won reelection seven times. He served as GOP whip in the House (1981–89).

In 1988 when veteran Democratic Sen. John Stennis retired, Lott won the seat for himself and for his party. He was reelected easily in 1994. In the House, Lott—through his operations as party whip—had created a tight system for maintaining party discipline; in the highly individualistic Senate, however, even he sometimes found it hard to maintain a firm grip on his colleagues—particularly the Democratic opposition. However, as the new majority leader, Lott broke a logjam, allowing the Senate to adopt the biggest GOP legislative achievement of 1996—a major welfare-reform bill.

Lott is married to the former Patricia Thompson of Pascagoula. The couple have a son, Chet, and a daughter, Tyler.

ROBERT SHOGAN

LUCID, Shannon W.

When U.S. astronaut Shannon W. Lucid stepped onto the tarmac at the Kennedy Space Center on Sept. 26, 1996, and proceeded to make the short walk to her waiting transporter, her legs were a bit wobbly. And no wonder: The 53-year-old biochemist had just spent 188 days in space, traveling about 75 million mi (121 million km) aboard the Russian space station *Mir* and setting new endurance records for the longest stay in orbit by a U.S. astronaut and by a woman. No one expected her to be able to stand, let alone walk, after such a protracted period in microgravity. That she did was a tribute to her grit and determination—qualities that have led one colleague to praise her (paradoxically, under the circumstances) as an extremely "down-to-earth" person.

Lucid spent much of her time in orbit studying how the space environment affects living tissue and how protein crystals grow in microgravity. But while the orbital research she conducted was important, it was Lucid herself who was the real test subject. With the assembly of a larger international space station scheduled to begin in 1997, extended stays in orbit could become routine. As a result, the National Aeronautics and Space Administration (NASA) has made studying the effects of long-term spaceflight on humans a top priority. For the six months following Lucid's return to Earth, medical personnel would examine everything from her bone loss and muscle tone to her heart rate and other bodily functions.

Throughout her record-breaking mission, Lucid maintained her sense of humor. In an interview conducted from

Shannon W. Lucid

© NASA/AP/Wide World Photos

Earth shortly before her return, she was asked what she missed most during her six months in orbit. "Obviously, I better say my family," she replied, "because they would feel really bad if they thought they came in second to some real gooey desserts." Upon her return to Earth, she was met with warm wishes from U.S. President Bill Clinton, who called her "a monument to the human spirit." The president also awarded her the Congressional Space Medal of Honor.

Background. Shannon W. Lucid was born on Jan. 14, 1943, in war-torn Shanghai, China, the daughter of Baptist preacher Joseph Oscar Wells and his wife Myrtle, a missionary nurse. When the future astronaut was only six weeks old, the family was interned in a Japanese prison camp, where they spent a grueling year before being released in a prisoner-of-war (POW) exchange.

The family eventually relocated to Bethany, OK, where Shannon was raised. She was graduated from Bethany High School in 1960, and went on to the University of Oklahoma, where she earned a bachelor's degree in chemistry (1963), a master's degree in biochemistry (1970), and a doctorate in biochemistry (1973).

In 1978, Lucid was selected by NASA as one of its first six female astronauts, along with Sally K. Ride, America's first woman in space, and Judith A. Resnick, who perished in the 1986 *Challenger* disaster. Lucid's first space launch came in 1985; the 1996 *Mir* mission was her fifth.

She is married to Michael Lucid of Indianapolis, IN; they have three grown children. In her spare time, Lucid enjoys flying, camping, hiking, and reading.

BRUCE JACOBY

MFUME, Kweisi

Former U.S. Rep. Kweisi Mfume was sworn in as president of the National Association for the Advancement of Colored People (NAACP) on Feb. 20, 1996.

Mfume's selection as head of the NAACP had been ratified by the organization's board on February 17. The board had amended its constitution so that Mfume would be the organization's president and chief executive officer. He also would report to a 17-member executive committee, not to the full 64-member board. The former Democratic congressman from Maryland promised to lead a "new NAACP, reinvented and reinvigorated." The organization had been facing financial and leadership difficulties. Mfume's predecessor at the NAACP, Benjamin F. Chavis, Jr., had been fired amid allegations that he used NAACP funds to settle a sexual-discrimination suit against him. In addition, the NAACP was suffering from a $3 million debt.

Mfume stated that his aim as NAACP president would be "to create and cultivate a movement that represents the best of America." He also said that "racial and religious tolerance and effecting change in government became the banner of NAACP some time ago and remains so today." Mfume also undertook a three-part "voter empowerment" drive—registration, education, and participation.

Background. Kweisi Mfume was born Frizzell Gray on Oct. 24, 1948, in Baltimore. As a boy, he was a good student and did well in sports. Following his mother's death when he was 16, the future civil-rights leader quit school and took on odd jobs. A few years later he went "kind of wild" and joined a gang. By the age of 22 he had fathered five sons by three different women.

Then, suddenly, he decided to turn his life around. After earning a high-school equivalency certificate, he was awarded a bachelor's degree, magna cum laude, from Morgan State University in 1976 and a master's degree from Johns Hopkins University in 1984. In 1972 he changed his name to Kweisi Mfume, a name of Ibo origin meaning "conquering son of kings."

Mfume also decided to pursue a career in politics. In 1979 he became a member of the Baltimore city council. He served as a council member for two terms, until his election to the U.S. House of Representatives from Maryland's 7th District in 1986. During the election campaign he projected himself as proof that anyone can change his or her lifestyle. His sons defended Mfume as a devoted father. He was elected with 87% of the vote and was reelected four times.

© Richard Ellis/Sygma

Kweisi Mfume

Mfume's voting record as a congressman was generally liberal. He opposed Presidents Ronald Reagan and George Bush on numerous issues, including cutting the capital-gains tax. He successfully sought the chairmanship of the Congressional Black Caucus in 1992. During his one term in the post, Mfume lobbied hard to have Jean-Bertrand Aristide, the deposed head of Haiti's government, returned to the presidency of that Caribbean nation.

Mfume's memoir, *No Free Ride: From the Mean Streets to the Mainstream*, written with journalist Ron Stodgill 2d, was published in 1996.

MURRAY, Eddie

Baseball star Eddie Murray is living proof that consistency counts. The 6'2" (1.88-m), 220-lb (100-kg) slugger had milestone hits in both the 1995 and 1996 seasons. On June 30, 1995, he became the 20th man to reach 3,000 hits when he singled against Mike Trombley in Minnesota. On Sept. 6, 1996, he became the 15th member of the 500-home-run club when he connected against Detroit's Felipe Lira in Oriole Park at Camden Yards. Murray joined Hank Aaron and Willie Mays as the only men in baseball history to notch 3,000 hits and 500 homers.

These two marks were the crowning achievements in a stellar career. With 79 runs batted in (RBIs) in the 1996 season, Murray became the first player to produce 20 consecutive seasons with at least 75 RBIs. Murray hit two grand-slam home runs in 1996, giving him a career total of 19, trailing only Lou Gehrig on the lifetime list. He also reached the 20-double plateau for the 20th consecutive year—a feat matched only by Tris Speaker. At the end of the 1996 season, Murray's career statistics were among the all-time leaders and tops among active players in a number of categories—hits (3,218), RBIs (1,899), home runs (501), and doubles (553).

Murray had a solid 1996 campaign. In the middle of the season he was traded from the Cleveland Indians to the Baltimore Orioles, the team with which he had played most of his career. He had 22 extra-base hits in 64 games for Baltimore, helping the team win the wild-card title and advance to the League Championship Series. (The previous season, Murray hit .323 to help the Indians compile the best record in baseball and reach the World Series.) Between the two clubs, he appeared in 152 games, the 16th time he has played at least 150 (one season short of the record held by Pete Rose). Murray's durability helps; he has been disabled only twice in his 20-year career.

Background. Born in Los Angeles on Feb. 24, 1956, Eddie Murray was the eighth of 12 children. Games of backyard stickball helped Murray learn to handle curves, sliders, and other hard-to-hit pitches. Four of his brothers played professional baseball, one of them in the majors. At Locke High School—where another baseball legend, Ozzie Smith, was a teammate—Murray played for the basketball team and doubled as a pitcher and first baseman in baseball. He had a 7-1 pitching record as a senior, but Baltimore liked his bat better. The Orioles drafted him in the 1973 free-agent draft. Just 17 when he signed, Murray spent four years in the minor leagues before reaching Baltimore.

In 1977, Murray played his first season in Baltimore as a designated hitter and captured American League (AL) rookie-of-the-year honors. The following year he moved to first base, winning Gold Gloves for his defensive play (1982–84). During his first dozen seasons, all with the Orioles, Murray led the team in RBIs nine times and in batting and home runs seven times each. Baltimore sportswriters named him the most valuable Oriole five straight seasons (1981–85), but he finished no better than second (twice) in the voting for AL most valuable player. With the Orioles, Murray played in two World Series (1979 and 1983).

He was dealt to the Los Angles Dodgers in December 1988 after the late Edward Bennett Williams, then owner of the Orioles, criticized his production and desire. Though Williams later apologized, it took eight years before Murray returned to Baltimore. In those interim years, Murray also played two years with the New York Mets.

Stoic and indifferent toward the press, Murray disdains interviews or individual attention, preferring to focus on winning games for his team. He lives in Los Angeles with his wife, the former Janice Zenon, and their daughter, Jordan Alexandra.

DAN SCHLOSSBERG

NETANYAHU, Benjamin

In the first direct election for the prime ministership on May 29, 1996, Israelis chose Benjamin Netanyahu for the post. The 46-year-old leader of the conservative Likud party narrowly edged incumbent Prime Minister Shimon Peres in a contest of competing ideologies. Netanyahu had stressed Israeli security in his media-savvy campaign; Peres, in contrast, had vowed to continue the Middle East peace process. With his election, Netanyahu became the youngest prime minister in Israel's history.

Background. Benjamin "Bibi" Netanyahu was born on Oct. 21, 1949, in Tel Aviv, Israel. In 1963, Netanyahu and his family moved to the United States after his father, a noted scholar of Jewish history and conservative Zionist, accepted a position at a Pennsylvania college. When the future prime minister finished high school in the United States, he served for five years (1967–72) in an elite Israel army antiterrorist unit, reaching the rank of captain. After completing his military service, Netanyahu attended the Massachusetts Institute of Technology, earning a bachelor's degree in architecture and a master's in business administration.

Netanyahu's entry into Israeli politics was precipitated by unfortunate circumstance. In 1976 his older brother Jonathan became a national hero in Israel after he was killed while leading a renowned operation in Entebbe, Uganda, to rescue passengers from an hijacked Air France plane. Netanyahu soon moved back to Israel and organized the Jonathan Institute in Jerusalem, which presented a series of seminars on terrorism that attracted considerable public attention. Although employed as a marketing manager at a furniture company, Netanyahu was chosen in 1982 by Israel's ambassador to the United States, Moshe Arens, to be his deputy in the post of consul general. From 1984 to 1988, Netanyahu served as Israel's permanent representative to the United Nations. Netanyahu, who speaks perfect English, acquired a reputation as one of Israel's most articulate spokesmen.

Elected to the Knesset (parliament) on the Likud list in 1988, Netanyahu soon rose to leading positions in the party, serving as deputy foreign minister (1988–91) and as deputy minister in the prime minister's office (1991–92). A member of the Israeli delegation and its spokesman during the 1991 Middle East peace conference in Madrid, he participated in subsequent peace negotiations in Washington during 1991–92. When Israel was struck by Iraqi missiles during the 1991 Gulf war, the telegenic Netanyahu became known internationally as his country's spokesman; he calmly conducted one interview during a missile attack while wearing a gas mask.

When outgoing Prime Minister Yitzhak Shamir announced in 1992 that he would not seek another term as Likud leader, Netanyahu became a leading contender for the post. In March 1993 he won a bitterly fought primary election for Likud leadership. As an opposition leader, Netanyahu was a forceful and frequent critic of the peace accord between Israel and the Palestine Liberation Organization (PLO). In particular, Netanyahu opposed Israeli territorial concessions and the recognition of the PLO and its president, Yasir Arafat, whom he accused of being a terrorist. After Prime Minister Yitzhak Rabin was assassinated by a Jewish right-wing extremist in November 1995, Netanyahu came under fire for allegedly fanning antigovernment extremism, a charge that the Likud leader denied.

As prime minister, Netanyahu was thrust into the middle of the Arab-Israeli peace process. Although he voiced clear objection to any changes in Israeli control of the West Bank and the Golan Heights, Netanyahu met soon after his election with Arafat and cautiously started direct negotiations with the Palestinians. Further diplomacy between the two leaders was necessary after violence between Palestinians and Israel erupted in September 1996.

Netanyahu and his third wife, Sara, a child psychologist, were married in 1991. The couple have two young sons. Netanyahu also has a daughter from his first marriage.

DON PERETZ

SARANDON, Susan

In 1996 actress Susan Sarandon at last took home the best-actress Oscar, after five nominations and more than 30 films. She won for her role as Roman Catholic nun Helen Prejean in *Dead Man Walking* (1995), a film directed and coproduced by her companion, Tim Robbins (who also wrote the screenplay). Her impressive turn as Prejean, who agrees to serve as spiritual adviser for a death-row convict (played by Sean Penn), was based on the story of the real-life Prejean and her work with death-row prisoners. Sarandon has become known in recent years for impressive performances in character roles—often those of so-called "martyr mothers" or strong, selfless women: for example, *Lorenzo's Oil* (1992), *Little Women* (1994), *Safe Passage* (1994), and *The Client* (1994). A notable exception was her role as one of the two gun-toting angry women in 1991's *Thelma & Louise*. She has received Oscar nominations for *Atlantic City* (1981), *Thelma & Louise*, *Lorenzo's Oil*, and *The Client*, as well as for *Dead Man Walking*.

As an actress, Sarandon has come into her own with middle age, and has grown to personify the prototypical

Benjamin Netanyahu

© Jeffrey Markowitz/Sygma

© King/Gamma-Liaison

Susan Sarandon

strong, intelligent, mature woman. She is unafraid to take risks such as appearing unattractive or old beyond her years on film. This quality has led to her achieving full-fledged stardom after age 40—a rarity in today's youth-obsessed Hollywood. She caught the public's attention with her sexy role in *Bull Durham* (1988), and first carried a major film in Robbins' adaptation of John Grisham's *The Client*. After her Oscar nomination for that role, she segued easily into *Dead Man Walking* and an Oscar win.

Background. Susan Abigail Tomalin was born Oct. 4, 1946, in New York City, the oldest of nine children. Her father, Philip, was a nightclub singer who later became an ad executive and TV producer. The family soon moved to Edison, NJ. At Catholic University of America in Washington, DC, the future actress majored in drama due to an academic interest in the field; she had no plans to act. This changed when she met graduate student and actor Chris Sarandon; the two were married when she was 20. (They divorced in 1979.)

Following her graduation, Sarandon began working with her husband in regional theater, and honed her acting skills with roles in soap operas. She unexpectedly got her first film role, in *Joe*, in 1970. The film that led to widespread recognition (if not critical praise) was *The Rocky Horror Picture Show* (1975), which became a cult hit. This was followed by several critical disasters. Sarandon resurfaced in *Pretty Baby* (1978), in which she earned favorable reviews playing the mother of Brooke Shields. Her following films, although not popular at the box office, garnered critical praise, as did the 1980–81 Off-Broadway production *A Coupla White Chicks Sitting Around Talking*.

Sarandon's films have always been a mixed bag. After her Academy Award nomination and best-actress award at the Venice Film Festival for *Atlantic City* (1981), she took a lesbian-vampire role opposite Catherine Deneuve in 1983's *The Hunger*. Her career perhaps hit its low point in the late 1980s, with a "humiliating" experience regarding the casting of *The Witches of Eastwick* (1987): After winning a meaty role, she found before shooting began that it was being transferred to Cher, and that she was being given a lesser role. Then, like an unknown, she had to audition for *Bull Durham* (1988), but unexpectedly got the role; her career has been on an upward trajectory ever since.

Susan Sarandon has three children—a daughter by Italian director Franco Amurri, and two sons by Robbins. Sarandon has made it clear that her principal priority is her children. She is known for her sometimes-controversial social activism.

WOODS, Eldrick (Tiger)

Surely no golfer ever has arrived on the professional golf scene with as much heraldry as did Eldrick (Tiger) Woods in 1996. And surely no player, at least for the moment, has done as much to fulfill—or exceed—such expectations.

Late in August, only days after winning the U.S. Amateur Golf Championship, the 20-year-old Stanford junior turned professional. While that decision surprised few, the size of his endorsement contracts with the Nike Corp. and other sponsors—thought to exceed $40 million—stunned even seasoned observers. Woods had his share of doubters who did not think he was ready for the rigors of the Professional Golfers' Association (PGA) Tour. Some said that he was too young and unpolished, while others noted that he had not played well in his previous professional events.

As a professional, however, Woods silenced his doubters with the fastest start in the history of the PGA. In eight starts at the end of the 1996 season, he had five top-five finishes, including two wins—at the Las Vegas Invitational and the Walt Disney World/Oldsmobile Classic. Not only did he earn his PGA Tour exemption for 1997, he qualified for the 1996 season-ending Tour Championship (reserved for the top 30 money winners). He ended the PGA season with $790,594 in earnings.

Woods, 6'2" (1.88 m) and a slim 155 lbs (70 kg), quickly established himself as the longest hitter on the Tour. Had he played enough rounds to be eligible, he would have led the Tour in driving distance, at 303 yds (277 m); birdies per round; and eagle frequency. With a 69.44 scoring average, he would have finished second in that category.

Perhaps even more significant than his success as a golfer was the sociological impact he was having on the game. Media attention was focused on his minority heritage—part black, part Native American, and part Thai. By year's end, his galleries were peopled increasingly by young African-American fans, an unusual occurrence for the sport. Handsome, personable, and articulate, Woods was considered by many to be a perfect role model.

Background. Eldrick Woods was born Dec. 30, 1975, in Cypress, CA. His father, Earl, is part black, part Native American; his mother, Kultida, is of Thai heritage. From an early age he was groomed, or perhaps pushed, by his father to excel at golf. The younger Woods—whose nickname "Tiger" was taken from one of his father's army buddies—was a golf prodigy by the age of 2, putting with Bob Hope on *The Mike Douglas Show*. He reportedly, at the age of 3, shot 48 for nine holes on a U.S. Navy course. And at age 5, he demonstrated his precocious talents on television's *That's Incredible*. He won his first significant amateur tournament at age 8 and became the youngest person (at 16) to play in a PGA tournament. Before leaving the amateur ranks in 1996, Woods had won virtually every possible title. His victories included an unprecedented three consecutive U.S. Amateur Golf Championships, three U.S. Golf Association Junior Championships, and the 1996 National Collegiate Athletic Association (NCAA) title.

LARRY DENNIS

Eldrick (Tiger) Woods

© Focus on Sports

BIOTECHNOLOGY

Each year approximately 120,000 people in the United States are faced with the critical need for a heart, liver, lung, or kidney to replace one of their own that no longer functions properly. Unfortunately, 102,000 of these patients die annually because of a lack of available human organs. This shortage has led to research on the possible use of animal organs for such transplants. The most-favored animal for such procedures is the pig, because it can be raised free of known diseases and has organs comparable in size to those of humans.

The critical problem in any organ-transplant procedure, especially between species, is rejection of the donor organ by the recipient's immune system. In an attempt to solve this problem, human genes that act to inhibit the body's immune response to its own tissues have been inserted into fertilized pig eggs. It is hoped that the organs of the subsequently developed animals, when transplanted to humans, will not trigger the activation of the recipients' immune systems. In one experiment involving the transplanting of such genetically altered pig hearts to monkeys, the animals lived for 60 days after receiving the pig hearts. When unaltered pig hearts were used, the survival time was 55 minutes.

Root-Growth Gene. Root growth is critical for a plant, determining its ability to obtain water and needed elements from the soil. Root growth also is important for humans, as a number of roots—including carrots, beets, and radishes—serve as food items, and other things (i.e., nutritional content and taste) being equal, the larger the root the better. Identification of the genes involved in root growth will permit their transfer to various food plants with a resultant increase in food production.

Working with a much-studied weed plant, *Arabidopsis thaliana*, Peter Dorner and his colleagues at the Salk Institute for Biological Studies in La Jolla, CA, were able through a gene-transfer procedure to cause the gene, cyclin 1, to produce its protein continuously rather than when it would do so normally, which is just before each cell division. They found that the cells of the genetically altered plants divided in a rapid and continuous fashion, resulting in much longer and thicker roots than those of unaltered plants. If this procedure can be developed commercially, it could contribute to the world's food supply.

Bone Glue. Human bone consists of both a mineral (65%) and an organic (35%) component. The mineral portion consists mainly of the compounds calcium phosphate (85%) and calcium carbonate (10%) plus small amounts of sodium, magnesium, and other elements. When a bone breaks, especially at the hip, knee, shoulder, or wrist, its repair is very difficult and may require the surgical attachment of a metal plate, screws, and pins to buttress the fracture against strain. The recovery process is usually a long one, is not always complete, and often requires an additional operation to remove the metal supports.

Brent R. Constantz and his colleagues at the biotechnology company Norian Corporation in Cupertino, CA, have developed a bonelike glue that could be injected directly into a fracture site. The injected material hardens in minutes, forming a bridge between the broken ends of the bone, thereby providing much-needed support for it. In addition, the bone glue is so similar in chemical composition to natural bone that the body treats it as such, gradually absorbing it and replacing it with new bone growth. The U.S. Food and Drug Administration (FDA) approved a trial of the new substance in various hospitals.

Light-Induced Fluorescence. A number of organisms, including fireflies and certain bacteria, have the gene that produces the enzyme luciferase. This enzyme catalyzes a reaction with the compound luciferin, resulting in the production of light. The luciferase gene has been transferred to other organisms, where it has been placed next to the controlling elements of a particular gene of interest. Under these conditions, whenever the gene of interest is activated, so is the luciferase gene. Although this system has been used to detect gene expression in a number of organisms, the wide application of this technique is limited by the need to supply luciferin for the reaction to occur.

Recently, Martin Chalfie and his colleagues at Columbia University, NY, and other institutions reported on their success in transferring the gene for the production of a fluorescent protein, called "Green Fluorescent Protein" (GFP), from the jellyfish *Aequorea victoria* to both a single-celled (bacterium) and a multicellular (roundworm) organism. GFP emits a green light when stimulated by exposure to blue light. This technique permits the monitoring of the gene expression without the need to add a compound, such as luciferin, that may interfere with the normal functioning of the organism. It is anticipated that this technique will have wide application in studying the efficiency of many biotechnological processes.

LOUIS LEVINE, *City College of New York*

BOLIVIA

Preparations for upcoming elections were under way in Bolivia during 1996. Also making headlines were new labor and land-reform protests, drug-fighting efforts, and slowed economic growth.

Government. Balloting for president, vice-president, and legislators in both houses of Congress was scheduled to be held in June 1997. President Gonzalo Sánchez de Lozada was barred constitutionally from seeking reelection, but as 1996 drew to a close, he had not expressed a preference as to his successor, and no candidate had emerged as the favorite.

The situation was complicated by the government's low popularity and the weakness of the opposition. The government had continued the ambitious reform programs launched by previous administrations, holding inflation in check, reducing the level of state participation in the economy, and decentralizing some aspects of public administration. But it failed to achieve rapid economic growth and reduce poverty. Both failures eroded the government's popularity and contributed to waves of street protests. In municipal elections held in December 1995, the ruling Free Bolivia Movement (MNR) lost many urban municipalities to opposition parties.

Strikes. A monthlong general strike that idled some 90,000 workers ended in April. The strike was called in protest of a government plan to privatize important state-owned businesses. The settlement covered a wage increase but left pending the labor opposition to privatization.

In September thousands of peasant farmers from all over the country undertook a monthlong march on La Paz, the capital, in protest of a proposed agrarian-reform law that would have strengthened government control over the distribution of land titles. Some 20,000 *campesinos* carried out daily protests and sometimes-violent confrontations with police before an accommodation was achieved. The accord, called the most important land law since the 1952 revolution, was reached on October 10; it guaranteed farmers title to the land they farmed and common titles to indigenous communities.

Drugs. Drugs continued to figure prominently in U.S.-Bolivian relations. In January the Bolivian Senate approved an extradition treaty that had been signed with the United States in 1995. The treaty, which was designed to deal mainly with drug-trafficking and terrorism cases, still required approval by the U.S. Senate. Under heavy U.S. prodding, the Bolivian government also stepped up its efforts to eradicate illegal coca fields and crack down on drug smugglers. Human-rights groups accused Bolivia of using antidrug efforts to cloak a "scorched earth" policy against coca farmers. A U.S. balance-of-payments loan was announced in July, part of which could used for drug-suppression efforts. In October, U.S. Ambassador Curt Kamman announced that in 1997, Bolivia would receive $50 million for antinarcotics programs.

Economy. The economy grew by only 3.8% in the first half of 1996, compared with 4% in 1995. Public-sector investment accounted for the main part of the growth. With an election coming, the government was expected to relax its tight money policies. In September, Bolivia joined Mercosur, the Southern Cone common market. As a member of the Andean Pact, Bolivia could accept the trade agreement, but could not accede to Mercosur's common external tariff.

RICHARD C. SCHROEDER, *Freelance Writer*

BOLIVIA • Information Highlights

Official Name: Republic of Bolivia.
Location: West-central South America.
Area: 424,162 sq mi (1 098 580 km²).
Population (mid-1996 est.): 7,600,000.
Chief Cities (1992 census): Sucre, the legal capital, 130,952; La Paz, the administrative capital, 711,036; Santa Cruz de la Sierra, 694,616; Cochabamba, 404,102.
Government: *Head of state and government,* Gonzalo Sánchez de Lozada, president (took office August 1993). *Legislature*—Congress: Senate and Chamber of Deputies.
Monetary Unit: Boliviano (5.105 bolivianos equal U.S.$1, July 1996).
Gross Domestic Product (1994 U.S.$): $18,300,000,000 (purchasing power parity).
Economic Indexes (1995): *Consumer Prices* (1991 = 100): all items, 145.7; food, 149.2. *Industrial Production* (1990 = 100): 128.
Foreign Trade (1995 U.S.$): *Imports,* $1,424,000,000; *exports,* $1,101,000,000.

BOSNIA AND HERZEGOVINA. *See* pages 96–101.

BRAZIL

During 1996, Brazil's President Fernando Henrique Cardoso began mobilizing support for a constitutional revision to permit his reelection in 1998. In the meantime, however, labor unions and Cardoso's political opponents protested against fiscal reforms that were part of the government's economic-stabilization package—the so-called *Plano Real* ("Real Plan"). Many of the plan's more aggressive provisions remained stalled in a skeptical Congress.

© Eraldo Peres/AP/Wide World Photos

Peasants throughout Brazil continued to organize as part of their campaign to push agrarian reform onto the national agenda during 1996. About 49% of Brazil's land was owned by 1% of the population; nearly 5 million families are landless.

Politics. Even after more than two years in office, Cardoso remained popular, thanks in large measure to his astute economic management and success in curbing inflation. In September he announced publicly what leaders of his Brazilian Social Democratic Party (PSDB) had been saying privately for months—that he would like to become his country's first president to win reelection. The 65-year-old chief executive would have to amend Brazil's constitution before he could stand for a second term. Such a change would require the approval of two thirds of the members of the 513-seat lower house and the 81-seat Senate. Most observers believed that the final bill, if passed, would allow all elected officials—including mayors and governors—to seek reelection.

To achieve the necessary votes, Cardoso's PSDB would need to obtain the backing of the Brazilian Democratic Movement Party (PMDB), the Brazilian Progressive Party (PPB), and the Liberal Front Party (PFL), none of which had committed themselves firmly as the year ended. Although a strong Cardoso ally, the highly disciplined, northeast-focused PFL—which was holding only two of 23 governorships—looked askance at extending the reelection principle beyond the presidency because it feared that such a move would impede its efforts to win new statehouses. Meanwhile, the support of the mercurial, opportunistic PPB was complicated by the presidential ambitions of Paulo Maluf, the outgoing mayor of São Paulo. In December delegates to the PPB's convention unanimously recommended reelecting the chief executive only after 2002.

Luiz Inácio (Lula) da Silva, the standard-bearer of the opposition Workers' Party (PT), whom Cardoso defeated in 1994, voiced outrage at the reelection initiative. "Fernando Henrique must think there are 150 million idiots in this country," Silva said, adding, "He is just using the reelection idea to divert attention from all the financial scandals."

At the other end of the spectrum, the business community bubbled with enthusiasm over the prospect of the market-oriented Cardoso occupying the Planalto presidential palace for another four years. The head of the São Paulo industrialists' chamber visited the incumbent to promise the support of at least 90% of the organization's members. "Despite all the sacrifices imposed on industry, the Real Plan is good and needs to be hurried through," he stated. The 27 constituent federations of the National Industrial Confederation reiterated similar sentiments. Moreover, newspapers reported in October that Petrobrás, the state oil company, would contribute funds to a $300 million "pro-reelection" advertising campaign on behalf of the reelection amendment.

An October national survey revealed that 51% of the respondents favored Cardoso's succeeding himself. Despite his popularity, Cardoso's PSDB failed to win key cities in local elections held in October and November. The party did obtain the lion's share of the votes nationwide, boosting its number of mayors to 910 from 513. Yet it suffered stinging losses in Belo Horizonte, Rio de Janeiro, and São Paulo. In the latter, the PPB's Celso Pitta's victory with 57% of the ballots cast signaled both voter satisfaction with Maluf's governance and an unparalleled political achievement for Pitto as an Afro-Brazilian.

Economics. The Brazilian economy was showing mixed signs of health in 1996. Inflation fell to approximately 10%, its lowest level in decades, while the gross domestic product (GDP) grew only an estimated 2.3%, compared with 4.2% a year earlier. In October, Finance Minister Pedro Malan announced plans to diminish spending by $6.5 billion in 1997 and increase tax collection in a move designed to address concerns over a mushrooming budget shortfall. Malan predicted that the measures would cut the operational deficit to below 2.5% of GDP in 1997, down from an expected 3.5% in 1996.

Malan and others in the government felt that additional efforts were needed to improve the economy—namely, a package of constitutional reforms that were being debated in Congress. These amendments would enable the government to prune the bloated federal bureaucracy, privatize more state assets, end lifetime employment and generous benefits for public employees, and boost tax receipts. The government also proclaimed its desire to extend the fiscal-stabilization fund—introduced in 1994 but due to expire in mid-1997—through the end of 1999. This fund, equivalent to 20% of the national budget, invested the finance ministry with control over monies allocated for specific purposes under the constitution.

The government's frustration over congressional foot-dragging on the constitutional reforms—introduced in early 1995 and unresolved as of October 1996—increased throughout the year. These sentiments surfaced in a midyear advertisement in *The Wall Street Journal*. According to the text, the president "has complied with his promise to propose reforms, but many in Congress—and those with vested interests—have been putting up serious resistance to modify or cancel many of his planned changes."

Cardoso's remarkable triumph as an inflation fighter gave him some leverage with recalcitrant lawmakers. His innovations helped slash monthly price increases from 50% in June 1994 to less than 1% in late 1996. Many observers feared that a failure to implement pending reforms would reverse this trend.

Foreign Affairs. U.S. Secretary of State Warren Christopher celebrated a warming in U.S.-Brazilian relations during a visit to Brazil in March. He expressed particular pleasure over the readiness of Brazil, once an opponent of nuclear nonproliferation ventures, to join Washington in working toward a worldwide ban on nuclear testing. The U.S. diplomat took part in a ceremony adopting a nuclear-cooperation agreement that would allow Brazil to buy materials for peaceful nuclear-power generation from the United States. In addition, Christopher lavished praise on Cardoso for ending Brazil's crippling inflation and opening his huge nation's market to U.S. imports, and called upon Brazil to help forge a free-trade zone spanning the Americas by 2005. The harmonious tone aside, Christopher disappointed his hosts by refusing to back fully Brazil's quest for a permanent seat on the United Nations (UN) Security Council. For its part, Brazil's foreign ministry still declined to sign the Nuclear Non-Proliferation Treaty on the grounds that the accord favored states already possessing nuclear weapons.

At midyear, Cardoso welcomed Bolivia as an associate member of the Mercosur common market.

GEORGE W. GRAYSON
College of William & Mary

BRAZIL • Information Highlights

Official Name: Federative Republic of Brazil.
Location: Eastern South America.
Area: 3,286,473 sq mi (8 511 965 km^2).
Population (mid-1996 est.): 160,500,000.
Chief Cities (mid-1993 est.): Brasília, the capital, 1,673,151; São Paulo, 9,842,059; Rio de Janeiro, 5,547,033; Salvador, 2,174,072.
Government: *Head of state and government,* Fernando Henrique Cardoso, president (sworn in Jan. 1, 1995). *Legislature*—National Congress: Senate and Chamber of Deputies.
Monetary Unit: Real (1.0390 reales equal U.S.$1, Dec. 31, 1996).
Gross Domestic Product (1994 est. U.S.$): $886,300,-000,000 (purchasing power parity).
Economic Indexes: *Consumer Prices* (1994, 1992 = 100): all items, 52,580.9; food, 54,510.9. *Industrial Production* (1995, 1990 = 100): 110.
Foreign Trade (1995 U.S.$): *Imports,* $53,783,000,000; *exports,* $46,506,000,000.

BULGARIA

The year 1996 proved to be critical in Bulgaria. The country experienced serious economic difficulties caused by the absence of systematic market reforms and widespread corruption by government officials. With social dissatisfaction growing, the ruling Socialist Party lost the presidential elections held in October–November and pressures increased for an early parliamentary election.

Political Turmoil. The Bulgarian Socialist Party (BSP) and its coalition partners, elected in December 1994, maintained a secure parliamentary majority despite growing pressures from the major opposition bloc, the Union of Democratic Forces (UDF). The political scene polarized between these two formations and their ideological differences were evident in all major issues affecting Bulgarian society—economic, social, and foreign-policy. The Socialists were determined to maintain the economic status quo and stalled the mass privatization program, leading to serious economic decline during the year.

Rifts also were evident within the Socialist Party between the harder-line members linked to Prime Minister Zhan Videnov and reformist elements critical of government policy. These divisions widened after the unsolved assassination of former Prime Minister Andrei Lukanov in early October. Lukanov had become an outspoken critic of the government's resistance to reform. Allegedly, he also possessed information on corruption at the highest levels of government that he was planning to make public. The presidential elections further undermined the Socialist administration. The UDF candidate, Peter Stoyanov, gained an overwhelming percentage of votes (44%) over Socialist Ivan Marazov (27%) in the first round of voting on October 27. Stoyanov was elected president in the second-round runoff on November 3, gaining 62% of the vote compared with 38% for Marazov. Although the post of president is primarily ceremonial, the UDF itself began pushing for a no-confidence vote in the government following the balloting.

Economic Distress. Bulgaria has been slow to shake off its communist economic legacy and some observers consider the country to have the worst-managed and most-corrupt administrations in the former Soviet bloc. During 1996, Bulgaria faced a major financial crisis. Its hard-currency reserves plummeted from about $1.5 billion to less than $600 million, and there were growing doubts that Sofia could meet its critical foreign-debt payments.

BULGARIA • Information Highlights

Official Name: Republic of Bulgaria.
Location: Southeastern Europe.
Area: 42,823 sq mi (110 910 km²).
Population (mid-1996 est.): 8,400,000.
Chief Cities (Dec. 31, 1992 est.): Sofia, the capital, 1,114,476; Plovdiv, 341,374; Varna, 308,601.
Government: *Head of state,* Peter Stoyanov, president (elected November 1996). *Head of government,* Zhan Videnov, prime minister (took office Jan. 25, 1995). *Legislature*—National Assembly.
Monetary Unit: Lev (135.0 leva equal U.S.$1, noncommercial rate, June 1996).
Gross Domestic Product (1994 est. U.S.$): $33,700,-000,000 (purchasing power parity).
Economic Indexes (1995, 1990 = 100): *Consumer Prices,* all items, 4,606.6; food, 4,936.1. *Industrial Production,* 68.
Foreign Trade (1994 U.S.$): *Imports,* $4,316,000,000; *exports,* $4,157,000,000.

The government continued to prop up obsolete and uncompetitive state-owned industries; only 5% of these enterprises were privatized. Moreover, the former communist *nomenklatura* controlled and exploited much of the economy through shady "economic groups" linked with the state, and corruption was rampant. An ambitious mass-privatization program remained stalled in parliament because of powerful vested interests.

As the financial crisis deepened, prices rose dramatically and the standard of living fell for much of the population. Bread shortages were reported in various parts of the country, while observers expected food and fuel shortages during the winter months. The central bank rapidly was running out of money to prop up the national currency (the lev) and to buy fuel and wheat. As a result of the economic crisis and official resistance to privatization, Bulgaria had the lowest level of foreign investment of any country in the region and more than one quarter of its insolvent banks were in receivership. A negative growth rate in the economy was forecast for 1996 and the annual inflation rate was estimated at about 240%. The victory of the reformist UDF in the presidential elections was unlikely to halt the economic decline.

Foreign Policy. Internationally, the Socialist government seemed to look more toward Moscow than to the West, signaling its support for the reintegration of the former USSR. Sofia was the only capital in the former Soviet bloc that was hesitant about membership in the North Atlantic Treaty Organization (NATO), even though it participated in NATO's Partnership for Peace program.

JANUSZ BUGAJSKI
Center for Strategic and International Studies

BURMA. *See* MYANMAR.

BUSINESS AND CORPORATE AFFAIRS

Strength in earnings and an overall favorable economic environment throughout 1996 disguised one of the most tumultuous years in recent corporate history in the United States. The earnings gains were consistent, ranged through businesses large and small, and were produced as much by efficient operations as economic strength. Through the third quarter, the return on equity of the Standard & Poor's 500-stock index averaged 22%, the highest for the period since the nation's economic recovery began in the early 1990s.

The performance was not sufficient to bring calm to the executive suite, however. The structures of old industries were changed radically, new companies emerged seemingly overnight, and old ones split up or changed product lines and marketing focus. As if pressures were not sufficient to test the agility and wisdom of management, corporate officials were pressured in ways unforeseen, and executive appointments and departures were everyday news. While at times the scene seemed one of disorder, academics suggested it was a creative ferment that would redesign markets for years to come. While most of the changes originated voluntarily within the private sector, some were imposed from without. Courts, regulators, and the U.S. Congress played major roles, with competition, discrimination, fraud, and health as concerns.

Legislation, Court Actions, Discrimination. The most momentous action came early with passage of a federal telecommunications bill that instantly changed that market, allowing local and long-distance phone companies to enter each other's provinces, freeing both to enter the cable-television business, and permitting cable companies to compete in the local phone area. After three years, cable-TV rates would be uncapped. And, in response to complaints, within two years new computers would include so-called "v-chips" to protect children from Internet pornography. (*See also* COMMUNICATION TECHNOLOGY.)

The tobacco industry faced problems of another sort. For one reason or another, it was in court and in the news all year long. Company executives swore to Congress that nicotine was not addictive, despite claims of medical authorities and at least one former high-level employee. (*See* SPECIAL REPORT, page 169.)

In another continuing investigation, Archer Daniels Midland Co. was fined $100 million after pleading guilty to charges that it fixed prices of two agricultural products. The company also agreed to assist the U.S. Justice Department in a continuing investigation into what the department said was an international conspiracy. Following the company's admission of guilt, executive vice-president Michael Andreas stepped down at least temporarily and corn-processing chief Terrance Wilson retired. Both were targets of the probe.

Discrimination, gender or racial, remained in the news for months, involving most prominently Mitsubishi Motors' manufacturing operation in Normal, IL, and Texaco Inc. The government filed charges of sexual harassment against Mitsubishi, as did 26 women workers in a class-action suit. An added stir was created by the company when it provided time off for workers to rally for the company. At Texaco the problems began later in the year with disclosure of a taped conversation among senior executives that led to a criminal investigation. It revealed not only a plot to destroy evidence sought in a discrimination suit by minority employees, but also belittling remarks made against these employees. Texaco agreed to pay more than $140 million to resolve the lawsuit and also said that it would make changes in its operations.

Prudential Insurance Co.'s continuing troubles were of another nature. It agreed in September to pay at least $410 million to settle lawsuits filed during the 1990s claiming it defrauded customers. The "no cap, unlimited settlement" could grow to more than $1 billion, but even that might not end the company's problems. Florida insurance regulators continued to probe the company's practices, alleging among other things that the company destroyed documents needed in their investigation. Still shocked by the extent of Prudential's violations, the public found its nerves strained further when it was discovered that Northeast Utilities, operator of five New England nuclear plants, regularly had practiced shortcuts to save money. The investigation revealed that supervisors delayed reporting violations of practices to the Nuclear Regulatory Commission (NRC), and then it was found that the NRC knew about the violations for a decade.

New Product Lines and Marketing Focus. Important as the court and regulatory issues were, they faded in relation to the changes resulting from voluntary actions and those dictated by private-sector market conditions. Many high-tech businesses burst upon the scene with new products and ways of doing things. The telecommunications industry and the delivery of information, of course, were changed forever by deregulation, and mergers and alliances followed. The medical-services and health-care industries continued to reposition themselves through agreements and mergers. And as spending on defense fell, companies such as Texas Instruments and Raytheon were compelled to reassess markets for their products. Innovation was in the air, and the competitive environment and relatively stable economy assured its continuation. Catalogue companies sold cars and even mansions. Seagram said it would deviate from the Distilled Spirits Council's self-imposed ban on TV ads. Even the used-car industry changed; car superstores—stressing fixed, "no haggle" pricing—sprang up around the country, competing not just with traditional used-car lots but with new-car dealers, too. Seeking to protect dealerships from losing their own used-car sales, the Big Three automakers and Honda created or tested used-car warranty programs.

Mergers and the Changing Marketplace. Evidence of other marketing changes were most obvious in mergers, but not exclusively so. Companies also divested themselves of operations. For example, late in the year, Texas Instruments sought bids on its defense-electronics holdings—valued at $2 billion or more—and some companies split into separate concerns. In October, Dun & Bradstreet became three companies: Cognizant Corp., a market-research company; A.C. Nielsen Corp., a provider of market information for consumer packagers; and a new D&B, whose assets included Moody's Investors Service and Reuben H. Donnelly, a publisher of yellow-page directories.

Still, mergers created the biggest news. The most electrifying was a $22 billion international agreement under which British Telecommunications PLC would acquire the 80% of MCI Communications Corp. it did not own already. Subject to regulatory hearings, the deal would be the largest foreign acquisition ever of a U.S. company, and the largest in the rapidly consolidating telecommunications industry. Earlier, Deutsche Telekom and France Télécom, two of Europe's biggest communications companies, had acquired 20% of Sprint Corp.; Bell Atlantic Corp. and Nynex Corp. had announced merger plans; and SBC Communications and Pacific Telesis Group—Southwest and California Bell units, respectively—made plans to join.

In October, CSX Corp. offered $8.5 billion for Conrail Inc., which was created by the government more than two decades earlier out of six bankrupt lines but now was the holder of a near monopoly of Northeast freight traffic. The bid quickly was topped by a $9.15 billion offer from Richmond-based Norfolk Southern Corp. Despite the higher

Bert C. Roberts, Jr., below left, *chairman of MCI Communications, and Sir Iain Vallance,* right, *chairman of British Telecommunications, oversaw the merger of their corporations, establishing the first transatlantic telephone carrier.*

© Bill Swersey/Gamma-Liaison

price, Conrail directors favored the CSX offer, and the year ended with the plan headed for the courts. In other mergers, Gillette Company announced that it had agreed to acquire Duracell International for some $7 billion, and Kohlberg Kravis Roberts planned to buy the nation's largest preschool and child-care company, Kindercare Learning Centers, for about $467 million. Still another industry, health and medical benefits, irreversibly was changed and challenged by a megamerger. Aetna Life & Casualty, cast in a century of tradition, moved strongly into a new area by merging with the smaller but highly experienced U.S. Healthcare, creating a network of 250,000 physicians and more than 2,500 hospitals. In December the Boeing Company announced that it planned to acquire McDonnell Douglas Corporation in a $13.3 billion deal.

Other than mergers, companies took multiple and original ways to deal with the changing marketplace. AT&T said it would eliminate 40,000 workers by the end of the year. Westinghouse Electric Corp., 110 years old, decided to spin off its old industrial businesses to concentrate on running CBS Inc., acquired in 1995. Westinghouse also announced that it would acquire Infinity Broadcasting for $3.9 billion. J.C. Penney Co., which had tried with only mediocre results to polish a dowdy image with high fashion, agreed to buy Eckerd Corp., a retail drugstore chain, for $2.5 billion. Federated Department Stores, the multistore chain, made plans for a first-time R.H. Macy's unit catalogue. America Online Inc., a provider of on-line computer services, reacted to competition from Internet providers by reorganizing into three divisions and writing off $385 million. Post Cereal, the industry's third-largest cereal company, countered competition by slashing wholesale prices 20%, compelling similar moves by Kellogg and General Mills. Quaker Oats—which lost heavily on its 1994, $1.7 billion purchase of Snapple, a natural-flavor-drink producer—sought vainly for an answer to big losses, but declined to retreat from hopes of having a nationally competitive product. Albert Dunlap, dubbed "Chainsaw Al" because of his reputation as a cost-cutter, announced plans to put home-appliance maker Sunbeam Corp. on track by eliminating half of its 12,000 jobs, by shrinking its number of factories from 26 to eight, and by dropping 87% of its products.

© Peter Morgan/Reuters Archive Photos

John R. Walter, the 49-year-old chairman of the commercial printers R.R. Donnelley & Sons, became president of AT&T and was expected to replace Robert E. Allen as chairman.

Management Changes. Understandably, change reverberated through top management layers. Ronald J. Burns of Union Pacific Railroad resigned and was replaced by Jerry Davis as president and by Dick Davidson as chief executive. Peter Bijur, a 30-year Texaco veteran, became chairman of the company in time to deal with the discrimination problem. Merrill Lynch, the nation's biggest broker, revealed plans to elevate David Komansky to chief executive officer from president and chief operating officer. At Motorola, Christopher Galvin, grandson of the founder, became chief executive officer. In December the Walt Disney Company announced that Michael Ovitz was resigning as president.

Tragedy rather than mere change also impinged on the executive suite. Weeks after the crash of Flight 800 with a loss of 230 lives, Trans World Airlines chief executive officer Jeffrey Erickson, widely credited with reviving the company's fortunes, announced his resignation. And in Russia, 41-year-old Paul Tatum—visionary founder of the Radisson Slavjanskaya Hotel and the adjoining Americom Business Center, widely used by American and European executives and diplomats—was gunned down gangland fashion in a Moscow subway station.

There was good news too. Aaron Feuerstein, owner of Malden Mills of Methuen, MA, who promised workers he would rebuild and maintain their paychecks and health insurance after a pre-Christmas 1995 fire almost destroyed the company, celebrated his 70th birthday in January with news that production would be back to 90% before midyear. Suppliers, workers, the local-area Chamber of Commerce, and others pitched in to help keep his promise.

JOHN CUNNIFF, *The Associated Press*

SPECIAL REPORT/BUSINESS AND CORPORATE AFFAIRS

The Tobacco Industry

On Aug. 9, 1996, in a suit against the Brown & Williamson Tobacco Corp., a state circuit-court jury in Jacksonville, FL, awarded $750,000 to a lung-cancer patient who had smoked cigarettes for 44 years. The jury found that cigarettes were a defective product and that makers were negligent in having failed to tell customers years ago that smoking was dangerous to their health. Although warnings were applied to cigarette packages in 1966, and cigarette companies by law could not be held liable after 1970 for alleged failure to warn smokers of hazards, millions of middle-aged and older Americans had begun smoking years earlier.

Court Suits. Those who had followed the tobacco wars over the previous three decades said the verdict—in favor of 66-year-old Grady Carter—was a landmark. Their view was supported by renewed interest in litigation by state officials seeking to recoup billions of dollars in Medicaid outlays they said were paid to treat smoking-related ailments. Fourteen states had suits pending at the time of the ruling.

While the industry, in 19 liability suits, had yet to pay a penny in damages, and Brown & Williamson indicated it would appeal the Jacksonville verdict, the joining of events made it especially significant. After seven tobacco-company chief executives swore to the U.S. Congress in March that cigarettes were not addictive, Liggett Group, smallest of the five major producers, broke ranks and entered into a first-ever settlement of lawsuits. Meanwhile, the U.S. Food and Drug Administration (FDA) proposed a ban on tobacco sales to minors under 18 years of age and sought to curtail industry advertising severely. That ban, which the companies opposed, was scheduled to take effect Feb. 28, 1997, and the industry had not countered it effectively. Then, bolstering the government's position, President Bill Clinton in August declared nicotine an addictive drug and sought to bring it under the control of the FDA.

Encouraged, the various antismoking organizations stepped up their attack. The National Center for Tobacco-Free Kids claimed that, each day, 3,000 youngsters began smoking, and that "one third of them would die from their addiction." It cited a University of Michigan study that showed teenage smoking had increased to the highest level in 16 years.

Tobacco Farmers and the Industry. Amid this powerful trend against smoking, a sense of anxiety was beginning to develop in the tobacco-producing states, where any major government action on tobacco likely would have substantial economic ramifications. Nationwide, 674 million acres (273 million ha) in the United States were planted with tobacco in 1995, down 10% from 1993. Tobacco is an especially lucrative crop for small farmers, who can realize profits as high as $1,000 per acre for tobacco; profits from other crops—including peanuts ($300 per acre), corn ($150 per acre), and soybeans ($100 per acre)—are much lower. Thus, tobacco farmers—as well as tobacco-company employees—worried that their economic livelihood was in jeopardy. Word of the award to Carter had sent tobacco-company stocks plummeting—at least momentarily. The stocks of the Philip Morris Companies and RJR Nabisco were affected particularly. However, both stocks rebounded in the months following and closed 1996 near their highest prices for the year. Both RJR Nabisco and Philip Morris are conglomerates that manufacture various consumer products in addition to tobacco, which contribute to their overall financial picture.

Powerful lobbies have evolved over the years that look after the interests of the tobacco companies and farmers. These lobbies and other tobacco interests have been the source of generous donations to the political campaigns of the elected officials who ultimately will be called upon to resolve the issue.

In May two U.S. companies—Philip Morris, the world's largest tobacco company, and U.S. Tobacco Co., the largest U.S. maker of smokeless tobacco—proposed legislation to counter the FDA advertising ban. As part of the proposed package, the tobacco industry would spend $250 million over five years to enforce youth antismoking campaigns. In return, they sought guarantees that the FDA would have no jurisdiction over tobacco products. The offer drew harsh criticism as nothing more than a public-relations ploy.

Overall, tobacco sales and profits increased in 1996, and cigarette sales abroad remained strong. The tobacco industry boasted a $45 billion business despite a sharp decrease in the number of smokers in the United States over the past several years. Exports of U.S. cigarettes, particularly to newly opened markets in Asia and Eastern Europe, accounted for the boom in sales.

JOHN CUNNIFF

CAMBODIA

In 1996 the political stability that had existed in Cambodia since the formation of the coalition government in 1993 was tested by growing factionalism. The weakened regime grappled with the unexpected fracturing of the Khmer Rouge and with accusations of human-rights abuses. But the government's commitment to economic reform helped retain critical foreign assistance and investment needed for reconstruction after decades of civil war.

Politics. A rift between First Prime Minister Norodom Ranariddh and Second Prime Minister Hun Sen erupted in March. Ranariddh vowed that his party would leave the ruling coalition if Hun Sen's party failed to divide power evenly at the district level. Hun Sen threatened to use the military force that he still largely controlled. Mediation by King Norodom Sihanouk helped the leaders reach a truce by midyear, but tensions remained high amid allegations that Hun Sen's supporters were harassing opposition politicians. A party office of Ranariddh was ransacked; members of the new Khmer Nation Party were arrested; and a prominent opposition newspaper editor was shot.

Reports that Khmer Rouge (KR) leader Pol Pot died in June appeared untrue. But the KR suffered a serious blow in August when one of the group's founders, Ieng Sary, defected with about half of the guerrillas' fighting force and control of lucrative gem mines and timber concessions. The defectors then declared a cease-fire and pledged to join the government army. King Sihanouk pardoned Ieng Sary, who had been under a 1979 death sentence for his part in the deaths of more than 1 million people. Royalists called for similar pardons for Princes Norodom Sirivudh and Norodom Chakrapong, who lived in exile after allegedly plotting to kill Hun Sen and stage a 1994 coup attempt, respectively.

CAMBODIA • Information Highlights

Official Name: Kingdom of Cambodia.
Location: Southeast Asia.
Area: 69,900 sq mi (181 040 km²).
Population (mid-1996 est.): 10,900,000.
Chief City (1991 est.): Phnom Penh, the capital, 900,000.
Government: *Head of state,* Norodom Sihanouk, king (acceded Sept. 24, 1993). *Head of government,* Prince Norodom Ranariddh, first premier (named Sept. 24, 1993); Hun Sen, second premier (named Sept. 24, 1993).
Monetary Unit: Riel (2,665.0 riels equal U.S.$1, August 1996).
Gross Domestic Product (1994 est. U.S.$): $6,400,000,000 (purchasing power parity).
Foreign Trade (1993 est. U.S.$): *Imports,* $479,300,000; *exports,* $283,600,000.

Economy. New foreign-investment projects, expanding trade, and additional foreign assistance fueled gross domestic product growth by about 7%. Asian foreign investors were encouraged by low import duties and Cambodia's plan to become a member of the Association for Southeast Asian Nations (ASEAN) and the ASEAN Free Trade Area. The United States' restoration of most-favored-nation status boosted prospects for trade with Western countries. Japan's $93 million pledge was the largest portion of $500 million promised by 16 nations attending a Tokyo aid conference. Other key donors included France, the United States, Australia, and Germany.

Economic growth, however, had an environmental cost and was distributed unevenly. International groups complained that logging was destroying Cambodia's forests at an alarming pace. Most people continued to live at subsistence levels with little or no electricity, a poor water supply, and rampant disease. Flooding and other disasters temporarily displaced 1 million people, and many others faced food shortages.

Foreign Affairs. Cambodian leaders reinforced plans to join ASEAN by visiting most ASEAN capitals. Visits by Thai and Vietnamese leaders, new economic agreements with Thailand, and the establishment of air and telephone links with Vietnam demonstrated the growing interconnection of the Southeast Asian peninsula.

Cambodian leaders had difficulty balancing political ties to China and North Korea with economic links to those countries' foes, Taiwan and South Korea. While reaffirming Phnom Penh's "one-China" policy, Hun Sen played down Taiwan's importance as a leading foreign investor. King Sihanouk highlighted his ties to North Korea when he blocked plans to establish full diplomatic relations with Seoul. Relations with the United States were marred by U.S. legislation criticizing Cambodia for human-rights abuses and by Washington's decision to put Cambodia on its list of drug-trafficking nations.

Social Issues. A survey of young people's sexual behavior suggested that they were unaware of or failed to consider the growing AIDS problem....Environmentalists and religious leaders warned that plans to expand the tourism sector near Angkor Wat would damage the religious site....Cambodians were disappointed when an international conference failed to ban land mines, which have maimed one in every 236 people in the country.

CHRISTINE VAN ZANDT
U.S. Government Analyst on East Asian Affairs

Canada

During 1996, Canada's federal and provincial governments cut services to reduce deficits and avoided consensus on how to respond to the narrow federalist victory in Quebec's 1995 referendum on sovereignty. Canadians worried about jobs, Quebec, and the weather.

Government. In Ottawa the Liberal government completed its third full year with majority public support in the polls. Prime Minister Jean Chrétien was blamed by many for the closeness of the Quebec referendum, for breaking promises to end the North American Free Trade Agreement (NAFTA) and the unpopular goods and services tax (GST), and for assaulting a separatist demonstrator in Hull. However, outside his native Quebec, Chrétien's popularity remained fairly high.

In a postreferendum shuffle in January, Montreal academic Stéphane Dion and lawyer Pierre Pettigrew entered the cabinet—the former as a hard-line, intellectual antiseparatist, and the latter as a link to provincial Liberals. Lucienne Robillard moved to the citizenship and immigration ministry with a promise to remove references to Canada's queen in the citizenship oath. Lloyd Axworthy left human resources for foreign affairs, leaving his portfolio to Douglas Young, who, as minister of transport, had privatized air control and the Canadian National Railways. Ret. Adm. Fred Mifflin replaced fellow Newfoundlander Brian Tobin in fisheries and oceans after the latter returned to become provincial premier.

Among pieces of legislation enacted in 1996 was a gay-rights amendment to the Human Rights Act. It passed in the House of Commons, 153–76, with the Bloc Québécois (BQ) and most Liberals in support, and all but one Reformer in opposition. Max Yalden, head of the Canadian Human Rights Commission, retired in 1996, citing paternalism in aboriginal policies, unemployment among the disabled, and a 30% gap in male and female earnings as unfinished business.

In March by-elections the Liberals won the five seats they had held formerly. The separatist BQ easily held the seat vacated by Lucien Bouchard when he became premier of Quebec in January. The following month, Michel Gauthier assumed BQ leadership. The by-election results gave the Reform Party—which finished a strong second in several contests—hope that it was beating the Conservatives for right-wing votes in eastern Canada.

The GST. In 1993 the Liberal Party had promised to replace the hated GST. That depended on "harmonizing" federal and provincial sales taxes, an idea that faced opposition in some provinces. Conservative Alberta, for example, had no provincial tax, while Ontario Premier Mike Harris opposed any tax increase. In contrast, Liberal governments in Newfoundland, Nova Scotia, and New

At their annual meeting in Jasper, Alta., in August 1996, Canada's provincial premiers agreed to establish a council to rewrite the rules governing social programs. Quebec's Lucien Bouchard did not attend the gathering.

© Dave Buston/Canapress

Brunswick agreed to cut merged rates from 18–19% to 15% but to allow books, fuel, and children's clothes to be taxed. When Ottawa promised C$1 billion to cover overall tax losses, richer provinces protested.

Deputy Prime Minister Sheila Copps—reminded of her 1993 pledge that the GST would be abolished—resigned from her seat in the Commons in May. However, she easily regained the seat with a by-election victory in June. Another Liberal, John Nunziata, was expelled from caucus for voting against the government's budget, which did not end the GST.

Provinces. At the annual first ministers' meeting in Ottawa in June, only Quebec and British Columbia (BC) opposed the creation of a national securities commission and all welcomed responsibility for job training, forestry, and mining. However, First Nations leader Ovide Mercredi complained that he had not been admitted as an equal of the premiers, and BC Premier Glen Clark emerged to denounce federal arrogance and intransigence.

Replacing Jacques Parizeau as Quebec premier gave Lucien Bouchard more power but it also saddled him with brutal choices. If, as he promised, his main purpose was to prepare Quebec economically for independence, many observers wondered who would be asked to make sacrifices. Unions and poverty organizations refused concessions to ease Quebec's serious financial shortfall, and language militants renewed their assault on English.

Meanwhile, more militant antisovereignist leaders insisted on their language rights, debated partitioning a sovereign Quebec, and insisted that Ottawa go to court to determine the constitutionality of secession. Aware that such notions offended many pro-federal, French-speaking Québécois, federal Attorney General Allan Rock held off until Quebec Justice Minister Paul Bégin declared that the province did not recognize Canada's 1982 constitution. By referring Quebec's right to secede to the Supreme Court, Rock pushed a furious Premier Bouchard to threaten a snap election to clear the way for a new sovereignty vote. In the end, however, Bouchard decided only to boycott the proceedings. Another Ottawa-Quebec row was avoided when the federally appointed lieutenant governor, Jean-Louis Roux, resigned on November 5 after an uproar over his admission that he had drawn a swastika on his lab coat and marched with right-wing nationalists in 1942.

In October, Newfoundland Premier Brian Tobin launched a new campaign to discredit the fixed-price contract that the province had signed in 1969 with Quebec to develop a hydroelectric facility at Churchill Falls. Claiming that Hydro-Quebec earned billions while its poorer neighbor paid to run the power project, Tobin gathered sympathy outside Quebec. The Bouchard government, however, secure in two Supreme Court decisions on the deal, refused to budge.

Budgeting. Unemployment, which sat at 9.9% in September, remained a tough issue for the ruling Liberal government. The government boasted of 600,000 new jobs created since 1993, but critics pointed to the estimated 1.4 million Canadians who were out of work. Some provinces tried tax cuts to stimulate job creation, but cuts to health, education, and other services added to the jobless total. Critics urged cuts to payroll taxes. Finance Minister Paul Martin insisted that deficit reduction and the resulting lower interest rates were the

THE CANADIAN MINISTRY

Jean Chrétien, prime minister
David Anderson, minister of transport
Lloyd Axworthy, minister of foreign affairs
Ethel Blondin-Andrew, secretary of state for training and youth
Don Boudria, minister of international cooperation and minister responsible for Francophonie
Martin Cauchon, secretary of state for the Federal Office of Regional Development—Quebec
Raymond Chan, secretary of state for Asia-Pacific
Sheila Copps, deputy prime minister and minister of Canadian heritage
David Dingwall, minister of health
Stéphane Dion, minister of intergovernmental affairs and president of the Queen's Privy Council for Canada
Arthur Eggleton, minister of international trade
Joyce Fairbairn, leader of the government in the Senate and minister with special responsibility for literacy
Hedy Fry, secretary of state for multiculturalism and the status of women
Alfonso Gagliano, deputy leader of the government in the House of Commons and minister of labor
Jon Gerrard, secretary of state for science, research and development, and western economic diversification
Ralph Goodale, minister of agriculture and agri-food
Herbert Eser Gray, leader of the government in the House of Commons and solicitor general of Canada
Ron Irwin, minister of Indian affairs and northern development
Lawrence MacAulay, secretary of state for veterans and the Atlantic Canada Opportunities Agency
John Manley, minister of industry, the Atlantic Canada Opportunities Agency, and western economic diversification, and minister responsible for the Federal Office of Regional Development—Canada
Sergio Marchi, minister of the environment
Diane Marleau, minister of public works and government services
Paul Martin, minister of finance
Marcel Massé, president of the Treasury board and minister responsible for infrastructure
Anne McLellan, minister of natural resources
Fred Mifflin, minister of fisheries and oceans
Douglas Peters, secretary of state for international financial institutions
Pierre Pettigrew, minister of human-resources development
Fernand Robichaud, secretary of state for agriculture and fisheries
Lucienne Robillard, minister of citizenship and immigration
Allan Rock, minister of justice and attorney general of Canada
Christine Stewart, secretary of state for Latin America and Africa
Jane Stewart, minister of national revenue
Douglas Young, minister of defense and veterans affairs

© Mark O'Neill/"Toronto Sun"/Canapress

Developments in Canada's labor movement in 1996 included a five-week strike by the Ontario Public Service Employees Union. Job security and severance terms were key issues in the walkout.

correct job-creation strategy, but he also promised a C$1 billion infrastructure fund and more money for a Working Income Supplement to low-income families.

Martin announced a new budget on March 6. The budget was designed to cut the deficit to C$24.3 billion for fiscal year 1997 and to C$17 billion for fiscal 1998, down from C$37.5 billion four years earlier. He promised more spending cuts, but few tax or spending changes. The government accepted a controversial 1995 court decision by forcing the contributor of alimony payments, not the recipient, to pay tax on them. Martin's most painful measure was reform of the Canada Pension Plan. Respectful of a powerful seniors' lobby, the budget reserved higher premiums and lower benefits for Canadians under age 60.

Business and Labor. Canada's labor movement, quiescent through much of the decade, awoke in Ontario in a series of daylong protests, including an October strike by 55,000 civil servants against a provincial government intent on downsizing public services. Tense labor negotiations also focused attention on the Canadian auto industry. In September the Canadian Auto Workers (CAW) signed a new labor agreement with Chrysler Canada. However, a tradition of pattern bargaining collapsed in October, when General Motors refused to accept the same contract, rejecting union demands on outsourcing and job protection. A long strike by the CAW threatened the central Canadian manufacturing economy but the dispute ended in compromise three weeks later. Ford accepted the pattern.

On the prairies farmers harvested record crops, though quality was cut by harvesttime snowfalls. With world prices high, some farmers demanded freedom from the Canadian Wheat Board's official monopoly on marketing their grain and some staged protests by trucking their crop to the United States. Agriculture Minister Ralph Goodale promised a vote to reform marketing practices affecting barley growers, but defended the board's control of wheat marketing. Alberta prepared a court challenge to a half century of orderly marketing.

The status of huge natural-gas deposits off Nova Scotia's Sable Island also was the source of controversy. Competing interests in several provinces were seeking support to transport the gas to either Boston or Quebec City.

Foreign Affairs. In January seven provincial premiers accompanied Chrétien on a Team Canada trade mission to India, Pakistan, Malaysia, and Indonesia, collecting

CANADA • Information Highlights

Official Name: Canada.
Location: Northern North America.
Area: 3,851,792 sq mi (9 976 140 km²).
Population (mid-1996 est.): 30,000,000.
Chief Cities (1991 census): Ottawa, the capital, 313,987; Toronto, 635,395; Montreal, 1,017,666.
Government: *Head of state,* Elizabeth II, queen; represented by Roméo LeBlanc, governor-general (took office February 1995). *Head of government,* Jean Chrétien, prime minister (took office Nov. 4, 1993). *Legislature*—Parliament: Senate and House of Commons.
Monetary Unit: Canadian dollar (1.3543 dollars equal U.S.$1, Dec. 4, 1996).
Gross Domestic Product (1994 est. U.S.$): $639,800,000,000 (purchasing power parity).
Economic Indexes: *Consumer Prices* (Oct. 1996, 1986 = 100): all items, 136.2; food, 128.3. *Industrial Production* (1995, 1990 = 100): 108.
Foreign Trade (1995 U.S.$): *Imports,* $168,055,000,000; *exports,* $192,204,000,000.

C$8.7 billion in firm and prospective deals and criticizing local human-rights records more overtly than they had in China in 1995.

A number of political and trade disputes continued with Washington, notably over the Helms-Burton Act, which punished foreign firms that did business with Cuba. Officials also debated Canadian regulation of so-called "split-run" editions of U.S. magazines, which receive the same content as U.S. editions but are filled with Canadian advertising. Washington also demanded that Ottawa open its borders to U.S. dairy, poultry, and eggs.

Canada played an active role regarding the refugee situation in Zaire. On November 6, Raymond Chrétien, a UN envoy from Canada, was named to seek a solution to the problem of some 1.2 million ethnic Hutu refugees threatened by starvation and disease in eastern Zaire. Canada later submitted to the UN Security Council a plan calling for the establishment of a peace force to provide food and protection to the threatened refugees. Canada's Lt. Gen. Maurice Baril was named to command the mission. (*See* REFUGEES AND IMMIGRATION.)

Defense. Some C$2 billion in budget cuts closed bases, ended careers, and stalled equipment programs for the Canadian Forces. In January, Defense Minister David Collenette announced the appointment of the youngest military chief of staff ever, Gen. Jean Boyle.

In October, however, both Collenette and Boyle resigned. A judicial inquiry into the 1993 murder of young Somalis by a Canadian airborne regiment on peacekeeping duties claimed that documents had been withheld. As the inquiry widened, Boyle ordered military personnel to conduct a one-day search for documents in April. Later that month, however, it was alleged that Boyle, as a public-relations chief in 1993, had shared in a cover-up of the events. When Boyle blamed subordinates for "lack of moral fiber" in giving him false documents, he became the target for politicians, journalists, and retired generals who denounced his leadership qualities. The Chrétien government initially defended Boyle, but when Collenette resigned on October 4 over an unrelated error of judgment, Boyle followed on October 8. Human Resources Minister Douglas Young replaced Collenette, proclaiming a goal of restoring morale and Canada's military reputation.

Justice. The year's most sensational judicial case was former Prime Minister Brian Mulroney's C$50 million libel suit against the federal justice department and the Royal Canadian Mounted Police for allegations made in a letter to Swiss authorities, seeking evidence about C$5 million in kickbacks. A Swiss accountant claimed that Mulroney received the money in 1988 for pressing Air Canada to buy Airbus aircraft for its fleet.

Corrections Canada Commissioner John Edwards resigned in April after a judicial inquiry blamed his organization for subjecting six women prisoners to strip searches by male guards and other abuse after a 1994 riot at the Prison for Women in Kingston, Ont.

Environment. The 1995–96 winter in most of Canada was long and harsh, and the summer was sodden. Particularly damaging were heavy floods in Quebec's Saguenay valley.

A happier story for the environment was the successful salvage of a sunken oil barge. The *Irving Whale* had leaked oil and PCBs since it sank near the Magdalen Islands in 1970. In July it was successfully raised and then shipped to Halifax. Scientists reported that tough measures seemed to be restoring Atlantic cod stocks, prompting demands for a return to fishing. A comparable overfishing crisis on the Pacific coast was aggravated by continuing battles between Ottawa and the British Columbian government and between Alaska and its southern neighbors.

Health. An inquiry by Ontario's Justice Minister Horace Krever into blood transfusions in the 1980s tainted with the human immunodeficiency virus (HIV) secured the right to criticize Red Cross and government officials in the blood system but not politicians who were not involved directly in the tragedy. Critics complained that the inquiry had cost more than C$13 million without providing a report. Meanwhile, Krever complained that federal and provincial health ministers were preparing a new system for blood products without waiting for his report.

DESMOND MORTON, *Director*
McGill Institute for the Study of Canada

The Economy

A lower dollar, falling interest rates, and dormant inflation fueled an export-led recovery for the Canadian economy in 1996. This recovery began during the first quarter, when households—buoyed by the creation of 129,000 jobs between November 1995 and March 1996 and the falling prices of old homes—began to spend again.

Growth and Trade. By March, sales of existing homes had posted solid growth, while sales of durable goods climbed after two flat months. In the meantime, economic funda-

© Jacques Boissinot/Canapress

Flash floods swept through eastern Quebec, including Chicoutimi (above), *during the summer of 1996. Some ten lives were lost and residential- and business-property damage was estimated at C$600 million as a result of the disaster.*

mentals conducive to growth improved significantly. The economy was almost free of inflation, while interest rates tumbled rapidly. By July, economic growth had gained some momentum when a surge in manufacturing helped in boosting gross domestic product at factor cost by 1.8%, the highest monthly growth since late 1994. Output increased in 18 of 21 major groups. Consequently, 25,000 manufacturing jobs were added.

Construction activity also became brisk when home building rose 1.6% in July. Higher demand for construction-related materials stimulated growth in wholesale trade, which rose 1.4% in August. By August, Canada's merchandise-trade surplus shot to C$4.02 billion, after recording monthly total exports of C$23.15 billion and imports of C$19.13 billion. This trade surplus, by rendering Canadian currency more attractive to foreigners, paved the way for further interest-rate reductions. The Bank of Canada lowered its trend-setting interest rate for the 20th time in a year and a half. Also, by August, output in mining, construction, and wholesale trade took another upturn; manufacturing and retail trade fell.

Housing Market and Employment. Similarly, the housing market, spurred by dwindling mortgage rates, was 20.5% stronger during the first nine months of the year than during the corresponding period of 1995. Such brisk housing markets got translated into C$3.9 billion worth of housing permits between July and September.

Overall, Canadians remained bullish on the economy as stock markets boomed and corporate profits rose dramatically. The irony, however, was that while people were feeling better about the economy, they remained gloomy about their own prospects. This became consistent for an economy where unemployment became double-digit, wage gains were modest, real incomes were declining, and governments were slashing transfers to people, including unemployment benefits and welfare payments. All this produced a lackluster growth in retail sales. Over the first eight months of 1996, nominal retail sales were 0.1% lower in real terms.

Modest economic growth of 1.3% over the first nine months failed to shake the lethargy from the labor market. Although 148,000 jobs were created from January to October, the seasonally adjusted unemployment rate rose from 9.9% in September to 10% in October. During that month manufacturing jobs fell by 30,000, followed by 14,000 job losses in transportation, communication, and other utilities. Employment growth (36,000) in the primary sector was negated by some of the job losses.

R. P. SETH, *Professor Emeritus*
Mount Saint Vincent University

Provinces and Territories

ALBERTA. Premier Ralph Klein's Progressive Conservative (PC) government in Alberta was awash in revenue in 1996. With every month that passed, provincial Treasurer Jim Dinning seemed to be announcing a higher budgetary surplus.

The Economy. In February the government unveiled a C$13.6 billion budget and predicted a surplus of C$23 million, giving the province its first forecast surplus budget in 12 years. The budget contained no new taxes or tax increases, but a variety of personal- and business-tax cuts spread over several years and intended to boost the economy. In August the government passed legislation to cut repayment of the accumulated debt to 13 years rather than the planned 25 years. The net accumulated debt was C$6.3 billion, but the province also had C$20 billion in liabilities it said was secured by assets of equal value.

Then, in September, the government announced it had reduced spending by more than C$1 billion and the 1995–96 surplus would be at least C$769 million. But in October, Klein predicted that if oil prices—from which the provincial government gets much of its revenue—stayed high, a C$1 billion surplus would be possible. By early November all signs pointed to the surplus being even higher than C$1 billion. Klein's success in cutting spending and producing surpluses could give him an edge in the election expected in 1997.

Politics. Liberal Opposition leader Grant Mitchell's hopes of undermining the popularity of Premier Klein's PC government waned in 1996, even though the Liberals launched all-out attacks on Klein's cost-cutting programs. Popularity polls showed Klein and his party well ahead of the Liberals. A number of Liberal members of the Legislative Assembly (MLAs) said they would not seek reelection. Government-cabinet ministers—including Treasurer Dinning, Justice Minister Brian Evans, Intergovernmental Affairs Minister Ken Rostad, Advanced Education Minister Jack Ady, and Science and Research Minister Dianne Mirosh—also announced they would not seek reelection. They claimed the government's aim of balancing the budget and revamping health, education, and welfare programs had been accomplished. Speaker of the Legislature Stanley Schumacher, also a government member, said he, too, would not seek reelection.

Justice. The story that dominated 1996 newspaper headlines and television newscasts centered on socialite Dorothy Joudrie, 61, who in 1995 had shot her husband, Earl Joudrie, six times and had been charged with attempted murder. Earl Joudrie is one of Canada's most prominent businessmen and has served as chairman of the board of such companies as Gulf Canada Resources, Algoma Steel, and Canadian Tire. At Mrs. Joudrie's trial in May, the defense convinced the jury that the accused had been in a "robotic state" when she shot her estranged husband and was not criminally responsible for her actions. The acquittal was greeted with outrage across much of the country. Mrs. Joudrie was ordered to spend some time at the Albert (psychiatric) Hospital, and to have ongoing psychiatric care.

Transitions. In March former Alberta Liberal Party leader and prominent oilman Nick Taylor was appointed to the Canadian Senate by Prime Minister Jean Chrétien. In April former federal Liberal cabinet minister H.A. "Bud" Olson was sworn in as lieutenant governor of Alberta. Both appointments were greeted with charges of patronage by Alberta's Progressive Conservatives.

PAUL JACKSON, *"The Calgary Sun"*

BRITISH COLUMBIA. British Columbia's 1996 provincial election was much anticipated, but few could have predicted the outcome.

Government and Politics. In February a New Democratic Party leadership convention chose Minister of Employment and Investment Glen Clark to replace retiring Mike Harcourt as party leader and premier. The exposure of personal share holdings by BC Hydro senior officials in a Pakistan public-private hydroelectric-power venture led the new premier to fire the chair and president of BC Hydro immediately.

In a brief spring legislative session, Bill 21 prevented any labor disruption in the health and education sectors during the upcoming election campaign by imposing industrial inquiry or mediation reports. Despite a loss of 11 seats, the New Democrats were returned to office on May 28 with 39 members of the Legislative Assembly (MLAs) and 39.45% of the vote. The Liberal opposition led by Gordon Campbell received the largest share of the vote, at 41.82%, but secured only 33 seats. The Reform Party retained two northern seats and the Progressive Democratic Alliance, one seat.

Public Policy. The 1996–97 provincial budget was reintroduced in the newly elected 36th Legislative Assembly, with expenditures of C$20.572 billion and revenues of C$20.659 billion. Personal- and small-business income taxes were cut by 1% in July 1996, with a further personal-income-tax point cut set for July 1997. College and university tuition, public auto insurance, and BC Hydro electricity rates were frozen. It later was revealed that the 1995–96 budget was not, as had been claimed, balanced, and balancing the current budget required expenditure cuts of C$750 million over the next 18 months. The budget controversy deepened in the fall when it was announced that C$400 million would be transferred from the BC Forest Renewal Fund, made up of dedicated stumpage revenues.

A royal commission was formed to examine workers' compensation. Concerns for child protection following the deaths of children under government care led to the creation of a new ministry for children and families and an independent children's commissioner.

Intergovernmental Relations. Early in 1996 the province successfully secured a constitutional-amendment veto for British Columbia in the federal government's constitutional-reform package. A C$80 million license-buyback plan for the Pacific-coast fishery by federal Fisheries Minister Fred Mifflin was not received well, but the provincial and federal governments formally agreed to pursue increased provincial participation in salmon-fishery management.

NORMAN J. RUFF, *University of Victoria*

MANITOBA. In Manitoba in 1996, the government of Gary Filmon produced its eighth successive budget with no significant tax increases; strikes were widespread; and Winnipeg lost its National Hockey League team. The province experienced an unusually harsh winter.

Labor and Privatization. A spending freeze by the government led to salary cuts for most government employees. In 1995–96, Manitoba experienced the most strikes since the general strike of 1919, with more than 250,000 days lost in all. Numerous government agencies experienced strikes. At the University of Manitoba, professors walked out for 23 days. Home-care workers, casino staff, and many other employees of government agencies were on the picket lines. In every case, the strikers had wages rolled back by from 2% to 3%. Manitoba's civil servants accepted a rollback without going on strike.

In November 1996 the Filmon government privatized the Manitoba Telephone System, after an attempted filibuster by the New Democratic Party opposition. The New Democrats claimed that privatization would lead to higher phone rates for rural customers, most of whom normally support the Conservatives. Despite the opposi-

© Chuck Stoody/Canapress Photo

Glen Clark, who took over from Michael Harcourt as leader of British Columbia's New Democratic Party and provincial premier in February 1996, saw his party returned to power—but with a trimmed majority—in May elections.

tion, the telephone system's shares quickly sold out, even before their price was announced.

Weather. Manitoba also had its worst winter since records were kept, with snow on the ground for more than five months. The month of January had the longest cold snap on record. On July 16 there was a severe hailstorm, with hailstones the size of golf balls. Losses—mostly to early planted crops and damaged cars—cost more than C$100 million. However, the remainder of the summer was one of the longest on record—with no major freezing until October—producing a bumper harvest.

Tourism and Sports. In July the Manitoba and Saskatchewan governments, with additional funding from a federal loan, committed more than C$1 million to the northern town of Churchill to boost it as a tourist attraction and port. In October the federally owned Canadian National Railways announced that it was selling its money-losing line to the town to a U.S.-based short-line conglomerate. Expectations were that this would make the line more viable.

Sports activities were dominated by the move of the Winnipeg Jets to Phoenix, AZ. Considerable public funding had gone to the campaign to keep the Jets in Winnipeg. An entertainment group, Mr. Canada's Touring Network, planned to purchase four historic theaters in central Winnipeg to be the base of "Nashville North." Some public funding was involved.

MICHAEL KINNEAR, *University of Manitoba*

NEW BRUNSWICK. A three-year plan to overhaul New Brunswick's health-care system—trimming administrative costs and raising user fees on subsidized prescription medicines—was made public on Feb. 12, 1996. Under the plan, adults on welfare would pay C$4 for a prescription—up from C$2—while children's prescriptions would double to C$2 from C$1. The blueprint also called for a ceiling on doctors' medicare billings.

The government of Premier Frank McKenna planned to invest C$50 million to help welfare recipients and young people crash the labor market. A four-year program announced on March 19 aimed to give 4,000 jobless people precious work experience and occupational skills. Participants would earn $250 a week for occupations ranging from out-of-doors maintenance work to studies in computer technology. Enrollment in the program was voluntary.

Finances. For the second straight year, the province's finances tipped into the black column. Presenting the fiscal 1996–97 budget in Fredericton on February 15, Finance Minister Edmond Blanchard forecast a surplus of nearly C$100 million on revenues of just less than C$4.5 billion and expenditures of C$4.4 billion. Seven hundred more public-sector jobs were being eliminated, bringing total cuts to 3,700 in four years.

Four months later, on June 25, Blanchard announced a C$51 million payment against the C$5.5 billion provincial debt. Conservative Opposition Leader Bernard Valcourt accused the Liberal government of juggling the books and claimed the actual debt payment was only about C$5 million.

Labor and Prisons. One of the longest and bitterest labor disputes in Atlantic Canadian history ended August 13 when employees of the Irving Oil Co. refinery in Saint John agreed to return to work after a 27-month strike.

A staggering 87% of New Brunswick jail inmates were repeat offenders. Solicitor General Jane Berry cited the statistic in announcing on April 10 the closure of four of the ten provincial jails. Most of the C$5.4 million savings would be plowed into rehabilitation programs.

JOHN BEST, *"Canada World News"*

NEWFOUNDLAND. The year 1996 was one of significant political change for Newfoundland.

Politics. Clyde Wells announced on Dec. 28, 1995, that he would retire as premier and leader of the provincial Liberal Party. By March 14, 1996, the province had a new premier, Brian Tobin, and a newly elected House of Assembly in which the standings were: 37 Liberals, nine Progressive Conservatives (PCs), one New Democrat, and one Independent. Lynn Verge, who lost her seat by seven votes, resigned as PC leader and was replaced by Loyola Sullivan. A record number of women—seven—was elected to the House on February 22, and four of them were appointed to the 16-member Liberal cabinet. The May budget brought no new taxes, but borrowing continued in the C$50 million range and about 1,000 civil servants faced layoffs.

The Liberal Member of Parliament, William Rompkey, was named to the Senate. In the subsequent by-election, another Liberal, Lawrence O'Brian, won by 1,000 votes over his Reform Party opponent. Arthur Max House was to take over as lieutenant governor in February 1997.

Educational Reform. The issue of educational reform failed to reach a conclusion in 1996. In July a provincial bill requesting amendment to Newfoundland's Terms of

CANADIAN PROVINCES AND TERRITORIES • Information Highlights

Province	Population in (millions)	Area (sq mi)	Area (km²)	Capital	Head of State and Government
Alberta	2.7	255,286	661 190	Edmonton	H.A. Olson, lieutenant governor Ralph Klein, premier
British Columbia	3.7	365,946	947 800	Victoria	Garde Gardom, lieutenant governor Glen Clark, premier
Manitoba	1.1	250,946	649 950	Winnipeg	Yvon Dumont, lieutenant governor Gary Filmon, premier
New Brunswick	7.6	28,355	73 440	Fredericton	Margaret Norrie McCain, lieutenant governor Frank McKenna, premier
Newfoundland	5.8	156,649	405 720	St. John's	Frederick W. Russell, lieutenant governor Brian Tobin, premier
Northwest Territories	.07	1,304,903	3 379 700	Yellowknife	Don Morin, government leader
Nova Scotia	9.3	21,425	55 491	Halifax	J. James Kinley, lieutenant governor John Savage, premier
Ontario	11.0	412,580	1 068 580	Toronto	Henry Jackman, lieutenant governor Mike Harris, premier
Prince Edward Island	1.4	2,185	5 660	Charlottetown	Gilbert Clements, lieutenant governor Pat Binns, premier
Quebec	7.3	594,857	1 540 680	Quebec City	Martial Asselin, lieutenant governor Lucien Bouchard, premier
Saskatchewan	1.0	251,865	652 330	Regina	John N. Wiebe, lieutenant governor Roy Romanow, premier
Yukon	.03	186,660	483 450	Whitehorse	Piers McDonald, government leader

Union with Canada (1949) so that the province's church-run schools could be reformed passed the House of Assembly unanimously. The legislation easily passed the federal House of Commons, but lost because the Senate refused to pass the bill. Subsequently the federal House of Commons passed the bill alone and the change in the constitution became final. In the meantime the province tabled a new education act that was expected to be implemented for September 1997. Chiefly, there would be a reduction in the number of elected school boards.

Nickel and Oil. Early in the year the size of the nickel find at Voisey's Bay, Labrador, was pegged at an astounding 150 million tons. In May, Inco Ltd. purchased the site for C$4.3 billion. No decision was made in 1996 on Premier Tobin's insistence that the smelter must be built in Newfoundland. Native land claims in Labrador have been put on a fast track by the provincial government and it was hoped that a settlement would be reached before the opening of the development stages of the mine in 1997.

The platform for Hibernia oil production was completed on time and under budget. That meant the final layoff of about 5,000 workers. The expected "tow-out" of the massive rig was set for June 1997.

SUSAN MCCORQUODALE
Memorial University

NORTHWEST TERRITORIES. During 1996, Canada's first diamond mine—to be constructed about 185 mi (300 km) north of Yellowknife in the Northwest Territories—received federal approval, and preparation continued for dividing the Northwest Territories into two new territories on April 1, 1999.

Mining. The go-ahead for Canada's first diamond mine followed environmental-review hearings and agreements on jobs, training, and benefits between BHP Canada and aboriginal organizations. BHP was expected to spend C$32 million in wages and provide 1,000 temporary construction jobs before the mine opens in 1998. During the expected 25 years of operation, the BHP diamond mine would have a workforce of 830 people.

The prospect of new mining jobs was welcomed by many residents during a year when the government of the Northwest Territories eliminated more than 345 positions as part of its deficit-cutting efforts. It also imposed five unpaid days of leave—known as "Donny Days" after Premier Don Morin—on its unionized employees.

Dividing the Territories. The Legislative Assembly invited the public to suggest names for the new western territory after the Northwest Territories is divided in 1999. Despite a campaign by a cabinet minister for a name that reflects the aboriginal cultures of the territory, and a tongue-in-cheek campaign for the name "Bob," the majority of suggestions supported keeping the name "Northwest Territories." A draft constitutional proposal for the western territory was released for public review.

Meanwhile, a proposal for gender parity in the new legislative assembly of Nunavut, as the new eastern territory will be called, received a positive response from Indian Affairs Minister Ron Irwin in December. The proposal, which would guarantee half of the legislative seats for women and half for men, was supported by 72% of the mostly male delegates at a November Nunavut leaders' meeting. Irwin said he was unsure his support would convince his federal colleagues to change the federal Nunavut Act to allow gender parity in the new territory.

AGGIE BROCKMAN
Freelance Writer, Yellowknife

NOVA SCOTIA. The John Savage government enacted 20 laws in 1996, touching municipal government, education, protection of adopted children, inspection and sale of meat and meat products, prevention of cruelty to animals, occupational health and safety, and health care. The government's preoccupation with developing cost-cutting measures was so strong that it enacted the Financial Measure Act, under which all future governments must balance their budgets and seek legislative approval whenever their expenditures exceed 1% of their budgeted amounts.

Cost Cutting. As part of the expenditure-reducing agenda, the government established the Queen Elizabeth II Health Sciences Center after amalgamating the existing four Halifax hospitals. The streamlined health-care-delivery system would cut 200 beds and 500 jobs over five years. Similarly, the municipalities of Halifax, Dartmouth, and Bedford were united into Halifax Regional Municipality to eliminate duplication and waste. Expenditures on postsecondary education were slashed, forcing the provincial universities to freeze their hirings of new faculty and rationalize spending by forming a consortium of Halifax universities. The number of school boards was chopped from 22 to seven and a dozen education bureaucrats were laid off.

The government also decided to restructure its civil service by downsizing the departments of finance, consumer affairs, housing, municipal affairs, transportation, public works and mines, and energy and resources. Consequently, the total number of provincial civil servants, compared with three years earlier, fell by 6,000.

Budget and the Economy. The provincial economy posted 1.2% annual growth. Factory shipments grew 5% during the first seven months over the same period of 1995. This was followed by brisk trade that touched the C$1.53 billion mark for the first half of 1996. Retail sales were up 3.9% for the first half. Housing starts were up 28% over the first seven months. Work started on the C$650 million Stora Forest Product Mill and the C$113 million Trans Canada Highway in northern Nova Scotia.

Such positive trends, however, failed to stimulate the labor market. Seasonally adjusted unemployment rose from 11.3% in January to 12.9% in November.

R.P. SETH
Mount Saint Vincent University, Halifax

ONTARIO. Undaunted by an increasingly vociferous opposition, Premier Mike Harris' Progressive Conservative government pressed forward with its program of deficit reduction and government restructuring. The May budget delivered the largest tax cut in provincial history. Reductions for upper-income earners, however, were offset by a new Fair Share Health Care Levy, a progressive tax to pay for the elimination of the payroll tax on small businesses. The deficit was estimated to fall to C$8.2 billion; a drop in revenues from tax cuts and reduced federal grants offset by cuts in program spending were responsible for the shortfall.

Social Welfare. A "workfare" scheme requiring all able-bodied welfare recipients to perform community service was announced in June and introduced in 20 communities in September. All municipalities would have to set up programs by 1998. Welfare recipients now are required to work a maximum of 17 hours per week, but single mothers with children under 3 years of age, seniors, and the disabled are exempt. To alleviate the problems of single mothers, new measures were introduced to force delinquent spouses to pay child support. These measures include denying the renewal of drivers' licenses to delinquents. The federal government was asked to cooperate by providing tax and residence information.

Cuts in health-care spending caused a bitter dispute with the province's 23,000 doctors. A reduction of fees paid to doctors and government contributions to malpractice insurance were key issues. Some obstetricians refused to take new patients and other doctors were threatening to do the same. The Ontario Medical Association and the Health Ministry reached a tentative agreement in mid-December that would allow doctors to keep more of the fees they charge patients.

Demonstrations. Plans to eliminate more than 13,000 jobs caused a five-week strike by provincial civil servants in February. Job security and severance terms were major issues. The strike turned violent when the provincial police clashed with pickets trying to prevent Conservative members from entering the legislature.

With the Liberal opposition awaiting a new leader, the main opposition to government social policy has passed to the streets. Increasingly angry demonstrations were organized by a coalition of antipoverty groups, unions, and social activists. Days of protest were organized in several cities, culminating in an attempt to shut down the city of Toronto in late October. Pickets forced the public-transit system to suspend operations. Anticipating difficulties, most commuters took the day off and the expected congestion never materialized.

PETER J. KING, *Carleton University*

PRINCE EDWARD ISLAND. A rejuvenated Conservative Party under new leader Pat Binns put an end to ten years of Liberal rule in Prince Edward Island (PEI) with a resounding provincial-election triumph on Nov. 18, 1996. The Tories won 18 of the 27 legislature seats, against eight for the Liberals and one—the first ever—for the New Democratic Party. Binns was sworn in as premier on November 27 at the head of a nine-member cabinet.

The election was called by Premier Keith Milligan shortly after he was chosen by the Liberals on October 5 to take over from Catherine Callbeck as party leader and premier. Callbeck had resigned suddenly on August 6 in the face of falling Liberal public-opinion ratings.

Island taxpayers were presented with a relatively easy-to-take budget for 1996–97 on March 14. It projected a C$3.4 million surplus on spending of C$797 million—and no tax increases. Several million dollars were to go to increased spending on schools and medical equipment.

Headliners. The strange odyssey of the oil barge *Irving Whale* came to an inglorious end on August 7 when it was piggybacked into Halifax harbor in Nova Scotia atop a submersible platform, 26 years after it sank off PEI's north coast in a storm. The previous week, the *Whale* had been raised from the floor of the Gulf of St. Lawrence in a major maritime-salvage operation and towed into Alberton for an initial cleanup. In Halifax it was turned over to its owner, New Brunswick's Irving industrial corporation, complete with 3,000 of the 4,300 tons of crude oil it was carrying when it went down. The rest of the oil had leaked into the gulf, raising environmental concerns.

The PEI and federal governments moved to cushion the economic blow to Borden-Carleton resulting from the scheduled 1997 opening of the new Confederation Bridge across Northumberland Strait. On October 4 they unveiled plans for a jointly funded C$7.3 million Gateway Village, aimed at stimulating commercial and tourism activity in the small community, the Island terminal of the PEI–New Brunswick ferry that would be replaced by the fixed link.

JOHN BEST

QUEBEC. The issue of Quebec's place in Canada—or outside it—dominated and at times convulsed affairs in the province in 1996. The near victory of the "yes" side in the late-1995 independence referendum left a legacy of political uncertainty, mixed with economic instability.

Lucien Bouchard was sworn in as premier on January 29 in succession to Jacques Parizeau, who had retired abruptly after the sovereignty vote. Bouchard vowed to hold another referendum if his separatist Parti Québécois (PQ) was returned to power in the next provincial election, expected in 1998. In the meantime, his regime would concentrate on restoring Quebec's faltering economy and providing good government.

Perhaps the main result of the federalist side's close brush with defeat in the Oct. 30, 1995, referendum was to spur the federal government into action. On September 26 in Ottawa, federal Justice Minister Allan Rock announced that the government had decided to ask the Supreme Court of Canada to rule on whether Quebec has the right under the Canadian constitution to separate from the rest of Canada. If the court said no, as the government obviously hoped, federal authorities would be in a strong position to state the conditions under which Ottawa would be prepared to negotiate a divorce, should Quebecers opt for one in a future referendum.

These conditions, entrenched in a so-called Plan B being hatched in Ottawa, would include a clear, concise referendum question as opposed to the convoluted question posed in 1995, and perhaps the margin of victory the separatists would need. The court's decision was not expected before late 1997. Bouchard dismissed the judicial reference as a federalist ploy and declared that Quebec's future will be decided by Quebecers alone.

The Budget and the Economy. The PQ government presented a budget on May 9 that held the line on personal-income and sales taxes while cutting tax credits for single persons and seniors with net incomes above C$26,000. Big business was hit with an additional C$233 million in taxes, but the government found C$42 million to help small business. Government spending was reduced by C$1.3 billion to C$40.9 billion, making for a 1996–97 deficit of C$3.3 billion—down C$600 million from fiscal 1996. In spending estimates tabled six weeks before the budget, the government reduced grants for health and education, welfare, and business development.

Quebec's ailing economy was the focus of a special four-day meeting of industrial, labor, and government leaders held in Montreal, October 29–November 1. Out of it came a three-year, C$2.6 billion recovery plan that Bouchard claimed would create 77,000 new jobs.

Language-Rights Issue. The long-festering issue of language rights erupted anew when the provincial government announced plans on June 10 to resurrect its so-called "language police" to help ensure the primacy of French on outdoor commercial signs. The police—otherwise known as the *Commission de Protection de la Langue Française*—had been disbanded a few years earlier by Premier Robert Bourassa's Liberal government. Two months later, on August 7, the government went a step further and announced the hiring of 15 additional inspectors to check on shops illegally posting indoor signs in English only. Both moves were denounced by groups representing the English-speaking minority.

JOHN BEST

SASKATCHEWAN. In 1996, Saskatchewan Premier Roy Romanow's New Democratic Party government sold off most of its shares in the privatized giant uranium company Cameco, eliminated 544 civil-service jobs, and took aim at reducing the number of rural governments and education districts as it continued its cost-cutting ways.

Government Action. With 847 municipal governments and 119 school-board divisions, Saskatchewan is "a very overgoverned province," Romanow said of the pressure to amalgamate rural municipalities to save money. In what amounted to a year of public and private reviews of most provincial institutions, the government also announced hearings into restructuring the education system from kindergarten through the university level and asked for public input in deciding the future of its Crown-owned utility companies.

In the 1996–97 budget, Finance Minister Janice MacKinnon projected revenues of C$5.34 billion, including a special dividend of C$350 million from the government's Crown Investments Corporation. The budget showed a surplus of C$8 million, with the province's total debt estimated at C$14.33 billion in March 1996. MacKinnon said her policies would ensure four more years of surplus budgets with no tax increases, with total accumulated debt decreasing to C$12.5 billion in fiscal year 2000.

The government also proposed changes to the welfare system and cracked down on drunk drivers. It wanted to make youths aged 18–21 whose parents could afford to support them no longer eligible for welfare, while those whose parents could not support them either would have to attend school or get jobs to collect social assistance. To reduce a drunk-driving rate that ranks among Canada's highest, the province legislated 24-hour license suspensions for drivers registering a .04 blood-alcohol content; extended the license suspension on a first .08 charge to one year from six months; and allowed the impoundment of vehicles—for a minimum of 30 days—of those caught driving while disqualified.

The Media, Crime, and the Economy. Conrad Black's Hollinger Inc. purchased all of the Armadale newspapers in the province and laid off 182 employees in Regina, Saskatoon, and Yorkton. The purchase ended seven decades of Sifton-family newspaper ownership and brought all of Saskatchewan's daily newspapers into the Hollinger fold. Despite widespread criticism, including a threat by a provincial cabinet minister to lobby the federal government for tighter laws governing media concentration, the federal Competition Bureau said the deal did not lessen competition for newspaper advertising in Saskatchewan.

By late 1996, six members of the Legislative Assembly (MLAs) of the Grant Devine administration had been found guilty of fraud, three had been acquitted, and three cases were before the courts....The Potash Corporation of Saskatchewan became the largest integrated fertilizer maker in the world by acquiring the assets of Arcadia Corp. in Memphis, TN, for C$1.18 billion.

SARATH PEIRIS
"The StarPhoenix," Saskatoon

YUKON. Yukoners went to the polls in the fall of 1996 and voted out the conservative Yukon Party (YP) government, replacing it with a socialist New Democratic Party (NDP) government. The NDP would form the government for the next four years with a landslide 11 seats in the 17-seat Yukon legislature. The Liberal and Yukon parties won three seats each. No Independents were elected. One riding—Old Crow, a First Nations village 100 mi (160 km) north of the Arctic Circle—voted to a tie. When a judicial recount failed to change the numbers, a name was drawn from a hat. The NDP candidate won the draw. The new government leader was veteran politician Piers McDonald. YP leader John Ostashek retained his Whitehorse seat, while Liberal leader Ken Taylor lost his and was expected to resign.

Economy. The election came as the territory's economy rested on the threshold of an unprecedented boom. Two gold mines were expected to come into production in central Yukon late in 1996. Loki Gold Corporation Limited and BYG Natural Resources Incorporated, both of Vancouver, BC, have gold properties with reserves of 17.4 million tons and 650,000 tons of gold and silver, respectively. Six other mining operations were in various stages of exploration and were going through their permitting stages with the federal government in Ottawa. They were expected to go into production within three to five years. Three may be in production in 1997 or 1998.

Government. Meanwhile, Ottawa offered the territorial government administrative control over the last remaining areas of responsibility traditionally controlled by the federal government—timber, mining, land, and oil and gas resources. The transfer to the Yukon government would place the territory, in effect, in a position of having fully responsible government, similar to that of the ten provinces, except for the name itself. A tentative transfer date was set for the spring of 1997, although the date could be extended to allow for negotiations among Ottawa, the territorial government, and the Yukon's First Nations people.

Some leaders of the 14 First Nations bands indicated they were not in favor of further devolution of political powers to the Yukon until all land-claims negotiations were completed. Seven native organizations had settled their claims. The seven outstanding claims were expected to be completed in 1997–98. The total package would amount to granting full First Nations government powers to 8,000 natives and would divide 16,000 sq mi (41 439 km^2) of land and C$242 million among the 14 bands.

DON SAWATSKY
Freelance Writer, Whitehorse

The Arts

The most radical change to the Canadian arts scene during 1996 was the federal government's decision to introduce sweeping changes to the Canadian Broadcasting Corporation (CBC) and to reduce its budget by almost one third (C$414 million) by 1998. The National Film Board was trimmed by C$20 million, resulting in job cuts and the closing of cinemas and libraries.

Architecture and Visual Arts. Vancouver's Patkau Architects, exploring architectural responses to natural and urban landscapes, represented Canada at the Venice Biennale International Exhibition of Architecture. Architects Kuwabara, Payne, McKenna, and Blumberg designed The Walter Carsen Centre, a functional and inviting new home for the National Ballet of Canada in Toronto.

The National Gallery of Canada marked the bicentennial of Jean-Baptiste Camille Carot with a huge retrospective—more than 135 paintings—of the popular French landscape painter's work. Carot's paintings anticipated modernism with gentle harmony and freedom of movement. The National Gallery also mounted an intriguing show of anatomical images, "The Ingenious Machine of Nature: Four Centuries of Art and Nature," consisting of 126 prints and drawings as well as beautifully illustrated books celebrating human anatomy from Raphael to today.

Thanks to diplomat Allan Gotlieb, who donated a major collection of prints by French painter James Tissot, the Art Gallery of Ontario (AGO) now has one of the most important collections of Tissot graphics. The AGO also mounted "Earthly Weathers/Heavenly Skies," a magnificent retrospective covering five decades of Paterson Ewen's drawings and paintings. Calgary's Glenbow Museum and Edmonton Art Gallery mounted the first "Alberta Biennial of Contemporary Art," surveying 23 artists. Stratford's Indigena Gallery featured some 20 sculptures by acclaimed Inuit artist Manasie Akpaliapik.

Performing Arts. The Stratford Festival launched the world premiere of William Luce's *Barrymore*, exploring the last year of the great American actor's life. Christopher Plummer played the lead with extraordinary talent and verve. Another highlight of the 1996 Stratford season included Shakespeare's *The Merchant of Venice*, set in the 1930s when anti-Semitism was on its dreadful rise. Directed by Marti Maraden, and with a fine performance by Douglas Rain as Shylock, Stratford's *Merchant* was an intelligent drama focusing on fascism and anti-Semitism. Also well-received was *King Lear*, directed by Richard Monette and starring William Hutt.

The flagship of the 1996 Shaw Festival was George Bernard Shaw's *The Devil's Disciple*, directed by Glynis Leyshon and with outstanding performances by Gordon Rand, Peter Hutt, Sara Orenstein, and William Webster. Oscar Wilde's *An Ideal Husband* appeared, even more successfully, for a second season. Duncan McIntosh's direction was superb, as were performances by Norman Browning, Brigitte Robinson, Jan Alexandra Smith, and Allan Gray. Also well-received was Harold Brighouse's *Hobson's Choice*, a

© Steve J. Sherman

Jukka-Pekka Saraste, a 39-year-old native of Finland, received high marks during his second season as conductor–music director of the Toronto Symphony Orchestra.

charming comedy set in an 1880s Lancashire boot shop. Faithfully reproducing the period, director Christopher Newton emphasized the class warfare and aspirations of social mobility of the times; Corrine Koslo as Maggie and Simon Bradbury as the illiterate bootmaker shone. Agatha Christie's murder mystery *The Hollow*, starring Jennifer Phipps, Tony van Bridge, Jan Alexandra Smith, and Peter Millard, rounded out a successful season.

The Atlantic Festival mounted a polished *She Stoops to Conquer* by Oliver Goldsmith, an antidote to the sentimental comedies of the late 1700s. The satire and social commentary were highlighted by superb performances by Megan Follows and Leon Pownall. Helen Burns' and Michael Langham's direction of Ibsen's *A Doll's House* produced a poetic and moving reinvestigation of Ibsen's feminist tract, helped considerably by a commanding performance by Megan Follows.

Toronto's Royal Alexandra Theatre brought in the acclaimed British production of Ibsen's *The Master Builder*, directed by Sir Peter Hall and starring Alan Bates, Gemma Jones, and Victoria Hamilton. Also hugely successful was *2 Pianos, 4 Hands* by Ted Dykstra and Richard Greenblatt, a two-person play based on the lives of the principals. It began its cross-country tour at Toronto's Tarragon Theatre. Toronto's Canadian Stage Company and the Vancouver Playhouse mounted a marvelous production of A.R. Gurney's *Later Life*, a comedy about two middle-agers who have a second chance to recapture lost love. Nicola Cavendish and Tom Woods romped through all 11 roles with the help of 12 quick-change artists.

The Canadian Opera Company (COC) opened its season with Richard Strauss' *Salome*, directed by innovative filmmaker Atom Egoyan, who added a multimedia dimension to the opera. The COC also mounted a playful *La Cenerentola*, starring Italian mezzo-soprano Caterina Antonacci in her Canadian debut. And soprano Susan Marie Pierson made her debut a great success in *Elektra*, directed by James Robinson. A stunning *Turandot*, featuring high-tech stagecraft, ended Opera Manitoba's 25th-anniversary season, with exceptional performances by Li Ping Zhang, Mary Jane Johnson, Craig Sirianni, and Ding Gao. Edmonton Opera produced a critically acclaimed *Die Fledermaus*, with a virtually perfect performance by Winnipeg coloratura Tracy Dahl. The Vancouver Opera produced an excellent *Marriage of Figaro*, with a stunning performance by Korean-born Jee Hyun Lim and fine work by Richard Bernstein and Peter Coleman-Wright. Also acclaimed was its production of Janacek's *Jenufa*, starring Judith Forst as Kostelnicka and Michaela Gurevich as Jenufa. After gaining international attention in her 1995 London debut as Anna in *Les Troyens*, mezzo-soprano Maria Popescu repeated her success in Milan's Teatro alla Scala.

The highlights of the 1996 Canada Dance Festival included several premieres, including Marie Chouinard's *The Almond and the Diamond* ("L'amande et le diamant"), an innovative work expressing primal energy; Ballet British Columbia's John Alleyne's *Sex Is My Religion*, which explores the relationship between a sex-addicted young man and his religious mother; and James Kudelka's *Cruel World*, with fine performances by Rex Harrington and Karen Kain.

The Royal Winnipeg Ballet's Evelyn Hart shone as the ethereal Giselle in the National Ballet of Canada's production, playing opposite Rex Harrington. The National Ballet also mounted an effective production, a Toronto premiere, of Sir Kenneth MacMillan's *Manon*, directed by Reid Anderson and starring Martine Lamy and Robert Tewsley. The ambitious fall season, under the directorship of James Kudelka, featured the dark, romantic *Onegin*, starring Karen Kain and Rex Harrington. Kain danced the role of Tatiana for the last time as a principal dancer with the National Ballet. John Cranko's powerful choreography was followed by *Cruel World, Paquita, and Voluntaries*, three works that tested the dancers' technical and dramatic abilities.

Film. After being awarded a special jury prize at Cannes in May, David Cronenberg's *Crash*, starring James Spader and Holly Hunter, continued to careen through the cinematic world. Also at Cannes, *Lulu*, a story about a Vietnamese refugee who becomes a mail-order bride, won high praise, especially for its star, Kim Lieu. Picked as best of festival at Toronto's International Film Festival, *Project Grizzly*, directed by Peter Lynch and starring Troy Hurtibise, relates Hurtibise's obsession with designing a protective suit for close encounters with *Ursus horribilis*. Also opening to rave reviews was Lynne Stopkewich's *Kissed*, starring Molly Parker in a tale about a young woman's passionate interest in death. *Hard Core Logo*—a fictitious documentary about a punk-rock band, directed by Bruce McDonald—was named best Canadian film and best Canadian screenplay at the Vancouver International Film Festival.

DOUGLAS R. CRONK
Open University of British Columbia

CARIBBEAN

The islands of the Caribbean experienced another difficult year in 1996. Particularly hard hit were the smaller economies of the eastern Caribbean, which struggled to recover from the devastating effects of 1995's hurricanes. A simmering dispute over the access of Caribbean bananas to the European market and the demand by Caribbean producers for parity with Mexico in the North American Free Trade Agreement (NAFTA) complicated the region's problems.

Tourism. During the first quarter of the year, tourism earnings fell by more than 30% in the eastern Caribbean, reflecting hurricane destruction of hotel infrastructure. Tourism receipts in the British colony of Montserrat, which also was affected by the yearlong rumblings of a volcano, dropped by more than 40%. Also showing significant decreases in tourist receipts from 1995 were Anguilla (–22.4%) and Antigua (–9.5%).

There was less storm damage in 1996, although Hurricane Bertha swept through the region for two days in July, causing six deaths and inflicting several million dollars' worth of damage in Antigua, St. Kitts-Nevis, Anguilla, the British and U.S. Virgin Islands, St. Martin, Puerto Rico, and the Turks and Caicos Islands. The physical destruction was accompanied by the economic impact of canceled visits by cruise ships, reduced hotel bookings, and wariness on the part of potential investors.

Agriculture. Agricultural production also fell in the first quarter. Dominica, whose sugar crop was destroyed almost completely by Hurricane Marilyn in September 1995, suffered the most, with its harvest down by more than 95%, to only 435 tons. Grenada and St. Vincent also were affected. In St. Lucia, the largest of the eastern Caribbean banana growers, export income declined due to falling prices in Great Britain and a decline in the quality of bananas. Grenada suffered a falloff in the production of nutmeg, and fruit and vegetable earnings in Grenada and Montserrat also fell.

Caribbean banana producers were upset by a U.S. decision to take a dispute over the European Union's (EU's) banana regime to the World Trade Organization (WTO). The EU gives preferential access to Caribbean bananas, and Latin American banana growers and the U.S.-based Chiquita Brands International claim that this treatment is discriminatory. Chiquita complained to the Office of the U.S. Trade Representative, which in turn filed a case with the WTO. Caribbean banana growers said they were shocked, insisting that the United States had agreed to negotiate a settlement of the dispute.

Manufacturing. Manufacturing output also was down in 1996. The production of soap in Dominica fell by 12.1% in the first quarter, and the production of flour, beer, and animal feed dropped in St. Vincent. In St. Lucia apparel output declined by 17.8%, electrical products by 15.1%, and rum by 6.3%. Construction, however, boomed, driven by post-hurricane reconstruction. Antigua began a remodeling of its hotel plant and St. Kitts-Nevis commissioned four new public-sector construction projects, including the building of a new cruise-ship facility.

Trinidad's Economy. The bigger economies of the Caribbean were not immune to the negative economic trends. Trinidad and Tobago, one of the healthier economies, grew by only 0.7% in the first quarter, compared with 1.7% in the last quarter of 1995. The nonpetroleum sector contracted by 0.4% during the quarter, dragging down the overall growth rate. Agriculture declined by 7.4% and government services by 7.0%. Manufacturing, which had been enjoying an export boom, declined by 1.9%. The petroleum sector, however, showed signs of healthy growth, posting an increase of 4.1%, based on higher crude production, an increase in refinery output, and continuing offshore exploratory drilling.

Caricom Summit. Caribbean heads of government ended an inconclusive meeting in Barbados on July 6. Little progress was made on the principal theme under discussion: the Caricom Single Market and Economy. The main stumbling block was Trinidad and Tobago's relatively large ($443.3 million) trade surplus with the rest of the Caribbean. Discussion of this issue was postponed for later consideration.

Limited progress was made in a number of other areas. Following a proposal by Trinidad and Tobago, there was agreement to set up a region-wide protection program for witnesses in drug-related cases. A Caribbean Investment Fund for stimulating private-sector investment in the region was set up with an initial target of $50 million. And the summit agreed to establish joint diplomatic offices abroad to represent the entire Caricom area.

Caricom and NAFTA. Twenty-four nations in the Caribbean Basin, including the nations of Central America, have been asking the United States, Canada, and Mexico for NAFTA parity to enable them to compete for markets in the trade bloc. The request, which

Caribbean leaders said they would pursue after the November 1996 U.S. presidential elections, would give the Caribbean nations preferential treatment until a hemisphere-wide free-trade area is established sometime after the year 2005. The proposal resonated well in Jamaica and Trinidad and Tobago, which indicated an interest in joining NAFTA. The United States, however, indicated that it would prefer that the 14 member states of Caricom approach NAFTA as a group rather than individually.

In Barbados, Prime Minister Owen Arthur said his country would not seek NAFTA membership but, however, would continue to press for NAFTA parity for Caribbean products. The Caribbean nations currently enjoy nonreciprocal trade preferences with the United States under the so-called Caribbean Basin Initiative (CBI), and has similar arrangements with Canada, but Caribbean governments contend they are losing markets to Mexico under NAFTA.

Drugs. During 1996 the islands of the Caribbean continued to witness a resurgence of drug trafficking accompanied by a sharp increase in money laundering by offshore banking operations in Antigua, Trinidad and Tobago, St. Kitts-Nevis, Jamaica, the Cayman Islands, Aruba, and the Dominican Republic. Puerto Rico was favored especially by the drug traffickers because of the ease of shipping merchandise free of customs inspections to the United States. Barry McCaffrey, President Bill Clinton's drug czar, estimated that as much as 154 tons of cocaine pass through the eastern Caribbean en route to the United States yearly. He also said that $50 billion from the sale of narcotics is laundered through Caribbean banks.

The United States has signed treaties with nine Caribbean nations permitting the U.S. Coast Guard to intercept shipments of narcotics bound for the United States in territorial waters around the islands. But despite the increase in drug trafficking, funds for U.S. interdiction efforts fell from $1.03 billion in 1992 to $569 million in 1995.

Suriname's New President. Jules Wijdenbosch, a leftist political scientist, was elected president of Suriname by the United People's Congress, an assembly of all Surinamese elected officials, on September 5. Wijdenbosch defeated Ronald Venetiaan, the incumbent president, by a vote of 436 to 408. The election result was proclaimed as a victory for former military dictator Desi Bouterse, who had backed Wijdenbosch.

RICHARD C. SCHROEDER, *Freelance Writer*

CENTRAL AMERICA

During four years in office, President Bill Clinton did not demonstrate much interest in Latin America in general, or Central America in particular. However, it seemed logical that the Clinton administration, having won a second term, would broaden its hemispheric interests during 1997. Meanwhile, newspaper coverage indicated that Washington's most significant concern with Central America was the region's drug business. Central America is not a major source of drugs, but its location between the growing fields and processing plants of South America and the consumers of the United States make it an important conduit. No state was untouched by the hemispheric efforts to curtail the business.

The president did send Secretary of State Warren Christopher for a nine-day visit to Latin America, including a few hours in El Salvador, beginning Feb. 25, 1996. Christopher met briefly with leaders of all the Central American countries except Panama. He praised the nations for ending the many bloody and prolonged civil wars that had torn at the region in the past decade. He could promise them little in U.S. assistance, but reported that the next budget would include proposals to give Central American states the same trade benefits that Mexico was receiving as a member of the North American Free Trade Agreement (NAFTA). The specific Central American exports probably would include shoes, clothing, textiles, and oil; keen international competition for the sale of all these items reduced the probability that any Central American state would join NAFTA soon, however.

A tragic consequence of the several Central American civil wars has been the economic, social, and even physical displacement of thousands of the region's young men. Most faced depressing unemployment pictures, ranging up to 50% in some places. Many men had spent their youth—almost their childhood—waging war. Now they had returned home totally unequipped to manage a trade, finding a society unable to afford training programs for such numbers of veterans. Some migrated to the United States, legally or otherwise, but employment conditions there proved little better for most of them because of language and training handicaps. Unfortunately, the heritage of these excursions often was indoctrination into gang life, little known throughout Central America until recently. During 1996, evidence was scant that these young men were entering the drug trade, but gang membership was becoming increasingly prestigious.

Belize. The Mayan heritage of Belize is less known than that of its neighbors—Mexico, Guatemala, and Honduras—but research may change a degree of that perception. Archaeologists from Boston University digging in northern Belize early in 1996 found an ancient tomb containing a man's skeleton. Because of the nature of the jewelry he wore, the scientists believe the man to have been a member of Mayan royalty. The site, which never had been looted, dates from about the fifth century A.D., putting it in the Classic period—well before the more famous finds of Palenque, Copán, and Tikal. The tomb, some 10 ft (3 m) underground, is located near an ancient city of about 50,000, dating from the beginning of the Christian era, but that disappeared about 1,000 years ago.

Since the early 1990s, Belize has become a favorite among international travelers. The spectacular Caribbean waters and the world's second-largest coral reef have made Belize a mecca for scuba divers who also can enjoy studying Mayan ruins. The increased tourism trend, accompanied by the nation's natural growth, has put pressure on the land and its resources. Fortunately, forward-looking Belizeans and international agencies have stepped in to preserve the past while trying to provide for future tourism. New resorts have been built near the best dive sites.

Perhaps two thirds of Belize is covered with rain forest and various kinds of pine-laden savanna. More than one half of the population lives in the two chief cities—Belmopán and Belize City; much of the rest of the population is composed of peasants who would like to make homes on the savanna. The government is trying to grant 40-acre (16-ha) homesteads to thousands of these campesinos, but the attendant problems are enormous.

Costa Rica. While Costa Rica's economy still had flaws, one strong piece of evidence declared that the nation had turned an important corner. In July, for the first time in 50 years, Costa Rica no longer was deemed in need of economic assistance from the U.S. Agency for International Development (AID) and related institutions. During those years the nation had been granted more than $2.7 billion, helping thousands of people and saving the nation's economy. A major goal of foreign aid has been to reduce Costa Rica's heavy dependency on the export of bananas and coffee; this colonial-type relationship reached its worst level about 1982, when coffee prices were very low and energy prices high. Largely through AID's efforts, nontraditional exports reached a high of 57% in 1995. Some poverty still existed in Costa Rica in 1996, but literacy had grown to an exceptional 94%, municipal water supplies had been clarified, the infant-mortality rate had fallen about 90% in 50 years, and the birthrate had been halved.

In recent years the government has expropriated thousands of acres of land for parks and admits owing some $15 million in compensation to the former owners. The issue is exacerbated by the actions of many squatters. Some of these are peasants staking title to lands they worked for now-departed U.S. banana firms. For example, when United Fruit left the Gulfito area in 1984, many campesinos began farming portions of the plantations as their own. Most were "legitimate" farmers, desperate for their own parcel of land; but recently groups of "armed pirates" have begun seizing lands and claiming title as a business. These latter groups have been opposed by human-rights agencies. Under some circumstances a squatter can clear legitimate title after one year and only a court judgment can displace him, so the "pirates" have found a moneymaking racket that complicates an already difficult national problem.

After a century of contribution to the Costa Rican economy, the banana was beginning to pose yet another national issue. Costa Rican environmentalists were concerned that the industry was detrimental to the nation's valuable forests; banana production requires the clearing of the natural forest. It also brings to the land fertilizers, pesticides, and acres of plastics. Local environmentalists have succeeded in forcing international growers and local governments to negotiate new contracts that will reduce some of the harm. Worker-safety regulations also are being reconsidered, partly as a consequence of lawsuits over pesticide use.

Between 1950 and 1990, Costa Rica lost almost one half of its national forest—the worst rate in Latin America. Many efforts were under way to reverse this process by replanting trees and expanding the limits of two national parks on the Pacific, which display spectacular scenery and an abundance of species of birds, mammals, and flora.

El Salvador. In 1996, Salvadorans finally could see preliminary steps taken to turn around some of the terrible destruction of the civil war (1979–92). The war, which killed 75,000, mostly civilians, brought near-total devastation to much of the environment.

Aside from personal losses, most peasants considered landownership their primary problem. In spite of years of planning and some action, perhaps 2 million campesinos still do not have title to land, even though they may be occupying what they consider their own parcel. A land-reform program instituted by former President José Napoleón Duarte in the 1980s had lacked financing needed for completion, and 80% of the farmland still is owned by only 20% of the farmers. But finally, in February 1996, the U.S. Congress approved a $10 million grant to clear titles, help peasants buy their land, and provide technical assistance—badly needed by people who never have managed their own crop production.

In addition to the lives torn by the war, the very earth of El Salvador has been broken. The nation's forests almost have disappeared. As a major step in reconstruction, the government employed workers from both sides of the conflict to make a park out of one of the war zones where the greatest number of lives were lost. In spite of the presence of unexploded mines, the workers were beginning to plant the first of some 75,000 trees in the "Monsignor [Oscar Arnulfo] Romero Forest of Reconciliation," named for the archbishop assassinated in 1980. In March the Roman Catholic Church of El Salvador formally declared its forgiveness of the killers of this most outspoken of the defenders of the nation's oppressed.

During a February visit to Latin America, Pope John Paul II spent one day in El Salvador. The pope visited Romero's tomb. Although the pope was received well, the church faced problems in El Salvador. Viewed by many as having supported the hard-line militarists, the church was losing members to evangelical Protestantism and even to a resurgence of Mayan beliefs. In addition, Pope John Paul II was criticized for not visiting the graves of the Jesuit priests massacred by government troops in 1989.

The Inter-American Development Bank lent $22 million to El Salvador to create an agency for improving the nation's judicial system and reducing juvenile delinquency.

Guatemala. Guatemala peacefully chose a new president in 1996. A runoff election in January resulted in victory for Alvaro Arzú Irigoyen, who received 51% of the small turnout, compared with 48.7% for Alfonso Portillo. Arzú is a wealthy businessman and former minister of foreign affairs. Politically he is probably a centrist; Portillo represented the right wing.

During Arzú's first week in office he cashiered more than 100 police officers and several military commanders suspected of criminal activity. Arzú inherited some serious problems. More than 30,000 Indian refugees still resided in Mexico, where they had fled from Guatemala's civil war. Some had lived in exile ten to 15 years; one half were children, born in Mexico and often unfamiliar with their parents' Indian language. Some who had returned to Guatemala faced torture and even massacre, creating a new fear among those left in Mexico. Treated reasonably by the Mexican government, most still preferred to return home if they had any assurance of getting their own land back. Two thirds of Guatemala's farmland still was owned by about 2% of the landowners. Many of the refugees lost their small parcels to friends of the military during the civil war. In three years about 2,300 families have been resettled, but

Alvaro Arzú Irigoyen and his wife, Patricia, became president and first lady of Guatemala in 1996. The leader of the center-right National Advancement Party (PAN) had been elected in a runoff vote.

CENTRAL AMERICA • Information Highlights

Nation	Population (in Millions)	Area (sq mi)	Area (km²)	Capital	Head of State and Government
Belize	0.2	8,865	22 960	Belmopán	Sir Colville Young, governor-general; Manuel Esquivel, prime minister
Costa Rica	3.6	19,730	51 100	San José	José María Figueres Olsen, president
El Salvador	5.9	8,124	21 040	San Salvador	Armando Calderón Sol, president
Guatemala	9.9	42,042	108 890	Guatemala City	Alvaro Arzú Irigoyen, president
Honduras	5.6	43,278	112 090	Tegucigalpa	Carlos Roberto Reina, president
Nicaragua	4.6	49,998	129 494	Managua	Violeta Barrios de Chamorro, president
Panama	2.7	30,193	78 200	Panama City	Ernesto Pérez Balladares, president

the process is slow and costly. Desperate for financial assistance, Guatemala could count on only $34 million from the U.S. government in 1996, compared with an annual average of $160 million in the 1980s.

Overt hostilities in Central America's longest war had ended, and in September the Arzú government and the rebels agreed upon a continuation of the cease-fire, as well as a reduction in military force. Counterinsurgency units were eliminated. But three decades of violence left its mark. Murder and kidnapping greatly increased in 1996; someone even tried to run over the president with a truck. The U.S. Central Intelligence Agency (CIA) declassified thousands of documents dating from the 1980s. They revealed that several agents took part in human-rights abuses and that high Guatemalan officials engaged in a massive cover-up, but the CIA still disclaimed responsibility in the death of a U.S. businessman and the husband of Jennifer Harbury. Violence even spilled over into sports; in October, 80 fans were killed and hundreds injured at a World Cup soccer qualifying match between Guatemala and Costa Rica. Apparently many tickets were counterfeit, and the disaster took place when far too many fans attempted to enter the stadium.

In November, President Arzú and rebel leaders finally reached an agreement about peace terms to be signed December 29. Both parties promised to settle the remaining details of Indian aid, human rights, and military power by that time.

Honduras. That some of the traditional power of Honduras' military finally was being limited became evident in a landmark decision of Honduras' supreme court. Overruling an appellate court, 9 to 0, the justices declared that ten military men could be tried for kidnapping and torture in a civilian court. The victims had been six leftist students. But army officers continued to wield considerable power. As in El Salvador, groups of them own many major businesses such as banks and factories, which are financed by their substantial retirement funds.

The military also got involved in a struggle for land. Claiming a need to cut costs and raise production, Chiquita Brands International used the army, police, and the government to evict 123 families of squatters from former banana lands; some of these families had resided on the land—without clear title—since the 1920s. Their homes and churches were destroyed and crops uprooted. Attacked by the church and civil-rights groups, the company replied that strikes and disease had cut production by two thirds in seven years. Wages range from about $3 to $8 per day. The matter was in the courts late in 1996.

Another dispute brought great unwanted publicity to the garment industry in Honduras and the United States. The charge was made in the U.S. Congress that a clothing line, bearing the name of talk-show hostess Kathie Lee Gifford and distributed by Wal-Mart Stores, was manufactured under sweatshop conditions in Honduras. Gifford tearfully denied knowledge of the conditions but admitted much truth in the charges. Although workers' pay averaged only $0.31 an hour, women and young children stood in line seeking these jobs. Wages often accounted for about 1% of the garments' selling prices. Gifford's clothing line was manufactured in a plant considered especially harsh, with workweeks of more than 70 hours typical. Legally, children between 14 and 16 could work only six hours a day. Repercussions were great; other companies such as Sears and J.C. Penney demanded an improvement in conditions. Gifford apologized and gave cash bonuses to workers. Unions, the Honduran government, and U.S. civil-rights workers all sought reforms. The question remained—would the reform spirit last? Honduras faced 40% unemployment, and corporations could buy clothing in Asia for even lower labor costs. (*See* LABOR—*The Reemergence of Sweatshops*.)

Human-rights activists were also upset by the appointment of Luis Alonso Discua Elvir, a general who had prevented civilian efforts to arrest officers on rights-abuse charges, as the nation's United Nations representative.

© Brennan Linsley/AP/Wide World Photos

In October 1996, Liberal Alliance leader José Arnoldo Alemán, 50, was elected to succeed Violeta Barrios de Chamorro as president of Nicaragua. He was to take office on Jan. 20, 1997.

Nicaragua. The shaky Nicaraguan democracy managed to weather a bitter presidential election in 1996. Among two dozen candidates, the chief contenders were Daniel Ortega Saavedra, former president and still leader of the Sandinista National Liberation Front (FSLN), and Liberal Alliance leader José Arnoldo Alemán, who had been an active and popular mayor of Managua. Campaign oratory was sharp, but there was little violence—the worst being an attack on Alemán's life. Ortega was branded a dangerous Marxist and Alemán a follower of the old Somoza dynasty. But Nicaragua's democracy survived. In the October election, Alemán won with about 50% of the vote to 39% for Ortega. A runoff was avoided. Alemán was to be inaugurated on Jan. 20, 1997.

As Managua's mayor, Alemán, 50, a lawyer and coffee grower, apparently earned grudging support from most citizens. He brought about significant upgrading of the infrastructure—particularly streets, parks, and markets—even in neighborhoods with substantial Sandinista support. In the 1980s he had become a spokesman for growers opposed to the Sandinista land program; he lost his own land and was sentenced to prison for seven years. During that period he lost his wife to cancer. Still undetermined was how well the nation's new chief executive could work with the strong FSLN presence in the Legislative Assembly.

The new government had much to do. Half the working force was unemployed or underemployed. The average annual income was running about $600. And the nation was tired of war. The World Bank reported that 85% of children under 14 were in poverty. An abundance of weapons had made crime a scourge. A reported 50% of Nicaraguan women were the victims of spousal abuse. Most of the land confiscations of the Sandinista era were under dispute. Outgoing President Violeta Chamorro claimed to have resolved almost all of the disputes, but few parties had accepted the judgments. Both rural development and judicial reform were needed badly. For more than a year terrorists had been bombing Catholic churches. The foreign debt was a crushing $12 billion. Cutbacks in free public education had increased gang membership greatly.

Panama. When the Panama Canal Treaties spelling out the future of the Panama Canal after 1999 were signed in 1977, most Panamanians rejoiced at the apparent end of a number of limitations on their sovereignty. By 1996 they were beginning to face some interesting new options. Oversized ships—mostly tankers—and the increasing efficiency of container shipping provoked possible change in the arrangements directed by the treaties. Some Panamanians wanted a new set of larger locks; Taiwan wants to build industrial parks and container terminals in the Canal Zone. Several Asian consortiums spoke of light-rail lines, perhaps even in Nicaragua.

The fact that Taiwan now was the third-largest user of the canal undoubtedly influenced the increase in Asian interest in the canal. A 1996 poll showed that most Panamanians wanted some U.S. presence after the change in ownership. President Clinton was "exploring" such possibilities with Panama's President Ernesto Pérez Balladares. By late 1996, 1,000 buildings and 22,000 acres (8 900 ha) of land—about one fourth of the total—had been turned over to Panama, and U.S. troop presence had been reduced to 7,500.

Several proposals have been made that certain bases be converted into international posts to cope with the heavy narcotics trade passing through the Isthmus, a function some bases already were providing. The United States did not believe such action was necessary. There was greater concern that some of Panama's many banks had engaged in laundering of drug money. This charge was aggravated by accusations that President Balladares' election had been supported by drug interests.

Human-rights groups actively campaigned against the government's pardoning of about 1,000 rights offenders, who had supported the regime of Manuel Noriega. They also protested the plans of a Canadian corporation to mine huge quantities of copper on land intended for an Indian reservation.

THOMAS L. KARNES
Arizona State University

CHEMISTRY

Important events in chemistry in 1996 included significant steps toward the development of plastic lasers, the discovery of new uses for huge molecules called dendrimers, the creation of a catalyst that effectively splits molecular oxygen, and progress in "environmentally friendly" chemistry.

Plastic Lasers. Polymers are very large molecules formed by repeatedly linking smaller molecules called monomers. Polymers have found wide usage as plastics, rubbers, and synthetic fabrics. Certain polymers have useful electrical and optical properties. Some, for example, glow when electrical current flows through them, and potentially can replace inorganic materials in many electronic and optical applications.

In 1996 three research groups announced that they had made a further stride, coming close to the long-sought goal of producing plastic lasers. Lasers are devices that produce coherent light of a single wavelength. Early attempts to make plastic lasers were thwarted by the propensity of polymers to absorb emitted light and degrade it into heat. Researchers carefully purified the polymers to diminish this problem and were able to observe laser-like emissions when thin films of the materials were "pumped" with intense light. Although the films are far from being practical devices—they cannot yet operate using only electrical energy and are prone to degradation—they have a number of potential advantages over alternative materials. They can be produced easily in different shapes, are flexible and mechanically stable, and produce light in a variety of colors.

Dendrimers. Dendrimers—first created in 1979 by Donald Tomalia, then a chemist at Dow Chemical Co.—are highly branched polymers, normally produced step by step by adding chemical groups to the tips of branches spreading from a central core. They were slow to gain attention. With potential applications including drug delivery, chemical sensors, and computer data-storage elements, dendrimers have become a hot area of chemical investigation in recent years because they can be tailored to perform specific tasks. In 1994, for example, Dutch chemists showed that dendrimers can be designed to entrap a variety of chemicals, and that their exteriors can be altered to release the chemicals selectively.

In 1996 a number of reports further demonstrated the potential of these unusual compounds. Test-tube experiments revealed that dendrimers can carry genetic material into animal cells, raising the possibility that they can be used to repair birth defects in humans. Chemists from Texas A & M University grafted dendritic polymers onto metal surfaces to form thin films, which can be used to inhibit corrosion or to detect metals or other materials. A Cornell University team synthesized a dendrimer that changes shape according to the polarity of the solvent in which it is placed, and a University of Illinois group designed chemical "wedges" that spontaneously organize into a six-unit dendrimer with a precisely defined structure.

Splitting Oxygen. Forming and splitting the chemical bond between the two oxygen atoms of molecular oxygen (O_2) is one of nature's most crucial chores. A number of key metal-containing enzymes perform this central task in animals and plants, but the mechanism of the reaction has been difficult to pin down. In the spring of 1996, a team from the University of Minnesota led by William Tolman reported the creation of a novel copper complex that cleaves the O-O bond in a reversible manner. The achievement appeared likely to provide new insights into how such so-called metalloenzymes act.

Green Chemistry. Chemists continued to seek ways to make chemical processes more environmentally friendly. Organic solvents used in many synthesis reactions present a major disposal and pollution problem. At a meeting of the American Chemical Society (ACS) in New Orleans, several research groups presented ways to carry out synthesis reactions in water using small amounts of metal catalysts, thereby eliminating the need for organic solvents. Other chemists described more drastic approaches that virtually would eliminate the use of any solvent, either by mixing only the ingredients for reaction, recycling solvents, or carrying out reactions in microwave ovens.

At the same ACS meeting, a team of chemists from the University of Idaho led by Chien Wai presented a method for using carbon dioxide under high pressure, called supercritical CO_2, to extract toxic metals. Metals such as mercury and plutonium pose an especially nasty environmental hazard, and are difficult to extract by conventional means. Supercritical CO_2 has the significant advantages of being both inexpensive and environmentally benign. The key to the technique's success is initial treatment of metals with chelating agents, which form specialized molecular ring structures.

PAUL G. SEYBOLD
Wright State University

CHICAGO

During 1996, Chicago hosted a successful Democratic National Convention and celebrated another National Basketball Association (NBA) title for the Chicago Bulls. In other news, several local aldermen were indicted in a sweeping federal corruption probe.

Events. In June the Bulls won their fourth NBA title in six years. Chicago police were geared up for potential problems, keeping in mind the rioting that had followed the Bulls' last title in 1993. The victory at the United Center over the Seattle SuperSonics brought tens of thousands of Chicagoans into the streets. They honked horns and set off fireworks into the night, but no major problems arose.

Similarly, Chicago police were prepared in August as the Democrats returned to the city for their presidential nominating convention for the first time since the tumultuous 1968 convention, when police and antiwar demonstrators clashed. Few arrests were made during the 1996 convention, which renominated President Bill Clinton for a second term. Chicago was all spruced up for the convention, as new trees and fresh coats of paint were evident throughout the city.

Corruption. Three Chicago aldermen were indicted in a federal probe of corruption known as Operation Silver Shovel. Two of the aldermen—who had received payoffs to permit dumping and other objectionable activities in their jurisdictions—pleaded guilty to charges of extortion, graft, and tax evasion, and resigned from office. U.S. Attorney James Burns said that, despite dozens of successful prosecutions of corrupt officials in recent years, Chicago's storied tradition of political corruption still remained a problem.

The Mayor. Mayor Richard M. Daley (D) won plaudits for a proposal to close Meigs Field, a small lakefront airport used by private pilots, corporate planes, and politicians. Daley's $27 million proposal would turn the airport, located on the edge of Lake Michigan, into a 90-acre (36-ha) park and nature preserve. Among the opponents to Daley's plan was Illinois Gov. Jim Edgar (R). The resulting dispute between the state and the city put the plan on hold and in litigation.

Daley also introduced a new plan to renovate Soldier Field, the home of the Chicago Bears. With many in Chicago debating the question of building a new sports stadium, Daley offered a $395 million proposal that would maintain the Romanesque facade of Soldier Field while revamping it as a combination sports center and exposition center with a retractable roof.

Other. A visit in June by Britain's Princess Diana brought out Chicago's elite and powerful to raise funds for breast-cancer research. On a sadder note, Cardinal Joseph Bernardin, Chicago's Catholic archbishop since 1982, died of cancer on November 14. The cardinal had been outspoken on social issues.

ROBERT ENSTAD, *"Chicago Tribune"*

Chicago hosted the 1996 Democratic National Convention and was proud as its Bulls won another National Basketball Association title. A statue of Bulls star Michael Jordan, below, *dominates the entrance to the United Center, site of the Democratic convention.*

© Porter Gifford/Gamma-Liaison

CHILE

Municipal elections were held in Chile in October 1996 in the face of widespread labor discontent, a nationwide economic slowdown, and a record drought.

Elections. The municipal elections—the second held since democracy was reestablished in Chile in 1990—were watched closely as a harbinger of both the upcoming balloting for Congress in 1997 and the 1999 presidential poll. Despite the country's problems, the ruling center-left coalition of President Eduardo Frei Ruíz-Tagle—the Concertation of Parties for Democracy—emerged triumphant in the election, taking 56% of the vote, up from its 53% share in 1992 municipal elections. One month before the election, President Frei had reshuffled his cabinet, naming four economists as ministers in a bid to spruce up the government's image.

Within the dominant coalition, Frei's own party, the Christian Democrats, fell from 29% to 25%, while the largest coalition partners, the Socialist Party and the Party for Democracy, raised their combined share to 23%. On the right, the Union for the Progress of Chile increased its voting percentage to 34%, from 28% in 1992. Much of the right's success was owed to the performance of Joaquin Lavín, the popular mayor of Las Condes, a rich Santiago suburb.

Labor Unrest. Chile experienced a full share of work stoppages and strikes in 1996. The troubles began on May 2 at the huge Chuquicamata copper mine, the world's largest, where workers demanded a 4% pay increase. The strike was settled on May 12 when workers accepted a 3% wage hike, a new 36-month contract, and a onetime bonus equivalent to $3,600.

On May 21 a strike broke out at the Lota coal mine, as workers struck in sympathy with 97 miners who had been laid off. The strike soon spread to all the nation's coal mines. In July, only days after the government threatened to close the Lota mine, the miners caved in. The government promised to seek money from the legislature to compensate any miners who were laid off or retired.

Late in September the beleaguered government faced more trouble when more than 100,000 teachers and at least that many sanitation, health, and transportation workers went on strike, seeking wage increases. Throughout the month of October, schools and hospitals were shuttered, garbage piled up in the streets, and there were clashes between police and demonstrators.

CHILE • Information Highlights

Official Name: Republic of Chile.
Location: Southwestern coast of South America.
Area: 292,259 sq mi (756 950 km²).
Population (mid-1996 est.): 14,500,000.
Chief Cities (June 30, 1995 est.): Santiago, the capital, 5,076,808; Concepción, 350,268; Viña del Mar, 322,220.
Government: *Head of state and government,* Eduardo Frei Ruíz-Tagle, president (took office March 1994). *Legislature*—National Congress: Senate and Chamber of Deputies.
Monetary Unit: Peso (422.00 pesos equal U.S.$1, official rate, Dec. 5, 1996).
Gross Domestic Product (1994 est. U.S.$): $97,700,-000,000 (purchasing power parity).
Economic Indexes (1995, 1990 = 100): *Consumer Prices,* all items, 191.1; food, 195.6. *Industrial Production,* 136.
Foreign Trade (1995 U.S.$): *Imports,* $15,914,000,000; *exports,* $16,039,000,000.

Economy. The Chilean economy began to show signs of a slowdown in May. Industrial production fell by 3.5% from a year earlier, the first drop in output since July 1994. Unemployment rose to 6.3% in March–May 1996, compared with 6.1% during the first four months of the year. The economy remained vibrant nonetheless, with high rates of consumer spending and company investment. Some fears of inflation were raised; inflation in July was 8.3%, against an official target of 6.5%. The central bank said no change in interest was contemplated, however, and by October inflation fell to 6.2%. Annual growth in gross domestic product (GDP) was predicted at 5% during the last quarter of the year, and was projected to pick up to 6% in 1997.

Drought. The country experienced its worst drought in a half century. In October the National Electricity Enterprise (Endesa) said the reservoirs of its hydroelectric plants were filled to only 32% of their capacity because of the drought, and that four new turbines would be required to cope with the emergency.

Mercosur. In 1996, Chile became an associate member of Mercosur, the Southern Cone free-trade agreement, after President Frei signed the Mercosur agreement in June and the Chilean Senate ratified it in September. Chile stood to benefit primarily from improved access to agricultural markets in Brazil and Argentina. Tariffs between Chile and other Mercosur members began to come down on October 1, but on a number of sensitive (mostly agricultural) items, they would be phased out over a period of ten to 18 years. The agreement permitted Chile to retain its standing external tariff structure and to make unilateral trade agreements with nonmember countries.

See LATIN AMERICA.

RICHARD C. SCHROEDER, *Freelance Writer*

CHINA

China exhibited a new assertiveness in its relations with the United States and its Asian neighbors in 1996. At the same time the government faced a range of intractable problems that appeared to grow more serious during the course of the year.

Paraphrasing the title of a recent book on Japan, a group of young Chinese intellectuals published a book entitled *China Can Say No* early in the year. It was followed soon afterward by the publication of two additional volumes, *China Can Still Say No* and *A Record of Confrontations between China and the United States*. These strong statements of anti-American and anti-Japanese nationalism were emblematic of a new strain of assertiveness in China's dealings with the outside world.

On the surface, the Chinese had much to be assertive about. The economy continued to grow at a rapid but controlled rate of just under 10% and inflation fell below 7%. Total foreign direct investment topped $40 billion during the course of the year, and China was well on the road to becoming one of the world's largest trading nations.

China confronted its neighbors in 1996. In February the People's Liberation Army (below) *began exercises meant to rattle Taiwan as it prepared for elections. Meanwhile, a "countdown" clock in Beijing* (right) *demonstrated China's disdain for the British-controlled government of Hong Kong by publicizing the July 1997 date that would mark the territory's transfer to China.*

© Forest Anderson/Gamma-Liaison

© Xinhua/Chine Nouvelle/Gamma-Liaison

The Chinese also had the wherewithal to be assertive. The People's Liberation Army (PLA) was an increasing source of concern to China's neighbors. Military exercises conducted by the PLA surprised many observers with the reliability of Chinese weapons and the accuracy of fire. During the year, China continued to augment its antiquated arsenal with military equipment purchased from abroad. It concluded a deal with Russia to purchase 72 high-performance SU-27 fighter aircraft; included in the deal was a licensing agreement to produce these aircraft in China. Also under discussion with Moscow was the purchase of SS-18 nuclear-missile technology. In October officials announced that negotiations were under way with France to purchase the carrier *Clemenceau*.

Taiwan. The promising trend toward closer relations across the Taiwan Strait was interrupted by China's reaction to the culmination of Taiwan's President Lee Teng-hui's campaign of "open diplomacy." Persuaded that Lee was embarked on a course that would result in his government's declaring its independence from China, Beijing attempted to influence the outcome of Taiwan's first direct presidential election in March, in which Lee was the front-runner.

China began by breaking off the two-year-old series of informal cross-Strait talks that it had hoped would lead to formal relations between the two governments. It then mounted a series of military exercises in the Taiwan Strait in February and March to demonstrate the PLA's capability to disrupt the island's maritime trade. Particularly troublesome was evidence that decisions about how to proceed with Taiwan were being made by China's military, not its civilian leaders.

China's saber rattling failed to sway Taiwan's voters, who returned Lee to office with a majority. By year's end, China's President Jiang Zemin, concerned about the effect of the confrontation on Taiwan's investment in and trade with the mainland, called for a meeting with President Lee and for opening direct communication and trade links across the Strait.

United States. While China's militant actions failed to sway Taiwan's voters, it did succeed inadvertently in bringing the United States back into the center of the Taiwan issue. A U.S. visitor to Beijing in December 1995 was told by his military hosts that U.S. leaders were unlikely to intervene because they "care more about Los Angeles than they do about Taiwan." China was prepared, they went on, "to sacrifice millions of men and entire cities" to ensure the unity of the Chinese state. Although denying that it was a response to this bluster, the U.S. Navy sent the carrier *USS Nimitz* through the Taiwan Strait later that month; it was the first U.S. warship to pass through those waters in many years. When the PLA's missile exercises threatened to disrupt the use of shipping lanes off Taiwan, the United States also stationed a carrier group in the vicinity.

Relations between Washington and Beijing reached a low point in 1996, exceeded in acrimony only by the period following the suppression of the Tiananmen demonstrations in 1989. The U.S. government threatened to impose economic sanctions on China in two separate instances during the year. The first was a response to the allegation that China had sold dual-use technology—5,000 ring magnets used to enrich uranium—to Pakistan in violation of the Nuclear Technology Control Regime (NTCR). U.S. law requires the government to suspend the sale of military and dual-use technology and to terminate Export-Import Bank loans to any country found in violation of the NTCR, even when, as in the case of China, it is not a party to the regime. In May the U.S. government determined that there was insufficient evidence to require the imposition of sanctions. Two months later, however, the U.S. government began a new investigation after information came to light indicating that China had transferred M-11 missiles to Pakistan between 1990 and 1994.

Intellectual-property rights were the second issue over which sanctions were threatened. A review of Chinese enforcement of its agreement to curb the illicit copying, marketing, and exporting of U.S.-made compact discs and computer software was begun in February. Despite Chinese press reports that enforcement measures had been stepped up, the U.S. government concluded that its agreement

CHINA • Information Highlights

Official Name: People's Republic of China.
Location: Central-eastern Asia.
Area: 3,705,390 sq mi (9 596 960 km²).
Population (mid-1996 est.): 1,217,600,000.
Chief Cities (Dec. 31, 1990 est.): Beijing (Peking), the capital, 7,000,000; Shanghai, 7,830,000; Tianjin, 5,770,000.
Government: *Head of state,* Jiang Zemin, president (took office March 1993). *Head of government,* Li Peng, premier (took office Nov. 1987). *Legislature* (unicameral)—National People's Congress.
Monetary Unit: Yuan (8.3282 yuan equal U.S.$1, Dec. 31, 1996).
Gross Domestic Product (1994 est. U.S.$): $2,978,800,-000,000 (purchasing power parity).
Foreign Trade (1995 U.S.$): *Imports,* $129,113,000,000; *exports,* $148,797,000,000.

with Beijing was being violated and threatened to impose tariffs on $2 billion in Chinese exports to the United States. The Chinese government retaliated immediately with even stiffer penalties on U.S. exports. Talks aimed at persuading the Chinese to close down more than 30 factories were unsuccessful right up to the June 17 deadline. At the very last moment an agreement was reached, with the Chinese committing to close 15 of the offending factories and to impose a new licensing arrangement on the production of music, film, and software discs.

Behind both of these episodes was U.S. concern about its mounting trade deficit with China. The deficit, which totaled about $35 billion in 1995, had reached that level by the end of October 1996 and was projected to approach $45 billion by year's end. On the basis of monthly figures, China overtook Japan in June as having the highest surplus in its trade with the United States. Wu Yi, China's minister of foreign trade and economic cooperation, presented the nation's perspective on the question of the deficit, noting that, by Chinese calculations, the 1995 deficit was $8.5 billion. The difference, Wu said, was accounted for by the fact that goods transshipped through Hong Kong were being counted by the U.S. government as exports from China, while their value was being determined on the basis of Hong Kong prices. Wu also noted that the rapid rise in the U.S. trade deficit with China largely was offset by a decline in the U.S. deficit with economies such as Korea and Taiwan, which had shifted much of their manufacturing operations to China. While Wu's arguments and figures were confirmed by U.S. economists, they did little to assuage concern in Congress.

Disturbed by the depth to which relations with China had fallen, the administration of President Bill Clinton launched an active policy of "constructive engagement" with Beijing in the spring. China's "most favored nation" trading status was renewed without serious opposition in Congress. U.S. Secretary of State Warren Christopher called for regular conversations between cabinet-level officials on the two sides. He followed up his proposal with three meetings with Chinese Foreign Affairs Minister Qian Qichen during the remainder of the year. U.S. National Security Adviser Anthony Lake, Arms Control and Disarmament Agency Director John Holum, Undersecretary of State Lynn Davis, and Central Intelligence Agency Director John Deutch all visited Beijing during the fall. The new policy culminated with a meeting between Clinton and Jiang in Manila in November, at which the two presidents agreed to an exchange of state visits in 1997 and 1998.

Japan. China's assertiveness toward Japan was triggered by a perceived revival of Japanese militarism. Making headlines was a continuing territorial dispute over islands—known to the Chinese as Diaoyu and to the Japanese as Senkaku—located between Okinawa and Taiwan and claimed by the governments of Japan, China, and Taiwan. When Japan's Prime Minister Ryutaro Hashimoto made a ceremonial visit in September to a shrine honoring Japanese soldiers killed in World War II, the Chinese government responded by formally protesting the erecting of structures on the islands by the conservative Japan Youth Federation. Although Beijing and Taipei took a reasonably low-key approach to the episode, public opinion on the mainland and in Taiwan and Hong Kong immediately was galvanized. Boatloads of Chinese attempting to land on and "reclaim" the islands were diverted by Japanese naval vessels.

Hong Kong. China also battled with the British-controlled government of Hong Kong. Chinese authorities professed a deep anger over Hong Kong Governor Christopher Patten's democratic reforms and over Hong Kong citizens' support for what remained of the democracy movement in China. China refused to recognize the legitimacy of the democratically elected Legislative Council created by the reforms, and insisted that it would be replaced by a legislature chosen by a 400-member selection committee when sovereignty over the territory shifted on July 1, 1997. Having made its point with the selection of Tung Chee-hwa as the prospective chief executive and the naming of the new legislature in December, Beijing retreated a bit and grudgingly acknowledged that Governor Patten might attend the transfer-of-sovereignty ceremonies in July. (*See* HONG KONG: A TIME OF DRAMATIC CHANGE, page 44.)

Economic Realities. Behind the facade of an assertive and nationalistic China, however, lay a myriad of difficult problems. On the economic front the two most serious issues were how to dismantle the decrepit and unprofitable state sector and how to ensure an adequate supply of grain for a growing population. While the share of the gross national product (GNP) produced by state-owned enterprises declined to less than 50%, the state sector continued to employ nearly 70% of the industrial workforce and to absorb two thirds of fixed-asset investment. This infusion

© Xinhua/Chine Nouvelle/Gamma-Liaison

Catastrophic flooding along the Yangtze River and other waterways left a wake of destruction in south and central China in July and August 1996. The region's worst flooding in decades caused the deaths of at least 2,500 persons and left millions more homeless.

of capital was augmented by subsidies that contributed to a 26% growth in the central government's budget deficit, and loans of such dubious quality that they caused the central bank's international credit rating to slip. Despite all of this costly support, the state sector continued to sink slowly into a pond of red ink. According to official figures, a quarter of the sector was operating in the red; unofficial estimates placed this figure much higher.

In some cases, officials simply closed unprofitable factories. Such steps were not put to broader use because there were not nearly enough jobs in the private and collective sectors to absorb the substantial number of workers that would be laid off if all unprofitable enterprises were shut down simultaneously. While the welfare of these workers certainly was a concern for the government, their disaffection and the possibility that they might act on that disaffection was foremost in the minds of decision makers.

The official unemployment figure of 3% did not include those on furlough or those who had been sent home on substantially reduced wages as a cost-cutting measure by ailing state-owned factories. Some 14 million workers—about 8% of the urban workforce—were affected by these measures. Planners forecast that to provide full employment for those unemployed, those laid off by bankruptcies in the state sector, and those entering the workforce anew, the economy would have to generate 40 million new jobs for the urban workforce in the next decade. They further estimated that the number of new jobs actually generated would fall short of that figure by as many as 16 million.

These figures also did not account for the migrant workforce of rural residents leaving their home villages in search of work. Their number was estimated to stand at 80 million and was projected to reach 110 million by the turn of the century. While somewhat less than half of these "floaters" were able to find work in collective enterprises located in their own home counties, the remainder moved into cities, where pay was substantially higher. Some argued that migrant labor was emerging as a positive force in Chinese society, providing a link to close the growing gap between the living standards of the rural majority and the urban minority and functioning as a safety valve for the rural economy, where nearly 140 million workers were unemployed or underemployed. However, others worried that "floaters" were adrift in what was once a highly regimented society. Troubled by this lack of control, the government proposed during the summer that the *hukou* (household registration) system be revived and revised. The system once functioned to keep every Chinese citizen glued to a specific *danwei* (work unit). The proposed system would preserve the free-

© Ajit Kumar/AP/Wide World Photos

During a visit to New Delhi, China's President Jiang Zemin (left) *met with India's Prime Minister H.D. Deve Gowda and signed a border pact and several other agreements on Nov. 29, 1996.*

dom to move from place to place in search of work, but would attempt to do a more effective job of keeping track of those choosing to exercise this freedom.

Feeding a growing population on a shrinking pool of arable land was a second problem that the government began to take very seriously. In 1994, Lester Brown, president of the U.S.-based Worldwatch Institute, predicted a shortfall in China's grain production by 2030 so large that it would exceed the world economy's capacity to fill it. He attributed the shortfall to an increase in the population, to increased per-capita grain consumption, and to a sharp decline in the amount of land under cultivation, brought on by economic development. The Chinese government dismissed Brown's predictions out of hand. More recently, however, it was clear that economic planners and agricultural economists in China were giving serious consideration to the facts on which Brown based his forecast.

In 1990 grain consumption in China was roughly 660 lb (300 kg) per person—about 38% of U.S. per-capita grain consumption. As China's standard of living increased, the Chinese people were expected not only to consume more grain per capita, but also to consume more meat and eggs—both of which exponentially increase per-capita grain consumption. Meanwhile, land was being drawn out of cultivation at a rate of about 460,000 acres (186 000 ha) per year as roads, railways, factories, and new housing were being built on land once used for crops. Planners set a target of 320,000 acres (130 000 ha) per year to limit the loss of arable land.

The 1996 grain harvest was predicted to reach an all-time high, despite extensive flooding in some of the country's most productive grain-producing areas. Ministry of agriculture planners expressed hopes of increasing annual production by increasing yields and multiple cropping on existing farmland, improving the quality of marginal land, and bringing new land under cultivation. Achieving these ambitious goals presupposed a substantial increase in state and private investment in the agricultural sector, as well as a committed and efficient workforce. The latter was expected to be difficult to create and sustain given the low incomes of rural residents, the erratic tax-collection system, and the land-tenure system that often obscures ownership rights.

The Political Realm. While Deng Xiaoping managed to confound prognosticators and live yet another year, there was mounting evidence that he and his views increasingly were being ignored by his putative successors. As his 92d birthday was about to be celebrated, his son, Deng Pufang, opened a meeting of the Chinese Federation for the Disabled with a speech attacking "policies that wholly negate the Deng Xiaoping line." His speech went unreported in the official press. Meanwhile Pufang and other members of Deng's family found themselves scrambling to defend themselves against mounting incursions on their positions and privileges.

The communiqué of the annual plenum of the Communist Party Central Committee, which met in October, paid only cursory lip service to Deng, calling instead for "socialist ethical and cultural progress" in combating "rampant individualism, lack of patriotism and moral decline," all of which it attributed to excessively rapid economic growth. When Deng last was heard from (in 1992), it was this very rapid growth that he was advocating. The new cautious line was associated closely with President and Party General Secretary Jiang Zemin, who spent the year at home and abroad attempting to consolidate his hold on the reins of power in preparation for the next party congress, scheduled to be held in 1997.

Corruption and crime continued to pose serious problems for the government. The National People's Congress in March adopted important legal reforms. The reforms, which were slated to go into effect on Jan. 1, 1997, called for the presumption of defendants' innocence until they are proven guilty, a greater role for defense lawyers in trial procedures, and a limit on the time suspects can be held in administrative custody before being brought to trial. All of these changes were hailed by proponents of the establishment of a rule of law in China. At the same time, however, observers noted an unseemly haste on the part of police and prosecutors to resolve long-standing investigations and conduct trials of dissidents long held in custody before the new procedures took effect.

In fact, by the end of December, virtually all of the remnants of the democracy movement were either in prison or under tightly supervised house arrest. The appeal of Wei Jingshen's 14-year sentence was denied in December 1995, and Wang Dan—who already had served three years in prison for his role in the Tiananmen demonstrations—was rearrested and sentenced to an additional 11 years for conspiracy to overthrow the government. Although Bao Tong, the only senior Communist Party official to be prosecuted in 1989, was released from prison in June for health reasons, he and other dissidents complained that the terms of the house arrest into which they were released were not only unduly restrictive, but also illegal.

Tibet was another of the government's problems that became considerably more complex during the year. A decision to crack down on Tibetan opposition to Chinese control, said to have been taken in July 1994, took the form in 1996 of a regulation preventing the display of pictures of the Dalai Lama. An article in the Chinese-controlled *Tibet Daily* in May referred to the struggle against the "Dalai Lama clique" as a "long-term, bitter, complex, you-die-I-live political battle with no possibility of compromise." There were four reports of bombings in Lhasa during the year and, by year's end, more than 600 Tibetans were being held in prison.

JOHN BRYAN STARR, *Brown University*

CITIES AND URBAN AFFAIRS

Unlike most of their European counterparts, U.S. cities have been afflicted by increased poverty, significant job loss, and growing numbers of abandoned buildings that once were sites of commerce, production, or residence. This has happened because ample land, ease of construction, federal tax and mortgage benefits, and fixed boundaries have led the affluent and those of middle income, as well as many businesses, to settle in suburban communities. This has eroded the tax base of central cities and left the poor, increasingly members of minority groups, at the core. Because of demographic and commercial shifts, central cities have struggled to achieve financial equilibrium and to define a raison d'être for themselves that does not include being home to the majority of the area's population and to middle-class families with children. Crime, battered school systems, and decay characterize many central cities in the mid-1990s.

Here, the focus is on certain key issues affecting major U.S. cities, such as crime, fiscal stress, development, community services, and education. Whatever the theme, the duality of urban existence—between an eviscerated core and a wealthy outer ring—is evident.

Crime. Many newspaper headlines heralded significant drops in major crimes in 1996. Incidences of crime, however, have been linked to the population of unemployed male youth, and as this population again would begin to increase in coming years, crime was expected to rise as well. The proliferation of firearms correlates with the crime rate, too. In Minneapolis, a city not particularly noted for social ills, the murder rate has soared, apparently because of a growing drug trade. Police, however, have become more aggressive in fighting crime. Baltimore, San Francisco, and other cities have installed cameras and listening devices at key places in order to monitor street activity and counteract random gunfire and gang shootings. Although the crime rate has fallen in many cities, crime has continued to present a challenge to urban living.

Fiscal Problems. The U.S. government's attempts to balance its budget have had ramifications for the nation's cities. Programs that cities have used for services and revitalization, including Community Development Block Grants, have been cut. Programs to employ teenage students have been slashed by 23%. Everywhere the costs of services have risen, while income has not. Changes to the nation's welfare programs will enhance the problems cities are facing; as 1996 ended the outlook for increased federal aid was bleak.

The fiscal crisis that Washington, DC, faced in 1996 was emblematic of the national problem. Its tax base has shrunk, while population flight has increased. Its services have declined and broken parking meters and uncollected trash have become visible symptoms of the crisis. In Montgomery, AL, and other communities, lower-income residents have worried about the decline and possible demise of public transportation.

Financial problems were a primary cause of a campaign in Miami, FL, to revoke the city's charter. Angered by a growing budget deficit and corruption scandals, many residents of Miami's wealthier districts were calling for the city to merge with the government of Dade county. A referendum on the question was expected to be held in 1997.

Development and Community Services. Because of a significant dependence on their own resources, cities have had to develop or die. This logic has guided many municipal projects since the 1950s. In recent years, tourism and often sports have been a central focus. For a city to remain in the "big leagues," it has to have major sports teams. Owners have used this premise to secure increasingly generous subsidies for new stadiums to keep existing sports franchises or to lure new ones. In 1996, Baltimore was building a $200 million stadium to house its Ravens, formerly the Cleveland Browns. Public debt was financing the new stadium, as it did the city's Camden Yards and the new Comiskey Park in Chicago.

Stadiums remained a jump start to redevelopment in Detroit, the nation's most depressed major city. There, new stadiums were to be built downtown for baseball's Tigers and football's Lions. Detroit was providing a new element for the equation: The team owners were paying a greater share of the costs themselves. Similarly, the Miami Heat basketball team agreed to fund the cost of its new arena. Although these cities will incur operating costs, their contribution to construction will be less than in the past. Detroit also will see a game of musical chairs, as General Motors moves its world headquarters to the Renaissance Center, while the city moves its offices to the former GM complex. Detroit, like other cities, was hoping that downtown development would restore the sparkle of a past era, perhaps emulating the success of Cleveland or Kansas City, MO.

In Kansas City, new buildings and important restorations have provided a distinct counterpoint to its continuing urban sprawl. Since the opening of Jacobs Field in 1994 and the Rock and Roll Hall of Fame and Museum in 1995, Cleveland has been many people's favorite comeback city. Its historic Warehouse District provides new homes to the upwardly mobile, and the Flats, an old industrial area, is turning into a nighttime entertainment district. New housing is going up to lure families back to the city. Cleveland's poverty population remains substantial and its school system is troubled. But the city has devoted considerable resources to planning and has a strong well-staffed business coalition supporting its efforts.

New York City, which also was contemplating a new home for its 1996-world-champion Yankees, was punctuating its development with an attention-getting display of public art that has been made possible by its "percent for art," collected during the heady building of the 1980s. Harlem was beginning to benefit from the Upper Manhattan Empowerment Zone, which brought $250 million to businesses and nonprofits for commercial development. Insurance companies that long had redlined central cities were appearing in Harlem and other minority areas in central cities.

A side benefit of declining federal aid to cities is the burgeoning of neighborhood groups that provide new volunteer-based service delivery, from tutoring to street patrols. They also lobby city officials for various improvements.

Education. Failing school systems in central cities increase middle-class flight and fail to provide the future workers needed in an increasingly technological society. The effect of poor schools on city viability was clear to a number of mayors and has led to drastic action in certain locations. Richard M. Daley, mayor of Chicago, pushed a bill through the state legislature that gave him control over the city's schools. Though the verdict was not yet in, changes were instituted quickly. In New York, Mayor Rudolph Giuliani also fought for greater control and replaced one school superintendent with someone more attuned to his aims. The move to charter schools, schools of choice, and site-based management are methods of reforming school districts. The linkage between schools and municipal well-being was clear; whether various attempts at reform would take hold was not certain yet.

Searching for Solutions. The basic problem of the urban tragedy is uneven development: Those people with means remain segregated, by and large, from those without. Opportunities expand on the periphery but those who need the opportunities most are at the core. Racial tensions continue to exacerbate the fundamental inequalities; indeed, the racial dimension is a fundamental factor in the isolation of central cities and in their neglect.

The problems of metropolitan areas generally, and especially those in less-developed countries, are likely to grow in the years to come, according to the second UN Conference on Human Settlements (Habitat II), which was held in Istanbul in June 1996. Urban populations in Africa, Asia, and Latin America are increasing so rapidly that some cities will become megacities of 20 million or more people, at least half of whom will live in dire poverty without access to basic sanitation and plagued by increasing violence and disease. This news from Habitat II reinforces the need to examine urban dualism everywhere and to search for intervention strategies.

LANA STEIN, *University of Missouri–St. Louis*

COINS AND COIN COLLECTING

A revamped U.S. $100 bill and two coins celebrating the Smithsonian Institution's 150th anniversary made 1996 an exciting year for collectors.

On Sept. 27, 1995, Federal Reserve Board Chairman Alan Greenspan and Treasury Secretary Robert Rubin announced the first comprehensive change in the design of U.S. paper money since 1929. In response to a serious threat of counterfeiting abroad, the new $100 bill was introduced early in 1996; lower denominations were to be revised over the next several years. Older series would not be demonetized, but would continue to circulate.

In addition to an extra letter in the serial number and a polymer thread running through it, the new $100 bill incorporates several counterfeit deterrents. The face, or front, of the note features two portraits of Benjamin Franklin: a large, intaglio-printed version, placed slightly off-center to reduce wear from folding; and, to the right, a watermark. Behind the large portrait of Franklin and around Independence Hall on the back of the note are fine concentric lines. The number at the lower right on the front is printed in color-shifting ink. Microprinting is found within the denomination at the lower left and on Franklin's lapel.

Besides gearing up to print the $100 bill, the Bureau of Engraving and Printing produced $2 bills for the first time since 1979. Printed at Fort Worth, TX, the bills will be issued only by the Federal Reserve Bank of Atlanta. The design of the Series 1995 notes remains unchanged.

For collectors of U.S. coinage, Jan. 10, 1996, was a memorable day: President Bill Clinton authorized a gold $5 and silver $1 coin commemorating the sesquicentennial of the Smithsonian Institution (*see* FEATURE ARTICLE). Founded with a bequest by British scientist James Smithson, the Smithsonian traces its origins to gold coins. Smithson's estate was converted to 104,960 British gold sovereigns; most were melted down by the U.S. Mint. Fortunately, two escaped the melting pot and now reside—along with almost 1 million other items—in the National Numismatic Collection at the Smithsonian. For each silver and gold coin sold, the Smithsonian will receive $10 and $35, respectively. Fifteen percent of the revenues will be credited to the National Numismatic Collection; the rest will support the Institution's educational outreach.

Collectors also were offered the second half of a 1995–96 coin series commemorating the Centennial Olympic Games in Atlanta, as well as a 1996 silver dollar recognizing national community service. In honor of the Roosevelt dime's 50th anniversary, the first 10-cent pieces to bear a "W" mint mark, for the West Point Mint, were made available in 1996 uncirculated sets.

MARILYN A. REBACK
American Numismatic Association

The year 1996 saw the release of a redesigned U.S. $100 bill and two commemorative coins celebrating the Atlanta Summer Olympics. The revamped $100 bill (top left *and* bottom left) *was designed to foil increasingly sophisticated counterfeiters; it features color-shifting ink, microprinting, a watermark, and an enlarged, off-center portrait. Meanwhile, the new U.S. coinage—a silver dollar* (top right) *and a half-dollar coin* (bottom right)*—paid special tribute to the 100th anniversary of the Olympic Games.*

© Bureau of Engraving and Printing

© Bureau of Engraving and Printing

© Courtesy, Krause Publications, Inc.

© Courtesy, Krause Publications, Inc.

COLOMBIA

In Colombia the first six months of 1996 were dominated by charges that President Ernesto Samper knowingly accepted some $6 million in contributions to his 1994 presidential campaign from the Cali drug cartel. Cries for Samper's resignation came from various quarters, including his former campaign manager and Minister of National Defense Fernando Botero Zea. Botero, who subsequently was convicted of fraud and illicit enrichment in connection with the contributions, implicated Samper in early January. Subsequently, charges of fraud, obstruction of justice, and illicit enrichment brought against Samper were considered by a congressional committee. On June 12 the Chamber of Deputies—a body dominated by Samper's Liberal Party—voted, 111–43, against sending the case to trial. That vote exhausted all of the measures allowed by Colombia's constitution to impeach the president.

Despite the outcry against the verdict and the subsequent revocation of Samper's visa by the U.S. government, national life soon returned to something close to normalcy. Even the September resignation of Vice-President Humberto de la Calle Lombana and his denunciation of Samper failed to roil the political waters further. By the end of the year, halfway through his term, Samper seemed more secure in the presidency than he had been in the previous two years.

Drugs continued to plague Colombia. In January the escape of a Cali drug kingpin from a Cali jail caused embarrassment to the government, as did the release from prison of a former Medellín drug lord after he had served only half of his five-year sentence. The lengthy debate in Congress over a new extradition law that would reinstate extradition of drug lords to the United States after a five-year hiatus was a further thorn in the government's side.

Guerrilla violence also continued throughout the year. An August attack by the Revolutionary Armed Forces of Colombia (FARC), the nation's oldest and largest rebel group, against several army and police posts in the south left more than 96 persons dead.

Economy. The economy rebounded after suffering during the first half of the year. Even so, the government estimate of a 4.9% increase in gross domestic product (GDP) was not met. Experts estimated that GDP growth would be between 2.5% and 3.8%. Inflation stayed relatively constant at roughly 21%. Unemployment rose from 8.7% in September 1995 to 12.1% in October 1996. Among economic sectors, construction was hardest hit. An October truckers' strike further damaged the economy by shutting down coffee exports for a short time.

Counterbalancing these trends was an unexpected dollar glut and a marked increase in international reserves, which totaled $8.1 billion at the end of September. In October the government began buying U.S. dollars in an effort to stop the plunge in the price of the dollar vis-à-vis the peso. The intervention had little effect, however, leaving Colombian exporters increasingly worried. Late in the year four new exploration contracts were signed by Ecopetrol, the national oil company, and foreign firms.

Foreign Relations. Relations between Colombia and the United States hit a new low during the year. In addition to the aforementioned visa cancellation, in March the United States decertified Colombia as a partner in the "war on drugs," a decision that made Colombia ineligible for most economic assistance from the United States.

Declarations by U.S. Ambassador Myles Frechette also angered Colombian officials on at least two occasions. Frechette first expressed displeasure in June over Samper's exoneration, and in October publicly threatened U.S. sanctions if a new extradition bill, complete with a retroactivity clause, was not approved by the Colombian Congress.

See also LATIN AMERICA.

ERNEST A. DUFF
Randolph-Macon Woman's College

COLOMBIA • Information Highlights

Official Name: Republic of Colombia.
Location: Northwest South America.
Area: 439,734 sq mi (1 138 910 km²).
Population (mid-1996 est.): 38,000,000.
Chief Cities (mid-1995 est.): Bogotá, the capital, 5,237,635; Cali, 1,718,871; Medellín, 1,621,356; Barranquilla, 1,064,255.
Government: *Head of state and government,* Ernesto Samper Pizano, president (took office August 1994). *Legislature*—Congress: Senate and House of Representatives.
Monetary Unit: Peso (995.50 pesos equal U.S.$1, Dec. 9, 1996).
Gross Domestic Product (1994 est. U.S.$): $172,400,-000,000 (purchasing power parity).
Economic Indexes (1995, 1990 = 100): *Consumer Prices,* all items, 302.4; food, 279.9. *Industrial Production,* 118.
Foreign Trade (1995 U.S.$): *Imports,* $13,853,000,000; *exports,* $9,764,000,000.

COMMONWEALTH OF INDEPENDENT STATES.

See RUSSIA AND THE COMMONWEALTH OF INDEPENDENT STATES.

COMMUNICATION TECHNOLOGY

The biggest news in communication technology in 1996 was the passage early in the year of legislation overhauling the U.S. telecommunications industry.

Telecommunications Reform. The first major revision of U.S. telecommunications law in 62 years had as a principal goal the promotion of competition among communications companies. It was hoped that more competition would lead both to better prices and services for U.S. consumers and to businesses' enhanced ability to compete abroad. Many barriers between categories of communications companies fell; cable-television providers now would be allowed to provide phone service, long-distance phone companies could compete in local markets, and the "Baby Bells" became able to offer long-distance service. Broadcasting companies now could own more TV and radio stations.

The point drawing the most controversy was the provision restricting the transmission of indecent material over computer networks. The law was challenged by civil-liberties groups, which filed a suit arguing that the act's broad definition of "indecency" would lead to infringements on free speech. In June a panel of three federal judges unanimously ruled the law's attempt to regulate on-line content unconstitutional.

In another attempt to regulate content and protect children, the reform bill mandated that a "v-chip"—which would allow viewers to block out violent or sex-oriented programming—be installed in all televisions manufactured in or imported for use in the United States.

At the beginning of August, the Federal Communications Commission (FCC) issued a comprehensive set of rules governing competition in local telephone markets. In October a federal court suspended key provisions of the rules that were being challenged by local carriers and state regulators.

New Directions. There soon were indications of the new developments made possible by the deregulation of the telecommunications industry.

In April 1996, two regional telephone companies, Bell Atlantic and Nynex, agreed to a merger. It would be one of the largest corporate mergers in U.S. history and would create the second-largest phone company in the United States, after AT&T. The new company would dominate telecommunications in the U.S. Northeast, operating in 12 states and serving about 36 million customers. Earlier in the year, SBC Communications had acquired the Pacific Telesis Group, creating a regional company providing service to more than 30 million customers in seven states.

By September, several major cable-television companies had begun offering Internet access, on a limited basis, through high-speed cable modems. Meanwhile, some telephone companies began marketing Internet access over special phone lines. Cable companies, however, would seem to have an advantage, since coaxial cable can transmit data hundreds of times faster than traditional copper telephone wires, and much faster even than high-speed ISDN (integrated-services digital network) lines. The transmission of full-motion video through cable modems, however, still was several years away. The phone companies, meanwhile, introduced a technology called ADSL (asymmetrical digital subscriber line) that allows faster and larger data transfers over regular copper lines. Several cable companies already were offering phone service.

Some of the fallout from deregulation was problematic. The increasingly fierce competition between phone companies led to consumers being unable to place calls in certain areas using calling cards from their chosen long-distance provider, as the Baby Bells sometimes refused access to their lines to AT&T. Eleven-digit access codes often had to be dialed in order to assure a call being carried by the correct company. The increased competition spelled trouble for AT&T, which announced in September that its profits for the rest of 1996 were likely to be as much as 10% below industry expectations. Hoping to strengthen its position, the company simultaneously announced a new flat rate of 15¢ per minute for all U.S. long-distance calls.

"Smart Phones." A product blurring the lines between telecommunications products and computers was the screen phone, or "smart phone." These phones feature small keyboards—usually about 4 inches (10.2 cm) high by 8 inches (20.3 cm) wide—and liquid-crystal display screens measuring about 3 inches by 4 inches (7.6 cm by 10.2 cm). Retailing at between $300 and $500, they allow users to send Internet E-mail; relay messages to pagers; and access stock quotes, sports scores, and other information. They also feature enhanced call waiting, in which the name and address of a person calling while the line is in use are displayed on the screen; the phone's user then can decide whether to take the second call or route it to a voice-mail system for message-taking.

The technological capabilities of "smart phones" are expected to increase dramatically and quickly. Most models are equipped with credit-card slots, which soon will be usable for electronic bill-paying and banking, and eventually for E-cash cards. Some are equipped to receive E-mail, once software is upgraded to make this possible—expected in 1997. Northern Telecom planned to incorporate Sun's Java software into its Powertouch model in 1997; this development would allow callers to see pictures of products they are ordering by phone.

Wireless Communications. Various forms of wireless communication continued their precipitous growth in 1996. Among these was a wireless Internet link, Ricochet, created by Metricom Inc., that allows computer users to access the Internet even when out of reach of traditional phone lines by using wireless modems. By late summer, Metricom had linked up several college and university campuses as well as the entire San Francisco Bay area; it was beginning to cover Seattle, WA, and Washington, DC.

Pacific Telesis, California's local phone company, showcased the state's first personal communications service (PCS) wireless phone system at the Republican National Convention in San Diego in August. Delegates and officials used the system to make calls from the convention floor.

In early October, AT&T introduced Digital PCS, a new wireless phone service, in 40 U.S. markets. Most current cellular phones use analog technology; digital phones would be expected to yield crisper, clearer sound and greater security. The service offered caller ID, voice mail, paging, and E-mail capabilities, negating the need for a separate pager. Competitors pointed out that it was not a true PCS system; AT&T, however, asserted that its new offering had almost all the same features as genuine PCS services, which some companies expected to introduce by year's end—months sooner than the expected debut of AT&T's true PCS system.

The U.S. Justice Department and the wireless industry went head-to-head in 1996. The government claimed it has the right—under 1994 legislation—to be able to determine the location of a cellular-phone caller within a half second and to monitor the status of other wireless-communication features. The industry and privacy advocates maintained the Justice Department was trying to obtain broader powers than the law intended.

ROBERT C. FIERO
Grolier Interactive

COMPUTERS

In 1996 the computer industry celebrated the 50th anniversary of ENIAC, the world's first general-purpose digital computer. Touted as being "faster than a speeding bullet," it could add 5,000 ten-digit numbers or multiply 333 of them in one second. The computer weighed 30 tons, and in one second used enough energy to meet the needs of a typical U.S. home for $1\frac{1}{2}$ weeks. Each time a different program was to be run, operators had to reset thousands of switches and reconnect hundreds of cables manually.

Developments in the succeeding decades have been amazing. Today's personal computers (PCs) weigh no more than a bag of groceries, are 1,000 times faster than ENIAC, and can switch quickly from one stored program to another. The pace of innovation continues at breathtaking speed, opening up new frontiers such as cyberspace (*see* FEATURE ARTICLE, page 62) and almost guaranteeing that today's products will be obsolete tomorrow.

Buyer's Market. The year saw the continuation of a familiar story: faster and more powerful machines coupled with falling prices. By mid-1996 desktop PCs were configured with Intel's superfast 200-MHz Pentium chips, eight-speed CD-ROM drives, and 1.6-gigabyte (GB) hard drives. Advances in miniaturization meant that the performance of notebook computers nearly matched that of desktop models. Sales of these lightweight machines were expected to reach almost 4.8 million units in 1996.

New, improved personal digital assistants (PDAs)—small, handheld pen-based PCs—continued to appear. The market for PDAs, however, had failed to match expectations, and analysts believed sales would not take off until prices declined and the devices could communicate, preferably wirelessly.

Throughout the industry, fierce competition created winners and losers. Microsoft continued to ride high, thanks in large part to the success of its Windows 95 operating system. Financially troubled Apple saw its U.S. market share dwindle from more than 10% in 1995 to about 7% in mid-1996. Netscape's Navigator dominated the market for browsers—software needed to access the Internet's World Wide Web—but Microsoft was fighting to gain customers for its Internet Explorer. To hook up to the Web, a PC user needs an account with an on-line service such as America Online or CompuServe, or with an Internet service provider (ISP). Increasingly, people were opting for the faster service

Courtesy, Unisys Corporation

Courtesy, Dell Computer Corporation

A study in contrasts: the room-filling, labor-intensive ENIAC computer of 1946 (top), *and today's powerful desktop PC* (above), *which allows users to issue commands with a single keystroke or mouse click.*

and better prices offered by ISPs. Adding yet more competition, Sony and Toshiba announced their entry into the PC market. Olivetti, however, said it intended to sell its PC division.

Mass Storage. The removable-mass-storage market traditionally has been dominated by magnetic tape. Up to 4 GB of data can be stored on a tape designed for use with a desktop PC. However, the tape drive must move through the reel to reach the data requested. CD-R, or compact disk-recordable, is a newer, faster option that allows a user to save up to 650 megabytes of data on a disk. Though comparatively high, CD-R prices declined as competition heated up. CD-R also can be used for creating multimedia presentations, distributing data to other computers, storing training videos that otherwise would overwhelm a hard disk, and other applications.

Another mass-storage technique expected to be introduced in late 1996 or early 1997 is the digital videodisc (DVD). Designed to replace videocassettes and CD-ROMs, DVDs can store at least 4.7 GB, the equivalent of a 133-minute movie. A new type of drive will be needed to read DVDs, but it is anticipated that such drives also will be able to read existing CD-ROMs.

Computer Telephony. An emerging technology was threatening in 1996 to replace traditional long-distance telephone services. It became possible—by using a multimedia PC and special software—to transmit voice over the Internet, and, during the same call, to send text, video, and other data. The caller speaks into the PC's microphone; the software digitizes and compresses the sounds and sends them via the Internet to the recipient's PC, which decompresses them and makes them audible. Unlike a phone conversation, only one person can speak at a time. Also, both computers must use the same software, though in mid-1996, Intel and Microsoft announced technical standards intended to promote compatibility among products.

Computer telephony has a major advantage: It is free. The caller avoids long-distance charges; the only cost is the monthly subscription fee to the ISP. Supporters envision numerous applications, including low-cost videoconferences and multiplayer computer games with voice capabilities. A group of long-distance phone companies, troubled by the potential competition, asked the Federal Communications Commission "to order the respondents to immediately stop their unauthorized provisioning of telecommunications services" and to levy charges on ISPs similar to those that long-distance carriers pay local phone companies for originating and terminating calls.

JENNY TESAR, *Author*
"The New Webster's Computer Handbook"

CONSUMER AFFAIRS

Involvement by the U.S. federal and state governments in consumer affairs was minimal in 1996. In a 1996 survey of more than 100 agency offices, most respondents reported that various state consumer-protection laws had been eliminated, while many others were under attack. Consumer groups were watching closely to determine if reductions in the role of federal and state agencies would have a substantive adverse effect on consumers or if the marketplace would perform better with reduced government oversight. Nevertheless, a few substantial laws and regulations involving the consumer were enacted or became effective during the year.

Meat and Poultry. In July, U.S. President Bill Clinton announced the first overhaul of federal meat-inspection regulations in 90 years. The new rules mandated that meat and poultry processors conduct scientific tests for disease-causing bacteria. Under the new regulations, processors would be required to install equipment to detect *E. coli* bacteria; the U.S. Department of Agriculture also would begin testing for the salmonella bacteria. The previously used system of visual, touch, and smell inspections could not uncover those deadly organisms. (*See also* FOOD.)

Telecommunications. Significant changes in telecommunications law were made in February with the passage of the Telecommunications Act of 1996. Lawmakers hoped that the legislation would increase competition among cable-television, radio, and local and long-distance telephone services. For example, the law opened the way for regional "Baby Bells" to enter the long-distance market and for other companies to enter the local market. Most cable rates were slated to be deregulated by the year 2000.

A portion of the law, the Communications Decency Act, included provisions that would penalize persons and communications providers who transmit indecent or offensive materials to minors over the Internet and other computer networks. In June and July, two federal courts found these provisions unconstitutional and blocked their enforcement; the Supreme Court was expected to issue a final ruling on the act's constitutionality. In any event, many observers believed that Congress would continue to play an active role in scrutinizing the burgeoning communications arena. The areas of decency, privacy, and fraud were expected to be targets for additional congressional action. (*See also* COMMUNICATION TECHNOLOGY.)

Telemarketing Rules. On Jan. 1, 1996, regulations mandated by the Telemarketing and Consumer Fraud and Abuse Prevention Act of 1994 were implemented. The regulations specify that material facts pertaining to goods or services offered for sale must be clearly and conspicuously disclosed to potential customers. For example, telemarketers must disclose that calls are for sales purposes and identify the name of the company selling the product or service. In addition, telemarketers are prohibited from calling consumers who do not want to be solicited and from making calls before 8:00 A.M. or after 9:00 P.M. local time. Finally, telemarketers are prohibited from withdrawing money from a customer's checking account without verifiable consent.

The Federal Trade Commission (FTC) has the power to enforce these regulations and to levy penalties of up to $10,000 per violation, and state law-enforcement agencies may prosecute telemarketers who operate across state lines and sue for nationwide injunctions in federal court. Individual consumers also are allowed to file lawsuits.

MEL J. ZELENAK
University of Missouri-Columbia

CRIME

U.S. crime rates continued to improve during 1996. Nonetheless, crime remained a prominent issue in the political arena, particularly in the presidential campaign.

Politics. Republican presidential nominee Robert Dole campaigned hard on the crime issue, accusing incumbent President Bill Clinton and his administration of contributing to a rise in illegal drug use among teenagers. Dole promised that if elected he would cut teen use of illicit drugs in half; Republicans also suggested the president tolerated drug use by White House aides. But President Clinton hardly shied from the debate. He blamed Republicans in Congress for cutting funds for fighting drug trafficking and advocated many anticrime proposals favored by his political opponents. Clinton endorsed expanding use of the federal death penalty and limiting death-row appeals; he also voiced support for new prison construction, curfews for minors, and more police on the streets.

In the U.S. Congress, legislation was passed and signed by the president that imposes criminal penalties for stalkers who cross state lines to harass or harm their targets. The measure closed a loophole in a 1994 comprehensive anticrime law that only covered interstate

© Alice Wheeler

The increased use of illegal drugs by teenagers became a concern of retired Gen. Barry McCaffrey (right) as he took over as director of the Office of National Drug Control Policy.

© John Gress/AP/Wide World Photos

stalking by current or former spouses or intimate partners. Individuals convicted under the new federal law would face five years in prison for harassment and a life term for killing a victim. Legislation outlawing Rohypnol and other so-called "date rape" drugs also was enacted. Rapists could get an extra 20 years in prison for using narcotics to incapacitate their victims.

An increasing number of states enacted laws against sexual offenders. Many states implemented various laws requiring sexual offenders released from prison to register with law-enforcement agencies. California became the first state in the nation to mandate the "chemical castration" of repeat child molesters. The state law would require anyone convicted of two sexual assaults on minors to be injected with a drug that reduces sex drive, unless the offender would agree to surgical castration at the government's expense.

Crime Rates. Continuing a trend that had begun several years earlier, the rate of violent crimes in the United States fell 4% and overall crime declined 2% in 1995, according to the Uniform Crime Report from the Federal Bureau of Investigation. The report also indicated that the nation's murder rate dropped 7% in 1995.

The National Crime Victimization Survey, a Justice Department report based on interviews of crime victims, also highlighted falling crime rates. The report found that about 9.9 million violent crimes occurred in 1995, one million fewer than in 1994. The survey also found that rape fell 18%, robbery declined 14%, assault dropped 8%, attacks causing injuries slid 24%, and purse snatching and pickpocketing dipped 18%. The number of property crimes fell 5.6%, while the rate of burglaries, theft, and theft of cars dropped 6.5%.

Criminologists attributed the declining crime rates to a variety of factors. Some experts cited economic expansion while others pointed to demographic trends that proportionately have reduced the number of young males, the group most prone to violent crime. Many warned that crime rates likely would climb in the next decade with an increased number of teenagers. In an effort to understand the decline in homicides among adults, some experts spotted an unusual contributing factor—a steep decline in the incidence of barroom brawls.

A report from the Justice Department found that the rate of juvenile crime fell slightly in 1995 for the first time in nearly a decade. Based on figures reported to the FBI by local police, the arrest rate for homicide of youths between the ages of 10 and 17 fell 23% from its peak in 1993.

The increasing use of juvenile curfews was credited by some with contributing to the improvement. Thousands of communities nationwide have adopted curfews despite criticism by civil libertarians, who contend that they violate the constitutional rights of the young. Of the 200 largest U.S. cities, at least 150 have established curfews—including 50 that have implemented them since 1990. In a related move, many states and cities have enacted new laws making parents responsible for their children's misbehavior. The National Conference of State Legislatures reported in 1996 that about half the states had passed such laws in the previous three years. In 1995 alone, at least ten states enacted legislation that imposes fines, and occasionally prison terms, on the parents of young offenders.

In the U.S. Congress, legislation was proposed to end federal mandates requiring states to segregate juveniles from adults in jails and prisons. The mandates were adopted in 1974 to prevent the abuse of young detainees. However, proponents of the legislation said that erasing the mandates was justified by the increasingly violent conduct of youthful offenders. Around the nation, so-called "three strikes" laws that allow or require life imprisonment or long sentences for three-time violent felons remained controversial. One study compiled by a group that is critical of the harsh penalties asserted that the laws rarely were used by the federal government or by most of the 22 states that had enacted them since 1993. The big exception was California, where the study estimated that the 15,000 offenders convicted under the law would require $4.5 billion in prison construction over five years.

A survey done for the Justice Department brought attention to the high costs of crime. The report found that crime costs Americans at least $450 billion per year. That total includes legal fees, lost work time, and the cost of police work (but not money spent running jails and prisons).

Major Crimes. One of the more highly publicized criminal cases in years reached a dramatic climax in a courtroom in San Jose, CA, when a judge sentenced Richard Allen Davis to death for the 1993 kidnapping and murder of Polly Klaas. Davis was convicted of abducting the 12-year-old girl from a slumber party in her Petaluma, CA, house and strangling her.

Equally notorious, Lyle and Erik Menendez were convicted in a Los Angeles retrial of killing their wealthy parents in 1989. Judge Stanley Weisberg, following the jury's recommendation, sentenced the brothers to life in prison without parole, stating that he believed that the defendants carefully had decided to kill both parents. At their first trial in 1994, which ended with hung juries, the brothers testified that they killed their parents in self-defense after years of abuse.

John E. du Pont, 57-year-old heir to the du Pont Co. chemical fortune, was judged unfit to stand trial in Pennsylvania for the murder of world-class wrestler David Schultz. A judge placed du Pont into a psychiatric facility for evaluation and treatment. Schultz, a former Olympic champion, was shot on the millionaire's estate in Newtown Square, PA, in January 1996.

In another case considering mental fitness, a federal judge ruled that reputed mob boss Vincent Gigante was competent to stand trial on murder and racketeering charges. The judge asserted that Gigante—who was known to wander through his New York City neighborhood in pajamas and who appeared feeble and incoherent in court—was feigning mental illness to avoid prosecution.

Mark Bechard was charged with fatally beating and stabbing two elderly nuns, Mother Superior Edna Mary Cardozo and Sister Marie Julien Fortin, after breaking into a small convent in Waterville, ME. Bechard, who had a

© Chick Harrity, "U.S. News & World Report"

Retailers lost some $30 billion to shoplifting and theft by their employees in 1995. Consequently, sales of increasingly advanced electronic article surveillance (EAS) systems—including those that monitor inventories, right—have increased significantly.

history of mental illness, was committed to the custody of state mental-health officials. A judge had ruled that he was not criminally responsible because of mental illness.

Mark Fuhrman pleaded no contest to felony perjury for denying at the trial of O.J. Simpson that he had used a racial slur in the past decade. The former Los Angeles police detective was fined $200 and given three years' probation. Simpson, acquitted of murder in 1995, went on trial on civil charges. The families of his former wife, Nicole Brown Simpson, and of her friend Ronald Goldman sued over the deaths of the two victims.

In October federal officials arrested seven individuals in what was described as a plot to plant bombs at several government sites in West Virginia, including the capitol in Charleston. All seven individuals allegedly belonged to a paramilitary group.

In New York City a woman who admitted working as a drug courier pleaded guilty in a case that brought heavy criticism upon federal judges perceived as soft on crime. Carol Bayless was charged after police found 75 lbs (34 kg) of cocaine and 4.5 lbs (2 kg) of heroin in the trunk of her rental car. Judge Harold Baer, Jr., tossed out the evidence, saying police had lacked sufficient reason to search her car. The Clinton administration called Baer's decision a mistake and Robert Dole and other prominent politicians called for the judge's impeachment. Baer reversed himself and allowed the evidence but insisted that he had not caved in to political pressure.

In another politically charged case, Susan McDougal, a former business partner of President Clinton, was sentenced in Little Rock, AR, to two years in prison for loan fraud related to the so-called Whitewater real-estate venture. In the same case, Arkansas Gov. Jim Guy Tucker was sentenced to 18 months of house arrest followed by 30 months of probation. McDougal's husband, James, also was convicted and faced sentencing but was said to be cooperating with prosecutors.

Former U.S. Rep.Walter R. Tucker 3d (D-CA) was sentenced in Los Angeles to 27 months in prison for extortion and income-tax fraud. Tucker claimed that he was set up by prosecutors trying to imprison black office-holders. He was accused of extortion for actions he took as mayor of Compton, CA, before his election to Congress in 1992.

Also in Los Angeles, investigators concluded there was insufficient evidence that tobacco heiress Doris Duke was murdered. She died in 1993 at age 80 in her Beverly Hills home a few months after suffering a stroke. A nurse charged that a former butler at the Duke estate and a physician conspired to kill the heiress with painkillers.

Steven Toney's 13-year stay in a Missouri prison was ended after DNA tests proved that he could not have raped a 21-year-old woman he had been convicted of assaulting. The DNA test was developed five years after Toney was sent to prison.

Larry Don McQuay, 32, who claimed to have molested scores of children, asked to be castrated surgically upon his April release from prison in Texas. Late in 1996, he was indicted in another 1989 molestation case.

A New York City jury awarded $43 million to Darrell Cabey, a young black man who was paralyzed when he was shot on a subway train in 1984 by Bernhard Goetz. The jury decided unanimously that the white gunman had acted recklessly and without justification in shooting Cabey, a teenager at the time of the attack, and three other youths. The chances of Cabey ever collecting the settlement, however, were slight; Goetz was working as a self-employed electronics expert and had little money.

Daniel Green and Larry Demery were convicted of killing James Jordan, the father of basketball star Michael Jordan, and were sentenced to life in prison. The elder Jordan was shot as he napped in his car along a North Carolina highway in 1993.

A pool mechanic and his employer were acquitted of charges related to the fatal carbon-monoxide poisoning of former tennis star Vitas Gerulaitis. He died in September 1994 while sleeping in a cottage on a friend's estate in Southampton, Long Island, NY. The mechanic, Bartholomew Torpey, was acquitted of criminal negligence on charges that he failed to read the installation instructions for a pool heater. The company he worked for was cleared of reckless manslaughter.

Rap star and actor Tupac Shakur died in Las Vegas, NV, from bullet wounds suffered in a drive-by shooting after he attended a boxing match. Shakur, 25, had been wounded in 1994 after being shot during an apparent robbery outside a New York recording studio.

In Texas two teenagers were charged with murder in a case that roiled two of the nation's military academies. David Christopher Graham of the U.S. Air Force Academy and Diane Zamora of the U.S. Naval Academy were accused of killing Adrian Jones, Graham's former girlfriend, in a brutal attack.

JIM RUBIN, *The Associated Press*

CROATIA. *See* pages 96–101.

CUBA

Two major, interconnected issues—the economy and relations with the United States—dominated Cuba's attention in 1996. The recovery of the island's seriously ailing economy continued, although slowly. The recovery's pace was retarded by new, harsher anti-Havana U.S. legislation and by Hurricane Lili, which cut a destructive swath in central Cuba in October.

The government of President Fidel Castro, whose efficient security apparatus easily kept in check the feeble internal opposition, appeared as firmly in power as ever. But there were signs that President Fidel Castro, who in August reached the age of 70, gradually was preparing a generational turnover. He was letting much younger officials run the government's day-to-day operations, spending more time than before in traveling outside the country. Abroad he was greeted politely as an elder, if not entirely mellowed, statesman. With 37 years as Cuba's "maximum leader," he was one of the world's longest-serving heads of state.

U.S. Relations. The event that hardened already strained Cuban-U.S. relations was the February 24 shooting down by Cuban air-force jets of two small civilian planes, killing their crews—four members of an anti-Castro group, Brothers To The Rescue. The incident, which occurred in international waters near the island, was preceded by several incursions into Cuban territory by the same group's Miami-based planes, which dropped anti-Castro leaflets over Havana. Pressured by the anti-Castro, Miami-based exiles, U.S. President Bill Clinton retaliated by agreeing to the passage by the U.S. Congress of stringent new anti-Cuban legislation, which he had opposed previously. Signed on March 12 and known as the Helms-Burton Act after its Republican sponsors, Sen. Jesse Helms (NC) and Rep. Dan Burton (IN), the law made permanent the 34-year-old U.S. embargo against Cuba, which previously had to be renewed every year. It gives U.S. citizens, including Cuban exiles nationalized after 1959, the right to sue non-American companies doing business in Cuba and "deriving benefit" from property worth $50,000 or more and seized without compensation by the Castro government.

The Helms-Burton Act punishes foreign companies doing business in Cuba by denying U.S. visas to foreign businessmen, their families, and stockholders who derive profit from, and traffic in, confiscated Cuban property. The act, which became effective on August 1, also gives the president the power to suspend some of its provisions for up to six months at a time if such action is in the national interest. Punished almost immediately were two companies—a Mexican telecommunications conglomerate, Grupo Domos, and a Canadian mining company, Sherritt International. Allowing the act to take effect, President Clinton suspended, at least until January 1997, the provision permitting the lawsuits against foreign companies. But Domos announced it would continue to upgrade Cuba's telephone system, and Wilton Properties, another Canadian firm, signed an agreement to build 11 hotels in Cuba.

© Zoran Milich/Gamma-Liaison

After two unarmed private planes belonging to Brothers To The Rescue—a Miami-based Cuban-exile pilots' organization—was shot down by Cuban MiG fighter jets in waters between Cuba and the United States on Feb. 24, 1996, some 60,000 people gathered at Miami's Orange Bowl to honor the four airmen killed in the attack.

While prospects of litigation in the United States discouraged a number of non-American companies from investing in Cuba or expanding their existing investments there, Helms-Burton was met by virtually unanimous and vociferous opposition abroad, even among Washington's traditional allies. In a stunning defeat for the United States, the Organization of American States (OAS) criticized the act as a violation of international law. Mexico and Canada passed retaliatory legislation.

In October the 15-nation European Union (EU) agreed on legislation to let companies countersue to recoup damages assessed in U.S. courts for trading in Cuba. The EU also was challenging Helms-Burton in a new world trade court created by the World Trade Organization to promote fair trading practices among its members, one of whom is the United States. These actions came after a tour of Europe and Latin America by U.S. Undersecretary of Commerce for International Trade Stuart E. Eizenstat, who tried unsuccessfully to assuage the areas' anger over the act.

Later in October the Vatican publicly condemned the law for the first time. The criticism underlined a marked warming of relations between Havana and the Holy See. President Castro and Pope John Paul II met privately for 35 minutes at the Vatican in mid-November. At the meeting, the pontiff accepted Castro's invitation to visit Cuba, most likely in mid-1997. The meeting between the anticommunist pope and the Jesuit-educated Cuban Marxist appeared to have been a success. Both septuagenarians have a strong sense of history and believe a papal visit to Cuba would serve their long-range goals. For Castro, John Paul in Havana would give his government a universal seal of legitimacy. The pope's view is that Havana's opening space to the church would give it a strong role in reshaping Cuba's post-Castro society.

At the United Nations the United States—unable to gain international support for a strong condemnation of Cuba over the plane-downing incident—agreed in July to a mild resolution that expressed regret for the action and, at the same time, urged states to prohibit civil aircraft from violating international laws. Cuba had sought the later provision.

Economy and Politics. Stating that Cuba had gained higher profits from its sugar and nickel production and tourism, Havana predicted an annual growth of 5.5% in mid-1996. Cuba announced that the 1996 output of sugar, its main cash export, was 4.45 million tons—1.1 million tons more than in 1995. In a sign of recovery—and an indication of increased hard-currency spending by tourists and dollar remittances by exiles—the value of one U.S. dollar declined from 22 Cuban pesos to 19 pesos. But the economy, Cuban officials conceded, continued to be beset by shortages of every kind and by unemployment and underemployment. The destruction caused to agriculture, dwellings, and some industrial installations by Hurricane Lili exacerbated these and other problems.

The hardening of U.S. policy toward Cuba resulted in a slowing down of the economic-liberalization process. There was no easing of the tight political controls exercised by the Castro regime. Hard-line ideologists again began preaching economic and political socialist orthodoxy, rhetoric that seemed to have waned by 1995. But many of the younger, more liberal Castro regime leaders and the Cuban intellectuals openly defied the hard-liners, accusing them of "intolerance" and producing an ideological stalemate by the end of the year. The "liberals" comprised for the most part a group of officials to whom Castro was delegating more authority in the government's decision making, as he told CBS correspondent Dan Rather in an August interview in Havana.

Robert Vesco. In August a Cuban court convicted Robert L. Vesco, a fugitive American businessman who fled the United States in the early 1970s and had lived in Havana for more than a decade, to 13 years in prison. Vesco was charged with having cheated the Cuban health ministry and other investors in a scheme to produce and market an unproven drug against cancer and arthritis. Also involved in the case was Donald Nixon, Jr., the nephew of the late President Richard M. Nixon, who testified in the trial but was not charged in the scheme.

GEORGE VOLSKY, *University of Miami*

CUBA • Information Highlights

Official Name: Republic of Cuba.
Location: Caribbean.
Area: 42,803 sq mi (110 860 km^2).
Population (mid-1996 est.): 11,000,000.
Chief Cities (Dec. 31, 1993 est.): Havana, the capital, 2,175,995; Santiago de Cuba, 440,084; Camagüey, 293,961; Holguín, 242,085.
Government: *Head of state and government,* Fidel Castro Ruz, president (took office under a new constitution, December 1976). *Legislature* (unicameral)—National Assembly of People's Power.
Monetary Unit: Peso (1.0 peso equals U.S.$1, noncommercial rate, June 1996).
Gross Domestic Product (1994 est. U.S.$): $14,000,000,000 (purchasing power parity).
Foreign Trade (1994 est. U.S.$): *Imports,* $1,700,000,000; *exports,* $1,600,000,000.

CYPRUS

During 1996, Cyprus went through its 22d year as a divided island republic—the result of a Turkish invasion in 1974, which had taken over about 40% of the island's territory in the north. Great Britain, under the terms of the 1960 settlement that had made Cyprus an independent state, retained two important sovereign military bases in the south—one at Akrotiri, the other at Dhekelia—comprising about 99 mi (160 km) of territory. The northern and southern parts of the island were separated by the "Green Line," manned by United Nations (UN) peacekeeping forces.

Island Animosities. In 1983 the northern Turkish-occupied lands had been proclaimed The Turkish Republic of Northern Cyprus, with Turkish Cypriot Rauf Denktash as president. This entity, however, has been recognized only by Turkey. In the rest of Cyprus the internationally recognized government of the Republic of Cyprus was headed by Greek Cypriot Glafkos Clerides. All efforts over 22 years to reconcile the Greek Cypriots and the Turkish Cypriots have failed. Some 200,000 Greek Cypriots had fled to the south from the north at the time of the 1974 invasion. Since then, Turkey has maintained a heavy military presence in the northern territories and brought mainland Turks to the island to strengthen the Turkish ethnic composition there.

Attempts—particularly by the United States, the United Nations, and Great Britain—continued to be made to bring the two communities together. Among those involved in these efforts was Madeleine Albright, U.S. permanent representative to the UN, who in July went to Nicosia, Athens, and Ankara. In June, President Clerides visited President Clinton at Washington.

Matters became more impassioned on the island in August. The Federation of European Motorcyclists planned a peaceful demonstration at the border of the Green Line. Despite President Clerides' call to cancel the demonstration, thousands of Greek Cypriots joined the bikers. A Turkish paramilitary group, the Grey Wolves, became involved. Greek Cypriots who crossed into the UN buffer zone were attacked by Turks armed with baseball bats and iron bars. One Greek Cypriot was beaten to death. His funeral three days later was attended by President Clerides. After the funeral, during a further demonstration in the buffer zone, another Greek Cypriot was shot to death from the Turkish side as he climbed a pole bearing the Turkish flag. The Turks then fired into the crowd, wounding two British soldiers and some civilians. Clerides presented evidence that two of Denktash's followers had been among those who shot at the pole. Though Denktash refused to accept responsibility, arrest warrants were issued for his two followers, along with others, for murder.

Turkey's Foreign Minister Tansu Ciller further inflamed Greek Cypriot passions the day after the second killing by emphasizing publicly the sanctity of the Turkish flag. In September the unsolved killing of a Turkish guard at his post near a British base caused countercharges from the Turkish Cypriot and Greek Cypriot sides. Then, in October, a third Greek Cypriot was killed when he strayed into Turkish-held territory while gathering snails. Coupled with the shooting in June from the Turkish Cypriot side of a Greek Cypriot soldier in the buffer zone, the five killings further compounded the finding of any viable solution to the island's division.

GEORGE J. MARCOPOULOS, *Tufts University*

CYPRUS • Information Highlights

Official Name: Republic of Cyprus.
Location: Eastern Mediterranean.
Area: 3,571 sq mi (9 250 km²).
Population (mid-1996 est.): 700,000.
Chief Cities (Dec. 31, 1993 est.): Nicosia, the capital, 186,400; Limassol, 143,400.
Government: *Head of state and government,* Glafcos Clerides, president (took office March 1, 1993). *Legislature*—House of Representatives.
Monetary Unit: Pound (0.459 pound equals U.S.$1, August 1996).
Gross Domestic Product (1994 est. U.S.$): $7,300,000,000 (purchasing power parity).
Economic Indexes (1995, 1990 = 100): *Consumer Prices,* all items, 126.0; food, 127.9. *Industrial Production,* 103.
Foreign Trade (1995 U.S.$): *Imports,* $3,690,000,000; *exports,* $1,229,000,000.

CZECH REPUBLIC

In 1996 the Czech economy continued its recovery. The economy grew by 5%, and industrial production increased by 10% in the first half of the year. Inflation was at 9.1% in October, and unemployment continued to be less than 3%. Foreign investment also grew. Foreign debt continued to be very low. Exports grew by 10.6%, but their growth was lower than that of imports, which grew by 28.5%. The country's trade deficit was $3.1 billion by midyear. Czech leaders cut spending in August to avoid a budget deficit. In October the government announced a new commission to speed up privatization and liberalization of the economy.

Politics. In the parliamentary elections held in late May and early June, the center-right coalition of Prime Minister Václav Klaus lost its majority in parliament. The center-right Civic Democratic Party gained the largest share of the vote (29.6%). Klaus' coalition partners, the Christian Democratic Union and the Civic Democratic Alliance, won 8.1 and 6.4%, respectively. Together, the three parties won 99 seats—two short of a majority.

The Social Democrats, led by Miloš Zeman, won 26.4% of the vote—a far larger share than the 6% they won in 1992. This increase allowed them to influence the formation of the government; Zeman, in return, became chair of the legislature. The Communist and Republican parties also won seats in parliament, with 10.3% and 8% of the vote. On July 25, Klaus' new government survived a vote of no confidence. As a result of the election, the smaller coalition parties gained more power in the coalition. Their number of ministers in the government increased, and they now could veto government decisions. Consequently the government agreed to the creation of regional governments, a step that Premier Klaus long had opposed.

Social reforms adopted in 1995, which were scheduled to go into effect gradually, were one of the factors that increased support for the Social Democrats. The shift from a universal to a needs-based welfare system proved to be unpopular with Czech citizens. Price increases of approximately 9%, which were especially marked in the areas of food and services, also eroded support for the ruling coalition, as did concerns about government scandals and corruption.

Prime Minister Klaus' coalition parties scored a victory in elections to the Senate in November. The coalition parties captured 52 of the 81 seats, while the opposition Social Democratic Party took 25. After the first elections, a third of the body would be elected every other year.

The collapse of several Czech banks cost the country $440 million and led to the commissioning of special investigators to look into the situation. Other controversial issues included the planned cut in the salaries of public officials and the country's citizenship law. Human-rights groups and outside governments, including the United States, continued to criticize the citizenship law, which left many Roma, or gypsies, without citizenship. In April the Czech parliament amended the law to waive the provision that required that applicants who are citizens of the Slovak Republic and Slovak citizens who have lived in the Czech Republic since Dec. 31, 1992, have no criminal record in the past five years.

CZECH REPUBLIC • Information Highlights

Official Name: Czech Republic.
Location: East-central Europe.
Area: 30,387 sq mi (78 703 km²).
Population (mid-1996 est.): 10,300,000.
Chief Cities (Dec. 31, 1994 est.): Prague, the capital, 1,213,299; Brno, 389,576; Ostrava, 325,827.
Government: *Head of state,* Václav Havel, president (took office Jan. 1, 1993). *Head of government,* Václav Klaus, prime minister (took office June 1992). *Legislature*—National Council: Senate and Chamber of Deputies.
Monetary Unit: Koruna (27.33 koruny equal U.S.$1, commercial rate, Dec. 31, 1996).
Gross Domestic Product (1994 est. U.S.$): $76,500,000,-000.
Economic Index (1995, 1991 = 100): *Consumer Prices,* all items, 161.7; food, 154.9.
Foreign Trade (1995 U.S.$): *Imports,* $25,308,000,000; *exports,* $21,640,000,000.

President Václav Havel underwent surgery for lung cancer in December.

Foreign Affairs. Top leaders continued to press for the inclusion of the Czech Republic as a full member of the North Atlantic Treaty Organization (NATO) and the European Union (EU). They also argued that Russia should not have a veto over NATO expansion. The Czech Republic was identified by the U.S. Congress as one of the countries—along with Hungary and Poland—that has progressed most toward NATO membership. As a result, the three countries were eligible to receive $60 million in military aid from the United States. Czech troops participated in NATO's Partnership for Peace program.

Some 850 Czech troops were to be sent to Bosnia as part of the international force that was to replace IFOR (implementation force). Czech officials welcomed the 1999 date set by President Clinton in an October speech as a target for the admission of new members to NATO. Approximately 42% of citizens surveyed in April supported the application for NATO membership; 21% did not; and 37% had no opinion.

Czech-Slovak relations were strained by Czech criticism of Slovak minority policies. The question of the rights of ethnic Germans of the Sudetenland region, who were expelled forcibly after World War II, continued to complicate Czech-German relations. Officials of the two countries continued to work on a joint declaration to resolve the issue. Such a declaration would include a Czech apology for the forced expulsion of some 3 million Sudeten Germans after World War II and a German commitment to compensate victims of Nazism. A declaration was initialed by the foreign ministers of both nations in December. It was to be signed in January 1997.

SHARON WOLCHIK
The George Washington University

© Paul Kolnik

The New York City Ballet's production of Peter Martins' "Reliquary" paid tribute to late choreographer George Balanchine and late composer Igor Stravinsky. It had its world premiere at New York City's Lincoln Center in January 1996.

DANCE

Despite fine premieres, the deaths of many dance-world leaders made 1996 seem to signal the end of a great era. An especially heavy blow was the death of the champion of American ballet, Lincoln Kirstein, who helped bring George Balanchine to the United States and with him cofounded the New York City Ballet. The year also saw the death of Gene Kelly, the Broadway and Hollywood tap star whose film dancing united choreography with innovative camera work. (*See* OBITUARIES.)

In an attempt to save choreographic treasures, the George Balanchine Foundation, under the supervision of the dance historian Nancy Reynolds, announced that it would preserve on tape examples of "lost" choreography by Balanchine—works that no longer are danced or that now are performed only in revised versions.

Ballet. Works by Balanchine and Jerome Robbins continued to dominate the New York City Ballet's repertory, augmented by competent, if not always inspired, contributions by other choreographers. Peter Martins honored Balanchine and Igor Stravinsky in *Reliquary*, which was indebted stylistically to such Balanchine-Stravinsky masterpieces as *Agon* and *Stravinsky Violin Concerto*; Charles Wuorinen based his score on music Stravinsky left unfinished at his death. Other 1996 premieres included David Parson's breezy *Touch*; Martins' virtuosic *Tchaikovsky Pas de Quatre*; Kevin O'Day's intricately patterned *Badchonim*; and Ulysses Dove's *Twilight*, the choreographer's last work before his death.

To bring dance to communities that could not afford the full ensemble of 81 dancers and to theaters with small stages, American Ballet Theatre toured with a group of 45 performers. Kevin McKenzie, Ballet Theatre's director, announced in December that in 1997 the company would become an affiliate of the new $180 million New Jersey Performing Arts Center in Newark, presenting December seasons there featuring Ben Stevenson's *Cinderella* and other holiday entertainments. Among the ambitious new productions of the company's 1996 engagement at the Metropolitan Opera House was Twyla Tharp's *The Elements*, which depicted the emergence of order out of chaos; the choreography looked still inchoate. Of greater interest was the U.S. premiere of Jiri Kylian's *Stepping Stones*, in which the Czech-born, Dutch-based choreographer invented what appeared to be mysterious rituals of an ancient civilization. Ballerina Marianna Tcherkassky, a member of Ballet Theatre for 26 years and acclaimed for her romantic style, gave her final New York performance on June 15 as a poignant Juliet in Kenneth MacMillan's *Romeo and Juliet*.

Eliot Feld's premieres for his Feld Ballets/NY ranged from the zany *Paper Tiger* to *Paean*, a choreographic ode to counterpoint.

The Joffrey Ballet, now based in Chicago, offered *Legends*, the latest attention-getting spectacle conceived by its director, Gerald Arpino. It featured an evening of dances by female choreographers (Joanna Haigood, Ann Reinking, Margo Sappington, Sherry Zunker Dow, and Ann Marie DeAngelo) to recordings by female pop stars. U.S. critics occasionally chided the company for overemphasizing such extravaganzas, while recognizing that *Billboards*, a similar collaboration, had aided the Joffrey considerably at the box office. British critics were less charitable. When the Joffrey presented a London season of *Billboards*, the reviews were scathing.

Pacific Northwest Ballet of Seattle continued to develop, and the San Francisco Ballet was maintaining its high level. The Paris Opéra Ballet's New York performances revealed this venerable organization to have a superbly trained ensemble.

Maya Plisetskaya, the Russian ballerina, celebrated her 70th birthday with gala performances, May 10–12, at New York's City Center. Dancers from eight American and European companies performed, as did Plisetskaya herself. Her fabled energy undiminished, she danced Michel Fokine's *Dying Swan* on point and Maurice Béjart's *Isadora*, a tribute to Isadora Duncan.

Modern Dance. The year 1996 was especially notable for grandly scaled modern-dance productions. Among them was Merce Cunningham's *Ocean*, a 90-minute piece rich in sweeping movements, which was staged outdoors in a park at the side of New York City's Lincoln Center complex as part of the new Lincoln Center Festival 96. Among the festival attractions indoors at the New York State Theater were Judith Jamison's *Sweet Release*, for the Alvin Ailey American Dance Theatre, and a new version of the 19th-century classic *Coppélia* by the enterprising Lyon National Opera Ballet. Maguy Marin, a French modern dancer who also works with ballet groups, rechoreographed the old story by setting it in a contemporary suburb, and inventively combined films with live action to suggest the characters' obsessions.

Another modern-dance updating of a familiar ballet was Donald Byrd's *Harlem Nutcracker*, which his company, Donald Byrd/The Group, toured in November and December. Set to jazz arrangements of Tchaikovsky by Duke Ellington and Billy Strayhorn, it showed an African-American grandmother remembering her youth. Retrospection also was a theme of *The Politics of Quiet*, a gentle meditation on the passage of time for which Meredith Monk provided both music and choreography.

Commissions from six producing organizations in the U.S. West and residencies in California and Texas enabled Pina Bausch to create her first new production outside her native Germany. The result was *Nur Du* ("Only You"), which Bausch's Tanztheater Wuppertal presented in four Western cities. Like most works by this neo-Expressionist choreographer, it examined heartbreak, yet did so with humor as well as pathos.

Susan Marshall directed and choreographed Philip Glass' *Les Enfants Terribles*, based upon a Jean Cocteau novel about a brother and sister who live in their own fantasy world. Glass called the piece "A Dance Opera Spectacle," and Marshall had each of the two leading characters played by a singer and three dancers. By having many performers represent only two people, she conveyed a sense of the characters' self-involvement.

Mark Morris, known for giving operas vivid choreographic interpretations, devised surprisingly bland movements in his production of Gluck's *Orfeo ed Euridice*, in collaboration with the Handel and Haydn Society Orchestra and Chorus.

Among the highlights of the American Dance Festival in Durham, NC, was Mark Dendy's *Ritual*. A large cast made an entire theater its shrine—dancing in the lobby and aisles as well as on the stage—in an exuberant hymn of praise to the wonder of live theater.

The ever-restless Twyla Tharp organized a new company called Tharp! that offered three premieres in Washington in October: *Sweet Fields* (to hymns), *66* (inspired by Highway 66), and *Heroes* (to music by Philip Glass). Reviews were mixed.

Musical Theater and Awards. The most talked-about dancing in a musical show was that in *Bring in da Noise, Bring in da Funk*. (*See* THEATER.)

Meredith Monk won the Samuel H. Scripps/American Dance Festival Award for lifetime achievement. The codirectors of the festival, Charles L. Reinhart and Stephanie Reinhart, were named artistic advisers for dance at the Kennedy Center in Washington. *Dance Magazine* Award winners were Savion Glover; Francia Russell and Kent Stowell, directors of Pacific Northwest Ballet; and Peter Boal of the New York City Ballet. The Japanese-born modern dancers Eiko and Koma received a MacArthur Fellowship. One of the Kennedy Center honors went to the ballerina Maria Tallchief.

JACK ANDERSON, *"The New York Times"*

DENMARK

Denmark's Supreme Court created new problems for the nation's already troubled European Union (EU) policies in 1996 by allowing a constitutional challenge to the existing Maastricht Treaty. Domestically, the economy continued its recovery, while turbulent relations between the Liberal and Conservative parties removed any immediate parliamentary threat to the coalition government led by Social Democratic Prime Minister Poul Nyrup Rasmussen.

European Affairs. Denmark's Supreme Court ruled in August that a district court should hear the case of 11 Danes who were challenging the constitutionality of the Maastricht Treaty. The plaintiffs claimed that the existing treaty usurped Denmark's sovereignty because it contained language that would allow the EU to take initiatives not specifically named in the treaty. The district court originally had refused to deal with the case on the grounds that the plaintiffs could not prove that their rights and interests as individuals were at stake. The courts promised to render a verdict before the anticipated 1997 completion of the EU intergovernmental conference (IGC). Although the Danish courts were not expected to overturn the ratification of the treaty, the case had an impact on Denmark's actions in the EU. In October, Denmark withheld initial support for an EU response to the U.S. Helms-Burton trade act, regarding Cuba.

Reversing a 1992 vote, Danes had ratified the Maastricht Treaty in 1993 after an agreement stipulated reservations allowing Denmark to "opt out" of economic and monetary union (EMU), the West European Union, and union citizenship. Popular opposition to the EU remained strong in 1996, with polls showing a majority of Danes insisting that the 1993 reservations regarding the Maastricht Treaty should not be compromised. The government promised to hold a referendum before Denmark would join the EMU.

Foreign Affairs. Denmark backed the aspirations of Estonia, Latvia, and Lithuania to become full members of the North Atlantic Treaty Organization (NATO), and Baltic military personnel joined Danish troops in NATO's implementation force (IFOR) in Bosnia. Following the unexplained June death in jail of Leo Nichols, the Danish honorary consul in Yangon, Myanmar, the Danish government called for economic sanctions against that country. A number of Danish companies, including the brewer Carlsberg, halted operations in Myanmar.

Economy. Following a weak start, the Danish economy revived sharply in the second half of 1996. Private consumption, business investment, and construction were growth leaders and helped lift gross domestic product (GDP) by 2% in 1996. Meanwhile, unemployment fell below 9% and interest rates dropped to within a percentage point of those in Germany.

Denmark was promised virtual membership in the EMU if politics prevented it from joining at the planned outset in 1999. Under the agreement, the krone would be linked to the EU's unified currency—the Euro—by a bilateral agreement limiting volatility. Danish telecommunications were liberalized in July 1996, 18 months ahead of EU requirements. French and Swedish companies soon after took advantage of the deregulation.

LEIF BECK FALLESEN, *Editor in Chief "Boersen," Copenhagen*

DENMARK • Information Highlights

Official Name: Kingdom of Denmark.
Location: Northwest Europe.
Area: 16,629 sq mi (43 070 km²).
Population (mid-1996 est.): 5,200,000.
Chief Cities (Jan. 1, 1995 est.): Copenhagen, the capital, 471,300; Århus, 277,477; Odense, 182,617.
Government: *Head of state,* Margrethe II, queen (acceded Jan. 1972). *Head of government,* Poul Nyrup Rasmussen, prime minister (took office Jan. 1993). *Legislature* (unicameral)—Folketing.
Monetary Unit: Krone (5.9695 kroner equal U.S.$1, Dec. 5, 1996).
Gross Domestic Product (1994 est. U.S.$): $103,000,000,000 (purchasing power parity).
Economic Indexes (1995, 1990 = 100): *Consumer Prices,* all items, 110.3; food, 108.0. *Industrial Production,* 116.
Foreign Trade (1995 U.S.$): *Imports,* $43,168,000,000; *exports,* $48,981,000,000.

DOMINICAN REPUBLIC

President Joaquín Balaguer of the Dominican Republic, perhaps the most enduring strongman in the Caribbean, relinquished his grip on power in 1996. The 89-year-old Balaguer, though legally blind and feeble, nevertheless retained the political acumen that had enabled him to remain the dominant force in Dominican politics for three decades.

He was succeeded by 42-year-old Leonel Fernández Reyna of the Dominican Liberation Party (PLD), who prevailed in a runoff election held on June 30. With 51.3% of the vote, Fernández narrowly defeated José Francisco Peña Gómez, warhorse and firebrand of the Dominican Revolutionary Party (PRD). Fernández—a political protégé of former President and PLD leader Juan Bosch—was born in the Dominican Republic but was raised and educated in New York City. The new president was inaugurated on August 16 along with Vice-President Jaime David Fernández Mirabal.

In the first round, Peña, the former mayor of Santo Domingo, gained 46% of the vote to outpoll Fernández (39%). Incumbent Vice-President Jacinto Peynado of the ruling Social Christian Reformist Party (PRSC), who campaigned with little support from Balaguer, finished last in the first round and did not qualify for the runoff.

For the second round of elections, Balaguer entered into a coalition—known as the National Patriotic Front—with his old rival Bosch to support Fernández. Balaguer asserted that the move would "prevent the country from falling into the hands of someone who is not truly Dominican," a reference to Peña's reputed origin as the child of Haitian immigrants. Peña's supporters denounced the move as racially motivated, since their man was black.

In spite of the political intrigue and maneuvering, the 1996 presidential election was the cleanest and least contentious in Dominican history. Both rounds took place under the watchful eyes of international observers from the United States, the Organization of American States, the United Nations (UN), and Europe. The contest was a far cry from those of 1990 and 1994, when Balaguer was thought to have cheated Peña of victory in national elections.

The long reign of Dominican strongman Joaquín Balaguer ended in 1996 when Leonel Fernández Reyna (below), *a 42-year-old lawyer born and raised in New York, was elected president.*

© C. Douce/E. Alonso/Sygma

DOMINICAN REPUBLIC • Information Highlights

Official Name: Dominican Republic.
Location: Caribbean.
Area: 18,815 sq mi (48 730 km²).
Population (mid-1996 est.): 8,100,000.
Chief Cities (1990 est.): Santo Domingo, the capital, 2,411,900; Santiago de los Caballeros, 489,500; La Vega, 192,300.
Government: *Head of state and government,* Leonel Fernández Reyna, president (inaugurated Aug. 16, 1996). *Legislature*—National Congress: Senate and Chamber of Deputies.
Monetary Unit: Peso (13.956 pesos equal U.S.$1, June 1996).
Gross Domestic Product (1994 est. U.S.$): $24,000,000,000 (purchasing power parity).
Foreign Trade (1995 est. U.S.$): *Imports,* $2,976,000,000; *exports,* $765,000,000.

Problems and Agenda. The tasks facing Fernández as president appeared nearly insurmountable. Control of the national legislature remained in the hands of Balaguer's PRSC. The PLD held only one out of 30 Senate seats and 13 of the 120 seats in the House of Deputies. New congressional elections were not scheduled until 1998. Many economic and social indicators remained grim. Unemployment hovered near 25% and illiteracy approached 30%. Other problems included frequent power failures, numerous stalled industries, the overvaluation of the Dominican peso, and a dependence on tourism and remittances from Dominicans living abroad.

Fernández vowed to rationalize public spending and shift the nation's priorities away from the massive public works favored by Balaguer to projects aimed at health and education. In an October address to the UN, Fernández announced a new package of economic and legal reforms. Later that month he began taking steps to trim the swollen upper ranks of the military, retiring 24 of the nation's 70 generals.

RICHARD C. SCHROEDER, *Freelance Writer*

DRUGS AND ALCOHOL

Assessments of the U.S. government's "war on drugs," first declared in 1971, played a prominent role in the 1996 presidential campaign. The Bill Clinton administration's effort against the importation and use of illicit drugs was a major campaign theme of Republican presidential nominee Robert Dole. From July to November, Dole strongly criticized the president, claiming that Clinton-administration drug policies were responsible for increasing use of marijuana among teenagers and that the president's positions on the issue sent an "an implicit message to parents and children" on drugs that was "casual, permissive, and liberal."

President Clinton and his supporters defended his administration's antidrug efforts, saying that an important factor in the rise in marijuana use was the Republican-controlled Congress' failure in 1996 to provide full funding for drug-prevention and drug-treatment programs. They also cited the efforts of retired Gen. Barry R. McCaffrey, who was sworn in as director (the so-called "drug czar") of the Office of National Drug Control Policy in March. The president's supporters also noted that the administration's $15.1 billion fiscal-year 1997 drug-fighting budget was a 9.3% increase compared with the previous year and the highest amount ever allocated to the federal war on drugs. (Congress later approved $15.3 billion for the war on drugs.)

There were two notable successes on the international drug interdiction front in 1996. In January, Mexican authorities arrested Juan García Abrego, a powerful drug lord who headed the Mexico Gulf cocaine cartel. Deported to the United States, Abrego was convicted in October in U.S. District Court in Houston on 22 counts of drug trafficking and money laundering. Prosecutors asserted that Abrego transported more than $1 billion worth of cocaine and marijuana into the United States. In May the U.S. Drug Enforcement Administration and other federal agencies concluded an eight-month operation that resulted in more than 130 arrests of alleged members of Colombian and Mexican cocaine-trafficking organizations. Despite those arrests, and the federal government's $3 billion interdiction effort, large quantities of cocaine and marijuana continued to be smuggled into the United States along the Mexican border.

In November voters in California and Arizona approved ballot initiatives legalizing the medical use of marijuana for sufferers of AIDS, cancer, and other chronic diseases. Advocates for the drug's use based their support on the experience of patients who found relief from the pain and nausea caused by their illnesses or by treatment for those illnesses. However, the passage of the measures brought a strong reaction from antidrug groups and law-enforcement officials who saw the initiatives as promoting greater use of marijuana and, possibly, as forerunners of laws legalizing the drug. "Just when the nation is trying its hardest to educate teenagers not to use psychoactive drugs," noted McCaffrey, "they are being told that marijuana and other drugs are good, they are medicine. The conflict in messages is extremely harmful."

Drug-Use Trends. Nationwide surveys released in 1996 indicated that marijuana use among young people continued a steady rise that had begun in 1992. The federal government's 1995 National Household Survey on Drug Abuse, released in August, found that 8.2% of those between the ages of 12 to 17 said they used marijuana monthly, more than double the number in 1992. The University of Michigan's Institute for Social Research's annual drug-use survey also reported increased use of marijuana among teenagers in 1995, as did a survey commissioned by the Partnership for a Drug-Free America released in February. Drug-abuse experts cited several factors—including concurrent increases in tobacco use by adolescents, growing drug use by teenagers in other countries, and the widespread belief among young people that marijuana is not as harmful as other drugs—in the increasing use of marijuana by young people.

Alcohol. One drug that received almost no attention during the presidential campaign was alcohol, the abuse of which continued to remain one of the nation's most serious public-health problems—for adults as well as teenagers. Alcohol use among teenagers dwarfed reported marijuana use, according to the University of Michigan's annual survey and the federal government's National Household Survey. The former reported that 81% of high-school seniors said they had tried alcohol at least once. The latter study reported that, of the 10 million teenagers who said they consumed alcohol during the previous month, some 4.4 million fit the category of "binge drinkers"—imbibing at least five drinks in one night.

Binge drinking also remained a problem on the nation's college campuses. According to studies conducted by the Harvard School of Public Health, some 44% of all college students engaged in binge drinking. The problem was most prevalent among those living in fraternity and sorority houses. A survey of 14,700 students at 115 colleges, the results of which were released late in 1995 in a Harvard study, found that 86% of fraternity men and 80% of sorority women were binge drinkers.

The National Highway Traffic Safety Administration reported in July that alcohol-related traffic fatalities rose by 4% in 1995—

the first increase in ten years. Alcohol was involved in about 41% of the more than 44,000 fatal driving accidents in 1995, the administration reported.

MARC LEEPSON, *Freelance Writer*

ECUADOR

The major event in Ecuador during 1996 was the transfer of the presidency in August from the conservative Sixto Durán Ballén to the populist Abdalá Bucaram Ortiz.

Politics. From March to August the presidential campaigns and elections dominated the news. In view of the deep unpopularity of President Durán, the Ecuadorian Conservative Party decided not to field a presidential candidate. Three candidates from other parties received most of the attention. The front-runner throughout the campaign was Jaime Nebot Saadi of the Social Christian Party (PSC). Nebot, who had come in second in the 1992 presidential election, advocated many of the same policies as the incumbent, but claimed to be more open to modifications to protect the poor and the middle class.

For many months the second candidate was Freddy Ehlers, a television personality backed by the diverse New Country coalition, which combined the Democratic Left Party of former President Rodrigo Borja, the Ecuadorian Socialist Party, several business groups, and an alliance of indigenous peoples' movements, including the Confederation of Indigenous Nationalities of Ecuador (CONAIE). To unite this unusual coalition, Ehlers' platform called for an "ethical, economic, educational, and ecological revolution." Ehlers was hurt by the fact that his wife was Peruvian—an awkward situation in a country so recently at war with Peru—and by early May, he dropped to third place in most polls. However, the coalition constituted an impressive first effort by the indigenous communities—an estimated 25% of the electorate—to participate in national electoral politics. Seven of the deputies elected in May were indigenous, and the New Country coalition supported CONAIE leader Luis Macas for president of the congress.

In the first round of the elections in May, Bucaram beat Ehlers for second place, and then went on to defeat Nebot in the second round in July. Bucaram, the candidate of the Roldista Party, was a former mayor of Guayaquil who had run second to Borja in 1988. Known popularly as "El Loco," he was an unpredictable candidate who once appeared in a Batman costume and was fond of cruelly mimicking his opponents and bursting into song during speeches. His rhetoric pitted the rich against the poor, which gave him the edge among poor highland Indians in the second round.

Once Bucaram was inaugurated, his commitment to the poor began to seem more symbolic than real, as his cabinet included several holdovers from Durán's administration. He also appointed billionaire banana magnate Alvaro Noboa as president of the monetary board and invited the architects of orthodox economic reforms in Argentina, Bolivia, and Chile to advise his government on an economic package. Because he simultaneously maintained consumer subsidies and talked about rescheduling Ecuador's foreign debt, business leaders claimed that his policies were incoherent. Despite such charges, a majority of Ecuadorians still approved of his performance late in the year.

Other News. Before the election, the lame-duck Durán administration had to deal with a strike in February that mobilized thousands of public employees to protest low wages, and nearly shut down the government before the president granted the workers a 35% salary increase. Late in March a magnitude-5.8 earthquake struck the already impoverished southern provinces of Cotopaxi and Tungurahua. At least 19 persons were killed and 70% of the buildings in the region reportedly were destroyed. In June, 112 indigenous communities brought suit against Texaco in a New York court, asking for $8 million in compensation for alleged environmental damage during the company's 25 years of oil production in the Amazon region. The suit, however, stalled after the Ecuadorian government refused to support the case in a foreign court.

MICHAEL COPPEDGE
University of Notre Dame

ECUADOR • Information Highlights

Official Name: Republic of Ecuador.
Location: Northwest South America.
Area: 109,483 sq mi (283 560 km^2).
Population (mid-1996 est.): 11,700,000.
Chief Cities (mid-1995 est.): Quito, the capital, 1,401,389; Guayaquil, 1,877,031; Cuenca, 239,896.
Government: *Head of state and government,* Abdalá Bucaram Ortiz, president (took office August 1996). *Legislature* (unicameral)—National Congress.
Monetary Unit: Sucre (3,490.00 sucres equal U.S.$1, floating rate, Dec. 5, 1996).
Gross Domestic Product (1994 est. U.S.$): $41,100,000,000 (purchasing power parity).
Economic Index (1995, 1990 = 100): *Consumer Prices,* all items, 521.7; food, 490.4.
Foreign Trade (1995 U.S.$): *Imports,* $4,193,000,000; *exports,* $4,307,000,000.

EDUCATION

Public education stepped onto center stage during 1996, becoming an issue that motivated action on the part of business leaders, considerable differences of opinion among political leaders, and sobering awareness on the part of school officials and reformers of the problems ahead.

Growing Enrollment, Inadequate Facilities. A major reason for education's move to the forefront was indisputable data—swelling school enrollments and decaying, inadequate school facilities. School enrollments set a record in the fall of 1996, with 51.7 million children in grades K–12 public and private schools. This was the "baby-boom echo," coming slightly more than 20 years after the peak post–World War II enrollment in the mid-1970s. The U.S. Department of Education (DOE) estimated that enrollment would continue to grow, reaching 54.6 million students by the year 2006.

Contradicting predictions of slow enrollment growth made by the U.S. Census Bureau less than a decade earlier, the new figures reflected some unanticipated demographics. Higher birthrates were occurring among women who delayed having children, among some minority groups, and among immigrant families. The DOE estimated that, within ten years, the nation would need an additional 6,000 schools and 190,000 additional teachers. The growth rate was also uneven. In Florida, Texas, and California, enrollments were swelling rapidly, but urban districts in other states and pockets of population growth faced similar problems. In Nevada's Clark county (which includes Las Vegas), for example, school enrollment doubled over the past decade to 179,000; 10,000 more students were enrolled in fall 1996 and another 10,000 more were expected in fall 1997. New York City began the 1996–97 school year lacking adequate classroom space for 90,000 students. California school districts scrambled to find up to 20,000 new classrooms in order to qualify for additional state funding, which was contingent on schools' limiting K–3 classrooms to no more than 20 students each.

School uniforms, below, *were gaining favor in an increasing number of public schools. It was hoped the use of uniforms would boost discipline and reduce violence.*

© Lynn R. Johnson/"Salt Lake Tribune"/AP/Wide World Photos

At the same time public-school officials realized they needed to plan for a considerable increase in new buildings, national studies of existing facilities revealed serious problems. The General Accounting Office (GAO), at the request of Sen. Carol Moseley-Braun (D-IL), conducted surveys and on-site visits of U.S. school facilities and issued a series of reports in 1995–96. The final report provided state-by-state data on the extent of facilities deficiencies, which the GAO estimated would cost $112 billion to repair or upgrade. In California, 87% of schools reported a need for major repairs or upgrading. In New York the figure was 90%. In the District of Columbia a federal judge delayed the opening of several schools because of unsafe conditions.

The Urban Problem. Enrollment growth and the poor condition of facilities deepened crisis conditions already felt by a number of U.S. urban districts. A report from the National Center for Education Statistics (NCES) described the barriers urban students face just from being in urban schools, with their high concentrations of poverty and unsafe environments. Even when accounting for poverty factors, urban students performed less well academically and had more behavioral problems. They were less likely to complete high school on time and, in later life, had much higher poverty and unemployment rates than their nonurban peers.

Poor achievement results and frequent financial mismanagement in urban districts produced unprecedented levels of concern among policy makers that led in several cases to major governance changes. In Chicago—where the mayor controls the schools through a four-year emergency power—the chief executive officer for the schools and school-board

© Sherman Zent/"The Palm Beach Post"

As U.S. school enrollment hit a new all-time high in the fall of 1996, concerns grew about overcrowded, inadequate school facilities and large class sizes—especially in urban areas. It was estimated the nation would need 6,000 new schools and 190,000 more teachers by 2006 as enrollment continued to grow.

chair put more than 100 schools on academic probation, giving the schools a year to shape up or face being shut down. Chancellor Rudolph Crew of New York City did the same with a group of consistently failing schools in his district. The Maryland state board discussed the possibility of taking over the floundering Baltimore school district, and the financial-control board for the District of Columbia considered a similar move. At a meeting on education issues, the nation's urban mayors produced a statement offering takeover of school systems by their offices as a viable alternative. Such legislation was proposed in Ohio, giving the Cleveland mayor control of the school system.

In some urban districts, reform efforts were beginning to show positive results. David Hornbeck, Philadelphia superintendent and architect of sweeping reforms in that district, weathered teacher-union opposition and court suits to attain progress on reforms, such as cluster organization of schools and a greater focus on standards-based staff development. Thomas Payzant, a former reform-minded superintendent in San Diego, took over the Boston schools. Deborah Meier, a nationally recognized school reformer in New York City and former principal of Central Park East Secondary School, left after 30 years of leadership to begin a new public school in Boston.

Standards-Based Reform. For only the second time in history, U.S. governors participated in a National Education Summit, this time organized by the chair of the National Governors' Association, Gov. Tommy Thompson (R-WI), and the chief executive of IBM, Louis Gerstner, Jr. The first summit, called by President George Bush and the nation's governors in 1989, established six National Goals to be reached by the year 2000. (The number of goals was expanded to eight by Congress.) The 1996 summit of governors and business leaders from each state was meant to renew sagging interest in reform based on higher standards for students and to promote technology use in schools.

The 1996 summit pledged to create a substitute for the original National Education Standards Improvement Council. Authorized in the Goals 2000 legislation, the council was to establish criteria for standards and assessments to be used voluntarily by states and districts. The council became a focal point of opposition to Goals 2000 by conservatives and was repealed by Congress. The 1996 Education Summit statement promised a new, voluntary clearinghouse on standards and assessments, and had raised about $5 million for the new effort, to be known as "Achieve." An office was to be established in Washington, DC. Business leaders also forged ahead. The Business Roundtable, National Alliance of Business, and U.S. Chamber of Commerce issued a joint statement supporting standards and urging their members to give importance to high-school transcripts.

In other ways, standards-based reform seemed to have established a firm stronghold. Every state except Virginia had agreed to accept Goals 2000 funding to help with the development of high content standards and new assessment systems linked to the standards. (Three states refused the money but allowed local school districts to apply directly for funds.) Preliminary studies of the use of Goals 2000 funds found a strong emphasis on professional development around new stan-

College Costs: Always Up

American youth want to go to college. According to the National Center for Education Statistics (NCES), 90% of 1992 graduating high-school seniors planned on attending college immediately or within a year after receiving a diploma (compared with 69% a decade earlier). Yet college costs continue to outpace inflation, and the value of grants for low-income students continues to decline.

One half of all students enrolled in postsecondary institutions receive some form of financial aid, primarily federal loans. Seventy-five percent of the aid that students receive is from federal sources as grants, loans, or work-study programs. Federal-loan programs alone accounted for $29 billion of the student aid distributed in the 1995–96 school year; the total aid for students amounted to more than $50 billion, or $3.3 billion higher than the year before.

Despite this huge investment, college costs probably will continue to grow. Students who complete a baccalaureate degree in four years can expect a 20% increase in their college costs during that time, if current trends continue. According to the 1996 report from the College Board, college tuition and fees had been increasing about 5% each year for the previous four years.

NCES reports that four of five students in higher education attend public institutions, where tuitions are much lower than at private ones. The College Board's survey of tuition and fees for the 1996–97 school year found that, on average, students in four-year public institutions were paying just under $3,000 a year. The one fourth of full-time undergraduate students who live on campus could expect an additional $4,200 in room-and-board charges. In contrast, students at four-year private institutions were paying more than $12,800 for tuition and an additional $5,400 for on-campus housing and meals. Tuition and fee costs at two-year institutions were much lower—$1,330 at public institutions and $6,339 at private institutions.

In addition to annual cost increases, students enrolling in higher education face other financial barriers. For example, a growing percentage of federal college loans are unsubsidized, meaning that students rather than the federal government pay the interest on the loans while they are in school. In 1995–96, more than one third of federal loans were unsubsidized. Another problem is the

dards and better use of technologies in classrooms.

According to the annual review by the American Federation of Teachers, 48 states were developing content standards. However, it considered only 15 of the states to have completed or be working on what it considered rigorous standards. Its definition tended to be proscriptive. Other experts emphasized the need for teachers to develop concepts and buy into standards through professional development centered on evaluating student work together. This was the approach of the Education Trust and the half dozen districts where it was developing K–16 reform efforts, as well as the Coalition of Essential Schools and the urban middle-grades reform network of the Edna McConnell Clark Foundation.

Fewer states were developing new assessment systems, but most were exploring alternative assessments requiring students to demonstrate how well they can use their knowledge. New Standards, a research-based assessment system benchmarked to global standards, gave its first reference exams in 1996, involving more than 60,000 students. New Standards is performance-based, but other researchers cautioned against large-scale use of performance assessments at this stage of their development. Kentucky returned to some multiple-choice test items and put its portfolio assessment on hold; California, whose performance-based assessment had been vetoed by the governor, began to rebuild a more traditional statewide testing system.

Teacher Issues. The standards-based reform movement shifted toward a focus on teachers. The National Board for Professional Teaching Standards was in its second year of certifying accomplished teachers. The board's emphasis on standards was embodied in a significant report on teaching quality. Prepared over two years by a 26-member commission, the report called for major changes in teacher recruitment, preparation, continuing development, and rewards. It would license teachers based on performance assessments rather than seat time or single-shot tests, require a yearlong internship for beginning teachers, close inadequate programs of teacher education, remove incompetent teachers, and growing inequity in student aid. Pell Grants were designed specifically to help disadvantaged students, but the purchasing power of Pell Grants has declined steadily. In the mid-1980s a Pell Grant covered 20% of the costs at a private campus and one half of the costs at a public campus. That proportion in the mid-1990s was 10% at private institutions, and one third at public institutions. According to a 1996 NCES analysis of access and choice issues of students who were in four-year institutions in 1994, a much larger percentage of black students (41%) than white students (19%) rated expenses as very important to their decision of where to go to college.

"NO, *WE'RE* THE PARENTS—THOSE ARE OUR *LOAN OFFICERS!*"

Donald Stewart, president of the College Board, pointed out that the expense of college costs may be overstated because of the focus on the highest-priced institutions. Less than 5% of all full-time undergraduates attend the pricey institutions. Almost three fourths of all students at four-year institutions were paying less than $6,000 a year for tuition and fees and one half were paying less than $4,000, according to Stewart. Also, at the same time that college costs are increasing, the total amount of aid available to students from all sources—federal, state, and institutional—has increased. It was up 4% in 1996–97 over the previous year. Altogether, students and families had $50.3 billion available to them to help with college costs.

ANNE C. LEWIS

reward teachers on the basis of knowledge and skills. Six states signed on as partners with the commission to pilot its recommendations.

Student Life. There was both good news and disturbing news about U.S. youth in 1996. Performance of high-school students on the SAT and ACT tests, barometers for achievement trends, was up slightly, and U.S. students performed well on an international assessment of reading. Also, the Census Bureau reported that, for the first time since data gathering on high-school graduation began 50 years earlier, black students were graduating at generally the same rates as white students. The graduation rate for Hispanic students, however, had slipped. Also, the graduation rate of Asian-Americans, who had been completing high school at higher rates than any other ethnic group, dropped approximately 5% since 1990, as did their college-degree rate. The biannual Youth Indicators report from NCES indicated that young people were getting the message about needing postsecondary education for job preparation. The percentage of high-school seniors planning to attend college jumped from 69% in 1982 to 90% in 1992 (the latest year for which statistics were available).

Despite a better academic picture, the public was alarmed by other aspects of student behavior, primarily increased drug use. According to the Department of Health and Human Services (HHS), marijuana use among teenagers more than doubled between 1992 and 1996, although drug use among adults stabilized. HHS also reported more experimentation by teenagers with cocaine, hallucinogens, and heroin. Drug abuse drew the attention of politicians, with Republican presidential candidate Robert Dole blaming the Bill Clinton administration for ignoring the problem, and President Clinton mounting a campaign against tobacco use by children and teenagers.

Values issues affected several other aspects of students' lives. The Salt Lake City (UT) school board suspended all school-sponsored student group activities rather than allow an organization for gay and lesbian students to use school space. Suits by gay students and by girls, charging that schools ignored harassment against them, were filed in several

SPECIAL REPORT/EDUCATION

Charter Schools

Charter schools—which had started modestly several years earlier in Minnesota—were the hottest item in school reform in 1996. More than 80,000 children were enrolled in more than 400 charter schools at the beginning of the 1996–97 school year. The schools existed in 13 states, but 25 states and the District of Columbia had approved the idea.

Ideally, charter schools are publicly funded autonomous schools chartered by a state, district, or certified agency. The charters agree to be accountable for certain results that must be documented within a time frame, usually three to five years. Depending on the legislation, groups of teachers and/or parents, community organizations, or outside groups can apply for charters.

People and groups are willing to run schools outside the public-school system primarily because of disillusionment with public education or a strong commitment to a particular philosophy or vision. Some reformers attach even more significance to the charter idea, seeing it as a way for state policy to allow for more than one organization in a community to run schools. Charter schools also fit in with reform trends that link state policies to local schools rather than districts and that provide more autonomy to individual schools.

Controversies. The charter-school idea has been controversial from its beginning. Opponents cite fears of public funds being used to support socially unhealthy environments, or of the potential for segregation of students along racial or ethnic lines. Some critics see the schools as part of an evolution toward vouchers. Teachers' unions have been particularly wary of the effect of the schools on contracts. Most charter-school legislation allows for waivers of union contracts but keeps regulations on safety and civil rights.

The controversies have resulted in a two-tiered picture of charter schools. Where opposition to proposed legislation was strong, the charter laws ended up being "weak"—that is, they imposed considerable restrictions. "Strong" legislation provides more autonomy. A review of state charter-school legislation by the Education Commission of the States (ECS) found that most of the newer laws are stronger than earlier ones. This was attributed to fewer compromises by supporters of the legislation and to a better understanding by legislators of how to provide autonomy. For example, more-recent bills allow for local sponsors other than school districts and include an appeals process when applications are rejected by school districts.

Preliminary Results and Obstacles. Studies of charter schools have found some unanticipated results. Instead of "creaming" more-advantaged children out of regular schools, charter schools are serving disproportionate numbers of minority students. Another ECS study found that half the charter schools in its sample were designed to serve "at-risk" students.

A Hudson Institute study found that charter schools tend to be either highly traditional or highly progressive, with a few combining both philosophies. None of the schools in its study "seemed outside the pale of defensible...educational thought and practice." Nor were they staffed by less-qualified teachers. Although many charter schools pay less than prevailing salaries, most teachers are certified, and most schools have waiting lists of teaching applicants.

Charter schools do, however, face many obstacles. In addition to autonomy problems, charter schools that did not inherit buildings may operate in makeshift environments. Also, while there is a perception that charter schools have the same per-pupil support as regular public schools, local school districts usually are allowed to subtract overhead costs, leaving the charters with as much as 20% less for operations. Financial problems have prompted state interventions in several instances.

Many charter schools face a philosophical difference with their states over accountability. Traditional testing programs do not fit with the schools' values, yet their charters require them to show results. The movement is too young for reliable data on student achievement, but the U.S. Department of Education, which was to spend $53 million on charter-school initiatives in fiscal 1997, launched a study of the effects of charter schools on academic achievement.

The charter-school movement can be unpredictable as well as dynamic. Detroit educators were chagrined that a suburban school district had set up a charter school in the inner city for school dropouts, anticipating that it would make money on the venture. And the National Education Association, often a critic of charter schools, launched its own initiative of teacher-formed charter schools, one each in six states.

ANNE C. LEWIS

places, but the sexual-harassment issue became a headliner because of action taken by schools against primary-grade boys accused of kissing classmates. The Office of Civil Rights in the Department of Education issued guidelines for school districts on the problem. Continuing concern over gender was evident in other actions: Virginia Military Institute became the last publicly funded institution to admit women, but in New York City an all-girls public school was opened amid controversy. The College Board also adjusted the Preliminary SAT, which determines the winners of National Merit Scholarships, to include non-essay writing tasks in order to improve girls' scores.

In an attempt to instill order and discipline and reduce violence in public schools, districts in several areas nationwide considered or began the use of school uniforms. The rationale behind the move was that, with the issue of fashionable clothing removed, students will be less likely to fight over clothes, and less likely to resort to violence to get desirable, "status" clothes from other students. Some students and adults objected to the uniforms; many did not agree that rivalry over clothes leads to violence. Nonetheless, President Clinton endorsed the concept—most notably in his State of the Union address—and the DOE issued manuals providing legal guidance to school districts considering uniforms.

Classroom Issues. Two almost diametrically different classroom issues dominated discussions in 1996. One was the renewed fight over the inclusion of creationism in the science curriculum, with organizations representing the Religious Right leading the effort to have creationism included as an alternative theory to evolution. Although the U.S. Supreme Court has rejected the teaching of creationism, it became an issue in legislatures in Tennessee and Alabama, as well as in school-board actions in several states. It was one piece of an agenda by the Religious Right that included returning prayer to the public schools and the assertion of parental rights. Proposed legislation in Congress on these issues failed, however.

The other major classroom issue concerned technology. What began as a single day of NetDay volunteer activity in California to wire classrooms for computers and Internet connections became a nationwide effort. The Clinton administration proposed connecting all schools and libraries to the Internet at little or no cost.

Education in Politics. Technology was not a political issue in 1996—in fact, Congress

© Tribune Media Services, Inc. Reprinted with permission.

approved $225 million more for various technology programs than in the previous budget—but other issues divided policy makers along partisan lines. The Republicans supported vouchers that could be used at private schools, and at least one voucher plan—for Cleveland—passed state-court muster but faced appeals to higher courts. A similar plan in Wisconsin also was in the courts. When a voucher plan was included in the appropriations for the District of Columbia by Congress, the bill was held up by Democrats until it was removed. In last-minute negotiations, a Republican-supported clause to deny education benefits to children of illegal immigrants was dropped from an immigration bill because of threats by President Clinton to veto the measure if it included that provision. While the Republicans stressed vouchers, parental issues, and less federal involvement, Clinton pushed for continuing Goals 2000 reforms and assistance to families for postsecondary education.

Republican candidate Dole also made teacher-union control an issue for his party; Clinton's response was to support teachers (he was endorsed by both major teacher unions). Throughout the year, the Republican-controlled Congress, as well as many Republican governors, criticized federal involvement in education, and the Republican Party platform called for elimination of the Department of Education. However, in the end, Congress not only funded all of the department's programs, but gave it $743 million more than the president requested, for a total of $26.3 billion. Still, the two major pieces of reform legislation that occupied a great deal of time on Capitol Hill—to create block grants for vocational education/training programs and to modify special-education legislation—died with the close of the congressional session.

ANNE C. LEWIS, *Education Policy Writer*

EGYPT

President Hosni Mubarak maintained Egypt's role as the leading Arab nation in the Middle East during 1996 by virtue of his centrist position on international affairs, especially in the Arab-Israel conflict; with his close ties with the West; and with his success in gaining the confidence of the International Monetary Fund (IMF). Despite continued clashes between Egyptian security forces and Islamic zealots, there was some improvement in domestic economic indicators and progress toward meeting demands from European creditors to privatize and decentralize the economy.

Domestic Affairs. The year began with Mubarak's appointment of a new government on January 2. The new prime minister was Kamal al-Ganzouri, a U.S.-educated economist who had served as minister of planning and deputy prime minister since 1987 under his predecessor, Atif Sidqui. With nine years on the job, Sidqui was the longest-serving prime minister in Egypt's modern history. Other notable appointments in the new government included Nawal al-Tatawi as minister of economy and international cooperation. Al-Tatawi, a U.S.-educated banker, was the first woman to head the economics portfolio.

Conflict between the government and Islamic radical groups continued, and Mubarak rejected an offer by the radicals in May to halt their violent attacks on security forces and tourists as part of a dialogue agreement. The minister of interior stated that any contacts with these "killers and criminals" would be rejected "by all means." The most serious incident occurred on April 18, when members of the largest militant faction, the Islamic Group, attacked a party of Greek tourists, killing 18 and wounding at least 15 others outside their Cairo hotel. The group stated that they had intended to kill Israelis in revenge for recent Israeli attacks on Lebanon. Much of the conflict between government forces and the Islamic radical factions was in Asyu't governorate in central Egypt.

In January the government registered a new political group, the Al Wasat (Center) party, established by mostly young, professional Islamists. Principal activists included former Muslim Brothers, Nasserists, and an evangelical Christian. Their platform called for reconciliation between Arab nationalists and Islamists and for implementing *sharia* (Islamic law) according to "modern legal thinking." In May, President Mubarak charged that Al Wasat was a front for the outlawed Muslim Brotherhood, and at least 12 of its leaders were accused of illegal party activity before a military tribunal.

Controversy over religious issues was a major focus of public and press attention. In July the ministry of health banned the ritual genital mutilation of girls, and the new head of al-Azhar University, the leading Islamic institution, refused to endorse the custom. Nevertheless several clerics defied the ban, insisting that it was ordained by Islam. Experts estimated that between 70% and 90% of Egyptian girls still were being subjected to the procedure, called female circumcision.

In May the Supreme Constitutional Court ruled that the *niqab* (veil) was not an "Islamic garment," thus making it possible to enforce the education ministry's ban on students wearing the veil to school without a parent's authorization. Contrary to expectations raised by the courts' trend toward liberalization, Egypt's highest judicial-review body, the Court of Cassation, upheld a lower-court ruling in August declaring a Cairo University professor an apostate from Islam because of his academic writings, and forcibly divorced him from his Muslim wife.

Economy. Under Mubarak the prime minister was largely responsible for managing the economy. Ganzouri accelerated privatization and substantially reduced import tariffs. These measures helped win the confidence of the IMF, which during October approved a $4.2 billion debt write-off from the Paris Club of creditor nations. This was the third and final

Egypt's President Hosni Mubarak (right) *met with Israel's new prime minister, Benjamin Netanyahu, for the first time in Cairo in July 1996. Egyptian-Israeli relations turned cool, however.*

© Nati Harnik/AP/Wide World Photos

tranche of Egypt's $11 billion debt-forgiveness plan.

The government announced that its economic-reform measures—such as lifting subsidies on food, energy, and services—led to a 32-year low in the inflation rate, which dropped from about 20% in 1991 to less than 7% in 1996. During that same period the budget deficit fell from 20% of gross domestic product (GDP) to less than 2%. Although government salaries and other wages remained stable, rising prices caused real wages to drop. The continued rapid population increase all but wiped out the rate of economic growth, which hovered close to zero.

From only three state companies sold off in 1994 and five in 1995, the number was increased by more than a dozen during 1996. Officials also reported plans to put 90 more firms up for privatization. Ganzouri won the confidence of Egyptian business at the expense of the state bureaucracy. Such privatization measures met opposition. In May the Social Labor, Nasserist Arab Democratic, and leftist Tagammu parties filed a court suit arguing that the cabinet's decree for privatization violated the constitution. Although Egyptian law did not acknowledge the right to strike, several workers' organizations staged small work stoppages and the Heavy Industries Syndicate created Egypt's first strike fund to prepare for opposition to the new measures. Labor and human-rights activists maintained that the ministry of manpower, which supervises elections for local labor-syndicate offices, assured that no opponents of privatization would be elected; the Center for Human Rights and Legal Aid filed 90 lawsuits against the ministry for excluding workers from the ballots and for other election improprieties. Clashes between workers and government authorities resulted in several riots.

Although the rise of Islamic militancy has discouraged Egypt's tourist trade, treasures such as the newly reopened ancient tomb in Luxor (above) *remain prime attractions.*

EGYPT • Information Highlights

Official Name: Arab Republic of Egypt.
Location: Northeastern Africa.
Area: 386,660 sq mi (1 001 450 km²).
Population (mid-1996 est.): 63,700,000.
Chief Cities (July 1, 1992 est.): Cairo, the capital, 6,800,000; Alexandria, 3,380,000; Giza, 2,144,000.
Government: *Head of state,* Mohammed Hosni Mubarak, president (took office Oct. 1981). *Head of government,* Kamal Ahmed al-Ganzouri, prime minister (took office Jan. 2, 1996). *Legislature*—People's Assembly.
Monetary Unit: Pound (3.3920 pounds equal U.S.$1, free-market rate, Dec. 31, 1996).
Gross Domestic Product (1994 est. U.S.$): $151,500,000,000 (purchasing power parity).
Economic Index (1995, 1990 = 100): *Consumer Prices,* all items, 178.7; food, 164.4.
Foreign Trade (1994 U.S.$): *Imports,* $10,218,000,000; *exports,* $3,475,000,000.

Foreign Relations. Egypt continued to be the site of several important international meetings and conferences. Leaders of 27 countries and the Palestinians participated in the March "Summit of the Peacemakers" at Sharm El-Sheik cosponsored by Egypt and the United States following terrorist incidents in Israel. Two months after his election in May, Israel's new Prime Minister Benjamin Netanyahu visited President Mubarak in Cairo, but relations between the two cooled due to Netanyahu's reluctance to further the Middle East peace process. An Arab summit in Cairo during June called for resumption of the peace talks and for Israel to implement its obligations according to previous agreements with the Palestinians.

After some hesitation, President Mubarak permitted the third annual Middle East–North Africa (MENA) Economic Summit to convene in Cairo in November, but attendance was lower than at the previous two economic conferences in Morocco and Jordan.

See also MIDDLE EAST.

DON PERETZ, *Professor Emeritus*
State University of New York, Binghamton

ENERGY

The U.S. energy picture for 1996 featured a continuation of recent trends: rising consumer demand, diminishing domestic resources, and growing reliance on foreign oil to meet the nation's energy needs. As year's end approached, it appeared likely that net imports of all energy sources would break the previous record of 18.6 quadrillion British thermal units (Btu), set in 1994. That was slightly more than the United States imported before the energy crises of the 1970s prompted conservation efforts to reduce the country's reliance on foreign fuels.

Oil. As in years past, oil and its refined products topped the list of energy sources consumed in the United States, accounting for nearly 40% of the total. Although the U.S. consumption of petroleum products had stayed within the 30 quadrillion–38 quadrillion Btu range since 1971, domestic production continued to decline. Domestic production of crude oil in 1996 was expected to fall below the 13.9 quadrillion Btu produced the previous year, continuing a steady decline from more than 19 quadrillion Btu registered in 1973. Following the first energy crisis of that year, imports rose as a share of U.S. oil consumption from 35% to about half.

The world's dependence on the Persian Gulf for much of its oil supplies 23 years after the first energy crisis continued to draw international attention to this volatile region, the source of almost a fifth of U.S. oil imports. To prevent any further interruption of the flow of Persian Gulf oil by the anti-American governments of Iran or Iraq, the United States maintained some 20,000 troops and a vast stockpile of arms in the region.

The main focus of concern remained the government of Iraqi President Saddam Hussein, whose invasion of neighboring Kuwait prompted the 1991 Persian Gulf war and subsequent United Nations (UN) sanctions barring Iraq from exporting oil, its main source of revenue. Under the UN-brokered deal permitting Iraq to export enough oil to feed its beleaguered population, limited Iraqi oil exports finally resumed in December with the reopening of an oil pipeline joining northern Iraq's oil fields and Turkey's Mediterranean coast. The oil-for-food agreement allowed Iraq to sell oil worth $2 billion over six months. Because Iraq's oil sales were not expected to exceed about 600,000 barrels per day—a small fraction of the 72 million barrels the world consumes daily—the resumption of Iraqi exports was not expected to affect world oil prices. Iraq was barred from resuming unlimited oil exports—which had exceeded 2.5 million barrels per day before the war—until the UN Security Council decided that the nation had abandoned plans to develop weapons of mass destruction.

Uncertainty about the conditions of Iraq's resumption of oil exports created turmoil in the world oil market for much of the year. Eager to prevent a glut in world oil supplies that might depress prices upon the return of Iraqi oil to the market, refiners slowed their purchases of crude oil early in the year. When negotiations for the UN deal stalled temporarily in the spring, crude prices jumped to a five-year high of more than $25 per barrel. In the United States the effect was a sudden rise in the price of heating oil, which more than 10% of Americans use to heat their homes.

Consumers recoiled at gasoline-price increases that also resulted from market uncertainties. The national city average retail price of unleaded regular gasoline stood at $1.23 per gallon in October, up 9% over October 1995. But gasoline prices later declined somewhat, and the real cost of gasoline, accounting for inflation, remained well below its peak of the early 1980s. This real decline in gasoline prices helped sustain a surge in consumer purchases of sport-utility vehicles and other energy-inefficient vehicles.

There was some optimistic news for the United States' energy future. Technological advances in equipment used to detect and tap oil reserves led to the discovery and exploitation of several new offshore sites in 1996. While onshore U.S. oil production slowed to less than 1,000 barrels per day, initial findings led experts to predict that reserves deep under the Gulf of Mexico eventually might produce more than 30,000 barrels per day. Although such an increase would not be enough to affect oil prices, analysis predicted that it could stem the fall in domestic oil production, perhaps even lessening U.S. dependence on oil imports.

Restructuring efforts begun in 1995 by the oil industry held the potential of lowering American drivers' future gasoline costs. Three of the world's largest oil companies announced in November that they were discussing plans to merge their so-called downstream operations—refining and marketing—in the United States. If the merger were completed, the new unit of Shell Oil Co., Texaco Inc., and Star Enterprises would account for 15% of the U.S. gasoline market. The announcement came on the heels of a September announcement by Diamond Shamrock Inc. and the Ultramar Corp. of a similar plan to merge their operations, concentrated in Texas and California, and an earlier merger between British Petroleum PLC and Mobil Corp. of their downstream operations throughout Europe.

Natural Gas. Continuing a decade-long trend, natural gas accounted for a growing portion of energy use in the United States—about a quarter of total energy consumption. Long used for home heating, natural gas became a leading alternative fuel for electric-power generation by utilities seeking to reduce the pollution associated with coal-fired plants. However, the country's reliance on imports continued to grow. Imported natural gas approached 3 quadrillion Btu in 1996, up from 0.7 quadrillion Btu as recently as 1986. The growing need for imported natural gas, however, was not considered as worrisome as the country's dependence on foreign oil. Unlike oil imports, which originate primarily in the Persian Gulf region, almost all of the natural gas imported into the United States comes from one of the country's most reliable trading partners—Canada.

The bitter cold that swept through the eastern United States in January and February 1996 came back to haunt consumers later in the year in the form of sharply higher natural-gas prices. Distribution companies whose gas supplies were drawn down during the cold wave competed to replenish their stocks over the summer, while another cold snap in early November signaled to the market that supplies could become tight again over the winter. As a result, the price of gas for home heating, which had held steady in recent years, rose by as much as 30% at the beginning of the fall heating season as compared to the previous year.

Coal and Electricity. Despite its implication in urban smog problems, coal continued to be a heavily used energy source, accounting for almost as much energy output as natural gas. Coal also remained a leading source of electricity generation as well as its uses in industry and in the heating of factories and other large buildings. Alone among the country's fossil fuels, coal reserves remained in abundance, providing export revenues as well as a relatively inexpensive energy source at home.

Despite efforts to replace coal with less-polluting fuels to produce electrical power, the country's electric utilities continued to rely on coal for more than half the electricity produced in 1996. While some utilities switched to natural gas, there was little change in the use of other alternative fuels. Since construction of new nuclear plants was halted more than a decade earlier, nuclear energy generated by the 110 plants in operation around the country continued to account for less than a quarter of generated electricity. Hydropower also remained static, at about 12% of the total, due to lack of appropriate new dam sites as well as concerns over hydroelectric plants' impact on fish migration and other damage to the environment.

With increasing gasoline prices a consumer concern throughout the United States, California was preparing to require that 10% of all new vehicles sold in the state be emission-free by 2003.

Sweeping power outages in the western United States called into question the reliability of the region's electrical-transmission system. A July 2 blackout cut power to 2 million residents of 15 states (as well as to locales in Mexico and Canada) covered by the largest power grid in North America. A second blackout on August 10 affected 4 million customers. In both cases, overburdened high-voltage lines drooped onto trees and short-circuited, sparking a chain reaction throughout the service area.

A concerted effort by Republican lawmakers to deregulate U.S. industry had a sweeping impact on the electric-power sector in 1996.

To prepare for the increased competition expected to come with the removal of price and supply regulations, some of the country's largest utilities proposed mergers that would expand their markets. Several merger proposals, such as those sought by the Brooklyn Union Gas Co. and the Long Island Lighting Co. and by the Potomac Electric Power Co. and Baltimore Gas and Electric Co., would bring large electric and gas companies under single ownership. Proponents of utility deregulation argued that a more efficient industry would pass along savings to consumers in the form of lower electricity and natural-gas rates. As the merger trend gained momentum, however, concern mounted that the new giant utilities might use their newfound monopoly status to charge even higher rates. The trend was expected to accelerate after the Federal Energy Regulatory Commission (FERC) moved in December to simplify and speed up the approval process for utility mergers.

Environmental Concerns. Efforts to reduce urban pollution, caused mainly by gasoline- and diesel-burning cars and trucks, led to the introduction of the first mass-produced electric car. The EV1, or Electric Vehicle 1, a two-seat passenger car produced by the General Motors (GM) Corp., went on sale in California and Arizona through GM's Saturn division. Though coal-powered utilities continued to feed the nation's electricity grid, electric cars were considered to be virtually nonpolluting because they do not produce tailpipe emissions, the culprit in most smog and ozone pollution.

Tougher clean-air standards, proposed on November 27 by the Environmental Protection Agency, were expected to prompt state and local officials in many parts of the country to raise parking fees and road tolls and take other measures to discourage driving. Cities along the U.S. east coast as well as in southern California already were struggling with standards limiting levels of ozone and other pollutants emitted primarily by gasoline-burning cars and trucks. The tougher standards, which must be approved by Congress, would force more drastic action in these regions.

Another by-product of oil, gas, and coal combustion—carbon dioxide—was the subject of international negotiation aimed at curbing global fossil-fuel consumption. Under a 1992 treaty signed at the Earth Summit in Rio de Janeiro, Brazil, the United States and about 150 other countries agreed to try to reduce fuel use in an effort to contain the release of excess carbon dioxide and other greenhouse gases. (Many scientists believe that an excess of greenhouse gases in the atmosphere could trigger a serious, long-term warming of Earth's climate.) Although the signatories agreed in 1996 that the treaty needed to be strengthened, they failed to resolve a disagreement over how to allocate the burden of cutting fuel consumption between developing countries and industrial countries.

Energy Policy. President Bill Clinton's first term in office ended with a mixed scorecard for the energy platform he ran on in 1992. The president abandoned his earlier promise to raise energy taxes significantly, but he thwarted efforts by the Republican-controlled Congress to expand oil drilling in Alaska, citing the threat it would pose to the environment.

Supporters of developing alternative sources of energy were dismayed when Congress approved, and the president signed, an energy and water appropriations bill for fiscal 1997 that cut funding for research into renewable energy sources, the only certain way to ensure the country's future energy independence. The $20.4 billion law funded $15.8 billion for the Department of Energy (DOE)—including $2.7 billion for programs to develop solar, wind, and other renewable energy sources—$16.5 million less than was allocated the previous year.

As President Clinton prepared for a second term in office, Secretary of Energy Hazel O'Leary was among a number of cabinet members to resign. The former utility executive had overseen a vast transformation of the DOE, from one of the most secretive federal agencies with responsibility for the country's nuclear arsenal during the Cold War to a more open bureaucracy focused on cleaning up the toxic waste remaining after 40 years of nuclear-weapons production. During O'Leary's four-year tenure, the DOE underwent a 41,000-person workforce reduction. At the same time the outspoken secretary came under criticism for excessive foreign travel. Before leaving office, O'Leary on December 9 unveiled a two-step plan for getting rid of 55 tons of excess plutonium from nuclear weapons being dismantled. In addition to calling for the burial of most plutonium, the plan would allow some of the lethal material to be used as fuel in civilian nuclear reactors.

In a surprise move, the president on December 20 named as O'Leary's successor Federico Peña, secretary of transportation during the first Clinton administration and a former mayor of Denver.

MARY H. COOPER
"The CQ [Congressional Quarterly] Researcher"

ENGINEERING, CIVIL

Several large civil-engineering projects aimed at improving transportation infrastructures commanded attention during 1996.

Ted Williams Tunnel. The Ted Williams Tunnel in Boston won the prestigious Outstanding Civil Engineering Achievement Award for 1996. The new tunnel, an immersed marine tube that lies in a trench as deep as 100 ft (30.5 m) below the surface of Boston Harbor, was designed for four lanes. Vehicular traffic will be limited to trucks, buses, taxis, and other commercial vehicles until 2001, when several highway interchanges and another tunnel will have been completed and the $1.3 billion Ted Williams Tunnel will be opened fully. The tunnel is the first completed component of Boston's ambitious $10 billion Central Artery/Third Harbor Tunnel project—the largest municipal infrastructure project in the United States.

More than 450,000 cubic yards (344 300 m^3) of concrete and 60,000 tons of rebar went into this cut-and-cover tunnel. It took four separate ready-mix plants in joint venture to supply the concrete. The ventilation buildings on either end of the tunnel house a total of 20 exhaust and 14 supply fans—each 120-in (3-m)-wheel centrifugal types—plus the associated variable-frequency drives, switch gear, generators, transformers, and electrical panels for tunnel lighting. In addition to carrying the roadway under the surface of the harbor, the tunnel also was designed to support a future airport terminal.

High-Speed Rail. Work was under way on Amtrak's new $877 million high-speed-rail plan, which will serve the Northeast Corridor. The all-electric system will run from New York to Boston and will consist of 18 high-speed train sets, 15 high-speed stand-alone electric locomotives, and three maintenance facilities. The system will be operational in 1999. To ensure passenger safety at speeds in excess of 150 mph (241 km/hr) without reconstructing the entire rail line, the new train sets will feature an electrohydraulic tilting system that anticipates the need to lean coaches into a curve to provide passengers with a comfortable ride. Additional safety features include advanced braking systems, antiwheel sliding systems, and new car-evacuation systems.

Washington, DC, Airports. The $2 billion renovation and expansion of National and Dulles International airports in Washington, DC, proceeded apace in 1996. The two airports were undergoing simultaneous $1 billion face-lifts in one of the most complex design, engineering, and construction programs in U.S. aviation history.

Construction at National includes a new $290 million, 35-gate terminal building. The first 24 gates are scheduled to open in 1997, with completion targeted for fall 1998. The 1-million-sq-ft (92 900-m^2) structure sits on an old shoal of the Potomac River, and construction crews encountered everything from hard cobblestone to spongy, soft clay fill used in the original airport construction in the 1940s. To overcome these soil conditions, crews drove 4,000 concrete piles to depths of 40 ft to 70 ft (12-21 m) under the main north-south concourse, as well as under each of the three east-west piers of the terminal building.

At Dulles an additional 320 ft (97.5 m) on both the east and west sides of the existing 600-ft (183-m) main terminal were built to match the appearance of the terminal, with the east end opening in late spring 1996 and the west end in summer 1996.

Advancing Composites. Advanced composite materials are becoming competitive with conventional structural materials, thanks to the ready availability of glass, aramid, and carbon fibers and epoxies, vinylesters, polyesters, and cementitious-bonding agents, as well as significant advances in manufacturing technologies. Improvements in the manufacturing of polymer-matrix composites in pultrusion, resin-transfer molding, and filament winding and the automated or semiautomated manufacturing of large components have reduced costs significantly. Designs of these various new materials in conjunction with conventional structural materials, rather than individual component replacement or complete advanced composite designs, have shown that technical efficiency can be achieved within competitive-cost constraints.

Advanced composites have shown significant promise in recent applications, particularly in the rehabilitation of existing structural systems. The seismic retrofitting of bridge columns with carbon-fiber wraps or preformed jackets has been demonstrated in California to be technically as effective as, and more cost-effective than, conventional steel jacketing. Strengthening of aging bridges with advanced composite overlays has been demonstrated successfully in Delaware and Florida, and building rehabilitation with composite wall overlays has shown significant enhancements to deformation capacities under lateral loads for both damaged and undamaged structures.

HARRY GOLDSTEIN
"Civil Engineering Magazine"

ENVIRONMENT

The environment sizzled as a major U.S. presidential-campaign issue and a Republican-controlled Congress chalked up some major victories in 1996, despite missteps a year earlier that energized opposition to their efforts to roll back environmental laws.

U.S. President Bill Clinton signed into law major environmental bills in 1996—including overhauls of pesticide, tap-water, and fishery regulations. But a number of big environmental initiatives languished and, eventually, were crushed in the end-of-session rush to adjournment. Trampled were bills to rewrite the nation's beleaguered superfund hazardous-waste and clean-water laws as well as endangered-species protections. Ironically, it was the Republican-controlled 104th Congress that resurrected the environment as a vibrant issue and succeeded in training President Clinton's attention on it.

The ground had begun to shift in the spring and summer of 1995 when the GOP committed two major political blunders. The Republicans in the House pushed through a rewrite of the clean-water act and endorsed environment-related legislative provisions in appropriation bills. Both moves were criticized roundly as regulatory rollbacks, and Republicans had to face the political fallout that followed. Clinton seized the opening, exploiting the Republicans' credibility gap to tar the Republican Congress as "extremists" and positioning himself as the chief protector of the environment.

That the political ground had shifted was exemplified most sharply by Clinton's signing of a sweeping bipartisan rewrite of the federal drinking-water law in August. It had been equally clear in the final rounds of the battle over fiscal 1996 domestic spending, as the GOP was forced to drop a handful of controversial environment-related legislative proposals attached to the spending bills. But the seesawing of environmental policy—seen in the shifts and divisions in the 103rd and 104th Congresses—have left environmental policy partly in limbo. For example, while many of the nation's environmental statutes were credited with success, the superfund program remained badly broken and, by some accounts, in a state of disrepair.

The Clinton administration ostensibly reflected an approach to environmental protection that favored consensus over confrontation, and a path away from prescriptive environmental laws. Indeed, there was a growing consensus in both parties that regulations need to be more flexible and that regulators should be given more leeway to take costs and benefits into account. But translating such principles into action is a delicate balancing act.

Efforts to overhaul the 1973 Endangered Species Act, for example, foundered over such issues as compensating landowners for restrictions that limit the use of their property. In addition, the environment, once a broadly bipartisan issue, took on a more partisan cast, as groups such as the Sierra Club pumped millions of dollars into efforts to defeat primarily Republican opponents. The series of events left many lawmakers chastened by their earlier attempts to overhaul federal regulatory policy, seen most clearly in the Republicans' congressional agenda. And as an issue once defined by national consensus grew more contentious, the future of environmental policy—a contested issue in the best of years—grew more uncertain.

Drinking Water. President Clinton on August 6 signed into law a sweeping rewrite aimed at protecting the nation's drinking-water supply, providing Congress with an important victory in environmental legislation. The new law takes a big step toward removing what critics called a regulatory straitjacket that hampered the nation's 185,000 regulated water systems. Establishing greater flexibility regarding the most urgent health needs, the new law authorizes billions of dollars for a state-administered loan and grant fund to help fiscally drained localities with the cost of compliance with the new rules. It also puts in place a new requirement that operators of community water systems must inform the public about the level of contaminants in drinking water and about the health effects of contaminants that exceed Environmental Protection Agency (EPA) standards.

Passage of the bill marked a high point for the Republican-controlled Congress and its efforts to reverse an image of favoring a rollback of environmental laws. Pressure had been building for years to shore up safeguards of the drinking-water supply, particularly after the 1993 outbreak of the deadly organism *cryptosporidium* in Milwaukee, WI, which resulted in several deaths. While many environmental groups did not issue an outright endorsement of the overhaul bill, they generally were supportive of many of its goals, and said it would help improve the quality of the nation's drinking-water supply.

Pesticides. For nearly two decades, Congress had been deadlocked over rewriting the

© Larry Downing/Sygma

Vice-President Al Gore joined Bill Clinton at the south rim of the Grand Canyon as the president designated nearly 2 million acres (810 000 ha) of southern Utah's red-rock wilderness as the Grand Staircase–Escalante National Monument.

nation's pesticide regulations. But on August 3, President Clinton signed into law a major overhaul endorsed by many environmental and industry groups. Passage of the law came with stunning speed, particularly given the logjam that had preceded it. The last major pesticide bill had passed in 1978, and further action had been stymied by fighting between environmentalists and industry.

The new measure—which would create a unified health standard for both raw and processed foods, with guidelines to protect children from pesticides—sailed through three congressional panels and the House and Senate within eight days. Congress was compelled to act quickly by recent court rulings that interpreted pesticide regulation so narrowly that the EPA faced the prospect of barring some pesticides. At issue was the so-called Delaney clause contained in the 1958 Federal Food, Drug and Cosmetic Act, which barred processed food from containing even minute amounts of cancer-causing chemicals. Since enactment of the Delaney clause, testing has become so advanced that the smallest amounts of cancer-causing chemicals can be detected, and many key pesticides would have been barred from the market under Delaney.

The new law imposes a less stringent, but more practical, safety standard. Residue from pesticides on both raw and processed food are allowed as long as they pose no reasonable risk of harm. That standard means that there likely would be no more than a one-in-a-million chance that the pesticide residue would cause cancer.

Fisheries. With many of the nation's fisheries badly depleted, President Clinton on October 11 signed a major overhaul of the 1976 Magnuson Fishery Conservation Act, which environmentalists and many in the fishing industry say will help bolster the domestic industry. The 1976 law had two main goals—to defend coastal fisheries against foreign competition and to protect against overfishing. At least in beating back the foreign threat, the act was a stunning success. But it was much less successful in protecting the fish supply. While the old law allowed regional councils to permit overharvesting to aid struggling communities, the new law would place a much greater emphasis on conservation. In overfished areas, management plans would have to be put in place that restore fish populations to sustainable levels and minimize the incidental kill of unwanted fish and other marine life. The bill almost foundered over a regional bout between Washington state and Alaska on divvying up the fish supply. But after a late-summer compromise, the broadly popular measure easily passed both the House and Senate.

Other Presidential Actions. During an election-year ceremony, President Clinton designated nearly two million acres (810 000 ha) of Utah land as a national monument, giving it new protected status. The establishment of the 1.7-million-acre (688 000-ha) Grand Staircase–Escalante National Monument set off fierce opposition in Utah, where many politicians accused Clinton of an election-year landgrab. In making the move, Clinton pleased environmentalists who were trying to protect the land from mining and other commercial enterprises, and reaped some political capital. The red-rock canyons of southern Utah have been at the center of a fierce battle between environmentalists and industry over their fate, and the decision did not play well with the home crowd. Many in Utah saw the move as emblematic of an overreaching federal government that showed little regard for local interests. Clinton announced the decision in nearby Arizona, rather than in Utah, to quiet the controversy.

On August 12 the president announced an agreement in principle between the federal government and the Canadian owners of the New World Mine by which the government would give $65 million worth of federal land in exchange for the company's ceasing claim to some $650 million worth of gold deposits in a section of the Yellowstone National Park.

In another action affecting the environment, President Clinton on October 12 signed a $3.8 million water-projects bill that authorized spending of up to$75 million to defend the Florida Everglades. The president later signed legislation creating or improving almost 120 national parks, trails, rivers, and historical sites.

Headwaters Forest. The federal government announced a deal to save 7,500 acres (more than 3 000 ha) of old-growth forests in California, including the Headwaters forest and the Elk Head Grove. Under the deal, Texas financier Charles Hurwitz received state and federal assets in exchange for the old-growth timber stands. Preserving the forest has been a top priority of environmentalists, who gave the deal lukewarm support. They asserted that the deal would not prevent Hurwitz from logging under the 1995 timber-salvage law.

Federal courts denied environmentalists' efforts to prevent salvage logging in ancient groves and surrounding forests. A federal judge ruled that the environmentalists had failed to prove their case that a threatened seabird, the marbled murrelet, would be endangered by the cutting.

Superfund. Created in 1980, the superfund hazardous-waste program was envisioned as a short-term effort to clean up the nation's worst toxic-waste sites. But it has fallen well short of its goal. And in 1996 the program continued to be mired in a morass of high-stakes politics and tussling over who should foot the billions of dollars in cleanup costs.

First, for the second time in two Congresses—the Democratic-led 103rd and the GOP-controlled 104th—lawmakers fell well short in their efforts to revamp the troubled program. What is more, the industry taxes that flow into the program's cleanup trust fund had been allowed to lapse at the end of 1995, and Republicans were balking at renewing them until a permanent fix of the program was in place. The Clinton administration took some steps to improve the program through a series of administrative actions, but EPA Administrator Carol M. Browner conceded that only a full-blown congressional revamp could fix the program.

In late 1996, there were a total of 1,227 superfund sites, but only 403 had been cleaned up or taken off the list. Those numbers are a testament to a program burdened by excessive litigation and snails'-pace cleanups. Neither party had come up with a solution that would pass muster in the Congress, leaving the program in limbo over such issues as liability for cleanup costs and how much the federal government should spend on such efforts.

Climate. The report from the United Nations' (UN's) Intergovernmental Panel on Climate Change (IPCC) provided fresh ammunition that Earth's climate is warming, as much as 6°F over the next 100 years. According to the UN group, made up of 2,500 scientists, the "balance of evidence" suggests that human activity is contributing to global climate change. Despite the finding, the group's report served to ignite further the controversial debate over global warming, with major environmental groups pushing to get the issue on the national agenda. *See also* METEOROLOGY.

ALLAN FREEDMAN, *"Congressional Quarterly"*

ETHIOPIA

During 1996, Ethiopia shored up its relations with the West, moved against its Islamic neighbors, and continued its crackdown against domestic opposition and intellectual critics of the government.

Foreign Affairs. After receiving plaudits from the West for the success of national elections held the previous year, Ethiopia moved rapidly to improve economic and security links with its Western supporters. In January, Germany agreed to loan Ethiopia $34 million for agricultural development. That same month the World Bank forgave $250 million of Ethiopia's commercial bank debt.

Ethiopian leaders held a series of high-level meetings with U.S. officials, and the appointment of David H. Shinn, a career diplomat, as the new U.S. ambassador to Ethiopia was confirmed. In April, John Deutch, director of the U.S. Central Intelligence Agency (CIA), visited Ethiopia and discussed national security in the Horn of Africa with Ethiopian Prime Minister Meles Zenawi. Following that meeting, Gen. Joseph Ralston, vice-chairman of the U.S. Joint Chiefs of Staff, met with Ethiopia's Defense Minister Tamrat Layne, discussing American assistance for the training and organization of Ethiopia's air force. U.S. and Ethiopian officials also discussed Islamic fundamentalism in Sudan and the prevailing anarchy in Somalia, and the effect of these situations on the security of Ethiopia.

In March, Ethiopian forces attacked border towns in eastern Sudan. Ethiopia had accused Sudan of organizing a 1995 assassination attempt on Egyptian President Hosni Mubarak while he was attending a meeting in Addis Ababa, Ethiopia's capital. Ethiopia's charge was endorsed officially by the United Nations in February 1996. The United States, which also accused Sudan of supporting international terrorism, stood by Ethiopia's assertions. In September three Egyptian militants were sentenced to death in Ethiopia for the abortive assassination attempt. All three reportedly were trained in Sudan and were members of Egypt's outlawed Islamic Group.

In response to the anarchy and power vacuum evident in Somalia in August after the death of Gen. Mohammed Farah Aidid, one of Somalia's most powerful warlords, Ethiopia attacked three border towns in Somalia's southwest, a stronghold of the fundamentalist Union of Islam. The group earlier had harassed Ethiopian civilians in the Ogaden region of Ethiopia in an attempt to stir up disorder and to gain control of the sector (to which Somalia lays historical claim). Although Ethiopian troops withdrew within two days, more than 200 persons were killed. Ethiopia clearly indicated that it would not tolerate the spread of Somalia's civil strife across its border.

Human Rights and Political Trials. In April the trials of officials of the former Marxist Dergue government resumed, as 71 high-ranking former Dergue representatives were charged with genocide and crimes against humanity. Meanwhile, another 1,700 people were awaiting trial. Prosecutors indicated that they had solid evidence of more than 1,800 politically motivated killings and many other crimes. Among those on trial were former Prime Minister Fikre-Selassie Wogderess, Capt. Legesse Asfaw (once the second-most-powerful man in the Dergue), and former Vice-President Fisseha Desta. After two weeks of testimony, the trials were adjourned, scheduled to resume early in 1997. According to *The New York Times*, the trial was shaping up to be the "most extensive judgment of war crimes since the Nuremberg trials of Nazis after World War II." Various relatives of those killed attended the 1996 court sessions.

The president of the Ethiopian Teachers' Association, Dr. Taye Woldesemayat, was arrested in May after returning from a conference in Europe. He was held on charges of subversion despite appeals for his release by the European Parliament, which claimed that the charges were fabricated to still a political opponent. Professor Asrat Woldeyes, the chairman of the All Amhara People's Organization—who was arrested in 1993 on charges of inciting war—remained incarcerated despite his claim that the charges against him were untrue.

PETER SCHWAB, *Purchase College*
State University of New York

ETHIOPIA • Information Highlights

Official Name: Ethiopia.
Location: Eastern Africa.
Area: 435,184 sq mi (1 127 127 km²).
Population (mid-1996 est.): 57,200,000.
Chief Cities (mid-1993 est.): Addis Ababa, the capital, 2,200,186; Dire Dawa, 173,588; Harar, 162,645.
Government: *Head of state,* Negasso Ghidada, president (took office May 1995). *Head of government,* Meles Zenawi, prime minister (took office May 1995). *Legislature*—Parliament (established 1995).
Monetary Unit: Birr (6.33 birr equal U.S.$1, May 1996).
Gross Domestic Product (1993 est. U.S. $): $20,300,-000,000 (purchasing power parity).
Economic Index (1995, 1990 = 100): *Consumer Prices,* all items, 183.9; food, 198.6.
Foreign Trade (1994 U.S.$): *Imports,* $1,033,000,000; *exports,* $372,000,000.

ETHNIC GROUPS, U.S.

Politics and court cases regarding discrimination dominated public-policy concerns for U.S. ethnic groups in 1996. Meanwhile, questions of sovereignty, cultural identity, and economic survival focused attention on Native Americans (*see* SPECIAL REPORT, page 235).

In two separate rulings the Supreme Court found that three Texan congressional districts with black or Hispanic majorities and a black-majority district in North Carolina were unconstitutional because they had been drawn with race as the predominant factor. In other rulings, the Supreme Court let stand a redrawn map in Georgia that reduced the state's black-majority districts from three to one; and a federal court ruled that a Florida congressional district was drawn unconstitutionally to create a black majority. Civil-rights activists worried that such decisions spelled the doom of black representation, but the elections proved otherwise. During U.S. elections held in November, every black candidate who had been pushed into a white-majority district by recent Supreme Court rulings that nullified racially gerrymandered congressional districts won reelection.

Political mobilization of new voters was a theme for several ethnic groups in 1996. Black professionals organized "National Freedom Day," taking time off from work to bring black voters to the polls on election day. In October tens of thousands of Hispanics marched on Washington to protest anti-immigrant and anti-Hispanic policies. Hispanic voters claimed a major victory in California's traditionally Republican Orange county when Democrat Loretta Sanchez, a Mexican-American, eked out a victory over a conservative incumbent for a seat in Congress. In an October runoff election, Cuban-American Alex Penelas defeated black candidate Arthur Teele to become mayor of Dade county, FL; earlier, Joe Corollo, also a Cuban-born American, had been elected mayor of the city of Miami. In November, Democrat Gary Locke won the governorship of Washington, becoming the first Chinese-American U.S. governor.

Affirmative Action. Affirmative action was a major issue during 1996. In January, Louisiana Gov. Mike Foster ordered an end to affirmative action and set-aside programs for women and minorities in the state, setting off protests in February. In November, in a much-watched campaign, voters in California passed Proposition 209, which banned affirmative action in hiring, contracting, and education. The American Civil Liberties Union (ACLU) and civil-rights groups filed suit to block the implementation of the bans, while other states began to consider similar prohibitions.

Several federal-court rulings also appeared to weaken affirmative action. The 5th U.S. Circuit Court of Appeals declared flatly that the University of Texas law school could not give preference to blacks and Hispanics in admissions and ordered immediate compliance (*Hopwood v. Texas*). The Supreme Court let the decision stand by refusing to hear an appeal in the case, thereby creating confusion by not issuing a ruling of its own or a comment on the validity of a 1978 case (*Regents of the University of California v. Bakke*) that allowed colleges to use race as "a factor" in admissions. The 3d U.S. Circuit Court of Appeals upheld a damage award to a white teacher from Piscataway, NJ, who had been laid off instead of an equally qualified black teacher. But in a landmark case, the Connecticut Supreme Court declared segregation in public schools in Hartford, CT, unconstitutional under terms of the state constitution. The ruling encouraged civil-rights organizations, which had been suing in state courts to achieve integration at a time when federal courts had been imposing stricter guidelines.

With the straitened budgets of the 1990s, ethnic groups had little success seeking redress in funding and contracts from government. In March the Clinton administration sought to comply with a 1995 Supreme Court ruling rejecting minority set-aside programs by proposing disparity studies to determine if racial discrimination kept minority-owned businesses from getting government contracts. The administration also proposed using incentives to get contracts for minority businesses rather than court-ordered remedies. Also in March, the Supreme Court unanimously rejected appeals by big cities to adjust the 1990 federal census because of a supposed undercount of minorities in inner cities.

Hostility toward immigrant and ethnic groups also grew in 1996. A new immigration bill, which was passed by Congress and signed into law in September, restricted illegal immigrants' access to public services, limited social benefits to legal immigrants, drastically curtailed judicial review for undocumented asylum seekers, and tightened border checks. Hispanic and Asian groups offered sharp criticism of the law. According to a National Asian Pacific American Legal Consortium study released in August, physical and verbal assaults on people of Asian and Pacific heritage rose in 1995. To counter the new legislation and to help immigrants help themselves,

Native Americans Today

Five hundred years after Europeans launched their conquest of North America, the continent's "first people" still are struggling to maintain a foothold in their homeland. As the 20th century nears its close, the Indian wars that decimated the indigenous population in years past have given way to a less bloody, but equally vital, battle for the economic and cultural survival of Native Americans today.

An Overview. Most of the country's 2.1 million Indians, more often called Native Americans in urban areas, suffer the highest poverty, unemployment, and disease rates of any group in the United States. Indians die from alcoholism at four and a half times the rate of the population as a whole. Tuberculosis, accidents, diabetes, suicide, and homicide also take a disproportionate toll among native Americans. While conditions on many reservations are dismal, Indians who move to cities in search of a better life often pay the price of cultural alienation and lost federal benefits, available only to reservation inhabitants.

Faced with these grim statistics, U.S. political leaders have done little to alleviate the Indians' plight. Even though the Indian population continues to grow, lawmakers have reduced funding of health, education, employment, and housing programs administered by the Interior Department's Bureau of Indian Affairs (BIA) over the past two decades. In fiscal 1996 alone, funding for Indian programs was cut by $160 million, a 9% cut from BIA's $1.7 billion budget in 1995. Spending for Indian programs again touched off debate between Congress and the Bill Clinton administration in 1996. Republican lawmakers tried to include in the fiscal 1997 Interior appropriations bill a provision that would have given states greater power to collect sales, fuel, and excise taxes on businesses run by Indian tribes. They said the tribes' ability to sell their goods tax-free at reservation convenience stores discriminated against non-Indian store operators just outside Indian lands. The provision ultimately was dropped after the administration backed the Indians' opposition to the provision as an attack on their treaty rights. An appropriation of $1.6 billion for Indian affairs was approved for fiscal year 1997.

Treaty, Adoption, and Public-Land Problems. Indian leaders see such challenges to the terms of long-standing treaties between the country's 552 federally recognized tribes and the U.S. government as nothing less than thinly disguised expressions of the racism that has permeated policy toward Indians throughout U.S. history. Decimated by disease and warfare and then uprooted from their ancestral lands, Indians were forced to trade their land for survival. Scores of treaties signed in the late 1800s consigned tribes to reservations, most of them remote and barren.

© Eastcott/Momatiuk/Woodfin Camp

Today, Indians invoke these same treaties as guarantees of their unique place in American society as both members of sovereign tribal nations and U.S. citizens. In their view, the Indian treaties have the same force of law as treaties with foreign countries. But some lawmakers—notably Sen. Slade Gorton (R-WA), chairman of the Senate Interior Appropriations Subcommittee—hold that the Indian treaties can be amended by Congress. Gorton tried unsuccessfully to include in the 1997 Interior appropriations bill a provision that would have given the nontribal 330,000 property owners on Indian lands new rights to sue the tribes over these rights.

Another controversial issue involves the role of Indian tribes in the adoption of members' children by non-Indians. For decades, so many Indian children were handed over to non-Indian adoptive parents that tribes feared for their own survival. To halt widespread abuses in the system, Congress in 1978 passed the Indian Child Welfare Act, which enabled tribes to prevent adoptions of tribal members. But the law itself proved flawed, as some parents were forced to relinquish custody of their adopted children long after the adoption process was complete. To rectify the problem, Sen. John McCain (R-AZ), one of the most outspoken advocates of Indian rights in Congress, led an effort to amend the law in 1996, which the Senate approved unanimously in September. The resulting bill would establish strict timetables for a tribe to be notified that an Indian child is up for adoption, for the tribe to intervene, and for the biological parents to withdraw consent for the adoption. The bill would impose criminal sanctions against anyone who lies about a child's Indian heritage and would require tribes to certify in court that the child is an Indian.

Disagreements over the proper use of public lands continue to plague Indian-federal relations. The National Park Service long has been at loggerheads with tribes over their access to park land. One of the treasured sites of the Grand Canyon is called Indian Gardens, but the Havasupai and neighboring tribes were evicted from the canyon when it became a park in the early 1900s. Today several tribes are contesting the Park Service's policies restricting Indian activities in public lands that comprise their ancestral homeland. In one hotly debated case, the Miccosukee Indians, who fled into the Florida's Everglades during the Seminole Wars more than a century ago, are challenging the Park Service over its opposition to a tribal housing project in their 333-acre (135-ha) special-use area in what is now the Everglades National Park.

A member of the Kiowa-Apache tribe dances in ceremonial dress at an intertribal powwow in Peoria, IL. With such activities, Native Americans maintain a link with their cultural heritage.

© Matt Dayhoff/"Peoria Journal Star"/AP/Wide World Photo

Gambling and Other Revenue Sources. Faced with declining federal support of Indian health and welfare programs, many tribes are seeking new ways to raise revenue to help themselves. But the most lucrative of these enterprises—casino gambling—is drawing some of the harshest criticism from non-Indians. They point to the Foxwoods Casino Resort in Ledyard, CT, the best known of some 220 Indian casinos across the United States. Owned by the small Mashantucket Pequot Tribe, Foxwoods brought in $319 million in 1995. Citing such huge profits, critics charge that Indians are enriching themselves with an immoral enterprise that often causes its customers to become hopelessly addicted to gambling and that attracts organized crime.

Indians counter that gambling operations have been much more effective at promoting economic development than any of the federal Indian programs, and at no cost to taxpayers. Many wonder why the antigambling offensive is not leveled against such non-Indian titans of the gambling industry as Donald Trump and suggest that the critics are more interested in protecting non-Indian gambling operations from competition than in the public at large.

While the widespread criticism of Indian gaming—a euphemism for gambling—focuses on the windfall profits gleaned at Foxwoods, most Indian casinos are far less profitable. Instead, they provide essential revenues, at a time of cuts in federal programs, to fund vital tribal services. In addition to granting tribes "the exclusive right to regulate gaming activity on Indian lands," the 1988 Indian Gaming Regulatory Act requires tribes to use casino revenues to "promote tribal economic development, tribal self-sufficiency, and strong tribal government." The Winnebago Nation of Nebraska, for example, has used casino profits to open a new tribal college, renovate the reservation hospital, and begin and organize other businesses.

© M.J. Okoniewski/Gamma-Liaison

Native Americans have turned to operating gambling casinos on their reservations as a prime source for raising revenue. By late 1996 there were some 220 Indian casinos across the United States.

Some tribes have run into further obstacles when they try to diversify their economies away from gambling by reinvesting their casino earnings into different businesses. The Viejas Indians, one of several small California tribes, have been stymied in their efforts to buy a controlling interest in Borrego Springs Bank, a small bank near the reservation outside San Diego. Charging that Indian gaming already is vulnerable to infiltration by organized crime, California's Attorney General Daniel Lungren opposed the deal, even after the Federal Deposit Insurance Corp. approved it in June 1996. Adding a bank to the tribe's casino business, he said, would provide an additional lure to criminals in search of money-laundering facilities.

The struggle between tribes and opponents to Indian gaming almost came to blows in 1995 after the New Mexico Supreme Court declared invalid agreements between 11 tribes and Gov. Gary E. Johnson allowing the tribes to open casinos. To protest the ruling, several tribes threatened to block major roads passing through reservation lands if authorities tried to shut down their casinos, the tribes' leading source of income. The crisis was defused somewhat in July when Judge Martha Vazquez of Federal District Court upheld the earlier ruling but then stayed her decision to allow Indian gambling operations to continue while the case is on appeal.

Many Indian tribes are unable to benefit from gaming revenues because their reservations are too remote to attract enough customers to profit from the business. Others—such as the Navajo Tribe of Arizona, New Mexico, and Utah—traditionally are opposed to gambling on moral grounds. Some of these tribes have found other sources of badly needed income. The Mississippi Band of Choctaws agreed to allow General Motors to build an electronics assembly plant on their reservation. The Salish and Kootenai tribes have earned enough revenue from a privately owned hydroelectric dam on their Montana reservation to invest in other businesses as well.

With the help of a nonprofit organization called the First Nations Development Institute, some tribes are finding it possible to turn their quest for cultural renewal into profit-making enterprises. The Nez Percé Indians, for example, are reviving the horse-breeding skills for which their tribe was once famous. Confined to a small Idaho reservation in the 1870s after their legendary leader, Chief Joseph, failed to lead them to safety in Canada, the Nez Percés now are producing a unique strain of riding horses they hope will bring the tribe badly needed income as well as a renewed sense of cultural identity.

If Indians are to win their struggle to survive in modern U.S. society, many of their leaders say, they must participate more fully in the political process that will determine the outcome of that struggle. The most prominent Indian government official in 1996 was Assistant Interior Secretary Ada Deer, a member of the Menominee Tribe of Wisconsin and the first woman to head the Bureau of Indian Affairs. But the only Native American member of Congress was Sen. Ben Nighthorse Campbell (R-CO), a Northern Cheyenne. Two Indian candidates—Bill Yellowtail, a Crow from Montana, and Georgianna Lincoln, an Athabascan Indian from Alaska—lost their bids to capture seats in the House of Representatives in November elections.

MARY H. COOPER

George Soros—a wealthy Hungarian-born financier—in September established the Emma Lazarus Fund with $50 million, to provide aid to community groups that help immigrants become citizens.

Anti-Bias Lawsuits. The recent reversals on affirmative action did not prevent successful lawsuits against governments and companies guilty of racial discrimination. In March a federal judge approved a settlement offered by the U.S. State Department to end a federal lawsuit dating back to 1986. The department agreed to pay $3.8 million in compensation to black foreign-service officers passed over in promotions because of race and to make its hiring and training procedures more sensitive to racial concerns. In July the Bureau of Alcohol, Tobacco, and Firearms agreed to a court settlement granting $5.9 million in a case brought by black agents who had charged the agency with discrimination; the agency also pledged to revise its hiring, training, discipline, and promotion policies.

In November, in the biggest corporate race-bias settlement in U.S. history, Texaco, Inc., agreed to pay $176.1 million to settle a two-year-old racial-discrimination suit. The case was brought by black employees who complained of being subjected to racial slurs and denied promotions in the company. The settlement came 11 days after tapes were released in which company executives were heard planning to destroy documents in the case. The settlement headed off a nationwide boycott of Texaco planned by the Rev. Jesse Jackson and other civil-rights leaders. In November, Avis, Inc.—conscious of the furor over the Texaco disclosures—also moved to address charges that franchises in North and South Carolina had refused to rent cars to blacks.

Education. In September the U.S. Census Bureau reported that, for the first time, black adults in their late 20s had high-school graduation rates equal to those of whites. An American Council of Education report released in June found that—although minority student enrollment in U.S. colleges rose by 4.9% in 1995—black, Hispanic, and American Indian college enrollment continued to lag behind that of whites. Between 1990 and 1994 the number of Hispanics enrolled in college increased by 35%, of Asians by 35%, of American Indians and Alaskan natives by 24%, and of blacks by 16%. According to reports issued by the U.S. Census Bureau and the National Coalition of Hispanic Health and Human Services Organizations in July, Hispanics made up the second-largest group of school-age children in the country, but Hispanic children were more likely than whites or blacks to lack health insurance, drop out of school, and die from injuries and accidents.

Health. In several health matters, blacks continued to suffer disproportionately. In May the Centers for Disease Control and Prevention (CDC) reported that young blacks were far more likely to die from asthma than were young whites, with the disparity largely due to the lack of quality health care for poor blacks. A major study released by Duke University Medical Center revealed that medical and cultural factors gave blacks significantly higher mortality rates from heart disease than whites.

Other Issues. Blacks' emphasis on self-help paid off in 1996. According to *Black Enterprise* magazine and the newsletter *Securities Pro*, the sales of top black businesses rose for the fourth straight year. As part of a continued effort to get mortgage money and investment capital into minority hands, the National Baptist Convention of America, Inc., and the National Baptist Convention USA, Inc., joined with the Federal Home Loan Mortgage Corporation to formulate a plan to make home loans available to at least 150,000 low- and moderate-income families in minority neighborhoods. In November the U.S. Treasury Department reported that home loans to minorities had increased at a rate three times faster than total mortgage lending since 1994.

After two years of internal crisis over leadership and direction and imminent bankruptcy, the National Association for the Advancement of Colored People, under the new leadership of Kweisi Mfume (*see* BIOGRAPHY), reported in October that it had returned to solvency and "the business of civil rights." With continued instances of the burning of rural black churches occurring through the summer of 1996, and with riots in St. Petersburg, FL, in October and November following the fatal shooting of a black motorist by a white policeman, civil-rights leaders had much work to do. Deval L. Patrick, the departing head of the U.S. Justice Department's civil-rights division, in November warned that "ambivalence on the question of [racial] integration" threatened "the vitality of American democracy."

In May the Pentagon named seven black U.S. soldiers from World War II to be recipients of the Congressional Medal of Honor for valor. No blacks who served during that conflict had been awarded the medal previously. Also in May, J. Paul Reason became the first black to be nominated for the rank of four-star admiral.

RANDALL M. MILLER, *Saint Joseph's University*

EUROPE

For the European Union (EU)—swollen to 15 members since January 1995 with the accession of Austria, Finland, and Sweden—1996 was a year of waiting and planning. Priority was given to preparation for the full economic and monetary union (EMU), including a common currency—planned in the Maastricht Treaty in 1991—and to the Intergovernmental Conference (IGC) opening in March, whose task was to renovate the Union's constitutional structure. But the national economies stubbornly refused to conform to government plans; and when new austerity programs were introduced in preparation for adoption of a common currency, social discontent escalated.

Preparing the EMU. At the Madrid summit of EU heads of state and government in December 1995, the EU leaders named the future common currency the euro; it was to have the same value as the present European currency unit (ecu) based on a basket of national currencies. The leaders also agreed that it should be used as an instrument of public debt from Jan. 1, 1999, and replace national currencies on Jan. 1, 2002. However, the EU previously had agreed that only countries meeting strict fiscal criteria—keeping their public debt at no more than 60% of gross domestic product (GDP) and their budget deficit at no more than 3% of GDP—would be permitted to join the currency union.

In 1995, only Luxembourg met those criteria. Among the larger members, Britain intended to opt out of EMU, and Italy appeared incapable of meeting the standards. If EMU were to be created on schedule, it, therefore, was essential for France and Germany to take the painful measures needed for them to lead the smaller members into the irrevocable currency fusion, even though the result would be a dangerous division in EU between participants and nonparticipants.

Yet the first serious attempt by French Prime Minister Alain Juppé in early December 1995 to cut pensions and health services had produced massive strikes, costing the country $1.6 billion and forcing the premier to modify the reforms sharply. Worse yet, both France and Germany entered 1996 with absolute falls in their GDPs. For that reason, both governments announced in concert in January that they were introducing multiple incentives to encourage new investment, spending, and economic growth.

Economic difficulties also led throughout the EU to a hardening of measures against immigrants, who increasingly were blamed—especially by far-right political parties—for at least some of Europe's high unemployment. Stricter rules adopted by the EU included refusal of political asylum to anyone entering the EU from a "safe country," which virtually cut off entry to asylum seekers reaching Germany and Austria by land. Airlines were punished for carrying passengers without entry papers. Fear of persecution by nongovernmental groups, such as Algerian fundamentalist guerrillas, no longer was a justification for asylum. Measures also were introduced to make it easier to expel illegal immigrants.

Although France had joined eight other EU members in signing the 1990 Schengen Agreement to abolish border controls, France refused to implement the policy, on the grounds that illegal immigrants were finding it easy to cross into the Union from some of the poorly policed southern borders. The success of the North Atlantic Treaty Organization (NATO)–led Implementation Force in bringing relative peace to Bosnia was regarded by Germany as justification for its announcement that it would begin repatriating some of the 320,000 Bosnian refugees it had accepted.

The Intergovernmental Conference (IGC) Opens. At the Maastricht summit in 1991, the EU had agreed to revise the Treaties of Rome to make its constitution more efficient and to prepare the mechanism for establishing common foreign and security policies. The large number of countries seeking EU membership—Bulgaria, Czech Republic, Cyprus, Estonia, Hungary, Latvia, Lithuania, Malta, Poland, Romania, Slovenia, and Slovakia—had been promised that accession negotiations would begin when these constitutional changes had been completed. And it was equally clear that the poorer countries of Eastern Europe could not be admitted unless the EU first changed two of its most costly programs—the payment of huge subsidies, expected to reach $50 billion a year, to farmers through the Common Agricultural Policy (CAP), and of regional aid to its economically backward regions.

Huge tasks faced the IGC, particularly the redefining of the voting strength of smaller members, the role of the Commission and the Court of Justice, and the powers of the European Parliament. Since these issues brought into the open the split in the EU between those, such as Britain, that opposed closer political integration and those, like Germany, that were determined to expand the Union's powers, the IGC was expected to last at least a year and to baffle the average European citizen with its complexity. For example, discussion in May on the possibility of making the Western European Union (WEU) into the military arm of the EU instantly foundered because EU's neutral members, such as Austria and Sweden, never had joined the WEU and still were unwilling to do so.

Florence Summit. The EU's summit in Florence, Italy, in June opened amid discouraging economic news. The European Commission forecast that the EU's GDP growth rate for 1996 would be a paltry 1.5%. But unless 2% growth were achieved, unemployment would continue to increase. In France it was surging inexorably from an already intolerable 11.5% in 1995 to 12.5%, while economic growth was not expected to exceed 1%. Italy, run by caretaker governments, was so burdened with government debt that its deficit had reached 7% of GDP. Even Germany had 4 million unemployed and a labor force so discontented that it mounted the largest demonstration of the post–World War II years in June to protest slashes in welfare payments. Rather than tackle general economic problems, however, the summit began by attempting to solve the crisis over "mad-cow disease" in Britain.

When British scientists announced in March that the cattle disease possibly could kill consumers of beef, the EU responded by banning the export of British beef worldwide, causing a loss to British farmers of up to $900 million annually, in addition to their losses from the collapse of their British market. European cattle farmers also suffered, however, as non-British beef sales also fell, compelling the Union to intervene by making purchases of surplus beef to keep up the price. The situation worsened in May when Britain attempted to force the Union to modify the ban by blocking the EU's normal business by vetoing any action where its consent was required. The effect, however, was merely to increase irritation that Britain's federalist-minded partners, such as Germany, already were feeling at British determination at the IGC to prevent adoption of measures that would increase the Union's powers.

At Florence compromise was reached. Britain agreed to end its policy of noncooperation, and the EU agreed to adopt a framework for the gradual lifting of the ban on British beef. But British Prime Minister John Major reiterated his position that, in the IGC, Britain would continue to oppose the extension of qualified voting in place of unanimous decision-making, and even would try to cut the powers of the Court of Justice. Unable to make substantive progress on rewriting the Maastricht Treaty, the summit instructed the IGC to produce a draft revision by the December summit in Dublin and the final version by 1997. By refusing Commission President Jacques Santer the $1.3 billion he requested for infrastructural investment for the purpose of cutting unemployment, the EU leaders dramatized how, after 18 months in office, Santer had not achieved the political prestige of his predecessor, Jacques Delors.

Renewed Enthusiasm for EMU. In the second half of the year, an unexpectedly large number of EU members, fearful of missing the economic stimulus and increased trade opportunities that possession of a common currency was expected to bring, began to take measures to meet the criteria necessary to join EMU in 1999. The new conservative government of Prime Minister José María Aznar in Spain, which took office in May, proposed in its September budget to cut spending by 1% in addition to raising taxes. The Italian government felt it necessary to follow suit, not least to foil the Northern League Party, which was pushing for northern Italy to secede and join EMU alone. Even Sweden brought in a cost-cutting budget to enable the country to meet the Maastricht criteria, although public opinion was against membership.

For France, where the far-right National Front was blaming the EU, as well as the 3 million Muslim immigrants, for French economic problems, Prime Minister Juppé nevertheless felt it necessary to make another effort in September to bring government spending down by across-the-board cuts in the budget of every ministry. The expected reaction of labor began at once with a teachers' strike, followed shortly by strikes of public servants and transport workers. Germany, too, risked confrontation with its unions by attempting again to cut welfare benefits. But it seemed that these efforts were showing results. Twelve of EU's members, the Commission announced in November, would have cut their deficits sufficiently to join EMU on schedule.

At the EU heads of state and government summit in Dublin in December, the leaders adopted a compromise on the "stability and growth pact" demanded by Germany for countries adopting the common currency, by permitting countries exceeding the permitted budget deficit to avoid fines by pleading more broadly defined "exceptional circumstances." No progress was made on the treaty revision required before the East European applicants could be admitted to the EU.

F. ROY WILLIS
University of California, Davis

FAMILY

Family values and such family-related needs as child care, Medicare, and education were rallying cries in the 1996 U.S. presidential election, as incumbent Bill Clinton and his Republican challenger, Bob Dole, courted the favor of a crucial voting bloc—women.

Children First. At the heart of many campaign messages was the effect of government action on children. A poll by *Time* magazine and Cable News Network (CNN) found that 73% of adult Americans favored spending more tax dollars on children. Leading the priority list for spending was health care, including free immunization shots, nutrition programs, and health insurance.

Marian Wright Edelman, founder of the Children's Defense Fund, called attention to the plight of children with a "Stand for Children" rally, held in June at Washington's Lincoln Memorial. Endorsed by more than 3,000 organizations, the event was attended by at least 200,000 people.

Income. The Census Bureau in September reported that median household income rose faster in 1995 than inflation, increasing 2.7% to $34,076. Also, the number of poor families dropped from 8.1 million to 7.5 million. Other statistics, however, tempered the good news. Median income had not yet returned to its 1989 high of $35,421; median earnings were down slightly; the number of people without health insurance was unchanged; and 49% of the nation's poor were either under 18 or over 65.

Children were affected most severely by the problems of poverty. According to the Department of Health and Human Services, the percentage of children living in families where the income was less than half the official poverty rate had doubled since 1975. And a June study found that the number of children in "working poor" families rose 30% between 1989 and 1994, to 5.6 million.

Family Structure. For the first time in nearly two decades, the birthrate among unmarried U.S. women dropped. In 1995 there were 44.9 births per 1,000 unmarried women, according to the National Center for Health Statistics; this was down 4% from 1994. The birthrate for teens declined for the fourth consecutive year, to 56.9 births per 1,000.

There also were indications that the "traditional" family was making a comeback. The number of two-parent households with children increased by 700,000 between 1990 and 1995 and the divorce rate slowed to 20.5 per 1,000 married women.

Debate about same-sex relationships continued. San Francisco took steps in 1996 to become the first major U.S. city to require that companies with which it does business offer health and other benefits to the unmarried partners of their employees. Meanwhile legislation was enacted to deny federal recognition of same-sex marriages. (*See* LAW—*Same-Sex Marriage*.)

Parental Rights. Just how much control parents should have over their children's upbringing is the issue at the heart of parental-rights amendments, which had been introduced in 28 states since 1994. Most recently, Colorado voters in November rejected a parental-rights amendment to the state constitution. Advocates of the amendments—many of whom are conservative, middle-class members of the so-called Christian Right—say they are needed to give parents the ability to challenge government involvement in what they say are family decisions. Opponents fear the proposals will put children at greater risk for abuse or neglect and could encourage parents to sue government agencies.

Meanwhile, faced with rising teen crime rates, some states were making parents responsible for their children's actions. Several states had passed laws holding parents responsible for damage caused by their children, for possession of firearms by their children, and for children's curfew violations or association with gangs.

Child Abuse. Child abuse and neglect nearly doubled between 1986 and 1993. The U.S. Department of Health and Human Services estimated that the number of abused and neglected children had risen to 2.81 million by 1993. Of confirmed cases, an estimated 14% involved sexual abuse.

Sexual abuse of children received international attention at the first World Congress Against Commercial Sexual Exploitation of Children, held in August in Sweden.

Child Care and Education. The number of children in organized day care continued to rise; by 1993, 30% of the 9.9 million children under age 5 who were in day care were in organized settings. The most popular form of child care was still leaving children with relatives (48%), while family day-care homes decreased by 18%.

The Family and Medical Leave Act, passed in 1994, proved popular among employees. Between 1.5 million and 3 million workers had taken family or medical leave, with only 14% of employers reporting a noticeable effect on productivity.

KRISTI VAUGHAN, *Freelance Writer*

FASHION

By 1996, fashion was regrouping; the trough was leveling off. The 1980s were regarded widely as fashion's high point in recent years, while the early 1990s were considered a disaster area beset with too many stores, too few ideas, and too-high prices. But now, small manufacturers, like small stores, were disappearing, and the megastars were taking over.

The Designers. Among U.S. designers, the big three were Calvin Klein, Donna Karan, and Ralph Lauren. Their clothes seemed to be everywhere. In stores, they were prominent in designer collections, in moderate-price areas, and in active-wear, sports, and jeans departments. This was predictable, but one also saw their labels in home-furnishings areas, accessories departments, and cosmetics sections. In addition to all this exposure, all three were opening their own stores, in locations from New York City to London, Paris, Hong Kong, and Seoul. "There is a lot of money in Seoul," said Klein after returning from a store opening there in the fall of 1996. "They are waiting for us." Films, pop music, television, and, of course, designer blue jeans had paved the way. Now designers were looking for worldwide acceptance of their clothes.

Although London did not quite repeat the success it had achieved in the 1960s as a center of youth-oriented fashion, it did produce two of the year's most important designers. One was John Galliano, who took over as designer for Christian Dior in Paris in October 1996, replacing Gianfranco Ferre. The other was Alexander McQueen, who generally was regarded as the most adventurous of the young British breed. He was named to be Galliano's replacement as designer at the Paris couture house of Givenchy.

Other designers who increased their reputations in 1996 were Tom Ford of Gucci and Miuccia Prada, both of Italy, and Jil Sander of Germany. All three are on the minimalist wave. In the United States, Tommy Hilfiger (*see* BIOGRAPHY), who had made his mark with casual clothes for men, added a women's collection and was aiming to join the Klein-

The prevailing look in women's fashion during 1996 featured a long, lean silhouette. Examples of this simple yet elegant style—appropriate for daytime or evening—were seen in the collections of Calvin Klein, below left, *and Donna Karan,* below right.

© Gregory Pace/Sygma

© Mantel/Sipa

© Frederic Nebinger/Sipa

Men's fashion was influenced by British-inspired styles popular in the 1960s and 1970s. Especially notable was the return of the three-piece suit, complete with a hat and dressy boots.

Karan-Lauren trio of world fashion leaders. The most popular European designers in the United States continued to be Karl Lagerfeld for Chanel and Giorgio Armani for both men's and women's clothes.

Designers continued to lean on the styles of the 1960s and the 1970s because they felt these decades would yield the simplicity for which they were searching. Missoni, an Italian knitwear company famous for its intricate patterns and minimal styles during those decades, enjoyed a serious revival. There was talk also of reviving the Halston label in 1997.

Trends. The dominant fashion trend of the past few seasons continued. The watchword has been "simple," or more pretentiously, "minimalist." This was a far cry from the ruffles, fringe, petticoats, and swooping panels formerly typified by European fashion, the pacesetter of the past. European designers as well as Americans endorsed a long, lean, no-frills look for fall 1996 and spring 1997. They also were permissive about hem lengths, with acceptable lengths ranging from mid-thigh to the ankle. This type of style—long associated with Calvin Klein—was based on American sportswear, which always has emphasized practicality and comfort.

A party given by Arnold Scaasi to celebrate a retrospective of his fashions from the past 40 years illustrated the change from more elaborate dressing. The invitations to the opening of the show at the New York Historical Society suggested women wear "Scaasi, if possible." Many—about 200—did. Richly colored silks, extravagantly curved shapes, bouffant skirts, and dashing necklines were prominent in the dresses displayed as well as worn by the women who came to the show. At other gatherings of the season, however, the prevailing style was a simple black dress with minimal jewelry. The contrast was apparent.

There was nonetheless a renewed interest in clothes, probably because women had bought so little in the past two years that it was now replacement time. The T-shirt and blue-jeans outfit that had seemed adequate for most occasions now seemed wanting. Narrow trousers, patterned leggings, leather jackets, and long coats were slightly more formal.

The coats were one of the few European ideas that crossed the ocean. They were suggested by Karl Lagerfeld in his collection for Chanel in Paris. Treated like suit jackets and shown with long skirts or pants, they were accepted eagerly, probably because they were not too radical in styling and fit in with the

The use of bright colors, as in the 1970s-influenced Prada pantsuit below, *helped enliven and add flair to the spare simplicity so evident in 1996's minimalist fashions.*

© Cavalli/Sipa

Real fur—which had been dropped by many designers due to protests by animal-rights activists—made a comeback in 1996. Most popular were luxurious, full-length coats, usually made using farmed and unendangered animals.

practical mood of fashion. They illustrated the "separates" principle, an integral part of the American sportswear theory of dressing. The principle is based on interchangeable parts and was developed during the Great Depression of the 1930s, when money was in short supply and a woman could get more mileage out of a skirt and two sweaters than out of a one-piece dress. With money, at least for fashion, again in short supply, women were interested in clothes that would serve multiple functions.

As the collections for spring 1997 were presented on the runways of Milan, the traditional suit received little attention. Instead, there were midriff-baring tops, skintight dresses, and oceans of chiffon. However, although designers may be bored with jackets, women were not. Certainly a see-through dress is no substitute for a woman who goes to work. Thus it seemed premature to mourn the passing of one of fashion's most enduring styles, the spring suit. Designers once again were sending the wrong message, one that was not likely to change women's insistence on casual, practical clothes.

Celebrity Fashion. Two social leaders were prominent on the world's fashion stage. Princess Diana attracted as much attention after her divorce as she had during her marriage to the Prince of Wales. She often wore clothes by British designer Catherine Walker, which helped call attention to London's revival as a fashion center. And Carolyn Bessette, after her marriage to John Kennedy, Jr., emerged as a fashion celebrity, immediately drawing comparisons to her late mother-in-law, Jacqueline Kennedy Onassis. Her wedding dress, designed by Narciso Rodriguez of Nino Cerrutti, brought her instant style status and was copied widely.

The Resurgence of Fur. Furs, along with fine jewelry, reflect status dressing. Fur sales were inhibited in recent years by animal-rights activists protesting the wearing of fur. Some designers, like Geoffrey Beene and Bill Blass, stopped making fur coats; others, however—among them Marc Jacobs, Yeohlee Teng, and other young designers—were eager to try their hand in a new area. They were careful to stay away from endangered species and usually worked with farmed animals, like mink. For some reason, sheepskin coats (fur on one side, leather on the other) escaped the wrath of the protesters. Called shearlings, these coats became popular as a means of achieving warmth in winter. They also fit into the prevailing casual look.

BERNADINE MORRIS
Freelance Fashion Journalist

FINLAND

Prime Minister Paavo Lipponen's so-called rainbow coalition government remained committed in 1996 to Finland's full participation in the European Union (EU). Finland joined the Exchange Rate Mechanism (ERM), taking another step toward gaining charter membership in the economic and monetary union (EMU) in 1999. Although elections to the European Parliament suggested that opposition to the EU was rising, popular support for Finnish participation remained strong. Membership in the North Atlantic Treaty Organization (NATO) also was the subject of debate.

Politics. The opposition Center Party won 24% of the votes in Finland's first direct elections to the European Parliament in October 1996, overtaking Lipponen's Social Democratic Party, which received 22% of the votes. Among the prominent candidates running on a platform of "Euro-skepticism" were former Foreign Minister Paavo Vayrynen of the Center Party and Esko Seppänen of the Leftist Alliance. When the 16 Finnish seats were distributed among the parties, however, little had changed. The Center Party lost a seat, while Seppänen and his party gained a seat. The Social Democrats retained their four seats, and the coalition partner, the Conservative Party, gained one seat to obtain a total of four.

European Affairs. Finland joined the ERM in October, paving the way for Finland to join France and Germany as founding members of the EMU. Many EU members asserted that a two-year membership in the ERM would be a political precondition of EMU membership (although Sweden and Great Britain disputed this position). The Finnish parliament would have to approve an application for EMU membership at the end of 1997, but a majority seemed assured. Finland considered full EU membership to be not only an economic issue, but also a vital security issue. Opinion polls showed that 60% of the electorate did not want to join the EMU in 1999, as the government vowed to do. But 55% of Finns still supported EU membership—one of the highest levels of popular support in Europe.

Minister of European Affairs Ole Norrback said in August 1996 that Finnish membership in NATO was more probable than improbable. But Prime Minister Lipponen and President Martti Ahtisaari both denied that membership was on the agenda. Finland warned the United States that NATO enlargement risked isolating the three Baltic states, of which Estonia has especially close links with Finland. Prime Minister Lipponen and his Swedish counterpart refused all suggestions that Finland and Sweden could create a Baltic regional security zone.

Economics. Finland's economy—which had one of the fastest growth rates in Europe in 1994 and 1995—had a moderate slowdown in the first half of 1996. However, the inflation rate fell below 1%, the lowest in the EU. Unemployment rates, which were as high as 18.4% in 1994, also dropped in 1996, to about 16%. Officials planned to stimulate growth with an income-tax cut equivalent to 1% of gross domestic product (GDP).

Eight directors of one of Finland's largest banks were indicted in September 1996 on charges of securities-market offenses. About 60 of the bank's small shareholders claimed that they were misled by marketing information during a large share offering in 1994, and demanded compensation. It was a strong sign of emerging shareholder activism in the Nordic countries.

LEIF BECK FALLESEN, *Editor in Chief "Boersen," Copenhagen*

FINLAND • Information Highlights

Official Name: Republic of Finland.
Location: Northern Europe.
Area: 130,127 sq mi (337 030 km²).
Population (mid-1996 est.): 5,100,000.
Chief Cities (Dec. 31, 1994 est.): Helsinki, the capital, 515,765; Espoo, 186,507; Tampere, 179,251.
Government: *Head of state,* Martti Ahtisaari, president (took office March 1, 1994). *Head of government,* Paavo Lipponen, prime minister (took office April 13, 1995). *Legislature* (unicameral)—Eduskunta.
Monetary Unit: Markka (4.6521 markkaa equal U.S.$1, Dec. 30, 1996).
Gross Domestic Product (1994 est. U.S.$): $81,800,000,000 (purchasing power parity).
Economic Indexes (1995, 1990 = 100): *Consumer Prices,* all items, 112.0; food, 94.7. *Industrial Production,* 116.
Foreign Trade (1995 U.S.$): *Imports,* $28,114,000,000; *exports,* $39,573,000,000.

FOOD

U.S. food supplies tightened during 1996 due to severe drought in parts of the Wheat Belt, strong exports, and record-low world grain stocks as a percent of utilization. Nevertheless, U.S. consumers enjoyed abundant food supplies, although costs accelerated some in the first half of the year. The food-supply situation was similar in Europe, Canada, and the stronger economies of Asia's Pacific Rim.

Consumers were purchasing an increasing amount of low-fat and no-fat foods. Nutritional specialists believed that these foods were of limited help to many consumers in controlling weight, because reduced fat content encour-

Fat-Free Foods

The 1996 approval by the U.S. Food and Drug Administration (FDA) of the fat substitute olestra highlighted a year in which no-fat foods gained great attention.

Background. Americans increasingly have become concerned about their fat intake for health reasons and due to a desire to look trim. Research has linked high-fat diets to increased risks of cancer, heart disease, and stroke. Despite efforts to cut fat consumption, U.S. consumers get an average of about 34% of their calories from fat—four percentage points above the recommended maximum. For individuals exceeding recommended fat consumption, a balanced diet including low-fat and no-fat foods can help reduce fat intake. (While lower fat consumption often is advisable for those exceeding dietary standards, zero-fat diets are not recommended. Some fat is necessary.)

No-fat foods always have been available through fruits, vegetables, and some pastas and cereals. These foods help reduce fat intake while providing other nutritional benefits. While some pastas and cereals have no fat, they contain starch that can cause body-fat formation.

In the 1950s, no-fat skim milk became available, bringing with it other lower-fat dairy products. These foods are made by manufacturing processes that eliminate or reduce fat content while retaining nutrients such as protein, calcium, vitamins, and minerals. Meat producers also have reduced the fat content of their products for health-conscious consumers.

Despite such steps, reducing fat consumption remains a difficult challenge for many individuals. Fats contribute texture, flavor, tenderness, and juiciness to foods and tend to provide a feeling of fullness after eating.

New Fat Substitutes. In January 1996 the FDA approved Procter & Gamble's olestra (marketed under the brand name Olean) for use in snack foods. Olestra is a human-made compound synthesized from sugar and fatty acids. It has fatlike qualities but passes through the body undigested and has no calories. Unlike other fat substitutes, olestra can withstand the high heat needed to fry potato chips and other snack foods; taste tests show similarities to items fried in traditional cooking oils.

Despite such positive attributes, Olestra was introduced amid great controversy. Some users report that olestra causes abdominal cramps or related digestive problems. In addition, research indicates that olestra may inhibit the body's absorption of fat-soluble vitamins and carotenoids—nutrients found in orange, red, and green fruits and vegetables. All manufacturers using olestra are mandated to provide a label indicating the digestive and vitamin-depletion concerns associated with the product.

Other no-fat foods are being made from water, soybean protein, starches, and fibers. In August 1996, researchers from the Agricultural Research Service (ARS) of the U.S. Department of Agriculture's (USDA's) National Center for Utilization Research in Peoria, IL, announced the development of a no-fat food, Z-Trim, made from agricultural by-products such as the hulls of oats, soybeans, peas, and rice, or corn or wheat bran. Researchers assert that this no-calorie, high-fiber fat substitute has a texture and consistency similar to those of animal and dairy fats, and is suitable for reduced-calorie cheese, meat products, and baked goods. Because it is made from food ingredients, researchers say modest consumption will not upset the digestive system.

Z-Trim's inventors believe it can help many Americans trim 20% of the calories from their diets without sacrificing flavor or satisfaction. For example, researchers assert that Z-Trim and water satisfactorily can replace up to 15% of the fat in ground beef, while increasing tenderness and juiciness. The ARS applied for a patent on Z-Trim and reported plans to license it to private firms. If the patent is approved, low-fat foods containing Z-Trim would be available to consumers.

Another no-fat product developed by the ARS, Oatrim-10, is derived from oats—as its name implies. Since the early 1990s, Oatrim has appeared in a number of low-fat meats, cheeses, and other food products. In 1996, USDA researchers developed a reduced-calorie chocolate bar using Z-Trim, oat fiber, Oatrim, and natural and artificial sweeteners. Taste tests indicate it may be an alternative to traditional chocolate bars. Other no-fat ingredients contain cornstarch, soybean protein, and gelatinized tapioca. These ingredients are used in such products as reduced-calorie dressings, margarines, sour cream, and dips. Despite the increasing variety of no-fat foods available, none have been found to be perfect replacements for dairy and animal fats. Thus, the search for new no-fat foods continues.

ROBERT N. WISNER

Meat Inspection

In July 1996, President Bill Clinton announced the most sweeping changes in the government's system of inspecting meat since the Federal Meat Inspection Act was passed in 1907. Since that time, meat inspection has been based on a "sniff and poke" method. The new, more scientific method was developed by the Food Safety and Inspection Service of the U.S. Department of Agriculture to improve meat safety. Called the Hazard Analysis and Critical Control Point (HACCP), it is designed to reduce pathogenic microorganisms in meat and poultry products through a five-step process. It will apply to all federally inspected plants.

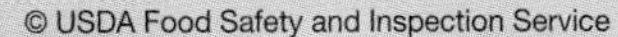
© USDA Food Safety and Inspection Service

The first step will be to identify clearly the responsibility of the company's management to ensure compliance with regulations. Plants must identify the significant hazards that might affect its products. Step two involves *E. coli* testing. All slaughter plants will be required to perform at least one antimicrobial treatment between slaughter and chilling of the carcass. Step three establishes a salmonella performance standard. The prompt chilling of the carcass and parts is required. Step four calls for standard sanitation operations that will improve plant operations. The latter step will be combined with daily microbial testing to see if targets are being met and whether company targets match federal goals.

As a final step, all federally inspected meat and poultry establishments will be required to implement an HACCP system to improve the safety of their products by a specific date. Secretary of Agriculture Daniel Glickman noted that the purpose of the new inspection plan was "to ensure that American families have the safest meat and poultry system possible."

Key details not completed as the year ended included: (1) sampling frequency needed to reach goals, (2) specific scientific tests to be administered, (3) the number of federal meat inspectors needed, (4) plans for scientific training of inspectors, and (5) how to implement and monitor details of each plant's HACCP system. Sources close to the industry noted that major meat companies already have their own HACCP systems in operation, but that the federal plan will standardize procedures nationwide.

Robert N. Wisner

aged some people to increase their food intake. (*See* Special Report, page 246.)

World Trends. Areas where food supplies tightened substantially and costs rose sharply included sub-Saharan Africa and parts of Southeast Asia and Latin America. With the transition from government-directed to market-oriented economies lagging, food remained expensive and supplies limited in the former Soviet republics. As the year ended, increased global grain harvests brought more abundant supplies, but world food reserves remained low.

The United States was a leading supplier of pork and beef to Pacific Rim markets and a big supplier of poultry to Russia. China and Mexico greatly increased imports of poultry. China's growing appetite for meat and livestock feed brought concern over a possible severe global grain shortage by the year 2020. It imported feed grains in 1996 for the second consecutive year. In 1993–94, China had been the world's second-largest exporter of corn, the leading feed grain. Also in 1996, China began importing soybeans, and soybean meal and oil.

Food Safety. Food safety remained a concern in the United States, Europe, and Japan. Contributing developments included bovine spongiform encephalopathy (BSE), also known as mad-cow disease, in British beef. In Japan food poisoning from *E. coli* bacteria left at least 11 persons dead and thousands ill. Late in the year a rash of illnesses caused by *E. coli* were reported in three western U.S. states; the infections were believed to be linked to a brand of organic fruit juice.

The USDA and the Food and Drug Administration developed science-based regulatory standards for proper cooling of shell eggs. Other areas of improved food safety included safer methods of transporting and storing raw meat, poultry, seafood, and eggs to prevent growth of harmful bacteria. The USDA also researched handling methods to reduce bacterial contamination of fresh vegetables and expanded educational efforts to inform consumers about retail purchasing, home handling, and preparation.

In Vermont consumers asked that milk produced with recombinant bovine somatotropin (rBST) be labeled clearly. Other groups requested that products derived from genetically altered soybeans be labeled as such and segregated in stores.

Robert N. Wisner, *Iowa State University*

FRANCE

In 1996, France emerged groggily from 1995's massive public-sector strikes without much hope of finding solutions to the grievances that had set off the historic work stoppages. Record-high unemployment rates and other grim economic news dominated headlines. The government's inflexible pursuit of austerity measures in order to abide by the rules for a single European currency continued to exasperate the electorate.

Despite ongoing economic anxiety, actions during the spring and summer by illegal immigrants from Africa protesting French immigration policies drew surprising public support. Leaving Prime Minister Alain Juppé and his cabinet to deal with these domestic land mines, President Jacques Chirac devoted himself to foreign affairs.

Domestic Affairs. When cancer-stricken former President François Mitterrand (*see* OBITUARIES—*Mitterrand, François*) died on January 8, it was as though he had timed his death—waiting out the end of the year, watching to see how the labor crisis of 1995 worked itself out. His passing drew an outpouring of emotion from ordinary citizens and, perhaps more surprisingly, from his successor, Jacques Chirac, who had been his bitter political rival for 20 years. In a moving eulogy, Chirac spoke of his "respect for the statesman, and admiration for the private citizen." Many members of Chirac's conservative majority bridled at what they saw as effusiveness, but commentators dated Chirac's full assumption of his presidency to this speech.

Relations between the French government and the violence-torn Mediterranean island of Corsica were troubled throughout the year. After a campaign of late-night bombings that caused tens of millions of dollars in damage to public buildings, Corsican separatists held a clandestine press conference on January 11, the eve of a visit by the interior minister, at which some 600 masked and heavily armed activists participated. Ostensibly called to announce a cease-fire, the event clearly was meant as a show of force.

Despite insistence that "republican order" must reign in Corsica, Paris pursued not-so-secret negotiations with outlawed separatists. Island judges and police officers were ordered to use the "utmost circumspection" in cases implicating suspected nationalists. Negotiating topics included increased official recognition of Corsican culture, a reorganization of the island's governing institutions, but especially the details of economic advantages for the island. Various nationalist groups were struggling to capture the benefits of whatever arrangement was agreed upon, and what once had been a political conflict with Paris took on distinctively moblike overtones. With the "negotiations" apparently not going its way, the main nationalist group broke its truce on October 5 with an ostentatious bombing of the city hall in Bordeaux, where Prime Minister Juppé also serves as mayor. Nighttime bombings of public buildings and officials' homes once again became daily fare.

In February, President Chirac announced a massive reform of the French armed forces. He called for ending conscription—a rite of passage that has marked French men's lives since the Napoleonic wars—reducing the standing army by almost one third, and phasing out France's land-based nuclear missiles. Chirac's argument that modern defense requirements called for a highly trained pro-

© Bernard Bisson/Sygma

Employees of French newspapers went out on strike on Oct. 15, 1996, to protest a government plan to repeal a 30% tax exemption for journalists. The walkout caused a one-day shutdown at several newspapers and halted operations at state-owned broadcasters of radio and television news.

fessional army won broad support, and critics focused on the impact on garrison towns and the loss of the citizen-building aspects of compulsory military service.

In the spring some 300 illegal immigrants from Africa, seeking to avoid deportation, began an unusual protest against France's stiff anti-immigration laws. Many were parents of children born in France unable to obtain residency permits for themselves; others had been denied political asylum. Arguing the historic contributions that their peoples had made to France—most had relatives who had served in the French army—and the role of French policies in the destitution of their African homelands, they called for an immediate solution to their own cases, as well as an overall reexamination of the so-called Pasqua laws (France's immigration laws, named after former Interior Minister Charles Pasqua) that had gone into effect in 1994. Early in July, after several months of impasse, ten of the immigrants began a hunger strike. On August 23, despite several hundred demonstrators holding a round-the-clock vigil outside the church where the Africans had taken refuge, riot police moved in, breaking down the church doors with axes and removing the immigrants.

What followed was judicial and administrative chaos. While 10,000 outraged Parisians demonstrated, most of the immigrants were released on street corners or miles outside Paris that evening. The prime minister and interior minister later asserted that the operation had been conducted with "humanity and heart," although television images broadcast across France suggested otherwise. Court cases revealed massive procedural violations; by the end of the year, 13 of the protesters were expelled, some 100 were granted residency status, and the rest regrouped to continue their action. In October the cabinet approved a revision of the Pasqua laws that would make them more coherent, if stricter.

France's National Front, the nationalist political party that won 16% of the popular vote in the 1995 presidential elections, remained conspicuously silent during the crisis. But in September, Front leader Jean-Marie Le Pen made headlines by declaring that "all of history proves" different races are inherently unequal. Amid the ensuing uproar, a Socialist Party leader called for the Front's dissolution; others demanded that the government file suit for "inciting racial hatred," a crime under French law. Justice Minister Jacques Toubon decided not to sue, but promised a stronger law against racist speech. In October he announced a bill that would make it illegal to "spread, by any means whatever, a message undermining the dignity of a person because of his or her connection to an ethnic group, a nation, a race, or religion." Many of the harshest opponents of the National Front criticized the proposed law for its potential impact on freedom of expression.

FRANCE • Information Highlights

Official Name: French Republic.
Location: Western Europe.
Area: 211,208 sq mi (547 030 km²).
Population (mid-1996 est.): 58,400,000.
Chief Cities (1990 census): Paris, the capital, 2,175,200; Marseilles, 807,726; Lyons, 422,444.
Government: *Head of state,* Jacques Chirac, president (took office May 1995). *Head of government,* Alain Juppé, prime minister (took office May 1995). *Legislature*—Parliament: Senate and National Assembly.
Monetary Unit: Franc (5.2440 francs equal U.S.$1, Dec. 30, 1996).
Gross Domestic Product (1994 est. U.S.$): $1,081,000,000,000 (purchasing power parity).
Economic Indexes (1995, 1990 = 100): *Consumer Prices,* all items, 111.6; food, 105.8. *Industrial Production,* 104.
Foreign Trade (1995 U.S.$): *Imports,* $274,335,000,000; *exports,* $286,536,000,000.

The government had little respite in 1996 from the corruption scandals that had rocked French politics for several years. Paris Mayor Jean Tiberi, in particular, was under continuing investigation for illegal practices as head of the Paris public-housing office. Though a minor figure himself, Tiberi represented a time bomb for the government, since his activities had been conducted under Chirac, then mayor of Paris. Prime Minister Juppé, Interior Minister Jean-Louis Debré, and Justice Minister Toubon also had been members of "Chirac's gang" at city hall. A judicial investigation of Tiberi's tenure at the public-housing office might prove not only that Chirac and his friends had helped themselves to prime city-owned real estate, but also that Chirac's Rally for the Republic (RPR) party had been financed by illegal kickbacks from Paris public-works contracts.

So dangerous did the government deem these investigations that it was willing to brook criticism by openly obstructing judicial procedures. Police officers received official approval after refusing to accompany an investigating judge on a search of Tiberi's apartment; a helicopter was sent in search of a "friendly" public prosecutor on vacation in the Himalayas after his deputy had opened an inquest into a payment received by Tiberi's wife; and a series of judicial appointments placed close friends of the administration in key investigating positions. Public reaction was limited to caustic remarks in the press and widespread cynicism among a population little used to interfering in judicial affairs.

On Feb. 1, 1996, French President Jacques Chirac told a joint session of the U.S. Congress that much of the decision-making authority of the North Atlantic Treaty Organization (NATO) should be shifted to its European members and that France would "take its full share in this renovation process."

© Tom Horan/Sygma

Despite predictions of an explosive autumn, widespread social unrest did not materialize, though a November truckers' strike further rattled an embattled government. A public-sector strike called in October, almost exactly a year after the civil-service walkout that sparked the 1995 movement, drew several hundred thousand participants. Other indicators of public exasperation with government economic policies were bitter localized strikes over a planned restructuring of Moulinex, a household-appliance manufacturer, and the privatization of the Thomson electronic firm. Truck drivers striking to obtain better pay and shorter working hours blocked fuel depots and other points across France for two weeks in late November, prompting gas rationing and massive backups at France's borders. The strike won strong support within France and focused attention on the need for harmonized labor standards throughout the European Union (EU).

By September, Prime Minister Juppé had garnered the highest dissatisfaction rating of any Fifth Republic prime minister. Newspaper headlines began raising questions about Juppé's ability to govern, and the ruling majority—increasingly concerned about 1998 elections—took frequent potshots at him from the National Assembly floor. Still, President Chirac—almost equally low in the polls—showed no signs of replacing his long-time political partner.

Economic Affairs. Despite France's consistently excellent foreign-exchange figures, a heavy pall continued to darken the overall economic picture. When, in October, a German institute published a report identifying France as one of only two European countries (excluding Germany) that fulfilled the strict criteria for a single European currency, the French did not applaud. The view had grown too widespread—even among past champions of European unification—that the criteria were excessively rigid and poorly adapted to the low-growth period France was experiencing. Former President Valéry Giscard d'Estaing was the most influential voice to join this argument, when he called for a devaluation in late November. So startling was this appeal, coming from a European purist, that Prime Minister Juppé and German Chancellor Helmut Kohl published an immediate joint communiqué saying the current franc-mark parity would not be altered. The move did not prevent a furious debate on France's present and future monetary policy.

In September, French unemployment topped an all-time record, at 12.6% of the workforce. Announced job cuts in the metallurgy, aeronautics, textile, and automobile industries presaged further bad news. Moreover, an increasing proportion of extant jobs were what the French considered "precarious," either part-time or of limited duration. Prime Minister Juppé's cautious exploration of increased labor flexibility as a means of combating unemployment seemed unlikely to be met with approval.

In an effort to infuse some hope into the economic picture and improve his own popularity ratings, Juppé announced a tax break totaling some $5 billion in the fall parliamentary session. However, reports indicated that the average employee would stand to gain a maximum of $100 per year, while those with higher incomes would receive larger absolute reductions. In addition, critics asserted that sharp rises in local taxes and alcohol and gasoline levies would more than erase the income-tax cut for most individuals.

In early December the government announced it was suspending the planned privatization of the Thomson electronics firm in the face of opposition. Anger had focused on the cession of Thomson home electronics to the Korean firm Daewoo, after recapitalization. Analysts agreed that the Juppé cabinet had mishandled the privatization process.

Foreign Affairs. After a final blast detonated on the Pacific atoll of Fangutaufa on January 27, President Chirac announced the definitive end of French nuclear testing. What he clearly had hoped would be a popularity-boosting display of French might and independence had turned into a public-relations fiasco. In the face of international opposition to his violation of Mitterrand's two-year moratorium, and marked acts of disapproval on the part of France's European partners, Chirac scaled back an originally scheduled eight tests to six, and scrambled in early 1996 to repair the damage to France's international reputation. On March 25, France—along with the United States and Great Britain—signed the Treaty of Rarotonga, making the South Pacific a nuclear-free zone.

After the wave of terrorist bombings in the summer of 1995, for which Algerian extremist groups claimed responsibility, Franco-Algerian relations were expected to dominate international news in 1996. With two exceptions, they did not. In March seven elderly Trappist monks were kidnapped from their monastery in the mountain town of Medea. When they were found killed in May in particularly gruesome fashion, demonstrations of grief and anger took place in France and Algeria. However, this event, as well as revelations that Paris might have undertaken and botched negotiations with the kidnappers, did not affect France's Algeria policy significantly. As the troubled North African country slid toward another miasma of violence in the weeks before a constitutional referendum in November, France was conspicuously silent.

On December 3 a bomb exploded aboard a crowded commuter train near Luxembourg Garden, killing four persons and injuring more than 80. The blast occurred on the same line and just two stops away from the deadly bomb of July 1995, which was attributed to the radical Algerian-based Armed Islamic Group. The explosion prompted the prime minister to retrigger security measures.

The year marked a turning point in France's relations with the North Atlantic Treaty Organization (NATO). While remaining an integral part of NATO's day-to-day operations, France had pulled out of the military-command structure in 1966 due to concerns that U.S. hegemony might force France into an unwanted conflict with the Eastern bloc. In December 1995, France discreetly began participating in meetings of the military committee, and in 1996 it pushed for a reorganization of NATO command structures that would give Europe a more "autonomous identity." France's insistence that a French general should be given control over NATO's southern command met stiff U.S. resistance.

In late June, the city of Lyons proudly hosted the summit of the world's seven most industrial democracies (G-7). Coming just after a terrorist attack on a U.S. air base in Saudi Arabia, the ostensibly economic meeting almost was swamped by U.S. President Bill Clinton's concern about terrorism.

President Chirac worked to increase French visibility in the Middle East. After Israel carried out air strikes against southern Lebanon in April, Foreign Affairs Minister Hervé de Charette worked toward a negotiated cease-fire, shuttling back and forth between Beirut, Tel Aviv, and Damascus—despite U.S. and Israeli irritation—until an accord finally was reached. In October, President Chirac embarked on a high-profile tour of the Middle East. Details such as Chirac's decision not to address the Knesset revealed the growing tension between France and the new Israeli government of Prime Minister Benjamin Netanyahu. Such tensions flared when, on a walking tour of East Jerusalem, Chirac practically came to blows with the omnipresent Israeli security forces. Later in the trip, Chirac was given a hero's welcome in the Palestinian territories. Chirac called for an "open Jerusalem"; he urged Israel to fulfill its signed commitments; and he argued that Europe's heavy financial commitment to peace in the region merited a permanent presence at ongoing talks.

On October 3, Serbian President Slobodan Milosevic and the head of Bosnia's new three-man presidency, Alija Izetbegovic, met in the French capital. They emerged from negotiations—in which both said Chirac had played a key role—with an agreement that included full diplomatic recognition. They both also signed on to the French idea for a two-year reconstruction plan, in which foreign aid would be contingent on their countries' application of the 1995 Dayton Accords.

SARAH CHAYES, *Paris Bureau*
The Christian Science Monitor Radio

GAMBLING

In many respects, 1996 was a watershed year for commercial gaming industries in North America. Their size, growth, and expanded presence, although significant, were not the main story of the year. These were overshadowed by an increasing degree of public scrutiny concerning the wisdom of permitted gambling.

Revenues. Such concerns notwithstanding, it was a record year for commercial gaming industries. U.S. revenues for casinos, lotteries, pari-mutuel wagering, sports betting, charity gaming, card clubs, bingo, and Indian gaming totaled $44.4 billion in 1995.

The non-Indian casino industry, legal and operating in ten states, generated gross revenues of $18.0 billion in 1995, a 17.2% increase over 1994. Casinos opened in Las Vegas, Mississippi, Iowa, Missouri, and Indiana. Most jurisdictions experienced moderate to strong economic performance in 1996, though increased competition eroded profit margins in regional markets.

Lotteries remained in second place among the commercial gaming industries, with sales (handle) of $38.9 billion and revenues after prize payment of $15.2 billion in the 36 states (plus the District of Columbia) where they operate. Video lottery terminals—casino-style electronic gaming devices—operated in four states and generated more than $600 million in revenues. Overall, year-to-year lottery growth was 7.9%.

Indian Gaming. Indian gaming increased 18.3% to $4.0 billion in 1995. As of mid-1996, there were 145 compacts for Indian gaming applying to tribes in 24 states. In October 1996 the second legal New England casino, the Mohegan Sun, opened in Connecticut only a few miles from the world's largest and most profitable casino, Foxwoods. In California and New Mexico, Indian casinos were operating without approved compacts, and their legal status was challenged. This resulted in closure of some casinos in New Mexico, but not in California.

Racing. The racing industry continued to be comparatively weak. Revenues generated by pari-mutuel wagering on horses and dogs grew by 2.8% in 1995 to about $3.7 billion. On-track revenues fell by 15.5%, with activity shifting to off-track and inter-track wagering. In Iowa, Louisiana, Rhode Island, and Delaware, racetracks were permitted to operate slot machines or other electronic gaming devices; in California, Hollywood Park was operating a card-club casino.

Regional Markets. Las Vegas and Atlantic City had record revenue years at $5.2 billion and $3.7 billion, respectively. Both cities were poised for major expansion. Two large casinos opened in Las Vegas in 1996, and several others were scheduled to open before the end of 1998. In Atlantic City the new convention center and a less restrictive regulatory environment had improved the economic climate for the casino industry substantially. Numerous major projects were announced.

New riverboat casinos began operation in Indiana and Iowa, and competition increased in northern and southern Mississippi, as well as in the metropolitan areas of Kansas City and St. Louis. Riverboats in western Louisiana performed well, but New Orleans casinos continued to disappoint. Negotiations on the bankrupt Harrah's Jazz land-based casino in New Orleans continued.

Nevada, New Jersey, Mississippi, Illinois, Louisiana, and Connecticut had casino industries with more than $1 billion in gross revenue, while Missouri, Minnesota, Iowa, and Colorado had approximately $500 million industries. In California card rooms and technically illegal Indian casinos combined for more than $1 billion in gross revenues.

In Canada, Ontario expanded the presence of government-owned casinos with the opening of a second casino in Windsor, one north of Toronto, and, late in the year, one near the U.S. border at Niagara Falls. These casinos created a "cross-border" effect that encouraged bordering U.S. states to consider casinos of their own. The success of the Windsor casinos—which generated more than $500 million in 1996, about 80% of it from U.S. residents—encouraged Michigan voters to authorize three Indian casinos for Detroit in the November 1996 election.

The Federal Government and Gaming. President Bill Clinton in August signed the National Gambling Impact Study Commission Act. The commission was to perform a study regarding benefits and costs associated with the spread of gambling. The nine-member commission was expected to complete its work by early 1999.

In March the U.S. Supreme Court decision declared part of the 1988 Indian Gaming Regulatory Act (IGRA) unconstitutional, ruling that Congress does not have the right to abrogate states' sovereign immunity. IGRA had stated that tribes could go to federal courts for mediation if states did not negotiate in good faith.

WILLIAM R. EADINGTON
University of Nevada, Reno

GARDENING AND HORTICULTURE

According to the National Gardening Association of Burlington, VT, the retail garden industry experienced a decline of 14% in sales in 1995, while consumer interest remained stable. The drop in sales—the first since 1990—was attributed to a wet spring followed by a hot, dry summer (especially in the northeastern United States); an 8% drop in single-family home completions; increased price competition among mass marketers; and decreased spending because some buyers had completed lawn and garden projects in 1994.

On-line and Computer Gardening. CD-ROMs and World Wide Web sites made their move into the gardening industry in 1996. Computer enthusiasts who enjoy gardening could tiptoe through the roses at a Web site called The Rose Resource. Created by All-America Rose Selections, the site—with more than 60 pages—was the first to offer a complete guide to rose gardening. Web surfers also could visit the Weekend Gardener by Chestnut Software, Inc., of Kunkletown, PA.

Sunset Garden Problem Solver, a CD-ROM by Sunset Publishing Corp., Menlo Park, CA, is a database of more than 400 pests, diseases, and weeds found in gardens throughout the United States and Canada. More than 130 step-by-step solutions and techniques are illustrated and described, including Safety Tips from the Plant Doctor—relating to everything from trees to houseplants, lawns to shrubs. *Problem Solver* is a companion to Sunset's *Western Garden* CD-ROM, a 6,000-entry encyclopedia of Western plants. The *Microsoft Complete Gardening* CD-ROM covers nearly 4,000 species; it features botanical names, with their correct pronunciation; plant-region maps; a problem solver; and tips for plant culture.

All-America Rose Selections 1997 Winners. Rose aficionados—as well as plain, ordinary rose lovers—will appreciate growing one or all of the three 1997 All-America Rose Selections (AARS) winners. "Artistry" is a coral-orange hybrid tea, "Timeless" is a deep rose-pink hybrid tea, and "Scentimental" is a burgundy and cream floribunda. "Artistry" and "Timeless" were hybridized by Keith W. Zary and introduced by Jackson & Perkins. "Scentimental" was introduced by Weeks Roses and hybridized by Tom Carruth from "Playboy" and "Peppermint Twist."

AARS winners are judged for bud and flower form, vigor, hardiness, growth habit, disease resistance, foliage, and fragrance during a two-year test program in rose gardens across the United States.

All-America Selections for 1997. Seven 1997 honorees were announced by All-America Selections (AAS). "Crystal White," a Zinnia Angustifolia, features blooming ability in 55 to 60 days from seeding on disease-resistant plants 4 to 5 inches (10.16 to 12.7 cm) high. "Dynamo" is a blue-green cabbage with a small, dense head weighing 2 to 2.5 lbs (0.9 to 1.13 kg). "Siam Queen" is a Thai basil with aromatic leaves on later-flowering plants with red-purple square stems. "Cajun Delight," a superior okra variety, boasts improved yield, tender pods, and earliness (50 to 55 days after transplanting into warm soil). "Prestige Scarlet," a Celosia cristata, has numerous side branches and cockscomb flowers that can be used fresh-cut or dried. Finally, "Gypsy" became the first Gypsophila, or baby's breath, to earn an AAS award. The winners were determined on the basis of tests conducted in 34 flower trial gardens and 27 vegetable trial sites across North America.

RALPH L. SNODSMITH
Ornamental Horticulturist

"Scentimental" and "Artistry" were winners of the 1997 All-America Rose Selections. "Scentimental," far left, *the first striped rose to win an AARS award, features a spicy fragrance. "Artistry,"* near left, *has long stems and a light fragrance that make it ideal for cutting.*

GENETICS

A person's overall temperament can be characterized as novelty seeking, harm avoiding, reward dependent, or persistent. Those individuals characterized as "novelty seeking" tend to enjoy exploring new environments, be excitable and quick-tempered, and seek thrilling sensations. In searching for the genetic basis of this behavior, scientists have examined the gene whose protein product is involved in the transmission of the molecule called dopamine from one brain cell to another. The gene, located on chromosome 11, is called the D4 dopamine receptor gene (D4DR). It determines the structure of the attachment site (receptor) through which dopamine enters a cell.

Two independent investigations reported that, depending on the person, the gene D4DR can be either shorter or longer in length, resulting in a differently structured dopamine attachment site. It was found that novelty seeking was associated with the longer form of the gene. The actual mechanisms by which the differently structured attachment sites have their effects were unknown in 1996. The discovery may prove to be the first step in identifying the genes that help determine human personality traits.

Plant-Pathogen Interaction. The resistance of many plants to particular pathogens is dependent on each organism having a specific genotype. For example, the common weed *Arabidopsis thaliana* is resistant to the pathogenic bacterium *Pseudomonas syringae* only if the host plant carries the dominant form of its gene RPM-1 and the bacterium a specific allele of its "avirulence" (avr) gene. In the absence of either allele, the bacterium attacks the leaves of the plant, destroying them and, ultimately, the plant. Resistance to infection was assumed to result from some direct interaction between the plant and bacterial gene products.

M.R. Grant at the Max Delbruck Laboratory in Germany and his colleagues at other institutions have discovered that *A. thaliana* plants carrying the RPM-1 mutation are resistant to *P. syringae* bacteria that carry either one of two avr alleles—namely, avrRpm-1 and avrB. This is the first time that a plant's resistance gene has been found to interact with more than one bacterial avr allele. The discovery was all the more unexpected because the nucleotide base sequences of avrRpm1 and avrB are very dissimilar, resulting in their gene products being quite different. This finding indicates that the RPM-1 gene product acts indirectly through a biochemical pathway that intercepts the biochemical pathways of more than one type of avr protein.

Premature Aging. A number of genetically caused premature-aging syndromes have been described. One such disorder is called Werner's syndrome. It is inherited as a recessive trait. Signs of aging appear when affected individuals still are in their 20s. Death usually occurs before age 50.

In the mid-1990s, G.D. Schellenberg at the Veterans Affairs Health Care System in Seattle, WA, and his colleagues at other institutions were able to isolate the gene involved in Werner's syndrome. They discovered that the biochemical defect in this disorder is an insufficient production of one type of helicase enzyme. Each type of helicase enzyme unwinds the DNA double helix in preparation for just one of the following processes: DNA replication, transcription, repair, or recombination. In Werner's syndrome, it is DNA repair that is faulty, resulting in the accumulation of spontaneous and environmentally induced chromosomal breaks and deletions. Such genetic damage leads to cancers and other medical problems. With the isolation of the Werner's-syndrome gene, it is hoped that studies will yield information on treating the diseases that characterize old age.

Genes and Mating Success. It has been hypothesized that mating success is dependent in many species upon interacting genetic variants that enhance the reproductive capabilities of one sex or the other. W.R. Rice at the University of California in Santa Cruz tested whether the above hypothesized situation could be demonstrated in males of the fruit fly *Drosophila melanogaster*. He did this by selecting for mating success in males while preventing the females' genes from affecting the situation.

Males were placed with females from a general population. The females that mated were isolated and maintained separately. Those females that had not mated were returned to the population. The male offspring of the mated females were used in a breeding program that weeded out the females' chromosomes, resulting in male descendants that carried only the genes from their male progenitors. The descendant males then were mated with females from the general population and the cycle was repeated for 41 generations. It was found that the selected males exhibited a significantly higher success rate in mating and also produced more offspring per mating.

LOUIS LEVINE, *City College of New York*

GEOLOGY

During 1996 scientists gained new insights into the structure and movement of Earth's layers, the lifestyle of predatory dinosaurs, and the mechanisms of volcanoes.

Inner Earth. Seismologists announced that Earth's solid inner core is rotating significantly faster than the rest of the planet—fast enough to lap the surface every 400 years. The researchers made the observation by measuring discrepancies in the time seismic waves took to travel through Earth's core in the 1990s compared to earlier decades. The scientists proposed that the core had changed its position relative to the crust over the decades, causing the seismic waves to take a slightly different path. Scientists expected that the observation would improve understanding of Earth's magnetic field.

Scientists also reported that Earth's middle layer, or mantle, may not be solid all the way through, as many seismologists have assumed. A dramatic drop in the velocity of certain seismic waves passing through the lower reaches of the mantle suggest that the rock there may be partially molten. The changes occur in a region beneath the South Pacific, although the scientists suspected that the soft layer extends around the globe. The layer may affect Earth's magnetic field strongly and may alter the transport of heat outward from the core. However, other scientists said that the seismic observations could be caused by changes in chemical composition at the bottom of the mantle.

Earth's Crust. Researchers obtained new evidence that Earth's seemingly rigid outer shell, or lithosphere, flows under its own weight. In mountainous areas, gravity pulls down on the raised areas, causing them to flatten out like cake batter poured into a pan. The process may explain the ongoing spreading of the crust in the Great Basin of the U.S. West, bordered by the Sierra Nevada mountains in the west and the Rockies in the east.

Geologists reported that a chunk of Argentina is a remnant of North America. The region, the Argentine Precordillera, split off from the continental mass called Laurentia (now North America) some 515 million years ago, rode across the ocean on a tectonic plate, and was welded to the western margin of Gondwana (the parent of South America) about 455 million years ago.

Two U.S. geologists found evidence that the presence of rock called schist may influence the size of earthquakes on certain faults in southern California. In areas underlain by schist basement rock, the researchers discovered, the depth of ruptures in the crust—and therefore the size of earthquakes—is smaller than in other areas. This may be because schist is softer at shallower depths than other rock types and is therefore less prone to sudden, deep ruptures along faults.

Paul C. Sereno, a paleontologist at the University of Chicago, inspects the fossil remains of the skull of the huge predatory dinosaur species "Carcharodontosaurus saharicus." Sereno led the expedition that found the skull in Morocco in the summer of 1995.

Paleontology. Researchers reported findings suggesting that *Tyrannosaurus rex* had a bite that apparently was as bad as its bark. The scientists estimated the strength of the creature's jaws by crunching cow bones in a hydraulic contraption fitted with simulated dinosaur teeth and comparing the bite marks to those found on the fossil remains of triceratops, whose bones were similar in structure to those of cows. The research adds weight to the case that *T. rex* was an active predator, not a scavenger of dead animals, as some paleontologists have argued. As powerful as *T. rex*'s jaws may have been, fossils discovered in Morocco show that the king of the dinosaurs had a rival—*Carcharodontosaurus saharicus*. The sheer size of the skull of this fearsome beast suggests it was as big as *T. rex*.

Paleontologists digging in Germany discovered fossils of a mouse equipped with skin flaps that allowed it to glide for short distances. The unusually well-preserved remains of the creature, which became extinct 5 million years ago, bring to four the types of rodents known to have evolved the ability to sail through the air.

Earthquakes. On February 17 a magnitude-8.1 quake shook the seafloor near Irian Jaya, Indonesia. The temblor unleashed a 23-ft (7-m) tsunami, or tidal wave, and left more than 100 persons dead and thousands more in temporary shelter. It was the region's 14th earthquake of magnitude 8.0 or larger since 1904. In June repeated earthquakes shook the Andreanof islands in the Aleutians, a chain of volcanic islands off Alaska. The action began with a magnitude-6.3 temblor on June 8. A magnitude-7.6 quake struck on June 10, followed by a magnitude-7.1 quake later the same day. No deaths or significant damage were reported on the remote islands, but the earthquakes did trigger moderate tsunamis that reached Hawaii and California.

Elsewhere, a strong magnitude-5.8 earthquake struck Ecuador on March 28, leaving 19 persons dead and significant damage in several southern provinces. On May 3 a magnitude-5.6 quake in Inner Mongolia, China, killed at least 18 and left 200,000 homeless.

Volcanoes. A number of significant eruptions drew the attention of volcanologists. The Soufrière Hills volcano on the Caribbean island of Montserrat, which came to life in 1995, continued to cause concern. Parts of the plug of congealed magma in the volcano's crater grew and collapsed repeatedly, loosing dangerous flows of hot debris, ash, and gas on low-lying areas around the volcano. Hot blocks of rock blasted from the crater damaged many homes near the volcano and forced thousands into temporary shelter.

In March, Popocatépetl, a volcano in central Mexico, began erupting after months of quietly venting gases. In April five mountain climbers were killed by an eruption of hot debris. Scientists were very concerned because about 30 million people live within 45 mi (72 km) of the volcano. Scientists studying ash deposits from previous eruptions determined that Popocatépetl may have contributed to the downfall of cities that flourished in the area from 100 B.C. to 750 A.D.

In July scientists detected the largest swarm of earthquakes ever to emanate from the Loihi Seamount, an underwater volcano 22 mi (35 km) southeast of the island of Hawaii. By the end of July, more than 4,000 individual earthquakes had been detected at Loihi. Scientists visited Loihi's summit in a small submarine to inspect a new crater formed during the eruption.

In August an explosive ash eruption from Canlaon volcano in the Philippines killed three hikers. The volcano ejected a dirty white plume of steam and ash some 4,800 ft (1 500 m) above its central summit crater.

On September 30 a volcano erupted beneath Iceland's Vatnajökull, the largest continental glacier in Europe, prompting fears that melting ice could unleash a catastrophic flood. Ash and gas spewed through the glacier by the erupting volcano, Grimsvotn, reached an altitude of 33,000 ft (10 060 m). The eruption ceased on October 13, but not before causing a huge amount of water to build up in a basin beneath the glacier. On November 5 the expected glacial outburst flood poured from beneath the glacier, unleashing an estimated 0.7 mi^3 (3 km^3) of meltwater on Sandur Plains. The flood destroyed bridges, toppled electric lines, and burst through levees.

Scientists announced a new theory to explain a 1986 volcano-related disaster in the African nation of Cameroon. That year, a dense cloud of carbon dioxide gas erupted from Lake Nyos, located in the crater of an old volcano, and asphyxiated more than 1,000 persons. Using computer simulations, the scientists determined that the gas fountained out of the water after the lake was stirred by an underwater landslide or by rainfall, both of which could have introduced vertical motion into the water. Scientists calculated that such an upward-flowing current could create a fountain of gas reaching heights of nearly 500 ft (150 m) above the water's surface.

DANIEL PENDICK, *Contributing Editor "Earth Magazine"*

GERMANY

Germans in 1996 struggled with a weak economy, the slow process of unification, and the country's future role in Europe and the international community. At the center of these developments stood Chancellor Helmut Kohl, Europe's senior statesman. In October, Kohl, after 14 years in office, overtook Konrad Adenauer as the longest-serving post–World War II chancellor.

Politics. Elections in 1996 were limited to three state elections in March and scattered local elections throughout the year. Chancellor Kohl's Christian Democrats maintained their leading position in most cases.

The major opposition party, the Social Democratic Party (SPD), was the big loser. The SPD continued to struggle over its program and leadership, appearing unable to offer convincing solutions for Germany's core economic problems. The question of who would be the party's chancellor candidate in the 1998 election remained unanswered. SPD leader Oskar Lafontaine was unsuccessful in 1990 and many in the party were reluctant to give him another chance.

While much smaller than the SPD, the other opposition party, the Greens, were more successful in criticizing the government. Led by Joschka Fischer, the Greens put the government on the defensive over questions of the environment and the stationing of German troops in Bosnia. The Greens also benefited from support among younger Germans. In 1996 the voting age for local elections was reduced to 16 in one state, Lower Saxony.

The former communists, the Party of Democratic Socialism (PDS), continued to receive the support of more than 20% of voters in the former East Germany. The PDS capitalized on easterners' dissatisfaction with the slow pace of unification and their perceived second-class status in the unified country.

In December, Chancellor Kohl's parliamentary majority actually increased when seven East German members of parliament left the opposition Greens and Social Democrats and joined the Christian Democrats. The seven all had been leading dissidents under the East German communist regime. They left the opposition to protest what they considered the growing tendency of the Greens and Social Democrats in the East to cooperate with the former communists.

Economy. For most of 1996 the economy stagnated. A modest recovery in the fourth quarter yielded an overall growth rate for the year of only 1%. In the East the economy grew by a disappointing 2%, the lowest level since the 1990 unification and a sharp drop from the robust 5.3% of 1995. This weak economy produced few new jobs in 1996 and unemployment rose to about 11%, the highest level in the postwar period. The modest growth that was achieved was due mainly to increased exports. For the first time since World War II, Germany's exports to Eastern Europe exceeded those to the United States. The other bright spot in the economy was the low inflation rate of less than 2%.

Another indicator of a troubled economy was the sharp rise in personal debt. Generally, Germans in the postwar period have avoided

A billboard welcomed German Chancellor Helmut Kohl to Lyon, France, for the major industrial nations (G-7) summit in June 1996. During the year, Kohl continued to play the role of Europe's senior statesman. There also were indications that, contrary to Kohl's 1994 statement that he would not run again, he would seek a record fifth term as chancellor in 1998.

In the fall of 1996, some 15,000 employees of Mercedes-Benz AG in Sindelfingen joined workers throughout Germany in protesting a reduction in sick-pay benefits.

© Camay Sungu/Reuters/Archive Photos

the credit-card, installment-payment culture common in other Western societies. Younger generations, however, have embraced the "buy now, pay later" philosophy. Between 1989 and 1996 personal short-term debt jumped by 700%. Personal bankruptcy was increasingly common as slowed economic growth and rising unemployment made it more difficult to manage personal debt.

In January, Kohl convened employers, union leaders, and governmental officials in an attempt to reach a consensus on how to deal with unemployment and the rising costs of the welfare state. Labor costs in Germany were among the highest in the world, due largely to generous fringe benefits—such as vacation and holiday pay, health and unemployment insurance, and pensions—that comprised about 80% of the average industrial worker's base wage.

Kohl in April announced plans for deep cuts in Germany's generous welfare state. The measures, most of which became law in October, were designed to lower the budget deficit and reduce the costs of doing business in Germany. State unemployment benefits, child allowances, and health-insurance benefits all were reduced. Even the fabled four-week "cure" at a health spa was not immune from the cutbacks. Instead of taking the waters for four weeks every three years, Germans would have to be content with a paid three-week stay every four years. The "savings package" also was designed to allow Germany to meet the 3% deficit criteria for the proposed unified European currency. In June, 300,000 demonstrators, led by the trade unions, traveled to Bonn to protest the cuts.

The new law also allowed employers to reduce sick-pay benefits from 100% to 80%. When in October several large firms, led by Daimler-Benz, announced plans to cut sick pay, thousands of workers throughout the country left their jobs and took to the streets in protest. In many cases the new law conflicted with collective-bargaining agreements that provided for full pay during illness. In an about-face, Chancellor Kohl announced shortly after the demonstrations that the law never was intended to invalidate existing labor contracts. Confronted with the government's retreat and the workers' protests, most firms agreed to postpone the cuts pending new labor-management negotiations.

In addition to high labor costs, excessive government regulation and a lack of venture capital frequently were cited by economists to explain Germany's economic malaise. To encourage investment and job growth, the parliament in November voted to abolish the so-called wealth tax on capital assets.

The parliament passed legislation in June, after decades of debate, to expand the hours retail stores may remain open. Since the 1950s, shops and stores had been required by law to close at 6:30 P.M. during the week and at 2:00 P.M. on Saturday. The new legislation, which took effect on November 1, expanded weekday hours to 8:00 P.M., bringing Germany closer to the more liberal policies of its European neighbors. The new policy was opposed by thousands of small shopkeepers who would have to work longer hours.

Unification Problems. The year saw little indication that the East was becoming less dependent on western subsidies. While wage levels in the former East Germany had climbed above 70% of the western level, productivity in the East continued to lag behind. East Germans produced only about 60% of what they consumed; the difference was being made up through subsidies from the West. This productivity gap could be closed only by greater capital investments in the East. Yet almost two thirds of the billions of marks transferred to the East were being spent on consumption rather than investment.

A further sign of unresolved East-West problems was seen in May, when voters in the eastern state of Brandenburg rejected a proposed merger with the city-state of Berlin. While most West Berliners approved the merger, voters in eastern Berlin and Brandenburg rejected it. Many easterners feared that the economic gap between prosperous West Berlin and poorer eastern regions would be widened by the merger.

In November the Federal Constitutional Court ruled that former top East German leaders could be tried on manslaughter charges for their approval of shoot-to-kill orders for East German border guards. The decision meant that three former top-ranking East German officials had to begin serving prison sentences. The decision also opened the way for the continuation of trials against several other former communist leaders. Previously, only low-level border guards had been convicted in the almost 600 deaths of East Germans who tried to flee the country between 1961 and 1989.

The Euro and the Mark. With Europe's strongest economy and currency as well as its most durable political leader, Germany assumed the leadership role in the currency-unification process. However, Germany's European partners were increasingly restive about the stringent monetary policies that they felt were being imposed upon them. Critics charged that the focus on inflation neglected the enormous social problems caused by 20 million jobless workers in the European Union (EU). In France two members of that nation's central bank openly questioned whether the policy of linking the franc to the mark had become an impossible burden for the French economy.

European critics of German economic policies received support in November when former Chancellor Helmut Schmidt accused Germany's central bank, the Bundesbank, of giving its European partners the impression that Germany "is imperious, power-hungry, and domineering." German central bankers replied by charging that their partners were attempting to use Bonn as a scapegoat for their own economic problems.

In December, at a meeting of EU finance ministers in Dublin, Ireland, agreement was reached on the introduction of the euro in 1999. EU members generally supported Germany's demand that the member countries pursue conservative fiscal and monetary policies to increase public confidence in the new currency.

The Troubled Past. Many Germans had hoped that the 50th anniversary of the end of World War II in 1995 would bring closure to painful discussions and revelations about the horrors of the Third Reich. Events in 1996 showed that this was not to be.

A U.S. scholar provoked yet another controversy over the Third Reich. Daniel J. Goldhagen, in his book *Hitler's Willing Executioners*, contended that hundreds of thousands of ordinary Germans willingly and enthusiastically took part in the murder of European Jewry because of a uniquely ingrained "eliminationist" anti-Semitism. Most historians on both sides of the Atlantic, but especially in Germany, charged that Goldhagen had indicted the entire German people and had resurrected long-discredited notions of German collective guilt. Upon publication in Germany in August, the book topped the best-seller list, where it remained for the remainder of the year. Younger Germans generally did not share the criticisms of the media and professional historians.

Unresolved problems from the Third Reich also were at the center of Germany's relations with the Czech Republic. For years the two countries had attempted to agree on a statement of reconciliation dealing with the Nazi annexation of 1938 and the behavior of Czechs toward German nationals after 1945. The Kohl government made compensation payments to victims of Nazism conditional upon a Czech apology for the 1945 expulsion of the Sudeten Germans. While conceding that the expulsions were not the best chapter

GERMANY • Information Highlights

Official Name: Federal Republic of Germany.
Location: North-central Europe.
Area: 137,931 sq mi (356 910 km^2).
Population (mid-1996 est.): 81,700,000.
Chief Cities (June 30, 1993 est.): Berlin, the capital, 3,471,500; Hamburg, 1,701,600; Munich, 1,256,300.
Government: *Head of state,* Roman Herzog, president (took office July 1994). *Head of government,* Helmut Kohl, chancellor (took office Oct. 1982). *Legislature*—parliament: Bundesrat and Bundestag.
Monetary Unit: Deutsche mark (1.55575 D. marks equal U.S.$1, Dec. 9, 1996).
Gross Domestic Product (1994 est. U.S.$): $1,344,600,000,000 (purchasing power parity).
Economic Indexes (1995, 1991 = 100): *Consumer Prices,* all items, 114.8; food, 108.4. *Industrial Production,* 95.
Foreign Trade (1995 U.S.$): *Imports,* $445,753,000,000; *exports,* $509,528,000,000.

in its history, Prague insisted that they were an understandable reaction to years of Nazi oppression.

Complicating the issue on the German side were the Sudeten Germans, many of whom settled in Bavaria after their expulsion. The group, an important interest group and staunch supporter of the Christian Social Union—the dominant party in the region and a national ally of Kohl's Christian Democrats—demanded a seat at the negotiating table. The issue also was complicated by Czech ambitions to become the first East European state to be admitted to the EU and the North Atlantic Treaty Organization (NATO). German support is critical for Czech admission, but little progress is possible until the two countries resolve their differences over the past. By year's end the two countries announced agreement on a joint resolution that would be presented to their respective parliaments in 1997.

Historical questions also played a role during the June visit of Pope John Paul II, the first papal visit since unification. The trip was designed to celebrate the end of the division between Europe and Germany. The pope led two Masses before very large crowds. But in Berlin thousands of protesters opposed to Catholic doctrine on birth control, sexual liberties, and traditional roles for women expressed open hostility to the pontiff. The pope also was criticized by Germany's small, but growing, Jewish community for failing to acknowledge publicly the failure of German Catholics to offer more resistance to the Nazi regime.

Foreign Policy. Germany continued its efforts to play a more prominent role in the international arena. In September, Foreign Minister Klaus Kinkel renewed Germany's claim to a permanent seat on the United Nations (UN) Security Council. The credibility and effectiveness of the body, Kinkel argued, required that it "look like the year 2000 and not the year 1945."

In December the parliament overwhelmingly approved the deployment of 3,000 combat troops to the Bosnian peacekeeping operation. It marked the first time since World War II that combat-ready German troops had been sent to an area outside of NATO. However, the deployment of German troops remained a controversial issue. There was substantial public opposition to military involvement, even under UN supervision. Opposition to the draft also was widespread. In 1996 more young Germans chose to be conscientious objectors, which involved a 13-month stint of alternative service in hospitals and welfare organizations rather than serving in the military.

© Laski Diffusion/Gamma-Liaison

In Moscow in February, Chancellor Kohl (left) *gave Russia's President Boris Yeltsin* (center) *what was considered an implicit reelection endorsement. Kohl called Yeltsin a "reliable partner."*

While willing to keep German troops in Bosnia, the Kohl government was less willing to keep Bosnian refugees in Germany. With more than 350,000 refugees, Germany was by far the largest receiving country in the EU. Citing the end of hostilities in the former Yugoslavia, many of the refugees in October were ordered returned to their homeland.

A diplomatic confrontation between Germany and China broke out in June when Beijing canceled the planned visit of Foreign Minister Kinkel to China in response to a parliamentary resolution that condemned China's human-rights record in Tibet. Previously the Bonn government had played down human-rights issues as German businessmen sought billion-dollar contracts from the Chinese. In the previous five years, trade between the two countries had more than doubled.

Germany's relations with Iran worsened in 1996, largely because of the trial of five Iranians charged with the 1992 assassination of four Kurdish separatist leaders at a Berlin restaurant. German prosecutors contended that the murders were planned at the highest levels of the Iranian government and the country's religious leadership. Tehran responded by calling the trial a defamation of Islam. Iranian religious leaders threatened the prosecutors with a *fatwa*, or death sentence. Iranian political leaders, however, distanced themselves from such pronouncements and the Kohl government continued its efforts to normalize relations with Tehran.

DAVID P. CONRADT, *East Carolina University*

GREAT BRITAIN

Throughout 1996 the Conservative government of British Prime Minister John Major faced challenges over domestic, economic, and foreign-policy issues. Particularly sharp conflict was brewing over accelerating moves toward greater unity by Great Britain's partners in the European Union (EU). Peace hopes in Northern Ireland were endangered in February by a massive bomb planted by the Irish Republican Army (IRA) in London. The marital troubles of the House of Windsor deepened as Queen Elizabeth II's first and second sons secured divorces.

Politics. Riding a tide of public approval in opinion polls, Labour Party leader Tony Blair kept up the pressure on Major and his government. The prime minister argued that the economy was buoyant and asserted that the Conservatives would win upcoming general elections, which must be held by May 1997.

In a January policy statement, Blair promised that Labour, if elected, would build an economy from which all citizens would benefit. Blair was reticent on policy details, but pledged that a Labour government would not be a "tax-and-spend" administration. In February he unveiled proposals for reform of the House of Lords, for a Freedom of Information Act, for incorporation of the European Convention of Human Rights into British law, and for the offer of parliamentary assemblies to Scotland and Wales. To underline his grip on Labour Party loyalty, Blair asked his party's rank-and-file members to vote on a draft manifesto. The outcome, announced in November, was an overwhelming majority in favor of the policy package.

Major attacked Labour's economic policies as unsound and likely to require increased taxes. He also said that constitutional changes were unnecessary and insisted that in calling for tough law-and-order policies, Labour was stealing the government's clothes. However, by proposing a steady stream of ideas and characterizing the Conservatives, in office for 17 years, as bereft of inspiration, Labour added to public perceptions that the government was on the defensive.

Such perceptions appeared to be confirmed in May, when local-government elections were held. The Conservatives won only about 27% of the vote and lost more than half of their council seats. In common with most other newspapers, the *London Times* said the

© "Scottish Daily Record"/Sipa Press

After a gunman killed 16 kindergarten children, their teacher, and himself in Dunblane, Scotland, on March 13, 1996, British Prime Minister John Major (right front) *offered his condolences to the mourning families and the shocked town.*

© Mike Sharpe/News Team/Sipa Press

result showed many people had voted for the opposition Labour and Liberal Democratic parties—which received roughly 43% and 26% of the vote, respectively—out of dissatisfaction with the Conservatives. Liberal Democrat leader Jeremy (Paddy) Ashdown said his party would be prepared to work with Labour if Blair formed the next government, but Blair shunned the offer.

Major's failure to dent Blair's confidence was reflected in parliamentary by-election results. For the fifth year in a row, the Conservatives lost all such contests. By the end of the year the government was heavily dependent on the votes of nine Ulster Unionist members of Parliament (MPs) for a majority in the House of Commons.

Major continued to be haunted by the long-term effects of political scandals in the ruling party. In February, Sir Richard Scott, who had been asked to investigate British arms sales to Iraq in the 1980s, produced a report critical of government ministers. As part of an energetic damage-limitation exercise, Major—who had one week to read the Scott report before its publication—denied senior opposition politicians access to it until three hours before it was debated in Parliament. In the Commons, Conservative MPs headed off by a single vote an attempt by Labour to condemn the government for selling arms to Iraq.

In September a scandal that had rocked the government two years earlier resurfaced when a senior Conservative MP, who in 1994 had been forced to resign as trade minister, suddenly dropped a defamation suit against the *Guardian*, which had published reports of his alleged financial improprieties. Neil Hamilton, together with a leading parliamentary lobbyist, claimed to be abandoning the case because of a lack of funds. But the *Guardian* then alleged that in 1994, another senior Conservative, while a government whip, had attempted to interfere in the investigation of the Hamilton case by a House of Commons committee. Major was left with no option but to ask the recently appointed parliamentary commissioner for standards to mount an urgent investigation.

Meanwhile, in July a solid majority of Britain's 651 MPs voted themselves a 26% pay raise while the government, without much dissent from Labour, continued to insist that public-sector workers should be content with raises no higher than 3%. One opinion poll showed that three quarters of voters opposed the MPs' pay increase.

Major's difficulties in keeping his party united were a feature of the year's politics. His problems were brought into relief by the murder in March in Dunblane, Scotland, of 16 children and their schoolteacher by a lone gunman. In October a judge's report on the massacre, which was committed with licensed weapons, proposed limited curbs on the sale and ownership of handguns. Amid widespread public disquiet, and with the families of the Dunblane victims vigorously campaigning for tougher measures, Major decided to go further than the report suggested, proposing that the government ban nearly all handguns above .22 caliber and restrict all legal firearms to secure gun clubs.

Blair and Ashdown pressed the prime minister to frame even tougher legislation, calling for a ban on all handguns, and to allow a free vote on the issue. But several Conservative MPs—some of them members of a gun club—expressed disagreement with Major's measures. Hoping to avert a party split that would allow passage of a Labour- and Liberal Democrat–backed total ban, Major said that Conservative MPs would be required to vote for the government's measure.

Major also drew disagreement from within his party in October, when, amid a flurry of cases of disruptive behavior in schools, he rebuked Education Secretary Gillian Shephard for advocating a return to corporal punishment for dealing with serious discipline problems. Despite Major's position, Home Secretary Michael Howard said that he too favored a return to corporal punishment in schools.

In October, Howard—who already had a reputation as a tough law-and-order minister—published a new crime bill that proposed to abolish judges' discretion in sentencing drug dealers and violent criminals, and that

GREAT BRITAIN • Information Highlights

Official Name: United Kingdom of Great Britain and Northern Ireland.
Location: Island, western Europe.
Area: 94,525 sq mi (244 820 km²).
Population (mid-1996 est.): 58,800,000.
Chief Cities (mid-1994 est.): London, the capital, 6,967,500; Birmingham, 1,008,400; Leeds, 724,400; Glasgow, 680,000; Sheffield, 530,100.
Government: *Head of state,* Elizabeth II, queen (acceded Feb. 1952). *Head of government,* John Major, prime minister and First Lord of the Treasury (took office November 1990). *Legislature*—Parliament: House of Lords and House of Commons.
Monetary Unit: Pound (0.5912 pound equals U.S.$1, Dec. 30, 1996).
Gross Domestic Product (1994 est. U.S.$): $1,045,200,-000,000 (purchasing power parity).
Economic Indexes (1995, 1990 = 100): *Consumer Prices,* all items, 118.2; food, 114.7. *Industrial Production,* 106.
Foreign Trade (1995 U.S.$): *Imports,* $265,320,000,000; *exports,* $242,038,000,000.

introduced mandatory life sentences for persistent offenders. Howard's measures, which included the building of 12 extra prisons, were attacked by leading jurists and by several former Conservative government ministers for being inflexible.

By far the most divisive and, for the prime minister, politically dangerous issue within the Conservative Party was Europe. Under the Maastricht Treaty, Britain was committed to furthering closer political and economic integration in the EU. However, Britain had secured arrangements allowing officials to "opt out" of joining the EU economic and monetary union (EMU), which would create a single European currency, and of accepting the EU's "social chapter" on workers' rights. Throughout the year the government was under pressure from a group of Conservative MPs, including a small group of cabinet ministers, either to reject outright British participation in a single currency or to let the issue be decided by a referendum. On the other hand, Chancellor of the Exchequer Kenneth Clarke continued to insist that it was in Britain's interests to join the EMU.

In a bid to avert a deep split in the cabinet, Major, with Clarke's concurrence, struck a compromise: Britain would continue to negotiate with the EU over a single currency, but would keep its options open until the last possible minute. If, at some date in the future, the government decided that Britain should join, it would hold a referendum to let the people decide. The compromise held until July 22, when David Heathcoat-Amory, a Treasury minister who had been at the heart of British policy-making on a single European currency, resigned and published a pamphlet attacking the concept, arguing that it would be "bad for Britain." Heathcoat-Amory drew support from John Redwood, who had resigned from Major's cabinet in 1995 and had challenged him for the Conservative Party leadership.

More ominously for the ruling party, Sir James Goldsmith, an Anglo-French billionaire and member of the European Parliament, announced that he was forming a party to campaign for a referendum on Britain's membership in the EMU. Goldsmith promised to spend £20 million (about $12 million) of his private fortune on the Referendum Party and pledged to put up candidates in up to 600 constituencies to fight Conservatives unwilling to support calls for a referendum. In October, Goldsmith called a well-attended national convention of the Referendum Party and pledged to do all in his power in the election campaign to loosen Britain's ties with the EU.

The Labour opposition remained reticent on the single-currency issue. In November, however, Robin Cook, the party's chief foreign-affairs spokesman, said he doubted whether Britain should join "in the first wave"—a more clear-cut position than any expressed by Tony Blair or Gordon Brown, Labour's "shadow" chancellor. Major accused Labour of papering over its own internal divisions on European policy, but for the most part, Blair appeared better able than the prime minister to impose discipline on his followers on the issue of Europe.

During the summer support for the Labour Party in opinion polls declined slightly, but a late October poll for the *London Times* indicated that Labour had bounced back, with 56% voicing support for the party (compared with only 28% expressing support for the Conservatives). In early December a Conservative MP withdrew his support for the party in an act of protest. Although the action caused the PCs to lose their one-seat majority in the House of Commons, the Tories still controlled 51 more seats than Labour, the body's second-largest party.

Economy. Chancellor of the Exchequer Clarke surprised financial markets in January by cutting interest rates for the second time in five weeks. He ordered further cuts in March and June. The moves highlighted disagreements between Clarke and Bank of England Governor Eddie George, who had argued for rate rises, citing underlying inflation. Clarke, however, contended that with unemployment continuing to fall (to 7.6% in July) and industry leaders calling for measures to boost consumer spending, an interest-rate cut was justified. Clarke resisted George's advice until October 30, when he raised base rates to 6%. In November, Chancellor Clarke reduced the standard rate of income tax by one penny to 23 pence in the pound.

Britain's cattle industry was thrown into turmoil in March, when the government issued a report indicating that a fatal human brain condition called Creutzfeldt-Jakob disease might be caused by eating beef affected by bovine spongiform encephalopathy (BSE), also known as mad-cow disease. The news prompted the EU to declare a worldwide ban on exports of British beef and demand that all British cattle likely to be suffering from BSE be culled. Britain protested vigorously, but the EU refused to relent. Faced with angry farmers demanding heavy compensation for their slaughtered cattle, Agriculture Minister Douglas Hogg became a familiar figure in Brussels as he tried without success to challenge the EU ban. In June the British government agreed to the selective slaughter of 147,000 cattle thought to be at the highest risk of BSE. The government reversed its position in September, however, citing British scientific evidence that BSE would die out by 2001 without a cull.

In pursuit of policies initiated in the 1980s, the Major government pressed ahead with plans for the Conservatives' last substantial privatization of a state-owned industry—British Rail (BR). Track and other infrastructure were consolidated as a separate company, Railtrack, and offered to shareholders in May. The rest of BR was split into more than 60 separate companies, with operators invited to bid for franchises. Winners of franchises were promised government subsidies at specified levels for up to 15 years. The government said it planned to have sold off 95% of BR by May 1997, and by year's end the target appeared certain to be met.

There were signs that a long period of comparatively strike-free industrial activity might be coming to an end. Starting in the summer, train drivers, along with London Underground workers, began taking action and demanding higher pay. Postal workers staged a series of nationwide one-day strikes to protest the Royal Mail's plans to rationalize delivery arrangements. The government said that if the strikes became persistent, the Royal Mail monopoly on postal deliveries would be abolished. In October the government proposed stricter controls on the conduct of strike ballots by industrial workers.

Throughout the year both opposition parties expressed concern about the National Health Service (NHS), claiming that, despite an annual budget of £42 billion (roughly $25 billion) and internal market reforms introduced in the Thatcher era, it was close to collapse. They were supported by the British Medical Association, whose chairman said in May that the NHS was facing its worst crisis in ten years and needed an immediate cash injection of £6 billion (about $3.6 billion) if it was not to sink "like the Titanic." In the government's annual public-spending review, the Treasury opposed extra money for the NHS as part of its attempt to contain overall state spending. Health Secretary Stephen Dorrell insisted that the NHS was "in good hands." Labour leader Blair said that a Labour government would get rid of the NHS internal market and ban tobacco advertising.

Other departments came under financial pressure. Education Secretary Shephard had to battle for a minimal budget increase, while spending on defense was frozen; also, the government ordered cuts in the budgets of the Transport, Environment, and National Heritage departments. Chancellor Clarke argued that money from the successful national lottery launched in 1995 made it possible for the government to cut spending on the arts.

Treasury demands for spending cuts threatened the British Broadcasting Corporation's (BBC's) highly regarded World Service, which derives most of its revenue from the Foreign Office. Faced with a real cut of 11% over three years, the BBC proposed the merger of the World Service's English-language news operations with the BBC's domestic news. MPs of all parties reacted angrily, claiming that the World Service's special character would be destroyed. In October the Foreign Office asked the BBC to accept 20 changes to its plan. The BBC agreed and began taking steps to merge the two units. However, BBC executives insisted that a shortage of money would force them to make deep cuts in the output of the World Service.

In May, British Telecommunications (BT), which had been privatized in 1984, failed in an attempted merger with Cable and Wireless, a telecommunications company with large interests in Asia. In November, however, BT announced agreement on a merger with MCI Communications Corp., a major U.S. telecommunications company. If approved by regulatory agencies in London, Brussels, and Washington, the merged company, to be called Concert, would become one of the world's four largest telecommunications operators.

Northern Ireland. Hopes that the peace process in Northern Ireland—initiated by a cease-fire declared in 1994—would yield results were shattered on February 9, when the IRA exploded a huge bomb near a busy London office complex, killing two persons. Other IRA attacks in the British capital, including an attempt to blow up a major bridge across the Thames, had little success, but another huge bomb in June injured more than 200 persons and destroyed a shopping center in Manchester.

On October 7, IRA terrorists struck with two car bombs at the British army's headquarters at Lisburn, near Belfast. This attack on the province's politically most sensitive—and supposedly most secure—target was the first IRA attack in Northern Ireland since the 1994 cease-fire. The bombings coincided with the opening of the Conservative Party's annual conference. Prime Minister Major declared: "If anybody thinks they can bomb the British government out of the policy stance we think

© Ian Jones/FSP/Gamma-Liaison

After Prince Charles, the heir to the British throne, and Princess Diana were divorced in August 1996, the princess announced that she would continue to travel, working for charities. In the fall, the princess visited Australia, left, *to raise funds for a cardiac-research institute in Sydney.*

is right, they are making a very serious and fundamental mistake." The Irish government condemned the attacks and said they were "aimed at undermining the multiparty talks in Belfast."

The talks already had been hampered by the IRA's refusal to denounce violence and to decommission its weapons. London and Dublin had demanded such a declaration as the price of letting Sinn Fein, the IRA's political wing, take part in talks already under way in Belfast.

The political atmosphere was soured further in the summer by Northern Ireland's annual "marching season," an occasion for Protestants and Roman Catholics to declare publicly their sectarian allegiances. In July members of the Protestant Orange Order demanded to be allowed to march through a mainly Catholic area in Drumcree. Police at first banned the march, then, after a lengthy confrontation, relented. Scuffles between marchers and Catholic residents triggered violent sectarian clashes in many parts of Northern Ireland. Later in the summer, Protestants attempted to march close to a Catholic district in Londonderry. Northern Ireland Secretary Sir Patrick Mayhew banned demonstrations, but marchers later held a more limited protest.

As a result of the renewed IRA bombing campaign, Sinn Fein President Gerry Adams, whom U.S. President Bill Clinton had invited to the White House in 1995, came under heavy pressure to urge the IRA to abandon violence and thus qualify for joining all-party talks. Adams, however, blamed the deteriorating peace process on the British government, claiming that Prime Minister Major was at the mercy of Ulster Unionist parliamentarians who held the balance of power in the House of Commons.

Other News. The marriage of Prince Andrew, Queen Elizabeth's second son, to Sarah Ferguson, duchess of York, was dissolved in May. Three months later the divorce of Charles, prince of Wales and heir to the throne, and Diana, the princess of Wales, was finalized in court. As part of a divorce settlement, estimated at $22.5 million, Diana was deprived of the title "Her Royal Highness" but was allowed to be called the princess of Wales. She said she would continue to travel the world, working for charities.

At an unprecedented private gathering of the royal family in the summer, the queen opened discussions about the future of the monarchy. Ideas considered included reducing the number of family members playing a prominent part in the life of the nation to about a dozen, cutting administrative costs at Buckingham Palace and other royal residences, and reviewing the monarch's status as supreme governor of the Church of England. A poll in the *Independent on Sunday* found that for the first time, fewer people thought that the monarchy had a long-term future than those who did not.

The government tightened rules for the processing of people arriving in Britain and claiming political asylum....The government said the Royal Air Force would withdraw from Germany in 2002....Kevin Maxwell, son of the late media tycoon Robert Maxwell, was found not guilty of conspiracy to defraud pension funds from the Maxwell empire...Prime Minister Major announced in July that the Stone of Scone—a 336-lb (153-kg) block of sandstone sitting beneath the coronation seat in London's Westminster Abbey and an ancient symbol of Scottish kingship—was going home to Scotland after 700 years.

ALEXANDER MACLEOD
"The Christian Science Monitor"

GREECE

The death of Greece's former Prime Minister Andreas Papandreou, the continued control of parliament by PASOK (the Panhellenic Socialist Movement) under new leadership, and serious strains between Greece and Turkey dominated the news in Greece in 1996.

Politics. A seriously ailing Andreas Papandreou, who had founded the PASOK party in 1974, remained as prime minister of Greece until January 1996, when he was replaced by PASOK member Costas Simitis. Papandreou, 77, died in June 1996. Simitis scheduled parliamentary elections for Sept. 22, 1996, which PASOK won. It gained 41.52% of the vote and 162 seats in parliament. The nearest opposition party, New Democracy, gained only 38.17% and 108 seats. The remaining 30 seats went to three other parties, including the Communists, who won 11. The leader of New Democracy, Miltiades Evert, resigned his post after the elections, but then was reelected as head of the party despite disaffection among some political figures in New Democracy.

Foreign Affairs. Greece, as in the past, steadfastly deplored Turkey's continued occupation of part of Cyprus. This matter was involved in other Greek-Turkish problems. In January the two countries almost went to war over the small, uninhabited Aegean Sea Imia islets. The crisis brought to the fore the continuing dispute between the two countries over control of territorial waters and the continental shelf around Greece's Aegean Islands, located geographically close to the Turkish mainland. The Greek government, basing its claim on past treaties, asserted that Imia was part of Greek territory; but Turkey did not accept that interpretation, and there was fear in Greece that Turkish actions and attitudes signaled a more aggressive Turkish policy toward Greek territory.

In November, Greek Foreign Minister Theodoros Pangalos stated that there was no possibility that Greece would enter into a single set of discussions with Turkey linking the issues of the Aegean sea with the Cyprus situation. Turkey, he asserted, by bringing forth claims to Greek territory in the Imia incident, had caused a severe change in the relations between the two countries.

Simitis then announced in mid-November 1996 that Greece was embarking on massive military expenditures—amounting to about $17 billion by 2007—to strengthen the military. The preponderant purchases for this project were scheduled to be from the United States. Both President Costis Stephanopoulos and Prime Minister Simitis met with U.S. President Bill Clinton in Washington in 1996.

Greece continued to refuse to recognize the name Macedonia for the Former Yugoslav Republic of Macedonia (FYROM) and continued to refer to the neighboring state as FYROM. It contended that Macedonia alone was not an acceptable name for the now-independent state for historical, political, and geographic reasons.

The Economy. Greece's economy lagged behind those of all other members of the European Union (EU). After the September elections, the Simitis government emphasized that it wanted to improve the economy so that Greece would qualify for European economic and monetary union (EMU) by the year 2000 or 2001. To achieve this, the governmental 1997 budget put forth late in 1996 foresaw a cut in state spending, a reduction of the high governmental deficit, a decrease in interest rates, and a cutting back of inflation.

The austerity plans had serious repercussions within the country. On November 28 the General Confederation of Greek Workers, which had been strike-prone earlier in the year, and the Civil Servants' Union staged a one-day immobilizing general strike. Also in November the farmers, who had made earlier protests, began a lengthy nationwide protest, blocking roads and rail lines and thus critically impeding the economy. Their demands included a lower value-added tax (VAT) on farm equipment, a restructuring of $1.3 billion in debts, less-costly fuel, and price supports. The farmers lifted their blockade on December 22, the same day that parliament presented the 1997 austerity budget.

Deposed Royal Family. In early 1996 the Supreme Court ruled by a vote of 25 to 15 that 1994 legislation taking away the property

GREECE • Information Highlights

Official Name: Hellenic Republic.
Location: Southeastern Europe.
Area: 50,942 sq mi (131 940 km²).
Population (mid-1996 est.): 10,500,000.
Chief Cities (1991 census): Athens, the capital, 772,072; Salonika, 383,967; Piraeus, 189,671.
Government: *Head of state,* Costis Stephanopoulos, president (took office March 1995). *Head of government,* Costas Simitis, prime minister (took office January 1996). *Legislature* (unicameral)—Chamber of Deputies.
Monetary Unit: Drachma (244.61 drachmas equal U.S.$1, Dec. 31, 1996).
Gross Domestic Product (1994 est. U.S.$): $93,700,000,000 (purchasing power parity).
Economic Indexes (1995, 1990 = 100): *Consumer Prices,* all items, 192.0; food, 189.2. *Industrial Production,* 98.
Foreign Trade (1994 U.S.$): *Imports,* $21,489,000,000; *exports,* $9,392,000,000.

and citizenship of the deposed Greek royal family was unconstitutional. Subsequently, the Council of State—by a vote of 17 to 10—ruled that the law was constitutional. This discrepancy meant that the question would have to be put before a specific court set up in accordance with the terms of the Greek Republic's 1975 constitution.

GEORGE J. MARCOPOULOS, *Tufts University*

HAITI

René Préval, 53, a former foreign minister, was inaugurated president of Haiti on Feb. 7, 1996, succeeding Jean-Bertrand Aristide, who had been overthrown by a military coup on Sept. 30, 1991, and was restored to power by a U.S. Army intervention three years later.

Peaceful though the transition was, Haiti remained a nation engulfed in turmoil. Domestic peace, if not tranquility, was preserved largely through the presence of a United Nations (UN) peacekeeping mission under Canadian leadership. The last U.S. combat troops were withdrawn in April, but U.S. security forces returned to Haiti three times during the year. Aristide still was a potent and visible political power in the country, hated and feared by his enemies—including elements of the former Haitian army, which Aristide had disbanded—and adored by his supporters in the Haitian masses.

Despite the withdrawal of its troops, the United States continued to be involved deeply in the day-to-day management of the country.

Foreign Troops. When the United States withdrew its troops from Haiti, it turned the peacekeeping mission over to a Canadian-led UN force of 1,900, backed up by soldiers from Argentina, Bangladesh, and Pakistan. After the UN presence was reduced to 1,200 soldiers and 300 police at the insistence of China—which was angry at Haiti's close ties to Taiwan—Canada said it would send the additional 700 troops at its own expense. The UN Security Council authorized the mission to stay in Haiti until July.

In June the Security Council voted unanimously to extend the mission for five months, through November, to "promote institutionalization and national reconciliation." On November 13, President Préval asked the Security Council to prolong the mandate another eight months, through the end of July, to give the nation more time to train its police force. In the meantime, independent of the UN force, the United States dispatched 165 members of the 82d Airborne Division on temporary duty to Haiti in July, and sent 50 Marines to Haiti on a "training mission" in August. In September, 40 security specialists from the U.S. Department of State were assigned to guard the national palace and to protect Préval when reports surfaced of a plot to assassinate the president and Aristide.

Seventeen officers from police forces across the United States joined the UN forces training Haitian police recruits at the end of October. The 5,300-member local police force was created after President Aristide disbanded the army in 1994. The U.S. police officers—the first to participate in the UN training mission—spoke French or Creole and were not expected to join in patrol missions or crowd-control duties.

Progress. Despite isolated incidents of violence—a police station burned to the ground in November; shots were fired at the national palace in August; a total of 50 persons were arrested for subversion, conspiracy, and illegal arms charges since April—relative stability had come to Haiti since the U.S. occupation in 1994. The military regime that was overthrown by the United States had killed with impunity at least 4,000 people and tortured many more. Now terror no longer ruled the streets. A free and open election brought a peaceful transition of power; the exodus of thousands of Haitian boat people had ended; and the armed forces had been disbanded.

By late 1996 much remained to be accomplished. Haiti still was a desperately poor nation. The newly installed police force had been unable to stop a crime wave. The parliament had yet to pass measures that were a condition for more than $300 million in foreign aid. The former army members, while demobilized, were still a problem. But the age-old cycle of violence with impunity appeared to have been checked.

RICHARD C. SCHROEDER, *Freelance Writer*

HAITI • Information Highlights

Official Name: Republic of Haiti.
Location: Caribbean.
Area: 10,714 sq mi (27 750 km^2).
Population (mid-1996 est.): 7,300,000.
Chief City (1987 est.): Port-au-Prince, the capital, 797,000 (incl. suburbs).
Government: *Head of state,* René Préval, president (took office Feb. 7, 1996). *Head of government,* Rosny Smarth, prime minister (took office March 1996). *Legislature*—National Assembly: Senate and Chamber of Deputies.
Monetary Unit: Gourde (14.10 gourdes equal U.S.$1, December 1994).
Gross Domestic Product (1994 est. U.S.$): $5,600,000,000 (purchasing power equivalent).
Economic Index (1995, 1990 = 100): *Consumer Prices,* all items, 227.6; food, 216.4.
Foreign Trade (1995 U.S.$): *Imports,* $696,000,000; *exports,* $154,000,000.

HONG KONG

Hong Kong continued in 1996 the transition from British to Chinese rule that would become effective in mid-1997. Overseeing the final stages of the transition was the Preparatory Committee (PC), a Chinese-appointed body of 150 members installed in January. In November the PC elected a 400-member Selection Committee, which on December 11 chose Tung Chee-hwa, a shipping tycoon and vice-chairman of the PC, as chief executive. Tung will succeed the British governor, Christopher Patton, when China resumes sovereignty. (*See* HONG KONG: A TIME OF DRAMATIC CHANGE, page 44.)

HOUSING

The housing market in the United States rebounded in 1996 after its 1995 setback. Sales of both new and previously occupied homes accelerated, starts of conventionally built single-family as well as multifamily structures strengthened, production of mobile homes held at a historically high level, and the residential remodeling market resumed positive growth after a downshift the previous year. The 1996 housing expansion was based broadly across the U.S. regions as both production levels and home prices rose, and the U.S. home-ownership rate approached an all-time high in the process.

On the international scene, both Canada and Japan enjoyed major housing expansion.

Market Segments Expand. The rebound in housing-market activity reflected a general pickup in the U.S. economy and an improvement in financial-market conditions. The U.S. Federal Reserve eased monetary policy during the latter half of 1995 and early 1996, reducing short-term interest rates. Long-term interest rates fell as well, and the rate on 30-year fixed-rate mortgages receded to a historically low level of 7% in early 1996. At the same time, the rate on one-year adjustable-rate mortgages receded to only 5.2%.

The declines in interest rates stimulated home buying and other types of economic activity. By midyear, both the housing market and the overall economy were expanding briskly, generating strong growth in national employment and national income. This strengthening process revived fears of inflation and put upward pressure on long-term interest rates during the summer, but the Federal Reserve held short-term rates steady throughout the year. Growth of housing and the economy subsided toward a more sustainable pace in the latter part of the year, and long-term interest rates receded as well. At year's end, fixed-rate mortgages were around 7.6% and adjustable-rate mortgages were about two percentage points lower.

For the year as a whole, sales of new and existing homes totaled 4.82 million—a U.S. record. Starts of new conventionally built housing units (excluding mobile homes) rose by 9% to 1.475 million, for the best year of the 1990s. Single-family units accounted for nearly 80% of total starts, while production of apartments in multifamily structures rose to 310,000 units—the best since 1989.

About 85% of new apartments in multifamily structures were built for the rental market in 1996. The rest were built for the condominium market, where individual units are owned by their occupants and there is common ownership of some open space and facilities. The condo share of the multifamily market peaked in the early 1980s at nearly 40%, and has been trending downward for more than a decade.

In addition to the large volume of conventionally built new housing units, about 300,000 mobile homes were placed for residential use in the United States during 1996, close to the record pace of 1995. About half of these were double- or triple-wide units that provided space comparable to that of many conventionally built homes; a decade earlier, only about 30% of new mobile homes were of this larger type. The average price of mobile homes was about $40,000 in 1996, compared with $165,000 for new conventionally built single-family homes.

Outlays for remodeling of existing housing units rose moderately in 1996, posting a record volume of about $116 billion. Spending for maintenance and repair accounted for roughly one third of total residential remodeling, while additions and alterations (including replacements of major items such as roofs and heating systems) made up the balance. In total, remodeling outlays were equivalent to about 75% of the dollar volume of outlays on new housing units, up from about 50% in the mid-1980s.

Housing Characteristics. More than 90% of conventionally built single-family homes started in the United States during 1996 were detached units on individual lots; as in previous years, attached (townhouse) units captured less than one tenth of the single-family market.

The average size of new single-family homes rose to a new record in 1996, exceeding

2,100 sq ft (195 m^2). Nearly one third of new homes had four or more bedrooms, and about half of the units had at least 2.5 bathrooms. More than four fifths of new homes had central air conditioning, nearly two thirds had fireplaces, and about three fourths had garages that could hold two or more cars.

The average size of apartments in multifamily structures also hit a new record in 1996, exceeding 1,100 sq ft (102 m^2). About 70% of new apartments had two or more bedrooms, and more than half of new units had at least two bathrooms.

Regional Balance. The geographic composition of U.S. housing-market activity changed little in 1996, as all regions posted good gains in absolute terms. Housing starts in the beleaguered Northeast region rose a bit faster than the national average, but this region still accounted for only about 8% of the national total—half the market share registered a decade earlier. On the other side of the country, the Pacific census division (including California) hung onto about one eighth of the national market, down from a record high of 23% as recently as 1989. The Mountain states also retained about one eighth of the national market, double the share claimed in the late 1980s. The huge South region accounted for about 45% of national housing starts, off marginally from 1995, while the Midwest edged up to nearly 22% of the total.

Average prices of single-family homes rose in all nine census divisions during the year. The U.S. average was up by 3.2%, with the most rapid rise in the East North Central division, where the average price shot up by 6.4%. As in other recent years, the weakest price performance occurred in the Northeast region (both New England and the Middle Atlantic states) and in the Pacific census division, where price increases barely averaged 1%. Indeed, average prices contracted somewhat in the states of Connecticut, Rhode Island, California, and Hawaii.

Home Ownership Rises. The U.S. home-ownership rate rose for the second consecutive year in 1996, averaging 65.4% for the first three quarters of the year. This rate was 1.4 percentage points higher than in 1994 and was close to the record high of 65.6% posted in 1980. By late 1996, there were more than 66 million U.S. home owners, up from 56 million a decade earlier.

Demographic factors and excellent affordability conditions in the single-family housing market contributed to the increase in the U.S. home-ownership rate in 1996. The National Home Ownership Strategy announced by the Bill Clinton administration in 1994 also contributed to the upward movements in both 1995 and 1996. This strategy enlists private industry, national nonprofit organizations, nonprofit community groups, and state and local groups in a concerted effort to help middle- and low-income families, racial and ethnic minorities, families with children, and young adults overcome a variety of barriers to home ownership. The strategy set a goal of 67.5% for the U.S. home-ownership rate by the year 2000. In view of recent progress, this target certainly seems attainable. Indeed, the target is below current home-ownership rates in some countries, including Australia, Great Britain, Ireland, and Israel.

International Comparisons. In the United States the real (inflation-adjusted) value of residential fixed investment—including production of new housing units as well as remodeling of the existing housing stock—grew by 5.2% in 1996, following a contraction of about 2% in 1995. This solid growth maintained the ratio of housing investment to total national investment (both public and private) at 22% and lifted the ratio of housing investment to gross domestic product (GDP) to 4%.

Housing investment also posted positive growth during 1996 in the other major industrialized countries. Growth was relatively slow in major European economies (Germany, France, Great Britain, and Italy) but the expansion was quite robust in Canada (9%) and Japan (15.4%), where housing investment had contracted sharply in 1995.

The share of housing in total national investment was quite similar to that in the United States in Canada, France, Great Britain, and Italy, ranging from 20.5% in France to 23.5% in Great Britain. This ratio was the highest in Germany, where housing accounted for one third of total national investment, up slightly from 1994 and 1995. The ratio of housing investment to GDP was also the highest in Germany, holding at 7.3% for the third consecutive year.

In Japan, where housing investment grew most rapidly in 1996, the housing share of GDP moved up to 5.5%. Even so, the housing share of total national investment was a relatively low 17.7% in Japan, reflecting the fact that nonresidential fixed investment (primarily plant and equipment) is a much larger share of total economic activity than in the other industrialized countries. This pattern largely reflects public policies that favor investment in the industrial sector.

DAVID F. SEIDERS
National Association of Home Builders

HUMAN RIGHTS

Aside from areas brutalized by ethnic strife, two countries in Asia—China and Myanmar (formerly Burma)—attracted the most intense international concern in 1996 because of recurring violations of basic rights. Other governments cited for perennial human-rights violations included Chad, Cuba, Guatemala, Indonesia, Iran, Iraq, Libya, Nigeria, North Korea, Saudi Arabia, Turkey, and Vietnam.

China. In its 1996 annual survey of human-rights practices worldwide, the U.S. State Department once again strongly indicted China for "widespread and well-documented human-rights abuses." The report pointedly rebutted a common view that China's economic growth automatically would reward China's people with basic freedoms—such as freedom of religion, the press, and assembly. "The experience of China in the past few years," the report said, "demonstrates that while economic growth, trade, and social mobility create an improved standard of living, they cannot by themselves bring about greater respect for human rights in the absence of a willingness by political authorities to abide by fundamental international norms."

In March, Amnesty International published a 121-page report titled "No One Is Safe: Political Repression and Abuse of Power in the 1990s," stating that despite economic gains, human-rights abuses continued in China on a "massive scale." Speaking in Hong Kong, Amnesty's Secretary-General Pierre Sane appealed to foreign businesspeople to use their leverage positively, not just out of altruistic motives but out for their own long-term commercial benefit.

Beijing accused both the State Department and Amnesty of interfering in China's internal affairs and fabricating falsehoods to "mislead world public opinion and damage China's prestige." Later, at the annual spring meeting of the United Nations (UN) Commission on Human Rights in Geneva, China succeeded in quashing a relatively mild resolution expressing concern over Beijing's violations of fundamental freedoms. It was the sixth year in a row that China escaped censure at the UN's main human-rights forum.

Myanmar. The military government that seized power in Myanmar in September 1988 and has ruled there since as the unelected State Law and Order Restoration Council (SLORC) won a measure of international legitimacy from its neighbors in July, when it gained observer status in the Association of Southeast Asian Nations (ASEAN). A renewed appeal for outside pressure on the SLORC was made by Aung San Suu Kyi, the 1991 Nobel Peace laureate and leader of the country's democratic forces, who was released from house arrest in mid-1995 but still was far from free. In a videotaped message smuggled out of Myanmar, she called for economic sanctions against the regime.

Though lacking in global strategic or economic significance, Myanmar has become a major test case of what the world community can or should do about a pariah government. Southeast Asian governments favor a policy of "constructive engagement," by which the SLORC would be persuaded to move away from authoritarianism in a gradual way that would not seriously disturb the status quo. Evidence cited against this approach was the SLORC's eight-year record of repression, including its wholesale arrests of pro-democracy activists in September.

A new U.S. law passed in September 1996 authorizes the president to block new private investment in Myanmar in case of "large-scale repression or violence against" the country's pro-democracy movement. Aware of Washington's traditional reluctance to impose sanctions, U.S. activists launched a boycott campaign at state and local governmental levels. The state of Massachusetts and seven municipalities adopted selective purchasing laws that bar contracts with corporations that do business in Myanmar. In addition, some institutional investors, coordinated in part by the New York–based Interfaith Center on Corporate Responsibility, persuaded a number of companies—including Levi Strauss, Eddie Bauer, and Amoco—to leave Myanmar.

Other News. A particular global problem—government-sponsored torture—was the focus of a Stockholm conference in October. Representatives—including medical doctors, police officials, and human-rights experts—from 50 nations participated....At its ministerial-level meeting in Singapore in early December, the World Trade Organization (WTO) again rejected setting up a committee to consider linking trade privileges to respect for certain human rights affecting the workforce, such as the abolition of child labor and bonded labor....Other problems that gained greater recognition were female genital mutilation—a practice common in some African countries that has spread with emigration—and the sale of children for prostitution, pornography, and adoption.

ROBERT A. SENSER, *Freelance Writer*

HUNGARY

During 1996, Hungary's governing coalition survived despite its tough austerity program, broad public disquiet, and a serious financial scandal concerning its privatization program. On the international front, Hungary signed important bilateral treaties with Slovakia and Romania and made significant progress toward future membership in the North Atlantic Treaty Organization (NATO) and the European Union (EU).

Politics. The government coalition between the Hungarian Socialist Party and the liberal Alliance of Free Democrats was maintained despite growing disputes and divisions over the radical austerity measures announced in March. In an effort to curtail state spending, Budapest cut back on its extensive social-security program, which led to protests by traditional socialists and trade-union leaders. Peter Medgyessy, who became finance minister after the resignation of Lajos Bokros, pledged to continued the tough economic measures. And the ruling Socialists, who reelected Prime Minister Gyula Horn as party chairman in April, reaffirmed their support for the economic-stabilization program.

A major government scandal was uncovered in October. Illegal financial dealings in the Privatization and Holding Company, which conducted the privatization program, led to the dismissal of the board of directors and the forced resignation of Finance Minister Bokros. The authorities vowed to make the privatization process more open to the public in order to avoid future scandals.

Although new general elections were not scheduled until 1998, the governing coalition was coming under increasing strain as the year came to a close. With the former governing party, the Hungarian Democratic Forum, splitting into two parliamentary factions, the nationalist opposition, the Hungarian Smallholders Party, increased its public influence.

Economy. Hungary's economy continued to perform reasonably well during 1996, although the growth rate slowed from 1.5% in 1995 to about 1% in 1996. Foreign capital investment in Hungary also was projected to decrease, although the authorities claimed that prospects for foreign investment would grow because of the country's improved credit rating in international financial circles. The year also saw some positive economic indicators. Inflation was expected to fall from 28% in 1995 to about 22% for 1996; and with the country's exports increasing by some 10%, the foreign-trade deficit was projected to decline.

HUNGARY• Information Highlights

Official Name: Republic of Hungary.
Location: East-central Europe.
Area: 35,919 sq mi (93 030 km²).
Population (mid-1996 est.): 10,200,000.
Chief Cities (Jan. 1, 1994 est.): Budapest, the capital, 1,995,696; Debrecen, 217,706; Miskolc, 189,655.
Government: *Head of state,* Arpád Goncz, president (elected August 1990). *Head of government,* Gyula Horn, prime minister (took office July 1994). *Legislature* (unicameral)—National Assembly.
Monetary Unit: Forint (165.13 forints equal U.S.$1, Dec. 31, 1996).
Gross Domestic Product (1994 est. U.S.$): $58,800,000,000 (purchasing power parity).
Economic Indexes (1995, 1990 = 100): *Consumer Prices,* all items, 309.7; food, 304.3. *Industrial Production,* 86.
Foreign Trade (1995 U.S.$): *Imports,* $15,046,000,000; *exports,* $12,435,000,000.

Budapest also continued to make progress in paying off its large foreign debt—the largest per-capita debt in Eastern Europe. On the domestic front, the government pledged to continue reforms in the pension and health-insurance systems and to scale down state expenditures on industry and welfare.

Foreign Affairs. In May, Hungary and Slovakia exchanged ratification documents on a bilateral treaty that helped to ease years of tension and mistrust, particularly over the status of the Hungarian minority in southern Slovakia. A treaty also was signed with Romania in September after years of tough negotiations. Budapest pledged to respect the inviolability of current borders between the two states, while Bucharest agreed to respect the rights of the large Hungarian minority in the Romanian province of Transylvania. Disagreements over this treaty had slowed down the progress of both countries in seeking NATO and EU membership.

Hungary had met most of the criteria for membership, including political stability, market reform, and the restructuring of civil-military relations in line with NATO standards. It was very active in NATO's Partnership for Peace program, and it was a participant in the NATO operation in Bosnia and Croatia.

JANUSZ BUGAJSKI
Center for Strategic and International Studies

ICELAND

In 1996, Iceland elected a new president, enjoyed a modest economic recovery, and witnessed a serious volcanic eruption.

Presidential Election. In June, Icelanders elected a new president, Ólafur Ragnar Grímsson. Grímsson received about 41% of the vote to defeat three other candidates—Pétur Hafstein, a high-court judge; Gudrún

Photos, © Michael Probst/AP/Wide World Photos

In the fall of 1996, a powerful volcanic eruption occurred beneath Iceland's Vatnajökull glacier, leading to heavy flooding. Rebuilding costs were estimated at more than $15 million.

Agnarsdóttir, a physician and former member of parliament for the feminist Women's Party; and businessman Ástthór Magnússon. Unlike his immediate predecessors in Iceland's apolitical presidency, Grímsson had a background in politics. A professor of political science at the University of Iceland, he was the former leader of the left-wing People's Alliance (1980–83) and minister of finance in a center-left coalition government (1988–91), as well as a ten-year veteran in the parliament.

Economy. The economy began to show signs of a slight but clear upturn. Gross domestic product (GDP) was expected to reach $7.5 billion in 1996—about 7% higher than in 1995. The purchasing power of disposable income was up 3% in 1995—the first rise in four years—and a similar rise was forecast for 1996. Unemployment fell to 4.4% in the second quarter of 1996, compared to 5.3% in the same period of 1995. Inflation rose slightly, running at about 2.5% in mid-1996.

Catch management via the quota system began to pay off. The quota for cod, Iceland's most important commercial species, was raised for the first time ever, from 155,000 tons during the 1995–96 fishing season to 186,000 tons in 1996–97. The quota was expected to be set at 200,000 tons for 1997–98, a rise that was expected to yield an estimated extra $30 million in export earnings. Quotas for other commercial species, however, generally were cut for 1996–97, with the exception of capelin, for which a record quota of 1.1 million tons was allowed. In spite of this improvement in fishing prospects in Icelandic waters, Icelandic fishery companies increasingly were looking to international waters for bigger catches and higher earnings.

Volcanic Eruption. On September 30 a powerful volcanic eruption began beneath Iceland's Vatnajökull, the largest continental glacier in Europe. The eruption melted a large cleft in the glacier, and by the time volcanic activity ceased on October 13, huge amounts of water had accumulated beneath the glacier. On November 5 the water forced its way from under the ice cap in a massive glacial "burst," causing major flooding. While minor bursts are a regular occurrence in the area, this was by far the most destructive of the 20th century; it swept away roads and destroyed bridges, cutting off the main route to the southeast.

ANNA YATES, *Freelance Writer, Reykjavík*

ICELAND • Information Highlights

Official Name: Republic of Iceland.
Location: North Atlantic Ocean.
Area: 39,768 sq mi (103 000 km²).
Population (mid-1996 est.): 300,000.
Chief City (December 1995): Reykjavík, the capital, 104,258.
Government: *Head of state,* Ólafur Ragnar Grímsson, president (took office August 1996). *Head of government,* Davíd Oddsson, prime minister (took office April 1991). *Legislature* (unicameral)—Althing.
Monetary Unit: Króna (66.62 krónur equal U.S.$1, selling rate, October 1996).
Gross Domestic Product (1994 est. U.S.$): $4,500,000,000 (purchasing power parity).
Economic Index (1995, 1990 = 100): *Consumer Prices,* all items, 119.0; food, 106.7.
Foreign Trade (1995 U.S.$): *Imports,* $1,755,000,000; *exports,* $1,803,000,000.

INDIA

National parliamentary elections in India in April–May 1996 brought a left-of-center coalition government to power. The new Parliament and cabinet, headed by Prime Minister H.D. Deve Gowda (*see* BIOGRAPHY), featured more low-caste members than ever before. Other notable 1996 events in India included widespread charges of corruption and indictments brought against major national politicians, including former Prime Minister P.V. Narasimha Rao. Peaceful elections were held in Jammu and Kashmir, and India refused to sign the Nuclear Test Ban Treaty.

National Politics. Elections for India's 11th Lok Sabha (lower house of Parliament) were held April 27 through May 7 with a 56.7% turnout. Enforcing strict guidelines established by the Supreme Court, the Election Commission exercised careful watch over party finances and use of official resources. "Divisive" slogans appealing to caste or religious intolerance were forbidden. In states such as Bihar where upper castes traditionally prevented lower castes from voting, the police and army were used to ensure that all registered voters could exercise their franchise. Many observed that these elections were India's fairest in years.

As predicted, no party won a majority of the 545 seats. The right-wing Hindu nationalist Bharatiya Janata Party (BJP) captured 160 seats and—with the support of the equally nationalist Shiv Sena and a few small groups—claimed a total of 194. The Congress Party, which has ruled for most of India's 49 years of independence, got only 136 seats and saw its popular vote drop from 36.5% in 1991 to 28%. The United Front (UF), a loose coalition of left-of-center parties headed by the Janata Dal and composed mainly of regional leaders, won 111 seats; the Marxists won 43. The remainder went to smaller regional parties and independent candidates.

In keeping with parliamentary tradition, President Shankar Dayal Sharma swore in BJP leader Atal Behari Vajpayee as prime minister on May 18. When it became apparent that the BJP could not win a vote of confidence that was scheduled for May 28, Vajpayee resigned. No other parties were willing to align themselves with the BJP's Hindu nationalist platform. The UF—with the support of Congress, the Marxists, and three smaller parties—then claimed a majority. On June 1, H.D. Deve Gowda, former Janata Dal chief minister of the southern state of Karnataka, became prime minister. Initially it was assumed this disparate coalition would be relatively short-lived. Given internal problems faced by both the Congress Party and BJP due to allegations of corruption and challenges to their national leadership, however, by year's end few expected major challenges in the immediate future.

Three main factors determined the electoral outcome. Three months prior to polling, the Central Bureau of Investigation (CBI) released results of several corruption investigations implicating top leaders from almost all parties except the Marxists. Among those named were BJP President L. K. Advani and members of the Congress government's cabinet, including former Prime Minister Rao's closest advisers. Rao himself escaped charges until after the elections. Corruption in the mainstream parties, a major issue in voters' minds over the previous several years, was

© Sondeep Shankar/Saba

An estimated 590 million Indian voters, below, *went to the polls in more than 543 constituencies in April–May 1996. The Congress Party, led by Prime Minister P.V. Narasimha Rao,* left, *suffered a major setback. Rao himself remained under investigation for political corruption.*

© Bartholomew/Gamma-Liaison

INDIA • Information Highlights

Official Name: Republic of India.
Location: South Asia.
Area: 1,269,340 sq mi (3 287 590 km²).
Population (mid-1996 est.): 949,600,000.
Chief Cities (1991 census): New Delhi, the capital, 301,297; Mumbai (Bombay), 9,925,891; Delhi, 7,206,704; Calcutta, 4,399,819.
Government: *Head of state,* Shankar Dayal Sharma, president (elected July 1992). *Head of government,* H.D. Deve Gowda, prime minister (took office June 1, 1996). *Legislature*—Parliament: Rajya Sabha (Council of States) and Lok Sabha (People's Assembly).
Monetary Unit: Rupee (35.700 rupees equal U.S.$1, official rate, Dec. 2, 1996).
Gross Domestic Product (1994 est. U.S.$): $1,253,900,000,000 (purchasing power parity).
Economic Indexes (1995, 1990 = 100): *Consumer Prices,* all items, 164.5; food, 173.3. *Industrial Production,* 131.
Foreign Trade (1995 U.S.$): *Imports,* $34,402,000,000; *exports,* $30,542,000,000.

associated primarily with the Congress Party. Never had its popular vote been so low. Although the BJP was expected to make stronger gains in India's Hindi-speaking heartland, Advani's fate—along with the public's reaction against fundamentalism—resulted in only a small increase in its support.

Additionally, in attempts to defeat the BJP, the Congress Party formed questionable alliances with regional parties, resulting in defections from its ranks. In Tamil Nadu it was allied with the AIADMK party of Chief Minister Jayaram Jayalalitha, which was renowned for flagrant abuses of power and public funds. Southern Congress members left, forming their own Tamil Maanila Congress and a coalition with the opposition Dravida Munnetra Kazagham (DMK), which was part of the UF. In Madhya Pradesh popular Congressman Madhav Rao Scindia was expelled from the party after being named in the CBI inquiries. Maintaining innocence, he formed the Madhya Pradesh Vikas Party, which successfully challenged the Congress Party in one of the latter's traditional strongholds. In the states of West Bengal, Maharashtra, Uttar Pradesh, Andhra Pradesh, and Bihar, local Congress Party leaders challenged Rao and his supporters.

Finally, there was a shift away from known national leaders to those with a regional base, who, according to polls, the electorate felt were closer to the nation's grassroots. In the new Parliament, almost 52% of the seats were held by farmers; "members of backward classes" occupied 23.3% of the seats; and 293 members were serving their first term. Analyses showed an erosion of the traditional "vote banks," including minorities and lower castes, on which the Congress Party relied. In essence, voters no longer could be "bought" with promises.

Disarray in the ranks of the Congress Party grew after the elections. Rao, who earlier had portrayed himself as above corruption, was implicated in several kickback schemes during the summer. Indictments were handed down in a major case brought against businessman Lakhubhai Pathak. Charges also were brought against Rao's son, P.V. Prabhakar Rao, for receiving illegal foreign payments. Other indictments were expected. Additionally, former Telecommunications Minister Sukh Ram was found holding more than $1 million in cash at his home. Though Ram maintained the funds were electoral contributions, inquiries—including evidence from Ram's own diaries—showed they were kickbacks from businesses bidding on government contracts. Though many in the Congress Party called for Ram's expulsion from the party, they also wondered when these revelations would end. Congress Party Treasurer Sitaram Kesri was named as the new party president, replacing Rao, who, however, retained his parliamentary seat. Rebuilding the party and public confidence were major concerns.

The BJP, too, faced problems. The party split in the state of Gujarat, where the assembly was dissolved in September and president's rule imposed until fresh elections could be held within the next six months. Similar problems emerged in the neighboring states of Maharashtra and Rajasthan as well as Uttar Pradesh. At issue were attempts by more radical Hindus to take over state cadres and also accusations of corruption against party members.

With two major parties facing internal problems, the outlook for the UF government's survival became brighter. However, Gowda's government would have to walk a fine line between its left and moderate flanks. The major sources of dissension could be center-state relations and economic liberalization. Center-state relations have been strained for the past three decades, with states complaining that India's federal system is too centralized. The UF promised a "new federalism" that would return programs and power to the states. However, because of states' reluctance to raise their own revenues despite initiating populist schemes, such as employment programs and free school lunches, many were virtually bankrupt. The central government, too, was under pressure to reduce its expenditures, and since states were unwilling to take on more programs without federal help, various observers felt little actually would be decentralized despite the strength of regional forces within the UF.

Second, Marxists, some members of the Janata Dal, and other UF participants were concerned about economic liberalization. Issues included whether and which public enterprises should be privatized, the extent to which foreign investment should be allowed to compete with Indian capital and in which areas, fear that liberalization would result in greater poverty and inequality, and a general concern over foreign pressure on what are seen as domestic-policy matters. Though the UF's program and the 1996–97 budget committed the government to continue the previous cabinet's policies, how far it would be able to do so was questionable.

State Politics. State Assembly elections were held in violence-torn Jammu and Kashmir in September. Despite intimidation by separatist militants, a remarkable 53% of voters turned out to elect a pro-union National Conference government. The election raised cautious hope that guns would be replaced by negotiation. New Delhi promised to work constructively with the new government to define specific forms of autonomy within Kashmir's "special status" in the constitution.

Elections also were held in the northern state of Uttar Pradesh in October. No party got a majority in the 425-seat state assembly. The BJP, which had hoped for a clear win, actually lost three seats from its 1993 total of 177. The Samajwadi Party was second with 110 seats, and the "low caste" Bahujan Samaj Party (BSP) got 67. Despite parliamentary convention, which would require the governor to ask the BJP to prove its majority as was done for the national Parliament in May, president's rule was imposed by New Delhi, which claimed no stable government could be formed. This was a controversial move since the UF had moved during the summer to restrict the center's powers to dismiss state governments. It accused the Congress Party of misuse of this constitutional provision, which should be a tool only in situations of extreme instability or a breakdown of law and order.

During the Uttar Pradesh (UP) campaign, statehood for the "hill districts"—called Uttarakhand—was agreed to by the UF but required passage by Parliament. This had been agreed to by the UP legislature in 1993 and, in principle, was supported by the center without any formal approval due to fears that similar demands in the states of Bihar, Assam, Madhya Pradesh, Maharashtra, and Andhra Pradesh would intensify. Though original states' boundaries were drawn along major linguistic lines, many included ethnic subgroups that in recent years have fought for autonomy mainly to control their own wealth and resources. The affected states are India's most populous, a fact that sympathetic observers feel has made them almost ungovernable. Uttarakhand's population is 6.5 million and that of other areas ranges from 3.5 million to more than 20 million, which could make them viable states. Few worry anymore about India's unity, but there is concern about a lack of clarity regarding autonomy issues.

The Economy. The nation's economic growth slowed from 7% in 1995 to about 6% in 1996. During the first half of 1996, exports declined somewhat due partially to aging infrastructure that made it difficult for exporters to meet deadlines. More importantly, the government's borrowing remained high at 10% of the gross domestic product (GDP), cutting into capital availability for the private sector. Forty-seven percent of all revenues went to debt servicing. Program commitments in the budget indicated little chance for reducing borrowing.

Agriculture received an increase, primarily for irrigation, and subsidies were raised on fertilizers. Loans to farmers through the National Bank for Agriculture and Rural Development were doubled. Investments in agriculture had stagnated over the previous several years; thus these increases were meant to increase productivity. Also important was Prime Minister Gowda's strong commitment to farmers. Though India now produced a surplus of wheat and rice, other food crops had not kept pace.

Despite a critical need, the budget did not allocate any significant additional funds for transportation, roads, or power. It was hoped that the private sector, with foreign collaboration, would fill the gap. The controversial agreement with Enron to build a power plant in Maharashtra was back on track, hopefully restoring foreign confidence in Indian investments. Especially problematic was the financial situation of most of the states. Though some states—such as Andhra Pradesh, Tamil Nadu, Haryana, and Madhya Pradesh—raised excise taxes and froze positions, these measures were not enough, especially since New Delhi probably would not increase its contributions to the state programs.

Budgetary constraints continued to raise serious questions about the state of India's military strength. Once a popular career choice, the services faced severe recruitment problems. Real funding had declined since 1990 and stood at 2.39% of the GDP, compared with the neighbors that India views as its main security threats—China (5.63%) and

Up-to-date military equipment, including Prithvi missiles (right), was displayed during the January 1996 Republic Day parade in New Delhi. India's military policy became a subject of conjecture after the nation refused to sign the Nuclear Test Ban Treaty.

Pakistan (6.88%). India still owed the former USSR just less than $100 billion for arms purchased in the 1980s. Parliament sanctioned a 20% military-pay increase, but did not add the funds to the military budget. This would cause further diversions from equipment acquisition and maintenance.

Social Issues. Women's groups around the country, particularly in rural areas, called for prohibitions against the sale and consumption of alcohol. As consumption has increased, these groups claim that more men waste hard-earned income on drink; domestic violence rises; and some families are abandoned. In Haryana state the Haryana Vikas (Development) Party captured the state assembly in May in part on a prohibition platform that went into effect in August. Most states do not ban alcohol, but those that do—such as Andhra Pradesh—face huge budget deficits from revenue losses and high enforcement costs as black marketeers meet demand. Consumption of illegal liquor frequently has resulted in blindness and death.

A UNICEF study published in June showed that more children in South Asia are malnourished than in either Africa or China. In India 53% are affected despite relatively good growth rates and food supplies. Contributing factors include mothers who themselves are undernourished and a general lack of education about infants' nutrition. As increased international attention focused on child labor, India faced strong pressure to enforce its laws that prohibit children from working before the age of 14.

Foreign Relations. India's refusal to sign the Nuclear Test Ban Treaty dominated foreign affairs. India has maintained that any treaty should include provisions to eliminate arsenals already held by the big nuclear powers. Two other factors strengthened India's resolve. First was the growth of China's nuclear power and its supply of weapons and technology to neighboring Pakistan. Second was Pakistan's continued nuclear-development program.

Despite speculation, there was no evidence that India has developed any nuclear weapons and, due to cost factors, it probably would not do so in the near future. Additionally, its rocket and space programs have been trimmed, making it even more unlikely. Given India's previous problems with both neighbors, supporting the treaty was considered risky business.

Relations with Bangladesh were "on hold" pending the outcome of Dhaka's June 1996 elections. Issues of concern continued to be the "Friendship Treaty" signed by India and Bangladesh and the sharing of Ganges River waters. The treaty provides for mutual collaboration in a wide range of matters but is seen by Bangladesh as providing its larger neighbor with advantages. Sharing of the Ganges' water revolves around charges that India uses too much during drought years and releases too much from its Farrakka Barrage during heavy monsoons, thus creating either drastic shortages or floods in Bangladesh. India tentatively agreed to adjust its use of the Ganges if Bangladesh provides a transit "corridor" that will permit more direct access to India's northeast states.

ARUNA NAYYAR MICHIE
Kansas State University

INDONESIA

Even though it was likely that Suharto would accept a seventh five-year term as president of Indonesia in 1998, the politics of succession dominated the political scene in 1996.

Politics. Two events in 1996 brought home forcefully the fact that Indonesia's long-serving President Suharto was mortal. On April 28 the president's wife died at the age of 72 after a heart attack. Questions arose as to whether the newly widowed Suharto would have the desire to stay on for a seventh term beginning in 1998, when he would be 77 years old. Rumors about the state of the president's health escalated when he traveled to Germany in July for a medical checkup. Although the procedures were described as routine and he was given a public clean bill of health, continuing concerns about his health and speculation about his intentions triggered an urgent debate over succession leading up to the 1997 parliamentary elections.

The government's resolve to prevent any real challenge to its electoral agenda sparked the worst political violence in Indonesia in two decades. The government sought to forestall the possibility that Megawati Sukarnoputri—leader of Indonesia's Democratic Party (PDI) and daughter of Indonesia's first president, Sukarno—might be offered as a presidential candidate herself. Army operatives engineered a PDI party coup to remove her from office. Her supporters refused to leave the PDI's headquarters in Jakarta, and on July 27 it was stormed by army-backed partisans of the new PDI leadership. Fighting spread into the streets, and the so-called "July 27 Affair" claimed at least five lives. Although Megawati was sidelined from politics, the affair underlined the pervasive uneasiness about Indonesia's future. The government quickly fastened blame on leftist subversives. In fact, the "July 27 Affair" was the latest of several violent incidents that suggested a more general sense of civil unrest.

Another element of the succession debate was the unprecedented rise to army prominence of President Suharto's son-in-law, Prabowo Subianto, who went from colonel to major general between September 1995 and August 1996. The 44-year-old Prabowo was placed in command of an augmented and expanded special-forces unit and was in line for a major regional command as the next step toward senior army leadership. He was credited with leading the May 1996 rescue by special forces of hostages being held in Irian Jaya.

Economy. Despite President Suharto's reiteration of Indonesia's adherence to a liberal trading regime and the World Bank's endorsement of Indonesia's latest deregulation package, the government's commitment to a free and open economy was called into question in 1996. The issue was raised by a presidential decree establishing a national car project—70% owned by the president's son, Hutomo "Tommy" Mandala Putra, and 30% owned by South Korea's Kia Motors. The enterprise was enjoying exclusive tax and tariff exemptions that gave it a great comparative price advantage over locally assembled foreign cars. Japanese automotive companies, now controlling 90% of the market, were particularly outraged. Rather than being "national," however, the first 45,000 units were imported directly from Korea. This set the stage for a major challenge to Indonesia's policy by Japan, the United States, and the European Union (EU) in the World Trade Organization (WTO).

At the macroeconomic level, Indonesia continued to demonstrate the robust growth that has led to its listing by the U.S. Commerce Department as one of the ten "big emerging markets." Real gross-domestic-product (GDP) growth in 1995 was 8.07%, up from 1994's 7.48%. Per-capita GDP was $1,023, compared with $920 in 1994.

Foreign Affairs. The international status of Indonesia's East Timor province came to world attention again in 1996 with the awarding of the Nobel Peace Prize jointly to East Timor's Roman Catholic Bishop Carlos Filipe Ximenes Belo and José Ramos Horta. Bishop Belo has been an open critic of Indonesian rule over the former Portuguese colony and a defender of the rights of the indigenous Timorese. Horta is a Sydney, Australia–based exiled spokesperson for Timorese independence. In making the award, the Nobel committee charged Indonesia with "systematically

INDONESIA • Information Highlights

Official Name: Republic of Indonesia.
Location: Southeast Asia.
Area: 741,097 sq mi (1 919 440 km²).
Population (mid-1996 est.): 201,400,000.
Chief Cities (1990 census): Jakarta, the capital, 8,222,515; Surabaya, 2,473,272; Bandung, 2,056,915; Medan, 1,730,052.
Government: *Head of state and government,* Suharto, president (took office for sixth five-year term March 1993). *Legislature* (unicameral)—House of Representatives.
Monetary Unit: Rupiah (2,362.00 rupiahs equal U.S.$1, Dec. 31, 1996).
Gross Domestic Product (1994 est. U.S.$): $619,400,000,000 (purchasing power parity).
Economic Indexes (1995, 1990 = 100): *Consumer Prices,* all items, 153.7; food, 156.3. *Industrial Production,* 107.
Foreign Trade (1995 U.S.$): *Imports,* $40,918,000,000; *exports,* $45,417,000,000.

oppressing" the East Timorese people and hoped that its action would lead to a diplomatic resolution of the problem of self-determination. By late 1996, however, the United Nations–sponsored meetings between Indonesia and Portugal had produced no Indonesian compromise on sovereignty.

Indonesia did compromise on a long-standing territorial dispute with Malaysia when it agreed to submit to the International Court of Justice the question of the islands of Sipadan and Ligatan on the border of Malaysia's Sabah state and Indonesia's East Kalimantan province.

Indonesian-U.S. relations became an issue in the U.S. presidential campaign. It was revealed that thousands of dollars had been funneled to the Democratic National Committee from the Sino-Indonesian Riady family's business conglomerate, the Lippo Group. Critics of the possibly illegal gifts quickly raised questions as to whether improper influence had been brought to bear on U.S. policy toward Indonesia, particularly a weakening of the U.S. stance toward Indonesia's human-rights policy.

DONALD E. WEATHERBEE
University of South Carolina

INDUSTRIAL PRODUCTION

Output of U.S. mines, factories, utilities, and farms rose solidly and even—in some instances—strongly during 1996, keeping supplies of raw materials and processed goods well ahead of demand and contributing greatly to a low inflation rate.

Excluding the output of farms, the level of production rose more than 3% over 1995, and was especially strong during the second quarter. Although production slid in October, most economists viewed it as a temporary event, tied to early snowstorms in the Midwest and a 21-day General Motors strike that caused a 7% month-to-month drop in assembly-plant activity. In spite of the overall solid performance, total industry capacity remained well below the 85% level at which bottlenecks were likely to appear.

Farm output was especially healthy, a somewhat surprising outcome after the year began with precariously low grain stockpiles and bad weather. In the fall, the U.S. Agriculture Department raised its estimate of corn production, the nation's biggest crop, to 9.27 billion bushels—26% greater than in 1995 and the third largest ever.

Technology Leads the Way. The star performance, however, was the powerful thrust of technology, much of it based on the electronic computer chip. It continued not just to transform the old industrial economy and the way people lived, but to breed products and applications undreamed of just a few years before. It left the mechanical age in what seemed the distant past, recreating industrial processes and finding its way invisibly into a range of products that included kitchen toasters, mining machinery, toys, singing greeting cards, hospital operating rooms, automobiles, and schoolrooms. In doing so, it created new possibilities that, experience showed, then would be the source of newer visions.

The number of transistors produced since 1971, according to *USA Today*, roughly equaled the world's population of ants; yet a sense existed that even more astounding things lay ahead. The Cray Research unit of Silicon Graphics introduced a supercomputer able to perform 1 trillion calculations per second, making it the world's fastest commercially available system, a machine that its creators said could compress a current three-month research project into a few days.

The evidence showed up everywhere in the home. A survey for the Conference Board showed that the percentage of families with home computers had climbed to 40%, from 22% in 1990. The survey indicated that more than half of all families had compact-disc players, up from 15% in 1990. About 60% had 25-inch (64-cm) or larger television sets, compared with 38% in 1990; and 70% had telephone answering machines, against only 38% in 1990. Another survey, this one by Find/SVP,

INDUSTRIAL PRODUCTION

Major Industrial Countries
1987 = 100 (seasonally adjusted)

	Canada	France	Germany	Great Britain	Italy	Japan	United States
1990	101.7	110.1	114.5	106.7	109.4	120.6	106.0
1991	97.4	108.7	117.8	102.8	108.4	122.9	104.2
1992	98.5	107.5	115.8	102.7	108.2	115.8	107.7
1993	102.9	103.4	107.1	104.9	105.5	111.0	111.5
1994	110.1	107.3	110.4	110.1	111.0	112.3	118.1
1995	113.8	109.0	111.5	113.0	117.0	115.8	121.9
1996*	116.3	110.0	112.0	114.6	115.0	119.1	127.1

*September preliminary

Source: National data as reported by Department of Commerce a market-research firm, found that households with access to the Internet more than doubled to 14.7 million in one year.

The television, personal computer, and telephone all raced to become a new all-purpose, home-entertainment, communications, master-control device—"smart" enough to operate large appliances, provide security, help with the shopping, allow access to the Internet, and provide assistance with banking and investing. In fact, personal computers already could handle long-distance telephoning, and television sets equipped to access the Internet were on sale at Christmastime. Meanwhile, satellite-delivered television was making competitive inroads into the pay-television industry, where cable companies had invested billions of dollars in what was essentially a 30-year monopoly.

Energy and Motor-Vehicle Production. All these products, magical as they seemed, were rooted in the old industrial base. Without electricity, they would not work; and without coal, hydraulic, and atomic-generating plants, there would be no electric power.

Energy production—80% of it electrical—rose for the fourth straight year to a level 7% higher than in the base measuring year of 1987. The rise was only slight because of increasingly effective usage. Partly reflecting the use of plastic substitutes in many products, the output of U.S. mines remained stuck in a decade-long pattern, neither growing nor shrinking. Coal production, however, ran at an annual rate 4% higher than in 1995, with 903 million tons excavated through October. And the number of rigs exploring for oil and natural gas numbered 841 early in December, 9% more than in the comparable period in 1995.

Reflecting the economy's emphasis on durable goods, the production of industrial machinery and equipment late in the year reached a rate more than double that of the base year. Motor-vehicle production remained strong and profitable, rising slightly—to more than 15 million units for the year. The growth was spurred by a growing household demand for light trucks and vans rather than conventional passenger cars. Because of its size, use of a vast array of other industrial products, and overall importance to the economy, the automotive industry continued as a major focus of attention. That focus was shifting, however, as electronics worked their way into every aspect of consumer and business products. DRI/McGraw-Hill economists put total growth of office and computing equipment at 39.3%, and as the holidays approached there was a waiting list for some models of laptop computers.

INDUSTRIAL PRODUCTION—MAJOR MARKET GROUPS

(1987 = 100; monthly data seasonally adjusted)

	1992	1994	1996*
Consumer Goods			
Total	106.0	113.7	117.8
Durable	103.0	124.2	125.3
Nondurable	106.9	111.2	116.0
Equipment			
Total	112.5	125.3	145.2
Business	123.4	144.9	175.2
Defense and space equipment	84.8	71.9	64.1
Intermediate Products			
Total	99.3	107.3	111.9
Construction	95.2	106.2	114.7
Business supplies	102.0	108.2	110.3
Materials			
Total	109.7	122.0	133.9
Energy	103.7	105.3	109.0
Primary Metals			
Total	101.9	116.4	120.1
Iron and steel	104.7	119.3	124.1
Fabricated Metal Products	99.0	110.5	118.3
Industrial Machinery and Equipment	124.0	157.7	214.5
Electrical Machinery	123.5	154.3	191.0
Transportation Machinery	104.8	115.3	119.0
Motor vehicles and parts	107.4	141.2	146.9
Lumber and Products	95.2	104.0	108.4
Nondurable Manufactures			
Apparel products	95.0	100.1	88.4
Printing and publishing	98.1	100.1	99.1
Chemical products	114.4	121.3	131.7
Food	106.9	113.2	117.5

*November preliminary

Source: Board of Governors of the Federal Reserve System

An Overview. Still, a mystery persisted: Why was the greater efficiency of office machinery and computers not showing up as greater productivity gains? For the first three quarters of 1996, the annual rate of productivity growth, or output per hour, was under 1%—a remarkable deterioration from the 2.7% average rate that existed from 1960 to 1973. Those who studied the problem blamed various factors; most often named was the difficulty of measuring quality improvements in a service economy. Adding credibility to this thesis was the fact that manufacturing productivity continued to grow at a long-term rate of 2.8%. Other causes cited were a slowdown in capital accumulation and the fact that many companies were reducing basic research.

Whatever the figures showed, U.S. industry continued to improve its production and distribution skills. Large manufacturers "outsourced" more parts production to suppliers and exerted increasing pressure on them to perform in terms of quality and price. The development of a global economy put a premium on continued innovation, and the ingenuity of entrepreneurial firms provided it, with start-up firms continually nipping at the heels of the giants.

JOHN CUNNIFF, *The Associated Press*

INTERIOR DESIGN

Casual elegance best described interior design in 1996. Following the dress-down trend prevalent in corporate America, furniture makers relaxed formal designs with low-luster finishes, antiqued hardware, even physical distressing (the intentional altering of a product to make it look older). At the same time, eclecticism retained its strong hold, with a growing number of consumers becoming comfortable with the mix-and-match concept of decorating.

Styles. Dominating the style scene were traditional—18th- and 19th-century—offerings with an emphasis in neoclassical and European country. Councill Craftsman's New Orleans Collection—licensed by the Preservation Resource Center in New Orleans—showed signs of French, English, West Indian, Spanish, even Chinese influences. Thus, a wide variety of designs ran the gamut from an American empire sofa to a pagoda-style china cabinet.

Meanwhile, Century's Towne & Country Collection focused on 18th-century English and French designs for inspiration, exemplified by such pieces as a stately slat-panel bed. (The latter also addressed another important trend of the year—statement beds.) Other traditional groupings of note included Hickory White's European Tour and Bernhardt's Embassy Row.

Contemporary design was not forgotten, however. It was the softer side of contemporary, though, that took the spotlight. Upholstery, for example, was decked out in softer, more tactile fabrics than ever before. Meanwhile, case goods featured fewer sharp angles, opting for more rounded corners and lighter finishes. For example, Ralph Lauren made a push for stainless-steel pieces.

Theme collections—a concept introduced several years earlier—were much in evidence and seemed to hit their stride in 1996. Casual lifestyles collections were offered by many a manufacturer. Richardson Brothers' Door County Collection, for instance, was inspired by Wisconsin's Door county peninsula—home to numerous artist colonies. Likewise, Hammary and Kincaid teamed up to present the Ducks Unlimited Collection. As its name suggests, this line had an environmental twist, too; a percentage of all of the manufacturer's sales was being donated to the foundation for which it was named.

In upholstery, there was an emphasis on comfort—often in the form of deep, low seating pieces. Overscaled, boxy sofas—specifically the high-backed shelter sofa—were found everywhere. Even the sectional—so popular some years back—seemed to make a comeback.

Colors. Green continued to be a hot decorating color in 1996, but it moved away from the sage tone that was so predominant in 1995. Instead, splashes of yellow and blue made olive, lime, eucalyptus, and even avocado the shades of choice. Likewise, red found its way onto a lot of furniture but it, too, was tinted. Red with a touch of orange or yellow, tomato, Spanish red, and barn red were particularly popular.

Meanwhile, as the 21st century approached, a continuing need for stability was calling for a return to the basics, too. The natural colors of the preceding year proved still to be popular, but they were warmed with the addition of deep brown and berry hues. The broadened focus on environmentalism brought metals and minerals into the palette, most notably translated in grays and golds.

Fabrics and Trimmings. The overall trend toward casual elegance also was reflected in upholstery offerings, with fabrics running the gamut from menswear looks to understated opulence. Chenille, in particular, retained its predominance, with some of the more impressive versions being formal chenille damasks that were washed for a more casual effect. Taking formality one step further were baroque-style offerings, characterized by scrollwork and heraldic icons.

There were some holdover favorites—especially in the area of leather—from 1995, too. In addition to the already popular broken-in, bomber-jacket styles, many leathers were teamed with fabrics for a fresh new look in design. As for the finishing touches, they took a more understated approach. Trimmings were selected carefully and used sparingly, making their occasional appearance all the more important.

Materials and Finishes. In 1996 wood finishes were less glossy and a bit darker in order to better achieve a relaxed formal look. This, perhaps, was most evident in solid-wood lines such as Century's Towne & Country and Kincaid's Ducks Unlimited partnership with Hammary.

Additionally, the back-to-nature movement still was apparent—most notably in wicker, iron, and stone pieces. There were some newcomers in terms of materials, however, including woven water hyacinth that was used in much the same way as wicker or rattan.

HEATHER J. PAPER
Freelance Interior Design Writer

INTERNATIONAL TRADE AND FINANCE

The world has slipped almost unnoticed into what Charles Dallara, managing director of the Institute of International Finance (IIF), called a "new era" in international finance. Private money has become far more important to economic development in many poorer countries than "official money."

In 1996 private flows exceeded by some 16 times the amount sent to "emerging markets" by rich nations as foreign aid and by numerous international development banks, such as the World Bank. The money comes, usually indirectly, from tens of millions of individuals in the United States and other industrial nations. Commercial and investment banks, mutual funds, and insurance companies are putting a small portion of their assets into developing countries and former communist nations. Some mutual funds, by design, invest practically all their assets in developing countries, hoping to benefit from the rapid growth in some of these nations.

International Investment. The flow of private money in 1996 into 31 "major" emerging markets reached about $225 billion, up from $208 billion in 1995, according to a forecast by the IIF, a group representing the world's most powerful financial institutions. That compares with $14.1 billion from all official sources—including the World Bank, the International Monetary Fund (IMF), United Nations (UN) agencies, and regional development banks such as the Asian Development Bank. All these numbers are "net," that is, with repayments of loans or income and dividends subtracted from the gross flow. The official net flow was depressed somewhat in 1996 by Mexico's advance repayment to the United States of a large portion of its crisis loan of 1995.

This flow is part of an even larger flow of funds across borders. According to the 1996 *World Investment Report* issued by the Geneva-based UN Conference on Trade and Development (UNCTAD), foreign direct investment—that is, money invested in such items as plant, equipment, offices, stores, and so on—surged by 40% in 1995 to reach $315 billion. This number indicated acceleration at a dramatic pace in the tempo of business globalization. In response to technological and competitive pressures, companies from every developed country and an increasing number of developing countries were making investments, acquisitions, or alliances in other nations. The growth of international investment was far faster than that of international trade. Tempted by rising stock prices, foreigners in addition bought a net $10.6 billion of U.S. stocks in the first half of 1996.

Foreign affiliates of "transnational" corporations now were generating annual sales well in excess of $6 trillion, about $1.5 trillion less than the entire annual output of the United States. Though numbers had not been gathered by late 1996, there apparently was no reversal of the globalization trend.

The rich industrial nations were the key force behind the record foreign-direct-investment flows. In 1995 they invested $270 billion in foreign countries (an increase of 42% over 1994) and received $203 billion (a 53% increase). But there also was a hefty rise in flows into developing countries, to $100 billion. (This sum was smaller than the IIF numbers because it did not include money invested in stock and bond portfolios or bank loans.) Outward investment from developing countries reached $47 billion. Investment flows to Central and Eastern Europe nearly doubled to $12 billion in 1995, after stagnating in 1994.

One implication of the new flow of private money into developing countries is that these countries have become subject to the rigors of private markets. If a nation messes up its economic policies or foreign-exchange rate, foreign private capital will rush to leave when possible or will cease to put in new investment. The result could be a financial crisis, as in Mexico in 1995, or economic stagnation. Another result of the trend has been to shrink the role of such multilateral institutions as the World Bank and IMF. "They are no longer the principal providers of finance to these countries," says Dallara. However, the World Bank remains highly important in the poorest nations of Africa and Asia, where there is a hesitancy to invest private capital. It continues to make loans for population control, health and education development, and some infrastructure. And the IMF helps some of its 181 member nations devise economic-reform programs and policies and comes to the rescue of nations in financial trouble. These two institutions played an important role in 1996 in helping the nations of Eastern Europe and the successor nations to the Soviet Union shift toward free enterprise. The IMF delayed a loan to Russia in an effort to force it to improve its tax-collection procedures.

The *World Investment Report* indicated that transnational corporations are using mergers and acquisitions in a big way to

© Apesteguy-Benainous/Gamma-Liaison

The leaders of the Group of Seven (G-7) industrial nations and of various organizations—including the World Bank and the International Monetary Fund—gathered in Lyon, France, in June 1996. World debt and trade issues were part of the summit's agenda.

become more active globally. Between 1988 and 1995, the value of all cross-border mergers and acquisitions doubled to $229 billion. If transactions involving only majority holdings—excluding those involving portfolio investment and minority-held direct investments—are counted, the sum reaches $135 billion. A large chunk of this took place in Western Europe as the "common market" moved forward. Some $50 billion of West European firms were sold. These firms bought $66 billion worth of foreign companies. U.S. firms were involved in $49 billion of sales and $38 billion of purchases. Japanese companies spent just $4.5 billion on foreign mergers and acquisitions.

Though 1996 numbers were not available by late 1996, mergers and acquisitions apparently continued at a hot pace in 1996. One planned acquisition alone—the purchase of MCI Communications Corp., the second-largest long-distance company in the United States—would cost British Telecommunications some $22 billion in stock and cash if approved. The deal was announced November 3. It brought the total amount of 1996 mergers and acquisitions announced in the United States (not necessarily cross-border deals) to $537 billion as of the start of November, according to Securities Data Company. That compares with $518 billion in all of 1995.

The Economic Picture. From an economic standpoint, 1996 was a modest success. Industrial nations grew about 2.3% on average after inflation, according to an IMF estimate. That was slightly above the pace of the year before, when a financial crisis in Mexico hurt U.S. growth somewhat. Growth in Germany, France, Italy, and Canada was between 1.1% and 1.4%, a slow rate that politically hurt these governments. Britain did better at about 2.2%. Inflation remained subdued in the industrial nations. The United States saw growth of about 2.4%, a bit better than 1995. Inflation ran about 3%, near the same rate as in 1995. The pace of U.S. growth varied considerably, from a 2% annual rate in the first quarter to 4.7% in the second quarter, and back to more modest rates in the second half. That prompted Wall Street to swing back and forth between calling on the Federal Reserve System (the Fed) to cut interest rates to making demands that it boost interest rates. The Fed itself took out some "insurance" against a recession. It dropped short-term interest rates in December 1995 and January 1996, by one quarter of a percentage point each time. Through the balance of the year, it did not yield to the pressures for an interest-rate hike from the 5.25% rate on funds commercial banks lend each other overnight.

U.S. unemployment measured 5.2% in October, and the federal deficit for fiscal 1996 came in at $107.3 billion, down $56.6 billion from the year before and the smallest since fiscal 1981. President Bill Clinton crowed about those statistics during his successful reelection campaign. The U.S. economic expansion passed the five-year mark in March. Clinton reappointed Alan Greenspan to a third term as chairman of the Fed in February, and the Senate confirmed the appointment in June.

Output in the world as a whole grew an estimated 3.8% in real terms in 1996, up from 3.5% in 1995, according to the IMF. The growth rate in Asia, at 8%, was off a little from 1995. China's economy, which had grown 10.2% in 1995, moved up at a less inflationary 9% rate in 1996. Africa, growing at a real 5%, improved from the 3% of 1995. Despite turmoil in Rwanda and surrounding nations, market reforms pushed growth above birthrates for the continent as a whole.

Countries in transition from communism to free enterprise moved, on average, from experiencing a shrinkage in their economies to real growth of 4%. Russia's economy, which shrank 4% in 1995, slipped 1.3% in 1996, according to the IMF projections. Official statistics indicated that the 28 transition countries lost about 50% of their output in the turmoil after the fall of communism. This may be an exaggeration, since private-sector activities likely are underreported. Nonetheless, notes the IMF, the transition has been "extremely costly" in terms of living standards and economic well-being. Thus, the IMF notes, it is "difficult to exaggerate the importance of the improvements" that have occurred or are expected in the transition nations.

The Economic Summit. At the annual meeting of leaders of the Group of Seven (G-7) industrial nations in late June in Lyon, France, six leaders took aim at U.S. President Clinton for supporting legislation that would punish countries that trade with nations the United States has designated as terrorist regimes, such as Iran and Libya. The six also condemned the U.S. Helms-Burton Act, which permits U.S. companies and citizens to sue foreign companies that own or operate properties in Cuba expropriated from U.S. citizens. The G-7 did approve a 40-point counterterrorism program, involving development of an international network for extradition to ensure criminals have nowhere to hide, a renewed fight against the spread of international firearms trafficking, and the exchange of financial information in money-laundering investigations. Pressure was put on Japan to keep interest rates low and government spending high to assure continued recovery in the Japanese economy. And the G-7 agreed to push for conclusion by the autumn of an action plan that would provide debt relief for the world's poorest countries.

Just prior to the joint annual meeting of the IMF–World Bank in early autumn in Washington, the finance ministers and central bankers of the G-7 reached a consensus on funding between $5.6 billion and $7.7 billion of relief for about 20 countries. The sum was to be spread over several years. These countries—including Burundi, Ethiopia, Mozambique, Nicaragua, and Sudan—have per-capita incomes of less than $865 per year. They also have relatively large amounts of "official" debt—that is, loans from governments of rich nations or from multilateral institutions, such as the World Bank and the IMF. The creditor nations, which meet as the so-called Paris Club, agreed on up to 80% relief on bilateral debt. Executive boards of the IMF and World Bank endorsed a program to use profits of the two institutions. The bank would provide $2 billion. Put off probably into the next century was a decision on whether the IMF would sell $2 billion of its $40 billion of gold and use the interest on that $2 billion for debt relief. Germany, Switzerland, Italy, and Finland opposed the gold sale.

To deal with Mexico-style financial crises, IMF policy makers made some progress on doubling an emergency bailout fund to about $50 billion. Further, IMF managing director Michel Camdessus asked that the fund's capital be doubled to $200 billion, or, at a minimum, increased by 50%. He also urged creation of 26 billion new special drawing rights, a type of IMF credit that, in effect, would provide $36 billion of free assets to nations that could be used in financial emergencies. The recipients mainly would be developing countries and former communist nations. Approval of the two proposals by the national legislatures could take two years or more.

Trade. The volume of goods and services moving across borders grew about 6.7% in 1996, down from 8.9% in 1995, according to the IMF. For the first time, more than $6 trillion in goods and services was traded. Imports grew especially robustly in developing nations, rising 11.3%, and at even a faster rate—12.3%—in transition countries. Exports from these two groups of nations grew 10.3% and 10.7%, respectively, slightly less than imports.

As usual, there were many trade fights. For example, the United States again threatened China over the protection of intellectual-property rights. In turn, by November, China was threatening the United States with retaliatory action for U.S. curbs on Chinese textile exports. Eastman Kodak Company wanted easier entry for its products in Japan. The relatively new World Trade Organization (WTO), the successor to the General Agreement on Tariffs and Trade (GATT), began to assert some authority. In April a three-judge panel ruled that regulations issued under the U.S. Clean Air Act discriminated against foreign oil refiners. This would force the U.S. Environmental Protection Agency to rewrite some rules concerning environmental standards for imported gasoline or face trade sanctions from the countries that filed the complaint, Venezuela and Brazil.

See also STOCKS AND BONDS.

DAVID R. FRANCIS
"The Christian Science Monitor"

IRAN

Iran in 1996 presented a spectacle difficult to summarize in succinct generalizations. In virtually every area of life or policy, conflicting tendencies were visible. It was unclear, for example, whether the religious-oriented state was relaxing, maintaining, or strengthening its grip on private life, dress and behavior, and the freedom of press. Likewise, in the economic sphere, observers debated whether free-enterprise ideas and policies were gaining ground, or still were being resisted. In foreign affairs, questions remained as to whether Iran was a menace to the flow of oil, to other states, and to international stability; or merely was pursuing an independent line and making some useful contributions without earning many thanks from the world.

Internal Developments. The overarching structure of the Islamic state, as established in 1979 by the fall of the shah and the assumption of power by the Ayatollah Khomeini, was not in question and was not permitted to be the subject of any public debate. Within that framework, however, there was room for much difference in interpretation and variation in policies. Moderates favored the gradual introduction of more liberal economic policies—their primary concern being prosperity rather than ideology; on the other side were the hard-core upholders of Islamic orthodoxy, who opposed any social or economic reform.

President Rafsanjani's daughter—Faezeh Hashemi, president of the Islamic Countries Women's Sports Solidarity Council—successfully sought a seat in Iran's 1996 parliamentary elections.
© Aladin Abdel/Reuters/Archive Photos

In some senses, there was a vigorous intellectual life in Iran with abundant debate. Tehran had eight daily newspapers and some 700 periodicals voicing different points of view. But the exercise, such as it was, of intellectual freedom was always precarious. This was demonstrated in January when Abbas Marufi, the editor of the cultural weekly *Gardun*—which had published an article that offended Ayatollah Ali Akbar Hoseini-Khamenei, Iran's supreme religious leader—was tried before a Tehran court. He was sentenced to six months in prison, 35 lashes of a cane, and a two-year suspension from journalistic activities; *Gardun* was shut down.

In January, for the first time in five years, Iran permitted a representative of the United Nations (UN) Commission on Human Rights to visit the country and conduct interviews. The UN representative, Canada's Maurice Copithorne, was a former judge and diplomat with some experience in Iran. His report, submitted along with two others to the commission in June, was debated and accepted by a majority vote. It reflected the ambiguities of the situation, was moderate in tone, and thus pleased neither the Iranian government, which had made unusual efforts to be conciliatory, nor the government's critics. While pointing firmly to many remaining abuses, the report detected an "atmosphere for change" that made wholesale denunciation no longer appropriate.

The rift between the two political rivals who clearly symbolized the opposing lines of thought—President Ali Akbar Hashemi Rafsanjani and the Ayatollah Khamenei—appeared to deepen in 1996. Political tensions grew in the spring with the approach of the general election to the Majlis (parliament) on March 8. An open letter to voters over the names of more than a dozen high officials, including ten cabinet ministers and the mayor of Tehran, urged voters to support candidates dedicated to the prosperity and modernization of Iran, described as the policy of the president. The letter evoked violent denunciations from the opposing forces.

The struggle for power to shape Iran's future possessed urgency in 1996 because Rafsanjani's second term was due to end in June 1997 and the existing constitution barred him from seeking a third term. Some observers thought that he might hope to amend the constitution to make a third term possible, but this would be opposed bitterly by Khamenei's ally, the speaker of the Majlis, Ayatollah Ali Akbar Nateq-Nuri, who also had presidential aspirations.

Officially recognized political parties did not exist yet in Iran—although there seemed a likelihood that they might be sanctioned formally within a year or two. This made describing the results of an election somewhat uncertain. However, most observers agreed that the Majlis election (which also required a second round of voting in April) represented a considerable advance for the more moderate forces. In the previous Majlis, the right-wing supporters of Speaker Nateq-Nuri had a clear majority; in the new one they and more moderate supporters of Rafsanjani were about equal in strength. Both sides were eager to court independent deputies who made up the remainder of the membership.

However, the early expectations of some observers after the election that there would be substantial policy changes were not borne out. The right, with a firm footing in a group called the Association of Combatant Clergymen, mounted a vigorous extraparliamentary counterattack that demonstrated their political strength. The right also enjoyed the support of the *Basij*, a paramilitary group composed of hard-line zealots.

The counterattack on the moderates took several forms. More women were harassed for failing to conform to the state-mandated dress code. In May the campaign of Islamic militants against what they dubbed "corrupting Western influences" included the shattering of the glass doors of cinemas in Tehran and other incidents. Also in May, right-wing pressure brought about the cancellation of a visit to Tehran University by Abdulkarim Sorush, a distinguished Islamic philosopher who advocated moderate reforms within the constitutional framework. The banning of the lecture evoked a petition in protest from some 500 students; this, in turn, yielded a demand from the Ayatollah Khamenei for an ideological purge at universities. As the phenomenon of student protests suggested, in the 17 years since the revolution a new generation had grown up with aspirations toward greater freedoms. This was the case even among the younger Islamic clergy, some of whom interpreted the Koran and Islamic law in ways different from their elders.

Physical conditions were better than they had been, even though the economy had not expanded to cope with the great increase in population and there was a high rate of inflation, estimated at 60% per year. Foreign travel increasingly was possible.

IRAN • Information Highlights

Official Name: Islamic Republic of Iran.
Location: Southwest Asia.
Area: 636,293 sq mi (1 648 000 km^2).
Population (mid-1996 est.): 63,100,000.
Chief Cities (1991 census): Tehran, the capital, 6,475,527; Mashad, 1,759,155; Esfahan, 1,127,050; Tabriz, 1,088,985.
Government: *Head of state and government,* Ali Akbar Hashemi Rafsanjani, president (took office August 1989). *Legislature* (unicameral)—Islamic Consultative Assembly (Majlis).
Monetary Unit: Rial (3,000.00 rials equal U.S.$1, official rate, Dec. 30, 1996).
Gross Domestic Product (1994 est. U.S.$): $310,000,-000,000 (purchasing power parity).
Economic Index (1995, 1990 = 100): *Consumer Prices,* all items, 353.3; food, 405.0.
Foreign Trade (fiscal year 1992–93 est. U.S.$): *Imports,* $18,000,000,000; *exports,* $16,000,000,000.

Foreign Relations. President Rafsanjani enjoyed a somewhat freer hand in foreign affairs than in domestic policy. In 1996 there were no great developments in foreign affairs, merely a range of matters of the second rank. Internationally, Iran remained somewhat isolated, although to a lesser degree than in the past. The United States continued to impose an embargo on dealings with Iran, and indeed stiffened its anti-Iranian policy, citing its record as a supporter of terrorism. However, many European countries, notably France and Germany, were more accommodating and diverged widely from U.S. policy.

The Iranian arms buildup continued to excite concern. In the fall, Iran took delivery of its third submarine purchased from Russia. There also were large purchases of other weapons, aircraft, and ships from sources such as China, North Korea, and Libya. Iranian support of terrorism in Lebanon and Israel, and murders of Iranian dissidents abroad, did not cease in 1996. Another source of long-term anxiety for many nations was that Germany was supporting the development of Iran's civilian nuclear-power program, which might have spillover benefits for weapons development.

A running dispute with Bahrain, which is located on the other side of the Persian Gulf, stemmed from the claim of the latter nation that Iran was fomenting disorder and sabotage there. In June officials in Bahrain claimed that Iran had sponsored an attempt to overthrow the ruling family. There also were repeated reports that Iran was forging and circulating throughout the Middle East nearly perfect U.S. $100 bills.

In August an agreement was made with Iraq—with which Iran had an eight-year war in the 1980s—to exchange bodies that were casualties of the war; otherwise, relations with Iraq remained cool. During Iraqi incursions into Kurdish districts in northern Iraq in September, Iran remained cautiously uninvolved in a military sense. Iran, however, was attempting to deal with some 200,000 Kurdish refugees who spilled over its borders.

On May 13, Rafsanjani formally inaugurated a railway link between Mashad, Iran, and Tedzhen, Turkmenistan. Iran made much of the event: The ceremony was attended by 11 heads of state and representatives from some 50 countries. The railroad was expected to further Iran's policy of strengthening links with the former Soviet republics of Central Asia.

ARTHUR CAMPBELL TURNER
University of California, Riverside

IRAQ

Despite a minor international crisis in September, the situation in Iraq changed little during 1996. The ruthless leadership of Saddam Hussein and his inner circle, the Revolutionary Command Council, survived another year; demonstrated how it dealt with defectors and dissidents; and in effect thumbed its nose with virtual impunity at the United States. However, there were indications in November that improvements in the material conditions of the long-suffering Iraqi population were on the way.

Two familiar themes—the dogged reluctance of Iraq to gain relief from United Nations (UN) economic sanctions by allowing the full inspection of its weapons and weapon-building facilities called for by UN resolutions; and the possible implementation under international control of a food-for-oil deal—carried over from past years.

The Political Climate. The peril for Iraqis of opposing Saddam Hussein was exhibited tellingly in February. Two high-ranking Iraqi officers—Lt. Gen. Kamel Hassan al-Majid and his brother Lt. Col. Saddam Kamel, who had defected in August 1995 with their wives (Saddam Hussein's two eldest daughters), and had been in frustrated exile in Jordan for six months—chose to return on the basis of what they believed to be a promise of pardon. Within three days they had been divorced by their wives and shot to death by family members. Their father also was killed.

Vain and disastrous as the defection and return were to the men themselves, the episode was not devoid of significant results. The general provided a wealth of hitherto unavailable information about Iraqi violations of UN arms conditions. These revelations foiled efforts by France and Russia to have UN sanctions against Iraq lifted. The incident also led Saddam Hussein to restrict the more obnoxious activities of his elder son, Uday, and to tidy up the domestic situation in other ways. Uday, who had many enemies, was wounded in an attempt on his life in December. The 32-year-old was shot as he drove his Porsche through a prosperous section of Baghdad. Two opposition groups abroad claimed responsibility for the attack.

The Iraqi regime presumably was strengthened, if only marginally, by parliamentary elections held in March—the first since 1989. The list of 689 candidates for the 250 seats was interesting in that a large number of "independent" candidates were permitted to run, and many were elected. However, all candidates allowed to run were obliged in advance to sign a declaration that the Iraqi-Iranian war and the Persian Gulf war had "crowned Iraq with glory," and to pledge allegiance to the 1968 coup that brought President Hussein's party to power.

The regime, however, manifestly still had enemies, even inside Iraq, as defections continued. The most important 1996 defector was Lt. Gen. Nazar Khazraji, who had been army chief of staff from 1988 to 1990. It was reported reliably in Israel that late in July a group of army officers made an attempt on Saddam Hussein's life. The plot failed, as a bomb exploded in one of Hussein's palaces only minutes after he had left; the incident led to hundreds of officers being arrested and dozens, including members of the elite Republican Guard, being executed.

Kurdish Crisis. In June 1991 the Western powers established a "safe haven" for Kurds in northern Iraq, and two "no fly" zones—one north of the 36th parallel, the other south of the 32d. Since Iraq's ground forces remained outside the northern zone, the area was thought to be a promising locale for the unfor-

IRAQ • Information Highlights

Official Name: Republic of Iraq.
Location: Southwest Asia.
Area: 168,754 sq mi (437 072 km²).
Population (mid-1996 est.): 21,400,000.
Chief City (1987 census): Baghdad, the capital, 3,844,608.
Government: *Head of state and government,* Saddam Hussein, president (took office July 1979). *Legislature* (unicameral)—National Assembly.
Monetary Unit: Dinar (0.311 dinar equals U.S.$1, principal rate, August 1996).

tunate Kurds, especially after the successful election in 1992 of a regional parliament. In fact it did afford them an opportunity—which they failed to seize. In May 1994 a factional conflict broke out between the Patriotic Union of Kurdistan (PUK), headed by Jalal Talabini, and the Kurdish Democratic Party (KDP), led by Massoud Barzani. The U.S.-sponsored cease-fire in 1995 turned out to be precarious and fighting broke out again in August 1996.

Barzani—hitherto known as more a friend to the West than his rival—surprisingly requested aid from the Iraqi government; on August 31, Iraqi troops seized the city of Erbil, north of the 36th parallel, from PUK forces. By September 2, however, Iraqi forces began to withdraw from the area. Most of the places lost by the PUK were retaken subsequently by them. The PUK had ties to Iran. Direct Iranian military intervention was feared, but did not occur.

The United States reacted immediately to Iraq's move, with cruise-missile strikes on southern Iraqi targets on September 3 and 4. These may have accelerated the Iraqi withdrawal, but otherwise had little military effect. The United States—with the concurrence of Britain alone—also extended the southern "no fly" zone north to the 33d parallel, only 30 mi (48 km) from Baghdad.

October talks held in Turkey by U.S. representatives with the two Kurdish factions achieved a cease-fire and, at the end of the month, an undertaking from both that they would not seek help from Iraq or Iran.

During the Iraqi occupation of Erbil, hundreds of opponents of the regime were hunted down and executed; a permanent network of informers and secret agents also presumably was established. The "Iraqi National Congress," an umbrella organization for various antigovernment forces, disintegrated. On September 19 the director of the U.S. Central Intelligence Agency (CIA), John M. Deutch, said that Iraq's confrontation with the West had left the Iraqi dictator stronger. International reaction showed that the anti-Iraqi coalition of 1991 largely had evaporated.

Economic Sanctions and Arms Inspection. The Iraqi dictator, perhaps driven by increasing internal problems, in February allowed talks to begin on implementing a 1995 UN Security Council resolution that envisaged permitting Iraq to sell $2 billion worth of oil per six months—provided that the money would be spent only on food and medical supplies. Iraq previously had rejected these terms as a humiliating infringement of sovereignty.

In September 1996, Iraqi women demonstrated their support for President Saddam Hussein amid U.S. missile attacks against Iraq in response to Iraqi offensive moves against the Kurds.

Finally, on November 25, Iraq agreed to meet such terms and an agreement was accepted. The sanctions were eased, and Iraq began selling oil for the first time since 1990 in December. UN Secretary-General Boutros Boutros-Ghali said that all the necessary procedures to monitor the sale were in place.

Iraq continued to evade and frustrate international inspection of its military power. In a series of incidents, UN monitoring teams were denied access to "sensitive" sites and then allowed in after several days. Prospects for effective arms inspection grew weaker, not stronger. Rolf Elkeus, head of the UN commission monitoring Iraq's arms, said in November that unless adequate funding were made available to support the inspectors inside Iraq and the operation's base in Bahrain, the whole program was in jeopardy.

ARTHUR CAMPBELL TURNER
University of California, Riverside

IRELAND

Despite the strenuous efforts of Ireland's coalition ministry—led by John Bruton of Fine Gael and Dick Spring of Labour—to promote a peace settlement in Northern Ireland, no visible progress occurred in 1996.

Peace Process. During the year, the so-called peace process designed to end sectarian unrest in Northern Ireland bogged down as a result of the intransigence of the opposing parties over the preconditions of any formal negotiations. Dependent for its survival on the votes of Ulster Unionist members of Parliament (MPs), Britain's Tory government acquiesced in the Unionists' demand that the Irish Republican Army (IRA) surrender its caches of weapons and explosives before they would take part in any formal peace talks. Meanwhile, hard-line elements in the Provisional IRA, frustrated by the stalemate in the peace process, abandoned their 17-month-long cease-fire and launched a series of bomb attacks in England, several of which proved abortive. During the summer and fall the Irish police discovered several large caches of weapons and explosives on remote farms from Donegal to Louth and arrested a number of IRA suspects.

Although Prime Minister (Taoiseach) Bruton hinted at the possibility of another IRA cease-fire after addressing the U.S. Congress on September 11, no such declaration emerged from a meeting of IRA leaders in early November. Although the British and Irish governments held secret talks with Gerry Adams, the president of Sinn Fein, their efforts to arrange a peace conference foundered over the refusal of Republican leaders and the three main Unionist parties to compromise on the preconditions.

IRELAND • Information Highlights

Official Name: Ireland.
Location: Island in the eastern North Atlantic Ocean.
Area: 27,135 sq mi (70 280 km²).
Population (mid-1996 est.): 3,600,000.
Chief Cities (1991 census): Dublin, the capital, 915,516 (incl. suburbs); Cork, 174,400; Limerick, 75,436.
Government: *Head of state,* Mary Robinson, president (took office Dec. 3, 1990). *Head of government,* John Bruton, prime minister (appointed Dec. 15, 1994). *Legislature*—Parliament: House of Representatives (Dail Eireann) and Senate (Seanad Eireann).
Monetary Unit: Pound (0.6037 pound equals U.S.$1, Dec. 31, 1996).
Gross Domestic Product (1994 est. U.S.$): $49,800,000,-000 (purchasing power parity).
Economic Indexes: *Consumer Prices* (1994, 1990 = 100): all items, 110.5; food, 107.0. *Industrial Production* (1995, 1990 = 100): 158.
Foreign Trade (1995 U.S.$): *Imports,* $32,430,000,000; *exports,* $43,940,000,000.

Society. Another top news stories of 1996 was the growth of organized crime and the failure of the police to arrest local gang lords involved in everything from protection rackets to drug trafficking. Veronica Guerin, who had written a series of articles about Dublin's rich crime bosses for the *Sunday Independent,* was shot to death on June 26. Although the police interrogated various suspects, they had charged only one man with conspiracy to murder by late in the year.

After intercepting a large amount of cocaine on board a Swedish-owned ship anchored at Moneypoint, county Clare, in August, the police found an even bigger cache of cocaine—worth about $80 million—on board a trawler in Cork harbor in October. On both occasions, three men were arrested.

In June the Irish Supreme Court dismissed a challenge by opponents of the 1995 referendum that had resulted in the legalizing of divorce by a 0.5% margin. Although the court criticized the government for having hired a public-relations firm to promote the cause of legalizing divorce, it found no evidence that the advertisements had influenced voters.

By mid-November some 50 Irish cattle had been diagnosed with "mad-cow disease," making a total of more than 160 cases since 1989, when the disease first came to light. The increase depressed not only a major sector of Irish agriculture but also the price of farmland in some areas.

Foreign Affairs. In a move interpreted by some observers as compromising Ireland's traditional neutrality in foreign policy, Minister of Foreign Affairs Dick Spring announced on March 26 that the government might support the North Atlantic Treaty Organization's (NATO's) Partnership for Peace program and was willing to cooperate with the European Union (EU) in undertaking humanitarian activities and peacekeeping efforts aboard. Spokesmen for Fianna Fail objected strenuously to placing Irish soldiers under NATO.

The Economy. The Irish economy showed impressive vitality in 1996, even though the unemployment rate hovered around 13%. Many overseas corporations had invested new capital in their Irish-based companies, creating many new jobs. In September the Irish stock market reached the 2,700 level for the first time. Overseas investors now owned 40% of Irish bonds. Typical of the robust state of the economy was the acquisition in March of the biotechnology company Athena Neurosciences by Elan, an Irish-based drug company, for some $600 million in shares.

L. PERRY CURTIS, JR., *Brown University*

ISRAEL

The campaign for the election of a prime minister dominated Israeli politics during the first half of 1996. Following the election of Benjamin Netanyahu (*see* BIOGRAPHY) and the 14th Knesset (parliament) on May 29, the new prime minister formed a center-right coalition led by his Likud Party, replacing Shimon Peres of the Labor Party and his center-left government. The principal issue during the election was which candidate better could assure the nation's security. After Netanyahu assumed office, security issues continued to dominate the political scene and were a major factor in the continuing peace negotiations between Israel, the Palestinians, and Syria.

Election. The election was among the most critical in Israel's history, the first with a two-ballot system approved by the Knesset in 1992; one ballot was for the direct election of the prime minister, and the second was for the election of Knesset members. In the previous system the leader of the party receiving the largest number of Knesset seats became the prime minister. The new procedure was intended to strengthen the premiership by diminishing its dependence on the bargaining usually required to form government coalitions. However, the result in 1996 was a more factionalized parliament. The two major parties, Labor and Likud, were weakened greatly and, surprisingly, the religious bloc and several new parties representing ethnic or special interests gained substantial influence.

During the bitter election campaign, Netanyahu accused Peres, who replaced assassinated Prime Minister Yitzhak Rabin as Labor leader in November 1995, of compromising national security in his negotiations with Yasir Arafat and the Palestine Liberation Organization (PLO). The security issue was underscored by a series of terrorist bombings in February and March that caused scores of Israeli casualties in Tel Aviv, Jerusalem, and other Jewish population centers. The terrorist suicide attacks, carried out by Palestinian Islamic fundamentalists, diminished popular support for Peres and were a major factor in Netanyahu's electoral victory.

Responding to the suicide attacks in April, Prime Minister Peres' government initiated construction of a hi-tech security barrier between Israel and the West Bank to prevent Palestinians from entering Jewish areas. This policy of "separation" entailed much stricter enforcement of the closure that kept Palestinian workers from earning their livelihood in Israel. Another tough policy adopted in April by Peres was the "Grapes of Wrath" campaign against Hezbollah (Party of God) guerrilla fighters who were attacking Israeli forces and their allies in southern Lebanon. The three-week pounding of southern Lebanon by Israel—which caused hundreds of Lebanese civilian casualties, the flight of thousands of Lebanese from their homes, and widespread destruction—was ended by a U.S.-brokered truce.

© Alain Buu/Gamma-Liaison

Clashes between Israeli and Palestinian forces broke out in 1996 after the Israeli government opened a new entrance to an archaeological tunnel under a mosque in Jerusalem's old city.

The race for prime minister was very close: Netanyahu won 1,501,023 votes (50.4%) and Peres received 1,471,566 votes (49.5%). Votes Peres received from Israel's Arab citizens helped close the gap; Netanyahu obtained about 60% of the Jewish votes compared with the 40% received by Peres. Eleven of the 20 parties participating in the election received the minimum 1.5% of votes required for a Knesset seat. Although Labor lost ten of its seats, it remained the largest party, with 34 of the 120 seats, gaining 26.8% of the vote. Netanyahu's Likud received 32 seats with 25.1% of the vote. The Likud election list was cobbled together from three right-wing factions: Likud; Gesher, formed early in 1996 by David Levy, a former Likud leader who broke with the party in 1995; and Tzomet, led by Rafael Eitan, a former army chief of staff.

Among the election's surprises was the strength of the three religious parties: SHAS, which emerged as the third-largest party, with ten seats; National Religious Party (nine seats); and United Torah Judaism (four seats). The 23 seats held by the religious bloc was the largest number it ever had obtained, giving it immense bargaining power in Netanyahu's new government. Other unanticipated election results included the support received by Natan Sharansky's Yisrael Ba-Aliya (Israel on the Ascent) party, largely backed by new Jewish immigrants from the former Soviet Union, with seven seats. The new Third Way party, formed mostly of former Labor supporters who disapproved of Peres' concessions in the peace negotiations, won four seats. The remaining seats went to the left-of-center Meretz (nine seats); the militantly nationalist Moledet (two seats); the Democratic Front for Peace and Equality (Hadash), made up of communists and several Arab factions (five seats); and the United Arab List (four seats).

In June the Labor Party, charging that there had been widespread ballot fraud, filed a motion in a Jerusalem court to have the election invalidated. However, the court rejected the appeal, maintaining that there were only insignificant violations.

Postelection Affairs. Following the election, Netanyahu had to form a new government coalition from eight diverse political factions representing the political center, the right, and the orthodox religious bloc. This meant that his own Likud was a minority, with fewer than half the cabinet members. Netanyahu could command a Knesset majority of at least 61 votes to back his hard-line policy in the peace process, but a majority was not assured in support of his domestic program, especially on matters concerning the status of religion and economics.

Issues of national security and the peace process continued to be salient after the election. Although Netanyahu asserted that he would honor agreements made by the Labor government with the Palestinians despite what he maintained were their shortcomings, his approach seemed to stymie further progress. Israeli withdrawal from the West Bank city of Hebron became a major issue in dispute between Israel and the Palestinians. Hebron was the last of six Arab cities that the previous Israeli government had agreed to turn over to the Palestinian Authority. However, following the terrorist attacks in February and March, Prime Minister Peres deferred withdrawal, which was to have occurred in March. Because of the presence of some 400–500 Jewish settlers who had moved into the city among its more than 100,000 Palestinian Arab inhabitants, the Israeli government demanded control of security measures that the Palestinians insisted infringed upon their sovereignty. Disagreement over the terms of Israeli withdrawal stalled the negotiations. However, the talks intensified late in the year and an agreement on Hebron was reported to be near.

During the election campaign, Netanyahu had denounced Labor and Peres for recognizing the PLO and the 1993 handshake between Rabin and Arafat. When first elected, Netanyahu seemed to shun contact with the Palestinian leader, but by September he met with Arafat and the two shook hands; at a subsequent news conference, they announced that they both were committed to the peace process. Prior to the election, Likud was adamantly opposed to the return of the Golan

An outbreak of fighting between Israeli and Palestinian forces in the West Bank and Gaza in late September not only resulted in casualties for both sides but also jeopardized the peace process. An emergency two-day White House summit meeting between Israel's Prime Minister Benjamin Netanyahu and Palestinian leader Yasir Arafat ended inconclusively.

Heights to Syria, but by the end of the year, Netanyahu seemed to moderate his stance; he still opposed returning all of the region to Syria, but there were reports that he might agree to a territorial compromise with Damascus. Syria, however, still opposed any agreement that did not include the full return of the Golan. (*See* MIDDLE EAST.)

Economy. Although Netanyahu's party promised to adopt a program fostering free-market and supply-side economic measures—including more rapid privatization of public-sector enterprises, fewer restrictions on business, and curtailment of government expenditures—his election was followed by a decline in economic indicators. After five years of economic growth (40% from 1990 to 1995) marked by more than 7% growth in 1995, there were indications that the increase would be half that in 1996. Shortly after taking office, Netanyahu warned that the economy was "on the edge of the abyss." Much of the decline was believed to be caused by fears among investors and businesspeople that the peace process would be suspended or would collapse.

Following Netanyahu's election and his statement of a more forceful foreign policy, many contacts that had been made with Arab entrepreneurs in the surrounding countries were brought to a halt and further negotiations on economic deals with Jordan, Egypt, Qatar, and other Arab states were suspended. Several Arab states called for reimposition of the boycott on products from Israel and on enterprises that had connections with the Jewish state.

By midyear tax collection fell off and the accumulated budget deficit for the first nine months exceeded the deficit planned for the entire year. By the end of the year, annualized inflation was higher than 11%, compared with 8% for 1995. Unemployment, which had fallen steadily in recent years, began to rise again with closures or cutbacks in several textile and hi-tech industries.

Netanyahu's government attempted to cope with the economic decline by cutting more than $1.6 billion in government spending. However, the distribution of the budget cuts became the source of acrimonious infighting among the various ministries and sparked a one-day general strike on July 17, shortly after the cuts were announced.

DON PERETZ
Professor Emeritus, Binghamton University

ISRAEL • Information Highlights

Official Name: State of Israel.
Location: Southwest Asia.
Area: 8,019 sq mi (20 770 km²).
Population (mid-1996 est.): 5,800,000.
Chief Cities (Dec. 31, 1993 est.): Jerusalem, the capital, 567,100 (including East Jerusalem); Tel Aviv–Jaffa, 357,400; Haifa, 246,500.
Government: *Head of state,* Ezer Weizman, president (took office March 1993). *Head of government,* Benjamin Netanyahu, prime minister (sworn in June 18, 1996). *Legislature* (unicameral)—Knesset.
Monetary Unit: Shekel (3.2808 shekels equal U.S.$1, Dec. 9, 1996).
Gross Domestic Product (1994 est. U.S.$): $70,100,000,-000 (purchasing power parity).
Economic Indexes (1995, 1990 = 100): *Consumer Prices,* all items, 182.7; food, 161.1. *Industrial Production,* 143.
Foreign Trade (1995 U.S.$): *Imports,* $29,632,000,000; *exports,* $19,028,000,000.

ITALY

Italy's political "revolution," which began in 1992, continued its feverish course in 1996. Parliamentary elections in April resulted in a swing to the left. In the new center-left government, former communists played a major role for the first time in 50 years. Meanwhile, Italy's national unity was challenged by the secessionist Northern League, which proclaimed independence for Padania in the Po Valley.

Political Crises. Following the forced resignation of the short-lived center-right government of Silvio Berlusconi in December 1994, Italy was administered from January 1995 until early in 1996 by an emergency government headed by Lamberto Dini, a former central banker and treasury minister. This was Italy's 54th government since World War II. It was composed of a nonpartisan group of technocrats, whose limited goal was to reduce the budget deficit.

When Premier Dini completed this task in December 1995, he urged Parliament to let him continue in office while Italy held the rotating presidency of the European Union (EU) from January to June 1996. But this ploy was rejected when the Democratic Party of the Left (PDS), heir to the old Communist Party, insisted on general parliamentary elections by spring. On January 11, Silvio Berlusconi, who long had opposed Dini, proposed a motion of nonconfidence in the government. Dini resigned at once rather than face certain defeat in that vote, but he agreed to continue as interim premier until a successor could be approved by Parliament.

In February, President Oscar Luigi Scalfaro asked Antonio Maccanico to form a government. Maccanico, like Dini, was a politically neutral bureaucrat. He was asked to initiate constitutional changes that would produce a

© Origlia/Pizzoli/Sygma

Romano Prodi

Romano Prodi, a distinguished professor of economics with little political experience, was sworn in as premier of Italy on May 18, 1996.

One of nine children, Prodi was born on Aug. 7, 1939, in the town of Scandiano in the northern province of Reggio dell'Emilia. After earning an economics degree at Milan's Catholic University in 1961, he worked as a researcher at the London School of Economics. In 1964, Prodi was elected (as a Christian Democrat) to the Communal Council of Reggio dell'Emilia. He quit in 1969 after gaining a professorship in economics and industrial policy at the University of Bologna. Specializing in industrial politics, Prodi reexamined the public sector of Italy's economy. In the 1970s, Prodi received a research grant from Stanford University. This was followed by a six-month appointment at Harvard University to teach a course on the Italian economy. Meanwhile, a Milan newspaper, *Corriere della Sera*, hired him to be its editorial commentator on economic issues.

In 1978–79 "il Professore" agreed to serve as minister of industry in the government of Prime Minister Giulio Andreotti, a Christian Democrat. In this post, Prodi helped design legislation to make it easier for the state to rescue ailing industries. From 1982 to 1989 (an era of center-left governments), Prodi served as president of the Institute for Industrial Reconstruction (IRI), a public-holding company that had become Italy's largest industrial conglomerate. He restored the IRI to profitability by privatizing various holdings. In May 1993, in the wake of scandals that brought down Italy's old political order, Premier Carlo Azeglio Ciampi named Prodi to head the IRI again. This time, Prodi sold off two of Italy's largest banks—Credito Italiano and Banca Commerciale Italiana. Prodi resigned in July 1994, two months after Silvio Berlusconi became premier.

Prodi is fluent in English and French and likes to bicycle and run. Married to the former Flavia Franzoni, he has two sons.

Charles F. Delzell

modified version of France's presidential system. Under that plan, Italy's president would be elected directly by the people rather than by Parliament. The president, in turn, would appoint the premier. Italy's system of proportional representation also would be altered to reduce the number of fringe parties. (There were then 26 parties in Parliament.) In his negotiations to form a government, Premier-designate Maccanico won support from all major parties except the far-right National Alliance (AN), whose leader, Gianfranco Fini, insisted on general elections.

On February 14, Maccanico informed President Scalfaro that a great and extraordinary opportunity had been lost for the future of the country, whose political and institutional system remained immersed in a grave crisis. After that announcement, leaders of the two major parties—the PDS' Massimo D'Alema and Forza Italia's Silvio Berlusconi—reversed themselves and declared that they, too, wanted general elections. President Scalfaro had no choice but to dissolve Parliament on February 16 and set new elections—the third in four years— for April 21. The outgoing Parliament had been elected in 1994. Lamberto Dini, the interim premier, continued in a caretaker role. This did not prevent Dini, however, from launching his own new centrist political party (Dini Italian Renewal) on February 23. He said his new party would give its support to the center-left bloc in Parliament. This bloc—composed of former communists, former Christian Democrats, and others—was referred to as the Olive Tree. It had been Dini's chief backer in several crucial votes. Dini's move infuriated rightist leaders, especially those of the Forza Italia ("Let's Go, Italy!") party and the National Alliance.

Meanwhile, on January 17 former Premier Berlusconi and several other defendants went on trial in Milan on charges of bribery and corruption. These stemmed from some 380 million lire ($241,000) in bribes that Berlusconi's Gruppo Fininvest media conglomerate had paid Italy's tax police after 1989 in exchange for favorable tax treatment. An investigation of this corruption (Operation Clean Hands) had been initiated in Milan in 1992 by Antonio Di Pietro, the city's chief magistrate. Soon, similar investigations were undertaken by magistrates elsewhere. Hundreds of indictments eventually were handed down. As a result, much of the old political class that had governed Italy since World War II was discredited fatally.

The bitter fight between the charismatic Berlusconi and the popular Di Pietro was one of several factors that had led to the crisis that forced Berlusconi to resign as premier in December 1994. That feud also had led to Di Pietro's own resignation as magistrate so that he could defend himself against criminal charges that Fininvest officials raised against him. On March 29 a court in Brescia cleared Di Pietro of these charges. The court also ruled that Silvio Berlusconi's brother Paolo, a Fininvest officer, and Cesare Previti, who had been defense minister in Berlusconi's government, would be tried on charges of blackmailing Di Pietro. The Brescia court's action not only rehabilitated Di Pietro but made it likely that this popular hero could become a powerful political player if he chose to be such.

Election Campaign and New Government. Active campaigning for the April 21 parliamentary election began on March 18. Two major blocs confronted each other. The center-left Olive Tree bloc consisted of the large, formerly communist Democratic Party of the Left (PDS), skillfully led by Massimo D'Alema; the Popular Party, heir to the once-ruling Christian Democratic Party and led by a newcomer to politics, Professor Romano Prodi, a distinguished economist; the environmentalist Green Party; and Dini Italian Renewal. D'Alema made it clear that the Olive Tree's choice for premier would be the Catholic centrist, Prodi.

On the center-right was the Freedom Alliance, composed of Berlusconi's conservative Forza Italia, Fini's post-Fascist National Alliance, and right-wing Christian Democrats. Umberto Bossi's conservative, secession-minded Northern League, whose withdrawal of support for the Berlusconi government had brought it down in December 1994, decided in 1996 to present its own separate slate in the election. The hard-line Refounded Communist Party, led by Fausto Bertinotti, also ran separately but pledged support to the Olive Tree except on the issues of cutting social spending and entering the European Union's economic and monetary union (EMU).

In the April 21 parliamentary elections, the Olive Tree coalition won 284 of the 630 seats in the Chamber of Deputies and 157 of the 315 seats in the Senate. The Freedom Alliance won 246 seats in the Chamber of Deputies and 116 seats in the Senate. Fifty-nine Chamber seats went to the Northern League, 35 to the Refounded Communist Party (PRC), and six to smaller parties. The Northern League also won 27 Senate seats, the Refounded Communists ten, and smaller parties five.

On May 9, after the opening session of the new Parliament, the center-left Olive Tree bloc won the speakerships of both houses. Nicola Mancino, a former Christian Democratic interior minister, assumed the gavel in the Chamber. In the Senate, Luciano Violante, a former anti-Mafia magistrate, became the presiding officer. As had been arranged, Prodi, the Popular Party economist and political newcomer, was appointed premier and was sworn in on May 18.

Prodi's center-left government lacked a clear majority in Parliament, however, and thus had to depend upon the tactical support of the far-left PRC. Luckily for Prodi, such PRC support was obtained "conditionally" in votes of confidence the new government won on May 24 in the Senate (173 to 139), and on May 31 in the Chamber of Deputies (322 to 299). The new government—Italy's 55th since 1945—was historic in that it included former communists for the first time since 1947.

Balancing the ministries in the Prodi government was a delicate task. The PDS was the largest party in the Olive Tree coalition; its leader, D'Alema, while not himself taking a cabinet post, exercised veto power over appointments. The PDS' Number 2 leader, Walter Veroni, became deputy premier, while the party's economic expert, Vincenzo Visco, took the finance portfolio and Giorgio Napolitano, who had engineered the transformation of the old Italian Communist Party into the PDS, became interior minister.

Prominent independents in the Prodi government included former Milan magistrate Di Pietro, who was assigned the public-works portfolio; the jurist Giovanni Maria Flick, who became justice minister; former Premier Carlo Azeglio Ciampi, who was given the treasury post; and Lamberto Dini, the outgoing caretaker premier, who became minister of foreign affairs and consequently handled the remaining two months of Italy's presidency of the EU.

Prodi's immediate task was to prepare a minibudget aimed at keeping the 1996 deficit below the target of 5.8% of gross domestic product (GDP). He also promised to whittle

ITALY • Information Highlights

Official Name: Italian Republic.
Location: Southern Europe.
Area: 116,305 sq mi (301 230 km²).
Population (mid-1996 est.): 57,300,000.
Chief Cities (Dec. 31, 1993): Rome, the capital, 2,687,881; Milan, 1,334,171; Naples, 1,061,583.
Government: *Head of state,* Oscar Luigi Scalfaro, president (sworn in May 28, 1992). *Head of government,* Romano Prodi, prime minister (sworn in May 18, 1996). *Legislature*—Parliament: Senate and Chamber of Deputies.
Monetary Unit: Lira (1,532.00 lire equal U.S.$1, Dec. 9, 1996).
Gross Domestic Product (1994 est. U.S.$): $998,900,000,-000 (purchasing power parity).
Economic Indexes (1995, 1990 = 100): *Consumer Prices,* all items, 127.7. *Industrial Production,* 108.
Foreign Trade (1994 U.S.$): *Imports,* $167,694,000,000; *exports,* $190,019,000,000.

the deficit to 3% of GDP by the end of 1997 in order to meet criteria for returning the Italian lira to the exchange-rate mechanism of the European Monetary System (EMS). Because of its weakened currency, Italy had had to pull out of it in 1992. This ambitious program, which came to include a onetime "tax for Europe," was hard to sell, but after much maneuvering won approval from Parliament on December 22. It cut $41 billion from the deficit. Anticipating this action, Europe's finance ministers, meeting in Brussels, permitted Italy to reenter the EMS on November 25 at the exchange rate of 900 lire to one German mark.

In an attempt to cut Italy's unemployment rate—12.3% nationally, but much higher in the South—the Prodi government signed a labor pact with unions and business leaders in September that would reduce the legal workweek from 48 to 40 hours, raise the minimum age for leaving school from 14 to 16, and provide new incentives for entrepreneurs.

Northern Independence Movement. The Prodi government's other great challenge was to design constitutional reforms that would change the electoral system and move Italy toward a federal system that would decentralize much of the decision-making. Such a reform might cut the ground away from Umberto Bossi's secessionist Northern League (LN), which insisted that Italy's prosperous and industrialized North no longer should be taxed to bail out the depressed South. Bossi argued that a separate northern Italian state could participate more competitively in the EU.

On May 12 the Northern League's breakaway 86 parliamentary deputies and senators announced in Mantua the formation of an 11-member government of the "Independent Republic of Padania" (named after the Po Valley), and of a ten-member "Committee for the Liberation of Padania" (an elastic geographical concept that embraced at least the regions of Piedmont, Lombardy, Liguria, Emilia-Romagna, and Venetia). Giancarlo Pagliarini, a former budget minister, was named prime minister of the shadow government, while Roberto Maroni, a former deputy prime minister, headed the government's liberation committee.

On September 13 the mystical Bossi began a theatrical three-day "March to the Sea" from the headwaters of the Po River to Venice on the Adriatic. There, on September 15, he declared to a crowd of 10,000 cheering separatists, "Padania is an independent, sovereign federal republic!" Italy's national leaders angrily denounced Bossi's "ridiculous" provocation and declared they could not tolerate incitement to illegal acts. In Milan on September 15, the far-right National Alliance staged a pro-unity counterdemonstration that attracted 150,000 people. On September 18 a police search of the Northern League's office in Milan ended in a scuffle that hospitalized Maroni.

Trials and Investigations. Erich Priebke, an 83-year-old former Nazi SS officer, was extradited from Argentina and indicted in Rome in April for his role in a massacre at the Ardeatine Caves outside Rome on March 24, 1944, in which 335 Italian civilians, 75 of them Jews, were shot in retaliation for an ambush by Italian partisans that had killed 33 German soldiers in Rome. An Italian military court freed Priebke in August, noting that a 30-year statute of limitations had run out on his crime, which had been reduced to one of multiple homicide. In the wake of a storm of protests in Rome, Italy's highest court nullified in October the military court's verdict and ordered Priebke to stand trial again, this time for crimes against humanity, a charge first used at the Nuremberg war-crimes trial in 1946.

On May 20 police arrested Giovanni Brusca, believed to be the top military figure in Cosa Nostra, the Sicilian Mafia. He was wanted especially for the killing of anti-Mafia prosecutor Giovanni Falcone, his wife, and three bodyguards in 1992. He also was accused of causing an explosion that damaged Florence's Uffizi Gallery.

Meanwhile, the trial of Giulio Andreotti, a seven-time Christian Democratic premier accused of conniving with the Mafia in return for the latter's electoral support, entered its second year. Andreotti also was involved in another trial in which he was accused of complicity in the 1979 murder of a journalist who was investigating the Mafia's political ties.

In another legal action, a judge in Milan on July 12 ordered two former premiers—Silvio Berlusconi (Forza Italia) and Bettino Craxi (Socialist)—as well as ten other people to stand trial in November for allegedly violating laws governing funding of political parties.

On November 13, when Antonio Di Pietro, the former Milan prosecutor who had joined Prodi's cabinet, was informed that he was a target of a judiciary investigation, he resigned his ministerial portfolio immediately. Then, on November 26, Premier Prodi was informed that he would face trial for an alleged conflict of interest dating to 1993, when he headed a giant holding company.

CHARLES F. DELZELL, *Vanderbilt University*

JAPAN

In 1996, Japanese leaders and the public paid less attention to foreign policy as they were absorbed in domestic political transition. All of Japan's political parties felt the impact of change as a new generation of politicians assumed positions of leadership. U.S. military bases in Okinawa became an issue that affected national politics, but adjustments between Tokyo and Washington removed the problem from election maneuvers.

Domestic Affairs

Japan entered the year under the leadership of an unusual coalition government. On January 5, Tomiichi Murayama, the nation's first socialist prime minister in 48 years, resigned. Six days later, Ryutaro Hashimoto, president of the once perennially dominant Liberal Democratic Party (LDP), formed a cabinet that still reflected the tentative nature of the coalition. After a general election was held on October 20, Hashimoto was able to form a second cabinet without a coalition, but his government failed to gain a majority.

Party Politics. In the post–World War II era from 1955 to 1993, the conservative LDP had dominated politics. The death of the LDP kingmaker Shin Kanemaru in March 1996 marked the end of his effort to cultivate second-generation figures in the party. These included Prime Minister Hashimoto and his rival, Ichiro Ozawa, who had left the LDP in 1994 to found the opposition New Frontier Party (Shinshinto).

A tactical truce between Hashimoto and Ozawa, necessary to pass the budget in May, angered third-generation leaders such as former Prime Minister Morihiro Hosokawa. As a result, on September 28 yet another dissident group was formed—the Democratic Party of Japan (DPJ). Members included Yukio Hatoyama, former head of the small New Party (Sakigake), which was part of the governing coalition; his brother Kunio Hatoyama, who defected from Shinshinto; and Naoto Kan, a popular politician who resigned from Hashimoto's cabinet.

The Socialists—who were traditional foes of the LDP, but coalition partners since 1994—also felt the impact of change. Just after Murayama resigned, in January, the party shortened its name to the Social Democratic Party (SDP). Negotiation with Sakigake toward forming yet another "nonconservative party" led nowhere. When the Diet convened in January 1996, the coalition (LDP, SDP, and Sakigake) held 292 of a total of 511 seats in

Yukio Hatoyama of the newly formed Democratic Party of Japan (DPJ) sought support prior to the Oct. 20, 1996, balloting. The DPJ won 52 seats on election day, and was expected to play a role in the balance of power in the new government.

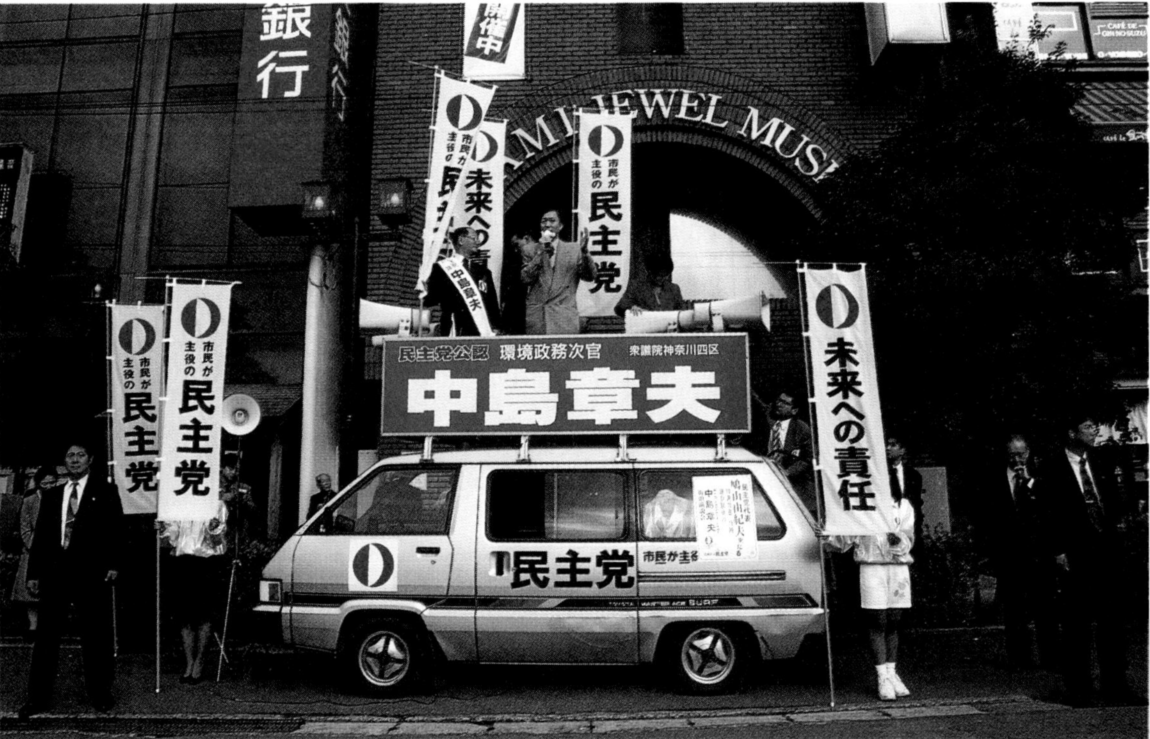

the (lower) House of Representatives. The opposition Shinshinto commanded 169 seats. In the (upper) House of Councillors the governing parties occupied only 140 of a total of 252 seats.

For weeks the Diet was caught in deadlock. Important legislation with regard to health insurance, deregulation of holding companies, and revision of the civil law went on the shelf. When in March the government introduced measures to liquidate housing loan-companies (*jusen*) that had failed in the tumultuous economy of the 1980s, Shinshinto mounted a three-week boycott of the House of Representatives Budget Committee. Opposition to the plan, to use almost $7 billion in public funds to rescue the firms, was expanded by a prior cabinet announcement that the national consumption tax would be raised from 3% to 5%, effective April 1, 1997.

On May 10, more than one month late, the Diet approved a $715 billion budget for fiscal year 1996, which had begun on April 1. By June 18, one day before the session closed, both houses had approved bills to liquidate the *jusen*. Only then did the public learn that half the "secondary losses," which totaled more than $12 billion, also would be covered by the government.

After budget passage, all parties prepared for a general election, which by law had to be held before July 1997. A *Kyodo News* poll revealed that the LDP retained the highest support rate (35%), more than three times that of Shinshinto (10.2%). Moreover, Hashimoto foresaw LDP success in an early vote under a new election law. It was designed to fill 300 seats from winner-take-all, single-seat (rather than the old multiseat) constituencies and 200 seats by proportional representation. Pundits predicted that smaller parties would not fare well in this scheme. On the other hand, the same public-opinion survey indicated that many voters (38%) supported no specific political party.

Prime Minister Hashimoto dissolved the lower house on September 27 and called a snap general election for October 20. The 59.6% turnout of eligible voters was a record low for any general election and confirmed predictions of apathy. The election marked progress of the LDP in its bid to return to power, but it also signaled victory for the status quo despite all the campaign talk about the need for reform and deregulation. In the lower house, Hashimoto's party expanded its plurality from 211 of 511 seats in the old house to 239 of 500 in the new, but was still a dozen short of a majority.

The prime minister immediately began an effort to win over partners for a new coalition. Difficulty lay in the fact that, although Shinshinto lost seats (down from 160 to 156), it remained a formidable opposition. The new DPJ (with 52 seats) was likely to play a role in the balance of power and ignored the LDP appeal. Moreover, partners in the previous government, the SDP (with only 15 seats, down from 30) and Sakigake (two seats), almost were wiped off the electoral map. They refused to enter another coalition and agreed to cooperate with the LDP only on a case-by-case basis to pass legislation.

Finally, on November 7, the lower house met in a special session to reelect Hashimoto with 262 votes, a slim but workable majority. He promptly formed his second cabinet, which was something more than a minority regime and something less than a coalition. In the new government, LDP members occupied all of the cabinet seats. Yukihiko Ikeda remained as foreign-affairs minister and Seiroku Kajiyama, as chief cabinet secretary. All other portfolios were given to veteran LDP figures. The prime minister promised to use skilled politicians to control and deregulate the bureaucracy.

Economy. In 1996, Japan continued a gradual recovery from the longest and deepest slump of the post–World War II era. After the overheated expansion of the 1980s, a nagging recession began in the second quarter of 1991. According to the Economic Planning Agency, the growth rate in gross domestic product (GDP) scraped bottom at 0.3% in 1993. Slowly the rate rose—to 0.5% in 1994 and 0.9% in 1995. In the last quarter of fiscal 1996 (to April 1996), an annualized rate of 2.3% marked the end of the three-year period of "no growth." The Bank of Japan estimated that Japan's annualized GDP was $4.519 trillion.

By the standards of other advanced economies, Japan's growing unemployment rate remained low. Despite the gain in GDP, the number of jobless reached 3.2 million in January. After several months of decline, the unemployment rate hit a record 3.5% in May, the highest level under current calculations since 1953. According to the Management and Coordination Agency, the sharpest rise in joblessness was among women between the ages of 25 and 34.

A major step toward deregulation was taken late in February, when a government advisory panel endorsed the breakup of the giant Nippon Telegraph and Telephone (NTT) Corp. The largely public firm would be split up into two regional telephone companies and a long-distance carrier that could enter the international market.

In July 1991, with the onset of a depression, the Bank of Japan had begun to lower the official discount rate to stimulate the economy—from a high of 6%. By September 1995 the rate reached 0.5%, the lowest level ever; it continued on that floor into 1996.

Society. To senior Japanese the low discount rate meant reduced returns on savings, traditionally used to supplement pensions. To all Japanese the dilemma lay in how a sharply declining cadre of working citizens would be able to support one of the world's most rapidly aging populations. In 1996 life expectancy at birth was at a "world-record" level, 83 years for females and 77 for males. The aged (65 and over) numbered about 15% of total population; this percentage that was predicted to exceed 30% by 2009. If so, the number of workers (aged 15–64) supporting each elder would continue to decline, dropping from 4.7 in 1996 to 2.2.

Two problems in the realm of public health attracted national attention and propelled a politician into prominence. On March 14, district courts in Tokyo and in Osaka imposed a compromise settlement in a lengthy legal case involving five drug firms and some 400 hemophiliacs who had filed suit against the companies in 1989. Earlier, the companies had apologized for distributing blood products that had been contaminated with the human immunodeficiency virus (HIV), which causes AIDS. Health and Welfare Minister Naoto Kan accepted the mediation for the government, pledging that 40% of the settlement (which totaled more than $170 million plus monthly stipends for AIDS victims) would be covered by public funds. He admitted the government's responsibility for poor supervision of drug distribution.

The second crisis arose in July from an outbreak of food poisoning that was centered in Sakai, Osaka prefecture. The Japanese, who had felt secure in their hygiene—particularly in handling foods—were alarmed over the epidemic, the first officially so declared in 20 years. The cause soon was determined to be a contagious strain of *E. coli* bacteria. Illness gripped the Osaka region for weeks and by mid-August produced 9,800 patients and at least 11 fatalities. Elementary schools were closed, food and water management were inspected, and medical examinations were conducted in sensitive areas. Once again HealthMinisteı Kan apologized publicly, stating forthrightly that the government had not responded in timely fashion.

Foreign Affairs

In a policy speech delivered to the Diet on January 22, Prime Minister Hashimoto endorsed an active foreign policy. He described the security arrangement with the United States as Japan's "most important bilateral relationship." He did, however, urge realignment and reduction of U.S. military bases in Japan.

U.S. Relations. In previous years, relations between Tokyo and Washington had been dominated by often-bitter trade disputes. At issue were Japanese exports of products such as textiles and imports of rice, computer chips, automobiles, and other goods. The Ministry of Finance announced that the customs-clearance trade surplus with the United States fell from $54.9 billion in 1994 to $45.5 billion in 1995. In April 1996 alone, the surplus dropped more than 55% from a year earlier, to $1.7 billion—the 14th consecutive monthly decline.

In June 1995, after a last-minute agreement on automobiles, U.S. President Bill Clinton predicted a sharp increase in sales of U.S.-made parts to Japan. In fact, a manufacturers' association in Tokyo announced that in fiscal 1995, major Japanese firms imported more than $21 billion in components. In August a successor agreement was signed providing that Japan would continue such imports voluntarily, but without numerical targets.

In similar fashion, settlement was reached in the sector of computer chips. The Ministry of International Trade and Industry announced that in December 1995, imported semiconductors totaled more than 30% of Japan's market for the first time. On August 2 the United States and Japan signed an agreement on computer chips, symbolically important because it abandoned, according to Tokyo, "managed trade."

JAPAN • Information Highlights

Official Name: Japan.
Location: East Asia.
Area: 145,882 sq mi (377 835 km²).
Population (mid-1996 est.): 125,800,000.
Chief Cities (March 31, 1995 est.): Tokyo, the capital, 7,836,665; Yokohama, 3,273,609; Osaka, 2,478,628; Nagoya, 2,086,745.
Government: *Head of state,* Akihito, emperor (acceded Jan. 9, 1989). *Head of government,* Ryutaro Hashimoto, prime minister (took office January 1996). *Legislature*—Diet: House of Councillors and House of Representatives.
Monetary Unit: Yen (113.88 yen equal U.S.$1, Dec. 17, 1996).
Gross Domestic Product (1994 est. U.S.$): $2,527,400,-000,000 (purchasing power parity).
Economic Indexes (1995, 1990 = 100): *Consumer Prices,* all items, 107.0; food, 106.1. *Industrial Production,* 95.
Foreign Trade (1995 U.S.$): *Imports,* $336,080,000,000; *exports,* $443,274,000,000.

In place of trade, security issues occupied the center of negotiations in 1996. On April 17, at the end of their summit meeting in Tokyo, Prime Minister Hashimoto and President Clinton reaffirmed the Japan-U.S. security alliance as "vital for stability and prosperity" in the entire Pacific region. An earlier cross-servicing pact expanded the scope of security, providing military cooperation in case of a threat even beyond Japan's borders.

On March 7 in Naha, Okinawa, three U.S. servicemen were convicted and sentenced for abduction and rape of a 12-year-old schoolgirl the previous September. The incident added to public sentiment against the U.S. military presence on Okinawa, a small island that was housing three quarters of U.S. bases in Japan. U.S. Ambassador Walter Mondale had helped quiet the uproar by promptly stating that, under the Status of Forces Agreement, alleged crimes by off-duty personnel would be judged under Japanese jurisdiction. In a brief meeting with President Clinton in California in February, Prime Minister Hashimoto raised the issue of Okinawa but agreed to postpone decision until their summit meeting in Tokyo. On April 15 a joint statement affirmed the U.S. promise to relinquish 20% of Okinawan land used for bases.

Even after the judgment and statement, a campaign to scale back the U.S. presence continued. It was under the direction of Okinawa Gov. Masahide Ota, who refused to exercise eminent domain to renew leases. After he lost two suits in district courts and an appeal to the Supreme Court, the governor still awaited a local plebiscite on the issue, held September 8. Results were in his favor, by a 10–1 ratio, but with a low turnout. Finally, on September 13 he gave up the legal fight and agreed to renew the land leases. On September 24 at the United Nations, Prime Minister Hashimoto and President Clinton reaffirmed the reduction of Okinawa bases and their relocation to elsewhere in Japan in five to seven years.

Russian Relations. On April 19 in Moscow, Prime Minister Hashimoto held a summit meeting with Russian President Boris Yeltsin. It was the first visit to Russia by a Japanese leader in a decade. The Japanese urged revitalization of talks toward a peace treaty, blocked since 1945 by a border dispute. At issue were four small islands in the Kurils, historically claimed by Japan but occupied by Russia since World War II. Almost in sight of Hokkaido, the islets were known by Japanese as the "Northern Territories." At the Moscow meeting, Yeltsin reaffirmed a promise made in the Tokyo Declaration (1993), which called for prompt resolution of the dispute. However, the Russian president was unable to make further concessions.

China. Small islands also disturbed relations between Tokyo and Beijing. When, in February, Tokyo announced plans to enforce a 200-mi (370-km) exclusive sea zone around Japan, China—as well as Taiwan and South Korea—protested. In China's case, the zone would include islands under Japan's control, the Senkaku (known to Chinese, who also claim the islands, as the Diaoyu). The Japanese built a lighthouse in the disputed area to symbolize ownership. Periodically, small, symbolic "invasions" by nationalist protesters were mounted by Chinese from the mainland, Taiwan, and Hong Kong.

More serious were differences over a larger island, Taiwan. Japan had recognized Beijing as the capital of one China but, like the United States, carried on informal contact with Chinese on Taiwan. In March the mainland regime carried out sensitive military maneuvers in the Taiwan Straits in the midst of a presidential election in Taiwan. On March 31 in Tokyo, Foreign Affairs Minister Ikeda in most strenuous terms informed his Chinese counterpart, Qian Qichen, that Japan disapproved of the military exercises. Qian responded sharply that Taiwan was a domestic Chinese issue, adding that China would uphold the policies of "one nation, two systems" and "peaceful unification," but would retain the option of applying force.

Most serious to Tokyo was China's policy with regard to nuclear weapons. On July 29, Prime Minister Hashimoto, voicing Japan's understandable nuclear allergy, expressed displeasure with China's latest nuclear experiments; these had come on the eve of talks in Geneva to negotiate a global test-ban treaty.

The Two Koreas. Although Japan normalized relations with South Korea in 1965, Tokyo still had no formal contact with North Korea. In March, Japan's media carried a flurry of reports on secret meetings in Beijing among foreign-affairs officials seeking to establish Japan–North Korea relations. On June 22–23 on Korea's island of Cheju, Prime Minister Hashimoto met with South Korea's President Kim Young Sam, agreeing to support talks among the two Koreas, the United States, China, and Japan to promote stability on the peninsula.

Tokyo's announcement of a 200-mi (370-km) sea zone affected relations with Seoul as well, since the zone included yet another island, which was controlled by the Koreans.

ARDATH W. BURKS, *Rutgers University*

JORDAN

In 1996, Jordan experienced its worst unrest in seven years, as rioting broke out over an increase in the price of bread. The nation also continued to deal with the ramifications of the peace treaty signed with Israel in October 1994. The basic line of cleavage remained between those who favored increasingly close economic and other links with Israel and those—at least a substantial minority—who held that such policies were being pursued much too fast or were entirely mistaken. The former policy also involved closer relations with the United States. For the first eight months of the year, King Hussein and his government appeared to be zealously pursuing close cooperation with the United States and with Israel; later, some criticisms were voiced.

JORDAN • Information Highlights

Official Name: Hashemite Kingdom of Jordan.
Location: Southwest Asia.
Area: 34,445 sq mi (89 213 km^2).
Population (mid-1996 est.): 4,200,000.
Chief Cities (Dec. 31, 1991 est.): Amman, the capital, 965,000; Zarqa, 359,000; Irbid, 216,000.
Government: *Head of state,* Hussein I, king (enthroned May 2, 1953). *Head of government,* Abd al-Karim al-Kabariti, prime minister (took office February 1996). *Legislature*—National Assembly: House of Notables and House of Representatives.
Monetary Unit: Dinar (0.71073 dinar equals U.S.$1, Dec. 31, 1996).
Gross Domestic Product (1994 est. U.S.$): $17,000,000,-000 (purchasing power parity).
Economic Indexes (1995, 1990 = 100): *Consumer Prices,* all items, 123.2; food, 126.3. *Industrial Production,* 124.
Foreign Trade (1995 U.S.$): *Imports,* $3,697,000,000; *exports,* $1,769,000,000.

Domestic Affairs. After little more than a year in office, Prime Minister Sharif Zayd bin Shakir was replaced in early February by Abd al-Karim al-Kabariti, who appointed a new cabinet. In office he made a point of giving a freer hand to the media and declined to follow up on previous hints of official action to curb professional associations. There, however, did not seem to be much change in basic policies. The Kabariti administration lost some popularity before year's end.

Serious discontent was manifested, as has happened before in Jordan, not over foreign policy or ideological issues but over something more basic—the price of necessities. In June and July the Kabariti government was considering reducing the bread subsidy—which had become more costly because of a steep rise in the world price of wheat—and thus reducing the government's $211 million budget deficit. The eventual phasing out of all food subsidies is a virtual International Monetary Fund (IMF) condition for continued international aid to Jordan. Donor countries meeting in Paris on July 10 pledged $1 billion to Jordan over the next two years.

However, when the price of bread was roughly tripled on August 16, widespread rioting broke out in southern Jordan, the poorest part of the country. The riots were centered in the town of Kerak. The course of events was strikingly similar to the riots of 1989. Stern military measures were instituted. King Hussein, in military uniform, toured Kerak on August 18, and order was restored by August 19. The summer session of parliament was dissolved. The king blamed "foreign circles," specifically Iraq, and the Jordanian Arab Socialist Baath Party for inciting the riots. In September it was announced that 145 people involved in the riots would be put on trial. In

© Yousef Allan/AP/Wide World Photos

In mid-August 1996, Jordanians lined up to purchase bread in the southern city of Kerak. An increase in the cost of bread, caused by a rise in the world price of wheat, had led to massive demonstrations. In turn, the government had imposed a curfew.

In October 1996, Jordan's King Hussein (left) *was received with full military honors when he met with Palestine leader Yasir Arafat* (right) *in Jericho in the West Bank. The monarch was the first Arab leader to visit a Palestinian-ruled area.*

© David Silverman/Reuters/Archive Photos

early November, Hussein gained in popularity after he asked his government to lower bread prices, since the world price of grain had declined again.

Economic Development. Plans went forward for various kinds of economic development, many in cooperation with Israel or the United States. In one of the most impressive, Jordan and Enron Corporation on March 27 signed a letter of intent to build a $300 million plant in Aqaba to supply Jordan as well as Israel with natural gas by the year 2000. The talks were completed by May 28.

External Relations. The marked reversal of Jordan's attitudes since the 1991 Persian Gulf war, when it refused to join the anti-Iraqi coalition and thus lost the friendship and financial support of Saudi Arabia, began to pay dividends in 1996. In January, Saudi Foreign Minister Prince Saud al-Faisal visited Amman, thus symbolizing the end of the breach. Saudi oil again became available to Jordan, but the nation continued to rely on imports from Iraq because of the advantageous prices. Also in January, the United States offered Jordan a $300 million military-modernization package that would include F-16 planes and M60 tanks.

The two sons-in-law of Saddam Hussein of Iraq—who had defected on Aug. 8, 1995, to Jordan—returned voluntarily to Iraq in February, and soon after were murdered. King Hussein condemned this action. Gen. Nizar al-Khazraji, former chief of staff of the Iraqi army, defected to Jordan on March 22. The same day, Jordan expelled a member of the Iraqi-embassy staff for harassing Iraqi exiles; Iraq retaliated by expelling a Jordanian diplomat. Between February and September, full diplomatic relations were reestablished between Jordan and all the Gulf states except Kuwait.

In early April, Jordan gave permission for U.S. planes to be based in Jordan to carry out patrols over southern Iraq, and Iraqi opposition leaders were allowed to open offices in Jordan. These were Jordan's most overtly anti-Iraqi actions to date. On May 26 daily commercial air service between Israel and Jordan was launched by Royal Jordanian Airlines and El Al.

King Hussein attended the antiterrorist conference on March 13 at Sharm El-Sheikh, flying there in U.S. President Bill Clinton's plane. The king paid his first state visit to Israel on January 10. He phoned Israeli Prime Minister Benjamin Netanyahu to congratulate him on his victory in the May Israeli general election, and the new Israeli premier visited Amman on August 5. At the Arab summit in Cairo, June 21–23, the king talked with Syrian President Hafiz al-Assad for the first time since May 1994.

After Saddam Hussein's largely successful and unpunished incursion into Kurdish northern Iraq in September, King Hussein "expressed concern" about the U.S. retaliatory measures. His brother, the crown prince, went further in criticizing U.S. policy in Iraq, including the continuance of sanctions. At the end of September, the king criticized the Israeli government for creating a new opening to an archaeological tunnel near Muslim holy sites in Jerusalem. The king contended that the Israeli actions violated the 1994 Washington agreements that had recognized Jordan's "special role" as interim guardian of Muslim holy sites in Jerusalem.

ARTHUR CAMPBELL TURNER
University of California, Riverside

KENYA

Kenya made substantial economic reforms in 1996, but the government's commitment to political reform remained questionable.

Political Reform. Elections were slated for sometime in 1997. Opposition parties asserted that major constitutional reforms would be necessary to ensure a democratic outcome. However, President Daniel arap Moi of the ruling Kenya African National Union (KANU) refused to consider constitutional reforms prior to elections.

The existing electoral system severely hampered the political opposition. For example, the government required that all parties be registered, but Moi refused to recognize any new parties. This policy left the status of Safina, a movement headed by paleontologist Richard Leakey and longtime opposition leader Paul Muite, up in the air. Existing laws also required that public meetings be licensed by the provincial administration, a task made all the more difficult by Moi's threat to sack any civil servant linked to the opposition. Should a party register and hold meetings, it still could be banned under the terms of the Registration of Parties Act. Finally, the Electoral Commission of Kenya was largely a bastion of support for the president, and abdicated responsibility for administering elections to Moi's office. Given the disarray of the opposition parties—FORD-Kenya's annual meeting dissolved into a factional brawl and FORD-Asili called for the expulsion of all Asians as the solution to corruption—KANU seemed poised to win the elections.

KENYA • Information Highlights

Official Name: Republic of Kenya.
Location: East Coast of Africa.
Area: 224,961 sq mi (582 650 km²).
Population (mid-1996 est.): 28,200,000.
Chief Cities (1990 est.): Nairobi, the capital, 1,505,000; Mombasa, 537,000.
Government: *Head of state and government,* Daniel T. arap Moi, president (took office Oct. 1978). *Legislature* (unicameral)—National Assembly.
Monetary Unit: Kenya shilling (56.922 shillings equal U.S.$1, August 1996).
Gross Domestic Product (1994 est. U.S.$): $33,100,000,000 (purchasing power parity).
Economic Index (1995, 1990 = 100): *Consumer Prices,* all items, 297.1; food, 309.8.
Foreign Trade (1995 U.S.$): *Imports,* $3,006,000,000; *exports,* $1,890,000,000.

KANU also expanded its control over the media beyond the state-run television and radio by purchasing a controlling interest in the *East African Standard*, one of the largest daily newspapers in Kenya. In an effort to control media it did not own, the government introduced a bill that would permit it to imprison any journalist and close any media operation that criticized the government. In the face of widespread domestic and international opposition, the government withdrew the bill.

Economic Reform. Kenya made progress in convincing international donors that it was serious about economic reform. President Moi drafted a policy framework that sought to decrease corruption, increase the pace of privatization, and decrease the public-sector deficit. He also established a presidential commission on economic reform to oversee the reform process. More importantly, the government took concrete steps to address the problem of corruption in the Port of Mombasa by sacking the minister for transportation, the head of the port authority, and 17 civil servants, who thereafter faced charges of defrauding the government. Minister of Finance Musalia Mudavadi introduced a balanced budget that sought to reduce inflation, rein in government-affiliated companies, and surpass the 5% growth rate achieved in 1995. Moreover, Kenya Airways was privatized in the largest stock issue in the history of the Nairobi Stock Exchange.

In March donors reacted positively by pledging $730 million to support the reforms—a figure that represented about half the amount of assistance Kenya received annually a decade earlier. Embarrassingly, after receiving $50 million from the World Bank for the rehabilitation of the Nairobi-Mombasa road, arguably the most important in the country, President Moi announced the purchase of a $60 million presidential jet—an expenditure that had not been included in the budget. Moreover, the principal suspect in the largest financial scandal in Kenya's history ran for parliament on the KANU ticket.

Human Rights. Amnesty International reported that torture was a principal tool of the police. Similar problems were identified by the U.S. Department of State. Given the importance of strengthening human rights and conducting free and fair elections, it appeared difficult to see how Kenya and its donors would maintain their current levels of cooperation.

WILLIAM CYRUS REED
The American University in Cairo

KOREA

In South Korea the 1996 trial of two former presidents and their aides for their roles in the 1979–80 power grab by the military and for subsequent corruption in office resulted in guilty verdicts for all defendants except one. Despite the modest success of the ruling party in the April 1996 general elections, the public image of the government under President Kim Young Sam was tarnished by allegations of bribery involving high officials. The intrusion by a North Korean submarine on the east coast of South Korea in September shocked—and angered—the people, but their daily concerns continued to focus on the economy.

For North Koreans, 1996 was another year of economic hardship. Politically, the suspense over Kim Jong Il's accession to official positions of supreme power continued. North-South relations reached a virtual breakdown over Pyongyang's unilateral dismantling of the military-armistice arrangement, the submarine incident, and the subsequent hardening of Seoul's position. The tension, however, eased somewhat late in the year when North Korea offered a vaguely worded apology for the act of submarine intrusion.

Republic of Korea (South Korea)

Politics and Society. Close on the heels of the arrest of former President Roh Tae-woo, his predecessor and mentor Chun Doo Hwan also was taken into custody in December 1995. He was charged with mutiny, insurrection, and extortion of bribery in connection with his seizure of power in 1979–80 and the brutal suppression of pro-democracy demonstrations in Kwangju in May 1980. He also was accused of amassing an illicit fortune of $900 million. The trial of the two former presidents, a score of their advisers and former colleagues, and several prominent business leaders produced, in August, guilty verdicts for all but one defendant. Chun received the death penalty (later reduced to life in prison), while Roh was sentenced to 22 ½ (later reduced to 17) years in prison. Most of the other defendants received shorter sentences; a few got suspended sentences.

The trial of the leaders of the preceding administrations obviously was on the mind of President Kim Young Sam when he called for a campaign to right the wrongs of history. In reaffirmation of Kim's resolve to distance himself from his predecessors, the name of the ruling party was changed to New Korea Party (NKP) from Democratic Liberal Party (DLP). The name change was clearly in preparation for the scheduled April general elections. Kim also reshuffled high NKP officials and invited well-known reform advocates to join the party in an effort to highlight the party's commitment to reform.

The voters gave the NKP 139 National Assembly seats out of a total of 299 (46%). The followers of longtime opposition politician Kim Dae Jung won only 79 seats (26%), well below their goal for their party, the National Congress for New Politics (NCNP). Kim himself failed to return to his assembly seat. Kim Jong Pil's United Liberal Democrats took 50 seats in the legislature.

A series of corruption cases tended to tarnish the image of President Kim as a reformist leader. In March a member of the presidential staff and longtime confidant of President Kim was charged with having accepted a huge bribe. Perhaps more damaging was the dis-

© Yun Jai-hyoung/AP/Wide World Photos

Lee Hoi-chang, center, *the chief campaign manager for the ruling New Korea Party (NKP), campaigned with parliamentary candidates in Seoul in March 1996. The NKP captured 139 of 299 National Assembly seats in South Korea's general elections in April.*

missal and indictment of the defense minister in October on charges of having offered a bribe to secure promotion while he was on active duty in the air force, as well as having accepted a large sum from a defense contractor. The revelation of the defense chief's misdeeds could not have come at a worse time. The combat readiness of the military then was being questioned in connection with the drawn-out manhunt for North Korean infiltrators who had landed from a submarine that ran aground on September 18 near the east-coast city of Kangnung. The 11-man crew and 15 passengers, including specially trained commandos, abandoned ship and made their way to the rugged mountain area near the coast. A massive manhunt by more than 60,000 South Korean troops took nearly two months. The troops killed 13 North Koreans and captured one, while 11 were found dead, possibly as the result of a suicide pact. The last one remaining at large was presumed dead. South Korean casualties were also considerable: 13 soldiers and policemen and three civilians dead.

The incident had far-reaching ramifications. The people in the South were alarmed that such a breach of their coastal defense could happen and that the mopping-up operations against the infiltrators were so sluggish. Above all, they were outraged by this armed provocation and by the North Korean attempt to deny any culpability. Pyongyang claimed that the ship had strayed into the South because of engine failure, and then went on to threaten retaliation against the South for the loss of its men.

The tense North-South relations also were involved when several thousand pro–North Korean students staged violent demonstrations in and around Yonsei University in Seoul in August after they had been denied permission to march to Panmunjom to meet their North Korean counterparts for a rally for Korean unification. Riot police occupied the campus and arrested more than 5,000 students, of whom nearly 450 were indicted.

As the year ended, there was no indication of who would be running in the December 1997 presidential election. Who was to get President Kim's blessing as the NKP candidate, as he himself could not run for a second term? Would the two Kims in opposition run one more time? Because of the enormous power of the president, and because of the widespread anticipation of some form of drastic change in inter-Korean relations during the five-year tenure of the next president, 1997 was slated to be a year of crucial decision for South Koreans.

Foreign Affairs. The most important task of South Korea's foreign policy in 1996 continued to be the management of its relations with the United States—a task that became all the more urgent due to the steady, albeit slow, growth in North Korean–U.S. contacts. The United States wanted to go ahead with the Korean Peninsula Energy Development Organization (KEDO) project to provide two light-water reactors to North Korea, and looked toward a gradual evolution of diplomatic and economic relations with the North. In contrast, South Korea was more interested in reactivating the dialogue with the North that had been dormant since 1992, and it considered the opening of a direct Pyongyang-Washington channel unhelpful for this purpose.

North Korea, for its part, sought better relations with the United States to end its

Dissident students and riot police clashed during demonstrations inside Yonsei University in August 1996. The students were demanding the reunification of South Korea with North Korea.

SOUTH KOREA • Information Highlights

Official Name: Republic of Korea.
Location: Northeastern Asia.
Area: 38,023 sq mi (98 480 km²).
Population (mid-1996 est.): 45,300,000.
Chief City (1990 census): Seoul, the capital, 10,612,577.
Government: *Head of state and government,* Kim Young Sam, president (formally inaugurated Feb. 25, 1993). *Legislature*—National Assembly.
Monetary Unit: Won (819.4 won equal U.S.$1, August 1996).
Gross Domestic Product (1994 est. U.S.$): $508,300,-000,000.
Economic Indexes (1995, 1990 = 100): *Consumer Prices,* all items, 135.1; food, 140.0. *Industrial Production,* 150.
Foreign Trade (1995 U.S.$): *Imports,* $135,216,000,000; *exports,* $125,453,000,000.

diplomatic and economic isolation and, at the same time, to drive a wedge between the South and the United States. Pyongyang's insistence on direct bilateral negotiations with Washington for a peace treaty to replace the 1953 armistice agreement, without South Korean involvement, was designed to undermine the legitimacy of the Seoul government. Seoul, wary of the North Korean stratagem, wished its U.S. ally to be cautious.

In April, on his way to Japan, U.S. President Bill Clinton made a stopover on the Korean island of Cheju to reaffirm U.S.–South Korean solidarity and cooperation. He joined President Kim in calling for a conference of four nations—the two Koreas, the United States, and China—to negotiate the political future of the peninsula. The two presidents met again in November in Manila, where Kim reportedly withdrew his earlier demand that Pyongyang should apologize for the submarine incident before the United States or South Korea would proceed with the plans for the four-power conference and the KEDO projects. Clinton, in return, agreed to go on record as demanding that North Korea take acceptable steps to resolve the submarine incident, reduce tension, and avoid future provocations. But when the moderate foreign minister of South Korea, Gong Ro-myung, resigned suddenly in early November, many observers took it as a sign of Seoul's tilt toward a hard-line position in dealing with Pyongyang, and with Washington as well.

Economic diplomacy was a salient theme in the high-level exchanges of visitors to and from South Korea. The presidents of Paraguay, Colombia, and Mexico visited Seoul, while President Kim, accompanied by a 40-man business delegation, journeyed to Guatemala, Argentina, Chile, Brazil, and Peru in September. Kim also traveled to Thailand, Malaysia, Singapore, Vietnam, and the Philippines and spoke of economic cooperation. He attended the first Asia Europe Meeting (ASEM), a summit meeting of ten Asian nations (the seven ASEAN members, Japan, China, and South Korea) and 15 European nations, held in Bangkok in March to promote a broad-based partnership with an economic emphasis. Visitors to Seoul included the prime ministers of Great Britain, the Netherlands, and Pakistan, as well as the king of Spain.

South Korea's growing international status was recognized by two events in 1996: its admission to the Organization for Economic Cooperation and Development (OECD) and the selection of South Korea and Japan as cohosts of the World Cup soccer competition in 2002.

Economy. South Korea had a record harvest in 1996, up 13% from 1995. Agricultural output helped the overall economic-growth rate to reach 6.9% instead of an earlier-forecast 6.8%. The same report put the per-capita gross national product (GNP) at $10,800, a 7% increase over 1995. Despite these encouraging statistics, there was a growing concern over a putative economic downturn, especially among business leaders. They pointed to a slowdown in manufacturing, rising prices, and a growing trade deficit. South Korea's export trade clearly was suffering. Statistics for July showed negative growth in exports for the first time since January 1993, while imports grew 13.7% over those of a year earlier. South Korea's trade balance was hurt by soaring labor costs and the growing demand for foreign consumer goods.

For the past several years, wages have been rising much faster than labor productivity. Combined with relatively high interest rates, these rapidly rising labor costs have undermined the competitiveness of South Korean products overseas. Belatedly, the government asked a commission to study possible labor-law changes. In another attempt to cut costs, many corporations tried to streamline their organizations and freeze the salaries of their executives. These developments were considered to be signs of hard times, and a vague sense of economic insecurity began to emerge.

Democratic People's Republic of Korea (North Korea)

Politics. The enigma surrounding Kim Jong Il's succession to the state and party posts left vacant by his father's death in 1994 continued for another year. The Supreme People's Assembly in 1996 still did not elect Kim president of North Korea, and the Central Committee of the Workers' Party did not vote to elevate him to general secretary. According to the great majority of outside observers, however, the 54-year-old Kim remained firmly in control.

The North Korean media continued to proclaim Kim Il Sung, father of Kim Jong Il, as the Great Leader and the savior of the nation two years after his death, even as they praised his eldest son. Whether this reliance on Kim Il Sung's charisma to legitimize the current leadership implied any weakness in his son's political standing was unclear. Nevertheless, the unexplained delay in succession amid conditions of severe economic difficulties gave rise to speculations about the future of North Korea. Some observers cited the steady flow of escapees from the North to the South, among them individuals from the privileged sectors of society, to forecast an implosion of North Korea. There were also warnings that North Korea, out of desperation, might resort to an all-out war that would end up in its absorption by the South. All things pointed to some form of change in North Korea in the not-too-distant future, but no solid evidence of any serious challenge to the existing regime or system surfaced in 1996.

Foreign Affairs. In 1996, North Korea increased its contacts with the United States. The United States, for its part, was interested in inducing Pyongyang to discard its self-imposed isolation and rejoin the international community. Negotiations began regarding the location and return of the remains of U.S. servicemen from the Korean War and produced an agreement that promised the payment of $2 million by the United States in return for North Korea's pledge of cooperation.

Working-level contacts for implementation of the KEDO agreement went on in New York and on the construction site in North Korea and involved U.S. managerial and technical staff. Two rounds of meetings took place in April and October to bring North Korea's development, production, and sale of ballistic missiles under international control. Test firing of the Rodong-1 missile with a reported 1,000-km (620-mi) range was a cause for alarm in Japan and the United States, as well as in South Korea.

© AP/Wide World Photos

The September intrusion of a North Korean submarine on the east coast of South Korea caused anguish in the South. The North expressed regrets for the incident as 1996 ended.

In August the U.S. State Department nominated a career diplomat to head the future U.S. liaison office in Pyongyang. Washington also pledged $2 million to provide grain for North Korea when South Korea chose to delay further food assistance until there was a change in the North's attitude toward the South. On the other hand, the United States continued to resist North Korea's demands for direct bilateral negotiations to conclude a peace treaty to replace the 1953 armistice. When North Korea announced in early April that it no longer would carry out its responsibilities under the 1953 accord for the maintenance and administration of the DMZ and proceeded to introduce heavily armed troops into the buffer zone for three days in violation of the agreement, the United States rebuffed this unilateral dismantling of the armistice regime. Washington condemned the submarine intrusion as a violation of the truce terms but it did extract from Pyongyang an expression of regret after weeks of negotiations.

North Korea's desire for better relations with the United States also was underlined in November when it released Evan C. Hunzik-

NORTH KOREA • Information Highlights

Official Name: Democratic People's Republic of Korea.
Location: Northeastern Asia.
Area: 46,540 sq mi (120 540 km²).
Population (mid-1996 est.): 23,900,000.
Chief Cities (1986 est.): Pyongyang, the capital, 2,000,000; Hamhung, 670,000.
Government: *Head of state and government,* president (vacant as of Dec. 31, 1996). *Legislature* (unicameral)—Supreme People's Assembly.
Gross Domestic Product (1994 est. U.S.$): $21,300,000,000.

© Katsumi Kasahara/AP/Wide World Photos

Evan C. Hunziker, 26, who spent three months in a North Korean prison on spy charges, apparently committed suicide shortly after his release and return to Tacoma, WA, in November 1996.

er, a self-styled U.S. missionary who had been detained and charged with spying.

North Korea's relations with China remained good and, in July, unconfirmed reports suggested that China might extend concessionary friendship prices for its sales to North Korea and that China also had agreed to supply millions of tons of grain, oil, and coal over the next five years. A potential kink in this relationship is North Korea's interest in economic and other exchanges with Taiwan.

Economy. The economy of North Korea remained very depressed, with continuing shortages of food and energy. The Bank of Korea in Seoul estimated that, in 1995, the North's GNP was $22.3 billion, or less than one twentieth that of the South; on a per-capita basis, the North's $957 was about one tenth that of the South's. The growth rates of major industries were mostly negative, with the lowest being –10.5% in agriculture, forestry, and fisheries. Foreign trade was about $2.05 billion, down 2.1% from the previous year.

Official North Korean delegations visited the United States, Japan, Hong Kong, Taiwan, and China asking for assistance. One highly placed North Korean official was quoted as having said in Washington, DC, that North Korea was interested in expanding economic cooperation with capitalist nations. The statement seemed to be credible, considering Pyongyang's interest in developing free-trade zones on both the east and west coasts.

Inter-Korean Relations

The year 1996 marked the lowest point in inter-Korean relations in decades. Even before the September submarine incident, it was clear that demands and counterdemands coming from the two Koreas were difficult to reconcile. The North demanded, as a precondition for the North-South dialogue, that Seoul apologize for not expressing its condolences at the death of Kim Il Sung. It also persisted in its demand for replacing the 1953 truce with a peace treaty that was to be negotiated directly with the United States, without the South's participation. The South, on the other hand, insisted on resumption of the dialogue as a precondition for any aid to the North. Seoul also asked Washington and Tokyo to join it in persuading Pyongyang to reopen the dialogue before they responded to Pyongyang's call for improving relations.

Mindful of Pyongyang's ungrateful behavior at the time of the delivery of 150,000 tons of rice from the South in 1995, President Kim, early in 1996, characterized the attitude of the North as one of betrayal. Kim's choice of the word set the tone for Seoul's hard-line position. Frigid North-South relations went from bad to worse as Pyongyang tore up the armistice agreement in the spring. The submarine incident in September further heightened the sense of crisis, at least in the South. Pyongyang's initial refusal to acknowledge and apologize for this truce violation, coupled with threats of retaliation, dashed hopes of easing the tension until the North expressed regret over the incident.

Chilly inter-Korean political relations spilled over into the fledgling economic exchanges between the two Koreas. South Korean statistics on inter-Korean trade showed a 25% decline in the two-way transactions during the first nine months of 1996 from the corresponding figures of the preceding year, or a decline in value from $253 million to $190 million. The change was particularly noticeable in the North's exports to the South: a 30% decline, from $193 million to $135 million. The setback was not confined to trade. Only days before the beaching of the submarine, Seoul decided not to send businessmen to a seminar in North Korea to brief prospective foreign investors about the operation of the Sonbong-Rajin free-trade zone, a pioneering economic-liberalization project in the North. The reason: The North invited only businessmen, excluding South Korean government officials and journalists.

HAN-KYO KIM, *University of Cincinnati*

LABOR

U.S. employment showed significant improvements in 1996 as compared to 1995. Unemployment for most age and ethnic groups fell during the year.

United States

Employment and Unemployment. U.S. employment in November 1996 was 2.6 million higher than in November 1995, while unemployment declined by 200,000, resulting in a decrease in the jobless rate to 5.3% as compared with 5.6% a year earlier. Unemployment for adult men and teenagers improved in 1996, dropping to 4.5% for men and to 16.8% for teenagers. The rate for women remained stationary at 4.8%. White and Hispanic workers showed significant decreases in unemployment, to 4.6% and 8.3%, respectively. Unemployment among black workers, however, rose to 10.6%. By region, the jobless rate was lowest in the Midwest, at 4.6%, and highest in the West, at 6.3%. All regions, however, fared better than a year earlier in terms of unemployment.

There was no evidence that the increase in the minimum wage, which became effective October 1, had any effect on employment. An interesting development noted in recent years was an increase in "contingent workers"—who include laid-off workers who remain "on call" by their former employers, temporary-help-agency workers, independent contractors, and workers provided to employers by contract firms. The Department of Labor only began to report statistics on these categories of workers in 1995.

Teamster Election. In a bitterly fought battle, Ron Carey, 60, was reelected in December to a second five-year term as president of the 1.4-million-member International Brotherhood of Teamsters, the largest union in the American Federation of Labor–Congress of Industrial Organizations (AFL-CIO). He received 52% of the votes cast, while his opponent, James P. Hoffa, received 48%.

Carey was criticized by some local union leaders for intervening too much in local affairs. Carey responded that such critics were angry because he limited their freedom to manipulate local union finances to their benefit. Even some Carey supporters complained, however, that he negotiated less than sterling contracts. But he countered that it was difficult to win generous contracts from tough employers who had benefited from the deregulation of the trucking industry.

Carey had earned a reputation as a clean leader who disassociated himself from the parent union's mob ties. He also avoided the

In December 1996, Ron Carey (below) *was elected to a second five-year term as president of the International Brotherhood of Teamsters. Carey outpolled James P. Hoffa, son of the famous teamster leader Jimmy Hoffa, to win the bitterly waged contest.*

luxurious lifestyle of his predecessors, selling the union's two private jets and conducting executive meetings in Washington instead of Hawaii, a location favored in the past.

Automobile Negotiations. The United Automobile Workers (UAW) and the three major U.S. auto manufacturers reached separate three-year agreements without a national strike at any company. The first agreement, which set a pattern for the other two, was reached in mid-September with the Ford Motor Company. It was followed by a contract with Chrysler two weeks later, and with General Motors in November. All three contracts were designed to maintain employment near existing levels, while allowing the companies to reduce labor costs in order to compete with nonunion Japanese and European auto plants in the southern United States.

The companies agreed to maintain employment at roughly 95% of late-1996 levels, with exceptions for market downturns and efficiency improvements. This represented a departure from a trend over 15 years, during which time the industry halved its workforce, partly by closing or selling parts factories while buying more parts from nonunion suppliers. In return for the employment guarantee, the companies would be allowed to pay lower wages in auto-parts factories that they buy or build. The contracts also provided for a $2,000 bonus in 1996, followed by 3% wage increases in the second and third years. Cost-of-living adjustments (COLA) would continue for the duration of the contracts, which covered roughly 400,000 UAW members.

Unions and the National Elections. The AFL-CIO spent $35 million on media advertisements in the 1996 presidential and congressional elections, with mixed results. It supported President Bill Clinton, who became the first Democrat to win reelection since Franklin D. Roosevelt. However, the Congress remained in the hands of the Republican Party, which generally is inimical to union legislative objectives. According to the AFL-CIO, union members and their families constituted 23% of the nation's voters. They supported Clinton over Republican nominee Bob Dole by 59% to 29%.

Alexis Herman, 49-year-old White House director of public liaison, was named to succeed Robert B. Reich as secretary of labor in the second Clinton term.

Minimum Wage. After months of debate, Congress passed a bill increasing the minimum wage from $4.25 to $5.15 an hour in two steps. The bill was signed into law in August. The first step, effective Oct. 1, 1996, increased the minimum by 50¢ per hour; a second increase of 40¢ would become effective Sept. 1, 1997. Taken together, the increases would translate into an annual pretax raise of $1,800 for millions of workers. To reduce the effect on small businesses, the measure provided for some tax breaks for small employers.

U.S. EMPLOYMENT AND UNEMPLOYMENT (Armed Forces Excluded)

	Nov. 1995	Nov. 1996
Labor Force	132,400,000	134,800,000
Participation Rate	66.4%	66.9%
Employed	125,000,000	127,600,000
Unemployed	7,400,000	7,200,00
Unemployment Rate	5.6%	5.3%
Adult Men	4.9%	4.5%
Adult Women	4.8%	4.8%
Teenagers	17.9%	16.8%
White	5.0%	4.6%
Black	9.4%	10.6%
Hispanic	9.4%	8.3%

Source: U.S. Bureau of Labor Statistics

Replacement Workers. The U.S. Court of Appeals in Washington, DC, dealt the Clinton administration and labor unions a setback in February by overturning a presidential order prohibiting companies with federal contracts exceeding $100,000 from hiring permanent replacements for striking workers. The order followed an unsuccessful attempt by the White House and congressional Democrats to pass legislation in 1993 that would have outlawed the hiring of permanent replacements of strikers in private labor disputes. The court ruled that the executive order violated the National Labor Relations Act, which guarantees employers the right to hire permanent replacements.

Professional-Baseball Agreement. After protracted and contentious negotiations, the club owners and the Major League Baseball Players Association reached a historic agreement that assured labor peace for at least four years. The owners voted, 26–4, on November 26 in favor of the same tentative agreement that they had rejected three weeks earlier. The new contract would provide for interleague regular-season games in 1997 and 1998 between American League and National League teams for the first time. Other provisions include a luxury tax (an assessment on team payrolls that exceed a specified amount), revenue sharing between rich and poor clubs, and a gradual increase in minimum salary from $109,000 in 1996 to $200,000 in 2001. The contract ended a destructive period of labor turmoil during which there was a 234-day players' strike affecting two seasons and causing the cancellation of a World Series. The contract was retroactive from the 1996

SPECIAL REPORT/LABOR

The Reemergence of Sweatshops

Factories in which persons worked long hours in unhealthy conditions for very low pay were especially widespread in the U.S. garment industry in the early 1900s. Such sweatshops have made a comeback in the United States and elsewhere in the latter years of the 20th century. Inspections of garment workshops across the United States have found increasing exploitation of recent immigrants in small workshops, particularly in the New York and Los Angeles areas.

According to U.S. Secretary of Labor Robert Reich, more than half of the 22,000 U.S. garment contractors were failing to pay the minimum wage. In May 1996 the U.S. Labor Department reported that 472 investigations of the garment industry and sweatshops revealed 222 labor-law violations nationwide. One of the worst cases was uncovered in August 1995 when law-enforcement officers freed 72 illegal Thai immigrants working as virtual slaves in a barbed-wire-enclosed compound near Los Angeles. A series of events in 1996 gave a tremendous boost to the campaign against this sweatshop trend and against a parallel one overseas—child labor.

Increased Publicity. The most publicized development involved Kathie Lee Gifford, celebrity cohost of a television talk show and successful businesswoman. In May it was revealed that some garments bearing her "Kathie Lee" brand label and sold at Wal-Mart stores were made in Honduran and New York City sweatshops. Upon learning of the exposés, Gifford became active, first with Wal-Mart in setting up a program to monitor Wal-Mart's contractors, and then with Secretary of Labor Reich in rallying support for reforms in the fashion industry. In August she joined officials of the clothing and footwear industries in a White House meeting with President Bill Clinton to announce private- and public-sector partnerships to inhibit reliance on sweatshops. Among the measures discussed was the creation of a "No Sweat" labeling system to identify products not made with sweatshop labor.

A coalition of investment companies issued a statement in September that they "will seek to invest in and monitor companies that take a leadership role in eradicating sweatshops" in the apparel, footwear, and toy industries worldwide. On Capitol Hill, Sen. Edward Kennedy (D-MA) and Rep. William Clay (D-MO) introduced the Stop Sweatshops Act to give U.S. garment workers greater protection against abuses.

Child Labor. Meanwhile, there were breakthroughs in the campaign against a common feature of sweatshops—child labor. According to the International Labor Organization (ILO), there were at least 73 million child laborers aged 10–14 and some 200 million child laborers of all ages. To combat the trend, the Brazilian government and business leaders in September made a public commitment to end what President Fernando Henrique Cardoso called an "unacceptable reality"—the 3.3 million Brazilian boys and girls under 14 who, instead of being in school, are working in mines, fields, and small workshops. In Europe the International Federation of Soccer Associations (FIFA) announced a new code that gradually would end the industry's dependence on soccer balls stitched by children as young as 5. In Geneva the ILO began updating its 1973 convention on the minimum age—now generally 14—for admitting children to employment. In New Delhi the South Asian Coalition on Child Servitude took the lead in creating a "Rugmark" label that identifies Indian and Nepalese hand-knotted carpets not made by children.

In Canada, Craig Kielburger, a 13-year-old schoolboy, launched Free the Children, an international movement of children led by children. At a congressional hearing in Washington, DC, Francoise Remington, a Virginia schoolteacher, charged that some World Bank–financed projects in India, monitored by herself and Indian colleagues, contribute to the growth of child labor.

At least in regard to public awareness, the world is "turning the corner in the struggle against sweatshops," said Neil Kearney, Brussels-based general secretary of the International Textile, Garment, and Leather Workers Federation. But, in a Washington talk in July, Kearney warned that there still was a long way to go because of global competition, in which 160 countries produce fashion goods for export to only about 30 nations. Kearney and others renewed efforts to have the World Trade Organization adopt a "social clause," linking trade benefits to minimal labor standards—such as a ban on child labor. At the same time, more U.S. businesses voluntarily were adopting codes of conduct limiting their purchases to domestic and overseas suppliers free of sweatshop taints.

ROBERT A. SENSER

season and would last through the year 2000, with the players having an option for a one-year extension.

International

Japan. A promise followed by large companies of lifetime employment for male employees was beginning to give way as Japanese employers tried to compete with the United States in the world market. While unemployment, which peaked at 3.5% in May, was much lower than in the United States and Europe, Japanese productivity lagged behind that of most Western economies. At the same time, Japanese wages were among the world's highest; one study found that the average wage increase in 1996 was 2.8% at 289 major enterprises. About one third of Japanese employers were trying to reduce their labor forces, according to Japan's labor ministry. But the pace of downsizing was slow as compared with companies from the United States and Western Europe. As the notion of a one-company career declined, workers were increasingly willing to consider changing jobs in order to fully exercise their talents and abilities, according to a government survey.

Belgium. In a reversal of previous practice, legislation was introduced in Belgium to move from decentralized wage bargaining to a centralized wage structure. Plans to reform the wage-bargaining system were founded on an agreement that wage growth would match that of Belgium's main trading partners—France, Germany, and the Netherlands. The legislative route was followed after one of the two largest trade unions failed to ratify a draft agreement reached by representatives of other unions, employers, and the government that contained similar elements. The move toward centralization was part of a legislative package designed to rein in public expenditure in order to meet criteria for entry into the economic and monetary union (EMU) and to reform the social-security system.

France. During November striking French truck drivers set up barricades blocking major highways for 12 days. The strike put a stranglehold on the economy of much of Western Europe. An agreement between the government and the truck drivers was reached on November 28, leading to a normalization of truck traffic. The settlement provided for a reduction of the retirement age for drivers from 60 to 55 after 25 years of service and a government promise to redefine work hours to include time spent waiting for cargo to be loaded and unloaded. The agreement also included a ban on Sunday driving by foreign truckers, bringing them in line with French drivers. Other provisions were the payment of expenses to truckers for nights away from home even if they sleep in their vehicles, and a reduction from ten to five unpaid days for sick leave before sick pay goes into effect. The settlement was another blow to the government's efforts to meet a series of stiff budget and public-debt targets to qualify France to join a single European currency in 1999. Great Britain, Spain, and Portugal—whose trucks have to cross France to reach other European countries—protested the effects of the strike.

Germany. Although national unemployment rose to about 11% and 200,000 construction workers were jobless, as many as 500,000 foreign legal and illegal workers were laboring on construction sites. Germany was troubled by the presence of many high-wage migrant workers, most of whom were British. A British construction worker could earn about twice as much as at home. Other migrant workers were coming from the Netherlands, Portugal, Poland, the Czech Republic, and Hungary. German employers said that foreigners cost less than German workers because of high wages, heavy taxes, and rigid work rules dictating how to pay nationals. In addition, many employers said that foreign workers were more flexible than their German counterparts.

The flood of foreign workers was particularly strong in the east, where German taxpayers were footing much of the bill. Since German unification occurred in 1990, the government had spent more than $600 billion to rehabilitate the formerly communist east. Much of that money went to subsidies and tax breaks for construction. As a member of the European Union (EU), Germany was required to let citizens of any EU country work and live within its borders. But workers from East European countries that were not part of the union also enjoyed relatively easy access to jobs in Germany.

German construction unions expressed great concern about the infusion of foreign workers. They succeeded in persuading the government to adopt a rule, effective Jan. 1, 1997, which would require construction companies to pay both foreign and German workers at least $10.07 an hour in the east and $10.95 in the west. In contrast, unionized workers receive $15.26 in the east and $16.07 in the west—as well as 22 vacation days (30 days under union contracts), one month's Christmas bonus, 14.82% of gross income for vacation money, $1.29 per hour extra winter pay, 125% of regular pay for overtime work, and 20% of gross wages for social-security taxes paid by the employer. British construction workers in Germany received none of these fringe benefits, except for an employer-paid social-security tax levied at less than half the rate paid for German workers.

High labor costs led many companies to set up factories in other countries. Automakers such as BMW, Volkswagen, and Daimler-Benz already had built plants in the United States, Asia, and Eastern Europe. The pressure on German employers was expected to become even more severe as the EU moved closer to becoming a single economic entity.

Great Britain. Britain's Prime Minister John Major promised to defy a November ruling by the European Court of Justice that rejected British objections to an EU directive mandating a maximum 48-hour workweek, including overtime, unless employers and unions agree otherwise. The work rules also would impose a minimum of a three-week paid vacation for employees and mandatory rest periods during long shifts. Major denounced the ruling as another attempt to restrain Britain's free-market economy, which was doing much better than the economies of the remaining 14 European Union members. Great Britain's unemployment, which stood at 6.9% in November, was one of the lowest in Europe. Some opponents to the EU saw the so-called working-time directive as the first in a set of unified rules and regulations issued by bureaucrats in Brussels that amounted to European "federalism" and "social engineering." The opposition Labour Party supported the maximum-hours work rule.

Spain. Spain's new conservative prime minister, José María Aznar, faced the challenge of reducing budget deficits and inflation in order to be eligible to adopt a single European currency by 1999 in accordance with EU policy. Economists agreed that unpopular measures—including layoffs in government agencies, a tightening of welfare spending, and the selling of government-owned companies—would have to be taken. The business community also demanded passage of a measure that would make the dismissal of workers less expensive. Under existing law, employers were required to provide 45 days' severance pay for every year of employment in order to dismiss an employee. The two main labor federations opposed privatization if it meant heavy job losses, cuts in pensions and health benefits, and any easing in the law regarding worker dismissals.

In an effort to reduce the number of strikes and working time lost, the unions and the employers' confederation agreed on a system of mediation and arbitration. Mediation would be compulsory in sector disputes and in companies that operate in multiple regions. Mediators would have a maximum of ten days to formulate proposals, which would not be binding. If mediation failed, an independent arbitrator could be called upon to resolve the dispute if both parties were agreeable. The arbitrator usually would have a maximum of ten days to make a decision, which would be binding on the parties with appeals allowed on points of law only. As an alternative to arbitration, the parties could seek a court ruling. The mediation-arbitration agreement would run until Dec. 31, 2000, and thereafter would be subject to review every five years.

Israel. Benjamin Netanyahu, the newly elected conservative prime minister of Israel, announced an economic program during the summer that would cut child allowances, impose fees for doctor visits, privatize some of the 140 enterprises under state control, and slash the number of government employees. The Histadrut, a labor organization representing nearly half of all Israeli workers, vowed to fight Netanyahu's proposed cutbacks in Israel's welfare state. The group called a three-day general strike in December to keep the program from being adopted by the Knesset (parliament), where even some members of Netanyahu's Likud Party expressed reservations about an ax that would fall too heavily on ordinary Israelis. Most of the proposed cuts were not included in the budget that the Knesset passed on Jan. 1, 1997.

Worldwide Unemployment. According to a report issued in November by the International Labor Organization (ILO), worldwide unemployment or underemployment rose to nearly 1 billion in 1995. Not since the Depression of the 1930s had unemployment been so high. In the 15 EU countries unemployment increased to 11.3% of the workforce, compared with 2% in the 1960s. France, Germany, Italy, and Sweden showed the largest increases, while Spain had the highest jobless rate, at nearly 22%. In Central and Eastern Europe unemployment remained in double digits. Unemployment also increased in many Latin American countries and, though few figures were available, joblessness was a large-scale problem in the developing world. Overall, the ILO report noted that about 30% of the world's labor force was either unemployed or underemployed.

JACK STIEBER, *Michigan State University*

LAOS

The Lao People's Democratic Republic's Sixth Party Congress in March 1996 highlighted the leadership's struggle to balance an authoritarian one-party political system with free-market economic reforms and a developing regional role. The party appeared particularly interested in limiting foreign influence, which it blamed for growing social problems, such as a rising crime rate.

Politics. Prime Minister Khamtay Siphandon and the Lao military appeared to have increased their power following the Party Congress. Khamtay was reelected Central Committee chairman. At least six of the new nine-member Politburo were serving or retired military men. Deputy Prime Minister Khamphoui Keoboualapha's ouster as economic czar and from the Politburo signaled Lao concern that he was pushing economic reforms too quickly and may have been growing too powerful.

President Nouhak Phoumsavan left the Politburo to become a special adviser, but the octogenarian retained the presidency despite rumors he would step down. The Congress failed to make a clear generational change; about 75% of the members of the Central Committee joined the party before the 1975 Communist takeover.

Economy. The economy grew and tight monetary policy stabilized the exchange rate, which depreciated sharply in 1995. Laos made progress on key infrastructure development projects necessary for long-term growth; at least two new sections of road, five bridges, and airports throughout the country were built or renovated. Nonetheless, flooding interfered with agricultural development in the mainly subsistence economy and double-digit inflation remained a concern. Vientiane's plan to serve as the crossroads of the Greater Mekong region and get off the underdeveloped-country list by 2020 remained a goal.

Foreign Relations. Laos invited representatives from China, Cambodia, Thailand, and Vietnam to the party congress. After submitting its membership application to the Association for Southeast Asian Nations (ASEAN) in March, Laos announced plans to open three embassies in Brunei, the Philippines, and Singapore—all ASEAN members. Foreign Minister Somsavat Lengsavat consolidated newly established relations with South Korea by making his first trip to Seoul in May. The minister also went to Iran and received the first Cuban delegation to visit in years. The United States and Laos signed the Overseas Private Investment Agreement in March.

CHRISTINE VAN ZANDT
U.S. Government Analyst on East Asian Affairs

LAOS • Information Highlights

Official Name: Lao People's Democratic Republic.
Location: Southeast Asia.
Area: 91,430 sq mi (236 800 km²).
Population (mid-1996 est.): 5,000,000.
Chief City (1990 est): Vientiane, the capital, 442,000.
Government: *Head of state,* Nouhak Phoumsavan, president. *Head of government,* Khamtay Siphandon, prime minister. *Legislature* (unicameral)—National Assembly.
Gross Domestic Product (1994 est. U.S.$): $4,000,000,000.
Foreign Trade (1995 est. U.S.$): *Imports,* $587,000,000; *exports,* $348,000,000.

LATIN AMERICA

During 1996, Latin American and Caribbean governments focused on three main issues in which they claimed to see evidence of cavalier treatment by the United States: the Cuban Liberty and Democratic Solidarity Act (the Helms-Burton law); the gridlock in the free-trade agenda flowing out of the 1994 Hemispheric Summit meeting in Miami, FL; and, to a lesser extent, U.S. policies toward Colombia, including revocation of the visa for entry into the United States of Colombia's President Ernesto Samper. The latter action produced an outcry against the United States throughout Latin America (*see* COLOMBIA).

Despite these irritants, 1996 was a good year for the hemisphere. The economic slowdown of 1995—which reduced overall economic growth to a meager 0.3%—was overcome, especially in Mexico and Argentina. A midyear estimate of the Latin economies by the UN Economic Commission for Latin America and the Caribbean (ECLAC) put the regional expansion rate at 3% for the year. In late September the World Bank issued an even rosier forecast for the region: a growth rate of 6% to 7%, provided "the government make an effort to achieve fiscal stability over the long term."

Helms-Burton. U.S. President Bill Clinton signed the Helms-Burton law on March 12, responding to a wave of anti-Castro feeling brought on when Havana shot down two unarmed light aircraft that had entered Cuban airspace. The act denies entry into the United States to foreign companies and family members judged by the U.S. State Department to be "trafficking" in U.S. property seized after the Cuban revolution. It also allows private claims to be filed through the U.S. court system for compensation against alleged "traffickers." The act provides for waivers of the legal provisions for up to six months at a time. Clinton issued such a waiver in July and again in early January 1997. According to the State Department, the act would "expedite a transition to democracy" in Cuba.

The Organization of American States (OAS) registered its disapproval of the act at its annual General Assembly in Panama in June. Latin American reaction was inflamed further when U.S. Ambassador to the OAS Harriet Babbitt accused General Assembly delegates of "diplomatic cowardice" for their vote. The Inter-American Juridical Commission, an OAS arm, claimed that Helms-Burton "did not conform to international law." The Rio Group of Latin American nations joined in the condemnation. (*See* CUBA.)

Free Trade. At the 1994 Miami summit meeting, the Clinton administration pledged to create a hemisphere-wide free-trade zone by the year 2005. Chile was to be the first country to be included in the existing North American Free Trade Agreement (NAFTA). In the contentious political climate of 1995 and in the election year of 1996, the administration did not move ahead with its plans, and talks with Chile ground to a halt. After the election, however, presidential counselor Thomas McLarty was sent to Latin America to reaffirm the Clinton administration's free-trade commitment and to prepare the way for a 1997 presidential trip.

The first task facing the administration would be to secure a "fast-track" agreement from the U.S. Congress. Fast-track authority would permit the government to restart negotiations with Chile and allow any resulting trade pact to go to Congress without being subject to unlimited amendments. Lack of a fast-track agreement undoubtedly would set back the free-trade goal.

The rapid expansion of Mercosur—the Southern Cone free-trade arrangement composed of Argentina, Brazil, Paraguay, and Uruguay—added some urgency to the administration's challenge. In 1996, Bolivia and Chile joined Mercosur as associate members; Colombia, Ecuador, and Venezuela were negotiating to sign a Mercosur free-trade pact; and Peru reportedly was considering the issue. The expansion of Mercosur seemed to represent a more promising route toward hemispheric integration than did incremental additions to NAFTA.

Economy. In 1996, Latin America and the Caribbean returned to a path of economic recovery. Chile showed the most dynamism, with an increase in gross domestic product approaching 7%. Argentina, Mexico, and Uruguay also experienced a turnaround. In several other countries, negative trends continued but at a lesser rate. The value of exports from the nine largest economies of the region increased by approximately 12% during the first half of the year, according to ECLAC. Private capital began returning to the region, after falling sharply. Per-capita income rose on a regional basis by 1%, after declining 1.5% in 1995.

Inflation continued to recede, reaching 22%, compared with 26% in 1995 and 60% between 1990 and 1994. The exception was Venezuela, with a 12-month inflation rate of 115% at the end of August. Unemployment was the most immediate negative feature of the Latin American economy. Real wages remained stationary and, in at least seven countries, unemployment was greater than it was in 1995.

The ECLAC report issued in October found that Latin American food exports have been declining steadily for more than two decades. Chile, Cuba, and Nicaragua were exceptions to the trend. Poverty was rising in the region. Another ECLAC study found more poverty in Latin America and the Caribbean in 1996 than there was in the 1980s. To eliminate poverty, the Latin American economies must grow by 6% per year.

Military Purchases. Under pressure from U.S. arms manufacturers, the U.S. Department of Defense signaled its intent to lift an arms embargo on Latin American nations, in effect since the Carter administration. Secretary of Defense William J. Perry told a meeting of Western Hemisphere defense chiefs in Argentina in October that the United States wants to allow the sale of advanced weapons—on a case-by-case basis and in a "very restrained fashion"—to help Latin American nations modernize their armed forces to fight drug trafficking and "narco-terrorism."

Meetings. In addition to its General Assembly in Panama in June, the OAS held specialized conferences on corruption (March 27–29, Caracas) and terrorism (April 23–26, Lima). In December a meeting on sustainable development in the Americas was held in Santa Cruz, Bolivia. After much wrangling, an agenda was agreed upon, including the state of the environment and social issues. Although the meeting initially was billed as a summit, only 13 Latin American heads of state and two prime ministers attended. Nineteen countries sent high-level delegations.

RICHARD C. SCHROEDER, *Freelance Writer*

Law

In its 1995–96 term, the U.S. Supreme Court charted a familiar course with a few dramatic detours. Under the leadership of Chief Justice William H. Rehnquist, completing his tenth term in that capacity, the high court has moved U.S. constitutional law to the right. The term that concluded on July 1, 1996, was, for the most part, no exception. But there were notable departures in key rulings affecting gay rights, gender bias, and criminal sentencing.

The justices occupying the court's ideological center—Sandra Day O'Connor and Anthony M. Kennedy—were the determining factors in many of the closely divided, high-profile cases. They were on the prevailing side in nine of the 12 cases decided by 5–4 votes. On the court's right, Justices Antonin Scalia and Clarence Thomas voted together 79% of the time in nonunanimous cases. On the liberal end of the spectrum, Justices David Souter and Stephen Breyer were in agreement in 84% of those cases. Justices Ruth Bader Ginsburg and John Paul Stevens were the other members of the more left-of-center wing.

A trend toward deciding fewer cases continued. The justices handed down signed opinions in 75 cases, the fewest in more than 40 years. Increasingly, the court seemed loath to inject itself into disputes it felt would be better left to Congress and state legislatures. To some commentators, the justices' diminished work product reflected a willingness to accept the outcome of cases heard in lower courts.

In the lower courts, cigarette smoking and the legal responsibility of tobacco companies for the health problems of smokers made headlines. A federal appeals court handed down an important affirmative-action ruling that could win Supreme Court review. The issue of doctor-aided suicide also was prominent, as was a dispute over the criminal liability of a woman accused of harming her fetus by taking drugs. The subject of same-sex marriage was gaining close scrutiny (*see* SPECIAL REPORT, page 316).

In international law, attentions were focused on the initiation of war-crimes tribunals in the former Yugoslavia and Rwanda.

United States

Supreme Court. One of the court's most prominent decisions broke new ground in the developing legal battle over gay rights. The justices held that states may not prevent local governments from writing ordinances that protect homosexuals from discrimination. The court struck down a Colorado provision banning local gay-rights laws, ruling that the measure violated the constitutional equal-protection guarantee (*Romer v. Evans*).

The justices ruled that the Virginia Military Institute's (VMI's) exclusion of women violates the constitutional guarantee of equal protection (*United States v. Virginia*). The justices said an alternative program that the state

© John Duricka/AP/Wide World Photos

Marchers supported the U.S. Supreme Court decision of June 26, 1996, that ruled that the Virginia Military Institute's exclusion of women violates the Constitution's equal-protection guarantee.

set up for women was an inadequate substitute for admitting women to the 157-year-old military college. In September, VMI's Board of Visitors voted to comply with the decision and admit women for the fall 1997 term.

The court ruled that three Texas congressional districts with black or Hispanic majorities and a black-majority North Carolina voting district were unconstitutional because the boundaries were drawn with race as the predominant factor (*Bush v. Vera* and *Shaw v. Hunt*). The twin 5–4 rulings appeared to leave some room for considering race among other factors in drawing voting districts. The justices agreed to hear related cases in the future.

In another 5–4 split, the court held that state political parties must obtain federal approval before charging a fee to participate in a nominating convention (*Morse v. Republican Party of Virginia*). But the justices said that political parties have a free-speech right to spend as much money as they desire to promote a candidate for the U.S. House or Senate as long as they do not coordinate the spending with the candidate (*Colorado Republican Committee v. Federal Election Commission*). In another battle over freedom of speech, the court ruled that independent government contractors cannot be fired for speaking out on public issues, a right already available to government employees (*Board of County Commissioners v. Umbehr*).

The justices also strengthened free-speech protection for advertisers, unanimously striking down a Rhode Island ban on advertising liquor prices (*44 Liquormart v. Rhode Island*). The decision cast doubt on the lawfulness of efforts to restrict cigarette promotions. The court struck down part of a 1992 federal law permitting cable-television systems to ban indecent programs from channels available to community groups. The justices upheld a provision permitting cable systems to ban such programs from channels leased to commercial programmers; they also struck down a section of the law requiring cable companies airing indecent programs to scramble the signal to all subscribers who do not, in writing, request access to indecent material (*Denver Area Consortium v. Federal Communications Commission*).

In the area of criminal law, the justices unanimously upheld a new law limiting federal-court appeals by state inmates, although the court affirmed its own jurisdiction to hear such petitions (*Felker v. Turpin*). The justices ruled that constitutional protection against double jeopardy is not violated when the government uses criminal law to prosecute drug offenders and then seizes a defendant's property in civil proceedings (*United States v. Ursery*). In another forfeiture case, the justices split 5–4 in ruling that the government may seize property used to commit a crime even if someone innocent owns the property (*Bennis v. Michigan*). A Michigan woman lost her claim to the family car used by her husband to solicit a prostitute.

The justices said that blacks who claim that they have been singled out for harsh prosecution must show that whites in similar circumstances have not been prosecuted (*United States v. Armstrong*). The court ruled that police officers may stop motorists for minor traffic violations, even if their real motive is to look for drugs (*Whren v. United States*).

The justices unanimously ruled in favor of judicial discretion in a sentencing case that arose from the videotaped police beating of Rodney King in Los Angeles. The court ruled that a judge was justified in departing from federal guidelines to reduce sentences for two police officers convicted of civil-rights offenses in the case (*Koon v. United States*). In another sentencing case, the court ruled that a federal law requiring a mandatory five-year sentence for using or carrying a firearm in the commission of a drug offense would not apply if the gun was not used to harm or threaten anyone (*Bailey v. United States*).

In one of several cases affecting the workplace, the justices unanimously ruled that federal labor law protects union organizers who take jobs at a company with the aim of unionizing workers (*National Labor Relations Board v. Town and Country Electric*). The court held that workers whose employers trick them into giving up benefits may sue to restore the coverage (*Varity Corp. v. Howe*). The court ruled unanimously that bosses can require workers to give up some legal claims as a trade-off for an early-retirement buyout with better pension benefits (*Lockheed v. Spink*). The court unanimously extended the Age Discrimination in Employment Act of 1967, ruling that the law can protect a worker who has been replaced by someone older than 40, the age at which the law's protections begin to apply (*O'Connor v. Consolidated Coin Caterers*).

The court ruled that consumers may sue the manufacturers of medical devices for damages under state law even if the instruments comply with federal safety rules (*Medtronic v. Lohr*). The justices were unanimous in rejecting broad claims of federal preemption urged by the maker of a cardiac pacemaker. However, the justices threw out a

SPECIAL REPORT/LAW

Same-Sex Marriage

With little debate, the U.S. Congress passed and President Bill Clinton signed into law in September 1996 a Republican-sponsored measure aimed at preventing marriages between homosexual couples. Under the Defense of Marriage Act—as the law was called by its key sponsors, Sen. Don Nickles (R-OK) and Rep. Robert L. Barr, Jr. (R-GA)—no state is required to recognize the validity of gay marriages performed in any other state. The act also defines marriage, under federal law, as the "legal union of one man and one woman" and a spouse as "a person of the opposite sex who is a husband or a wife." That provision makes it impossible for gay couples to share spousal benefits from Social Security and other federal programs, even if the state they live in were to sanction same-sex marriage.

No U.S. state allowed same-sex marriage in 1996; indeed, at least 15 states specifically barred such unions. But Republican lawmakers brought the measure to a vote after a surprise ruling by the Hawaii Supreme Court in May 1993 that the state may not deny same-sex couples marriage licenses without a "compelling" reason. The court ruled on a case in which three homosexual couples sued the state of Hawaii for permission to be married.

In December 1996 a circuit-court judge in Hawaii ruled that state officials had failed to demonstrate any compelling reasons for the existing ban on same-sex marriages. Calling the ban unconstitutional, the judge ordered the state to stop denying marriage licenses to gay couples. However, lawyers representing the state filed an appeal to the Hawaii Supreme Court; a decision was not anticipated until at least mid-1997. The circuit-court ruling was put on hold until the state's high court issued a ruling.

Constitutional considerations prompted lawmakers opposed to gay marriage to preempt the Hawaii state court's 1993 decision with federal legislation. The U.S. Constitution requires each state to recognize all other states' "public acts, records, and judicial proceedings"—including marriage licenses. But the Constitution also empowers Congress to modify that requirement, which it chose to do in this instance.

Congress also narrowly rejected a related bill that would have banned job discrimination on the basis of sexual orientation—a practice that is legal in 41 states. Supporters of the measure asserted that it was only fair to include gays and lesbians among the protected classes of citizens. Pointing to the fact that homosexual acts are still

---

jury's $2 million punitive-damage award to a BMW owner who sued the automaker because he was not told that his new car had received a paint touch-up job (*BMW v. Gore*). The majority opinion stated that the money was "grossly excessive," in violation of constitutional due-process protections.

The justices ruled that the federal government broke contracts with three savings-and-loan companies and must pay for damages incurred by the institutions (*United States v. Winstar*). At issue was a change in accounting rules that the companies said had devastating financial impact. The ruling applied to more than 90 similar breach-of-contract cases.

The court unanimously ruled that the Census Bureau did not violate the U.S. Constitution when it decided in 1990 not to adjust its figures to help undercounted minorities (*Wisconsin v. New York*). New York and other big cities had sued to force an adjustment.

In a 5–4 ruling, the court curbed the authority of Congress to subject states to federal lawsuits. The justices struck down part of the Indian Gaming Regulatory Act of 1988 permitting Indian tribes to sue states to force them to bargain over terms for opening casinos (*Seminole Tribe v. Florida*).

Local Law. Cigarette companies faced some 200 lawsuits alleging that they hid tobacco's dangers from the public. A man stricken by lung cancer after smoking cigarettes for 44 years was awarded $750,000 by a jury in Jacksonville, FL. The verdict against Brown & Williamson Tobacco Corp. found that cigarettes were a defective product and that the company was negligent for not warning consumers about the dangers. Analysts said the ruling was a significant setback for the tobacco industry. In a similar case, an Indianapolis jury found cigarette companies not responsible for a smoker's cancer death, ruling against the widow of a man who began smoking at age 5 and died from cancer at age 52.

The 3d U.S. Circuit Court of Appeals in Philadelphia ruled that school officials in Piscataway, NJ, should not have laid off a white teacher instead of an equally qualified black

© Stephen Jaffe/Reuters/Archive Photos

Protesters held a prayer vigil on the steps of the U.S. Supreme Court in September 1996 after federal legislation aimed at preventing marriages between same-sex couples was enacted.

illegal in many states, opponents warned that the measure ran counter to the public will and that its approval would result in unwarranted government intrusion in private business decisions.

For his part, President Clinton—with his quiet signing of the Defense of Marriage Act—signaled his desire to avoid stirring up debate over the controversial issue just weeks before the election. The first presidential candidate to court the gay vote openly—during his 1992 campaign—Clinton long had supported the antidiscrimination bill while opposing same-sex marriage. Opinion polls showed continuing opposition to same-sex marriage among a large majority of voters.

While Congress moved to halt the expansion of rights for homosexual couples during 1996, corporate America took steps in the opposite direction. In September, International Business Machines Corp. (IBM) announced it would extend health-care coverage and other company benefits to the partners of its homosexual employees. IBM, the nation's sixth-largest company, joined several hundred other U.S. employers in offering benefits to their workers' unmarried domestic partners. Most of these companies are in the high-technology sector. To receive IBM's medical, dental, and vision-care benefits, same-sex couples would be required to sign a statement declaring that they are in a long-term relationship and live in the same household.

MARY H. COOPER

for the sake of racial diversity. The ruling appeared likely to end up as a new Supreme Court test case for affirmative action.

The 9th U.S. Circuit Court of Appeals ruled that mentally competent, terminally ill adults have the constitutional right to a doctor's help to hasten death. The appeals court said that a Washington state law making physician-assisted suicide a felony violated due-process protections. The 2nd U.S. Circuit Court of Appeals struck down two laws that barred doctor-assisted suicide, ruling that they unconstitutionally failed to treat people equally. In October the Supreme Court agreed to review both appellate rulings.

The South Carolina Supreme Court ruled that women who take illegal drugs during pregnancy can be prosecuted for child abuse. The decision was believed to be the first by any state appellate court to hold that a pregnant woman can be criminally liable for endangering the health of a viable fetus.

A Florida appeals court upheld the ruling of a trial judge who transferred custody of a 12-year-old girl from her lesbian mother to her father, a convicted murderer who had served eight years for killing his first wife. Both the original trial judge and the appeals court said that their rulings were not based merely on the mother's sexual orientation.

At a Honolulu court-martial, two U.S. Marines were convicted of refusing an order to have their blood screened for a DNA registry (the registry was created to help identify the remains of service personnel killed in the line of duty). The defendants argued that the DNA samples could be used to discriminate against them. In contrast, prosecutors said the case was about the soldiers' refusal to obey orders, not the lawfulness of genetic testing.

Gaining attention late in the year was an ongoing civil case against O.J. Simpson. The families of his former wife, Nicole Brown Simpson, and of her friend, Ronald Goldman, were suing over the "wrongful deaths" of the two victims. The former football star was acquitted in criminal proceedings in 1995.

JIM RUBIN, *The Associated Press*

International Law

The most important activity in international law in 1996 focused on cases deriving from the collapse of the former Yugoslavia that were heard in two courts in The Hague. Meanwhile, trials related to the 1994 Rwandan genocide also began.

First Cases in Former Yugoslavia. The International Court of Justice (ICJ), a United Nations (UN) body, accepted jurisdiction in a case that Bosnia and Herzegovina had filed in 1993, charging Yugoslavia (Serbia and Montenegro) with responsibility for genocide. The decision meant that the ICJ accepted the principle that the Genocide Convention protects states as well as individuals, although there was dissent on this point. The case was scheduled to continue until July 1997 in order to provide Serbia and Montenegro with the opportunity to respond to the charges.

The other major events in international law took place in the International Criminal Tribunal for the former Yugoslavia (ICTY). The first trial in the ICTY, of Bosnian Serb Dusan Tadic on 31 charges of war crimes and crimes against humanity, began on May 7, with closing arguments heard late in November. No decision was announced by the end of the year, however.

The Tadic trial revealed weaknesses in the structure of the ICTY. First, the trial took far longer than had been anticipated, and thus cost much more than expected. Considering that the ICTY had only one courtroom (another was planned), it seemed impossible that speedy trials could be held for the more than 70 people indicted by the court if all of them were to be arrested. Thus the fact that, as of late November 1996, only seven defendants were actually in custody may have saved the ICTY from collapsing under its workload.

A major perjury scandal at the Tadic trial also revealed serious flaws in the ICTY's rules. At the start of the trial the court had decided to permit anonymous testimony against defendants, keeping the identity of witnesses secret, even from the defense lawyers, in order to protect such witnesses and their families from retaliation. Near the end of the Tadic trial, however, the defense was able to show that one of the anonymous witnesses against Tadic had lied about some aspects of his testimony. Upon investigation by the tribunal itself, it was shown not only that this witness had lied, but that he had been trained to give false testimony by the Muslim-led government of Bosnia and Herzegovina, which threatened him with execution if he did not perform as required. The defense had uncovered the perjury by chance, and the anonymity of the witness otherwise made it virtually

On May 31, 1996, Drazen Erdemovic, below, *a 24-year-old Bosnian Croat who had served in the Bosnian Serb army of Gen. Ratko Mladic, pleaded guilty to participating in the mass murders of Bosnian Muslims in 1995. Erdemovic cooperated with the prosecution, however, and received a ten-year prison sentence in November. Meanwhile, indictments were issued for numerous other suspected war criminals,* left.

impossible to cross-examine him effectively. While the specific charge against Tadic that this testimony was meant to prove was dropped, the perjury of the witness drew into question the ability of defendants to receive a fair trial.

In other actions at the ICTY, the first conviction was obtained by the confession of a Bosnian Croat who had served in the Bosnian Serb army to atrocities at the time of the fall of the UN-designated "safe area" of Srebrenica in July 1995. The confession of Drazen Erdemovic caused an ethical dilemma for the ICTY, because the prosecution argued for a light sentence for the defendant to reward his cooperation, while some judges were concerned about striking deals with a confessed mass murderer. However, a ten-year sentence proposed by the prosecution was accepted by the judges late in November.

Other ICTY Developments. In July the ICTY engaged in a novel public "review of indictments" against Bosnian Serb leaders Radovan Karadzic and Ratko Mladic, who had been charged by the tribunal but not arrested. The review gave the prosecution an opportunity to present in a public hearing its evidence against the accused. An attempt by Karadzic to appoint an attorney to represent him was rejected by the court, which noted that it was not empowered to hold trials in absentia and that a defendant would have to appear if he wished to defend himself. At the end of the review the tribunal reconfirmed its original indictments against the accused and issued international arrest warrants against them.

Despite these moves, however, the entire ICTY enterprise remained clouded. Many Serbs regarded the public review of indictments of Serb leaders to be a propaganda exercise aimed against them. Only 10% of the persons indicted by the ICTY actually were arrested, and many of those not apprehended were living openly in Serbia, Croatia, and Serb- or Croat-controlled parts of Bosnia. The failure to arrest those indicted became a political issue, with North Atlantic Treaty Organization (NATO) forces in Bosnia refusing to take the risks involved in such actions, and the major powers not able to pressure Croatian and Serbian leadership to crack down on people who were, in many cases, the supporters of these leaders. Further, it seemed unlikely that these leaders themselves would be indicted, even though they were the ones responsible for the war, because they were seen as essential to fulfilling the peace settlement for Bosnia that was reached in November 1995.

Perhaps because of frustration with the lack of arrests of those indicted, the ICTY took actions straining the limits of propriety in a court bound by law. In February the tribunal demanded that two Bosnian Serb army officers who were captured by the Muslim-led government be transferred to the ICTY, even though neither had been indicted or investigated by the tribunal. Faced with a deadline for either releasing or charging the men, the prosecutor indicted one of them, even while acknowledging that there might have been insufficient evidence to do so. (The accused later was found to be dying of cancer and was released on humanitarian grounds.) The president of the ICTY, Justice Antonio Cassese, also seemed at times to be at the limits of judicial propriety in his public appearances with the chief prosecutor, and with a news conference in October at which Cassese seemed to be calling for the indictment of specific individuals.

Broader Problems. The war-crimes tribunal for war crimes and genocide committed in Rwanda was in an even worse position than the ICTY, with thousands of potential defendants but only primitive facilities for conducting trials. Nevertheless, the first trial was begun in this court late in 1996.

The experiences of the ICTY and Rwanda tribunals during the year indicated that the ideal of international criminal tribunals for crimes committed in ethnic or civil wars might not be obtainable. The problems preventing the indictment of the highest leaders of the nations of the former Yugoslavia or the arrest of those indicted indicated that the ICTY was driven at least as much by international politics as it was by abstract standards of law. Its legitimacy appeared unlikely to be accepted widely by Serbs and Croats, who saw the tribunal as ignoring crimes committed against them. The daunting prospects of trying even 70 people in the ICTY were dwarfed by the situation of the Rwanda tribunal, confronted with thousands of potential defendants.

Civil wars inevitably produce mass casualties, and it is extremely unlikely that all who inflict them can be tried. On the other hand, Nuremberg-like trials of leaders require that the accused be out of power, and probably that their countries be under military occupation. Since such a situation did not exist in either the former Yugoslavia or in Rwanda, it seemed unlikely that these international war-crimes tribunals would have the moral impact or stature hoped for when they were formed.

ROBERT M. HAYDEN
University of Pittsburgh

LEBANON

During 1996, Lebanon was the site of a military conflict in March and April between Israel and Hezbollah, the Lebanese fundamentalist Muslim movement. In addition, the nation held parliamentary elections in August and September. Lebanon continued to possess working political institutions and all the external trappings of sovereignty, but was in substance a puppet state under Syrian control. Syria also continued to kidnap and imprison Lebanese political opponents without trial.

Israeli Conflict. A new round of conflict arose in March as Hezbollah and Israeli forces began trading blows. The situation escalated in April as attacks became more frequent and Hezbollah forces fired rockets into Israeli territory. In retaliation for the latter action, Israel launched a large-scale military attack—dubbed "Operation Grapes of Wrath"—against much of Lebanon. During the operation, Israeli forces mistakenly shelled a United Nations (UN) refugee camp near Tyre, killing at least 107 civilians and wounding more than 100. The entire conflict left some 150 Lebanese dead, forced the evacuation of hundreds of thousands, and caused massive property damage.

On April 26, Lebanon and Israel agreed to a U.S.-brokered cease-fire pact. Although Syria was not formally a party to the accord, officials in Damascus were consulted throughout the negotiations. The pact formalized a 1993 agreement that restricted military engagements to Israel's self-declared security zone in southern Lebanon. The pact also created a monitoring group—composed of Lebanon, Israel, Syria, the United States, and France—to enforce the agreement. The southern Lebanon front was relatively quiet for the remainder of 1996.

A Quasi-Sovereign State. The restrictions on Lebanese sovereignty were not limited to the omnipresent Syrian domination. The security zone occupied by Israel since 1978 removed about 10% of the country's territory from the control of the Beirut government. The security zone was guarded by some 1,000 Israeli soldiers and the 2,500-strong "South Lebanon Army," collaborators with Israel. The armed Hezbollah group, supported by Iran and tolerated by Syria as a device through which to keep up pressure on Israel,

Conflict between Israel and Lebanon's fundamentalist Muslim movement, Hezbollah, resumed in 1996. On April 18 at least 107 civilians were killed by Israeli artillery at a United Nations refugee camp near Tyre in southern Lebanon.

had its base in the Bekaa Valley just northeast of the Israeli-controlled zone. Other forces in Lebanon included a large contingent of Iranian Revolutionary Guards; several thousand Palestinians opposed to any dealings with Israel; and 5,000 UN peacekeepers.

Domestic Affairs. The most important domestic event in Lebanon in 1996 was the parliamentary general election held in August and September. The presidential election that should have been held in November 1995 at the end of President Elias Hrawi's first six-year term had been canceled at Syria's behest (with the concurrence of the Lebanese parliament), and his term was extended by three more years. The parliamentary general election due in 1996, however, went forward normally, if with some bumps. The election was preceded by constitutional squabbles. Calls from exile for a Maronite boycott, however, largely were disregarded.

Lebanon's complicated electoral law had divided the country into five traditional constituencies. On July 10 a change was approved by parliament that carved one constituency, the Maronite stronghold of Mount Lebanon, into six electoral districts. This was done mainly to secure the reelection (in the Shuf district) of Walid Jumblatt, the Druze leader and an ally of Prime Minister Rafiq al-Hariri. The change evoked criticism, not all from exiles: One critic was Maronite Foreign Minister Faris Buwayz. The law was challenged before the semiofficial Lebanese Constitution Council, which declared it "invalid" and in need of amendment. The Hariri government brushed off this evaluation and proceeded with the election under a slightly amended version of the law. Another preelection squabble arose between the two leading Shiite factions, Hezbollah and its rival Amal, which at first were unable to cooperate on an electoral coalition. A compromise, however, was achieved as a result of lengthy discussions—held in Damascus.

The results of the election for the 128-seat house were satisfactory both for Premier Hariri and for Syria. The personnel of the new parliament suggested a body that would be even more amenable to Syrian influence. The election, however, was smirched by numerous well-established cases of corruption and manipulation.

The election produced a slight decrease in Hezbollah's parliamentary representation—to nine from the 12 seats (including allies) that it had held since 1992. However, there was a growing perception that Hezbollah's role probably would be redefined in the near future, especially if a general regional peace were achieved. Hezbollah already had established itself as a welfare state within the state, operating efficient hospitals and welfare programs. In 1996 it began to foster tourism in the Bekaa Valley.

The dominating political figure in Lebanon in 1996 continued to be Hariri, prime minister since October 1992. Some postelection bickering over the distribution of cabinet portfolios—between President Hrawi, Premier Hariri, and Speaker of the National Assembly Nabi Birri—delayed the confirmation of Hariri by parliament until the end of October. On November 8 the reconfirmed premier announced the formation of a new cabinet.

Hariri pushed ahead with his ambitious plans to reestablish Lebanon as the region's great financial center, with a reconstructed Beirut as its showplace. The tireless vitality of the Lebanese in rebuilding their country already had achieved remarkable results, and this progress continued in 1996. However, the Israeli incursion into Lebanon in April, with its physical destruction (estimated at $500 million) and discouragement of foreign investment, occasioned a setback. Previous estimates of a 6% economic growth in 1996 were scaled back thereafter by the finance minister to a more modest 3%, and an active search was launched for foreign aid from the European Union and other possible donors.

Foreign Affairs. President Jacques Chirac of France made a significant visit to Lebanon, April 4–6, in the course of the first of several Mideast tours he made in 1996. Chirac's travels had a particular significance for Lebanon, so recently (along with Syria) a French-mandated territory, and with historic links going back to the Middle Ages. Chirac firmly enunciated the French view that total Israeli withdrawal from Lebanon was essential.

ARTHUR CAMPBELL TURNER
University of California, Riverside

LEBANON • Information Highlights

Official Name: Republic of Lebanon.
Location: Southwest Asia.
Area: 4,015 sq mi (10 400 km^2).
Population (mid-1996 est.): 3,800,000.
Chief Cities (1982 est.): Beirut, the capital, 509,000; Tripoli, 198,000.
Government: *Head of state,* Elias Hrawi, president (took office November 1989). *Head of government,* Rafik al-Hariri, premier (named Oct. 22, 1992). *Legislature* (unicameral)—National Assembly.
Monetary Unit: Lebanese pound (1,552.75 pounds equal U.S.$1, Dec. 17, 1996).
Gross Domestic Product (1994 est. U.S.$): $15,800,000,-000 (purchasing power parity).
Foreign Trade (1993 est. U.S.$): *Imports,* $4,100,000,000; *exports,* $925,000,000.

LIBRARIES

Libraries throughout the United States were rethinking their services and even their purpose during 1996.

Funding and the Internet. Library-funding news was mixed in 1996. When President Bill Clinton and Congress finally agreed on a fiscal year 1996 federal budget, libraries were appropriated $133 million—an 8% drop from 1995. On the local level, libraries in several states experienced gains in successful election-day referenda.

The Internet was foremost on the agenda for most of the nation's libraries in 1996. A survey by the National Commission on Libraries and Information Services (NCLIS) found that 45% of public libraries were connected to the Internet; this was more than double the 21% connected when NCLIS conducted the same survey in 1994. The number was expected to rise to 60% by 1997. (*See* FEATURE ARTICLE, page 62.)

Taking seriously their role in providing Internet access to the public, libraries found a variety of ways to fund the necessary technology and equipment. Many sought out local-government funding, private community resources, grants administered through state- or federal-library sources, or a combination of these. Bill Gates, head of the Microsoft Corporation, formed a partnership with the American Library Association (ALA) in the "Libraries Online!" project, which provided $3 million to nine public-library systems in 1996 to help link patrons to the Internet. In March, Microsoft announced a donation of $1 million to the Chicago Public Library to facilitate Internet access and training. In other corporate-funding news, 1996 marked the second year of "LibraryLINK," a joint project of ALA and MCI, in which MCI provided grants to libraries to implement technology projects that would enhance reference and information services.

LIBRARY AWARDS IN 1996

Beta Phi Mu Award for distinguished service to education for librarianship: Robert N. Broadus, Chapel Hill, NC (retired)

Randolph J. Caldecott Medal for the most distinguished picture book for children: Peggy Rathmann, *Officer Buckle and Gloria* (edited by Arthur Levine)

Grolier Award for unique contributions to the stimulation and guidance of reading by children and young people: Patricia S. Siegfried, youth-services director, Public Library of Charlotte and Mecklenburg County, NC

Joseph W. Lippincott Award for distinguished service to the profession of librarianship: F. William Summers, professor, School of Library and Information Studies, Florida State University

John Newbery Medal for the most distinguished contribution to literature for children: Karen Cushman, *The Midwife's Apprentice*

In February, President Clinton signed into law the Telecommunications Act of 1996. Librarians applauded the concept of universal service contained in the legislation, as well as the provision of preferred telecommunication rates for libraries, schools, and rural health-care providers. A part of the legislation known as the Communications Decency Act (CDA) stipulated that anyone found responsible for the display or transmission of "indecent" materials via the Internet could be prosecuted. A coalition of organizations led by ALA filed suit challenging the CDA's constitutionality; this suit was consolidated with one brought by an American Civil Liberties Union (ACLU)–led coalition. The result was a unanimous federal-district-court decision in June declaring the act unconstitutional and blocking its enforcement.

Other News. On April 18, San Francisco's New Main Library opened. A bond measure had been passed in 1988 to construct the building; the San Francisco Library Foundation, using an innovative campaign, had raised an additional $35 million. The foundation set up ten community "affinity groups" among various constituencies; each set its own fund-raising goals. The groups were encouraged to split funds raised between special collections and the New Main Library as a whole. The concentration of the new library on computerization led to controversy, with critics accusing the library of shortchanging its printed collections in favor of the computer.

As a centerpiece to its centennial celebration, the New York Public Library opened the new Science, Industry and Business Library on the site of the old B. Altman building.

Karin Trainer became the first woman to hold the top librarian post at Princeton University. The appointment was effective in May.

Associations. ALA's 115th annual conference, held July 5–10 in New York City, drew almost 24,000 attendees. ALA President Betty Turock presided over the conference, which had as its theme "Equity on the Information Superhighway." Mary Somerville, director of the Miami-Dade Public Library System, was inaugurated as ALA's new president. Executive director Elizabeth Martinez announced her resignation. In her 18 months with ALA, she had made sweeping changes, but had come under fire for her management style.

"Reinventing Libraries" was the theme of the Canadian Library Association's 51st annual conference, held June 5-9 in Nova Scotia.

RENÉE PRESTEGARD, *Edmonds Community College Library, Lynnwood, WA*

© Eric Risberg/AP/Wide World Photos

Two major libraries opened in large U.S. cities in 1996. The San Francisco New Main Library was unveiled in April. The 375,000-sq-ft (34 839-m²) building (above) *combines a classic Beaux Arts front facade with strongly contemporary elements. The library can seat more than 2,000 patrons and boasts 400 computer workstations, 100 with Internet access. The sculpture "Cyclone Fragment," by Alice Aycock, is displayed in the five-story skylit atrium* (right)*. Meanwhile, in New York City the Science, Industry and Business Library* (below) *opened, occupying about 160,000 sq ft (14 864 m²) in the former B. Altman building. The $100 million project was the largest undertaken by the New York Public Library since 1911; it features 250 computers, as well as 500 workstations equipped for laptop connection.*

© Peter Laurence Photography/Courtesy, San Francisco Library

Courtesy, The New York Public Library

LIBYA

A United Nations (UN) boycott on air travel to and from Libya and the U.S. government's classification of the country as a supporter of international terrorism, which precludes U.S. firms from doing business there, strained Libya's economy in 1996. Allegations that Libya was developing a chemical-weapons capability played a role in the enactment of U.S. legislation calling for the punishment of foreign companies that invested in Libya's energy industry. Within the country, outbreaks of antigovernment violence revealed the persistence of opposition to Libya's leader Col. Muammar el-Qaddafi. Despite these problems, however, Libya completed work on extensions of its Great Man-Made River project to carry water to densely populated coastal regions.

Foreign Relations. Reports in April that Libya was building an underground complex near Tripoli for the manufacture and storage of chemical weapons produced threats of a U.S. military strike. However, the inability to prove categorically that the plant was not intended for peaceful civilian purposes, as the Libyan government contended, forestalled retaliation. A few weeks later, however, U.S. President Bill Clinton signed an antiterrorism bill that took particular aim at Libya by its inclusion of provisions allowing relatives of American victims of the 1988 Pan Am bombing over Lockerbie, Scotland (in which Libyans have been implicated), to sue Libya. Shortly afterward, a $10 billion suit was filed in a New York court.

Also in April, a Libyan plane violated the UN ban on international air travel, imposed to pressure Libya to turn over the alleged perpetrators of the Lockerbie bombing, by flying passengers to Saudi Arabia to participate in a Muslim pilgrimage. In June, Qaddafi himself defied the ban by flying to Cairo for an Arab summit meeting. In July, Qaddafi demanded that the economically damaging ban be lifted, but the UN refused to reconsider its position.

In August the United States sought to stifle Libya's economy further by enacting a law enabling the president to impose a variety of penalties on foreign corporations that make new investments worth more than $40 million in the Libyan energy sector. The bill evoked a storm of criticism from many U.S. allies, who argued that the legislation unfairly restricted free trade. Libya also lodged a formal protest against the law at the UN General Assembly in September.

Domestic Affairs. The escape from a prison near Benghazi in March of hundreds of political detainees, including members of militant Islamist organizations, highlighted the underground opposition's capability to challenge the Qaddafi regime. The dispatch of military forces to recapture the prisoners triggered a period of intense fighting in the remote areas to which the escapees had fled. A July soccer match in Tripoli between teams sponsored by two of Qaddafi's sons degenerated into a riot when fans began chanting slogans critical of the widely disliked heir apparent, Muhammad Qaddafi. Shots were fired by supporters of both factions, resulting in eight fatalities, according to government officials, although other observers reported several times that number of deaths. Less violent forms of criticism were also in evidence. At the February session of the General People's Congress, representatives posed pointed questions about the government's allocation of revenues from oil sales.

Early in the year, Qaddafi pursued a policy, initiated in 1995, of expelling 1 million foreign laborers, noting that they filled jobs needed by Libyans, were often in the country illegally, and—particularly in the case of the Sudanese—frequently were agents of extremist Islamist organizations. Detention camps sprang up around Libyan cities and, owing to the ban on air travel, deportees were transported overland across harsh desert terrain to Libya's borders.

A new segment of the Great Man-Made River, which brings water supplies to Tripoli, was inaugurated in September to mark the 27th anniversary of the military coup that brought Qaddafi to power. The massive civil-engineering project carries fresh water from aquifers in the south to the more densely populated northern regions.

KENNETH J. PERKINS
University of South Carolina

LIBYA • Information Highlights

Official Name: Socialist People's Libyan Arab Jamahiriya ("state of the masses").
Location: North Africa.
Area: 679,359 sq mi (1 759 540 km^2).
Population (mid-1996 est.): 5,400,000.
Chief Cities (1988 est.): Tripoli, the capital, 591,062; Benghazi, 446,250.
Government: *Head of state and government,* Muammar el-Qaddafi (took office 1969). *Legislature* (unicameral)—General People's Congress.
Monetary Unit: Dinar (0.364 dinar equals U.S. $1, June 1996).
Gross Domestic Product (1994 est. U.S.$): $32,900,000,000 (purchasing power parity).
Foreign Trade (1994 est. U.S.$): *Imports,* $6,900,000,000; *exports,* $7,200,000,000.

Literature

Overview

© Laski Wojtek/Gamma-Liaison

Wislawa Szymborska

Wislawa Szymborska, a Polish poet whose work celebrates life's daily quirks, won the 1996 Nobel Prize for literature....Robert Hass was named to a second term as the U.S. poet laureate as the poetry genre was in the midst of a revival....For the first time the National Book Foundation included a Young People's Literature Award among its standard award categories.

Meanwhile, the memoir was a dominant force in American literature, the trend toward multiculturalism remained prevalent in children's literature, and books on varying political views were common in English literature.

Nobel Prize. Polish poet Wislawa Szymborska was awarded the Nobel Prize for literature at the age of 73. Little known outside of Poland, she was the second consecutive poet to win the award and the fifth Polish author to be so honored. The Swedish Academy cited Szymborska as a "Mozart of poetry" and for "poetry that with ironic precision allows the historical and biological context to come to light in fragments of human reality." Czeslaw Milosz, who won the award in 1980, called her winning "a great triumph for Polish poetry in the 20th century." The new Nobelist is considered deeply political and very witty.

Robert Hass

Courtesy, Ecco Press

Szymborska was born on July 2, 1923, in a small Polish town near Poznan. She moved with her parents to Kraków when she was 8 and attended Jagiellonian University there. Her first marriage to Adam Wlodek, also a poet, ended in divorce. Her second husband, Kornel Filipowicz, was a writer. He died in the early 1990s.

Her first poem was published in a Kraków newspaper in 1945. Much of her early work embraced the Socialist Realism of the Stalinist era. She since has renounced that work and become a critic of Stalin, likening him to the "Abominable Snowman." Her more recent work stresses the quirks and unexpected nature of daily life and personal relations.

Szymborska's early works include *Questions Put to Myself* (1954) and *Calling Out to Yeti* (1957). Her second husband's death inspired a collection, *The End and the Beginning* (1993). She also has written *Salt* (1962), *No End of Fun* (1967), *A Large Number* (1976), and *People on the Bridge* (1986).

U.S. Poet Laureate. In April 1996, Robert Hass was reappointed as the Library of Congress' poet laureate. A member of the faculty of the University of California, Hass had been appointed to the post nearly a year earlier. In his first term he took on the cause of improving education and increasing literacy by volunteering to speak at dozens of community-based business and service organizations. He also brought to Washington, DC, many poets from Western states who read at the Library of Congress. He initiated a regular column in *The Washington Post Book World* called "Poet's Choice." In the column he weekly introduced and discussed a poem.

National Book Awards. The first-ever National Book Award for Young People's Literature was awarded to Victor Martinez for his first novel, *Parrot in the Oven: Mi Vida.* Also winning 1996 National Book Awards were *An American Requiem: God, My Father, and the War that Came Between Us* by James Carroll in nonfiction; *Ship Fever And Other Stories* by Andrea Barrett in fiction; and *Scrambled Eggs & Whiskey: Poems 1991–1995* by Hayden Carruth in poetry.

KRISTI VAUGHAN

American Literature

To many observers, 1996 was the year of the memoir. As baby boomers faced middle age, they summed up their early years and confronted their mortality through autobiography and family history. Even when authors wrote fiction, poetry, and other genres, the writing often seemed deeply rooted in their own lives.

Novels. In a prefatory note, Paul Theroux calls *My Other Life* "an imaginary memoir" written from the viewpoint of a second Paul Theroux "who looks just like me." In episodes that vary in quality, the fictional Theroux meets the queen of England, spends a night in a housing project with some teenaged yahoos who wonder if he is the author of *Walden* (Henry David Thoreau), and emerges as one of the real Theroux's best drawn, if least likable, characters.

William Kennedy's *The Flaming Corsage* is the sixth in his impressive cycle of novels about marriage, betrayal, and ghosts from the past among the Irish-Americans of Albany, NY. A father tries to solve the mystery behind his son's death in Ron Hansen's *Atticus*. Jessica Hagedorn examines individual, family, and cultural identity as she moves the reader briskly from the Philippines to San Francisco to New York in her supercharged *Gangster of Love*. Joyce Carol Oates offers depictions of family life gone awry in the fully realized *We Were the Mulvaneys* and the stagier, less successful *First Love: A Gothic Tale*. Steven Millhauser's *Martin Dressler: The Tale of an American Dreamer* is a feverish, magical evocation of life in 19th-century New York.

© Sam McCracken/Courtesy, The Dial Press

Courtesy, The Dial Press

Courtesy, W.W. Norton and Company

Courtesy, W.W. Norton and Company, Photo by Barry Goldstein

Elemental violence is the subject once again in veteran novelist Larry Brown's *Father and Son*. The protagonist of Gary Eberle's fey and funny *Angel Strings* is a guitarist who plays in a Las Vegas "Dead Superstar Revue." Daniel Woodrell transcends the crime genre in *Give Us a Kiss: A Country Noir*, a fast-paced tale set in the Ozarks that focuses on a drug deal but takes on the worlds of writing and academe as well. *The Distance from the Heart of Things* is Ashley Warlick's funny, finely detailed story of a fetching young woman's coming of age. Duff Brenna's *The Holy Book of the Beard* bids for underground cult status with its Ken Kesey–style look at slacker life in California.

In *John's Wife*, Robert Coover pushes his well-established postmodern tendencies in this tricky, parodic look at the mysterious disappearance of an alluring woman in an American prairie town. Paul Beatty also provides parody as well as an irreverent analysis of African-American history in *The White Boy Shuffle*. One of the year's most imposing titles was David Foster Wallace's satire *Infinite Jest*, a 1,088-page behemoth that includes nearly 400 footnotes.

Short Stories. Love is the main focus of Andre Dubus' *Dancing After Hours*, luminous, graceful new work from one of the most accomplished American writers of short fiction. The 22 stories in Joyce Carol Oates' *Will You Always Love Me? and Other Stories* provide ample servings of the well-known author's trademark subjects—the sex, violence, crime, guilt, and madness her characters almost seem to hunger for.

AMERICAN LITERATURE MAJOR WORKS • 1996

NOVELS

Alexie, Sherman, *Indian Killer*
Beatty, Paul, *The White Boy Shuffle*
Bell, Madison Smartt, *Ten Indians*
Berger, Thomas, *Suspects*
Brenna, Duff, *The Holy Book of the Beard*
Brown, Larry, *Father and Son*
Coover, Robert, *John's Wife*
Didion, Joan, *The Last Thing He Wanted*
Ditchoff, Pamela, *The Mirror of Monsters and Prodigies*
Friedman, Bruce Jay, *A Father's Kisses*
Gibson, William, *Idoru*
Hagedorn, Jessica, *The Gangster of Love*
Hansen, Ron, *Atticus*
Homes, A. M., *The End of Alice*
James, Kelvin Christopher, *Fling with a Demon Lover*
Janowitz, Tama, *By the Shores of Gitchee Gumee*
Jones, Matthew F., *A Single Shot*
Kennedy, William, *The Flaming Corsage*
Lord, Bette Bao, *The Middle Heart*
Major, Clarence, *Dirty Bird Blues*
McCracken, Elizabeth, *The Giant's House*
McInerney, Jay, *The Last of the Savages*
McMillan, Terry, *How Stella Got Her Groove Back*
Mendelsohn, Jane, *I Was Amelia Earhart*
Millhauser, Steven, *Martin Dressler: The Tale of an American Dreamer*
Murray, Albert, *The Seven League Boots*
Oates, Joyce Carol, *First Love: A Gothic Tale; We Were the Mulvaneys*
Peery, Janet, *The River Beyond the World*
Piercy, Marge, *City of Darkness, City of Light*
Powell, Padgett, *Edisto Revisited*
Sayers, Valerie, *Brain Fever*
Smith, Martin Cruz, *Rose*
Suarez, Virgil, *Going Under*
Theroux, Paul, *My Other Life*
Tilghman, Christopher, *Mason's Retreat*
Updike, John, *In the Beauty of the Lilies*
Wallace, David Foster, *Infinite Jest*
Warlick, Ashley, *The Distance from the Heart of Things*
Wideman, John Edgar, *Cattle Killing*
Woodrell, Daniel, *Give Us a Kiss: A Country Noir*
Yglesias, Rafael, *Dr. Neruda's Cure for Evil*

SHORT STORIES

Barrett, Andrea, *Ship Fever and Other Stories*
Barth, John, *On with the Story*
Butler, Robert Olen, *Tabloid Dreams*
Castillo, Ana, *Loverboys*
Dubus, Andre, *Dancing After Hours*
Egan, Jennifer, *Emerald City*
Everett, Percival, *Big Picture*
Falco, Edward, *Acid*
Goran, Lester, *Tales from the Irish Club*
Grayson, Richard, *I Survived Caracas Traffic*
Lawrence, Starling, *Legacies*
LeGuin, Ursula K., *Unlocking the Air and Other Stories*
Maslow, Jonathan, *Torrid Zone: Seven Stories from the Gulf Coast*
McGraw, Erin, *Lies of the Saints*
Morrow, James, *Bible Stories for Adults*
Oates, Joyce Carol, *Will You Always Love Me? and Other Stories*
Pfeil, Fred, *What They Tell You to Forget: A Novella and Stories*
Piazza, Tom, *Blues and Trouble*
Robinson, Roxana, *Asking for Love and Other Stories*
Shepard, Sam, *Cruising Paradise*
Watson, Brad, *Last Days of the Dog-Men*
Wolff, Tobias, *The Night in Question*

HISTORY AND BIOGRAPHY

Ambrose, Stephen E., *Undaunted Courage*
Arax, Mark, *In My Father's Name: A Family, a Town, a Murder*
Baker, Carlos, *Emerson among the Eccentrics: A Group Portrait*
Barnett, Louise, *Touched by Fire: The Life, Death, and Mythic Afterlife of George Armstrong Custer*
Barnouw, Erik, *Media Marathon: A Twentieth-Century Memoir*
Breslin, Jimmy, *I Want to Thank My Brain For Remembering Me*
Brookhiser, Richard, *Founding Father: Rediscovering George Washington*
Cantwell, Robert, *When We Were Good: The Folk Revival*
Carroll, James, *An American Requiem: God, My Father, and the War That Came Between Us*
Clark, Thekla, *Wystan and Chester: A Personal Memoir of W. H. Auden and Chester Kallman*
Crowley, Monica, *Nixon in Winter: The Last Campaign*
Davenport-Hines, Richard, *Auden*
Doty, Mark, *Heaven's Coast: A Memoir*
Duberman, Martin, *Midlife Queer: Autobiography of a Decade, 1971–1981*
Gordon, Mary, *Losing My Father*
Greene, Melissa Fay, *The Temple Bombing*
Harris, David, *Our War: What We Did in Vietnam and What It Did to Us*
Harrison, Barbara Grizzuti, *An Accidental Autobiography*
Hendrickson, Paul, *The Living and the Dead: Robert McNamara and Five Lives of a Lost War*
Kazin, Alfred, *A Lifetime Burning in Every Moment*
Kehoe, Louise, *In This Dark House*
Kennan, George F., *At a Century's Ending: Reflections, 1982–1995*
Kincaid, Jamaica, *The Autobiography of My Mother*
Leavitt, David, and Mitchell, Mark, *Italian Pleasures*
Matousek, Mark, *Sex Death Enlightenment: A True Story*
McCourt, Frank, *Angela's Ashes*
Meyers, Jeffrey, *Robert Frost: A Biography*
Middlekauff, Robert, *Benjamin Franklin and His Enemies*
Morris, Roy, Jr., *Ambrose Bierce: Alone in Bad Company*
Mura, David, *Where the Body Meets Memory: An Odyssey of Race, Sexuality, and Identity*
Reich, Cary, *The Life of Nelson A. Rockefeller: Worlds to Conquer 1908–1958*
Robertson-Lorant, Laurie, *Melville*
Van Slyck, Abigail A., *Free to All: Carnegie Libraries and American Culture, 1890–1920*
Wharton, William, *Houseboat on the Seine: A Memoir*
Wineapple, Brenda, *Sister Brother: Gertrude and Leo Stein*

CULTURE AND CRITICISM

Bloom, Harold, *Omens of Millennium: The Gnosis of Angels, Dreams, and Resurrection*
Bly, Robert, *The Sibling Society*
Denby, David, *Great Books: My Adventures with Homer, Rousseau, Woolf, and Other Indestructible Writers of the Western World*
Di Piero, W. S., *Shooting the Works: On Poetry and Pictures*
Dobyns, Stephen, *Best Words, Best Order*
Ellison, Ralph, *The Collected Essays of Ralph Ellison*
Gates, Henry Louis, Jr., and West, Cornel, *The Future of the Race*
Irving, John, *Trying to Save Piggy Sneed*
Joe, Rita, *Song of Rita Joe: Autobiography of a Mi'kmaq Poet*
Kammen, Michael, *The Lively Arts: Gilbert Seldes and the Transformation of Cultural Criticism in the United States*
Levine, Lawrence W., *The Opening of the American Mind: Canons, Culture, and History*
Murray, Albert, *Blue Devils of Nada: A Contemporary American Approach to Aesthetic Statement*
Nussbaum, Martha C., *Poetic Justice: The Literary Imagination and Public Life*
Ozick, Cynthia, *Fame and Folly*
Roiphe, Anne, *Fruitful: A Real Mother in the Modern World*
Winchell, Mark Royden, *Cleanth Brooks and the Rise of Modern Criticism*

POETRY

Brodsky, Joseph, *So Forth*
Carruth, Hayden, *Scrambled Eggs and Whiskey: Poems 1991–1995*
Clifton, Lucille, *The Terrible Stories*
Hass, Robert, *Sun under Wood*
Hull, Lynda, *The Only World*
Lesser, Rika, *All We Need of Hell: Poems*
Mathis, Cleopatra, *Guardian*
Norris, Kathleen, *Little Girls in Church*
Olds, Sharon, *The Wellspring*
Ostriker, Alicia Suskin, *The Crack in Everything*
Pinsky, Robert, *The Figured Wheel: New and Collected Poems, 1966–1996*
Pope, Deborah, *Mortal World*
Simic, Charles, *Walking the Black Cat*
Smith, Charlie, *Before and After*

Courtesy, Simon & Schuster
Photo by Darlene H. Olivo

Courtesy, Simon & Schuster

As the book's title suggests, the stories in Ana Castillo's *Loverboys* are about lovers, although not all of them are boys. Middle-aged women with strong survivor instincts are featured in Roxana Robinson's *Asking for Love*. In contrast, women and cars usually spell trouble for the men in Tom Piazza's *Blues and Trouble*. The otherwise ordinary characters in Starling Lawrence's *Legacies* always are discovering the peril that surrounds them. Family life is grubby and desperate in *Lies of the Saints*, but somehow author Erin McGraw makes it seem appealing.

Lester Goran's *Tales from the Irish Club* reads like a transcript of hilarious, moving anecdotes told after a holiday dinner. Bizarre twists abound in Edward Falco's *Acid*. The God who appears in James Morrow's *Bible Stories for Adults* is not the familiar Creator and, in fact, plays something more like a supporting role in these dark, funny fantasies. Natural beauties and off-the-wall characters get equal billing in Jonathan Maslow's *Torrid Zone: Seven Stories from the Gulf Coast*.

History and Biography. Vietnam continues to haunt private lives in James Carroll's *An American Requiem: God, My Father, and the War That Came Between Us*. Paul Hendrickson attempts to capture the psyche of the war's chief architect in *The Living and the Dead: Robert McNamara and Five Lives of a Lost War*. Nonetheless, in *At a Century's Ending: Reflections, 1982–1995*, George F. Kennan argues that the United States' historical reluctance to extend its empire sets it apart from other world powers.

Monica Crowley, Richard Nixon's research assistant until his 1994 death, portrays her subject as a hard worker, serious thinker, and thin-skinned brooder in the much-publicized *Nixon in Winter: The Last Campaign*. Robert Cantwell's *When We Were Good: The Folk Revival* is an academic study of the folk-music revival of the 1960s. A 1958 bombing in Atlanta is the focus of Melissa Fay Greene's *The Temple Bombing*, an examination of race, ethnicity, and grassroots fascism that seems strangely contemporary.

In *Auden*, Richard Davenport-Hines takes a fresh look at W. H. Auden and discusses the moral engagement of a writer perpetually launched on a search for justice. Thekla Clark recalls the poet and his longtime companion in *Wystan and Chester: A Personal Memoir of W. H. Auden and Chester Kallman*. Two remarkable if fractious siblings are portrayed in Brenda Wineapple's *Sister Brother: Gertrude and Leo Stein*, the story of a pair who were constant companions for nearly 40 years but then, following a quarrel over Picasso's work, shunned each other for more than three decades.

Losing My Father, novelist Mary Gordon's examination of the life of her late father, deals with the devastating discovery that her adored parent had a secret life as an anti-Semite and soft-core pornographer. Mark Arax turns personal tragedy into a wide-ranging meditation on individual and community in *In My Father's Name: A Family, a Town, a Murder*.

Expatriate Americans weigh in with David Leavitt and Mark Mitchell's *Italian Pleasures*, whose title speaks for itself, and William Wharton's *Houseboat on the Seine: A Memoir*, where the reader learns that the bohemian life is anything but carefree. In *Where the Body Meets Memory: An Odyssey of Race, Sexuality, and Identity*, David Mura examines what he sees as his barely tenable place in the country that interned so many of his Japanese-American countrymen during World War II. The gay life before and after AIDS is examined in Martin Duberman's *Midlife Queer: Autobiography of a Decade, 1971–1981* and Mark Matousek's *Sex Death Enlightenment: A True Story*.

Culture and Criticism. In *Blue Devils of Nada: A Contemporary American Approach to Aesthetic Statement*, novelist and blues expert Albert Murray argues that fundamental universalities underlie the work of musicians, artists, and writers regardless of race or color. A slightly different take is offered by David Denby, who argues in *Great Books: My Adventures with Homer, Rousseau, Woolf, and Other Indestructible Writers of the Western World* that while classic authors favor Western values over others, many of them bring out the individual best in every reader, regardless of race and gender. Meanwhile, Lawrence W. Levine champions multiculturalism in *The Opening of the American Mind: Canons, Culture, and History*, a reaction to Allan Bloom's conservative polemic *The Closing of the American Mind*. And in *Poetic Justice: The Literary Imagination and Public Life*, Martha Nussbaum argues that literature can and should lead to a greater understanding of the richness and complexity of ordinary people's lives.

Michael Kammen argues that one man was largely responsible for the serious treatment of populist mass culture in *The Lively Arts: Gilbert Seldes and the Transformation of Cultural Criticism in the United States*. Cynthia Ozick, on the other hand, concentrates mainly on such undisputed masters as T. S. Eliot, Henry James, and Saul Bellow in the savvy, well-wrought essays gathered in *Fame and Folly*. Peer influence gets a bad rap in Robert Bly's *The Sibling Society*, a provocative, uneven indictment of a high-tech, pop-cult, and increasingly parentless society. The old-fashioned Dickensian novel is defended vigorously in John Irving's *Trying to Save Piggy Sneed*.

Stephen Dobyns discusses two types of poems in *Best Words, Best Order*, the "light" shone on the reader by an academic maestro and the friendlier "small machine" that effectively recreates emotions and ideas. In Rita Joe's *Song of Rita Joe: Autobiography of a Mi'kmaq Poet* and W.S. Di Piero's *Shooting the Works: On Poetry and Pictures*, two very different poets reveal how their poetry is rooted in rich ethnic experience.

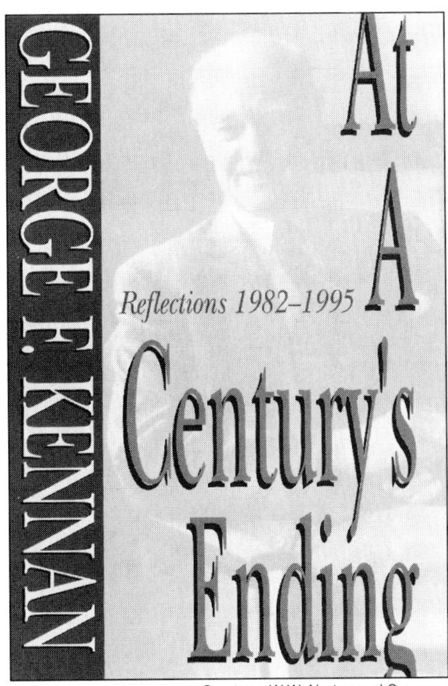

Courtesy, W.W. Norton and Company

Poetry. Joseph Brodsky, the Russian emigré and 1987 Nobel Prize winner, died in 1996 after writing the poems that appear in *So Forth*, his final collection. Translated from the original Russian and also composed directly in English, the poems are rich in both American pop culture and Old World history; these are poems by a survivor, resigned yet still buoyant.

Other collections are even more intimate: For example, much of Deborah Pope's *Mortal World* chronicles a failed marriage. In *Little Girls in Church*, Kathleen Norris retools her lost faith in orthodox religion to make it highly personal and thus fulfilling again. There is a strong elegiac tone to the poems in Lynda Hull's *The Only World*, where death and disease are con men always on the lookout for another victim. Sharon Olds traces the arc of her life in *The Wellspring* with poems about her mother, father, lovers, husband, children, and self. One of the most memorable collections of the year, Charlie Smith's *Before and After*, looks at the life of one woeful, crabby family through radiant metaphors that show how, as in a sad but beautiful love song, harrowing emotion is brightened through the optimism of craft.

DAVID KIRBY, *Florida State University*

The Poetry Revival

Poets used to dread the question: "Whatever happened to poetry?" But they need fear no longer. True, the number of poetry books published in the United States dropped from a high of nearly 1,400 titles in 1979 to less than 900 in 1990, but the total is rising again. More than 1,000 poetry titles were published in 1996.

The new color in poetry's cheeks is due partly to its recent honeymoon with film and other electronic media. The romance began in 1989, with the release of the motion picture *Dead Poets Society*, in which Robin Williams, as a charismatic English teacher at a prim New England prep school, persuades his impressionable students that poetry will fill their lives with passion and romance. Then, the poetry work of W. H. Auden (1907–73) enjoyed a vigorous revival after an elegy of his was read in the 1994 hit movie *Four Weddings and a Funeral*.

Yet neither of these films had the impact of the 1995 release *The Postman* ("Il Postino"), the story of a fictional friendship between Pablo Neruda, the Nobel Prize-winning Chilean poet, and an unpretentious postman who delivers his mail. *The Postman* was one of the most successful foreign-language films of that year and was the first foreign-language film in 23 years to be nominated for an Academy Award as best picture. The film captured an Oscar for best soundtrack. To coincide with the release of the film, Miramax Films joined forces with Hyperion to rerelease the novel on which the film is based, Antonio Skarmeta's *The Postman*—originally published as *Burning Patience* in the United States but retitled to capitalize on the film's popularity—as well as a collection called *Love: Ten Poems by Pablo Neruda*. The two books quickly sold out their 25,000-copy first print run and were in their third printing—with more than 45,000 copies of each sold—by fall 1996. At the same time, Copper Canyon Press, publisher of seven collections of Neruda's work, reported a 35% increase in sales of Neruda titles since the film's release.

In addition, Miramax/Hollywood Records released a CD soundtrack with music from the movie as well as readings of Neruda poems by such stars as Wesley Snipes, Andy Garcia, Julia Roberts, and Madonna. And in March 1996 the American Academy of Poets awarded Miramax Films its first Frank O'Hara Citation for *The Postman* "in recognition of the tremendous contribution the film and its producers have made to the appreciation of poetry in America." Hereafter the O'Hara Citation, named for the poet who championed film so enthusiastically in his writing, will be awarded annually to the feature-length film that makes the most notable contribution to the appreciation of modern poets and poetry.

Other media events have brought poetry to the attention of those otherwise unlikely to encounter it. For example, MTV, the music-video channel, aired performance poets reciting their own work, and the Poetry Society of America sponsored the program Poetry in Motion, which displayed short poems on buses and other forms of public transportation. In addition, public-television host Bill Moyers introduced such venerated poets as Donald Hall and Sharon Olds on his 1995 "Language of Life" series. As the same time, celebrity wannabes pushed their own poetic work in coffeehouse "slams." Such sessions often were noisy competitions with all the subtlety of a wrestling match. More staid events were organized by students and faculty at the countless writing workshops that dot the United States.

With all of this renewed interest in an ancient craft, it hardly is surprising that 1996 was the year President Bill Clinton declared April to be National Poetry Month. Clinton already had helped nudge poetry back into the spotlight by inviting Maya Angelou to read at his 1993 inauguration. The Academy of American Poets, with whom the idea for National Poetry Month originated, sent a media kit with suggestions for readings and other activities designed to promote poetry to more than 4,000 booksellers, librarians, and members of the press.

Meanwhile, as politicians, media figures, and corporate executives seemed bent on outdoing each other to embrace poetry and restore it to a central position in the public's mind, so too was a quieter and, in the end, possibly even more effective group—the devotees of the World Wide Web. Scores of Web sites—from individual home pages to such comprehensive resources as the Electronic Poetry Center, the home of 14 on-line poetry magazines—exist already.

Although no single poet represents the consciousness of the nation as, say, Walt Whitman did in the 19th century, the future of poetry actually may be healthier, insofar as more people seem to be reading and writing poems of every kind today.

DAVID KIRBY

Children's Literature

Although the number of U.S. children's books continued to decrease in 1996 after the artificial boom of several years earlier, the market also continued to attract attention. Hollywood had discovered children's books and, in the previous two years, films had been made from such well-known favorites as Chris Van Allsburg's *Jumanji*, Roald Dahl's *James and the Giant Peach* and *Matilda*, and Louise Fitzhugh's *Harriet the Spy*.

Children's literature continued to reflect the push toward multiculturalism. Picture books regularly featured racially mixed characters and a sizable percentage of fiction and nonfiction books concentrated on the stories of African-Americans and other minorities.

An interesting 1996 publishing event was the publication of two new versions of *Little Black Sambo*. Long banished for its racial stereotypes, the story by Helen Bannerman was given new life in these very different editions. Illustrator Fred Marcellino stuck with the original story, changed the title to *The Story of Little Babaji*, and set it in India, where Bannerman lived for 30 years. With *Sam and the Tigers*, folklorist Julius Lester and illustrator Jerry Pinkney set the tale in the imaginary land of Sam-sam-sa-mara. By getting rid of racial stereotypes and retaining the essence of the story, Lester and Pinkney redeemed it. Both their version and Marcellino's were praised widely.

The 1996 Newbery Award went to Karen Cushman for *The Midwife's Apprentice*. Set in the Middle Ages, it is the story of a girl who is able literally to pull herself out of the dung heap by finding meaning in her work. The Caldecott Medal was won by Peggy Rathmann for her delightful *Officer Buckle and Gloria*, about a policeman and his dog who turn school visits upside down.

Picture Books. Picture books in 1996 were at their best when they focused on the experiences of their target audiences. An outstanding example was Kevin Henkes' *Lilly's Purple Plastic Purse*, in which a little mouse-girl who adores her teacher is mischievous and temporarily earns his disapproval. In Amy Hest's *Baby Duck and the Bad Eyeglasses*, the subject of how it feels to get glasses is explored from the young wearer's perspective.

Middle-Grade Books. While series books were not proliferating the way they once did, one series—the Goosebumps series by R.L. Stine, which features creepy stories in the tradition of Stephen King—continued to influence other areas of publishing. Middle graders could not seem to get enough of Stine's gore. Its popularity spawned a series of imitators, none of which duplicated Stine's success.

Happily, there were other offerings for middle-graders from some of juvenile literature's best writers. Karen Cushman turned her attention to the U.S. West in *The Ballad of Lucy Whipple*; Lois Lowry wrote a new book about everyone's favorite little brother, *See You Around, Sam!*; and Katherine Paterson produced a dramatic story of abandonment and hope in *Jip, His Story*.

Junior High and Young Adult. Books for older children and teens continued to receive attention from publishers, who tried to cultivate an audience among young people who already may have moved on to adult books. One successful effort was Philip Pullman's fantasy, *The Golden Compass*, which also was marketed for adults. Avi wrote Books One and Two of *Beyond the Western Sea*, a saga in

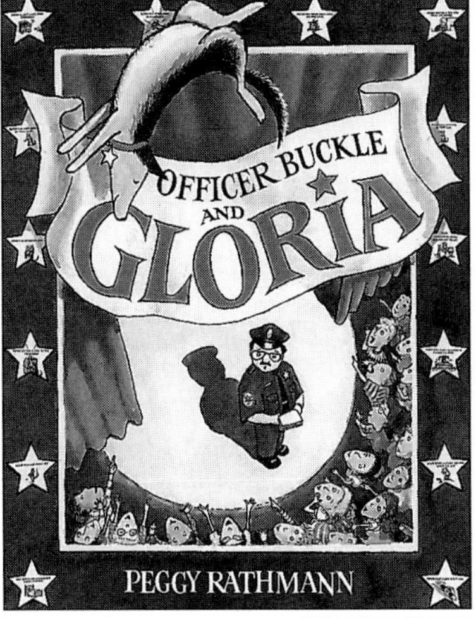

© Courtesy, Putnam

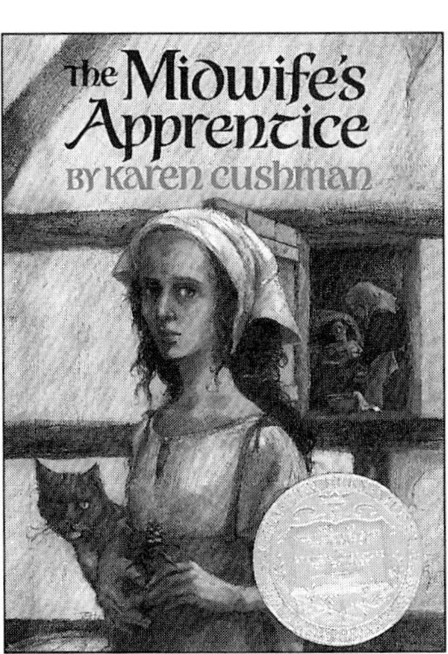

© Courtesy, Clarion Books

Peggy Rathmann's "Officer Buckle and Gloria" was awarded the 1996 Caldecott Medal as the best illustrated children's book, while Karen Cushman won the Newbery Award for "The Midwife's Apprentice."

SELECTED BOOKS FOR CHILDREN

Picture Books

Cooney, Barbara, *Eleanor*
Egan, Tim, *Metropolitan Cow*
Erdrich, Louise, *Grandmother's Pigeon*
Grimes, Nikki, *Come Sunday*
Kellogg, Steven, *I Was Born About 10,000 Years Ago*
Kleven, Elisa, *Hooray, A Piñata!*
Opie, Iona, *My Very First Mother Goose*
Pilkey, Dav, *The Paperboy*
Waber, Bernard, *A Lion Named Shirley Williamson*

The Middle Grades

Blumberg, Rhoda, *Full Steam Ahead*
Dickinson, Peter, *Chuck and Danielle*
Fleischman, Sid, *The Abracadabra Kid*
Hahn, Mary Downing, *Following My Own Footsteps*
Krull, Kathleen, *Wilma Unlimited*
McGraw, Eloise, *The Moorchild*
McKissack, Patricia and Fredrick, *Red-Tail Angels*
Prelutsky, Jack, *A Pizza the Size of the Sun*
Sanfield, Steve, *The Great Turtle Drive*
Wallace, Barbara Brooks, *Cousins in the Castle*

Junior High

Marrin, Albert, *Plains Warrior*
Myers, Anna, *Fire in the Hills*
Nix, Garth, *Sabriel*
Paulsen, Gary, *Brian's Winter*
Staples, Suzanne Fisher, *Dangerous Skies*
Thomas, Rob, *Rats Saw God*
Voigt, Cynthia, *Bad Girls*

the style of Charles Dickens, and Donna Jo Napoli authored *Zel*, a different take on the fairy tale *Rapunzel*.

ILENE COOPER, *Editor*
Children's Books, "Booklist" Magazine

Canadian Literature: English

In 1996 subjects in Canadian nonfiction ranged from politics to the social impact of the global economy. Historical fiction was brought to new heights, and finely crafted first novels received acclaim.

Nonfiction. Laurier La Pierre charts the career of Canada's most admired prime minister in *Sir Wilfrid Laurier and the Romance of Canada*, while Denis Smith documents the public life of one of the nation's most fiery leaders in *Rogue Tory: The Life and Legend of John G. Diefenbaker*.

Ideology is the subject of two books from opposite sides of the political spectrum. James Laxer's *In Search of a New Left* traces the rise of the New Democratic Party and its subsequent demise federally, and challenges what the author considers to be the neoconservative dismemberment of the social conscience. In *What's Right: The New Conservatism and What It Means for Canada*, David Frum promotes neoconservatism and the preeminence of the marketplace. Pollster Angus Reid analyses the economic problems that unbridled capitalism creates in *Shakedown: How the New Economy Is Changing Our Lives*, and proposes a series of compromises.

John Ralston Saul followed up the success of his *Voltaire's Bastards—The Dictatorship of Reason in the West* and *The Doubter's Companion—A Dictionary of Aggressive Common Sense* with *The Unconscious Civilization*, which won the Governor-General's Literary Award for nonfiction. Mel Hurtig, champion of Canadian culture and sovereignty, takes an optimistic view in his *At Twilight in the Country: Memoirs of a Canadian Nationalist*.

Montreal-born journalist Jan Wong records her initial enthrallment with revolutionary China and her attempts to come to terms with the Cultural Revolution, as well as her disillusionment after the Tiananmen Square massacre, in *Red China Blues: My Long March from Mao to Now*. In *A History of Reading*, Alberto Manguel draws on his wide reading experience to celebrate this passionate and personal act. On a different note, Paul Grescoe dissects the billion-dollar romance industry in *The Merchants of Venus: Inside Harlequin and the Empire of Romance*.

Poetry. Al Purdy's highly readable *Rooms for Rent in the Outer Planets: Selected Poems 1962–1996* presents a range of provocative poems. The late Alden Nowlan is well represented in *Alden Nowlan: Selected Poems*, edited by Patrick Lane and Lorna Crozier. Nowlan wrote about ordinary people and ordinary lives, but with great compassion, understanding, and honesty.

Renowned for his political poems, Gary Geddes gathered much of his best work in *Active Trading: Selected Poems 1970–1995*. Charles Lillard's poems in *Shadow Weather: Poems, Selected and New* are rooted firmly in the west coast, evoking its mystery and mythology. *John Thompson: Collected Poems and Translations*, edited by Peter Sanger, contains many previously unpublished works by this eccentric and charismatic New Brunswick poet.

Apostrophes: Woman at a Piano won E.D. Blodgett high praise—as well as a Governor-General's Award—for his innovative images and keen insights. Marya Fiamengo's *White Linen Remembered* covers a wide range of work from the meditative to the passionate.

Fiction. Margaret Atwood's first historical novel, *Alias Grace*, set in Victorian Ontario, recounts the life of a 16-year-old housemaid convicted as an accomplice to a double murder, investigating her claim of innocence while maintaining a detailed vision of the times. The book was shortlisted for the prestigious Booker Prize, as was Rohinton Mistry's *A Fine Bal-*

© Andrew MacNaughton/Courtesy, Nan A. Talese/Doubleday
© Courtesy, Nan A. Talese/Doubleday

ance, which gave a Dickensian account of the turbulent India of the 1970s. *The Englishman's Boy* by Guy Vanderhaeghe took a Governor-General's Award; its plot centers on the Cypress Hills massacre of peaceful Indians by American wolfers in 1873.

Claudia Casper's first novel, *The Reconstruction*, is an intelligent portrayal of a woman who works to create a lifelike model of Lucy, a 3-million-year-old human ancestor, and puts her own life back together in the process. Anne Michaels' stunning first novel, *Fugitive Pieces,* set in Greece and Canada from World War II to the present, depicts the lives of two men whose lives have been scarred by the Holocaust. Timothy Findley's *You Went Away* also deals with World War II, but from the perspective of the home front of southern Ontario.

Award-winning playwright Ann-Marie Macdonald's first novel, *Fall On Your Knees*, won the writer praise for her fresh style and dramatic narration of the lives of three Cape Breton families from World War I to the Depression.

Two of Canada's most renowned short-story writers produced 1996 collections: Alice Munro's *Selected Stories* contains 28 brilliantly crafted tales, while *The Collected Stories* of Mavis Gallant draws on her long career and displays a richness and depth that is nothing short of astonishing.

Douglas R. Cronk
Open University of British Columbia

English Literature

English literature in 1996 was marked by an unusual lack of controversy in the awarding of the Booker Prize, as well as by a thorough new biography of Queen Elizabeth II on the occasion of her 70th birthday, and several works debating varying political views.

The Booker Prize and Other Fiction. Among the British literary awards given each year, the Booker Prize stands preeminent; in 1996 it was awarded to Graham Swift for *Last Orders*, a novel about a journey taken to Kent by four Londoners to scatter a deceased friend's ashes into the ocean. This tale of a dead man's bequest is told in ways that allow landscape and plot to merge and thereby enliven characters whose voices ring with clarion authenticity. The six-book shortlist also mentioned Beryl Bainbridge's *Every Man for Himself*, which recounts the tragic voyage of the *Titanic*; *Reading in the Dark*, the first novel of poet Seamus Deane, which captures an Irish youth in Catholic Derry in prose both wincing and haunting; *The Orchard on Fire* by Shena MacKay, following a mature woman from London to her childhood home in a village in Kent; and two works by Canadian authors—*A Fine Balance* by Rohinton Mistry and *Alias Grace* by Margaret Atwood (*see* LITERATURE—*Canadian*).

There were many other notable voices in English fiction during 1996. Barry Unsworth's novel *After Hannibal* treats mishaps that attend a successful British novelist who, with his wife, is moved to buy a house in Italy. Muriel Spark's 20th novel, *Reality and Dreams*, pursues her penchant for the philosophical. Colin Thuburn's *Distance* charts the disturbing recovery of a scientist who suffers at the outset from amnesia, allowing the novelist to explore the intertwining themes of memory, time, and love. Jane Gardam's *Faith Fox*, which follows the fate of an abandoned baby, reveals a special gift for characterization in its portrayal of an old English woman of considerable pluck. *A Perfect Execution* by Tim Binding centers around the deeds and relationships of a compassionate hangman, and is told with a disquieting intensity.

Doris Lessing's *Love Again* ends a long hiatus in her distinguished career, and Ben Okri's *Dangerous Love* reveals a young man in Nigeria facing his confrontations. *Admiring Silence* by Abdulrazak Gurnah explores a post-colonial English theme of the exile in suburban London, with characters graphically torn between competing concepts of home, while *Asylum* by Patrick McGarth astutely

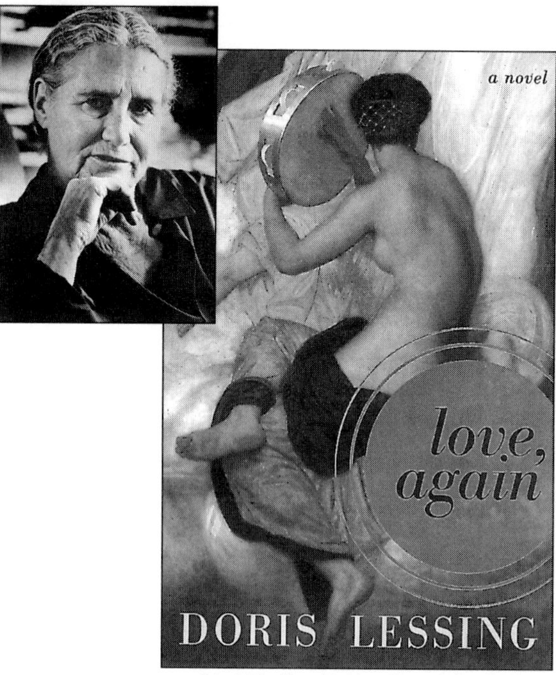

© Ingrid Von Kruse/Courtesy, HarperCollins Publishers
© Courtesy, HarperCollins Publishers

explores a world of competing obsessions. Philip Hensher uses former Prime Minister Margaret Thatcher as narrator in *Kitchen Venon*, a story about a hunchback who plays an important role in the House of Commons; these devices are ripe for a blend of the political and symbolic. Meanwhile, high on the list of 1996's good short-story groupings is Jamie Galloway's *Where You Find It*, a collection realistic in detail and surreal in syntax.

Nonfiction. In general, the British love coverage of the royalty; in 1996 the exhaustive *The Queen, A Biography of Elizabeth II* offered interested readers more than scandal. Ann Thwaite treats an earlier period with her biography *Emily Tennyson, The Poet's Wife*; a new critical biography, *The Life of Samuel Taylor Coleridge* by Rosemary Ashton, leaves readers in awe of the poet's brilliance.

Mark Kinkead-Weekes' biography *D.H. Lawrence: Triumph to Exile, 1912–1922* focuses on the writer in his most creative period. James Knowlson's *Damned to Fame: The Life of Samuel Beckett* covers the life of the quizzically engaging Irish exile. In *The Stations of the Sun: A History of the Ritual Year in Britain*, Ronald Hutton explores the establishment and maintenance of social as well as religious traditions within the calendar year.

Among books treating political subjects, *The Liberal Political Tradition: contemporary reappraisals*, edited by James Meadowcroft, focuses on the expanded role of government in the life of the citizen, while John Charmley's *A History of Conservative Politics, 1900–1996* provides an alternate picture. Several books appeared during the year on Wales and its political and cultural status; among these were R.S. Thomas' *Cymru or Wales?* and Clive Betts' *The Political Conundrum*. And for background on English relations with Scotland, Robert Clyde provides a critical perspective in *From Rebel to Hero: The Image of the Highlander, 1745–1830*.

Collected letters and travel books provide access to remote minds and faraway countries, and 1996 produced four notable examples of such works. *The Letters of Charles Dickens, Volume Eight: 1856–1858*, edited by Graham Storey and Kathleen Tilotson, chronicle the period of the author's break with his wife. Thomas Pinney, editor of *The Letters of Rudyard Kipling, Volume Three: 1900–1910*, provides insight into Kipling's several masks of fancy and the exotic. Peter Levi's *A Bottle in the Shade* recounts his visits to sites ancient and modern in western Greece in the company of a Greek fellow poet. And John Pemble's *Venice Rediscovered* serves as more than a travelogue; it offers a critique of the Italian Republic, and an assessment of Venice in the cultural milieu of the world.

Poetry. Among the poetic voices introduced to a wider audience during the year was that of Michael Haslam, whose *A Whole Bauble (Collected Poems, 1977–1994)* contains musical poems, many of which push the limits of language. The *Collected Poems* of Eavan Boland celebrate the singular voice of an Irish poet with a resourceful, compelling feminine vision. In *Slattern*, poems by Scottish poet and onetime Eric Gregory Award winner Kate Clanchy study man from disconcerting angles, revealing a keen visual image and musical detail. Declan Kiberd surveys and critically assesses the cultural and political settings of Irish literature in *Inventing Ireland*; Patrick Crotty edits an anthology, *Modern Irish Poetry*, that celebrates the variety of voices and visions that comprise the people of that rich, soil- and language-tied tradition.

In *The Dow Low Drop, new and selected poems*, Roy Fisher explores the idea of history without a sense of place, casting a critical yet lyrical eye over the effects of a city personified. Seamus Heaney, the 1995 winner of the Nobel Prize for literature, produced a new work, *The Spirit Level*, which offers readers down-to-earth poems in vivid detail that at the same time are structured around Greek myths that parallel the war and wounds of contemporary northern Ireland.

DONALD L. JENNERMANN
Indiana State University

World Literature*

The year 1996 in world literature was not one of the brightest in recent memory, but it did bring a good harvest of new works and important translations from a broad range of established and emerging writers.

Romance Languages. The prolific, multilingual J. M. G. Le Clézio, widely regarded as one of the dominant figures of contemporary French fiction, produced his 20th novel in 24 years with *The Quarantine*. This sprawling family saga is based loosely on the author's own forebears, who resettled from Brittany to the island colony of Mauritius in the late 19th century. The novel is set on Flat Island, a quarantine station for passengers on the way to Mauritius.

The multitalented Italian polymath Umberto Eco brought out the much-awaited sequel to *The Name of the Rose* and *Foucault's Pendulum*, the intriguingly titled novel *The Island of the Day Before*. Set in the 17th century and filled with metafictional allusions to a host of literary, cultural, social, and philosophical artifacts that all relate to that baroque/picaresque era, the narrative charts the mental and physical course of the young sailor Roberto della Griva, shipwrecked off the coast of a small Pacific island from which he is separated by what is now known as the International Date Line (hence the title). Eco's venerable countryman Mario Rigoni Stern presented his legion of fans and admirers with a somewhat more traditional novel, *Giacomo's Seasons*, re-creating the life of a small mountain town as it struggled to survive and adapt during the Fascist era between the two world wars without sacrificing its integrity and its strong sense of community.

From the eminent Mexican novelist Carlos Fuentes came *The Glass Curtain* (the Spanish title literally means "The Crystal Border"), "a novel in nine stories" focused on the oligarchic Barroso family but ultimately concerned with the larger themes of love and perfidy, hope and disillusionment, idealism and corruption, and the problematic relations between Mexico and the United States. *It's a Crime to Dance the Chachacha* by Guillermo Cabrera Infante showcased the Cuban émigré's characteristically mordant wit and incessant wordplay in three interlinked stories about a young couple dining at a Havana restaurant in the late 1950s with bolero and cha-cha music blaring in the background.

German. Far and away the most significant new work of German literature published in 1996 was Martin Walser's novel *Fink's War*. Based, like much of Walser's earlier fiction, on a true event, the work follows the agonizing six-year legal battle of a mid-level government official forcibly transferred to another office so that a patronage appointee might have his cherished position. Resistance brings only damaging (and untrue) slanders about his past performance and further outrage to his sense of honor and duty, and each defeat and indignity only increases his obsession with obtaining justice. The grinding process of the case ultimately produces in Fink utter exhaustion or transcendent wisdom, for by the time he finally wins on appeal, he no longer seems really to care about either rehabilitation or remuneration, having found in an idyllic Swiss abbey the inner peace that so long had eluded him.

A drastically different but equally strong literary impact was made by the Austrian novelist and playwright Peter Handke with the journal/pamphlet *A Winter Journey to the Danube, Sava, Morava, and Drina Rivers, or Justice for Serbia*. As the subtitle indicates, Handke was aiming to redress a perceived imbalance in the European- and world-press coverage of the Balkan conflict, coverage that often had cast the Serbs in the role of aggressors and the Muslims and Croats as victims. Public readings from the text in several German and Austrian cities only heightened the controversy that the work had sparked upon publication.

Russian. With *Dust and Ashes*, Russian writer Anatoli Rybakov concluded his monumental trilogy, *Children of the Arbat*. This time he portrays the horrors of the Stalinist purges of the 1930s and early 1940s down to the fateful battle of Stalingrad and concludes the sad tale of the ill-fated young lovers Sasha and Varya. Stalin himself occupies nearly a third of the book, and the resulting portrait of the tyrant is bloodcurdling, matched perhaps only by Aleksandr Solzhenitsyn's depiction of Stalin in the novel *The First Circle* published a quarter century earlier.

Mark Kharitonov's novel *Lines of Fate*, a powerful and charmingly oddball metafictional detective story that won the first Russian Booker Prize for fiction in 1992, was made available to readers in the West in an excellent translation by Helena Goscilo. Admirers of Ludmilla Petrushevskaya's dark, pessimistic plays and fiction welcomed her new collection of stories and monologues, *Immortal Love*, a title typically ironic in its counterpoint to the often abortive loves and strangling intimacies depicted in the tales themselves. That the sto-

*Some titles are translated.

ries possess such strong interest and fascination is due in no small measure to the manner of storytelling, a relentlessly oral, colloquial, and largely uninflected style perfectly suited to the women whose experiences are recounted.

Czech. The exuberant and accessible Czech novelist Josef Skvorecky treated his international audience to his first big novel in several years, *The Bride of Texas*, a colorful saga that mixes historical fact with invention in following the fortunes of some 300 Czech soldiers who fought with the Union army's Wisconsin Battalion under Gen. William Tecumseh Sherman in the U.S. Civil War. A parallel plotline traces the life and loves of the strong-willed Lida, a sort of Czech-born Scarlett O'Hara who time and again manages to choose the wrong men. Also new to Skvorecky's Czech readers in 1996 was his *New Canterbury Tales*, written in the 1950s but never before published until its release as part of a 20-volume collected edition of his works. Although the author has dismissed the nine tales as sentimental juvenilia, readers and critics have embraced their lively inventiveness and irreverent humor, reminiscent of Skvorecky's now-classic first novel, *The Cowards*.

The West Indies. Nobel Prize winner Derek Walcott brought out *The Bounty*, his first new collection of verse since the book-length epic poem *Omeros* appeared in 1990. The biggest literary impact of the year 1996 in the Caribbean region, however, was made by *Jonestown*, Wilson Harris' fictionalization of the events surrounding the 1978 mass suicide in his native Guyana by hundreds of followers of the Rev. Jim Jones. As usual in Harris' fiction, heavy doses of philosophy and mysticism almost overwhelm the narrative line (the narrator is a survivor of Jonestown), and the events are subsumed within a larger context, one of postcolonial excesses and antihumanism challenged by the unbridled spirit of the "sovereign" imagination.

The Middle East. The ancient practices of vendettas and blood feuds are at the heart of Egyptian writer Bahaa Taher's latest novel, *Aunt Safiyya and the Monastery*. In this work, the author's first to appear in English, a Muslim elder and a Coptic monk join forces to oppose and end the vengeance sworn by the eponymous Safiyya against the man who killed her husband. In *A Beggar at Damascus Gate*, the Palestinian writer and archaeologist Yasmine Zahran links the story of her people's 20th-century struggle for a place to call home with an evocation of the ancient worlds of their ancestors. *Until the Dawn's Light*, by the Israeli novelist Aharon Appelfeld, follows the tragic fortunes of a brilliant young East European Jewish girl in the first decade of this century as she abandons her faith out of love for a Gentile, suffers unbearable abuse at his hands, and eventually murders him.

Asia and the Pacific. The young Indian expatriate Rohinton Mistry produced perhaps the finest single work of 1996 about the Asian subcontinent with *A Fine Balance*, the tale of four ordinary people struggling to survive and make ends meet during the 1975–76 state of emergency declared by Indira Gandhi. Indonesian writer Pramoedya Ananta Toer's extraordinary "Buru Quartet" was brought to completion for Western readers with the publication of *House of Glass*.

The late Shen Congwen, considered by many critics as China's most serious Nobel prospect during the 1970s and 1980s, was presented to the West in 1996 with an excellent and representative collection of his short fiction, *Imperfect Paradise*. Most of the 24 tales, which were written during the 1920s and 1930s, involve provincial folk and pastoral settings, but as the volume's title implies, the "paradises" presented in the collection are far from vapid idealizations of bucolic charms and peasant wisdom.

In Japan, Akira Yoshimura's *Shipwrecks* also avoids the pitfalls of romanticized idealism in its lean, graceful account of the poverty-stricken life in a medieval fishing village. The late Kobo Abe's final novel, *Kangaroo Notebook*, indulges in typically dark, surreal fantasy in its imaginative and vigorous account of an office-products developer sent careening on a hospital gurney through bleak realms of memory, barren alienating wastelands, and fearful underground encounters with creatures and images of the wildest kind imaginable. And lastly, Japan's 1994 Nobel laureate Kenzaburo Oe offered readers two new books in 1996—the first English translation of his novel *An Echo of Heaven*, which follows the path to sainthood of a Japanese woman who salves her personal losses and tragedies through ministering to the needs of the poor and downtrodden in Mexico; and the new novel *On the Day of Grandeur*. The latter completes his "Burning Green Tree" trilogy with the convoluted but ultimately uplifting tale of another saintly figure, Brother Gii, whose sacrificial death reunites the warring factions within his church and sets them back on the road to salvation for themselves and for humankind.

WILLIAM RIGGAN
"World Literature Today"

LOS ANGELES

Los Angeles had a quiet year in 1996, although both the city and the county continued to operate under severe financial constraints.

Personnel. Mayor Richard Riordan delivered his State of the City message in April in a tone of optimism, seemingly anticipating a campaign for a second term in 1997. His approval level in the *Los Angeles Times* poll held steady at about a 45% overall rating among those with an opinion. His approval rating among Latinos and blacks, however, was less than 35%. The mayor refused to either sign or veto several measures to prevent veto overrides by the City Council. The mayor and the council also squabbled over personnel for the patronage-rich Community Development Agency.

Councilman Marvin Braude, a supporter of environmental causes, retired after almost 32 years in office. County Supervisor Dean Dana retired after 16 years in office. County Chief Administrative Officer Sally Reed left in May to head the state department of motor vehicles. Sid Thompson announced he would leave as school superintendent in 1997. Mark Finucane took over as director of the health department and said he would confront issues of ethnic imbalance in the department.

Development and Finances. Rebuild L.A. (RLA), a program designed to spur economic development after the 1992 riots, began to dissolve as required. It never had been able to attract large business firms to low-income areas and settled for expediting small-business and industrial location. Its resources were turned over to a nonprofit organization.

The subway under construction reportedly had numerous problems of sinking ground, water leaks, and inadequate materials. A huge digging machine became stuck in a tunnel for six weeks. Further, the project faced at least $14 million in cost overruns and a reduction in federal support.

The city budget already had been shrunk by earlier Riordan budgets, but the mayor was stymied in efforts to reclaim idle resources. The mayor proposed selling some of 7,000 city-owned parcels of vacant land and developing a plan for regular sell-offs. The council added a provision assigning half of the proceeds to be divided equally for improvement projects in each district. The $11.9 billion county budget, in far worse condition than that of the city, was pasted together again with small cuts, onetime revenues, no pay raises, and hoped-for federal funds.

© J. Markowitz/Sygma

Former football great O.J. Simpson (left) *faced new charges late in 1996 in a civil suit brought by the families of his former wife, Nicole Brown Simpson, and of her friend, Ronald Goldman.*

Police and the Simpson Case. The police department and its chief, Willie L. Williams, remained involved in matters of controversy. Mayor Riordan provided for 710 new recruits in his budget, depending in part upon temporary federal funds. Fearing later funding problems, the council cut back to 450 recruits, then overrode the mayor's veto. In the last year of his five-year term as chief, Williams faced deteriorating relations with the mayor and the council. Arrests dropped in five years from 290,000 to 189,000, while the force grew in size and reported crimes dropped slightly, but the meaning of these trends was controversial. The county sheriff's department also had problems, especially of finance, and could not afford to open the new Twin Towers, a $373 million jail downtown.

Also gaining attention late in 1996 was the ongoing civil "wrongful death" suit brought against former football star O.J. Simpson by the families of his former wife, Nicole Brown Simpson, and of her friend, Ronald Goldman. In December a judge awarded Simpson custody of his two children, removing the parents of Nicole Brown Simpson as their legal guardians.

Schools. Surveys showed a majority of respondents favored breaking up the huge Unified School District. Whether bilingual education was failing was also at issue. An influx of state money to reduce class size just before the school year began created problems of quickly finding adequate classrooms and qualified teachers.

CHARLES R. ADRIAN
University of California, Riverside

MACEDONIA. *See* pages 96–101.

MALAYSIA

Prime Minister Mahathir bin Mohamad and his ruling National Front coalition dominated the political landscape of Malaysia in 1996. Mahathir continued to be the architect-designer of Malaysia with bold proposals for the future. He also showed political courage in facing troubling radical Muslim groups within Malaysia.

Economy. The economic environment was much improved in 1996. Swift government action to increase interest rates cooled off an overheating economy. Even so, projected growth in per-capita gross domestic product (GDP) was 8.2%; it was the ninth straight year in which GDP growth exceeded 8%. Unemployment was under 3%, with inflation under 4%. The current-account deficit equaled about 6% of GDP—a significant improvement over 1995. A strong domestic market cushioned a downturn in exports.

Malaysia launched programs to improve shipping, banking, and aviation in an attempt to win back business lost to Singapore. In August, Mahathir made public plans for a $2 billion multimedia "corridor" that would connect Kuala Lumpur, the proposed government center at Putrajaya, and the new international airport at Sepang. Meanwhile, the $6 billion Bakun hydroelectric project in Sarawak was held up due to a failure to follow environmental-impact procedures. In August a 12-hour national power blackout put more pressure on the government to speed up power development and privatization.

The government struggled to cope with some 1.75 million foreigners in Malaysia's workforce, half of whom were thought to be illegal. Bangladesh was the largest supplier of migrants. Incidents of violence between migrants and Malays prompted strong action on the part of the government. New laws imposed harsh penalties on departed illegals who reenter the country and those assisting them, anyone employing or housing five or more illegals, and illegals who marry locals.

Foreign Relations. Malaysia was criticized for the August state visit of Myanmar's State Law and Order Restoration Council (SLORC) Chairman Than Shwe, who was responsible for that country's crackdown on pro-democracy forces. In an attempt to improve its image, Kuala Lumpur sent Foreign Minister Abdullah bin Ahmad Badawi to Yangon (Rangoon) to press SLORC to change its ways.

Society. Kuala Lumpur was concerned about the spread of Shiite theology among the mostly Sunni Muslim population, and was considering a constitutional amendment stating that Sunni Islam is the national religion. In May and June, 18 members of the banned Al-Argam Islamic group were detained under the Internal Security Act. Iranian-trained Shiite teachers were suspected of spreading their brand of Islam in the universities. Prime Minister Mahathir was especially critical about the treatment of women under Islamic law, as well as other aspects of fundamentalist teachings.

Politics. The big political event of the year was an April meeting between Mahathir and his old rival, Tengku Razaleigh Hamzah. Razaleigh left Mahathir's United Malay National Organization (UMNO), the dominant Malay party, in 1987 after a leadership struggle and formed his own party, Semangat '46. The two agreed in May to allow Semangat '46 members to rejoin the UMNO, thus weakening the opposition. As a result of these events, the fundamentalist Parti Islam (PAS) broke with Semangat '46, its coalition partner in Kelantan, the only opposition-controlled state.

The reconciliation did little for Razaleigh and his followers, who received no seats on the 45-person UMNO Supreme Council in a selection process held in November. Deputy Prime Minister Anwar bin Ibrahim remained the likely successor to Mahathir if the prime minister should retire.

PATRICK M. MAYERCHAK
Virginia Military Institute

MALAYSIA • Information Highlights

Official Name: Malaysia.
Location: Southeast Asia.
Area: 127,317 sq mi (329 750 km^2).
Population (mid-1996 est.): 20,600,000.
Chief Cities (1991 census): Kuala Lumpur, the capital, 1,145,342; Ipoh, 382,853; Johor Baharu, 328,436.
Government: *Head of state,* Sultan Jaafar bin Abdul Rahman, king (selected February 1994). *Head of government,* Mahathir bin Mohamad, prime minister (took office July 1981). *Legislature*—Parliament: Senate and House of Representatives.
Monetary Unit: Ringgit (Malaysian dollar) (2.5226 ringgits equal U.S.$1, Dec. 30, 1996).
Gross Domestic Product (1994 est. U.S.$): $166,800,000,000 (purchasing power parity).
Economic Indexes (1995, 1990 = 100): *Consumer Prices,* all items, 121.4; food, 129.3. *Industrial Production,* 168.
Foreign Trade (1995 U.S.$): *Imports,* $77,615,000,000; *exports,* $73,715,000,000.

Medicine and Health

Mad-cow disease and a variety of other infectious diseases often dominated medical headlines during 1996. Though the top three causes of disability and premature death worldwide were infectious diseases, a five-year study by the World Health Organization and other medical groups found that vaccination drives and other steps have made significant inroads in combating these diseases. These groups cautioned that noncommunicable diseases and accidents were threatening to replace infectious diseases as primary causes of disability and shortened life.

In the United States noncommunicable diseases long have headed the list. Heart disease has been the nation's leading cause of death for more than 50 years, followed by cancer. But as a result of improved detection and treatment, coupled with healthier lifestyles, the death rate from these diseases has declined. Particularly encouraging was the report in 1996 that the cancer mortality rate had dropped 3% in the first half of the 1990s—the first sustained drop since at least the 1930s (*see* FEATURE SECTION, page 51).

During the year scientists identified genes associated with epilepsy and premature aging, as well as a gene that appeared to offer protection against acquired immune deficiency syndrome (AIDS). New research also implicated faulty genes in the onset of cancer, Alzheimer's disease, and many other ailments. Mental-health experts reported new findings about schizophrenia and genetic links to obesity and depression, while medical ethicists continued debate on patient-assisted suicide, the implications of managed care, and organ-donor procedures. Health-care costs remained very much an issue, and the U.S. Congress enacted the health-insurance-reform bill.

Overview

AIDS. By late 1996 nearly 23 million people worldwide were infected with the human immunodeficiency virus (HIV), which causes AIDS; an additional 8,500 people, including 1,000 children, were infected each day. Sub-Saharan Africa and South and Southeast Asia accounted for most cases. In North America an estimated 780,000 people were infected. In the United States, AIDS was the leading cause of death among blacks aged 25 to 44; the Harvard AIDS Institute projected that by the year 2000, more than half of U.S. AIDS cases would be among blacks.

Some people appear to be immune to HIV despite repeated exposure to the virus. One reason was reported by U.S. and Belgian scientists: They discovered a mutation in the CC-CKR-5 gene that prevents HIV from gaining a foothold in the body. A normal CC-CKR-5 gene controls production of a protein receptor

About 15,000 people from some 125 countries attended the 11th International Conference on AIDS in Vancouver, BC, Canada, July 7–11, 1996. More than 5,000 research papers were presented at the meeting. Demonstrators, right, *encouraged a greater awareness of the magnitude of the disease.*

that is needed by HIV to enter a cell. People who have inherited the mutation from both parents cannot make the protein and seem to be fully protected against the virus. People who inherited the mutated gene from one parent and a normal gene from the other parent may have limited protection. The discovery may be useful in developing vaccines or drugs to block the protein receptor.

The standard test for determining the progression of AIDS measures the quantity of CD4 cells in patients' blood. A new test approved by the U.S. Food and Drug Administration (FDA) measures the viral load, or amount of HIV in the blood; studies indicated that the higher the viral load, the greater the risk of disease progression. The new test appeared to provide quicker, more precise results than the CD4 test. It was being used to monitor therapy and to indicate patients' five-year survival rates.

New drug therapies appeared to be so effective against HIV that some experts expressed optimism that AIDS could be changed from a usually fatal disease into one that is chronic and manageable. A class of drugs called protease inhibitors, when used in combination with older anti-HIV drugs known as nucleoside analogs, produced dramatic declines in viral loads. In many cases, viral replication was so suppressed that it became virtually impossible to find any HIV in the bloodstream (though it was believed to be present in other body tissues). The drug combinations were effective for both early- and late-stage infections, but they were expensive and involved taking numerous pills daily on a rigid time schedule.

Alzheimer's Disease (AD). AD is a degenerative illness most common among the elderly. It is characterized by abnormal brain-cell tangles and the slow death of brain cells; inheritance of genes for the protein ApoE-4 appears to increase the risk of AD. Growing evidence suggests that AD is a lifelong disease that progresses slowly, manifesting itself only after significant brain damage has occurred.

Using a brain-scanning technique called positron-emission tomography, doctors found that asymptomatic people who had two ApoE-4 genes showed low brain activity in the same areas as AD patients, though the spots were not as intense or as broad as in AD patients. Autopsies performed by German researchers showed that AD's pathological cell tangles can be present as early as age 20. An intriguing study that compared the autobiographies of 93 young women about to become nuns more than 50 years ago found that the women who had weak language skills were much more likely to develop AD than those with good linguistic abilities.

Certain substances may lower significantly the risk of developing AD. A study of 1,124 elderly women found that women who had taken estrogen supplements after menopause had a reduced risk of AD; the longer they had taken estrogen, the less their risk. A study of 2,065 elderly people gave support to earlier findings that ibuprofen, the drug contained in nonsteroidal anti-inflammatory drugs (NSAIDs) such as Advil, helped reduce the risk of developing AD by up to 60%.

In November the FDA approved a new drug for Alzheimer's developed by a Japanese company. The drug, called Aricept, has been found to slow the memory-robbing symptoms of AD in many patients by inhibiting the breakdown of a key brain chemical.

Respiratory Ailments. Some 4.8 million children in the United States have asthma; it is the most common chronic illness in children. The Centers for Disease Control and Prevention (CDC) reported that the asthma death rate among people from birth to age 24 more than doubled between 1980 and 1993. Some of the increase simply may be due to improved diagnosis, but epidemiologists noted that 25% of U.S. children live in areas where levels of ozone, a known lung irritant, exceed federal standards. Black youths were six times more likely than whites to die of asthma in 1993, possibly due to socioeconomic factors, including poor access to medical care.

A study of 182 women, including girls as young as 13, who required emergency treatment for asthma found a correlation between the attacks and the patients' menstrual cycles. Of the women studied, 46% were in the perimenstrual phase, which begins about three days before the start of a period. Researchers concluded that the asthma attacks may result from hormonal changes, particularly the decrease in estrogen that occurs during this phase of the cycle.

Emphysema is a degenerative lung disease characterized by overinflation of the lungs, which pushes the diaphragm downward, giving the patient's chest a barrel-shaped appearance; breathing is shallow and difficult. Lung-volume-reduction surgery is a relatively new procedure that removes 20% or more of the damaged lung tissue, enabling the diaphragm to move upward slightly and at least temporarily improving breathing. The procedure is not without controversy. It is very costly, and while some patients have benefited, others have not.

Tick-Borne Diseases. Each year, more than 10,000 cases of Lyme disease are reported to the CDC. Eight states—Rhode Island, Connecticut, New York, New Jersey, Pennsylvania, Maryland, Wisconsin, and Minnesota—account for about 90% of all cases. A study conducted by researchers at the University of Maryland School of Medicine suggested that the disease may occur much more often than reported. Their random survey of 1,200 Maryland physicians found that 1,900 to 2,400 cases were being diagnosed each year—significantly more than the 180 to 340 cases reported annually by the state health department.

A study led by Michael A. Gerber at the University of Connecticut found that Lyme disease is easy to diagnose and treat in children. He studied 201 children who were treated with antibiotics for two to four weeks; all the children were cured, including the 10% who were in later stages of the disease and had arthritis.

Like Lyme disease, human granulocytic ehrlichiosis (HGE) is a bacterial disease spread by ticks and is characterized by flulike symptoms. Unlike Lyme disease, it does not produce a distinctive bull's-eye rash. HGE, which first was recognized in 1991, is believed to be widespread in Minnesota, Wisconsin, and several northeastern states. Some ticks carry the infective agents for both Lyme disease and HGE, putting anyone bitten by these ticks at risk of contracting both ailments. Different drugs are needed to treat the two diseases.

Gulf-War Syndrome. Thousands of veterans of the 1991 Persian Gulf war have reported an array of medical and psychological symptoms—including nausea, cramps, skin rashes, headaches, and short-term memory loss—that collectively have been called Gulf-war syndrome. Medical experts have been unable to attribute the problem to known causes, and they have found no unique, consistent pattern of diseases or symptoms among Gulf-war veterans. Also, studies that compared hospitalization and mortality rates of Gulf-war veterans with those of other veterans found no significant differences.

Exposure to chemical or biological weapons was considered a possible cause by some investigators, but the U.S. Department of Defense insisted that there was no evidence to indicate that troops had been exposed to such agents. Late in 1996, however, the department reported that more than 20,000 troops may have been exposed to nerve gas when combat engineers blew up an ammunition depot in southern Iraq; other troops may have been exposed to mustard gas released by an Iraqi missile. Investigators for the Presidential Advisory Committee on Gulf War Veterans' Illnesses, created by President Bill Clinton in 1995, criticized Defense Department investigations as "superficial." The committee said that the department's failure prior to mid-1996 to fund research into the health effects of low-level chemical exposure had "done veterans and the public a disservice."

Mad-Cow Disease. By late 1996 at least 12 people—11 in Great Britain and one in France—had died from a newly identified strain of Creutzfeldt-Jakob disease, a degenerative ailment belonging to a group known as spongiform encephalopathies. These diseases, whose causative agent is unknown, are found in various mammals. Typically, Creutzfeldt-Jakob disease develops in midlife, apparently after a long period of incubation. Once symptoms appear, the disease progresses swiftly toward dementia and death.

Many of the latest cases occurred in teenagers and young adults. There were indications that they may have become infected by ingesting contaminated beef. Cattle are susceptible to bovine spongiform encephalopathy (BSE), popularly known as mad-cow disease. British cattle are believed to have con-

Beef products, especially those from Britain, became the focus of attention after 12 people died from a newly identified strain of Creutzfeldt-Jakob disease. There were suggestions that the victims may have been infected by ingesting contaminated beef.

© John Redman/AP/Wide World Photos

tracted BSE from feed supplements, which until 1988 were made from brains and other offal from sheep, including sheep that had died of scrapie, a spongiform encephalopathy.

Faced with a worldwide ban on beef exports, Britain reluctantly began a program of slaughtering cows that were at risk of contracting mad-cow disease. Most of those killed were older cows, which had been thought to be at greatest risk of getting BSE. Later in 1996, however, British scientists found that BSE could be passed directly from a cow to her calf. Some researchers thought that this could explain why more than 28,000 cows born after the 1988 ban had contracted the disease.

Many nations have monitoring systems to detect mad-cow disease. According to the U.S. Department of Agriculture, the disease never has been identified in the United States. Among monitoring nations, BSE has been detected only in ten nations to which Britain exported cattle in the 1980s.

New Medications. The FDA approved Xalatan (latanoprost), a new drug that fights glaucoma—a disease in which fluid pressure inside the eyes rises, leading to vision loss. Latanoprost, based on the natural chemical prostaglandin, helps drain fluid, thereby reducing pressure. But it has a side effect: It turns some blue or green eyes brown.

The first antibiotic treatment for fighting *Helicobacter pylori*, the bacteria associated with ulcers, received approval. The treatment involves taking Biaxin (clarithromycin), an antibiotic previously approved for other purposes, in combination with Prilosec (omeprazole), an antacid.

Tissue plasminogen activator (TPA), a clot-dissolving drug widely used to treat heart attacks, was approved for use in treating ischemic strokes, which are caused by clots that block the flow of blood to the brain. To be effective, TPA must be used within three hours of the onset of an ischemic stroke; used later, it may cause bleeding in the brain.

Dexfenfluramine was approved for weight loss and maintenance of weight loss in obese patients; it was the first diet pill approved by the FDA in 22 years. The drug causes the brain to release serotonin, a chemical that reduces appetite and cravings. Meanwhile, the drug-approval process received renewed interest (*see* SPECIAL REPORT, page 344).

In recent years, one of the options for people eager to stop smoking has been the use of bandage-like nicotine patches, which release nicotine through the skin in ever-decreasing doses. In July 1996, Nicotrol, the first nonprescription nicotine patch, was approved for sale. Unlike prescriptive patches, Nicotrol was available in only one strength, for use for up to six weeks. A competing company was seeking approval to offer over-the-counter patches in three strengths, to enable smokers to wean themselves of the habit over ten weeks. Patch users are warned not to smoke while wearing patches, not to wear several patches at once, and not to use any other nicotine product, including nicotine-laced chewing gum; doing so could cause heart palpitations, nausea, and other problems.

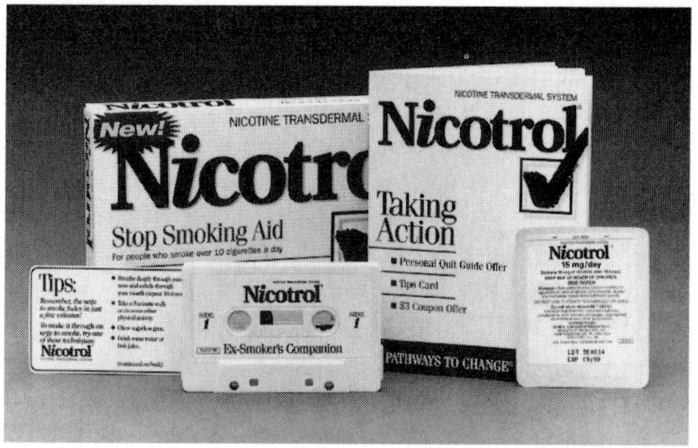

McNeil Consumer Products

In July 1996, Nicotrol—the first nonprescription nicotine patch, which is intended to help cigarette smokers give up the habit—was approved. It can be used for up to six weeks.

In November, despite the opposition of medical groups and government officials, voters in California and Arizona approved propositions that would legalize the medical use of marijuana for sufferers of cancer, AIDS, glaucoma, arthritis, and other chronic diseases; such patients in Florida and Ohio already had the right to use marijuana. Advocates for the drug's use based their support on the experience of patients who found relief from the pain and nausea caused by their illnesses or by treatment for those illnesses.

Melatonin. Books, magazines, and television talk shows touted melatonin pills as a cure for dozens of ailments, including schizophrenia and cancer. Little evidence supported these claims, however. Melatonin is a hormone secreted by the pineal gland in the brain. Secretion follows a daily rhythm, peaking at night and at its lowest during daytime. For reasons not completely understood, melatonin has a sleep-inducing effect. Because of this, some people take melatonin supplements to adapt to jet lag and changes in work schedules. The supplements have been sold as dietary aids, not as drugs, which means they do not have to be approved by the FDA or demonstrate that they are safe and effective.

JENNY TESAR
Freelance Science Writer

SPECIAL REPORT/MEDICINE AND HEALTH

"Physical Activity and Health"

"Americans, take a walk!" encouraged Vice-President Al Gore in July 1996, as he helped introduce *Physical Activity and Health*, the first-ever surgeon general's report on physical fitness and health. Issued as athletes were preparing for the Summer Olympics, the 278-page report detailed the benefits that everyone can derive from physical activity: reduced risk of premature death; lower chances of developing coronary heart disease, hypertension, colon cancer, diabetes, and other ailments; and improved mental health, with fewer symptoms of depression and anxiety.

Donna E. Shalala, secretary of health and human services, who commissioned the report, noted its key finding: "People of all ages can improve the quality of their lives through a lifelong practice of moderate physical activity." Shalala and other officials hoped that the report would be as effective in changing public attitudes as was the 1964 surgeon general's report on smoking and health. They received enthusiastic support from the health and fitness industries, as well as positive publicity from fitness publications.

The Report's Recommendations. *Physical Activity and Health* stressed the value of daily exercise that burns at least 150 calories, referring to "an emerging consensus. . .that physical activity need not be of vigorous intensity for it to improve health." Examples of moderate activities include a 15-minute run, a 30-minute brisk walk, 30 minutes of raking leaves or fast social dancing, and 45 to 60 minutes of washing windows or playing volleyball.

© Phil McCarten/Photo-Edit

A report issued in 1996 by the U.S. surgeon general detailed an abundance of health and quality-of-life benefits that people can gain by including moderate physical activity in their daily lives.

People who already are moderately active on a daily basis were advised that increasing the duration, frequency, or intensity of their activities would produce added health benefits. Sedentary people who are unaccustomed to strenuous activity were told to start with short exercise sessions of five to ten minutes and gradually build up to the desired level of activity, in order to avoid musculoskeletal injuries and other health problems associated with activities for which the body is not conditioned.

Americans and Exercise. Though numerous studies over the years have shown the health benefits of exercise, many Americans continue to resist a more active lifestyle. Data from national- and state-based surveillance systems sponsored by the Centers for Disease Control and Prevention (CDC) indicate that more than 60% of U.S. adults do not exercise regularly. Inactivity is more prevalent among women than men, among blacks and Hispanics than whites, among older than younger adults, and among the less affluent than the more affluent. Among young people, "participation in all types of physical activity declines strikingly as age or grade in school increases." The impact of this sedentary lifestyle is significant: About one third of Americans are seriously overweight, and the CDC estimates that 250,000 deaths a year can be linked to a lack of regular physical activity.

Officials recognize that couch potatoes are not going to change overnight. Commented Shalala, "Much work will need to be done so that we can determine the most effective ways to motivate all Americans to participate in a level of physical activity that can benefit their health and well-being."

JENNY TESAR

The Drug-Approval Process

On March 14, 1996, the U.S. Food and Drug Administration (FDA) approved a new drug called indinavir, just 42 days after pharmaceutical manufacturer Merck & Co. had submitted its application. The approval was the latest in a string of speedy decisions regarding a new class of medications called protease inhibitors that are targeted to battle acquired immune deficiency syndrome (AIDS). Within the previous six months, the FDA had approved two other protease inhibitors—Hoffman LaRoche's saquinavir and Abbott Laboratories' ritonavir—in less than 100 days. These rapid actions were a far cry from the beginning of the decade, when the FDA took an average of 25 months to process a new-drug application.

While such faster approvals were applauded by many observers, the entire FDA drug-approval process was under debate—in the public, industry, and government. Critics claimed that the FDA had moved beyond its role as a consumer protector to become a bureaucratic regulator and was endangering human lives by delaying the approval of potentially lifesaving drugs. In addition, pharmaceutical companies charged that millions of dollars were being spent unnecessarily in order to bring a new product to market. Proponents of reforming the FDA pointed to the example set by many European nations, where much simpler review procedures were in place and drugs were approved in far less time.

In contrast, many interested parties—including some congressional Democrats, consumer groups, and patients'-rights organizations—charged that an FDA overhaul would be an ill-advised move that would place Americans at risk. Some noted that European nations pay for their faster drug approvals with a higher rate of adverse drug reactions than in the United States. For instance, remoxipride, which appeared to be a promising new treatment for schizophrenia, was approved in Great Britain during the early 1990s but failed to gain FDA approval. However, the drug was taken off the world market after physicians found that it caused the bone marrow to shut down in some patients, causing aplastic anemia, a life-threatening blood disease.

Meanwhile, consumer-rights advocates predicted that an FDA overhaul would lead to the approval of unsafe drugs, pointing to the controversial 1996 approval of dexfenfluramine, marketed by Wyeth-Ayerst Laboratories under the name Redux. Some scientists asserted that Redux, the first antiobesity drug to be approved by the FDA in 23 years, posed several serious health risks to some patients. Other officials questioned whether radical reform of the FDA was needed, pointing out that voluntary administrative changes at the agency already were yielding substantial improvements in approval time.

Nevertheless, Congress debated a number of sweeping reforms for the FDA during 1996. At the end of the legislative session, several bills were under consideration in both the Senate and the House of Representatives. All of the bills would force the FDA to accelerate the review process by reducing the amount of research that drug manufacturers must submit and instituting third-party product reviews. Some proposals also would allow seriously ill patients to get experimental drugs more easily. While the concept of FDA reform had bipartisan support, the extent of change needed remained the subject of substantial dispute.

Background. The FDA was established as the Department of Agriculture's Bureau of Chemistry by the Food and Drug Act of 1906. Initially, the act required only that drugs meet official standards of strength and purity. In 1938, however, after 107 people died from using an untested new drug called sulfanilamide, Congress passed a stronger law—the Federal Food, Drug, and Cosmetic Act—requiring manufacturers to prove the safety of a drug before marketing it. The Drug Amendments of 1962 further required firms to prove a drug's effectiveness for its intended use, to send adverse-reaction reports to the FDA, and to provide complete information on both risks and benefits in all drug advertisements. Today, the FDA also manages postmarketing surveillance of drugs and reviews data if a manufacturer seeks to develop new uses for a drug.

In order to help the FDA speed the approval process, Congress passed the Prescription Drug User Fee Act of 1992, which requires drug companies to pay fees when submitting new drug applications and, in some instances, provides FDA funds to hire more reviewers. By 1994, 96% of new drug applications were being reviewed within 12 months. In the following two years, approval times declined further, especially for AIDS and cancer drugs. At the same time, the debate over reform of the FDA accelerated.

JENNY TESAR

Health Care

The U.S. Congress in 1996 took its first significant action on health insurance since its high-profile failure to revamp the nation's health-care system in 1993–94, enacting a modest measure that would make it easier for those with insurance to keep it. In separate actions, Congress also took small steps to expand insurance coverage for those with mental illness and to guarantee new mothers at least a two-day hospital stay following childbirth.

But none of the legislation was predicted to have much effect on the spiraling number of Americans without health insurance, which grew to some 40.6 million individuals, according to the Census Bureau. The percentage of Americans under age 65 without insurance (virtually all of those 65 and over are covered by the federal Medicare program) grew from 15.2% in 1988 to 17.3% in 1995. Among those losing coverage the fastest were children. In 1995 nearly 10 million of the uninsured were under age 18.

Managed Care. The managed-care phenomenon continued to sweep both the public and private health-insurance systems. According to the American Association of Health Plans, a trade association for network-based health plans, the number of Americans in managed-care plans grew to an estimated 149 million in 1995, up 13% from 1994. Of that total, an estimated 58 million people received care through health-maintenance organizations (HMOs), up from 51 million people the year before and double the total in 1987. The other 91 million Americans were covered by somewhat less restrictive preferred-provider organizations (PPOs).

Managed-care enrollment grew even faster in the federal Medicare and joint federal-state Medicaid programs. In Medicare—where HMOs were until 1996 the only form of managed care available, and where enrollment was strictly voluntary—the number of beneficiaries in managed care doubled between 1993 and 1996, with about 13% of the program's patients covered. While Medicare HMOs restricted patients' choices of hospitals and doctors, they were attractive to beneficiaries because they offered little paperwork and lower out-of-pocket expenses, and often featured popular benefits, notably prescription-drug coverage, that Medicare otherwise did not provide. Managed-care enrollment also spiraled for beneficiaries of Medicaid, the health program for the poor, although in most cases the decision to move to managed care was made by state officials rather than patients. In 1995, nearly 30% of Medicaid beneficiaries were covered by a managed-care plan, more than double the enrollment of two years earlier.

The pace of U.S. health-care spending began to slow down dramatically. In 1994 national health spending totaled $949.4 billion, an increase of 6.4% over the previous year, according to the federal Health Care Financing Administration. That represented the lowest percentage growth in more than three decades. Per-capita spending grew to $3,510 in 1994 from $141 in 1960.

While businesses and government officials hailed the lower spending rise and its beneficial effects on their bottom lines, many con-

© Brad Markel/Gamma-Liaison

On Aug. 21, 1996, President Bill Clinton signed into law the Health Insurance Portability and Accountability Act, allowing workers who change or lose their employment to retain their health-insurance coverage and limiting the ability of insurance companies to withhold coverage because of preexisting medical conditions. The legislation's Senate sponsors, Nancy Kassebaum (R-KS) and Edward Kennedy (D-MA), were directly behind the president at the White House South Lawn ceremony.

sumers felt the move in a less positive way. Managed-care policies intended to promote efficiencies by having less care provided in hospitals and more care provided by primary-care physicians rather than specialists produced a backlash that ultimately forced lawmakers at both the state and federal levels to respond. In the first six months of 1996 alone, 33 states passed laws to regulate the practices of managed-care plans, according to a survey by Families USA, a consumer-advocacy organization. Among the most popular targets was what came to be called "drive-through delivery," the practice of requiring new mothers and babies to leave the hospital only 24 hours, and sometimes even sooner, following delivery. But anecdotal horror stories involving complications that could have been detected during a longer stay prompted lawmakers to step in. By mid-1996, 28 states had enacted legislation on the subject, most requiring managed-care plans to pay for at least a 48-hour hospital stay following a normal delivery and four days following a cesarean section. Congress in September passed its own law on the subject, thus protecting those covered by so-called "self-insured" health plans, which are exempt from state regulation.

Other managed-care issues addressed by state laws and discussed although not acted on in Congress included whether managed-care plans may charge patients extra for using an emergency room if a condition turns out to be less urgent than the patient feared, and so-called "gag clauses" that restrict physicians from telling patients about other doctors or procedures not covered by their health plan. In December the Department of Health and Human Services decreed that HMOs may not use gag clauses to limit the medical options of Medicare patients. The federal government subsequently informed HMOs of a new policy limiting the type of bonuses that can be paid to doctors for controlling the cost of services from Medicare and Medicaid patients.

A thorny controversy also brewed over the use of a popular managed-care payment mechanism called capitation, which provides physicians a set monthly fee to cover a patient's care. Managed-care organizations asserted that capitation promoted an efficient use of resources, since physicians were financially responsible for all care provided. However, consumer advocates protested that capitation provided too much of an incentive for doctors to withhold needed care. In Oregon, a state that pioneered managed care, voters rejected a ballot initiative that would have banned capitation arrangements.

New Legislation. By far the most significant action at the federal level was enactment of the Health Insurance Portability and Accountability Act of 1996. The measure, cosponsored by Sen. Nancy Kassebaum (R-KS) and Sen. Edward Kennedy (D-MA), was signed into law by President Bill Clinton at a White House ceremony on August 21. The centerpiece of the measure made it easier for those with health insurance to keep it, by barring insurance companies from dropping coverage for people who get sick and by limiting waiting periods for people with preexisting conditions who change insurers. The law also required that insurers provide individual coverage for those who lose their group coverage, although it did not guarantee that such coverage would be affordable. Other notable features of the law sought to crack down on health-care waste and fraud, increased the percentage of health-insurance premiums that self-employed individuals may deduct on their income taxes, and granted tax-deductible status to certain long-term-care insurance and expenses.

While Democrats and Republicans had few disagreements over the centerpiece "portability" provisions, disputes over other portions of the bill nearly scuttled the measure. Among the most contentious issues was whether to allow the creation of medical savings accounts (MSAs)—tax-preferred plans that would permit people to pay their own routine medical bills and carry only catastrophic insurance coverage. Proponents argued that MSAs would hold down costs by making consumers more sensitive to actual prices, while opponents charged that they would provide tax shelters for the wealthy and healthy, while raising premiums for those with traditional insurance. In the end, the law called for a four-year test of the accounts, with a limit of 750,000 policies.

Much to the chagrin of mental-health advocates, left out of the Kassebaum-Kennedy law was a provision passed unexpectedly by the Senate calling for parity between insurance benefits for mental and physical ailments. Many policies, for example, pay 80% of bills for surgery and other medical procedures, but only 50% of bills for mental illness. The advocates did find some solace in September, when Congress, as part of a separate bill, required insurers to impose the same annual and lifetime benefit limits for mental illness as for physical ailments. The measure, however, did not require that insurers offer mental-health benefits.

JULIE ROVNER, *Health-Policy Writer*

Medical Ethics

In 1996 a number of medical-ethics issues faced clinicians, attorneys, public-policy makers, and ordinary citizens, as radical changes in the structure of health-care institutions, the potential for enhancement of humans, and problems in human experimentation surfaced. In addition, important legal developments in euthanasia and physician-assisted suicide loomed on the horizon.

Capitation. In an attempt to cut ever-increasing health-care costs, U.S. employers have invested more than $20 billion in managed-care plans, and tens of millions of U.S. workers are enrolled in health-maintenance organizations (HMOs). One important ethical issue in managed care is the use of a program called capitation. In capitated care, physicians are allocated a set amount of funding per patient per month. At the end of each year, through a variety of programs, managed-care physicians are reimbursed some percentage of the money not spent on plan patients during the year. One resulting financial incentive is to do less for patients, potentially placing the interests of the physician and the patient in direct conflict. Concerns about this issue led the U.S. Congress to consider—but not pass—legislation that would force health plans to justify and disclose capitation rates and incentives. Also coming under scrutiny during the year were attempts by some managed-care companies to prevent physicians from discussing plans or their benefits through so-called "gag clauses." (*See also* MEDICINE AND HEALTH—*Health Care*.)

Enhancement. News reports described dramatic increases in the rate of prescription of the drug Ritalin, used since the 1970s to treat attention deficit disorder, a neurological dysfunction that prevents children from concentrating and learning. Earlier, the nationwide best-seller *Listening to Prozac* (1993) had described the increasing use of Prozac and other antidepressant drugs.

According to 1996 research, psychiatrists and parents were beginning to move toward the utilization of such drugs to increase children's performance in school and on standardized tests. Ethicists worried that such moves would create a pharmacological underclass of children who not only would be at a socioeconomic disadvantage in school, but who also would be unable to concentrate as well as their affluent, pharmacologically improved classmates.

New genetic tests for susceptibility to diseases such as breast and prostate cancer—and an ever-increasing variety of genetic linkages to things like risk-seeking behavior, homosexuality, and a wide range of psychiatric disorders—sparked ethicists to wonder about the potential for genetic enhancement. Parents already had the ability to use preimplantation genetic diagnosis to select embryos with desirable characteristics, and in vitro fertilization remained virtually unregulated. As a result, ethicists worried that a free market in genetic improvement would be generated. New studies indicated that more than 44% of parents would improve their children's genetic inheritance if it were possible.

Physician-Assisted Suicide. Ought physicians be obligated to help their patients die? Who should regulate assisted suicide? During the 1996–97 session, the U.S. Supreme Court was expected to wrestle with these and other questions relating to physician-assisted suicide. The court agreed to hear two cases in which a ban on physician-assisted suicide had been struck down.

In March 1996 the 9th Circuit Court of Appeals held in *Compassion in Dying v. Washington* that preventing a competent adult from seeking physician assistance in committing suicide interferes with liberty and, therefore, violates an individual's substantive due-process rights. The following month the 2d Circuit Court of Appeals in *Quill, Klagsbrun, and Grossman v. New York* held that the New York statutes criminalizing assisted suicide violate the equal-protection clause of the 14th Amendment. The court reasoned that the state has no rational or legitimate interest in preventing a mentally competent, terminally ill patient in the final stage of illness from taking a lethal dose of a physician-prescribed medication. Its reasoning was that there is no difference between withdrawing care from the dying and administering a deadly dose, as both are intended to allow death.

Human Experimentation. Even though 1996 saw the 50th anniversary of the Nuremberg trials of Nazi clinicians, who experimented on their subjects without consent, and of the Nuremberg code, commemorating the rights of research subjects, scandal and debate abounded in 1996 concerning informed consent in human research. Two major commissions held hearings and issued findings on abuses of research subjects in radiation studies and in the Persian Gulf war. At the same time, debate continued over the protection and compensation of research subjects, including the homeless.

GLENN MCGEE and MATTHEW WEINBERG
University of Pennsylvania

Mental Health

During 1996 researchers reported new insights into schizophrenia, the children of trauma sufferers, Tourette syndrome, and genetic links to obesity and depression. Also gaining notice was a controversy about the increasing rate of diagnosis and treatment of attention deficit disorder (*see* SPECIAL REPORT, page 349).

Clues to Schizophrenia. Scientists reported evidence that some pregnant women experience an immune reaction that contributes to higher rates of schizophrenia in their offspring. The researchers suspect that the occurrence of this immune response in an expectant mother causes as yet poorly understood fetal brain damage that may lie at the root of some cases of schizophrenia. About one in 100 people suffers from schizophrenia, usually beginning in late adolescence or young adulthood. Symptoms include severely disorganized thinking, an inability to communicate with others or function in social situations, the belief that one is hearing taunts or instructions from disembodied voices, and the holding of bizarre beliefs.

J. Megginson Hollister of the University of Pennsylvania and her colleagues theorized that a biological mismatch between mother and child raises the youngster's likelihood of developing schizophrenia. The scientists focused on women's antibodies to the Rhesus (Rh) D antigen. RhD is a substance carried in the blood that tells the immune system to attack foreign bodies. RhD-negative mothers can become sensitized to RhD-positive blood through miscarriage, abortion, or delivery of an RhD-positive child. In later pregnancies, an RhD-negative mother's immune system can cause jaundice, anemia, or brain damage in RhD-positive babies.

Hollister's group reviewed Danish medical and psychiatric records for 1,867 men born between 1959 and 1961. Of that number, 535 were Rh incompatible (RhD-positive individuals born to RhD-negative mothers); the rest would not have provoked immune responses by their mothers. Through 1994, the average rate of schizophrenia for Rh-incompatible men was 160% greater than for Rh-compatible men. Schizophrenia most often occurred in second- and later-born men who were Rh incompatible.

Trauma's Generational Legacy. People who develop persistent psychological symptoms in response to severely traumatic experiences may pass on to their children a vulnerability to the same reactions, according to a study conducted by researchers and led by Rachel Yehuda at Mount Sinai School of Medicine in New York City. The study also indicated that parents' traumatic experience can become a source of trauma for their children.

The group studied 80 Jewish adults born to survivors of World War II's Holocaust—who either had endured internment in concentration camps or had hidden for years from Nazi authorities—and 20 Jewish adults of comparable age whose parents had not been exposed to Nazi persecution. At some time in their lives, nearly one in three offspring of the Holocaust survivors had suffered from post-traumatic stress disorder (PTSD), a condition that is characterized by nightmares, repeated flashbacks of distressing events, and fears of any reminders of those experiences. Distressing images of their parents' wartime traumas often intruded into their thoughts. No instances of PTSD were uncovered among participants whose parents had not faced Holocaust-related trauma.

Yehuda proposed that the children of those who suffer from PTSD may carry a genetic vulnerability to the disorder or acquire some features of PTSD through extended exposure to their parents' traumatic symptoms. Disturbances of brain growth in the womb or shortly after birth also may influence PTSD.

Inside Tourette Syndrome. Images of living brains provided scientists with a glimpse of the biological influences on Tourette syndrome, a condition that affects some 200,000 people in the United States. Prominent features of Tourette syndrome include head jerks, facial grimaces, eye blinks, and involuntary vocal outbursts.

Drugs that block activity of the chemical messenger dopamine in the brain are used frequently as a treatment for Tourette syndrome. A 1996 study by a team at the National Institute of Mental Health Neuroscience Center in Washington, DC, has linked the disorder to an oversensitivity of a certain class of molecular gateways for dopamine in the caudate nucleus, a brain structure that has been implicated in the control of intentional actions.

The investigators studied brain scans of five pairs of identical twins in which one had moderate symptoms and the other had severe symptoms of Tourette syndrome. Each twin received an injection of a drug labeled with a minute amount of radioactive substance that attaches to specific dopamine receptors in the brain. A brain scanner then measured how much of the substance accumulated in those receptors.

Attention Deficit Disorder

At home or in the classroom, the boy cannot sit still. He fidgets constantly and jumps up repeatedly from his seat. His teacher says he seldom follows instructions, rarely completes a task, and often interrupts lessons. Outside school, he chatters nonstop, breaking into conversations, asking questions and not waiting for the answers. He rushes to pick up a game and then, just as quickly, leaves it for something else.

Such children—who might simply have been labeled in the past as troublemakers—more often are diagnosed today as suffering from attention deficit disorder (ADD), a complex condition marked by poor concentration, impulsive actions, and, usually, hyperactivity. In the United States and Canada, 3% to 5% of all school-age children may have ADD. That figure has risen steadily since the condition was identified in the 1970s. And increasingly, treatment for ADD includes powerful psychostimulant drugs. Use of Ritalin (methylphenidate), the most widely prescribed drug, grew 150% in North America from 1990 to 1995. The increase was sharp enough to prompt a United Nations (UN) report, released in February 1996, expressing concern about possible misuse and overuse of the drug.

The report added fuel to a controversy over ADD and its treatment. Drug therapy has proved an enormous help to many ADD sufferers. But some experts charge that doctors, teachers, and parents are too quick to blame behavior on ADD—and too quick to turn to drugs to quiet unruly children. As one Iowa pediatrician told *Newsweek* magazine, "It takes time for parents and teachers to sit down and talk to kids. It takes less time to get a child a pill."

A Difficult Diagnosis. ADD can be difficult to identify because the diagnosis is based chiefly on behavior. Children and Adults with Attention Deficit Disorder (CHADD), an advocacy and support group for victims and their parents, lists these signs: fidgeting with hands or feet; difficulty remaining seated; difficulty awaiting turns in games; difficulty following instructions; shifting from one uncompleted task to another; difficulty playing quietly; interrupting conversations; intruding into other children's games; appearing not to listen to what is being said; and taking dangerous actions without considering the consequences.

Children with ADD often are quite smart, but they do poorly in school because they cannot concentrate. ADD also can lead to social failure.

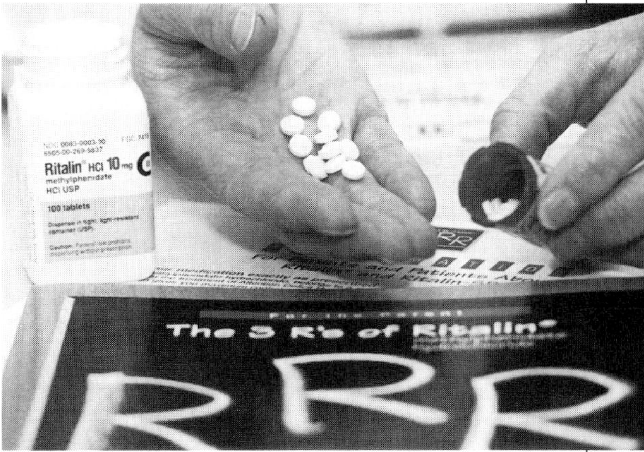

© Joe Raymond/AP Photo

Talking too much, interrupting others, not listening, and disrupting, dominating, or quitting games are traits that make it difficult to keep friends. Boys are affected more often than girls, who, when they have ADD, are less likely to be hyperactive. (When hyperactivity is a prominent symptom, the condition often is called attention deficit/hyperactivity disorder, or ADHD.) Signs usually appear before age 7. ADD once was thought to disappear as children grew up, but increasing numbers of teens and adults are being diagnosed with the disorder.

Researchers believe that the disorder has biochemical roots. Positron-emission-tomography (PET) scans show that the brains of ADD sufferers use less glucose, and thus less energy, in areas associated with attention, inhibition, and motor control. Scientists do not yet know how and why these differences arise. ADD once was blamed on diet, but few experts hold that view today. Some suggest that problems during pregnancy, including fetal exposure to substances such as alcohol and lead, may play a role. Other studies point to hereditary links. One study found that more than one third of children with ADHD have a sibling who suffers from the disorder.

Controversial Treatment. Ritalin, which increases levels of dopamine in the brain, has been the drug of choice for treating ADD since the early 1980s. It reduces impulsiveness and hyperactivity, and helps children concentrate. Occasional side effects include difficulty falling asleep, loss of appetite, headaches, and stomachaches. On the whole, though, the drug is considered safe. Several other psychostimulants, as well as antidepressants, are prescribed less often for ADD.

Experts caution that drugs should be only part of the treatment. Parents need to work with children to help them modify their behavior; counseling may be called for; and schools can adopt individualized instruction, short work periods, or other measures. Under a 1991 federal law, children with ADD are eligible for special-education services.

As part of a broad treatment program, drug therapy has turned out to be a real boon. But too often, some experts say, children with ADD get little more than medication. Moreover, the sharp increase in use of drugs has raised concerns that parents and educators are seeing ADD everywhere and that children are being misdiagnosed. Many children show some classic signs at one time or another. Even when the signs are strong and consistent, ADD may not be the culprit. Learning disabilities, depression, anxiety, neglect, abuse, or even an undiagnosed hearing problem may be the cause.

Growing Concerns. The 1996 UN report estimated that 1.5 million to 2.5 million American children were taking Ritalin. Some pediatricians feel that as many as one third of those children should not be on the drug, while other contend that far more children could be helped by the drug.

Some parents reportedly ask pediatricians to prescribe the drug for children who lack clear signs of ADD to help them do better in school. The picture is even more muddled for adult ADD, a form of the disorder that was not recognized until the 1990s. By 1996 psychiatrists were fielding calls from adults wondering if their depression, anxiety, and even procrastination and marital problems might be caused by ADD—and helped by Ritalin.

The increase in diagnosis of ADD has been unique to North America, a fact that some experts find odd. Drug abuse is also a concern. In high doses, Ritalin, which is a relative of amphetamine, produces a sense of euphoria. A black market has developed for the drug, with children crushing the pills and snorting Ritalin like cocaine, or cooking and injecting it like heroin. At least one death from the unauthorized use of Ritalin was reported in 1995. In 1996, Ciba Pharmaceuticals, the drug's maker, began an education program aimed at curbing abuse.

Concerned about the risks associated with drug therapy, some parents have turned to alternative therapies, such as biofeedback, to treat ADD. But scientific evidence for the effectiveness of these treatments is scant. Careful diagnosis seems to be the best defense against inappropriate therapy. Experts say that a child who may have ADD should be evaluated by a specialist, such as a child psychologist or a behavioral pediatrician. The evaluation should include screening for physical conditions and learning disabilities that could account for inattention and similar problems. Only after other possible causes have been ruled out should drug therapy begin.

ELAINE PASCOE

Twins with severe symptoms displayed much greater accumulations of the substance in dopamine receptors at the front of the caudate nucleus. This finding suggests that in cases of severe Tourette syndrome, receptors in the caudate nucleus prove overly sensitive to naturally occurring dopamine.

Obesity, Depression Genes. Researchers located two genetic sites where chemical changes may contribute jointly to obesity, depression, and anxiety, especially in young women. However, the controversial findings were expected to require confirmation in independent laboratories.

Altered chemical sequences in regions adjacent to the so-called obesity (*ob*) gene appear much more often in obese women between the ages of 16 and 40, compared with women in the same age range without weight problems, reported David E. Comings of the City of Hope National Medical Center in Duarte, CA, and his colleagues. In particular, this altered version of the *ob*-gene region showed up in obese women between the ages of 26 and 30 who also exhibited symptoms of depression and anxiety. The scientists asserted that the psychiatric symptoms were not simply reactions to being overweight, but reflected a genetic influence. Comings theorized that changes near the *ob* gene subtly may transform the actions of its protein product in the brain, which could boost appetite and feelings of depression and anxiety.

Ob-gene-related alterations that occurred in combination with a version of the dopamine D2 receptor gene known as the A1 allele raised the likelihood of obesity in young women even further. Comings theorized that the A1 allele disturbs the workings of reward centers in the brain and creates a vulnerability to a broad spectrum of related disorders, including substance abuse, severe alcoholism, obesity, and pathological gambling.

BRUCE BOWER, *"Science News"*

METEOROLOGY

Scientists continued research and debate on climate conditions in 1996, while major new weather systems were initiated or upgraded.

Global Warming. Researchers continued to refine their estimates of the climatic effects due to the ongoing buildup of greenhouse gases—atmospheric gases that tend to increase air temperatures for an unchanged input of sunlight. In 1996 the Intergovernmental Panel on Climate Change developed a range of scenarios for greenhouse-gas and aerosol concentrations for the period 1990 through 2100, then analyzed the climatic consequences. According to that analysis, by the year 2100 the average global temperature likely would increase by 1.8–6.3° F (1–3.5° C). During the same period the report projected that the average sea level would rise (due to the thermal expansion of the oceans and the melting of glacial ice) an estimated 6–37 in (15–95 cm).

The U.S. government moved on several fronts to combat the perceived threat of global warming due to greenhouse gases. For example, a second round of projects were selected to participate in the U.S. Initiative on Joint Implementation. The eight projects selected joined seven previously chosen; all were international pilot programs aimed at encouraging the private sector to reduce greenhouse gases. On the regulatory side, advisers to U.S. President Bill Clinton promoted the concept of specifying target levels of pollutants for industry, rather than prescribing the means of achieving the goals. At the international level, U.S. representatives proposed binding, rather than voluntary, agreements on reducing emissions, a departure from past U.S. policies.

The economic costs associated with curbing greenhouse gases continued to drive a vigorous international debate over the state of scientific understanding of global warming. In general, scientific panels assembled by the United Nations pressed for stronger action, while major energy-producing and -consuming industries and some scientists argued for more certainty before increased regulation.

Air Chemistry. The ozone hole—a patch of the stratosphere marked by extremely low concentrations of ozone—over Antarctica was about the same size in 1996 as the record-setting hole of 1993. However, the ozone amounts measured in 1996 were substantially higher than the record low amounts observed in 1993. The observed ozone amounts seemed to result from above-average amounts in the mid-stratosphere that partially offset low values in the main ozone belt in the lower stratosphere.

A significant stratospheric ozone depletion also was reported in the Northern Hemisphere in early 1996. The ozone layer over the region stretching from Greenland to western Siberia was thinned by an average of 20% to 30%, and briefly by a record 45%. This event highlighted the global nature of the ozone-depletion problem.

Although the process by which anthropogenic chemicals, principally chlorofluorocarbons (CFCs), destroy stratospheric ozone is well understood, the year-to-year fluctuations in ozone have remained puzzling. A new study showed that many of these changes, including changes as a function of height, could be explained by including data on the occurrence of tiny particles called aerosols injected into the stratosphere by volcanic eruptions. Such aerosols apparently accelerate the destruction of ozone by providing the solid surfaces (however minute) that the chemical cycle requires to operate.

Satellites. Early in 1996 a Geostationary Operational Environmental Satellite, dubbed GOES-9, was placed in its permanent location over the U.S. West Coast. However, in late summer researchers discovered that excessive heat buildup during periods when the Sun was shining into the imager had caused the backup motor on the main imaging mirror to fail. As a result, operations were modified to point the satellite away from the Sun at certain times of day during critical seasons of the year. This move reduced the data coverage provided, but NOAA was hopeful that the lower temperatures inside the spacecraft would prevent further loss of systems on the satellite.

Japan launched the Advanced Earth Observing Satellite (ADEOS) into a low-earth, circular polar orbit in August; this was the first in a series of major collaborative efforts between the National Aeronautics and Space Administration (NASA) and Japan's National Space Development Agency (NASDA). Instrumentation included the NASA Scatterometer (to measure wind speed at the ocean's surface), NASA's Total Ozone Mapping Spectrometer, and NASDA's Ocean Color and Temperature Sensor. The first operational data were collected in November.

Meteorology on the World Wide Web. The distribution of meteorological data, images, and documentation historically has been a problem due to their volume and changeability. This situation changed rapidly in 1995 and 1996 as the part of the Internet global computer network known as the World Wide Web grew explosively. By providing text, graphics, and images on demand to users anywhere on the network, the Web inaugurated a new level of access to current meteorological data.

Wildfires and Wind. Scientists have coupled a numerical model of a small region of the atmosphere with a numerical model of forest fires in dry eucalyptus forests to explore the complicated relationship between the local wind and fire. They found that weak large-scale winds made the modeled fire more susceptible to unstable, "blow-up" conditions, while stronger large-scale winds favored a more predictable, but faster-moving, fire. As well, under weak large-scale winds the model indicated that a main fire line is likely to break up into "fingers" of flame spaced about 0.6 mi (1 km) apart. Such fingers had been attributed to variations in fuel or local geography, but the study found that they are an instability of the wind circulation driven by fire.

New Tools. The 1996 Summer Olympics were held in Atlanta, GA, and surrounding areas. Given the climatology of the area, with its relatively high probabilities of thunderstorms and hot, humid weather, the National Weather Service (NWS) applied new tools coming on-line as part of its modernization and restructuring plan to provide detailed forecasts for all Olympic venues. Special fine-resolution numerical models were run twice daily, with even-finer-resolution models being run as needed for local areas. New generations of computer-aided analysis and forecasting tools also were made available to forecasters. Besides providing the meteorological information to safeguard participants and spectators, this special effort provided valuable experience in coordinating the use of the new tools.

After 35 years as a mainstay of real-time forecasting, the WSR-57 weather-surveillance network was decommissioned totally in late 1996 as the new network of Doppler weather-surveillance radars (WSR-88D) became fully functional. Implementation of the new system was a cornerstone of the NWS plan to leapfrog several generations of electronic and computational improvements in radar technology. The Doppler capabilities, improved accuracy, and digital communications built into the WSR-88D already were enabling improved forecasts and warnings.

Summary of Weather Events. The hurricane season in the Atlantic was above average, with 13 named storms, including nine hurricanes. Although this number was below the near-record pace of 1995, a number of locations were hit hard. Both hurricanes Bertha (in mid-July) and Fran (in early September) took a track that made landfall near Wilmington, NC, and then moved up the eastern slope of the Appalachian Mountains. Some 750,000 persons were evacuated in coastal areas for Bertha, while nearly 500,000 were evacuated for Fran. Fran proved to be much stronger, causing an estimated $3.2 billion in damage, mostly in North Carolina. Immediately after Fran, some 4.5 million people in the Carolinas and Virginia were without power. Bertha also wreaked havoc in parts of the Caribbean, including the Virgin Islands, which were damaged badly in the 1995 hurricane season. Another notable event was the passage of Hurricane Cesar across Nicaragua (causing at least 51 deaths in the Caribbean and Central America). After emerging in the eastern Pacific, it was renamed Douglas and again gained hurricane strength. The last such crossing of Central America occurred in 1988.

Weather in the United States was consistent for much of 1996, with the East and Northwest having wet, cool weather, while hot, dry weather dominated the Central Plains and Southwest. Many locations in the East experienced record or near-record snowfalls during early 1996. Then hurricanes Bertha and Fran brought excessive rainfall and flooding to the Mid-Atlantic states during the summer. The drought that dominated the Southwest and Central Plains early in the year eased in summer, partly due to rains associated with Hurricane Dolly. The late fall brought stormy conditions to much of the country.

Around the globe, a severe drought struck Mongolia. Wildfires consumed some 23 million acres (9.3 million ha) of forests and grasslands, taking 800 lives and 7,800 head of livestock. U.S. officials rushed a satellite receiving station to Mongolia to help officials there track fire activity. Conversely, heavy summer rains and flooding plagued Afghanistan, Pakistan, Nepal, Bangladesh, and eastern China, where thousands were reported killed in heavy flooding. The summer storms in Bangladesh included a tornado that tore through villages and inflicted heavy casualties. Southern Africa and southeastern Australia suffered through unusually cold and snowy winters, and Western Europe started the winter with unusually cold, stormy weather.

U.S. tornado activity for 1996 was slightly behind 1995, but well above average. Deaths (23) were about 30% of the average, extending a recent trend for relatively large numbers of tornados with relatively few fatalities.

George J. Huffman
Science Systems and Applications, Inc.

© Paul VanDevelder/Gamma-Liaison

© Tony Dejak/AP/Wide World Photos

The United States received its fair share of extreme weather conditions during 1996. In February heavy rains and an early snowmelt swelled Oregon's Willamette River (left) *and other waterways in the Pacific Northwest to their highest levels in three decades. In September the year's most destructive tropical storm—Hurricane Fran—wreaked havoc throughout the Carolinas and Virginia after making landfall near Topsail Beach, NC* (below)*. Wintry conditions came unseasonably early to the Great Lakes region with a "lake-effect" snowstorm in mid-November. The area surrounding Cleveland, OH* (above)*, was particularly hard hit, receiving as much as 4 ft (1.2 m) in three days.*

© Cramer Gallimore/Gamma-Liaison

MEXICO

During 1996, President Ernesto Zedillo Ponce de León pointed to rising economic growth and diminished inflation as proof that Mexico's economy had weathered the storm precipitated by a bungled peso crisis late in 1994. Opposition groups lambasted the watering down of a comprehensive reform designed to ensure the integrity of elections, whose outcome once was manipulated by Zedillo's Institutional Revolutionary Party (PRI). The PRI's ardor for sweeping constitutional changes cooled after the governing party suffered setbacks in state elections late in the year. In the south, guerrilla violence grew as a new group, the People's Revolutionary Army (ERP), took its place with the Zapatista National Liberal Army (EZLN or Zapatistas).

Politics. In late July, after 19 months of desultory negotiations, Mexico's major parties agreed to ambitious electoral reforms that Zedillo had proposed soon after he took office in December 1994. The parties engaged in the protracted negotiations were the PRI, the center-right National Action Party (PAN), the nationalist left Democratic Revolutionary Party (PRD), and the tiny left-leaning Workers Party (PT).

The modifications included enlarging the number of deputies chosen by proportional representation so that no single party could capture more than 300 seats, down from 315, in the 500-member lower house; prohibiting unions and other organizations from joining parties on a collective basis; providing more public financing of elections, while imposing new ceilings on party funding and campaign spending; specifying that, beginning in 1997, residents of Mexico City would elect their mayor, previously appointed by the president; and ending the executive branch's control of the Federal Electoral Institute (IFE), which oversees the electoral process. In addition, the authority to rule on electoral appeals would be shifted from the executive branch to the Supreme Court.

On August 5 the Chamber of Deputies and the Senate gave final approval to the reforms, which involved amending some 20 sections of the constitution. Although the amendments gained rapid passage, Congress had more difficulty crafting the regulatory statutes necessary to implement specific provisions. By mid-November, lawmakers had agreed only on the composition of the IFE.

The PRI exhibited mixed emotions about the electoral innovations. On the one hand, the party felt obliged to back the hard work that Government Secretary Emilio Chuayffet Chemor and PRI President Santiago Oñate Laborde had invested in the negotiations. On the other hand, warhorses privately decried curbs on campaign outlays and excoriated the ban on unions, peasant groups, and other organizations affiliating en masse with the party. At the PRI's National Assembly, held in September, party stalwarts gave abundant lip service to the constitutional changes, heaping praise on Oñate and Chuayffet. At the same time, they allowed members of the labor, peasant, and popular sectors to vote with both their state delegations and their corporatist entities. In addition, the 4,423 delegates indirectly expressed disdain for Zedillo, former President Carlos Salinas de Gortari,

© Roberto Velazquez/AP/Wide World Photos

Mexico's President Ernesto Zedillo (center) of the Institutional Revolutionary Party (PRI) was greeted by supporters as he and Santiago Oñate (right), the PRI president, left the party's 17th convention on Sept. 22, 1996. The majority of convention delegates had agreed that future PRI candidates for president and other high posts would have to have served in an elected post for the party. Zedillo and his four predecessors as president would not have met such a requirement.

and other foreign-educated technocrats by requiring future PRI candidates for major posts to have been active in the party for at least ten years and to have held an elective post. Such provisos would have prevented the last five PRI chief executives—and all but three of Zedillo's cabinet members—from seeking the presidency.

Before the July reform took effect, voters cast ballots in local elections in Guerrero, the poor southern state where the ERP first had appeared on June 28 and where, a year earlier, state police had killed 17 peasants. Rather than disrupt the contests as many observers feared, the ERP observed a unilateral cease-fire "in order to promote" participation. For their part, government troops remained in the barracks lest their presence incite violent confrontations. In view of the uncertain climate, some 65% of the 1.3 million eligible citizens stayed at home. The low turnout redounded to the advantage of the well-organized PRI, which captured 53 of the beleaguered state's 76 mayoral contests. The PRI also won a majority in the state legislature.

The PRI's luck ran out on November 10, when the party suffered stinging reversals in Mexico state, Coahuila, and Hidalgo. Although retaining control of the legislature and a majority of municipalities, the PRI lost mayoral races in five of Mexico state's largest cities. This outcome could serve as a harbinger of the mid-1997 Mexico City election, when voters will select their mayor for the first time. The setbacks persuaded PRI legislators to attenuate the electoral initiative. They boosted the ceiling on political contributions; eliminated criminal penalties on excess campaign spending; reduced media coverage for the opposition; and prohibited coalition candidates from Mexico's City's mayoral contest.

Early in December, President Zedillo dismissed Attorney General Fernando Antonio Lozano Gracia, who had become entangled in controversy for mishandling a number of high-profile political crimes. Lozano had been the only member of Zedillo's cabinet who belonged to an opposing party. The PRI also replaced Oñate as party president with Humberto Roque, the leader of the PRI deputies, who had engineered the turnabout on electoral reform.

Economics. On the heels of the 1995 disaster, economic growth was expected to exceed 4% in 1996 as exports of oil, minerals, auto parts, and products of *maquiladora* plants—where foreign-made components are assembled into completed parts—spearheaded the recovery. Finance Secretary Guillermo Ortiz

MEXICO • Information Highlights

Official Name: United Mexican States.
Location: Southern North America.
Area: 761,602 sq mi (1 972 550 km²).
Population (mid-1996 est.): 94,800,000.
Chief Cities (March 1990 census): Mexico City (Federal District), the capital, 8,235,744; Guadalajara, 1,650,042; Nezahualcóyotl, 1,255,456.
Government: *Head of state and government,* Ernesto Zedillo Ponce de León, president (took office Dec. 1, 1994). *Legislature*—National Congress: Senate and Chamber of Deputies.
Monetary Unit: Peso (7.885 pesos equal U.S.$1, floating rate, Dec. 31, 1996).
Gross Domestic Product (1994 est. U.S.$): $728,700,000,000 (purchasing power parity).
Economic Indexes (1995): *Consumer Prices* (1994 = 100): all items, 135.0; food, 139.2. *Industrial Production* (1990 = 100): 104.
Foreign Trade (1995 U.S.$): *Imports,* $46,756,000,000; *exports,* $48,430,000,000.

Martínez also stressed that price increases, which reached 52% in 1995, dropped to 30% late in 1996—with 15% projected for 1997. In November, Zedillo announced substantially higher federal spending on roads, ports, and other infrastructure projects. Clearly, he wanted to boost the economy and generate jobs as political contests approached—including elections for Congress, Mexico City's mayor, and six governors in 1997.

A medley of economic problems continued to demand the government's attention and resources—namely, a heavily indebted banking system, delays in creating individual social-security accounts for workers, and a persistent drought in the nation's northern and central regions. In October and November a falling peso added to Ortiz' woes. Explanations for the decline of the peso vis-à-vis the U.S. dollar ranged from a low trade surplus in August to a flare-up in inflation in September to the beginning of another chapter in the Salinas family tragicomedy as investigators discovered a body buried on the estate of Raúl Salinas, the immensely wealthy brother of the former president.

With oil prices approaching $25 per barrel, officials hoped that Petróleos Mexicanos (Pemex), the national petroleum monopoly, would privatize its secondary petrochemical holdings to boost exploration and production. The sell-off constituted a vital step toward eventually opening Mexico's oil sector to private companies, which eventually might provide the investment required to boost output well above the 1996 levels of 2.8 million barrels of crude oil per day and earn critically needed revenue for the energy sector and the economy as a whole.

Raw politics forced Pemex to modify its ambitious proposal. A deal struck with leaders of the oil workers' union (STPRM) allowed Pemex executives to reconfigure the mammoth corporation along functional lines, spin off air-transport and other peripheral activities, buy into a Texas refinery, and stimulate earnings. In early 1995, traditional top-down control succumbed to rank-and-file agitation as activists vehemently opposed Pemex's announced plans to auction off ten petrochemical complexes embracing 61 plants, in hopes of raising some $1.5 billion. As the STPRM balked at the initiative, opposition escalated to the point that Zedillo and his entourage of technocrats found themselves on the defensive, since the Confederation of Mexican Workers, the PRI, and political parties across the spectrum cast their lot with the union. The firestorm of protest persuaded the market-oriented chief executive to withdraw the sell-off scheme. In November he revised the plan to say that while private entrepreneurs could own 100% of any new plants constructed, their equity in existing facilities would be limited to 49%. The union-inspired brouhaha chilled investor enthusiasm for the project.

Society. Once renowned for its tranquility, Mexico City witnessed an alarming upswing in violent crime, apace with the growing unemployment and misery exacerbated by the 1995 recession. The number of violent crimes reported per day shot up from 290 in 1982 to 600 in 1995—with the daily rate mounting to 676 for the first eight months of 1996. Every public-opinion poll highlighted "public safety" as the paramount concern of the 18 million inhabitants in the city's metropolitan area, an astounding two fifths of whom told pollsters that they or a close family member were victimized in 1995.

The police, whose monthly salaries hovered around $200, contributed to the problem. Long infamous for extracting bribes to drop trumped-up charges, law-enforcement officers increasingly became involved in car thefts, burglaries, assaults, murders, narcotics trafficking, and even protection of drug lords. In a public-opinion survey, the newspaper *Reforma* found that most Mexico City residents voiced little or no confidence in the municipal police. This lack of trust prompted Zedillo to replace the city's top 17 public-safety officials with army generals and colonels. He hoped that they could reverse the city's crime rate and extirpate police corruption before local voters elected their first mayor in July 1997.

The emergence of ERP rebels posed another challenge to the armed forces and Zedillo, who quickly drew a distinction between "good" and "bad" guerrillas. The former were the Zapatistas, who surfaced on Jan. 1, 1994. Although originally violent, the EZLN soon revealed themselves to be pragmatic performers of guerrilla theater, who sought not military victory but simply to dramatize the oppression suffered by indigenous peoples. By contrast, the better-financed, armed-to-the-teeth ERP doggedly attempted to ring down the curtain on a regime that had ruled Mexico for 67 years. By late 1996, they had killed or wounded dozens of people, concentrating their fire on police and army officers. Moreover, the EZLN chief, ski-masked Subcommander Marcos, exhibited a self-deprecating sense of humor, soft-spoken avoidance of ideological cant, and even poetic musings. For their part, the ERP protagonists displayed the demeanor of true believers determined to accomplish a radical upheaval.

At year's end, it appeared that the Zapatistas would form or join a political party to take part in the upcoming federal legislative elections. Meanwhile, the ERP showed no sign of trading bullets for ballots. Equally frustrating from Zedillo's perspective was the confusion over the source of ERP funding.

Foreign Policy. Efforts to diversify its foreign relations aside, Mexico's interests were becoming even more intertwined with those of the United States, especially since the North American Free Trade Agreement (NAFTA) had taken effect on Jan. 1, 1994. The thorniest bilateral issue in 1996 involved the Helms-Burton Act, which included a provision authorizing U.S. citizens to take legal action in U.S. courts against foreign "traffickers" in properties that had been confiscated by Castro's regime in Cuba. In late August the U.S. State Department notified Mexico's Grupo Domos SA that it was in violation of the law and that failure to divest its Cuban holdings promptly would lead to a ban on its executives entering the United States. Grupo Domos denied that it "directly or indirectly" owned any nationalized assets in Cuba. Yet U.S. officials insisted that the Mexican firm owned a 37% stake in the Cuban state telephone company, the heart of which had been owned by the U.S. firm ITT before Castro's revolution.

The Mexican Congress passed a measure in December that would grant dual citizenship to Mexicans living abroad. The law was expected to affect millions of Mexican citizens living in the United States, encouraging such people to seek U.S. citizenship.

GEORGE W. GRAYSON
College of William and Mary

MICROBIOLOGY

A critical event in the life cycle of an infectious organism is its entry into a host cell. If the mechanism by which this entry occurs can be discovered, it may be possible to avoid infection by interfering with the process. One bacterial species in which this event has been studied in the 1990s is *Listeria monocytogenes*. It invades epithelial cells and is responsible for human food-borne infections leading to meningitis and spontaneous abortion, with accompanying high mortality rates. If a bacterium is to be able to invade a cell, the bacterium must possess a surface protein that can serve as an attachment site to a protein on the cell's membrane. The joining of the two proteins then must induce the cell's membrane to encircle the bacterium and bring it into the cell. Jerome Mengaud and his colleagues at the Pasteur Institute, Paris, discovered that the protein interaction involving *L. monocytogenes* was between a bacterial protein called internalin and a cell-membrane protein called E-cadherin. E-cadherin is a molecule that binds intestinal epithelial cells together to form intestinal tissue. It is worth noting that *L. monocytogenes* has evolved a molecular strategy for entry into a host cell.

Radiation-Surviving Bacteria. Ionizing radiation (X rays, gamma rays) kills organisms by fragmenting their chromosome material beyond the ability of the organism to repair the damage. This led to the idea that packaged food could be preserved indefinitely by exposing it to high levels of radiation that would kill all organisms within the package. However, in rare cases, it was found that some organisms survived, reproduced, and spoiled the food.

Experiments by Michael J. Daly and Kenneth W. Minton of the Uniformed Services University in Bethesda, MD, have demonstrated that *Deinococcus radiodurans* can survive exposure to as many as 3 million rads of ionizing radiation (500 rads is lethal for human beings). This bacterium—generally harmless to humans—has four to ten chromosomes, depending on the stage of its life cycle. The organisms were found to have an unusually efficient DNA-repair machinery that can reassemble hundreds of chromosomal fragments into their original arrangements without any indication of damage or mutagenic change. It is hypothesized that these bacteria even could survive passage across interstellar space and be capable of establishing themselves on some very distant planet.

Living on Geochemical Energy. It has been considered axiomatic that all food chains are dependent ultimately on the energy obtained from sunlight through the process of photosynthesis. However, Todd Stevens and James McKinley from the Pacific Northwest Laboratory in Richland, WA, have discovered a community of bacteria that are able to obtain all the energy they need from a purely geochemical reaction. The bacteria are found in the volcanic rocks (basalt) that underlie the Columbia River near Hanford, WA, at a depth of more than 3,300 ft (1 000 m). At this depth, oxygen is not available. The bacteria derive the energy they need for their metabolism from hydrogen that is produced as a by-product of the spontaneous chemical reaction between the iron-rich minerals found in the basalt and the surrounding water.

Evidence for the independence of these populations from photosynthesis is seen in the results of an experiment in which basalt rock, deoxygenated water, and the bacteria were placed in a sealed container for one year. The bacteria were able to maintain a viable community under these conditions. The discovery of these bacteria may explain how organisms survived on Earth from the time they first appeared—estimated to be about 3.5 billion years ago—to the time of the development of photosynthesis, about 2.8 billion years ago.

Tail Formation in Bacteria. It is not unusual for an intracellular parasite to take possession of a host structure and incorporate it into one of its own subcellular parts. An example of this occurs when the bacterium *Shigella flexneri*—the causative agent of dysentery—enters the intestinal-tract cells of a human. The bacterium has a tail-like structure that it uses for locomotion. Upon entering cells, the bacteria divide many times. Each resultant bacterium forms its own tail by absorbing the rigid protein filaments that maintain the shape of the cell and reorganizing them into the propelling elements of its tail. The protein is called actin. The *S. flexneri* bacteria posses a gene called IcsA that controls tail production.

Julie Theriot of the Whitehead Institute for Biomedical Research in Cambridge, MA, and Marcia Goldberg of the Albert Einstein College of Medicine in New York transferred the IcsA gene into *Escherichia coli* bacteria, which are normally nonmotile. They then placed these genetically altered bacteria in dishes containing human-cell extracts that included actin filaments. The *E. coli* promptly developed actin-containing tails and began moving about. This demonstrates the ease with which motility can be gained, and presumably lost, by bacterial species.

LOUIS LEVINE, *City College of New York*

© Brad Markel/Gamma-Liaison

On Oct. 1–2, 1996, Palestinian leader Yasir Arafat, Israeli Prime Minister Benjamin Netanyahu, and Jordan's King Hussein (left to right) *were at the White House for an emergency summit, which was hosted by President Bill Clinton.*

MIDDLE EAST

The bright hopes of 1993 and the following years were dimmed in 1996 as a number of events diminished the apparent chances of achieving a general regional peace in the Middle East. There was a mounting spiral of outrage and retaliation. Shimon Peres, committed to the pursuit of peace, was replaced as prime minister of Israel by Benjamin Netanyahu, a hard-line upholder of Israel's concerns with security. There was a major bomb attack in Saudi Arabia on U.S. personnel. There was a daring and successful challenge by Saddam Hussein to existing arrangements limiting his authority over the Kurdish area of northern Iraq; a sharp worsening of Israeli-Arab relations over a seemingly minor archaeological issue; and an impasse in the scheduled withdrawal of Israeli forces from certain areas in the West Bank. All of these events were negative, with a formidable cumulative effect.

Such negative events appeared to weigh much more heavily in the balance than the positive developments. The year's promising developments included an antiterrorist summit organized by U.S. President Bill Clinton; a Palestinian-authority election, which strengthened Arafat's hand in leadership of the Palestinians; and repeated efforts on the part of U.S. mediators to defuse dangerous situations and bring about cease-fires.

Despite such efforts, however, attitudes hardened on all sides and the possibilities of fruitful compromises seemingly were lessened. The historic 1993 "Declaration of Principles," made by Israel and the Palestine Liberation Organization (PLO), and the subsequent "Oslo II" agreement of 1995 in large part depended for their apparent success on the assumption that difficult points could be dealt with later, when the impetus of initial success would create a climate favorable to compromise. Among the difficult questions at issue between Israel and the PLO thus relegated were the actual details of Israeli withdrawal from the West Bank, and particularly from Hebron. The still more intractable issues, not yet faced and certainly not resolved, loomed: the undetermined future status of the Palestinian entity in the West Bank and Gaza, and the question of sovereignty over Jerusalem.

Arafat Strengthened. Two terrorist actions in early January did not disrupt the January 20 elections for the Palestinian National Authority (PNA). The two violent incidents were the assassination on January 5, in the Gaza Strip, of Yahya Ayyash, a Palestinian who allegedly built bombs used against Israel; and the fatal shooting in the West Bank on January 17 of two Israeli soldiers. The second incident possibly was a retaliation for the first, blamed on Israel. In the PNA elections, Yasir Arafat, chairman of the PLO, easily won the presidency of the new PNA. He obtained nearly 90% of the votes; his only opponent was a leftist woman candidate, Samiha Khalil. In the legislative-council elections, Al-Fatah, the mainstream group that Arafat headed, gained about three quarters of the seats in the 88-member legislature. There had been an attempt to boycott the elections on the part of two militant Islamic groups, Hamas and Islamic Jihad, and by the Syrian-based Popular Front for the Liberation of Palestine. These attempts did not succeed; the voting turnout was about 75% of the 1 million registered voters. There were, however, sufficient independents and opponents of Arafat elected to provide dissent in the new legislature.

Arafat hailed the election as "the foundation for our Palestinian state"—a sentiment totally unwelcome to most Israelis. However, in a show of goodwill, Shimon Peres, who had replaced the assassinated Yitzhak Rabin as Israeli prime minister in November 1995, telephoned Arafat to congratulate him on the election. The election had been monitored by two large teams of foreign observers. Numerous irregularities and cases of intimidation led the observers to qualify their approval of the election procedures, but to conclude that the results were reasonably representative.

Hamas Bombings: Peace Process in Jeopardy. These promising prospects were put in disarray by a series of suicide bombings in Israel on February 25 and March 3–4 that resulted in all in the deaths of 61 persons, all civilians but not all Israelis. The bombings were the work of the militant wing of Hamas, a longtime opponent of the Israeli-PLO peace process, and were said to be in retaliation for the January death of Ayyash. The objective clearly was to provoke Israelis into hardening their attitude and thus make Peres less likely to win the coming Israeli elections.

Peres never had been a soldier—in contrast to his predecessor, the general-turned-peacemaker Rabin. Peres, under pressure to demonstrate a serious concern for Israeli security, declared that his government would respond with a war against Hamas to eradicate it. Peace talks with Syria, which had been going on in Maryland, were suspended. Peres closed Israel's borders and barred Palestinians from working in Jewish settlements in the West Bank and Gaza. However, in succeeding days, Israeli and PNA police cooperated in raids on Islamic militants.

Antiterrorism Summit. The international response to the shocking murders of civilians in Israel by the Hamas bombings was the one-day summit meeting of world leaders held in Egypt on March 13. The meeting was organized hastily on the initiative of the U.S. government and—at least as far as immediate appearances went—was a striking success and demonstration of abhorrence of terrorism and support for the peace process. President Clinton and Egyptian President Hosni Mubarak, the host, were the cosponsors. Leaders of 27 states, including Egypt and 13 other Arab states, and the Palestinians attended. Iran, Iraq, Sudan, and Libya—all notorious as supporters and sponsors of terrorism—apparently were not invited; Syria and its puppet state Lebanon, although invited, chose not to attend. The conferees, ironically, met at Sharm El-Sheik, at the southern tip of the Sinai Peninsula—the same spot whose occupation by Egyptian forces occasioned the 1967 Arab-Israeli War.

This "summit of peacemakers" actually glossed over considerable differences of focus

Under the stipulations of the September 1995 agreement on Palestinian autonomy, some 750,000 Arab voters went to the polls on Jan. 20, 1996. Yasir Arafat overwhelmingly defeated Samiha Khalil for the presidency of the Palestinian National Authority (PNA).

and opinion. However, the agreed-upon joint communiqué vowed to cooperate in combating terrorism by preventing fund-raising by such organizations and by preventing recruiting and arms traffic for terrorism within their borders. Also, a continuing working group was established to formulate concrete measures to implement the declared purposes of the summit. It would, however, be difficult to point to any substantial achievements of the group in the months that followed.

The conference day also saw several conciliatory gestures by Peres. The Israeli border closing—which had been protested bitterly by Arafat—was eased; communication with the PNA was reopened; and Israeli trucks carried foodstuffs into the Gaza Strip.

Israeli Actions in Lebanon. The next jolt to endanger the peace process arose with Israel's actions in Lebanon. Trouble began on March 5, when four Israeli soldiers in the Israeli "security zone" in southern Lebanon were killed by Hezbollah forces. Other outrages committed by both sides followed in April, including the firing of rockets by Hezbollah into settlements on the Israeli side of the border. Events showed that the 1993 informal agreement—under which both sides undertook to restrict armed encounters to south Lebanon and to refrain from targeting civilians—had broken down.

In declared retaliation for the Hezbollah attacks on Israel itself, in mid-April, Israeli planes and helicopters conducted an offensive against wide areas of Lebanon, including Beirut suburbs. On April 13, Israeli warships off the Lebanese coast imposed a virtual blockade. In an unhappy event on April 18, Israeli artillery aiming at a Hezbollah camp near Tyre mistakenly hit a United Nations (UN) refugee camp, killing at least 107 civilians and wounding more than 100.

International opinion mostly condemned Israel's actions. A French attempt at diplomatic intervention was rebuffed by Israel, but—after some 150 Lebanese had been killed, hundreds of thousands had fled their homes, and much property damage had occurred—a U.S.-brokered cease-fire was achieved that became operative on April 27. The Lebanese-Israeli accord endowed Syria with considerable importance. It specifically was said to be written "in consultation with Syria"—although Syria was not a signatory. The pact was the achievement of U.S. Secretary of State Warren Christopher, capping a week of shuttle diplomacy.

In substance, the April pact essentially formalized the 1993 agreement; but it also created a monitoring group composed of Lebanon, Israel, Syria, the United States, and France. The monitoring group did not meet with any regularity before the late summer, but the south Lebanon front was relatively quiet for the rest of the year. The April pact also authorized the establishment of a consulting group, with a membership of the five nations in the monitoring group plus Russia and the European Union (EU), to explore ways of gaining reconstruction funds for Lebanon.

PLO Revokes Anti-Israeli Clauses. On April 24 the Palestine National Council (PNC) supported Yasir Arafat by a substantial majority in agreeing to rescind clauses in its 1964 charter calling for the destruction of Israel and for the waging of guerrilla war against it. The four-day session of the PNC, regarded as the parliament of the whole Palestinian movement, marked the first time the body had met since 1991. Although the vote to rescind the clauses was 504–54, with 14 abstentions, it was by no means certain that it accurately reflected Palestinian opinion in general. Technically, the resolution put forward by Arafat was a declaration of the intention to replace the existing charter with a new document that would embody these changes. Arafat's own readiness to accept the legitimacy of Israel's existence had been declared in an exchange of letters with Prime Minister Rabin in September 1993. The charter revision had been delayed noticeably.

Victory of Netanyahu. The whole approach to peace, as it had been forwarded since 1993 by Rabin and his successor Peres, was thrown into some doubt by Peres' narrow defeat in the election for prime minister by the Likud Party candidate, Benjamin Netanyahu (*see* BIOGRAPHY). The May 29 contest was the first time in Israel that there had been a direct election for the post of prime minister. The parallel but separate elections for the Knesset (parliament) produced a membership from which Netanyahu was able to select a coalition government (*see* ISRAEL).

Netanyahu's campaign had stressed his concern with Israel's security and had striven to depict his opponent as inadequately concerned with that basic matter. In the months that followed the election, the new Israeli prime minister often seemed to act in an unnecessarily abrasive way—in addition to following substantive policies that the PLO, as well as the wider Arab world, found offensive. However, in the victory speech he had made on June 2, he adopted a conciliatory tone, saying that he would advance the peace and the negotiating process with all of Israel's neighbors—and that he sought "a stable peace, a real peace—with security." King Hussein of Jordan personally congratulated Netanyahu on his victory and spoke optimistically of the prospects for peace.

However, the Arab League summit held in Cairo on June 22–23 took a less sanguine view. This Arab League meeting, the first since 1990, brought together all members except Iraq, which was not invited. The final communiqué called on Israel to withdraw from all occupied lands and permit the establishment of a Palestinian state in the West Bank, Gaza, and East Jerusalem. If not, it warned, there would be increased tension and a reconsideration of the whole process. Netanyahu responded jauntily that "one-sided demands that harm security are not reconcilable with peace talks." On his first official U.S. visit, when he addressed Congress on July 10, the prime minister portrayed Israel as a democracy under threat from "unreconstructed dictatorships whose governmental creed is based on tyranny and intimidation."

On September 4 a long-delayed first meeting between Netanyahu and Arafat took place at the Erez checkpoint on the Israel–Gaza Strip border; and thereafter the suspended talks between the two sides resumed. Netanyahu also stoutly faced down criticism from his own right wing at a Likud meeting the next day. The reopened talks reportedly were making progress as the year ended, however. The sticking point was the question of Israeli withdrawal from the city of Hebron, the only major West Bank town where Israeli troops still were stationed. Hebron had a few hundred Israeli settlers among an otherwise totally Palestinian population. The Israeli pullout, scheduled for March, had been postponed by Peres.

Israeli-PLO relations were exacerbated in the fall by at least two matters. The Israeli decision in September to open a new entrance to an archaeological tunnel in Jerusalem that ran under or near two mosques sparked gunfire between Palestinian police and Israeli soldiers in the West Bank and Gaza that left at least 50 persons dead. Secondly, the Israeli government made a number of moves in the fall that presaged more Israeli settlement in the West Bank. Any enlargement of settlements had been suspended for the previous two years. President Clinton hosted an emergency summit in Washington, DC, in early October, between Arafat and Netanyahu, but little progress was made.

The Gulf Region. A new north-south axis was created in February with the conclusion of an agreement on military cooperation between Israel and Turkey—an agreement much resented by all Arab states. Turkey has common borders with Syria, Iraq, and Iran. The assistance given in late August and early September by Saddam Hussein of Iraq to one of the Kurdish factions in its warring with the other enabled him largely to end the status of northern Iraq as a "safe haven." This success for Iraq raised new questions about the security of all the oil-rich Gulf states and impelled the United States to enlarge the southern "no fly" zone in Iraq. (*See also* IRAQ.)

© Agence France Presse/Corbis-Bettmann

Libyan leader Muammar el-Qaddafi attended the Arab League summit meeting in Cairo, Egypt, in June 1996, despite a UN-imposed ban prohibiting him from traveling internationally by air.

Other Matters. The U.S. policy of maintaining an economic embargo on terrorist states—particularly new legislation signed into law August 5 that would impose sanctions on foreign companies that invest in Iran or Libya—was opposed strongly by France and Germany. The increasing assertion of France's intention to play a significant role in the Middle East also was a notable feature of the year, symbolized in a number of visits to the region by Prime Minister Jacques Chirac and his foreign minister. The French moves were particularly forceful, and successful, in regard to Lebanon.

ARTHUR CAMPBELL TURNER
University of California, Riverside

MILITARY AFFAIRS

International arms-control and disarmament efforts highlighted military affairs during 1996. Also making headlines were continued troubles in the Russian military, growing opposition to land mines, and questions about expanding the North Atlantic Treaty Organization (NATO). In the U.S. military, attentions focused on a deadly bombing in Saudi Arabia, a sex-abuse scandal in the army, and renewed tensions in Iraq. New revelations about so-called Gulf-war syndrome also were prominent (*see* MEDICINE AND HEALTH).

Arms Control and Disarmament. The first international treaty banning the testing of nuclear weapons was signed in 1963 by Great Britain, the Soviet Union, and the United States. The treaty prohibited tests conducted in the atmosphere, underwater, and in space (but not underground). Thirty-three years later, a new pact—the Comprehensive Test-Ban Treaty (CTBT)—forbids the testing of all nuclear weapons, regardless or size or location. The treaty was passed on September 10 by the United Nations (UN) General Assembly by a 158–3 vote. Two weeks later, the five declared nuclear powers—Britain, China, France, Russia, and the United States—signed the CTBT.

While most nations sided with the nuclear-weapons states, several voiced objections. Leading those that opposed the treaty was India, which detonated a nuclear device in 1974. New Delhi asserted that it would not sign until the treaty included a provision and a date for the total elimination of nuclear weapons. Neighboring Pakistan indicated that it would not sign if India did not sign.

The CTBT was not scheduled to become operational for two years. The U.S. State Department expressed hope that during that time, India and other treaty opponents could be persuaded to sign. Without adoption by India, Pakistan, and all other nations possessing nuclear reactors, the treaty would not enter into force, although signatory nations would be expected to abide by its terms.

In accordance with the U.S. Constitution, the treaty would have to be ratified by a two-thirds vote of the Senate. This did not appear to be assured, since the 1996 Republican Party platform rejected the treaty as "inconsistent with American security interests." The GOP platform also stated that the United States would "require the continuing maintenance and development of nuclear weapons and other periodic testing" in order to deter the threat of mass-destruction weapons from so-called rogue nations—a term generally used in reference to states such as Iraq, Iran, Syria, and North Korea.

In a September address to the UN General Assembly, U.S. President Bill Clinton called for new measures to "further lift the threat of nuclear-weapons destruction and the threat of weapons of mass destruction and to limit their dangerous spread." The president decried the fact that the U.S. Senate had failed to ratify the Chemical Weapons Convention—banning the use of poison gas and similar weapons—and promised that he would not let the treaty die. He called for the adoption of a treaty to freeze the production of fissile materials for use in nuclear weapons to help prevent outlaw nations from acquiring weapons-grade uranium and plutonium. The president stated his intention to continue the reduction of nuclear weapons and said that when Russia ratified the second Strategic Arms Reduction Treaty (START II), further cuts could be discussed with Moscow. Clinton also called for strengthening the Nuclear Non-Proliferation Treaty (NPT) by providing the International Atomic Energy Agency with stronger inspection practices; for law-enforcement and customs officials to cooperate more fully in the effort to stop the smuggling of nuclear materials; and for those nations that had not signed the NPT to do so.

Although ratified by the U.S. Senate, the START II agreement—which calls for deep and permanent reductions in the strategic nuclear forces of the United States and Russia—remained stalled in Moscow. The problem with START II from the Russian perspective was the fear of the Kremlin's military that the agreement, coupled with a possible antiballistic-missile (ABM) deployment by Washington in the future, would result in strategic advantages for the United States. U.S. Secretary of State Warren Christopher and Russian Foreign Affairs Minister Yevgeniy Primakov worked on means to allay Russian concerns. In the fall they indicated that an agreement had been reached that would permit the United States to build "theater missile defenses" to protect forces in the field against tactical missile systems. However, work remained on defining clearly the line of demarcation between such defenses and high-velocity ABM defenses that could appear threatening to Moscow if Russia substantially reduced its number of intercontinental ballistic missiles (ICBMs) and submarine-launched ballistic missiles (SLBMs).

Action on the Chemical Weapons Convention, which had been before the Senate since

Land Mines

Land mines ostensibly are produced to kill or maim soldiers who are not deterred by their presence. In recent decades, however, land mines have taken an increasingly steep toll on civilians, often children, living in areas where minefields remain as deadly relics of past conflicts. Officials estimate that land mines kill or hurt some 2,000 persons per month. Such devastation has helped fuel a steadily increasing public demand for an international ban on the manufacturing and use of these weapons.

Land mines come in a variety of sizes and categories. All types explode when they detect the pressure of a foot or a vehicle. Newer models are made of plastic to foil metal detectors. The majority of mines today are "dumb," meaning that they remain active indefinitely. "Smart" mines automatically deactivate or self-destruct after a set period of time.

Long employed by major military nations to defend international borders, demilitarized zones, and the perimeter of exposed military positions, land mines today are concentrated in poorer nations—such as Angola, Afghanistan, Cambodia, and Bosnia—that have suffered through long civil wars. In all, experts estimate that more than 100 million land mines are found in 64 nations.

In Geneva, Switzerland, in May, delegates from 55 nations attended a United Nations (UN) conference to consider revision of the land-mines protocol of the 1980 convention on certain conventional weapons. The participants approved new provisions that banned the use and export of "dumb" mines and placed tighter restrictions on "smart" mines. The revised protocol also extended its scope to include civil (internal) as well as international conflicts. Many member nations and humanitarian groups criticized the revised protocol. Some were disappointed by the failure of the conference to approve a total ban on land mines. Others were unsatisfied by the long implementation period—nine years—and the lack of enforcement and verification mechanisms.

Before the UN in the fall, U.S. President Bill Clinton renewed his "appeal for the swift negotiation of a worldwide ban on the use, stockpiling, production, and transfer of antipersonnel land mines." Officials reported that Washington annually was spending $90 million in mine-clearing efforts, and was developing new technology to reduce the costs and hazards of this work. These initiatives followed numerous efforts by the Vietnam Veterans of America Foundation and other domestic groups to ban land mines.

© David Brauchli/Sygma

The U.S. commander in the Persian Gulf war, Gen. Norman Schwarzkopf, and other prominent retired officers wrote and published a letter to President Clinton that stated that, "Given the wide range of weaponry available to military forces today, antipersonnel land mines are not essential." Sen. Patrick J. Leahy (D-VT) has been a leading proponent of legislation barring or limiting the use of land mines. In 1992, President George Bush signed a bill sponsored by Leahy that outlawed the export of U.S. land mines for one year. Later, Leahy won acceptance for the prohibition to be extended through 1997. In 1996, President Clinton signed into law Leahy's proposal to impose a moratorium on the use of antipersonnel land mines beginning in 1999.

Although the Defense Department long had opposed a ban on land mines, Gen. John Shalikashvili, the chairman of the U.S. joint chiefs of staff, ordered a review of this policy and indicated that he would support a ban. The boundary between North and South Korea and the Persian Gulf region were considered possible exceptions to a land-mine ban.

ROBERT M. LAWRENCE

1991, was postponed until after the 1996 election. Former Sen. Robert Dole, the Republican presidential candidate, cited two reasons to oppose the treaty. He said that the agreement would permit too much intrusion by international inspectors at private U.S. chemical companies. Secondly, Dole voiced concerns that states such as Libya, Syria, and North Korea would not be parties to it.

A disarmament problem that previously had seemed solved reappeared in 1996. While Ukraine and Kazakhstan handed over their ICBMs to Russia for dismantling, Belarus had not done so by the end of the year as promised. Belarussian President Alyaksandr Lukashenko held onto 18 mobile ICBMs that had been left in Belarus after the Soviet Union disintegrated five years earlier. Although nominally under the control of Russian officers, President Lukashenko's reneging on his agreement with Washington caused concern in the United States.

The Russian Military. The Russian military establishment had another tough year in 1996. On the fighting front, Russian soldiers were unable, in spite of a number of attacks, to defeat rebel forces in Chechnya. Financially, the Russian military continued to suffer from a stagnant economy that was unable to produce the revenues necessary to provide full pay and allowances to both officers and enlisted personnel. President Boris Yeltsin's campaign promises to streamline the military and replace conscription with an all-volunteer army by the year 2000 appeared unlikely to be realized.

Blunt-speaking retired Gen. Alexander Lebed, whom President Yeltsin appointed as his national security chief in June, and who personally brokered a peace agreement to end the war in Chechnya, was fired by Yeltsin in October. At the time, accusations were made by Kremlin officials that Lebed was involved in a possible coup attempt. For his part, Lebed said he would abide by the constitution and would run for president in four years, or earlier if Yeltsin died or became unable to govern due to illness. Ivan Rybkin, a former speaker in the Duma, the lower house of the Russian parliament, assumed many of Lebed's duties. Rybkin was named the secretary of the Russian National Security Council and Yeltsin's personal representative to Chechnya, but he was not given Lebed's former title.

In the West concern was voiced over the plight of the Russian military. The worry was that disaffected officers and soldiers, poorly housed and paid, could be attracted to a right-wing nationalist leader who might work to undermine the relatively recent Russian efforts to develop a democratic society. The national-security community in the West also remained aware that despite the paucity of financial support for the Russian military, their long-range rocket forces and missile-carrying submarines remained capable of initiating enormous nuclear destruction.

The U.S. Military. On June 25 a housing complex for U.S. Air Force personnel near Dhahran, Saudi Arabia, was the target of a truck-bomb attack. Nineteen airmen were killed in the explosion, which heavily damaged the Khobar Towers, where they were quartered. A Department of Defense investigation of the bombing chaired by retired Army Gen. Wayne A. Downing was critical of the local air-force commander, Brig. Gen. Terryl J. Schwalier, for ignoring warnings of terrorist threats and for subsequently failing to initiate security precautions. However, a later air-force inquiry cleared General Schwalier of any wrongdoing in the incident. As a result of the bombing, U.S. Secretary of Defense William Perry announced new measures would be taken to protect U.S. service personnel stationed overseas from terrorist attacks. In November the Saudis arrested some 40 persons for involvement in the attack, and Saudi officials said they believed the bombing attack was instigated by Iran.

Ongoing tensions between the United States and Iraqi President Saddam Hussein erupted into violence in September. Following Iraqi troop incursions into Kurdish enclaves in northern Iraq, President Clinton ordered cruise-missile attacks against Iraqi air defenses in southern Iraq. In a prepared statement the president said, "Our missiles sent the following message to Saddam Hussein: When you abuse your own people or threaten your neighbors you must pay a price." Then he added, "We must reduce Iraq's ability to strike out at its neighbors, and we must increase America's ability to contain Iraq over the long run." To that end, the United States announced that the southern "no-fly" zone that had been maintained since the end of the Persian Gulf war would be moved north from the 31st parallel to the 33rd parallel, only 30 mi (48 km) from the Iraqi capital of Baghdad. Reaction to the U.S. attack ranged from verbal support by the British and condemnation by the Chinese and Russians to silence from some of the United States' Arab partners in the Gulf war.

Local opposition to the continued presence of U.S. forces on the Japanese island of Okinawa produced a nonbinding referendum in September calling for a reduction of U.S. forces and a change in their legal status. About 89% of voters supported a reduction in the U.S. military presence, which numbered about 27,000 troops. The referendum was a culmination of resentment stemming most immediately from the rape of a 12-year-old Okinawan girl by three U.S. servicemen in 1995. In spite of the results, both Tokyo and Washington reemphasized their intent to maintain a strong U.S. military force in Japan. However, the United States agreed to close a Marine helicopter base located in a heavily populated area.

Early in November the public learned of a major sex-abuse scandal in the U.S. Army. The situation came to light after a number of male officers at the Aberdeen Proving Ground in Maryland were charged with raping, assaulting, sexually harassing, or having improper relations with female recruits. However, the scandal soon expanded to raise much broader questions—about incidents at other training facilities, about the extent of sexual harassment throughout the armed forces, and about the failure of the chain of command to stem such problems. Army officials quickly set up a toll-free hot line to serve anyone with questions about sexual harassment or assault. Within two weeks, the line fielded about 4,500 complaints of sexual misconduct, including nearly 600 calls that were considered credible enough to warrant further criminal investigation. Army leaders promised the swift prosecution of all offenders and other steps to protect its servicewomen.

In September, President Clinton signed a $256.6 billion military-spending bill for the fiscal year that began October 1. According to the president, the bill's highlights were the inclusions of a 3% salary raise for military personnel and a 4.6% increase in the allowance provided for off-base living quarters.

President Clinton later named William S. Cohen, who did not seek reelection as a Republican U.S. senator from Maine, to serve as secretary of defense in his second term.

NATO. Two major issues faced NATO members in the waning days of 1996. One was what to do with the 60,000 NATO troops that had been sent to Bosnia the previous year to maintain peace in that part of the former Yugoslavia. The mandate for the NATO force had been scheduled to expire on Dec. 20, 1996. In November, however, President Clinton announced that the mission would be extended, with a reduced force of 8,500 U.S. troops staying on. He also said that he expected the U.S. force to be reduced by about half before the end of 1997 and to be withdrawn fully by June 1998. The U.S. contingent initially totaled 20,000 troops and was reduced to 14,000 by late 1996.

© Martin Smith-Rodden/Sygma

Adm. Jay L. Johnson, 50-year-old U.S. vice-chief of naval operations, was appointed chief of naval operations following the suicide of Adm. Jeremy M. Boorda in May 1996.

The other major issue before NATO members was when, and how, to open up the organization to Central European nations that formerly had belonged to the Warsaw Pact. In an October campaign speech, delivered in Detroit, President Clinton suggested that NATO extend full membership to some Eastern European nations by the spring of 1999, a date that would mark the 50th anniversary of the military alliance. President Clinton did not name which countries he had in mind, but for some months it had been known that the State Department strongly favored an initial list that included Poland, the Czech Republic, and Hungary, with Romania and Slovenia as other possible candidates. Latvia, Lithuania, and Estonia—the Baltic states, which were accused by Moscow of treating their Russian minority populations unfairly—were not expected to be admitted in the near future. The most immediate problem facing the eastward expansion of NATO was a fear expressed by some Russians that the expanded alliance would pose a threat to their security. Complicating the situation with Moscow was the question of what role Ukraine—in view of its geographical location—would play in an expanded NATO.

ROBERT M. LAWRENCE
Colorado State University

MINING

Coal[a] (thousand metric tons per month average)

	1994	1995
China	100,508	107,624
United States[b]	86,125	85,808
India	20,974	23,232[c]
Australia	18,912	20,255[c]
South Africa	15,208	N/A
Russia	14,622	13,866
Poland	11,136	11,347
Ukraine	7,650	7,900[c]
Kazakhstan	8,696	6,933
Germany	4,802	4,905

Lignite[a] (thousand metric tons per month average)

	1994	1995
Germany	17,261	16,058
Russia	6,917[c]	6,917
Poland	5,564	5,296
Czech Rep.	N/A	4,829
Turkey	4,526	4,714[c]
Greece	4,728	4,539
Australia	4,165	4,013[c]
Yugoslavia	3,128	3,328[c]
Canada	3,618	3,028
Romania	2,936	2,901

Natural Gas[a] (terajoules per month average)

	1994	1995
Russia	1,525,232	1,936,092
United States	1,700,081	1,700,100[d]
Canada	438,335	607,608
Indonesia	193,583	274,382[c]
United Kingdom	203,875	213,987
Netherlands	207,317	209,229
Mexico	97,285	137,540[c]
Uzbekistan	130,816	137,540[c]
Saudi Arabia	122,592	N/A
Argentina	99,366	106,952[c]

Crude Oil[f] (thousand barrels per day average)

	1994	1995
Saudi Arabia	8,147	8,231
United States	6,662	6,560
Russia	6,135	5,768
Iran	3,635	3,643
China	2,939	3,015
Norway	2,521	2,768
Venezuela	2,588	2,750
Mexico	2,689	2,618
United Kingdom	2,375	2,489
United Arab Emirates	2,263	2,274
World total[g]	61,358	62,230

Aluminum (primary smelter) (thousand metric tons)

	1994	1995
United States	3,299	3,375
Russia	2,670	2,722
Canada	2,255	2,172
China[e]	1,450	1,600
Australia	1,317	1,297
Brazil	1,185	1,188
Norway	858	847
Venezuela	585	630
Germany	505	500[e]
India[h]	472	463
World total[g]	19,200	19,400

Bauxite (thousand metric tons)

	1994	1995
Australia	41,733	42,655
Guinea[e,i]	14,400	14,400
Jamaica[i]	11,564	10,857
Brazil	8,673	8,761
Venezuela	4,419	5,184
China[e]	3,700	5,000
India	4,809	4,800
Kazakhstan	2,425	3,300
Suriname	3,772	3,300
Russia	3,000[e]	3,100[e]
World total[g]	107,000	109,000

Cement (thousand metric tons)

	1994	1995
China	421,180	445,610
Japan	91,624	90,474
United States	79,353	78,320
India[e]	60,000	70,000
Korea, Republic of	50,730	55,130[e]
Germany	40,380	40,000[e]
Russia	37,200	36,400[e]
Italy	33,192	35,000[e]
Turkey	29,493	33,153
Thailand[e]	28,000	26,500
World total[e,g]	1,380,052	1,421,342

Copper (mine) (metric tons copper content)

	1994	1995
Chile	2,219,900	2,488,000
United States	1,813,000	1,849,000[e]
Canada	617,300	728,680[e]
Russia	573,300	591,000[e]
Indonesia	322,190	443,618
Australia	391,000	437,000
Poland	378,000	383,600
Peru	343,600	380,700[e]
China[e]	396,000	370,000
Mexico	305,500	331,900
World total[g]	9,490,000	10,000,000

Copper (refined primary and secondary) (metric tons)

	1994	1995
United States	2,230,000	2,280,000
Chile, primary	1,277,000	1,485,000
Japan	1,119,168	1,187,959
China[e]	736,000	843,000
Germany	591,859	616,300
Canada	550,000	559,997
Russia	516,000	521,000[e]
Poland	425,000[e]	436,000
Belgium	375,200	393,000[e]
Kazakhstan[e]	347,000	353,000
World total[g]	11,200,000	11,700,000

Iron Ore (thousand metric tons metal content)

	1994	1995
Brazil	108,800	120,900
Australia[e]	80,900	88,653
China[e]	72,050	75,000
Russia[e]	40,000	43,200
United States	36,762	39,577
India	37,368	37,800[e]
Ukraine[e]	22,700	24,800
Canada	24,235	24,651
South Africa	18,903	19,806
Sweden	12,587	13,880[e]
World total[g]	517,112	554,846

Iron (raw steel) (thousand metric tons)

	1994	1995
Japan	98,295	101,640
United States	91,200	95,200
China[e]	92,600	93,000
Russia	48,812	51,300
Germany	40,847	42,100
Korea, South	33,745	36,772
Italy	26,114	27,800
Brazil[e]	25,700	25,100
Ukraine	24,111	22,300
India	19,285	20,291
World total[g]	730,000	752,000

Lead (mine) (metric tons)

	1994	1995
Australia	537,000	455,000
China[e]	462,000	430,000
United States	370,000	394,000
Peru	233,510	232,540
Canada	167,584	210,415
Mexico	170,322	164,348
Sweden	112,787	100,000
South Africa	95,824	87,965
Korea, North[e]	80,000	80,000
Morocco	73,164	73,000[e]
World total[g]	2,810,000	2,710,000

Lead (refined) (metric tons)

	1994	1995
United States	1,260,000	1,350,000
France[e]	444,000	425,000
China[e]	467,900	420,000
United Kingdom	352,466	350,000[e]
Germany	331,684	335,000[e]
Japan	292,262	286,534
Canada	251,640	277,372
Australia	232,500	235,400
Italy	205,900	205,000[e]
Mexico	180,000	174,000[e]
World total[g]	5,380,000	5,400,000

Phosphate rock (thousand metric tons)

	1994	1995
United States	41,100	43,500
China[e]	24,000	21,000
Morocco	19,764	20,200
Russia[e]	8,000	8,800
Tunisia	5,699	7,241
Jordan	4,217	4,984
Israel	3,961	4,063
Brazil	3,530	3,530[e]
South Africa	2,545	2,790
Kazakhstan[e]	2,000	2,200
World total[g]	128,000	131,000

Salt (thousand metric tons)

	1994	1995
United States	39,800	42,100
China[e]	29,700	25,000
Canada	11,700	10,893
Germany	10,532	10,800[e]
India[e]	9,500	9,500
Australia (brine and marine)	7,685	8,480
Mexico	7,458	7,670
France	7,536	7,350[e]
United Kingdom[e]	7,000	7,100
Brazil	6,043	6,100[e]
World total[g]	190,000	189,000

Sulfur (all forms) (thousand metric tons sulfur content)

	1994	1995
United States[e]	11,500	11,800
Canada	8,850	9,010
China[e]	6,900	6,530
Russia[e]	3,510	4,000
Mexico	2,890	2,880[e]
Japan[e]	2,820	2,860
Poland	2,435	2,440[e]
Saudi Arabia	2,300	2,200
Germany	1,240	1,230[e]
France	1,180	1,100[e]
World total[g]	54,100	54,300

Zinc (mine) (metric tons zinc content)

	1994	1995
Canada	984,000	1,111,497
China[e]	990,000	950,000
Australia	995,000	930,000
Peru	690,017	688,619
United States	598,000	644,000
Mexico	381,689	363,658
Korea, North[e]	210,000	210,000
Kazakhstan[e]	190,000	190,000
Ireland[e]	195,000	182,000
Spain	150,425	170,000[e]
World total[g]	7,020,000	7,120,000

Zinc (smelter) (metric tons)

	1994	1995
China[e]	1,010,000	1,050,000
Canada	690,965	720,145
Japan	713,300	716,900
United States	356,000	363,000
Germany	359,878	360,000[e]
Australia[e]	328,000	337,000
Spain	300,600	325,000[e]
France[e]	310,000	306,000
Belgium	306,200	300,000[e]
Italy (primary and secondary)	242,000	250,000[e]
World total[g]	7,370,000	7,480,000

[a]Source: *Monthly Bulletin of Statistics*, UN Dept. for Economic and Social Information and Policy Analysis. [b]Source: U.S. Dept. of Energy; includes lignite. [c]Average of monthly information published for 1995. [d]Estimate based on data published by the U.S. Dept. of Energy. [e]Estimated. [f]Source: *International Petroleum Statistics Report*, U.S. Dept. of Energy, October 1996. [g]May include other countries not listed. [h]Primary ingot. [i]Dry bauxite equivalent of crude ore. [p]Preliminary.

Source: U.S. Geological Survey, U.S. Department of the Interior, unless otherwise indicated.

Note: Numerals are annual production unless otherwise indicated.

MOROCCO

Morocco took a step toward liberalizing its political system in September 1996, when 99.56% of the voters in a referendum on an amended constitution supported King Hassan's plan to replace the partially elected assembly with a two-chamber parliament.

Domestic Affairs. Under the new legislative system, and after elections scheduled for the first half of 1997, parliament would be composed of a directly elected lower chamber and an upper house in which deputies would be elected indirectly by local councils, professional bodies, and trade unions. The reforms opened the way for the next government to be formed by the two largest opposition parties—Istiqlal and the Socialist Union of Popular Forces (USFP). The king, however, would retain his considerable influence over the political process through the upper house, which will have the power to dissolve the government. Under the new constitution, Morocco's disadvantaged rural population was expected to have a bigger say in politics because regional representation was enhanced in the upper house.

In March, King Hassan celebrated 35 years on the throne, but a bout of ill health in late 1995 raised much informal speculation about Morocco's future. The king was believed to want to strengthen the institutions of the country and to forge a greater consensus among political forces to ensure a smooth transition when his son succeeds him.

Morocco also has been trying to put its house in order, and 1996 saw wide-ranging campaigns against the drug trade and corruption. The Moroccan authorities said that they broke up more than 25 international drug-trafficking rings. There also were several widely publicized trials. Morocco's northern Rif region was the source of most of the cannabis sold on Europe's streets, and the European Union (EU) had put pressure on the kingdom to stem the flow. The authorities also mounted an anticorruption crackdown.

Western Sahara. In December 1995 the United Nations suspended the process of registering voters for the much-postponed referendum on the future of Western Sahara. The process had been bogged down constantly as a result of disagreements between Morocco and the Polisario Front over who was eligible to vote. Delegations representing Morocco and Polisario met in August. Both sides said they were willing to resume talks.

Foreign Relations. Spain's Prime Minister Felipe González made an official visit to Rabat in February, which set the seal on the improvement in the relationship between the two countries after 1995's dispute over Spanish fishing rights in Moroccan waters. González announced that Spain was giving its southern neighbor $1.3 billion in soft credits. Spain and Morocco also decided to seek European Union (EU) financing for the construction of an underwater tunnel to link their two countries. González' successor, José María Aznar, was in Morocco in May.

In May, King Hassan went on a high-profile state visit to France, where he addressed the National Assembly. Communist deputies and some left-wing members walked out, and human-rights groups criticized the visit. In June the European Parliament ratified the EU-Morocco association agreement, with the proviso that the European Commission should monitor human rights in Morocco.

The Economy. Plentiful rainfall raised expectations of a 10% growth rate—a vast improvement over 1995, when drought shrank this predominantly agricultural country's gross domestic product (GDP) by 7.6%. The World Bank said the country needed a sustainable growth rate of 6% to 7% in order to resolve fiscal and social problems and absorb new entrants into the labor market.

Morocco was pursuing an ambitious privatization program, which saw the flotation of the state-owned steel giant Sonasid on the Casablanca stock exchange. Morocco wanted to complete the sale of 112 state enterprises by 1998, and there were plans to privatize the telecommunications industry as well as sugar refineries and a fertilizer company. Morocco signed a $500 million agreement with the South Korean group Daewoo. It involved projects in telecommunications and tourism.

HEBA SALEH
BBC North Africa Correspondent

MOROCCO • Information Highlights

Official Name: Kingdom of Morocco.
Location: Northwest Africa.
Area: 172,413 sq mi (446 550 km²).
Population (mid-1996 est.): 27,600,000.
Chief Cities (1994 census): Rabat, the capital (incl. Salé), 1,385,872; Casablanca, 2,940,623; Fez, 774,754; Marrakech, 745,541.
Government: *Head of state,* Hassan II, king (acceded 1961). *Head of government,* Abdellatif Filali, prime minister (appointed May 1994). *Legislature* (unicameral)—Chamber of Representatives.
Monetary Unit: Dirham (8.649 dirhams equal U.S.$1, August 1996).
Gross Domestic Product (1994 est. U.S.$): $87,500,000,000 (purchasing power parity).
Economic Indexes (1995): *Consumer Prices* (1991 = 100): all items, 134.0; food, 142.5. *Industrial Production* (1990 = 100): 112.
Foreign Trade (1995 U.S.$): *Imports,* $8,539,000,000; *exports,* $4,665,000,000.

MOTION PICTURES

Occasionally a film emerges that taps into public taste and not only elicits a huge financial return but generates audience response and media discussion that goes beyond the film's worth as art or entertainment. Two major examples occurred in 1996. *The First Wives Club*, directed by Hugh Wilson and based on Olivia Goldsmith's novel, touched a nerve in championing former wives with grievances against bad treatment by their men. The spirited, amusing trio of Bette Midler, Goldie Hawn, and Diane Keaton as women who decide to get even proved to be immensely popular. The other example was the blockbuster *Independence Day*, directed by Roland Emmerich. Brimming with eye-catching special effects, it was part of the revived interest in science fiction (*see* FEATURE ARTICLE, page 84) and made audiences feel good about seeing the United States defeat a deadly foe from outer space, even though American cities were wrecked severely in the process.

The year also was marked by actors going beyond their customary boundaries. Emma Thompson, for example, gained recognition as a screenwriter for the 1995-released *Sense and Sensibility* with an Oscar for best screenplay from a work in another medium. The film itself, which was directed by Ang Lee and in which Thompson starred, won the top Golden Bear award at the Berlin International Film Festival. Actor Mel Gibson won the best-director Oscar for *Braveheart*.

Actors Turn to Directing. The unusual number of actors who directed feature films for the first time was highlighted when about a dozen such works were showcased at the Toronto International Film Festival. Al Pacino ventured into directing with *Looking for Richard*, his appealing exploration of Shakespeare pegged to *Richard III*. Actor Nick Cassavetes, son of the late innovative director John Cassavetes, made his first feature, *Unhook the Stars*, casting his mother, Gena Rowlands, in the lead as a woman trying to cope with life after the death of her husband. Rowlands was very affecting in the role.

Kevin Spacey, fresh from his best-supporting-actor Oscar triumph for *The Usual Suspects*, unveiled his directorial effort, *Albino Alligator*, about a robbery gone wrong. Anjelica Huston, daughter of the late director John Huston, followed in her father's path with *Bastard Out of Carolina*, about child abuse. Cher directed part of a Home Box Office television film concerning abortion, *If These Walls Could Talk*. Stanley Tucci and Campbell Scott teamed on *Big Night*, a warm comedy about immigrant brothers struggling in the restaurant business.

Tom Hanks demonstrated his ability to direct with *That Thing You Do!*, a lively 1960s story about a fictional Pennsylvania rock group. Matthew Broderick directed *Infinity*, about the life of physicist Richard Feynman, who worked on developing the atom bomb. Other actors-turned-directors featured at the Toronto festival included Kevin Bacon with *Losing Chase*, about relations between two women; Armin Mueller-Stahl, who also played Hitler in *Conversations with the Beast*; and Steve Buscemi, whose *Trees Lounge* is set in a small-town bar.

The Everett Collection

In "The First Wives Club," Goldie Hawn (left), *Diane Keaton* (center), *and Bette Midler portray three wives who take revenge after being dropped by their husbands for younger women. The movie was very popular with women, and its subject matter was the basis of a "Time" magazine cover story.*

The Everett Collection

Debbie Reynolds returned to the screen in Albert Brooks' "Mother." Brooks (above right) *also starred in the film as Reynolds' twice-divorced son who decides to live with Mom again.*

Outstanding Films. Audiences had an extensive menu of substantial films in 1996—whether studio products, independent productions, or imports. The New York Film Festival opened with a preview of *Secrets and Lies*, one of the year's most compelling dramas. Directed by Mike Leigh, the film from England delved into the upheaval that occurs in a family when a white woman, extraordinarily acted by Brenda Blethyn, and a young black woman, superbly played by Marianne Jean-Baptiste, discover they are mother and daughter. The festival closed with *The People vs. Larry Flynt*, Milos Forman's flamboyant story of the sex-magazine publisher, colorfully acted by Woody Harrelson.

Shine, a powerful Australian import directed by Scott Hicks, brilliantly captured the true story of the troubled life of classical pianist David Helfgott. *Lone Star*, the latest from John Sayles, spun a mystery yarn while illuminating the complex social fabric along the Texas-Mexico border. *Fargo*—another accomplished work by brothers Joel and Ethan Coen—was a fascinating crime story that generated complaints from Minnesotans who did not appreciate the satirical look at their locale. The film yielded a memorable performance by actress Frances McDormand as a homespun but effective cop. Another skillful and popular film was *Emma*, spotlighting actress Gwyneth Paltrow and providing another example of Jane Austen's revived popularity. John Schlesinger's version of the 1930s British novel *Cold Comfort Farm* also merited high marks as a witty comedy. *Angels and Insects*, directed by Philip Haas, proved to be a sophisticated drama implicitly comparing the human species with the insect world.

Irish revolutionary zeal provided strong material for Neil Jordan's *Michael Collins*, a prime vehicle for Liam Neeson in the title role, and also was the basis for *Some Mother's Son*, directed by Terry George and starring Helen Mirren and Fionnula Flanagan in tour de force performances. With its revenge plot for abuses at a reform school for boys, *Sleepers*—directed by Barry Levinson and starring Robert De Niro, Kevin Bacon, Brad Pitt, and Dustin Hoffman—revived the controversy over the source book by Lorenzo Carcaterra and succeeded as a harrowing if not always convincing tale. Spike Lee applied his talent to *Get on the Bus*, which emotionally dramatized the lives and viewpoints of African-Americans who set off for the 1995 Million Man March in Washington.

In a lighter vein, Woody Allen made his first musical, *Everyone Says I Love You*, a charming, entertaining compendium of old songs, dance routines, humorous characters, and Allen as a loser seeking romance. Albert Brooks' *Mother* hilariously examined a mother-son relationship enhanced by a memorable performance by Debbie Reynolds as the mom, with Brooks himself playing the son. Herb Gardner recycled his hit play *I'm Not Rappaport* into an entertaining film version that teamed Walter Matthau and Ossie Davis in sterling performances. Shakespeare's comedy *Twelfth Night* received a classy well-cast production directed by Trevor Nunn and gained from a towering performance by Nigel Hawthorne as Malvolio.

Other Standouts. Commendable performances included those by Sissy Spacek, Piper Laurie, Walter Matthau, and Mary Steenburgen in *The Grass Harp*, directed by Charles Matthau, the actor's son. Audiences warmed to the performance of Richard Dreyfuss in the uplifting *Mr. Holland's Opus*. The riveting acting of Lili Taylor sparked Mary Harron's musing on the Andy Warhol era in *I Shot Andy Warhol*. Alison Elliott merited remembrance as a woman trying to start her life anew in *The Spitfire Grill*, a hit at the Sundance Festival. Nick Nolte was outstanding as a troubled man whose secret mission to become a Nazi results in moral ambiguity in *Mother Night*, adapted from Kurt Vonnegut's novel. Although *The Chamber* was wanting, Gene Hackman's acting as a condemned Southern bigot was powerful. Ralph Fiennes and Kristin Scott Thomas brought intense passion to the grandly atmospheric epic tale of love and betrayal set against the background of World War II in

The Everett Collection

Chris Cooper is the reluctant sheriff of a small town on the Texas-Mexico border and Elizabeth Peña is his former girlfriend in John Sayles' issue-oriented, highly praised film "Lone Star."

The English Patient, based on Michael Ondaatje's novel and impressively directed by Anthony Minghella. Terry Gilliam's *12 Monkeys*, which was highlighted at the Berlin Film Festival, was underappreciated despite its engrossing science-fiction plot and the performance by Bruce Willis as a man desperately trying to prevent a world health debacle. Billy Bob Thornton scored a coup by writing, directing, and effectively starring in *Sling Blade*.

Many high-profile films were scheduled for late-year release, including Nicholas Hytner's *The Crucible*, based on the durable Arthur Miller play about the Salem witch trials. Alan Parker's *Evita*, spawned by the Andrew Lloyd Webber–Tim Rice stage work about Argentine legend Eva Perón, starred Madonna in a role that was a major challenge for her. Other stage-based films included Kenneth Branagh's version of Shakespeare's *Hamlet*, in which he starred as well as directed, and Scott McPherson's play *Marvin's Room* as adapted by John Guare and directed by Jerry Zaks, with a top cast led by Diane Keaton and Meryl Streep. Major book adaptations included the Henry James classic *The Portrait of a Lady*, brought to the screen by Jane Campion and starring Nicole Kidman.

Foreign-Language Films. French films showed strength after years of relative decline. Many vital films—whether by well-established directors or newcomers—made their way in limited venues. André Téchiné's *Ma Saison Préférée* ("My Favorite Season") paired Catherine Deneuve and Daniel Auteuil in an intense, sensitive drama about a sister and brother. Téchiné also directed the taut drama *Les Voleurs* ("Thieves"), teaming the same stars. Auteuil shared the acting prize at the Cannes Film Festival with Pascal Duquenne for *Le Huitième Jour* ("The Eighth Day"), Belgian director Jaco Van Dormael's heartwarming story of an unusual friendship. Numerous other worthy French imports—such as *Ridicule*, *Nelly and Monsieur Arnaud*, and *Salut Cousin!* ("Hello Cousin!")—reflected the upsurge of quality.

The Netherlands' *Antonia's Line*, written and directed by Marleen Gorris, won enthusiasts for its depiction of women who showed courage and independence in facing life's problems. Hungary, which continued its tradition of an annual Hungarian Film Week in Budapest to introduce its product to the world's critics and distributors, unveiled Judit Elek's profound *To Speak the Unspeakable: The Message of Elie Wiesel*, involving a trip by Wiesel to his pre-Holocaust town and the retracing of his anguished story of survival.

Unusual Events. The oldest complete feature film made in the United States, a version of Shakespeare's *Richard III* made in 1912 that was assumed lost, surfaced in Oregon in the collection of William Buffum, a former movie projectionist. Buffum gave the film, which starred Frederick Warde, to the American Film Institute. *The Rolling Stones Rock and Roll Circus*, made in 1968 but left to languish because the Stones were unhappy with it, finally emerged to be presented at the New York Film Festival prior to its release. Its scenes between Mick Jagger and John Lennon held nostalgic appeal. The insect world was explored with unusual effect in an amazing film, *Microcosmos*, directed by Claude Nuridsany and Marie Perennou. *The Line King*, directed by Susan W. Dryfoos, celebrated the special talent of Al Hirschfeld, who has spent his life drawing entertainment celebrities in his unique style.

Industry News. Even more than in the past, the fate of films could be sealed within a day or two after their openings. The initial box-office results in a competitive market led companies to decide to spend more on advertising and promotion or cut projected losses by virtually abandoning a film. The situation made it increasingly difficult for worthy films without such drawing power to compete.

A long-expected leadership upheaval occurred in the Japan-based Sony Corporation's Hollywood operation. Sony, beset by high spending on films that failed, appointed respected producer John Calley as president and chief operating officer of Sony Pictures Entertainment, which encompasses the Columbia and Tristar Studios.

WILLIAM WOLF, *New York University*

MOTION PICTURES • 1996

ALBINO ALLIGATOR. Director, Kevin Spacey; screenplay by Christian Forte. With Matt Dillon, Faye Dunaway, and Gary Sinise.

AMERICAN BUFFALO. Director, Michael Corrente; screenplay by David Mamet, based on his 1975 play. With Dustin Hoffman and Dennis Franz.

ANGELS AND INSECTS. Director, Philip Haas; screenplay by Philip Haas and Belinda Haas, based on the novella *Morpho Eugenia*, by A.S. Byatt. With Mark Rylance.

ANTONIA'S LINE. Written and directed by Marleen Gorris. With Willeke van Ammelrooy and Els Dottermans.

BEAVIS AND BUTT-HEAD DO AMERICA. Director, Mike Judge; screenplay by Judge and Joe Stillman, based on MTV's *Beavis and Butt-head*, created by Judge. Voices by Judge.

BEFORE AND AFTER. Director, Barbet Schroeder; screenplay by Ted Tally, based on the book by Rosellen Brown. With Meryl Streep and Liam Neeson.

BEYOND THE CLOUDS. Director, Michelangelo Antonioni, assisted by Wim Wenders; screenplay by Antonioni, Wenders, and Tonio Guerra, based on *That Bowling Alley on the Tiber*, by Antonioni. With John Malkovich, Fanny Ardant, and Sophie Marceau.

BIG NIGHT. Directors, Stanley Tucci and Campbell Scott; screenplay by Joseph Tropiano and Tucci. With Tony Shalhoub and Tucci.

THE BIRDCAGE. Director, Mike Nichols; screenplay by Elaine May, based on the stage play *La Cage aux Folles*, by Jean Poiret, and the screenplay by Francis Veber, Eduoard Molinaro, Marcello Danon, and Jean Poiret. With Robin Williams, Nathan Lane, Gene Hackman, and Dianne Wiest.

BREAKING THE WAVES. Written and directed by Lars Von Triers. With Emily Watson and Stellan Skarsgard.

BROKEN ARROW. Director, John Woo; screenplay by Graham Yost. With John Travolta and Christian Slater.

THE CABLE GUY. Director, Ben Stiller; screenplay by Lou Holtz, Jr. With Jim Carrey, Matthew Broderick, and Leslie Mann.

THE CHAMBER. Director, James Foley; screenplay by William Goldman and Chris Reese, based on the book by John Grisham. With Chris O'Donnell and Gene Hackman.

COLD COMFORT FARM. Director, John Schlesinger; screenplay by Malcom Bradbury, based on the novel by Stella Gibbons. With Kate Beckinsale, Eileen Atkins, and Ian McKellan.

COURAGE UNDER FIRE. Director, Edward Zwick; screenplay by Patrick Sheane Duncan. With Denzel Washington and Meg Ryan.

THE CRUCIBLE. Director, Nicholas Hytner; screenplay by Arthur Miller, based on his play. With Daniel Day-Lewis, Winona Ryder, Paul Scofield, and Joan Allen.

DAYLIGHT. Director, Rob Cohen; screenplay by Leslie Boehm. With Sylvester Stallone, Amy Brenneman, and Claire Bloom.

D3: THE MIGHTY DUCKS. Director, Robert Lieberman; screenplay by Steven Brill and Jim Burnstein, based on a story by Kenneth Johnson and Burnstein and characters created by Brill. With Emilio Estevez, Jeffrey Nordling, and Paul Kariya.

THE EIGHTH DAY. Written and directed by Jaco Van Domael. With Daniel Auteuil and Pascal Duquenne.

EMMA. Written and directed by Douglas McGrath, adapted from the Jane Austen novel. With Gwyneth Paltrow, Jeremy Northam, and Juliet Stevenson.

THE ENGLISH PATIENT. Written and directed by Anthony Minghella, based on Michael Ondaatje's novel. With Ralph Fiennes, Willem Dafoe, and Kristin Scott Thomas.

ERASER. Director, Charles Russell; screenplay by Tony Puryear and Walon Green. With Arnold Schwarzenegger and Vanessa Williams.

THE EVENING STAR. Written and directed by Robert Harling, based on a Larry McMurtry novel. With Shirley MacLaine; appearance by Jack Nicholson.

EVERYONE SAYS I LOVE YOU. Written and directed by Woody Allen. Musical with Allen, Goldie Hawn, Julia Roberts, and Tim Roth.

EVITA. Director, Alan Parker; screenplay by Parker and Oliver Stone, adapted from the Andrew Lloyd Webber–Tim Rice play. With Madonna, Jonathan Pryce, and Antonio Banderas.

FARGO. Director, Joel Coen; screenplay by Joel and Ethan Coen. With Frances McDormand, William Macy, and Steve Buscemi.

THE FIRST WIVES CLUB. Director, Hugh Wilson; screenplay by Robert Harling. With Bette Midler, Goldie Hawn, and Diane Keaton.

FLY AWAY HOME. Director, Carroll Ballard; screenplay by Robert Rodat and Vince McKewin, based on autobiography of Bill Lishman. With Jeff Daniels, Anna Paquin, and Dana Delany.

THE FUNERAL. Director, Abel Ferrara; screenplay by Nicholas St. John. With Chris Penn, Christopher Walken, Annabella Sciorra, and Isabella Rossellini.

GET ON THE BUS. Director, Spike Lee; screenplay by Reggie Rock Bythewood. With Ossie Davis, Andre Braugher, and Charles Dutton.

GHOSTS OF MISSISSIPPI. Director, Rob Reiner; screenplay by Lewis Colick. With Alec Baldwin, Whoopi Goldberg, and James Woods.

THE GRASS HARP. Director, Charles Matthau; screenplay by Stirling Silliphant and Kirk Ellis, based on the Truman Capote novel. With Sissy Spacek, Piper Laurie, Walter Matthau, and Mary Steenburgen.

HAMLET. Directed and adapted by Kenneth Branagh, based on the play by William Shakespeare. With Branagh, Derek Jacobi, Julie Christie, Kate Winslet, Jack Lemmon, Charlton Heston, Billy Crystal, Robin Williams, and Gérard Depardieu.

HARRIET THE SPY. Director, Bronwen Hughes; screenplay by Douglas Petrie and Theresa Rebeck, with adaptation by Greg Taylor and Julie Talen, based on the novel by Louise Fitzhugh. With Michelle Trachtenberg and Rosie O'Donnell.

HOMEWARD BOUND 2: LOST IN SAN FRANCISCO. Director, David R. Ellis; screenplay by Chris Hauty and Julie Hickson, based on characters from *The Incredible Journey* by Sheila Burnford. With the voices of Michael J. Fox, Sally Field, and Ralph Waite.

THE HUNCHBACK OF NOTRE DAME. Directors, Gary Trousdale and Kirk Wise; animation story by Tab Murphy; screenplay by Murphy, Irene Mecchi, Bob Tzudiker, Noni White, and Jonathan Roberts, based on the Victor Hugo novel *Notre Dame de Paris*. With the voices of Tom Hulce, Demi Moore, and Jason Alexander.

I'M NOT RAPPAPORT. Written and directed by Herb Gardner, adapted from his stage comedy. With Walter Matthau, Ossie Davis, Amy Irving, Martha Plimpton, and Craig T. Nelson.

INDEPENDENCE DAY. Director, Roland Emmerich; screenplay by Emmerich and Dean Devlin. With Will Smith, Jeff Goldblum, Harvey Fierstein, and Harry Connick, Jr.

INFINITY. Director, Matthew Broderick; screenplay by Patricia Broderick, based on autobiographies of Richard Feynman. With Patricia Arquette, Peter Riegert, Jeffrey Force, and Broderick.

I SHOT ANDY WARHOL. Director, Mary Harron; screenplay by Harron and Daniel Minahan. With Lili Taylor, Jared Harris, and Stephen Dorff.

JACK. Director, Francis Ford Coppola; screenplay by James DeMonaco and Gary Nadeau. With Robin Williams, Bill Cosby, and Fran Drescher.

JAMES AND THE GIANT PEACH. Director, Henry Selick; screenplay by Karey Kirkpatrick, Jonathan Roberts, and Steve Bloom, based on the book by Roald Dahl. With Joanna Lumley, Miriam Margoyles, voices of Richard Dreyfuss and Susan Sarandon.

With her title role in "Emma," Gwyneth Paltrow achieved new star status. The movie was one of three major films of 1995 and 1996 adapted from the novels of 19th-century writer Jane Austen.

© David Appleby/Miramax Films

JANE EYRE. Director, Franco Zeffirelli; screenplay by Hugh Whitemore and Zeffirelli, based on the novel by Charlotte Brontë. With William Hurt, Anna Paquin, Geraldine Chaplin, and Charlotte Gainsbourg.

JERRY MAGUIRE. Written and directed by Cameron Crowe. With Tom Cruise, Kelly Preston, and Cuba Gooding, Jr.

JINGLE ALL THE WAY. Director, Brian Levant; screenplay by Randy Kornfield. With Arnold Schwarzenegger, Sinbad, Phil Hartman, and James Belushi.

THE JUROR. Director, Brian Gibson; screenplay by Ted Tally, based on the book by George Dawes Green. With Demi Moore and Alec Baldwin.

KANSAS CITY. Director, Robert Altman; screenplay by Altman and Frank Barhydt. With Jennifer Jason Leigh, Miranda Richardson, and Harry Belafonte.

LONE STAR. Written and directed by John Sayles. With Kris Kristofferson, Matthew McConaughey, and Chris Cooper.

THE LONG KISS GOODNIGHT. Director, Renny Harlin; screenplay by Shane Black. With Geena Davis and Samuel L. Jackson.

LOOKING FOR RICHARD. Director, Al Pacino; narration written by Pacino and Frederic Kimball. With Pacino, Alec Baldwin, Kevin Spacey, Estelle Parsons, Winona Ryder, and Aidan Quinn.

LOSING CHASE. Director, Kevin Bacon; screenplay by Ann Meredith. With Helen Mirren, Kyra Sedgwick, and Beau Bridges.

MARS ATTACKS!. Director, Tim Burton; screenplay by Jonathan Gems, based on *Mars Attacks!* by TOPPS. With Jack Nicholson, Glenn Close, Annette Bening, Pierce Brosnan, and Danny DeVito.

MARVIN'S ROOM. Director, Jerry Zaks; screenplay by Scott McPhearson, based on his play. With Diane Keaton, Meryl Streep, Robert De Niro, Leonardo DiCaprio, Hume Cronyn, and Gwen Verdon.

MARY REILLY. Director, Stephen Frears; screenplay by Christopher Hampton, based on the novel by Valerie Martin. With Julia Roberts and John Malkovich.

MATILDA. Director, Danny DeVito; screenplay by Nicholas Kazan and Robin Swicord, based on the book by Roald Dahl. With DeVito, Rhea Perlman, and Mara Wilson.

MICHAEL. Director, Nora Ephron; screenplay by Ephron, Delia Ephron, Pete Dexter, and Jim Quinlan, based on a story by Dexter and Quinlan. With John Travolta, Andie MacDowell, and William Hurt.

MICHAEL COLLINS. Written and directed by Neil Jordan. With Liam Neeson and Julia Roberts.

THE MIRROR HAS TWO FACES. Director, Barbra Streisand; screenplay by Richard LaGravenese, based on the film *Le Miroir A Deux Faces*. With Streisand, Jeff Bridges, Lauren Bacall, Pierce Brosnan, and Mimi Rogers.

MISSION: IMPOSSIBLE. Director, Brian De Palma; screenplay by David Koepp and Robert Towne; story by Koepp and Steven Zaillian, based on the television series by Bruce Geller. With Tom Cruise, Jon Voight, and Vanessa Redgrave.

MR. HOLLAND'S OPUS. Director, Stephen Herek; screenplay by Patrick Sheane Duncan. With Richard Dreyfuss, Glenne Headly, Olympia Dukakis, and Jean Louisa Kelly.

MOLL FLANDERS. Written and directed by Pen Densham, based on the novel by Daniel Defoe. With Robin Wright, Morgan Freeman, and Stockard Channing.

MOTHER. Written and directed by Albert Brooks. With Debbie Reynolds and Albert Brooks.

MOTHER NIGHT. Director, Keith Gordon; screenplay by Robert B. Welde, adapted from Kurt Vonnegut's novel. With Nick Nolte, Alan Arkin, and John Goodman.

MULHOLLAND FALLS. Director, Lee Tamahori; screenplay by Pete Dexter, based on a story by Dexter and Floyd Mutrux. With Nick Nolte and Melanie Griffith.

MULTIPLICITY. Director, Harold Ramis; screenplay by Chris Miller, Mary Hale, Lowell Ganz, Babaloo Mandel, and Ramis, based on a short story by Miller. With Michael Keaton and Andie MacDowell.

MY FELLOW AMERICANS. Director, Peter Segal; screenplay by E. Jack Kaplan, Richard Chapman, and Peter Tolan. With Jack Lemmon, James Garner, and Dan Aykroyd.

THE NUTTY PROFESSOR. Director, Tom Shadyac; screenplay by David Sheffield, Barry W. Blaustein, Shadyac, and Steve Oedekerk, based on the 1963 movie written by Jerry Lewis and Bill Richmond. With Eddie Murphy.

ONE FINE DAY. Director, Michael Hoffman; screenplay by Terrel Seltzer and Ellen Simon. With Michelle Pfeiffer and George Clooney.

101 DALMATIANS. Director, Stephen Herek; screenplay by John Hughes, based on the novel by Dodie Smith. With Glenn Close, Joely Richardson, and Jeff Daniels.

THE PEOPLE VS. LARRY FLYNT. Director, Milos Forman; screenplay by Scott Alexander and Larry Karaszewski. With Woody Harrelson and Courtney Love.

PHENOMENON. Director, Jon Turteltaub; screenplay by Gerald DiPego. With John Travolta and Kyra Sedgwick.

THE PORTRAIT OF A LADY. Director, Jane Campion; screenplay by Laura Jones, adapted from Henry James' novel. With Nicole Kidman, John Malkovich, and Barbara Hershey.

THE PREACHER'S WIFE. Director, Penny Marshall; screenplay by Nat Mauldin and Allan Scott, a remake of the 1947 film *The Bishop's Wife*. With Whitney Houston and Denzel Washington.

PRIMAL FEAR. Director, Gregory Hoblit; screenplay by Steve Shagan and Anne Biderman, adapted from the novel by William Diehl. With Richard Gere, Edward Norton, Laura Linney, and Frances McDormand.

RANSOM. Director, Ron Howard; screenplay by Richard Price and Alexander Ignon, based on a story by Cyril Hume and Richard Maibaum. With Mel Gibson and Rene Russo.

RICH MAN'S WIFE. Written and directed by Amy Holden Jones. With Halle Berry, Christopher McDonald, and Clive Owen.

RIDICULE. Director, Patrice Laconte; screenplay by Remi Waterhouse, Michel Fessler, and Eric Vicaut. With Fanny Ardant and Charles Berling.

THE ROCK. Director, Michael Bay; screenplay by David Weisberg, Douglas Cook, and Mark Rosner, based on a story by Weisberg and Cook. With Sean Connery, Nicolas Cage, and Ed Harris.

SCREAM. Director, Wes Craven; screenplay by Kevin Williamson. With David Arquette, Neve Campbell, and Courtney Cox.

SECRETS AND LIES. Written and directed by Mike Leigh. With Brenda Blethyn and Marianne Jean-Baptiste.

SHINE. Written and directed by Scott Hicks. With Armin Mueller-Stahl, Noah Taylor, Geoffrey Rush, Lynn Redgrave, and John Gielgud.

SLEEPERS. Written and directed by Barry Levinson, based on a book by Lorenzo Carcaterra. With Brad Pitt, Robert De Niro, Dustin Hoffman, Jason Patric, and Kevin Bacon.

SLING BLADE. Written and directed by Billy Bob Thornton. With Thornton.

SOME MOTHER'S SON. Director, Terry George; screenplay by George and Jim Sheriden. With Helen Mirren and Fionnula Flanagan.

SPACE JAM. Director, Joe Pytka; screenplay by Len Benvenuti, Steve Rudnick, Timothy Harris, and Herschel Weingrod. With Michael Jordan and Looney Tunes characters.

THE SPITFIRE GRILL. Written and directed by Lee David Zlotoff. With Alison Elliott, Ellen Burstyn, and Marcia Gay Harden.

STAR TREK: FIRST CONTACT. Director, Jonathan Frakes; screenplay by Brannon Braga and Ronald D. Moore. With Patrick Stewart, Frakes, and Brent Spiner.

STEALING BEAUTY. Director, Bernardo Bertolucci; screeenplay by Susan Minot, based on a story by Bertolucci. With Liv Tyler, Jeremy Irons, Sinead Cusack, and Jean Marais.

STRIPTEASE. Written and directed by Andrew Bergman, based on the novel by Carl Hiassen. With Demi Moore and Burt Reynolds.

SURVIVING PICASSO. Director, James Ivory; screenplay by Ruth Prawer Jhabvala. With Anthony Hopkins and Natascha McElhone.

THAT THING YOU DO!. Written and directed by Tom Hanks. With Hanks, Tom Everett Scott, Steve Zahn, Liv Tyler, and Jonathan Demme.

A TIME TO KILL. Director, Joel Schumacher; screenplay by Akiva Goldsmith, based on the novel by John Grisham. With Sandra Bullock, Samuel L. Jackson, and Matthew McConaughey.

TIN CUP. Director, Ron Shelton; screenplay by John Norville and Shelton. With Kevin Costner and Rene Russo.

TO GILLIAN ON HER 37TH BIRTHDAY. Director, Michael Pressman; screenplay by David E. Kelley, based on the play by Michael Brady. With Peter Gallagher, Claire Danes, and Michelle Pfeiffer.

TRAINSPOTTING. Director, Danny Boyle; screenplay by John Hodge, based on the novel by Irvine Welsh. With Ewan McGregor, Ewen Bremner, and Jonny Lee Miller.

TREES LOUNGE. Written and directed by Steve Buscemi. With Buscemi, Anthony La Paglia, Elizabeth Bracco, and Samuel L. Jackson.

THE TRUTH ABOUT CATS AND DOGS. Director, Michael Lehmann; screenplay by Audrey Wells. With Uma Thurman and Janeane Garofalo.

TWELFTH NIGHT. Written and directed by Trevor Nunn, based on the play by William Shakespeare. With Helena Bonham Carter, Richard E. Grant, Nigel Hawthorne, Ben Kingsley, and Imogen Stubbs.

12 MONKEYS. Director, Terry Gilliam; screenplay by David Peoples and Janet Peoples. With Bruce Willis, Brad Pitt, and Madeleine Stowe.

TWISTER. Director, Jan de Bont; screenplay by Michael Crichton and Anne-Marie Martin. With Helen Hunt and Bill Paxton.

TWO DAYS IN THE VALLEY. Written and directed by John Herzfeld. With James Spader, Eric Stoltz, Danny Aiello, Jeff Daniels, Keith Carradine, Glenne Headly, Marsha Mason, and Greg Cruttwell.

UNHOOK THE STARS. Written and directed by Nick Cassavetes. With Gena Rowlands, Marisa Tomei, and Gérard Depardieu.

UP CLOSE AND PERSONAL. Director, Jon Avnet; screenplay by Joan Didion and John Gregory Dunne. Suggested by the book *Golden Girl*, by Alanna Nash. With Michelle Pfeiffer, Robert Redford, and Stockard Channing.

THE WAR AT HOME. Director, Emilio Estevez; screenplay by James Duff, adapted from his play. With Estevez, Martin Sheen, and Kathy Bates.

WHITE SQUALL. Director, Ridley Scott; screenplay by Todd Robinson. With Jeff Bridges and Caroline Goodall.

WILLIAM SHAKESPEARE'S ROMEO AND JULIET. Director, Baz Luhrmann; screenplay by Craig Pearce and Luhrmann, based on the Shakespeare play. With Leonardo DiCaprio and Claire Danes.

Music

Overview

For classical music, 1996 meant strikes and celebrations; Alanis Morissette was the new "big" pop star; and jazz fans mourned the death of the legendary Ella Fitzgerald.

Classical

The year 1996 was a tumultuous and trying one in the world of classical music, a year in which business concerns far outweighed artistic ones. A hard blow to the recording industry seemed to take many by surprise, though it was long in the making. The great boom years of recording that had followed the 1980s introduction of the compact-disc (CD) format seemed to come suddenly to an end in 1996, as one by one the major record labels started issuing markedly fewer recordings. Release schedules were cut dramatically, and often focused on crossover repertoire. Music lovers, who once were bombarded with multiple new recordings of the same repertoire pouring forth on a monthly basis, suddenly had to make do with a greatly reduced diet of new issues.

To a certain extent, the recording bust rippled through the rest of the classical-music world. Major U.S. symphonies such as the Philadelphia Orchestra, that once had taken for granted that they always would have long-term recording contracts with major record labels, instead found themselves with no contracts at all. That, in turn, became a labor issue with their players, who often received bonuses for recording and broadcasting work. The loss of recording income—and a general move by orchestra managements to rein in salary increases and health-care costs—led to one of the most divisive and bitter years of labor negotiation in memory. Crippling strikes silenced orchestras in Atlanta, on strike for ten weeks; and Philadelphia, on strike for nine weeks. Eleventh-hour negotiations led others, including the New York Philharmonic, to the brink of crisis. Labor woes also plagued the Oregon and San Francisco symphonies. Ironically, all of this occurred in a year that marked the 100th anniversary of the American Federation of Musicians.

Labor difficulties made the most memorable headlines during the year. Yet, as it has for a generation or more, the industry carried on despite threats that once again the sky was falling. The National Endowment for the Arts, though vastly reduced in size and influence, continued to survive; signs that there might be a warming of attitude toward the necessity of arts education began to crop up around the country; a Louis Harris public-opinion survey revealed the not surprising, but often ignored, fact that Americans indeed do support federal (57%) and state (63%) funding for the arts; and one survey found opera attendance had

© Osamu Honda/AP/Wide World Photos

James Levine (center), *conductor and artistic director of the Metropolitan Opera, celebrated his 25th anniversary at the Met with an eight-hour conducting marathon. The gala, held in April, included performances by dozens of opera stars from around the world.*

increased by 10% in recent years, though symphonic and chamber performances suffered a decline.

Opera-Company News. In the world of opera, performing space was as much in the news as performance itself. The San Francisco Opera began its 1996–97 season by vacating its home of the last 64 years, the War Memorial Opera House. The venerable hall needed serious renovations, including "seismic retrofitting." The company decided to present its usual season, but in two unusual locations—the Bill Graham Civic Auditorium and the Orpheum Theatre. Company officials put a cheery face on the inconvenience of being homeless, offering more tickets at lower prices and highlighting the creative challenge and opportunity of working in unconventional spaces.

The Washington Opera, which welcomed renowned tenor Plácido Domingo as its new artistic director in 1996, announced in March that its chairman of the board, local philanthropist Betty Brown Casey, had donated the $18.05 million Woodward and Lothrop department-store building to the company. Although the company has been performing for a quarter century in the Kennedy Center, the gift of the bankrupt department-store facility was announced as a first step toward its building its own downtown opera house. The move inspired skepticism among some, especially when the price tag for the project was announced: $105 million.

For considerably less, the Michigan Opera Theatre made news by renovating an old vaudeville house in Detroit. The company moved into the new theater—its first full-time home—in March, amid much jubilation that it was participating in a general renaissance of the city's long-plagued downtown. The cost for the facility—which combines a historic auditorium with a newly built stage facility—was a remarkably frugal $27 million–$30 million. Artistically, the major events of the year included a completed Wagner *Ring* cycle at the Lyric Opera of Chicago. The Lyric announced that its general director, Ardis Krainik, would step down in 1997. Krainik had been a powerful force in developing the Lyric into a world-respected company; earlier in the year, her role as a musical leader was acknowledged by the French government, which honored her with the title of *Officier des Arts et Lettres*. She would be succeeded by William Mason, who, like Krainik, had worked his way up through the ranks over a long career with the company.

At the flagship of U.S. opera companies, New York's Metropolitan Opera, James Levine celebrated his 25th anniversary with the company. Under his tutelage, the Met had become an efficient machine, criticized in some quarters for its conservative, curatorial approach, but praised almost universally for the quality of its orchestra, the musical insight of Levine himself, and the professionalism of its stagings. Levine's anniversary was celebrated in April with the conductor in the orchestra pit, leading an hours-long marathon performance with a cast of 61 singers central to the Met during Levine's tenure; virtually

The Spoleto Festival in Charleston, SC, featured the first professional production in the United States of Leoš Janáček's opera "The Excursions of Mr. Broucek." The opera starred (left to right) *Penelope Lusi, soprano; Peter Kazaras, tenor; and Raymond Aceto, bass.*

Courtesy, Spoleto Festival. Photo by William H. Struhs.

every major opera star in the world was represented. The event was broadcast live nationwide by the Public Broadcasting System.

New Productions. New productions at the Met in calendar year 1996 included, among others, Mozart's *Così fan tutte*, Giordano's *Fedora*, Bizet's *Carmen*, and Britten's *Midsummer Night's Dream*. New operas premiered in the United States during the year included Tobias Picker's *Emmeline* (Santa Fe Opera), Tod Machover's *Brain Opera* (Lincoln Center Festival '96) and Daniel Catan's *Florencia en el Amazonas* (Houston Grand Opera). The young American composer Lowell Lieberman saw his new opera, *Dorian Gray*, premiered in Monte Carlo in May.

New orchestral works continued to pour forth. Among premieres in 1996 were Augusta Read Thomas' *Words of the Sea* (Chicago Symphony Orchestra); David Diamond's *Night Thoughts for Small Orchestra* (New York Chamber Symphony); Peter Lieberson's *Fire* (New York Philharmonic); George Perle's *Transcendental Modulations* (New York Philharmonic); and John Williams' Concerto for Trumpet (The Cleveland Orchestra).

Courtesy, Metropolitan Opera. Photo by Winnie Klotz.

On April 10, 1996, 32-year-old French tenor Roberto Alagna debuted at the Metropolitan Opera. A 1988 winner of the Pavarotti Competition, he sang the role of Rodolfo in "La Bohème."

Departures and Milestones. Also of note in the orchestra world were several departures. Ernest Fleischmann, longtime managing director of the Los Angeles Philharmonic, announced his intended retirement, effective June 1997; the announcement came at a time when plans to build a new Walt Disney Concert Hall were in jeopardy due to soaring costs and unsecured funds. The orchestra had something to celebrate nonetheless in 1996—its 75th anniversary, marked with a marathon concert in July. Also in California, Michael Tilson Thomas enjoyed wide-ranging attention in his new post at the helm of the San Francisco Symphony; the symphony toured the country in the spring and held an eclectic festival of American music in June. Other milestones included the departures of Leonard Slatkin as musical director of the St. Louis Symphony, and of Loren Maazel as music director of the Pittsburgh Symphony Orchestra. Their final concerts took place on the same day in May. Slatkin then began his new position with the National Symphony Orchestra in Washington, DC; Maazel remained principal conductor of the Bavarian Radio Symphony Orchestra. In Baltimore, David Zinman announced his intention to retire as music director of the Baltimore Symphony Orchestra.

Sadder passings included the death of Jacob Druckman, in May, at the age of 67. Druckman cut a wide swath through the music world, holding major positions with the Yale University School of Music, the Aspen Festival, and the Aaron Copland Fund. A piano concerto, scheduled to be premiered in November, remained unfinished at his death. Morton Gould, a composer of popular and accessible classical works, died in February. Berthold Goldschmidt, a composer whose early career was derailed by Nazi censorship and harassment, died in October at age 93. Austrian composer Gottfried von Einem died in July at the age of 78—less than a year shy of a major new production of his opera *The Visit of the Old Lady* at the New York City Opera. The soprano Pilar Lorengar also died.

Other News. The advent of the Lincoln Center Festival marked a major change in the concert life of the country's busiest musical city. Under the direction of former *New York Times* music critic John Rockwell, the new festival was organized as a multidisciplinary affair, featuring ensembles brought in from around the world. Musical events at the first festival included a Beethoven series by the Orchèstre Revolutionnaire et Romantique, a four-performance series by the Kirov Orchestra and Chorus, and a major retrospective of the music of U.S. composer Morton Feldman.

Finally, music popped up in popular culture in various ways. The U.S. mezzo Jennifer Larmore used the occasion of the 1996 Summer Olympics in Atlanta to launch her first national recital tour.

PHILIP KENNICOTT
Music Critic, "St. Louis Post-Dispatch"

Popular and Jazz

As rock 'n' roll entered its fifth decade of existence, a number of 1996 events showed how popular music, like history, has a habit of repeating itself. The enduring popularity of the Beatles was emphasized by the successful release of three two-CD sets consisting of some of the band's unreleased music, as well as alternate versions of familiar songs. After the Broadway musical based on The Who's *Tommy* closed, composer Pete Townshend reconvened his old bandmates for concert performances of his other decades-old extended work, *Quadrophenia*. And the Eagles continued to mount lucrative concerts by reviving their hits of the 1970s.

The most pointedly ironic revival, however, was the reunion of the Sex Pistols, the band that personified the anarchistic spirit of the punk rock of the late 1970s, and that presumed to spit on the graves of "dinosaurs" like the Eagles and The Who. In the 1990s, many of the styles and attitudes embraced by punk rock have entered the mainstream within the rather elastic (and extremely popular) genre known as alternative rock. In that context, the Sex Pistols' "Filthy Lucre Tour" was just another example of how the more things change, the more they stay the same.

Rock. The Grammy Awards gave prizes to two of the year's most commercially successful performers. Alanis Morissette's *Jagged Little Pill*, a debut album that by late 1996 had sold a staggering 13 million copies in the United States alone, was named album of the year. Morissette is a particular favorite of young women, who appreciate her lyrical take on the vagaries of life and relationships. Hootie & the Blowfish, winner of the best-new-artist Grammy for the equally popular *Cracked Rear View*, reprised their collegiate folk-rock for a second release, *Fairweather Johnson*.

Canadian native Alanis Morissette, below, *was one of 1996's most popular rock singers. The 22-year-old surprised some with her raw, emotional performances.*

© Jay Blakesberg/Retna

Morissette was far from the only woman on the charts. Joan Osborne, a bluesier singer than Morissette, sold millions of copies of her own debut, *Relish*, which featured a hit single, "One of Us," musing about whether Jesus would be recognized riding on a bus. The year also saw the high-profile return of Tracy Chapman, who—a decade after her celebrated debut album—enjoyed a comeback hit with a sultry blues song, "Give Me One Reason," from a collection prophetically titled *New Beginnings*.

The use of heroin among alternative musicians, a trend that had been evident since the 1994 suicide death of Nirvana's Kurt Cobain, became a very public issue in 1996. Smashing Pumpkins, a Chicago band led by guitarist Billy Corgan, sold more than 6 million copies of an ambitious two-disc collection called *Mellon Collie and the Infinite Sadness*. The Pumpkins made news when a keyboard player touring with the band died of a heroin overdose after taking the drug with the band's drummer, who later was fired. Also, the Stone Temple Pilots—poised to mount a summer tour in support of their successful third album *Tiny Music. . .From the Vatican Gift Shop*—had to cancel when singer Scott Weiland was busted for heroin and sentenced to drug rehabilitation.

Oasis, a British band who shamelessly boasted of being the new Beatles, established a U.S. following for their relatively ornate pop-rock with their second album, *(What's the Story) Morning Glory?*. The U.S. band Metallica pleased heavy-metal fans with the release of *Load*. But the bohemian rock community was stunned when the group was signed to headline the keynote alternative-rock package tour of the summer, the Lollapalooza Festival. The debate over what constitutes "alternative" underscored the blurry nature of the lines separating various musical genres.

Few could escape contact with the dance fad of the year, the macarena. The tune that sparked the dance, "Macarena (Bayside Boys Mix)," was a souped-up version of a song recorded by Los Del Rio, a pair of middle-aged Spanish singers known in their native country for traditional folk songs. The tune topped the charts in the United States, Germany, France, Austria, Switzerland, Denmark, Israel, and the Philippines.

© Phil Smith/Redferns/Retna

The British group Oasis drew fans with their pop-rock songs, and created controversy with their sometimes raucous behavior. The band, hailed in England as the most popular since the Beatles, abruptly canceled the last few stops on its three-week U.S. tour in September 1996, reportedly due to "internal differences" among its members.

Rap and Rhythm & Blues. The violence implicit in the music known as gangsta rap was underscored by the gangland-style murder of rap star Tupac Shakur. Shakur—known musically as 2Pac—was also an occasional actor (he appeared in the film *Poetic Justice*). His run-ins with the police were reflected by his rap lyrics, his rap sheet, and his tattoo reading "Thug Life." His most recent album, the hugely popular *All Eyez on Me*, had been recorded while he was free on bail pending appeal of a sexual-abuse conviction. The work made no apologies for his behavior and pointed fingers at his rap-world enemies. Shakur was gunned down on the Las Vegas strip.

The Fugees represent a style of rap that features more live instruments and offers a more positive view of life than that portrayed by gangsta rap. The success of *The Score*, the trio's second album, was due in large measure to singer Lauryn Hill's interpretation of Roberta Flack's romantic hit of the 1970s, "Killing Me Softly." The impact of rap on rock—and vice versa—was evident in one of the year's most critically acclaimed recordings, *Odelay*, a dense and canny mix of rap rhythms and rock dynamics by the musician known as Beck.

More traditional styles of rhythm and blues continued to find success alongside rap. Babyface, a singer, songwriter, and producer, solidified his reputation as one of pop music's great talents. His production of songs by performers like Whitney Houston and Toni Braxton made the *Waiting to Exhale* film soundtrack one of the year's biggest hits. Babyface's range was underscored further by his production of blues-rock guitarist Eric Clapton's "Change the World," a hit single from the soundtrack to the film *Phenomenon*. Babyface's success shows the enduring appeal of vocal soul music, a path followed by successful performers like Tony Rich and D'Angelo.

Country. Garth Brooks became history's top-selling solo artist with record sales totaling 58 million units. (By contrast, Elvis Presley's music has sold 41 million.) Shania Twain was country's biggest female star with *The Woman in Me*, which won the Grammy for best country album and spent most of the year at the top of the country charts—a run helped in no small part by saucy videos for songs like "(If You're Not in it For Love) I'm Outta Here!." LeAnn Rimes, 13, was the year's youngest hit maker with "Blue," a torchy ballad prompting some to think of her as a teenage Patsy Cline.

Rock fans were drawn to the work of Nashville's more adventurous artists, including singer-songwriters like Steve Earle, Iris DeMent, and Dwight Yoakam, and groups like the Mavericks. Emmylou Harris defied genre considerations with *Wrecking Ball*, a mesmerizing collection that placed the country singer within a dense, rocklike production. *Wrecking Ball* won the Grammy for best contemporary folk album.

Jazz. The jazz world lost one of its all-time greats with the passing of singer Ella Fitzgerald (*see* OBITUARIES). Meanwhile, Cassandra Wilson, one of contemporary jazz's finest vocalists, released an album called *New Moon Daughter* that challenged jazz purists by including songs by writers like Hank Williams and Neil Young. Eclectic producer and musician Quincy Jones enjoyed a long run at the top of the contemporary jazz charts with *Q's Jook Joint*, an all-star album featuring everything from hip-hop to bebop. Jones, who produced the 1996 Academy Awards broadcast, also signed a $1.1 million book deal to write his autobiography.

An intriguing trend in jazz was for musicians to apply their skills to classical music. Trumpeter Wynton Marsalis, head of the jazz program at New York's Lincoln Center, was among the first jazz musicians to mount such a double play. In 1996 pianist Marcus Roberts, who got his start playing with Marsalis, simultaneously released a jazz trio album, *Time and Circumstance*, and an interpretation of George Gershwin's *Rhapsody in Blue* called *Portraits in Blue*. Similarly, pianist Keith Jarrett, famous for his ruminative solo performances, was backed by a full orchestra for a set of Mozart piano concertos.

© Gerard Schachmes/Regards/Retna

Romantic ballads retained their popularity in 1996, as evidenced by the triple-Grammy-winning "Kiss From a Rose," written and performed by British-born singer Seal, above.

Deaths. American music lost a giant with the passing of Bill Monroe, generally credited with inventing the bluegrass style. Others who died in 1996 included blues musician Brownie McGhee; country music comedienne Minnie Pearl; Lola Beltran, the "queen of Mexican ranchera"; Bernard Edwards, cofounder of the disco band Chic; blues and soul musician Johnny "Guitar" Watson; and Chas Chandler, bassist for the 1960s group the Animals who went on to discover and manage legendary guitarist Jimi Hendrix.

JOHN MILWARD, *Freelance Writer and Critic*

42 songs "every American should know..."

During 1996 the 65,000-member Music Educators National Conference (MENC) and Hal Leonard Publishing selected 42 songs "every American should know." The purpose of the campaign was to "get America singing...again." Folk singer Pete Seeger was named honorary national chair of the campaign.

According to Will Schmid, president of MENC, "we have a whole generation that has grown up without singing songs...that are part of our culture, part of who we are." Schmid believes "we need to...start singing again in our neighborhoods, homes, churches, schools, ballparks, scout troops, and summer camps." The 42 songs are:

Amazing Grace
America
America the Beautiful
Battle Hymn of the Republic
Blue Skies
Danny Boy
De colores
Dona Nobis Pacem
Do-Re-Mi
Down by the Riverside
Frère Jacques
Give My Regards to Broadway
God Bless America
God Bless the U.S.A.
Green, Green Grass of Home
Havah Nagilah
He's Got the Whole World in His Hands
Home on the Range
If I Had a Hammer
I've Been Working on the Railroad
Let There Be Peace on Earth
Lift Ev'ry Voice and Sing
Michael (Row the Boat Ashore)
Music Alone Shall Live
My Bonnie Lies Over the Ocean
Oh! Susanna
Oh, What a Beautiful Mornin'
Over My Head
Puff the Magic Dragon
Rock-A-My Soul
Sakura
Shalom Chaverim
She'll Be Comin' Round the Mountain
Shenandoah
Simple Gifts
Sometimes I Feel Like A Motherless Child
The Star-Spangled Banner
Swing Low, Sweet Chariot
This Land Is Your Land
This Little Light of Mine
Yesterday
Zip-A-Dee-Doo-Dah

MYANMAR

The struggle by Myanmar's ruling junta for political legitimacy and economic development continued in 1996. The international community remained divided over how to interact with the regime, but Myanmar took an important step toward international respectability when it won observer status from the Association of Southeast Asian Nations (ASEAN) in July.

The State Law and Order Committee (SLORC) that has ruled Myanmar since 1988 maintained its totalitarian hold on the country. Every household had to register its members with the police and get permission for overnight guests. Censorship excluded all references to poverty, corruption, AIDS, or political opposition. The SLORC felt that achieving cease-fires with 15 dissident groups that have struggled for 48 years against the dominant Burmese was a major achievement. Contingents of Karen Christians still were fighting on the Northwest Thai border.

The Political Front. The SLORC continued its long-running constitutional convention. Key decisions such as the role of the military were not debatable. The opposition National League for Democracy (NLD) had walked out in protest in November 1995. The SLORC wanted a new constitution because it lost the 1990 election to the NLD. It then nullified the results. A new made-to-order constitution was expected to avoid any risks for the junta. In May, on the sixth anniversary of the elections, the NLD held a convention to draft an alternative constitution. More than 270 of its delegates were jailed. The SLORC announced prison sentences of five to 20 years for criticizing the official constitutional convention.

Opposition leader Aung San Suu Kyi continued until mid-September to hold weekend meetings by the gate of her home for up to 10,000 who crowded the busy street. Though "freed" in 1995 after more than six years of house arrest, she could not travel within the country, and foreign officials risked the wrath of the government if they attempted to meet with her. In late September soldiers and riot police sealed off approaches to her home and arrested hundreds of her supporters. Responding to weeklong student protests in December, the government ordered classes suspended at Rangoon University and Mandalay Institute of Medicine. The government blamed Suu Kyi for inciting the students and confined her to her home.

Economy. Myanmar's gross national product (GNP) grew by 7% in 1995, fueled in large part by soaring heroin production. The regime was indifferent to the spread of heroin since it needed the revenue; but it also found the drug useful domestically as a "pacifier" of rebellious youth. Domestic consumption was leading to a major AIDS epidemic.

The SLORC has received 65% of its revenues since 1990 from foreign oil companies. A $1.2 billion pipeline for shipping natural gas to Thailand was under construction in 1996. France's Total and the United States' Unocal were the chief investors. Unocal was being sued by Myanmar's government-in-exile in U.S. district court. Damages were being sought for the slave labor being utilized. Pepsico announced in May it no longer would hold assets in Myanmar.

International Affairs. In May the SLORC sentenced James Nichols, the honorary consul in Myanmar for the Scandinavian countries, to three years in prison for having two fax machines. When Nichols died five weeks later under mysterious circumstances, Denmark and other members of the European Union (EU) called for economic sanctions.

On July 21, ASEAN voted unanimously to admit Myanmar to observer status in the organization. Members argued they were pursuing a policy of "constructive engagement" with Myanmar's renegade regime, but they also were rebuffing Western critics of its human-rights record, positioning themselves for lucrative investments in Myanmar.

Economic sanctions were discussed by the EU and within the U.S. Congress. In late September, President Bill Clinton signed legislation that authorizes sanctions against nations that practice massive repression. The law also barred members of the SLORC and their families from entering the United States. The United States used its influence to prevent the International Monetary Fund (IMF) and the World Bank from making loans to the nation.

LINDA K. RICHTER, *Kansas State University*

MYANMAR • Information Highlights

Official Name: Union of Myanmar.
Location: Southeast Asia.
Area: 261,969 sq mi (678 500 km²).
Population (mid-1996 est.): 46,000,000.
Chief Cities (1983 census): Yangon (Rangoon), the capital, 2,513,023; Mandalay, 532,949.
Government: *Head of state and government,* Gen. Than Shwe (took power April 23, 1992). *Legislature* (unicameral)—People's Assembly.
Monetary Unit: Kyat (5.941 kyats equal U.S.$1, May 1996).
Gross Domestic Product (1994 est. U.S.$): $41,400,000,000 (purchasing power parity).
Economic Index (1995, 1990 = 100): *Consumer Prices,* all items, 330.3; food, 353.9.
Foreign Trade (1995 U.S.$): *Imports,* $1,272,000,000; *exports,* $847,000,000.

NETHERLANDS

The year 1996 in the Netherlands was marked by increased employment in the private sector abetted by government programs. Steps were taken to restrict drug usage.

Labor Affairs. Strong job growth occurred in small businesses and in the service sector of the Dutch economy. Employment expansion by such big firms as Philips and DAF helped to counter the effects of the collapse of the 77-year-old Fokker aviation company. When rescue negotiations between Fokker and Samsung Group of South Korea failed, Daimler-Benz AG of Germany, the controlling shareholder of Fokker, chose to end further support. Termination of the firm's core aircraft business meant the loss of some 5,600 jobs—the largest such loss in the history of the Netherlands. Nearly 2,000 other jobs were saved when other aspects of the firm's business were diverted to a new holding company.

Government investment in infrastructure improvements—including harbor, airport, and rail expansion—created jobs. Thus despite the Fokker collapse, the official unemployment rate in May was 6.7%, far better than in neighboring Belgium and almost a half point lower than during the previous year. Given the increase of the labor supply, this achievement was noteworthy. Growth came from heavy immigration, including many refugees, and an accelerating flow of women into the labor market. (Dutch women traditionally have been slower than their European counterparts in joining the job force.)

The government also persuaded workers to accept low-income jobs rather than rely on social-security payments. Such payments were reduced, making low-paying jobs more attractive. As demand for social security stabilized and government spending slowed, social-security taxes took a smaller bite from each paycheck. New regulations increasing flexibility in work rules, hiring, and firing were tolerated by unions, which also restrained their price demands. As a result, Dutch goods became more competitive throughout Europe and temporary employment opportunities expanded dramatically.

Foreign Affairs. The Dutch firmly support the Schengen Convention (1990), which is intended to eliminate border controls among several of the European Union (EU) member states. Thus when the Netherlands' neighbors, especially France, insisted that the Netherlands tighten its drug laws, the small country responded. In April the legislature reduced from 30 grams to five grams (1 oz to .17 oz) the amount of marijuana that could be sold openly and legally in so-called "coffee shops." Action also was taken to reduce these shops in number to 1,000, to increase penalties for drug users guilty of petty crimes, and to discourage "drug tourism" by foreigners. These steps were part of an envisioned series designed to persuade neighboring states to continue implementation of the Schengen Convention.

In March the government supported an EU ban on the importation of cattle from Britain, following detection there of "mad-cow disease." A month later, the government initiated the slaughter of some 64,000 British cows imported prior to the start of the disease scare. Despite British protests, the Dutch in May backed German determination to maintain the EU ban on the import of British beef.

The United States criticized the sale by Russia of highly enriched uranium to the EU for use in the Netherlands, Germany, France, and Belgium. Such a sale was contrary to U.S. efforts to reduce the shipment or production of weapons-grade uranium.

Other. The legislature's vote supporting permission of homosexual marriage changed no laws but encouraged the government to revise existing laws....In July a Belgian Air Force plane carrying a Dutch army band crashed at Eindhoven, killing 32 passengers and crew members....The new European Police Office (Europol) opened its headquarters in the Hague.

JONATHAN E. HELMREICH
Allegheny College

NETHERLANDS • Information Highlights

Official Name: Kingdom of the Netherlands.
Location: Northwestern Europe.
Area: 14,413 sq mi (37 330 km²).
Population (mid-1996 est.): 15,500,000.
Chief Cities (Jan. 1, 1994): Amsterdam, the capital, 724,096; Rotterdam, 598,521; The Hague, the seat of government, 445,279.
Government: *Head of state,* Beatrix, queen (acceded April 30, 1980). *Head of government,* Willem Kok, prime minister (took office Aug. 22, 1994). *Legislature*—States General: First Chamber and Second Chamber.
Monetary Unit: Guilder (1.7172 guilders equal U.S.$1, Dec. 6, 1996).
Gross Domestic Product (1994 est. U.S.$): $275,800,000,000 (purchasing power parity).
Economic Indexes (1995, 1990 = 100): *Consumer Prices,* all items, 114.4; food, 109.2. *Industrial Production,* 106.
Foreign Trade (1995 U.S.$): *Imports,* $146,150,000,000; *exports,* $165,572,000,000.

NEW YORK CITY

New York City was snowed under—literally, but not figuratively—in 1996. Beginning with a blizzard in January, a record 75 inches (1.9 m) of snow was recorded for the season. It taxed even the legendary resilience of New Yorkers. By several measures, though, the city rebounded. Double-digit annual percentage declines in crime continued to outpace the decreases in many other major cities, although a number of horrific crimes tempered the good news. A surge in Wall Street profits generated a tax windfall for the city budget, although the blip was a reminder of how much the city's fortunes depend on a single economic engine. Tens of thousands more students enrolled than the public schools could accommodate, affirming the city's role as a magnet for immigrants, but also producing some severe classroom overcrowding. And New York capped the year with an artificial blizzard of ticker tape on lower Broadway to celebrate the Yankees' first World Series victory since 1978.

The Mayor. Mayor Rudolph W. Giuliani basked in the national spotlight, positioning himself to seek a second term as a Republican opposed to the harshest provisions of federal welfare and immigration revisions. Typical of New York's mayors, he also injected himself into other controversies, too. For example, he championed Rupert Murdoch's Fox News Channel in a local cable war against Time Warner and accused airline officials of callousness in how they informed families and friends of the passengers killed on TWA Flight 800, which crashed into the Atlantic Ocean on July 17 shortly after takeoff from New York to Paris.

Crime. Overall crime in New York City kept falling—even after the resignation of William Bratton, the popular police commissioner, who largely was credited with the decline. But as the number of murders plunged to levels not seen in more than a quarter century, several spectacular crimes dominated the news. City officials revamped the Administration for Children's Services after criticism that the beating death of a 6-year-old girl could have been prevented by authorities. A drifter was charged in four brutal assaults on women, including the stabbing death of a Park Avenue dry cleaner and the beating of a piano teacher in Central Park. A man was arrested for the so-called Zodiac attacks, which left three persons killed and five wounded in the early 1990s. Three men, including the accused mastermind of the 1993 World Trade Center bombing, were convicted of a plot to bomb U.S. airliners overseas.

No executions resulted from the state's new death-penalty law, which was enacted in 1995. No one even was convicted in a capital case. But prosecutors promised to seek the death penalty in more than one case—particularly after the Bronx district attorney, who opposes capital punishment, was superseded in one murder case that Gov. George Pataki said merited the death penalty.

On Oct. 29, 1996, an estimated 3.5 million people honored New York City's latest heroes—the Yankees—with a giant ticker-tape parade after the team won its first World Series since 1978.

Other News. An estate auction of Jacqueline Kennedy Onassis' personal possessions signaled the final curtain for Camelot....The New York Public Library opened a vast Science, Industry, and Business Library on the site of the former B. Altman department store....In a referendum, New Yorkers rejected an appeal from most elected officials and voted not to loosen term limits approved previously....A 7-year-old boy from Queens was suspended from school for sexual harassment, then pardoned by his local school board, after kissing a fellow second grader....And as the city's most supportive Yankee fan, Mayor Giuliani, was poised to run for reelection in 1997, still unresolved was whether the team would remain in the Bronx when its lease on Yankee Stadium expires in 2002.

SAM ROBERTS
"The New York Times"

NEW ZEALAND

In October 1996, New Zealand's first general election under a new mixed-member proportional-representation system that is similar to Germany's left no party holding close to an absolute majority of seats in parliament. Protracted negotiations over the formation of a coalition government followed. Finally, late in the year the New Zealand First party, under Winston Peters, chose to ally itself with the National Party. The comprehensive policy agreement included significant increases in spending on health and education. Although Jim Bolger remained prime minister, Peters became his deputy, as well as treasurer. New Zealand First was allocated five ministerial posts in an enlarged 20-member cabinet.

Politics. Although the former National Party cabinet of Prime Minister Bolger remained technically a minority government, it always headed all preelection opinion polls comfortably. The Labour and New Zealand First parties seesawed in second position. One National member of parliament (MP) resigned after a scandal without precipitating a by-election, and there were rumbles of dissatisfaction over the Labour hierarchy. Eventually, Michael Cullen became Labour's deputy leader.

With the campaign itself revolving more around style than substantive issues, Helen Clark led Labour to a late surge. Meanwhile the National Party, belatedly trying to reduce its vulnerability over health-care services, saw its support leaching away. A NZ$1 billion sale of cutting rights to the vast state forests on election eve, for which polls showed only 25% backing, probably cost the National Party many votes. The election outcome vindicated the final polls. National won 34% of the vote and 44 seats, only seven seats ahead of Labour. Insofar as coalition cards were concerned, the clear victor was the centrist New Zealand First Party with its 17 seats. Out on the ideological flanks, the left-wing Alliance was as disappointed with its 13 seats as the right-wing ACT, making its political debut, was elated with its eight seats. Turnout among the 2.4 million voters was 86%—almost identical with 1993's turnout.

Economy. The essential buoyancy of New Zealand's economy was reflected in preelection polls in which only one voter in seven believed that either the economy or unemployment were the most important issues facing the country. Notwithstanding that the 2% annual inflation target was breached in the March–June quarter, the market was little concerned against a broader backdrop of confidence. The New Zealand dollar continued to advance against major currencies throughout the year, to the point where it was regarded as dangerously overvalued.

In January, Standard & Poor assigned an AA+ rating to New Zealand—the first time it had surpassed Australia's rating. The principal reasons cited for New Zealand's new rating were prudent financial management and the contriving of a budget surplus equaling 3% of gross domestic product (GDP). With a substantial reduction in the base income-tax rate to 21.5 cents to the dollar and other tax adjustments already announced, the May budget of Finance Minister Bill Birch excited few but economists. Partly because of Treasury's warning that the economy was on the verge of overheating, spending initiatives were few. Spending for education was boosted by 5%, however. Public debt dropped.

Other Events. New Zealand's election to the Finance Committee of the United Nations attested to the nation's responsible and independent reputation....The September visit of the Tibetan spiritual leader, the Dalai Lama, and his meeting with Prime Minister Bolger drew protests from China....In March, Sir Michael Hardie Boys, a former lawyer and judge, was sworn in as the 17th governor-general....Kiwi International Airline collapsed in September, leaving 3,000 passengers stranded and debts of NZ$4.4 million.

G. W. A. BUSH, *University of Auckland*

NEW ZEALAND • Information Highlights

Official Name: New Zealand.
Location: Southwest Pacific Ocean.
Area: 103,737 sq mi (268 680 km²).
Population (mid-1996 est.): 3,600,000.
Chief Cities (March 1994 est.): Wellington, the capital, 326,900; Auckland, 1,002,000; Christchurch, 312,600; Hamilton, 151,800.
Government: *Head of state,* Elizabeth II, queen, represented by Sir Michael Hardie Boys, governor-general (sworn in March 21, 1996). *Head of government,* James Bolger, prime minister (took office November 1990). *Legislature* (unicameral)—House of Representatives.
Monetary Unit: New Zealand dollar (1.4162 N.Z. dollars equal U.S.$1, Dec. 31, 1996).
Gross Domestic Product (1994 est. U.S.$): $56,400,000,000 (purchasing power parity).
Economic Indexes (1995, 1990 = 100): *Consumer Prices,* all items, 110.8; food, 103.1. *Industrial Production,* 112.
Foreign Trade (1995 U.S.$): *Imports,* $13,957,000,000; *exports,* $13,746,000,000.

NIGERIA

During 1996, Nigeria's dictatorial regime led by Gen. Sani Abacha attempted to mollify negative world opinion by arranging for the first cycle of elections, releasing a few political prisoners, and easing some restrictive economic practices.

Political and Internal Developments. The military government—while still holding Moshood Abiola, the proclaimed winner of the 1993 presidential election; Olusegun Obasanjo, former head of state; and other important political leaders—released some from detention. It put into effect its transition program, the first steps toward an elected government. The constitution that was approved in October 1995 established a modified presidential system in which the main offices would be rotated. Ward elections were held in March. No political parties were allowed and the turnout was very large. The government deployed 50,000 police to keep order. The next step in implementing the planned return to civilian control in October 1998 was to lift partially the ban on political activity. The rules for recognition of political associations were stringent; by July, 16 political associations were certified.

Ethnic and religious differences continued to spawn violence. Communal fighting in Enugu state in March rendered an estimated 10,000 people temporarily homeless. In September in Kaduna, Shiite fundamentalists rioted. The universities remained hostile to the regime. Violence was endemic. General Abacha's jet exploded under mysterious circumstances in January. Later there were explosions at Kano airport and at the Durbar Hotel. Important persons were targeted for assassination. Kudirat Abiola, wife of the imprisoned president, was murdered in June, and an attempt was made on the life of Emeka Ojukwu, who formerly had served as the leader of Biafra.

Economic Developments. The national deficit at the end of 1995 was about $1 billion, or 1.4% of the gross domestic product. The inflation rate was 47%. The budget for 1996 targeted inflation to be only 30% and fixed the exchange rate at 22 naira to the dollar. External debt was $32.5 billion, mostly in short-term loans to the Paris Club. Service on the debt amounted to an average of $2 billion per year. At midyear the central bank indicated that revenues had increased by more than 100%, with petroleum sales accounting for most of the rise. However, service on the nation's debt reduced the revenue amount to a $300 million deficit for the year.

Much of the work on major projects—such as the Katsina and Ajokuta steel mills, a paper mill, and a large-scale water project—was not finished. Nigeria Airways, which had its flagship seized by Britain following nonpayment of $2 million in fines, was reorganized. The cost of goods to the consumer increased drastically and there were shortages of key supplies. In February there was a two-week fuel shortage in Lagos. Corruption permeated all levels of society despite government attempts to eradicate it. In late November the government formed Vision 2010, a program initiative to improve the living standards of Nigeria's populace.

NIGERIA • Information Highlights

Official Name: Federal Republic of Nigeria.
Location: West Africa.
Area: 356,668 sq mi (923 770 km²).
Population (mid-1996 est.): 103,900,000.
Chief City (1993 unofficial est.): Abuja, the capital, 250,000.
Government: *Head of state and government,* Gen. Sani Abacha, military leader (took over November 1993). *Legislature* (suspended)—National Assembly: Senate and House of Representatives.
Monetary Unit: Naira (21.887 naira equal U.S.$1, July 1996).
Gross Domestic Product (1994 est. U.S.$): $122,600,000,-000 (purchasing power parity).
Economic Index (1995, 1990 = 100): *Consumer Prices,* all items, 687.9; food, 379.9.
Foreign Trade (1993 U.S.$): *Imports,* $7,513,000,000; *exports,* $9,923,000,000.

Foreign Policy. Nigeria was suspended from the Commonwealth in 1995 and was not readmitted, despite several meetings with Commonwealth leaders. Border problems with Chad were resolved in March. However, the conflict with Cameroon over control of the oil-rich Bakassi Peninsula remained. The question was referred to the International Court of Justice. Nigeria continued as the main support for peacekeeping in Liberia.

Economic pacts were signed with Russia and China. Later, a bilateral agreement on culture and education was signed with Iran.

See also AFRICA.

HARRY A. GAILEY
San Jose State University

NORWAY

Norway's Prime Minister Gro Harlem Brundtland resigned in 1996 and was succeeded by Labor Party leader Thorbjoern Jagland. The nation's strong economy was sustained by growth in oil and gas exports and private consumption.

Politics. Brundtland, who had been prime minister since November 1990 and previously had served in the post from February 1981 to October 1981 and from May 1986 to October 1989, resigned in October. Her resignation fueled rumors, which she denied, that she wanted to be the next secretary-general of the

© Bjorn Sigurdsoen/AP/Wide World Photos

Norwegian Labor Party leader Thorbjoern Jagland, above, *was named in October to head the government after the resignation of Prime Minister Gro Harlem Brundtland.*

United Nations (UN). She was replaced by Thorbjoern Jagland, longtime favorite as her successor and chairman of the Labor Party since 1992.

Though no major policy changes were proclaimed, Jagland was considered to be further to the left in the Labor Party than Brundtland, most notably in his view that state ownership is a means of preserving Norwegian control of major companies and banks. Norway lacks not only the ideological motive to participate in the general European trend toward privatization, but also the financial incentive. At the start of 1996, Norway became the world's second-biggest oil exporter, after Saudi Arabia, and oil and gas income continued to create large and growing revenues for the government. Income from this source was expected to grow to $15.4 billion by the year 2000—four times the income in 1994.

Economy. Before leaving office, Prime Minister Brundtland engineered a budget compromise with the Conservative Party, increasing taxes on food and providing a budget surplus of $3.8 billion, or 3.8% of gross domestic product. The Norwegian economy grew by more than 5% in the first half of 1996, more than expected. The prime movers were exports, with oil and gas rising by 17%. But private consumption also rose sharply and unemployment dropped to 92,000, or about 4.7%—by far the lowest level among the Nordic countries and less than half that of the average of the European Union (EU) nations. Employment rose in the mainland non-oil sector of the Norwegian economy for the first time in more than 25 years, igniting fears of inflation that were shown to be partly justified in the second half of 1996.

Kvaerner, a major business conglomerate that includes oil and gas interests, acquired the British group Trafalgar House. The purchase included the faltering Cunard Line.

Foreign Affairs. Russian President Boris Yeltsin visited Norway in March 1996, and negotiations between Norway and Russia intensified on a number of issues. Among them was the division of the Barents Sea, an area that may have rich deposits of oil and gas, into economic zones. The Norwegians asked for a midline division, but the Russians demanded two thirds of the area, including virtually all promising prospecting sites. No final solution was found by year's end. Agreements were signed between the two nations, however, on taxes, economic and trade cooperation, and an effort to reduce pollution from Russian nickel works at Pechenga, an area close to the Norwegian border.

In her first official visit to a Baltic country, Prime Minister Brundtland visited Lithuania in March 1996, signaling Norwegian support of Baltic aspirations for membership in North Atlantic Treaty Organization (NATO). A major NATO exercise was conducted to the north of Norway, provoking protests from Russia prior to the Yeltsin visit.

Norway and the EU agreed on the tariff regime for a number of processed foods. High Norwegian tariffs had created friction, especially with Sweden.

LEIF BECK FALLESEN, *Editor in Chief*
"Boersen," Copenhagen

NORWAY • Information Highlights

Official Name: Kingdom of Norway.
Location: Northern Europe.
Area: 125,182 sq mi (324 220 km²).
Population (mid-1996 est.): 4,400,000.
Chief Cities (Jan. 1, 1995 est.): Oslo, the capital, 483,401; Bergen, 221,717; Trondheim, 142,927; Stavanger, 103,590.
Government: *Head of state,* Harald V, king (acceded January 1991). *Head of government,* Thorbjoern Jagland, prime minister (sworn in Oct. 25, 1996). *Legislature*—Storting: Lagting and Odelsting.
Monetary Unit: Krone (6.4438 kroner equal U.S.$1, Dec. 31, 1996).
Gross Domestic Product (1994 est. U.S.$): $95,700,000,000 (purchasing power parity).
Economic Indexes (1995, 1990 = 100): *Consumer Prices,* all items, 112.5; food, 105.1. *Industrial Production,* 128.
Foreign Trade (1995 U.S.$): *Imports,* $32,707,000,000; *exports,* $41,744,000,000.

Obituaries

MITTERRAND, François

French politician: b. Jarnac, France, Oct. 26, 1916; d. Paris, Jan. 8, 1996.

With the possible exception of Charles de Gaulle, no French president has been the subject of more books than François Mitterrand, who died of cancer on Jan. 8, 1996. This may be because Mitterrand—with his ambiguities, his complex intelligence, his love of the land, and his terrible need to control his destiny—more closely mirrored France itself than any of the men who preceded him.

Mitterrand's history joined that of France in 1943 when, after escaping from a Nazi prison, he met General de Gaulle in Algiers. He served in the first Free France government council before being elected to the National Assembly in 1946. Mitterrand's war years are deeply controversial, and he never provided more than a veiled picture of them. It now is known that he backed the Vichy government, in which he served until he joined the Resistance in late 1943. This capacity to shift allegiances at an appropriate moment has been seen as unflatteringly representative of the period.

Beginning in 1947, Mitterrand held cabinet posts under successive center-right Fourth Republic governments. A relatively liberal attitude toward the independence aspirations of the French African colonies was marred by his attachment to French Algeria, even at the price of barbaric practices by the French police during his term as justice minister (1956–57).

Mitterrand's early political career was marked by a ferocious opposition to de Gaulle, who returned to power in 1958. Ironically, Mitterrand—whom many analysts see as the most kingly of French presidents—was opposed to the Fifth Republic that de Gaulle ushered in, because of the increased powers it accorded the presidency. It is in this context of opposition to the person of de Gaulle that Mitterrand's shift to the left must be understood.

His political tour de force was to bring together the disparate French left into an uncomfortable "union," consecrated in 1971. Successfully siphoning allegiance away from the then-powerful Communist Party, he left the Socialists as the only credible governing party on the French left. It was as head of this union that Mitterrand was elected president in 1981, after two narrowly unsuccessful bids (1965, 1974).

© Chip Hires/Gamma-Liaison

François Mitterrand

After keeping such campaign promises as the appointment of Communists as cabinet ministers and the nationalization of key industries, Mitterrand executed an economic about-face in 1983. Thenceforth, France's policies stayed solidly in the Western mainstream. Mitterrand was elected for a historic second term in 1988, although for two two-year intervals he governed with a conservative cabinet. He will be remembered as a complex, sphinx-like man, of extraordinary—even Machiavellian—political deftness, who was preoccupied by history and his own place in it. His principal ideological constant was his commitment to European unification.

Background. François Mitterrand was the fifth of eight children. His father was a railway-station chief. After eight years in a local Catholic boarding school, he went to Paris at 17 to study law and political science. World War II, his escape from prison after being wounded, and his role in the Resistance opened the door to his political career. Mitterrand was a representative in the National Assembly (1946–58 and 1962–81), and a senator (1959–63), as well as mayor of Chateau-Chinon (1959–81). Among his Fourth Republic cabinet posts were the ministries of veterans' affairs, overseas territories, interior, and justice.

He was survived by Danielle Gouze, whom he married in 1944; their two sons, Jean-Christophe and Gilbert; and Mazarine, his daughter with longtime mistress Anne Pingeot. The former French president was the author of numerous books.

SARAH CHAYES

JORDAN, Barbara Charline

U.S. lawyer, legislator, and educator: b. Houston, TX, Feb. 21, 1936; d. Austin, TX, Jan. 17, 1996.

Barbara C. Jordan, the first black woman to be elected to the U.S. Congress from the Deep South, was known for her deep devotion to the U.S. Constitution and her eloquent speaking ability. In fact, she carried a copy of the Constitution in her purse, and was judged the world's best living orator by the International Platform Association in 1984.

As a member of the Judiciary Committee of the U.S. House of Representatives in 1974, she drew national attention as she voted to approve articles of impeachment against President Richard M. Nixon. At the time, the Democratic congresswoman from Texas stated that her "faith in the Constitution is whole, it is complete, it is total, and I am not going to sit here and be an idle spectator to the diminution, the subversion, the destruction of the Constitution." She later was selected to deliver the keynote addresses at the 1976 and 1992 Democratic national conventions.

As chair of the Commission on Immigration Reform (1995), Jordan spoke against a proposal to deny automatic citizenship to the children of illegal immigrants born in the United States. "To deny birthright citizenship would derail the engine of American liberty," she argued.

Background. Barbara Charline Jordan, whose father was a Baptist minister, attended Houston's segregated public schools and was graduated with honors from Texas Southern University in 1956. After earning a law degree from Boston University in 1959 and being admitted to the bar, she engaged in private law practice, was an administrative assistant to a county judge, and became active in Democratic politics. After unsuccessful campaigns to win election to the Texas House of Representatives in 1962 and 1964, she was elected to the state Senate in 1966. She served in that body for six years.

In 1972, Jordan was elected to the first of three terms in the U.S. House from Texas' 18th District. During those years she worked closely with her fellow Texans. Her mentor, former President Lyndon B. Johnson, helped her gained a seat on the Judiciary Committee. In 1979, Jordan retired from the House and began teaching public policy at the Lyndon B. Johnson School of Public Affairs at the University of Texas. In her later years the former legislator was confined to a wheelchair by multiple sclerosis.

Barbara C. Jordan

JAMES E. CHURCHILL, JR.

KELLY, Gene

U.S. dancer, actor, choreographer, and director: b. Pittsburgh, PA, Aug. 23, 1912; d. Beverly Hills, CA, Feb. 2, 1996.

Gene Kelly liked to call himself a "sweatshirt dancer." In contrast to Fred Astaire, who was sophisticated and debonair in white tie and tails, Kelly was earthy and athletic. He fused tap, jazz, and ballet into an energetic style all his own that set a fresh standard for contemporary dance on stage and screen in the 1940s. He was a major force in the colorful, celebrated era of the Hollywood musical, and his intimate, easygoing singing style added to his charm as an ordinary-guy type of leading man with whom audiences could identify.

The image of Kelly most familiar to audiences was one of him dancing joyfully in the rain in the defining number of what many regard as the peak of Hollywood musicals, the 1952 hit *Singin' in the Rain*, which Kelly and Stanley Donen codirected. He also danced with an animated mouse in *Anchors Aweigh* (1945), broke ground by doing musical numbers on actual locations in New York for the film *On The Town* (1949), and wrote and choreographed a jazz ballet, playfully titled *Pas de Dieux*. The latter was set to George Gershwin's *Concerto in F* and was performed in 1960 by the Paris Opera Ballet.

Background. Eugene Curran Kelly was one of five children whose mother saw to it that

© Archive Photos

Gene Kelly

they all took music and dance lessons. He studied economics at the University of Pittsburgh and after graduation took odd jobs during the Depression era. In 1938 he headed for Broadway. "Several of us in New York were trying to create a new style of dance," he recalled 40 years later. "I wanted it to be an athletic style based on the popular music I grew up with in Pittsburgh—Cole Porter, Rodgers and Hart, Jerome Kern, and Irving Berlin."

His first Broadway opening was as a dancer in the chorus of *Leave It to Me*, starring Mary Martin. Next he was cast in William Saroyan's play *The Time of Your Life*. His big break came when he starred in the musical *Pal Joey* (1940), followed by *Best Foot Forward* (1941). Hollywood took notice, and Kelly became a film star. He teamed with Judy Garland in *For Me and My Gal* (1942). After a series of films, including *Du Barry Was a Lady* (1943) and *Cover Girl* (1944), his career was interrupted when he served in the U.S. Navy.

Among Kelly's many later films—some successful, some not—was the especially remembered *An American in Paris* (1951). In addition to winning eight Academy Awards, the movie was the occasion for a special Oscar for Kelly for his contributions to screen choreography. His other honors included the National Medal of Arts and lifetime achievement awards from the Kennedy Center and the American Film Institute. As his advancing age eliminated him as a dancer, he concentrated on acting, directing, and producing. He directed the lavish film *Hello Dolly!* with Barbra Streisand in 1969, but by then the movie musical was no longer in vogue. Kelly also co-narrated a series of three nostalgic *That's Entertainment* movies, featuring sequences from bygone MGM hits.

Kelly, who died at 83, was married three times—first to actress Betsy Blair, with whom he had a daughter, Kerry. They were divorced in 1957. His second wife, Jeanne Coyne, who died in 1973, was his assistant choreographer. They had two children, Timothy and Bridget. In 1990 he married writer Patricia Ward.

WILLIAM WOLF

BURNS, George

U.S. comedian, actor, author, and show-business icon: b. New York, NY, Jan. 20, 1896; d. Beverly Hills, CA, March 9, 1996.

George Burns lived an entire century, and for most of it—ever since the age of 7—he was in show business. Although illness prevented him from his much-publicized goal of performing on his 100th birthday in London or Las Vegas as he had planned, he was able to watch a televised tribute on the occasion that featured many notables in the entertainment world.

Burns' fame sprang from vaudeville and grew from the radio and early TV shows on which he played "straight man" to the ditsy responses of his partner and wife Gracie Allen, who died in 1964. His reputation as a master entertainer, however, grew with age. Performing well into his 90s, he won new audiences with his wit, impeccable timing, amusing ditties, and gags based on his age. Trademark cigar in hand, he would tell a

George Burns

© Marc Biggins/Gamma-Liaison

crowd, "It's nice to be here. At my age, it's nice to be anywhere."

At age 79, when it seemed as if Burns would remain no more than a beloved survivor of the golden era of show-business comedians, he was cast in the movie version of Neil Simon's *The Sunshine Boys* (1975) and won a best-supporting-actor Oscar, leading him into a whole new career.

Background. Born on Jan. 20, 1896, Burns was the ninth of 12 children. His original name was Nathan Birnbaum. Growing up in poverty on the Lower East Side of Manhattan, he had to scrounge for a living. Burns rose through the hard knocks of vaudeville; at one point he even performed with a trained seal.

The turning point came in 1922 when he met another vaudevillian, Gracie Allen. They teamed up professionally, and married in 1926. At first Allen was the "straight man" in the act. But Burns soon realized that the act was funnier with him feeding the straight lines and Allen getting the laughs with her innocently dumb responses.

The couple honed the formula and, as Burns and Allen, became a hit on radio with a show that ran from 1932 to 1950. Their radio success led to appearances as themselves in numerous films, including *The Big Broadcast* series. The pair made a successful transition to television at CBS in 1950, but Allen retired in 1958. Burns subsequently toured nightclubs in an act with Carol Channing.

After his coup with *The Sunshine Boys*, Burns played God in the film *Oh, God!* (1977) and in two sequels. He wrote the best-sellers *Gracie: A Love Story* (1988) and *All My Best Friends* (1989), as well as numerous other books, and received Kennedy Center honors in 1988. He never remarried, and was survived by a son, a daughter, seven grandchildren, and five great-grandchildren.

WILLIAM WOLF

Edmund Muskie

MUSKIE, Edmund Sixtus

U.S. politician: b. Rumford, ME, March 28, 1914; d. Washington, DC, March 26, 1996.

When Edmund S. Muskie died of a heart attack at the age of 81, President Bill Clinton praised him as a "leader in the best sense." Indeed, Muskie's leadership qualities were much in evidence during his 35 years in politics as state legislator and governor of Maine, U.S. senator, secretary of state, and Democratic vice-presidential and presidential candidate. A big man—6′4″ (1.93 m) tall—with craggy features, he had a reputation for honesty.

During his 21 years in the U.S. Senate, Muskie supported such liberal programs as President Lyndon Johnson's Great Society initiatives, but at the same time fought to keep government spending in check. And, as befits an outdoorsman from the Pine Tree State, he was a pioneer environmentalist.

Background. Edmund Muskie was graduated from Bates College in Lewiston, ME, and went on to earn a law degree in 1939 from Cornell Law School. But soon, the United States entered World War II, and Muskie entered the U.S. Navy, serving on destroyer escorts. At war's end, he turned to politics, winning election to the Maine House of Representatives in 1946 and 1948. In 1954 he defeated his Republican opponent to become Maine's first Democratic governor in 18 years. Mainers reelected him in 1956, and two years later they elected him to the U.S. Senate. This was the first time a Maine Democrat had been elected popularly to that body. In the Senate, where he was the architect of the 1963 Clean Air Act and the 1965 Water Quality Act, Muskie's abilities became apparent, and in 1968, Hubert Humphrey chose him as his

© Cynthia Johnson/Gamma-Liaison

Ronald H. Brown

vice-presidential running mate in the Democrats' unsuccessful bid to defeat Richard Nixon and Spiro Agnew.

In 1972, Muskie was the leading candidate for the Democratic presidential nomination. But this bid was foiled when the conservative *Manchester Union Leader* ran a series of articles attacking Muskie and his wife. When he defended her during a speech, he appeared to some reporters to be crying, and this seeming weakness resulted in a drop in his popularity and his withdrawal from the presidential race. It was later revealed that Nixon aides had engineered the newspaper attacks. In the meantime, Muskie had become a member of the Senate Foreign Relations Committee and was the first chairman of the Senate Budget Committee. In 1980, during the Iranian hostage crisis, President Jimmy Carter named Muskie secretary of state. After Carter was defeated in his reelection bid that year, Muskie returned to the practice of law. The former senator later served on the presidential panel that investigated the National Security Council during the Iran-contra affair in the late 1980s.

Muskie was survived by his wife, Jane; five children; and seven grandchildren.

WILLIAM E. SHAPIRO

BROWN, Ronald Harmon

U.S. public official: b. Washington, DC, Aug. 1, 1941; d. near Dubrovnik, Croatia, April 3, 1996.

He "walked and ran and flew through life, and he was a magnificent life force," said President Bill Clinton of Commerce Secretary Ron Brown after his death in a plane crash in Croatia on April 3, 1996. "If there was ever a guy who had the capability to walk with kings and queens and not lose the common touch, Ron was the guy," said David Dinkins, New York City's first African-American mayor. These were some of the qualities and abilities that brought Ron Brown to the pinnacle of power in the U.S. government. But there were many others.

An African-American, he was equally at home in the presence of civil-rights leaders and CEOs of major corporations. A master politician with supreme confidence, he was able to mediate among disparate Democratic factions. A dynamic innovator, he made trade and the creation of jobs an integral part of U.S. foreign policy.

Background. Ronald Harmon Brown grew up during the 1940s and 1950s in Harlem in New York City. He lived in the Hotel Theresa, which his father managed, and met many prominent African-Americans. Brown went to Middlebury College in Vermont, did a stint in the army, and then studied law at night at St. John's University, being graduated in 1970. At the same time, he ran a youth program for the National Urban League in New York City, and in 1972 he became the League's spokesperson in Washington. There he met Sen. Edward Kennedy of Massachusetts, who hired him as deputy head of his unsuccessful 1980 presidential bid. In 1982, Brown was named deputy chairman of the Democratic National Committee.

Brown left politics in 1985 to work full-time with the high-powered Washington lobbying firm of Patton, Boggs & Blow, becoming its first black partner. In 1988, however, he returned to politics, first as Jesse Jackson's campaign manager and then as the manager of the 1988 Democratic National Convention. The following year he was named chairman of the Democratic National Committee, becoming the first African-American to head a national party. In this role he was able to unite the various Democratic factions behind Bill Clinton in 1992. President-elect Clinton later named Brown his secretary of commerce.

As commerce secretary, Brown undertook 19 overseas missions to promote U.S. trade. The spring 1996 mission to the former republics of Yugoslavia, to promote U.S. investment and involvement in the reconstruction of that war-torn area, ended in tragedy.

Brown was survived by his wife, Alma; a son, Michael; and a daughter, Tracey.

WILLIAM E. SHAPIRO

© Metronome/Archive Photos

Ella Fitzgerald

FITZGERALD, Ella

U.S. jazz singer: b. Newport News, VA, April 25, 1917; d. Beverly Hills, CA, June 15, 1996.

Ella Fitzgerald earned the title "the first lady of song" with a vocal style that defined the art of interpretation. "I never knew how good our songs were," commented Ira Gershwin, "until I heard Ella Fitzgerald sing them."

Fitzgerald's professional career began in the mid-1930s with Chick Webb's Big Band. With Webb, she transformed the nursery rhyme "A-Tisket, A-Tasket" into a swing hit. The tune became a showcase for the wordless style of improvisatory singing known as "scat," a technique that Fitzgerald refined in the 1940s as she used her voice to suggest the revolutionary bebop solos of such influential instrumentalists as trumpeter Dizzie Gillespie and saxophonist Charlie Parker.

Scat was the style that insured Fitzgerald an exalted position in the world of jazz, but it was the series of "songbook" albums recorded in the 1950s that established her as a mainstream treasure. *The Cole Porter Songbook*, released in 1956, was followed by volumes devoted to the songs of Harold Arlen, Irving Berlin, Duke Ellington, Jerome Kern, Frank Loesser, Johnny Mercer, Rodgers and Hart, and George and Ira Gershwin. Instead of improvising upon the tunes—the typical strategy of the jazz singer—Fitzgerald embraced the melodies with sophisticated abandon. Critics praised the songbooks.

Background. Ella Fitzgerald's refined artistry belied her tough beginnings. Born in Newport News, VA, on April 25, 1917, she never knew her natural father. Fitzgerald grew up in Yonkers, NY, lost her mother at the age of 15, and fled an abusive stepfather to live with an aunt in Harlem. Life in the city led to a brief stint in a reformatory, but also to the Apollo Theater, where she entered an amateur competition and sang a song made famous by her idol, Connee Boswell—"The Object of My Affection." Fitzgerald won the contest, and a career was born that produced more than 200 recordings as well as concerts around the world. Most often, however, she performed with a small group, the setting best showcasing the voice that set a new standard.

Fitzgerald had married twice, and had one adopted son and a granddaughter. In recent years her health had suffered, and she was forced to curb her legendary enthusiasm for touring. As well as 13 Grammys (one for lifetime achievement), she received Kennedy Center Honors in 1979 and was awarded a Presidential Medal of Freedom in 1992.

JOHN MILWARD

PETERSON, Roger Tory

U.S. naturalist and illustrator: b. Jamestown, NY, Aug. 28, 1908; d. Old Lyme, CT, July 28, 1996.

To identify an unfamiliar bird, millions of people page through a pocket-sized field guide. Chances are that guide was written by Roger Tory Peterson. His books introduced simplified drawings and brief text that focused on a species' essential features and distinguishing characteristics. For example, he succinctly described the male common goldfinch in easy-to-remember terms: "The only small yellow bird with black wings."

Peterson's guides were the first to use little arrows to point out a bird's distinctive markings. They also were the first to group birds by appearance, rather than by scientific classification. Today, Peterson is the best-known ornithologist of the 20th century. More importantly, he is credited with making bird-watching a hobby easily accessible to all. Initially, however, his radical departures from traditional bird books were not greeted enthusiastically by publishers. At least four publishers rejected Peterson's original *A Field Guide to the Birds*. But when Houghton-Mifflin finally brought out the first edition in 1934, the general public was quick to appreciate its value. The edition sold out in two weeks. Since then, Peterson's two major field guides, covering birds in the eastern and western United States, have sold more than 7 million copies.

Peterson also wrote or edited books about other animals, plants, and nature in general. In addition, he created richly detailed paintings

Alfred Eisenstaedt/"Life" Magazine/© Time Inc.

Roger Tory Peterson

of his feathered friends. He also was a noted photographer and filmmaker.

Background. Roger Tory Peterson's fascination with birds began at age 11, when one of his teachers started a Junior Audubon Club. Peterson never attended college and had no formal training in the study of birds. He developed his vast ornithological knowledge through careful observation.

After high school, Peterson worked briefly, then began to study art. Encouraged by friends and naturalists, he wrote his first field guide. After it became a success, he joined the staff of the Audubon Society, where he worked for nine years. During his lifetime, he visited all seven continents and saw or at least heard some 4,700 species of birds.

Married three times, Peterson was survived by his third wife and two sons.

JENNY TESAR

SAGAN, Carl Edward

U.S. astronomer: b. New York, NY, Nov. 9, 1934; d. Seattle, WA, Dec. 20, 1996.

As an astronomer, Carl Sagan made important contributions to human knowledge of the planets and outer space. As a gifted storyteller, he became a celebrity, communicating his knowledge about the cosmos and his enthusiasm for space exploration.

Sagan first gained a public following with television audiences in the 1970s, when he started to appear on *The Tonight Show* with Johnny Carson. In 1980 he hosted *Cosmos*, a 13-part series on public television exploring the universe's evolution; it was watched by some 400 million people in 60 countries. Sagan also wrote hundreds of scientific papers and more than a dozen books, including *The Dragons of Eden*, for which he was awarded the Pulitzer Prize in 1978.

Sagan's ability to interpret and explain complex principles in ways that enthralled lay people sometimes was criticized by scientists who felt that he oversimplified matters. But Sagan commented that he proudly wore the badge of science popularizer.

Background. From the time he was a young child in New York City, said Sagan, "the only thing I really wanted to be was a scientist, to actually do the science, to interrogate nature, to find out how things work." He studied at the University of Chicago, receiving a doctorate in astronomy and astrophysics (1960). Sagan's first major scientific contributions were made while he was still in his 20s, when he deduced that Venus is extremely hot and that Mars is a cold, desertlike world. In 1968—after stints at Stanford and Harvard—he moved to Cornell, where he set up a laboratory for planetary studies.

He was instrumental in establishing exobiology as a scientific discipline and helped create the Search for Extraterrestrial Intelligence, a nonprofit corporation that funds studies looking for signs of life in the universe. Sagan also was involved with the National Aeronautics and Space Administration's (NASA's) planetary missions, including the Voyager 1 and 2 craft that visited the outer planets and then left the solar system. He conceived the idea of including messages aboard the Voyager spacecraft, in case they were found by extraterrestrial beings.

Married three times, Sagan was survived by his wife Ann Druyan and four children.

JENNY TESAR

Carl Sagan

© Tony Korody/Sygma

The following is a selected list of prominent persons who died during 1996. Articles on major figures appear in the preceding pages.

Agnew, Spiro T. (77), U.S. Republican vice-president (1969–73) and governor of Maryland (1967–69); resigned from his vice-presidential office in disgrace, pleading no contest to charges of income-tax evasion. To his death, he denied any wrongdoing. While vice-president, his reputation as a sharp-tongued defender of the Nixon administration struck a receptive chord among the U.S. electorate but caused him to be disliked deeply by many: d. Berlin, MD, Sept. 17.

Aidid, Mohammed Farah (59–61), Somali clan leader and warlord; helped overthrow Somalia's government in 1991, and fomented continuing civil war in the nation since then. He declared himself president in June 1995: d. Mogadishu, Somalia, Aug. 1.

Albrecht, Prince Luipold Ferdinand Michael (91), duke of Bavaria and heir to the Bavarian throne; grandson of King Ludwig III, the last king of Bavaria: d. Castle Berg, Starnberg Lake, Germany, July 8.

Allen, Mel (83) (born Melvin Allen Israel), sports announcer; known for his exuberant, talkative style. With Red Barber, was one of the first two inductees into the National Baseball Hall of Fame's broadcasting wing, in 1978: d. Greenwich, CT, June 16.

Ames, Louise Bates (88), child psychologist; her pioneering work in the 1930s and 1940s with fellow researchers Frances Ilg and Arnold Gesell introduced the theory of predictable stages of child development. She wrote several best-selling books, including *Child Behavior* (1981): d. Cincinnati, OH, Oct. 31.

Amsterdam, Morey (81), comedian; well known for his role on *The Dick Van Dyke Show* (1961–66): d. Los Angeles, CA, Oct. 28.

Ayres, Lew (88), actor; following his acclaimed performance in the film *All Quiet on the Western Front* (1930), became one of America's most famous leading men. He was especially well known for his role in *Young Dr. Kildare* (1938) and eight sequels: d. Los Angeles, CA, Dec. 30.

Azikiwe, Nnamdi (91), lawyer, journalist, and Nigerian government figure; served as the nation's first president (1963–66): d. eastern Nigeria, May 11.

Badr, Imam Mohammed al- (67), former Yemeni ruler; ascended the throne in 1962 but was overthrown one week later. After escaping the country, he led a civil war against the rebels that ended in 1969 in defeat: d. Kent, England, Aug. 6.

Balsam, Martin H. (76), film and stage actor; won a best-supporting-actor Oscar in 1965 for his role in *A Thousand Clowns* and a Tony Award in 1967 for Broadway's *You Know I Can't Hear You When the Water's Running*: d. Rome, Italy, Feb. 13.

Baltzell, E(dward) Digby (80), sociologist and writer; his analytical books discuss questions of class in the United States, particularly the lives of WASPs (white Anglo-Saxon Protestants): d. Boston, MA, Aug. 17.

Baroody, William J. (58), top aide to President Gerald Ford (1974–76); also served as president of the conservative American Enterprise Institute for Public Policy Research (1978–86): d. Alexandria, VA, June 8.

Barr, Joseph W. (78), bank executive and government official; a member of the U.S. House of Representatives (D-IN) from 1959 to 1961. He was chairman of the Federal Deposit Insurance Corporation (FDIC) from 1963 to 1965, and served briefly as secretary of the treasury from 1968–69: d. Playa del Carmen, Mexico, Feb. 21.

Beattie, Mollie H. (49), forester; the first woman to serve as director of the U.S. Fish and Wildlife Service (1993–96): d. Townsend, VT, June 27.

Bell, Terrel H. (74), educator; served as the top U.S. education official under Presidents Richard Nixon, Gerald Ford, and Ronald Reagan. He commissioned the 1983 report "A Nation at Risk," which drew attention to declining U.S. educational standards: d. Salt Lake City, UT, June 22.

Belli, Melvin (88), trial lawyer; his flamboyance and eloquence made him a controversial celebrity. His famed clients included Jack Ruby and Jim and Tammy Faye Bakker: d. San Francisco, CA, July 9.

Beradino, John (79), television actor; played a lead role on the soap opera *General Hospital* (1963–96). He earlier had been a major-league baseball player: d. Los Angeles, CA, May 19.

Berman, Pandro (91), film producer; among his films were *Of Human Bondage* (1934), *The Hunchback of Notre Dame* (1939), *National Velvet* (1944), and several Fred Astaire–Ginger Rogers musicals. He was presented with the Irving G. Thalberg Memorial Award (1977) and the David O. Selznick Lifetime Achievement Award for Motion Pictures (1992): d. Beverly Hills, CA, July 13.

Bernardin, Cardinal Joseph (68), *see* RELIGION—*Roman Catholicism*.

Bessell, Ted (57), actor and director; costarred with Marlo Thomas in the television series *That Girl* (1966–71). He later directed *The Tracey Ullman Show* (1987–90), which won an Emmy: d. Los Angeles, CA, Oct. 6.

Blanton, Ray (66), Democratic governor of Tennessee (1975–79) and member of the U.S. House of Representatives (1967–72); was ousted from his gubernatorial office three days ahead of schedule due to a scandal. In 1981 he was convicted of conspiracy to sell liquor licenses while in office. He was credited with recruiting industry from overseas, including Japan's Nissan automaker: d. Jackson, TN, Nov. 22.

Bokassa, Jean-Bedel (75), leader of the Central African Republic (1965–79). He was chosen by France to overthrow the Central African Republic's first president, David Dacko. Bokassa declared himself emperor for life in 1977. Reports of atrocities led to his overthrow by French paratroopers in 1979. He was tried in 1986 but was acquitted of all charges related to alleged killings: d. Bangui, Central African Republic, Nov. 3.

Bombeck, Erma (69), humor columnist and best-selling author; her column, "At Wit's End," appeared in hundreds of newspapers nationwide. She wrote more than a dozen books and appeared on television: d. San Francisco, CA, April 22.

Boorda, Jeremy M. (57), chief of U.S. naval operations since 1994; the first man in the U.S. Navy's history to rise from the lowest rank, sailor, to become a four-star admiral. He committed suicide as questions were being raised about some of the combat decorations he wore: d. Washington, DC, May 16.

Bourassa, Robert (63), Canadian political figure; Quebec's premier (1970–76; 1985–94): d. Montreal, Quebec, Oct. 2.

Brennan, Peter J. (78), U.S. secretary of labor (1973–75) and labor-union leader: d. Massapequa, NY, Oct. 2.

Broccoli, Albert Romolo (Cubby) (87), film producer; produced 16 of the 17 James Bond movies. He received a special Academy Award in 1982 for his work on the hit series. He also produced *Chitty Chitty Bang Bang* (1968): d. Beverly Hills, CA, June 27.

Brodkey, Harold (born Aaron Roy Weintrub) (65), author; his first short-story collection, *First Love and Other Stories* (1958), won the Prix de Rome. His first and best-known novel, *The Runaway Soul* (1991), took 32 years to complete: d. New York City, Jan. 26.

Brodsky, Joseph (55), Russian poet; he was exiled to the United States in 1972 by the Soviet authorities. His intense, emotional writings won him a MacArthur Award (1981), a National Book Critics Circle Award (1986), and the Nobel Prize in literature (1987). He was appointed U.S. poet laureate in 1991: d. Brooklyn Heights, NY, Jan. 28.

Brown, Edmund G. (90), Democratic politician; governor of California (1959–67). His son later served as California's governor: d. Beverly Hills, CA, Feb. 16.

Brownell, Herbert, Jr. (92), U.S. atttorney general under President Dwight Eisenhower (1953–57); as chairman of the Republican National Committee (1944–46), engineered Eisenhower's first nomination for the presidency: d. New York City, May 1.

Bundy, McGeorge (77), foreign-policy adviser to U.S. Presidents John F. Kennedy and Lyndon B. Johnson; strongly urged the escalation of U.S. involvement in the Vietnam war: d. Boston, MA, Sept. 16.

Burke, Arleigh A. (94), U.S. Navy admiral; chief of U.S. naval operations (1955–61). He was awarded the Medal of Freedom (1977). In 1991 he was the first living person to have a ship named after him: d. Bethesda, MD, Jan. 1.

© UPI/Corbis-Bettmann

Spiro Agnew

© Camera Press (Camerapix)/Globe Photos

Mohammed Farah Aidid

© Charles Tasnadi/AP/Wide World Photos

Joseph Brodsky

© Douglas Kirkland/Sygma

Erma Bombeck

Burke, James (Jimmy the Gent) (64), gangster; suspected mastermind behind the 1978 "Lufthansa theft," in which almost $6 million was stolen. His career was the subject of the book *Wiseguy*, later made into the film *Goodfellas*: d. Buffalo, NY, April 13.

Cahill, William T. (84), Republican governor of New Jersey (1970–74); reformed the state's tax structure. He also served six terms in the U.S. House of Representatives (1957–69): d. Haddonfield, NJ, July 1.

Ceauşescu, Nicu (45), son of Romanian communist dictator Nicolae Ceauşescu; a powerful figure in Romania until the 1989 overthrow and execution of his parents: d. Vienna, Austria, Sept. 26.

Chancellor, John W. (68), television journalist; a reporter for NBC News since 1950, he served as an anchor of the *NBC Nightly News* (1970–82). In 1993 the Overseas Press Club presented him an award for his "distinguished and exemplary service" and "long-term dedication": d. Princeton, NJ, July 12.

© Everett Collection
John Chancellor

Chiriaeff, Ludmilla (72), Latvian-born Canadian dance director and teacher; founded Les Grands Ballets Canadiens of Montreal in 1958. She received the Governor-General's Medal of the Order of Canada and the Governor-General's Award for Performing Arts: d. Montreal, Quebec, Sept. 22.

Clampitt, Robert H. (69), founder of Children's Express, a U.S. children's nonprofit news service created in 1975: d. Washington, DC, Aug. 8.

Clark, Eleanor (82), author; won the National Book Award in 1964 for *The Oysters of Locmariaquer*. She was the widow of Robert Penn Warren: d. Boston, MA, Feb. 16.

Clark, Ossie (born Raymond Oswald Clark) (54), British fashion designer; his "mod" designs and high-profile lifestyle helped set worldwide trends—including the midi skirt—in the 1960s: d. West London, England, Aug. 6.

Clurman, Richard M. (72), journalist; in his career at *Time* magazine, served in various posts including as head of the Time-Life News Service. He also served as editorial director at *Newsday* (1955–58): d. Quogue, NY, May 15.

Cohen, Audrey (64), educator; her emphasis on "purpose-centered" instruction attracted interest and support from institutions and educators. She founded Audrey Cohen College in New York City in 1964, and Audrey Cohen schools enroll about 20,000 students: d. New York City, March 10.

Colbert, Claudette (born Lily Claudette Chauchoin) (92), French-born U.S. stage and film actress; won the best-actress Oscar in 1934 for her role in the comedy *It Happened One Night*. She appeared in more than 60 films and in many Broadway productions, as well as on television. She received Kennedy Center Honors in 1989: d. Barbados, July 30.

Colby, William E. (76), former director of the Central Intelligence Agency (CIA) (1973–76); led the agency during its worst crisis, when a list of many serious violations of the CIA charter was released during a congressional investigation. Colby cooperated with the investigators, leading to strong criticism from many intelligence officials and eventually to his dismissal: d. Rock Point, MD, April 27.

Colley, Russell (97), mechanical engineer; helped design a pressurized suit for aviator Wiley Post to fly above 40,000 ft (12 192 m) and later helped create the suits for the Mercury astronauts: d. Springfield, OH, Feb. 4.

Collins, Tommy (67), professional boxer; in 1953 his violent pummeling by an opponent spurred calls for boxing reform that eventually led to the "three-knockdown rule": d. Boston, MA, June 3.

Condon, Richard (81), novelist; his best-known works were *The Manchurian Candidate* (1959) and *Prizzi's Honor* (1982) and its sequels: d. Dallas, TX, April 9.

Conerly, Charlie (74), professional football player; a quarterback for the New York Giants (1948–61), he led the team to the 1956 NFL championship and set many long-standing team records. He was inducted into the College Football Hall of Fame in 1966: d. Memphis, TN, Feb. 13.

Connal, Allan B. (Scotty) (68), television producer; won an Emmy Award for his work as executive producer of NBC's coverage of the 1975 World Series. He later helped create the cable sports network ESPN: d. Atlanta, GA, July 30.

Connolly, Thomas (86), U.S. Navy admiral; helped design the F-14 Tomcat plane, which was named for him: d. Holland, MI, May 24.

Conover, Willis (75), radio broadcaster for the Voice of America; had an estimated 30 million listeners at the Cold War's peak: d. Alexandria, VA, May 17.

Cray, Seymour R. (71), computer scientist; led the team that created the first commercially used computer to use transistors instead of vacuum tubes, in 1957. He created the first supercomputers during the 1960s and 1970s: d. Colorado Springs, CO, Oct. 5.

Cruzan, Lester (62), pivotal figure in a landmark U.S. Supreme Court ruling. His daughter was left in a vegetative state by a 1983 auto crash. Her parents fought to remove her feeding tube in a case that eventually led to a 1990 Supreme Court ruling affirming, in specific cases, a constitutional "right to die": d. Carterville, MO, Aug. 17.

Danzig, Sarah Palfrey (83), former tennis champion; won 18 Grand Slam titles. She was inducted into the Tennis Hall of Fame in 1963: d. New York City, Feb. 27.

Davies, Ronald N. (91), U.S. district-court judge; issued the 1957 order to integrate the schools of Little Rock, AR, and sought an injunction against Arkansas Gov. Orval Faubus, who had assigned the National Guard to a school to prevent black students from entering; the students finally entered under the protection of federal troops: d. Fargo, ND, April 18.

Davis, Hugh J. (69), gynecologist; inventor of the Dalkon Shield intrauterine device, introduced in 1971. The shield was found to be responsible for scores of infections and miscarriages, as well as 18 deaths: d. Gibson Island, MD, Oct. 23.

Day, J. Edward (82), U.S. postmaster general (1961–63); inaugurated the Zoning Improvement Plan, or ZIP code system, in 1963: d. Hunt Valley, MD, Oct. 29.

Debré, Michel (84), French politician; the Fifth Republic's first prime minister (1959–62). He also held other high government posts: d. Montlouis-sur-Loire, France, Aug. 2.

Djukic, Djordje (62), Bosnian Serb army officer; charged by the UN war-crimes tribunal with committing atrocities during the war in Bosnia. He was arrested in January 1996, and pleaded not guilty to charges that he had helped direct the siege of Sarajevo (1992–96): d. Belgrade, Yugoslavia, May 18.

Dominguín (born Luis Miguel González Lucas) (69), Spanish celebrity bullfighter; a leading matador in the 1940s and 1950s: d. Soto Grande, San Roque, Spain, May 8.

Donoso, José (72), Chilean novelist; noted for his dark, surrealistic themes. His best-known book was *The Obscene Bird of Night* (1971; English translation, 1973): d. Santiago, Chile, Dec. 7.

Draper, Paul (86), tap dancer; teamed with Larry Adler, a harmonica player, he became an international star in the 1940s, but the two were blacklisted in 1949: d. Woodstock, NY, Sept. 20.

Druckman, Jacob (67), musical composer, conductor, and teacher; his first large-scale work for an orchestra, "Windows," won the Pulitzer Prize in music in 1972: d. New Haven, CT, May 24.

Dubroff, Jessica (7), pilot; was attempting to become the youngest pilot ever to fly across the United States when her plane crashed: d. Cheyenne, WY, April 11.

Dugmore, Edward (81), abstract painter; received an award from the American Academy and Institute of Arts and Letters in 1980, and the Pollock-Krasner Foundation's Lifetime Achievement Award in 1995: d. Minneapolis, MN, June 13.

Dulles, Eleanor L. (101), economist, diplomat, and author; as an economic specialist for the U.S. State Department after World War II, played a major role in planning the postwar reconstruction of West Berlin: d. Washington, DC, Oct. 30.

Dunn, Robert Ellis (67), choreographer; helped establish the field of modern dance. He received an American Dance Guild conference award in 1988: d. New Carrollton, MD, July 5.

Duras, Marguerite (born Marguerite Donnadieu) (81), French author, playwright, and screenwriter; her best-known work was *The Lover* (1984), an international best-seller that was made into a 1992 film. She also wrote the screenplay for the classic film *Hiroshima, Mon Amour* (1960): d. Paris, France, March 3.

© UPI/Corbis-Bettmann
Claudette Colbert

Duval, Cardinal Léon-Étienne (92), Algerian Roman Catholic cardinal; served as archbishop of Algiers (1946–88): d. Algiers, Algeria, May 30.

Edwards, Vince (born Vincenzo Eduardo Zoino) (69), actor; known for playing the title role in the television series *Ben Casey* (1961–66): d. Los Angeles, CA, March 11.

Ellington, Mercer (76), jazz composer, trumpet player, and bandleader; led his father's Duke Ellington Orchestra for 20 years after the older man's death in 1974. He won a 1988 Grammy for *Digital Duke*: d. Copenhagen, Denmark, Feb. 8.

Elytis, Odysseus (born Odysseus Alepoudhelis) (84), Greek poet; awarded the 1979 Nobel Prize for literature: d. Athens, Greece, March 18.

Emerson, William (58), member of the U.S. House of Representatives (R-MO, 1981–96): d. Bethesda, MD, June 22.

Erdos, Paul (83), Hungarian mathematician; considered one of the 20th century's most brilliant mathematicians. He founded the field of discrete mathematics, the foundation for computer science. He was awarded the Wolf Prize in 1983: d. Warsaw, Poland, Sept. 20.

Factor, Max (born Francis Factor, Jr.) (91), film makeup artist and cosmetics executive; he and his father developed pancake makeup in 1935, and he later developed waterproof mascara and smudge-proof lipstick: d. West Los Angeles, CA, June 7.

Finley, Charles O. (77), owner of the Oakland Athletics major-league baseball team (1960–80); moved the team from Kansas City to Oakland in 1968. He pioneered night games during the World Series, colorful uniforms, and the designated hitter: d. Chicago, IL, Feb. 19.

Fish, Hamilton, Jr. (70), member of the U.S. House of Representatives (R-NY, 1969–94); was a major figure in the passage of the Voting Rights Act extension of 1982, the Americans With Disabilities Act of 1990, and the Civil Rights Act of 1991: d. Washington, DC, July 23.

© Photofest

Greer Garson

© AP/Wide World Photos

Morton Gould

Fleming, James F. (81), television news director and producer; helped begin the *Today* show on NBC in 1952. His 1967 ABC documentary *Africa* won an Emmy Award for best news documentary: d. Princeton, NJ, Aug. 10.
Flemming, Arthur S. (91), U.S. Republican government official; secretary of health, education, and welfare (1958–61) under President Dwight Eisenhower. He later was U.S. commissioner on aging (1973–78) and chairman of the U.S. Commission on Civil Rights (1974–81). He was awarded the Presidential Medal of Freedom in 1994: d. Alexandria, VA, Sept. 7.
Forte, Chet (born Fulvio Chester Forte, Jr.) (60), television director; director of ABC's *Monday Night Football* from its start in 1970 until 1987. He won 11 Emmy Awards: d. San Diego, CA, May 18.
Fox, Harold (86), clothier and musician; claimed credit for creating and naming the "zoot suit" popular during the early 1940s: d. Siesta Key, FL, July 28.
Franey, Pierre (75), French-born chef, restaurant critic, and writer; with *New York Times* food writer Craig Claiborne, he wrote a *Times* column, "60-Minute Gourmet." He and Claiborne cowrote five popular cookbooks: d. Southampton, England, Oct. 15.
Gad al-Haq, Sheikh Gad al-Haq Ali (78), Egyptian Islamic cleric; served as Egypt's mufti (the highest government post for a religious figure) from 1978 to 1982: d. Cairo, Egypt, March 15.
García, Hector Pérez (82), physician and activist for the civil rights of Hispanic Americans; in 1948, founded the American G.I. Forum. He was awarded the Presidential Medal of Freedom in 1984: d. Corpus Christi, TX, July 26.
Garson, Greer (92), British-born actress; among her films were *Good-bye, Mr. Chips* (1939); *Mrs. Miniver* (1942), for which she won an Oscar; and *The Valley of Decision* (1945). She made her Broadway debut in *Auntie Mame* in 1958: d. Dallas, TX, April 6.
Geisel, Ernesto (89), president of Brazil (1974–79); head of a military dictatorship that ran the nation from 1964–85: d. Rio de Janeiro, Brazil, Sept. 12.
Gilpatric, Roswell L. (89), attorney and U.S. government official; as deputy secretary of defense (1961–64), he played an important role in the 1962 Cuban missile crisis: d. New York City, March 15.
Gladwyn, Lord (born Hubert Miles Gladwyn Jebb) (96), British diplomat; helped draft the charter of the United Nations (UN) and was appointed the UN's acting secretary-general in 1946. He served as Britain's representative to the UN (1950–54), as British ambassador to France (1954–60), and as a member of the European Parliament (1973–75): d. Halesworth, England, Oct. 24.
Gould, Morton (82), musical composer; served as president of the American Society of Composers, Authors and Publishers (ASCAP) from 1986–94. He received Kennedy Center Honors in 1994 and won the 1995 Pulitzer Prize in music, and had won a Grammy in 1966: d. Orlando, FL, Feb. 21.
Grosz, Karoly (65), Hungarian politician; as the then communist nation's premier (1987–88), helped bring about democratic reform. He was ousted as leader of Hungary's Communist Party in 1990: d. Hungary, Jan. 7.
Gullikson, Timothy E. (44), tennis player and coach of Number 1–ranked Pete Sampras. During his playing career he had won four singles and 16 doubles titles: d. Wheaton, IL, May 4.
Gurney, Edward (82), U.S. congressman from Florida (House of Representatives, 1963–69; Senate, 1969–75); Florida's first Republican senator since Reconstruction. He resigned from the Senate in 1974 amid charges of corruption, of which he later was exonerated: d. Winter Park, FL, May 14.
Hanson, Duane (70), sculptor; his realistic, life-size sculptures of people in everyday situations often were mistaken for being real: d. Boca Raton, FL, Jan. 6.
Heinemann, George (78), television executive; developed several children's and educational programs during in the 1950s, among them *Ding Dong School*, *Shari Lewis and Lambchop*, and *Dr. Joyce Brothers*. His programs won seven Peabody Awards, and he received a special Peabody Award in 1972: d. Canaan, NY, Aug. 21.
Hemingway, Margaux (41), actress and model; a granddaughter of author Ernest Hemingway, she gained fame as a supermodel during the 1970s and later moved on to acting: d. Santa Monica, CA, July 1.

© G. Salis/Sygma

Margaux Hemingway

Henderson, Virginia (98), nurse, researcher, and teacher; helped transform nursing into a respected and independent profession. She received nursing's highest honor, the Christiane Reimann Prize of the International Nursing Council, in 1985: d. Branford, CT, March 19.
Hiss, Alger (92), diplomat and lawyer; his appearances before the House Un-American Activities Committee in 1948 and in two subsequent trials, where he denied accusations of having been a communist spy when he was working in the U.S. State Department in the 1930s. He was convicted of perjury in 1950: d. New York City, Nov. 15.
Howard, Chuck (63), television sports producer; credited with pioneering the use of the split screen and isolated camera work in sports coverage. He won 11 Emmy Awards: d. Pound Ridge, NY, Nov. 21.
Hughes, Harold E. (74), Democratic governor of Iowa (1963–69) and U.S. senator (1969–75): d. Glendale, AZ, Oct. 23.
Hummert, Anne (born Anne Schumacher) (91), credited with being the creator of the soap-opera genre; she and her husband began creating radio serials in the 1930s: d. New York City, July 5.
Huncke, Herbert (80), inspiration for writers of the 1950s' "Beat Generation"; a petty criminal, street hustler, and drug addict, he was also intelligent and well-read: d. New York City, Aug. 8.
Iharos, Sandor (65), Hungarian athlete; a middle- and long-distance runner, he set 11 world records, breaking seven world records in 14 months from 1955–56: d. Budapest, Hungary, Jan. 23 or 24.
Israel, Franklin D. (50), architect; noted especially for his private residences in southern California. He received the Rome Prize in 1973: d. Los Angeles, CA, June 10.
Jacobs, Bernard B. (80), president of the Shubert Organization, the largest theater owner in the United States. He received an Actors' Fund Medal in 1992: d. Roslyn, NY, Aug. 27.
Jayewardene, J.R. (Junius Richard) (90), prime minister (1977–78) and president (1978–89) of Sri Lanka; worked to dismantle the island nation's socialist economic system and move toward a free market: d. Colombo, Sri Lanka, Nov. 1.
Jenco, Lawrence M. (61), Roman Catholic priest; was one of several U.S. hostages held by Islamic radicals in Lebanon from 1985–86: d. Hillside, IL, July 19.
Johnson, Ben (born Francis Benjamin Johnson) (75), actor; won an Academy Award and a New York Film Critics Award for his supporting role in the 1971 film *The Last Picture Show*: d. Mesa, AZ, April 8.
Kabua, Amata (68), president of the Marshall Islands (1979–96); he served as the nation's first and only president: d. Honolulu, HI, Dec. 19.
Kallai, Gyula (85), Hungarian intellectual and politician; prime minister in the late 1950s and 1960s. He and Communist Party chief Janos Kadar were arrested in 1951 for allegedly being "Titoists," but later were rehabilitated: d. Budapest, Hungary, March 12.

© UPI/Corbis-Bettmann

Alger Hiss

Kanemaru, Shin (81), Japanese politician; Diet member (1958–92) and deputy premier (1986–87), he long was considered the nation's most powerful politician. A 1992 scandal led to his Liberal Democratic Party's fall from power in 1993: d. Shiranecho, Japan, March 28.
Karmal, Babrak (67), president of Afghanistan (1979–86); a Soviet-backed communist, he was installed after the Soviet invasion of 1979: d. Moscow, Russia, Dec. 1.
Kennedy, David M. (90), U.S. secretary of the treasury (1969–70): d. Salt Lake City, UT, May 1.
Kerr, Walter (83), theater critic; his opinions strongly influenced U.S. theater. He was awarded a Pulitzer Prize in 1978 for "the whole body of his critical work": d. Dobbs Ferry, NY, Oct. 9.
Khariton, Yuli B. (92), Russian physicist; directed the creation of the first Soviet atomic bomb in the late 1940s. He later revealed that the bomb was constructed using plans from the U.S. bomb obtained by at least one spy: d. Sarov, Russia, Dec. 19.
Kieslowski, Krzysztof (54), Polish film director; internationally praised for his trilogy "Three Colors": *Blue*, *White*, and *Red*. The latter film was voted best foreign film in 1994 by the National Society of Film Critics and the New York Society of Film Critics, and brought the director an Oscar nomination: d. Warsaw, Poland, March 13.
King, John W. (79), Democratic governor of New Hampshire (1963–69). He also served as chief justice of the state's supreme court (1980–86): d. Manchester, NH, Aug. 9.
Kirk, Samuel A. (92), expert in mental retardation and learning disorders; did pioneering research as the founding director of the Institute for Research on Exceptional Children. He served as the U.S.

Office of Education's Division of Handicapped Children (1963–64): d. Tucson, AZ, July 21.

Kirstein, Lincoln (88), ballet promoter; founded the School of American Ballet in 1933. With George Balanchine, cofounded the New York City Ballet in 1948. He was awarded the Presidential Medal of Freedom in 1984 and the National Medal of Arts in 1985: d. New York City, Jan. 5.

Kitchell, Alma (born Alma Hopkins) (103), pioneering radio and television personality; a radio singer from 1927. She made TV history as the star of the first commercial network series in 1947: d. Sarasota, FL, Nov. 13.

Knutson, Coya (born Coya Gjesdal) (82), member of the U.S. House of Representatives (D-MN, 1955–59): d. Edina, MN, Oct. 10.

Kosterlitz, Hans W. (93), German-born neuropharmacologist; shared the Albert Lasker Award in 1978 for his work in discovering and researching natural opiate-like substances in the brain called endorphins, as well as neuroreceptors for those substances: d. Aberdeen, Scotland, Oct. 26.

Kraus, Hans (90), physician; considered the originator of U.S. sports medicine. He helped establish the President's Council on Physical Fitness in the 1950s: d. New York City, March 6.

Krol, Cardinal John (85), head of the Roman Catholic archdiocese of Philadelphia (1961–88); appointed a cardinal in 1967. He was president of the National Conference of Catholic Bishops (1971–74): d. Philadelphia, PA, March 3.

Kubelik, (Jeronym) Rafael (82), Czech musical conductor; a champion of Czech works. He conducted the Czech Philharmonic (1941–48) and the Chicago Symphony (1950–53): d. Lucerne, Switzerland, Aug. 11.

Kubly, Herbert O. (81), author and playwright; won a National Book Award in 1956 for his first book, *American in Italy*: d. New Glarus, WI, Aug. 7.

Lacoste, (Jean) René (92), French tennis champion; nicknamed "the Crocodile," he was one of the "Four Musketeers" who dominated world tennis in the 1920s. He won ten major titles. He later designed the first metal tennis racket and developed a popular line of clothing: d. St. Jean-de-Luz, France, Oct. 12.

Lafferty, Bernard (51), Irish-born butler-millionaire; the butler of tobacco heiress Doris Duke, he became a controversial millionaire when he inherited $5 million at Duke's death and was named co-executor of her estate: d. Bel Air, CA, Nov. 4.

Lamour, Dorothy (born Mary Leta Dorothy Slaton) (81), actress; best remembered for seven "road" films she made during the 1940s through the early 1960s with Bob Hope and Bing Crosby, and for the sarong she often wore in those films: d. Los Angeles, CA, Sept. 22.

Lanusse, Alejandro Agustín (77), former military ruler of Argentina; took power in a March 1971 coup. He scheduled elections in March 1973 that led to the return of civilian government: d. Buenos Aires, Argentina, Aug. 26.

LaPrise, Larry (83), singer and songwriter; credited with writing the novelty song and dance called "The Hokey-Pokey": d. Boise, ID, April 11.

Larina, Anna (82), possible widow of Nikolai Bukharin, an architect of Russia's Bolshevik Revolution. Her best-selling 1988 autobiography, *This I Cannot Forget*, included Bukharin's final testament: d. Moscow, Russia, Feb. 24.

LaRue, Lash (born Albert LaRue) (78), star of more than 20 film Westerns; he was known for his skill with a bullwhip and tough-guy persona: d. Burbank, CA, May 21.

Leakey, Mary (born Mary Douglas Nicol) (83), paleolithic archaeologist; with her husband, Louis Leakey, and other members of the Leakey family, worked in Africa to discover fossil clues regarding the origin of mankind. Among her finds was the first known member of *Homo habilis*. She received awards from the National Geographic Society, the Geological Society of London, and the Royal Swedish Academy: d. Nairobi, Kenya, Dec. 9.

© Bob Campbell/Sygma

Mary Leakey

Lear, Frances (73), media figure and magazine founder; the former wife of television producer Norman Lear. In 1988 she founded *Lear's* magazine, which folded in 1994: d. New York City, Sept. 30.

Learson, T. Vincent (84), former chairman of the International Business Machines (IBM) Corporation (1971–73); led the company in the early 1960s in developing the revolutionary 360 mainframe computer: d. New York City, Nov. 4.

Leary, Timothy (75), clinical psychologist and advocate of LSD use during the 1960s; became a spokesman for the hippie movement, urging young people to "tune in, turn on, drop out": d. Beverly Hills, CA, May 31.

Lee, J(oseph) Bracken (97), Republican governor of Utah (1949–57); also served as mayor of Salt Lake City (1960–72): d. Salt Lake City, UT, Oct. 20.

Levine, Mickey (born Milton Levine) (83), veterans' advocate; helped organize the American Veterans Committee after World War II: d. North Miami Beach, FL, Nov. 22.

Luening, Otto C. (96), musical composer, conductor, and flutist; directed a noted opera program at Columbia University (1944–70) where some 40 modern operas debuted: d. New York City, Sept. 2.

Lukanov, Andrei (58), Bulgarian premier (1990); the nation's first premier of the postcommunist era, he was a member of the Socialist Party (formerly the Communist Party). He was assassinated: d. Sofia, Bulgaria, Oct. 2.

MacPhail, Bill (76), television executive; served as sports director and vice-president of sports during 18 years at CBS. He influenced the use of the instant replay and CBS' purchase of TV rights to the 1960 Olympics. He later helped create CNN's sports division: d. Atlanta, GA, Sept. 4.

Madison, Guy (born Robert Ozell Moseley) (74), actor; starred in the television series *The Adventures of Wild Bill Hickok* (1951–58). Among his films were *Honeymoon* (1947), *The Command* (1954), and *Bullwhip* (1958): d. Palm Springs, CA, Feb. 6.

Manning, Ernest (87), Canadian goverment official; longtime leader of the Social Credit Party, he served as premier of the province of Alberta (1943–68). He was the father of Canadian right-wing opposition leader Preston Manning: d. Calgary, Alta., Feb. 19.

Manoogian, Alex (95), Armenian-born designer of the first successful single-handled faucet; gave away many of the millions he earned from his invention to cultural, charitable, and educational institutions. He received the Ellis Island Medal of Honor in 1990: d. Detroit, MI, July 10.

Manz, Esther S. (88), founder of the TOPS (Take Off Pounds Sensibly) weight-loss support group: d. Milwaukee, WI, Feb. 26.

Mastroianni, Marcello (72), Italian actor; among his best-known movies were Federico Fellini's *La Dolce Vita* (1960) and *8½* (1963). He won the best-actor award at Cannes for his role in *Dark Eyes* (1987): d. Paris, France, Dec. 19.

© Sunset Boulevard/Sygma

Marcello Mastroianni

Maynor, Dorothy (85), operatic soprano and founder of the Harlem School of the Arts; performed at the inaugural galas of Presidents Harry Truman and Dwight Eisenhower: d. West Chester, PA, Feb. 19.

McLamore, James W. (70), a founding partner of Burger King, which became the world's second-largest fast-food chain: d. Coral Gables, FL, Aug. 9.

Meadows, Audrey (69), actress; best-known for her role as Alice Kramden on the 1950s television series *The Honeymooners*. She won an Emmy for the role in 1955: d. Los Angeles, CA, Feb. 3.

Méndez Montenegro, Julio César (80), president of Guatemala (1966–70): d. Guatemala, April 30.

Meyers, Stephen (53), lawyer; with his partner, Leonard Jacoby, created the first U.S. mass-market law firm: d. New Fairfield, CT, April 19.

Miller, F. Don (75), former head of the U.S. Olympic Committee; helped save the committee, which was in danger of extinction after the boycott of the 1980 Moscow Olympics. He received the Olympic Order from the International Olympic Committee in 1984: d. Colorado Springs, CO, Jan. 17.

Milne, Christopher Robin (75), British bookseller; the son of A.A. Milne, creator of the Winnie the Pooh children's stories. He was the model for the fictional Christopher Robin character in the books: d. England, April 20.

Minnesota Fats (born Rudolf Walter Wanderone, Jr.) (82 or 95), pool hustler; became famous after reinventing himself as "Minnesota Fats" after the character in the 1961 film *The Hustler*: d. Nashville, TN, Jan. 18.

Mitchell, Hugh (89), Democratic member of the U.S. Senate (1945–47) and U.S. House of Representatives (1949–53): d. Seattle, WA, June 10.

Mitford, Jessica (78), British-born nonfiction writer; her best-selling work *The American Way of Death* (1963) exposed many unsettling aspects of the U.S. funeral industry: d. Oakland, CA, July 23.

Molnar, Charles (61), computer scientist; in 1962, codeveloped what is considered the first personal computer: d. Mountain View, CA, Dec. 13.

Monroe, Bill (84), musician; generally credited with inventing the acoustic mountain style known as bluegrass: d. Springfield, TN, Sept. 9.

Montana, Patsy (born Rubye Blevins) (81), country-music singer; her biggest hit, "I Want to Be a Cowboy's Sweetheart" (1935), was the first million-selling hit by a female country singer: d. San Jacinto, CA, May 3.

Morris, Robert J. (82), anticommunist crusader; chief counsel to the U.S. Senate Judiciary Subcommittee on Internal Security (1951–53; 1956–58), which was considered more powerful than the better-known House Committee on Un-American Activities: d. Santa Monica, CA, Dec. 31.

Moshoeshoe II, King (born Constantine Bereng Seeiso) (57), king of Lesotho; he succeeded his father as chief of the then British protectorate in 1960, becoming king at independence in 1966. He was deposed in 1989 and reinstated in 1994, but with no political power: d. Maseru, Lesotho, Jan. 15.

Mott, Sir Nevill Francis (90), British theoretical physicist; his work in solid-state physics helped lay the groundwork for today's electron-

© Archive Photos

Minnie Pearl

ic devices. He shared the Nobel Prize in physics in 1977: d. Milton Keynes, England, Aug. 8.

Najibullah (Najib) (born Najibullah Ahmadzi) (49), Afghanistan's president (1987–92); he earlier had served as chief of the secret police (1979–86) in the Soviet-supported communist government that took control in 1978. His government fell in 1992 following an abortive UN peace initiative. He took refuge in Kabul, where he was executed by Islamic Taliban forces: d. Kabul, Afghanistan, Sept. 27.

Nannen, Henri (82), German journalist; cofounder in 1948 and editor (1948–80) of the German current-affairs magazine *Stern*. His reputation was damaged when, in 1983, *Stern* published the "Hitler diaries," found to be a hoax: d. Hamburg, Germany, Oct. 13.

Ngor, Haing (45 or 55), Cambodian physician turned actor; his experiences as a prisoner of Cambodia's Khmer Rouge and his escape to the United States led to a new career. He won a 1984 Academy Award for his debut role in *The Killing Fields*: d. Los Angeles, CA, Feb. 25.

Niarchos, Stavros S. (86), Greek shipping magnate; an archrival of Aristotle Onassis, he built up a personal fortune of some $4 billion: d. Zurich, Switzerland, April 15.

Noel, Emile (73), French civil servant; one of the founders of the European Union. He served as executive secretary of the Commission of the European Economic Community (1958–67) and as secretary-general of the Commission of European Communities (1968–87): d. Viareggio, Italy, Aug. 24.

Okello, Tito (82), Ugandan military figure; served briefly as the nation's leader (1985–86) after a military coup. He was overthrown by Yoweri Museveni: d. Kampala, Uganda, June 3.

Overmyer, Robert F. (59), U.S. Marine Corps colonel, test pilot, and astronaut; commanded one of the space shuttle *Challenger*'s last successful missions, in 1985, and piloted *Columbia*'s first fully operational flight, in 1982: d. Duluth, MN, March 22.

Packard, David (83), cofounder in 1938 of the Hewlett-Packard Company; it grew into the world's second-largest computer company: d. Palo Alto, CA, March 26.

Packard, Vance (82), journalist and social critic; among his best-selling books was *The Hidden Persuaders* (1957): d. Martha's Vineyard, MA, Dec. 12.

© Camera Press/Globe Photos

Andreas Papandreou

Papandreou, Andreas George (77), premier of Greece (1981–89, 1993–96); founded the Panhellenic Socialist Movement (Pasok) in 1974. He had become a U.S. citizen after fleeing Greece during World War II, and entered Greek politics in 1963 after his father became premier. He was defeated in 1989 amid an embezzlement scandal, but regained power after his acquittal in 1992: d. Athens, Greece, June 23.

Patterson-Tyler, Audrey (69), Olympic athlete; in earning a bronze medal in the 200-m dash in the 1948 Olympics, became the first U.S. African-American woman to win an Olympic medal: d. San Diego, CA, Aug. 23.

Pearl, Minnie (born Sarah Ophelia Colley) (83), radio, television, and stage personality; created the character of "Cousin Minnie Pearl" in the 1930s. She became a member of the Grand Ole Opry in 1940 and was inducted into the Country Music Hall of Fame in 1975: d. Nashville, TN, March 4.

Poher, Alain (87), French politician; twice served as interim president of France (1969, 1974). He was head of the French Senate and president of the European Parliament (1966–69): d. Paris, France, Dec. 9.

Prowse, Juliet (59), British-born dancer and actress; best-known for her role in the movie musical *Can-Can* (1960): d. Los Angeles, CA, Sept. 14.

Quinlan, Joseph (71), father of coma victim Karen Ann Quinlan; a pioneer of the "right-to-die" movement in the 1970s. A ruling by New Jersey's Supreme Court gave the Quinlans the right to have their daughter taken off a respirator: d. Wantage, NJ, Dec. 7.

Rankin, J(ames) Lee (88), lawyer; as an assistant U.S. attorney general in 1953, he argued before the U.S. Supreme Court in the *Brown v. Board of Education* case that resulted in the outlawing of segregated schools. He served as U.S. solicitor general (1956–61): d. Santa Cruz, CA, June 26.

Reddy, Neelam Sanjeeva (83), president of India (1977–82): d. Bangalore, India, June 1.

Reese, J. Terence (82), British bridge champion and writer; regarded as the world's best player during the 1940s and 1950s. He wrote *Reese on Bridge* (1948) and *The Expert Game* (1958). In 1965, a cheating scandal ended his tournament career: d. Hove, England, Jan. 28.

Reichstein, Tadeus (99), Polish-born Swiss organic chemist; developed a process in 1933 for the synthesis of vitamin C, leading to its mass production. In 1950 he shared the Nobel Prize in physiology or medicine for groundbreaking work in cortisone research: d. Basel, Switzerland, Aug. 1.

Rey, Margret (90), German-born artist and writer; with her husband, created the popular series of "Curious George" children's books in 1941, featuring an inquisitive and mischievous monkey: d. Cambridge, MA, Dec. 21.

Rico, Guillermina (63), Mexican street vendor and labor organizer; organized Mexico City street vendors into an influential political bloc: d. Mexico City, Mexico, Sept. 4.

Ridley, Walter N. (86), educator; in 1953 was the first African-American to obtain a doctorate from a state-supported university in the South—the University of Virginia. As president of the American Teachers Association, he helped achieve its merger with the National Education Association in 1966: d. West Chester, PA, Sept. 26.

Rollins, Howard (46), actor; his role in the 1981 film *Ragtime* earned him an Academy Award nomination. He later had a leading role in the hit TV series *In the Heat of the Night* (1988–93): d. New York City, Dec. 8.

Rouse, James W. (81), real-estate developer; created the towns of Cross Keys, MD, and Columbia, MD, in the 1960s. He also developed "festival marketplaces" like Faneuil Hall in Boston, MA, and South Street Seaport in Manhattan. He was awarded the Presidential Medal of Freedom in 1995: d. Columbia, MD, April 9.

Royster, Vermont Connecticut (82), journalist; former editor at *The Wall Street Journal*. He was awarded two Pulitzer Prizes, in 1953 and 1984, and received the Presidential Medal of Freedom in 1986: d. Raleigh, NC, July 22.

Rozelle, Pete (70), National Football League (NFL) commissioner (1960–89); a former public-relations executive, he transformed pro football into an integral part of U.S. culture. He engineered the 1966 merger of the NFL with the American Football League, and created the Super Bowl. He was elected to the Pro Football Hall of Fame in 1985: d. Rancho Santa Fe, CA, Dec. 6.

© Bill Crespinel/Globe Photos

Pete Rozelle

Rudolph, Arthur (89), German rocket scientist; after emigrating to the United States during World War II, led the development of the Saturn V rocket, which carried astronauts to the Moon for the first time in 1969. In 1982 he was accused of war crimes in Germany and left the United States: d. Hamburg, Germany, Jan. 1.

Ruppe, Loret Miller (60), head of the Peace Corps (1981–89); the longest-serving director of the organization. She later served as U.S. ambassador to Norway (1989–93): d. Bethesda, MD, Aug. 6.

Safir, Nathan (83), pioneer in Spanish-language broadcasting in the United States; manager and general manager of KCOR-AM in San Antonio, TX—the first full-time Spanish-language station in the United States. He was inducted into the National Association of Broadcasters' Broadcasting Hall of Fame in 1989: d. San Antonio, TX, Sept. 7.

Salam, Abdus (70), Pakistani physicist; shared the 1979 Nobel Prize in physics for research on the fundamental forces of nature: d. Oxford, England, Nov. 21.

Salter, Andrew (82), psychologist; helped develop the field of behavior therapy during the 1940s: d. New York City, Oct. 7.

Samora, Julian (75), sociologist; helped found the National Council of La Raza, regarded as the foremost civil-rights organization for Mexican-Americans: d. Albuquerque, NM, Feb. 2.

Samuels, Ernest (92), author; best-known for his three-volume biography of Henry Adams. The second volume won a 1958 Bancroft Prize and the Francis Parkman Prize, while the final volume was awarded a Pulitzer in 1964: d. Evanston, IL, Feb. 12.

Sandefur, Thomas E., Jr. (56), tobacco executive; chairman of the Brown & Williamson Tobacco Corp. (1993–95). He drew fire when he testified in 1994 U.S. House subcommittee hearings that he did not believe nicotine to be addictive: d. Louisville, KY, July 14.

Santos, Benvenido N. (84), Philippine-born novelist; his writings about the troubles of Filipino immigrants won him a Guggenheim Foundation fellowship and an American Book Award: d. Legaspi, Philippines, Jan. 7.

San Yu, U (78), president of Myanmar (Burma) from 1981 to 1988; a close associate of dictatorial leader U Ne Win: d. Yangon, Myanmar, Jan. 28.

Sawyer, Grant (77), governor of Nevada (1959–67); a Democrat, he created the state's Equal Rights Commission and the Nevada Gaming Commission: d. Las Vegas, NV, Feb. 19.

Schapiro, Meyer (91), Lithuanian-born art historian, teacher, and critic; considered one of the most influential art scholars of the 20th century: d. New York City, March 3.

Scherer, Cardinal Alfredo Vicente (93), Brazilian Roman Catholic cardinal; appointed a cardinal in 1969: d. Pôrto Alegre, Brazil, March 10.

Schine, G(erard) David (69), hotel heir and pivotal figure in the U.S. Army-Sen. Joseph McCarthy hearings of 1954, which were intended to resolve the question of whether McCarthy had used

Tupac Shakur

pressure to obtain an army commission for Schine: d. Burbank, CA, June 19.

Shakur, Tupac (25), rap-music performer and actor; his albums, two of which reached Number 1 on the Billboard chart, were criticized for their violent lyrics. He appeared in several films: d. Las Vegas, NV, Sept. 13.

Shenandoah, Leon (81), Native American leader; head of New York's Onondaga Indians and chief of chiefs (*Tadadaho*) since 1969 of the Six Nations of the Iroquois Confederacy: d. Onondaga reservation, NY, July 22.

Siegel, Jerry (81), creator of the Superman comic-book character; with his partner, sold the rights to the character to DC Comics for $130: d. Los Angeles, CA, Jan. 28.

Siles Zuazo, Hernán (83), president of Bolivia (1956–60; 1982–85); cofounded the Nationalist Revolutionary Movement in 1941, and was a leader of the nation's 1952 revolution: d. Montevideo, Uruguay, Aug. 6.

Silliphant, Stirling (78), screenwriter; his screenplays included *In the Heat of the Night* (1967), for which he won an Academy Award; *Charly* (1968); *The Poseidon Adventure* (1972); and *The Towering Inferno* (1974): d. Bangkok, Thailand, April 26.

Simpson, Don (52), film producer; coproduced box-office hits of the 1980s, among them *Flash Dance* (1983), *Top Gun* (1986), and *Beverly Hills Cop II* (1987): d. Los Angeles, CA, Jan. 19.

Sleet, Moneta, Jr. (70), photographer; won a Pulitzer Prize for his photo taken at the funeral of Martin Luther King, Jr., showing King's widow and daughter: d. New York City, Sept. 30.

Snell, George Davis (92), geneticist; shared the 1980 Nobel Prize in physiology or medicine for work providing the theoretical basis for human tissue and organ transplants: d. Bar Harbor, ME, June 6.

Snyder, Jimmy ("Jimmy the Greek") (born Emetrios Synodinos) (76), sports analyst and oddsmaker; was the betting analyst on CBS' *The NFL Today* for 12 years. He was fired in 1988 after making racially offensive remarks: d. Las Vegas, NV, April 21.

Spínola, António Sabastião Ribeiro de (86), Portuguese president (1974) and military officer: d. Lisbon, Portugal, Aug. 13.

McLean Stevenson

Stevenson, McLean (66), television actor; best-known for his role (1972–75) as Lt. Col. Henry Blake on the television series *M*A*S*H*. He won a Golden Globe Award for the role in 1973: d. Tarzana, CA, Feb. 15.

Stokes, Carl B. (68), mayor of Cleveland, OH (1967–71); was the first African-American mayor of a major U.S. city. He later became a television news anchor in New York City and was U.S. ambassador to the Seychelles (1995–96): d. Cleveland, OH, April 4.

Stone, Toni (born Marcenia Lyle Stone) (75), first woman to play major-league baseball on a regular basis; was inducted into the Women's Sports Foundation's International Women's Sports Hall of Fame in 1985: d. Alameda, CA, Nov. 2.

Sudoplatov, Pavel A. (89), former Soviet spymaster; headed the USSR secret police's political-assassination branch from the 1930s to the 1950s. He arranged the death of Communist Party enemies, including Leon Trotsky: d. Moscow, Russia, Sept. 24.

Suenens, Cardinal Leo Joseph (91), Belgian Roman Catholic cardinal; a leader at the Second Vatican Council (1962–65): d. Brussels, Belgium, May 6.

Sullivan, Walter (78), science writer; science editor for *The New York Times* (1964–87). He wrote several books—including the best-selling *We Are Not Alone*. He won the George Polk Award and the Public Service Medal of the National Academy of Sciences: d. Riverside, CT, March 19.

Synar, Mike (45), member of the U.S. House of Representatives (D-OK, 1979–95): d. Arlington, VA, Jan. 9.

Talbot, Lyle (born Lyle Henderson) (94), film and television actor; appeared in more than 150 films. For ten years he appeared on the television series *The Adventures of Ozzie and Harriet*: d. San Francisco, CA, March 3.

Ter-Pogossian, Michel M. (71), French-born nuclear physicist and radiology researcher; led the development of the positron emission tomography (PET) scanner: d. Paris, France, June 19.

Tesich, Steve (born Stoyan Tesich) (53), Yugoslavian-born U.S. playwright and screenwriter; his film *Breaking Away* (1979) won an Academy Award for best screenplay: d. Sydney, Nova Scotia, Canada, July 1.

Thompson, Mary (120), believed to be the oldest living American; the daughter of slaves, she had no birth certificate, but her life was traced back to 1876 by Social Security officials: d. Orlando, FL, Aug. 3.

Tiny Tim (born Herbert Khaury) (64), singer and ukulele player; known for his 1968 hit "Tiptoe Through the Tulips," which made him a pop-culture figure, due largely to his quavery falsetto and unusual appearance. He even got married on the *Tonight* show in 1969. He died while performing his signature song: d. Minneapolis, MN, Nov. 30.

Todorov, Stanko (76), communist prime minister of Bulgaria (1971–81); in 1989, helped overthrow the nation's longtime dictator, Todor Zhivkov: d. Sofia, Bulgaria, Dec. 17.

Tordella, Louis W. (84), mathematician; helped break the German military code during World War II. He later helped create the National Security Agency. He pioneered the use of computers for code-breaking: d. Bethesda, MD, Jan. 9.

Touvier, Paul (81), French war criminal; the only Frenchman to be convicted of crimes against humanity after World War II. He was found guilty in absentia of ordering the execution of seven Jews: d. near Paris, France, July 17.

Tra, Tran Van (77), Vietnamese army general and communist government figure; helped launch the Tet offensive in 1968, and directed the final assault on Saigon (now Ho Chi Minh City): d. Ho Chi Minh City, Vietnam, April 20.

Travers, P(amela) L(yndon) (born Helen Lyndon Goff) (96), Australian-born English writer; wrote *Mary Poppins* (1934) and its six sequels. The book was made into a Disney musical in 1964: d. London, England, April 23.

Trilling, Diana (born Diana Rubin) (91), literary critic and writer; despite her considerable talents, she was known best as the wife of literary figure Lionel Trilling: d. New York City, Oct. 23.

Tuttle, Elbert P. (98), U.S. circuit-court judge; known for enforcing civil-rights laws and for his long term of service—he retired in 1995. He was awarded the Presidential Medal of Freedom in 1980: d. Atlanta, GA, June 23.

Carl Stokes

Upton, Richard F. (81), New Hampshire lawyer and politician; known for his 1952 alteration of the state's primary to show the names of the candidates themselves rather than those of prospective delegates to the national nominating conventions. The primary gained national influence: d. Concord, NH, Aug. 12.

Uys, Jamie (74), South African filmmaker; best-known for writing, producing, and directing the 1981 film *The Gods Must Be Crazy*, which became a worldwide hit: d. Pretoria, South Africa, Jan. 29.

Van Fleet, Jo (81), actress; won an Oscar for her first screen appearance, in *East of Eden* (1955), and was awarded a Tony as best featured actress for *Trip to Bountiful* (1957): d. New York City, June 10.

Vassall, John (71), British government clerk found to be a Soviet spy; his exposure in 1962 created a sex scandal that helped bring down the government of Prime Minister Harold Macmillan: d. London, England, Nov. 18.

Vickrey, William S. (82), Canadian-born economist; died, apparently of a heart attack, two days after being awarded the Nobel prize in economics (*see* PRIZES AND AWARDS): d. Harrison, NY, Oct. 10.

Wallenda, Angel (born Elizabeth Pintye) (28), circus performer; after part of her leg was amputated in 1987 due to cancer, she continued walking the high wire, using an artificial limb: d. Sayre, PA, May 3.

Wallenda, Helen K. (85), circus performer; the last surviving member of the original high-wire troupe The Great Wallendas: d. Sarasota, FL, May 9.

Wang Li (75), Chinese radical; a leading figure during the Cultural Revolution of the 1960s and 1970s. He helped Mao Zedong overthrow many of his rivals, but fell out of favor with Mao and was imprisoned from 1967–82: d. Beijing, China, Oct. 21.

Watkins, Perry (48), U.S. Army sergeant; a homosexual, he was allowed to reenlist three times before the army forced a discharge on him in 1984. A court ruling allowing Watkins to reenlist was upheld by the U.S. Supreme Court in 1990: d. Tacoma, WA, March 17.

Watson, Johnny (Guitar) (61), pioneering rhythm-and-blues musician; popular in the 1950s and 1960s, he had found new admiration in the mid-1990s: d. Yokohama, Japan, May 17.

Weston, Paul (born Paul Wetstein) (84), musical arranger, conductor, and composer; his pioneering 1944 album *Music for Dreaming* was considered the first example of "mood music." He was a founder of the National Academy of Recording Arts and Sciences and was its first national president: d. Santa Monica, CA, Sept. 20.

Whittle, Sir Frank (89), British inventor of the jet engine; he was knighted in 1948, and he and German jet inventor Hans von Ohain received the Charles Stark Draper Prize in 1991: d. Columbia, MD, Aug. 8.

Wiegand, Clyde E. (81), physicist; helped design the detonators for the first atomic bomb. In 1955 he and two colleagues proved the existence of the antiproton: d. Oakland, CA, July 5.

Wilkinson, Sir Geoffrey (75), British inorganic chemist; shared the 1973 Nobel Prize for chemistry for his work with organometallic compounds: d. England, Sept. 26.

Williams, Garth (84), children's-book illustrator; illustrated E.B. White's *Stuart Little* (1945) and *Charlotte's Web* (1952), several of the "Little House" series by Laura Ingalls Wilder, and several books by George Selden: d. Guanajuato, Mexico, May 8.

Yarborough, Ralph W. (92), U.S. senator (D-TX, 1957–71): d. Austin, TX, Jan. 27.

OCEANOGRAPHY

The year 1996 was an eventful one for oceanography, with some exciting new discoveries—including a possible confirmation of a global climatic change.

Earth's Rotation. An important discovery for oceanography and earth science was made in 1996 by two scientists from the Lamont-Doherty Earth Observatory. Drs. Xiaodong Song and Paul Richards determined that Earth's inner core, which is surrounded by an outer liquid core, rotates in the same direction as Earth, and, most importantly, that it does it a little faster than the rest of the planet. They studied seismic waves generated by earthquakes, and determined that the inner core moves 12 mi (19 km) more per year than the surface of Earth's crust. At this rate, the difference in movement would be equivalent to a quarter-turn of the planet in 100 years. This is an extremely fast motion; for example, it is about 100,000 times faster than that of the drift of the continents due to plate tectonics. The finding of such a difference in speed between the movement of the inner core and the rest of Earth may explain how our magnetic field is generated and maintained. The latter is an especially important phenomenon in understanding many of the processes that affect the ocean—such as plate tectonics—and that are used to define and date past oceanographic conditions when such evidence is found in marine sediments.

Global Climate Change. The uncertainty of whether a global climate change or warming is in progress continued to be an important scientific, economic, and political question. Several recent observations indicated that such a change indeed may be occurring; for example, 1995 was—on a worldwide basis—the warmest year since records were started in the 1860s. The National Aeronautics and Space Administration (NASA) found an error in its satellite measurements of global sea level. A downward revision of its estimated annual rate of recent rise in sea level—due to glacial melting and warming and expanding seawater volume—from 5.8 mm to 8 mm (.22 inches to .31 inches) to a measurement more reasonable and consistent with others—1 mm to 3 mm (.039 inches to .11 inches)—was required. A positive statistic was that the rate of world population growth slowed compared with 1994. The role of the ocean in affecting or even controlling global climate change still is one of conjecture, but is being studied heavily. One important study is the Global Ocean Ecosystem Dynamics (GLOBEC) program, whose goal is to understand how the animals and plants in the ocean vary due to marine physical processes and thus how they would respond to any change in global climate.

Decreasing Fishery Resources. The decline of marine-fish resources continued to be a worldwide problem. The increasing human population, combined with a growing appetite for seafood, have caused numerous fisheries to collapse or reach near-critical conditions. In 1994—the most recent year for which there is adequate data—the harvest of finfish increased about 8 million tons over 1993, to a total of 109 million tons. Although much of the increase came from aquaculture, most experts agreed that such a harvest was not sustainable, especially in light of anticipated future increases in demand for fish products. Without increased activities in aquaculture and better management of existing fish stock, the prospects for fish being available cheaply around the world are small.

Ships and Budgets. Oceanography is a very expensive science. The daily costs of a research vessel can exceed $15,000. Worldwide budget problems have affected numerous programs. For example, the main U.S. agency concerned with the ocean—the National Oceanic and Atmospheric Administration (NOAA)—had its budget reduced $97 million from final 1995 levels.

The research vessel *Atlantis II* formally ended its oceanographic career in July 1996 after 33 years of use by scientists from the United States and elsewhere. From its first cruise in February 1963 until its retirement, the vessel sailed more than 1 million miles, visited 112 ports in 78 nations, and spent 8,115 days conducting various oceanographic and engineering research. In February 1983, *Atlantis II* became the support ship for the deep-diving submersible *Alvin*. *Atlantis II* will be replaced in 1997 by a new AGOR (Auxiliary General Oceanographic Research) ship, to be called the *R/V Atlantis*. A similar vessel, the *R/V Roger Revelle*, was delivered to the Scripps Institution of Oceanography in 1996.

"Red Tide." Manatees, or sea cows, are an endangered species native to tropical regions. Although efforts have been made to protect them and their estuarine habitat, more than 150 manatees died in Florida in early 1996. Scientists eventually identified their deaths as being due to a neurotoxin that comes from "red tide," a large bloom of algae that sometimes can give the water a red color.

DAVID A. ROSS
Woods Hole Oceanographic Institution

PAKISTAN

Having completed barely three years of her five-year term, Prime Minister Benazir Bhutto and her government were dismissed Nov. 5, 1996, by President Farooq Leghari, concluding a year of political and economic crises.

Political Unrest. The dismissal of the Bhutto government was accompanied by accusations of corruption, economic mismanagement, and abuse of powers by the prime minister, her husband Asif Ali Zardari, and others. President Leghari appointed Malik Meraj Khalid, former National Assembly speaker, as acting prime minister, and scheduled general elections for Feb. 3, 1997. Like Bhutto and Leghari, Khalid is a member of the Pakistan People's Party (PPP). The president also dismissed the Parliament and the various provincial assemblies.

Pressures against the Bhutto government had been building for months. In June the *Sunday Express*, a British newspaper, reported that Prime Minister Bhutto and her husband had purchased a $4 million mansion in southern England, with property that spread over 350 acres (142 ha). Despite rigorous denials, this and other alleged scandals led to calls by both press and opposition politicians for a judicial inquiry into government corruption. In July, 13 opposition parties joined forces in an alliance for the purpose of toppling the Bhutto government.

Another set of issues concerned relations between the prime minister and the judiciary. Supreme Court judgments in March and April severely limited the government's prerogatives in the making of judicial appointments. In June the court invalidated the government's 1993 dissolution of local councils in Punjab. Delays in implementing either decision fueled open confrontation between the prime minister and the nation's chief justice, Sajjad Ali Shah.

The prime minister and Zardari also were suspected of involvement in the death in September of Bhutto's brother, Mir Murtaza Bhutto, who had sought since 1993 to challenge her for party and national leadership. The Bhuttos' mother and Mir Murtaza Bhutto's widow both blamed the prime minister and Zardari for the killing.

Army complaints against the government included the decision to purchase 32 French Mirage 2000-5 fighter aircraft for $4 billion. Though it was reluctant to hazard another martial law, the army was seen as an obvious advocate of Bhutto's ouster.

© B.K. Bangash/AP/Wide World Photos

Concern for the economy and charges of government corruption led Pakistan's President Farooq Leghari to dismiss Benazir Bhutto (above) *as prime minister in November 1996.*

President Leghari, who came to power under Bhutto's sponsorship in 1993, also became more independent throughout 1996. His appointment of Lt. Gen. Jehangir Karamat as the new chief of army staff in December 1995 generally was praised for its selection of professional competence over political patronage. As subsequent political and economic issues arose in 1996, President Leghari distanced himself from the prime minister. Finally, the inability of the government to deal effectively with the economy, other government institutions, or the many charges of corruption apparently outweighed old loyalties, and the president moved to exercise the same powers by which his predecessor had dismissed Bhutto in 1990 and Mian Nawaz Sharif in 1993.

In anticipation of the early 1997 general elections—the fourth elections in less than a decade—the two major parties continued to be Bhutto's PPP and Nawaz Sharif's Pakistan Muslim League. The Jamaati Islami and other Islamic parties were likely to be prominent in the elections, as was the Mohajir Qaumi Movement (MQM), based in urban Sindh. In April 1996 the cricket star Imran Khan, captain of Pakistan's 1992 World Cup championship team, initiated a new political movement, called Tehreeq-e-Insaaf ("Movement

PAKISTAN • Information Highlights

Official Name: Islamic Republic of Pakistan.
Location: South Asia.
Area: 310,402 sq mi (803 940 km^2).
Population (mid-1996 est.): 133,500,000.
Chief Cities (1981 census): Islamabad, the capital, 204,364; Karachi, 5,180,562.
Government: *Head of state,* Farooq Leghari, president (elected Nov. 13, 1993). *Head of government,* Malik Meraj Khalid, prime minister (sworn in Nov. 5, 1996). *Legislature*—Parliament: Senate and National Assembly.
Monetary Unit: Rupee (39.54 rupees equal U.S.$1, Dec. 31, 1996).
Gross Domestic Product (1994 est. U.S.$): $248,500,000,000 (purchasing power parity).
Economic Index (1995, 1992 = 100): *Consumer Prices,* all items, 138.8; food, 144.3.
Foreign Trade (1994 U.S.$): *Imports,* $8,889,000,000; *exports,* $7,365,000,000.

for Justice"); he hoped to make his new party a viable third force against government corruption. His financial backing was from his father-in-law, British billionaire financier James Goldsmith.

Violence in Karachi abated in 1996, so that the year's final death count was likely to be less than the approximately 2,000 in 1995. A strong governmental crackdown on the militant MQM was credited with much of the reduction in intergroup violence in Karachi, but charges of police repression and officially sanctioned violence mounted. Meanwhile, violence increased in Punjab, Pakistan's largest province. Bombings of buses, markets, and a hospital in Punjab killed more than 70 people. It was not clear who was responsible for the bombings, which hit both government and antigovernment targets. In July a bomb blast at the Lahore airport killed four and injured nearly 70. There also was a rise in sectarian violence between majority Sunni groups and the minority Shias. In August gunmen fired on a Shia procession near Multan, in southern Punjab; 18 people were killed, including three of the gunmen.

The Economy. Economic crises exacerbated the prime minister's political problems. In December 1995, the International Monetary Fund (IMF) had agreed to provide Pakistan with a $600 million emergency loan, following cancellation the previous June of a $1.5 billion 1993 loan agreement. Pakistan had agreed to bring down domestic bank borrowing, raise foreign-exchange reserves, lower the budget deficit, and meet revenue-collection targets. However, in May 1996 the IMF suspended the current loan because of alleged governmental corruption and deception. Bhutto's dismissal was welcomed by the IMF and the World Bank, and both promised additional support beyond reinstatement of the suspended loan. Confidence was boosted by Khalid's appointment of senior World Bank official Shahid Javed Burki as financial adviser.

The annual budget, presented June 13, called for 41 billion rupees ($1.2 billion) in new taxes—including 26 billion rupees ($760 million) in new sales taxes—out of a total budget of 500 billion rupees ($14.6 billion). Meanwhile, there remained no income tax on agricultural income and no increase in the modest wealth taxes on the wealthy rural landlords who constitute a backbone of political support for Bhutto's PPP. Business, workers, and urban consumers all found common cause to protest the increased inequities.

A report early in the year suggested that growth in the gross domestic product would exceed the target of 6%, but subsequent strikes and other economic and political problems adversely affected growth. Inflation remained in double digits. The new taxes were intended to bring the budget deficit down from more than 5% to 4%, but tax receipts appeared to be no more than half of what had been projected. Exports also appeared to be falling, leading some economists to predict that Pakistan's trade deficit—a record $3 billion in 1995—might be still larger in 1996. The Karachi Stock Exchange fell about 15%.

International News. Nuclear and arms-sales issues dominated Pakistan's foreign relations throughout most of 1996. On January 27, U.S. President Bill Clinton signed the Brown Amendment, ending a five-year moratorium on U.S. arms sales to Pakistan. Despite concern over nuclear issues, implementation of the amendment released $386 million in military equipment already paid for by Pakistan.

Nuclear confrontation with India remained a major concern. On January 27, India conducted the 15th test of its Prithvi short-range missile, which is capable of carrying nuclear warheads, and threatened deployment along its border with Pakistan. The United States considered sanctions against China and Pakistan for Pakistan's apparent acquisition of Chinese-made M-11 missiles, but ultimately held off.

In neighboring Afghanistan, Pakistan-supported Taliban forces captured Kabul in September. However, Taliban's subsequent oppressive actions, including hanging former leaders and banning women from appearing in public, created widespread alienation, and Bhutto's downfall removed from power Taliban's strongest Pakistani advocate, Home Minister Naserullah Babar.

WILLIAM L. RICHTER
Kansas State University

PARAGUAY

Challenges from the army, organized urban and rural labor, and impeachment-minded legislators tested Paraguay's fledgling democracy in 1996.

Abortive Coup and Politics. A political disagreement between Gen. Lino Oviedo and his commander in chief, President Juan Carlos Wasmosy, led the latter to ask for Oviedo's resignation in April. The general countered by threatening to overthrow the elected regime. Unable to assert his authority over Oviedo, President Wasmosy considered stepping down, but international support for constitutional order soon surfaced from the Organization of American States (OAS), the United States, and neighboring governments. Wasmosy then offered a powerless ministry of defense to the stubborn general, conditional on his resignation from the military. Even though Oviedo accepted the offer, the public did not. While Wasmosy accepted the resignation, he soon withdrew the offer of a cabinet post, purging those officers closest to Oviedo. Retaliating, Oviedo appeared before Congress to denigrate Wasmosy and demand reinstatement. The former officer was taken into custody in June and charged with rebellion. However, an appeals-court judge released Oviedo in August, freeing him to pursue his presidential ambitions, even though a lesser charge of sedition remained.

Election for chairman of the highly factionalized, but dominant, Colorado Party was held in April. Luis María Argaña, a holdover from former dictator Alfredo Stroessner's regime, easily won. The victory moved Argaña closer to the party's 1998 presidential nomination and forced cabinet changes. Argaña's Colorado Reconciliation faction in Congress has opposed both Oviedo and Wasmosy since 1993.

Local-government contests were held on November 18. While the Colorado Party remained dominant, it was unable to recapture the Asunción city hall, which was won by Martin Burt of the opposition Authentic Liberal Radical Party, allied with the National Encounter Party.

General Strikes and the Economy. General strikes took place on March 28, May 2–3, and August 28, triggered by price increases on utilities in February. Pressed for a 31% across-the-board wage boost and an end to the government's neoliberal policies, price controls, and war against corruption within the public sector, the president offered only a minimum-wage hike of 10% and a U.S.5¢ per 2.2 lbs (1 kg) subsidy to cotton growers. The agriculture minister resigned, and the justice minister was replaced. Some leaders called for an impeachment of the chief executive. Coincidentally, a Supreme Court ruling allowed the expropriation of a 40,000-acre (16 187-ha) farm for distribution to some 5,000 rural families.

About 62% of Paraguayan exports during the first six months of the year went to Mercosur, the four-country Southern Cone common market, with Brazil taking an 87% share. Export earnings through May amounted to $426 million, with soya accounting for almost half of the sales abroad. Wasmosy readied a second phase of privatization, targeting telecommunications, social security, and two banks. Planners estimated in March that privatization would involve dismissing 100,000 public employees, and it was opposed by Argaña and organized labor.

While foreign investment was negligible, Inter-American Development Bank (IDB) loans included $150 million for social-security-system reform. Paraguay's foreign debt reached $1.3 billion in June. An inflation rate of 9.7% was forecast in October. Economic growth continued, with a rate of 2.7% expected for the year.

International Affairs. The Declaration of Viña del Mar, signed in November by Ibero-American governments, incorporated a plan for multilateral action by states in defense of threatened democracies. An agreement was announced in November between Bolivia and Argentina on utilization of Pilcomayo River water. Obligated by membership in Mercosur, Paraguay would pave 150 mi (241 km) of its Trans-Chaco highway. After 36 years, consular relations were reestablished with Cuba in August.

LARRY L. PIPPIN
University of the Pacific

PARAGUAY • Information Highlights

Official Name: Republic of Paraguay.
Location: Central South America.
Area: 157,046 sq mi (406 750 km²).
Population (mid-1996 est.): 5,000,000.
Chief Cities (1992 census): Asunción, the capital, 502,426; Ciudad del Este, 133,896; San Lorenzo, 133,311.
Government: *Head of state and government,* Juan Carlos Wasmosy, president (sworn in Aug. 15, 1993). *Legislature*—Congress: Chamber of Senators and Chamber of Deputies.
Monetary Unit: Guaraní (2,095.0 guaraníes equal U.S.$1, market rate, August 1996).
Gross Domestic Product (1994 est. U.S.$): $15,400,000,-000 (purchasing power parity).
Economic Index (1995, 1992 = 100): *Consumer Prices,* all items, 164.2; food, 173.0.
Foreign Trade (1994 U.S.$): *Imports,* $2,370,000,000; *exports,* $817,000,000.

People, Places, and Things

The following four pages recount the stories behind a selection of people, places, and things that may not have made the headlines in 1996 but that drew attention and created interest.

© Bob Strong/Sipa

Addressing the Democratic National Convention in August 1996, actor Christopher Reeve (above), who is a quadriplegic as the result of a 1995 horseback-riding accident, spoke of the need for increased funding for medical research. In February, Russian chess great Gary Kasparov (below) won a well-publicized chess match against the IBM computer "Deep Blue." Kasparov captured three games and scored a draw in two; "Deep Blue" took the first game.

© H. Rumph, Jr./AP/Wide World Photos

© Mike Fiala/AP/Wide World Photos

© Steve Helber/AP/Wide World Photos

The new twin Petronas Towers (top), *the headquarters of Malaysia's oil monopoly in Kuala Lumpur, became the world's tallest buildings at 1,483 ft (452 m), exceeding Chicago's Sears Tower. A statue of the late African-American tennis great Arthur Ashe was unveiled on Monument Avenue—a Richmond, VA, street famous for its statues of Confederate heroes. Objects belonging to Jacqueline Kennedy Onassis, including items from her years as U.S. first lady, were auctioned off at Sotheby's in the spring. The four-day sale earned $34.5 million.*

© Justin Sutcliffe/Sipa

© Denis Reggie/AP/Wide World Photos

In a private ceremony in a tiny church on Georgia's remote Cumberland Island on September 21, John F. Kennedy, Jr., the son of the late president and Jacqueline Kennedy Onassis, married Carolyn Bessette, 30, who has worked in fashion public relations. The 35-year-old Kennedy, the founder of the magazine "George," had been called "America's most eligible bachelor."

© William Mercer McLeod

With corporate downsizing continuing in the U.S. business world in 1996, the Dilbert cartoon strip—created by Scott Adams (right), *a former middle manager for Pacific Bell—was appearing in more than 1,000 newspapers. In the cartoon, corporate ineptitude is rewarded with advancement to management. Meanwhile, "The Dilbert Principle," a collection of Adams' cartoons and observations, was a 1996 nonfiction best-seller, and the Dilbert Zone Web site was receiving 1.6 million hits daily.*

© Renato Rotolo/Gamma-Liaison

© Liaison

Also during 1996, the theme restaurant remained as popular as ever, the woman's two-piece bathing suit (the bikini) turned 50, and the macarena was the new dance craze at weddings, parties, and ballparks (below). *Peter Morton, who began the theme-restaurant trend by cofounding the Hard Rock Cafe chain* (above left) *in 1971, and his partners sold their interest in the chain to a British entertainment company in 1996. The first two-piece bathing suit was unveiled by France's Louis Réard at a Paris swimming pool on July 5, 1946. Actress Marilyn Monroe* (above right) *helped publicize it. The macarena—a line dance done to a tune recorded by Los Del Rio, a Spanish guitar-playing duo, in 1993—was featured at the Summer Olympics and the Democratic National Convention.*

© Michael Clevenger/AP/Wide World Photos

PERU

Peru's President Alberto Fujimori watched his popularity decline slowly but continuously throughout 1996, the first year of his second term. The reasons for the decline—from more than 70% approval to 50%—were a deliberate economic slowdown, resistance to privatization, opposition to a presidential adviser, and a resurgence of political violence. However, Fujimori's supporters maintained a commanding majority in Congress, which succeeded in blocking opposition to government initiatives.

Economics. One of the most important reasons for Fujimori's high initial popularity was his success at transforming a collapsing economy with 7,000% inflation in 1990 into the fastest-growing economy in Latin America in 1995, with inflation down to almost 10%. However, Economy and Finance Minister Jorge Camet agreed with the International Monetary Fund that inflation would accelerate if such rapid growth continued. The resultant policies, adopted in late 1995, produced negative growth in the first quarter of 1996.

The poor economic performance led to the resignation of Prime Minister Dante Córdova Blanco. He was replaced by Alberto Pandolfi Arbulu, who was more in agreement with Camet. Pandolfi supported a new wave of budget cuts, tax hikes, and wage restraint, which succeeded in slowing the pace of inflation to a 4% annual rate by September. However, the austerity moves increased the anxieties of the underemployed and unemployed waiting for higher-paying jobs to be created.

Opposition also was galvanized by an announcement in January that the state-owned oil company, Petroperu, would be sold to private investors. The leftist General Confederation of Peruvian Workers and the broad-based Union for Peru (which had backed former United Nations Secretary-General Javier Pérez de Cuéllar for president in 1995) immediately launched a petition drive to call a referendum to stop the privatization. Labor leaders feared that a privatized oil company would fire many workers; indeed, more than 4,000 had been laid off already. (Government officials asserted that such moves were needed to ensure the company's profitability.) Public-opinion polls showed that the public overwhelmingly opposed the move at first, although opinion became more evenly divided as the year progressed.

Politics. Some observers interpreted the resignation of Minister of the Presidency Jaime Yoshiyama in September as a sign of disenchantment within the president's own camp, as Yoshiyama had been considered a possible successor to Fujimori. Yoshiyama himself, however, claimed that his resignation was a personal decision to retire from politics.

Peru faced a resurgence of political violence in 1996. In August, security commandos (below) *countered advances made by the Maoist Shining Path, while Marxist guerrillas gained headlines in December after taking hundreds of hostages at an embassy in Lima.*

© Vera Lentz/Reuters/Archive Photos

PERU • Information Highlights

Official Name: Republic of Peru.
Location: West coast of South America.
Area: 496,224 sq mi (1 285 220 km^2).
Population (mid-1996 est.): 24,000,000.
Chief Cities (mid-1991 est.): Lima, the capital, 6,414,500 (metropolitan area); Arequipa, 624,500; Trujillo, 521,200.
Government: *Head of state,* Alberto Fujimori, president (took office July 28, 1990). *Head of government,* Alberto Pandolfi Arbulu, prime minister (sworn in April 3, 1996). *Legislature* (unicameral)—Congress.
Monetary Unit: New sol (2.577 new sols equal U.S.$1, official rate, Dec. 31, 1996).
Gross Domestic Product (1994 est. U.S.$): $73,600,000,000 (purchasing power parity).
Economic Index (Lima, 1995; 1990 = 100): *Consumer Prices,* all items, 1,806.4; food, 1,483.4.
Foreign Trade (1995 U.S.$): *Imports,* $9,224,000,000; *exports,* $5,575,000,000.

Despite Fujimori's increasing vulnerability to criticism, he still could count on the support of his loyal Change 90–New Majority Party majority in the unicameral Congress. In April he declared a state of emergency—without congressional opposition—in the coca-growing regions of the country. During the same month, his congressional supporters threw an obstacle in the path of the antiprivatization petition drive by requiring the support of 40% of the Congress, in addition to a petition of 10% of the electorate, before any referendum would be authorized.

In June, Congress gave Fujimori decree powers for three months on a limited range of economic issues. Most significantly, in August the pro-Fujimori majority approved an interpretation of the 1993 constitution that would allow Fujimori to run for a third term in the year 2000, on the grounds that his first term was served under the 1979 constitution. Court challenges to the decision were not exhausted, however.

Violence and Corruption. The resurgence of political violence was another blow to Fujimori's prestige because one of his most-heralded accomplishments was the arrest of much of the leadership of the Shining Path, a Maoist guerrilla organization. Many Shining Path cadres responded to an offer of amnesty after 1992, when the founder of the movement was captured. But in mid-1996 it became clear that the organization had not been defeated, as a surviving faction led by Oscar "Feliciano" Ramírez Durand carried out several car bombings in urban areas and brief occupations of several towns in the upper Huallaga Valley.

The year's most dramatic rebel attack occurred on December 17, when roughly 25 Marxist guerrillas with the Túpac Amaru Revolutionary Movement stormed the Japanese embassy in Lima during a major diplomatic party. The rebels held hostage more than 400 international dignitaries, demanding the release of hundreds of their comrades in prison. Diplomatic efforts by the Red Cross, Peruvian government, and officials from other nations in the following two weeks helped secure the release of hundreds of hostages, but made little progress toward a broader solution. As the new year began, the rebels still held about 80 captives and were sticking to their original demands.

In September opposition politicians drew attention to a former drug trafficker named Demetrio "El Vaticano" Chávez Peñaherrera, who charged that the president's top adviser had protected cocaine traffickers in 1991 and 1992. The accused adviser, Vladimiro Montesinos, was regarded as being extraordinarily influential in the Fujimori administration despite having served as an attorney for drug traffickers and having been tried for treason (but acquitted) in 1984 due to alleged ties to the U.S. Central Intelligence Agency. Congressional hearings on the matter ended when three cabinet ministers testified on Montesinos' behalf and the U.S. State Department denied any knowledge of links between government officials and drug traffickers.

MICHAEL COPPEDGE, *University of Notre Dame*

PHILIPPINES

During 1996 the Philippines celebrated 50 years of independence from the United States with elaborate festivities marking the July 4th date. Other causes for the nation to celebrate were striking economic growth and an August peace accord with longtime Muslim secessionists in the south.

Peace Accord. The peace accord between the Moro National Liberation Front (MNLF) and the Ramos administration—formally signed on September 2—capped a lengthy government effort to end the three-decade military struggle in the south. There was hope that a lasting peace could accelerate the long-delayed development of the southern Philippines and limit the immense economic and human costs of the prolonged struggle.

At one time, the southern Philippines was predominantly Muslim, but political policies in this century have diluted Muslims' strength by facilitating Christian migration to the resource-rich areas. In 1972 a major guerrilla secessionist effort led by the MNLF and its leader Nur Misuari forced the regime of Ferdinand Marcos to keep much of the Philippine army fighting in the region for years. Libya helped to broker the Tripoli Accord in 1976, which called for elections and regional autonomy. While some efforts to implement the Tripoli Accord were made, the peace process broke down and sporadic fighting resumed. Complicating the peace talks of the successor regime of Corazon Aquino was the breakdown of Muslim resistance into several groups.

The 1996 peace accord honored many of the stipulations of the 1976 agreement. The pact scheduled a plebiscite to approve a new regional government to be headed by Misuari and outlined plans to integrate some MNLF troops into the national army. Minority Muslim factions and Christian settlers in the region were not represented at the talks, generating some concerns that the agreement could unravel.

Another group, the New People's Army—the military arm of the Communist Party of the Philippines (CPP)—also was on the wane. Without the Cold War and the presence of U.S. military bases to oppose, the communists had lost much of their appeal. Reports indicated that the CPP was attempting to negotiate a settlement with the Philippine government late in 1996.

Domestic Affairs. On the overall political scene, the chronic and serious problems of corruption and crime kept Manila's tabloids filled with lurid tales of wrongdoing during the year. A study reported that the Philippines ranked 11th among the 45 countries studied in terms of corruption. Most of the countries with severe corruption problems were far more underdeveloped, both politically and economically, than the Philippines. Even the ombudsman selected to deal with the unresponsive system became embroiled in charges of corruption and of failing to investigate allegations of abuse. An effort to impeach him failed, reputedly after congressmen were bought off.

The scandal that most captured the news was the misuse of the so-called "Pork-Barrel Fund," used by members of Congress for costly infrastructure projects and payoffs to important constituents. The use of such money was not believed to be new, but the investigative reporting of it was. Several of the accused legislators threatened a massive lawsuit against the newspaper that had publicized the scandal. The public reacted with unprecedented fury against the congressmen, who soon after dropped the suit. As the issue lingered, editorials cheered the public anger against corruption as a hopeful sign that Philippine democracy was maturing.

Meanwhile, a year after 1995 congressional elections, postelection irregularities continued to gain attention. Many members of the commission on elections resigned due to persistent questions about a number of Senate races and the lackluster performance of the commission's chairman.

Crime also remained a serious concern. Kidnappings of wealthy businesspeople and their children were a growing problem. Such crimes often went unreported because of assumptions about the dishonesty or ineffectiveness of the police. Many kidnappings were targeted at wealthy Chinese, who have little political clout. In general, most ransoms were paid and few kidnappers were caught. As a result, kidnappings were beginning to affect more middle- and working-class families.

As the 1998 presidential election grew nearer, politicians were jockeying for power. President Ramos was limited to a single six-year term under the 1987 constitution. Though the president was having the most successful administration in modern memory, his past association with discredited dictator Ferdinand Marcos and the democratic but troubled term of President Corazon Aquino made many wary. Ramos repeatedly said that he would not seek a constitutional amendment to permit him to run for reelection. However, with the scars of Marcos' 20-year rule still fresh and with only one peaceful transfer of power under the new constitution, people remained dubious.

Economy. The first half of 1996 saw robust economic growth. The nation's gross national product (GNP) grew at an annualized rate of 7.7% in the second quarter, exceeding even the most optimistic forecasts. Overall gross-domestic-product (GDP) growth was forecast to surpass 4.7% for the year, while inflation was running at 8.5%. Agriculture, which had

PHILIPPINES • Information Highlights

Official Name: Republic of the Philippines.
Location: Southeast Asia.
Area: 115,830 sq mi (300 000 km^2).
Population (mid-1996 est.): 72,000,000.
Chief Cities (1990 census): Manila, the capital, 1,601,234; Quezon, 1,669,776; Davao, 849,947; Caloocan, 763,415, Cebu, 610,417.
Government: *Head of state and government,* Fidel V. Ramos, president (sworn in June 30, 1992). *Legislature* (bicameral)—Senate and House of Representatives.
Monetary Unit: Peso (26.30 pesos equal U.S. $1, floating rate, Dec. 31, 1996).
Gross Domestic Product (1994 est. U.S.$): $161,400,-000,000 (purchasing power parity).
Economic Indexes (1995, 1990 = 100): *Consumer Prices,* all items, 163.9; food, 155.1. *Industrial Production,* 152.
Foreign Trade (1995 U.S.$): *Imports,* $28,337,000,000; *exports,* $17,502,000,000.

© Enny Nuraheni/Reuters/Archive Photos

In 1996 the Moro National Liberation Front (MNLF), a Muslim separatist group, and the Philippine government concluded a peace accord to end three decades of military conflict. MNLF leader Nur Misuari (left) *and Indonesian Foreign Minister Ali Alatas* (right) *were leading players in the historic agreement, which was signed formally on September 2.*

done poorly in 1995, leading to shortages in rice and other commodities, was doing much better in 1996. Even the old nemesis, tax collection, was improving, from a disgraceful 9.6% of GNP in the 1970s to a less dismal 15.5% in 1996.

In April the World Bank reported further evidence of economic strength. Exports were soaring while investor confidence was growing. There was a 500% increase in investment between 1994 and 1995. Even the poverty rate declined (though some critics charged that it had been redefined to assure rosier figures). Once a sordid monument to Philippine poverty, a towering garbage dump called Smokey Mountain was leveled. For years, hundreds had lived and scavenged among the 5,000 tons of Manila's trash dumped there daily. In its place, low-income housing was rising.

Remittances from Filipinos working abroad soared in 1996, but the number of people working overseas declined slightly. The government more aggressively was protecting the rights of overseas workers and monitoring their living conditions. On several occasions, officials intervened diplomatically in the Middle East to reduce sentences against overseas Filipinos accused of capital crimes.

The economy still faced major challenges. The World Bank identified many systemic problems. The agrarian reform targeted to be finished in 1988 was stalled. Landlessness and tenancy problems continued to haunt efforts at rural development. The budget was bloated by an overblown bureaucracy and crushing debt. The domestic savings rate was the lowest in Asia and income distribution remained among the most unequal in the world. Studies estimated that one third of Manila's residents were living as illegal squatters on public or private land.

Many officials asserted that these problems were linked to the nation's 2.1% population growth. Though the Ramos government achieved modest success with population-planning campaigns, it came at a high political cost. The Roman Catholic Church, which claims 83% of the population as parishioners, has been relentless in its opposition to the first Protestant president's initiatives in this area.

Even though national law prohibits children under the age of 14 from working, the Philippines was reported to have more than 15% of its 30 million children working as child laborers. Roughly 1 million reportedly were working in hazardous conditions or at full-time jobs.

Foreign Relations. Against the recommendation of the United States and most European governments, the Philippines voted with all other members of the Association of Southeast Asian Nations (ASEAN) in July to admit Myanmar to observer status. In September, President Ramos nominated his sister, Leticia Shahani, a veteran diplomat, for the position of secretary-general of the United Nations. The Philippines hosted the fourth annual summit of the Asia-Pacific Economic Cooperation (APEC) forum in November.

During 1996 the president traveled to Brunei, Japan, and Thailand, and requested funds for travel to 11 nations in 1997. Though often criticized for his trips abroad, Ramos justified the trips in terms of encouraging foreign investment. The dramatic increases in foreign investment helped blunt much of the criticism.

LINDA K. RICHTER, *Kansas State University*

PHOTOGRAPHY

The year 1996 saw the arrival of dramatic new photographic technology. Highlighting the hardware and software developments was the long-awaited introduction of the Advanced Photo System (APS).

The field of electronic photography continued to garner attention. Contradicting predictions that an affordable digital camera would not be available until after the year 2000, Kodak introduced its DC20, a compact point-and-shoot (P/S) camera good enough for most amateurs, for a cost of less than $300. And Corbis Corporation, a firm owned by Microsoft chairman Bill Gates, purchased the electronic rights to make the images of Ansel Adams and other prominent photographers available in nonprint form.

In the world of auctions, traditional photographs were still the center of attention. Of particular import was a large collection of 19th-century American daguerreotypes auctioned in April at Sotheby's in New York City. The collection of 440 gilt-edge mirror images, all from the estate of Brooklyn, NY, collector Abraham Stransky, brought in $745,864. Some of the well-known Victorians pictured were Jenny Lind and Peter Cooper.

Advanced Photo System (APS). Developed by a consortium of five companies—film manufacturers Kodak and Fuji and camera manufacturers Canon, Minolta, and Nikon—the APS roared in with a wave of nearly 30 cameras and a slew of film products introduced at the annual Photo Marketing Association trade show. The manufacturers positioned this system to give silver-halide photography a new lease on life and to challenge the rapidly emerging field of electronic imaging.

A 24mm-wide film—thinner and stronger than the current 35mm film emulsion—is the key to the new system. Magnetic striping and optical data located on the film edges contain useful information about the film, including its speed, latitude, color aim point, and frame numbers. Such imprinted on-film information can be read by the camera or by a photofinisher. The APS provides photographers with a choice of three picture formats—producing conventional, wide-screen, or panoramic prints.

The new system provides easy-to-load, drop-in, leaderless cassettes that contain 15, 25, or 40 exposures. Processed APS film is returned to customers and stored in the original cassettes, along with an index print of thumbnail-sized images for convenient reprinting reference. Only big film processors initially could handle the photofinishing because the necessary machinery was not available to local developers.

APS camera equipment was designed primarily for amateurs and includes both P/S and single-lens reflex (SLR) models. Basic models were available for less than $100, while top-of-the-line units cost $500 or more. The tiny proportions of the 24mm film format have allowed manufacturers to make more-compact cameras.

The most notable of the new APS cameras designed for P/S photographers was Canon's ELPH, which was only the size of a deck of cards. The ELPH featured a 24–48mm zoom, a space-age look, and hybrid autofocusing, combining the advantages of both active and passive focusing.

Courtesy, Kodak

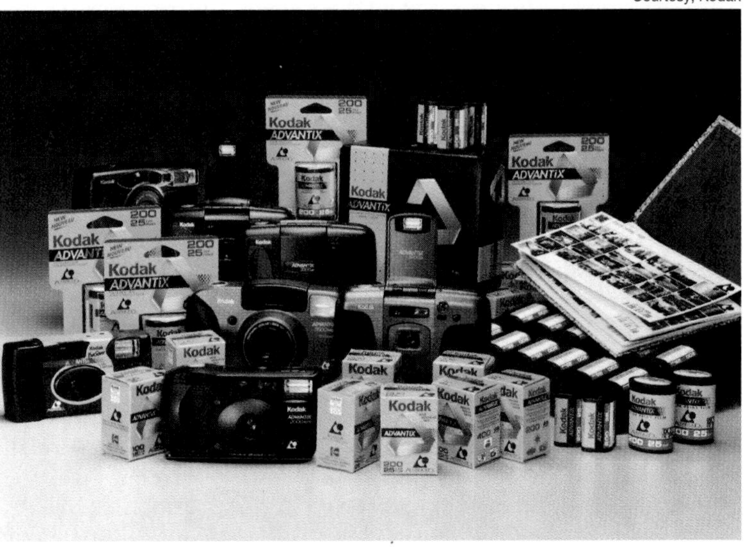

The long-awaited Advanced Photo System (APS) was unveiled in 1996. Featuring a new film format, the APS offers extremely compact cameras, flexible processing, and foolproof film loading. It was developed by Kodak, Fuji, and three camera manufacturers—Canon, Minolta, and Nikon.

Courtesy, Whitney Museum of American Art

Alexander Gardner's images of the California desert were shown in 1996 at New York City's Whitney Museum as part of "Perpetual Mirage: Photographic Narratives of the Desert West," a multimedia exhibition tracing 150 years of photography in the region.

Minolta's Vectis S-1 was the first interchangeable-lens SLR camera designed for the new APS. Thanks to the compact APS film cassette, the camera was roughly half the size of comparable 35mm SLRs, and its body weight was a mere 13 oz (368 g). Among other manufacturers, Canon came out with the EOS IX and Nikon introduced the Pronea 6i, while Fuji brought out the Endeavor 4000 SL, an SLR with a noninterchangeable lens.

Among single-use APS cameras, Fuji's QuickSnap Super Slim contained 400-speed APS film, weighed just 1.4 oz (40 g), and was less than 0.8 inch (2 cm) thick, while the Agfa Easy was the first single-use camera to take advantage of APS multiformatting capabilities.

Nearly every film manufacturer—including Agfa, Fuji, Kodak, and Konica—introduced APS color-print films with great fanfare. Cautiously worded press releases implied that these emulsions are inherently superior to 35mm film emulsions of the same speed; early magazine tests seemed to verify the claims. It was expected that all APS films initially would be about 10 percent higher in cost than 35mm films.

Other Hardware and Software. In the non-APS 35mm market, the trend in P/S cameras toward longer telephoto lenses persisted, extending to 160mm in the Pentax IQZoom 160. Black camera bodies continued to go out of style as gray, brushed-metal, and colorful finishes grew increasingly popular.

The SLR camera arena saw two big introductions. The Contax AX provided autofocus operation with any Zeiss manual-focus lens, doing so by moving not the lens but the film, via the Automatic Back Focusing (ABF) system, a camera within a camera. The other new camera, Nikon's new flagship F5, was the first SLR with a built-in database that adjusts automatically via 1,005 discrete color-sensitive picture elements (pixels). The F5 also included a blazing built-in motor drive capable of advancing eight frames per second. The Pentax ZX-5 typified the still-big retro look in SLRs. Though compact and lightweight, the camera featured dials, buttons, switches, levers, and a chrome finish that were reminiscent of models from the 1960s.

Another noteworthy product introduction was the first 35mm returnable with black-and-white film—the Ilford XP2 single-use camera.

In the video-camera revolution, Sony's Digital Handycam camcorders were the first models to feature the new digital video (DV) format, recording on 6mm tape housed in a tiny 2-inch x 2-inch (5-cm x 5-cm) cassette.

Exhibitions and Publications. New York City hosted a number of noteworthy photo exhibitions. The 100th anniversary of the first publication of photographs in *The New York Times* was celebrated with several exhibits, including one at the Museum of Modern Art (MoMA), where the pictures will be permanently housed. (*See* PUBLISHING—*"The New York Times" at 100.*) "Roy DeCarava: A Retrospective" also was shown at MoMA. This exhibit featured 200 black-and-white prints, including many published in DeCarava's 1955 book on Harlem, *The Sweet Flypaper of Life*.

Also in New York City was a gallery showing of William Klein's black-and-white pictures of the city taken in 1954 and 1955. Many of these hard-edged, fiercely alive, and funny photographs also appeared in a book that was an entirely new version of one published in Paris in 1956 (but never published in the United States). The Whitney Museum of Art hosted "Perpetual Mirage: Photographic Narratives of the Desert West." The show exhibited more than 300 original photographs, books, and albums to explore the social context and implicit messages in photographical campaigns in the American West from 1840 to the present. Also at the Whitney was "Nan Goldin: I'll Be Your Mirror," the first in-depth retrospective of Goldin's photography. Earlier in the year, *I'll Be Your Mirror*, a British film portraying the life and work of the art photographer, made its U.S. debut at the New Festival in New York City.

The Corcoran Gallery of Art in Washington, DC, hosted the show "Hospice: A Photographic Inquiry." It was accompanied by a book of the same title. The traveling show "Harry Callahan," surveying the artist's contribution to American photography, was at the National Gallery of Art. Exhibited at the Museum of Modern Art in San Francisco, CA, was "Crossing the Frontier: Photographs of the Developing West, 1849 to the Present."

The 1996 Summer Olympics in Atlanta, GA—the 100th anniversary of the modern Games—were captured on 175,000 rolls of film by some 900 professional photographers. Also during the Games, an exhibition called "Picturing the South: 1860 to the Present" was shown at Atlanta's High Museum of Art. It contained the work of more than 100 photographers whose images have shaped the nation's view of the South. Former *Rolling Stone* photographer Annie Leibovitz turned images of U.S. Olympic athletes into art in her book *Annie Leibovitz: Olympians*.

BARBARA LOBRON
Writer, Editor, Photographer

PHYSICS

In 1996 physicists confirmed the discovery of a new state of matter called the Bose-Einstein condensate, while new studies explored neutrino oscillation and the substructure of the proton.

Bose-Einstein Condensation. A Colorado research team became the first to observe a new state of matter first predicted in 1924 by Albert Einstein. Einstein's prediction concerned the behavior of atoms chilled to near-absolute-zero temperatures—0°K (-460°F or -273°C). Under such conditions, the atoms slow down dramatically. According to a property called the Heisenberg uncertainty principle, if the momentum of an atom is well defined—in this case, nearly zero—uncertainty in the atom's position grows large. The wave function, which describes the atom's position in terms of probabilities, spreads out. Einstein reasoned that if enough atoms could be cooled, their wave functions would merge and overlap, so that individual atoms no longer would be distinguishable. This effect in a gas became known as Bose-Einstein condensation long before it ever was seen.

Similar quantum phenomena have been observed in solids (superconductivity) and liquids (superfluidity). However, because Bose-Einstein condensates are still gases, their behavior is easier to study than comparable effects in solids and liquids, where chemical interactions between particles are more significant. However, these same properties make the formation of a Bose-Einstein condensate exceptionally difficult. Scientists must cool the material to extremely low temperatures, trap the atoms, and then find some way to observe the condensation.

Eric Cornell, Carl Wieman, and colleagues at the Joint Institute for Laboratory Astrophysics (JILA) at the National Institute of Standards and Technology (NIST) and the University of Colorado were the first to observe a Bose-Einstein condensate. They reached the ultralow temperature by a combination of laser cooling (using laser light to slow down atoms) and evaporative cooling (using magnetic fields to trap atoms in a shallow well and to repel faster-moving, and thus hotter, atoms out of the trap). Using these procedures, the scientists produced a cloud of rubidium-87 atoms, with a few thousand atoms in one quantum state, which lasted for 15 seconds. Researchers also were able to generate images of the condensate.

Within a few months, the new state of matter was observed again by physicists at the Massachusetts Institute of Technology (MIT) in Cambridge. They reported condensates with more than 250 times the number of atoms observed in the first experiment.

Neutrino Oscillations. New data and improved analysis announced in 1996 by scientists from Los Alamos National Laboratory (LANL) in New Mexico provided strengthened evidence that neutrinos have a mass and can change form. Similar, though more preliminary, results reported the previous year implied such a large and unexpected neutrino mass that much criticism was directed at the experimental results. The issue is so important that two new large-scale projects to detect neutrino oscillations have been planned.

Detecting neutrinos—neutral, nearly massless particles that interact very weakly with matter—is exceptionally difficult, and finding their mass is even more challenging. The particles have other puzzling characteristics. The solar neutrino problem, for example, refers to the discrepancy between the number of neutrinos expected to be emitted by the Sun and the number actually measured. Another difficulty—the atmospheric neutrino problem—concerns the smaller-than-expected number of neutrinos generated by cosmic rays striking the upper atmosphere. One proposed explanation of these problems is that neutrinos change in flight from one type of neutrino to another—a phenomenon known as neutrino oscillation.

In the LANL experiment, physicists used a particle accelerator to generate many subatomic particles, including muon neutrinos. (Neutrinos come in three types—electron, muon, and tau—along with their antimatter counterparts.) Significantly, particles known as electron neutrinos were not produced by the reaction. The newly created neutrinos were aimed into a massive neutrino detector containing baby oil and surrounded by photodetectors. This apparatus, the liquid scintillator neutrino detector (LSND), was designed to detect only electron neutrinos. The observation of electron neutrinos thus would imply that the neutrinos changed or oscillated in flight.

New analysis of a data set twice as large as the one first presented in 1995 was consistent with the initial results, indicating that neutrinos do oscillate and thus have mass. However, the implied mass difference between the electron and muon neutrinos from the LSND experiment fails to solve the solar neutrino or atmospheric neutrino problems.

Two new experiments on neutrino oscillations have been planned, both with a much longer distance separating the source and detectors. U.S. scientists plan to create neutrinos at Fermi National Accelerator Laboratory (Fermilab) in Batavia, IL, and to detect them in an unused iron mine in northern Minnesota some 460 mi (740 km) away. This project was expected to be operational by about 2001. Meanwhile, in Japan there were plans to generate neutrinos at the KEK proton synchrotron in Tsukuba and detect neutrinos at Super-Kamiokande—a detector located in an old zinc mine some 155 mi (250 km) away.

Quark Structure of Proton. In 1995, after years of experiments at Fermilab, the definitive observation of the top quark was announced. According to the Standard Model—a broad theory that explains elementary particles and their interactions—all matter is composed of quarks and particles called leptons (of which the electron and the neutrino are most familiar). Quarks are classified into six types—up, down, strange, charm, bottom, and top. These particles have many remarkable properties, including fractional charge.

With the existence of the top quark established, focus has shifted to remaining questions. In 1987 scientists with the European Muon Collaboration at CERN, the European high-energy laboratory in Geneva, announced that very little of the proton's spin is due to the three quarks that make up the particle. This result led to the so-called "spin crisis." Further studies indicated that the proton contains not only three quarks from the first generation (up and down), but also a number of strange quark-antiquark pairs.

These results led to a number of experiments, both by U.S. researchers at the Stanford Linear Accelerator Center (SLAC) in California and by a new collaboration at CERN called the Spin Muon Collaboration. After several years of apparent discrepancies, both sets of experiments have yielded similar data. These studies indicate that neither the three up and down quarks nor the quark-antiquark pairs carry much of the spin. As a result, scientists were planning more studies to further their understanding of the proton and to solve the spin crisis.

GARY MITCHELL
North Carolina State University

POLAND

During 1996, Poland experienced remarkably rapid economic growth, accompanied by some familiar political and social conflicts. The nation's foreign-policy efforts largely were focused on achieving greater integration with Western Europe.

Government and Politics. On the political front, the year began with the dramatic resignation of Premier Józef Oleksy, a former communist who was accused of having been a spy for the Soviet Union and Russia between 1990 and 1995. Oleksy, who had served as premier since February 1995, resigned on January 24, when he made a television speech to the nation simultaneously announcing his resignation and protesting his innocence. Treasonous ties to a former Soviet intelligence official, Col. Vladimir Alganov, were alleged. However, according to some prominent former Solidarity dissidents—notably Jacek Kuron and Karol Modzelewski—Oleksy was being framed by officials supportive of former President Lech Walesa who were seeking to discredit and undermine the regime of newly elected (and also formerly communist) President Aleksander Kwasniewski. Oleksy was elected as the leader of the Social Democratic Party, the principal component of the SLD, on January 27.

On February 7, Wlodzimierz Cimoszewicz was sworn in as Oleksy's replacement. Cimoszewicz, 45, had been deputy speaker of the Sejm (lower house of parliament) and also was a former communist. His elevation to the premiership resulted from cooperation between the formerly communist Alliance of the Democratic Left (SLD) and the leftist Polish Peasant Party, which together controlled a majority in the Sejm. The new cabinet consisted of 20 ministers, most of them holdovers from the Oleksy administration and largely drawn from the SLD.

On April 22, Col. Slawomir Gorzkiewicz, the military prosecutor who headed the official investigation of the spy charges against Oleksy, announced that there was "no direct proof" against the former premier. Meanwhile, former President Walesa denounced this finding as a political cover-up. The "Oleksy affair" illustrated a continuing sharp cleavage in Polish society over its communist past.

On May 30 the parliament passed a law granting pensions to former presidents of Poland. The pension amounted to roughly half of the salary of the sitting president and various additional benefits. The legislation granted pensions to Lech Walesa, who had served from 1990 to 1995; Ryszard Kaczorowski, who served as the last president of the London-based government in exile; and, somewhat surprisingly in view of the 1995 criminal charges against him, Gen. Wojciech Jaruzelski, the last leader of communist Poland and the man who had directed the use of force against the Solidarity freedom movement in the 1980s. (In late October the parliament voted to abandon all criminal charges against Jaruzelski.) Since leaving the office of president, Lech Walesa frequently had protested the lack of presidential pensions in Poland and, in fact, returned in April to his old job as an electrician at the Gdansk shipyard. Late in November, prosecutors in Warsaw began conducting an investigation that allegedly concerned the unlawful seizure and destruction of state documents by Walesa shortly before the end of his term in 1995.

Economy. Poland continued to experience robust economic growth. In October industrial production stood 13.9% higher than it had a year earlier. There was also good news on the inflation front, with prices rising about 19.4% in the 12 months ending in November 1996. That figure was in marked contrast to several previous years, when the pace of inflation exceeded 30%. It appeared likely in the fall that Poland would continue to lead all European nations in its rate of growth, which stood at about 7%. There was continuing substantial investment throughout the year by large U.S. and other foreign companies—such as General Motors, Philip Morris, and Texaco—in the Polish economy. While economic development and privatization continued at a brisk pace, not all sectors of the Polish economy benefited from the new emphasis on profitability and competition.

In a development full of historical irony, the Gdansk shipyard, birthplace of Lech

POLAND • Information Highlights

Official Name: Republic of Poland.
Location: Eastern Europe.
Area: 120,726 sq mi (312 680 km²).
Population (mid-1996 est.): 38,600,000.
Chief Cities (Dec. 31, 1994 est.): Warsaw, the capital, 1,640,700; Lodz, 828,500; Kraków, 746,000.
Government: *Head of state,* Aleksander Kwasniewski, president (took office December 1995). *Head of government,* Wlodzimierz Cimoszewicz, prime minister (took office Feb. 7, 1996). *Legislature*—National Assembly: Senat and Sejm.
Monetary Unit: Zloty (2.87 zlotys equal U.S.$1, Dec. 31, 1996).
Gross Domestic Product (1994 est. U.S.$): $191,100,000,000 (purchasing power parity).
Economic Indexes (1995, 1990 = 100): *Consumer Prices,* all items, 556.7; food, 461.6. *Industrial Production,* 124.
Foreign Trade (1995 U.S.$): *Imports,* $29,050,000,000; *exports,* $22,892,000,000.

© Joe Marquette/AP/Wide World Photos

During a July 1996 visit to the White House, Polish President Aleksander Kwasniewski (left) *and U.S. President Bill Clinton discussed military affairs and Poland's pursuit of North Atlantic Treaty Organization (NATO) membership.*

Walesa's Solidarity movement of 1980, became a victim of bankruptcy in postcommunist Poland. The government declared in June that the shipyard, 60% state-owned, would be closed within 12 months because it had become debt-ridden and unprofitable. The facility was supposed to reorganize eventually and reopen, largely under private auspices. Concerned with loss of jobs, shipyard workers staged a sit-down strike July 12–13. Government officials brought the strike to an end by promising transitional assistance and future opportunities to shipyard employees.

Church and State. While the year did not produce any dramatic clashes between the Catholic Church and the government, the presidency of former communist Aleksander Kwasniewski, with a government and a parliament led by former communists, all contributed to increased estrangement between the two entities. The continued availability and practice of abortion were frowned upon by church leaders. Measures relaxing Poland's abortion guidelines were signed into law in November. The church offered strong criticism of the new guidelines, which would allow doctors to perform abortions through the 12th week of pregnancy, legalize abortions for financial or emotional reasons, and let private clinics perform abortions.

In October, Catholic circles in Poland experienced great anxiety over the health of the Polish-born pontiff, Pope John Paul II, who underwent an appendectomy, was reported to be suffering from a form of Parkinson's disease, and generally appeared to be in frail health. Fears were eased somewhat by the pope's subsequent strong recovery.

Polish-Jewish Issues. In July the government undertook two measures intended to improve Polish-Jewish relations. On July 7, Premier Cimoszewicz attended ceremonies acknowledging and commemorating the 50th anniversary of the pogrom in the southern town of Kielce, where 42 Jews who had survived the Holocaust were murdered by members of the local Polish population. This and other similar events helped precipitate the mass flight of remaining Jews from Poland after World War II. On July 9, President Kwasniewski presented a plan prohibiting commercial development on the site of the Auschwitz-Birkenau death camp, where more than 1.5 million Jews were exterminated by the Nazis. Construction of business facilities, begun in the camp and in the nearby town of Oswiecim in November 1995 under the Walesa presidency, was halted in April. The appropriate preservation and recognition of places of Jewish martyrdom in Poland had been an issue of contention between Polish and Jewish communities for a number of years.

Foreign Relations. Poland continued to seek membership in the North Atlantic Treaty Organization (NATO) and the European Union (EU), in part at least as a hedge against the possible revival of Russia's hegemonic aspirations. Poland also was pursuing substantial investments from abroad. While no dramatic breakthroughs occurred in 1996, policy makers in Western Europe and the United States appeared to be moving closer toward the full acceptance of Poland within the framework of their international institutions. The year 1999 was considered as a likely entrance date by many observers.

Poland participated in the May 30–31 Geneva meeting of some 80 countries to discuss the problem of forced migrations within the Commonwealth of Independent States (CIS), an organization of former Soviet republics. The United Nations (UN) and the Organization for Security and Cooperation in Europe (OSCE) were among the organizations taking part in the event. The conference recommended that CIS countries voluntarily grant citizenship rights to and protect the welfare of all their minorities, thus presumably easing large-scale population movements and international conflicts with spillover effects for Poland and other nations.

In July, President Kwasniewski made his first official visit to the United States where he met with President Bill Clinton and other officials at the White House. Kwasniewski sought early admission of Poland into NATO, and he also discussed acquisition of U.S. aircraft for the Polish military. In July the U.S. Senate passed a resolution favoring the admission of Poland—along with Hungary, Slovenia, and the Czech Republic—into NATO. Poland was recognized as having met membership criteria of civilian control of the military, and serious commitment to human rights and to political democracy. In late October, President Kwasniewski traveled to Britain to confer with Prime Minister John Major on Poland's integration into the Western economic and security systems. In December, Kwasniewski traveled to France, collecting public pledges of support for Poland's entry into NATO and the EU from President Jacques Chirac.

ALEXANDER J. GROTH, *Professor Emeritus*
University of California, Davis

POLAR RESEARCH

Important scientific studies reported in 1996 yielded new findings about the climate, geography, ecology, and geologic history of the polar regions. In addition, the United States approved an international protocol that would extend new environmental protections to Antarctica.

Antarctic. On October 2, President Bill Clinton signed into law a bill giving U.S. approval to the Protocol on Environmental Protection to the Antarctic Treaty. The protocol, which was drafted by 26 nations in 1991, established specific rules for human activities in the region. The measure would allow scientific research in Antarctica, but would limit the discharge of pollutants and ban any mineral extraction. The international pact would not become effective and enforceable until all 26 nations enacted legislation implementing it; as of the October U.S. signing, five countries—Belgium, Finland, India, Japan, and Russia—had not done so yet.

A drilling project in Antarctica yielded the deepest ice-core sample ever extracted from Earth. In January a team of Russian, U.S., and French scientists brought up a 10,984-ft (3 348-m) core using a tubular drill. That length, paired with the extreme density of the Antarctic ice pack, translates into a climatic record stretching back an unprecedented 400,000 years, through at least three ice ages. Glaciologists can deduce climatic information by measuring the concentration of certain element isotopes or identifying the presence of specific types of ash at different depths. Scientists were hopeful that such historical data would provide new insights into Earth's cycles of glaciation.

In June a team of glaciologists reported the discovery that one of the world's largest and deepest freshwater lakes is located 2.5 mi (4 km) beneath the icy Antarctic surface. Although that body, Lake Vostok, first was located in the 1970s, scientists had been unable to measure its size. By analyzing seismic data, researchers calculated that Lake Vostok has a maximum depth of 1,675 ft (510 m) and is as large as Lake Ontario. Many biologists were interested in the announcement because the lake appeared likely to contain microbes that had lived undisturbed for hundreds of thousands of years.

Arctic. A team of Norwegian and U.S. geologists announced in September the discovery of an unusually well-preserved crater on the Arctic seafloor beneath the Barents Sea. Scientists estimated that the large crater, which is about 25 mi (40 km) wide, was formed by a meteorite impact some 130 million years ago. Geologists regarded the presence of shocked quartz and iridium in and near the crater as solid indicators of an extraterrestrial collision.

In February microbiologists led by James Staley of the University of Washington presented evidence refuting a widely held theory that environments with similar conditions should support identical bacterial species. Over a five-year period, the scientists collected bacteria from sea ice from both the North and South poles—and found no common species. The microbiologists also reported that very few of the organisms had been identified previously.

PETER A. FLAX

PORTUGAL

Portugal's Prime Minister António Guterres, a pragmatic socialist, watched his popularity grow in 1996 as he laid the groundwork for his country's participation in the European economic and monetary union (EMU).

Politics. Elections in October 1995 had given Guterres' Socialist Party (PS) 112 of 230 seats in the nation's unicameral legislature. Thus, on controversial questions, the prime minister was forced to seek support from the centrist Social Democratic Party (PSD), which held power from 1985 to 1995. One such issue was the new government's ambitious domestic proposal to decentralize economic-planning functions to yet-to-be-created regions. The initiative remained under study as experts pondered the boundaries of the regions, the functions to be devolved, and the means to obtain approval of the initiative.

In most endeavors, Guterres enjoyed the support of fellow Socialist Jorge Sampaio, who was elected president on January 14. He captured 53.8% of the vote to defeat the PSD candidate, former Prime Minister Aníbal Cavaco Silva, who attained 46.2% of the ballots cast in a contest that drew two thirds of the country's 9 million eligible voters to the polls. For the first time since the restoration of democracy in Portugal in 1974, the nation's president and prime minister hailed from the same party—an outcome that Cavaco Silva decried as a "dictatorship of the majority" in which the PS could ignore other parties.

For their part, Sampaio and Guterres insisted that their having been chosen in tandem enhanced economic stability. They believed that the dour Cavaco Silva would have tried to play the role of "alternative" prime minister if he had won. PSD activists also alleged that the chief executive seldom would use the veto to keep his Socialist brethren in check. Not only can the president exercise veto power, he also can dissolve parliament. Should Guterres have difficulty forging coalitions to pass legislation, Sampaio could call general elections to provide his party with a chance to achieve a working majority.

In a minor embarrassment to the government, Public Works Minister Murteira Nabo resigned on January 12 in reaction to charges of tax evasion.

Economics. In October, Prime Minister Guterres unveiled a budget that, if adhered to, would bolster Portugal's chances of qualifying for a single European currency, the euro. The document anticipated a 3% growth in gross domestic product (GDP), up slightly from 1996, and a drop in inflation from 4.1% to 2.5%. The central financial goal, however, was to reduce the fiscal deficit from 4% of GDP in 1996 to 2.9% in 1997—a figure that falls within the 3% minimum set by the Maastricht Treaty, which governs admission to the EMU. Meanwhile, the government forecast a fall in public debt to 63% of GDP by 1996—only three points above the Maastricht target. Unemployment was at 7.1%, almost four points below the European Union's average.

"The EMU goals are within our reach," Guterres told parliament. "We can achieve them with measures that are in themselves beneficial to the economy and without provoking the social confrontations that have occurred in much richer countries." Luis Marti, vice-president of the European Invest-

© Gamma-Liaison

Supporters of Jorge Sampaio were jubilant as the Socialist Party candidate defeated former Premier Aníbal Cavaco Silva of the Social Democratic Party in Portugal's presidential vote in January 1996.

PORTUGAL • Information Highlights

Official Name: Portuguese Republic.
Location: Southwestern Europe.
Area: 35,552 sq mi (92 080 km^2).
Population (mid-1996 est.): 9,900,000.
Chief Cities (1991 census): Lisbon, the capital, 681,063; Oporto, 309,485; Vila Nova de Gaia, 247,499.
Government: *Head of state,* Jorge Sampaio, president (took office March 1996). *Head of government,* Antonio Guterres, prime minister (took office October 1995). *Legislature* (unicameral)—Assembly of the Republic.
Monetary Unit: Escudo (156.52 escudos equal U.S.$1, Dec. 31, 1996).
Gross Domestic Product (1994 est. U.S.$): $107,300,-000,000 (purchasing power parity).
Economic Indexes (1995): *Consumer Prices* (1991 = 100): all items, 127.1; food, 119.9. *Industrial Production* (1990 = 100): 99.
Foreign Trade (1995 U.S.$): *Imports,* $32,435,000,000; *exports,* $22,632,000,000.

ment Bank, shared the prime minister's optimism: "Outside the core European economies, Ireland and Portugal are the two countries near enough to be included." Investors seemed to agree. In response to Lisbon's success in reducing the deficit and paring the budget shortfall, the differential between Portuguese and German interest rates on ten-year bonds plummeted from 520 to 165 basis points between early 1995 and late 1996.

Guterres' energetic, articulate advocacy of EMU admission contributed to an 80% public support for affiliation. Yet, even noneconomists understood that eliminating foreign-exchange risk within the euro bloc would enhance investor interest in Portugal, thanks to its low labor rates and generous government incentives. The government has made adoption of a European currency "socially tolerable" by boosting outlays on investment and social programs. At the same time officials in Lisbon, mindful of the resentment sparked by a continuing freeze on public-employee salaries in Spain, promised Portuguese civil servants a modest wage increase in 1997.

On the other hand, Cavaco Silva was less sanguine about Portugal's getting in on the EMU's ground floor. The delay in Spain's entry would make Portugal's admission "totally unrealistic," he stated. For his part, Guterres insisted that any decision on the issue should be based on his nation's own merits—separate from consideration of Spain's eligibility. Some observers contended that failure to gain EMU entry would relegate Portugal to the same position as Poland, Hungary, and the Czech Republic, which are only candidates to join the European Union (EU) to which Lisbon has belonged for a decade. "We would lose influence over the future of Europe," a senior official in Cavaco Silva's administration told the *Financial Times.*

Foreign Relations. In October the 185-member UN General Assembly elected Portugal as one of five countries to serve a two-year term on the powerful UN Security Council, beginning Jan. 1, 1997. Portugal attracted votes from scores of Third World states because of its cultural and economic ties to Brazil and former African territories.

In Lisbon in July the Community of Portuguese-Language Countries (CPLC) was formed to enhance commerce and cooperation among Portuguese-speaking nations.

GEORGE W. GRAYSON
College of William and Mary

PRISONS

Continuing a long-term upward trend, more than 5,375,000 people were under the control of the U.S. criminal-justice system in 1996. Official figures at the beginning of the year revealed 1,078,357 in state and federal prisons; 507,044 in local jails; 3,090,000 on parole; and another 700,000 on probation. These growing numbers put considerable economic and legal strains on federal, state, and local governments. Since the mid-1970s, as a public passion to get tough on crime has grown, the number of people in prisons has increased by more than 300%. At the same time the percentage increase in expenditures for corrections has been considerably less. Prison administrators have been increasingly under pressure to eliminate programs, downsize staff, and decrease expenditures wherever possible, while admitting more prisoners.

Economic Strains. Traditionally the vast majority of prisoners in the United States have been the responsibility of state and local jurisdictions, with the federal government offering guidelines and recommendations, but relatively little in federal financial aid. Consequently, most states long have had substantial budgets for prisons. Those budgets have been increasing—slowly but consistently. In 1980 corrections amounted to 1% of state expenditures. By 1996 the figure was 5%. In 1996, at the very point when U.S. prisons were more overcrowded than at any other time in history, the federal government was giving state governments a greater voice in determining just where public funds, including federal support, would be targeted. This includes such crucial areas of direct concern to the public at large—and especially to the poor—as medical care, welfare, education, and prisons.

In 1996, on the average, states increased spending on public and higher education by 5%, on Medicaid by 7%, and on corrections by 13%. California, which once had a higher-education system acknowledged throughout the world for its excellence, now ranked 46th among states in higher-education funding per student. The standard pay for corrections officers exceeded $55,000 per year, considerably higher than salaries in education. Florida, also with an extremely large prison system, spent more in 1996 on incarceration than on education. Texas, presently in the process of building more prisons than any other state, ranked last in public-high-school graduation rates. Ironically, 85% of those imprisoned in Texas were high-school dropouts.

Prisoners' Rights. The year also saw the enactment of federal legislation that curtailed the legal rights of prisoners. The Antiterrorism and Effective Death Penalty Act of 1996, signed into law in April, provided that no death-row inmate may present more than one habeas corpus petition in federal court, except in extraordinary circumstances. Habeas corpus is the sole means through which a prisoner can make a constitutional challenge in his or her case.

In addition, the Prison Litigation Reform Act of 1996, passed as part of the 1996-budget legislation, includes strict and shorter time limits for court orders regarding prison conditions, termination of existing decrees and court orders, and sharp reductions in the availability of attorney fees. The latter act makes it extremely difficult for all inmate plaintiffs to bring cases to the courts. In effect, the act renders void the court orders and decrees that were in place in 36 states, plus the District of Columbia, Puerto Rico, and the Virgin Islands, to limit population or improve conditions in the entire system or in major facilities. Such essential areas of prison life as medical care, mental-health care, legal access, religious freedom, and issues regarding sexual harassment and abuse now must be relitigated and with much less chance of success. The current impasse in prison conditions reflects the growing numbers of prisons and prisoners in the correctional system, as well as pressures to hold the line on correction budgets and the curtailment of the legal rights of prisoners.

In light of these conditions, many experts predict that penal practices will become even more punitive. Several states have revived chain gangs. Recreation and entertainment programs have been eliminated almost entirely. Vocation, education, and training programs have been cut severely. While many of these measures have been encouraged by politicians eager to respond to what they see as public demand, the result is that prisons now are populated by large numbers of idle people, increasingly full of tension and extremely more likely to revolt.

During the past years, Sheriff Joseph M. Arpaio in Arizona, for example, has attracted considerable media attention with his tough tactics, including putting women on chain gangs and housing prisoners in tents. In November some 300 to 400 prisoners under Arpaio took 11 guards hostage and set fire to their tents in protest against what they argued were inadequate medical care, bad food, brutality by the guards, and discomfort at living in overcrowded tents. The prisoners were transferred for several days to other county jails, while negotiations over the conditions were carried out.

New Approaches. There were a few alternatives that could portend a somewhat more positive scenario for the otherwise bleak prison future. One is prison industry—through which prisoners manufacture products or services for the financial benefit of the locale. The practice increasingly is being allowed to operate as a private business in competition with outside businesses. Several states, including New York, are expanding in this area as a way of offsetting the high costs of housing, feeding, and overseeing the burgeoning prison population. The potential profits to governments for the manufacture of such items as furniture and even prefabricated prison cells appear attractive. But the wages paid to inmates, ranging from 15 cents to 50 cents per hour, are attracting the ire of local unions and the affected businesses.

Still another alternative being explored is the privatization of prisons. While services of many types—including food, security equipment, and medical care—long have been provided to prisons by outside contractors, a few private contractors recently have built and run entire correctional facilities. While the privatization movement has affected relatively small numbers of prisoners, the pressure to move further in this direction appears strong. The legal and constitutional issues involved in private companies confining large numbers of convicted citizens barely have reached the courts. The economic benefits to state and local governments so far have been minimal. To date, the main benefit of privatization is a slight lowering of costs, with little change in conditions and methods of imprisonment.

DONALD GOODMAN and ROBERT L. BONN
John Jay College of Criminal Justice

PRIZES AND AWARDS

NOBEL PRIZES[1]

Chemistry (shared): Harold Kroto, Sussex University, England; Robert F. Curl, Jr., and Richard E. Smalley, Rice University, Houston, TX; for their 1985 discovery of fullerenes, or "buckyballs"—unusually shaped molecules of carbon that now are aiding in the development of new medicines and other materials; "No physicist or chemist had expected that carbon would be found in such a symmetrical form other than those already known."

Economics (shared): James A. Mirrlees, Cambridge University, England; William Vickrey, Columbia University, New York, NY; for separate work that made "fundamental contributions to the economic theory of incentives under asymmetric information"

Literature: Wislawa Szymborska, Poland, for "poetry that with ironic precision allows the historical and biological context to come to light in fragments of human reality" (*See* LITERATURE—*Overview*.)

Peace (shared): Bishop Carlos Filipe Ximenes Belo and José Ramos Horta, East Timor, Indonesia, for "their work toward a just and peaceful solution to the conflict in East Timor"

Physics (shared): David M. Lee and Robert C. Richardson, Cornell University, New York; Douglas D. Osheroff, Stanford University, California; for "their discovery of superfluidity in helium-3," which was a "breakthrough in low-temperature physics"

Physiology or Medicine (shared): Peter C. Doherty, St. Jude's Research Hospital, Memphis, TN; Rolf M. Zinkernagel, Institute of Experimental Immunology, Zurich, Switzerland; their research—which uncovered how the immune system's T-cells recognize virus-infected cells—"fundamentally changed our understanding of the development and normal function of the immune system" and led to the development of improved vaccines and new disease therapies

[1]approx. $1,120,000 in each category

ART

American Academy and Institute of Arts and Letters Awards
- Academy-Institute Awards: architecture—Maya Lin; art—Jack Beal, Kerry James Marshall, John Moore, Jim Nutt, Otto Piene; music—Ronald Caltabiano, Richard Danielpour, Anthony Davis, Scott Lindroth
- Award for Distinguished Service to the Arts: Ethelyn Atha Chase
- Award of Merit for Sculpture: George Trakas
- Arnold W. Brunner Memorial Prize in Architecture: Tod Williams and Billie Tsien
- Jimmy Ernst Award in Art: Pat Adams
- Gold Medal for Architecture: Philip Johnson
- Walter Hinrichsen Award in Music: Jing Jing Luo
- Charles Ives Fellowship in Music: Pablo Ortiz
- Goddard Lieberson Fellowships in Music: Richard Campanelli, Chen Yi
- Wladimir and Rhoda Lakond Award in Music: Justin Dello Joio
- Louise Nevelson Award in Art: Debra Bermingham
- Richard and Hinda Rosenthal Foundation Award: Diana Horowitz

Hans Christian Andersen Illustration Award: Klaus Ensikat, Germany

Capezio Dance Award ($10,000)**:** Charles L. Reinhart, president, American Dance Festival

Ditson Conductor's Award for the advance of American music ($1,000)**:** James Bolle, founder and conductor, New Hampshire Symphony Orchestra

George and Ira Gershwin Award for lifetime musical achievement: Tom Petty

Dorothy and Lillian Gish Prize for outstanding contribution to the arts ($200,000)**:** Robert Wilson

Glenn Gould Prize: Toru Takemitsu, Japan (posthumous)

Grawemeyer Award for musical composition ($150,000)**:** Ivan Tcherepnin, *Double Concerto for Violin, Cello, and Orchestra*

John F. Kennedy Center Honors for career achievement in the performing arts: Edward Albee, Benny Carter, Johnny Cash, Jack Lemmon, Maria Tallchief

National Academy of Recording Arts and Sciences Grammy Awards for excellence in phonograph records
- Album of the year: *Jagged Little Pill*, Alanis Morissette
- Classical album: *Debussy: "La Mer"*, Pierre Boulez conducting the Cleveland Orchestra
- Country album: *The Woman in Me*, Shania Twain
- Country song: "Go Rest High on That Mountain," Vince Gill
- Country vocalist: (female)—Alison Krauss, "Baby, Now That I've Found You"; (male)—Vince Gill, "Go Rest High on That Mountain"; (group or duo)—The Mavericks, "Here Comes the Rain"
- Jazz vocalist: Lena Horne, *An Evening with Lena Horne*
- Lifetime achievement: Dave Brubeck, Marvin Gaye, Sir Georg Solti, Stevie Wonder
- New artist: Hootie and the Blowfish
- Pop album: *Turbulent Indigo*, Joni Mitchell
- Pop vocalist: (female)—Annie Lennox, "No More I Love Yous"; (male)—Seal, "Kiss From a Rose"; (group or duo)—Hootie and the Blowfish, "Let Her Cry"
- Record of the year: "Kiss From a Rose," Seal
- Rock album: *Jagged Little Pill*, Alanis Morissette
- Rock song (songwriters' award): "You Oughta Know," Glen Ballard, Alanis Morissette
- Rock vocalist: (female)—Alanis Morissette, "You Oughta Know"; (male)—Tom Petty, "You Don't Know How It Feels"; (group or duo)—Blues Traveler, "Run-Around"
- Song of the year (songwriter's award): "Kiss From a Rose," Seal

National Medal of Arts (presented by President Bill Clinton on Jan. 9, 1997)**:** Edward Albee, Sarah Caldwell, Harry Callahan, Zelda Fichandler, Eduardo "Lalo" Guerrero, Lionel Hampton, Bella Lewitzky, Vera List, Robert Redford, Maurice Sendak, Stephen J. Sondheim, Boys Choir of Harlem

Praemium Imperiale for lifetime achievement in the arts ($150,000 ea.)**:** Tadao Ando, Japan (architecture); Luciano Berio, Italy (music); Cy Twombly, United States (painting); César, France (sculpture); Andrzej Wajda, Poland (theater and film)

Pritzker Architecture Prize ($100,000)**:** José Rafael Moneo (Spain)

Pulitzer Prize for Music: George Walker, *Lilacs*

Samuel H. Scripps/American Dance Festival Award ($25,000)**:** Meredith Monk

JOURNALISM

Maria Moors Cabot Prizes ($1,000 ea.)**:** Dudley Quentin Althaus, Mexico City bureau chief, *Houston Chronicle*; Ramón Alberto Garza García, editor in chief, *Reforma*, Mexico City, and *El Norte*, Monterrey, Mexico; Timothy Jay Johnson, Bogotá bureau chief, *The Miami Herald*; Eduardo Ulibarri Bilbao, editor in chief, *La Nación*, San José, Costa Rica

National Magazine Awards
- Design: *Wired*
- Essays and criticism: *The New Yorker*
- Feature writing: *GQ*
- Fiction: *Harper's Magazine*
- General excellence: *Business Week*, *Outside*, *Civilization*, *The Sciences*
- Hall of Fame awards: Helen Gurley Brown, *Cosmopolitan*; Osborn Elliot, *Newsweek*; Clay Felker, *New York Magazine*; Richard Stolley, *People*; Ruth Whitney, *Glamour*
- Personal service: *SmartMoney*
- Photography: *Saveur*
- Public interest: *Texas Monthly*
- Reporting: *The New Yorker*
- Single-topic issue: *Bon Appétit*
- Special interest: *Saveur*

Overseas Press Club Awards
- Newspaper or wire service reporting from abroad: David Rohde, *The Christian Science Monitor*
- Interpretation of foreign affairs: Susan Sach, *Newsday*
- Photographic reporting: Anthony Suau, *Time*
- Photography: (magazines and books)—David Turnley, Black Star, for *Time*; (newspapers and wire services)—Mindaugas Klilbis, The Associated Press

© Karin Cooper/AP/Wide World Photos

© Muchtar Zakaria/AP/Wide World Photos

José Ramos Horta (left) *and Bishop Carlos Filipe Ximenes Belo* (right) *of East Timor shared the 1996 Nobel Peace Prize for their efforts toward bringing an end to the ongoing conflict between East Timor and Indonesia.*

© Mike Theiler/Reuters/Archive Photos

Recipients of the prestigious John F. Kennedy Center Honors were given their awards at the annual Trustees Dinner in December 1996. The honorees were (left to right) *country musician Johnny Cash, playwright Edward Albee, former ballerina Maria Tallchief, actor Jack Lemmon, and jazz musician Benny Carter.*

Radio news or interpretation of foreign affairs: *All Things Considered*, National Public Radio
Television spot news reporting from abroad: CBS News
Television interpretation or documentary: ABC News
Magazine reporting from abroad: *Time*
Cartoons on foreign affairs: Jack Ohman, *The Oregonian*
Business reporting: *The Wall Street Journal*
Madeline Dane Ross Award (for foreign correspondent in any medium showing a concern for the human condition): Laurie Garrett, *Newsday*
Reporting on human rights: *The Baltimore Sun*
Reporting on international environmental issues: Michael Parfit, *National Geographic*
President's Award: Walter Cronkite, CBS

George Polk Memorial Awards
Business writing: Kurt Eichenwald, *The New York Times*, for series on the failings of the U.S. kidney-dialysis business
Career achievement award: John K. Cooley, ABC News
Consumer reporting: Lea Thompson, Jack Cloherty, Sandra Surles, "Optical Illusion," *Dateline* (NBC)
Education reporting: Steve Stecklow, *The Wall Street Journal*, for series exposing a fraudulent investment scheme
Foreign reporting: David Rohde, *The Christian Science Monitor*, for reports on the Srebrenica massacre of Bosnian Muslims
Health-care reporting: Chris Adams, *The Times-Picayune*, New Orleans, LA, for exposing Medicaid fraud in Louisiana
Local reporting: Elizabeth Llorente, *The Record*, Hackensack, NJ, for exposing inhumane conditions at an Elizabeth, NJ, immigrant detention center
Local television reporting: Tom Grant, KREM-TV, Spokane, WA, for an investigation of an alleged child-sex ring in Wenatchee, WA, that eventually led to the exonerations of the accused participants
Magazine reporting: Richard Behar, "Stalked by Allstate," *Fortune*
Medical reporting: *The Orange County Register*, Santa Ana, CA, for investigating a scandal involving the theft and implantation by fertility doctors of eggs harvested from patients
Metropolitan reporting: Frank Bruni, Nina Bernstein, Joyce Purnick, Lizette Alvarez, *The New York Times*, for coverage of the role of New York City's Child Welfare Administration in the case of Elisa Izquierdo
National reporting: Michael Weisskopf and David Maraniss, *The Washington Post*, for series on the Republican-controlled U.S. House of Representatives
Network television reporting: Jim Clancy, *Rwanda: Cry Justice* (CNN)

Pulitzer Prizes
Beat reporting: Bob Keeler, *Newsday*, Long Island, NY
Commentary: E.R. Shipp, *New York Daily News*
Criticism: Robert Campbell, *The Boston Globe*
Editorial cartooning: Jim Morin, *The Miami Herald*
Editorial writing: Robert B. Semple, Jr., *The New York Times*
Explanatory journalism: Laurie Garrett, *Newsday*, Long Island, NY
Feature photography: Stephanie Welsh, freelance photographer; distributed by Newhouse News Service
Feature writing: Rick Bragg, *The New York Times*
International reporting: David Rohde, *The Christian Science Monitor*
Investigative reporting: staff of *The Orange County Register*, Santa Ana, CA
National reporting: Alix M. Freedman, *The Wall Street Journal*
Public service: *The News & Observer*, Raleigh, NC
Special award: Herb Caen, *San Francisco Chronicle*
Spot news photography: Charles Porter 4th, freelance photographer; distributed by The Associated Press
Spot news reporting: Robert D. McFadden, *The New York Times*

LITERATURE

American Academy and Institute of Arts and Letters Awards
Academy-Institute Awards: Whitney Balliett, Carol Brightman, Robert Fagles, Robert Hughes, August Kleinzahler, Larry Kramer, Paul Muldoon, David Quammen
Witter Bynner Prize for Poetry: Lucie Brock-Broido
E.M. Forster Award in Literature: Jim Crace
Gold Medal for History: Peter Gay
Sue Kaufman Prize for First Fiction:Peter Landesman, *The Raven*
Rome Fellowship in Literature: Randall Kenan
Richard and Hinda Rosenthal Foundation Award: David Long, *Blue Spruce*
Harold D. Vursell Memorial Award: A.J. Verdelle, *The Good Negress*
Morton Dauwen Zabel Award: J.D. Landis, *Lying in Bed*

American Book Awards: Sherman Alexie, *Reservation Blues*; Stephanie Cowell, *The Physician of London*; Chitra Banerjee Divakaruni, *Arranged Marriage*; Maria Espinosa, *Longing*; William Gass, *The Tunnel*; Kimiko Hahn, *The Unbearable Heart*; E.J. Miller Laino, *Girl Hurt*; Chang-rae Lee, *Native Speaker*; James W. Loewen, *Lies My Teacher Told Me: Everything Your American History Textbook Got Wrong*; Glenn C. Loury, *One by One from the Inside Out*; Agate Nesaule, *Woman in Amber: Healing the Trauma of War and Exile*; Joe Sacco, *Palestine*; Ron Sakolsky and Fred Wei-han Ho, eds., *Sounding Off! Music as Subversion/Resistance/Revolution*; Arthur Sze, *Archipelago*; Robert Viscusi, *Astoria*
Children's Book Award: Paul Owen Lewis, *Storm Boy*
Editor/Publisher Award: (book)—Alexander Taylor and Judith Doyle, Curbstone Press; (newspaper)—Niall O'Dowd, *The Irish Voice*
Lifetime Achievement/Journalist Award: Herb Caen
Lifetime Achievement Award: Janice Mirikitani

Anisfield-Wolf Book Award for nonfiction: Jonathan Kozol, *Amazing Grace: The Lives of Children and the Conscience of a Nation*

Hans Christian Andersen Author Award: Uri Orlov, Israel

Bancroft Prizes in American history ($4,000 ea.): David S. Reynolds, *Walt Whitman's America: A Cultural Biography*; Alan Taylor, *William Cooper's Town: Power and Persuasion on the Frontier of the Early American Republic*

Rebekah Johnson Bobbitt National Prize for Poetry ($10,000): Kenneth Koch, *One Train*

Canada's Governor-General Literary Awards ($10,000 ea.)
English-language awards
Children's literature (illustration): Eric Beddows, *The Rooster's Gift*
Children's literature (text): Paul Yee, *Ghost Train*
Drama: Colleen Wagner, *The Monument*
Fiction: Guy Vanderhaeghe, *The Englishman's Boy*
Nonfiction: John Ralston Saul, *The Unconscious Civilization*
Poetry: E.D. Blodgett, *Apostrophes: Woman at a Piano*
French-language awards
Children's literature (text): Gilles Tibo, *Noémie—Le Secret de Madame Lumbago*
Drama: Normand Chaurette, *Le Passage de l'Indiana*
Fiction: Marie-Claire Blais, *Soifs*
Nonfiction: Michel Freitag, *Le Naufrage de l'université—Et autres essais d'épistémologie politique*
Poetry: Serge Patrice Thibodeau, *Le Quatuor de l'errance*; *La Traversée du désert*

Lannan Foundation prizes for distinctive literary merit ($50,000 ea.)
Fiction: Howard Norman, Tim Pears, William Trevor, David Foster Wallace
Lifetime achievement: R.S. Thomas
Nonfiction: David Abram, Charles Bowden
Poetry: Anne Carson, Lucille Clifton, Donald Justice
Medal of Honor for Literature: E.L. Doctorow
Mystery Writers of America/Edgar Allan Poe Awards
Critical or biographical work: Robert Polito, *Savage Art: A Biography of Jim Thompson*
Fact crime: Peter Earley, *Circumstantial Evidence*
First novel: David Housewright, *Penance*
Novel: Dick Francis, *Come to Grief*
Grandmaster award: Dick Francis
Motion-picture screenplay: Christopher McQuarrie, *The Usual Suspects*
Original paperback: William Heffernan, *Tarnished Blue*
Short story: Jean Cooper, "The Judge's Boy"
Television series or miniseries: Chris Gerolmo, *Citizen X* (HBO)
National Book Awards ($10,000 ea.)
Body of work: Toni Morrison
Fiction: Andrea Barrett, *Ship Fever And Other Stories*
Nonfiction: James Carroll, *An American Requiem: God, My Father, and the War That Came Between Us*
Poetry: Hayden Carruth, *Scrambled Eggs & Whiskey: Poems 1991–1995*
Young people's literature: Victor Martinez, *Parrot in the Oven: Mi Vida*
National Book Critics Circle Awards
Biography/autobiography: Robert Polito, *Savage Art: A Biography of Jim Thompson*
Criticism: Robert Darnton, *The Forbidden Bestsellers of Pre-Revolutionary France*
Fiction: Stanley Elkin, *Mrs. Ted Bliss* (posthumous)
Nonfiction: Jonathan Harr, *A Civil Action*
Poetry: William Matthews, *Time and Money*
National Book Foundation Medal for Distinguished Contribution to American Letters ($10,000)**:** Toni Morrison
PEN Literary Awards
Ernest Hemingway Foundation Award for first fiction ($7,500): Chang-rae Lee, *Native Speaker*
PEN/Faulkner Award for fiction ($15,000): Richard Ford, *Independence Day*
L.L. Winship/PEN New England Award: Jane Brox, *Here and Nowhere Else: Last Seasons of a Farm and Its Family*
Pulitzer Prizes
Biography: Jack Miles, *God: A Biography*
Fiction: Richard Ford, *Independence Day*
General nonfiction: Tina Rosenberg, *The Haunted Land: Facing Europe's Ghosts After Communism*
History: Alan Taylor, *William Cooper's Town: Power and Persuasion on the Frontier of the Early American Republic*
Poetry: Jorie Graham, *The Dream of the Unified Field*
Rea Award for the Short Story ($30,000)**:** Andre Dubus, *Dancing After Hours*
Tanning Prize for Poetry ($100,000)**:** Adrienne Rich
Kingsley Tufts Poetry Award ($50,000)**:** Deborah Digges, *Rough Music*
Whiting Writers' Awards for outstanding talent and promise ($30,000 ea.)**:** Christine Garcia, Anderson Ferrell, Brigit Pegeen Kelly, Brian Kiteley, Molly Gloss, Chris Offutt, Elizabeth Spires, Patricia Storace, Judy Troy, A.J. Verdelle

MOTION PICTURES

Academy of Motion Pictures Arts and Sciences ("Oscar") Awards
Actor—leading: Nicolas Cage, *Leaving Las Vegas*
Actor—supporting: Kevin Spacey, *The Usual Suspects*
Actress—leading: Susan Sarandon, *Dead Man Walking*
Actress—supporting: Mira Sorvino, *Mighty Aphrodite*
Cinematography: John Toll, *Braveheart*
Costume design: James Acheson, *Restoration*
Director: Mel Gibson, *Braveheart*
Documentary feature: *Anne Frank Remembered*
Documentary short subject: *One Survivor Remembers*
Film: *Braveheart*
Foreign-language film: *Antonia's Line* (Netherlands)
Honorary awards: Kirk Douglas, Chuck Jones
Original musical or comedy score: Alan Menken and Stephen Schwartz, *Pocahontas*
Original dramatic score: Luis Bacalov, *Il Postino* (*The Postman*)
Original song: Alan Menken and Stephen Schwartz, "Colors of the Wind" (from *Pocahontas*)
Screenplay—original: Christopher McQuarrie, *The Usual Suspects*
Screenplay—adaptation: Emma Thompson, *Sense and Sensibility*
Special achievement award: John Lasseter, *Toy Story*
American Film Institute's Life Achievement Award: Martin Scorsese
Cannes Film Festival Awards
Caméra d'Or (best first film): Shirley Barrett, *Love Serenade* (Australia)
Chevalier of the Legion of Honor for lifetime achievement: Robert Altman (United States)
Palme d'Or (best film): Mike Leigh, *Secrets and Lies* (Great Britain)
Grand Jury Prize: Lars von Trier, *Breaking the Waves* (Denmark)
Jury Prize: David Cronenberg, *Crash* (Canada)
Best actor (shared): Daniel Auteuil and Pascal Duquenne, *Le Huitième Jour* (*The Eighth Day*) (Belgium)
Best actress: Brenda Blethyn, *Secrets and Lies*(Great Britain)
Best director: Joel Coen, *Fargo* (United States)
Best screenplay: Alain le Henry and Jacques Audiard, *Un Heros Très Discret* (*A Self-Made Hero*) (France)
Best short film: Lynne Ramsay, *Small Deaths* (Great Britain)
Technical Grand Prize: Claude Nuridsany and Marie Perennou, *Microcosmos* (France)
Directors Guild of America Awards
Documentary: Terry Zwigoff, *Crumb*
Feature film: Ron Howard, *Apollo 13*
D.W. Griffith Award: Woody Allen
Golden Globe Awards
Actor—drama: Nicolas Cage, *Leaving Las Vegas*
Actress—drama: Sharon Stone, *Casino*
Actor—musical or comedy: John Travolta, *Get Shorty*
Actress—musical or comedy: Nicole Kidman, *To Die For*
Director: Mel Gibson, *Braveheart*
Drama: *Sense and Sensibility*
Musical or comedy: *Babe*
National Society of Film Critics Awards
Actor: Nicolas Cage, *Leaving Las Vegas*
Actress: Elisabeth Shue, *Leaving Las Vegas*
Cinematography: Tak Fujimoto, *Devil in a Blue Dress*
Director: Mike Figgis, *Leaving Las Vegas*
Documentary: *Crumb*
Film: *Babe*
Foreign-language film: *Wild Reeds* (France)
Screenplay: Amy Heckerling, *Clueless*
Supporting actor: Don Cheadle, *Devil in a Blue Dress*
Supporting actress: Joan Allen, *Nixon*

PUBLIC SERVICE

Africa Prize for Leadership for the sustainable end of hunger ($100,000 shared)**:** Amadou Toumani Toure, Mali; Bisi Ogunleye, Nigeria
Charles A. Dana Foundation Awards for pioneering achievements in health and higher education ($50,000 ea.)**:** health (shared)—Michael I. Posner, Institute of Cognitive and Decision Sciences, University of Oregon; Marcus E. Raichle, Washington University, St. Louis; education—Sharon K. Darling, National Center for Family Literacy, Louisville, KY; distinguished achievement—Baruj Benacerraf, Dana-Farber Cancer Institute
American Institute for Public Service Jefferson Awards
Benefiting the Disadvantaged: Rosalynn Carter
Public Official: U.S. Sen. Sam Nunn (D-GA)
Private Citizen: Brian Lamb, C-SPAN
Citizen 35 or Younger: Andrea Jaeger
Templeton Prize for Progress in Religion ($1,100,000)**:** Bill Bright, founder and president, Campus Crusade for Christ
U.S. Congressional Gold Medal: Billy and Ruth Graham
U.S. Presidential Medal of Freedom (awarded by President Clinton on Sept. 9, 1996)**:** Cardinal Joseph Bernardin, James Brady, Millard Fuller, David Alan Hamburg, John H. Johnson, Eugene M. Lang, Jan Nowak-Jezioranski, Antonia Pantoja, Rosa Parks, Ginetta Sagan, Morris K. Udall

SCIENCE

Bristol-Myers Squibb Awards for distinguished achievement in medical research ($50,000 ea.)**:** cancer: Henry T. Lynch, Creighton University School of Medicine; cardiovascular (shared): Tadashi Inagami, Vanderbilt University School of Medicine; John H. Laragh, Cornell University Medical College; infectious diseases: Louis Miller, National Institute of Allergy and Infectious Disease,

Mel Gibson, below, *gained new respect as a director when his film "Braveheart" won two Oscars in 1996—one for best film and one for Gibson as best director.*

© Blake Sell/Reuters/Archive Photos

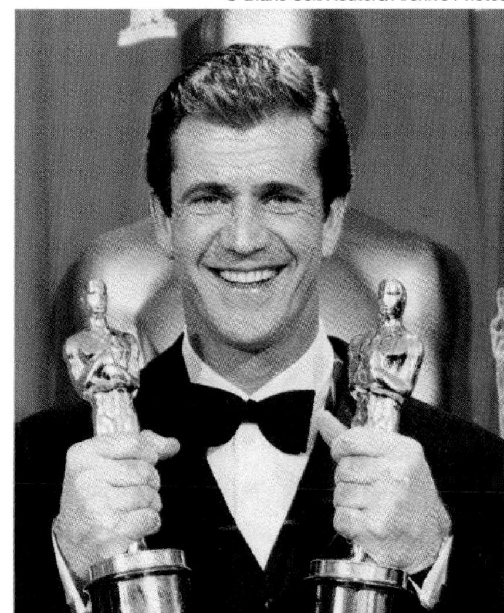

National Institutes of Health; neuroscience: Solomon H. Snyder, Johns Hopkins University School of Medicine; nutrition: Irwin H. Rosenberg, Tufts University–Jean Mayer USDA Human Nutrition Research on Aging; orthopedic: Jorge O. Galante, Rush-Presbyterian St. Luke's Medical Center, Chicago

U.S. Congressional Space Medal of Honor (presented by President Bill Clinton on Dec. 2, 1996): Shannon W. Lucid

Louisa Gross Horwitz Memorial Prize for research in biology or biochemistry ($22,000 shared): Clay M. Armstrong, University of Pennsylvania; Bertil Hille, University of Washington

General Motors Cancer Research Foundation Awards ($100,000 ea.)

Kettering Award (shared): Malcolm A. Bagshaw, Stanford University School of Medicine; David Hall McConnell, Brady Urological Institute, Johns Hopkins University School of Medicine

Mott Award (shared): Richard David Kolodner, Harvard University Medical School and Charles Dana Division of Human Cancer Genetics, Dana-Farber Cancer Institute; Paul L. Modrich, Duke University Medical School and Howard Hughes Medical Institute

Sloan Award (shared): Tak Mak, Ontario Cancer Institute; Mark Davis, Stanford University

Albert Lasker Medical Research Awards:

Basic Research ($25,000 shared): Robert F. Furchgott, State University of New York Health Science Center, New York, NY; Ferid Murad, Molecular Geriatrics Corporation, Lake Bluff, IL

Clinical Research ($10,000 ea.): John B. Robbins and Rachel Schneerson, National Institute of Child Health and Human Development, Bethesda, MD; Porter W. Anderson, Jr., University of Rochester; David H. Smith, New York, NY

Special Achievement in Medical Science ($25,000): Paul C. Zamecnik, Worcester Foundation for Biomedical Research, Shrewsbury, MA

National Medal of Science (presented by President Bill Clinton on July 26, 1996): Wallace S. Broecker, Norman Davidson, James L. Flanagan, Richard M. Karp, C. Kumar N. Patel, Ruth Patrick, Paul A. Samuelson, Stephen Smale

National Medal of Technology (presented by President Bill Clinton on July 26, 1996): Charles H. Kaman, Stephanie Louise Kwolek, James C. Morgan, Peter H. Rose, Johnson & Johnson

TELEVISION AND RADIO

Academy of Television Arts and Sciences ("Emmy") Awards

Actor—comedy series: John Lithgow, *3rd Rock From the Sun* (NBC)
Actor—drama series: Dennis Franz, *NYPD Blue* (ABC)
Actor—miniseries or a special: Alan Rickman, *Rasputin* (HBO)
Actress—comedy series: Helen Hunt, *Mad About You* (NBC)
Actress—drama series: Kathy Baker, *Picket Fences* (CBS)
Actress—miniseries or a special: Helen Mirren, *Prime Suspect: Scent of Darkness* (PBS)
Comedy series: *Frasier* (NBC)
Directing—comedy series: Michael Lembeck, "The One After the Superbowl," *Friends* (NBC)
Directing—drama series: Jeremy Kagan, "Leave of Absence," *Chicago Hope* (CBS)
Directing—miniseries or a special: John Frankenheimer, *Andersonville* (TNT)
Directing—variety or music program: Louis J. Horvitz, *The Kennedy Center Honors* (CBS)
Drama series: *ER* (NBC)
Guest actor—comedy series: Tim Conway, "The Gardener," *Coach* (ABC)
Guest actor—drama series: Peter Boyle, "Clyde Bruckman's Final Repose," *The X-Files* (Fox)
Guest actress—comedy series: Betty White, "Here We Go Again," *The John Larroquette Show* (NBC)
Guest actress—drama series: Amanda Plummer, *The Outer Limits* (Showtime)
Individual performance—variety or music program: Tony Bennett, *Tony Bennett Live By Request: A Valentine Special* (A&E)
Miniseries or a special: *Gulliver's Travels* (NBC)
Movie made for television: *Truman* (HBO)
President's Award: *Blacklist: Hollywood on Trial* (American Movie Classics)
Supporting actor—comedy series: Rip Torn, *The Larry Sanders Show* (HBO)
Supporting actor—drama series: Ray Walston, *Picket Fences* (CBS)
Supporting actor—miniseries or a special: Tom Hulce, *The Heidi Chronicles* (TNT)
Supporting actress—comedy series: Julia Louis-Dreyfus, *Seinfeld* (NBC)
Supporting actress—drama series: Tyne Daly, *Christy* (CBS)
Supporting actress—miniseries or a special: Greta Scacchi, *Rasputin* (HBO)
Variety, music, or comedy series: *Dennis Miller Live* (HBO)
Variety, music, or comedy special: *The Kennedy Center Honors* (CBS)
Writing—comedy series: Joe Keenan, Christopher Lloyd, Rob Greenberg, Jack Burditt, Chuck Ranberg, Anne Flett-Giordano, Linda Morris, Vic Rauseo, "Moon Dance," *Frasier* (NBC)
Writing—drama series: Darin Morgan, "Clyde Bruckman's Final Repose," *The X-Files* (Fox)
Writing—miniseries or a special: Simon Moore (teleplay), *Gulliver's Travels* (NBC)
Writing—variety or music program: Dennis Miller, Eddie Feldmann, David Feldman, Mike Gandolfi, Tom Hertz, Leah Krinsky, Rick Overton, *Dennis Miller Live* (HBO)

Golden Globe Awards

Drama series: *Party of Five* (Fox)
Musical or comedy series: *Cybill* (CBS)

Humanitas Prizes (for film and TV scripts that enrich the lives of the viewing public):

Feature film ($25,000): Tim Robbins, screenplay, *Dead Man Walking*
Cable- or public-television production ($25,000): John Hopkins and Toshiro Ishido, *Hiroshima* (Showtime)
Children's animated television production ($10,000): Alex Taub, episode of *Life With Louie* (Fox)
Children's live-action television production ($10,000): Betty G. Birney, "Fast Forward," *ABC Afterschool Special*
Network television production (90-minute or longer) ($25,000): Simon Moore, *Gulliver's Travels* (NBC)
Network television production (60-minute) (15,000): Nick Harding and David E. Kelley, episode of *Picket Fences* (CBS)
Network television production (30-minute) ($15,000): Steve Levitan, episode of *Frasier* (NBC)

George Foster Peabody Awards

Radio: WJR Radio, Detroit, MI, *Blind Justice: Who Killed Janie Fray?*; Minnesota Public Radio, St. Paul, MN, *St. Paul Sunday*; Canadian Broadcasting Corporation, Toronto, Ont., *Kevin's Sentence*; Oscar Brand, WNYC, New York City, for helping preserve folk music; National Public Radio, Washington, DC, and Sony Classical Film and Video for PBS, *Wynton Marsalis: Making the Music/Marsalis on Music*

Television: CBS News, for coverage of the assassination of Israeli Prime Minister Yitzhak Rabin; three Oklahoma City stations for coverage of the terrorist bombing there; Barbara Walters, ABC News, interview with Christopher Reeve; Oprah Winfrey, ABC, for her work on talk shows; PBS, *Hoop Dreams*; NBC, *Homicide*; WFAA-TV, Dallas, TX, *The Peavy Investigation*; ABC News, *20/20*, "Truth on Trial"; WXYZ-TV, Detroit, MI, *Target Seven: Armed and Angry*; WCBS-TV, New York City, *New York City School Corruption*; Television Broadcasts Ltd., Kowloon, Hong Kong, *50 Years After the War*; Cinemax Reel Life Presentation of a Lauderdale Production for Channel 4, London, and Cinemax, New York, *The Dying Rooms*; Public Policy Productions Inc. in association with Thirteen/WNET, New York City, presented on PBS, *Road Scholar*; WGBH-TV, Boston, MS, and BBC Bristol, *Rock-and-Roll*; ABC News, *Peter Jennings Reporting: Hiroshima: Why the Bomb Was Dropped*; Discovery Journal Special, Discovery Channel, Bethesda, MD, and Brian Lapping Associates for BBC London, *Yugoslavia: Death of a Nation*; CBS News, *CBS Reports: In the Killing Fields of America*; P.O.V./Deborah Hoffman, New York City, presented on PBS, *Complaints of a Dutiful Daughter*; Turner Original Productions, Tollin/Robbins and Mundy Lane in association with Television Production Partners, *Hank Aaron: Chasing the Dream*; Turner Original Productions and BBC Natural History, London, *The Private Life of Plants*; Deep Focus Productions, Los Angeles, CA, presented on PBS, *Coming Out Under Fire*; Aardman Animations in association with Wallace & Gromit Ltd., BBC Children's International, BBC Bristol, and BBC Lionheart, animation, *Wallace and Gromit*; WGBH-TV, Boston, MA, *Frontline: Waco: The Inside Story*

THEATER

American Academy and Institute of Arts and Letters Awards

Richard Rodgers Award in Musical Theater: James McBride and Ed Shockley, *Bobos*; Peter Foley and Kate Chisholm, *The Hidden Sky*; Karole Foreman and Andy Chukerman, *The Princess and the Black-Eyed Pea*

Outer Critics Circle Awards

Actor—play: George C. Scott, *Inherit the Wind*
Actor—musical: Nathan Lane, *A Funny Thing Happened on the Way to the Forum*
Actress—play: Zoe Caldwell, *Master Class*
Actress—musical: Julie Andrews, *Victor/Victoria*
Choreography: Savion Glover, *Bring in da Noise, Bring in da Funk*
Musical: *Victor/Victoria*
Play: *Master Class*
Revival—play: *Inherit the Wind*
Revival—musical: *The King and I*

Antoinette Perry ("Tony") Awards

Actor—play: George Grizzard, *A Delicate Balance*
Actor—musical: Nathan Lane, *A Funny Thing Happened on the Way to the Forum*
Actress—play: Zoe Caldwell, *Master Class*
Actress—musical: Donna Murphy, *The King and I*
Choreography: Savion Glover, *Bring in da Noise, Bring in da Funk*
Director—play: Gerald Gutierrez, *A Delicate Balance*
Director—musical: George C. Wolfe, *Bring in da Noise, Bring in da Funk*
Featured actor—play: Ruben Santiago-Hudson, *Seven Guitars*
Featured actor—musical: Wilson Jermaine Heredia, *Rent*
Featured actress—play: Audra McDonald, *Master Class*
Featured actress—musical: Ann Duquesnay, *Bring in da Noise, Bring in da Funk*
Musical: *Rent*
Musical—book: Jonathan Larson, *Rent*
Musical—score: Jonathan Larson, *Rent*
Play: *Master Class*
Regional theater award: Alley Theater, Houston, TX
Reproduction of a musical: *The King and I*
Reproduction of a play: *A Delicate Balance*

Pulitzer Prize for Drama: Jonathan Larson, *Rent* (posthumous)

PUBLISHING

The publishing industry faced uneven prospects in 1996. For the first time in the 1990s, magazines and newspapers enjoyed both growing advertising revenues and dropping paper prices. In contrast, only modest growth developed in the book industry. Publishers won some important legal battles but also encountered potentially costly forms of new regulation. The industry continued to introduce experimental services via the Internet, often without knowing from where the revenues to support them would come.

Books. The year appeared to be a largely mediocre one for books. In July the Book Industry Study Group (BISG) predicted that sales would grow only by 3.8%, to $20.1 billion, in 1996. Prospects looked somewhat brighter for 1997. The BISG predicted a 4.7% total increase, to $23.5 billion. An August report by Veronis, Suhler and Associates—an investment-banking firm that specializes in publishing industries—reflected caution about the long-term prospects of the industry. It predicted only a 5.3% compound annual growth in book sales from 1995 to 2000.

In March books by three attorneys involved in the O.J. Simpson murder trial hit the shelves: *In Contempt* by prosecutor Christopher Darden, *Reasonable Doubts* by defense attorney Alan Dershowitz, and *In Search of Justice* by defense attorney Robert Shapiro. All quickly hit the *Publishers Weekly* nonfiction best-seller list. Another best-seller was *Primary Colors*, an anonymously written novel inspired by Bill Clinton's 1992 presidential campaign and often seen as the work of an insider. *Newsweek* columnist Joe Klein eventually admitted authoring the tale of political intrigue. Also among the year's most popular titles was *Bad As I Wanna Be* by flamboyant professional basketball star Dennis Rodman.

Acquisition activities continued. In March the Tribune Company completed the purchase of supplemental school publisher Educational Publishing and textbook publisher NTC Publishing Group for an estimated $282 million. The deals established the Tribune Co. as a major player in the K–12 market. In March the Thomson Corp. agreed to acquire West Publishing for $3.45 billion, which would join two of legal publishing's largest companies. A government-proposed antitrust settlement required West and Thomson to divest more than 50 legal publications valued at $275 million. However, a legal challenge to this settlement later was filed, alleging that antitrust regulators had not been tough enough.

Large bookstore chains continued to increase market share, fueled by the popularity of chain superstores. Total sales for the four largest U.S. bookstore companies increased 17.4% for the year ending in January 1996, accounting for 44% of the total retail market. Superstore sales grew by about 45%, along

In July 1996, "Newsweek" columnist Joe Klein confessed to authoring the political satire "Primary Colors." The revelation ended speculation about who had authored the anonymously written best-seller and spurred debate over Klein's journalistic credibility.

Courtesy, Random House

© Jacques M. Chenet/Gamma-Liaison

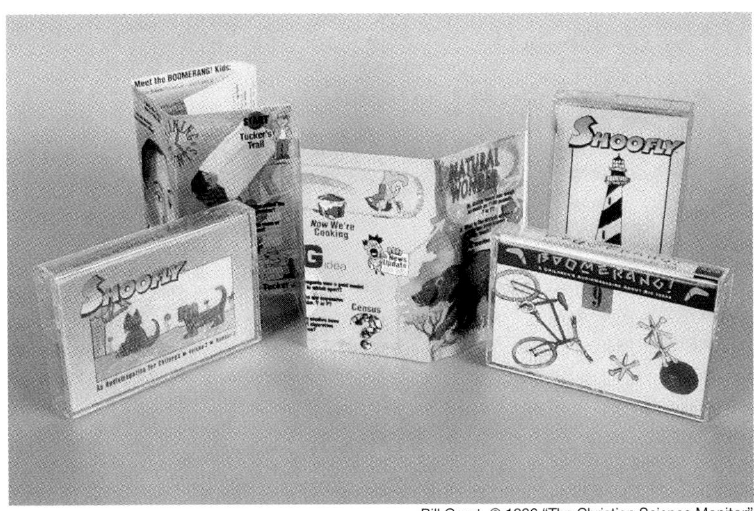

Bill Grant, © 1996 "The Christian Science Monitor"

During 1996 several children's publishers were marketing or developing so-called audiomagazines—products akin to books on tape that contain stories, poems, and other informative material on cassettes.

with a 36% increase in new outlets. Also booming were audio books, which were generating about $1.4 billion in annual sales.

Legal issues continued to arise. In April, Random House announced plans to appeal a court decision that allowed actress Joan Collins to keep a $1.2 million advance for manuscripts that the publisher had deemed unpublishable. Later, the attorney for Collins claimed Random House editors were threatening to publish the work without editing in an effort to humiliate her.

The pricing practices of large publishers faced continued challenges. In January the American Booksellers Association (ABA) filed an antitrust suit against Random House, in an effort to force the largest U.S. trade publisher to provide independent bookstores with the same wholesale price and promotional allowance it provides to major chains. The action resembled a 1994 suit that the ABA filed against five others. During late 1995 and 1996, the remaining four defendants in that case—Houghton Mifflin, Penguin, Rutledge Hill Press, and St. Martin's Press—reached similar out-of-court agreements with the ABA. In September 1996 the Federal Trade Commission shocked some observers by dismissing a pricing case against Random House, Simon & Schuster, Macmillan, Hearst, Harper & Row, and Putnam Berkley. The case involved a 17-year investigation of practices that favored large chains. The decision left publishers with the ABA settlements as the only precedent for pricing policies.

Magazines. The magazine industry faced a qualifiedly hopeful future during 1996. Magazine spending grew 6.4% in 1995, according to the Publishers Information Bureau. For the first six months of 1996, advertising revenues rose 8.3% in comparison with the same period in 1995. Ad pages dropped a somewhat disappointing 1.9%, however. In mid-1996, Veronis, Suhler and Associates predicted that advertising and circulation revenues for consumer and trade titles would reach $31.5 billion in the year 2000, up from $23.4 billion in 1995. Spending was projected to increase at a 6.2% compound annual rate, as compared with 3.8% during the previous five years.

A total of 10,387 U.S. titles were being published during 1995. Two publications received by members of the American Association of Retired Persons (AARP)—*NRTA/AARP Bulletin* and *Modern Maturity*—remained circulation leaders during the first half of 1996, with more than 20 million each. *Reader's Digest*, *TV Guide*, and *National Geographic* followed.

In June, McDonald Communications acquired *Working Woman*, *Working Mother*, and *Ms.* from Lang Communications Corp. and its major creditor. During the late summer and fall, *U.S. News & World Report* underwent a makeover, complete with editorial-staff changes, designed in part to have the magazine deemphasize its political coverage. Andrew Sullivan resigned as editor of the *New Republic* in April and disclosed that he was HIV-positive. *Adweek* magazine named Sullivan its editor of the year for 1996.

Many magazines continued to introduce on-line services, and some notable "webzines," distributed primarily or exclusively on the Internet's World Wide Web, appeared. For example, former *New Republic* staffer and *Crossfire* cohost Michael Kinsley was editing Microsoft's *Slate*. The title featured political commentary and articles about culture and public policy.

Forbes magazine editor in chief Steve Forbes' unsuccessful bid for the Republican presidential nomination set off an apparent battle between business publications. In February rival *Fortune* accused Forbes of seeking office to increase ad pages at his magazine and alleged that *Forbes* advertisers could command changes in articles. In May, *Forbes* ran an article describing Time Warner, the parent of *Fortune*, as loaded with debt and management turmoil.

In January, *Money* magazine fired famed financial journalist Dan Dorfman after he refused to reveal names of sources to the managing editor of the magazine. Federal authorities reportedly were investigating his friendship with a public-relations executive whose clients had been touted by Dorfman. In August the cable channel CNBC, which also carried Dorfman reports, announced that an internal probe found no evidence that Dorfman had violated any law.

Legal issues remained prominent. In April the 6th Circuit Court of Appeals overturned a prior-restraint order that had blocked *Business Week* from running a story based on sealed court documents. Many magazine titles faced lost revenues because of federal rules classifying nicotine as a drug. According to the rules, only black-and-white, text-only tobacco ads would be permitted in publications with a youth readership of more than 15% or with more than 2 million readers younger than age 18. The regulations could take effect as early as September 1997. Legislation introduced in the U.S. Congress could extend similar regulations to the advertising of alcoholic beverages.

Many publishers expressed concern about certain provisions of the Communications Decency Act, adopted in February as part of the 1996 Telecommunications Act. In June a federal appeals court in Philadelphia cited 1st Amendment concerns and threw out a section of the act banning the distribution of indecent material on the Internet. The U.S. Department of Justice appealed the decision to the U.S. Supreme Court.

Newspapers. The newspaper industry appeared mostly healthy during 1996, amid revenue growth and falling newsprint prices. After peaking at about $750 per ton in late 1995, paper prices fell to $650 per ton at midyear. Through June most public newspaper companies reported significant gains in profits and revenues. Ad spending rose about

A Milestone for "The New York Times"

Aug. 18, 1996, marked the 100th anniversary of the acquisition of *The New York Times* by Adolph S. Ochs, a Tennessee newspaper publisher. To honor the milestone, four New York City museums featured exhibitions, and a book and keepsake editions of *The Times'* Sunday magazine and book review were published. The celebrations focused on the history of what many consider the world's finest and most influential newspaper.

The Times was founded in 1851, but Ochs largely was responsible for its longevity and success. He coined the famous phrase "All the News That's Fit to Print" and promised to pursue truth "without fear or favor" as an alternative to the notoriously sensationalized press of the day. He envisioned *The Times* as a "newspaper of record" that would feature superior coverage of local, national, and international events. Journalists working for him made the paper one of the world's most prestigious. Scholars have documented the enormous influence *The Times* exerts on other news organizations, which often imitate its judgments.

The Times flourished under Ochs. In 1896 the nearly bankrupt newspaper—for which Ochs had paid $75,000 to gain a controlling interest—had a circulation of about 9,000. A century later, its U.S. weekday circulation exceeded 1.1 million and Ochs' heirs controlled a company worth roughly $3 billion.

The high points of the paper's history include the 1971 publication of the so-called Pentagon Papers—a secret government study that documented and criticized the U.S. policies that led to the Vietnam war—that the Department of Justice had attempted to suppress. As a defendant in the 1964 *New York Times Co. v. Sullivan* suit, the paper also helped remake U.S. libel law. In that case, the U.S. Supreme Court ruled that public officials can collect damages for libel only if false statements are made with "actual malice." Despite its prestige, the paper also has had low points. To many, these include the favorable portrayal of the Stalin regime during the 1930s, the sparse coverage of the Holocaust, and admiring stories about Fidel Castro in the 1950s.

DAVID K. PERRY

5.3% during the first half of the year. The paper prices suggested that even better news might be forthcoming in late 1996. In August, Veronis, Suhler and Associates predicted that total spending on newspapers would grow to $65.8 billion by the year 2000, up 31% from 1995. The report also forecasted that advertising would grow about 5.7% per year during this period, soaring to $53.2 billion. The firm also foresaw slight increases in daily and Sunday circulation during this time.

The total number of dailies fell slightly during 1995 to 1,533. Daily circulation also fell, totaling about 58.3 million at the end of 1995, down from 59 million the previous year. The declines occurred among afternoon papers, which fell in number from 947 to 928, in part because some switched to morning publication. *The Wall Street Journal* continued as the daily circulation leader, with about 1.84 million copies, followed by *USA Today*, *The New York Times*, and *The Los Angeles Times*. Sunday circulation fell modestly. The Newspaper Association of America (NAA) reported that 8,453 weeklies, with 79.5 million total circulation, were being published.

Newspapers continued to experiment with on-line information. By the fall, more than 1,400 newspapers worldwide had sites on the Internet's World Wide Web, almost double the number that existed at the start of the year and a 15-fold increase from early in 1995. Many of the sites offered free news services to browsers. Publishers wondered, however, whether sufficient revenue would materialize, perhaps from advertising, to support these online services.

Acquisition activity continued during 1996. In March, Central Newspapers, Inc., completed its acquisition of the *Alexandria* (LA) *Daily Town Talk*, which had been family-owned since 1883, for $62 million. In February one of the last family-owned papers in California, the *San Mateo Times*, was sold to the Alameda Newspaper Group. During the summer, Pulitzer Publishing Company paid about $214 million for 16 dailies from the Scripps League chain.

In June, Media General purchased the *Danville* (VA) *Register and Bee* for $38 million. The following month, Media General announced that it would pay $710 million to acquire the parent company of Park Communications, Inc., owner of 28 dailies and 82 weeklies. In August, Thomson Newspapers agreed to acquire six Arizona dailies from Cox Enterprises in part for two Thomson dailies in North Carolina. The deal remained subject to regulatory approval. A. H. Belo

The Freedom Forum Journalists Memorial (above) *in Arlington, VA, was dedicated in May 1996. The glass and steel structure was built to honor journalists who died in pursuit of the news.*

Corp., publisher of *The Dallas Morning News*, agreed in September to buy the Providence Journal Co., publisher of *The Providence Journal-Bulletin* and owner of nine television stations, for $1.5 billion. The deal was expected to be completed early in 1997.

A strike begun in July 1995 against the *Detroit News* and *Detroit Free Press* continued into the fall of 1996 with no end in sight. The National Labor Relations Board charged that neither side had obeyed labor laws during the strike. The Audit Bureau of Circulations estimated that the combined circulation at the two papers had dropped by more than 30% by early 1996.

Newspaper publishers celebrated some legal victories. They generally praised the federal telecommunications bill passed in early 1996. The law requires regional telephone companies to offer electronic publishing services through a separate subsidiary. This apparently eased fears about electronic classified advertisements that telephone companies would offer. (Classifieds account for an estimated 50% of newspaper profits.)

See THE WORLD OF THE INTERNET, page 62.

DAVID K. PERRY, *The University of Alabama*

REFUGEES AND IMMIGRATION

Two events—a series of new legislative initiatives by the U.S. government to deal with the growing problem of illegal immigration and continuing refugee disasters in Central Africa—dominated national and international attention regarding immigration and refugee matters in 1996.

New U.S. Legislation. Through new laws on welfare, immigration, and counterterrorism, the U.S. government imposed new restrictions affecting most immigrants. For example, a new welfare-reform bill, which was signed into law in August, made illegal immigrants ineligible for most public-assistance programs financed by the federal government or the states. In addition, the law greatly restricted public benefits such as food stamps and Supplemental Security Income for most legal immigrants.

A new illegal-immigration bill was signed into law in September. The law was designed to curb illegal immigration, providing a number of new enforcement provisions to enable the Immigration and Naturalization Service (INS) to fulfill this mission. The law included provisions to nearly double the number of border-patrol agents (to 10,000) by the year 2001 and to allow the INS to add 1,200 workers to investigate the smuggling and unlawful hiring of illegal aliens. The law also increased the penalty for smuggling people into the United States to a prison term of up to ten years; meanwhile, the criminal penalties for fraud or misuse of government-issued identification documents were increased to 15 years' imprisonment, from five years. The law also contained provisions providing for the summary exclusion of those arriving without proper documents.

These procedures, and those contained in a provision in a counterterrorism bill approved by Congress, also would affect prospective asylum seekers. If someone seeking asylum was found to have no credible fear of persecution after an initial hearing with an INS officer, the person would be subject to removal after a hearing before an immigration judge. Such appeals would have to take place within seven days, with no further appeals or reviews allowed. Anyone suspected of terrorism would be rejected immediately. The immigration law also provided initial steps for the establishment of a national employee-verification system. Pilot programs were scheduled to be established in five states with high populations of illegal immigrants, allowing employers voluntarily to check the legal status and validity of prospective workers on INS databases. Finally, the illegal-immigration law altered the income guidelines for those who sponsor legal immigrants for citizenship, requiring sponsors to earn at least 125% of the poverty level.

Critics of the new legislation argued that the laws focused unduly on eliminating the attractiveness of public benefits for illegal immigrants rather than addressing the magnet of U.S. jobs through tougher sanctions against employers who hire illegal aliens. Opponents of immigration also were disappointed that the new welfare law did not bar illegal immigrants from public primary or secondary schools or from emergency health care. Others argued that it would be unfair to deny food stamps and other social benefits to most legal immigrants, especially since these very same people pay taxes and contribute their work and energy to their communities. Other critics claimed that the new income restrictions for those wishing to sponsor immigrants, whether they be family members or others, represented a mean-spirited and backhanded way of limiting future immigration. Finally, human-rights advocates maintained that summary exclusion decisions made solely and independently by poorly trained INS agents at border crossings and ports of entry (as stipulated in the counterterrorism and illegal-immigration laws) would deny many asylum seekers a fair hearing of their claims. They also decried the provisions in these laws that would close the courts to lawsuits challenging INS policies and practices.

The Future of U.S. Immigration Policy. Many in Congress felt that the annual numbers of immigrants were too high and planned to push for renewed legislative efforts to reduce that number greatly. The 1996 presidential campaign also highlighted national anxiety over the rapidly increasing numbers of immigrants naturalized each year. During fiscal year 1996 nearly 1.1 million immigrants became citizens, roughly doubling the record set the year before. The high numbers of new citizens appeared likely to continue in future years. According to the INS, there were about 10 million legal residents in the United States, of whom about 7 million, including 1 million children, were eligible to apply for citizenship. Many of these people were worried not only that they soon would lose their benefits under the new welfare-reform law, but also that—in the nationwide crackdown against immigrants—they might lose the opportunity to apply for naturalization if they did not do so soon.

Photos, © Nanzer/Sipa Press

In the fall of 1996, international attention was drawn to the refugee situation in Central Africa, as the horrible living conditions in Hutu refugee camps in Zaire came to light. Before the year ended, hundreds of thousands of these refugees had returned to Rwanda.

Continuing Crises. In Africa and other parts of the world, the refugee situation did not improve markedly during the year. Faced with mass influxes of displaced people and a greater share of the world's refugee burden because of restrictionist policies in the developed countries, many governments in Africa that in the past had responded humanely to the needs of the millions who were forced from their homelands now closed their borders to new arrivals. In early 1996 boatloads of Liberian refugees were stranded at sea for weeks until neighboring states reluctantly agreed to provide them with refuge. Tanzania, host to hundreds of thousands of refugees from neighboring countries, expelled and refused entry to tens of thousands of asylum seekers and refugees fleeing violence in Burundi and Rwanda. In Bosnia, despite provisions in the so-called Dayton Accords allowing for the repatriation of some 2 million Bosnian refugees and internally displaced persons, only a few thousand persons were permitted to return to their prior homes.

The plight of some refugees, particularly those in Central Africa, worsened. During the second half of the year, a power struggle between ethnic Hutu and Tutsi fueled a conflict in eastern Zaire that caused hundreds of thousands of Hutu refugees to flee the camps in which they had resided since leaving Rwanda in mid-1994. For the previous two years, Hutu militia had used the camps as bases from which to attack Tutsi in Rwanda and Burundi, and had intimidated Hutu refugees living in the camps and prevented many of them from returning to their home countries.

By mid-1996, Hutu militia groups allied with local Zairian officials tried to expel Tutsi who had lived in eastern Zaire for more than 200 years. A rebel force of Zairian Tutsi known as the Banyamulenge resisted and, armed by neighboring Rwanda and allied with groups from a neighboring region, pushed the Zairian army out of most of eastern Zaire. In the battles that ensued, refugee camps came under attack and international aid workers were evacuated, severing roughly 1 million Hutu refugees from the outside world and creating a major new refugee crisis. The situation was eased in mid-November when a major repatriation occurred, with some 500,000 Hutu refugees streaming back to Rwanda in four days. A few weeks later the United Nations High Commissioner for Refugees (UNHCR) supported the expulsion of more than 200,000 Rwandans from camps in Tanzania. The UNHCR had concluded that the refugees would be better off in Rwanda than in camps under Hutu militia control and that the host governments and the government in Rwanda were eager to see the camps closed and the refugees returned home. But human-rights organizations criticized the UNHCR for supporting forced repatriation.

GIL LOESCHER, *University of Notre Dame*

Religion

Overview

Religious groups were divided on several issues during 1996. Christians debated various foundational teachings of their faith, including the identity and mission of Jesus and the nature of hell. At the same time, Christians drew attention to religious persecution and martyrdom throughout the world. There was concern about a rash of arsons hitting churches in the United States.

Disputed Issues. In April, when President Bill Clinton vetoed a bill banning a late-term abortion procedure, U.S. Catholic leaders called the action "shameful" and urged Congress to override it. In the Southern Baptist Convention (SBC), Clinton's denomination, President Jim Henry and ten past presidents urged him to apologize for the veto. In contrast, 36 religious leaders in the interfaith Religious Coalition for Reproductive Choice said that, although they held human life sacred, they supported the president's action "in standing with women and their families who face tragic, untenable pregnancies."

At its annual meeting in New Orleans in June, the SBC called for new efforts to evangelize Jewish people and announced that a new home missionary, Jim Sibley, had been appointed for that task. While the action won praise from such Hebrew-Christian groups as Jews for Jesus, it was denounced by mainstream Jewish organizations—including the Anti-Defamation League of B'nai B'rith, which called it an insult to the Jewish people.

Nobel Peace Prize winner Elie Wiesel, a Holocaust survivor, stirred another Christian-Jewish dispute in July when he described the presence of crosses at the concentration-camp site of Birkenau, Poland, as an "insult" and "blasphemy." His demand that they be removed was denounced by Bishop Tadeusz Pieronek, secretary-general of the Polish Catholic Bishops' Conference, as "unbelievable and excessive."

Doctrine. Jesus appeared on the covers of three major weekly newsmagazines for the issues of April 8. The accompanying articles discussed scholarly controversies over the historical Jesus and whether the Bible could be trusted on such matters as the physical nature of his resurrection. The subject drew the attention of 17 scholars later that month at a Resurrection Summit in New York called to discuss the importance of that doctrine to the Christian faith and its relevance to issues like violence and women's rights.

The doctrine commission of the Church of England issued a report in January saying that hell should be viewed as a state of total non-being rather than a place of eternal torment. Two months later the Barna Research Group issued the results of a U.S. survey that found that 31% of adults view hell as a place of physical torment, while 37% believe it to be a "state of permanent separation from the presence of God."

Religious Persecution. At a Washington gathering in January, leaders of more than 40 evangelical and Roman Catholic organizations urged Congress to take up the cause of Christians persecuted for their faith around the world. In September both the House of Representatives and the Senate adopted resolutions deploring such persecution. The Senate urged President Clinton to "initiate a thorough examination of all U.S. policies that affect persecuted Christians" and to appoint a special adviser on religious persecution. Two such cases were the abduction and murder of seven Trappist monks in Algeria by Islamic terrorists and the conviction in Kuwait of Robert Hussein, a Muslim who converted to Christianity, by an Islamic court on a charge of apostasy. Hussein left Kuwait in August.

Church Arsons. A wave of arson attacks on churches in the United States—including numerous black churches in the Southeast—led Congress to enact the Church Arson Prevention Act. The new legislation makes it easier to prosecute those charged with setting church fires and establishes a fund to provide loans and grants to rebuild burned churches. While groups encompassing a wide variety of faiths contributed money and muscle to help rebuild the houses of worship, there was some disagreement on how much of the arson represented racism.

Diane Knippers, president of the Institute on Religion and Democracy, said in August that arson at black churches accounted for just a fraction of the 600 churches torched every year, and that approximately the same number of black and white churches had burned since 1995. She accused the National Council of Churches (NCC) of promoting a "great church-fire hoax" to promote its racial agenda. In response, NCC General Secretary

Joan Brown Campbell said the rate of white church arsons had not increased in the previous 18 months, while that of black church arsons was more than double what it had been in previous years. Campbell also said that black churches were burning in proportion to their number at four times the rate of white churches.

Church-State. An appeals court in St. Louis ruled in May that the Religious Freedom Restoration Act enabled a church in New Hope, MN, to keep money it had received in tithes from a couple who later filed for bankruptcy. But in a June case involving a dispute over whether a church in Cumberland, MD, could raze property that the city wanted preserved, a Baltimore judge said the 1993 law was unconstitutional because it "usurped the Supreme Court's authority to determine the scope and meaning of the First Amendment." A major overhaul of the federal welfare system enacted in August provided for the first time that the U.S. government could give money to churches and other sectarian organizations to carry out some of their ministries.

© Tim Rasmussen/Sygma

Templeton Prize. Bill Bright, the Presbyterian layman who founded Campus Crusade for Christ in 1951, was the recipient of the 1996 Templeton Prize for Progress in Religion. The group's pamphlet, "The Four Spiritual Laws," has appeared in almost 200 languages since its original publication in 1956, and the ministry's feature-length film on the life of Jesus has been translated into more than 300 languages and viewed by people in more than 200 countries. Bright said he would use the $1 million prize for a program to educate church leaders around the world on fasting and prayer.

DARRELL TURNER, *Religion Writer*
"Journal Gazette," Fort Wayne, IN

Far Eastern

In February 1996 an international team of archaeologists announced that they had discovered rooms believed to be the birthplace of the historical Buddha. The excavation was located at a site in Lumbini, Nepal, near the Indian border. The Indian prince named Siddhartha who researchers believe was born at the site became a traveling monk in the 6th century B.C. and became known as "Buddha" ("the enlightened one"). Inscriptions on an ancient pillar above the chambers in the 2,000-year-old temple proclaim it to be Buddha's birthplace.

Four months later a British library reported that it had acquired ancient bark scrolls believed to be the oldest surviving Buddhist manuscripts. The scrolls were dated to the period between the 1st and 2nd century A.D.—within five or six centuries of Buddha himself. Written in Gandhari, the language of the ancient region of Gandhara—located in north Pakistan and east Afghanistan of today—the

© Les Stone/Sygma

A wave of arson attacks against churches in the United States, including the Southeast, in 1995–96 led to campaigns to rebuild the edifices (left) *and to prosecute those guilty of arson.*

manuscripts are believed to be part of the long-lost canon of the Sarvastivadin sect that helped to spread the Buddhist faith into Central and East Asia.

In the United States the Odiyan Buddhist Center in Stewarts Point, CA, opened to the public in June after being under construction for 21 years. The center, located north of San Francisco, features six large temples, a holy shrine, and 6 acres (2.4 ha) of formal gardens, as well as thousands of statues, prayer wheels, and other sacred objects. The center is designed to preserve the Nyingma tradition of Tibetan Buddhism, an 8th-century movement that predates three other schools, including that of the Dalai Lama.

China's communist government continued efforts to discredit the Dalai Lama. Authorities in Tibet banned photographs of the Dalai Lama in monasteries and public places during the year and launched a campaign to try to convince Tibetans that he was no longer a religious leader. The Chinese press published articles declaring that the Dalai Lama lacked the qualifications to lead the dominant school of Tibetan Buddhism. Another source of conflict was the year-old dispute between the Dalai Lama and the Chinese government begun in 1995 over the selection of the Panchen Lama, the second-highest leader of Tibetan Buddhism.

Authorities in Myanmar began a new tourist campaign promoting excursions to the country's centuries-old pagodas. The nation's most important temple, a golden pagoda called Shwedagon located in the capital city of Yangon, was built 2,500 years ago to enshrine eight hairs of the Buddha's head. On the plains of Pagan, more than 2,000 pagodas remain, survivors of a rampage by the Mongol emperor Kublai Khan in the 13th century that destroyed more than 10,000 of these structures.

Dilip Singh Judeo, a Hindu fundamentalist serving as a member of the Indian Parliament, announced in January a campaign to reconvert 100,000 Christians in the central Indian state of Madhya Pradesh back to Hinduism. He declared 1996 to be "the year of reconversion."

DARRELL J. TURNER

With interest in the Buddhist religion increasing in the United States, the Odiyan Buddhist Center in Stewarts Point, CA, opened to the public in June 1996. Overlooking the Pacific Ocean, the center serves lay students of Tibetan Buddhism.

Islam

During 1996 adherents of movements advocating the incorporation of Islamic principles into public life campaigned against secular regimes and Muslim leaders whose policies they judged unacceptable in the Middle East. Elsewhere, Shiite Muslims clashed with a Sunni-dominated government over political participation. In Asia, Chinese authorities curbed a protest movement within the country's Muslim minority population while, in the Philippines, a lengthy conflict between Muslims and the government came to an end. In the United States the steadily growing Muslim population was receiving increased public recognition.

Algeria. In Algeria the Armed Islamic Group (GIA) and other guerrilla organizations carried out attacks against officials of the secular government, foreign residents, and Algerian citizens deemed to have violated Islamic behavioral norms. The GIA is an extremist offshoot of the Islamic Salvation Front (FIS), the political party banned in 1992 following the cancellation of parliamentary elections in which its candidates won an unanticipated victory.

In September, President Lamine Zeroual organized a Conference of National Understanding attended by representatives of some, but not all, Algerian political parties and other national organizations. The FIS was excluded, but another important Islamist party, Hamas—whose leader Mahfoud Nahnah had run second to Zeroual in presidential elections in late 1995—did participate. At the conclusion of the conference, President Zeroual promised to hold new elections early in 1997 and a referendum on constitutional reforms designed to separate religion and politics.

Saudi Arabia and Bahrain. Islamist criticism of the government of Saudi Arabia, although less forceful than in Algeria, created an atmosphere of tension there. Exiled dissidents accused Saudi rulers of failing to maintain Islamic standards and values, particularly criticizing their willingness to allow the kingdom's use as a base for foreign, non-Muslim forces. Even within the country, some Muslim leaders warned that the spread of Western cultural influences, made more accessible by modern technology, threatened Islamic values. The May execution of four men allegedly linked to Islamist opposition groups for the 1995 bombing of a U.S. military installation heightened tensions, as did the destruction a few weeks later of a U.S. military housing complex. Officials viewed both acts as attempts to embarrass the government and diminish Western support.

On the neighboring Persian Gulf island nation of Bahrain, Shiite Muslims, who comprise some 70% of the population but never have enjoyed comparable political influence, organized a series of protests and demonstrations. In June the Sunni-controlled government claimed to have thwarted an Iranian-supported plot to overthrow it.

Turkey, China, and the Philippines. Turkey's Islamic-oriented Welfare Party outpolled each of its competitors in parliamentary elections in late 1995, but was prevented from forming a government when its two main rivals forged a coalition in March. Within months, however, the arrangement collapsed and Welfare leader Necmettin Erbakan became prime minister. To the relief of many Turks who valued the separation of politics and religion, the Islamist philosophy of the Welfare Party did not produce dramatic changes in the social fabric of Turkish life nor did it alter significantly the country's foreign policy, as some of its critics had feared.

In the late spring, China claimed that Muslims in the country's far western provinces were organizing antigovernment groups with the objective of attaining some form of autonomy. In the crackdown that followed, several thousand Uighurs, a Turkic minority group, were arrested.

In August, Philippine President Fidel Ramos signed an agreement with the Moro National Liberation Front, which had waged a guerrilla campaign against the government for almost 25 years. The accord granted Muslims autonomy in 14 southern provinces where they are either a majority or a significant minority. Many Christians in the region denounced the accord, vowing to overturn it in a final status referendum scheduled for 1999.

United States. Early in 1996, U.S. Muslims were invited to the White House for the first time to mark the end of the sacred month of Ramadan. A U.S. Army Muslim chaplain (imam) presided over prayers, further symbolizing the integration of Muslims into American life. At the same time, ironically, the unsubstantiated association of U.S. Muslims with international terrorists sparked a series of attacks on mosques and individual Muslims, with more than 300 such incidents reported in the year following the April 1995 bombing of the Oklahoma City federal building.

KENNETH J. PERKINS
University of South Carolina

Judaism

Long-standing tensions between Judaism's liberal movements and the Orthodox were heightened during 1996. Among the causes of these strains were the assassination of Israeli Prime Minister Yitzhak Rabin late in 1995 by an Orthodox student; the election—with strong Orthodox backing—of Benjamin Netanyahu as prime minister in May 1996; and the onset of violence between Palestinians and Israelis in September. (*See* ISRAEL.)

In March, Rabbi Simeon Maslin, president of the Central Conference of American Rabbis, a Reform organization, publicly attacked Orthodox Judaism, comparing it to the ancient Sadducee sect, which interpreted scripture literally without regard for the changing needs of the people. After the Israeli election, some non-Orthodox denominations warned that infringement on religious pluralism in the Jewish state could lead to a cutoff of donations from American Jews.

Reform Judaism itself was caught between the forces of tradition and change. The demographic erosion of American Jewry generated pressures to ensure Jewish "continuity," and thus the newly installed leaders of Reform Judaism—Rabbi Eric Yoffie, president of the Union of American Hebrew Congregations; and Rabbi Sheldon Zimmerman, president of Hebrew Union College—both called for increased study and ritual. Yet the Reform commitment to egalitarianism led the movement to approve officially—and lobby the government for—the right of homosexual couples to civilly recognized marriage, which was anathema in the eyes of traditional Judaism. A good number of Reform rabbis were willing to perform Jewish marriage, or "commitment," ceremonies for such couples.

As for mixed-religion families—traditionally welcomed by Reform—the movement for the first time adopted a policy of exclusion: Any child who was being educated in another religion could not study in a Reform school. While this guideline was adopted to forestall the spread of religious syncretism, many Reform leaders felt that it contradicted Reform principles of openness.

Within Orthodox Judaism, the controversy over Lubavitch Hasidism escalated. Two years after the death of Rabbi Menachem Schneerson, the leader of the sect, followers who thought that he was the messiah and would yet arise from the dead continued a media campaign to convince both Jews and Gentiles of their belief. In June 1996 the Rabbinical Council of America, the largest Orthodox rabbinical body in the United States, effectively declared the messianists schismatics by passing a resolution that the idea of a resurrected messiah has no place in Judaism.

Conservative Judaism faced an institutional challenge when the University of Judaism in Los Angeles, CA, announced the opening of a full-fledged rabbinical school. Movement leaders feared that it would compete for students and funding with the Jewish Theological Seminary of America in New York City, previously the only Conservative rabbinical school. But proponents of the West Coast seminary argued that the scholarly emphasis of the New York institution was inappropriate for the West, which needed rabbis who valued spirituality over textual expertise. Once the new seminary became a fait accompli, negotiations were held to coordinate policies and standards between the two schools.

A new problem concerned the infiltration of "messianic" Jews, who believe that they can accept Jesus and remain Jews, into mainstream Jewish bodies. Some "messianics" were using subterfuge to become members and even officers of mainstream synagogues and Jewish organizations. Since Jewishness traditionally has been determined by birth rather than belief, the Jewish community lacked guidelines on whether "messianics" could or should be ejected. Jewish concern mounted in June, when the Southern Baptist Convention announced a missionary campaign targeted at the Jewish community.

LAWRENCE GROSSMAN
The American Jewish Committee

Orthodox Eastern

Archbishop Spyridon become the first U.S.-born primate of the Greek Orthodox Archdiocese of America in 1996. He succeeded Archbishop Iakovos, who retired in July after holding the position for 37 years. With millions returning to the church after the fall of communism, the number of Orthodox Christians worldwide was estimated to be 250 million.

Archbishop Spyridon. Chosen primate of the Greek Orthodox Church of America by the Holy Synod of the Ecumenical Patriarchate of Constantinople, Archbishop Spyridon was born George Papageorgiou in Warren, OH, in 1944. The new primate was graduated from the Patriarchal School of Theology in Halki, Turkey, in 1966. He served as a deacon until 1976, when he was ordained as a priest for the Greek Orthodox Church in Rome,

© Bebeto Matthews/AP/Wide World Photos

Archbishop Spyridon was installed as the first U.S.-born primate of the Greek Orthodox Archdiocese of America at the Cathedral of the Holy Trinity in New York City on Sept. 21, 1996. He succeeded Archbishop Iakovos, who held the position for 37 years.

Italy. In 1985 he was consecrated a bishop and in 1991 was appointed the first Greek Orthodox metropolitan in Venice.

Ecumenical Patriarch Bartholomew stated that Spyridon's "crowning qualification" for the position was his "unlimited fidelity and devotion" to the "ecumenical throne." The patriarch's statement, together with the establishment of three new metropolitanates—one for Canada; one for Central America, Mexico and the Caribbean; and one for South America—indicate a new policy for Greek Orthodoxy in North and South America. Prior to Spyridon's appointment, all three metropolitanates were part of one archdiocese under Archbishop Iakovos.

Estonia and Albania. The Russian Orthodox Church broke relations with the Church of Constantinople when the ecumenical patriarchate, responding to pleas from Orthodox Estonians, reclaimed ecclesiastical jurisdiction in Estonia after having transferred the Estonian Orthodox Church to the Moscow patriarchate in 1978. A permanent split between the patriarchates was avoided when they agreed that Orthodox in Estonia may choose their ecclesiastical allegiance. Some churches remained within the Moscow patriarchate and others were reestablished into an autonomous Orthodox Church of Estonia under the ecumenical patriarchate.

The ecumenical patriarchate also consecrated and appointed three metropolitans for sees in Albania. The new metropolitans were elected when the Autocephalous Orthodox Church of Albania was reestablished by Constantinople after the collapse of communism, but were refused entrance into the country. The Albanian government persisted in forbidding these bishops, who are of Greek nationality, to occupy the dioceses. Archbishop Anastasios of Tiräne, also of Greek nationality, declined to participate in the consecrations.

Balkans, Bulgaria, Ukraine, Slovakia. The Holy Synod of the Serbian Orthodox Church continued to censure the actions of former communist nationalist leaders and to call the Serbian people to "reconciliation and repentance," urging them to "make peace with the peoples with whom we have lived for centuries." The episcopate also continued to demand justice for Serbians expelled from their homelands, especially the victims of the complete "ethnic cleansing."

Divisions among the Orthodox in Bulgaria were solved, with schismatic groups being reintegrated into the patriarchate. Divisions among the Orthodox in Ukraine persisted, but significant steps were taken toward reunification of the Ukrainian Orthodox Church and the Ukrainian Autocephalous Orthodox Church. Disputes between Orthodox and Greek Catholics in Ukraine and Slovakia quieted as the divided churches continued to organize their separate lives. Many new seminaries have opened on both sides. Orthodox in Slovakia were constructing new churches in major cities and towns.

Orthodox and Catholics. The Russian Orthodox Church and the Roman Catholic Church renewed pledges not to interfere with each other's members in Russia or to encourage transfer from one church to the other. Patriarch Aleksy II of Moscow refused an invitation to meet with Pope John Paul II in Hungary, saying that the time was not yet ripe for such an encounter. The pope and the patriarch of Constantinople, who met again in Rome, received a party of Catholic and Orthodox bishops and theologians from North America. The delegation was part of a celebration of the 25th anniversary of the Roman Catholic–Orthodox dialogue in the United States and Canada.

THOMAS HOPKO
St. Vladimir's Orthodox Seminary

Protestantism

During 1996, Protestants disagreed on such thorny questions as ordination of homosexuals and women and even on the doctrine of salvation. A nationwide survey by the Barna Research Group found that attendance at church services in the United States was at an 11-year low, with only 37% of Americans attending in a given week.

The Ordination of Homosexuals. During the 1996 quadrennial General Conference of the 8.6-million-member United Methodist Church in Denver in April, 15 bishops issued a statement of dissent against the denomination's ban on ordaining homosexuals to the ministry. However, delegates voted 577–378 against changing the church's 24-year-old position that the practice of homosexuality is "incompatible with Christian teaching."

Bishops of an Episcopal Church court voted 7–1 in Wilmington, DE, in May to dismiss heresy charges against retired Bishop Walter Righter for ordaining a gay man as a deacon. They said a 1979 General Convention resolution deeming it "not appropriate" to ordain a practicing homosexual or anyone engaging in heterosexual relationships outside of marriage was a recommendation that did not have the full force of church law in the 2.1-million-member denomination.

A document in support of a group that favors the ordination of homosexuals to the Anglican priesthood was issued in February with the signatures of 300 bishops, including Archbishop Desmond Tutu of South Africa and the heads of Anglican bodies in Canada, Scotland, and the United States.

The General Assembly of the Presbyterian Church (U.S.A.), meeting in Albuquerque, NM, in July, voted 313–236 for a measure that would require fidelity in marriage and chastity in singleness for all officers of the 2.7-million-member denomination, thus barring practicing homosexuals from ordination. The amendment was sent to the presbyteries for approval. Earlier the Permanent Judicial Commission of the church's Cincinnati Presbytery declared the ordination of an allegedly gay man "null and void." A similar action reversing the ordination of a homosexual was taken in June by the General Assembly of the 800,000-member Presbyterian Church of Canada, meeting in Charlottetown, P.E.I.

In October the Atlanta presbytery of the Presbyterian Church (U.S.A.) voted to uphold the ordination of Erin Swenson, a transsexual who had undergone a sex-change procedure.

New Positions for Women. In August, Ruth Hofman of Toronto became the first woman

Rev. Tom Elliff of Del City, OK, and his wife attended the 1996 annual meeting of the Southern Baptist Convention (SBC) in New Orleans, at which he was elected SBC president.

© Judi Bottoni/AP/Wide World Photos

ordained to the full ministry in the 211,000-member Christian Reformed Church (CRC) of North America. At its annual synod in Grand Rapids, MI, in June, the denomination declined 24 petitions challenging its 1995 decision to allow regional church groups to ordain women. That led the 20,000-member Orthodox Presbyterian Church to suspend fellowship with the CRC.

Other strides for women in Protestant bodies in 1996 included the election of Claire Elgersma of Kitchener, Ont., as first clerk of the Reformed Ecumenical Council. It marked the first time the organization of 30 Calvinist bodies with 5 million members had elected a woman officer. Frances Alguire of New Buffalo, MI, was elected to chair the World Methodist Council, the first time a woman or a layperson had been chosen to head the 32-million-member organization of Methodist churches.

Other Controversies. The Rev. Richard A. Rhem came into conflict with the 200,000-member Reformed Church in America for saying he no longer believes that faith in Jesus is the only way to salvation. A regional governing body of the church censured him in July, and his nearly 1,000-member congregation, Christ Community Church in Spring Lake, MI, then voted to leave the denomination. In May two congregations were expelled from the Florida Baptist Convention for charismatic tendencies in what was believed to be the first time a state Southern Baptist body had used the denomination's 1963 "Baptist Faith and Message" statement to exercise discipline against a local church.

Southern Baptist Convention. The Rev. Tom Elliff of Del City, OK, was elected president of the 15.6-million-member Southern Baptist Convention (SBC) at its annual meeting in June in New Orleans, marking the first time since 1942 that a nonincumbent president was elected without opposition. The convention criticized several policies of the Walt Disney Co., including providing insurance for same-sex partners of employees, opening theme parks to homosexual groups during gay and lesbian theme nights, and releasing films like *Priest*, which the resolution said "disparages Christian values and depicts Christian leaders as morally defective." The resolution said Southern Baptists would be urged to boycott the company unless it changed such policies. In a similar action, the General Presbytery of the Assemblies of God called in August for that denomination's 2.5 million members to boycott Disney for "abandoning the commitment to strong moral values."

Other Developments. Two major changes in the life of Protestant bodies came about at the beginning of 1996. The first step toward separation of the Church of Sweden and the government occurred January 1, when children born to at least one Lutheran parent were no longer given automatic membership in the state Lutheran church. And in the United States the overseas mission boards of the 1.5-million-member United Church of Christ and the 1-million-member Christian Church (Disciples of Christ) were merged into a Common Global Ministries board.

In September leaders of Anglican churches in Great Britain and Lutheran churches in Scandinavia signed a plan for full communion. A month later bishops of the Episcopal Church and the Evangelical Lutheran Church in America met in White Haven, PA, to hash out a similar agreement to be voted on by their conventions in 1997.

DARRELL J. TURNER

Roman Catholicism

For the second year in a row, the health of Pope John Paul II was at the forefront of concern for the world's 1 billion Catholics.

The Pope. After several bouts with fever and nausea caused by "recurring episodes of inflammation of the appendix," according to the Vatican, the 76-year-old pontiff had his appendix removed in October. But even after the surgery, the public was left wondering about the ongoing tremor in the pope's left arm. The Vatican has described it as a "extrapyramidal" disturbance, a term that can include Parkinson's disease. Despite his health problems, the pope traveled throughout the year, urging true peace and solidarity in the Latin American countries of Guatemala, Nicaragua, El Salvador, and Venezuela. He also visited Tunisia, Slovenia (his first visit there since the breakup of Yugoslavia in 1991), Germany, Hungary, and France. In a move signaling a thawing in the relationship between the Catholic Church and Cuba, the pope met with Cuba's President Fidel Castro in November for the first time.

Pope John Paul celebrated his 50th anniversary of priestly ordination on November 1. In October the pope made world headlines when he said it was time the Catholic Church recognized the theory of evolution "as more than a hypothesis." He said evidence now supports the idea that humans developed along an evolutionary line. John Paul II also made some minor changes to the centuries-

© Porter Gifford/Gamma-Liaison

CARDINAL JOSEPH L. BERNARDIN

Cardinal Joseph L. Bernardin, the archbishop of Chicago since 1982, died of cancer on Nov. 14, 1996. The cardinal had gained wide respect for the way he confronted his illness. He was awarded the Presidential Medal of Freedom shortly before his death.

Born in Columbia, SC, on April 2, 1928, he was ordained a priest in 1952. He was the first general secretary of the National Conference of Catholic Bishops and the U.S. Catholic Conference (1968–72), and was chosen archbishop of Cincinnati in 1972.

old, secretive tradition of electing a pope. Up to 120 cardinal electors will be housed in a newly constructed guest house inside Vatican City, from where they will be taken to the Sistine Chapel for voting. In the past, they had stayed in the ancient rooms surrounding the chapel. The Vatican reported a $1.7 million surplus for 1995. It was the third straight year in which operating expenses were kept under budget after years of million-dollar deficits.

Church Reform. Bishop Fabian Bruskewitz of Lincoln, NE, stirred debate in March when he threatened Catholic members of groups supporting legal abortion or euthanasia—which are against Catholic teaching—with excommunication. Vatican officials were studying the pastoral and legal ramifications of the action. Archbishop John R. Quinn, a retired San Francisco archbishop, sparked controversy when he called for major reforms in the Roman Curia, the church's network of central administrative agencies, as well as new ways of selecting bishops. He also said a new ecumenical council should open the millennium and let the world's bishops discuss frankly and openly key issues facing the church. Cardinal Joseph L. Bernardin of Chicago and a group of U.S. Catholic leaders announced a Catholic Common Ground Project to promote dialogue to overcome divisions among Catholics on such issues as the changing roles of women, the declining numbers of priests and nuns, and religious education for children. The project drew varied reaction from church officials. Some said that it could become a forum for dissent.

U.S. Developments. In November the U.S. bishops agreed on a plan for ministry to young adults, a statement of economic-justice principles, and a document that applies papal norms to U.S. institutions of Catholic higher education. They approved the final two segments of the Sacramentary, the book of prayers and instructions used during Mass. The Sacramentary changes would go to the Vatican for approval. They discussed but did not finalize a plan to restructure their twin conferences.

The sacred seal of confession came under scrutiny after Oregon jailers taped a murder suspect's confession to a priest without informing either party. Church officials asked a court to order destruction of the tape, but as of late November the court had refused. U.S. Catholic leaders and lay people unsuccessfully pushed for a ban on "partial-birth abortion," a late-term abortion procedure. In an unprecedented move, all eight active U.S. cardinals wrote a letter to President Bill Clinton, condemning his veto of the legislation. They later led a prayer service on the steps of the U.S. Capitol, urging members of Congress to override the president's veto. The override vote failed. Catholic leaders also spoke out against proposals legalizing physician-assisted suicide.

People. Mother Teresa, the 1979 Nobel Peace Prize winner who widely is considered a living saint because of her work with the poor, was hospitalized several times. At 86, she became one of only five persons in U.S. history to receive honorary U.S. citizenship. Meanwhile, the Missionaries of Charity, the religious order she founded and has led since 1950, planned to hold an election for a new superior general in late 1996 or early 1997. Bishop Carlos Filipe Ximenes Belo of East Timor became the first Catholic bishop to win the Nobel Peace Prize. The 48-year-old cleric shared the 1996 prize with an exiled East Timorese activist for their struggle for peace on the Indonesian island.

The Numbers. While the number of priests, religious sisters, and brothers worldwide dropped slightly in 1995 from 1994, the number of men studying for the priesthood reflected a 1.3% increase and the number of permanent deacons grew by almost 4%, according to the 1997 *Catholic Almanac*. The almanac also reported a slight increase in the number of U.S. Catholics, which stood at more than 57.4 million—about 22% of the population.

JILL JASUTA
"The Catholic Review"

RETAILING

U.S. retail sales were robust during the first half of 1996, then weakened in the third quarter. The third-quarter uncertainty was caused in part by the highest level of consumer debt load since 1975. Concomitantly, there was a significant increase in credit-card delinquencies and personal bankruptcies in 1996. Nonetheless most analysts predicted a moderate boost in retail sales for 1996 overall compared with 1995 levels. Rising incomes, low unemployment, and high consumer confidence led to the optimistic assessments.

Consumer Confidence. When consumer confidence and optimism are high, consumer spending—which accounts for approximately two thirds of the U.S. economy—is usually brisk. Consumer confidence, as measured by the Conference Board index, hit a six-year high in the summer of 1996, then tapered off somewhat. In November another established indicator of consumer sentiment, a monthly survey conducted by the University of Michigan, indicated that consumer optimism had surged to a ten-year high.

Retail Sales. Through the first three quarters of 1996, the five largest retailers (Wal-Mart, Kmart, Sears, Dayton Hudson, and J.C. Penney) posted moderate sales gains. Retail sales were particularly strong in the areas of apparel, home goods, and general merchandise. Wal-Mart, the nation's largest retailer, continued its expansion efforts by announcing plans to open 185 additional stores worldwide. Wal-Mart would have more than 2,000 stores worldwide, more than 350 Supercenters, and approximately 450 Sam's Clubs by the end of 1997.

Dayton Hudson, the fourth-largest retailer, sold four of its Marshall Field stores in August and expressed interest in selling off more stores outside the Midwest, its core market. Dayton Hudson is the parent company of Dayton, Hudson, Mervyn's California, and Target stores. Target continued to be the strength of the company with more than 70% of Dayton-Hudson's operating profit. Kmart, near bankruptcy in 1995, continued to have its difficulties, yet overall it was a good year for the second-largest retailer in the United States. Kmart broke a streak of 13 consecutive quarters of declines or losses in the second quarter of 1996. Most of the progress, however, was due to the sale of assets and substantial cost-cutting measures. The company continued to have revenue problems.

Cyberspace Shopping. In 1996 the emphasis in cyberspace was beginning to turn from marketing and advertising of products to direct sale of these products. Widespread acceptance of this direct-sales innovation may not occur for a few years, in part because of the problems with fraud, privacy issues, and credit-card-security issues.

© Godlewski/Gamma-Liaison

After facing near-bankruptcy in 1995, Kmart rebounded in 1996. The second-largest U.S. retailer opened its first store in downtown Manhattan, New York City, above, *in the fall.*

Nonetheless the future success of cyberspace shopping is assured. Retailer benefits include the reduction of inventories and locations for their products. Fewer employees also are required. Consumer benefits include convenience, prices that are typically 10% to 30% off regular retail prices, and the virtually unlimited selection of goods and services that can be offered. By late 1996 there were 40 million users of this technology, and the numbers were increasing rapidly. It was expected that hundreds of other large and small retailers would enter the cyberspace marketplace in the years immediately ahead.

MEL J. ZELENAK
University of Missouri-Columbia

ROMANIA

Romania's domestic political situation underwent dramatic changes during 1996. President Ion Iliescu's governing coalition of socialists and nationalists unraveled, and reformer Emil Constantinescu led his opposition coalition, the Democratic Convention, to victory in local, parliamentary, and presidential elections. Meanwhile, the country's economic performance barely improved, but Romania signed an important treaty with neighboring Hungary.

Political Changes. During 1996, Romania experienced major political turmoil. The ruling Party for Social Democracy of Romania (PDSR), a postcommunist formation that had been in power for seven years, began to shift toward the political center because of rising public discontent and the government's desire to move the country closer to the North Atlantic Treaty Organization (NATO). Despite this shift, the PDSR suffered a major setback in local elections in June, when the opposition Democratic Convention (CD) and its ally, the Social Democratic Union (USD), won a majority of mayoral and local-council seats in the larger cities. Following the elections, the PDSR broke with several nationalist groupings in its ruling coalition, including the extremist anti-Hungarian Party of Romanian National Unity (PUNR). Major cabinet reshuffles also took place in preparation for the November elections.

As the country's economic situation worsened, the anti-incumbent mood grew. As a result, in the November parliamentary elections, the CD and USD combined to win 76 of the 143 seats in the Senate and 175 of the 343 seats in the Chamber of Deputies, enabling them to form a governing coalition. In the presidential ballot, Constantinescu won 54.4% of the vote to 45.6% for Iliescu. Victor Ciorbea, who earlier had defeated former tennis star Ilie Nastase in the Bucharest mayoral election, was named prime minister.

Economic Problems. Romania's economy grew slowly during the year, and the economic-reform program continued to lag. The country entered the next stage of its mass privatization program—designed to sell off about 60% of state-owned companies—but vested political interests and widespread corruption prevented the emergence of genuine competition or a free market. Inflation rose to 45% by year's end, while exports dropped by about 10%. The new government would face a severe challenge in closing obsolete industries, curtailing spending, limiting the wasteful bureaucracy, privatizing banks, developing capital markets, and modernizing the inefficient agricultural sector, which continued to be subsidized.

Romania also experienced an energy crisis. To prevent major energy shortages, the government increased its oil and other fuel imports, while subsidizing energy prices. Numerous strikes and industrial actions were staged during the year, with workers demanding wage increases. Further protests could be expected if the new government scaled down its subsidies to obsolete and uncompetitive industries.

Foreign Successes. With the goal of preparing Romania for eventual membership in NATO, Bucharest pursued a very active foreign policy in 1996. Officials held a series of high-level meetings in NATO countries, and the government sponsored a series of Partnership for Peace military exercises with NATO members on Romanian territory. The authorities also undertook broad measures to reform and modernize the armed forces to bring them up to NATO standards.

After several years of dispute over its provisions, a treaty was signed by Romania and Hungary that gave minority-rights guarantees to the 1.6 million ethnic Hungarians who live in Romania's province of Transylvania. The treaty also guaranteed Romania's borders. Bucharest signed an agreement with the European Union (EU) that established a bilateral free-trade area and gave Romania favorable trade concessions. However, most of the Romanian economy still needed to be harmonized with EU standards before economic integration could be considered. The United States granted Romania "most favored nation" trade status.

JANUSZ BUGAJSKI
Center for Strategic and International Studies

ROMANIA • Information Highlights

Official Name: Romania.
Location: Southeastern Europe.
Area: 91,699 sq mi (237 500 km²).
Population (mid-1996 est.): 22,600,000.
Chief Cities (July 1, 1993 est.): Bucharest, the capital, 2,066,723; Constanța, 348,985; Iași, 337,643.
Government: *Head of state,* Emil Constantinescu, president (elected November 1996). *Head of government,* Victor Ciorbea, prime minister (named November 1996). *Legislature*—Parliament: Senate and Chamber of Deputies.
Monetary Unit: Leu (3,028.0 lei equal U.S.$1, June 1996).
Gross Domestic Product (1994 est. U.S.$): $64,700,000,000 (purchasing power parity).
Economic Indexes (1995): *Consumer Prices* (1991 =100): all items, 3,461.4; food, 3,657.3. *Industrial Production* (1990 = 100): 65.
Foreign Trade (1995 U.S.$): *Imports,* $9,424,000,000; *exports,* $7,548,000,000.

Russia and the Commonwealth of Independent States

The year 1996, the fifth since the end of the Soviet Union, was one of the most dramatic of Russia's brief existence as a free society. It was a year dominated by elections, an internal war that waxed and waned, a presidential health crisis, and a gradually improving economy. Shaping most of these events were strong public personalities—particularly President Boris Yeltsin, who was reelected, and retired Gen. Alexander Lebed, whose year ran the gamut from rival to protégé to political outcast. The presidential campaign dominated the first half of the year, while regional elections throughout nearly two-thirds of the Russian Federation were a central preoccupation of the last four months of 1996. Russia's war against its breakaway republic of Chechnya became an issue in the presidential race as fighting flared and subsided amid patchwork peace talks, until what appeared to be a durable peace was reached during the summer. Yeltsin's heart condition, also an election issue, reached a crisis state in late spring, necessitating his temporary withdrawal from public life during the summer and much of the fall, until successful surgery apparently brought him relief. Finally, foreign affairs remained on a steady course, while the economy showed modest signs of bottoming out and beginning to turn up. (*See also* FEATURE ARTICLE, page 34.)

Political Developments. The year opened with the Communist Party and its nationalist allies holding the majority in the State Duma, the lower house of parliament, in the wake of the December 1995 parliamentary elections. As a result, the Communists were able to place their people in the Duma's key leadership positions. However, the campaign to elect the president, which kicked off in January, overshadowed the legislative branch for much of the next six months. Gennadi Zyuganov, leader of the Communist Party and its parliamentary faction, was the early front-runner in the presidential race, and hence was on the campaign trail much of the time. Yeltsin, the trailing incumbent, in turn was struggling to regain popularity with a flood of executive decrees, high-profile state visits, and various grand gestures, all of which commanded the front pages and the top of the news.

In March the Duma did come center stage in a dramatic move that the majority soon came to regret. Trying to capitalize on what they perceived as the politics of nostalgia, the Communist leadership of the Duma pushed through a resolution nullifying the treaties signed in December 1991 that formally disbanded the USSR. Although the poorly thought-out resolution had no legal force, it aroused a furor—both domestically and in many former Soviet republics. By implication, the Communists had declared illegitimate the Russian Federation as an independent state, along with most of its governing institutions—including the parliament itself. As Yeltsin

Reuters/Archive Photos

After undergoing a multiple-bypass heart operation in Moscow on Nov. 5, 1996, Russia's President Boris Yeltsin took a much-publicized recuperative walk with his wife and granddaughter on the hospital grounds on November 20. The president's health was a subject of great speculation in the West during the spring and summer.

On Aug. 31, 1996, retired Gen. Alexander Lebed (left), who served as President Yeltsin's national security adviser from mid-June until October 17, signed an agreement with the commander of secessionist troops in Chechnya to end the conflict in the breakaway Russian republic. Late in the year, President Yeltsin ordered all of Russia's remaining garrison troops out of Chechnya.

pointed out in ironic rebuttal, he as president was the only legitimate figure left standing by the misguided resolution, since he had been elected in June 1991, before the demise of the Soviet Union. Many observers thought that the Communists had overreached and subjected their presidential candidate, Zyuganov, to public derision. Added to the chorus of protests were the outraged voices of the leaders of the former Soviet republics whose independent statehoods since 1991 had been called into question by the Duma's symbolic action.

In what was rated as an impressive political comeback, Yeltsin won reelection as president in a runoff election on July 3, after he narrowly outpolled Zyuganov in the initial June balloting. A surprise third-place finisher in the first round of voting was Lebed, who, with little prior political experience, ran as a law-and-order candidate. As it turned out, the Yeltsin campaign—which was awash in campaign funds, both legal and illegal, and had much of the press on its side—quietly had assisted Lebed's candidacy with advisers, funds, and media attention, with the purpose of drawing voters away from Zyuganov. Since Yeltsin only edged out Zyuganov by a few points in the first round, the strategy appeared successful. Then, to ensure victory in the runoff, President Yeltsin struck a deal with Lebed, bringing him into the administration in return for his support.

Yeltsin's electoral success nearly became a Pyrrhic victory, almost costing him his life. His vigorous efforts on the campaign trail brought on cardiac problems—either a heart attack or a milder attack of ischemia—in June that largely kept him out of the public eye between the first round and the July runoff. Then, after winning a second term, the president-elect dropped out of sight except for a brief appearance at his inauguration in August. Behind the scenes, doctors were evaluating his condition to determine if surgical intervention would be safe. A decision was made, and Yeltsin in September broke the Kremlin's silence, announcing he would be out of action for several months in connection with heart surgery. A key medical player in the high drama was the visiting Dr. Michael DeBakey, a renowned U.S. cardiovascular surgeon who, by voicing optimism about Yeltsin's prognosis, helped stabilize Russian elite politics during the fall. After a long preoperative period, the president underwent multiple-bypass surgery in early November. The operation proved a success, and President Yeltsin returned to work in the Kremlin during Christmas week.

The Chechen Crisis and Russian Federalism. The crisis in the republic of Chechnya, one of the 89 components of the Russian Federation, had waxed and waned since Russian troops began assaulting the secessionist province in December 1994. Negotiations had occurred in 1995, with peace accords and truces brokered and broken in quick succession. By the start of the presidential campaign in early 1996, polls indicated Chechnya was a burning issue for a majority of the public, which wanted an end to the fighting. Responding to this concern, Yeltsin at the last minute managed to preside over yet another peace agreement on the eve of the June election. Then, after bringing Lebed in as his national security adviser, Yeltsin assigned him the task of negotiating a political settlement to the Chechen crisis.

During the summer, Lebed did just that, but with a seriously ill chief executive in seclusion, he found little support among the president's staff back in Moscow. Lebed had brought an end to what one Russian human-rights leader called "the dirty war in Chechnya," securing a politically face-saving exit for Russia, but many Russian politicians and journalists criticized him for selling out Russia's interests. The blunt and combative former general struck back at his critics with harsh words. Although the peace held, by the fall Lebed's outspokenness got him in trouble with many of Yeltsin's aides, and the president dismissed him in October. After his surgery, however, a recuperating Yeltsin acknowledged the new political reality and ordered all remaining garrison troops out of Chechnya.

Politically and legally, the Yeltsin administration had justified the invasion of Chechnya by stressing the need to preserve Russia's territorial integrity. Yet, by the end of 1996, the Chechen rebels had prevailed politically and were on their way to de facto sovereignty, well ahead of the five-year waiting period negotiated by Lebed. Meanwhile, none of the other 20 republics of Russia had shown any signs of seceding from the federation. On the contrary, the central government, recognizing the need for some decentralization, had begun an orderly process of devolving authority by signing a bilateral treaty with the republic of Tatarstan in early 1994. Subsequently, similar power-sharing treaties with other republics followed. By early 1996 the administrative regions also were included in the treaty devolution process, with Sverdlovsk oblast being the first to sign an agreement with Moscow. Then, in the course of the presidential campaign, Yeltsin quickened the process, signing bilateral treaties with a number of other federation components, especially those in vote-rich areas of the country.

By late fall, indications of an embryonic "state's rights" trend could be observed. A much-needed bill on the structure of the judicial system passed the Duma and was sent to the upper house, the Federation Council, where the republics and regions are represented most heavily. There, the bill initially failed by two votes as its opponents argued that it denied the republics' right to organize subnational judicial systems. Compromises were reached and the bill was signed into law on December 31. The regional and local elections, beginning in September and running through the end of 1996—and including 52 gubernatorial races as well as 26 big-city mayoral contests—were expected to strengthen the trend toward the federalization of Russia.

The Economy. By the end of Russia's fifth year of economic reform, several international and Western financial institutions cautiously were forecasting the end of the country's great depression and projecting the first signs of modest growth for 1997. The International Monetary Fund (IMF), the Organization for Economic Cooperation and Development (OECD), and the credit-rating agencies Moody's and Standard and Poor's all expressed guarded optimism about Russia's economic future. The IMF acted first by extending a three-year, $10.2 billion loan to Russia on March 26. However, concerned over weakening economic indicators, the IMF suspended the October disbursement of $336 million. After some improvement, the transfer was made in December, bringing the total disbursed to $2.7 billion. At year's end, the OECD concluded that the Russian economy had stopped contracting and at last might experience marginal growth. From the credit agencies came a similar vote of confidence. For the first time, they rated Russia's corporate debt, giving it the equivalent of U.S. junk bonds—a debt grade below Poland's corporate-debt rating, but higher than that of Brazil.

COMMONWEALTH OF INDEPENDENT STATES • Information Highlights

Nation	Population (in millions)	Area (sq mi)	Area (km^2)	Capital	Head of State and Government
Armenia	3.8	11,506	29 800	Yerevan	Levon Akopovich Ter-Petrosyan, president
Azerbaijan	7.6	33,436	86 600	Baku	Geidar A. Aliyev, president
Belarus	10.3	80,154	207 600	Minsk	Aleksandr Lukashenko, president
Georgia	5.4	26,911	69 700	Tbilisi	Eduard Shevardnadze, president
Kazakhstan	16.5	1,049,151	2 717 300	Alma-Aty	Nursultan A. Nazarbayev, president
Kyrgyzstan	4.6	76,641	198 500	Bishkek (Frunze)	Askar Akayev, president
Moldova	4.3	13,012	33 700	Chisinau (Kishinev)	Petru Lucinschi, president
Russia	147.7	6,592,741	17 075 200	Moscow	Boris Yeltsin, president
Tajikistan	5.9	55,251	143 100	Dushanbe	Emomili Rakhmonov, president
Turkmenistan	4.6	188,456	488 100	Ashkhabad	Saparmurad Niyazov, president
Ukraine	51.1	233,089	603 700	Kiev	Leonid Kuchma, president
Uzbekistan	23.2	172,741	447 400	Tashkent	Islam Karimov, president

Both Russian and foreign economists tended to agree that, statistically, 1996 had been a relatively good year. Russia had a favorable balance of trade, privatization continued with 70% of the economy in private hands, gross-national-product (GNP) decline was leveling off at approximately 4%, and inflation had fallen from over 100% in 1995 to a consensus figure of 22% in 1996. On the other hand, falling tax revenues and growing payment arrearage represented serious problems during 1996. The presidential campaign had disrupted tax collection as candidate Yeltsin handed out tax breaks, while many large firms withheld payments just in case the anti-market Zyuganov won the election. During the summer and early fall, tax revenues were down 25%, causing the IMF twice to delay its loan payments to Russia. Only through tough enforcement measures, including threatening some of the biggest tax scofflaws with bankruptcy proceedings, were collection levels partially restored. Wage and salary arrears constituted the other major crisis, with arrearages growing to $8 billion by November, twice the midsummer level. As of late December, more than 62% of the labor force still was waiting for September wages. In response to personal hardship, hundreds of thousands of coal miners, teachers, and government employees struck throughout the country in the most massive labor upheaval since the end of the Soviet regime. Ominously, the miners no longer confined their demands to economic issues, but included a call for the cabinet's resignation as well.

Foreign Affairs. Russia's foreign relations throughout the year continued past trends. President Yeltsin in January appointed a new foreign minister, Yevgeniy Primakov, an experienced diplomat of a more conservative bent than his liberal predecessor Andrei Kozyrev. Primakov continued Russia's diplomatic opposition to the North Atlantic Treaty Organization's (NATO's) enlargement into Eastern and Central Europe, but also gave priority to strengthening the Commonwealth of Independent States (CIS), and particularly Russia's role in it. To this end, Russia signed an economic-integration agreement with three other CIS members—Kazakhstan, Kyrgyzstan, and Belarus. In addition, in April, Russia and Belarus signed an accord to bring the two countries together gradually into an economic and political union called the Community of Sovereign Republics. On the other side of the ledger, Russia maintained pressure on Ukraine over the division of the Black Sea fleet and control of its port facilities, as well as on both Latvia and Estonia over the legal status of the large Russian minorities in those two Baltic states. Finally, relations with the United States remained stable, with the U.S. government discreetly supporting Yeltsin's successful bid for reelection.

ROBERT SHARLET, *Union College*

The Commonwealth of Independent States

During 1996 the leaders of the 12 member nations of the Commonwealth of Independent States (CIS) held their 18th and 19th summit meetings since the organization of former Soviet republics was established in December 1991. The 18th summit, held in Moscow, Russia, on January 19, dealt with strife in Georgia, with the CIS states agreeing to impose sanctions on the rebellious republic of Abkhazia; and with the revolt in Tajikistan, with the CIS agreeing to extend the mandate of its Russian-dominated peacekeeping force.

The 19th summit, also held in Moscow, on May 17, seemed to have a political agenda, with the member nations endorsing Boris Yeltsin's bid for reelection in Russia's June presidential election. An early June meeting between Yeltsin and the leaders of Armenia, Azerbaijan, and Georgia also was political in intent, with Yeltsin trying to assure Russian voters that solutions to the ethnic conflicts in the Caucasus were in the process of being resolved.

Three important CIS pacts were signed during the year. In March, Belarus, Kazakhstan, Kyrgyzstan, and Russia signed a treaty to create a community of integrated states for the purpose of furthering economic cooperation. In April, Belarus and Russia signed a treaty that provided for closer political and economic ties and possible future reintegration. And in August, Kazakhstan, Kyrgyzstan, and Uzbekistan signed an agreement to create a single economic market by 1998.

Despite these efforts to improve economic relations, many CIS member states continued to falter in their efforts to reform their economies. Exacerbating the situation was such internal strife as voting violations, increasingly authoritarian rule, antigovernment demonstrations, civil war, and secessionist movements.

ARMENIA. Armenia faced considerable unrest in the fall after President Levon Ter-Petrosyan won reelection to a second five-year term; opposition forces, calling the election a fraud, staged massive demonstrations and demanded Ter-Petrosyan's resignation.

Presidential Election. On September 22, in Armenia's first presidential election since it became independent after the 1991 collapse of the Soviet Union, Ter-Petrosyan won 52% of the vote, while his main opponent, former Prime Minister Vazgen Manukian of the National Democratic Union (NDU), won 41%. There were very serious irregularities in the election, according to observers from the Organization for Security and Cooperation in Europe (OSCE). Opposition parties went even further, saying that the election was rigged to give Ter-Petrosyan more than 50% of the vote so that he would not have to face Manukian in a runoff election. One day after the vote, some 40,000 people staged demonstrations against Ter-Petrosyan's election in the capital city of Yerevan. On the following day, when opposition forces attempted to storm the parliament building, the government labeled the action as an attempted coup. It not only ordered riot police and other security forces to disperse the crowds, but also raided opposition-party headquarters and arrested several opposition leaders. NDU leader Manukian and others went into hiding.

Azerbaijan Conflict and the Economy. The Armenian-Azerbaijani cease-fire, in effect since May 1994, held in 1996, and peace talks between Armenia and Azerbaijan over Nagorno-Karabakh, the Armenian-controlled enclave within Azerbaijan, continued.

On the economic front, Armenia had a budget deficit of about $86.8 million, or 7% of gross domestic product (GDP), for 1996. Early in the year, the International Monetary Fund (IMF) approved a three-year, $148 million loan. It was, however, contingent upon the government's enforcement of stricter discipline in banking and the reformation of the power sector.

AZERBAIJAN. In February runoff elections for 15 parliamentary seats, the New Azerbaijan Party, aligned with President Geidar Aliyev, picked up 12 seats to add to the majority it had won in the November 1995 elections. As they had in 1995, opposition parties accused the government of voting violations.

Also in February, former Foreign Minister Tofik Gasymov was given a 15-year prison sentence for his role in the March 1995 coup attempt involving a rebel paramilitary unit north of Baku, the capital. Twenty-five other people received sentences of between 10 and 15 years.

In July, in the wake of President Aliyev's accusations of economic mismanagement by the government, Prime Minister Fuad Quliyev resigned and was replaced on an interim basis by First Deputy Prime Minister Artur Rasizade. Three other senior ministers with economic responsibilities were dismissed. Rasizade was appointed prime minister by a presidential decree in November.

Budget, the Economy, and the Armenia Conflict. The 1996 Azerbaijani budget, which included a 50% increase in social spending, was expected to have a deficit of $116.3 million. Good economic news was the signing in January of an agreement with Russia to pipe Azerbaijani

After opposition forces in Armenia claimed that the Sept. 22, 1996, reelection of President Ter-Petrosyan was rigged and sought to storm parliament, riot police and government security forces took up positions at the building, left, *and dispersed the crowds.*

In late October 1996 a large crowd in Minsk, Belarus, protested the forthcoming referendum on the nation's new constitution. The new constitution, which was approved in the referendum and signed on November 28, increased President Aleksandr Lukashenko's control over the legislative and judicial branches of the government.

© Robert King/Sygma

crude oil from Caspian Sea fields to a Russian port on the Black Sea, from which it could reach world markets. The signing of the agreement was welcomed by the consortium of U.S. and British oil companies that in 1994 had agreed to develop the Caspian Sea oil fields.

There were no reports of border clashes between Azerbaijan and Armenia during 1996. But Armenians continued to consolidate their hold on their Nagorno-Karabakh enclave in Azerbaijan.

BELARUS. On April 2, 1996, Belarussian President Aleksandr Lukashenko and Russian President Boris Yeltsin signed a treaty establishing a Community of Sovereign Republics. It provided for increased political, military, and economic cooperation, as well as further—as yet unspecified—steps toward eventual reintegration. Thousands of Belarussians protested the pact on the grounds that it would give Russia an opportunity to suppress Belarussian culture. In November, Belarus turned over to Russia the last of the former Soviet Union's nuclear weapons that had remained in Belarus after the 1991 breakup of the Soviet Union.

Politics and New Constitution. On the political front, President Lukashenko held a referendum in November to amend Belarus' constitution in a way that would give him near-absolute power. His efforts to turn his already authoritarian rule into what many feared would be a Soviet-style dictatorship met with harsh condemnation by the Belarus parliament, as well as the nations of Eastern Europe and the West. Lukashenko wanted to extend his term to the year 2001 and expand his power over the legislative and judicial branches of government. The parliament, on the other hand, wanted to abolish the presidency and increase the power of the prime minister and his cabinet. Despite efforts by Russia to bring about a compromise between Lukashenko and the parliament, Lukashenko went ahead with the referendum. According to government sources, more than 70% of the voters approved Lukashenko's proposals, but government opponents and neutral observers said there were serious voting irregularities. On November 28, Lukashenko signed the new constitution—which the Council of Europe said violates the separation of powers.

The new constitution allows Lukashenko to rule by decree and to create a new upper house of parliament, to which he can appoint 20 of the 60 members. He also formed a new 110-deputy lower house that contained his supporters from the former parliament. The constitution also gave Lukashenko the power to appoint half the members of the constitutional court. Three senior judges earlier had protested Lukashenko's actions by resigning their posts. Prime Minister Mikhail Chigir also had resigned in November and was replaced by Sergey Ling.

Western Aid and the Economy. In January, in an effort to ensure continuing aid from Western donors, Lukashenko approved plans to privatize 1,700 government-owned businesses during 1996, increasing the proportion of industries under private control from 10% to 20%. Nevertheless, the Belarus economy remained in trouble. It shrank 22% in 1994 and 10% in 1995, forcing Russia to write off $1.4 billion in debts early in 1996.

GEORGIA. President Eduard Shevardnadze's government continued to deal with the problems created by Georgia's two breakaway regions, South Ossetia and Abkhazia. In April a meeting sponsored by the OSCE brought South Ossetian leader Ludvig Chibirov together with Georgian Foreign Minister Irakli Menagharishvili to discuss ways to achieve peace in the region. The two leaders met again in late August.

Abkhazia. In Abkhazia, where ethnic Abkhazis have been in rebellion against Georgian rule since 1992, the May 1994 cease-fire remained in effect, but little progress was made in resolving the situation. The 1,500 CIS peacekeeping troops in Abkhazia, most of them Russians, remained in place. And the mandate of the United Nations Observer Mission in Georgia (UNOMIG) was extended by the UN Security Council until Jan. 31, 1997. In August it was reported that more than 3,300 Georgian soldiers and some 5,000 Abkhazi fighters had been killed since the start of the conflict.

Economy. On the economic front, Georgia continued along its path toward privatization and reform, including the passage of legislation enabling individuals to purchase arable land. In February the IMF approved a three-year loan worth about $246 million.

KAZAKHSTAN. The most positive economic news to come out of Kazakhstan during 1996 was the announcement in April that it had signed a treaty with Russia and the Sultanate of Oman to build a $1.2 billion, 900-mi (1 400-km) oil pipeline from Kazakhstan's Tengiz oil field on the Caspian Sea to a new Russian port on the Black Sea. Eight oil companies, including Mobil and Chevron from the United States, also would be involved in the construction, which was expected to be completed by the year 2001. The Tengiz field was estimated to have more than 6 billion barrels of recoverable oil reserves.

Other Economic and Diplomatic News. The IMF approved in July a three-year, $446 million credit for the implementation of Kazakhstan's 1996–98 economic-reform program. In June the United States pledged $40 million to help the nation complete the destruction of ballistic-missile silos and other nuclear-weapons structures. Kazakhstan already had destroyed or transferred to Russia all nuclear weapons on its territory.

In the spring, Kazakhstan signed two treaties, one economic and one political, with other members of the CIS. In March it joined with Belarus, Russia, and Kyrgyzstan in a treaty that pledged them to increased economic cooperation. And in April, in an effort to improve security along its borders, Kazakhstan signed a nonaggression pact with Kyrgyzstan, Tajikistan, Russia, and China.

New Capital. Even as the new Kazakh parliament, elected in December 1995, met for the first time in January 1996, President Nursultan Nazarbayev was making plans to move the entire government from Alma-Aty to Akmola, a city of 270,000 in the northern part of the country, by 1998. His plans, in addition to the erection of government buildings, include the construction of a new business center, luxury hotel, and residential areas.

KYRGYZSTAN. Following his reelection to a second five-year term as president in December 1995, Askar Akayev moved to increase his power further. In a Feb. 10, 1996, referendum, the people of Kyrgyzstan approved a constitutional amendment that gave the president substantially increased authority, including the right to appoint all senior government officials except for the prime minister.

New Treaties and Chinese Relations. In the spring, Kyrgyzstan signed two treaties, one economic and one political, with other members of the CIS. In March it joined with Belarus, Russia, and Kazakhstan in a treaty that pledged them to increased economic cooperation in the areas of industry, agriculture, energy, transportation, and information systems. In April, in an effort to improve security along its borders, Kyrgyzstan signed a nonaggression pact with Kazakhstan, Tajikistan, Russia, and China.

During the year, President Akayev moved to improve relations with China. In July he welcomed Chinese President Jiang Zemin to the Kyrgyz capital city of Bishkek, where the two pledged to increase political and economic cooperation. And in September the two countries opened a new frontier checkpoint on their common border, and President Akayev pledged that Kyrgyzstan never would establish official links with Taiwan.

MOLDOVA. Moldova, like many other members of the CIS, continued to deal with the problems of a secessionist region during 1996. The Dnestr region, called the republic of Trans-Dnestr by the secessionists, lies along Moldova's eastern border with Ukraine and is populated by ethnic Russians and Ukrainians. Following the collapse of the Soviet Union and Moldovan independence in 1991, ethnic Slavs in the region refused to accept the rule of the nation's Romanian-speaking majority. A brief civil war was fought in 1992, before Russian peacekeeping troops brought an end to the fighting, but no resolution of the problem.

Presidential Election. On December 1, in a runoff election, Moldovan voters elected Petru Lucinschi president. The speaker of the parliament won 54% of the vote, compared with 46% for incumbent Mircea Snegur. The main issues debated during the election campaign were the dramatic decline of the Moldovan economy since the nation's independence, relations with Russia and Romania, and the tense situation in Trans-Dnestr, where secessionist leader Igor Smirnov had refused to allow the people to vote, except those in 13 ethnic Romanian enclaves.

Immediately after his election, Lucinschi said he would initiate talks with Smirnov's regime with a view to granting Trans-Dnestr a measure of autonomy. He also said that Moldova would not seek to join the North Atlantic Treaty Organization (NATO), but that it would take part in NATO's Partnership for Peace program.

Economy. Moldova's largely agricultural economy continued to decline, with the nation's GDP down 60% since 1990. The inflation rate, however, was reduced to just 15% in 1996, from more than 500% in 1994; and all banks and about 66% of the nation's businesses were privatized by 1996.

In May, Moldova received a much-needed $195 million credit from the IMF for the period 1996–98.

TAJIKISTAN. The civil war between the Russian-backed government of President Emomili Rakhmonov and Islamic rebels based in Afghanistan continued throughout much of 1996. Early in the year, the situation was exacerbated by the murder of Mufti Fatkhulla Sharipov, the spiritual leader of the nation's Muslims, and by the threatened revolt of two powerful warlords who had been loyal followers of the president. In late January and early February, the warlords, Makhmud Khudoberdyev and Ibodullo Boimatov, took control of the city of Tursun-Zade and marched to within 10 mi (16 km) of the capital city of Dushanbe. When they demanded that Rakhmonov dismiss a number of senior government officials on the grounds of corruption, the president complied, and the warlords, given amnesty, ended their rebellion. Prime Minister Jamshed Karimov, who resigned following the uprising, was replaced by Yahyo Azimov, a newcomer to politics.

Even as the warlords laid down their arms, Islamic rebels renewed their efforts to topple the government by seizing a town just 90 mi (145 km) east of the capital. A UN-sponsored cease-fire, signed on July 21, halted the fighting for only a few weeks, and in mid-August rebel forces seized control of the town of Tavildara in central Tajikistan. Another cease-fire in December also was ignored, as rebel forces in northern Afghanistan fired at Russian troops on the Tajikistan side of the border. Later in December, gunmen loyal to yet another warlord seized 23 hostages, including seven UN observers, and threatened to detonate bombs they had placed in Dushanbe. All but two of the hostages were released unharmed the following day.

Nonaggression Pact. In April, in an effort to improve security along its borders, Tajikistan signed a nonaggression pact with Russia, China, Kazakhstan, and Kyrgyzstan. The pact called on these nations not to attack any of the other signatories, and to inform their neighbors about major military exercises or troop movements within 60 mi (100 km) of their common borders.

TURKMENISTAN. In an effort to counteract the effects of a steadily deteriorating economy that had yet to see any signs of movement toward reform, Turkmen President Saparmurad Niyazov and other government officials made efforts to woo potential economic partners. In July, Deputy Prime Minister Boris Shikmuradov traveled to India, a country very interested in Turkmenistan's huge oil and natural-gas reserves, to discuss economic cooperation. In November, Niyazov visited Turkey at the invitation of Turkish President Suleyman Demirel, and the two discussed further Turkish cooperation with Turkmenistan, especially in the areas of the environment, transportation, energy, education, and training. By 1996, Turkish firms already had begun 21 projects and invested

© Anatoly Kleschuk/Sygma

The control room of the Chernobyl nuclear-power plant in Pripyat, Ukraine, was in operation in 1996, ten years after the world's worst nuclear accident. Ukraine's president said that the remaining Chernobyl reactors would be shut down by the year 2000.

$1.2 billion in the country, and nine Turkish banks had set up operations there. Another project, the construction of a $110 million cellulose plant, was awarded to a Turkish firm in December.

Natural-Gas Pipeline. Turkmenistan agreed to construct a $2 billion, 870-mi (1 400-km) natural-gas pipeline to Pakistan by way of war-torn Afghanistan. Its partners in the venture, which would be a boon to Turkmenistan's energy sector, would be Russian, U.S., and Saudi Arabian oil and natural-gas firms. However, because of the continuing strife in Afghanistan and potential Russian opposition, analysts predicted that the venture would not get off the ground for some time.

UKRAINE. Ukraine's government underwent considerable changes in 1996. President Leonid Kuchma dismissed Prime Minister Yeuben Marchuk on May 27, blaming him for the country's deteriorating economy. He replaced him the following day with Pavlo Lazarenko, a close political ally with experience in the energy sector. In July, Lazarenko was injured slightly in an assassination attempt by unknown parties who exploded a remote-controlled bomb near his car.

New Constitution. On June 28, Ukraine's parliament approved a new constitution that substantially increased presidential power and made Ukrainian the nation's only official language, an action strongly condemned by Ukraine's large Russian-speaking minority. Following the approval of the constitution, Kuchma appointed new defense, agriculture, and finance ministers.

Chernobyl, Nuclear Warheads, and Relations with the West. Ukraine marked the tenth anniversary of the April 26, 1986, explosion and fire at Chernobyl—the world's worst nuclear accident. President Kuchma repeated his pledge to shut down the remaining Chernobyl reactors by the year 2000. Just three days before the anniversary, a forest fire broke out not far from Chernobyl and scattered decade-old radioactive dust. At a June 1 ceremony attended by U.S. Defense Secretary William Perry and his Russian counterpart, Kuchma announced that Ukraine had sent the last of the Soviet-era nuclear warheads on its territory to Russia for destruction.

President Kuchma met with U.S. President Bill Clinton in Washington, DC, in February, and in March, Kuchma welcomed U.S. Secretary of State Warren Christopher to Kiev. President Kuchma told Christopher that Ukraine would not join NATO, but that it would continue to take part in NATO's Partnership for Peace program.

Economy. Ukraine, whose GDP declined by some 50% between 1992 and 1996, continued to face economic difficulties during the year. Its problems—high inflation, budget deficits, and mismanagement—forced the IMF to freeze loans on two occasions. In May, however, the IMF approved an $867 million standby loan to help cover Ukraine's budget deficit. In June, Ukrainian and IMF officials sat down to discuss Ukrainian adherence to IMF guidelines, as well as future loans.

UZBEKISTAN. President Islam Karimov, who in a 1995 referendum had won a three-year extension of his term—from 1997 to 2000—was accused in May 1996 of various human-rights abuses by the New York–based Human Rights Watch. The group accused Karimov's government of arresting government opponents arbitrarily, dismissing them from their jobs without reason, tapping their telephones, and placing their homes under surveillance. Other opponents simply disappeared.

Human Rights. A month later, however, the president seemed to do an about-face in his harsh treatment of political opponents—perhaps, many believed, because of his trip that month to the United States for a meeting with U.S. President Bill Clinton. Just prior to that meeting, Karimov amnestied some political prisoners and even met with Abdumannob Polatov, the government's main opposition leader and human-rights activist, who then was living in exile in the United States. Karimov invited Polatov to return to Uzbekistan. In August, with Polatov back in his country, the president announced to parliament that he not only would protect human rights but also would allow opposition to the government. Many observers, including those from the OSCE, reported that there were indeed signs of change in the government's attitude toward human rights, but they also questioned whether these political reforms were designed to impress the nations of the West, whose financial aid was needed for economic reform.

See also BALTIC REPUBLICS.

WILLIAM E. SHAPIRO, *Freelance Writer*

SAUDI ARABIA

Concerns about Saudi Arabia's stability increased in 1996 as a result of a new terrorist attack on U.S. soldiers, the illness of King Fahd, and budgetary imbalances.

International Relations. On Nov. 13, 1995, terrorists exploded a bomb at a Saudi National Guard training facility in Riyadh, killing five Americans and two others. U.S. President Bill Clinton sent Federal Bureau of Investigation (FBI) agents to help Saudi authorities catch those responsible for the attack. The confession of four Saudi suspects arrested on April 22, 1996, for the bombing was broadcast on television, and they were executed on May 31, giving rise to threats of revenge by their sympathizers.

On June 25 a powerful truck bomb exploded near a military housing complex in Khobar, killing 19 U.S. servicemen and wounding hundreds of other people, including many Saudis who lived nearby. U.S. victims had worked in the King Abdul Aziz Air Base at Dhahran, from which they patrolled the airspace of southern Iraq and enforced the no-fly zone. Suspicion centered on Saudi Islamic fundamentalists who objected to the presence of non-Muslim foreign troops. While visiting Saudi Arabia in August, U.S. Secretary of Defense William Perry hinted that Iran might be partially responsible for the attack. Perry agreed with the Saudis on the relocation of U.S. forces away from Riyadh, Khobar, and Dhahran to Prince Sultan Air Base at al-Kharj, 60 mi (100 km) southeast of the capital.

Saudi Arabia and the United States launched investigations into the bombing and jointly offered a $5 million reward for information, but little progress was made in discovering the identity of the attackers. Some analysts criticized Saudi authorities for not taking sufficient precautions, while a Pentagon report put much of the blame on a failure of U.S. commanders to inform Washington about the need for heightened security measures. A later inquiry by the U.S. Air Force exonerated the U.S. officers of any wrongdoing, and Secretary Perry announced new measures to protect U.S. military personnel stationed abroad from terrorist attacks.

Saudi Arabia supported U.S. policy in Bosnia, and Saudi officials attended the U.S.-initiated antiterrorism summit held in March in Egypt, thereby demonstrating Saudi backing of the Israeli-Palestinian peace process.

When Iraqi troops marched into the Kurdish-held area in northern Iraq, the United States responded on September 3–4 with attacks on Iraqi antiaircraft facilities in southern Iraq. Saudi Arabia, which had not given the United States permission to use Saudi territory or facilities, quietly criticized this action, arguing that it was too little to hinder Saddam Hussein seriously and only would stir up sympathy for him in the Arab world. Nevertheless, the United States sought to reassure the Saudis of continuing U.S. support by sending two Patriot antimissile batteries to Saudi Arabia, along with soldiers trained to operate them.

Political Affairs. After suffering a minor stroke on Nov. 30, 1995, King Fahd left the hospital on December 7. However, his health continued to be impaired, so on Jan. 1, 1996, he temporarily ceded power to his half brother, Crown Prince Abdullah. Fahd reassumed full authority on February 21 but remained

© Gamma-Liaison

The deteriorating health of Saudi Arabia's King Fahd increased tensions about the nation's leadership. Among those jockeying for power were Fahd's half brother and heir apparent, Crown Prince Abdullah (left), *and the king's full brother, Prince Sultan* (center).

SAUDI ARABIA • Information Highlights

Official Name: Kingdom of Saudi Arabia.
Location: Arabian peninsula in southwest Asia.
Area: 756,981 sq mi (1 960 582 km^2).
Population (mid-1996 est.): 19,400,000.
Chief City (1993 est.): Riyadh, the capital, 3,000,000.
Government: *Head of state and government,* Fahd bin 'Abd al-'Aziz Al Sa'ud, king and prime minister (acceded June 1982). *Legislature*—consultative council.
Monetary Unit: Riyal (3.7505 riyals equal U.S.$1, Dec. 31, 1996).
Gross Domestic Product (1994 est. U.S.$): $173,100,000,000 (purchasing power parity).
Economic Index (1995, 1990 = 100): *Consumer Prices,* all items, 111.1; food, 111.7.
Foreign Trade (1993 U.S.$): *Imports,* $28,198,000,000; *exports,* $42,395,000,000.

frail thereafter, delegating many activities to Abdullah, the heir apparent since 1982.

Abdullah could count on the loyalty of the National Guard, which had been under his command since 1963. Prince Sultan, minister of defense and a full brother to King Fahd, was a rival for current influence and future power, using as his base of support the regular armed forces. On September 27 the king replaced the chief of staff, Lt. Gen. Mohammed Saleh al-Hammad, with Maj. Gen. Saleh ibn Ali al-Mohaya.

Princes Abdullah and Sultan were both worried about the growing opposition to the Saudi royal family and its policies, as witnessed in attacks on Americans and also in public criticism from Saudi exiles living abroad, such as Mohammed al-Masaari, a leader of the London-based Committee for the Defense of Legitimate Rights. The British government, acting in response to pressure from Saudi Arabia, sought judicial consent to expel the former physics teacher, but al-Masaari successfully opposed this.

Economy. In 1996, Saudi Arabia remained the world's largest oil exporter, selling about 8 million barrels per day, which represented about one third of oil sales by the Organization of the Petroleum Exporting Countries (OPEC) and about 12% of world production. On Oct. 21, 1995, Saudi-owned Delta Oil Co., in partnership with the U.S.-based Unocal Corp., signed an $18 billion agreement to finance an oil pipeline from Turkmenistan to Pakistan via civil-war-plagued Afghanistan. This deal was part of Saudi economic strategy to invest in oil throughout the world.

Oil prices rose in March 1996 and remained higher than expected for the rest of the year, thereby unexpectedly increasing Saudi government revenues. On June 7, OPEC agreed to keep the Saudi production quota at 8 million barrels per day, even though it then appeared the United Nations (UN) would grant Iraq the right to sell oil abroad. Overcoming opposition from Algeria and Iran, Saudi Arabia succeeded in convincing OPEC that no adjustment to production quotas should be made until it became clear that Iraq's government would comply with all aspects of the UN agreement.

The Saudi budget announced on January 1 called for fiscal caution, with about $40 billion of expenditures—the same as in 1995—and a slightly decreased revenue projection of about $35 billion. The budget continued the nearly one-third cut in total spending enacted between 1993 and 1995, although it increased funding of education, transportation, and communications. Higher revenues from oil sales enabled the government to erase the budget deficit, pay back bills to contractors and foreign creditors, and slightly increase foreign reserves, which had fallen to about $8.6 billion at the end of 1995.

King Fahd was able to turn his attention to other issues, such as unemployment and education. In September the king called on Saudi employers to hire more Saudis and fewer foreign workers, and in October the government banned foreigners from working in more than a dozen private-sector jobs. This action was in keeping with a government plan to eliminate 300,000 of the 5 million foreign workers in the nation by the year 2000 and to create 650,000 jobs for Saudi citizens.

On September 14 a record 4 million Saudi students began the school year, a number reflecting the 60% of the population that was under the age of 20.

WILLIAM OCHSENWALD
Virginia Polytechnic Institute and State University

SINGAPORE

In 1996, Singapore's leaders worked hard to show the rest of the world that the country was not a "tired tiger." By Western standards, the economy enjoyed another good year. Senior Minister Lee Kuan Yew was involved in a real-estate controversy, and the political arena heated up in anticipation of the 1997 national elections.

Politics and Government. On December 16, President Ong Teng Cheong dissolved Parliament in preparation for national elections in early January 1997. As usual, the People's Action Party (PAP) went all out to secure a convincing victory. In his August National Day speech, Prime Minister Goh Chok Tong raised international eyebrows when he said that if Singapore should falter, the country would be forced to "ask Malaysia to take us back." In June, Senior Minister Lee stated that a "remerger" with Malaysia would be possible if that country became a meritocracy like Singapore. Malaysia's Prime Minister Mahathir bin Mohamad charged that Goh was trying to frighten Singaporeans into voting for the PAP in the upcoming elections.

The political climate changed little in 1996. People remained reluctant to talk about national politics with foreigners, and it remained risky to be in the political opposition. In June the Singapore Democratic Party (SDP), holding three of four opposition seats in Parliament, was banned from distributing a video as part of its election campaign. The SDP head, Chee Soon Juan, was charged with contempt of Parliament after incorrectly stating government statistics about health-care subsidies in August. In December, Parliament fined Chee S$25,000 (about $17,900), but left him free to run in the 1997 general election. The Workers Party also was being sued for libeling five members of Parliament (MPs) who were PAP members.

On the assumption that the Singaporeans would not trust the opposition enough to turn the government over to it but that they were tired of the PAP, the Singapore People's Party called for the opposition to field no more than 30 candidates for Parliament. A victory of this magnitude by the opposition would send shock waves through the PAP while leaving it in control.

In October the PAP-dominated Parliament amended the constitution to increase the number and size of group-representation constituencies (multimember electoral districts). Both changes could make it harder for opposition parties, which must field a full slate to contest these constituencies. Another amendment reduced the powers of the elected president, allowing the government to use a referendum to set aside a presidential veto under carefully defined circumstances. Parliament also was given the power to override a presidential veto of top civil-servant appointments if the president was found to have acted contrary to the recommendation of the Council of Presidential Advisers.

While Senior Minister Lee remained the country's dominant political figure, he and his son, Deputy Prime Minister Lee Hsien Loong, were cast in a negative spotlight in May when it became known that they had obtained the right to purchase several luxury condominiums at discounted prices. The Lees donated the value of the discounts to charity, but the question of how they obtained the right to purchase the properties in the first place remained unanswered.

SINGAPORE • Information Highlights

Official Name: Republic of Singapore.
Location: Southeast Asia.
Area: 244 sq mi (632.6 km^2).
Population (mid-1996 est.): 3,000,000.
Chief City: Singapore City, the capital.
Government: *Head of state,* Ong Teng Cheong, president (took office September 1993). *Head of government,* Goh Chok Tong, prime minister (took office November 1990). *Legislature* (unicameral)—Parliament.
Monetary Unit: Singapore dollar (1.4003 S. dollars equal U.S. $1, Dec. 31, 1996).
Gross Domestic Product (1994 est. U.S.$): $57,000,000,-000 (purchasing power parity).
Economic Index (1995, 1990 = 100): *Consumer Prices,* all items, 113.5; food, 109.8.
Foreign Trade (1995 U.S.$): *Imports,* $124,502,000,000; *exports,* $118,263,000,000.

Economy. The economy remained strong, with growth of roughly 6%. Inflation was in the 2% range, with unemployment under 3%. One study predicted that Singapore could be seventh in the world in per-capita gross domestic product (GDP) by 1999. However, a global slump in the home-electronics market, which accounts for almost 45% of manufactured output, sent the Singapore stock market to an eight-month low near the end of the year. Both manufactured output and non-oil exports were down for the year. In addition, Singapore's middle- and low-middle-income citizens were finding it harder to obtain affordable housing. And grumbling about the huge salaries for the prime minister and his cabinet was not uncommon.

Singapore's leaders continued to make international investments. The country's biggest overseas investment, the Suzchow Industrial Park, topped $7 billion for the year. In June the government announced a joint venture with the city of Shanghai for a housing development for up to 50,000 families. Singapore also was a major trader and investor in China's Liaoning province.

Society. The government initiated a "save water" campaign and ordered the Singapore Armed Forces (SAF) to cut consumption by 5%. While the population had tripled since 1950, water consumption had increased sevenfold. Singapore receives half of its water from Malaysia's Johore state, under an agreement set to expire in 2011. A new agreement was made to provide up to 1 billion gal (3.8 billion l) per day from Indonesia's Bintan Island, but this water was quintuple the cost of water from Johore. Singapore was expected to require desalinated water within a decade.

PATRICK M. MAYERCHAK
Virginia Military Institute

SLOVAKIA

In 1996 political life in Slovakia reflected continued tension between President Michal Kovač and Prime Minister Vladímir Mečiar. There were also significant strains within the ruling coalition. Several of the government's policies were criticized by outside governments and organizations.

Domestic Affairs. One of the most controversial steps taken by the government was the passage of the so-called "law on the protection of the republic." Opposition activists and leaders of the Hungarian minority argued that the law, which made critics liable to criminal persecution and jail sentences, would be used for political reasons against Mečiar's opponents. Although President Kovač vetoed the law in May, a revised version of the bill passed in parliament in December. Leaders of the nonprofit sector also protested against a law on foundations, which the president also vetoed but which was passed again by parliament on June 20.

The reorganization of Slovakia into eight new administrative regions also created controversy. The reorganization made Bratislava, which had the status of an independent region, part of a larger region. Hungarian leaders also claimed that the new regions benefited Mečiar's party and that the plan, by dividing heavily Hungarian districts, was a disadvantage to the Hungarian minority.

Opposition activists protested the sale of an opposition newspaper to an enterprise closely connected to the government and a draft law on universities that would limit university autonomy. They also charged that secret-service agents were following opposition leaders. In September representatives of opposition parties met to discuss their plans for the upcoming parliamentary session.

SLOVAKIA • Information Highlights

Official Name: Slovak Republic.
Location: East-central Europe.
Area: 18,859 sq mi (48 845 km²).
Population (mid-1996 est.): 5,400,000.
Chief Cities (Dec. 31, 1994 est.): Bratislava, the capital, 450,776; Kosice, 239,927.
Government: *Head of state,* Michal Kovač, president (took office February 1993). *Head of government,* Vladimir Mečiar, prime minister (took office December 1994). *Legislature* (unicameral)—National Council.
Monetary Unit: Koruna (30.69 koruny equal U.S.$1, Dec. 31, 1996).
Gross Domestic Product (1994 est. U.S.$): $32,800,000,-000 (purchasing power parity).
Economic Index (1995): *Consumer Prices* (1991 = 100): all items, 168.9; food, 168.7.
Foreign Trade (1995 U.S.$): *Imports,* $8,488,000,000; *exports,* $8,549,000,000.

Conflict between the president and the prime minister continued in regard to the activities and kidnapping of the president's son, Michal Kovač, Jr., who was charged with fraud in Slovakia in January. In May the president sued the prime minister in response to charges that he had violated the constitution by his actions regarding the case. In April a former policeman who had testified in the case died in a car-bomb explosion.

Prime Minister Mečiar's governing coalition was threatened in June when his coalition partners, the Slovak National Party and the Association of Workers of Slovakia, stopped supporting the government. They did not withdraw from the coalition, however, and talks in late June and early July led to an agreement to support it once again.

Economy. Slovakia's economy continued to grow in 1996. Gross domestic product (GDP) increased by 7.1% in the first half of 1996. Inflation was 6.0% in August. Unemployment was 12% in September. Foreign investments increased by 7.7% in the first quarter of 1996 but were lower than political and economic leaders wished.

Foreign Affairs. Slovak leaders completed the country's questionnaire for European Union (EU) membership in July. A parliamentary commission on European integration that included opposition members was set up in September. However, EU officials criticized the country's press and minority policies several times in 1996 and warned that these problems could delay Slovakia's inclusion in the EU. U.S. officials also criticized political developments in Slovakia and omitted it from the list of countries slated to be admitted in the first wave of the expansion of the North Atlantic Treaty Organization (NATO). In November, Slovak leaders discussed holding a referendum on NATO membership.

Slovak relations with Hungary continued to be troubled, despite the ratification of the Slovak-Hungarian Treaty by the Slovak parliament in March. In May a declaration in Hungary calling for autonomy for Hungarian minorities abroad led to renewed tensions between the two countries. Prime Minister Mečiar met in November with his Hungarian and Austrian counterparts to discuss regional cooperation. He also discussed the Gabčikovo dam and implementation of the basic treaty with Hungarian Prime Minister Gyula Horn.

SHARON L. WOLCHIK
The George Washington University

SLOVENIA.

See pages 96–101.

SOCIAL WELFARE

The social conditions faced by the millions of Americans living in poverty eased moderately for a second consecutive year in 1996, largely due to the nation's relatively healthy economic situation. Outside the United States, meanwhile, dire social conditions continued unabated for hundreds of millions of people, especially in developing countries in South Asia, sub-Saharan Africa, and Central America.

U.S. Developments

Income and Poverty. The annual Census Bureau survey of family income and poverty reported two positive pieces of news: the first increase in six years in overall household income, and a significant decrease—of about 1.6 million people—in the number of Americans living below the poverty line. The report, released September 26, found that in 1995 the nation's median household income, when adjusted for inflation, rose 2.7% to $34,074, and that about 13.8% of the population—some 36.5 million people—lived below the poverty line, defined as a total cash income of $15,569 for a family of four. That compared with 14.5% of the population living in poverty in 1994 and 15.1% in 1993. For the first time since the Census Bureau began keeping such statistics, the percentage of African-Americans living below the poverty line—29.3% in 1995—dropped below 30%.

The poverty rate for Hispanic Americans, on the other hand, reached an all-time high of 30.3%, a figure that for the first time was higher than the poverty rate for African-Americans. The percentage of children living in poverty—20.8 in 1995—represented a one-percentage-point decrease compared with 1994. Still, the country's child-poverty rate was the highest among the world's industrialized nations and remained an extremely serious national social problem.

The picture of America's poorest children was illuminated further in two 1996 reports. The Baltimore-based Annie E. Casey Foundation's annual "Kids Count" report, released in June, noted that the number of U.S. children in working-poor families rose 65% from 1974 to 1994, to 5.6 million. The advocacy group Bread for the World's 1996 annual report, released in October, estimated that some 4 million U.S. children were hungry and that an additional 9.6 million children were at risk of hunger.

The annual "Index of Social Health," issued in October by social scientists at the Fordham Institute for Innovation in Social Policy in Tarrytown, NY, also indicated that the social welfare of U.S. children and young people was disproportionately low compared to that of the total population. The survey, which measures 16 different social problems, reported that four of the six social problems faced by American children under 18—child abuse, teenage suicide, drug abuse, and the high-school dropout rate—worsened in 1994.

Surrounded by national political leaders and former welfare recipients, President Bill Clinton signed the welfare-reform bill into law in a White House Rose Garden ceremony on Aug. 22, 1996. The act abolishes federal guarantees of welfare benefits and gives block grants to the states to establish aid for the poor.

"The decline in the social health of children and youth tells us something about the future shape of our society," said Marc L. Miringoff, director of the Fordham study.

Welfare Reform. During 1996 the highest-profile social-welfare issue in the United States was the effort to reform the national welfare system. In 1996 nearly 13 million Americans received federal welfare benefits and more than 25 million received food stamps. The high-stakes debate began in January when President Bill Clinton vetoed a wide-ranging welfare bill that had been approved by the Republican-controlled Congress late in 1995. That bill called for ending the 60-year-old federal guarantee of assistance to needy families by turning the national welfare program over to the states in the form of block grants. That bill, the president said, did "too little to move people from welfare to work," and "was soft on work and tough on children. It imposed deep and unacceptable cuts in school lunches, child welfare, and help for disabled children."

Following the president's veto, both houses of Congress immediately began structuring new, but similar, welfare-reform measures. On July 18 the House of Representatives approved a slightly different version of the 1995 welfare-reform measure by a 256–170 vote that reflected party lines. Five days later the Senate passed a similar measure, 74–24, in a largely nonpartisan vote. Both bills retained the main feature of the 1995 welfare-reform bill: turning the welfare system over to the states. The bills also contained provisions that would reduce lifetime welfare assistance to five years, require the head of every family on welfare to work within two years or lose all benefits, deny welfare benefits and food stamps to most legal immigrants until they are U.S. citizens, restrict childless adults aged 18 to 50 to three months of food stamps every three years unless they fulfill certain work requirements, and establish a national child-support-payment system. Observers characterized the changes as the biggest in U.S. social policy since the Depression.

Analysts estimated that those measures would reduce federal welfare spending by some $54 million over six years. The main savings would come from cutting back or abolishing many federal programs, including the largest, Aid for Families with Dependent Children (AFDC), which was created by the Social Security Act and signed into law by President Franklin D. Roosevelt in 1935 during the Depression. Under AFDC, some 12.8 million Americans—including more than 8 million children—received a monthly average benefit of $400. The legislation passed by Congress in 1996 replaced AFDC and other federal welfare programs with direct cash payments to individual states, which would be allowed to create their own independent welfare systems.

The final conference agreement that was passed by the Senate and the House included provisions to increase funding to provide day care for the children of welfare recipients and to help single mothers while they sought work. The final bill also eliminated provisions that would have cut federal programs that provided school lunches and food stamps for children on welfare. Citing these changes, President Clinton signed the 1996 welfare-reform bill into law on August 22. In doing so, the president said, he fulfilled a promise he had made during the 1992 presidential campaign that, if elected, he would make radical changes in the nation's welfare system—or, as he said: "end welfare as we know it." The president said that the new law would "transform a broken system that traps too many people in a cycle of dependence to one that emphasizes work and independence." Republican presidential nominee Robert Dole endorsed the bill, which he characterized as a Republican-shaped measure. "My only regret," Dole said, "is that President Clinton did not join with us sooner in helping end a welfare system that has failed the taxpayers and those it was designed to serve."

The sweeping new law went into effect October 1. The states were given until July 1, 1997, to submit new welfare plans to the federal government. On October 1, 11 states had submitted outlines for new welfare plans. The other states announced that they would continue to operate their existing welfare programs in the short term or continue recently adopted changes that made significant reforms in their welfare programs that were aimed at cutting welfare rolls and putting welfare recipients in jobs. Some states—including Arizona, Kentucky, Maine, Michigan, Minnesota, New Jersey, Ohio, Oregon, and Wisconsin—announced new, experimental proposals that included paying moving expenses for welfare families willing to relocate to find work, and requiring virtually every adult on welfare to hold down a job.

The law was criticized by liberal congressional Democrats, some religious groups (including the National Council of Churches), labor unions, women's groups, and advocates for the poor, mainly because of fears that state and local governments would not be able to pay for programs to help the nation's poorest families. Sen. Christopher J. Dodd (D-CT) characterized the bill as "an unconscionable retreat from a 60-year commitment that Republicans and Democrats, ten American presidents, and Congress have made on behalf of America's children." Sen. Daniel Patrick Moynihan (D-NY), a longtime proponent of welfare reform who strongly opposed the new legislation, characterized the law as "not welfare reform, but welfare repeal" and "the first step in dismantling the social contract that has been in place in the United States since at least the 1930s."

The Disabled. The U.S. Department of Justice took significant steps in 1996 to enforce the landmark 1990 Americans With Disabilities Act (ADA), which for the first time prohibited discrimination, in the workplace and public facilities, against the nation's estimated 43 million to 49 million physically and mentally disabled persons.

In February the department filed a civil suit against the Days Inns of America, Inc., contending that the hotel chain violated several of the law's provisions in five newly built hotels. The suit alleged, among other things, that the newly constructed hotels' ramps were too steep for wheelchairs, that the hotels lacked visual fire alarms for the hearing impaired, and that their rest rooms were too narrow for wheelchair users. "Not only do these violations impede access, in many cases it is unsafe for guests with disabilities to stay at these hotels," said Deval L. Patrick, the Justice Department's assistant attorney general for civil rights.

In April the Justice Department announced an agreement with United Artists Theatre Circuit Inc., one of the nation's biggest movie-theater chains, that would make the chain's facilities more accessible to the disabled, primarily the approximately 5 million Americans who use wheelchairs. United Artists, which operates 420 movie theaters and 2,300 screens across the country, agreed to make its rest rooms, concession stands, telephones, and drinking fountains accessible to those in wheelchairs and to install special seats for the disabled. The Justice Department also was investigating four other large movie-theater chains in 1996. "We can now tell moviegoers with disabilities, access is coming soon to a theater near you," Patrick said.

Under pressure from the Justice Department, the National Collegiate Athletic Association (NCAA) proposed two measures in April designed to make college athletics more accessible to the learning disabled. Under the ADA, educational institutions were required to make "reasonable accommodations" to allow the disabled to learn on an equal basis with other students. Colleges and universities across the nation have set up an array of programs since 1990 to comply with the law. These have included giving learning-disabled students extra time to complete exams and offering school-year and summer tutoring programs. The NCAA measures, which required approval of the association's full membership, would give learning-disabled prospective college athletes extra time to meet NCAA minimum academic standards.

International Conditions

Poverty. In 1996, U.S. social problems again seemed less significant when compared to the severe poverty, malnutrition, and social dislocation faced by hundreds of millions of people in other countries. Noting that reducing poverty "is the most urgent task facing humanity today," a report issued in June by the World Bank found that more than one fifth of the world's population—some 1.3 billion people—live on less than $1 per day.

Every year, the report also said, some 8 million children die from poverty-related diseases caused by dirty water, air pollution, and other environmental problems; 50 million children are "mentally or physically damaged" due to inadequate nutrition; and 130 million children (80% of them girls) are denied the opportunity to go to school. "The shocking fact is that a child born in sub-Saharan Africa today is still more likely to be malnourished than to go to primary school and is as likely to die before the age of five as to enter secondary school," the report noted.

The survey found that the incidence of poverty, between 1987 and 1993, was on a downward trend in East Asia, the Middle East and North Africa, and South Asia. Poverty was more or less stable in Latin America and sub-Saharan Africa; and increased from very low levels in Eastern Europe and Central Asia. The report found that roughly 90% of the poor people in the developing world lived in Brazil, Central America, China, Indochina, Mongolia, South Asia, and sub-Saharan Africa.

The report noted that poverty was primarily a rural phenomenon, but predicted that within a decade, the number of urban poor would exceed the number in rural areas. The urban poor "generally live in appalling conditions," the report said. "Infrastructure facilities lag far behind what is needed, and local governments do not have the resources to provide even the most basic services."

Regional Conflict. Another significant and widespread international social problem, regional conflict, put some 42 million people in danger of starvation or life-threatening disease, according to a multiagency U.S. government survey presented to the United Nations (UN) in April. The survey, called "Global Humanitarian Emergencies, 1996," reported that the number of regional conflicts increased from four in 1985 to more than 20 in 1995 and that the number of people at risk increased by 60% in that time period. The study said the problem was most acute in Afghanistan, Angola, Bosnia, Ethiopia, Eritrea, Haiti, Liberia, Rwanda, Sierra Leone, Somalia, Sudan, and Tajikistan. Governmental repression, the study said, also caused severe social problems, including widespread food shortages, in North Korea and Iraq.

In the last three months of 1996, international attention focused on the worsening social dislocation in Central Africa that affected millions of citizens in Rwanda, Burundi, and Zaire. In 1994, a vicious civil war had broken out between the Hutu and Tutsi tribal ethnic groups in Rwanda, during which an estimated 500,000 Rwandans were killed and more than 5 million of the nation's 8 million people were forced from their homes. Two million fled to neighboring Zaire, where in 1996 some 700,000 Hutu refugees remained.

Late in October open warfare broke out between Zaire and the Tutsi-led Rwandan army, aided by Tutsi rebels in Zaire and Burundi. The fighting caused workers with the UN and other international relief agencies to leave the area and brought the threat of famine and epidemics to some 1.1 million ethnic Hutu refugees. In mid-November officials announced that Canada would be leading an international mission to bring water and food to refugees in eastern Zaire and to those who returned to Rwanda. (*See also* REFUGEES AND IMMIGRATION.)

MARC LEEPSON, *Freelance Writer*

SOMALIA

In 1996, Gen. Mohammed Farah Aidid, Somalia's foremost clan leader, died. His leadership position was filled by his son. Yet the civil strife that had engulfed the country since 1991 continued, throwing Somalia ever deeper into anarchy.

Clan Leader Dies. General Aidid, the warlord who virtually single-handedly forced United Nations and U.S. troops to evacuate from Somalia after they failed in their peacekeeping efforts, died in late July due to wounds suffered during a street battle with a rival clan in the capital city of Mogadishu. Aidid had been the most powerful clan leader in the country and had tried without success to vanquish other clan leaders and have himself declared president of Somalia.

In August, Aidid's group selected Hussein Mohammed Aidid, the son of the fallen leader, as its new head. A former U.S. marine holding dual citizenship, Hussein promptly vowed to continue battling other clans, rejecting peace overtures from Ali Mahdi Mohammed, leader of an opposing clan and the nation's second-most-important leader. In the following months international aid workers were harassed by the forces of both clans.

Anarchy and Fighting Prevails. In the wake of Aidid's death and escalating battles among various clans throughout the country, a political vacuum was created. In August, Ethiopia, in a two-day attack, struck three border towns in southwestern Somalia that are strongholds of Islamic fundamentalism, killing more than 200 persons. Ethiopia claimed that the attack was in response to attempts by local Islamic groups to stir disorder in Ethiopia's Ogaden region, an area Somalia historically has claimed. In October cross-border shelling occurred intermittently.

Islamic leaders throughout Somalia also attempted to fill the vacuum by trying to coopt public support, seeing Islam as a way to restore order to the country. A legal system based on the Koran, the establishment of *sharia* courts, and the creation of an alternate system of political authority were among the moves taken. In September clan leaders announced their opposition to the establishment of Islamic authority, and the anarchy evident for the past five years appeared to deepen. Social disorder also increased in 1996 as drought, floods, famine, and hunger, as well as the ongoing warfare, continued.

PETER SCHWAB, *Purchase College State University of New York*

SOMALIA • Information Highlights

Official Name: Somalia.
Location: Eastern Africa.
Area: 471,776 sq mi (637 660 km²).
Population (mid-1996 est.): 9,500,000.
Chief City (1984 est.): Mogadishu, the capital, 600,000.
Government: No functioning government as of December 1996.
Monetary Unit: Shilling (approx. 5,000 shillings equal U.S.$1, January 1995).
Gross Domestic Product (1994 est. U.S.$): $3,300,000,000 (purchasing power parity).

SOUTH AFRICA

South Africa moved closer to a final constitution in 1996 after two years of drafting and public debate. The coalition between the African National Congress (ANC) and National Party (NP) ended, in part, because of the NP's rejection of some of the terms of the new constitution. Urban crime continued to plague the country and discourage foreign investment; in response, the government promised to increase funding for crime prevention. The Truth and Reconciliation Commission began its task of public review of the atrocities and tragedies of the apartheid era. In July, President Nelson Mandela stated officially that he would not seek another term. Although his successor ultimately would be chosen by the ANC, Mandela indicated that he would recommend Executive Deputy President Thabo Mbeki for the position.

New Constitution. In May, after two years of deliberations, South Africa officially adopted a new constitution when the Constitutional Assembly agreed to a 140-page document by a vote of 421 to 2 with ten abstentions. The right-wing Freedom Front, which seeks to establish an Afrikaner homeland, abstained, and the Inkatha Freedom Party (IFP), led by Mangosuthu Buthelezi, did not participate in the session.

Until the last minute there was some uncertainty whether there would be agreement between the two principal parties, Mandela's ANC and Executive Deputy President F. W. de Klerk's NP. Compromise was reached on such issues as property rights and the protection of the language and cultural rights of whites. There were significant areas in which the new constitution moved away from the interim constitution negotiated in 1993, most significantly in departing from a coalition government to a "winner take all" system, in which the majority party in the National Assembly would choose the president who, in turn, would select the cabinet. The new constitution established a federal system with a strong central government, a presidency, and a two-chamber legislature; excluded any discrimination based on race, gender, age, or sexual orientation; abolished the death penalty; and replaced the existing Senate with a Council of Provinces. The new constitution kept many of the features of the interim arrangement, including a 400-member National Assembly, and the current structure of nine provinces.

In September, the Constitutional Court declined to certify the new constitution because it did not meet requirements originally agreed to regarding the allocation of powers to provincial governments. Judge Arthur Chaskalson, the court's president, declared that while the basic structure was sound, the nine provinces were given substantially fewer powers than the interim constitution required. In addition, the court ruled that the restructuring of the Senate that the ANC had advocated diminished the powers of this important body. Members of the Constitutional Assembly made appropriate changes to meet the court's requirements and the new constitution was then certified on December 4. It was signed on December 10, Human Rights Day, by President Mandela at the symbolically important site of Sharpeville, where a mas-

© Adil Bradlow/Pool/AP/Wide World Photos

South Africa's President Nelson Mandela (right) *and Cyril Ramaphosa, chairman of the Constitutional Assembly, displayed the nation's new constitution after it was signed into law in Sharpeville on Dec. 10, 1996. The signing completed South Africa's transition from white-minority rule to a nonracial democracy.*

© Reuters/"The Argus"/Archive Photos

Njongonkulu Winston Ndungane (right) *was chosen to succeed Desmond Tutu* (left), *who was retiring as archbishop of Cape Town and head of the Anglican church in southern Africa.*

sacre of antiapartheid demonstrators occurred in March 1960.

In a separate ruling, the court refused to approve the KwaZulu/Natal provincial constitution because it exceeded the powers it could claim rightly. These rulings clearly indicated the strength and independence of the Constitutional Court.

Other Political Developments. One day after the adoption of the new constitution, de Klerk's NP announced that it would split from the coalition government as of June 30. The NP was concerned that the new constitution did not provide mechanisms for executive-level power sharing or any form of joint decision-making. While the party's departure was seen as a factor in further discouraging foreign investors, many considered that the coalition had served its purpose. Many in the party also hoped that by leaving the government, the NP would be able to establish itself as a viable opposition party.

Local elections held at the end of May in Western Cape firmly established the NP as an opposition party. It won a majority of seats in five out of six district councils in metropolitan Cape Town and 23 of the 27 rural councils. While the ANC increased its percentage of the vote from 9% in the previous election to 32%, it was clear that it had not won over the so-called Coloured population. In local elections in KwaZulu/Natal late in June, the IFP won about 45% of the votes cast, down from more than 50% in the 1994 provincial election. The ANC maintained its 33% share of the votes cast. The NP received about 13% of the vote, with most of its support coming from white and Indian voters.

On March 28, Minister of Finance Chris Liebenberg resigned his portfolio, citing personal reasons. That same day, President Mandela chose Trevor Manuel, the minister of trade and industry, to replace Liebenberg. In May, with the withdrawal of the NP from the government, the president made further changes to the cabinet, effective July 1. The president brought back into the cabinet Pallo Jordan—whom he had dismissed in late March as minister of posts, telecommunications, and broadcasting—to become minister of environment affairs and tourism. Former Home Affairs Minister Penuell Maduna replaced Pik Botha (longtime foreign-affairs minister under the NP) as minister of mineral and energy affairs. The president decided not to replace the second deputy presidency left vacant by NP leader de Klerk. The cabinet was reduced from 28 to 26 ministries with the merging of agriculture with land affairs under Derek Hanekom and the abolition of the general-affairs ministry.

Alleged Scandal, Truth and Reconciliation Commission, and Magnus Malan Trial. At the end of August, Gen. Bantu Holomisa, former leader of the Transkei homeland and subsequently deputy minister of the environment, was expelled from the ANC for having accepted a 1994 campaign donation from developer Sol Kerzner, who was under investigation on charges of bribery. Holomisa, who refused to participate in the disciplinary hearing, said that he intended to appeal the expulsion and alleged that high-ranking ANC members, including Executive Deputy President Mbeki and President Mandela, were aware of the contribution. Expulsion from the ANC by the party's disciplinary committee meant that Holomisa no longer would retain his seat in the South African parliament.

On April 15 the 17-member Truth and Reconciliation Commission began its hearings, presided over by Nobel Peace Prize winner Archbishop Desmond Tutu. The commission, which was slated to operate for two years, was established in order to collect and investigate victims' accounts of apartheid for the period 1960–93, to consider amnesty for those who confessed their participation in atrocities, and to make recommendations for reparations. In July the Constitutional Court unanimously rejected a case brought by three families of murdered antiapartheid activists who asserted that the granting of amnesty was unconstitutional.

Throughout the year, the commission continued to investigate activities of both the apartheid regime and its opponents. In October the former chief of the South African police force, Gen. Johan van der Merwe, admitted that he had ordered acts of terror with the approval of the cabinet. The admission was an important breakthrough because no previous investigation had been able to link directly the highest levels of government to acts such as the 1988 bombing of Khotso House—the Johannesburg headquarters of the South African Council of Churches—and the sending of booby-trapped grenades to student activists in 1985. Van der Merwe indicated that he had received approval from the minister of law and order at the time and that he believed that final approval had been given by then President P.W. Botha. In November former President Botha met with Tutu and issued a statement in which he defended his record in government and insisted that he had not done anything that would warrant him applying for amnesty.

In March former Defense Minister Magnus Malan and 19 other former military and police officers were placed on trial for political crimes committed during the apartheid era. The 20 men were charged with organizing a 1987 raid on the home of Victor Ntuli, an ANC leader in what is now KwaZulu/Natal. The raid, which was aimed at assassinating Ntuli, who was not home at the time, left 13 persons dead, most of whom were women and children. Malan, a former general who had been defense minister from 1980–91, was accused of conspiring to arm and train the hit squad of Inkatha gunmen who participated in the raid. Prosecutor Timothy McNally tried to connect Malan to "Operation Marion," which sought to train Inkatha supporters to attack identified targets with the ultimate purpose of fomenting conflict between the ANC and Inkatha. However, the trial ended in October with all of the accused being acquitted. The ruling judge said that the state's key witnesses had been unconvincing.

Crime. South Africa continued to experience soaring urban crime rates. In September, President Mandela publicly acknowledged the seriousness of the situation but assured the country that the government was dealing with it. He said that the provinces of Western Cape and Gauteng were the major areas of concern. ANC national and provincial leaders recommended that the party reconsider its policy on the death penalty as one way of dealing with the problem. Another response was the formation of People Against Gangsterism and Drugs (PAGAD), a largely Muslim-based community organization, which originally was started to demonstrate against the worsening crime problem, but over the course of the year began to take the law into its own hands. Early in August, for example, in a confrontation between PAGAD and drug members in Athlone, near Cape Town, drug lord Rashaad Staggie was killed brutally. PAGAD, whose slogan is "one gangster, one bullet," issued a number of ultimatums to drug lords demanding that they cease their activities. The government was put in the difficult position of trying to control the rising crime rate while, at the same time, preventing the rise of militant vigilante activity. In August troops and police used rubber bullets and tear gas in a tense situation in which gangs staged counterdemonstrations against PAGAD.

Economic Issues. While South Africa's economic growth of more than 3% was the highest in 20 years and inflation was relatively low at 9%, unemployment remained the major problem, with nearly half of the country's 17 million workers unemployed. In the last quarter of the year, agriculture did extremely well because of an outstanding maize harvest. Manufacturing was down because of uncertainties on the part of consumers and there was a decline in the production of gold. The South African Reserve Bank saw this slowdown as positive because of the need to keep inflation under control; the rise in consumer prices had to be checked to avoid returning to double-digit inflation.

The budget for the 1996–97 fiscal year, which was presented in March by Finance Minister Chris Liebenberg, showed an increase of 10.4% over the previous year in total expenditures. It included funds for the restructuring of the public service in order to make it more efficient by downsizing and by providing incentives for skilled workers to remain in government service. There was increased funding for education and defense, while there was a drop in the amount allocated for housing because nearly $800 million was carried over from the previous year. The

SOUTH AFRICA • Information Highlights

Official Name: Republic of South Africa.
Location: Southern tip of Africa.
Area: 471,008 sq mi (1 219 912 km^2).
Population (mid-1996 est.): 44,500,000.
Chief Cities (1991 census, city proper): Pretoria, the administrative capital, 525,583; Cape Town, the legislative capital, 854,616; Durban, 715,669; Johannesburg, 712,507.
Government: *Head of state and government,* Nelson Mandela, president (took office May 10, 1994). *Legislature—*Parliament: National Assembly and National Council of Provinces.
Monetary Unit: Rand (4.6790 rands equal U.S.$1, Dec. 31, 1996).
Gross Domestic Product (1994 est. U.S.$): $194,300,000,000 (purchasing power parity).
Economic Indexes (1995, 1990 = 100): *Consumer Prices,* all items, 170.6; food, 197.9. *Industrial Production,* 103.
Foreign Trade (1995 U.S.$): *Imports,* $29,608,000,000; *exports,* excluding exports of gold, $26,912,000,000.

© Jacques Witt/Sipa Press

South Africa's President Nelson Mandela made state visits to Great Britain and France in July 1996. In France he was honored at the Bastille Day military parade and was awarded an honorary doctorate at the Sorbonne (above).

surplus highlighted the fact that many of the problems faced by the government were not financial but ones of implementation and delivery. The overall goals of the budget included job creation, land reform, support for small farmers, the promotion of exports, vocational training, and the development of small businesses. The budget was seen as more of a holding operation rather than one that made substantial efforts to alleviate poverty or address other pressing social issues within the nation.

The value of the rand continued to decline, and by year's end stood at about R4.7 to the U.S. dollar. In addition, in December the price of gold dropped below $370 per ounce, its lowest level in three years.

With the completion of the work of the Constitutional Assembly, its chair, Cyril Ramaphosa, became deputy chairman of New African Investments Ltd. (NAIL), a major consortium of black business leaders chaired by Nthato Motlana. NAIL, which owns the *Sowetan* newspaper and the Metropolitan Life insurance company, sought to buy the Anglo American Corp.'s 47.4% share in Johnnic, one of South Africa's major industrial conglomerates. The National Empowerment Consortium (NEC), of which NAIL is the major partner, succeeded in making a deal in September in which it agreed to purchase 20% and then to proceed to a 35% share in 18 months. This was the largest black economic-empowerment deal in South Africa's history. NAIL was said to be preparing to bid for Johannesburg Consolidated Investments (JCI), one of the country's largest mining houses.

Foreign Relations. In May, President Mandela made a three-day state visit to Germany where he addressed parliament and held meetings with government and business leaders. In July he paid a four-day state visit to Great Britain accompanied by a delegation of 100 business and government leaders. During the visit he addressed the British Parliament and received eight honorary doctorates from British universities. After the visit to Britain, President Mandela went to France, where he met with President Jacques Chirac.

In November, Mandela announced that South Africa would terminate diplomatic relations with Taiwan. While he was grateful for the long relationship with Taiwan, Mandela said that this would open the way for diplomatic relations with the People's Republic of China, which he believed would be in the better long-term international interests of South Africa. Mandela later said that a committee would be set up to find a formula for continued bilateral relations of some kind with Taiwan.

Graça Machel. In March the 38-year marriage of Nelson Mandela and Winnie Mandela ended when the Rand Supreme Court granted them a divorce. In September the president's office confirmed that he had entered a romantic relationship with Graça Machel, the widow of the former president of Mozambique.

PATRICK O'MEARA and N. BRIAN WINCHESTER
Indiana University

SPACE EXPLORATION

Space science in 1996 was marked by a number of provocative discoveries, from the possible find of primitive life in a Martian meteorite and the prospect of ice being found at the Moon's south pole to puzzling observations by the Galileo spacecraft orbiting Jupiter. The Hubble Space Telescope (HST) continued to relay stunning images of the birth and death of stars and of galaxies in the process of development. Meanwhile, the United States and Russia completed several joint missions in preparation for building a future International Space Station (ISS). Russia's continuing financial woes, however, threatened the stability of that country's involvement in the venture.

Shuttle Program. The National Aeronautics and Space Administration (NASA) launched seven shuttle missions in 1996—its 15th year of shuttle operations. In October, as a hoped-for cost-saving move, United Space Alliance (USA)—a commercial joint venture of the Lockheed Martin Corp. and Rockwell International Corp.—began operating the shuttle fleet. Under a six-year, $7 billion contract, USA formally took over that function from NASA. In July, NASA selected Lockheed Martin to build the X-33, a reusable launch vehicle. A commercial single-stage-to-orbit version of the X-33 was being eyed as a shuttle replacement for early in the 21st century.

© NASA

On the STS-80 mission of the space shuttle "Columbia," 61-year-old astronaut Story Musgrave (far left) *became the oldest person to fly in space and the first to travel on all five shuttles.*

Endeavour's STS-72 mission (January 11–20) carried a six-person crew, including Japanese astronaut Koichi Wakata. *Endeavour* snagged the Japanese Space Flyer Unit (SFU)—a satellite platform that carried an infrared telescope, a furnace for materials-science research, and life-science experiments. The SFU had been lofted into orbit in March 1995. Using the shuttle's robotic arm, the SFU was tucked safely into *Endeavour*'s cargo bay for transport back to Earth. To accomplish this, however, two SFU solar panels that would not retract had to be jettisoned. Later in the mission, NASA's Office of Aeronautics and Technology (OAST) Flyer was deployed from the shuttle for a two-day solo flight. The OAST Flyer, loaded with test hardware, then was retrieved. A set of astronaut space walks tested assembly tools to be utilized in building the ISS.

Columbia's STS-75 mission (February 22–March 9) focused on testing the concept of space tethers. Tethers were being considered for a number of potential uses, including to gather electrical current as they slip through space and to transfer momentum to toss satellites into higher orbits. The tether test was a repeat of a 1992 shuttle mission that ran into technical problems. *Columbia*'s seven-person crew was successful in deploying an Italian Space Agency satellite at the end of nearly 12.5 mi (20 km) of narrow Teflon cord. Instruments aboard *Columbia* reported that electrical energy was being generated by the tether and that the electrical current collected was many times the level predicted before the mission. During the test, electrical arcing caused the tether to snap, losing the Italian satellite. The frustrated crew continued their work in space by completing numbers of experiments in the U.S. Microgravity Laboratory (USML), studying protein-crystal growth and flame propagation in microgravity.

Atlantis' STS-76 mission (March 22–31) carried out the third docking between a U.S. shuttle and the Russian *Mir* space station. Once the two spacecraft were linked, astronaut Shannon Lucid, one of the six shuttle crew members, transferred over to *Mir* to begin a projected 140-day stint aboard the

Russian complex, joining cosmonauts Yuri Onufrienko and Yuri Usachev. As a biochemist, Lucid was tasked with dedicated experiments that evaluated physiological changes due to long-term exposure to the space environment. Before *Atlantis* undocked, astronauts performed a space walk, testing equipment destined for use on building the future ISS. The two spacecraft were docked together for five days.

The liftoff of *Endeavour* on its STS-77 mission (May 19–29) saw the first test of an inflatable structure from a space shuttle. Tagged the Inflatable Antenna Experiment (IAE), the device was carried inside the Spartan satellite. With the six-person crew watching, the IAE slowly filled with gas. The inflatable antenna took shape until fully deployed at 50 ft (15 m) in diameter. Although the IAE did not inflate itself fully, as hoped for, the test was considered a success. With the test complete, the inflated structure was ejected from the Spartan. After several orbits of Earth, the IAE reentered the atmosphere. A small satellite also was released into space during the mission, demonstrating that it could stabilize itself using the natural magnetic field of the Earth rather than costly fuel-powered rocket thrusters. Returning to the Kennedy Space Center in Florida at mission's end, *Endeavour* entered an extensive overhaul period to ready it for use in assembling the ISS.

Columbia's long STS-78 mission (June 20–July 7) permitted extensive medical experiments to be performed in space. The 16-day, 22-hour mission set a record for the longest shuttle mission to date. Mounted within the shuttle's cargo bay, the pressurized Spacelab module allowed the crew to study microgravity effects on humans, animals, and plants. The seven-person shuttle crew worked around the clock, completing complex life-science experiments. The astronauts used themselves as subjects to study the effects of microgravity on human physiology. Along with numerous life-science studies, a variety of materials-processing experiments were done, several of them making use of a high-temperature furnace. The astronauts also tested new ways for a shuttle to boost itself using its set of small vernier thrusters. The technique was under consideration to boost the orbiting HST to a higher altitude without damaging the observatory's large solar panels.

The six-person crew of *Atlantis* flew the STS-79 mission (September 16–26), marking the fourth docking with *Mir*. The mission was to have been launched July 31, but tropical storms and concern over problems discovered with booster rockets led to a delayed liftoff. Once airborne, *Atlantis* suffered a failure of one of its auxiliary power units, but the problem did not threaten the mission. STS-79 was the first shuttle-*Mir* mission to carry a double-module Spacehab. Use of the commercial Spacehab, positioned directly behind the crew compartments in the cargo bay, permitted the crew to carry out experiments before, during, and after docking with the Russian space station. Also housed in the Spacehab were food, clothing, experiment supplies, and spare equipment for transfer to *Mir*. A key event of this mission was the replacement of astronaut Shannon Lucid on *Mir* with astronaut John Blaha. Lucid's 188-day stay on *Mir* was a record-setting sojourn in space for a woman. Following the landing of *Atlantis*, Lucid began six months of intensive medical evaluations. She was awarded the Congressional Space Medal of Honor at a White House ceremony on December 2 (*see* BIOGRAPHY).

Columbia's STS-80 mission (November 19–December 7) was a record-long flight for the shuttle program, adding up to 17 days, 16 hours. Among the five-person crew was the oldest person to fly in space, 61-year-old Story Musgrave. Two platforms were released from

As part of a renewed effort to explore the fourth planet, the Mars Pathfinder spacecraft was launched on Dec. 4, 1996. The probe (depicted below) *was slated to touch down in July 1997.*
© NASA/Science Photo Library/Photo Researchers

the shuttle's cargo bay during the flight. The Wake Shield Facility floated free of the shuttle to produce innovative semiconductor chips in microgravity. Also deployed was the Orbiting and Retrievable Far and Extreme Ultraviolet Spectrograph–Shuttle Pallet Satellite II (ORFEUS-SPAS II). A joint program of NASA and the German Space Agency, ORFEUS-SPAS II made measurements of ultraviolet radiation from stars and interstellar gases. Both platforms later were retrieved for return to Earth. The mission was marred when the shuttle's airlock door to exit into space jammed. The door problem scratched two scheduled space walks and prevented a test of construction equipment designed for building the ISS. The stuck door, it was determined later, was jammed by a loose screw that was embedded in gears.

Space Stations. Russia's *Mir* space station was in use throughout the year. European Space Agency (ESA) astronaut Thomas Reiter completed a 180-day stay aboard *Mir*, returning to Earth February 29 with cosmonauts Yuri Gidzenko and Sergei Avdeyev. They were replaced by cosmonauts Yuri Onufrienko and Yuri Usachev, who blasted off in a Russian Soyuz spacecraft on February 21 to board the station. In March, U.S. astronaut Shannon Lucid was transported to *Mir* via a space shuttle. She lived aboard the station for 188 days, and was replaced by astronaut John Blaha in September. On August 17 a Soyuz rocket carried Valery Korzun and Alexandr Koleri to *Mir* to replace long-duration crew members Onufrienko and Usachev. Also on board the Soyuz was France's first female astronaut, Claudie André-Deshays, who lived on *Mir* for two weeks. The space station was completed with the addition of its final module. Launched April 23, the Priroda module was loaded with hardware, including Russian remote-sensing equipment.

Despite budget pressures, the U.S. Congress continued to support funding for the ISS. U.S. elements for the multinational project—as well as Japanese, Canadian, and European segments—moved closer to completion during 1996. The first U.S. component, called Node 1, reached critical milestones in preparation for its launch in December 1997. A U.S.-financed Russian Functional Energy Block (FGB) was scheduled to be orbited in November 1997, marking the first step in building the ISS.

Money shortfalls, however, appeared likely to delay Russia's building of a critical service module for the ISS. In December, NASA officials began discussing alternative plans to counter the Russian difficulties. Whether or not the timetable for a completed six-person station by June 2002 could be met remained unknown. Furthermore, the financial impact of Russian difficulties on the program remained uncertain.

Space Science. A banner year for space science was highlighted by the announcement in August by NASA scientists of evidence of primitive biology within a meteorite believed to have been from Mars (*see* ASTRONOMY). Yet another potential discovery—the indication of ice at the Moon's south pole—was reported in December using data gleaned by the Clementine satellite that orbited the Moon in 1994.

Throughout 1996, the U.S. Galileo spacecraft sent back close-up images of a number of moons circling Jupiter. Images indicated that Ganymede supports a thin oxygen atmosphere; that Io seems to be resurfacing itself due to volcanic eruptions; and that Europa may have a subsurface ocean below its cracked cover of ice. Meanwhile, NASA's HST also captured startling views of such things as quasars, the most energetic objects in the universe.

ESA's Infrared Space Observatory (ISO) and Solar and Heliospheric Observatory (SOHO), both launched in late 1995, produced a spate of new findings. ISO detected evidence that stars formed at a prodigious rate in some of the most distant galaxies known in the universe. New details regarding the Sun's internal composition were undertaken by SOHO.

A privately financed Search for Extraterrestrial Intelligence (SETI) by the SETI Institute in Mountain View, CA, began in October. A long-term scanning effort using a radio telescope situated at Green Bank, WV, started looking for transmissions from intelligent life elsewhere among the stars.

On February 17 the U.S. Near-Earth Asteroid Rendezvous (NEAR) mission was launched by NASA; it was set to start orbiting the asteroid Eros in February 1999. On the way to Eros, NEAR was scheduled to pass by another asteroid, Mathilde, in June 1997. The U.S. Polar space-physics spacecraft was lofted into Earth orbit February 24. Polar was designed to measure magnetospheric hot plasma, electric and magnetic fields, and plasma waves, and to map auroral displays with ultraviolet cameras.

To better determine the state of Earth's protective cover of ozone, NASA successfully lofted on July 2 the Total Ozone Mapping Spectrometer (TOMS). Yet another U.S.

spacecraft dedicated to investigating auroral phenomena was orbited in August—the Fast Auroral Snapshot (FAST) Explorer.

In August, Russia launched the second component of its Interball Project, the Auroral Probe, along with the Magion 5 subsatellite. Launched from the Plesetsk Cosmodrome in Russia, the Auroral Probe was carrying instruments to monitor the magnetic field, plasma, and energetic particles in Earth's magnetosphere as they relate to the auroral phenomena. The smaller Czech-built Magion was designed to measure properties of the magnetosphere, although it ran into problems when it failed to be released from Interball Aurora.

A new era of Mars exploration began with the November 7 launch of the U.S. Mars Global Surveyor. The spacecraft was set to reach Mars in September 1997, then would take about four months to adjust its orbit to begin mapping the red planet for a total of 687 Earth days.

Russia's Mars 96 was launched November 16 from the Baikonur Cosmodrome in Kazakhstan. Intended to orbit Mars, then to dispatch dual landers and penetrators, Mars 96 crashed to Earth due to a fourth-stage-booster problem. The out-of-control interplanetary probe, carrying plutonium fuel to power spacecraft elements, was thought to have impacted in or near northern Chile or Bolivia.

NASA's Mars Pathfinder roared skyward December 4 on a Delta 2 booster, heading toward a July 4, 1997, touchdown on Martian terrain. Once on Mars, the Pathfinder lander was slated to release the Sojourner mini-rover to wheel itself across Mars' landscape. The renewed effort to explore Mars was centered on assessing the prospects that life once existed on the fourth planet.

Applications Satellites. The year also saw the orbiting of an Indian Remote Sensing (IRS) spacecraft on March 21. Blasting off from the Sriharikota launch station in India, the IRS-P3 spacecraft was outfitted with a Wide Field Scanner capable of working in visible light and infrared to study crop conditions, geology, and snow cover. The spacecraft also was expected to help study oceanic chlorophyll, sediment transport, and ocean dynamics.

Japan lofted its Advanced Earth Observation Satellite (ADEOS) on August 17 using the country's powerful H-2 rocket from Tanegashima Space Center. ADEOS carried instruments to monitor wind and temperature on ocean surfaces and aerosols, ozone, and greenhouse gases in the atmosphere.

Meanwhile, France's SPOT 3 Earth-observation satellite stopped sending signals in mid-November. The problem put a crimp on selling SPOT data services to worldwide customers, forcing backup use of the older SPOT 1 and SPOT 2 satellites.

Communications Satellites. The launching of communications satellites remained a booming business for commercial companies selling launch services. The French firm Arianespace had a banner year with successful launches of its rocket-for-hire Ariane 4 booster. Launches of ten Ariane 4 rockets orbited a company record of 15 satellites. However, the ESA suffered a major blow June 4 during the maiden voyage of its heavy-lift Ariane 5 booster, which exploded just 40 seconds after takeoff from Kourou, French Guiana. ESA had spent ten years and $8 billion to build the Ariane 5. The mishap later was attributed to a software problem that led to the launcher's destruction. Four scientific satellites were destroyed along with the rocket. A second flight of the booster was slated for 1997.

On January 14 a McDonnell Douglas Delta 2 booster placed South Korea's Koreasat 2 into geostationary orbit. A Delta 2 also orbited, on May 24, the U.S. Galaxy 9 satellite to provide voice and vision communications to North America.

Indonesia's Palapa C-1, built to provide voice and television coverage to the thousands of islands of Indonesia and the nearby Asia-Pacific region, was orbited February 1 atop a Lockheed Martin Atlas 2AS rocket. The 79-nation International Mobile Satellite Organization (Inmarsat) consortium used a similar booster to loft the Inmarsat 3-F1 on April 3; a U.S. GE-1 on September 8; and a Hot Bird 2 on November 21 for Eutelsat, the Paris-based consortium of 45 member nations and signatories.

Russia's Proton-K rocket also was offered commercially, with the booster placing the U.S.-built Astra 1F in orbit on April 8 to provide direct-broadcast television to Europe. Similarly, a Proton rocket hurled into space on September 6 an Inmarsat 3 F2 satellite to provide communications among objects on land, sea, or in the air.

China continued its struggle to gain acceptance in the commercial booster business. In 1996, Chinese-built Long March rockets suffered two failures in four launches, including a tragic crash at liftoff on February 14 that killed numerous onlookers and destroyed an Intelsat spacecraft.

Leonard David
Space Data Resources & Information

SPAIN

On May 5, 1996, Spain's King Juan Carlos swore in José María Aznar, the leader of the center-right Popular Party (PP), as the nation's new prime minister. He replaced Felipe González of the Socialist Workers' Party (PSOE), which narrowly had been defeated in elections for the Cortés (parliament) in March. Still, the absence of a legislative majority forced Aznar to bargain with opposition groups to achieve reforms designed to boost the country's flagging economy.

Politics. Despite the killings of two prominent civilians by Basque extremists in February, more than 25 million Spaniards—77.5% of those eligible—cast ballots in the legislative contests that took place on March 3. As predicted in public-opinion surveys, the PP ousted the Socialists, who had held power since 1982. The margin of victory, however, was a scant 350,000 votes as the PP barely outpolled the PSOE—38.9% to 37.5%. The United Left coalition (IU) finished a distant third (10.6%). Many voters, especially in rural areas and among the elderly, apparently believed Socialist claims that a PP regime would slash Spain's generous social-welfare system and revive the authoritarian practices of Gen. Francisco Franco, who died in 1975.

All told, the PP expanded its presence in the 350-member Cortés from 141 to 156 seats; the Socialists declined from 159 to 141 seats; and the IU increased its delegation from 18 to 21 members. The PP registered more impressive results at the local level, capturing majorities in 11 of 17 regional parliaments and in 32 of 52 provincial capitals, while winning pluralities in another ten.

José María Aznar

Spain's new Prime Minister José María Aznar was born on Feb. 25, 1953, and was raised in the wealthy Madrid neighborhood of Salamanca. Both his father and one of his grandfathers were prominent conservative journalists who held political posts in Gen. Francisco Franco's regime. Aznar received his law degree from Complutensian University. A passion for politics led him to devote more time and energy to the conservative cause than to his work as a tax lawyer. He assiduously worked his way up the party ladder, advocating a shift to the political center and a severing of ties to Franco's former supporters. In the process, he won election to parliament (1982) and led the PP's efforts to oust the Socialist Party from power in the 1989 national contests. In 1990 his hard work garnered him the Popular Party's presidency. He quickly earned a reputation for running the PP as a tight, highly organized ship. Observers credit his no-nonsense leadership with the party's success in May 1995 regional elections, in which the PP gained majorities in 11 of Spain's 17 regional parliaments.

Aznar is married to a former law-school classmate, Ana Botella. The couple have three children.

GEORGE W. GRAYSON

A medley of factors—splits with PSOE labor allies, corruption suffusing González' administration, and economic stagnation—helped ring down the curtain on his 13-year rule. During the campaign, observers had complained that Aznar preferred generalities to specific proposals—a strategy designed to take advantage of the Socialists' mounting unpopularity. The PP leader told the electorate that Spain needed a "clean" party. If elected, "his great party of the center" would streamline the bureaucracy, balance the budget, extirpate corruption, crack down on Basque terrorists, cut taxes, and spur employment.

José María Aznar, 43-year-old leader of Spain's conservative Popular Party (PP), cast his ballot in parliamentary elections in March 1996. The Popular Party scored a tight win over the Socialist Workers' Party, which had been in power since 1982.

Younger Spaniards held the key to the outcome of the parliamentary contests, as 40% of voters between the ages of 18 and 30 opted for the PP. They seemed to cast their ballots less because of enthusiasm for the 43-year-old Aznar than out of protest against the corruption-plagued PSOE. Although exonerated of any guilt, González watched his public-approval rating dwindle as detractors accused him of complicity in death-squad slayings of Basque separatists in the 1980s.

The PP's failure to win an outright majority in the Cortés led Aznar to hammer out an alliance with Catalan nationalists (CiU), Basque nationalists (PNV), and deputies from the Canary Islands. Together, these four parties held 181 seats. In exchange for throwing support to the PP, CiU leader Jordi Pujol extracted promises that Aznar would bestow greater powers on Catalonia and the other 16 semiautonomous regions that comprise Spain. The pact with Pujol also would shift substantial control of law enforcement, transportation, and tax revenues from the federal government to Catalonia—with similar accords likely with other regional governments. Previously, the PP had opposed initiatives to attenuate the power of the central government. Aznar justified his latest action by pointing to putative savings arising from local handling of tax monies.

Aznar appointed four women to his cabinet—the most ever to hold ministerial portfolios in Spain. He also named three independents, but no representatives of the regional parties that ensured him a working legislative majority.

The Economy. Spain's economy grew just 2% in 1996, down a point from the previous year. Meanwhile, prices rose nearly 4%, down from 4.6% in 1995. Efforts to curb inflation would make it even more difficult for Minister of Economy and Finance Rodrigo Rato to reduce the nation's 22.7% unemployment rate, the highest in Western Europe. Of course, extremely generous benefits mitigate the hardship of joblessness and, critics assert, diminish the incentive to seek work.

Several factors—namely, soft consumer demand, anemic competition in some domestic sectors, and an abundance of goods on the continental market produced in Poland, the Czech Republic, and other low-wage East European countries—impeded job creation. In midyear, Aznar introduced a package of fiscal and deregulation measures to spur economic growth and competition. A cut in the capital-gains tax highlighted this plan. The new government also pledged to accelerate the privatization program begun by González, stressing telecommunications, power generation, and the petroleum industry.

At the same time, Rato vowed to lower the fiscal deficit to 3% of gross domestic product (GDP) in 1997—down from 4.4% in 1996 and 5.9% in 1995—to meet the criteria of the Maastricht Treaty for Spain's participation in a single European currency. Achieving this goal would require trimming a bloated bureaucracy, while reducing the growth of popular social programs that the trade unions had vowed to defend. Labor protests aside, Aznar affirmed his commitment to continue the public-sector wage freeze through 1997.

Foreign Policy. In April a member of the Civil Guard died when his helicopter crashed while chasing drug traffickers. Authorities captured two of three suspects. When the third escaped by power boat to Gibraltar, Spain's foreign ministry imposed stricter controls around its frontier with Gibraltar and warned that it would close the border completely if Britain could not control unlawful activities in its colony. In October discussions over Gibraltar reached an impasse when the Madrid government insisted that any talks involve only Great Britain and Spain, excluding a separate Gibraltan delegation. Contributing to the sensitivity of such parleys were Spain's efforts to join the military structure of the North Atlantic Treaty Organization (NATO) with a mandate to oversee the defense of the entire Iberian peninsula, including Gibraltar.

In spite of budget constraints, Spain agreed to fund the country's participation in the Eurofighter 2000 program to construct an advanced combat jet. Britain, Germany, and Italy also were involved in the construction.

GEORGE W. GRAYSON
College of William and Mary

SPAIN • Information Highlights

Official Name: Kingdom of Spain.
Location: Iberian Peninsula in southwestern Europe.
Area: 194,884 sq mi (504 750 km²).
Population (mid-1996 est.): 39,300,000.
Chief Cities (March 1991 est.): Madrid, the capital, 3,010,492; Barcelona, 1,643,542; Valencia, 752,909.
Government: *Head of state,* Juan Carlos I, king (took office Nov. 1975). *Head of government,* José María Aznar, prime minister (took office May 5, 1996). *Legislature*—Cortés Generales: Senate and Congress of Deputies.
Monetary Unit: Peseta (126.16 pesetas equal U.S.$1, Nov. 11, 1996).
Gross Domestic Product (1994 est. U.S.$): $515,800,-000,000 (purchasing power parity).
Economic Indexes (1995, 1990 = 100): *Consumer Prices,* all items, 128.6; food, 120.7. *Industrial Production,* 103.
Foreign Trade (1995 U.S.$): *Imports,* $114,972,000,000; *exports,* $91,533,000,000.

Sports

Overview

In 1996 sports enthusiasts were treated to classic struggles between perennial powerhouses and to the emergence of exciting new champions.

As compelling as these performances were, however, business issues and other nonsporting distractions continued to vie for headlines. The dizzying pace of player trades, team movement and expansion, stadium and arena construction, product merchandising, and salary escalation left many fans yearning for simpler days. In addition, disturbing new questions about player conduct—highlighted by Roberto Alomar's spitting at an umpire, Mahmoud Abdul-Rauf's refusal to sing the national anthem, and a major gambling scandal at Boston College—surfaced during the year as front-page news.

Luckily, sports fans could find solace in the drama on the field of play. In the National Basketball Association (NBA), Michael Jordan and the Chicago Bulls returned to championship form by putting away a spirited Seattle Supersonic squad. Elsewhere on the hardwood, the Kentucky Wildcats won that school's fifth National Collegiate Athletic Association (NCAA) title, while the consistently strong Lady Volunteers of Tennessee captured a national championship. In the World Series, the New York Yankees—the most storied franchise in baseball—defeated the team of the 1990s, the Atlanta Braves. The city of Denver gained its first professional champion when the Colorado Avalanche defeated the Florida Panthers to take hockey's Stanley Cup.

In other sporting action, the golf world was captivated by the sensational professional debut of Eldrick (Tiger) Woods; Major League Soccer enjoyed a strong first season; the horse Cigar (*below*) matched a 46-year-old record with 17 consecutive victories; Evander Holyfield recorded a shocking defeat of Mike Tyson to take the heavyweight title for the third time; Pete Sampras and Steffi Graf defended their Number 1 rankings in tennis; Denmark's Bjarne Riis outrode a field that included five-time champion Miguel Indurain to capture the Tour de France; and Alaskan Jeff King won his second title at the Iditarod Trail Sled Dog Race.

Finally, Atlanta hosted the 1996 Summer Olympics in July and August. The Games featured outstanding performances on the track, in the pool, and in women's team events.

PETER A. FLAX

© Focus on Sports

Auto Racing

Great Britain's Damon Hill, son of the late racing legend Graham Hill, overcame another second-generation driver, Canada's Jacques Villeneuve, to win the 1996 Formula One championship. Hill captured eight events and accumulated 97 points to 78 for his teammate Villeneuve, the 1995 Indianapolis 500 winner and IndyCar champion who switched to the world circuit in 1996. The son of the late Gilles Villeneuve won four Grand Prix events and finished ahead of defending champion Michael Schumacher of Germany, who won three races.

Terry Labonte outpointed defending Winston Cup stock-car champion and Hendrick Motorsports teammate Jeff Gordon to win his second championship. Gordon posted ten victories and Labonte won twice. Dale Jarrett, who was third on the points list, was a four-time winner, including three of the circuit's most prestigious events—the Daytona 500, the Coca-Cola 600, and the Brickyard 400.

A split between the established IndyCar circuit and the fledgling Indy Racing League (IRL) threw U.S. top open-wheel racing into conflict. The IRL, founded by Indianapolis Motor Speedway President Tony George, conducted five oval-track races and limited the bulk of the Indianapolis 500 field to IRL competitors. Buddy Lazier won the Indianapolis 500 by .695 seconds over Davy Jones, and Buzz Calkins and Scott Sharp tied for the IRL points title. IndyCar rebelled with its own U.S. 500 at Brooklyn, MI, on the same day. Jimmy Vasser won the U.S. 500 and three other events to take the IndyCar season championship, outpointing five-time winner Michael Andretti 154–132. Alex Zanardi won three times and finished third in points, while winning rookie-of-the-year honors. Six days after winning the pole at Indianapolis, veteran driver Scott Brayton was killed in a practice accident.

STAN SUTTON
"Louisville Courier-Journal"

AUTO RACING

Major Race Winners, 1996

Indianapolis 500: Buddy Lazier, United States
Marlboro 500: André Ribeiro, Brazil
Daytona 500: Dale Jarrett, United States
Brickyard 400: Jarrett

1996 Champions

Formula One: Damon Hill, Great Britain
NASCAR: Terry Labonte, United States
IndyCar: Jimmy Vasser, United States
Indy Racing League: Buzz Calkins, United States; and Scott Sharp, United States

Grand Prix for Formula One Cars, 1996

Australian: Damon Hill, Great Britain
Brazilian: Hill
Argentinian: Hill
European: Jacques Villeneuve, Canada
San Marino: Hill
Monaco: Olivier Panis, France
Spanish: Michael Schumacher, Germany
Canadian: Hill
French: Hill
British: Villeneuve
German: Hill
Hungarian: Villeneuve
Belgian: Schumacher
Italian: Schumacher
Portuguese: Villeneuve
Japanese: Hill

Baseball

The 1996 baseball season was the first in three years not to be shortened or terminated due to labor problems. Although players and owners failed to reach a new labor agreement until after the end of the World Series, the game won back many of the fans turned off by a 234-day player strike that ended in March 1995. The average attendance of 26,889 was an increase of 6.4% over the previous year.

Spurring the revival at the turnstiles was an unprecedented offensive explosion. The 28 teams combined for 4,962 home runs, erasing the 1987 record of 4,458. A record 17 players hit 40 home runs, while 43 hit at least 30 homers and 82 men hit 20 or more. The Baltimore Orioles hit 257 homers, and was one of three teams to break the major-league mark of 240 set by the 1961 New York Yankees.

On October 26 negotiators Donald Fehr of the Players Association and Randy Levine, representing club owners, announced that they had finalized a new labor agreement. The new contract would introduce interleague play, as well as revenue sharing between teams and a payroll "luxury" tax.

Play-Offs and World Series. With a week left in the season, only two teams—the Atlanta Braves and the Cleveland Indians—had clinched play-off spots, as ten teams were in contention for the remaining six spots. For the second straight year, Cleveland (99–62) led the majors in victories. However, the Indians fell to Baltimore in the American League (AL) Division Series in four games. The Birds won at home, 10–4 and 7–4, then lost Game 3 in Cleveland, 9–4, before clinching with a 4–3 win in Game 4. Cleveland pitchers fanned a record 23 Orioles in the finale but a homer by Roberto Alomar in the 12th inning made the difference.

Alomar's emergence as the team's savior was ironic; he had been the center of fan antagonism after spitting in the face of umpire John Hirschbeck during an altercation in Toronto on September 27. Only a court order

© Focus on Sports

John Wetteland earned World Series MVP honors after helping New York to its first championship in 18 years. The hard-throwing closer notched saves in all four Yankee victories.

kept major-league umpires from boycotting postseason games, while Alomar agreed to serve a five-game suspension at the start of the 1997 season.

In the other AL Division Series, the Yankees defeated the Texas Rangers in four games. In their first 25 years, the Rangers never had reached the play-offs. But their blend of pitching, power, and defense enabled them to win the AL West by 4½ games. Although Juan Gonzalez hit five homers in four games against Yankee pitching, New York won three straight, 5–4 in 12 innings, 3–2, and 6–4, after dropping a 6–2 opener at Yankee Stadium. Yeoman work by the Yankee bullpen consistently bailed out struggling starting pitchers.

In the American League Championship Series, the Yankees and Orioles split the first two games at Yankee Stadium. In Game 1, New York received some unexpected help from a 12-year-old fan who deflected a Derek Jeter drive into the right-field stands above the waiting glove of Oriole outfielder Tony Tarasco. Umpire Rich Garcia ruled it a home run, tying the game in the eighth inning. When Bernie Williams hit a legitimate homer leading off the 11th, the Yankees won, 5–4. Williams, who went on to hit five postseason homers, later was named most valuable player (MVP) of the American League play-offs. Baltimore's only win was a 5–3 verdict in Game 2 at Yankee Stadium. Once the series shifted to Oriole Park at Camden Yards, the Yankees won three straight, 5–2, 8–4, and 6–4, to take their first pennant since 1981.

That set the stage for a World Series meeting with the Braves, who had forged a 96–66 record en route to their fifth straight divisional title. While the Braves swept the wild-card Los Angeles Dodgers—2–1 in ten innings, 3–2, and 5–2—in the National League (NL) Division Series, in the other Division Series the St. Louis Cardinals, champions of the NL Central, swept the NL West–champion San Diego Padres, 3–1, 5–4, and 7–5. The Dodgers had lost the NL West title by one game after they dropped a season-ending series at home to San Diego.

Atlanta won the opener of the National League Championship Series (NLCS) at home, 4–2, but dropped Game 2, 8–3, when Gary Gaetti hit a grand slam against Greg Maddux. A pair of home runs by former Brave Ron Gant gave St. Louis a 3–2 win in Game 3, while Brian Jordan's solo shot won Game 4, 4–3, to give the Cards a 3–1 series edge. However, the Braves' moribund offense suddenly ignited with a 22-hit, 14–0 victory in Game 5 that sent the series back to Atlanta, where the Braves took a 3–1 verdict before burying the Cardinals, 15–0, in the finale. Although the big hit was a two-out, three-run triple by Glavine, teammate Javier Lopez was named MVP.

Atlanta's onslaught continued in the opener of the 92d World Series in New York, as the Braves breezed to a 12–1 win behind John Smoltz. When Greg Maddux and closer Mark Wohlers combined for a 4–0 shutout in Game 2, Atlanta seemed on track to win its second straight world championship.

But the Braves were victimized by a leaky bullpen, spotty defense, and unexpected contributions from lightly regarded Yankee catchers Jim Leyritz and Joe Girardi. After winning five straight postseason games, Atlanta lost its last four: 5–2, 8–6 in 10 innings, and 1–0 in Atlanta and 3–2 at Yankee Stadium. The turning point was Atlanta's inability to hold a 6–0, sixth-inning lead in Game 4, tied when Leyritz hit a three-run, eighth-inning homer against Wohlers. Three days later, Girardi's triple off Maddux was the biggest hit in the series-clinching Game 6.

Closer John Wetteland, who saved all four Yankee wins, was named World Series MVP as the Yankees won their first world championship since 1978. The victory was especially sweet for first-year Yankee manager Joe Torre, who won his first World Series title in a 36-year career as player and pilot.

Regular Season. The "Year of the Homer" began when Frank Thomas of the Chicago White Sox hit the 14th pitch of the season out of the ballpark on March 31, baseball's earliest Opening Day. Although several players made runs at Roger Maris' single-season record of 61 homers, only Brady Anderson of the Baltimore Orioles and Mark McGwire of the Oakland Athletics finished with at least 50—the first pair of players to reach that level in a season since Maris and Mickey Mantle did so in 1961. McGwire led the majors with 52 home runs, a .730 slugging percentage, and a .467 on-base percentage. Andres Galarraga of the Rockies led the National League in homers (47) and topped the majors with 150 runs batted in (RBIs)—two more than AL leader Albert Belle of the Indians.

The AL MVP award went to Juan Gonzalez, who had 47 homers and 144 RBIs for the Rangers. He outpolled Mariners shortstop Alex Rodriguez in a very close vote. Rodriguez topped the AL in batting (.358), runs (141), and doubles (54). In the NL, San Diego's Ken Caminiti became the fourth unanimous MVP selection in league history. The Padre third baseman batted .326 and collected 40 home runs and 130 RBIs.

Also producing big numbers was three-time NL MVP Barry Bonds of San Francisco, who hit .308 with 42 homers, 122 runs scored, 129 RBIs, an NL- record 151 walks, and 40 stolen bases. The NL's first 40/40 man (with 40 home runs and 40 stolen bases) also became the fourth player with at least 300 career homers and 300 career steals. Also notching 30/30 seasons were Dante Bichette and Ellis Burks of Colorado and Cincinnati shortstop Barry Larkin. Burks joined Hank Aaron as the only men ever to have 40 homers, 30 stolen bases, and 200 hits in one season.

Lance Johnson of the Mets led the majors with 227 hits. The first man to lead both leagues in hits, Johnson also hit 21 triples, the NL's most since 1930. The NL batting king was no surprise: San Diego's Tony Gwynn won for the seventh time with a .353 mark. Eric Young of the Rockies led the NL with 53 stolen bases, 22 less than major-league leader Kenny Lofton of the Indians.

Though Greg Maddux was unable to win his fifth straight Cy Young Award, the Braves managed to keep the trophy. It went to John Smoltz, who had a 24–8 record, 2.94 earned-run average (ERA), and a major-league-leading 276 strikeouts. Florida's Kevin Brown posted the best ERA (1.89) in the majors. Toronto's Juan Guzman had the AL's best ERA (2.93), while teammate Pat Hentgen

BASEBALL

Professional—Major Leagues

Final Standings, 1996

AMERICAN LEAGUE

Eastern Division	W	L	Pct.
New York	92	70	.568
Baltimore	88	74	.543
Boston	85	77	.525
Toronto	74	88	.457
Detroit	53	109	.327
Central Division	**W**	**L**	**Pct.**
Cleveland	99	62	.615
Chicago	85	77	.525
Milwaukee	80	82	.494
Minnesota	78	84	.481
Kansas City	75	86	.466
Western Division	**W**	**L**	**Pct.**
Texas	90	72	.556
Seattle	85	76	.528
Oakland	78	84	.481
California	70	91	.435

NATIONAL LEAGUE

Eastern Division	W	L	Pct.
Atlanta	96	66	.593
Montreal	88	74	.543
Florida	80	82	.494
New York	71	91	.438
Philadelphia	67	95	.414
Central Division	**W**	**L**	**Pct.**
St. Louis	88	74	.543
Houston	82	80	.506
Cincinnati	81	81	.500
Chicago	76	86	.469
Pittsburgh	73	89	.451
Western Division	**W**	**L**	**Pct.**
San Diego	91	71	.562
Los Angeles	90	72	.556
Colorado	83	79	.512
San Francisco	68	94	.420

Play-offs—American League: Division Series—Baltimore defeated Cleveland, 3 games to 1; New York defeated Texas, 3 games to 1. Championship Series—New York defeated Baltimore, 4 games to 1. National League: Division Series—Atlanta defeated Los Angeles, 3 games to 0; St. Louis defeated San Diego, 3 games to 0. Championship Series—Atlanta defeated St. Louis, 4 games to 3.

World Series—New York defeated Atlanta, 4 games to 2. First Game (Yankee Stadium, New York, Oct. 20, attendance 56,365): Atlanta 12, New York 1; Second Game (Yankee Stadium, Oct. 21, attendance 56,340): Atlanta 4, New York 0; Third Game (Fulton County Stadium, Atlanta, Oct. 22, attendance 51,843): New York 5, Atlanta 2; Fourth Game (Fulton County Stadium, Oct. 23, attendance 51,881): New York 8, Atlanta 6; Fifth Game (Fulton County Stadium, Oct. 24, attendance 51,881): New York 1, Atlanta 0; Sixth Game (Yankee Stadium, Oct. 26, attendance 56,375): New York 3, Atlanta 2.

All-Star Game (Veterans Stadium, Philadelphia, PA, July 9, attendance 62,670): National League 6, American League 0.

Most Valuable Players—American League: Juan Gonzalez, Texas; National League: Ken Caminiti, San Diego.

Cy Young Memorial Awardsoutstanding pitchers—American League: Pat Hentgen, Toronto; National League: John Smoltz, Atlanta.

Managers of the Year—American League: Joe Torre, New York, and Johnny Oates, Texas; National League: Bruce Bochy, San Diego.

Rookies of the Year—American League: Derek Jeter, New York; National League: Todd Hollandsworth, Los Angeles.

Leading Hitters—(Percentage) American League: Alex Rodriguez, Seattle, .358; National League: Tony Gwynn, San Diego, .353. (Runs Batted In) American League: Albert Belle, Cleveland, 148; National League: Andres Galarraga, Colorado, 150. (Home Runs) American League: Mark McGwire, Oakland, 52; National League: Galarraga, 47. (Hits) American League: Paul Molitor, Minnesota, 225; National League: Lance Johnson, New York, 227. (Runs) American League: Rodriguez, 141; National League: Ellis Burks, Colorado, 142. (Slugging Percentage) American League: McGwire, .730; National League: Burks, .639.

Leading Pitchers—(Earned Run Average) American League: Juan Guzman, Toronto, 2.93; National League: Kevin Brown, Florida, 1.89. (Victories) American League: Andy Pettitte, New York, 21; National League: John Smoltz, Atlanta, 24. (Strikeouts) American League: Roger Clemens, 257; National League: Smoltz, 276. (Shutouts) American League: Pat Heutgen, Toronto, 3; National League: Brown, 3. (Saves) American League: John Wetteland, New York, 43; National League: Jeff Brantley, Cincinnati, and Todd Worrell, Los Angeles, 44. (Innings) American League: Heutgen, 265.2; National League: Smoltz, 253.2.

Professional—Minor Leagues, Class AAA

American Association: Oklahoma City
International League: Columbus
Pacific Coast League: Edmonton

Amateur

NCAA: Louisiana State University
Little League World Series: Kao-Hsiung, Taiwan

and New York's Andy Pettitte were the league's only 20-game winners. Hentgen—who led the league in innings pitched and complete games (10) and ranked second in ERA (3.22)—narrowly outpolled Pettitte to win the AL Cy Young Award. Three-time Cy Young Award winner Roger Clemens of the Boston Red Sox had a 20-strikeout game, tying his own record, against Detroit on September 18 and won his third AL strikeout crown with 257.

Jeff Brantley of the Reds and Todd Worrell of the Dodgers saved 44 games each, tops in the majors and one more than New York's John Wetteland, the AL leader. Yankee shortstop Derek Jeter, whose .314 average included 41 extra-base hits, was a unanimous choice for AL rookie-of-the-year honors. Dodger outfielder Todd Hollandsworth won NL freshman honors after hitting .291 with 21 steals, marking the fifth straight year that a Dodger had won the award.

Twice the Rockies fell victim to no-hitters. They lost to Al Leiter in Florida, 11–0, on May 11, and 9–0 to Hideo Nomo of the Dodgers at Coors Field on September 17. The year's only other no-hitter was Dwight Gooden's 2–0 victory over Seattle at Yankee Stadium May 14.

Dodger Mike Piazza was named All-Star Game MVP after delivering a home run and RBI double in the National League's 6–0 win at Philadelphia's Veterans Stadium on July 9.

Baltimore's Eddie Murray hit his 500th career homer September 6, joining Willie Mays and Hank Aaron as the only men with 500 homers and 3,000 hits. On September 16, Minnesota's Paul Molitor tripled in Kansas City for his 3,000th career hit. By season's end, Cal Ripken, Jr., of the Orioles had stretched his consecutive-game playing streak to 2,316.

In July, Dodger manager Tommy Lasorda retired after suffering a minor heart attack the previous month. Lasorda was one of only four men to manage the same team for 20 years—and his teams won seven division titles, four pennants, and two World Series. Kirby Puckett, a ten-time All-Star for the Minnesota Twins, also retired in midseason after developing a serious eye problem. Baseball also said farewell to Ozzie Smith, Andre Dawson, and Alan Trammell. Two other veterans made miraculous returns from life-threatening ailments. Brett Butler of the Dodgers, diagnosed with throat cancer in May, returned in September, while David Cone of the Yankees needed surgery in May to remove a shoulder aneurysm, but was pitching again in September. John McSherry was not so fortunate. At age 51, the veteran National League umpire suffered a fatal heart attack while working home plate in Cincinnati on Opening Day.

© Focus on Sports

Third baseman Ken Caminiti—who led San Diego into the playoffs with a .326 batting average, 40 home runs, and 130 RBIs—was a unanimous choice for National League MVP.

Marge Schott, the controversial owner of the Reds, was criticized roundly for complaining about the cancellation of the game at which McSherry died. In June, under threat of suspension by the game's ruling executive council, she agreed to give up control of the club through 1998. Schott, previously suspended for comments considered racially insensitive, angered baseball officials with statements about Hitler, Asians, and working women during interviews.

On August 4, pitchers Jim Bunning and Bill Foster and managers Earl Weaver and Ned Hanlon were enshrined in the Baseball Hall of Fame at Cooperstown, NY.

DAN SCHLOSSBERG, *Baseball Writer*

Basketball

After a two-year absence, the Chicago Bulls resumed their dominance of the National Basketball Association (NBA). The Bulls, led by Michael Jordan, beat the Seattle SuperSonics in six games to win the final round of the league play-offs and capture their fourth title in six years. The Bulls also set an NBA record by winning 72 games during the regular season.

In college basketball, the University of Kentucky, one of the premier basketball schools in the United States, won its first National Collegiate Athletic Association (NCAA) championship in 18 years by defeating Syracuse in the final of the NCAA tournament. The women's basketball title went to Tennessee, which used an impressive team effort to run over Georgia and take its first title since 1991.

The Professional Season

Headliners. The season began with questions surrounding Michael Jordan of the Bulls. Could he regain the form that made him the NBA's dominant player before he retired prior to the 1993–94 season? Or would he continue the inconsistent play that characterized his performance during the spring of 1995, when he returned to the league after a failed attempt to become a major-league-baseball player?

Jordan answered every question quickly and positively. He elevated his game and in the process became the catalyst—along with Scottie Pippen—of the Bulls' historical season. The Bulls were bolstered by the addition of Dennis Rodman, the best rebounder of his time, who was not retained by his 1994–95 employer, the San Antonio Spurs, because of his controversial lifestyle and unwillingness to follow team rules. Rodman is frequently temperamental and always individualistic—he was suspended at one point during the 1995–96 season for head-butting a referee—but he gave Chicago a much-needed rebounding boost. He wound up leading the league in rebounding for the fifth straight time, matching Moses Malone's league mark. Jordan led in scoring—winning his eighth title, which broke Wilt Chamberlain's NBA record of seven.

© Barry Gossage/NBA Photos

Michael Jordan (23) was the dominant force as Chicago defeated the Seattle SuperSonics in the play-off finals. The Bulls had set an NBA record by winning 72 regular-season games.

PROFESSIONAL BASKETBALL

National Basketball Association (Final Standings, 1995–96)

Eastern Conference

Atlantic Division	W	L	Pct.	Games Behind
*Orlando	60	22	.732	—
*New York	47	35	.573	13
*Miami	42	40	.512	18
Washington	39	43	.476	21
Boston	33	49	.402	27
New Jersey	30	52	.366	30
Philadelphia	18	64	.220	42
Central Division				
*Chicago	72	10	.878	—
*Indiana	52	30	.634	20
*Cleveland	47	35	.573	25
*Atlanta	46	36	.561	26
*Detroit	46	36	.561	26
Charlotte	41	41	.500	31
Milwaukee	25	57	.305	47
Toronto	21	61	.256	51

Western Conference

Midwest Divison	W	L	Pct.	Games Behind
*San Antonio	59	23	.720	—
*Utah	55	27	.671	4
*Houston	48	34	.585	11
Denver	35	47	.427	24
Minnesota	26	56	.317	33
Dallas	26	56	.317	33
Vancouver	15	67	.183	44
Pacific Division				
*Seattle	64	18	.780	—
*Los Angeles Lakers	53	29	.646	11
*Portland	44	38	.537	20
*Phoenix	41	41	.500	23
*Sacramento	39	43	.476	25
Golden State	36	46	.439	28
Los Angeles Clipppers	29	53	.354	35

*In play-offs

Play-offs

Eastern Conference

First Round	Atlanta	3 games	Indiana	2
	Chicago	3 games	Miami	0
	New York	3 games	Cleveland	0
	Orlando	3 games	Detroit	0
Second Round	Chicago	4 games	New York	1
	Orlando	4 games	Atlanta	1
Finals	Chicago	4 games	Orlando	0

Western Conference

First Round	Houston	3 games	L.A. Lakers	1
	San Antonio	3 games	Phoenix	1
	Seattle	3 games	Sacramento	1
	Utah	3 games	Portland	2
Second Round	Seattle	4 games	Houston	0
	Utah	4 games	San Antonio	2
Finals	Seattle	4 games	Utah	3

Championship Chicago 4 games Seattle 2
All-Star Game East 129, West 118

Individual Honors

Most Valuable Player: Michael Jordan, Chicago
Most Valuable Player (championship): Michael Jordan
Most Valuable Player (All-Star Game): Michael Jordan
Rookie of the Year: Damon Stoudamire, Toronto
Coach of the Year: Phil Jackson, Chicago
Defensive Player of the Year: Gary Payton, Seattle
Sixth-Man Award: Toni Kukoc, Chicago
Leader in Scoring: Michael Jordan, 30.4 points per game
Leader in Assists: John Stockton, Utah, 11.2 per game
Leader in Rebounds: Dennis Rodman, Chicago, 14.9 per game
Leader in Field-Goal Percentage: Gheorghe Muresan, Washington, .584
Leader in Three-Point-Shooting Percentage: Tim Legler, Washington, .522
Leader in Free-Throw Percentage: Mahmoud Abdul-Rauf, Denver, .930
Leader in Steals: Gary Payton, 2.85 per game
Leader in Blocked Shots: Dikembe Mutombo, Denver, 4.49 per game

Chicago lost only ten games all season and broke the 1971–72 regular-season record of the Los Angeles Lakers—69 victories and 13 losses. That achievement stimulated comparisons between the Bulls and other great teams in NBA history.

The schedule also was highlighted by the brief return of Magic Johnson, who came back to the Lakers in late January 1996, ending a retirement that began in 1991 after he announced he was HIV-positive. Since then, he also had coached the team briefly. After the season ended, Johnson announced he was retiring again—this time for good.

The Regular Season. Houston began the season trying to defend its back-to-back championships. But the Rockets were slowed by a series of injuries during the season and wound up finishing third in the Midwest Division behind Utah, which once again was led by Karl Malone and John Stockton, and first-place San Antonio, which featured a big season from center David Robinson. Seattle's outstanding play in the Pacific Division was overshadowed by Chicago's performance. The SuperSonics had the NBA's second-best record—64–18—to secure home-court advantage in the Western Conference.

The Orlando Magic, which were expected to challenge Chicago for the best record in the Eastern Conference, had problems winning on the road and never really came close to equaling the Bulls. But the Magic did win the Eastern Division. The second-place New York Knicks showed their age and also survived a coaching change. Veteran coach Don Nelson was fired in March and was replaced by Jeff Van Gundy, who was given a new contract after the season ended. Miami had expected to receive a spark from new coach Pat Riley, but the Heat barely made the play-offs despite a trade during the season for Charlotte center Alonzo Mourning. The season also marked the debut of expansion teams in Vancouver and Toronto.

Besides Jordan and Rodman, other league leaders included Dikembe Mutombo of the Denver Nuggets, who became the first NBA player to finish first in block shots for three straight seasons. Utah's Stockton won his

The NBA Draft

In the relationship between professional and college basketball, easily the most controversial aspect is the National Basketball Association (NBA) college draft. The draft was instituted in 1947, at the very start of the NBA as we now know it, to provide an organized method of distributing the best college players among the pro teams. The object was to allow the worst squads to have the first chance at the selections, so they would be able to improve by adding better players. But little did the NBA founders realize how the draft would evolve.

NBA rules once stopped any team from drafting a player whose college class had not finished its final season of eligibility. But challenges to the legality of the draft led the league to adopt its current rules. Undergraduate players with eligibility remaining now can declare themselves available for the draft. They have an option of withdrawing their names from the draft pool prior to the draft and maintaining their eligibility, but few have exercised that choice. Instead, a steady stream of elite undergraduate players have left college over the past few years, weakening that level of basketball. This has created major problems for college coaches, who now find it difficult to keep their best players for a full four seasons. Some of those coaches now complain that the college game is losing its appeal because of the exodus.

The draft also has changed in other ways. Instead of seven rounds, it now has only two. And to prevent bad teams from intentionally losing at the end of the season to secure a more advantageous position in the draft, the league now conducts a random lottery among the teams with the first seven picks.

The NBA correctly says that it legally cannot prevent undergraduates from stepping up to the pros. The league discourages the movement but its teams lure the best of these undergraduates with the prospect of million-dollar contracts. Some draft foes believe the draft should be abolished, allowing NBA teams to compete in an open market for all available college players. But that would negate the object of the draft, which is to distribute talent more equitably among league teams; thus it is likely the current controversial system will continue.

PAUL ATTNER

ninth consecutive assist title and also broke the league record for steals, breaking the mark held by Maurice Cheeks. Bob Cousy had held the NBA assist record for eight straight years. Jordan easily was chosen as the league's most valuable player (MVP) for the fourth time, and his coach, Phil Jackson, was picked as coach of the year. Seattle's Gary Payton was the defensive player of the year; Chicago's Toni Kukoc won the sixth-man award; and Washington center Georghe Muresan, who led the league in field-goal percentage, was selected as the most improved player. The all-NBA team included Jordan, Robinson, Orlando's Penny Hardaway, Utah's Malone, and Pippen. The members of the second team were Shawn Kemp and Payton of Seattle, Grant Hill of the Detroit Pistons, Hakeem Olajuwon of the Rockets, and Stockton. Making up the third team were Charles Barkley of Phoenix, Juwan Howard of Washington, Mitch Richmond of Sacramento, Reggie Miller of Indiana, and Orlando's Shaquille O'Neal.

Two star players were involved in regular-season trades: Derrick Coleman of the New Jersey Nets was sent to the Philadelphia 76ers for center Shawn Bradley and Kenny Anderson of the Nets was traded to Charlotte. Coaches who were fired included John Lucas of the 76ers, Butch Beard of New Jersey, Brendan Malone of Toronto, and Allan Bristow of Charlotte. Dick Motta of Dallas retired, and Paul Westphal of Phoenix was released during the season.

The Play-offs. Based on their regular-season record, the Bulls were seen as overwhelming favorites to capture the championship. It was considered more a matter of how many games they would be extended before ending their play-off quest.

As it turned out, Chicago romped about as easily as expected through the early play-off rounds. The Bulls beat Miami in three straight, took four of five from the New York Knicks, and swept past Orlando in four straight. The defeat of the Magic was most impressive, considering Orlando's talent and the presence of O'Neal and Hardaway. But the Bulls had too much depth and experience for the Magic to overcome. That victory set up a league-title showdown with Seattle. The SuperSonics got to the final by downing Sacramento—three games to one—and by ending Houston's hopes of a third straight title. In the conference finals, they won a spirited seven-game series against Utah, taking the final game 90–86.

In the championship series, the Bulls opened with an impressive 107–90 triumph. Chicago's Kukoc was the hero, scoring 12 of his 18 points in the fourth period to halt a Seattle rally. In Game 2, the Sonics crept closer, losing by only 92–88. Again the game was determined in the fourth period. Chicago had an 84–76 lead early in the quarter but could score only eight more points the rest of the way; that still was enough to win. In Game 3 at Seattle, the Bulls raced out to a 22-point lead in the first quarter and the Sonics never challenged. Jordan finished with 36 points after scoring 28 points in the first game and 29 in the second. It appeared the Bulls would sweep this series, too, but the Sonics rallied in the next two games, both at home, to add some excitement to the finals. Seattle's Kemp and Payton finally were able to raise their games and counter the abilities of Jordan and Co. The Sonics won Games 4 and 5, returning the series to Chicago. The Bulls, who were showing fatigue, found enough energy to wrap up the series in six games. Rodman was the hero, pulling down 19 rebounds and refusing to allow his teammates to falter. Jordan wound up being the series MVP, although Rodman probably was more consistent. The Bulls' triumph in the series was even more impressive considering that Pippen did not play particularly well.

The College Season

The 1995–96 collegiate-basketball season eventually evolved into a tale of two teams connected by a friendship between their coaches. The University of Kentucky Wildcats, coached by Rick Pitino, and the Massachusetts Minutemen, coached by John Calipari, emerged as the elite squads. Their coaches were friends and had worked together earlier. Their teams played similar full-court press, fast-break, up-tempo basketball. In the preseason, Kentucky was the odds-on choice to win the national title, while Massachusetts was ranked among the second echelon of clubs. Other strong teams were Villanova, defending champion UCLA, Georgetown, Connecticut, Iowa, Mississippi State, and Utah.

But Massachusetts quickly claimed the Number 1 spot with an early-season victory over Kentucky. The Minutemen, behind standout center Marcus Camby, lost only to George Washington during the regular season and wound up ranked Number 1 entering postseason play. By then, well-balanced and deep Kentucky was performing up to expectations and was considered on the same level as Massachusetts. But they were not the only talented teams. Connecticut, behind outstanding guard Ray Allen, was the Big East's best team, nosing out both Villanova and Georgetown. Purdue again won the Big Ten, while Kansas emerged as the Big Eight's most impressive squad. Wake Forest, with dominant big man Tim Duncan, reigned over the Atlantic Coast Conference (ACC). UCLA repeated as the Pac-Ten champion. The strongest conferences were the Big East, ACC, and Southeastern.

Marcus Camby of Massachusetts was the best player in the nation, but he had stiff competition. Tim Duncan of Wake Forest and guard Allen Iverson of Georgetown both had outstanding seasons. They made first-team consensus All-American along with Camby, Allen of Connecticut, and forward Kerry Kittles of Villanova. Other elite players included Keith Van Horn of Utah, Tony Delk of Kentucky, Danny Fortson of Cincinnati, Jacque Vaughn of Kansas, John Wallace of Syracuse,

With Syracuse's John Wallace defending, Kentucky's Tony Delk tries for two in the NCAA tournament final. The Kentucky Wildcats won, 76–68, for their first championship since 1978.

COLLEGE BASKETBALL

Conference Champions

American West: Cal Poly-San Luis Obispo[r]; Southern Utah[t]
Atlantic Coast: Georgia Tech[r]; Wake Forest[t]
Atlantic 10: Massachusetts (Eastern Division)[r], Virginia Tech, George Washington (tied, Western Division)[r]; Massachusetts[t]
Big East: Connecticut (Big East 6)[r], Georgetown (Big East 7)[r]; Connecticut[t]
Big Eight: Kansas[r]; Iowa State[t]
Big Sky: Montana State[r,t]
Big South: North Carolina-Greensboro[r,t]
Big Ten: Purdue
Big West: Long Beach State[r]; San Jose State[t]
Colonial: Virginia Commonwealth[r]
Conference USA: Tulane (Red Division)[r], Memphis (White Division)[r], Cincinnati (Blue Division)[r]; Cincinnati[t]
Ivy League: Princeton
Metro Atlantic Athletic: Iona, Fairfield (tied)[r]; Canisius[t]
Mid-American: Eastern Michigan[r,t]
Mid-Continent: Valparaiso[r,t]
Mid-Eastern Athletic: South Carolina State, Coppin State (tied)[r]; South Carolina State[t]
Midwestern: Wisconsin-Green Bay[r]; Northern Illinois[t]
Missouri Valley: Bradley[r]; Tulsa[t]
North Atlantic: Drexel[r,t]
Northeast: Mount St. Mary's[r]; Monmouth[t]
Ohio Valley: Murray State[r]; Austin Peay[t]
Pacific Ten: UCLA
Patriot: Colgate[r,t]
Southeastern: Kentucky (Eastern Division)[r], Mississippi State (Western Division)[r]; Mississippi State[t]
Southern: Davidson (Northern Division)[r], Western Carolina (Southern Division)[r]; Western Carolina[t]
Southland: Northeast Louisiana[r,t]
Southwest: Texas Tech[r,t]
Southwestern Athletic: Jackson State, Mississippi Valley (tied)[r]; Mississippi Valley[t]
Sun Belt: Arkansas-Little Rock, New Orleans (tied)[r]; New Orleans[t]
Trans America: College of Charleston (Eastern Division)[r], Samford, Southeastern Louisiana (tied, Western Division)[r]; Central Florida[t]
West Coast: Santa Clara, Gonzaga (tied)[r]; Portland[t]
Western Athletic: Utah[r]; New Mexico[t]

[r]regular-season winner
[t]conference-tournament winner

Tournaments

NCAA Division I: Kentucky
NCAA Division II: Fort Hays State
NCAA Division III: Rowan, NJ
NIT: Nebraska
NAIA Division I: Oklahoma City University
NCAA Division I (women): Tennessee
NCAA Division II (women): North Dakota State
NCAA Division III (women): Wisconsin-Oshkosh

Stephon Marbury of Georgia Tech, and Shareef Abdur-Rahim of California. Camby, Iverson, Allen, and Marbury were among a large group of underclassmen who decided to pass up their remaining eligibility and join the pro ranks. (*See* SIDEBAR.)

The NCAA Tournament. Along with Massachusetts and Kentucky, the top seeds in the NCAA tournament were Purdue and Connecticut. But neither the Boilermakers nor the Huskies could survive their respective regionals. Instead, Mississippi State—which had played in the shadow of the Kentucky Wildcats in the Southeastern Conference but had managed to capture the conference's tournament—wound up winning the Southeast Regional to join Kentucky in the Final Four. Purdue could not win the West regional; instead that section went to upstart Syracuse, the fourth seed and an also-ran in the Big East. The Orangemen joined Massachusetts as the other two teams in the Final Four.

In the Final Four, the semifinal game between Massachusetts and Kentucky was considered the real showdown for the national title. The Wildcats had won games by an average of 28.3 points in the tournament but had problems with Massachusetts. Kentucky led by eight at halftime and quickly opened a 43–28 lead in the second half. But the Wildcats went cold and Massachusetts got back into the game, closing the lead to three points in the final minutes. Kentucky eventually pulled out an 81–74 victory. In the other semifinal, Mississippi State played horribly, committing too many mistakes to stay with Syracuse, which won 77–69. Mississippi State had 21 turnovers to Syracuse's five.

Kentucky was favored heavily to win the championship game and ultimately did, 76–67. But Syracuse made the contest much closer than expected. Guard Tony Delk, chosen the Final Four's outstanding player, scored 24 points; he and freshman Ron Mercer were the only Kentucky players who performed well at the end. Their teammates seemed tired and tense in the second half. The Wildcats led by 13 with 11 minutes left, then had to hold off a Syracuse rally that was hindered by poor foul shooting. It was Pitino's first national title after producing a number of outstanding Kentucky teams in previous years.

The Women. In the women's tournament, all eyes were on defending national titleholder Connecticut, which had another outstanding season despite the loss of Rebecca Lobo, the 1994–95 player of the year. The Huskies were trying to become the second team in 15 years to win back-to-back titles. They were matched in the Final Four with Tennessee, which had not won a national crown since 1991 despite a string of contending teams. The semifinal game between Connecticut and Tennessee lived up to every expectation. It took overtime before Tennessee was able to come away with an 88–83 victory. In the other semifinal, Georgia outdistanced Stanford, 86–76. In the tournament final, Tennessee held Saudia Roundtree, the player of the year, to eight points and romped to an 83–65 victory over the Southeastern Conference rival. Starring for Tennessee was freshman Chamique Holdsclaw, who had 16 points and 14 rebounds. Georgia shot only 38% as Tennessee reversed a regular-season defeat to the Lady Bulldogs. Tennessee also had won titles in 1987, 1989, and 1991. All-Americans, in addition to Roundtree, included Kara Wolters and Jennifer Rizzotti of Connecticut, Vickie Johnson of Louisiana Tech—the Number 1 team in the regular season—and Latasha Byears of DePaul.

PAUL ATTNER, *"The Sporting News"*

Boxing

One of the biggest upsets in boxing history highlighted the 1996 fight scene when Evander Holyfield knocked out Mike Tyson, the sport's most heralded champion.

Tyson and Holyfield. Tyson, who had served three years in prison for rape and had returned to the sport in 1995, was seeking to unify the heavyweight division in 1996. This quest started on March 16, when he knocked out Frank Bruno of Britain in the third round to win the World Boxing Council (WBC) title in Las Vegas, NV. Tyson gained a second title on September 7 when he stopped Bruce Seldon, the World Boxing Association (WBA) titleholder, in 109 seconds at Las Vegas in a bout that was so unpopular that charges of fixing were widespread. Later that month, rather than face Lennox Lewis, the mandated Number 1 challenger, Tyson gave up the WBC title.

Tyson's pursuit of a unified championship came to a halt in his next title fight—the WBA heavyweight championship, held on November 9 in Las Vegas—as Holyfield, an 8–1 underdog who once had been diagnosed with heart problems, had other plans. In the sixth round the 30-year-old Tyson was knocked down for only the second time in his career. He got into more trouble in the tenth round, reeling against the ropes, but was saved by the bell. In the 11th round, Holyfield hit Tyson with a series of punches to the head that sent Tyson into the ropes. Referee Mitch Halpern stopped the fight 37 seconds into the round. With the victory, Holyfield, 34, joined Muhammad Ali as the only boxers to win the heavyweight title three times.

Holyfield's share of the purse was $11 million. Tyson's purse was $30 million, zooming his 1996 earnings to $75 million. However, Tyson's former trainer, Kevin Rooney, was awarded more than $4.4 million when a federal jury decided in September that Tyson had broken a lifetime contract with him.

Other Heavyweights. On the undercard of the Tyson-Holyfield bout, Michael Moorer retained the International Boxing Federation (IBF) heavyweight crown with a 12th-round knockout of Frans Botha of South Africa.

Two other heavyweights—George Foreman and Tommy Morrison—silenced some of their doubters in November in Tokyo. Foreman, at 47 years of age and 253 lbs (115 kg), scored a unanimous 12-round decision over the unheralded Crawford Grimsley. Meanwhile, Morrison—infected with the human immunodeficiency virus (HIV), which causes AIDS—floored Marcus Rhode three times in the first round to win. When his infection was diagnosed in February, Morrison had vowed to quit boxing. But he changed his mind, saying that he wanted to fight to earn money for Knockout AIDS, a foundation he established for children infected with HIV.

Lighter Divisions. In the lighter weights, two unbeaten fighters, Oscar De La Hoya and Roy Jones, Jr., kept their records intact. In June, De La Hoya, 23, a former Olympic champion, raised his record to 22–0 with a convincing victory over Julio César Chávez for the WBC super-lightweight title in Las Vegas. De La Hoya used his jab as a weapon and opened a cut on Chávez' left eye in the first round. Chavez never recovered and the American dethroned the Mexican, whose record fell to 97–2–1, in the fourth round.

At Tampa, FL, on November 22, Jones scored a unanimous decision over Mike McCallum to win the vacant WBC light-heavyweight title. Jones, 27, remained unbeaten in 34 fights and added a new title to his portfolio, which already had included the IBF super-middleweight title.

GEORGE DE GREGORIO, *"The New York Times"*

WORLD BOXING CHAMPIONS*

Heavyweight: World Boxing Council (WBC)—vacant; World Boxing Association (WBA)—Evander Holyfield, United States, 1996; International Boxing Federation (IBF)—Michael Moorer, United States, 1996.
Cruiserweight: WBC—Marcelo Dominguez, Argentina, 1996; WBA—Nate Miller, United States, 1995; IBF—Adolpho Washington, United States, 1996.
Light Heavyweight: WBC—Roy Jones, Jr., United States, 1996; WBA—Virgil Hill, United States, 1992; IBF—Henry Maske, Germany, 1993.
Super Middleweight: WBC—Robin Reid, Britain, 1996; WBA—Frank Lyles, United States, 1995; IBF—Roy Jones, Jr., United States, 1994.
Middleweight: WBC—Keith Holmes, United States, 1996; WBA—William Joppy, United States, 1996; IBF—Bernard Hopkins, United States, 1995.
Junior Middleweight: WBC—Terry Norris, United States, 1995; WBA—Laurent Boudouari, France, 1996; IBF—Norris, 1995.
Welterweight: WBC—Pernell Whitaker, United States, 1993; WBA—Ike Quartey, Ghana, 1994; IBF—Felix Trinidad, Puerto Rico, 1993.
Junior Welterweight: WBC—Oscar De La Hoya, United States, 1996; WBA—Khalid Rahilou, France, 1997; IBF—Kostya Tszyu, Australia, 1995.
Lightweight: WBC—Jean-Baptiste Mendy, France, 1996; WBA—Ulzubek Nazarov, Russia, 1993; IBF—Phillip Holiday, South Africa, 1995.
Junior Lightweight: WBC—Azumah Nelson, Ghana, 1995; WBA—Yongsoo Choi, South Korea, 1996; IBF—Arturo Gatti, United States, 1995.
Featherweight: WBC—Luisito Espinosa, Philippines, 1995; WBA—Wilfredo Vazquez, Puerto Rico, 1996; IBF—Tom Johnson, United States, 1993.
Junior Featherweight: WBC—Daniel Zaragoza, Mexico, 1995; WBA—Antonio Cermeno, Venezuela, 1995; IBF—Vuyani Bungu, South Africa, 1994.
Bantamweight: WBC—Wayne McCullough, Ireland, 1995; WBA—Daorung Siriwat, Thailand, 1996; IBF—Mbulelo Bottle, South Africa, 1995.
Junior Bantamweight: WBC—Hiroshi Kawashima, Japan, 1994; WBA—Yoktha Sith Oar, Thailand, 1996; IBF—Danny Romero, United States, 1996.
Flyweight: WBC—Yuri Arbachakov, Russia, 1992; WBA—San Sow Ploenchit, Thailand, 1994; IBF—Mark Johnson, United States, 1996.
Junior Flyweight: WBC—Saman Sorjaturong, Thailand, 1996; WBA—Pitchinoi Siriwat, Thailand, 1996; IBF—Mauricio Patrana, Colombia, 1997.
Strawweight: WBC—Ricardo Lopez, Mexico, 1990; WBA—Rosendo Alvarez, Nicaragua, 1995; IBF—Rataanpol Vorapin, Thailand, 1993.

*As of Jan. 18, 1997. Date indicates year title was won.

Football

The championship game of the 1996–97 National Football League (NFL) season featured a showdown between the Green Bay Packers, a former league power, and the New England Patriots, a former member of the old American Football League (AFL) who never had won an NFL title. Both teams reached the Super Bowl with wins over impressive second-year squads. The Packers beat the Carolina Panthers in the National Football Conference (NFC) title game, while the Patriots got by the Jacksonville Jaguars to win the American Football Conference (AFC) championship.

In Super Bowl XXXI, Green Bay capitalized on big plays to top New England before 72,301 fans at the Super Dome in New Orleans. The Packers' 35–21 victory gave that storied franchise its first NFL title in 29 years and extended a long streak of NFC domination in the Super Bowl. At the end of a high-scoring first quarter, the Patriots held a 14–10 edge, but the momentum soon shifted in Green Bay's favor. Quarterback Brett Favre, with two long touchdown strikes and a 2-yard scoring dive, helped the Packers stake a 27–14 halftime lead. New England narrowed the contest to 27–21 with a third-quarter score, but this comeback effort was deflated on the following kickoff as Desmond Howard zipped to a 99-yard touchdown. Howard, who finished with a Super Bowl–record 244 yards on kickoff and punt returns, became the first special-teams player to earn most-valuable-player honors in the title game. Under great pressure from Reggie White and the rest of the Packer defense, the Patriots never reestablished an offensive rhythm.

Quarterback Brett Favre (4) led the Green Bay Packers to a 30–13 victory over the Carolina Panthers in the NFC championship and to a 35–21 win over New England in Super Bowl XXXI.

© Mark Duncan/AP/Wide World Photos

In college competition, the Florida Gators won their first national title by beating Florida State in the Sugar Bowl and avenging an earlier loss to the Seminoles. Florida's quarterback Danny Wuerffel was awarded the Heisman Trophy.

In the Canadian Football League (CFL), the Toronto Argonauts topped the Edmonton Eskimos, 43–37, to win the Grey Cup. Argonaut quarterback Doug Flutie was judged the outstanding player of the game as well as the league's most valuable player.

The Professional Season

NFL Developments. Some stability returned to the NFL after a tumultuous 1995 season. The most notable development was the debut of the Ravens in Baltimore, which had lacked an NFL team since 1984, when owner Robert Irsay moved the Colts to Indianapolis. The Ravens were the former Cleveland Browns, who were moved from that city by owner Art Modell after the 1995 season. The city of Cleveland was promised a new NFL team by 1999 and began building a new stadium. Seattle Seahawks owner Ken Behring attempted to move his team to southern California but was stopped by the league. Behring was considering selling the franchise to Paul Allen, owner of the Portland Trailblazers basketball franchise and cofounder of the Microsoft Corp. Tampa Bay voters approved a stadium-construction proposal that would keep the Bucs in that city.

Former NFL commissioner Pete Rozelle passed away on December 6. Rozelle led the league when it merged with the AFL and he was responsible for signing the NFL's first landmark television contract. He also was credited with turning the NFL into the nation's dominant sports organization.

The league was rocked by the arrest in March of Dallas receiver Michael Irvin for cocaine possession. After Irvin terminated his trial with a plea of no contest, league officials suspended him for the first five games of the 1996 season. Packers quarterback Favre spent time during the off-season in a clinic to end an addiction to painkillers. The Pittsburgh Steelers, the defending AFC champions, suffered the biggest off-season free-agency loss when quarterback Neil O'Donnell signed with the New York Jets.

Regular Season and Play-offs. Defending champion Dallas faced numerous internal problems during the season. Besides Irvin's troubles, tight end Jay Novacek sat out the season with back problems; defensive end Charles Haley's back problems sidelined him the last half of the season; and defensive tackle Leon Lett was suspended in December for violating the league's drug-abuse policies. (NFL officials said that the suspension would last at least one year.) Still, the Cowboys overcame a slow start and played well enough to win the NFC East title, despite a below-par season from star running back Emmitt Smith and a struggling showing from quarterback Troy Aikman. The rest of the division was a disappointment. Washington failed to qualify for the play-offs despite winning seven of its first eight games and Philadelphia, which made the play-offs, did not improve on an impressive 1995 performance.

Green Bay ran away with the NFC Central title, compiling the best record in the league behind the stellar play of Favre at quarterback. The Packers had home-field advantage throughout the play-offs. Minnesota squeezed into the play-offs thanks to the play of backup quarterback Brad Johnson.

PROFESSIONAL FOOTBALL

National Football League
Final Standings, 1996

AMERICAN CONFERENCE

					Points	
Eastern Division	**W**	**L**	**T**	**Pct.**	**For**	**Against**
New England	11	5	0	.688	418	313
Buffalo	10	6	0	.625	319	266
Indianapolis	9	7	0	.563	317	334
Miami	8	8	0	.500	339	325
N.Y. Jets	1	15	0	.063	279	454
Central Division						
Pittsburgh	10	6	0	.625	344	257
Jacksonville	9	7	0	.563	325	335
Cincinnati	8	8	0	.500	372	369
Houston	8	8	0	.500	345	319
Baltimore	4	12	0	.250	371	441
Western Division						
Denver	13	3	0	.813	391	275
Kansas City	9	7	0	.563	297	300
San Diego	8	8	0	.500	310	376
Oakland	7	9	0	.438	340	293
Seattle	7	9	0	.438	317	376

PLAY-OFFS

Jacksonville 30, Buffalo 27
Pittsburgh 42, Indianapolis 14
Jacksonville 30, Denver 27
New England 28, Pittsburgh 3
New England 20, Jacksonville 6

NATIONAL CONFERENCE

					Points	
Eastern Division	**W**	**L**	**T**	**Pct.**	**For**	**Against**
Dallas	10	6	0	.625	286	250
Philadelphia	10	6	0	.625	363	341
Washington	9	7	0	.563	364	312
Arizona	7	9	0	.438	300	397
N.Y. Giants	6	10	0	.375	242	297
Central Division						
Green Bay	13	3	0	.813	456	210
Minnesota	9	7	0	.563	298	315
Chicago	7	9	0	.438	283	305
Tampa Bay	6	10	0	.375	221	293
Detroit	5	11	0	.313	302	368
Western Division						
Carolina	12	4	0	.750	367	218
San Francisco	12	4	0	.750	398	257
St. Louis	6	10	0	.375	303	409
Atlanta	3	13	0	.188	309	465
New Orleans	3	13	0	.188	229	339

PLAY-OFFS

Dallas 40, Minnesota 15
San Francisco 14, Philadelphia 0
Green Bay 35, San Francisco 14
Carolina 26, Dallas 17
Green Bay 30, Carolina 13

SUPER BOWL XXXI: Green Bay 35, New England 21

The biggest surprise came in the NFC West. The San Francisco 49ers, long the dominant team in that division, lost two regular-season games to the Carolina Panthers, who won the title. The Panthers sent seven players to the Pro Bowl and won 12 games. The 49ers, who also finished the season with a 12–4 record, qualified as a wild-card team.

In the AFC East, the Buffalo Bills, who had played four straight Super Bowls in the early 1990s, seemed good enough entering the 1996 season to return for a fifth time. But injuries to quarterback Jim Kelly and running back Thurman Thomas stalled their offense and they lost the division title to the New England Patriots, who rallied at the end of the schedule behind an improved defense. The Indianapolis Colts, who had made it to the AFC title game the previous season, qualified as a wild-card entry.

The Steelers overcame the loss of O'Donnell—relying on an aggressive defense and the running of Jerome Bettis—to win the AFC Central title for a third straight year. Jacksonville, another second-year expansion team, squeezed into the play-offs with a narrow win over Atlanta in their season finale.

The Denver Broncos emerged as the AFC's best team, dominating the AFC West and finishing with the conference's best record (13–3). The Broncos' offense featured quarterback John Elway and running back Terrell Davis. Kansas City, which had been viewed as a strong championship contender, failed to qualify for the play-offs after losing its last game to Buffalo.

In the play-offs, the biggest shock came in the second round, when visiting Jacksonville beat the Broncos in Mile High Stadium, where Denver had not lost all season. The Broncos could not stop either Jaguar quarterback Mark Brunell or running back Natrone Means. That upset put the Jaguars in the AFC final against New England, which had trounced Pittsburgh in the second round. The Patriots held Jacksonville without a touchdown and their defense and special teams generated enough points and turnovers to send New England to its second Super Bowl.

The NFC play-offs went according to form. The Packers crushed San Francisco during a heavy rainstorm and then hosted Carolina in the championship game at Lambeau Field. The Panthers had overcome the Cowboys in the second round, beating Dallas in Charlotte. The Green Bay–Carolina game was close for two quarters, but the Packers' explosive offense, helped by an efficient running game, dominated the second half as Green Bay cruised to a victory.

Individual Performances. For the second straight season, Brett Favre was the NFL's most valuable player. He threw for 39 touchdowns to set an NFC season record and finished second to the 49ers Steve Young as the highest-rated passer in the league. Barry Sanders of Detroit won the rushing title, gaining 1,553 yards. He beat out Terrell Davis of Denver on the final game of the regular season. Jerry Rice of the 49ers had another remarkable season, leading the league with 108 catches—two more than Herman Moore of Detroit and eight more than Carl Pickens of Cincinnati. Terry Glenn of New England and running back Eddie George of Houston were among the top rookies.

Off the Field. NFL coaches had a tough time in 1996. In December, Jim Mora of New Orleans quit after his team got off to a slow 2–6 start, while David Shula of Cincinnati was fired and replaced by Bruce Coslett. At season's end, the following coaches resigned or were fired: Wayne Fontes of Detroit, Dan Reeves of the New York Giants, Bobby Ross of San Diego, Mike White of Oakland, June Jones of Atlanta, Rich Kotite of the New York Jets, and Rich Brooks of St. Louis. In a surprising move, George Seifert retired from the 49ers after leading the team to a 108–35 record and two Super Bowl wins. He was replaced by Steve Mariucci, the coach at the University of California. Two of the departing coaches found work quickly—Ross was hired in Detroit and Reeves took over the Falcons. Jacksonville aide Kevin Gilbride went to San Diego, while Jim Fassel, offensive coordinator of the Arizona Cardinals, took over the Giants. Dick Vermeil, who had not coached since retiring as coach of the Eagles after the 1982–83 season, was hired to coach the Rams.

Admitted to the Pro Football Hall of Fame were coach Joe Gibbs, offensive tackle Dan Dierdorf, receiver Charlie Joiner, defensive back Mel Renfro, and tackle Lou Creekmur.

The College Season

Entering the season, Florida State was considered the best team, followed by defending national champion Nebraska and Florida. Other contenders included Ohio State, Tennessee, Colorado, Southern California, Notre Dame, and Miami. The biggest surprise proved to be Arizona State, who finished undefeated and won the Pac-10 title behind the exciting play of quarterback Jake Plummer.

Danny Wuerffel of Florida won the 1996 Heisman Trophy. In the closest finish since 1989, Wuerffel—who set 47 school, Southeast-

COLLEGE FOOTBALL

Conference Champions

Atlantic Coast—Florida State
Big Ten—(tie) Northwestern, Ohio State
Big Twelve—Texas
Big West—(tie) Nevada, Utah State
Pacific Ten—Arizona State
Southeastern—Florida
Western Athletic Conference—Brigham Young

NCAA Champions

Division I-AA—Marshall
Division II—Northern Colorado
Division III—Mount Union (Ohio)

NAIA Champions

Division I—Southwestern Oklahoma State
Division II—Sioux Falls (SD)

Individual Honors

Heisman Trophy—Danny Wuerffel, Florida
Lombardi Award—Orlando Pace, Ohio State
Outland Trophy—Orlando Pace

Major Bowl Games

Alamo Bowl (San Antonio, TX, Dec. 29)—Iowa 27, Texas Tech 0
Aloha Bowl (Honolulu, HI, Dec. 25)—Navy 42, California 38
Blue-Gray Classic (Montgomery, AL, Dec. 25) Blue 44, Gray 34
Carquest Bowl (Miami, FL, Dec. 27)—Miami 31, Virginia 21
Citrus Bowl (Orlando, FL, Jan. 1)—Tennessee 48, Northwestern 28
Copper Bowl (Tucson, AZ, Dec. 27)—Wisconsin 38, Utah 10
Cotton Bowl (Dallas, TX, Jan. 1)—Brigham Young 19, Kansas State 15
Fiesta Bowl (Tempe, AZ, Jan. 1)—Penn State 38, Texas 15
Gator Bowl (Jacksonville, FL, Jan. 1)—North Carolina 20, West Virginia 13
Heritage Bowl (Atlanta, GA, Dec. 31)—Howard 27, Southern 24
Holiday Bowl (San Diego, CA, Dec. 30)—Colorado 33, Washington 21
Independence Bowl (Shreveport, LA, Dec. 31)—Auburn 32, Army 29
Las Vegas Bowl (Las Vegas, NV, Dec. 19)—Nevada 18, Ball State 15
Liberty Bowl (Memphis, TN, Dec. 27)—Syracuse 30, Houston 17
Orange Bowl (Miami, FL, Dec. 31)—Nebraska 41, Virginia Tech 21
Outback Bowl (Tampa, FL, Jan. 1)—Alabama 17, Michigan 14
Peach Bowl (Atlanta, GA, Dec. 28)—LSU 10, Clemson 7
Rose Bowl (Pasadena, CA, Jan. 1)—Ohio State 20, Arizona State 17
Sugar Bowl (New Orleans, LA, Jan. 2)—Florida 52, Florida State 20
Sun Bowl (El Paso, TX, Dec. 31)—Stanford 38, Michigan State 0

© Gary Hershorn/Reuters/Archive Photos

Florida's standout quarterback Danny Wuerffel—winner of the 1996 Heisman Trophy—threw three touchdowns and ran for another to lead the Gators past Florida State, 52–20, in the Sugar Bowl. The big victory gave Florida its first national championship.

ern Conference, and NCAA records—edged out Iowa State running back Troy Davis, who became the first major college player to rush for 2,000 yards twice, including 2,185 yards in 1996. Jake Plummer was third and Ohio State tackle Orlando Pace was fourth. Other standouts included Tennessee quarterback Peyton Manning, Florida State running back Warrick Dunn, Florida receiver Ike Hilliard, running back Darnell Autry and linebacker Pat Fitzgerald of Northwestern, defensive lineman Darrell Russell of Southern California, Texas Tech running back Byron Hanspard, linebacker Matt Russell of Colorado, and cornerback Bryant Westbrook of Texas.

The biggest off-field news was the decision by Notre Dame coach Lou Holtz to retire. Holtz had coached the Irish to one national title and consistently had kept them among the country's best teams. He was replaced by Bob Davie, who had been on the Notre Dame staff. Another outstanding coach with a national title, Gene Stallings of Alabama, retired in 1996. He was replaced by Mike Dubose, who was promoted from defensive coordinator. Grambling coach Eddie Robinson, the school's coach since 1941 and the winningest football coach in history, agreed to stay for one more season before retiring. He had been under pressure to retire.

The Bowl Games. In the second season under the new so-called Bowl Alliance, the Number 1–ranked and undefeated Florida State and third-ranked Florida met for the national title in the Sugar Bowl. Florida State had beaten Florida during the regular season, 24–21, in a game that was not as close as the final score. Florida had been unable to control Florida State's running game and pass rush. But in the rematch, the Gators contained the Seminole running backs, while Florida quarterback Danny Wuerffel enjoyed great protection and threw three touchdowns. With a 52–20 victory, Florida won its first national championship and vindicated coach Steve Spurrier, whose team had been routed a year earlier by Nebraska in the Fiesta Bowl.

Meanwhile, Arizona State missed an opportunity to complete an undefeated season and contest for a top ranking by losing to Ohio State in the Rose Bowl. The Sun Devils appeared to have won the game when quarterback Jake Plummer scored on an 11-yard rush with 1:40 left in the game. But Ohio State rallied and registered the winning touchdown with 19 seconds remaining, to win 20–17.

In the Cotton Bowl, Brigham Young, which felt that it should have received a bid to a larger bowl, set a major college record by winning its 15th game of the season, 19–15, over Kansas State. Gene Stallings won his last game with Alabama when the Crimson Tide defeated Michigan, 17–14, in the Outback Bowl. In other action, Tennessee rode the strong arm of quarterback Peyton Manning to overwhelm Northwestern, 48–28, in the Citrus Bowl; Penn State topped Texas, 38–15, in the Fiesta Bowl; and Nebraska overwhelmed Virginia Tech in the Orange Bowl, 41–21.

Other Divisions. In Division I-AA, Marshall crushed Montana, 49–29. Northern Colorado claimed its first Division II title with a 23–14 win over Carson-Newman. In the Division III championship, Mount Union amassed 682 yards in offense to top Rowan, 56–24.

PAUL ATTNER, *"The Sporting News"*

Golf

The professional debut of Eldrick (Tiger) Woods overshadowed the golf world late in 1996 (*see* BIOGRAPHY), but over the course of the year, a bevy of big names provided one moment of excitement after another.

PGA Tour. At the age of 37, Tom Lehman came late to success. He was playing on the Nike Tour (primarily for players unable to qualify for the PGA Tour) as recently as 1991. Since then he had won twice on the PGA Tour, and in 1996 he roared to the top. In June he finished tied for second, losing by one stroke to Steve Jones, in the U.S. Open. He was victorious the following month at the British Open, becoming the first U.S. professional to win that title at Royal Lytham and St. Annes. And at the season-ending Tour Championship at Southern Hills in Tulsa, OK, he won by six shots and wrapped up the money title, the Vardon Trophy with a 69.32 scoring average, and player-of-the-year honors. Phil Mickelson led all multiple winners with four tournament victories.

In April, Nick Faldo shot a steely final-round 67 to overcome Greg Norman's six-stroke lead and win the Masters by five as Norman stumbled to a 78 in one of history's biggest collapses. In the PGA Championship, the last of the year's majors, Mark Brooks won in a play-off over Kenny Perry at Valhalla in Louisville, KY. It was Brooks' third victory of the year.

Fred Couples, who won the prestigious Players Championship early in April, resurfaced in September to birdie the 17th hole in the final match to beat Vijay Singh and give the United States a 16½–15½ victory over the International Team in the second President's Cup. The biennial event pits U.S. players against non-European international golfers.

Senior Tour. On the Senior PGA Tour, Jim Colbert won two of his five victories in the last seven weeks of the season to win his second consecutive money title as well as his second straight Senior PGA Tour Player of the Year award.

Hale Irwin, who won the Byron Nelson Trophy with a 69.47 scoring average, won two tournaments, including the PGA Seniors' Championship in April. South African John Bland won four times and easily captured rookie-of-the-year honors on the Senior Tour. Raymond Floyd also won four times in 1996.

Irwin was a key figure in all the senior major championships. In addition to his PGA Seniors' victory, he finished second behind Jack Nicklaus at the Tradition, Dave Stockton in the U.S. Senior Open, and Raymond Floyd in the Ford Senior Players Championship.

LPGA Tour. Australian rookie Karrie Webb burst onto the Ladies Professional Golfers Association scene with four victories, including the rich ITT LPGA Tour Championship at year's end that gave her the money title. She became the first LPGA player to top $1 million in winnings in one season and was select-

Nick Faldo (right) *gained his third green jacket at Augusta National with a remarkable come-from-behind victory in the 1996 Masters. Faldo's steady final round of 67 vaulted him past a collapsing Greg Norman, who had entered the day with a seemingly unbeatable six-stroke lead.*

GOLF

PGA Tour

Mercedes Championships: Mark O'Meara (271)
Nortel Open: Phil Mickelson (273)
Bob Hope Chrysler Classic: Mark Brooks (337)
Phoenix Open: Phil Mickelson (269)
Buick Invitational of California: Davis Love III (269)
United Airlines Hawaiian Open: Jim Furyk (277)
Nissan Open: Craig Stadler (278)
Doral Ryder Open: Greg Norman (269)
Honda Classic: Tim Herron (271)
Bay Hill Invitational: Paul Goydos (275)
Freeport-McDermott Classic: Scott McCarron (275)
Players Championship: Fred Couples (270)
BellSouth Classic: Paul Stankowski (280)
Masters: Nick Faldo (276)
MCI Classic: Loren Roberts (265)
Andersen Consulting U.S. Championship: Scott Hoch
Greater Greensboro Chrysler Classic: Mark O'Meara (274)
Shell Houston Open: Mark Brooks (274)
GTE Byron Nelson Classic: Phil Mickelson (265)
Mastercard Colonial: Corey Pavin (272)
Kemper Open: Steve Strickler (270)
Memorial Tournament: Tom Watson (274)
Buick Classic: Ernie Els (271)
U.S. Open: Steve Jones (278)
Federal Express St. Jude Classic: John Cook (258)
Canon Greater Hartford Open: D. A. Weibring (270)
Motorola Western Open: Steve Stricker (270)
Michelob Championship: Scott Hoch (265)
Deposit Guaranty Golf Classic: Willie Wood (268)
CVS Charity Classic: John Cook (268)
Buick Open: Justin Leonard (266)
PGA Championship: Mark Brooks (277)
Sprint International: Clarence Rose (+31)
NEC World Series of Golf: Phil Mickelson (274)
Greater Vancouver Open: Guy Boros (272)
Greater Milwaukee Open: Loren Roberts (265)
Bell Canadian Open: Dudley Hart (202)
Quad City Classic: Ed Fiori (268)
B.C. Open: Fred Funk (197)
Buick Challenge: Michael Bradley (134)
Las Vegas Invitational: Eldrick (Tiger) Woods (332)
Lacantera Texas Open: David Ogrin (275)
Merrill Lynch Shootout: Craig Stadler
Walt Disney World/Oldsmobile Classic: Eldrick (Tiger) Woods (267)
Tour Championship: Tom Lehman (268)

Senior PGA Tour

Tournament of Champions: John Bland (207)
Senior Skins Game: Raymond Floyd
Royal Caribbean Classic: Bob Murphy (203)
Greater Naples Challenge: Al Geiberger (202)
GTE Suncoast Classic: Jack Nicklaus (211)
American Express Invitational: Hale Irwin (197)
FHP Health Care Classic: Walter Morgan (199)
Senior Slam: Raymond Floyd (140)
Toshiba Senior Classic: Jim Colbert (201)
Liberty Mutual Legends of Golf: Mike Hill/Lee Trevino (198)
SBC Dominion Seniors: Tom Weiskopf (207)
Tradition: Jack Nicklaus (272)
PGA Seniors Championship: Hale Irwin (280)
Las Vegas Senior Classic: Jim Colbert (207)
PaineWebber Invitational: Graham Marsh (206)
Nationwide Championship: Jim Colbert (206)
Cadillac NFL Golf Classic: Bob Murphy (202)
BellSouth Senior Classic: Isao Aoki (202)
Bruno's Memorial Classic: John Bland (208)
Pittsburgh Senior Classic: Tom Weiskopf (205)
du Maurier Champions: Charles Coody (271)
Bell Atlantic Classic: Dale Douglass (206)
Kroger Senior Classic: Isao Aoki (198)
U.S. Senior Open: Dave Stockton (277)
Ford Senior Players Championship: Raymond Floyd (275)
Burnet Senior Classic: Vicente Fernandez (205)
Ameritech Senior Classic: Walter Morgan (205)
VFW Senior Championship: Dave Eichelberger (200)
First of America Classic: Dave Stockton (206)
Northville Long Island Classic: John Bland (202)
Bank of Boston Senior Classic: Jim Dent (204)
Franklin Quest Senior Classic: Graham Marsh (202)
Boone Valley Classic: Gibby Gilbert (203)
Bank One Classic: Mike Hill (207)
Brickyard Crossing Championship: Jimmy Powell (134)
Vantage Championship: Jim Colbert (204)
Merrill Lynch Shootout: Walter Morgan
Ralphs Senior Classic: Gil Morgan (202)
The Transamerica: John Bland (204)
Raley's Gold Rush Classic: Jim Colbert (202)
Hyatt Regency Maui Kaanapali Classic: Bob Charles (198)
Emerald Coast Classic: Lee Trevino (207)
Energizer Senior Tour Championship: Jay Sigel (279)

LPGA Tour

Chrysler-Plymouth Tournament of Champions: Liselotte Neumann (275)
Healthsouth Inaugural: Karrie Webb (209)
Cup Noodles Hawaiian Ladies Open: Meg Mallon (212)
Ping-Welch's Championship (March): Liselotte Neumann (276)
Standard Register PING: Laura Davies (284)
Nabisco Dinah Shore: Patty Sheehan (281)
Twelve Bridges LPGA Classic: Kelly Robbins (273)
Chick-fil-A Charity Championship: Barb Mucha (208)
Sara Lee Classic: Meg Mallon (210)
Sprint Titleholders Championship: Karrie Webb (272)
McDonald's LPGA Championship: Laurie Davies (213)
LPGA Corning Classic: Rosie Jones (276)
JCPenney/LPGA Skins Game: Laura Davies
U.S. Women's Open: Annika Sorenstam (272)
Oldsmobile Classic: Michelle McGann (272)
First Bank Presents the Edina Realty LPGA Classic: Liselotte Neumann (207)
Rochester International: Dottie Pepper (206)
ShopRite LPGA Classic: Dottie Pepper (202)
Jamie Farr Kroger Classic: Joan Pitcock (204)
Youngstown-Warren LPGA Classic: Michelle McGann (200)
Friendly's Classic: Dottie Pepper (279)
Michelob Light Heartland Classic: Vicki Fergon (276)
du Maurier Classic: Laura Davies (277)
Ping-Welch's Championship (August): Emilee Klein (273)
Weetabix Women's British Open: Emilee Klein (277)
Star Bank LPGA Classic: Laura Davies (204)
State Farm Rail Classic: Michelle McGann (202)
The Safeway LPGA Golf Championship: Dottie Pepper (202)
Fieldcrest Cannon Classic: Trish Johnson (270)
Safeco Classic: Karrie Webb (277)
JAL Big Apple Classic: Caroline Pierce (211)
CoreStates Betsy King Classic: Annika Sorenstam (270)
Samsung World Championship of Women's Golf: Annika Sorenstam (274)
Nichirei International: United States
Toray Japan Queens Cup: Mayumi Hirase (212)
ITT LPGA Tour Championship: Karrie Webb (272)

Other Tournaments

British Open: Tom Lehman (271)
U.S. Women's Amateur Public Links: Heather Graff
U.S. Men's Amateur Public Links: Tim Hogarth
U.S. Junior Girls: Dorothy Delasin
U.S. Junior Boys: Shane McMenamy
U.S. Women's Amateur: Kelli Kuehne
U.S. Men's Amateur: Eldrick (Tiger) Woods
U.S. Women's Mid-Amateur: Ellen Port
U.S. Men's Mid-Amateur: John Miller
U.S. Senior Women's Amateur: Gayle Borthwick
U.S. Senior Men's Amateur: O. Gordon Brewer
World Cup of Golf: Team: South Africa (547); Individual: Ernie Els, South Africa (272)
NCAA Men: Individual: Eldrick (Tiger) Woods, Stanford (285); Team: Arizona State (1186)
NCAA Women: Individual: Marisa Baena, Arizona (296); Team: Arizona (1240)
British Amateur: Warren Bladon
British Senior Amateur: Joe Hirsch (210)
British Senior Open: Brian Barnes (277)
Toyota World Match Play: Ernie Els
Lincoln-Mercury Kapalua International: Paul Stankowski (269)
Dunhill Cup: United States
Mastercard PGA Grand Slam of Golf: Tom Leaman (134)
Franklin Funds Shark Shootout: Jay Haas/Tom Kite (187)
JCPenney Classic: Donna Andrews/Mike Hulbert (197)
The Skins Game: Fred Couples
Sun City Million Dollar Challenge: Colin Montgomerie (274)
Diner's Club Matches: PGA Tour—Tom Lehman/Duffy Waldorf; Senior PGA Tour—Jim Colbert/Bob Murphy; LPGA—Dottie Pepper/Juli Inkster
President's Cup: United States 16.5, International 15.5
Curtis Cup: Great Britain–Ireland 11.5, United States 6.5
The Solheim Cup: United States 17, Europe 11
Sarazen World Open Championship: Frank Nobilo (272)

ed as the LPGA Rolex Rookie of the Year. Other multiple winners included Dottie Pepper (four) and Liselotte Neumann (three).

Laura Davies was the LPGA's Rolex Player of the Year with victories in two major championships—the McDonald's LPGA Championship and the du Maurier Classic—and three other tournaments. She had the lowest LPGA scoring average at 70.32. However, she did not play enough rounds to qualify for the Vare Trophy, which went to Annika Sorenstam, who had a 70.47 average. Sorenstam won the U.S. Women's Open in a runaway. Patty Sheehan won the other women's major, the Nabisco Dinah Shore.

Betsy King won two doubles matches and another in singles as the United States outscored Europe, 17–11, to retain the biennial Solheim Cup.

Amateur. Only days before turning professional, Tiger Woods defeated Steve Scott at Cornelius, OR, to gain an unprecedented third U.S. Amateur Golf Championship title.

LARRY DENNIS, *Editor, "Senior Golfer"*

Horse Racing

During 1996, Cigar tied Citation's 46-year-old record with 16 consecutive victories. The streak began at an allowance race at New York's Aqueduct on Oct. 28, 1994, and continued through the Citation Challenge at Arlington Park in Arlington Heights, IL, on July 13, 1996. During the string, Cigar won such prestigious stakes races as the Donn Handicap, Hollywood Gold Cup, Jockey Club Gold Cup, Dubai World Cup, and 1995 Breeders' Cup Classic.

The streak ended Aug. 10, 1996, at Del Mar, CA, when the long shot Dare and Go posted a $3^1/_2$-length victory over Cigar in the Pacific Classic. The winning time of $1{:}59^4/_5$ was two fifths of a second off the track record for 1.25 mi (2 km). Cigar then lost to 3-year-old Skip Away in the Jockey Club Gold Cup at Elmont, NY, and finished third in the $4 million Breeders' Cup Classic, held on October 26 at the Woodbine racetrack in Toronto, Ont. Alphabet Soup, ridden by Chris McCarron, ran the 1.25-mi (2-km) in 2:01.

The $2 million Breeders' Cup Turf went to Pilsudski. He was ridden by Walter Swinburn, who had suffered near-fatal skull injuries in a race earlier in 1996. Storm Song, daughter of 1990 Preakness winner Summer Squall, won the Juvenile Fillies and gave trainer Nick Zito his first victory in the Breeders' Cup. Boston Harbor withstood a late run by Acceptable to win the $1 million Breeders' Cup Juvenile for trainer D. Wayne Lukas, who marked his fifth victory in the Juvenile. The $1 million Breeders' Cup Mile saw Da Hoss avenge a 13th-place finish in the previous year's race by posting a $1^1/_2$-length victory over Spinning World. Jewel Princess' stretch run overcame Serena's Song by $1^1/_2$ lengths in the Breeders' Cup Distaff. Lit de Justice captured the Breeders' Cup Sprint. Lit de Justice was trained by Jenine Sahadi, the first woman to saddle a Breeders' Cup winner.

The 122d Kentucky Derby at Churchill Downs in Louisville, KY, was won by Grindstone, who finished a nose ahead of Cavonnier with favored Unbridled's Song fifth. In the second Triple Crown race, Louis Quatorze captured the 1.19-mi (1.9-km) Preakness Stakes at Pimlico in Baltimore, MD, after coming in 16th in the Kentucky Derby. Editor's Note then won the 1.5-mi (2.4-km) Belmont Stakes at Elmont, NY.

Harness Racing. Continentalvictory won the Hambletonian, the top event for trotters, and also captured the World Trotting Derby and Yonkers Trot. The Little Brown Jug, the showcase event for pacers, was won by Armbro Operative.

STAN SUTTON

HORSE RACING

Major U.S. Thoroughbred Races

Arlington Million: Mecke, $1 million (total purse)
Arkansas Derby: Zarb's Magic, $500,000
Belmont Stakes: Editor's Note, $729,800
Blue Grass Stakes: Skip Away, $700,000
Breeders' Cup Classic: Alphabet Soup, $4 million
Breeders' Cup Turf: Pilsudski, $2 million
Breeders' Cup Juvenile: Boston Harbor, $1 million
Breeders' Cup Juvenile Fillies: Storm Song, $1 million
Breeders' Cup Mile: Da Hoss, $1 million
Breeders' Cup Distaff: Jewel Princess, $1 million
Breeders' Cup Sprint: Lit de Justice, $1 million
Champagne Stakes: Ordway, $400,000
Donn Handicap: Cigar, $300,000
Florida Derby: Unbridled's Song, $500,000
Haskell Invitational: Skip Away, $750,000
Hollywood Gold Cup: Siphon, $1 million
Iselin Handicap: Smart Strike, $300,000
Jim Beam Stakes: Roar, $600,000
Jockey Club Gold Cup: Skip Away, $1 million
Kentucky Derby: Grindstone, $1,169,800
Kentucky Oaks: Pike Place Dancer, $500,000
Pacific Classic: Dare and Go, $1 million
Pimlico Special: Star Standard, $582,000
Preakness Stakes: Louis Quatorze, $704,800
Santa Anita Derby: Cavonnier, $1 million
Strub Stakes: Helmsman, $500,000
Swaps Stakes: Victory Speech, $500,000
Travers Stakes: Will's Way, $750,000
Wood Memorial: Unbridled's Song, $500,000
Woodward Stakes: Cigar, $500,000

Major North American Harness Races

Breeders Crown Open Pace: Jenna's Beach Boy, $300,000
Breeders Crown Open Trot: CR Kay Suzie, $500,000
Breeders Crown Mare Pace: She's a Great Lady, $300,000
Breeders Crown 2-year-old Filly Pace: Before Sunrise, $576,533
Breeders Crown 2-year-old Colt Pace: His Mattjesty, $700,153
Breeders Crown 2-year-old Filly Trot: Armbro Prowess, $406,200
Breeders Crown 2-year-old Colt Pace: Malabar Man, $428,267
Breeders Crown 3-year-old Filly Pace: Mystical Maddy, $390,000
Breeders Crown 3-year-old Colt Pace: Armbro Operative, $400,000
Breeders Crown 3-year-old Filly Trot: Personal Banner, $350,000
Breeders Crown 3-year-old Colt Trot: Running Sea, $400,000
Cane Pace: Scoot to Power, $326,429
Hambletonian: Continentalvictory, $1 million
Little Brown Jug: Armbro Operative, $347,020
Meadowlands Pace: Hot Lead, $1 million
Peter Haughton Memorial: Yankee Glide, $500,000
Sweetheart Pace: Sternam's Place, $665,400
Woodrow Wilson Pace: Jeremy's Gambit, $800,000
World Trotting Derby: Continentalvictory, $535,000
Yonkers Trot: Continentalvictory, $334,700

Ice Hockey

The 1995–96 National Hockey League (NHL) season was memorable for two wildly improbable reasons. Individually, Wayne Gretzky, the greatest scorer in NHL history, was traded from Los Angeles to St. Louis—the second time the 35-year-old center had been dealt. Gretzky, who had campaigned for a trade to get to a team with a better chance to win a Stanley Cup, had been sent to Los Angeles from Edmonton in the biggest trade in NHL history in 1988. In an even stranger scenario, a team from Miami—in only its third NHL season—made it to the championship final against a team from Denver that was not in existence the year before.

The heavily favored Detroit Red Wings, who set an NHL record with 62 wins in the 82-game season, once again crashed and burned when it counted most, in the play-offs. In the regular season, the Red Wings surpassed the 1976–77 Montreal Canadiens, who won 60 games that season, but they failed in their quest for their first Stanley Cup title since 1955.

While the Wings' fans continued with their long tradition of throwing octopuses onto the ice in Detroit to cheer goals, the fans of the Florida Panthers came upon a new celebration—throwing plastic rats. The idea came about after Panther player Scott Mellanby killed a live rat in the team dressing room early in the season, then scored two goals that night. After that, toy rats were the constant theme in Miami, as fans threw hundreds of them onto the ice. However, by season's end, the NHL had decided to ban the practice for the 1996–97 season because it was disruptive and fans in other cities had taken to throwing objects onto the ice, too.

On a more positive note, Pittsburgh's Mario Lemieux, who sat out the entire 1994–95 season to recuperate from his battle with Hodgkin's disease and a chronic back problem, came back to win the scoring title for the fifth time. The Pittsburgh center also won his third Hart Trophy as the league's most valuable player, beating out two-time winner Mark Messier of the New York Rangers and Philadelphia's Eric Lindros, the 1995 winner. Lemieux played only 70 games and seldom played in games on back-to-back nights early in the season, but nevertheless had 69 goals—the most in the league. He raced past the 500-goal plateau, continuing a remarkable run that has seen him score 563 goals in only 669 games. It was the best goals-to-games ratio in NHL history.

The other amazing story in the season came from Grant Fuhr, the St. Louis goalie, who started 76 consecutive games, setting an NHL record; the old mark was 70. Although the 34-year-old Fuhr was considered a major risk going into the season because he had been relegated to backup duty for the previous three years in Toronto, Buffalo, and Los Angeles, he challenged Lemieux as the comeback player of the year.

Regular Season. The 1995 league-champion New Jersey Devils did not make the postseason, becoming the first team since the 1969–70 Canadiens to win the Stanley Cup one year and not compete the next year.

The Wings were the flip side of the story. Twice they won nine straight games. In March they played 13 games without a loss, establishing the longest unbeaten streak of the season. They lost only three times in 41 games at their home rink, Joe Louis Arena, and gave up only 80 goals at home. They had 131 total points and were so dominant—losing only 13 times

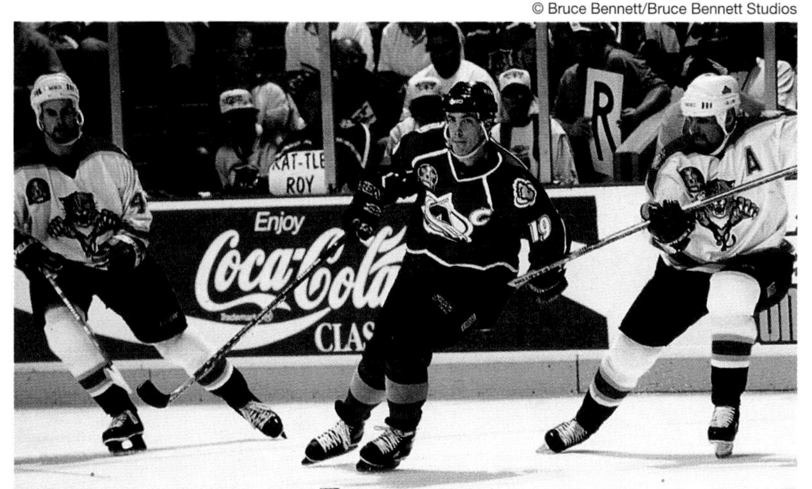

Joe Sakic (19) led the Colorado Avalanche to victory in the 1996 Stanley Cup finals. The Colorado center and team captain scored 18 play-off goals and received the Conn Smythe Trophy as the most valuable player in the play-offs.

ICE HOCKEY

National Hockey League (Final Standings, 1995–96)

Eastern Conference

Atlantic Division	W	L	T	Pts.	Goals For	Goals Against
*Philadelphia	45	24	13	103	282	208
*N.Y. Rangers	41	27	14	96	272	237
*Florida	41	31	10	92	258	230
*Washington	39	32	11	89	234	204
*Tampa Bay	38	32	12	88	238	248
New Jersey	37	33	12	86	215	202
N.Y. Islanders	22	50	10	54	229	315
Northeast Division						
*Pittsburgh	49	29	4	102	362	284
*Boston	40	31	11	91	282	269
*Montreal	40	32	10	90	265	248
Hartford	34	39	9	77	237	259
Buffalo	33	42	7	73	247	262
Ottawa	18	59	5	41	191	291

*In play-offs

Western Conference

Central Division	W	L	T	Pts.	Goals For	Goals Against
*Detroit	62	13	7	131	325	181
*Chicago	40	28	14	94	273	220
*Toronto	34	36	12	80	247	252
*St. Louis	32	34	16	80	219	248
*Winnipeg	36	40	6	78	275	291
Dallas	26	42	14	66	227	280
Pacific Division						
*Colorado	47	25	10	104	326	240
*Calgary	34	37	11	79	241	240
*Vancouver	32	35	15	79	278	278
Anaheim	35	39	8	78	234	247
Edmonton	30	44	8	68	239	304
Los Angeles	24	40	18	66	256	302
San Jose	20	55	7	47	252	357

Stanley Cup Play-offs

Eastern Conference

	Winner	Games	Loser	Games
Quarterfinals	Florida	4 games	Boston	1
	N.Y. Rangers	4 games	Montreal	2
	Philadelphia	4 games	Tampa Bay	2
	Pittsburgh	4 games	Washington	2
Semifinals	Pittsburgh	4 games	N.Y. Rangers	1
	Florida	4 games	Philadelphia	2
Finals	Florida	4 games	Pittsburgh	3

Western Conference

	Winner	Games	Loser	Games
Quarterfinals	Chicago	4 games	Calgary	0
	Colorado	4 games	Vancouver	2
	Detroit	4 games	Winnipeg	2
	St. Louis	4 games	Toronto	2
Semifinals	Colorado	4 games	Chicago	2
	Detroit	4 games	St. Louis	3
Finals	Colorado	4 games	Detroit	2

Stanley Cup Finals

Colorado 4 games Florida 0

Individual Honors

Hart Trophy (most valuable player): Mario Lemieux, Pittsburgh
Ross Trophy (leading scorer): Mario Lemieux
Vezina Trophy (top goaltender): Jim Carey, Washington
Norris Trophy (best defenseman): Chris Chelios, Chicago
Selke Trophy (best defensive forward): Sergei Fedorov, Detroit
Calder Trophy (rookie of the year): Daniel Alfredsson, Ottawa
Jennings Trophy (fewest goals allowed): Chris Osgood and Mike Vernon, Detroit
Lady Byng Trophy (most gentlemanly player): Paul Kariya, Anaheim
Conn Smythe Trophy (most valuable in play-offs): Joe Sakic, Colorado
Adams Award (coach of the year): Scotty Bowman, Detroit
King Clancy Trophy (humanitarian service): Kris King, Winnipeg
Bill Masterton Trophy (perseverance, dedication, and sportsmanship): Gary Roberts, Calgary
Lester B. Pearson Award (outstanding player, voted by peers): Mario Lemieux

all year—that they finished 27 points better than their closest pursuer, the eventual NHL-champion Colorado Avalanche. The latter team was born in Denver after the Quebec Nordiques were sold.

Detroit won the Western Conference's Central Division by 37 points, with Chicago second. Colorado topped the Pacific Division with 104 points; Philadelphia took the Atlantic title in the Eastern Conference with 103 points; and Lemieux's Penguins won the Northeast Division with 102 points.

Lemieux, with 69 goals, beat teammate Jaromir Jagr by seven, as seven players scored at least 50 goals. Vancouver's Alexander Mogilny was third with 55. The Rangers' Messier, 35, looked likely to become the oldest player to score 50 goals, but he was injured in the last three weeks and fell three goals short. Brett Hull, who had had five straight 50-goal seasons, struggled to 43. Jagr and Lemieux waged a torrid scoring-race battle, with Lemieux beating Jagr, the 1994–95 champion, 161–149. Colorado captain Joe Sakic—who went on to win the play-off most-valuable-player (MVP) award—edged another Pittsburgh forward, Ron Francis, 120–119, for third, stopping the Penguins from having the top three scorers. In all, 12 players, including Gretzky, had 100 or more points. Gretzky had 102 to run his career total to 2,608 points—758 more than the Number 2 scorer Gordie Howe.

Play-offs. There were no surprises in the first round of the play-offs, although Lemieux and the Penguins almost went down to Washington. Trailing two games to one in the series, they survived four terrific overtime periods in Game 4 and took a six-game series win. Florida blew out Boston in five games. The Rangers lost the first two games at home but rallied to beat Montreal in six games. Philadelphia got a scare, but beat Tampa Bay in six.

In the Western Conference, Colorado got past Vancouver in six, as did Detroit over Winnipeg. The Jets relocated to Phoenix after the season ended. St. Louis beat Toronto in six games, even though Fuhr ripped up his knee and the team had to use backup goalie Jon Casey. Chicago swept Calgary four straight in the other Western series.

In the second round, Florida surprised the Flyers in six games and Pittsburgh whipped the Rangers in five. In the West, Detroit got a huge scare against St. Louis but captain Steve Yzerman scored in the second overtime in Game 7 for the win. Colorado won two overtime games against Chicago to take its series in six.

In the third round, the Panthers rallied from being down three games to two in their series with the Penguins to take it in seven. Tom Fitzgerald's long shot late in the third period was the winner. The Avalanche knocked off the Red Wings in six, with Sakic leading the way. Colorado lost winger Claude Lemieux, the 1995 play-off MVP, however, for the first two games of the finals when he was suspended for hitting Detroit's Kris Draper into the boards, breaking his jaw and nose.

In the finals, the Avalanche took the first game in Denver, 3–1, with three second-period goals in a four-minute span. Colorado was sparked by checking center Mike Ricci, who had a goal. In Game 2, Peter Forsberg scored three goals in the game's first 15 minutes as Colorado ripped Florida, 8–1. Sakic had four assists in the game. The games were much closer in Miami. In Game 3, Colorado goalie Patrick Roy was superb as the Avalanche hung on for a 3–2 win. Lemieux, in his first game back after the suspension, scored three minutes into the contest; Sakic got the winner, his sixth of the play-offs and an all-time record, in a 3–2 win. In Game 4, Roy and Florida goalie John Vanbiesbrouck were sensational. Roy made 63 saves and Vanbiesbrouck 54 in a thrilling game that was not decided until four minutes into the third overtime. Uwe Krupp, the only NHL player who was born in Germany and played there, beat Vanbiesbrouck with a long slap shot to give Colorado a 1–0 win and a sweep of the series.

ICE SKATING

World Figure-Skating Championships

Men: Todd Eldredge, United States
Women: Michelle Kwan, United States
Pairs: Marina Eltsova and Andrei Bushkov, Russia
Dance: Oksana Gritschuk and Yevgeny Platov, Russia

U.S. Figure-Skating Championships

Men: Rudy Galindo
Women: Michelle Kwan
Pairs: Jenni Meno and Todd Sand
Dance: Elizabeth Punsalan and Jerod Swallow

Speed Skating World Cup—Final Points

Men's 500 meters: Nanabu Horij, Japan
Men's 1,000 meters: Adne Sondral, Norway
Men's 1,500 meters: Hiroyuki Noake, Japan
Men's 5,000 meters: Rintje Ritsma, Netherlands
Women's 500 meters: Svetlana Zhurova, Russia
Women's 1,000 meters: Christine Witty, United States
Women's 1,500 meters: Gunda Niemann, Germany
Women's 3,000 meters: Gunda Niemann

It was the second straight year the final ended in four games. New Jersey whipped Detroit in 1995. The win for Colorado was Denver's first-ever professional-sports championship. Sakic finished with 18 play-off goals, only one off the postseason record, which was set by Jari Kurri and Reg Leach.

Following the season, Gretzky, now a free agent, signed a contract to play for the New York Rangers in 1996–97. He would join his former teammate Mark Messier.

Collegiate Season. U.S. collegiate hockey celebrated its centennial in 1996. The first college-hockey game saw Johns Hopkins University and Yale University play to a tie on Feb. 1, 1896. One hundred years later, the University of Michigan defeated Colorado College for the National Collegiate Athletic Association (NCAA) crown, and Brian Bonin of Minnesota took the Hobey Baker Award as college-hockey player of the year.

JIM MATHESON
"The Edmonton Journal"

Ice Skating

For the first time since 1986, Americans captured both the men's and women's singles titles at the World Figure-Skating Championships in Edmonton, Alberta, in March 1996. Michelle Kwan, a 15-year-old Californian who earlier had been crowned with the U.S. women's singles championship, took the world title. She edged out defending champion Chen Lu of China. Irina Slutskaya of Russia was awarded the world bronze medal. At the 1996 U.S. nationals, Tonia Kwiatkowski, 24, and Tara Lipinski, 13, captured the silver and bronze medals, respectively.

Meanwhile, Todd Eldredge, 24, gained the world men's singles crown. Russia's Ilia Kulik and Rudy Galindo of the United States were awarded the world silver and bronze medals, respectively. Eldredge, who had won the U.S. nationals for a third consecutive time in 1995, lost the U.S. title to Galindo in 1996. Dan Hollander finished third at the U.S. nationals.

Speed Skating. Christine Witty of the United States won the women's championships at the 27th world sprint speed-skating championships in Heerenveen, the Netherlands, in February. Norway's Edel Theres Hoiseth was second. Sergei Klevchenja of Russia went home with the men's title as he outpointed Hiroyasu Shimizu of Japan.

Veteran German skater Gunda Niemann continued to win titles in World Cup competition.

Olympic Games

The XXVI Summer Games, which marked the centennial of the modern Olympic movement, were held in Atlanta, GA, from July 19 through Aug. 4, 1996. They wound up being the most expensive and biggest—in terms of number of countries represented and total participants—in the 100-year history of the quadrennial event.

A total of 10,750 athletes from 197 countries—every nation that was eligible to attend—showed up in Atlanta. Organizers of the Games spent $1.7 billion to stage the event, the most extravagant sporting presentation in history. More than 9 million tickets, double the total sold in the 1988 and 1992 Games combined, were distributed. But everything was marred when, during the early-morning hours of July 27, a bomb exploded in Centennial Olympic Park—an open-to-the-public area that became the centerpiece of the Olympic celebration. One person was killed; a Turkish cameraman suffered a fatal heart attack; and 111 persons were injured. The park eventually reopened, but the incident—the first act of violence at the Olympics since the Munich Games in 1972—detracted considerably from the joyous atmosphere that had marked the first days of the competition.

The Atlanta Games also were hindered in their early days by an unreliable transportation system highlighted by bus drivers who did not know how to get to their assigned destinations. And the computerized information system was marred by inaccurate results and slow reporting of events and lineups for future activities. The International Olympic Committee (IOC) wound up reprimanding the Atlanta organizers on both fronts. But from a political standpoint, things were more encouraging. The protests and boycotts that had hindered many previous Games were absent this time around.

French sprinter Marie-José Pérec scored an impressive double triumph at the 1996 Summer Games in Atlanta, GA, becoming the first woman to win both the 200-m and 400-m dashes.

© Mike Hewitt/Allsport

With the former Soviet Union now represented by a number of nations, the United States was expected to be the dominant power and, indeed, it turned out that way. The United States wound up winning 101 total medals, including 44 gold. Germany finished second with 65 medals, including 20 gold. Russia was third, with 63 medals and 26 gold, and China was fourth—16 gold and a total of 50. But for many other countries without the superior athletic numbers of these nations, the Games still were memorable. For example, Josia Thugwane became the first black South African to win a gold medal when he finished first in the marathon on the closing day of the Games, and Nigeria became the first African nation to win gold in men's soccer.

Track and Field. Michael Johnson of the United States provided the Games with some of their most emotional high points. Johnson came into the Games attempting to win both the 200-m and 400-m events, a feat never accomplished in the Olympics. He was the dominant runner in both events prior to the Games, and he lived up to expectations. First, he took the 400-m easily, winning with a near-world-record time of 43.49 seconds. Then, three days later, he sprinted away from a quality field in the 200-m dash and romped to a second gold, this time in world-record time—19.32 seconds. It was an astonishing time, breaking his former mark of 19.66, set in the Olympic trials.

Johnson's feat was duplicated by Marie-José Pérec of France, who quietly took gold in both the 400-m and 200-m. She was almost as dominant in her triumphs as Johnson was in his. Another difficult double was turned in by Svetlana Masterkova of Russia, who won both the women's 800-m and 1,500-m races.

American Dan O'Brien could boast of the title "world's greatest athlete" after winning the decathlon, beating Frank Busemann of Germany. O'Brien had been a gold-medal favorite in the 1992 Barcelona Games, but he did not make the U.S. team after failing to register a height in one of the ten events, the pole vault. But fellow American Jackie Joyner-Kersee failed in her quest to defend her heptathlon title. She pulled out because of a hamstring muscle pull, then later finished third in the long jump. Ghada Shouaa won the

Michael Johnson of the United States sprinted into the record books with dominating Olympic victories in the 400-m and 200-m races. In the latter event (right)*, the 28-year-old Texan obliterated a quality field and his own world record with a time of 19.32.*

© Gary M. Pryor/Allsport

heptathlon to become the first Syrian woman to capture an Olympic medal. Donovan Bailey of Canada defeated a terrific field to win the 100-m dash in world-record time.

The most controversial track participant was American Carl Lewis. Winner of eight previous gold medals spread over three Olympics, Lewis was not expected to do well at these Games. Instead, on his last jump, he captured the long jump, beating out James Beckford of Jamaica and Joe Greene of the United States. He then expressed a desire to run on the U.S. 400-m-relay team, so he would have a chance at a tenth gold—a total no previous Olympian had obtained. (Four athletes, including Lewis, have won nine.) But Lewis had finished eighth in the 100-m at the U.S. Olympic trials and was not put on the team, which lost to Canada. The U.S. team finished second.

Decathlete Dan O'Brien of the United States captured a gold medal at the 1996 Games. A favorite to win the decathlon four years earlier, O'Brien had failed to qualify for that Olympiad.

© Mike Hewitt/Allsport

Gymnastics. The women's gymnastics competition was highlighted by perhaps the most heroic individual performance of the Games. During the competition for the team title, the U.S. team was down to its final performer—Kerri Strug on the vault apparatus. The team thought it needed her to score at least a 9.6 to wrap up a gold medal. On her first vault she badly injured an ankle. She was unsure if she wanted to continue but did so anyway. On her second vault, she scored 9.712. She somehow remained standing on her landing before collapsing to the mat in severe pain. As it turned out, the Americans would have won the gold even if she had not taken the second vault. Later, she was carried to the medal-awards ceremony by her coach Bela Karolyi. It was the first time the United States had won gold in the team standings. Russia was second and Romania was third.

Lilia Podkopayeva of the Ukraine won the all-around title. Americans Dominique Dawes and Shannon Miller both were vying for first place in this event until they made major mistakes late in the competition. Podkopayeva also won a gold in floor exercise and a silver on the balance beam. Miller finished first on the beam and Dawes was third in floor exercise. Teammate Amy Chow tied for second in the uneven bars.

In the men's competition, Vitaly Scherbo, who had won an astonishing six gold medals

ARCHERY

Men's Individual: Justin Huish, U.S.
Men's Team: United States
Women's Individual: Kim Kyung-wook, South Korea
Women's Team: South Korea

BADMINTON

Men's Singles: Poul-Erik Hoyer-Larsen, Denmark
Men's Doubles: Indonesia
Women's Singles: Bang Soo-hyun, South Korea
Women's Doubles: China
Mixed Doubles: South Korea

BASEBALL

Cuba

BASKETBALL

Men: United States
Women: United States

BEACH VOLLEYBALL

Men: United States
Women: Brazil

BOXING

Light Flyweight: Daniel Petrov, Bulgaria
Flyweight: Maikro Romero, Cuba
Bantamweight: Istvan Kovacs, Hungary
Featherweight: Somluck Kamsing, Thailand
Lightweight: Hocine Soltani, Algeria
Light Welterweight: Hector Vinent, Cuba
Welterweight: Oleg Saitov, Russia
Light Middleweight: David Reid, U.S.
Middleweight: Ariel Hernández, Cuba
Light Heavyweight: Vassili Jirov, Kazakhstan
Heavyweight: Félix Sávon, Cuba
Super Heavyweight: Vladimir Klitchko, Ukraine

CANOEING

Men's 500-m Canoe Singles: Martin Doktor, Czech Republic
Men's 500-m Canoe Pairs: Hungary
Men's 1,000-m Canoe Singles: Martin Doktor, Czech Republic
Men's 1,000-m Canoe Pairs: Germany
Men's Single Canoe Slalom: Michal Martikan, Slovakia
Men's Double Canoe Slalom: France
Men's 500-m Kayak Singles: Antonio Rossi, Italy
Men's 500-m Kayak Pairs: Germany
Men's 1,000-m Kayak Singles: Knut Holmann, Norway
Men's 1,000-m Kayak Pairs: Italy
Men's 1,000-m Kayak Fours: Germany
Men's Single Kayak Slalom: Oliver Fix, Germany
Women's 500-m Kayak Singles: Rita Koban, Hungary
Women's 500-m Kayak Pairs: Sweden
Women's 500-m Kayak Fours: Germany
Women's Single Kayak Slalom: Stepanka Hilgertova, Czech Republic

CYCLING

Men's Pursuit: Andrea Collinelli, Italy
Men's Points Race: Silvio Martinello, Italy
Men's Time Trials: Miguel Indurain, Spain
Men's 1-km Time Trial: Florian Rousseau, France
Men's Road Race: Pascal Richard, Switzerland
Men's Sprint: Jens Fiedler, Germany
Men's Mountain Bike: Bart Jan Brentjens, Netherlands
Men's Team Pursuit: France
Women's Pursuit: Antonella Bellutti, Italy
Women's Points Race: Nathalie Lancien, France
Women's Time Trials: Zulfiya Zabirova, Russia
Women's Sprint: Felicia Ballanger, France
Women's Road Race: Jeannie Longo-Ciprelli, France
Women's Mountain Bike: Paola Pezzo, Italy

EQUESTRIAN

3-Day Event: Blyth Tait, New Zealand
Team 3-Day Event: Australia
Dressage: Isabell Werth, Germany
Team Dressage: Germany
Jumping: Ulrich Kirchhoff, Germany
Team Jumping: Germany

FENCING

Men's Epée: Aleksandr Beketov, Russia
Men's Team Epée: Italy
Men's Foil: Alessandro Puccini, Italy
Men's Team Foil: Russia
Men's Individual Saber: Stanislav Pozdnyakov, Russia
Men's Team Saber: Russia
Women's Epée: Laura Flessel, France
Women's Team Epée: France
Women's Foil: Laura Badea, Romania
Women's Team Foil: Italy

FIELD HOCKEY

Men: Netherlands
Women: Australia

GYMNASTICS

Men's All-Around: Li Xiaoshuang, China
Men's Floor Exercises: Ioannis Melissanidis, Greece
Men's Horizontal Bar: Andreas Wecker, Germany
Men's Parallel Bars: Rustam Sharipov, Ukraine
Men's Pommel Horse: Li Donghua, Switzerland
Men's Rings: Yuri Chechi, Italy
Men's Vault: Alexei Nemov, Russia
Men's Team: Russia
Women's All-Around: Lilia Podkopayeva, Ukraine
Women's Balance Beam: Shannon Miller, U.S.
Women's Floor Exercises: Lili Podkopayeva, Ukraine
Women's Uneven Parallel Bars: Svetlana Chorkina, Russia
Women's Vault: Simona Amanar, Romania
Women's Team: United States
Women's Rhythmic: Yekaterina Serebryanskaya, Ukraine
Women's Team Rhythmic: Spain

HANDBALL

Men: Croatia
Women: Denmark

JUDO

Men's Extra Lightweight: Tadahiro Nomura, Japan
Men's Half-Lightweight: Udo Quellmalz, Germany
Men's Lightweight: Kenzo Nakamura, Japan
Men's Half-Middleweight: Djamel Bouras, France
Men's Middleweight: Jeon Ki-young, South Korea
Men's Half-Heavyweight: Pawel Nastula, Poland
Men's Heavyweight: David Douillet, France
Women's Extra Lightweight: Kye Sun, North Korea
Women's Half-Lightweight: Marie-Claire Restoux, France
Women's Lightweight: Driulis Gonzalez, Cuba
Women's Half-Middleweight: Yuko Emoto, Japan
Women's Middleweight: Cho Min-sun, South Korea
Women's Half-Heavyweight: Ulla Werbrouck, Belgium
Women's Heavyweight: Sun Fuming, China

MODERN PENTATHLON

Individual: Aleksandr Parygin, Kazakhstan

ROWING

Men's Single Sculls: Xeno Mueller, Switzerland
Men's Double Sculls: Italy
Men's Quadruple Sculls: Germany
Men's Pairs Without Coxswain: Great Britain
Men's Fours Without Coxswain: Australia
Men's Lightweight Double Sculls: Switzerland
Men's Lightweight Four Without Coxswain: Denmark
Men's Eights: Netherlands
Women's Single Sculls: Yekaterina Khodotovich, Belarus
Women's Double Sculls: Canada
Women's Quadruple Sculls: Germany
Women's Pairs Without Coxswain: Australia
Women's Lightweight Double Sculls: Romania
Women's Eights: Romania

SHOOTING

Men's Air Pistol: Roberto Di Donna, Italy
Men's Free Pistol: Boris Kokorev, Russia
Men's Rapid-Fire Pistol: Ralf Schumann, Germany
Men's Running Game Target: Yang Ling, China
Men's Air Rifle: Artem Khadzhibekov, Russia
Men's Rifle, 3 Positions: Jean-Pierre Amat, France
Men's Rifle, Prone: Christian Klees, Germany
Men's Open Skeet: Ennio Falco, Italy
Men's Open Trap: Michael Diamond, Australia
Men's Double Trap: Russell Mark, Australia
Women's Air Pistol: Olga Klochneva, Russia
Women's Sport Pistol: Li Duihong, China
Women's Air Rifle: Renata Mauer, Poland
Women's Rifle, 3 Positions: Aleksandra Ivosev, Yugoslavia
Women's Double Trap: Kim Rhode, U.S.

SOCCER

Men: Nigeria
Women: United States

SOFTBALL

United States

SWIMMING AND DIVING

Men's 100-m Backstroke: Jeff Rouse, U.S.
Men's 200-m Backstroke: Brad Bridgewater, U.S.
Men's 100-m Breaststroke: Fred Deburghgraeve, Belgium
Men's 200-m Breaststroke: Norbert Rozsa, Hungary
Men's 100-m Butterfly: Denis Pankratov, Russia
Men's 200-m Butterfly: Denis Pankratov, Russia
Men's 50-m Freestyle: Alexander Popov, Russia
Men's 100-m Freestyle: Alexander Popov, Russia
Men's 200-m Freestyle: Danyon Loader, New Zealand
Men's 400-m Freestyle: Danyon Loader, New Zealand
Men's 1,500-m Freestyle: Kieren Perkins, Australia
Men's 400-m Freestyle Relay: United States
Men's 800-m Freestyle Relay: United States
Men's 200-m Individual Medley: Attila Czene, Hungary
Men's 400-m Individual Medley: Tom Dolan, U.S.
Men's 400-m Medley Relay: United States
Men's Platform Diving: Dmitry Sautin, Russia
Men's Springboard Diving: Xiong Ni, China
Women's 100-m Backstroke: Beth Botsford, U.S.
Women's 200-m Backstroke: Krisztina Egerszegi, Hungary
Women's 100-m Breaststroke: Penny Heyns, South Africa
Women's 200-m Breaststroke: Penny Heyns, South Africa
Women's 100-m Butterfly: Amy Van Dyken, U.S.
Women's 200-m Butterfly: Susan O'Neill, Australia
Women's 50-m Freestyle: Amy Van Dyken, U.S.
Women's 100-m Freestyle: Le Jingyi, China
Women's 200-m Freestyle: Claudia Poll, Costa Rica
Women's 400-m Freestyle: Michelle Smith, Ireland
Women's 800-m Freestyle: Brooke Bennett, U.S.
Women's 400-m Freestyle Relay: United States
Women's 800-m Freestyle Relay: United States

Women's 200-m Individual Medley: Michelle Smith, Ireland
Women's 400-m Individual Medley: Michelle Smith, Ireland
Women's 400-m Medley Relay: United States
Women's Platform Diving: Fu Mingxia, China
Women's Springboard Diving: Fu Mingxia, China

SYNCHRONIZED SWIMMING

United States

TABLE TENNIS

Men's Singles: Liu Guoliang, China
Men's Doubles: China
Women's Singles: Deng Yaping, China
Women's Doubles: China

TENNIS

Men's Singles: Andre Agassi, U.S.
Men's Doubles: Todd Woodbridge and Mark Woodforde, Australia
Women's Singles: Lindsay Davenport, U.S.
Women's Doubles: Gigi Fernandez and Mary Joe Fernandez, U.S.

TRACK AND FIELD

Men's 100-m Dash: Donovan Bailey, Canada
Men's 200-m Dash: Michael Johnson, U.S.
Men's 400-m Run: Michael Johnson, U.S.
Men's 400-m Relay: Canada
Men's 800-m Run: Vebjoern Rodal, Norway
Men's 1,500-m Run: Noureddine Morceli, Algeria
Men's 1,600-m Relay: United States
Men's 5,000-m Run: Venuste Niyongabo, Burundi
Men's 10,000-m Run: Haile Gebrselassie, Ethiopia
Men's 20-km Walk: Jefferson Pérez, Ecuador
Men's 50-km Walk: Robert Korzeniowski, Poland
Men's 110-m Hurdles: Allen Johnson, U.S.
Men's 400-m Hurdles: Derrick Adkins, U.S.
Men's 3,000-m Steeplechase: Joseph Keter, Kenya
Men's Marathon: Josia Thugwane, South Africa
Men's Decathlon: Dan O'Brien, U.S.
Men's Discus: Lars Riedel, Germany
Men's Hammer Throw: Balazs Kiss, Hungary
Men's High Jump: Charles Austin, U.S.
Men's Javelin: Jan Zelezny, Czech Republic
Men's Long Jump: Carl Lewis, U.S.
Men's Pole Vault: Jean Galfione, France
Men's Shot Put: Randy Barnes, U.S.
Men's Triple Jump: Kenny Harrison, U.S.
Women's 100-m Dash: Gail Devers, U.S.
Women's 200-m Dash: Marie-José Pérec, France
Women's 400-m Run: Marie-José Pérec, France
Women's 400-m Relay: United States
Women's 800-m Run: Svetlana Masterkova, Russia
Women's 1,600-m Relay: United States
Women's 1,500-m Run: Svetlana Masterkova, Russia
Women's 5,000-m Run: Wang Junxia, China
Women's 10,000-m Run: Fernanda Ribeiro, Portugal
Women's 10-km Walk: Yelena Nikolayeva, Russia
Women's 100-m Hurdles: Ludmila Enquist, Sweden
Women's 400-m Hurdles: Deon Hemmings, Jamaica
Women's Marathon: Fatuma Roba, Ethiopia
Women's Heptathlon: Ghada Shouaa, Syria
Women's Discus: Ilke Wyludda, Germany
Women's High Jump: Stefka Kostadinova, Bulgaria
Women's Javelin: Heli Rantanen, Finland
Women's Long Jump: Chioma Ajunwa, Nigeria
Women's Shot Put: Astrid Kumbernuss, Germany
Women's Triple Jump: Inessa Kravets, Ukraine

VOLLEYBALL

Men: Netherlands
Women: Cuba

WATER POLO

Spain

WEIGHT LIFTING

Flyweight: Halil Mutlu, Turkey
Bantamweight: Tang Ningsheng, China
Featherweight: Naim Suleymanoglu, Turkey
Lightweight: Zhan Xugang, China
Middleweight: Pablo Lara, Cuba
Light Heavyweight: Pyrros Dimas, Greece
Middle Heavyweight: Aleksei Petrov, Russia
Heavyweight: Akakide Kakhiashvilis, Greece
Second Heavyweight: Timur Taimazov, Ukraine
Super Heavyweight: Andrei Chemerkin, Russia

WRESTLING, FREESTYLE

Paperweight: Kim Il, North Korea
Flyweight: Valentin Jordanov, Bulgaria
Bantamweight: Kendall Cross, U.S.
Featherweight: Tom Brands, U.S.
Lightweight: Vadim Bogiev, Russia
Welterweight: Bouvaisa Satiev, Russia
Middleweight: Khadzhimurad Magomedov, Russia
Light Heavyweight: Rasul Khadem, Iran
Heavyweight: Kurt Angle, U.S.
Super Heavyweight: Mahmut Demir, Turkey

WRESTLING, GRECO-ROMAN

Paperweight: Sim Kwon-ho, South Korea
Flyweight: Armen Nazaryan, Armenia
Bantamweight: Yuri Melnichenko, Kazakhstan
Featherweight: Wlodzimierz Zawadzki, Poland
Lightweight: Ryszard Wolny, Poland
Welterweight: Feliberto Ascuy, Cuba
Middleweight: Hamza Yerlikaya, Turkey
Light Heavyweight: Vyacheslav Oleynyk, Ukraine
Heavyweight: Andrzej Wronski, Poland
Super Heavyweight: Aleksandr Karelin, Russia

YACHTING

Laser: Robert Scheidt, Brazil
Soling: Germany
Star: Brazil
Tornado: Spain
Men's Finn: Mateusz Kusznierewicz, Poland
Men's Mistral: Nikolaos Kaklamanakis, Greece
Men's 470: Ukraine
Women's Europe: Kristine Roug, Denmark
Women's Mistral: Lee Lai-shan, Hong Kong
Women's 470: Spain

FINAL MEDAL STANDINGS

Country	Gold	Silver	Bronze	Total
United States	44	32	25	101
Russia	26	21	16	63
Germany	20	18	27	65
China	16	22	12	50
France	15	7	15	37
Italy	13	10	12	35
Australia	9	9	23	41
Cuba	9	8	8	25
Ukraine	9	2	12	23
South Korea	7	15	5	27
Poland	7	5	5	17
Hungary	7	4	10	21
Spain	5	6	6	17
Romania	4	7	9	20
Netherlands	4	5	10	19
Greece	4	4	0	8
Czech Republic	4	3	4	11
Switzerland	4	3	0	7
Denmark	4	1	1	6
Turkey	4	1	1	6
Canada	3	11	8	22
Bulgaria	3	7	5	15
Japan	3	6	5	14
Kazakhstan	3	4	4	11
Brazil	3	3	9	15
New Zealand	3	2	1	6
South Africa	3	1	1	5
Ireland	3	0	1	4
Sweden	2	4	2	8
Norway	2	2	3	7
Belgium	2	2	2	6
Nigeria	2	1	3	6
North Korea	2	1	2	5
Algeria	2	0	1	3
Ethiopia	2	0	1	3
Britain	1	8	6	15
Belarus	1	6	8	15
Kenya	1	4	3	8
Jamaica	1	3	2	6
Finland	1	2	1	4
Indonesia	1	1	2	4
Yugoslavia	1	1	2	4
Iran	1	1	1	3
Slovakia	1	1	1	3
Armenia	1	1	0	2
Croatia	1	1	0	2
Portugal	1	0	1	2
Thailand	1	0	1	2
Burundi	1	0	0	1
Costa Rica	1	0	0	1
Ecuador	1	0	0	1
Hong Kong	1	0	0	1
Syria	1	0	0	1
Argentina	0	2	1	3
Namibia	0	2	0	2
Slovenia	0	2	0	2
Austria	0	1	2	3
Malaysia	0	1	1	2
Moldova	0	1	1	2
Uzbekistan	0	1	1	2
Azerbaijan	0	1	0	1
Bahamas	0	1	0	1
Latvia	0	1	0	1
Philippines	0	1	0	1
Taiwan	0	1	0	1
Tonga	0	1	0	1
Zambia	0	1	0	1
Georgia	0	0	2	2
Morocco	0	0	2	2
Trinidad and Tobago	0	0	2	2
India	0	0	1	1
Israel	0	0	1	1
Lithuania	0	0	1	1
Mexico	0	0	1	1
Mongolia	0	0	1	1
Mozambique	0	0	1	1
Puerto Rico	0	0	1	1
Tunisia	0	0	1	1
Uganda	0	0	1	1

© Tony Duffy/Allsport

In the women's gymnastics team competition, a gritty U.S. squad defeated the favored Russian and Romanian teams to win gold. The competition was highlighted by a gutsy vaulting performance by an injured Kerri Strug (second from right).

at the 1992 Games, came back for these Games hoping to add to his gold total. Instead, he settled for bronze medals in the vault, parallel bars, horizontal bars, and all-around. The all-around title went to Li Xiaoshuang of China, who also won a silver in floor exercise. The team gold went to Russia, with China second and Ukraine third.

Basketball. The U.S. men's basketball team, otherwise known as the "Dream Team," once again dominated the basketball competition. The Dream Team first came about at the 1992 Games, when players from the National Basketball Association (NBA) were allowed to play in the Olympics despite their professional status. The 1996 version of the Dream Team was not quite as strong as its 1992 predecessor, which had featured Michael Jordan, Larry Bird, and Magic Johnson. Still, the Americans had little trouble cruising to the gold medal. They won the gold-medal game by racing past Yugoslavia, 95–69. Stars of the team included Reggie Miller, David Robinson, Shaquille O'Neal, Karl Malone, Hakeem Olajuwon, and Scottie Pippen.

The competition was much closer for the women's gold medal. The U.S. team entered the competition with a long unbeaten streak and ultimately came away with a first-place finish. The Americans saved their best game for last, rolling past an experienced Brazil team, the defending world champions, 111–87. The United States was led by Lisa Leslie, Teresa Edwards, Sheryl Swoopes, and Katrina McClain.

Swimming and Diving. Unlike 1992, when the women's swimming and diving competition was dominated by the Chinese team amid questions about its use of steroids, the 1996 Games were a forum for a comeback by U.S. competitors. But there was still controversy. Michelle Smith of Ireland emerged the standout individual swimmer. She improved her best times considerably while swimming for gold in the 200-m and 400-m individual medleys and the 400-m freestyle. Some U.S. swimmers questioned whether she was helped by steroids, but she passed all Olympic drug tests. Amy Van Dyken of the United States also was a standout. She earned individual gold medals in the 100-m butterfly and the 50-m freestyle and was a member of two gold-medal-winning relay teams—the 400-m freestyle and the 400-m medley. She became the first U.S. woman to win four gold medals in the same Olympics, winter or summer. Krisztina Egerszegi of Hungary won the 200-m backstroke for the third straight Olympics, a record. American Janet Evans, who had hoped to win a fifth gold medal, which would have been an Olympic record for the United

© Ross Kinnaird/Allsport

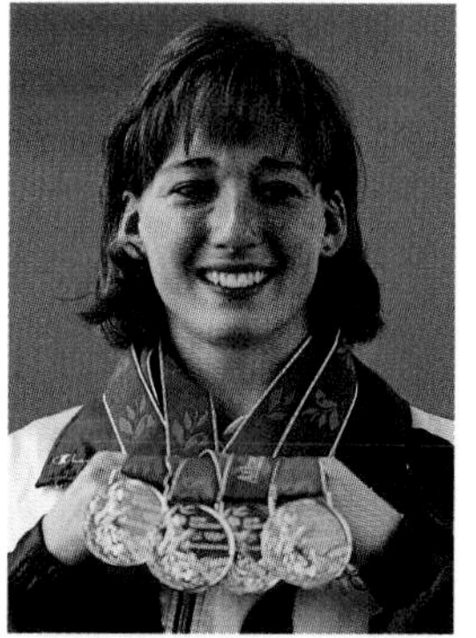

The golden exploits of Amy Van Dyken spearheaded a strong comeback for the U.S. swimming program. The 23-year-old Coloradan became the first U.S. woman to win four gold medals at one Olympics.

States, failed to win a medal and retired once the competition ended.

The glamour figure of the men's swimming competition was Russia's Alexander Popov, who held off American Gary Hall, Jr., in both the 50-m and 100-m freestyles to win the gold. Hall is the son of Gary Hall, a dominant swimmer in the 1970s. One of the most touted swimmers was American Tom Dolan, a heavy favorite to win the 400-m individual medley. He wound up taking the gold medal, barely beating out fellow American Eric Namesnik. Both Dolan and Namesnik swam for the University of Michigan.

The diving was marked by a stellar showing from the Chinese performers, who won gold in three of the four events. Fu Mingxia won gold medals in the women's springboard and platform, while countryman Xiong Ni took the men's springboard. Russia's Dmitri Sautin came away with a gold medal in the men's platform.

Boxing. Cuba had hoped to repeat its domination of boxing. But the Cuban team failed to match its 1992 total of seven gold medals. This time, it won four gold and three silver medals. The most dramatic match came between light middleweights David Reid of the United States and Alfredo Duvergel of Cuba. Duvergel was winning handily going into the third and final round, only to be knocked down by Reid. The referee stopped the bout, giving Reid the gold medal. That was the only gold taken by the Americans in boxing. Scoring once again was done by judges using a computer to mark every time they decided one of the boxers landed a punch. As in 1992, the system for scoring remained controversial.

Baseball. What was supposed to be a close competition between the Cuban and U.S. teams turned into a one-sided domination by the talented squad from Cuba. The Cubans breezed to a gold medal, defeating Japan in the championship game. The United States lost in the semifinals to Japan, then came back to take the bronze. Bad pitching hampered the U.S. team.

Other Sports. U.S. women's teams had an especially successful Olympics. Besides winning the basketball competition and the team title in gymnastics, American women won the gold medal in softball—which was an Olympic sport for the first time—and in soccer. A crowd of 76,481 fans saw the United States defeat China in soccer's thrilling championship game.

Weight lifter Naim Suleymanoglu of Turkey won a stunning third straight gold medal by taking the 64-kg (141-lb) class. The Greco-Roman wrestling competition was dominated by Russian heavyweight Aleksandr Karelin, who won a decision over Matt Ghaffari of the United States to take the gold. The imposing Karelin never has lost an international match. Poland won three gold medals in Greco-Roman wrestling, while the United States took three golds in freestyle wrestling. The latter were won by Kendall Cross in the 57-kg (126-lb) class, Tom Brands in the 62-kg (137-lb) class, and Kurt Angle in the 100-kg (220-lb) class. Russian wrestlers also won three golds in freestyle.

The U.S. women's team (in blue) *defeated China to take the first-ever Olympic gold in softball. American women also won gold—and new fans—with victories in basketball and soccer.*

The tennis gold medals went to American Andre Agassi on the men's singles side and American Lindsay Davenport on the women's singles side. The latter upset Arantxa Sánchez Vicario of Spain in the title match. Agassi downed Sergi Bruguera of Spain to win gold.

Among the sports introduced for the first time in the Olympics was beach volleyball. Americans Karch Kiraly and Kent Steffes won the men's gold, while Jackie Silva and Sandra Pires of Brazil won the women's gold. (*See* SIDEBAR.)

Overall. The organizers of the Atlanta Games had wanted them to be especially memorable, considering the event marked the 100th anniversary of the Olympics. Despite criticism about their size and the obvious commercialism that dominated the streets throughout Atlanta, the Games provided excellent athletic competition and functioned smoothly after an uneven start. Even the unfortunate bombing incident did not halt the

Beach Volleyball—A New Olympic Sport

When the U.S. men's beach-volleyball team of Karch Kiraly *(below)* and Kent Steffes and the Brazilian women's beach-volleyball team of Jackie Silva and Sandra Pires won gold medals at the 1996 Summer Olympics, history was made. The foursome were the first to be awarded gold medals in the world's fastest-growing sporting event. For Kiraly, it was the third time that he had captured a gold medal. However, his earlier medals—in 1984 and 1988—were for the traditional indoor game of volleyball.

Rules. The rules of beach volleyball differ from those of its indoor cousin, although the court size and net height remain the same. Although the court's surface is sand, man-made artificial courts have become common. As in traditional volleyball, players may touch the ball only three times on one side of the net. But with two players per team instead of six, players must do it all—serve, dig, set, spike, and kill. And with no substitutions allowed, they have to do it without protracted rests and usually covered with sweat and sand.

Two-man or two-woman teams play one set to 15 points, but victory must be by two points. The finals take the form of a two-out-of-three-set contest, with the first two games played to 12 points and the third, if necessary, to 15. Normally, only the serving team can score points; but in the third set of the finals, both teams can score. Shirts are mandatory; sunglasses, visors, and hats—usually festooned with corporate logos—are permitted. Footwear is optional, and most players go barefoot even though sand temperatures can reach 110° F (43° C).

Criticism and Popularity. Some volleyball purists have questioned whether fans are drawn to the beach version of the sport by the action or by the scantily clad, suntanned bodies flying through the air. The latter theory gains credibility when one reads the promotional material touting "beach-bound bombshells." But beach volleyball has succeeded in accomplishing something the indoor game never could: It has attracted millions of fans, as well as television sponsors, endorsement contracts, and big prize money. In fact, from its roots in southern California in the 1920s to its current pro circuit, beach volleyball has become so popular that it was one of the first events to be sold out at the Atlanta Games.

BRUCE JACOBY

competition. The 2000 Games will be held in Sydney, Australia.

See also THE OLYMPIC GAMES: 1896–1996.

PAUL ATTNER

Skiing

Lasse Kjus of Norway and Katja Seizinger of Germany emerged as the overall champions of the men's and women's 1996 World Cup circuit, respectively.

Alberto Tomba captured the slalom and giant slalom at the World Alpine Championships. The Italian said that he "suffered more for these wins than [for] the Olympics."

Picabo Street became the first U.S. woman to win an event at the World Alpine Championships. The 24-year-old resident of Idaho captured the downhill. She also successfully defended her World Cup downhill crown and took the downhill and super-giant slalom at the U.S. Alpine Championships.

SKIING

World Cup

Men's Downhill: Luc Alphand, France
Men's Slalom: Sebastien Amiez, France
Men's Giant Slalom: Michael von Gruenigen, Switzerland
Men's Super-Giant Slalom: Atle Skaardal, Norway
Men's Overall: Lasse Kjus, Norway
Women's Downhill: Picabo Street, United States
Women's Slalom: Elfi Eder, Austria
Women's Giant Slalom: Martina Ertl, Germany
Women's Super-Giant Slalom: Katja Seizinger, Germany
Women's Overall: Katja Seizinger

U.S. Alpine Championships

Men's Combined: Chris Pucketts
Men's Downhill: Chad Fleischer
Men's Slalom: Chip Knight
Men's Giant Slalom: Daron Rahlves
Men's Super-Giant Slalom: Kyle Rasmussen
Women's Combined: Kirsten Clark
Women's Downhill: Picabo Street
Women's Slalom: Kristina Koznick
Women's Giant Slalom: Jennifer Collins
Women's Super-Giant Slalom: Picabo Street

World Alpine Championships

Men's Downhill: Patrick Ortlieb, Austria
Men's Slalom: Alberto Tomba, Italy
Men's Giant Slalom: Alberto Tomba
Men's Super-Giant Slalom: Atle Skaardal
Men's Combined: Marc Girardelli, Luxembourg
Women's Downhill: Picabo Street
Women's Slalom: Pernilla Wiberg, Sweden
Women's Giant Slalom: Deborah Compagnoni, Italy
Women's Super-Giant Slalom: Isolde Kostner, Italy
Women's Combined: Pernilla Wiberg

NCAA Championships

Men's and Women's Team: University of Utah

Soccer

Major League Soccer (MLS)—a new U.S. professional league—made its successful debut in 1996. The inaugural season came to a close on October 20 with the MLS Cup championship. A crowd of 34,643 braved torrential rains at Foxboro (MA) Stadium to watch D.C. United rally from a two-goal deficit to defeat the Los Angeles Galaxy in overtime, 3–2. United midfielder Marco Etcheverry, who notched two assists in the game, was named the most valuable player (MVP).

MLS officials had reason to be cautiously optimistic at season's end. The level of play in the league widely was regarded as good, perhaps a notch beneath first-division competition in Europe and South America. The teams were composed primarily of U.S. players, including John Harkes, Cobi Jones, Alexi Lalas, and other veterans of the 1994 U.S. World Cup team. Lending international credibility to the MLS were such top foreign stars as Bolivia's Etcheverry, Mexico's Jorge Campos, Italy's Roberto Donadoni, and Colombia's Carlos Valderrama, who was voted the league's regular-season MVP. Each team was allowed to sign no more than four foreign players; however, league officials announced plans to raise that number to five for the 1997 season. Attendance and sponsorship also were somewhat better than expected. The league averaged 17,416 paid fans per game.

© Rick Stewart/Allsport

At the inaugural MLS Cup championship, held in soggy conditions at Foxboro, MA, Raul Diaz Arce (21) and his D.C. United teammates won, 3–2, in overtime over the Los Angeles Galaxy.

International Play. Germany captured the year's most important tournament, the quadrennial European Championship. In the title game, Germany scored a controversial 2–1 sudden-death victory over an unheralded squad from the Czech Republic. New champions were crowned in the two most prestigious European competitions. In the European Champions Cup, Juventus of Turin outscored defending champion Ajax Amsterdam in a 4–2 overtime shoot-out. In the Cup Winners Cup, Paris–St. Germain edged Rapid Vienna, 1–0. Juventus and Paris–St. Germain were slated to meet in the European Super Cup—which pits the victors of the Champions Cup and the Cup Winners Cup—early in 1997. Ajax Amsterdam had won the 1996 Super Cup with a 4–0 victory over Spain's Real Zaragoza in February.

Shared World Cup. In an unprecedented decision, officials awarded the 2002 World Cup to two nations—South Korea and Japan. Both countries had mounted contentious bids to bring the World Cup to Asia for the first time. Late in 1996, officials had not yet reached final decisions about which of the two nations would host the championship game, whether both countries would get automatic bids into the tournament, and if North Korea would have any involvement as a cohost.

Women's Soccer. In the year's most important tournament, the United States swept the competition to capture the U.S. Cup championship. In other news, the United States was awarded the right to host the 1999 women's World Cup after Chile and Australia failed to submit formal bids.

Collegiate Champions. The Red Storm of St. John's University gave that school its first National Collegiate Athletic Association (NCAA) championship in any sport with a 4–1 victory over Florida International. In women's action, the perennially powerful Tarheels of the University of North Carolina regained the NCAA title with a 1–0 overtime victory over defending champion Notre Dame.

PETER A. FLAX

Swimming

U.S. swimmers who either were overshadowed or did not qualify for the 1996 Summer Olympics in Atlanta redeemed themselves in August at the Phillips 66 Senior National Championships in Fort Lauderdale, FL.

U.S. Champions. Josh Davis of San Antonio, TX, who won three Olympic gold medals and virtually was overlooked because they were all in relays, swam to three titles in the nationals. An hour after winning the 200-m freestyle (1:49.18 seconds), he anchored the Athletes in Action team to victory in the 400-m freestyle relay. Davis also captured the 400-m freestyle title. Lenny Krazelburg of Studio City, CA, who finished fifth in the 200-m backstroke in the Olympic trials, took the national title in 1:59.37. Neil Walker of Verona, WI, also missed an Olympic spot—by .01 second in the 400-m freestyle relay—but won the 100-m freestyle title in 50.07.

Misty Hyman of Phoenix, AZ, captured the 200-m butterfly title in 2:10.95, having missed an Olympic berth by .03 second in the 100-m butterfly. Tom Wilkens of Middletown, NY, and Jennifer Parmenter, 15, of Granada Hills, CA, easily won the 400-m individual-medley (IM) titles. Wilkens won by 5.52 seconds in 4:18.76, and Parmenter, who missed a shot at the Games by finishing third in the 400-m IM at the trials, won the national title by 4.44 seconds with 4:43.48. Parmenter also won the 400-m freestyle with a time of 4:13.24.

Among other winners of national titles were: Lauren Thies of Portland, OR, 200-m freestyle (2:01.45); Lea Loveless of Crestwood, NY, 100-m backstroke (1:02.50) and 200-m backstroke (2:12.11); Annemieke McReynolds of Wildwood, GA, 200-m breaststroke (2:29.71); Matt Hooper, San Antonio, TX, 200-m butterfly (1:59.64); Liesl Kolbisen, Half Moon Bay, CA, 100-m freestyle (56.50); Lawrence Frostad, Sacramento, CA, 800-m freestyle (8:02.64); and Ashley Whitney, Jacksonville, FL, 800-m freestyle (8:36.62).

U.S. Diving Champions. Young divers excelled at the Phillips 66 National Diving Championships at Moultrie, GA. Troy Dumais, 16, from Ventura, CA, won the 1-m and 3-m springboard titles, and Becky Ruehl, 18, of Lakeside Park, KY, took top honors on the 10-m platform. In other events, Russ Bertram of Fort Lauderdale, FL, won the 10-m platform; Erica Sorgi of Mission Viejo, CA, won on the 3-m springboard; and Doris Glenn Easterly of Fort Lauderdale, FL, captured the 1-m springboard title.

GEORGE DE GREGORIO

Tennis

During 1996, Steffi Graf continued her relentless assault on the peaks of tennis, as she and Pete Sampras maintained Number 1 rankings in their respective precincts.

In team competition, Monica Seles and Lindsay Davenport helped the United States beat Spain, 5–0, to win the Federation Cup. On the men's side, France took the Davis Cup in a gripping final over Sweden, 3–2. The U.S. squad fell to the Czech Republic in quarterfinal action.

The Women. Graf, overriding the pain of back and knee injuries as well as the trauma of her father's jailing and trial for income-tax evasion in Germany, left few scraps for her rivals. Kept from the Australian Open by a leg injury, she won the other three majors: a fifth French, 6–3, 6–7 (4–7), 10–8 over Arantxa Sánchez Vicario of Spain, who twice served for victory; a seventh Wimbledon, 6–3, 7–5, over Sánchez Vicario; and a fifth U.S., 7–5, 6–4, over Seles.

Graf, with 21 major singles crowns at the end of 1996, was approaching Margaret Court's all-time record (24). During the year, Graf won 54 of 58 matches and seven titles. At the season-concluding WTA Tour finale, the

TENNIS

Davis Cup: France
Federation Cup: Spain

Important Tournaments

Australian Open—men's singles: Boris Becker (Germany); men's doubles: Stefan Edberg (Sweden) and Petr Korda (Czech Republic); women's singles: Monica Seles; women's doubles: Chanda Rubin and Arantxa Sánchez Vicario (Spain); mixed doubles: Larisa Neiland (Latvia) and Mark Woodforde (Australia).

Lipton International Players Championships—men's singles: Andre Agassi; men's doubles: Todd Woodbridge (Australia) and Mark Woodforde (Australia); women's singles: Steffi Graf (Germany); women's doubles: Jana Novotna (Czech Republic) and Arantxa Sánchez Vicario (Spain).

Italian Open—men's singles: Thomas Muster (Austria); men's doubles: Byron Black (Zimbabwe) and Grant Connell (Canada); women's singles: Arantxa Sánchez Vicario (Spain); women's doubles: Arantxa Sánchez Vicario (Spain) and Irina Spirlea (Romania).

French Open—men's singles: Yevgeny Kafelnikov (Russia); men's doubles: Yevgeny Kafelnikov (Russia) and Daniel Vacek (Czech Republic); women's singles: Steffi Graf (Germany); women's doubles: Lindsay Davenport and Mary Joe Fernandez; mixed doubles: Patricia Tarabini (Argentina) and Javier Frana (Argentina).

Wimbledon—men's singles: Richard Krajicek (Netherlands); men's doubles: Todd Woodbridge (Australia) and Mark Woodforde (Australia); women's singles: Steffi Graf (Germany); women's doubles: Martina Hingis (Switzerland) and Helena Sukova (Czech Republic); mixed doubles: Cyril Suk (Czech Republic) and Helena Sukova (Czech Republic).

U.S. Open—men's singles: Pete Sampras; men's doubles: Todd Woodbridge (Australia) and Mark Woodforde (Australia); women's singles: Steffi Graf (Germany); women's doubles: Gigi Fernandez and Natasha Zvereva (Belarus); mixed doubles: Lisa Raymond and Patrick Galbraith; masters men's doubles: Tom Gullikson and Dick Stockton; masters women's doubles: Anne Hobbs (Great Britain) and Virginia Wade (Great Britain).

ATP Finals—singles: Pete Sampras; doubles: Todd Woodbridge (Australia) and Mark Woodforde (Australia).

WTA Tour Championship—singles: Steffi Graf (Germany); doubles: Lindsay Davenport and Mary Joe Fernandez.

NCAA (Division I)—men's singles: Cecil Mamiit, Southern Cal; men's doubles: Justin Gimelstob and Srdjan Muskatirovic, UCLA; women's singles: Jill Craybas, Florida; women's doubles: Dawn Buth and Stephanie Nickitas, Florida.

N.B. All players are from the United States unless otherwise noted.

© Richard Martin/Vandystadt/Allsport

Yevgeny Kafelnikov demonstrated an overpowering baseline game while defeating Germany's Michael Stich in the French Open final. The 22-year-old became the first Russian to win a Grand Slam title.

Chase Championships in New York, Graf beat 16-year-old Martina Hingis of Switzerland, 6–3, 4–6, 6–0, 4–6, 6–0 (the lone best-of-five final on the women's tour). Hingis won two tournaments and became (at 15 years, 283 days) the youngest of all Wimbledon champs by taking the doubles with Helena Sukova of the Czech Republic.

Seles, 22, in her first full season since being stabbed by a deranged German in 1993, started splendidly. She won her fourth Australian title, beating Germany's Anke Huber, 6–4, 6–1. It was Seles' ninth singles major; she also won four other tournaments and 48 of 56 matches. But, hampered by an injured left shoulder, she dropped from her co–Number 1 ranking with Graf to share the Number 2 ranking with Sánchez Vicario, who won two tournaments and 54 of 76 matches.

At the Summer Olympics in Atlanta, the singles gold went to the 6' 3" (1.91-m) Davenport, who beat Sánchez Vicario, 7–6 (8–6), 6–2. The U.S. Fernandez coalition, composed of the unrelated Mary Joe and Gigi, did a gold repeat of 1992 in the doubles, 7–6 (8–6), 6–4, over Czechs Novotna and Sukova.

The Men. Germany's Boris Becker, 28, made a startling resurgence to win his first major in seven years—and second Australian title—6–2, 6–4, 2–6, 6–2, over Michael Chang of the United States, the only occupant of two major finals. Two of the remaining major singles titles went to first-time winners: Russia's Yevgeny Kafelnikov at the French and the Netherlands' Richard Krajicek at Wimbledon. Kafelnikov took the title bout from Germany's Michael Stich, 7–6 (7–4), 7–5, 7–6 (7–4), while Krajicek's bold serving and backhand beat MaliVai Washington of the United States, 6–3, 6–4, 6–3, in the tournament's first unseeded final. Both Kafelnikov and Krajicek defeated Sampras on the way to their respective victories.

Sampras, however, won the year's final major, the U.S. Open, 6–1, 6–4, 7–6 (7–3), over Chang; it was his fourth U.S. and eighth major. But Sampras' monumental test of the year was a quarterfinal U.S. Open win over Spaniard Alex Corretja. Ill and vomiting at the climax, Sampras survived a match point in a thrilling tiebreaker to win, 7–6 (7–5), 5–7, 5–7, 6–4, 7–6 (9–7). Bouncing back from a defeat by Becker in the round-robin phase of the ATP Tour World Championship, Sampras outlasted Boris in a rousing final, 3–6, 7–6 (7–5), 7–6 (7–4), 6–7 (11–13), 6–4, winning his eighth title of the year on a 65–11 record.

Andre Agassi of the United States, who had battled Sampras for Number 1 in 1995, did win Olympic gold—6–2, 6–3, 6–1, over Spain's Sergi Bruguera. But he played only fairly elsewhere, sliding to Number 8. The Olympics doubles were taken by Australia's Todd Woodbridge and Mark Woodforde.

BUD COLLINS, *"The Boston Globe"/NBC*

Track and Field

The outstanding efforts of U.S. sprinter Michael Johnson (*see* BIOGRAPHY) during 1996 highlighted a year in which many track-and-field records were broken.

Sprint Events. Even before he made history at the 1996 Summer Olympics, Michael Johnson served notice that his quest for track immortality was not an idle wish. On June 23 in Atlanta at the Olympic trials, on the same surface that would host the Olympic competition in July, Johnson broke track's oldest major world record when he clocked 19.66 seconds for the 200-m. That time shattered the 17-year-old mark of 19.72 set by Pietro Mennea of Italy in Mexico City. The mark was all the more impressive in that, unlike Mennea's, it was achieved at sea level and was Johnson's eighth race in nine days. Earlier in the week, he had won the 400-m event in 43.44, the third-fastest time ever run at that distance.

The trials produced one of the most powerful U.S. teams ever sent to the Olympics, although Gwen Torrence, a gold medalist in 1992, finished fourth at 200-m and was denied a chance of going for a coveted double. Earlier in the trials she had qualified with a 10.82 victory at 100-m.

Twice during the year, Johnson was defeated at 200-m. On July 5 in Oslo, Norway, he suffered his first defeat in two years and 21 races at that distance, falling to Frankie Fredericks of Namibia, who shot to an African-record 19.82, beating Johnson by .03 second. Johnson again was beat by Fredericks on August 30 in Berlin, Germany. Fredericks' 19.97 beat Johnson by .05.

Fredericks also defeated another world-record holder and Olympic champion at the season's final meet, the Toto Super International in Tokyo, Japan, beating Canada's Donovan Bailey at 100-m. At the same meet, Jamaican Merlene Ottey gained a bit of revenge against her U.S. nemesis, Gail Devers, in the 100-m, reversing their Olympic finish with a narrow win.

Distance Records. The Grand Prix meet in Zurich, Switzerland, on August 14, in which 17 Olympic champions competed, produced a world record in the mile by Svetlana Masterkova of Russia, winner of two gold medals in Atlanta. The 28-year-old's time of 4:12.56 erased the mark of 4:15.61 set by Paula Ivan in 1989. Nine days later, Masterkova erased the 1,000-m mark with a time of 2:28.98.

The 10,000-m record fell to Salah Hissou of Morocco on August 23 in Brussels, Belgium. Hissou was timed in 26:38.08, clipping 5.45 seconds from the 1995 mark of 26:43.53 set by Haile Gebrselassie of Ethiopia. Daniel Komen, a Kenyan who failed to make his national Olympic team, broke the world standard for 3,000-m on September 1 in Rieti, Italy, with 7:20.67, bettering the 7:25.11 registered by Noureddine Morceli of Algeria in 1994. The 20-year-old Komen also set a world record in July in the infrequently run two-mile event (8:03.54).

Kerry Saxby-Junna of Australia set a world record in the 5,000-m walk (20:13.26) on February 25 at Sydney, Australia.

Field Events. Jan Zelezny of the Czech Republic threw the javelin 323' 1" (98.48 m) on May 25 at Jena, Germany. In the women's pole vault, Emma George of Australia vaulted 14'7 1/2" (4.45 m) on July 14 in Sapporo, Japan, and Mihaela Melinte of Romania threw the hammer 227' 9" (69.42 m) on May 12 in Cluj, Romania.

GEORGE DE GREGORIO

Yachting

The sailing world focused its attentions on regattas and long-distance races in 1996.

At the biennial Kenwood Cup, held in August in Hawaii, a three-boat Australian squad took top honors, with a U.S. team finishing second. Winning the maxi-class competition was the 78-ft (24-m) *Sayonara*, a U.S. entry skippered by Chris Dickson of New Zealand. In other events, Zack Leonard, Pete Alarie, and Josh Adams skipped the *Pablo Picasso* team to victory in the U.S. Team Race Championship, sailed on Lake Erie in July. At the annual Rolex Cup Regatta, contested in April in St. Thomas, Tom Hill of Puerto Rico won the overall title on *Titan*.

In the June Newport-to-Bermuda Race, George Coumantaros' *Boomerang II* established a new standard of 2 days, 9 hours, and 31 minutes for the 635-mi (1 020-km) course. That mark, however, fell in November when Jean-Pierre Mouligné of Newport, RI, shaved about three hours off that record on the 50-ft (15-m) monohull *CCP/Cray Valley*.

Another record was set in the 2,308-mi (4 714-km) Victoria-Maui Race. Roy Disney sailed *Pyewacket* from British Columbia to Hawaii in 9 days, 19 hours, and 36 minutes, pruning some four hours off the old mark. U.S. adventurer Steve Fossett broke the solo transpacific record by three days in August, sailing his trimaran *Lakota* from Yokohama, Japan, to San Francisco in 20 days, 12 hours, and 53 minutes. In June, Loick Peyron of France won the single-handed transatlantic race in 10 days, 10 hours, missing the existing mark by 50 minutes.

In the year's biggest match-racing series—the Brut Cup—Russell Coutts of New Zealand won three straight events, after losing the first, to claim a $250,000 prize, the largest cash jackpot in yachting history.

The 100th Boston Marathon

The 100th Boston Marathon was celebrated in appropriately grand fashion on April 15, 1996. At precisely noon, the crack of a starter's pistol sent more than 40,000 runners—the largest field in marathoning history—surging eastward from the tiny town of Hopkinton, MA, toward Boston along a course steeped in tradition.

The 1996 Event. A crowd of some 1.5 million spectators was treated to a festive afternoon of competitive racing. On the men's side, Moses Tanui led a crowd of fellow Kenyans to the finish line, claiming victory on the 26.2-mi (42.2-km) course with a time of 2:09:16. Tanui and his countrymen took seven of the first eight places in the race. In the women's field, Germany's Uta Pippig won in 2:27:12, earning her third consecutive victory at Boston.

Behind Tanui, Pippig, and the other elite racers followed a massive field of recreational athletes eager to take part in the historic event. Some 38,000 official entrants were joined by at least 10,000 unregistered competitors—locally known as "bandits."

History. The Boston Marathon grew to such prominence from relatively humble roots. Inspired by the first modern Olympic marathon (at the 1896 Athens Games), the Boston Athletic Association sponsored a 25-mi (40-km) race along the dirt roads between Ashland and Boston. In the inaugural 1897 event, a New York lithographer named John McDermott outran a 15-man field to gain victory.

The race grew slowly and steadily. In 1924 race officials moved the starting line to Hopkinton in order to lengthen the course to the traditional marathon distance. Women officially were excluded from the event until 1972. Five years earlier, however, Kathrine Switzer—entered as K.V. Switzer—had gained fame when a race official tried unsuccessfully to force her off the course.

The rolling hills between Hopkinton and Boston have yielded a rich history of running legends. Bill Rodgers' four victories in the 1970s, for example, elevated Rodgers to folk-hero status and helped spur a nationwide jogging boom. Boston's most prolific champion, Clarence DeMar, won the race seven times over a 29-year span. But perhaps even more incredible is the lifetime performance of John A. Kelly, who ran his first Boston Marathon in 1928 at the age of 20. After running the 1992 event, an 84-year-old Kelly drew the curtains on a Boston Marathon career that included two victories, 18 top-ten placings, and a mind-boggling 58 finishes. In a fitting tribute to two enduring legends, John Kelly served as the grand marshal of the marathon's 100th running.

PETER A. FLAX

With a courageous come-from-behind effort at the 1996 Boston Marathon—the 100th running of the race—Uta Pippig (right) *of Germany became the first woman to win the storied event for three consecutive years.*

SPORTS SUMMARIES[1]

ARCHERY—World Champions: men: barebow: Rensco Van Wees, Netherlands; compound bow: Jeff Button, Cottage Grove, WI; women: barebow: Odile Boussière, France; compound bow: Petra Ericsson, Sweden.

BADMINTON—U.S. Champions: men's singles: Steve Butler, Miller Place, NY; women's singles: Tang Yeping, Gaithersburg, MD.

BIATHLON—World Champions: men's 10K: Vladimir Dratshev, Russia; men's 20k: Sergei Tarasov, Russia; women's 7.5k: Olga Romasko, Russia; women's 15k: Emmanuelle Claret, France.

BOBSLEDDING—World Champions: 2-man: Christoph Langen and Olaf Hampel, Germany; 4-man: Christoph Langen.

BOWLING—Professional Bowlers Association Tour: BPAA U.S. Open: Dave Husted, Milwaukie, OR; Tournament of Champions: Dave D'Entremont, Middleburg Heights, OH; PBA National Championship: Butch Soper, Lake Havasu City, AZ; **Ladies Professional Bowlers Tour**: BPAA U.S. Open: Liz Johnson, Niagara Falls, NY; Sam's Town Invitational: Carol Gianotti-Block, Australia.

CANOEING—U.S. Champions: men: 500m kayak: Mike Herbert, Rogers, AR; 1,000m kayak: Mike Herbert; 500m canoe: Jim Terrell, Milford, OH; 1,000m canoe: Jim Terrell; women: 500m kayak: Alexandra Harbold, Rockaway Beach, NY.

CASTING—World Champions: men's all-around: Steve Rajeff, Woodland, WA; women's all-around: Alice Gillibert, Oakland.

CHESS—Professional Chess Association: Gary Kasparov, Russia.

CRICKET—World Cup: Sri Lanka.

CROSS-COUNTRY—World Champions: men: Paul Tergat, Kenya; women: Gete Wami, Ethiopia; **U.S. Champions:** men: Reuben Reina, Fayetteville, AR; women: Lynn Jennings, Newmarket, NH; **NCAA Division I:** men: Stanford; women: Stanford.

CURLING—World Champions: men: Jeff Stoughton, Canada; women: Marilyn Bodogh, Canada.

CYCLING—World Champions: men's pro road: Johan Museeuw, Belgium; men's sprint: Florian Rousseau, France; men's time trial: Alex Zülle, Switzerland; men's pursuit: Chris Boardman, Britain; women's pro road: Barbara Heeb, Switzerland; women's sprint: Felicia Ballenger, France; women's time trial: Jeannie Longo-Ciprelli, France; women's pursuit: Marion Clignet, France; **Tour de France:** men: Bjarne Riis, Denmark.

DOG SHOWS—Westminster: best in show: Ch. Clussexx Country Sunrise, clumber spaniel, owned by Richard and Judith Zaleski, Sorrento, FL.

EQUESTRIAN—U.S. Champions: Dressage: Peron TSF, Michelle Gibson, Roswell, GA; Show Jumping (tie): Crown Royal Legato, Peter Leone, Greenwich, CT, and Caras J., Tim Grubb, Bridgehampton, NY.

FENCING—U.S. Champions: men's foil: Nick Bravin, New York, NY; men's saber: Adam Skarbonkiewicz, Portland, OR; men's épée: Ben Atkins, New York, NY; women's foil: Felicia Zimmermann, Rochester, NY; women's épée: Leslie Marx, Pittsford, NY.

FIELD HOCKEY—NCAA Division I: North Carolina.

GYMNASTICS—World Champions: men's floor exercise: Vitaly Scherbo, Belarus; men's parallel bars: Rustam Sharipov, Ukraine; men's still rings: Yuri Chechi, Italy; men's vault: Aleksei Nemov, Russia; men's pommel horse: Gil Su Pae, North Korea; men's horizontal bar: Jesus Carballo, Spain; women's floor exercise (tie): Gina Gogean, Romania, and Yuan-Yuan Kui, China; women's uneven bars (tie): Svetlana Chorkina, Russia, and Yelena Piskun, Belarus; women's balance beam: Dina Kochetkova, Russia; women's vault: Gina Gogean, Romania.

HANDBALL—U.S. Handball Association: men's one-wall: Eddie Maisonet, New York, NY; men's three-wall: Vincent Munoz, Commerce, CA; men's four-wall: David Chapman, Long Beach, CA; women's one-wall: Karen McConney, New York, NY; women's three-wall: Anna Engele, St. Paul, MN; women's four-wall: Anna Engele.

HORSESHOE PITCHING—World Champions: men: Alan Francis, Defiance, OR; women: Beverly Nathe, St. Stephen, MN.

JUDO—U.S. Champions: men's heavyweight: Damon Keeve, San Francisco, CA; women's heavyweight: Colleen Rosensteel, Colorado Springs, CO.

LACROSSE—NCAA Division I: men: Princeton; women: Maryland.

LUGE—U.S. Champions: open men: Robert Pipkins, Bloomfield, NJ; junior men: Adam Heidt, Lake Placid, NY; open women: Cammy Myler, Lake Placid, NY; junior women: Maryann Baribault, La Canada, CA; **World Champions:** open men: Markus Prock, Austria; junior men: Markus Kleinheinz, Austria; open women: Jana Bode, Germany; junior women: Maryann Baribault.

MODERN PENTATHLON—U.S. Champions: men: James Gregory, Killeen, TX; women: Jessica Lisagor, San Antonio.

PADDLE TENNIS—U.S. Champions: men's singles: Scott Freedman, Venice, CA; men's doubles: Sol Hauptman, Los Angeles, CA, and Scott Freedman; women's doubles: Ingrid Fields, Culver City, CA, and Jamie Murphy, Rolling Hills Estates, CA.

PLATFORM TENNIS—U.S. Champions: men's singles: Scott Staniar, Greenwich, CT; men's doubles: Scott Mansager, Rochester Hills, MI, and Flip Goodspeed, Grand Rapids, MI; women's doubles: Robin Fulton, Stamford, CT, and Diane Tucker, Bedford, NY.

POLO—U.S. Open: Outback Steak House, Tampa, FL; **U.S. Gold Cup:** White Birch, Greenwich, CT; **World Cup:** Isla Carroll, Atlanta, GA; **Argentina Open:** Marlboro, Argentina.

RACQUETBALL—U.S. Champions: men's pro: Ruben Gonzalez, New York, NY; women's pro: Michelle Gould, Boise, ID.

RODEO—World Champion: men's all-around: Joe Beaver, Huntsville, TX.

ROWING—World Champions: men's eights: Germany; women's coxless fours: United States; **U.S. Collegiate Champions:** men: Princeton; women: Brown.

RUGBY—U.S. Champions: men's club: Old Mission Beach, San Diego, CA; women's club: Beantown, Boston, MA.

SHOOTING—U.S. Champions: men's trap: Brian Ballard, Bennington, NE; men's skeet: Joe Buffa, Flushing, MI; women's trap: Joetta Novinski, Renton, WA; women's skeet: Colleen Rumore, Glastonbury, CT.

SLED DOG RACING: Iditarod (Anchorage to Nome): Jeff King, Denali Park, AK.

SOFTBALL—U.S. Champions: men's fast pitch: All Car, Green Bay, WI; women's fast pitch: California Commotion, Woodland Hills, CA.

SURFING—World Champions: men: Kelly Slater, Cocoa Beach, FL; women: Lisa Andersen, Cocoa Beach, FL.

TRIATHLON—World Champions: men's ironman: Luc Van Lierde, Belgium; women's ironman: Paula Newby-Fraser, Zimbabwe.

VOLLEYBALL—U.S. Open Champions: men: POL-AM VBC, New York, NY; women: Pure Texas Nuts, Austin, TX; **NCAA Division I Champions:** men: UCLA; women: Stanford.

WATER POLO—U.S. Champions: men's outdoor: Harvard Water Polo Foundation; men's open: United States; women's outdoor: Sunset, Los Angeles, CA.

WEIGHT LIFTING—U.S. Champions: men: 54kg: Chad Ikea, Honolulu, HI; 59kg: LeGrand Sakamaki, Hilo, HI; 64kg: Thanh Nguyen, Pacifica, CA; 70kg: Tim McRae, Daytona Beach, FL; 76kg: David Santillo, Colorado Springs, CO; 83kg: Dean Goad, Sumner, WA; 91kg: Thomas Gough, Colorado Springs, CO; 99kg: Peter Kelley, St. Joseph, MO; 108kg: Robert Wentlejewski, Gilbert, AZ; 108kg-plus: Mark Henry, Sibley, TX; women: 44kg: Sibby Flowers, Alabaster, AL; 50kg: Tara Nott, Atlanta, GA; 54kg: Robin Goad, Sumner, WA; 59kg: Christina Wilson, Flagstaff, AZ; 64kg: Lea Rentmeester, Savannah, GA; 70kg: Kerri Hanebrink, Austin, TX; 76kg: Stacey Ketchum, Austin, TX; 83kg: Decia Stenzel, St. Paul, MN; 83kg-plus: Vikki Scaffe, Marietta, GA.

WRESTLING—U.S. Champions: men's freestyle: 105.5 lbs: Rob Eiter, Clarion, PA; 114.5 lbs: Lou Rosselli, Edinboro, PA; 125.5 lbs: Kendall Cross, Raleigh, NC; 136.5 lbs: Tom Brands, Iowa City, IA; 149.5 lbs: Towsend Saunders, Phoenix, AZ; 163 lbs: Kenny Monday, Phoenix, AZ; 180.5 lbs: Les Gutches, Corvalis, OR; 198 lbs: Melvin Douglas, Phoenix, AZ; 220 lbs: Kurt Angle, Pittsburgh, PA; 286 lbs: Bruce Baumgartner, Edinboro, PA.

[1]Sports for which articles do not appear in pages 467–499.

SRI LANKA

The bloodiest fighting in the history of Sri Lanka's 13-year-old ethnic conflict took place in 1996. Major military campaigns by the government alternated with well-executed raids by the Liberation Tigers of Tamil Eelam (LTTE). The People's Alliance government headed by President Chandrika Bandaranaike Kumaratunga continued its policy of combining military action with discussion of political concessions.

The Civil War. The government's military victory in December 1995—taking Jaffna and dispersing the LTTE forces from their headquarters—was answered January 31 by a suicide truck bomb that left 88 persons dead and 1,400 injured in downtown Colombo. In late March and early April the LTTE carried out several raids that left dozens of government soldiers dead. On April 4 a state of emergency was extended to the entire country. Two weeks later the army began a large-scale offensive to clear the entire Jaffna Peninsula; the operation appeared complete by May 16.

In July the LTTE launched a series of devastating attacks. In the east rebel fighters wiped out a platoon, killing 32; and in Jaffna a suicide bomber killed 26 and injured 60. On July 18 the military base at Mullaitivu in the northeast apparently was taken by surprise and 1,400 troops were killed or captured, in the government's worst defeat of the war. A week later, two bombs on a commuter train in a suburb of Colombo killed more than 70 and injured at least 400. A government offensive begun shortly afterward on Kilinochchi, the new LTTE headquarters, succeeded September 29 with the fall of the city at a reported cost of about 250 soldiers and 700 rebels killed.

Politics. A proposal to devolve power to a union of regions, which had been presented in August 1995, was announced in codified form in January 1996 by Justice and Constitutional Minister G. L. Peiris. In March it was presented to a parliamentary committee, which immediately became deadlocked. From the start, the plan met Buddhist resistance and seemed unlikely to win the necessary two-thirds vote in Parliament, followed by a popular referendum. President Kumaratunga's People's Alliance was 13 votes short and needed the support of other parties. The leading opposition party, the United National Party, remained silent on the plan. During the year the provisions for devolution were watered down considerably to meet Sinhala objections, thereby losing the lukewarm support it had received from moderate Tamil parties. After the LTTE was driven from the Jaffna Peninsula, government officials hoped that some support could be built up in the Tamil community, but such shifts did not appear to occur.

Under the state of emergency, press control was extensive. When Sri Lankan journalists finally were allowed back into Jaffna in May, they remained subjected to censorship. The army was accused by the Tigers of widespread human-rights abuses, some of which were confirmed by independent observers. Other security concerns also had political consequences. The appearance of Colombo was transformed by barbed wire, sandbags, and security checks. In the south there were signs of renewed activity by the Janatha Vimukthi Peramuna (JVP), a radical movement whose ideology mixes Sinhalese nationalism and Marxist orthodoxy.

Economy. The war caused serious economic deterioration. Very large arms orders placed during the year distorted the budget and drove up the cost of living. Foreign aid and private investment from overseas were put on hold for security reasons, as was the tourist trade.

Foreign Affairs. Sri Lanka continued to participate in the South Asian Association for Regional Cooperation (SAARC). Relations with India were complicated by the flight to that country of Tamil refugees from the fighting, with the encouragement of the LTTE. At least 150,000 people who fled the offensives in Jaffna and Kilinochchi were living in temporary camps and suffering from severe shortages of food and medical facilities. Also on the agenda for talks with India was the status of 160,000 stateless people of Indian origin living in plantation areas in the south of Sri Lanka.

LELAH DUSHKIN, *Kansas State University*

SRI LANKA • Information Highlights

Official Name: Democratic Socialist Republic of Sri Lanka.
Location: South Asia.
Area: 25,332 sq mi (65 610 km²).
Population (mid-1996 est.): 18,400,000.
Chief Cities (mid-1990 est.): Colombo, the capital, 615,000; Dehiwala–Mount Lavinia, 196,000; Moratuwa, 170,000.
Government: *Head of state,* C.B. Kumaratunga, president (took office November 1994). *Head of government,* S. Bandaranaike, prime minister (appointed November 1994). *Legislature* (unicameral)—Parliament.
Monetary Unit: Rupee (55.947 rupees equal U.S.$1, August 1996).
Gross Domestic Product (1994 est. U.S.$): $57,600,000,-000 (purchasing power parity).
Economic Index (Colombo, 1995; 1990 = 100): *Consumer Prices,* all items, 163.1; food, 162.1.
Foreign Trade (1995 U.S.$): *Imports,* $5,192,000,000; *exports,* $3,798,000,000.

STAMPS AND STAMP COLLECTING

Athletes and animals topped the list of subjects for stamps in 1996. Many countries issued stamps to mark the 100th anniversary of the modern Olympic Games, as well as the 1996 Summer Games, held in Atlanta, GA. Meanwhile, concern about endangered animals prompted dozens of new stamps on environmental and wildlife themes.

Among the 124 new issues from the United States Postal Service (USPS) was a pane of twenty 32-cent stamps for the Atlanta Games, depicting events that ranged from basketball to wrestling. The USPS also released a single 32-cent stamp showing a statue of an ancient Greek discus thrower, honoring the Olympic anniversary. Several other countries marked the anniversary with stamps depicting modern athletes alongside athletes from the past—from ancient Greece, or from the first modern Olympics in 1896. Canadian stamps saluted five of the nation's past gold medalists. Australian stamps honored the 1996 Games and those of the year 2000, to be held in Sydney.

The USPS highlighted endangered wildlife with a sheet of 32-cent stamps depicting 15 species, from the California condor to the Florida manatee. Birds such as the blue jay and the redheaded woodpecker were featured on other U.S. stamps of various denominations. And extinct prehistoric animals, such as the mastodon and fierce saber-toothed tiger, appeared on four 32-cent stamps.

Canada began a three-year series on native birds. Mexico issued a pane of 24 stamps that together depicted the full range of its endangered wildlife, while Britain released a group of five stamps showing birds that live in wetland habitats. A German semipostal issue, issued to promote conservation, showed tropical animals.

Courtesy, U.S. Postal Service

Several other notable stamps were inspired by the silver screen. Fifties film idol James Dean appeared on a 32-cent stamp in the USPS Legends of Hollywood group. Dominica honored fictional film detectives with a sheet of $1 stamps. The nine sleuths ranged from Sam Spade (actor Humphrey Bogart) to Dick Tracy (Warren Beatty).

One of the most colorful offerings from the USPS was a 32-cent stamp showing Georgia O'Keeffe's spectacular painting "Red Poppy." Keith Birdsong, a Cherokee/Creek artist, designed a sheet of 32-cent stamps depicting five Native American dances. Another group of four U.S. stamps featured fictional American folk heroes.

Canada's 1996 Canada Day issue, a 45-cent self-adhesive, was based on a handcrafted patchwork quilt with a maple-leaf design. Canada also drew attention to the disease AIDS with a 45-cent stamp, and it completed its four-year series on historic land vehicles with seven stamps. Finally, a Finnish booklet of 12 stamps added a twist to the popular concept of greeting stamps—stamps that send a message. Each stamp in the booklet showed a different letter, allowing people to spell out their own greetings.

ELAINE PASCOE, *Freelance Writer*

SELECTED U.S. STAMPS FOR 1996

Subject	Denomination	Date
Utah Statehood	32¢	Jan. 4
Winter Garden Flowers	32¢	Jan. 19
Dr. Ernest E. Just	32¢	Feb. 1
Smithsonian Institution	32¢	Feb. 7
Year of the Rat	32¢	Feb. 8
Pioneers of Communication	32¢	Feb. 22
Fulbright Scholarships	32¢	Feb. 28
Marathon	32¢	April 11
Olympic Games	32¢	May 2
Georgia O'Keeffe	32¢	May 23
Tennessee Statehood	32¢	May 31
American Indian Dances	32¢	June 7
Prehistoric Animals	32¢	June 8
Breast-Cancer Awareness	32¢	June 15
James Dean	32¢	June 24
Folk Heroes	32¢	July 11
Iowa Statehood	32¢	Aug. 1
Rural Free Delivery	32¢	Aug. 7
Riverboats	32¢	Aug. 22
Big-Band Leaders	32¢	Sept. 11
Songwriters	32¢	Sept. 11
F. Scott Fitzgerald	23¢	Sept. 27
Endangered Species	32¢	Oct. 2
Computer Technology	32¢	Oct. 8

States, U.S.

During 1996, U.S. states were engrossed in presidential primaries, political conventions, and finally in the November general election. As it turned out, the election did not change much, since—for the most part—the status quo prevailed. Republicans kept both houses of Congress, while a Democratic president remained in the White House. Among the 11 state governors' races, only two saw a change in party, as West Virginia elected a Republican and New Hampshire, a Democrat. There was a record number of initiatives on the ballots, however, totaling 90—a number that tied the previous record, set in 1914. The most frequent topics addressed were term limits, hunting, the environment, taxes, and legalized gambling.

Meanwhile, it was a good year economically in most of the states. In November the national unemployment rate was 5.4%, but in some states the rate during the year was less than 3%.

Other newsworthy events involved the weather and natural disasters, tragic airline crashes, and both revitalization and fiscal and social upheaval in some major cities.

ALABAMA. In a state with a long history of racial tensions and long recognized as a focal point of the civil-rights movement, 1996 saw new chapters being written on famous—and infamous—events that occurred during the volatile 1960s.

When 77-year-old former governor and segregationist George Wallace apologized to Vivian Malone Jones, he demonstrated how far he had come toward the goals of tolerance and equality. Speaking of the black woman he tried to keep out of the University of Alabama with his "stand in the schoolhouse door" protest of June 1963, the state's former chief executive declared, "Vivian Malone Jones was at the center of the fight over states' rights and conducted herself with grace, strength, and, above all, courage. She deserves to be rewarded for her actions in that air of uncertainty." The apology was issued along with an award—named in honor of Wallace's wife—given to acknowledge women who have made major improvements in the state.

Also in 1996, the U.S. Congress designated the 54-mi (86-km) route of Dr. Martin Luther King's Selma-to-Montgomery march as a national historic trail. The march, which catapulted King to the forefront of the civil-rights movement, took place in March 1965, but only after President Lyndon Johnson mobilized the National Guard and ordered U.S. troops to protect the participants.

Elections and the Economy. The big election news in Alabama was the race to succeed retiring Democratic U.S. Sen. Howell Heflin. The race was won by Republican Jeff B. Sessions, who, interestingly, had been nominated in 1986 to a federal judgeship by President Ronald Reagan, only to have his nomination denied by the Senate Judiciary Committee, with Heflin voting against him. Republicans also picked up two additional U.S. House

The United States experienced a high number of western wildfires in 1996; some 6 million acres (2.4 million ha) had burned by late October. More than 8,400 acres (3 400 ha) were destroyed in California's Lamb Canyon, near Jacinto, below, *in August.*

seats, giving Republicans in the Alabama House delegation a 5–2 majority.

Alabama residents had good news on the economic front in 1996. Unemployment dropped two full percentage points—to 4.5%—marking the largest drop in the nation and also the lowest unemployment rate the state had seen since tracking began in 1978. Also, Alabamans learned that they enjoy the status of having the earliest "tax freedom day" in the country, with the average taxpayer's burden of federal, state, and local taxes fulfilled by April 23. B. J.

ALASKA. Oil production, medical experiments, and an active volcano were among the top news stories in Alaska in 1996.

Oil, Medical Experiment. BP Exploration Alaska, Inc., a subsidiary of British Petroleum, announced that it was increasing by $1 billion the amount of investment funds devoted to North Slope oil production. The Prudhoe Bay output had dropped to about 830,000 barrels per day, down from 1.5 million barrels in the late 1980s, and was forecast to drop even further. The injection of funds signified BP's commitment to enhanced recovery projects and the development of new oil fields in order to reverse the downward trend.

Alaska's residents each received more than $1,100 as their share in the state's oil wealth; an annual dividend actually was written into the state constitution.

The U.S. government admitted that it was wrong for conducting medical experiments on unsuspecting Alaskans during the 1950s. The experiments, which involved administering radioactive iodine to determine whether the thyroid gland helps humans adjust to Arctic climates, were performed on 102 Alaska natives, many of them children whose parents were not consulted. The National Research Council claimed that no physical harm was done.

Election and Other News. Republican Ted Stevens easily won reelection to his fifth term in the U.S. Senate; his Democratic challenger, Theresa Obermeyer, did not help her own chances when she spent 30 days in federal custody after assaulting a security guard; with 10% of the vote, she received fewer votes than Jed Whittaker, the Green Party candidate, who took 13% of the vote. Voters approved a measure designed to promote congressional term limits and also chose to ban the hunting of wolves from airplanes.

Unemployment rose to 7.3%, the highest rate among the 50 states. A second consecutive near-record salmon harvest was blamed for plummeting prices and overflowing warehouses, a situation that has most fishing-industry watchers concerned.

In December the Pavlof Volcano, 590 mi (950 km) southwest of Anchorage, showed a marked increase in activity, sending ash 15,000 ft (4 572 m) into the air and prompting the Alaska Volcano Observatory to issue a red alert. The volcano has erupted 40 times since 1790, making it one of the most active on the Pacific rim. B. J.

ARIZONA. In the November 5 elections, all six of Arizona's U.S. House incumbents—five Republicans and one Democrat—were reelected. Arizonans also approved a ballot measure that legalizes medicinal use of marijuana, while requiring violent drug offenders to serve their full sentences and mandating drug treatment rather than prison for nonviolent offenders. Other approved ballot measures required violent criminals 15 or older to be tried as adults, expanded the state health-insurance system to cover more low-income residents, and instructed the governor to negotiate gambling compacts with Indian tribes. Arizona's February 27 presidential primary failed to attract the national attention that its supporters had promised, despite being the first in the western United States.

Republican Gov. Fife Symington refused to step down after he was indicted June 13 by a federal grand jury on 23 counts of fraud and extortion related to his business dealings before becoming governor. His trial was set for 1997. The governor also faced creditor lawsuits after he filed for personal bankruptcy. In November a TV station in Phoenix revealed that a state-prison inmate had stolen millions of dollars' worth of military equipment. The inmate was in a work program in which he was supposed to sell unwanted equipment and turn over the proceeds to the state.

Legislation. In its 1996 session, the legislature enacted a $200 million property-tax cut for home owners and businesses. Out of the total $4.8 billion budget, about $1.8 billion would go to education. The session provided $30 million to build and repair schools and $20 million for rapidly growing schools. The session provided $5.4 million for a program to counsel parents on how to head off child abuse, to teach parents to read, and to immunize children. The state would not recognize same-sex marriages. State judges now may impose life sentences for acts of terrorism when there is an aggravating factor. About 50,000 acres (20 234 ha) of state trust land was set aside for open-space use. A new law made it more difficult for cities to place moratoriums on new developments, as Scottsdale attempted to do in 1995.

The state funded a program to fingerprint all welfare applicants. Penalties were increased for cruelty to animals. The governor vetoed a bill aimed at limiting lobbyist gifts to state officials. The state established a water-banking authority, allowing it to store its unused allocation of Colorado River water in the Central Arizona Canal. The measure is seen as a way to keep other states from getting Arizona's share of Colorado River water. The legislature allowed Pima county to raise its local hotel tax from 1% to 2% to pay for a baseball stadium in Tucson. A federal district judge on September 14 stopped the state from implementing a 1996 law to require teens to get parental consent for abortions. E. S.

ARKANSAS. Although the reelection of native son Bill Clinton as U.S. president was no surprise to many residents of this small state, the 1996 election had many interesting twists and turns at the state level.

The state elected its first Republican U.S. senator since Reconstruction. Tim Hutchinson, who has been a U.S. representative since 1993, defeated Attorney General Winston Bryant by six percentage points in the heavily Democratic state. Political pundits attributed Hutchinson's victory to his superior political organization and debating skills. However, a gaffe by Bryant—who many thought was unbeatable—also contributed to the GOP win. When Bryant was chief prosecutor, his office failed to file an appeal in the case of two suspects who had confessed to a murder in Fort Smith, and the two suspects were released and could not be tried. Hutchinson exploited this issue. The 1996 voting put two brothers in federal office: Hutchinson and his brother, Asa, who was elected to Tim Hutchinson's former seat in the U.S. House.

The national debate over the Whitewater controversy filtered down into state politics in 1996. Gov. Jim Guy Tucker, a Democrat, had said he would resign after he

Editor's Note. The initials of the contributors of the state articles follow each entry: L.B., Lane Beauchamp; M.L.C., Mary Lou Cooper; S.F., Saundra France; B.J., Bruce Jacoby; C.S., Christopher Schwarz; E.S., Elaine Stuart. Their affiliations are listed on pages 591–94.

THE U.S. STATES

	Population* (in millions)	Area (sq mi)	Area (km²)	Capital	Governor
Alabama	4.3	52,423	135 776	Montgomery	Fob James, Jr. (R)
Alaska	.6	656,424	1 700 138	Juneau	Tony Knowles (D)
Arizona	4.4	114,006	295 276	Phoenix	J. Fife Symington III (R)
Arkansas	2.5	53,182	137 741	Little Rock	Mike Huckabee (D)[1]
California	31.8	163,707	424 001	Sacramento	Pete Wilson (R)
Colorado	3.8	104,100	269 619	Denver	Roy Romer (D)
Connecticut	3.3	5,544	1 359	Hartford	John Rowland (R)
Delaware	.7	2,489	6 447	Dover	Tom Carper (D)
Florida	14.4	65,758	170 313	Tallahassee	Lawton Chiles (D)
Georgia	7.4	59,441	153 952	Atlanta	Zell Miller (D)
Hawaii	1.2	10,932	28 314	Honolulu	Benjamin J. Cayetano (D)
Idaho	1.2	83,574	216 457	Boise	Philip Batt (R)
Illinois	11.8	57,918	150 008	Springfield	Jim Edgar (R)
Indiana	5.8	36,420	94 328	Indianapolis	Evan Bayh (D)
Iowa	2.9	56,276	145 755	Des Moines	Terry E. Branstad (R)
Kansas	2.6	82,282	213 110	Topeka	Bill Graves (R)
Kentucky	3.9	40,411	104 664	Frankfort	Paul Patton (D)
Louisiana	4.4	51,843	134 273	Baton Rouge	Mike Foster (D)
Maine	1.2	35,387	91 652	Augusta	Angus King, Jr. (I)
Maryland	5.1	12,407	32 134	Annapolis	Parris N. Glendening (D)
Massachusetts	6.1	10,555	27 337	Boston	William F. Weld (R)
Michigan	9.6	96,705	250 466	Lansing	John Engler (R)
Minnesota	4.7	86,943	225 182	St. Paul	Arne Carlson (R)
Mississippi	2.7	48,434	125 444	Jackson	Kirk Fordice (R)
Missouri	5.4	69,709	180 546	Jefferson City	Mel Carnahan (D)
Montana	.9	147,046	380 849	Helena	Marc Racicot (R)
Nebraska	1.7	77,358	200 357	Lincoln	E. Benjamin Nelson (D)
Nevada	1.6	110,567	286 369	Carson City	Bob Miller (D)
New Hampshire	1.2	9,351	24 219	Concord	Stephen Merrill (R)
New Jersey	8.0	8,722	22 590	Trenton	Christine Todd Whitman (R)
New Mexico	1.7	121,598	314 939	Santa Fe	Gary Johnson (R)
New York	18.2	54,556	141 300	Albany	George Pataki (R)
North Carolina	7.3	53,821	139 396	Raleigh	James B. Hunt, Jr. (D)
North Dakota	.6	70,704	183 123	Bismarck	Edward Schafer (R)
Ohio	11.2	44,828	116 105	Columbus	George V. Voinovich (R)
Oklahoma	3.3	69,903	181 049	Oklahoma City	Frank Keating (R)
Oregon	3.2	98,386	254 820	Salem	John Kitzhaber (D)
Pennsylvania	12.1	46,058	119 290	Harrisburg	Tom Ridge (R)
Rhode Island	1.0	1,545	4 002	Providence	Lincoln Almond (R)
South Carolina	3.7	32,008	82 901	Columbia	David Beasley (R)
South Dakota	.7	77,121	199 743	Pierre	William Janklow (R)
Tennessee	5.3	42,146	109 158	Nashville	Don Sundquist (R)
Texas	19.1	268,601	695 677	Austin	George W. Bush (R)
Utah	2.0	84,904	219 901	Salt Lake City	Michael O. Leavitt (R)
Vermont	.6	9,615	24,903	Montpelier	Howard Dean (D)
Virginia	6.7	42,777	110 792	Richmond	George F. Allen (R)
Washington	5.5	71,302	184 672	Olympia	Mike Lowry (D)
West Virginia	1.8	24,231	62 758	Charleston	Gaston Caperton (D)
Wisconsin	5.2	65,499	169 642	Madison	Tommy G. Thompson (R)
Wyoming	.5	97,818	253 349	Cheyenne	Jim Geringer (R)

*July 1, 1996 estimate

[1]Appointed July 15, 1996, to replace Gov. Jim Guy Tucker.

was convicted on fraud charges in May stemming from the Whitewater case. Tucker's resignation would make Lt. Gov. Mike Huckabee the state's first Republican governor since the early 1980s. After Tucker's conviction, he refused to resign, saying his conviction had been tainted. He said he would step down temporarily during his appeal. Tucker changed his mind, resigning in July after the legislature threatened to begin impeachment charges against him and the attorney general said he would sue to have him removed from office.

Tornado. On April 21 a large twister touched down in Fort Smith, the state's second-largest city, and cut a large swath through the town's historic district. Though only four people were killed, the tornado caused nearly $500 million in damage, left 1,000 people homeless, and destroyed about 200 businesses. C. S.

CALIFORNIA. Control of the California state Assembly shaped up as the biggest plum of the 1996 election season. Democrats retook the Assembly, which they had lost in 1994 elections, and selected Cruz Bustamante of Fresno to become their next speaker. Bustamante was the first Latino speaker in California history. Democrats kept control of the state Senate. Gov. Pete Wilson was not up for reelection. State legislative term limits kicked in for the first time in 1996, with almost 30% of the Assembly and

25% of the Senate forced to leave their elected posts. Democrats won 29 U.S. House seats and Republicans captured 23.

Of the 15 statewide ballot issues faced by California voters, Proposition 209—to eliminate state and local affirmative-action programs in employment, education, and contracting—garnered national publicity. The measure won hands down, and opponents went to court immediately to block implementation, while student protests broke out on several California campuses. Voters also approved a $995 million bond issue to clean up the San Francisco Bay/Sacramento–San Joaquin Delta estuary. An increased minimum wage, limits on campaign contributions, and the use of marijuana to relieve pain won voters' support, as did a proposal to require a majority of property owners, not just voters, to approve all new fees. Voters rejected a proposition to make it easier for shareholders to sue for securities fraud involving retirement savings, and they also said "no" to stiff regulations of managed health care and to higher income taxes for California's wealthiest individuals.

Legislation. Lawmakers set aside $1 billion to reduce the size of public-school classes, to deregulate electric utilities, and to make it easier for home owners to buy earthquake insurance. Chemical castration of repeat child molesters was adopted, and a $279 million tax cut was approved for high-tech industries, multinational corporations, aerospace manufacturers, and start-up companies grossing less than $1 million.

Other News. A federal judge ruled that the new federal welfare-reform law allows California to deny prenatal care to pregnant women who immigrate illegally. In southern California a civil wrongful-death suit opened against O.J. Simpson. Simpson was acquitted in 1995 of murdering his former wife and her friend.

Pacific Gas and Electric's chief economist, Tappan Munroe, reported that after the 1990s recession, when California lost 500,000 jobs, the state's economy experienced massive restructuring from defense and aerospace into computers, software, and entertainment. Munroe said that Hollywood makes 80% of the world's movies and is home to 57% of the nation's multimedia firms and half the U.S. biotechnology jobs. While employment and personal income grew faster than California's population, the state's economic health was not geographically uniform. The Federal Reserve noted that unemployment in southern California was 7%, while northern California's unemployment rate was just 4.6%. After 18 months of bankruptcy, Orange county in June sold $880 million in securities and was to use the proceeds to repay its creditors and county employees.

M. L. C.

COLORADO. Colorado made national news in the realm of gay rights when the U.S. Supreme Court struck down the state's banning of laws that protect gays from discrimination. The state made national news in the realm of sports, too, as the Colorado Avalanche won the 1996 Stanley Cup. The Christmastime murder in Boulder of JonBenet Ramsey, a 6-year-old who had participated in various children's beauty pageants, also made national headlines.

Politics. A bevy of ballot issues were acted on in the Rocky Mountain State in 1996. Among those that passed were a ban on certain types of hunting, a congressional term-limits initiative, and a cap on campaign contributions in state and local elections. Among those defeated were a gambling proposition and a measure to impose taxes on certain properties used for religious purposes. Another issue that voters rejected was a controversial state constitutional amendment that would have given parents ultimate rights in matters of education and discipline of their children. Proponents of the amendment, sponsored by a conservative Christian organization, said it would protect families and act as a buffer against government interference. Opponents claimed it would hamper investigations of alleged child abuse and also would make it harder to devise school curriculums.

B. J.

CONNECTICUT. In the November 5 election balloting, Democrats regained the majority control of the Connecticut Senate that they had lost in 1994. The Senate now would be composed of 19 Democrats and 17 Republicans. Republican Gov. John Rowland would face a solidly Democratic legislature in 1997.

Connecticut's 3.9%, $268 million reduction in personal-income, corporation-income, and hospital taxes was the second-largest tax cut in the nation in 1996, according to the National Conference of State Legislatures. The bulk of the tax cut was part of a multiyear measure first adopted in 1995, however. Connecticut's gas tax increased to 38 cents per gallon on October 1.

Budget and the Economy. Connecticut finished fiscal year 1996 with its largest budget surplus in a decade. Connecticut's improved fiscal situation was largely due to its improving economy. However, the state's employment-growth rate of 1.12% lagged slightly behind the national average of 1.9%. Aiding the state's economic growth was the Mohegan Sun Casino, opened by the Mohegan tribe in Montville in October. Foxwoods Resort Casino, run by the Mashantucket Pequots, was Connecticut's first casino. In the fall, Six Flags Theme Parks Inc. proposed a $200 million amusement park on 200 acres (81 ha) off Interstate 95 in North Stonington.

Education and Legislation. Thousands of volunteers wired public schools for Internet connections in the fall. The Connecticut Supreme Court July 9 ordered the state to desegregate Hartford public schools, which are 95% nonwhite.

In its 1996 legislative session, Connecticut eliminated its general cash-assistance program for people able to work. As a result of other new legislation, the state would allow nonsectarian charter schools beginning July 1, 1997, and the schools would receive state aid but would be free of many rules and regulations; child support would be easier to collect; and biotechnology companies would receive a tax break. Property-tax and corporate-tax breaks would be given to service firms in enterprise zones, which are poor areas targeted for development by the state. Banks, insurers, and investment companies could escape sales and corporate taxes and state regulations by locating in a section of Hartford designated as an export zone. A new law phased out coin-operated cigarette-vending machines available to minors and increased fines for selling cigarettes to minors. Another law required 16- and 17-year-olds to be accompanied by an adult when learning to drive. Drivers under age 21 who misuse their licenses to obtain liquor would receive a 90-day license suspension. A law aimed at preventing child abuse expanded the grounds for terminating parental rights. A tighter domestic-violence law allowed longer court orders to protect family members. Insurers must offer mothers and newborns at least 48-hour hospital care following delivery and must cover applicants who have been cancer-free for five years after suffering from breast cancer. Housing assistance would be given to local and state police officers to live in certain areas.

E. S.

DELAWARE. The big story in Delaware in 1996 was the arrest in November of two 18-year-old college students for allegedly murdering their newborn infant.

Criminal News. According to charges, Brian Peterson, Jr., and Amy Grossberg checked into a Newark, DE, motel, where the baby was born and then killed. The body was found in the motel's trash bin, and autopsy

© Oscar Sosa/AP/Wide World Photos

Residents of Jacksonville, FL, went wild as their Jaguars—an expansion team in its second season in the National Football League—advanced to the American Football Conference championship game. Although the game was played in Foxboro, MA, more than 10,000 Jaguars fans watched their club go down to defeat on a giant screen at Jacksonville Municipal Stadium.

reports indicated that it was born healthy, then died of a skull fracture and brain injuries. It was not determined whether the injuries occurred before or after the baby was thrown in the dumpster. Peterson and Grossberg, both children of wealthy New Jersey families, were charged with first-degree murder and could face the death penalty.

In January 40-year-old convicted murderer Billy Bailey was executed. The event became more newsworthy because Bailey chose hanging as the method of his execution. It was the first use of the gallows in Delaware since 1946 and only the third in the nation since the death penalty was reinstated in 1976. Bailey had been convicted of murdering an elderly couple in 1979. Although Delaware offers condemned prisoners their choice of death by hanging or lethal injection, state officials prefer the latter method, conceding they are out of practice with the former.

Elections. Incumbents had an easy time in Delaware. President Bill Clinton carried the state without any local campaigning; Gov. Thomas Carper and Sen. Joseph Biden, both Democrats, were reelected in landslides, as was the state's lone congressional representative, Michael Castle, a Republican. Even the party breakdown in the state House and Senate remained the same, with Republicans holding onto the House and Democrats keeping control of the Senate. B. J.

FLORIDA. In the November general election, all of Florida's 15 Republican and five Democratic U.S. House incumbents were reelected, and Democrats won the three open House seats being vacated by retiring members. President Bill Clinton won the state's 25 electoral votes, but garnered less than a majority (48%) of the vote in the three-way presidential race. In addition, for the first time in the 20th century, there would be a GOP majority (61–59) in the Florida House. In ballot initiatives, voters passed a constitutional amendment requiring that any new state taxes be approved by a two-thirds majority of the popular vote.

The Everglades. Voters rejected a tax on sugar grown in the Everglades, but passed two other propositions relating to protection and cleanup of the Everglades. In other news relating to the Everglades, President Clinton in April had signed legislation that would provide $200 million to purchase and protect sensitive Everglades land. (An additional $100 million was provided for protection of other Florida land.) A second piece of legislation, signed in October, provided $75 million to restore and protect the Everglades. Disaster struck the area in May when a ValuJet airliner crashed in the Everglades, killing 110 people.

Native Americans and Urban Affairs. In a U.S. Supreme Court ruling upholding states' rights, the Seminole Indian tribe lost its case against the state of Florida, filed after talks had broken down regarding the establishment of a casino on tribal land. The court indicated that the disputed portion of the 1988 Indian Gaming Regulatory Act violated states' sovereignty rights granted under the U.S. Constitution's 11th Amendment.

Two major Florida cities experienced difficulties in 1996. Following the death in June of Miami Mayor Stephen Clark, Cuban-born Joe Carollo was elected mayor in July. In September a budget crisis involving a $68 million shortfall was discovered after three officials resigned in a corruption scandal. In December, Gov. Lawton Chiles declared a fiscal emergency in Miami. In St. Petersburg rioting erupted in October following the fatal shooting of a black motorist by a white police officer. The apparently speeding motorist was stopped by the police and was shot when he refused to get out of his car. A grand jury in November cleared the officer, provoking further disturbances in the city. S. F.

GEORGIA. Atlanta hosted the 26th Summer Olympic Games in July, an event that attracted visitors and participants from around the world. During the Games, the state helped respond to a bomb blast in Olympic Park that killed one person.

Elections. On November 5, Democrat Max Cleland won the U.S. Senate seat vacated by retiring Democrat Sam Nunn, despite Republican presidential candidate Bob Dole outpolling President Bill Clinton. All U.S. House incumbents were reelected, including two black representatives who won reelection after their districts were redrawn at the direction of the U.S. Supreme Court. The court had ruled their districts could not be drawn on the basis of race. As a result, these districts were redrawn so that they were predominantly white rather than black.

Legislation. In its 1996 session, the Georgia state legislature approved a law doing away with merit-system job protections for state employees hired after July 1, 1996.

The law did not eliminate the merit system for the state's existing 64,000 employees. The $11.3 billion state budget cut social services and Medicaid, but increased spending on education. The 4% state sales tax on food was to be phased out in 1998. A 3% tax on car rentals in Atlanta was to fund improvements for the Atlanta Hawks basketball arena. The state raised the speed limit to 70 mph (113 km/hr) on rural interstates and required drivers to wear seat belts and place children in safety seats.

State corrections officials were authorized to hire private firms to build and operate prisons. Insurers must provide minimum two-day hospital coverage for normal childbirths. Employees enrolled in health-maintenance organizations (HMOs) may pick doctors outside their networks for an extra fee, and HMOs must tell patients what they do and do not cover before the patients sign up. Women in HMOs may get access to obstetric and gynecologic care without getting a referral from another doctor.

Deadbeat parents who do not pay child support may lose their professional and driver's licenses. The state now would recognize only marriages between a man and a woman and no longer would recognize common-law marriages. Teens must show proof of age when purchasing cigarettes. Telemarketers who defrauded the elderly would be subject to greater penalties.

Kindergarten funding was boosted so that no preschooler would be turned away. Teachers would receive pay increases averaging 6%. English became the state's official language. A new law, which applied to the Internet, made it a misdemeanor for anyone to transmit data that falsely identified the sender of the data. E. S.

HAWAII. The presidential-election results in Hawaii came as a surprise to no one: President Bill Clinton carried the state with 57% of the vote to 32% for Bob Dole. Clinton had been considered the overwhelming favorite; neither candidate campaigned in the state; and no polls were conducted by local newspapers. One of the two congressional races proved more lively, however, with Democratic incumbent Neil Abercrombie winning a narrow victory over Republican rival Orson Swindle. The race, considered one of the nastiest in state history, resorted to name-calling at one point. The other congressional seat was kept by incumbent Democrat Patsy Mink.

A sovereignty movement was gaining momentum, seeking redress for the illegal overthrow of the monarchy in 1893. Although the U.S. Congress in 1988 had apologized for the event, publicity surrounding the centennial of the event sparked a grassroots movement. A plebiscite in the summer was sponsored by the state, and by a margin of three to one, descendants of the original Polynesian denizens voted in favor of a resolution that would take the next step toward some form of native government. That next step called for a constitutional convention in 1998 to decide exactly what kind of government was wanted.

Economy. The unemployment rate in Hawaii fell slightly—from 6.1% to 6.0%. But what was once the state's biggest industry suffered another blow as the last sugarcane plantations on the islands of Oahu and Hawaii closed to make room for other cash crops. The closure left only four sugar producers active in the state: two on Maui and two on Kauai.

Same-Sex Marriages. The big story of the year occurred in December, when a circuit-court judge in Honolulu ruled that lawyers for the state had failed to show any compelling reason for a ban on gay and lesbian unions, and declared the ban unconstitutional. The ruling paved the way for the legalization of same-sex marriages, although the state was expected to appeal the decision. There were national repercussions to the ruling even before it was handed down. Just the prospect prompted the U.S. Congress to pass the Defense of Marriage Act, which President Clinton signed into law in September. The act declared that individual states were not required to recognize gay marriages performed elsewhere; it also allowed states to withhold federal tax, pension, health, and other benefits from homosexual partners. B. J.

IDAHO. Two disasters—one natural, the other not—made news in Idaho in 1996. In February floods ravaged parts of the state. The towns of St. Maries, Cataldo, and Orofino were described as "devastated," "underwater," and "cut in half," respectively. Gov. Phil Batt requested that President Bill Clinton declare the region a federal disaster area, with damages estimated at more than $100 million. The man-made disaster occurred in January, when a corporate plane carrying four Coca-Cola executives and four other people crashed and burned in a canyon during a flight from Salt Lake City, UT, to Pocatello, ID. There were no survivors.

Election and Other News. A November referendum approved a deal with the federal government that allowed nuclear waste to be stored in the state, provided it be cleaned up by the year 2035. Another ballot issue rejected limits on bear hunting, while a third gave support to a move toward enacting congressional term limits. As expected, Republicans won big in Idaho, with presidential candidate Bob Dole carrying 52% of the vote and Sen. Larry Craig being reelected easily. Both U.S. House seats, too, were won by the Republican incumbents—Helen Chenoweth and Michael Crapo.

Governor Batt called upon the legislature to provide migrant farm laborers with a workers'-compensation package. The request had the support of the Cattleman's Association as well as other businesses. Leaders in both houses of the state legislature vowed to consider any and all proposals. B. J.

ILLINOIS. While the Democratic National Convention in Chicago may have captured the most attention in Illinois in 1996, the lifesaving efforts of a zoo gorilla captured hearts all around the state—and the nation.

Headlines. In August, Binti Jua, a 160-lb (72.6-kg) western lowland gorilla housed at a suburban Chicago zoo, protectively cradled a 3-year-old boy who had fallen 18 ft (5 m) into her gorilla pit. Binti Jua, with her own baby on her back, carried the boy to a door for keepers to rescue him. The boy later was released from the hospital. A few days later, Democrats from around the country returned to Chicago for their national convention for the first time since the tumultuous, riot-filled convention of 1968.

In the November elections, state Democrats narrowly regained control of the Illinois House of Representatives, although Republicans retained the state Senate. Democratic Rep. Richard J. Durbin won the U.S. Senate seat vacated by the retiring Paul Simon.

Other Stories. Archer Daniels Midland Co. in Decatur pleaded guilty to federal price-fixing charges and was fined $100 million....In November, 14 people died when a United Express flight and a private plane collided on the ground at an airport near Quincy....The federal government pursued charges against Mitsubishi Motor Manufacturing of America Inc., based in Normal, for allegedly ignoring sexual-harassment claims.

In November the death of Chicago Cardinal Joseph Bernardin, 68, affected much of the state. Bernardin, the nation's highly respected and most senior Roman Catholic clergyman, died of pancreatic cancer. L. B.

INDIANA. The Hoosier state elected its first African-American to Congress in 1996 as Julia Carson, a Democrat from Indianapolis, won a seat in the U.S. House of

Representatives by 7 percentage points in the November elections. A former dress-shop owner and human-resources manager, Carson made her political mark after being elected Center Township trustee in 1991. She worked to revamp the welfare assistance distributed by the township. Carson returned the nearly bankrupt system to solvency, largely by putting aid recipients to work. Carson would take the seat that was held by Andrew Jacobs, Jr., her former boss and political backer. But observers did not expect her to be a Jacobs clone. She is far more liberal than he and comes from a very different background.

Indiana voters also elected a new governor, as Frank O'Bannon, the Democratic lieutenant governor, defeated Stephen Goldsmith, the highly regarded Republican mayor of Indianapolis. Goldsmith was best known for turning over city services to private companies.

Economy and Weather. It was a very good year for the state economically. Two major industrial plants announced that they would build factories in the southwestern part of the state. Toyota Motor Corp. announced it would build a truck plant in Gibson county near Evansville. The plant was viewed widely as one of the plum economic development projects in the nation. And AK Steel announced it would build a finishing plant in Spencer county.

The state experienced heavy snow in the winter of 1996 but averted any major climatological disasters. C. S.

IOWA. In a state dominated by Republican officeholders, two Democrats made news in this election year. The first was U.S. Sen. Tom Harkin, who became the first Iowa Democrat ever reelected to a third term. And in the race to fill the vacancy in the House of Representatives left by Harkin's opponent, Democratic State Sen. Leonard Boswell won a close battle to break the GOP's monopoly on the Iowa contingent; he would join four Republican representatives in Washington.

President Bill Clinton fared well in Iowa, too, capturing the state's seven electoral votes with a 50%–40% victory over Bob Dole. However, Republicans maintained their majority in the state House, and also captured the state Senate, no doubt pleasing GOP Gov. Terry Branstad.

Crime and Other Headlines. In a macabre story that came to light in October, a young woman named Kimmi Hardy was arrested and charged with murder in an elaborate scheme to become a mother. According to charges, Hardy faked being pregnant, then announced the "birth" of her child, when she actually had murdered the baby's real mother and took the child to claim as her own. Hardy's story became suspect when guests invited to her baby shower alerted police that the infant looked too old to be a newborn; Hardy's husband eventually confessed to the plot.

Unemployment for the year ending in August 1996 fell from 3.5% to 3.0%. The government announced new programs to assist prospective home buyers in a state that already enjoys one of the largest per-capita figures for home ownership.

The U.S. Supreme Court let stand a ruling that Polk county violated religious freedoms by firing an employee who held prayer meetings at work. Iowa showed itself to be an innovator in health-care legislation by enacting a law in July that guaranteed continued coverage for people switching jobs; this legislation preceded the national Kennedy-Kassebaum bill, and was used as a model for the federal law. B. J.

Jim Ryun, a former Olympic runner who once held the world record for the mile, made a successful bid for the U.S. House. The 49-year-old Republican was elected in Kansas' 2d District.

© Steve Zuk/AP/Wide World Photos

KANSAS. The national spotlight shone brightly on Kansas in 1996 as the Sunflower State's favorite son, Bob Dole, won the Republican nomination for president.

Politics and Court Case. Dole used his hometown of Russell as the feel-good backdrop for much of his ultimately unsuccessful campaign. In June he gave up his Senate seat to campaign for the White House, ending a 35-year career in Congress.

The year also brought to an end the political career of Kansas' other senator, Nancy Kassebaum. Kassebaum, also a Republican, chose not to run for reelection. In the November elections, Republicans had little difficulty holding onto both Senate seats and all House seats, and also easily maintained a majority in the state legislature.

Kansas Attorney General Carla Stovall argued before the U.S. Supreme Court in favor of the state's sexual-predator law. The law, which had been overturned by the state's highest court, allowed Kansas officials to keep violent sex offenders in custody even after their criminal sentences had concluded. The case, which the Supreme Court had not ruled on at year's end, was expected to affect several other states as well.

Other News. The Kickapoo Tribe opened the first Indian casino in the state....Elected officials refused to help out financially troubled horse- and dog-racing tracks by allowing additional types of gambling....And the legislature ended an open-admissions policy at Kansas universities, meaning that, starting in 2001, high-school graduates would not be admitted automatically for classes; instead, they would have to meet certain academic requirements. L. B.

KENTUCKY. In 1996, Kentucky became one of a growing number of states to allow its citizens to carry concealed weapons. The state's General Assembly easily approved the measure, sponsored by Democratic Rep. Bob Damron, after about two decades of debate.

Legislation. Under the new law, businesses were allowed to prohibit people from carrying concealed weapons, though many gun advocates said that they would organize boycotts of those businesses. The people who fought against the bill said it would result in more gun-related homicides, though supporters said it actually would lower crime. Nearby Indiana, which has allowed concealed weapons for decades, has experienced neither of these effects.

As the year ended, Democratic Gov. Paul Patton was headed toward a showdown with labor unions over special legislation that would attempt to reform the state's workers'-compensation laws. Ironically, many political insiders credited the efforts of labor unions as the single factor that gave Patton his slim victory in 1995 over Republican Larry Forgy. Supporters of the reform said that workers'-compensation costs were suffocating many of the state's businesses, fattening the wallets of attorneys, and preventing new businesses from moving to the state. Labor unions said the reform would take money away from truly injured workers.

Elections. The 1996 elections had only a few surprises. State Rep. Anne Northup defeated incumbent U.S. Rep. Mike Ward in a tight race in Louisville's 3d District. Northup's victory increased the Republican grip on Kentucky's federal offices, though Democrats still controlled the governor's mansion, the state legislature, and most of the local offices in this traditionally Democratic stronghold. President Bill Clinton won Kentucky in 1996, despite strong opposition from the state's tobacco farmers to his administration's plan to regulate nicotine as a drug. Republicans in the state Senate increased their numbers slightly in 1996, after many speculated that they actually might take control of the state's upper chamber—an event that never has occurred in the history of the Commonwealth. C. S.

LOUISIANA. When the counting was done, about 12,000 votes—less than 1% of the total—separated the two candidates, and Louisiana had elected its first woman to the U.S. Senate. The winner was Mary Landrieu, succeeding fellow Democrat J. Bennett Johnston, who had announced his retirement earlier in the year.

Court Ruling and Church Burnings. In a decision that garnered national attention, the Louisiana Supreme Court ruled that laws prohibiting the sale of alcohol to those under 21 constituted age discrimination. Highway-safety groups around the country feared that the ruling might start a trend, particularly since it came at a time when members of Congress were inclined to oppose the federal government's attempts to mandate state actions by threatening to withhold federal funds. The nationwide drinking age of 21 was instigated during the 1980s, in part by just such a threat.

The rash of arson cases involving southern black churches continued in 1996. In June a suspicious fire heavily damaged a boarded-up church in a predominantly African-American neighborhood in Shreveport. Meanwhile, in Baton Rouge, officials were asked to investigate a macabre offering left outside the Shiloh Baptist Church—a knotted hangman's noose was found at the door by church workers. B. J.

MAINE. Environmental issues played a major role in the nation's northeast corner in 1996. In September the oil tanker *Julie N* rammed into a Portland drawbridge, spilling 170,000 gal (643 520 l) of oil into the Fore River, affecting the inner harbor and nearby estuaries. Happily, damage was limited, and far less wildlife was killed than originally feared.

Elections and the Environment. The election, too, was highlighted by the environment, as a major issue was whether 10.5 million acres (4.2 million ha) of northern forest would be protected from clear-cutting. Although polls in the spring showed 70% in favor of an outright ban, a compromise referendum proposed by the multinational paper companies and backed by Independent Gov. Angus King managed to sway voters away from the more drastic restrictions.

On the political front, the U.S. Senate seat vacated by retiring three-term Republican William Cohen was won by a former aide, fellow Republican Susan Collins. However, both House seats were won by Democrats, marking a loss for the GOP, as incumbent James Longley, Jr., was defeated by Tom Allen. The state voted heavily in favor of President Bill Clinton, and the Democrats carried the state legislature. Maine became one of nine states to enact a measure that asked congressional candidates to pass term-limit legislation. Officials who declined to do so would have their positions noted on the ballot in forthcoming elections. Voters also approved public funding for candidates. In December, President Clinton nominated retiring Senator Cohen to be secretary of defense in his second term.

Other News. The University of Maine learned it could keep its 1993 men's hockey championship, as the National Collegiate Athletic Association (NCAA) ruled in August that players who received stipends in the 1992 Olympics had been misled....Figures for the 1995 lobster harvest were released, marking it as the largest in history—37 million lbs (16.8 million kg), valued at more than $100 million....Elizabeth Noyce, one of the state's top philanthropists, invested millions of dollars in downtown Portland, hoping to stem the flight to the suburbs....The Hathaway shirt factory in Waterville, which dated back to 1837, was shut down by its parent company, the Warnaco Group, even though workers had given up raises to hire consultants and had doubled their productivity....The Brunswick Naval Air Station announced the permanent relocation to Brunswick of two naval-reserve aviation squadrons and a dozen supporting units. The move would provide employment for up to 1,000 full- and part-time personnel. B. J.

MARYLAND. There were few surprises in the November elections in Maryland: All eight U.S. House incumbents—four Democrats and four Republicans—ran for reelection and all eight won. The victors included Democrat Elijah Cummings of Baltimore's 7th District, who was elected to his first full term; he had won his seat in April in a special election mandated by the retirement of Rep. Kweisi Mfume. Mfume left Congress to head the National Association for the Advancement of Colored People (NAACP). President Bill Clinton won the state's ten electoral votes with a 54%–38% margin over Republican challenger Bob Dole.

Welfare Program. In the wake of the federal government's decision to allow states to design their own welfare programs, a Maryland legislative panel proposed a law linking entitlements to drug testing. The proposal was considered unique, and the message it offered was simple: If you do drugs, you do not get money. Under the law, the Temporary Cash Assistance program (which once was called Aid to Families with Dependent Children) would demand drug testing of its recipients. Anyone who tested positive would be sent to a drug-treatment program at the state's expense. If the person refused treatment, they would lose their portion of assistance, and although money still would be provided for minor children, it would be given to a third party to ensure that it was not spent on drugs. The proposal, although supported by both conservatives and liberals on the panel, upset many civil libertarians, who claimed it violated the U.S. Constitution's 4th Amendment guarantees against illegal search and seizure. B. J.

MASSACHUSETTS. A Democratic sweep in the November 5 elections resulted in U.S. Sen. John Kerry's keeping his seat in a tough fight with Republican Gov. William Weld. Democrats gained two more congressional seats to attain control of all of the state's 12 seats in Congress. In state legislative races, Democrats increased their solid majorities. Also, a ballot measure to outlaw trapping passed by a wide margin.

Politics. Governor Weld signed a $150 million reduction in income taxes, made possible by unexpected tax revenues. Individuals were to be allowed a higher personal exemption on their 1996 returns, saving about $40 each.

© Charles Krupa/AP/Wide World Photos

In a closely watched race, Massachusetts Democrat John Kerry captured a third term in the U.S. Senate. He defeated the state's popular governor, William Weld, by a margin of 52%–45%.

The tax break came because the state's stabilization fund—also called the rainy-day fund—had a $540 million balance, enough to trigger an automatic tax cut. A new law provided from $40 million to $50 million in tax relief to the mutual-fund industry.

The legislature overrode the governor's veto of a 25-cent cigarette-tax hike. The higher tax was to fund health-insurance coverage for 150,000 uninsured children and prescription-drug assistance for 65,000 low-income adults. A new law made Massachusetts the first state to require tobacco makers to publicly disclose product information by listing the additives and nicotine yield ratings in cigarettes, snuff, and chewing tobacco. The industry pledged a court fight.

A $17.5 billion budget was approved for fiscal 1997, including $2.58 billion for educational funding from kindergarten through high school. The budget included $200 million to increase the amount of state aid going to less wealthy school districts. The legislature approved a rivers-protection law, reformed the disability pension system, and consolidated the state's two retirement funds. A new law called for establishing a sex-offender registry. The state provided an $86 million bond for school technology.

The state Department of Revenue resumed seizing boats and other property of parents who refused to pay court-ordered child support. E. S.

MICHIGAN. Despite a strike by more than 80,000 General Motors workers in March, the labor and economic news in Michigan was good in 1996, supported by a vigorous upsurge in the auto industry. Unemployment fell to 4.5%, the lowest in 20 years, as the state claimed the largest back-to-work figures in the nation.

Elections and the Economy. All this good news translated to victory for most incumbents in the fall elections; Sen. Carl Levin won reelection, as did 14 of 16 congressmen. President Bill Clinton won the state easily, and on his coattails the state House was captured by the Democratic Party, although the Senate remained in the hands of Republicans.

The good economic news was apparent in downtown Detroit, which was enjoying a revitalization. General Motors announced it had purchased the landmark Renaissance Center there for its corporate headquarters, and the National Football League's Detroit Lions unveiled plans to move back to the city after 20 years in suburban Pontiac. A new $245 million domed stadium was to be built next door to the planned $240 million open-air stadium previously designated as the new home of baseball's Detroit Tigers. The two stadiums, if completed as planned, would comprise one of the largest U.S. sports and entertainment complexes.

Dr. Kevorkian and Crime News. Perennial headliner Dr. Jack Kevorkian was arrested again on the occasion of his 46th physician-assisted-suicide case, in which he ignored a court order barring the practice.

Other lawbreakers—both documented and alleged—made big news in Michigan in 1996. A University of Michigan graduate student injured by a letter bomb filed a civil suit against Unabomber suspect Theodore Kaczynski. Ferdinand Hammer, 74, was stripped of his U.S. citizenship and faced deportation after it was determined he was an SS guard at the Auschwitz concentration camp during World War II. Jonathan Schmitz was found guilty of second-degree murder after a sensational trial. Schmitz shot and killed Scott Amedure after the two appeared together on a syndicated television talk show, during which Amedure claimed he had a gay crush on Schmitz.

Federal authorities claimed that they had "driven a stake through the heart" of the Detroit Mafia, after 17 members of an alleged crime family were indicted. B. J.

MINNESOTA. An eclectic variety of news made headlines in Minnesota during 1996.

Election Results. Incumbent U.S. Sen. Paul Wellstone won reelection against Republican Rudy Boschwitz, who waged what was considered one of the nation's most negative campaigns. Interestingly, results of a poll conducted about the effect of negative advertising showed that many voters indeed were influenced by the negativity, but not in the way intended—the ads actually may have convinced them to vote for Wellstone. In what was almost an anticlimax, Wellstone won, 50%–41%. To no one's surprise, the state was carried by President Bill Clinton, thus making it the only state to vote Democratic in presidential elections each of the last six campaigns. In a referendum, Minnesotans approved that bonuses be given to Persian Gulf war veterans.

Court Cases, Mall Curfew. In a Minnesota case, the U.S. Supreme Court ruled that states could limit charitable soliciting to local charities, maintaining that a "local presence" for solicitations is constitutional. Minnesota's Supreme Court, meanwhile, ruled that Blue Cross/Blue Shield could sue tobacco companies for alleged false advertising and deceptive trade practices, seeking to recoup money that they had had to spend in health care.

The United States' largest shopping center, the Mall of America, instituted a curfew for teenagers under the age of 16 after numerous incidents of rowdy behavior, including chases, practical jokes, and fistfights. The move raised questions that troubled civil-liberties groups, however. Opponents claimed the curfew infringed on the rights of young people and, furthermore, could be interpreted as being racially motivated—many black teens complained that they were being handed copies of the new rules, while white teens were not. B. J.

MISSISSIPPI. In the November 5 election, the state voted for Republicans Bob Dole for president and Thad Cochran for the U.S. Senate. Republican Charles W. Pickering, Jr., won the U.S. House seat vacated by retiring Rep. G.V. Montgomery. Voters rejected casinos in De Soto county, near Memphis, TN. Gov. Kirk Fordice suffered injuries in a crash when he drove his jeep off the road on election night. The governor was not up for reelection.

The U.S. Supreme Court in November rejected Mississippi's bid to appeal a ruling that denied student-led, voluntary prayer at various public-school events under a 1994 law. A U.S. district judge on September 27 struck down the state's attempt to impose restrictions on abortion clinics that had been established in a 1996 law.

Mississippi, unlike most of the nation, had no growth in employment from August 1995 to August 1996.

Legislation. In the 1996 session, the legislature approved a budget of $2.76 billion and increased funding for schools by $8 million. A new law required speedy state intervention for schools facing financial or academic emergencies.

Another new law mandated that any student bringing a deadly weapon to school could be expelled for a year. A new college-savings plan allowed parents to contract to pay tuition in advance for children younger than 18. The $182 million corrections budget included an additional $23 million for operating new prisons, authorized in 1994. The state approved allowing inmates to contract to work for private enterprises. Victims of sex crimes were to be notified ten days before their attacker was released from prison. The speed limit was raised to 70 mph (112 km/hr) on the interstate. Parents who did not pay court-ordered child support could have their driver's or professional licenses suspended.

The legislature passed, over the governor's veto, a measure that allowed only state residents to collect signatures for ballot petitions. A *Wall Street Journal* editorial on March 28 accused state House Speaker Tim Ford of trying to restrict the initiative process with the law. In 1994 a term-limit proposal for legislators was petitioned to the ballot, but was defeated after legislators campaigned against it. E. S.

MISSOURI. Former Missouri House Speaker Bob Griffin, for years one of the most powerful politicians in the state, was indicted in October on federal public-corruption charges. Griffin, a Democrat who held the speaker's post longer than anyone in Missouri history, left the state legislature early in 1996 as allegations against him mounted. Three of Griffin's colleagues also were indicted by the federal grand jury.

November Elections. Voters sent Democratic Gov. Mel Carnahan back to the state capital for a second term, while also reelecting five other Democrats to the U.S. House. Meanwhile, Republican Kenny Hulshof, a former special prosecutor for the Missouri attorney general, upset longtime Democratic Congressman Harold Volkmer in Missouri's 9th District.

Aerospace Industry and Other News. Also in 1996, aerospace giant McDonnell Douglas Corp., based in St. Louis, suffered problems. Despite winning a $16 billion contract from the U.S. Air Force, the company lost in its bid for an important fighter-jet program, and its machinists walked off the job in a 99-day strike. At year's end, the company's fiercest competitor, Boeing Co., announced plans to buy McDonnell Douglas.

Two instructors at the U.S. Army's Fort Leonard Wood admitted to abusing female trainees and faced courts-martial....A 10-year-old reportedly was kept alive by wild dogs after he got lost in the woods in below-freezing weather, though some officials questioned the tale told by the boy's mother....A new collegiate conference, the Big 12—a combination of the Big 8 Conference and four teams of the Southwest Conference—debuted. L. B.

MONTANA. In terms of national rankings, Montana may have the seventh-smallest population, but it had two of the biggest news stories in 1996—the capture of the suspected Unabomber and the armed siege at "Justice Township."

Unabomber and "Justice Township." With the arrest of Theodore Kaczynski in a remote cabin near the Montana town of Lincoln on April 3, the Federal Bureau of Investigation (FBI) asserted it had stopped the terror of mail bombings that had claimed the lives of three people and injured 23 others between 1978 and 1995. The former mathematics professor put up no struggle and, according to officials, there was much incriminating evidence found, including two live bombs. The big break in the case came when the suspect's brother, David Kaczynski, alerted authorities of the strong similarities between the Unabomber's published manifesto and his brother's writings. Kaczynski's California trial on a ten-count indictment was set to begin in November 1997, and may be only the first of many; he could face charges in seven other states.

The year's other big story concerned the so-called Freemen group, which instigated an 81-day standoff against local, state, and federal forces on a farm complex outside Jordan, which the Freemen renamed "Justice Township." The siege began on March 25, when two of the group's leaders were arrested on charges of fraud and making death threats. The Freemen, although not part of any known organized militia group, rejected all government controls, including taxes. For more than two months, they managed to keep authorities at bay. President Bill Clinton and Attorney General Janet Reno praised the FBI and local officials for using restraint during the long ordeal, which ended peacefully.

Elections. Gov. Marc Racicot (R) was expected to win reelection and did; what made it unusual was that his opponent, State Sen. Chet Blaylock, died of a heart attack two weeks before the election, while driving to a scheduled debate. Blaylock, 71, had a history of heart problems. The Democratic Party scrambled to find a replacement for Blaylock and chose Judy Jacobson, who was running for lieutenant governor, to run against the incumbent. Racicot won with 80% of the vote. B. J.

NEBRASKA. Nebraska enjoyed fine weather and bumper crops in 1996, recording one of the best harvests in state history. Stable farm prices and a surge in agricultural exports assured the state's prosperity and contributed to a low unemployment rate—2.6%.

Elections. No doubt the economic good news affected the polling in November, with all three incumbent U.S. representatives winning reelection. But Ben Nelson, the popular governor, lost in his bid to replace retiring U.S. Sen. Jim Exon, a three-term Democrat. Both Nelson and his opponent, Chuck Hagel, a Republican businessman, ran on conservative, antiabortion platforms; Hagel, however, was an early supporter of Bob Dole's tax-cut plan, and as the state gave Dole his third-strongest showing in the country—53% of the popular vote—Hagel won the Senate seat easily.

Native Americans. The year marked a landmark split among Native American tribes, as the Santee Sioux of northern Nebraska petitioned the U.S. Congress for their share of a $400 million fund the government had put aside to settle long-standing land disputes. The request was significant in that eight other Sioux tribes refused to touch any of the money, preferring to maintain their claim on the land instead—a claim that includes the Black Hills of South Dakota. Spokesmen for the Santee claimed that the tribe was in dire financial straits, with unemployment on the reservation at 85% and with the federal government trying to shut down the tribe's casino.

Other News. John Joubert, a convicted child killer, was executed in July. Also in July, an explosion at a sugar factory injured 12 people and sent debris flying as far as a mile away. B. J.

NEVADA. If 1996 was any indication, Nevada was facing the good news/bad news dilemma of rapid growth. Statistics showed it was the fastest-growing state in the nation; in the year between July 1995 and July 1996, the estimated population grew an astonishing 4.5%, as compared to nationwide growth of less than 1%. In Las Vegas alone, $7 billion worth of new hotels were under construction or in the planning stage, which would add 29,000 rooms to the tourist mecca.

But the rapid growth presented problems, too. The booms in population, jobs, and construction came with a rise in litigation against builders and an increase in violent crime, notably homicides. Furthermore, the Clark County School District, which includes Las Vegas, was the nation's tenth largest, and it was running out of classrooms.

Politics and Mother Nature. Voters approved a referendum that would ask congressmen to attempt to pass term-limits legislation and publicly would identify congressional candidates who failed to do so. Nevada was one of nine states to approve some action on term limits. Also approved was a plan to limit campaign contributions in state and local races. Democrats won a majority in the state House, which previously had been tied. Republicans, however, kept control of both the state's U.S. House seats.

Mother Nature made her presence known, from the August wildfires that destroyed 6,000 acres (2 428 ha) of forest to the December blizzard that dumped as much as 3 ft (1 m) of snow and shut down the state government in Carson City. B. J.

NEW HAMPSHIRE. Voters on November 5 elected the state's first woman governor, Democrat Jeanne Shaheen. A former state senator, Shaheen beat Republican candidate Ovide Lamontagne. Popular GOP Gov. Stephen Merrill chose not to seek a third term. New Hampshire voted for Republican candidates to fill a U.S. Senate seat—Robert C. Smith—and two House seats—Charles Bass and John E. Sununu, the son of the former governor. Republicans also held onto the state legislature, keeping a majority in both chambers.

Legislation. In its legislative session, the state banned exclusive contracts between doctors and managed-care companies. The measure was intended to increase competition, lower premium costs, and provide consumers better access to health care. A new law to deregulate the electric-utility industry was aimed at Public Service Company of New Hampshire, which had some of the highest electric rates in the country. The pilot program was intended to open competition for electricity consumers. Another new law sought to help communities establish kindergartens. About one third of the state's school districts offer kindergarten, which is not mandatory. The legislature promised to grant districts $500 per kindergarten-age child to help pay for the classes. E. S.

NEW JERSEY. The highlight of the year in New Jersey was, by all accounts, the nastiest political campaign ever run in the state, and one of the worst in the country. It pitted two U.S. representatives—Democrat Robert Torricelli and Republican Richard Zimmer—vying for the Senate seat vacated by retiring Bill Bradley. Torricelli won by ten points, but some observers called it a Pyrrhic victory at best: His credibility was so damaged during the campaign that he would have a hard time establishing himself in Washington.

Gov. Christine Todd Whitman (R) was mentioned early on as a possible running mate for presidential nominee Robert Dole, until she took herself out of the running, claiming her commitment to continue governing the state. She lowered taxes for the third consecutive year, mostly by slashing government spending; environmental-protection plans suffered the severest cuts.

Environmental News. In May, 40 mi (64 km) of beaches along the Jersey shore remained opened despite a 30,000-gal (113 562-l) oil spill. Even wild turkeys had their 15 minutes of fame, with the announcement that their population—which had been wiped out in the 1970s due to hunting and deforestation—was making a comeback, now numbering approximately 13,000.

Judicial Front. Deborah T. Poritz was sworn in as the first woman to serve as state Supreme Court chief justice, replacing Robert Wilentz, who retired due to illness. Poritz, 50, was also the state's first female attorney general, and her appointment to the bench marked the first time in the state's history that a Republican "affiliate" had served as chief justice. Meanwhile, the judicial system labored under a severe shortage of trial judgeships, with 30 vacancies throughout the state, causing massive overloads and backlogs.

Other News. The battle against New York over who owns Ellis Island continued....New Jersey finally was going to have a state song, with "New Jersey, My Home"—written and composed by a high-school music director—the leading contender....State officials claimed that the Genovese crime family had infiltrated the health-care business....Big storms in January and June wreaked havoc throughout the state. B. J.

NEW MEXICO. Republican Sen. Pete Domenici, chairman of the powerful U.S. Senate Budget Committee, easily won reelection to his fifth term. And despite less-than-perfect economic news—New Mexico's unemployment rate climbed to 7.1%, the second highest of the 50 states—it was a good year for incumbents. The three U.S. House incumbents were reelected, and President Bill Clinton won the state's five electoral votes.

Judicial Rulings. To the delight of animals-rights activists and Native American groups, a federal district-court judge blocked implementation of a controversial plan to allow buffalo hunting on army land. In January, Judge Martha Vasquez ordered an environmental-impact

In New Hampshire, Democrat Jeanne Shaheen (left)*, a three-term state senator, was chosen to succeed Republican Gov. Stephen Merrill* (center)*. Merrill had decided not to run again.*

© Jim Cole/AP/Wide World Photos

study, an action that could establish a precedent for the banning of hunts on other military properties.

Judge Vasquez made news again in September when she forced the closing of a gambling casino run by the Mescalero Apaches. The action came after a long dispute between the state and 11 Indian-run casinos, which had been ruled illegal by three federal judges and the New Mexico Supreme Court. In January the ten other casinos had signed an agreement with the U.S. Attorney that allowed them to remain open while they appealed the ruling; the Mescaleros had refused to join the tribes in signing that agreement.

Drought and Forest Fire. A drought, one of the worst of the century, scorched millions of acres of sheep-grazing land on the vast Navajo Reservation....In April a fire destroyed more than 16,000 acres (6 475 ha) of forest, damaging 800-year-old ruins at some Anasazi Indian archaeological sites within Bandelier National Monument and for a time threatening the National Laboratory at Los Alamos. B. J.

© Porter Gifford/Gamma-Liaison

Gov. Christine Todd Whitman (left), *who continued to lower taxes in New Jersey, campaigned hard for GOP presidential nominee Robert Dole* (center) *and his 15% tax-cut plan.*

NEW YORK. Although it still laid claim to the largest city in the nation, New York state continued its decline in overall population, being one of only two states to lose population during 1996. It now was the third-largest U.S. state in terms of population, behind California and Texas. Statewide unemployment fell to 6.1% during the year ending in August, although New York City's rate rose to 8.5% during the same period.

Politics. As expected, President Bill Clinton carried the state easily with 59% of the vote, despite New York's former U.S. representative Jack Kemp running as vice-president on the Republican ticket. One of the more publicized election races, however, occurred on Long Island, where Carolyn McCarthy, a lifelong Republican, switched parties and ran as a Democrat for Congress against freshman incumbent Dan Frisa. What made the story newsworthy is that McCarthy switched parties after her husband was killed and her son wounded in a 1993 Long Island Railroad massacre. Frisa—who had voted to repeal the assault weapons ban—lost easily, and was the only incumbent congressman in the state not to be reelected.

Continuing a long and ignominious tradition of tardiness, Gov. George Pataki and the state legislature took until July to finally pass a $66 billion budget. Due on April 1, it marked the 12th straight year that the budget was late. B. J.

NORTH CAROLINA. Democratic Gov. James Hunt, Jr., handily beat Republican Robin Hayes in the November 5 election to win a fourth term. Voters also agreed to amend the state constitution to give the governor veto power. North Carolina's governor was the only one in the country without the power to veto bills. Republican U.S. Sen. Jesse Helms beat Democrat Harvey Gantt, an African-American, for the second time. Democrats won two more U.S. House seats for a split of six Republicans and six Democrats. Democrats also increased their numbers in the state legislature, winning four more seats in the state Senate—which now would have 30 Democrats and 20 Republicans—and gaining seven seats in the state House, with 61 Republicans and 59 Democrats. Stock-car-racing legend Richard Petty lost his bid to become the state's first Republican secretary of state, however. Voters approved a $1.8 billion school bond issue and a $950 million bond issue to speed highway construction, and approved constitutional amendments to give new rights to crime victims and allow judges to impose alternative sentences.

Legislation. Action in the state legislature in 1996 reduced the sales tax on food, raised salaries for teachers and state workers, and boosted funding for Smart Start—Governor Hunt's program aimed at helping preschool children with better day-care services. The legislature increased public-school funding by more than 7%. The session approved establishment of charter schools, which are innovative public schools free from many regulations. A new law, which took effect in July, gave the state more power in collecting child support, including suspending or revoking the professional or business licenses or driver's licenses of deadbeat parents. The session increased funding for the environment and voted restrictions on massive hog farms to curb pollution.

Court News. The U.S. Supreme Court in June 1996 ruled that the state's 12th congressional district was unconstitutional. In the 1997 session, lawmakers would be faced with an April 1 deadline for drawing congressional districts.

The North Carolina Supreme Court in March approved a law allowing local governments to offer tax incentives to attract industry.

The U.S. Supreme Court in February 1996 ruled unconstitutional an exemption from the state intangibles tax for stocks and bonds of North Carolina companies. However, the state had anticipated the decision and repealed the intangibles tax in 1995. The state said it would refund $123 million to residents who paid the tax on shares of stock under protest.

Other News. Hurricane Fran hit the coast of Wilmington, NC, in September; it was the second storm in two months to prey on North Carolina....The North Carolina Medical Board in October endorsed the use of powerful narcotics, prescribed by doctors, to manage chronic pain such as arthritis or back pain. E. S.

NORTH DAKOTA. Republican Bob Dole carried the state in the November 5 election, and Republican Gov. Edward Schafer won reelection in a landslide. Voters in North Dakota approved a ballot measure lengthening the term of state representatives to four years. There was something new in how some elections were conducted, with the state being one of two in the nation—along with Oregon—that allowed a national election by mail; the method was used in the Republican presidential primary. Supporters of the policy claimed that it cost less than traditional polling methods and that voter participation was significantly higher because of the convenience. Political scientists saw the move as a transitional phase leading to the eventual use of electronic voting by computer or telephone.

Meteorology, the Economy, and *Fargo*. A November blizzard dumped as much as 13 in (33 cm) of snow in one night in many parts of the state. The snow—along with wind gusts of more than 50 mph (80 km/hr)—shut down large portions of the interstate highway system....The state's unemployment level fell to 2.7%.

In the entertainment world, the state received a big dose of publicity as filmmakers Joel and Ethan Coen released their thriller *Fargo*, which earned rave reviews and was expected to garner numerous Academy Award nominations in 1997. The movie depicts a fact-based case of a series of grisly murders in and around Fargo. B. J.

OHIO. Ohio passed legislation that banned so-called "partial-birth" abortions, an issue that also came before the U.S. Congress in 1996.

Politics. Voters soundly defeated a ballot issue that would have permitted casino gambling in the state. Some pundits credited Gov. George Voinovich's leadership with the initiative's defeat, while others argued it was voters' historically rocky relationship with such ballot issues. Casino gambling was a hot issue because neighboring Indiana has riverboat gambling, and many observers feared that the rise of riverboat gambling would drain the coffers of Ohio's state lottery. Republicans strengthened their grip on Ohio's state House of Representatives and Senate, picking up one seat in the state Senate and four in the House.

Perhaps the biggest news in Ohio state government was Senate President Stanley Aronoff's announced retirement from the legislature. After 36 years in the state legislature, Aronoff was seen as the Republicans' voice of moderation. Sen. Richard Finan, Aronoff's fellow Cincinnati Republican and longtime lieutenant, won Aronoff's leadership position.

The legislature completed the second year of its biennium with a heavy emphasis on crime bills. A constitutional challenge over the way school systems were funded made its way to the Ohio Supreme Court, and education surpassed crime as voters' top concern.

Economy and the Weather. It was a year of steady, moderate economic growth for the state. The legislature completed a pro-business overhaul of the Ohio workers'-compensation system engineered by the Voinovich administration.

It was a tough year for farmers in terms of weather. A wet spring, dry summer, and early freeze made it difficult for farmers to get their crops in and out of the ground on time. Huge winter snowstorms gripped northern Ohio—Cleveland in particular—in November. C. S.

OKLAHOMA. The big story of 1995—the Oklahoma City bombing of the Alfred P. Murrah Federal Building—continued to make news throughout 1996, primarily on the legal front. Colorado became the state of choice as a change in venue was ordered for the trial that was expected to begin in 1997. A federal judge ruled that a fair trial could not be expected in Oklahoma, so suspects Timothy McVeigh and Terry Nichols were moved to Denver to await their day in court. Meanwhile, lawyers for the defense filed motions for separate trials, even as the prosecution looked into the possibility of pursuing the death penalty.

In a related story, the Oklahoma City Council voted to close permanently the street in front of the former site of the Murrah building, where 168 people lost their lives in the explosion.

Other News. Governor Keating proposed an $11 million bonus-pay plan for teachers. Voters opposed a plan that would have changed school funding fundamentally, much like California's Proposition 13 did in 1978....A meteorological phenomenon called a "heat burst" hit ten Oklahoma counties on the evening of May 22; during the event, temperatures soared from 88° F (31° C) to 102° F (39° C) in the space of 25 minutes. High winds toppled trees and knocked down power lines. B. J.

OREGON. The most hotly contested race of Oregon's 1996 election season was for the U.S. Senate seat vacated by veteran Republican Sen. Mark O. Hatfield. Republican candidate Gordon Smith edged out Democrat Tom Bruggere. Both men were multimillionaires. Smith served as president of the Oregon Senate, but it was Bruggere's first run for political office. Of Oregon's five U.S. House seats, Democrats took four slots and Republicans garnered one. The 1996 elections left Republicans in control of both houses of the state legislature. Gov. John Kitzhaber, a Democrat, was not up for reelection.

Almost 50% of those voting in the November general election did so by absentee ballot. In January 1996, Oregon held the nation's first all-mail-in special election to replace former U.S. Sen. Bob Packwood. U.S. Rep. Ron Wyden defeated Gordon Smith to become the state's first Democratic U.S. senator in more than 30 years.

Initiatives. The state legislature did not meet in 1996, but voters themselves took up ballot measures in record

The National Weather Service issued flood warnings for numerous rivers in Oregon, left, *as heavy rain and melting snow caused extensive flooding in the U.S. Northwest late in the year.*

© Jeff Christensen/Sipa Press

The barge the "North Cape" struck a sand bar off Point Judith, RI, in January 1996, spilling more than 800,000 gal (3 028 329 l) of heating oil into Block Island Sound. Federal funds were made available for the cleanup.

numbers. Twenty-three statewide proposals qualified for the general election, the most of any state in the nation. Oregonians said "yes" to measures that increased the minimum wage, eliminated unanimous verdicts in murder trials, increased cigarette taxes, and limited property taxes. They rejected proposals to expand Oregon's bottle bill, to eliminate flat fees for doctors, to remove free-speech protections for obscenity, to test fourth- through 12th-graders in math and verbal skills, and to raise the retirement age of state workers. Voters refused to require their state and federal legislators to vote for congressional term limits.

Welfare, Economy, Weather. As a result of an innovative system—known as the Oregon Option—to move welfare recipients into jobs, the state ranked third in the nation in welfare-caseload reductions, and it did so before federal welfare reform became a law.

Oregon continued to experience strong economic growth, prompting state economist Paul Warner to report that Oregon is "running out of labor." High-tech manufacturing and service industries were fueling the state's economy, with exports to Asia particularly significant.

In terms of weather, Oregon experienced the worst flood since 1964 in February, causing thousands to flee their homes and closing hundreds of roadways. M. L. C.

PENNSYLVANIA. Republicans increased their majorities in the General Assembly in November 5 voting and also were elected to two statewide offices—attorney general and treasurer. Robert Casey, Jr., son of the former governor, was the only Democrat to win a statewide race, with his election as auditor general. President Bill Clinton, however, won the state's electoral votes.

Judiciary. The state Supreme Court in July ruled for the second time since 1987 that the state should take over the costs of county courts. This time the court decided to appoint a special master to set up a funding mechanism by 1998 for the change to a unified state-court system. In September the high court ruled in a dispute between the state and a commonwealth court over desegregation costs of Philadelphia schools, striking down an order that the state must pay $45 million to Philadelphia. The city of Philadelphia and the state each contended that the other should pay for the cost of complying with court-desegregation orders in the schools.

Legislation. The legislative session approved a general-fund budget of $16.4 billion, more than 40% of which was to go to fund education in the state. A reform of the state's welfare laws replaced previous work requirements with a new program requiring all welfare applicants to work or seek job training or education. Applicants also must agree to keep their children in school, immunize their children, and prepare to support themselves. Applicants could receive welfare for two years only. In addition, the residency requirement for applying for welfare increased from two to 12 months. The welfare law also eliminated Medicaid coverage for 230,000 medically needy adults with no dependent children. A new law required insurers to offer mothers of newborns at least 48 hours in the hospital for childbirth.

The legislature funded $33 million to upgrade technology at schools and libraries. The state outlawed same-sex marriages. Newly passed workers'-compensation reforms cut benefits for some and made it easier to deny aid to malingerers. A new law forbade insurers from denying medical coverage to victims of domestic abuse. Corrections funding increased by more than $102 million, for a total budget of $933 million. The 1996 legislative session also authorized construction of a new state prison to hold 1,000 inmates. E. S.

RHODE ISLAND. The nation's smallest state began the year with the largest oil spill in its history, as more than 800,000 gal (3 028 329 l) of heating oil flowed into Block Island Sound from a ruptured barge near Matunuck. More than 43,000 lbs (19 504 kg) of lobsters and 189 seabirds were known to have perished in what was termed "a disaster and a tragedy." A 250-sq-mi (647-km^2) area around the spill was closed to fishing.

Environment. In August there was more bad environmental news, but this time the culprit was the lowly mosquito. Gov. Lincoln Almond ordered the spraying of saltwater ponds and other mosquito breeding grounds, as fear spread that a rare virus was being carried by the buzzing insects. The virus, eastern equine encephalitis, which can be deadly to humans, had been found in mosquitoes in Rhode Island and Connecticut, prompting the governor's actions. Similar measures were ordered in Connecticut by Gov. John Rowland. It was stressed that the spraying was precautionary, and that no cases of human infection had been reported.

Court Rulings. Two U.S. Supreme Court rulings made headlines in the state during 1996. In one, the high court ruled that Native American tribes could not sue states that refused to allow gambling. The Narragansett tribe of Rhode Island had been trying to establish a casino to rival those in nearby Connecticut. In another case, the court voted unanimously to strike down a Rhode Island ban on advertising liquor prices, claiming it impinged on 1st Amendment rights of free speech. Court watchers expected this particular ruling to have broader implications, especially as President Bill Clinton continued his campaign against cigarette advertising.

Election News. Rhode Island went solidly Democratic, giving the party landslide victories in all four national races. For the presidency, Clinton garnered 60% of the vote to Bob Dole's 27%; Congressman Jack Reed easily won the Senate seat vacated by retiring six-termer Claiborne Pell, defeating Nancy Mayer 63%–35%, and both U.S. House seats were won easily by Democratic candidates. Incumbent Rep. Patrick Kennedy took 69% of the vote in his race, and Robert Weygand won Reed's seat with 64%. B. J.

SOUTH CAROLINA. It appeared that the Civil War, which began in South Carolina more than 130 years ago, finally might be ending in that state. Republican Gov. David Beasley announced in late November that he wanted to take the Confederate flag down from the flagpole over the statehouse.

According to observers, the move, which would need approval from the General Assembly, would end an era of racial insensitivity and acknowledge that South Carolina is definitely part of the New South. Supporters of the Confederate flag long have said that it is an integral part of the state's heritage and a memorial to the lives of thousands of South Carolinians who gave their lives in battle during the Civil War. However, the people who want the so-called "Stars and Bars" removed point out that the flag was raised over the statehouse in 1962 as a symbol of defiance toward the federal government, which at the time was forcing the state to desegregate; it was not raised in remembrance of Confederate dead.

Economy, Race Relations, and Politics. Since the 1960s, South Carolina had begun to imitate its more prosperous neighbor, North Carolina, and had become home to many international manufacturers, including Bavarian Motor Works (BMW) and its many suppliers. As an example of development efforts, one of the major pieces of legislation to come out of the General Assembly in 1996 was the Rural Development Act. This new law offered tax incentives to companies moving to poorer counties in the state, though richer counties also would benefit from the act.

Despite this pro-business attitude, some observers contended that South Carolina had a long way to go with regard to race relations, as black legislators held the Rural Development Act hostage until legislation could be passed creating a black-heritage monument on the Capitol grounds. The General Assembly adjourned sine die without passing either piece of legislation. The governor later called the legislature into a special session to get both passed.

In the November election, Republican Sen. Strom Thurmond—at age 93 the oldest senator in U.S. history—was reelected to his seventh full term. The nation's longest-serving legislator, Marshall Williams, passed away in 1996. C. S.

SOUTH DAKOTA. The big news of 1996 in South Dakota occurred in the November elections, when U.S. Sen. Larry Pressler became the only incumbent of that body to lose reelection. Pressler, a three-term Republican, lost to Democratic U.S. Rep. Tim Johnson in a tight race marked by heavy negative campaigning. Fewer than 10,000 votes separated the two. Johnson's House seat was won by a Republican.

Another nationally important story involved the refusal of the U.S. Supreme Court to hear an appeal regarding abortion rights in a South Dakota case. The high court in effect thus refused to reinstate certain abortion-restriction laws that had been struck down by a lower court. The laws—if reinstated—would have required doctors to notify the parents of any minor seeking an elective abortion. Opponents claimed the laws put an excessive burden on many minors.

South Dakotans enjoyed another drop in their unemployment rate—to 2.8%. They also could look forward to more state money being spent on education programs, according to Gov. William Janklow, who said the majority of increased spending in his new $1.9 billion budget would be so designated. B. J.

TENNESSEE. The 1996 elections set into motion a chain of events that could result in three Tennesseans running for president in 2000.

Politics. Vice-President Al Gore was positioning himself to succeed President Bill Clinton in four years. Lamar Alexander, who ran unsuccessfully for the Republican nomination for president in 1996, became a much-discussed contender for 2000. And U.S. Sen. Fred Thompson of Nashville was thought to be considering a run for the top position.

Democrats regained a majority and control of the state Senate following the November election. The GOP had controlled the body for less than a year, although it kept the same leadership structure intact because of a coalition of Republicans and conservative Democrats.

Economic Front. Nashville sealed the deal to become the new home to the Houston Oilers football club. The move had the approval of the National Football League, and bonds were being sold to finance a new stadium. The team was expected to play its first season in 1998, but the name of the team was still an unknown. Nashville is not renowned for its oil business.

The health-care industry was booming in the capital city, however. Health-management megagiants like Columbia/HCA were active and expanding in the city, as were other medical-insurance companies. On the western edge of the state, Memphis continued to become a mail-order hub in the United States, thanks to Federal Express' presence. Large mail-order companies such as Williams-Sonoma had moved some operations to Memphis to save shipping time to their customers. C. S.

TEXAS. In the November general election, Texas Republican Sen. Phil Gramm was reelected to a third term.

Politics. Earlier in the year, Gramm had been a GOP presidential-primary contender. Candidates for 13 Texas U.S. House seats ran in congressional districts that had been redrawn in August after the U.S. Supreme Court ruled that three of the districts were unconstitutional because they had been drawn primarily on the basis of race. Three districts had December runoff elections, as no candidate had received a majority. In the final tally, Democrats won 17 and Republicans won 13 House seats; about two thirds of the incumbents won. Republicans gained control of the state Senate. In a referendum, voters in Harris county approved public funding for a $265 million Houston baseball stadium. The stadium, which would house the Astros, would have a retractable roof.

During a successful campaign for the post of treasurer of Texas in 1994, Martha Whitehead had promised to dissolve the office and have its functions taken over by the state comptroller. Voters approved the action in a 1995 constitutional amendment, and Whitehead (right) oversaw the elimination of the office in August 1996.

© "Austin American Statesman," Larry Murphy/AP/Wide World Photos

Two prominent Texas politicians died in January: Ralph Yarborough, 92, had been a U.S. senator from 1957 to 1971; Barbara Jordan, 59, a U.S. representative from 1973 to 1979, had been the first black and the first woman elected to Congress from Texas.

Other Headlines. The U.S. Supreme Court in July let stand a March appeals-court ruling that had struck down an admission policy based on race at the law school of the University of Texas. The Texas school had amended its admission policy to reduce the role of race.

A study conducted at the University of Houston and released in March estimated that from 1985 to 1994, 3,200 illegal aliens had drowned in attempting to enter the United States by crossing the Rio Grande. The figure, higher than that reported by Texas state officials, was thought by researchers to be the result of stricter border enforcement that forced aliens to cross the river at more dangerous spots.

In a case that had attracted national attention, Wanda Webb Holloway was sentenced in September to ten years in prison for plotting a murder to secure a cheerleading-squad spot for her daughter. She originally was convicted in 1991, but that conviction had been overturned. S. F.

UTAH. Was it election-year politics or real environmental concern? That was the question on many an observer's mind as President Bill Clinton designated a vast swath of desert as a national monument—ending, with a stroke of his pen, plans for mining concessions and oil drilling. The new park is designated as the Grand Staircase–Escalante National Monument, its 1.7 million acres (687 966 ha) making it almost as large as Yellowstone National Park. If the move was motivated by politics, it certainly did not help in local races; with prospects of a healthy economic boost dimmed by the act, residents were upset, and Republican presidential challenger Bob Dole carried the state easily. Indeed, the backlash even may have influenced the vote that defeated the state's sole Democratic representative, Bill Orton, who lost to Republican Christopher B. Cannon.

Enid Greene, once a rising young star in the Republican Party, decided not to seek reelection after her freshman term in Congress. The reason was severe criticism of her handling of financial and family affairs. She blamed her then husband, Joe Waldholtz, who acted as her campaign manager in 1994. In November, Waldholtz was sentenced to 37 months in prison after pleading guilty to charges of bank, election, and tax fraud. According to Greene, Waldholtz had forged checks, embezzled campaign funds, and stolen money from her father. The couple were divorced in 1996.

Economy. The state of Utah did rather well economically in 1996. Unemployment fell to 2.9%, the fourth lowest in the nation and the lowest in the state since tracking began in 1978. Tourism flourished, new residents poured in, and the state seemed set to enjoy the status of an ongoing boom for many years to come. Perhaps as a reflection of good economic news, Gov. Michael Leavitt, a Republican, won reelection easily. B. J.

VERMONT. This sparsely populated New England state was named the safest in the nation by an independent research agency, which based its finding on 14 factors, including several types of violent crime. With Vermont's unemployment remaining steady at 4.3%—along with the state's claim to some of the prettiest scenery in New England—there was the question about how sparse the population would remain.

Politics. In election results, the state backed President Bill Clinton's reelection with 54% of the vote and reelected Gov. Howard Dean in a landslide, 71% to 23%, over Republican challenger John Gropper. For the state's sole U.S. House seat, Socialist/Independent incumbent Bernard Sanders easily won reelection, defeating both Republican Susan Sweetser and Democrat Jack Long.

Governor Dean made national news when he suggested a federal health-insurance plan based on a successful model implemented in his state in 1992. Dean, a physician, claimed his program had seen teenage-pregnancy and infant-mortality rates drop, while immunization rates had climbed. His proposed plan would cost $6.5 billion annually. B. J.

VIRGINIA. The U.S. Supreme Court ruled June 26 that the Virginia Military Institute's all-male enrollment policy violated the U.S. Constitution. The state-funded college indicated that female applicants would be eligible for admission in the fall of 1997. The state boosted aid to education at all levels by $1 billion, linked to higher academic standards and regular student testing. Gov. George Allen announced March 29 that he would impose a "freeze" on in-state college-tuition costs through 2000. The governor vetoed federal Goals 2000 education money in the budget, saying it represented federal intrusion into local education. The veto meant the state would not seek nearly $7 million in federal funds for teacher training.

Elections and Legislation. U.S. Sen. John Warner (R) won a fourth term in November elections, and voters passed a victims'-rights amendment to the state constitution. Under new state laws, violent teen criminals would be treated as adults; they would be kept in jail longer, and rehabilitation would be promoted. Sentencing options for teens now included boot camps. Anyone 14 or older accused of murder or aggravated malicious wounding would be tried as an adult. To combat graffiti, a new law made parents responsible for up to $2,500 in property damage caused by their children. The governor launched a series of community-work projects for nonviolent offenders. Sex offenders were required to register with the police. Young drivers with learning permits must be accompanied by an adult driver or family member.

Other new laws required insurers to pay for standard hospital stays of 48 hours or more for new mothers and infants and made it easier for insured women to get annual mammograms and pap smears to detect cancer. The state eliminated abortion coverage for state employees in its health-insurance plan. Also enacted were laws that promoted economic development by rewarding companies with state grants and incentives for investing in the state. IBM/Toshiba, for example, was to receive grants of up to $38.4 million for building a $1.2 billion semiconductor-manufacturing plant and creating 4,000 jobs.

Other Developments. Virginia's welfare caseload dropped by 16% in October, a year after a 1995 welfare-reform measure took effect. More than 30% of the state's 63,000 welfare recipients were working in exchange for their benefits. The law required able-bodied recipients to go to work within 90 days, placed a two-year time limit on benefits, required minor mothers on welfare to live with a parent or guardian, and banned additional benefits for recipients who have more children while on welfare.

Virginia opened a high-tech toll-payment system on the Dulles Toll Road in April. The system allows motorists to have accounts deducted electronically each time they drive past the toll booth.

President Bill Clinton declared several areas of Virginia eligible for federal aid following damage caused by Hurricane Fran in early September. E. S.

WASHINGTON. The 1996 Washington elections produced a landslide for Democratic gubernatorial candidate Gary Locke, who grabbed 59% of the vote to defeat Republican conservative Ellen Craswell. Locke became the first Chinese-American governor in the nation. Until his election, he served as King county executive and as a state legislator for 11 years.

Republicans took over the state Senate and kept a majority in the House to give the party control of both chambers for the first time in 14 years. More women served in the state legislature in the 1995–96 term than in any other state, holding 40% of the seats—almost double the national average.

Candidates for the U.S. House of Representatives fought hard over the state's nine district seats, resulting in the election of six Republicans and three Democrats. Voters said "no" to slot machines and video poker on Indian reservations and rejected proposals to create school vouchers and charter schools and for term limits for members of Congress.

Economy and an Earthquake. Washington's economy accelerated in 1996, with employment growth approximately twice that of 1995. Much of the growth was due to Boeing's resurgence, as the company planned to add more than 13,000 jobs. Software companies led by Microsoft and computer makers also contributed to the state's economic health. The decline in the forest-products industry persisted. Washington maintained strong ties to Asian markets. *Fortune* magazine rated Seattle as the best city in the United States for work and family.

In May an earthquake of magnitude 5.4 jolted western Washington but was described as relatively insignificant compared with major quakes.

Legislation. The 1996 state legislature approved more than 300 laws, but retiring Gov. Mike Lowry vetoed all or part of 49 of them. Lawmakers continued to get tough on crime, especially sex crimes. Persistent sex offenders would be sentenced to life imprisonment without possibility of parole after convictions. Corrections officials could reject placement of sex offenders near vulnerable populations. School employees with unsupervised access to children must undergo record checks. Penalties for domestic violence were increased, and although some persons convicted of misdemeanors may qualify to possess firearms, those convicted of domestic violence may not. The primary method of execution was changed from hanging to lethal injection.

Lawmakers also took aim at managed health care and increased the required disclosure of services and options. Health-care providers, not insurers, must decide how long mothers should be hospitalized for childbirth. The governor vetoed a bill to repeal those portions of the 1993 school-reform law that required a certificate of mastery for high-school graduation. He also vetoed legislation to prohibit organ transplants for offenders on death row. The legislature overrode his veto of legislation to reduce the state's business and occupation tax. M. L. C.

WEST VIRGINIA. Cecil Underwood made West Virginia history in 1996, becoming the oldest person, at age 74, ever elected governor of the state. It would be the Republican's second term as governor in the predominantly Democratic state. His first term was from 1957 to 1961, when he was the youngest person ever elected to the post. Underwood defeated Democrat Charlotte Pritt, the first woman in the state to win a party's nomination for governor. Pundits said that voters in the socially conservative state were not ready to elect a woman as governor, especially one who was fairly liberal politically, as Pritt was perceived to be.

Utah's Gov. Michael Leavitt (R), who based his campaign on his record of increasing salaries for teachers and cutting taxes, won reelection overwhelmingly, defeating Democrat Jim Bradley.

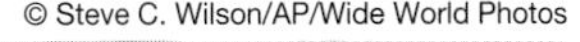
© Steve C. Wilson/AP/Wide World Photos

In West Virginia in November 1996, Republican Cecil Underwood (right) not only celebrated his election to the governorship but also his 74th birthday. He had been chosen for the post once before—40 years earlier—becoming the youngest person ever to be the state's governor. Now he would be the oldest.

© "The Journal," Todd Hartless/AP/Wide World Photos

The state's longtime speaker of the House, Chuck Chambers, announced that he would step down from the legislature after serving as speaker for 12 years, the longest consecutive term as speaker in the state's history. Both the state House of Representatives and Senate remained in the control of Democrats.

Legislation and the Economy. One of the more significant legislative initiatives was the passage of a "workfare" bill. The pilot program set up by the legislation eventually would require that 10% of the state's welfare recipients be enrolled in a program that ultimately would lead to employment. The move was an effort by the state to anticipate federal changes in welfare that would require aid recipients to work.

The legislature also called two special sessions in 1996 devoted to using surplus revenue for flood relief. On three different occasions, there was heavy flooding in the mountainous parts of the state. The first was the result of the rapid thaw of heavy snow during the winter, and the others were the result of heavy rain in the summer months. Charleston set a record for snowfall in the state, getting more snow than Buffalo, NY, during the winter of 1996.

In economic news, Toyota Motor Corp. announced it would build an engine plant in Putnam county, 35 mi (56 km) from Charleston. The plant was expected to be a $300 million investment in the state. C. S.

WISCONSIN. News from the sports world dominated headlines in Wisconsin in 1996. The Green Bay Packers football team, the pride of the entire state, reached Super Bowl XXXI in January 1997, with the National Football League's most valuable player, quarterback Brett Favre, leading the way. After an off-season rehabilitation for an addiction to painkillers, Favre—perhaps the most popular person in the state—returned to quarterback the team. In baseball news, the Milwaukee Brewers broke ground on a $250 million stadium in November. The construction came about only after months of political controversy and financial wrangling. The stadium was due to open in the year 2000.

In November, four Republican and three Democratic U.S. House incumbents retained their seats, and Democrats picked up the two open House seats. Wisconsin's 11 electoral votes went to President Bill Clinton.

Other News. Pabst Brewing Co. closed its 150-year-old brewery in Milwaukee....The state enacted a groundbreaking new program designed to move people from welfare to work that several other states considered adopting as a solution to welfare reform....Seven persons were charged with stealing $13 million worth of equipment from Fort McCoy, a military base in western Wisconsin....A freight train carrying propane derailed in March in the central Wisconsin town of Weyauwega. The fuel burst into flames, prompting an evacuation of the entire town of about 1,700 residents. Most were forced out of their homes for 19 days during the cleanup. L. B.

WYOMING. Americans watched and listened in April as Jessica Dubroff, a 7-year-old girl, made the rounds of national television and radio news shows, discussing her impending attempt to become the youngest pilot to fly across the continent.

Air Disasters. Jessica Dubroff took off from Half Moon Bay, CA, on April 10, heading for Falmouth, MA, and a spot in the record books. With her in the single-engine Cessna 177B were her father, Lloyd Dubroff, and her flight instructor, Joe Reid. The first leg of her trip went smoothly, and the three aviators spent the night in Cheyenne. Early the next morning, only moments after taking off in high winds and heavy rain and sleet, the plane stalled and plummeted nose-first into a residential area near the airport. All three on board were killed.

Another airplane tragedy in Wyoming made national news when, in August, a U.S. Air Force Lockheed C-130 cargo plane crashed near Sheep Mountain a few minutes after taking off from Jackson Hole. The significance of the accident was that the plane was part of the White House entourage; President Bill Clinton had left the area only a few hours before for a New York City celebration, and the C-130 was bound for the same destination. One Secret Service employee and all eight air-force crew members were killed.

Elections. In the November election, Republican State Sen. Michael B. Enzi won the U.S. Senate seat being vacated by retiring Sen. Alan K. Simpson. The Republican House incumbent, Barbara Cubin, retained her seat. Presidential candidate Bob Dole carried the state with 50% of the vote. Wyoming voters in a referendum backed congressional term limits. B. J.

STOCKS AND BONDS

Confounding its many doubters on Wall Street and Main Street, the great bull market in U.S. stocks took another leap forward in 1996, carrying the Dow Jones industrial average above 6,000, and then past 6,500, for the first time. That headline-grabbing performance helped inspire the biggest year yet for the booming mutual-fund industry.

The "Dow" celebrated its 100th anniversary (*see* SPECIAL REPORT, page 523) with a rise of 1,331.15 points, or 26.01%, to 6,448.27, on top of a 33.45% jump in 1995, when it broke 4,000 and 5,000. Standard & Poor's 500-stock composite index posted a 1996 rise of 124.81 points, or 20.26%, to 740.74, and the composite index of the Nasdaq market gained 238.9 points, or 22.71%, to 1,291.03.

The stock market spent the winter and early spring climbing to a succession of new highs, reaching 5,778 in the Dow on May 22, as enthusiasm for stocks and stock mutual funds carried over from the prosperous year of 1995. Then, in a spell of about eight weeks, the market averages suffered a sharp setback of nearly 10% to as much as 20% as talk spread that the economy was gathering strength, raising the specter of revived inflation and possible moves by the Federal Reserve to tighten credit conditions. After mid-July, however, the market rallied as those fears eased and ultimately proved unfounded. Statistical measures of the economy showed it remaining in what Wall Streeters came to call a "Goldilocks" condition—neither too hot nor too cold—with slow to moderate growth and low inflation. After the November 5 election, when the voters returned both Bill Clinton, the Democratic president, and a Republican congressional majority to office, stock investors staged another celebration, concluding that no political shifts were likely to disrupt Wall Street's good times.

The bond market also followed a zigzag pattern through the year, but with much more subdued results. The yield on 30-year Treasury bonds, which began the year just under 6.25%, climbed above 7% as worries increased about inflationary pressures, but then fell back below 6.5% as the economy cooled in the second half. In the closing weeks of the year, long-term government bonds showed a small positive total return (including interest payments and price changes) since New Year's.

Falling interest rates had been cited widely as a prime force pushing stock prices higher through much of their long climb in the 1980s and 1990s. Stocks were able to do well in 1996 without much help from interest rates, analysts said, because corporate profits kept

George Stewart

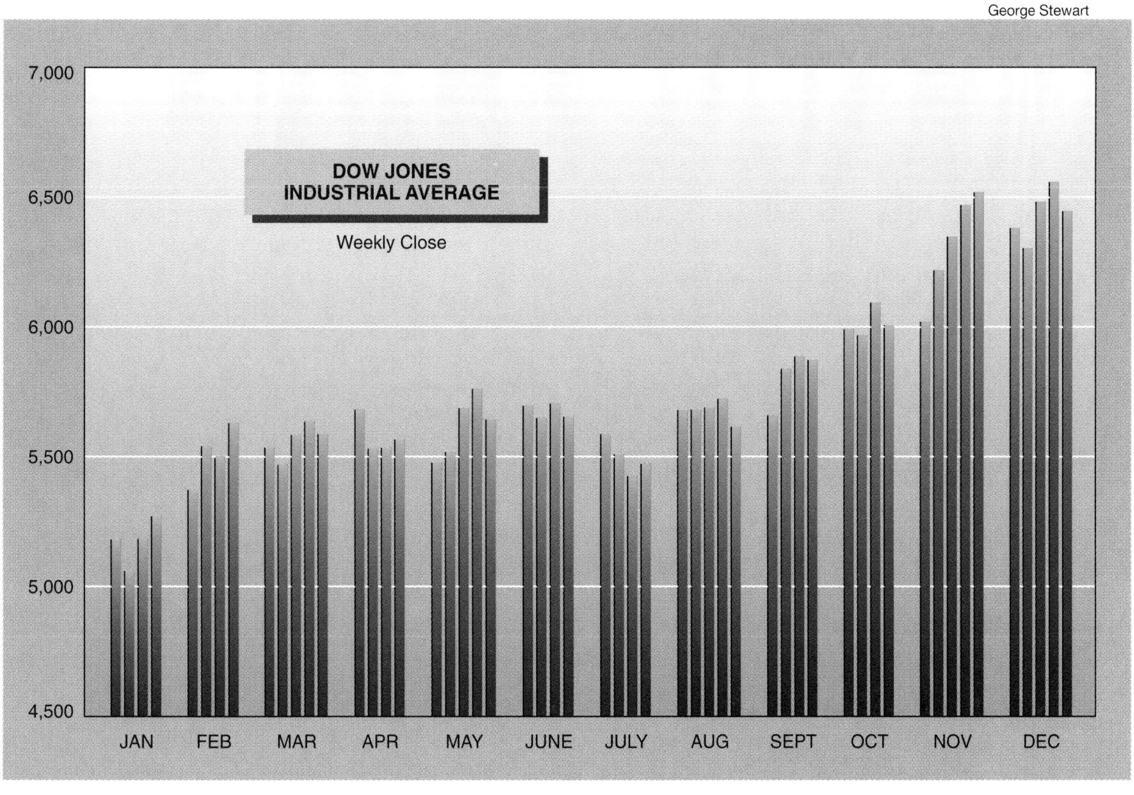

DOW JONES INDUSTRIAL AVERAGE
Weekly Close

7,000
6,500
6,000
5,500
5,000
4,500

JAN FEB MAR APR MAY JUNE JULY AUG SEPT OCT NOV DEC

improving strongly even in a sluggish economic environment, and U.S. industry seemed to be extending its impressive competitive gains in world markets.

The world price of gold, often considered a good gauge of anxiety about inflation and other economic uncertainties, briefly spiked above $400 an ounce in early 1996. But the rally quickly faded, and gold settled back to the neighborhood of $380 an ounce, within a few dollars of where it finished both 1994 and 1995. However, it began 1997 at about $360 an ounce—the lowest level since 1993.

Among the year's strongest-performing stocks were oil-drilling and other energy issues—bolstered by a rise in oil demand and prices—and bank and brokerage stocks. Bank shares benefited from a continuing consolidation of the industry through mergers, while all financial-services stocks rode the wave of enthusiasm generated by the stock bull market and growing concern for savings and investment among an aging population unsure of how much future help it could expect from Social Security in retirement.

Mutual Funds. No financial-services business exhibited more prosperity than the mutual-fund industry, which rolled up some of its most impressive statistics yet in a generation-long spell of dramatic growth. By mid-November, stock mutual funds had piled up cash inflows from investors of a record-shattering $200 billion. Bond and income funds, by contrast, showed inflows of less than $10 billion. At the end of October, total assets in the nation's 6,000-plus mutual funds of all types stood at almost $3.4 trillion—up about $700 billion from 12 months before—according to the Investment Company Institute, the funds' main trade association. Assets, of course, are increased by rising values of funds' portfolio investments as well as by new money invested in funds.

The exuberant demand for funds intensified a debate that had been simmering for years. Skeptics said the boom was setting investors and the markets up for a nasty retrenchment when the stock market lost its forward momentum. Fund partisans countered that investors demonstrated their steady nerves and perseverance in the early-summer market correction. Stock funds, in any case, were not the only popular type of mutual fund. Money-market funds, with yields hovering at or just below 5% from the short-term interest-bearing investments in their portfolios, boasted assets of more than $875 billion at the end of October, according to the ICI, up from about $733 billion a year earlier.

World Markets. For the third consecutive year, domestic stock funds outperformed international and global stock funds, which have been touted widely in the 1990s as a way for U.S. investors to increase opportunities and diversification at the same time. But many world funds enjoyed a respectable year, as most markets around the world gained ground. Through late November, Hong Kong, up 30.9%, was the best performer in a tally of world markets by Morgan Stanley Capital International Perspective in Geneva. That market was aided by increasing confidence among investors as Hong Kong approached its scheduled reversion at mid-1997 from British to Chinese control.

Also besting or rivaling Wall Street's gains, as tracked in local currencies, were the stock markets of Canada, up 29%, and France, up 24%. Germany gained 18.1%; Switzerland, 15.4%; Britain, 10.2%; and Australia, 3.6%. The laggard was Japan, up 1.1%, still struggling to recover from a multiyear recession that followed the collapse of its financial boom of the late 1980s.

Debate Over Values. As mutual-fund coffers swelled and stock prices rose, worried analysts said most traditional measures of domestic-stock values had reached levels suggesting danger. Aggregate dividend yields of U.S. stock-market averages and indexes, already at record or near-record lows as the year began, fell to the neighborhood of 2%. By some analysts' measurements, the typical domestic stock traded for the first time ever at more than four times its book value, or theoretical liquidating value. Bull-market believers said there were special reasons for these extreme readings. Dividend payments, for one thing, had lagged in recent years as many corporate boards elected to earmark a share of profits for stock buybacks. Book-value measures were said to have fallen behind the pace of technological change—which, meanwhile, produced important productivity improvements that were hard to measure statistically.

Besides, said the optimists, traditional valuation measures might be outmoded in an era marked by real progress in smoothing out the ups and downs of business conditions. Since the beginning of the 1980s, the U.S. economy had suffered just one traditional recession—a relatively brief period of declining output in late 1990 and early 1991. Indeed, as 1996 drew to a close, a lively debate broke out on Wall Street over whether the Federal Reserve and other policy makers had succeeded in taming the business cycle altogether.

CHET CURRIER, *The Associated Press*

SPECIAL REPORT/STOCKS AND BONDS

The Dow Jones Index Turns 100

As widely known and as controversial as ever, the Dow Jones average of 30 industrial stocks marked its 100th anniversary in 1996 by reaching new highs. The average passed 6,000, seven and one half times its level of 777 in August 1982, when one of the greatest bull markets in financial history began on Wall Street.

History. The average, introduced by Dow Jones & Co. in 1896, began with just 12 component stocks. That early roster reflected an economy dominated by industrial commodity companies like American Cotton Oil; American Sugar Refining; Tennessee Coal, Iron & Railroad; U.S. Leather; and U.S. Rubber. The list was expanded to 20 companies in 1916 and 30 in 1928, with the adding of such modern corporate giants as American Telephone & Telegraph, General Motors, Sears Roebuck, and Standard Oil of New Jersey (later to be renamed Exxon).

Originally the "Dow" was a simple average, determined by adding up the prices of its component stocks and dividing the sum by the number of those components to get their average price. But with substitutions in the average's makeup over time, stock splits, and other changes, it became necessary to recompute the divisor frequently to maintain the average's continuity. Today the Dow is calculated with a divisor that, instead of 30, is less than 1%—.33792816 as of July 16, 1996. So a rise or fall of one point in any component stock now translates into a gain or loss of about three points in the average.

Criticism and Clout. Critics complain that the shrinkage in the divisor, combined with the high nominal level of the average, gives an exaggerated impression of stock-market volatility. It also is pointed out frequently that the average is not strictly "industrial" anymore, considering that its modern components include businesses far from the old smokestack-and-factory tradition of U.S. industry.

For some time now the Dow has been supplanted by other indicators—such as Standard & Poor's 500-stock composite index—as a formal measure used by professional investors and money managers of the behavior of the stock market. It is dismissed widely as too narrow a sample and too mathematically unsophisticated in other ways to represent the real-world fortunes of the investing public. Nevertheless the Dow remains the common coinage by which the market's ups and downs are described. It endures as the single image of Wall Street most widely recognized worldwide.

Certainly the milestones it has passed to mark the stock market's modern progress have been celebrated widely. From the mid-1960s through the early 1980s, it wavered uncertainly each time it approached or briefly surpassed 1,000. Since then, it has soared. Membership in the Dow 30 roster, moreover, continues to stand as a certification of blue-chip status. The list of Dow companies as of mid-1996 included: Allied Signal, Aluminum Company of America, American Express, AT&T, Bethlehem Steel, Boeing, Caterpillar, Chevron, Coca-Cola, Disney, du Pont, Eastman Kodak, Exxon, General Electric, General Motors, Goodyear, International Business Machines, International Paper, McDonald's, Merck, Minnesota Mining & Manufacturing, J.P. Morgan, Philip Morris, Procter & Gamble, Sears Roebuck, Texaco, Union Carbide, United Technologies, Westinghouse Electric, and F.W. Woolworth.

CHET CURRIER

THE DOW JONES INDUSTRIAL AVERAGE—HISTORICAL MILESTONES

May 26, 1896	The Dow Jones Industrial Average is published for the first time.
January 12, 1906	The Dow closes over 100 points for the first time.
October 28, 1929	The average falls more than 38 points, signaling the beginning of the Great Depression of the 1930s.
March 12, 1956	For the first time, the Dow Jones average breaks 500.
November 14, 1972	The Dow breaks 1,000 points.
January 8, 1987	The Dow breaks another record, closing above 2,000 points.
October 16, 1987	The average falls more than 108 points—the first time it has ever lost more than 100 points in a day.
October 19, 1987	In a crashing end to the 1980s bull market, the Dow falls 508 points.
January 2, 1990	The first new high is set since the 1987 crash, as the Dow closes at 2810.15.
April 17, 1991	The average breaks the 3,000-point mark.
February 23, 1995	Continuing its steady climb, the Dow Jones average closes over 4,000.
November 21, 1995	The Dow reaches another milestone, closing over 5,000 points.
October 14, 1996	The Dow closes above 6,000—6,010—for the first time.

SUDAN

In 1996 the Sudanese government remained under the control of military officers led by Omar Hassan Ahmed al-Bashir and the National Islamic Front (NIF), led by Hassan al-Turabi. In March elections were held in which Bashir won 76% of the votes for president and the NIF gained total control of the National Assembly. Al-Turabi became speaker of the Assembly, accepting an official role in the government for the first time since the regime came to power in 1989. The elections represented a new stage in the political system based on the NIF's program of Islamization. In October, Khartoum city authorities promulgated rules calling for the separation of the sexes in public places.

Continuing economic difficulties were reflected in demonstrations protesting the rise in prices of basic commodities. The government removed subsidies on gasoline and other products as a part of its economic program, but this resulted in further inflation. There were contradictory reports late in the year about the financial prospects of the Arakis Energy Corporation, which had been developing Sudanese oil resources in the south-central regions. Relatively significant production was reported reliably and some southern armed groups were working with the government to provide security for the oil fields.

Student demonstrations were the primary expression of internal opposition as NIF groups lost in some student elections. Omdurman University was closed following clashes between students supporting the NIF and those affiliated with the opposition. The government also reported attempted military coups, led by retired officers associated with the opposition in exile, in March and August.

Civil War. The civil conflict continued during 1996 with major issues being the government's program of Islamization and the future of the southern regions. In April the government signed a peace agreement with two southern Sudanese military groups—the Southern Sudan Independence Movement (SSIM), led by Riak Machar, and a faction of the Sudan People's Liberation Army (SPLA) led by Kerbino Kuanyin Bol. However, the leader of the largest SPLA faction, John Garang, and the northern opposition groups in exile rejected this agreement.

The coalition of northern Muslim antigovernment groups in exile and the opposition SPLA—the National Democratic Alliance (NDA)—received important international recognition early in the year. The Eritrean government turned over the Sudanese embassy building in Asmara to the NDA in February. The NDA announced a campaign of military opposition to the NIF regime but this had few visible results by late in the year.

Representatives of the NIF, NDA, SPLA, and Sudanese Christian officials joined together in Rome in March for the ceremonies involved with the beatification of Bishop Daniel Comboni, a 19th-century Roman Catholic missionary who served in central Africa in the 1870s. However, Catholic bishops from SPLA-controlled areas were among the most articulate international critics of the NIF regime, and there were tensions between SPLA officers and church officials. One local SPLA commander imprisoned six Catholic priests and religious in August, accusing them of hindering SPLA recruitment and secretly working to spread Islam.

International Affairs. Sudan remained at odds with its neighbors, who feared possible Sudanese support for domestic opposition groups. At the same time, some progress was made in reducing tensions. In September an agreement was signed with Uganda—with the help of Iranian mediation—to establish ways of monitoring borders. Good relations with Iran were maintained, and Saudi leaders engaged in friendly discussions with Bashir.

Relations with Egypt were less tense than in the previous year, and Egypt's President Hosni Mubarak welcomed Bashir to the Arab League summit in Cairo in June. Relations with Egypt continued, however, to have a negative impact upon Sudan's broader international position. Accusations that the Sudanese government harbored terrorists, specifically people accused of attempting to murder Mubarak in 1995, led to international condemnation. The UN Security Council passed three U.S.-supported resolutions (in January, April, and August) condemning Sudan for its sheltering of terrorist suspects.

JOHN O. VOLL, *Georgetown University*

SUDAN • Information Highlights

Official Name: Republic of the Sudan.
Location: Northeast Africa.
Area: 967,494 sq mi (2 505 810 km^2).
Population (mid-1996 est.): 28,900,000.
Chief Cities (1993 census—provisional): Khartoum, the capital, 924,505; Nyala, 1,267,077; Sharg en-Nil, 879,105.
Government: *Head of state and government,* Omar Hassan Ahmed al-Bashir, president (took power June 30, 1989). *Legislature*—Transitional National Assembly.
Monetary Unit: Pound (434.8 pounds equal U.S.$1, official rate, January 1995).
Gross Domestic Product (1994 est. U.S.$): $23,700,000,000 (purchasing power parity).
Foreign Trade (fiscal year 1993–94, U.S.$): *Imports,* $1,700,000,000; *exports,* $419,000,000.

SWEDEN

In 1996 the Swedish government, under new leadership, was completing its financial-consolidation program, and the nation's membership in the European economic and monetary union (EMU) was put on hold.

Politics and the Economy. Finance Minister Göran Persson took over from Ingvar Carlsson as leader of the Social Democratic Party and prime minister in March 1996. The government continued the four-year consolidation program—of which Persson was the principal original architect—to cut public expenditure by $18.8 billion. The public-sector deficit was about 4% of gross domestic product (GDP) in 1996, down from 13% in 1994 and projected to be in balance by 1998.

Erik Asbrink, who took over from Persson as finance minister and is considered to be a fiscal hard-liner, said that Sweden might require a permanent budget surplus, if the nation were to remain outside a single European currency and if EMU starts on schedule in 1999. The priority of the government was to reduce open unemployment from the 1996 level of 8% to 4% in the year 2000. Total unemployment, which includes persons in various publicly funded training jobs, is almost twice as high.

Exports and investments grew fast in Sweden in 1996, and—with a small increase in private consumption—total GDP growth approached 2%, well below the 3% that Finance Minister Asbrink deemed necessary to meet government job-creation targets. More than 30% of the equity on the Stockholm stock exchange was owned by foreigners in 1996, prompting discussions about the future of Swedish industry. General Motors obtained an option to buy all or part of the shares in SAAB Auto that it did not own.

SWEDEN • Information Highlights

Official Name: Kingdom of Sweden.
Location: Northern Europe.
Area: 173,732 sq mi (449 964 km²).
Population (mid-1996 est.): 8,800,000.
Chief Cities (Dec. 31, 1994 est.): Stockholm, the capital, 703,627; Göteborg, 444,553; Malmö, 242,706; Uppsala, 181,191.
Government: *Head of state,* Carl XVI Gustaf, king (acceded Sept. 1973). *Head of government,* Göran Persson, prime minister (took office March 1996). *Legislature* (unicameral)—Riksdag.
Monetary Unit: Krona (6.8050 kronor equal U.S.$1, Dec. 5, 1996).
Gross Domestic Product (1994 est. U.S.$): $163,100,000,000 (purchasing power parity).
Economic Indexes (1995, 1990 = 100): *Consumer Prices,* all items, 122.7; food, 103.0. *Industrial Production,* 115.
Foreign Trade (1995 U.S.$): *Imports,* $64,446,000,000; *exports,* $79,918,000,000.

© Dan Van Der Zwalm/Sygma

Sweden's Prime Minister Göran Persson was among those who addressed the World Congress against Commercial Sexual Exploitation of Children, held in Stockholm, Aug. 27–31, 1996.

The monarchy in Sweden, especially Queen Silvia, is usually reticent in political matters. But in July she frontally attacked Sweden's liberal child-pornography laws in a television interview. She complained that nothing was being done to stop the sexual exploitation of children and proposed that newspapers protect children rather than criminals by publishing the names of convicted pedophiles. Police supported her, noting that Sweden is one of the few countries in the world where owning child pornography is not a crime. A parliamentary commission had been working on the issue for some two years.

European Affairs. An opinion poll published in October 1996 showed that only 32% of Swedes had a positive view of the European Union (EU)—the lowest percentage of any member country. And though the government expected Sweden to qualify for membership in the EMU by 1999, such membership was put on hold. Prime Minister Persson did not exclude the possibility that Sweden would be among EMU's charter members, but Sweden, unlike Finland, did not join the Exchange Rate Mechanism in 1996. It, therefore, would not meet the formal requirement of two years in the mechanism by 1999.

Foreign Policy and Defense. Foreign Minister Lena Hjelm-Wallen and Defense Minister Thage G. Peterson stated in June 1996 that

Sweden has no intention of joining the North Atlantic Treaty Organization (NATO). They were responding to a debate in the wake of Prime Minister Persson's visit to the Baltic states, where he had expressed support for the right of the Baltics to join NATO.

Swedish defense expenditures were being cut by 10%, though the defense staff said that the cut was actually bigger. There now was independent confirmation from former Swedish and Soviet naval officers that Sweden had been the target of Soviet intrusions by mini U-boats in large numbers as late as 1992.

LEIF BECK FALLESEN, *Editor in Chief*
"Boersen," Copenhagen

SWITZERLAND

Swiss concerns in 1996 were dominated by an escalating banking scandal that turned into a national "crise de conscience."

Holocaust Victims' Accounts. In 1934 the Swiss government enacted bank-secrecy laws to protect the identities of German Jewish depositors. With the outbreak of World War II, deposits in Swiss bank accounts by European Jews rapidly escalated. After the war, it became apparent that many of the depositors had died in Nazi concentration camps. In recent years identification and disposition of the dormant accounts has generated tension between the Swiss banking industry and the international Jewish community. On Feb. 7, 1996, the Swiss Bankers Association reported that it had identified 775 accounts totaling $32 million that "could" have belonged to Holocaust victims. This figure was rejected by the World Jewish Congress, which maintained the correct figure might be as much as $7 billion.

On April 23, Hans Baer, a director of the Swiss Bankers Association, told the U.S. Senate Banking Committee that his group would support the establishment of an independent investigatory commission to seek out funds belonging to Holocaust victims. Representatives of the association, the World Jewish Congress, and the Jewish Agency in Israel agreed to form a panel to perform this task. The resultant commission announced in November that an audit of Swiss banks, to be conducted by three major U.S. accounting firms, would seek out accounts and assets belonging to victims of the Nazis and would turn evidence over to the Swiss authorities.

Nazi Gold Sales. The actions of Swiss banks during World War II again came under further scrutiny and condemnation later in the year. The British Foreign Office asserted that Swiss banks had bought and sold gold looted by the Nazis from occupied countries. Also sold, it was alleged, were gold and jewels confiscated from those in concentration camps. The British maintained that Swiss banks had returned only 10% of this wealth to its rightful owners. The Swiss National Bank conceded in December that it had made a substantial profit on wartime dealings in gold bullion with Germany's central bank; it denied, however, that gold stolen from Holocaust victims had passed through the bank and insisted the bank was holding no gold marked by the Reichsbank. Revelations from declassified U.S. documents cast doubt on these assertions, however. Critics also charged that Switzerland had used assets deposited by East European Jews to compensate Swiss citizens who had lost property nationalized by the communist regimes in Poland, Hungary, and Czechoslovakia. In late September the Swiss government announced it would establish an independent commission of historians and judges to investigate all wartime banking and insurance transactions. The parliament in December approved the commission's creation and ordered the nation's banks to lift their secrecy rules.

For Switzerland's populace the scandal raised moral questions of collusion with the Nazis and of the degree to which Switzerland had "bought" its neutrality during the war—questions that struck at the very foundation of Swiss citizens' perception of themselves and of their country's unique historical tradition of neutrality.

Other News. The nation agreed in principle to join the Partnership for Peace plan of the North Atlantic Treaty Organization (NATO)....The government announced that 230,000 cattle would be destroyed in an effort to eliminate "mad-cow disease."

PAUL C. HELMREICH, *Wheaton College, MA*

SWITZERLAND • Information Highlights

Official Name: Swiss Confederation.
Location: Central Europe.
Area: 15,942 sq mi (41 290 km²).
Population (mid-1996 est.): 7,100,000.
Chief Cities (Dec. 31, 1994 est.): Bern, the capital, 128,422; Zurich, 342,872; Basel, 175,561.
Government: *Head of state and government,* Jean Pascal Delamuraz, president (took office January 1996). *Legislature*—Federal Assembly: Council of States and National Council.
Monetary Unit: Franc (1.3137 francs equal U.S.$1, Dec. 5, 1996).
Gross Domestic Product (1994 est. U.S.$): $148,400,000,000 (purchasing power parity).
Economic Indexes (1995, 1990 = 100): *Consumer Prices,* all items, 116.8; food, 107.0. *Industrial Production,* 111.
Foreign Trade (1995 U.S.$): *Imports,* $77,006,000,000; *exports,* $77,670,000,000.

SYRIA

Syrian affairs were notably immobile in 1996. This was not necessarily to be regarded as a failure, however. The regime of President Hafiz al-Assad evidently considered that the status quo was sufficiently favorable.

Domestically, it was easy to understand the rationale of such an attitude. Assad's control of domestic affairs was virtually absolute, and had been so for more than a quarter of a century. Despite some democratic gestures, normal political life remained virtually nonexistent. On the other hand, the basis of his power could not be regarded as completely secure. He and his immediate associates are Alawite Muslims—members of a small Shiite sect constituting no more than 15% of the population of Syria and regarded as semiheretical by both Sunni and mainstream Shiite Muslims. But the regime's grip continued to be tight and stability widely was regarded as a blessing.

Domestic Affairs. Damascus was hit by a series of bomb blasts in June. Although the identity of the perpetrators remained unknown, it seemed likely that the bombings had been carried out by opponents of the government. It also was said credibly that a number of arrests had been made in the wake of the blasts. Neither the bombings nor the arrests were mentioned in the controlled Syrian press, although they were, cautiously and a little later, in the press of Lebanon.

Economic policy continued to loosen government controls. Oil production, though small by Middle Eastern standards, continued to rise; and Syria received adequate subsidies from richer Arab states to compensate for the disappearance of Syria's former patron, the Soviet Union.

Foreign Relations. In 1996, Assad made some trips within the Middle East, and there was a spectacular procession of Damascus-bound diplomatic pilgrims, but virtually no change in Syria's position or policies eventuated. When U.S. President Bill Clinton sponsored a one-day antiterrorism summit in Sharm El-Sheik, Egypt, on March 13—convened in response to the series of Hamas bombings in Israel—Syria and its satellite state, Lebanon, declined to attend.

In March the annual report to the U.S. Congress on the antinarcotics efforts of foreign countries again listed Syria as one of six "noncooperative" nations in the war on drugs. Also in March, the annual U.S. State Department report on human-rights violations listed Syria as guilty of significant breaches. In April the State Department listed Syria as one of seven states that were sponsors of terrorism.

Syria's already strained relations with Turkey grew worse in 1996 as a result of Turkey's military-cooperation agreement with Israel, concluded in February. The chronic issue of new Turkish dams, thought to imperil Syrian water supplies from the Euphrates, remained unresolved.

The key question of a possible peace with Israel saw no progress. The unproductive U.S.-sponsored Israel-Syrian negotiations that had been in progress since December 1995 were broken off by Israel in March because of Syria's refusal to condemn the Hamas terrorist acts in Israel. On April 23, Assad delivered a spectacular snub to his frequent visitor, U.S. Secretary of State Warren Christopher, when he refused to see Christopher although a meeting had been arranged. They did, however, meet on succeeding days.

The Israeli election in May of Prime Minister Benjamin Netanyahu appeared to lessen chances of agreement. Assad adhered adamantly to his reiterated demand that total Israeli withdrawal from the Golan Heights must precede any other Israeli-Syrian topics. The peacemaking example of Egypt, Jordan, and the Palestine Liberation Organization (PLO)—as well as the blandishments of the United States—all were ineffective in modifying the rigidity of this stance.

In June, Assad attended the Pan-Arab summit in Cairo, but was unsuccessful in his attempts to persuade Arab leaders to break economic and other links with Israel, or to adopt friendlier policies with Iran....On September 10, Syria abstained in the UN General Assembly vote approving the Comprehensive Test Ban Treaty.

See also MIDDLE EAST.

ARTHUR CAMPBELL TURNER
University of California, Riverside

SYRIA • Information Highlights

Official Name: Syrian Arab Republic.
Location: Southwest Asia.
Area: 71,498 sq mi (185 180 km²).
Population (mid-1996 est.): 15,600,000.
Chief Cities (June 30, 1994 est.): Damascus, the capital, 1,444,138; Aleppo, 1,542,000; Homs, 558,000.
Government: *Head of state,* Gen. Hafiz al-Assad, president (took office officially March 1971). *Head of government,* Mahmoud Zubi, prime minister (took office November 1987). *Legislature* (unicameral)—People's Council.
Monetary Unit: Pound (11.225 pounds equal U.S.$1, August 1996).
Gross Domestic Product (1994 est. U.S.$): $74,400,000,000 (purchasing power parity).
Economic Index (Damascus, 1994; 1990 = 100): *Consumer Prices,* all items, 143.8; food, 130.4.
Foreign Trade (1995 U.S.$): *Imports,* $4,616,000,000; *exports,* $3,970,000,000.

TAIWAN

In 1996, Taiwan saw its first-ever direct presidential election, a sharp deterioration in relations with China, a setback in efforts to secure international recognition, and a slowing of economic growth.

Politics. Lee Teng-hui, who had been serving as president since 1988, was elected to the office on March 24 in the nation's first direct election for the presidency. In fact, it was the first such election in any Chinese society and was regarded by many as a major milestone in the emergence of Chinese democracy. More than three quarters of those eligible participated in the election. Lee and his running mate, Lien Chan, received 54% of the vote. The opposition Democratic Progressive Party (DPP), which campaigned on a platform of independence for Taiwan, received 21%, and the conservative New Party, a splinter of Lee's Nationalist Party, received 15%.

Despite the substantial margin of victory, President Lee found himself thwarted in his attempt to make good on his mandate. Legislative elections in December 1995 left his Nationalist Party with a majority of only three seats, and the opposition was quick to accuse the ruling party of inefficacy and corruption. In July and August serious damage resulted from Typhoon Herb, the worst storm to hit the island in 30 years. The storm revealed the government's failure to implement flood-control plans.

With the political system midway through a fundamental reform, the balance of power among the executive branch, the Legislative Yuan, and the National Assembly remained undetermined. The conflict between the executive branch and the legislature came to a head with Lee's decision to keep Lien, his newly elected vice-president, in the position of prime minister. Arguing that it was not a new appointment, he refused to submit Lien's name to the legislature for confirmation. Opposition legislators—known for a proclivity to turn to physical action when words fail—blocked the entrance when the prime minister came in October to deliver a scheduled report on the development of a new nuclear reactor. While some argued that the largely ceremonial National Assembly should be abolished, others advocated that it be transformed into a second chamber of a bicameral legislature.

Relations with the Mainland. China's leaders appeared to believe that, despite his statements to the contrary, Lee was a closet advocate of independence for Taiwan. Moreover, they found the contrast between the rapid expansion of democracy on Taiwan and their

LEE TENG-HUI

Taiwan's first democratically elected president, Lee Teng-hui, was born in northern Taiwan on Jan. 15, 1923. He was educated in Taiwan and Japan and began his career teaching at National Taiwan University. After he earned a doctorate in agricultural economics at Cornell University in 1968, he returned to Taiwan and joined the government.

In 1978, Lee was appointed mayor of Taipei, and three years later he became governor of the province of Taiwan. Lee was the first Taiwanese-born politician to occupy these positions. The Nationalist Party, which took control of Taiwan in 1946, was for many years controlled by a mainland-born minority. To enhance the legitimacy of the Nationalist Party and its government, President Chiang Ching-kuo began appointing native-born politicians to important positions.

In 1984, President Chiang selected Lee as his running mate. Soon after his term began, however, Chiang's health began to deteriorate, and he died in office in 1988. It surprised no one when Lee succeeded him. Many assumed that he would finish out Chiang's term and be replaced by a mainland-born successor. However, despite vigorous opposition, Lee was elected to head the Nationalist Party. In 1990 he was elected by the National Assembly as president. This term was marked by the vigorous pursuit of a policy of opening ties with the People's Republic of China and by efforts to secure diplomatic recognition for his government.

Lee is married to Tseng Wen-hui, whom he has known since childhood. The couple have two daughters.

JOHN BRYAN STARR

© AFP/Corbis-Bettmann

own hardening resistance to political liberalization highly distasteful and potentially embarrassing. As a result, Beijing worked actively to bring about Lee's defeat in the presidential election or at least to cut the size of his majority. The official press carried blistering denunciations. More alarming, officials with the People's Liberation Army (PLA) had dropped hints to a U.S. visitor to Beijing in December 1995 that, should Lee be elected, it would conduct daily missile strikes on the island for 30 days. Fueling the rumors, the PLA moved more than 150,000 troops into Fujian province opposite Taiwan in late February and began a series of missile test firings into the Taiwan Strait in early March. The exercises were meant to demonstrate China's capability to interrupt the island's maritime commerce.

Generally speaking, the reaction among Taiwan's population was the opposite of that anticipated by Beijing. Although Taiwan's stock market fluctuated even more wildly than usual, support remained strong for Lee and for those advocating a more extreme anti-Chinese position than he did. The U.S. government, though it did not take seriously the threat of an actual attack on Taiwan, denounced the military exercises as "unnecessarily provocative," moved a carrier group into the vicinity, and agreed to the sale to Taiwan of Stinger air-defense missiles and other "defensive" weapons.

Following the election, Beijing attempted to put a good face on the outcome. Pointing to the decline in support for the DPP between the 1995 legislative elections (in which the party received 41% of the vote) and the presidential elections, the Chinese press said that the election results offered proof that the people of Taiwan had rejected independence. It advocated an early meeting between President Lee and Chinese President Jiang Zemin and the opening of direct air, shipping, and mail links across the Taiwan Strait. At his inauguration in May, President Lee, too, proposed an early meeting with President Jiang. Three months later, however, Lee called for voluntary limits on Taiwan's investments in the mainland—which, by year's end, totaled some $25 billion in more than 30,000 projects. China denounced Lee's limits as creating obstacles to the free operation of market forces.

Diplomatic Setbacks. Taiwan's campaign to secure international recognition was dealt a serious blow in late November when the government of South Africa announced that it would sever diplomatic ties with Taipei in December 1997 and extend recognition to the People's Republic of China. Foreign Affairs Minister John Chang visited Pretoria but was unsuccessful in persuading his hosts to maintain some form of downgraded formal ties. The following week, Taiwan announced that it would end all aid to South Africa, suspend most treaties between the two nations, and recall its ambassador.

TAIWAN • Information Highlights

Official Name: Taiwan.
Location: Island off the southeastern coast of mainland China.
Area: 13,892 sq mi (35 980 km²).
Population (mid-1996 est.): 21,400,000.
Chief Cities (Dec. 31, 1994 est.): Taipei, the capital, 2,653,578; Kaohsiung, 1,416,248; Taichung, 832,654; Tainan, 702,658; Panchiaio, 539,115.
Government: *Head of state,* Lee Teng-hui, president (took office January 1988). *Head of government,* Lien Chan, prime minister (appointed Feb. 1993). *Legislature* (unicameral)—Legislative Yuan; (unicameral)—National Assembly.
Monetary Unit: New Taiwan dollar (27.50 NT dollars equal U.S.$1, Dec. 31, 1996).
Gross Domestic Product (1994 est. U.S.$): $257,000,000,000 (purchasing power parity)

Taiwan's Latin American friends once again proposed that the United Nations appoint an ad hoc committee to study modes for granting Taiwan representation, but, with strong pressure from the Beijing government, the measure was excluded from the General Assembly's agenda.

The Economy. The economy generally remained healthy, though the growth rate was projected to fall below 6% for the first time in many years. The unemployment rate—3.2% at year's end—was at its highest level in a decade. Foreign-exchange reserves were slightly higher than $80 billion, down from a high of $100 billion in 1995.

JOHN BRYAN STARR, *Brown University*

TANZANIA

Despite the flawed elections that brought Benjamin Mkapa to power in 1995, Tanzania's president succeeded in consolidating his control over the ruling Chama Cha Mapinduzi (CCM) Party and gaining the confidence of international donors. In Zanzibar, however, he had little influence, and the government and opposition remained at loggerheads.

On May 21, Tanzania experienced the worst maritime disaster in its history when a ferry on Lake Victoria capsized, killing more than 500 persons.

Politics. Even though he won 62% of the vote in the 1995 election, Mkapa came to power with little legitimacy, domestically or internationally. Many people voted for him because of the enthusiastic support he received from former President Julius Nyerere. Nevertheless, in July, Mkapa was elected chairman of the CCM and was able to marginalize the old guard still further. This was critical given events in Zanzibar and Pemba. There, CCM candidate Salmin Amour was declared the victor over Civic United Front (CUF) candidate Sief Harif Hamad by only 1,500 votes in an election marred by fraud. Both Hamad and Amour ruled out any cooperation, so with CUF holding nearly 50% of the seats in the Zanzibar parliament, that body became hamstrung. Also, Amour detained CUF members, stopped all opposition meetings, and banned all but the most sympathetic journalists. In return, CUF initiated a school boycott, and there were several arson attacks on the parliament and on residences of CCM officials. With this deterioration of human rights, Sweden, Norway, and Denmark suspended foreign assistance to the islands.

Foreign Affairs. Because nearly 40% of Tanzania's economy is based on international assistance, which had been cut off prior to the elections, gaining the confidence of donors was critical. This Mkapa did by reducing the size of the cabinet and filling it with new faces, tightening up on government spending, increasing revenue collection, and reducing patronage and corruption in parastatals. Seven months after being elected, Mkapa received pledges of $1.2 billion at a donors' conference in Paris.

Former President Nyerere continued to play a major international diplomatic role, working closely with former U.S. President Jimmy Carter to convene a series of Great Lakes summits aimed at ending conflicts in the nations surrounding the Great Lakes region—Zaire, Burundi, Rwanda, Tanzania, and Uganda. Following the coup in Burundi that brought Gen. Pierre Buyoya to power, Nyerere was invited to pursue a negotiated settlement, but talks soon stalled.

Economy. Cashew exports increased in both value and volume and emerged as the bright spot in Tanzania's export economy. Increased levels of gem and gold production made little contribution to the country's official economy. To remedy this, the government set up purchasing centers in mining areas. Tourism, whose future development is to be led by the private sector, continued to thrive.

WILLIAM CYRUS REED
The American University in Cairo

TANZANIA • Information Highlights

Official Name: United Republic of Tanzania.
Location: East coast of Africa.
Area: 364,900 sq mi (945 090 km²).
Population (mid-1996 est.): 29,100,000.
Chief Cities (1985 est.): Dar es Salaam, the capital, 1,096,000; Mwanza, 252,000; Tabora, 214,000.
Government: *Head of state,* Benjamin Mkapa, president (took office Nov. 23, 1995). *Head of government,* Frederick Sumaye, prime minister (appointed November 1995). *Legislature* (unicameral)—National Assembly.
Monetary Unit: Tanzanian shilling (590.740 shillings equal U.S.$1, August 1996).
Gross Domestic Product (1994 est. U.S.$): $21,000,000,000 (purchasing power parity).
Economic Index (Tanganyika, 1995; 1990 = 100): *Consumer Prices,* all items, 335.7; food, 346.7.
Foreign Trade (1995 U.S.$): *Imports,* $1,678,000,000; *exports,* $683,000,000.

TAXATION

Federal tax-reform proposals framed much of the debate in the 1996 U.S. presidential election. One candidate for the Republican nomination—Steve Forbes—championed a proposal for a flat tax (*see* SIDEBAR, page 531), as well as reductions in the tax rate imposed on capital gains. However, rather than proposing major structural changes, most of the candidates' debate centered on the size and form of tax cuts to the existing system.

Robert Dole, as the Republican presidential nominee, proposed more-modest changes to the existing federal income-tax system. The centerpiece of his tax proposal was a 15% across-the-board cut of marginal individual income-tax rates. Incumbent President Bill Clinton also proposed changes to the federal tax code, including targeted cuts in the capital-gains tax, tuition tax credits, and an expansion in allowable contributions to Individual Retirement Accounts (IRAs). Reform Party candidate Ross Perot urged tax simplification as well as the dismantling of the Internal Revenue Service (IRS), the main federal tax-collection agency.

For the second consecutive year, net state-tax revenue fell as legislatures in nearly 30 states passed modest individual- and business-tax cuts. Additional changes in state and local taxes resulted from ballot initiatives, most of which were designed to cut taxes or restrict the future growth of taxes or tax bases. There also were tax changes in other countries.

United States

Federal. Three taxes dominated total U.S. federal receipts for fiscal year (FY) 1996 (Oct. 1, 1995–Sept. 30, 1996), making up more than 90% of federal tax revenue. Of the estimated

$1,426,800,000,000 in federal tax collections, about 44% ($630.9 billion) came from individual income taxes, 35% ($507.5 billion) from social-insurance taxes and contributions for Social Security and Medicare, and 12% ($167.1 billion) from corporate taxes. Excise taxes, estate and gift taxes, customs duties, and miscellaneous receipts made up the remaining federal tax collections.

Compared to the contentious debate between the Republican-controlled Congress and Democratic President Clinton that characterized the eventual passage of the FY 1996 federal budget, the FY 1997 budget passed with little acrimony. Although disagreements remained, legislators were eager to begin reelection campaigns and few wanted to repeat the federal-government shutdowns that occurred prior to the passage of the FY 1996 budget.

During FY 1996, the federal income tax was structured into five marginal tax rates. Taxable family income between $0 and $38,000 faced a 15% marginal tax rate; income between $38,001 and $91,850 was taxed at 28%; family income between $91,851 and $140,000 was taxed at 31%; income between $140,001 and $250,000 was taxed at 36%; and income greater than $250,000 faced the top marginal tax rate of 39.6%. The progressivity of the income tax was increased further with the federal Earned Income Tax Credit (EITC), a tax-credit subsidy to the earnings of low-income families.

The 1996 presidential campaign was shaped in large part around tax reform. Armed with his proposal for a flat tax, Steve Forbes ran a surpassingly effective campaign for the GOP nomination. The basic structure of the Forbes flat tax was to replace the existing structure of five marginal tax rates with a single rate of 17%.

In part because of the success of the Forbes campaign on this issue, Dole proposed major changes to the existing individual-income-tax system in his fall campaign against President Clinton. The major Dole proposal was an across-the-board cut of 15% in the individual income-tax rate, with a continued commitment to balance the federal budget by the year 2002. Dole also proposed a $500-per-child tax credit for families, a repeal of the 1993 Social Security tax increase on upper-income individuals, a cut in the tax rate on capital gains from 28% to 14%, and IRS reforms. President Clinton's campaign proposals took the form of targeted tax breaks, including a targeted capital-gains-tax cut for middle-income families who sell their home, an annual tuition tax credit of $1,500 for the first two years of college, credits to businesses that hire welfare recipients, and a $5,000 tax credit for parents who adopt children.

The fastest-growing portion of total federal revenue in 1996 remained the social-insurance tax (payroll taxes). Given the projected growth in the social-insurance programs that this tax funded, this status was expected to

The Flat Tax

The 1996 U.S. presidential campaign, particularly the candidacy of Republican Steve Forbes, called attention to the concept of a flat tax.

The basic flat-tax structure would replace the existing five-tier structure with a single tax rate of about 20%, applied equally to businesses and to individuals exceeding a specified exemption. Under this basic structure, taxable individual income would include wages and pension/retirement benefits. Each person or family would get a personal allowance based on marital status and number of dependents, but other deductions from taxable individual income—such as mortgage interest, charitable contributions, and medical expenses—would be eliminated. However, variations on this basic structure would allow some of these deductions. The more deductions included in the structure, the greater the tax rate required to achieve a given level of tax revenue.

Supporters of the flat tax argued that a lower tax rate would increase work and savings because after-tax dollar earnings by workers and savers would rise. Others said that a single low tax rate would improve the fairness of the tax system by removing major preferences that often benefit upper-income individuals. Finally, proponents touted the simplicity of the flat tax, which would replace complex tax documents with a postcard-sized form.

Opponents argued that supporters were overstating the increased economic activity that would result from lower tax rates. They also predicted that upper-income taxpayers would benefit disproportionately from the flat tax, and that eliminating deductions would reduce charitable giving and housing values. Finally, the critics argued that since most taxpayers did not itemize deductions, few would benefit from the simplicity of the flat-tax plan.

THOMAS A. HUSTED

continue. Indeed, without specifying specific solutions, Dole and Clinton debated the fiscal problems related to the growth of the Social Security and Medicare programs. In 1996 the social-insurance tax was a flat statutory tax rate of 6.2% applied to all labor income—e.g., interest and capital gains were not covered by this tax. No tax was paid on individual income beyond $57,900. In addition to the employee's share, the employer also was responsible for 6.2% of the employee's labor income. An additional flat tax on the employer and employee of 1.45% on all labor income was designated for the medical-insurance program (Medicare) for the elderly. Since the combined 7.65% total payroll tax rate did not vary by income level and the 6.2% rate went to zero beyond $57,900, the social-insurance tax was considered regressive—individuals with higher income pay a smaller tax as a proportion of their total income. The progressivity of this tax was restored, however, when the payments from these taxes (Social Security, Medicare, and unemployment insurance) were taken into consideration.

State and Local. State- and local-government tax revenues were projected to be about $1 trillion in FY 1996. The major sources of state tax revenue were from taxes on individual income, sales, and corporate income. Local governments received the bulk of their revenue from property taxes and, in a few localities, from income and sales taxes.

Many differences in tax structures and burdens existed across the states and localities. Fourteen states did not impose a personal income tax in 1996, and, in the states that did, the numbers and levels of income-tax brackets varied widely, as did the levels of personal exemptions and deductions. In addition, a few states did not impose a general sales tax, and most other states exempted food and/or prescription drugs as well as other items. Large differences also existed at the local-government level with regards to the property-tax rate as well as the property that was taxed.

Twenty-nine state legislatures reduced tax revenue in FY 1996, while only eight states increased taxes; the net tax reduction equaled roughly $4 billion. The largest decrease was a $2 billion cut in New York's personal- and corporate-income-tax revenue. New York's personal-income-tax cut was accomplished through a reduction in the top marginal tax rate, an increase in the standard deduction, and an expansion in the state's earned income tax credit. Connecticut, Delaware, Ohio, and Utah also cut tax rates, and five other states—Iowa, Kentucky, Massachusetts, Ohio, and South Carolina—increased their standard deduction. The total reduction in personal-income-tax revenue for all states surpassed $2.7 billion. Twenty-one states changed their sales-tax structure and revenues fell in all but four states—Louisiana, Vermont, Virginia, and Wisconsin. The most significant changes occurred as the sales-tax rates on food purchased for home consumption were cut in Georgia and North Carolina. The total net reduction in sales-tax revenue in all states was more than $432 million. Seventeen states changed their taxes on corporate income, with a net reduction in tax revenue equal to about $625 million. Revenue obtained from state taxes on health care and cigarettes and tobacco increased, while taxes on motor fuel and alcohol decreased.

State and local tax reform also took place on election day, as many states had tax initiatives on the November ballot. Measures were passed in California, Florida, and Nevada that make it more difficult for state and local lawmakers to raise state and local property taxes. Florida voters also rejected a proposed tax on sugar grown in the Everglades. Caps on property taxes were passed in Illinois and Oklahoma. Voters did not always pass tax decreases and limitations, however. In Arkansas voters approved a minimum property tax to be used to fund the state's public schools; they also increased the state's sales tax to fund conservation and tourism. Sales-tax hikes were passed in several Kansas counties and a cigarette-tax rate increase was approved by Oregon voters. Nebraskan voters rejected efforts to pass a property-tax cap.

International

Other countries changed their tax systems in response to changing political and economic events. Bulgaria, for example, imposed an emergency economic-reform program in response to the requirements of a loan from the International Monetary Fund (IMF). The program relied on increased gasoline taxes and on an increase in the value-added tax (VAT) from 18% to 22%. The government also imposed a 5% tax on imported goods.

Russia also made several changes in its tax system. The Russian government increased the VAT from 20% to 21% to replace lost revenue from dropping an excess-wage tax and a temporary VAT surcharge on coal and farm subsidies. After much public dissent, Russian President Boris Yeltsin dropped plans to impose a broad-based tax-withholding plan.

THOMAS A. HUSTED, *American University*

TELEVISION AND RADIO

At least when compared to the chaos of 1995, television had a quieter, more stable year in 1996. There was no phenomenon on the scale of 1995's O.J. Simpson trial to generate TV-related controversy, and the continuing criticism of TV's sex and violence—as well as its sleazy talk shows—was somewhat more muted, as several shows moved to clean up their acts. The acknowledged pioneer of audience-participation TV talk shows, Phil Donahue, retired during the year after a 30-year run and nine Emmy awards.

In fact, the debate over criticism of sex and violence—along with the slow-building successes of *Touched by an Angel* and *Dr. Quinn, Medicine Woman* on the Columbia Broadcasting System (CBS)—prompted that network in the fall to introduce more such life-affirming series with positive family values. These included *Early Edition*, about a man using newspapers from the future to warn others of tragedies; and *Promised Land*, with Gerald McRaney as a man who loses his job and takes his family on a tour of a still-hopeful America. A *New York Times* analysis piece found that series such as these were competing with another strain of programs—like the American Broadcasting Companies' (ABC's) *Spin City* and Home Box Office's (HBO's) *Arli$$* (the portrait of an unprincipled sports agent)—that catered to a "nation of cynics."

Aaron Spelling, veteran producer of many sex-spiced series (e.g., *Melrose Place*), boarded the modest bandwagon of wholesomeness with *7th Heaven*, a Warner Brothers network (WB) drama starring Stephen Collins as a pool-playing preacher and devoted family man.

Also hinting at a more family-friendly future for television was the passage—after a six-year battle—of federal rules requiring broadcasters to offer at least three hours of educational programming a week beginning in September 1997. In addition, the TV industry formally unveiled a controversial planned rating system for most programming. The voluntary system would use age-based ratings similar to those utilized by the film industry, ranging from "TV-G" to indicate a show suitable for all ages to "TV-M" to indicate material meant for mature audiences only. All programming except sports and news—including newsmagazines and children's shows—would carry ratings, which would be given by the programs' originators (producers, networks, or syndicators, for example). Critics complained the system was too vague and would be of little help to parents who needed to know specifics about violence, bad language, or depictions of sex in a program. The ratings system—slated to be in use by early 1997—was subject to approval by the Federal Communications Commission (FCC).

The 1995–96 Broadcast Season. The National Broadcasting Corporation (NBC) took an inspired gamble on *Third Rock From*

Photos, © Photofest

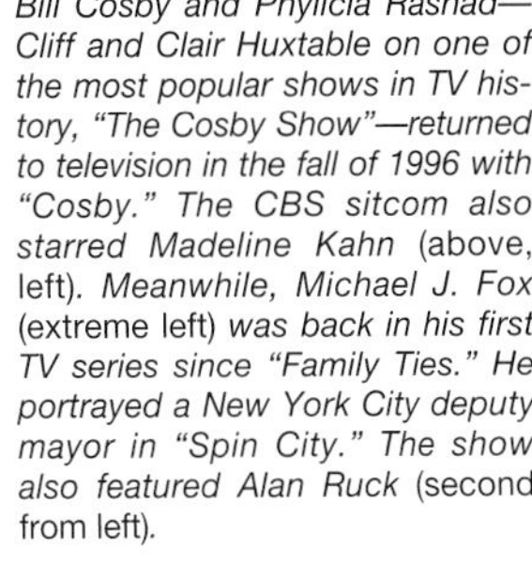

Bill Cosby and Phylicia Rashad—Cliff and Clair Huxtable on one of the most popular shows in TV history, "The Cosby Show"—returned to television in the fall of 1996 with "Cosby." The CBS sitcom also starred Madeline Kahn (above, left). *Meanwhile, Michael J. Fox* (extreme left) *was back in his first TV series since "Family Ties." He portrayed a New York City deputy mayor in "Spin City." The show also featured Alan Ruck* (second from left).

the Sun—after ABC rejected the idea—and ended up with the freshest hit comedy of the season. Written by the team of Bonnie Turner and Terry Turner (responsible for the "Wayne's World" and "Church Lady" sketches on *Saturday Night Live*), *Rock* profiled a group of aliens posing as earthlings to study human behavior. *The New York Times* called the show "a brilliantly idiotic, ribald pastiche of farce, burlesque and satire." Respected theater and film thespian John Lithgow showed a new dimension of wackiness as the alien patriarch and picked up an Emmy for best actor on a comedy.

NBC won the Nielsen ratings race for the season that ended in May—the network's first such victory since 1990–91—with several of the highest-rated shows on TV, including the medical drama *ER* (Emmy for best drama), *Frasier* (Emmy for best comedy), and perennial favorite *Seinfeld*. NBC was up from the previous season with a 11.7 rating (percentage of TV sets in the country) and a 19 share (percentage of sets turned on).

ABC, showing no immediate creative benefits from its acquisition by the Disney Company, was down with a 10.6 rating and an 18 share, although its core comedies *Home Improvement*, *Grace Under Fire*, and *Ellen* remained popular. Adding interest were published reports that *Ellen*'s heroine would "come out" as a lesbian on the show during the 1996–97 season. CBS was down for the season with a 9.6 rating and 16 share. *Variety* calculated that CBS' strategy to woo younger demographics not only had failed but also had driven away some of the network's older core audience. Fox, in its tenth season, was also down, with a 7.5 rating and 12 share, although the network won some rare appreciation from critics with *Profit*, its glossy drama on the cutthroat world of big business.

Cumulatively, the four major networks continued to slide, losing another 5 million viewers from the previous year.

Cable. New respect flowed to cable programmers after they held their own against the broadcast networks, winning an unusually large number of 1996 Emmy awards. American Movie Classics (AMC) won the Emmys' first President's Award for its documentary *Blacklist: Hollywood on Trial*. HBO was honored for best TV movie—*Truman*, with Gary Sinise in the title role—and also took awards for lead actor in a miniseries (Alan Rickman in *Rasputin*), supporting actor in a comedy (Rip Torn in *The Larry Sanders Show*), and writing on a variety program (*Dennis Miller Live*). Meanwhile, Arts & Entertainment (A&E) was honored for performance on a variety program (*Tony Bennett: Live on Request*), while Turner Network Television (TNT) won for direction of a miniseries (John Frankenheimer, *Andersonville*) and for supporting actor in a special (Tom Hulce, opposite Jamie Lee Curtis in *The Heidi Chronicles*, a Wendy Wasserstein play).

In the cable industry's ACE awards, there were honors for TNT in cinematography (*Riders of the Purple Sage* with Ed Harris and Amy Madigan); for A&E in special writing (the *Biography* segment on Martin Luther King); for Comedy Central in talk-show series (*Politically Incorrect with Bill Maher*); and for the Disney Channel in art direction (*Adventures in Wonderland*).

Rosie O'Donnell

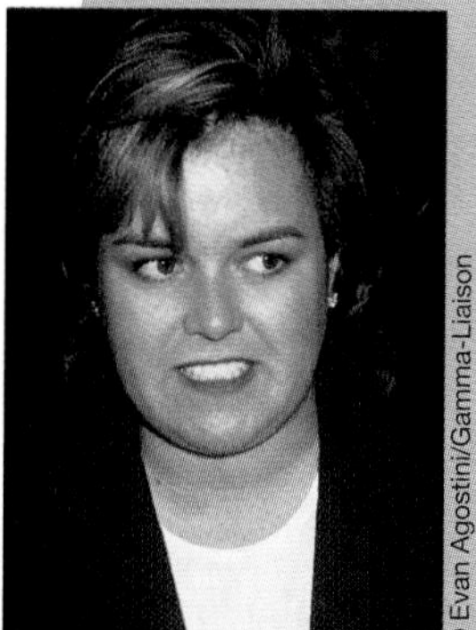

Proving that nice still can attract TV viewers, comedian Rosie O'Donnell burst onto the daytime talk-show scene in 1996 with *The Rosie O'Donnell Show*. *Rosie* focuses on good old-fashioned celebrities and entertainment. Combining wit and down-home charm, O'Donnell has a knack for putting people at ease.

The former stand-up comedian got her start while still a teen in Commack, Long Island, NY. Determined to become a movie star, she discovered comedy while performing in a high-school skit. A member of the audience was so impressed that he suggested she audition at his comedy club. She went on tour at age 17, and became a five-time comedy champion on *Star Search*. She moved to Los Angeles in 1984.

Spotted by Brandon Tartikoff—at the time the head of NBC's entertainment division—while performing at a club, O'Donnell was cast in the NBC sitcom *Gimme a Break* in its final season. She appeared on VH-1 and hosted and produced *Stand-Up Spotlight*. Her acting credits include *A League of Their Own* (1992), *Sleepless in Seattle* (1993), *The Flintstones* (1994), and *Now and Then* (1995). In 1994 she appeared on Broadway in *Grease*. O'Donnell's talk-show break came in June 1996 when Warner Brothers syndicated *The Rosie O'Donnell Show*.

As an actress, O'Donnell cited as her idols Barbra Streisand, Carol Burnett, Lucille Ball, and Bette Midler. But it was from talk-show hosts of years past that O'Donnell—a fan of Merv Griffin and Mike Douglas—drew inspiration for her own show.

O'Donnell lives in New York City with her son, Parker Jaren.

Kristi Vaughan

© Terry Ashe/ABC News

After longtime newsman David Brinkley (right) *retired in 1996 as host of "This Week With David Brinkley," Cokie Roberts and Sam Donaldson* (both left) *took over as hosts of "This Week." The commentary of George Will* (second from right) *remained a feature.*

Despite the various awards, however, cable continued to be criticized for depending heavily on reruns of series from the broadcast networks. Only rare cable series drew ratings comparable to those of an average broadcast-network show.

One new series with a particularly original premise was *The High Life* (HBO), a fall entry produced by David Letterman's World-wide Pants Inc. Shot in black and white, the offbeat comedy "is set in 1950s Pittsburgh but truly lives in a dark parallel universe," said the *Times*. The *Times* concluded that—with its bumbling buddies reminiscent of the *Honeymooners* characters played by Jackie Gleason and Art Carney—"*Life* at its best is cranky and innovative."

HBO also was praised for its handling of *If These Walls Could Talk*, a TV movie with Demi Moore, Sissy Spacek, and Cher representing three generations in the history of abortion controversy. And *Bastard Out of Carolina*, a TV movie based on the novel about parental abuse and incest, was purchased and aired by Showtime. The movie had been produced by Turner Broadcasting System (TBS) but then was rejected by Ted Turner himself as too explicit.

M2, a new MTV-spinoff channel targeting more-sophisticated alternative-rock fans, was the first channel to offer a 24-hour link with computer users, called Intercast.

News. A new study showed that only 42% of the U.S. viewing public regularly watched news programs (not including magazine shows), representing a loss of one third of the news audience since 1993. As if to underline the groping for new leadership and direction in TV news, David Brinkley retired after a distinguished anchor career at NBC and ABC; and NBC anchor Tom Brokaw, not realizing his microphone was turned on, accused CBS rival Dan Rather of reporting false stories fed to him by the Nixon White House 20 years earlier.

CBS' *60 Minutes* continued to be a respected performer as it closed in on its 30th anniversary, but the venerable newsmagazine lost viewers and had a tumultuous year. In a decision that brought criticism of CBS, the show was ordered by network lawyers not to air an interview with tobacco-industry whistle-blower Jeffrey S. Wigand for fear of a lawsuit from Wigand's former employer, Brown & Williamson Tobacco Corp. Two months later, after Wigand's allegations became public anyway (through a court deposition published in *The Wall Street Journal*), *60 Minutes* aired the interview, in which Wigand claimed that Brown & Williamson executives lied to Congress about their knowledge of the health hazards of cigarettes and threatened his life. In addition to the tobacco snafu, *60 Minutes* faced stiff new ratings competition when NBC boldly rescheduled its somewhat trendier magazine, *Dateline NBC* with Jane Pauley and Stone Phillips, directly against the CBS show on Sundays.

Launched in 1996 was *Access Hollywood*, a syndicated show-business/gossip tabloid along the lines of *Entertainment Tonight*. Cable News Network (CNN) moved to cover poli-

TELEVISION • 1996

Some Sample Programs

Alien Empire—Three-part "Nature" series about the bizarre universe of the 30 million species of insects that inhabit the Earth. PBS, Jan. 11.

The American Experience: "Daley, the Last Boss"—Portrait of Chicago's late mayor, Richard J. Daley. PBS, Jan. 22.

America on Wheels—Three-part series chronicles 100 years of automobile history. PBS, June 10.

America's Dream—Three African-American short stories. With Danny Glover, Wesley Snipes, and Jasmine Guy. HBO, Feb. 17.

Andersonville—Two-part epic about the Confederate prison camp. TNT, March 3.

Arctic Kingdom: Life at the Edge—"National Geographic" special about the struggle for survival in the far north. NBC, May 15.

Born Free: A New Adventure—New show on Elsa, the tamed lioness who needs to be reeducated to survive in the wilderness. ABC, April 27.

Caesar's Writers—Sid Caesar and writers from his popular 1950s TV shows reminisce. PBS, Aug. 19.

Captains Courageous—Adaptation of Rudyard Kipling's 1897 sea adventure. Family Channel, April 21.

The Celluloid Closet—Documentary on homosexual images in the movies. Lily Tomlin narrates. HBO, Jan. 30.

The Cherokee Kid—Comedy about multicultural Wild West. With Sinbad. HBO, Dec. 17.

The Cold Equations—Adaptation of Tom Goodwin science-fiction short story about a doomed spacecraft. Sci-Fi Channel, Dec. 14.

Crazy Horse—TV movie on the Sioux warrior who led his people to victory at the Battle of Little Big Horn. TNT, July 7.

Dead Man's Walk—Adaptation of Larry McMurtry's Western novel. With Keith Carradine and Harry Dean Stanton. ABC, May 12.

The Final Cut—Two-part British thriller about a diabolical prime minister. With Ian Richardson. PBS, Feb. 4.

Galápagos: Beyond Darwin—Scientists photograph never-before-seen species. Discovery Channel, Aug. 18.

Genesis: A Living Conversation with Bill Moyers—Ten-part weekly series exploring the relevance of the Genesis stories for today's world. PBS, Oct. 16.

Gone in the Night—TV movie about a daughter abducted from her home while the family sleeps. With Shannen Doherty and Kevin Dillon. CBS, Feb. 25.

Gotti—Biography of the fallen mob chief John Gotti. HBO, Aug. 17.

The Great War and the Shaping of the 20th Century—Eight-hour historical documentary on the social impact of World War I. PBS, Nov. 10.

Gulliver's Travels—Four-hour adaptation of Jonathan Swift's classic 1726 fantasy satire about the adventures of Lemuel Gulliver. With Ted Danson. NBC, Feb. 4.

Hidden in America—TV movie about struggling assembly-line worker and his family. Showtime, Dec. 1.

In Search of the Oregon Trail—Three-hour chronicle of the great migration along the Oregon Trail. PBS, April 29.

The Limbic Region—Thriller about a policeman hunting a serial killer. Showtime, June 30.

Mark Russell Comedy Special—The comedian takes aim at politicians and others in the news. PBS, Jan. 10.

Marlon Brando: The Wild One—Documentary on the movie star. AMC, May 28.

Moses—Two-part movie about the biblical leader. With Ben Kingsley. TNT, April 7.

Muhammad Ali: The Whole Story—Documentary about the famous boxer. TNT, Sept. 3.

Mumia Abu-Jamal: A Case for Reasonable Doubt?—Documentary on the controversy surrounding the African-American journalist and activist who is on death row for the 1982 murder of a Philadelphia policeman. HBO, July 23.

Nature: "Jane Goodall's Wild Chimpanzees"—Three generations of a ruling family of chimpanzees. PBS, March 2.

No One Would Tell—Fred Savage plays an abusive teenage boyfriend. With Candace Cameron. NBC, May 6.

Norma Jean and Marilyn—Pseudobiography of movie star Marilyn Monroe. HBO, May 18.

100 Years of Olympic Glory—Three hours on the legendary sportsmen and -women of the Olympics. TBS, April 15.

Passion—Stephen Sondheim musical. PBS, Sept. 8.

The Politician's Wife—Two-part "Masterpiece Theatre" drama about British politics and infidelity. With Juliet Stevenson. PBS, Jan. 7.

Positive: Life with HIV—Four-part series viewing life through the eyes of people with the virus. PBS, Jan. 7.

Pride and Prejudice—Six-hour adaptation of Jane Austen's novel. Arts & Entertainment, Jan. 14.

Prime Suspect: Inner Circles—Scotland Yard mystery. With Helen Mirren. PBS, Feb. 11.

Radiant City—TV movie about a woman who grows restless with life in the housing projects of post–World War II New York. ABC, March 31.

Ralph Emery on the Record with Waylon Jennings—The singer discusses his friendship with Buddy Holly, his image as an outlaw, and his cocaine addiction. TNN, Sept. 25.

Rasputin—TV movie on the man who was the spiritual adviser to the Russian royal family. With Alan Rickman. HBO, March 23.

Riders of the Purple Sage—Adaptation of Zane Grey's 1912 classic parable of love and revenge. With Ed Harris and Amy Madigan. TNT, Jan. 21.

Riverdance—Television premiere of the megahit stage show based on Irish lore, featuring dancing and music. PBS, Dec. 7.

Rodgers & Hammerstein: The Sound of Music—Two hours of movie-musical highlights. A&E, April 7.

Ruby Ridge: An American Tragedy—Docudrama about the 1992 siege at Ruby Ridge, ID. CBS, May 19.

Run for the Dream: The Gail Devers Story—True-life movie about the U.S. track star. Showtime, June 16.

Russia's Last Tsar—Documentary on Nicholas II and Alexandra. NBC, March 6.

Savage Skies—Meteorologist Al Roker hosts a four-part series on the power and beauty of the world's most severe weather. PBS, May 6.

A Season in Purgatory—Two-part TV-movie adaptation of Dominick Dunne's book about a fictional Catholic political dynasty. CBS, May 5.

Seduced by Madness: The Diane Borchardt Story—Fact-based story of a teacher who seduces a student and convinces him to kill her adulterous husband. With Ann-Margret. NBC, Feb. 25.

Shattered Mind—TV movie about a woman with multiple personalities. With Heather Locklear. NBC, May 27.

Steve Earle: To Hell and Back—Program by formerly heroin-addicted country rocker who served two months in prison for drug possession. MTV, August 17.

The Summer of Ben Tyler—TV movie about a southern family's experiences in 1942 when they take in the retarded orphan son of their late African-American housekeeper. With James Woods and Elizabeth McGovern. CBS, Dec. 15.

Talk to Me—TV movie about a sleazy TV talk show and an idealistic young woman who tries to save a heroin-addicted prostitute. ABC, Oct. 20.

The Thorn Birds: The Missing Years—Sequel to the 1983 miniseries. With Richard Chamberlain. CBS, Feb. 11.

Titanic—Miniseries about the 1912 disaster. CBS, Nov. 17.

The Trial of O.J. Simpson: An Insider's View with Dominick Dunne—Hour-long interview with journalist and author Dominick Dunne. The Learning Channel, July 14.

Two Mothers for Zachary—Fact-based TV movie about a Virginia custody case in which a lesbian fights her mother for custody of her son. ABC, Sept. 22.

The Typewriter, the Rifle and the Movie Camera—Documentary on Sam Fuller. Tim Robbins narrates. Independent Film Channel, June 24.

An Unfinished Affair—TV movie about a professor who has an affair with a student. With Tim Matheson and Jennie Garth. ABC, May 5.

VH1 Presents the '70s—Five-part series on the music of the 1970s. VH1, Aug. 19.

The Way of the Wizard—Best-selling author Deepak Chopra presents a guide to using spiritual alchemy to create a life rich in self-expression. PBS, March 1.

The West—Twelve-and-one-half-hour series by Ken Burns and Stephen Ives brings the saga of the American West to life. PBS, Sept. 15.

Whose Death Is It Anyway?—Documentary and audience discussion about tough choices at the end of life. PBS, June 3.

The Wrecker's Ball: Three Dances by Paul Taylor—Popular songs from the 1940s, 1950s, and 1960s set the background for dances about longing, love, and war. PBS, Oct. 30.

Photofest

Produced by Aaron Spelling and created by Brenda Hampton, the Warner Brothers network's family-oriented "7th Heaven" offered Stephen Collins as a minister and father of five children.

tics seriously for younger viewers (so-called Generation X) with reporters Jonathan Karl, 28, and Farai Chideya, a 27-year-old African-American; their fresh perspectives on the Republican and Democratic conventions were praised by *The New Yorker*. To compete with CNN, two new 24-hour news channels were introduced: MSNBC, a co-venture of NBC and computer giant Microsoft; and Fox News, with a brash tone embodied by conservative commentator Sean Hannity and Fox News chairman Roger Ailes.

Sports. Fox earned new respect for its burgeoning sports coverage. Although there had been gloomy predictions in the press when the ten-year-old network outbid CBS for National Football League broadcast rights in 1993, *Time* magazine saluted the coverage as irreverently entertaining. Also noting innovative coverage of baseball and hockey (including a computer-enhanced, easy-to-spot puck), *Time* declared, "Fox Sports has made imitators out of skeptics."

Critics chided NBC for its heavily theatricalized, super-patriotic coverage of the Centennial Olympic Games in Atlanta, exemplified in soft-focus profiles about the athletes' personal lives. *The New Yorker* called it "an artificial construct designed for maximum sentiment and ratings." The strategy succeeded, however, scoring the highest ratings in Olympics history (more than 200 million Americans watched some part of the 14-day coverage of the Games) with the highest ratio ever of women viewers (50%) and children and teenagers of both sexes (15%).

The Fall 1996 Network Season. For fall 1996, a tidal wave of 40 new prime-time series on the six broadcast services—the four major networks plus newcomers WB and United Paramount Network (UPN)—failed for the second straight season to produce "a single verifiable breakout hit," *The New York Times* reported. Indeed, no show had created immediate, sustained nationwide impact since the 1994–95 debuts of NBC's *ER* and *Friends*.

The newly intensified strategy of building series around well-known stars (as opposed to original ideas) did not pay quick dividends. There were, at best, only modestly encouraging ratings from such new series as *Cosby* (CBS), reuniting Bill Cosby and Phylicia Rashad; *Ink* (CBS), from *Murphy Brown* creator Diane English, with Ted Danson and his real-life wife Mary Steenburgen as skirmishing formerly married journalists; and *Spin City* (ABC), with Michael J. Fox as a crafty politico. *Suddenly Susan* (NBC), with Brooke Shields attempting to recast herself as a daffy, down-to-earth comedienne, performed better than most star vehicles, thanks to having the most secure slot in TV—between ratings powerhouses *Seinfeld* and *ER*.

One reason for the flat fall, said Leslie Moonves, president of CBS Entertainment, was that the explosion in TV channels was spreading creative talent thin: "There are 70 sitcoms in production this year—that's ridiculous," Moonves told the *Times*. "There are only 29 good comedy directors in TV. And how many good writing staffs can there be?"

The *Times* observed, "Evidence points to a slower gestation for hits in the multichannel era." The newspaper cited shows that started far down in the rankings and rose in subsequent seasons, including Fox's *The X-Files*, CBS' *Touched by an Angel*, NBC's *Law and Order*, and ABC's *The Drew Carey Show*.

While the total of shows with predominantly African-American casts increased from 14 in 1995 to 17 a year later, the four major networks' share of these shows fell from nine to six, with the increase appearing on the low-rated WB and UPN networks.

The Alien Trend. The success of extraterrestrial themes in *The X-Files* and *Third Rock From the Sun*—not to mention the continuing syndicated *Star Trek* sequels *Deep Space 9* and *Voyager*—opened the hatch for more programming of this ilk throughout 1996 (*see also*

THE SCIENCE FICTION INVASION, page 84). There was great anticipation for *Millennium*, the high-priced new Fox series from *X-Files* creator Chris Carter about a former policeman with supernatural visions. It had a highly rated debut, but some critics found the show too dark, and viewership fell off.

Meanwhile, NBC packed its Saturday lineup with new alien-theme shows: *Dark Skies* and *The Pretender*. UPN managed to graft two vogues—interplanetary fantasy and raucous urban comedy—in its *Homeboys in Outer Space*.

Radio. A study by the Annenberg School for Communication at the University of Pennsylvania showed that nearly one in five U.S. adults listened to a radio talk show at least twice a week. Those listeners were "more knowledgeable and more involved in politics" (especially conservative causes) than nonlisteners, the study found.

Despite the continuing popularity of legitimate and informative talk shows, scandals, stunts, and charges of hate-mongering nevertheless continued to plague the talk-radio universe. WLQY-AM, a station targeted toward Haitian immigrants in Fort Lauderdale, FL, announced that AIDS is a myth. Long-embattled talk host Bob Grant was fired by WABC-AM in New York after a joke about Ron Brown, the African-American secretary of commerce who was killed in a plane crash in Croatia; Grant quickly was hired by WOR-AM. U.S. Sen. Bill Bradley was ambushed by two topless dancers in KLOL-AM's Houston studios and refused to be escorted by them to his on-air interview. Sacramento Mayor Joe Serna, Sr., called for the resignation of KSTE-AM morning host Jeff Katz after he proposed that motorists be awarded a sombrero-shaped bumper sticker for every illegal immigrant hit while attempting to cross the border from Mexico. (In response, Katz said his remark was meant as a joke.)

The most notorious episode did not occur on the air but did involve one of radio's most famous "shock jocks": Don Imus, who—at a broadcast-industry banquet—roasted the present President Clinton and First Lady Hillary Rodham Clinton in what many felt was a tasteless fashion.

DAN HULBERT
"The Atlanta Journal and Constitution"

TERRORISM

Terrorism continued to be a major concern for the United States in 1996. From a truck bombing at a U.S. military housing complex in Saudi Arabia to a pipe bombing during the Summer Olympic Games in Atlanta, Americans again were reminded of the diverse nature of this global threat. Terrorist incidents both in the United States and abroad led President Bill Clinton to sign a new antiterrorism bill, while the Group of Seven (G-7) summit of industrialized nations pledged unity in the fight against terrorism. The year also was characterized by the capture of a man believed to be one of the most wanted terrorists in the United States, the infamous Unabomber. Meanwhile, the midair explosion of TWA Flight 800 off Long Island, NY, led to speculation that a missile or a bomb may have brought down the plane, although the exact cause of the crash remained unknown as the year drew to a close.

New Developments. With memories of the 1995 Oklahoma City bombing still fresh in the public's mind, the 1996 Summer Olympic Games in Atlanta were conducted under tight security. Nevertheless, a bomb hidden in a backpack exploded at Centennial Olympic Park during a concert in the early-morning hours of July 27, killing an American woman and injuring more than 100 others. A Turkish cameraman covering the explosion died from a heart attack. The bombing was the first terrorist incident at an Olympic Games since the massacre of 11 Israeli athletes at the 1972 Games in Munich, Germany. Since Centennial Park had been designed to allow people without tickets or credentials for the Olympics to gather for music and other activities, it was the least secure site and provided an easy target for terrorists. The initial suspect in the bombing was a security guard at the park, but the U.S. Federal Bureau of Investigation (FBI) stated a few months later that he was no longer under investigation. By the end of 1996 there were no arrests for the crime.

The Atlanta bombing came only ten days after TWA Flight 800 exploded in midair off Long Island, killing all 230 persons on board. The July 17 crash fueled immediate speculation that a bomb or missile may have caused the Boeing 747 to explode shortly after takeoff from John F. Kennedy International Airport in New York. Several eyewitnesses told authorities that they saw streaks of light in the sky before the jet, which had been bound for Paris, exploded. However, after recovering 95% of the jet's wreckage, the authorities could not find any evidence that a missile struck the plane. There was also no evidence that a bomb caused the explosion. By the end of 1996, investigators were giving more weight to the theory that mechanical failure caused the central fuel tank to explode, although the bomb and missile theories had not been ruled out officially.

The activities of militia groups added to the threat of terrorism in the United States. In November three members of a group called the 112th Georgia Militia, including its leader, Robert Starr 3d, were convicted of conspiracy for stockpiling pipe bombs for use against the federal government. According to authorities, the men had planned to rob armories and drug dealers to finance a terrorist campaign. They also had planned to stage terrorist activities during the Summer Olympics in Atlanta, but were arrested a few months before the Games began.

Meanwhile, one of the longest sieges in FBI history occurred in 1996 when members of the so-called "Freemen," a right-wing group that rejects all authority of the federal and state governments, barricaded themselves on a farm near Jordan, MT. The tense situation began on March 25 after two members of the Freemen were arrested on charges of threatening public officials, conspiracy, and fraud. Several other members of the group, who faced various charges, then barricaded themselves in the farmhouse. The FBI surrounded the farm, but did not launch a raid. Prior federal raids against antigovernment groups in Waco, TX, and Ruby Ridge, ID, led to fatalities and widespread criticism of government strategies and tactics. The 81-day standoff ended peacefully on June 13 when the last of the Freemen in the farmhouse surrendered.

A man believed to be one of the most infamous terrorists in U.S. history was captured in 1996. Theodore Kaczynski, 53, the alleged Unabomber, was arrested in a remote cabin near Lincoln, MT, on April 3. Officials hoped that the arrest would end a 17-year reign of terror in which the Unabomber sent mail bombs to various people associated with universities, airlines, computers, and other industries. Three persons were killed and 23 others injured in the multiple bombings. Kaczynski's brother, David, contacted the FBI after discovering writings by Kaczynski that resembled the Unabomber's antitechnology manifesto that had been published in the newspapers. Federal agents found explosive chemicals and other bomb-making material in Kaczynski's cabin, as well as a manual typewriter believed to be the one used to write the Unabomber's manifesto. Kaczynski, a Harvard graduate and former assistant professor of mathematics at the University of California at Berkeley, could face the death penalty for the bombings.

In another major development, Ramzi Ahmed Yousef was convicted by a federal jury on September 5, along with two other defendants, of plotting to blow up 12 U.S. airliners flying to the United States from Asia over a two-day period. The case illustrated how terrorists had become more daring and creative in their violence. Authorities asserted that Yousef, who also was facing a trial as the alleged mastermind of the World Trade Center bombing, learned how to make bombs from unsuspicious-looking types of objects that could pass easily through airport security. These included a digital wristwatch that was modified to serve as a timer, and a plastic contact-lens-solution bottle that was filled with liquid components for nitroglycerine.

© Elaine Thompson/AP/Wide World Photos

During June 1996 a federal grand jury in Sacramento, CA, charged Theodore J. Kaczynski (center) with ten felony counts, involving the deaths of two persons and the injuries of two others that authorities connected to the so-called Unabomber case. The 53-year-old former university professor had been arrested on April 3 after a raid on a remote Montana cabin.

Pretrial proceedings continued during 1996 in the Oklahoma City bombing case. Lawyers for the two defendants, Timothy J. McVeigh and Terry Lynn Nichols, were granted a change in venue as they argued that their clients could not receive a fair trial in Oklahoma because of the vast amount of news coverage in that state about the bombing. The trial was moved to Denver and was expected to begin sometime in 1997. The courts decided that McVeigh and Nichols would be tried separately for the April 19, 1995, bombing of the Alfred P. Murrah Federal Building in Oklahoma City, which resulted in 168 deaths.

The worst anti-U.S. terrorist incident overseas in 1996 was the bombing of a U.S. military housing complex in Dhahran, Saudi Arabia. The June 25 truck bombing at the Khobar Towers, which housed about half of the 5,000 U.S. troops in Saudi Arabia, killed 19 U.S. servicemen and wounded many others. The truck bomb exploded within about 100 ft (30 m) of the complex. A Pentagon investigative report by retired Gen. Wayne A. Downing faulted U.S. military commanders for lax security around the complex. However, a subsequent U.S. Air Force inquiry cleared the commanders of any blame for the tragedy. In October the Saudi government reported that it had caught about 40 persons that it claimed were responsible for the bombing and contended that they had been supported by Iran. Some of the militants detained reportedly had ties to four men who had been beheaded for a November 1995 car bombing of a building in Riyadh that killed five Americans and two Indians. Following the June bombing, U.S. troops were moved to Al Kharj, a remote Saudi air base, to provide better security against a terrorist attack. There was growing opposition in Saudi Arabia to the U.S. military presence in the country and to the Saudi regime.

In other developments, Spain extradited to Italy Magied Youssef al-Molqi, a Palestinian terrorist who had been convicted by an Italian court for the murder of a U.S. citizen, Leon Klinghoffer, during the 1985 *Achille Lauro* cruise-ship hijacking. Molqi had been given a 12-day furlough to leave prison in Rome in February, but did not return and fled to Spain, where he was captured in March.

Antiterrorism. Several high-profile international summits were held during the year to deal with the growing threat of terrorism. A wave of suicide bombings in Israel in late February and early March that had threatened to derail the Mideast peace process led to an emergency one-day summit meeting in Sharm El-Sheik, Egypt, attended by the leaders of 27 nations and the Palestinians. The March 13 meeting was more symbolic than substantive, but succeeded in presenting, at least for one day, a united stance against terrorism. In a communiqué issued after the summit, the group agreed to bring terrorists to justice and to identify and cut off the sources of financing for terrorist groups. Following the summit, President Clinton visited Israel and pledged $100 million in technical assistance to combat terrorism in that country, including training, bomb-detection scanners, X-ray systems, and robotics for handling suspicious packages.

Terrorism was also a major topic at the G-7 summit in Lyon, France, in June. The leaders of the G-7 countries—the United States, Japan, Germany, Britain, France, Italy, and Canada (nonmember Russia also participated in the summit)—approved in principle a package of recommendations to combat terrorism and crime. One month later, the G-7 foreign and interior ministers met in Paris and adopted 25 measures to fight terrorism. These included extradition of terrorists, intelligence sharing, cutting off the supply of money and weapons to terrorists, monitoring terrorist attempts to communicate over the Internet, and accelerating research and development of methods of detection of explosives and other harmful substances. They pledged to carry out these measures by the end of 1996. In a separate development, President Clinton signed a law on August 5 that would impose sanctions on foreign companies that invest heavily in Iran or Libya, two state sponsors of terrorism. The new legislation drew criticism from France and Germany.

Meanwhile, President Clinton signed antiterrorism legislation on April 24 that enhanced law-enforcement capabilities to fight terrorism. The bill, which had been drafted in the aftermath of the 1995 Oklahoma City bombing, authorized about $1 billion in funding over four years for federal antiterrorism law-enforcement efforts, including the hiring of more than 1,000 new law-enforcement officers. It also would require manufacturers to place chemical tracing agents known as "taggants" in plastic explosives so the terrorists who use them could be tracked. Among other measures included in the bill—known as the Antiterrorism and Effective Death Penalty Act for 1996—were the creation of a federal death penalty for terrorist murders, a curbing of the number of appeals by death-row inmates, and permission for the president to designate certain groups as terrorist organizations and to ban their fund-raising efforts in the United States.

© Eyal Warshavsky/AP/Wide World Photos

After a series of suicide bombings in Israel, leaders of 27 nations as well as the Palestinians gathered in Sharm El-Sheik, Egypt, for a one-day conference, March 13, 1996. The meeting, cosponsored by Egypt and the United States, established a working group to formulate measures to fight terrorism. Following the summit, President Bill Clinton traveled to Israel for meetings with Israeli leaders (left).

Aviation security received high priority in the United States in 1996. Even though the cause of the midair explosion of TWA 800 remained a mystery late in the year, the tragedy increased the public's apprehension about airport security. President Clinton established a commission to reevaluate security at airports that was headed by Vice-President Al Gore. The White House Commission on Aviation Safety and Security, also known as the Gore Commission, issued an interim report in September that included several recommendations for enhancing airport security. These were included in an aviation bill—the Federal Aviation Administration (FAA) Reauthorization Act of 1996—that President Clinton signed on October 9. The new bill would provide for additional baggage screeners to detect explosives, more teams of bomb-sniffing dogs, background checks on airport and airline employees who have access to security areas, continued development of computer-assisted passenger-profiling programs to identify potential terrorists, and a doubling of the FAA's security force over three years. The bill also called for the FAA to conduct a study and report to Congress on potential sources of funding for security measures, and on whether, and if so how, to transfer certain responsibilities for aviation security from the airlines to airport operators or the federal government.

Meanwhile, despite a September directive by President Clinton to the FAA to begin live trials at a major airport on the best way to match passengers and luggage on domestic flights—and thereby identify potentially bomb-laden luggage checked in by a person who then did not board the plane—the plan was scaled back to the development of a computer model to simulate such matches. Airlines had objected to live tests of bag-matching on domestic flights, fearing it would cause long lines, reduction in scheduled flights, and loss of customers. (*See also* TRANSPORTATION—*The Safety Issue*.)

JEFFREY D. SIMON, *Author, "The Terrorist Trap: America's Experience with Terrorism"*

THAILAND

During 1996, Thailand celebrated the golden anniversary of the reign of King Bhumibol Adulyadej, who came to the throne in 1946. Through a period of rapid change and a succession of military dictators, juntas, and weak democratic regimes, the king had stood as a symbol of unity, continuity, and moral rectitude and as a bulwark for a secure national identity.

Politics. The government of Chart Thai party leader Prime Minister Banharn Silpa-archa—buffeted by charges of incompetence, mismanagement, and corruption and under siege even from within his coalition on allegations of personal dishonesty—collapsed in September after only 14 months in power. The six-party coalition was fragile from the outset, with the head of the New Aspiration Party (NAP), retired Gen. Chawalit Yongchaiyut, playing the role of prime-minister-in-waiting. In advance of a no-confidence vote targeted against him personally, Banharn promised to resign within a week if the coalition would stick together on the confidence vote. After winning the vote, however, the coalition could not agree on who would suc-

© Patrick Aventurier/Gamma-Liaison

Ceremonies marking the 50th anniversary of the monarchy of Thailand's King Bhumibol Adulyadej were held in Bangkok in 1996. Bhumibol, 68, was the world's longest-serving monarch.

ceed Banharn as prime minister. Angry at what he saw as Chawalit's effort to undermine him, Banharn exercised his legal prerogative and, without warning, dissolved the parliament on September 27 rather than see his rival in the coalition become prime minister. A snap election was called for November 17.

Fifteen parties contested the election, with 2,310 candidates seeking 393 seats in the parliament. The campaign issues polarized around the potential formation of a coalition government led either by former Prime Minister Chuan Likphai's opposition Democrat Party or Chawalit's NAP. The election campaign was characterized as the dirtiest and most violent in 20 years. It was estimated that more than $1.2 billion was spent in campaigning and vote-buying.

On election day, the NAP captured 125 seats, more than doubling its strength in the previous parliament. The Democrats won 123 seats, up from 86. Using the old coalition as his base, Chawalit moved quickly to form a government, only replacing Banharn's Chart Thai—which lost nearly 60% of its seats—with the Chart Pattana party, led by former Prime Minister Chatichai Choonhavan. The process of coalition making was fought out over control of the economy, with Chatichai's Chart Pattana the seeming winner. Prime Minister Chawalit's new government, with 221 seats, had a comfortable 49-seat majority.

The first major hurdle confronting the new government was to continue the process of constitutional reform begun in the previous parliamentary-session government. A 99-member Constituent Assembly had to be picked by the end of 1996 to replace the constitution sponsored by the military junta. Prime Minister Chawalit promised to call new elections once a new constitution was in place. After two very expensive elections in 15 months, however, no political party appeared anxious to go to the polls again soon.

Economy. Part of the public dissatisfaction with the Banharn government stemmed from a sharp slowdown of the economy. Rather than the 8% real growth averaged over the past decade, forecasters warned of less than 7% in 1996. In part, Thailand was experiencing the same decline that other newly industrializing Asian economies were encountering. Thailand's economic problems were exaggerated by ballooning current-account deficits, scandal-ridden bank failures, a slumping stock market, and the business community's lack of confidence in the government's fiscal policies. The concerns of investors were not put to rest by the formation of what looked like a "Banharn II government" without Banharn.

Foreign Affairs. In March 1966, Thailand hosted the first Asia-Europe Meeting (ASEM) bringing together the leaders of the European Union (EU) member states and of East Asia and the Pacific. In November, President Bill Clinton became the first U.S. leader since Richard Nixon to visit Thailand.

DONALD E. WEATHERBEE
University of South Carolina

THAILAND • Information Highlights

Official Name: Kingdom of Thailand (conventional); Prathet Thai (Thai).
Location: Southeast Asia.
Area: 198,456 sq mi (514 000 km²).
Population (mid-1996 est.): 60,700,000.
Chief City (1991 est.): Bangkok, the capital (metropolitan area), 5,620,591.
Government: *Head of state,* Bhumibol Adulyadej, king (acceded June 1946). *Head of government,* Chawalit Yongchaiyut, prime minister (elected November 1996). *Legislature*—National Assembly: Senate and House of Representatives.
Monetary Unit: Baht (25.64 baht equal U.S.$1, Dec. 31, 1996).
Gross Domestic Product (1994 est. U.S.$): $355,200,000,-000 (purchasing power parity).
Economic Index (Bangkok, 1995; 1990 = 100): *Consumer Prices,* all items, 126.6; food, 132.9.
Foreign Trade (1994 U.S.$): *Imports,* $54,438,000,000; *exports,* $45,236,000,000.

THEATER

In the 1995–96 season, Broadway made one of its most impressive comebacks in a quarter century of troubled times.

There were 38 new productions, as compared with 29 for the previous season. Attendance grew by almost 5% from 1994–95, to 9.47 million, continuing a gradual six-year trend. Under the headline, "Banner Year," *Variety* reported, "By every measure...and, most important, production of shows actually worth seeing...there were substantial improvements over last season."

And yet there were signs of strain. Julie Andrews—who at 60 seemed agelessly ebullient as a woman impersonating a man impersonating a woman in *Victor/Victoria* (based on her 1982 film)—refused to accept her Antoinette Perry (Tony) Award best-actress nomination to protest the exclusion of many of her *Victoria* colleagues from the nominations. In effect, Andrews symbolized the old guard of Broadway artists and their aging audience, going head-to-head with a Tony nominating committee with a less commercial, more artistic, more youth-oriented outlook.

Broadway's Spring Productions. There was no surprise or debate over the fact that, for best musical, the committee nominated *Rent*, the acclaimed Jonathan Larson rock musical (which went on to win the Tony) that paralleled Puccini's *La Bohème* in its gritty portrait of bohemians grappling with AIDS, drugs, and alternative sexual lifestyles; and *Bring in da Noise, Bring in da Funk*, by writer-director George C. Wolfe, which illuminated African-American history through the brilliant dance of Savion Glover.

Andrews, however, was outraged that her own hit was passed over in the other two best-musical nominations in favor of quick flops: *Swinging on a Star* (a revue of Johnny Burke songs) and the artistically daring *Chronicle of a Death Foretold*. Most critics agreed with the committee that *Victoria* and *Big* (another large-scale musical snubbed in the nominations) were artistically mediocre, and should not have been nominated simply because they were the only new musicals besides *Rent* and *Funk* that had managed to stay open. Missing the nomination was a factor in the costly, premature closing of *Big*, based on the Tom Hanks film comedy about a grown man with the mind of a boy. That failure helped focus attention on the finances of Broadway (*see* SPECIAL REPORT).

Also hanging like clouds over the so-called "banner year" were the brevity of several previous "recoveries" of the Great White Way (for instance, the premature "Broadway's Back" headlines that accompanied the *Guys and Dolls* revival in the spring of 1992). Not every critic agreed that the season's work

"Rent"—a rock opera based on Puccini's "La Bohème," with Jonathan Larson as composer, writer, and lyricist—became the first musical since "A Chorus Line" to win both a Tony Award and a Pulitzer Prize. The show was a major Broadway hit.

© Joan Marcus

© Joan Marcus

A new production of Edward Albee's "A Delicate Balance," starring George Grizzard and Rosemary Harris, took a Tony for best revival of a play. Grizzard was judged best actor in a play.

lived up to the glowing reviews. Some argued that the powerful *New York Times* was taking a softer critical line. The much-hyped *Rent*, while original and energized, was not really as revolutionary as the extravagant *Times* coverage suggested; and Vincent Canby, the *Times*' Sunday theater critic, was far more generous to some scripts (Edward Albee's *A Delicate Balance*) and some stagings (Oscar Wilde's *An Ideal Husband*) than might be expected from such rigorous *Times* predecessors as Frank Rich.

Buried Child, Sam Shepard's 1979 Pulitzer Prize–winning drama (with streaks of dark comedy), profiled a bizarre heartland family so wildly forgetful that they embodied denial as a national psychic disorder. It was Shepard's first play on Broadway. The risky revival attracted financial backing because of the prestige and marketability of Shepard and director Gary Sinise (both movie stars), and the outstanding track record of Chicago's Steppenwolf Theatre Company (1993's *The Grapes of Wrath*), which originated the revival. Unfortunately, the haunting production with Lois Smith and James Gammon could not parlay its glowing reviews into a long Broadway transfer.

August Wilson, along with Shepard and David Mamet the most admired of American playwrights, returned to the Great White Way with *Seven Guitars*. The title referred to the seven African-American characters in 1940s Pittsburgh and their almost musical style of storytelling; among them is a blues guitarist (Keith David) who is dangerously desperate for success. Despite a slow-developing story and overlap with previous Wilson works, *Guitars* had power. It was acted splendidly by an ensemble under perennial Wilson director Lloyd Richards.

It was neither the Tony nominees *Guitars* nor *Child* that won for best play, however, but rather Terrence McNally's more crowd-pleasing *Master Class*, which had opened in the fall of 1995. The production also won a best-actress award for Zoe Caldwell as opera legend Maria Callas.

With his sterling revival of *A Delicate Balance*, director Gerald Gutierrez and the Lincoln Center Theater Company pulled off another surprising coup on the order of 1995's *The Heiress*, winning the Tony for best revival. Albee's wry but intellectually shallow 1966 study of upper-middle-class suburbanites suddenly shaken by existential panic featured elegant designs and performances by George Grizzard (Tony for best actor), Rosemary Harris, and Elaine Stritch.

Another top revival was *A Funny Thing Happened on the Way to the Forum*, the ingenious 1962 grafting of Roman farce and American burlesque by playwrights Larry Gelbart and Burt Shevelove and composer-lyricist Stephen Sondheim. The madcap show reunited principals of the memorable 1992 *Guys and Dolls*: Dodger Productions, director Jerry Zaks, and actor Nathan Lane (finally a full-fledged star by virtue of his 1996 film *The Birdcage*).

Just as many critics were impressed by the Australia-based revival of Rodgers and Hammerstein's *The King and I*. Lou Diamond Phillips played the King of Siam. But it was the splendid Donna Murphy as the governess Anna Leonowens (taking the Tony that otherwise would have gone to the protesting Julie Andrews) who restored the happy balance that existed between Gertrude Lawrence and Yul Brynner in the original 1951 production, before Brynner made the show a one-star vehicle in revival tours.

New York's Fall Productions. *Chicago* was reborn, much as *Carousel* was in 1994, in a production so good that it made critics realize the musical had been underrated when it premiered in 1975. The key talent was Ann Reinking, who adapted the near-erotic choreography of the late Bob Fosse and played the leading role, a 1920s chorus girl accused of murder who becomes a celebrity by converting her testimony into musical numbers in front of a jury. James Naughton and Bebe Neuwirth excelled in other key roles. *Chicago* lyricist Fred Ebb, who with composer John

BROADWAY OPENINGS • 1996

MUSICALS

BIG, book by John Weidman; music by David Shire; lyrics by Richard Maltby, Jr; directed by Mike Ockrent; with Daniel Jenkins, Crista Moore, Jon Cypher, Brett Tabisel, Patrick Levis; April 28– Oct. 13.

BRING IN DA NOISE, BRING IN DA FUNK, book by Reg E. Gaines; music by Daryl Waters, Zane Mark, Ann Duquesnay; conceived and directed by George C. Wolfe; with Savion Glover, Jeffrey Wright, Ann Duquesnay; April 25– .

CHICAGO, book by Bob Fosse and Fred Ebb; music by John Kander; lyrics by Ebb; directed by Walter Bobbie; with Ann Reinking, Bebe Neuwirth, James Naughton, Joel Grey; Nov. 14– .

A FUNNY THING HAPPENED ON THE WAY TO THE FORUM, book by Burt Shevelove and Larry Gelbart; music and lyrics by Stephen Sondheim; directed by Jerry Zaks; with Nathan Lane, Mark Linn-Baker; April 18– .

JUAN DARIEN: A CARNIVAL MASS, by Julie Taymor and Elliot Goldenthal; music and original lyrics by Goldenthal; directed by Taymor; with Daniel Hodd, Martin Santangelo; Nov. 24– .

THE KING AND I, book and lyrics by Oscar Hammerstein 2d; music by Richard Rodgers; directed by Christopher Renshaw; with Donna Murphy, Lou Diamond Phillips, Jose Llana, Joohoe Choi; April 11– .

ONCE UPON A MATTRESS, book by Jay Thompson, Marshall Barer, and Dean Fuller; music by Mary Rodgers; lyrics by Barer; directed by Gerald Gutierrez; with Sarah Jessica Parker, David Aaron Baker, Mary Lou Rosato, Heath Lamberts; Dec. 19– .

RENT, book, music, and lyrics by Jonathan Larson; directed by Michael Greif; with Daphne Rubin-Vega, Adam Pascal, Jesse L. Martin, Wilson Jermaine Heredia, Fredi Walker, Idina Menzel, Anthony Rapp, Taye Diggs; April 29– .

STATE FAIR, book by Tom Briggs and Louis Mattioli; music by Richard Rodgers; lyrics by Oscar Hammerstein 2d; directed by James Hammerstein and Randy Skinner; with John Davidson, Kathryn Crosby, Andrea McArdle, Ben Wright, Donna McKechnie; March 27–June 30.

PLAYS

THE APPLE DOESN'T FALL..., by Trish Vradenburg; directed by Leonard Nimoy; with Margaret Whitton, Florence Stanley; April 14–April 15.

BURIED CHILD, by Sam Shepard; directed by Gary Sinise; with Jim True, Lois Smith, James Gammon, Terry Kinney, Leo Burmester, Kellie Overbey; April 30–June 30.

BUS STOP, by William Inge; directed by Josephine R. Abady; with Mary-Louise Parker, Ron Perlman, Billy Crudup, Patricia Dunnock; Feb. 22–March 17.

A DELICATE BALANCE, by Edward Albee; directed by Gerald Gutierrez; with Rosemary Harris, Elaine Stritch, George Grizzard, Mary Beth Hurt; April 21–July 21.

THE FATHER, by August Strindberg; adapted by Richard Nelson; directed by Clifford Williams; with Frank Langella, Angela Bettis, Gail Strickland, Ivar Brogger, Tom Beckett; Jan. 11–Feb. 18.

GETTING AWAY WITH MURDER, written and directed by Harvey Miller; with Dan Aykroyd, Jack Lemmon, Lily Tomlin, Bonnie Hunt; March 17–March 31.

GOD SAID "HA!" written and performed by Julia Sweeney; directed by Beth Miles; Nov. 19–Dec. 8.

HUGHIE, by Eugene O'Neill; directed by Al Pacino; with Al Pacino, Paul Benedict; Aug. 22–Nov. 2.

AN IDEAL HUSBAND, by Oscar Wilde; directed by Peter Hall; with Anna Carteret, Martin Shaw, David Yelland, Penny Downie, Dulcie Gray; May 1– .

INHERIT THE WIND, by Jerome Lawrence and Robert E. Lee; directed by John Tillinger; with George C. Scott, Charles Durning; April 4–May 12.

JACK: A NIGHT ON THE TOWN WITH JOHN BARRYMORE, devised by Nicol Williamson and Leslie Megahey; directed by Megahey; with Nicol Williamson; April 24–May 5.

A MIDSUMMER NIGHT'S DREAM, by William Shakespeare; directed by Adrian Noble; with Desmond Barrit, Alex Jennings, Lindsay Duncan; March 31–May 26.

THE NIGHT OF THE IGUANA, by Tennessee Williams; directed by Robert Falls; with William Petersen, Marsha Mason, Cherry Jones; March 21–May 19.

PRESENT LAUGHTER, by Noel Coward; directed by Scott Elliott; with Frank Langella, Lisa Emery, Tim Hopper; Nov. 18– .

THE REHEARSAL, by Jean Anouilh; directed by Nicholas Martin; translated by Jeremy Sams; with Roger Rees, Anna Gunn, David Threlfall, Frances Conroy, Kathryn Meisle; Nov. 24– .

SEVEN GUITARS, by August Wilson; directed by Lloyd Richards; with Keith David, Viola Davis, Ruben Santiago-Hudson, Tommy Hollis, Michele Shay, Rosalyn Coleman, Roger Robinson; March 28–Sept. 8.

SEX AND LONGING, by Christopher Durang; directed by Garland Wright; with Sigourney Weaver, Dana Ivey, Peter Michael Goetz, Jay Goede, Guy Boyd; Oct. 10–Nov. 19.

SKYLIGHT, by David Hare; directed by Richaed Eyre; with Michael Gambon, Lia Williams; Sept. 19–Dec. 29.

SUMMER AND SMOKE, by Tennessee Williams; directed by David Warren; with Mary McDonnell, Harry Hamlin; Sept. 5–Oct. 20.

TAKING SIDES, by Ronald Harwood; directed by David Jones; with Daniel Massey, Ed Harris, Elizabeth Marvel, Michael Stuhlbarg; Oct. 17–Dec. 29.

TARTUFFE: BORN AGAIN, by Molière; adapted by Freyda Thomas; directed by David Saint; with John Glover, Haviland Morris, David Schramm, Kevin Dewey, Alison Fraser; May 23–June 23.

A THOUSAND CLOWNS, by Herb Gardner; directed by Scott Ellis; with Judd Hirsch, David Margulies, Dov Tiefenbach; July 14–Aug. 11.

OTHER ENTERTAINMENT

DAVID COPPERFIELD: DREAMS AND NIGHTMARES, adapted by David Ives; with David Copperfield; Dec. 5–Dec. 29.

LOVE THY NEIGHBOR, with Jackie Mason; March 24– .

"Bring in da Noise, Bring in da Funk," a musical created by Savion Glover and George C. Wolfe that utilizes the rhythms and energies of tap dancing, was awarded four Tonys.

The Finances of Broadway

The story of the 1995–96 Broadway theater season—and a vision of Broadway's future—might be summed up in the opposite financial fates of two musicals—*Rent*, a smash hit, and *Big*, a flop.

Only six months after its April 1996 opening, the modestly budgeted ($3.5 million) *Rent* issued its first checks to investors—a year or more ahead of the usual break-even date for bigger, splashier musicals that cost three times as much. The rocking musical portrait of downtown bohemians anticipated a long stage run and a movie version. With breakthrough exposure, *Rent* and *Bring in Da Noise, Bring in Da Funk*—the nearly-as-hot dance musical—were pulling in younger baby boomers and Generation Xers who never venture onto Broadway, where prime weekend tickets cost around $60 to $75 each.

Also in mid-October, at roughly the same time that *Rent* went into the black, *Big* closed and lost its entire investment of $10.5 million—one of the costliest flops ever. And *Big*, the family musical adapted from the fantasy film of the same name, was hardly the most expensive production on the Great White Way. Musicals such as *Sunset Boulevard* ($12 million) and *Beauty and the Beast* ($13 million) managed to get into the black only by running for 18 months or more.

There was much ballyhoo about 1995–96 being a "banner season" for Broadway, with a record $436 million in box-office sales. However, the sum was more attributable to ticket inflation than to the modest 5% rise in attendance over the previous season. Clearly, *Rent*—with its rare artistic freshness and its relatively cheap running costs—is a rarity, not yet representative of a trend. The financial risks of the so-called main stem remained as intractable as ever.

The gamble is even bigger in the 1990s, with five out of six productions losing money. Good, serious, new drama has been financially problematic on Broadway since the days of Eugene O'Neill. Regional and off-Broadway theaters, with lower union contracts, have taken on the role of preserving and celebrating American theater classics. The Broadway situation for new drama appeared to be all but hopeless when even Tony Kushner's *Angels in America*, the most honored play in a generation, failed to recoup its investment after a 20-month run in 1993–94. The defection of Neil Simon—Broadway's highest-earning playwright since the 1960s—to off-Broadway with *London Suite* proved that not even a work by a comedy genius was a safe bet anymore.

Theater—simply by its exclusive nature of being created from scratch each day for a limited audience—is like any labor-intensive industry trying to compete with larger economies of scale. Movies and television, for example, repeatedly can exploit their initial investment, but each theater performance is a fully-staffed event. The theater's intimacy and its unique fleetingness are its economic liabilities.

But even this long-established trend does not explain completely the extreme increases in theatrical costs. For instance, even when the original 1927 cost of *Showboat* ($150,000) is adjusted to 1995 dollars ($1.3 million), it comes up far short of the $7 million price tag of the musical's 1994 revival, which planned to close in January 1997 with a modest profit. One reason for this balloon effect is the audience hunger for impressive designs and scenic opulence; without them, audiences might have ignored the new *Showboat* as just an old chestnut not worth the admission price. While some musicals have stories and scores so compelling that they conceivably could work on a bare stage—for example, *Les Misérables*—others are heavily dependent on spectacle (*Phantom of the Opera* and *Big*) or star power (*Victor/Victoria*). The sales of the latter 1995 musical dipped alarmingly when Julie Andrews took a badly needed rest.

Another root reason for the inflation spiral is, ironically enough, rent. In 1996 the major theater-owning groups—the Shubert, Nederlander, and Jujamcyn organizations—were charging $20,000 per month for such prime theaters as the Palace, where *Beauty and the Beast* was running. This expense—along with the rising costs of advertising and the inflated "featherbed" wages and benefits for stagehands, technicians, and musicians—trickle down to the consumer in the form of exorbitant ticket prices. Such prices were topping out at $75 in 1996, as compared with $15 in 1968.

The good news for Broadway in 1996 was that *Rent* was a miracle, generating business and excitement. The freshness of the writing and performance meant that it could afford a bare-bones, industrial-chic set and a bargain budget of $3.5 million. The bad news was that for each *Rent* there is liable to be a *Big*, trying to mask its weaknesses in expensive glitter.

DAN HULBERT

Courtesy, The Alley Theater

Those associated with Houston's Alley Theater were delighted when it was given the 1996 Special Tony Award for regional theater. The Alley Theater also celebrated its 50th anniversary during the year. To mark the occasion, members of the famed Redgrave family delighted audiences by appearing in a Shakespeare repertory.

Kander created *Kiss of the Spider Woman*, said, "The show used to be considered too dark to be a major Broadway hit, but now—in the age of O. J. Simpson—it looks like its time has come." Even Joel Grey—the long-absent veteran of the Kander-Ebb *Cabaret*—enjoyed a comeback role in *Chicago*.

Once Upon a Mattress, the fairy-tale musical that launched the career of Carol Burnett in the early 1960s, had its first major Broadway revival. With the exception of Sarah Jessica Parker in the princess role, it was a disappointment.

The 1996–97 season was a slow starter for plays (such as Christopher Durang's panned *Sex and Longing*, with Sigourney Weaver), and the closing of the Circle Repertory Theater, one of the most fertile off-Broadway companies of the 1970s and 1980s, cast a pall. A rare piece of exciting good news was *Skylight*. In addition to the literate, politically edged script by David Hare (*Racing Demon*), the London import was notable as the overdue New York debut of Michael Gambon, one of Britain's most distinguished actors, who was compellingly unpredictable as a wealthy restaurateur striving to rekindle an old romance with a self-sacrificing liberal woman.

Another brilliant London star, Irishwoman Fiona Shaw, had a New York debut with deeply respectful notices for her off-Broadway reading of T. S. Eliot's *The Waste Land*. A much more surprising one-woman tour de force on Broadway came from Julia Sweeney, best known as the sexually ambiguous "Pat" on *Saturday Night Live*. Sweeney's *God Said "Ha!"*was a funny and moving account of how her family bonded against deadly illnesses (including her own cervical cancer). Its run was short, however.

Director Scott Elliott, whose sexually provocative style drew kudos in the previous off-Broadway season (*Ecstasy* and *Curtains*), brought that style to his Broadway debut, an unorthodox revival of Noel Coward's *Present Laughter*. It was the second acclaimed starring role of 1996 for Frank Langella (*The Father*).

David Henry Hwang, whose brilliant *M. Butterfly* was one of the finest plays of ideas in the late 1980s, finally scored again with *Golden Child*. Produced off-Broadway by the New York Shakespeare Festival, *Child* explored a young Asian-American man's struggle to come to terms with the ghosts of his polygamist ancestors. The Brooklyn Academy of Music continued its proud tradition as an importer of important work with new plays by Wole Soyinka of Nigeria and Robert Lepage of Canada.

The off-Broadway Signature Theatre Company continued the rediscovery of Sam Shepard with an all-Shepard season. It included a double bill (lauded by *The New York Times*) of the one-acts *Chicago* (1965) and *When the World Was Green (A Chef's Fable)*, which had debuted at the Olympic Arts Festival in Atlanta; and a revised version of the 1972 play *The Tooth of Crime*, about the deadly rivalry of futuristic rock stars.

Regional Theater. Members of the Redgrave theatrical dynasty dazzled Houston in a Shakespeare repertory. As part of the 50th-anniversary celebration of that city's Alley

Theatre, Vanessa Redgrave played Cleopatra in *Antony and Cleopatra* (also her U.S. directing debut), while her brother Corin Redgrave directed and played the title role in *Julius Caesar*. Also at the Alley, *The Young Man From Atlanta*, the 1995 Pulitzer Prize winner by Horton Foote—whose lifetime home was close to Houston—made its regional debut. The tingling family drama, revolving around an unspoken theme of forbidden homosexuality in the 1950s, featured its original off-Broadway stars, Ralph Waite and Carlin Glynn. The stellar Alley season clinched its win of the 1996 Special Tony Award for achievement by a regional theater.

Sharon Ott, who over 13 years built the Berkeley Repertory Theater into what many felt was the leading theater of the Bay Area, resigned at the end of 1996 to become the artistic director of the Seattle Repertory Theatre. Her move symbolized a shift of artistic prestige from San Francisco (once a leading city in regional theater) to the 1990s theatrical hotbed of Seattle. One hugely successful homegrown production in San Francisco, however, was John Fisher's campy extravaganza, *Medea: The Musical*, which at year's end had been running 17 months at the Stage Door Theatre.

Another popular phenomenon of the Far West was the Oregon Shakespeare Festival, whose spring-summer repertory of 11 plays virtually was sold out; the festival was the center for the thriving tourist industry in Ashland, OR. The Shakespeare Theatre of Washington, DC, similarly renowned for stately treatments of the Bard, also continued to capitalize on America's sudden rediscovery of Shakespeare onstage and in the movies.

The original musical *Time and Again*, based on the popular time-travel fantasy novel by Jack Finney, debuted at the Old Globe Theatre of San Diego and underwent further revisions for a future New York mounting. Also considered a future candidate for Broadway was Randy Newman's irreverent musical *Faust*, which originated at La Jolla (CA) Playhouse in 1995 and had a second, revised production at the Goodman Theatre of Chicago in 1996.

The Olympic Arts Festival, which overlapped with the centennial Olympic Games in Atlanta, featured world premieres by two Pulitzer Prize–winning playwrights, Sam Shepard and Alfred Uhry (*Driving Miss Daisy*). Shepard teamed with writer/director Joseph Chaikin for *When the World Was Green*, a tingling mystery fable about a chef (the masterful Alvin Epstein) whose act of ethnic vengeance evoked the butchery in Bosnia. Uhry again mined his Atlanta upbringing for *The Last Night of Ballyhoo*, a warm romantic comedy framed against class prejudices within that city's Jewish community in 1939. Featuring two of Uhry's *Daisy* alumni—Dana Ivey and director Ron Lagomarsino—*Ballyhoo* was slated for a New York transfer in 1997. Another work launched by the Olympic festival was *Hip 2: Birth of the Boom*, a musical of a young black man's coming-of-age by Tom Jones and Atlanta's Jomandi Productions that transferred to a critically acclaimed run at the Studio Theatre in Washington, DC.

American Theatre magazine's annual survey of the most frequently produced plays in regional nonprofit theaters in 1996–97 included: *Sylvia*, A.R. Gurney, Jr.'s comedy in which a middle-aged man's beloved dog is played by a woman (28 productions); *Arcadia*, Tom Stoppard's brilliant time-traveling play of ideas (13 productions); *The Glass Menagerie* by Tennessee Williams (12); *To Kill a Mockingbird*, adapted from Harper Lee's novel by Christopher Sergel (12); *Having Our Say*, adapted from the book of African-American sisters Bessie and Sadie Delany's memoirs by Emily Mann (ten); *A Tuna Christmas*, a holiday edition of the small-town Texas satire by Jaston Williams, Joe Sears, and Ed Howard (eight); *Love! Valour! Compassion!*, the 1995 Tony Award winner for best play by Terrence McNally (eight); *The Diary of Anne Frank* (eight); *The Woman in Black*, adapted from Susan Hill by Stephen Mallatratt (seven); and *The Cryptogram*, a chilling child's-eye view of family disintegration by David Mamet (seven).

It was a very sluggish fall for the commercial touring circuit after a series of flush seasons; for instance, *Applause* with Stefanie Powers canceled several cities after poor reviews and sales.

One commercial bright spot, in terms of national attention, was the pre-Broadway tryout of Andrew Lloyd Webber's *Whistle Down the Wind* at the National Theatre of Washington, DC. Adapted from a 1961 film with Hayley Mills and transplanted to the American South, the family tale of a mysterious drifter and the children who believe he is Jesus was the first Lloyd Webber musical to premiere in the United States since *Jesus Christ Superstar* in 1971. The tryout was panned by *The Washington Post* but received an encouraging review from *Variety*.

DAN HULBERT
"The Atlanta Journal and Constitution"

TRANSPORTATION

Safety issues and corporate restructuring actions eclipsed other events in the transportation industry in 1996.

Airlines. The airline industry enjoyed robust growth in traffic. Between January and July 1996, total domestic and international passengers carried on the ten largest U.S. passenger airlines increased 5.0% above the same period in 1995, while revenue passenger-kilometers rose 6.3% and freight-ton kilometers (on the 12 largest passenger and cargo carriers) grew 1.6%. Among 21 smaller U.S. airlines, total passengers carried jumped 11.1%, revenue passenger-kilometers grew 9.5%, and freight-ton kilometers climbed 10.8%. Between January and August 1996, revenue passenger-kilometers on international routes of the Association of European Airlines rose 7.5% over the same interval in 1995, while freight-ton kilometers grew 4.1%.

Revenues from this traffic growth—along with the favorable impacts on an eight-month lapse in the 10% federal ticket tax and continuing moderation in fare competition—helped boost profitability in the U.S. airline industry (despite a jump in fuel costs in the fall), which returned in 1995 following five years of losses totaling at least $13 billion. Between Jan. 1 and Dec. 31, 1996, the industry's scheduled-service carriers earned estimated total net profits of about $3.5 billion, up 49% from full-year results for 1995.

Some companies did not share in this prosperity. During the first four months of the year, newer airlines in the so-called low-fare sector enjoyed strong actual and expected traffic growth. However, their fortunes plunged following the May 11 crash of a ValuJet DC-9 in the Florida Everglades. Immediately afterward, Secretary of Transportation Federico Peña flew to the crash scene and declared that ValuJet's operations were safe. His subsequent reversal of that judgment, coupled with the Federal Aviation Administration's (FAA's) grounding of all ValuJet flight operations on June 17, intensified a decline in consumers' confidence in the newer low-fare carriers. Concerns about air safety grew even more following the July 17 loss of TWA flight 800 off the coast of Long Island, NY (*see* SPECIAL REPORT, page 551). ValuJet resumed limited operations on September 30, shortly after receiving final approval to do so from the federal government.

The year's worst crash was a midair collision in November of two passenger planes near New Delhi, India, that claimed 349 lives. Worldwide, air-transport fatalities for the year totaled 1,597, up 73% from 924 in 1995, and 40% above the yearly average of 1,136 deaths during the 1980s.

An erosion of passenger traffic and revenues contributed to several corporate failures. Nations Air Express Inc., the earliest casualty, suspended its scheduled services just eight days after the ValuJet crash. Kiwi Inter-

The initial phase of the new $860 million Dallas Area Rapid Transit system—the first modern rail-transit line in the U.S. Southwest—opened in Dallas, TX, in June 1996.

national Air Lines filed for protection under Chapter 11 of the federal bankruptcy laws on September 30, and terminated all scheduled flight operations in October. JetTrain, Inc., which reported a decline of more than 25% in traffic following the ValuJet grounding, ceased operation in November. JetTrain alleged that cutthroat competitive tactics by larger airlines contributed to its demise. Battling for survival, Vanguard Airlines, Inc., announced a major restructuring of its network in November, after aggressive fare cutting and competition from American Airlines and other major carriers forced it to withdraw from routes that it had entered recently. Pursuit of an expensive program of rapid expansion, together with costly responses to a major competitor, burdened Western Pacific Airlines with a net loss of almost $3 million during the first three quarters of the year. Hurt by rising competition from Southwest Airlines and Delta Express, and by a traffic drop-off sparked by the ValuJet disaster, American Trans Air (AmTran) announced in the fall that it would make large cuts in its schedule and concentrate primarily on charter traffic. AmTran, the largest U.S. charter airline, stepped into the scheduled-service realm in 1993, but found it far less profitable than its original charter niche.

Amidst this gloom, Reno Air, Inc., offered a beacon of hope as it continued to develop its network around hubs at Reno, NV, and San Jose, CA, and reported net profits for six successive quarters. Late in September a legendary corporate name in commercial aviation took wing again with the inaugural flight of Pan Am Corp. Investors who formed the new company had purchased the Pan Am name and its famous blue globe logo for $1.3 million in 1993, in the bankruptcy court charged with overseeing the liquidation of Pan American World Airways, Inc., which ceased operation in 1991.

Elsewhere, a downturn in earnings threatened the survival of Canadian Airlines near year's end, forcing the company to seek cash savings through reductions in wages for its unionized employees, deferral of loan payments to creditors, and other measures. Air France reported a profit of about $158 million for the six months ending on Sept. 30, 1996, compared with a loss of $66 million during the same period in 1995. In an effort to bolster revenues in the important transatlantic market in competition with other major European carriers, Air France entered into marketing alliances with Continental Airlines and Delta Air Lines in October.

In June, Northwest Airlines agreed to purchase 6,654 shares of Northwest preferred stock held by KLM Royal Dutch Airlines for $378 million. The shares had been acquired by KLM in 1989. British Airways and American Airlines opened negotiations to establish a strategic alliance, which precipitated action by USAir to dissolve an existing marketing alliance between itself and British Airways. British Airways moved to sell its holdings of USAir stock.

Bus. First-quarter ridership on Greyhound Lines, Inc., the only nationwide carrier, rose 16.5% above the ridership during the same period in 1995. Greyhound's financial performance also continued to improve. During the first half of 1996, total revenue rose 6.7% compared to the same period in 1995, to $172 million. Over that same time period the company's net loss (after interest and taxes) declined 44%, to $5.53 million. Late in the year, Greyhound anticipated that it would earn its first fourth-quarter profit since 1992. Passenger-ticket sales in October were 6.8% above those for the same month in 1995, and the company estimated that it could handle growth in traffic without a significant increase in operating expenses.

January-March traffic on the nine largest regional intercity bus lines rose 1.3% above the same period in 1995. However, their first-quarter net operating loss increased 9.2%, to $40.2 million.

Greyhound's appointment in May of a former Amtrak executive to the post of director of intermodal alliances signaled an end to the antagonism that Greyhound long had manifested toward Amtrak, and underscored a drive to develop new sources of revenues through the establishment and maintenance of connections with passenger carriers in other modes of transportation. By November, Greyhound had entered into at least eight new code-sharing schedules with Amtrak involving through ticketing, coordinated scheduling, and use of joint terminal facilities at bus-rail connecting points. Greyhound also pursued efforts to take advantage of the impending Jan. 1, 1997, opening to cross-border bus operations under the North American Free Trade Agreement (NAFTA).

Rail. Changes in industry structure dominated the rail scene. On July 3 the U.S. Surface Transportation Board (STB) approved the merger of the Southern Pacific Rail Corp. into the Union Pacific Railroad Co. The $5.4 billion transaction created a network of roughly 37,000 mi (59 500 km) in 25 states, Mexico, and Canada. In an effort to moderate

SPECIAL REPORT/TRANSPORTATION

The Safety Issue

While travel in the United States remained safer than in most countries of the world, a number of high-profile accidents in 1996 focused public attention on the weaknesses in transportation systems—particularly in the air.

Air. The year 1996 was one of the worst years for airline crashes in more than a decade. As of the end of November, 1,929 U.S.-owned aircraft were involved in 1,897 accidents. Of those, 356 resulted in 1,488 fatalities. The most dramatic were the May 11 crash of ValuJet's Flight 592 in the Florida Everglades, and the July 17 crash of TWA's Flight 800 into the Atlantic off the coast of Long Island, NY. Both incidents led to changes in the government's and airlines' procedures.

ValuJet's DC-9 apparently caught fire when expired oxygen generators, which mistakenly had been loaded in the cargo hold of the plane without the proper safety caps, ignited. The accident, which killed all 110 aboard the plane, led to the June 17 shutdown of the airline for an intensive review by the Federal Aviation Administration (FAA). The incident focused public attention on the FAA and its oversight of low-cost, start-up carriers. After the shutdown, Secretary of Transportation Federico Peña requested that Congress change the FAA's mandate from its dual role of promoting and regulating airlines to regulation only. The FAA also issued new requirements for airlines in the area of training, repairs, and outsourcing maintenance, and increased its level of scrutiny over low-cost start-ups. After an intensive review and compliance with all FAA requests, ValuJet was permitted to resume operations on August 29.

The National Transportation Safety Board (NTSB), the independent government agency charged with investigating transportation accidents, publicly criticized the airline's and a subcontractor's treatment of hazardous materials, and the FAA's oversight of the airline. The NTSB also criticized the FAA for not acting on a 1988 recommendation to install fire-detection devices in all aircraft. The FAA later stated its intent to implement that recommendation.

As the end of the year approached, the cause of the TWA crash, which killed all 230 passengers aboard, still was a mystery. Because the downing originally appeared to be the result of a criminal act, the Federal Bureau of Investigation and the NTSB conducted a joint investigation. Even after more than 95% of the Boeing 747 had been recovered, the cause of the crash remained elusive. Investigators knew that the center fuel tank exploded, but did not know what ignited the blast. Investigators said they were considering three possibilities: a bomb, a missile, or mechanical failure. Immediately after the crash, President

Following devastating airline crashes in the first seven months of 1996, measures, including new security procedures at airports—such as the security advisory at Boston's Logan Airport, below*—were taken to make air travel safer.*

© Brooks Kraft/Sygma

Bill Clinton appointed a commission to be led by Vice-President Al Gore to look into airport and airline security and safety. That committee later recommended enhanced security procedures at airports, many of which were implemented later in 1996.

Boeing Co., the world's largest supplier of commercial jets, released a study in 1996 predicting that, if accident rates remained constant over the next ten years, the number of accidents would increase as the number of flights increased. The report projected that air travel would increase by 50% between 1996 and 2006, at which time one major accident would occur every eight days. The study analyzed data on the world's accidents since 1959. It found that an accident is usually the result of a chain of events, with an average of four factors contributing to each accident. If one of those links in the chain is circumvented, the accident will not happen.

Several steps have been taken to remove those links. One is the Flight Operations Quality Assurance (FOQA) program, in which airlines make use of computers already on board their aircraft that measure up to 150 parameters of the airplane. In contrast to flight data recorders, or "black boxes," which measure only about 17 to 25 parameters and are removed only after an accident, FOQA measurements are recorded constantly and can be downloaded from a plane after each flight to determine if any irregularities or patterns are developing that need attention.

Other new technologies also have been tested. Some airlines were experimenting with new Controlled Flight into Terrain (CFIT) systems that experts say could have prevented the December 1995 crash of an American Airlines aircraft into a mountain in Cali, Colombia. Existing jet cockpits are equipped with electronic signals that work off the radar altimeters. The signal screams "pull up" if the plane approaches a steep mountain. But the pilot only has about ten seconds to adjust. In the experimental CFIT program, a computer memory chip can provide pilots with a continuous display of the terrain that is 7 to 10 mi (11 to 16 km) away on a cockpit monitor.

Automobiles. In 1995, 41,798 persons were killed in auto accidents, a 2.8% rise from 1994. But government statistics indicated that the number of miles traveled increased, so the 1995 fatality rate, 1.7 per 100 million vehicle miles traveled, was the same as it had been since 1993. About 3,386,000 were injured in auto accidents, and 4,409,000 crashes involved property damage only. The economic cost of accidents in the United States was estimated to top $150 billion per year.

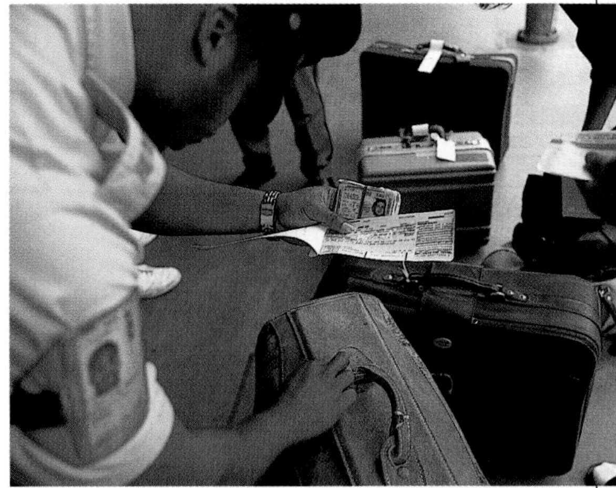

© Steve Lehman/Saba

A more thorough check of luggage at airports, including the matching of bags with passengers, was recommended by the 1996 White House Commission on Aviation Safety and Security.

Safety experts called for tougher enforcement of speed-limit, drunk-driving, and seat-belt laws. The use of safety belts—required in every state except New Hampshire—rose to 68% in 1995, but a 1996 study showed that 32% of drivers and passengers still do not use them. Alcohol-related fatalities fell in 1995 to 41.3% of all traffic fatalities (compared with 55.1% in 1985). However, the number of alcohol-related traffic fatalities rose to 17,274 in 1995, up from 16,589 in 1994.

Two new studies reported that air bags cut the fatality rate for adults by 11%, but that they increased the fatality rate for children under 12 and seated in the front seat by 28% to 33%. The National Highway Transportation Safety Administration (NHTSA) called for new measures to enhance air-bag use. First, the NHTSA called for a phase-in schedule for "smart" air bags, which can be tailored to fit the occupant and the circumstances of a crash, beginning in 1999. The NHTSA also recommended that children be placed in safety seats in the backseat of vehicles and extended a provision permitting automakers to install cutoff switches in vehicles without backseats. It also asked auto manufacturers to warn owners of cars with air bags of their risks.

Railroad. Accidents at highway-rail crossings are the top cause of deaths in the rail industry. The Federal Railroad Administration (FRA) reported that 579 persons were killed and 1,894 were injured in 4,633 rail-crossing accidents in 1995. FRA statistics showed that rail-crossing fatalities decreased in the first half of 1996 by 31% compared to the same period in 1995, due mainly to safety measures implemented in 1994–95.

FAYE BOWERS, *"The Christian Science Monitor"*

anticompetitive effects, the STB required that the merged company grant access to Burlington Northern Santa Fe on more than 3,500 mi (5 600 km) of track. On October 15, Conrail, Inc., stunned industry observers by announcing an agreement to merge its 11,700-mi (18 800-km) network with CSX Corporation's 18,000-mi (29 000-km) system. Eight days later, CSX rival Norfolk Southern launched a competing bidding effort for Conrail that escalated to $10 billion by year's end and sparked fierce debate among the three rail carriers, investors, rail-freight shippers, employees, and other interested parties.

In December the parent company of the 2,900-mi (4 700-km) Kansas City Southern Railway announced plans to purchase all outstanding stock of the 402-mi (647-km) Gateway Western Railway, and was named the winning bidder (in partnership with a Mexican company) for a 50-year concession to operate 2,400 mi (3 900 km) of rail line in northeast Mexico. Acceptance of the $1.4 billion bid marked the first firm step in the Mexican government's plan to privatize the Ferrocarriles Nacionales de Mexico. In January, Illinois Central acquired the Chicago, Central & Pacific, a line that it had sold in 1985. Burlington Northern Santa Fe repurchased and rebuilt trackage it had sold or taken out of service in the 1980s running over its Stampede Pass line in order to relieve congestion on its other two routes linking eastern Washington with Seattle and Tacoma.

Other larger railways continued to sell numerous light- and medium-density lines to regional and short-line carriers. Notable transactions included Canadian Pacific–owned Soo Line Railroad's sale of its Kansas City–Chicago line and so-called "corn lines" in Iowa and Minnesota. The Canadian Pacific Railway (CPR) placed its operations between Montreal, Toronto, Chicago, and the U.S. Northeast into a new subsidiary, the St. Lawrence & Hudson Railway, in an effort to restore profitability to the eastern end of its network.

Freight traffic on major U.S. railways remained almost flat. During the first 49 weeks of the year, ton-miles increased about 1.9%, total carload shipments declined 0.5%, and intermodal traffic rose 2% in comparison with levels for the same period in 1995.

Amtrak struggled to maintain and improve service in the face of inadequate revenues and federal funding. Developments that were considered positive included final environmental approval and groundbreaking for the electrification of its New Haven–Boston line. In March, Amtrak placed an order for 15 high-horsepower electric locomotives and 18 high-speed train sets. The train sets, scheduled to enter service in 1999, would operate in the Boston-Washington Northeast Corridor at speeds up to 150 mph (240 km/hr). Amtrak and the state of Washington moved toward the acquisition of three Spanish-design train sets for use in the corridor between Vancouver, BC, and Eugene, OR.

Amtrak closed the year with no passenger fatalities. However, eight passengers and three crew members on a commuter train died in a February 16 collision with an Amtrak train in Silver Springs, MD; and one passenger and two crew members perished in the collision of two New Jersey Transit trains on February 9. These accidents, together with a series of high-profile freight-train derailments and collisions, made rail safety a political issue and sparked several congressional hearings.

Truck. The intense rate competition and unused capacity that decimated the profitability of both less-than-truckload (LTL) and truckload (TL) carriers in 1995 moderated somewhat by the end of 1996, but earnings for most carriers remained relatively weak. Of the four largest LTL carriers, only Roadway Express reported a profit ($11.3 million on revenue of $1.59 billion) during the first nine months of 1996. The other three carriers—ABF Freight System, CF Motor Freight, and Yellow Freight System—reported collective losses of about $60 million on $4.78 billion in revenue during that period. Unionized CF Motor Freight was spun off (and renamed Consolidated Freightways Corp.) by its corporate parent, which retained ownership of profitable nonunion trucking subsidiaries. Dissatisfaction over financial performance caused Yellow Freight System's board of directors to initiate a major management change.

Water. Seeking greater economic strength in the competitive market for ocean container service, the London-based Peninsular and Oriental Steam Navigation Co. and the Royal Nedlloyd Group, which is based in Rotterdam, declared in midyear that they would merge to create the world's largest containership fleet. Near year's end, Canadian Pacific Limited and its subsidiary, CP Ships, announced an intention to bid for purchase of Lykes Brothers Steamship Co., which had been operating under the protection of Chapter 11 of the federal bankruptcy code since October 1995. Many observers of the maritime industry saw CP's bid as the only hope for the survival of Lykes.

JOHN C. SPYCHALSKI
The Pennsylvania State University

TRAVEL

Preliminary figures for 1996 showed an increase in international tourism of 3.8% worldwide, according to the World Tourism Organization. U.S. travel increased slightly. A record number of U.S. passports was issued even though passport offices were closed for six weeks during government shutdowns in late 1995 and early 1996. Leisure travel drove the growth, accounting for 60% of total U.S. domestic sales and 69% of the international pie. Corporate travel was level again.

Packaged adventure tours accounted for half of all leisure travel. Also popular was "soft adventure," an expanded ecotour that combines exotic locations with some physical activity and opportunities for learning about both a region's environment and its culture.

The International Scene. Despite a breakdown in the peace process, the Middle East was the world's fastest-growing travel region, with Egypt experiencing a 95% increase in tourism revenues. Southeast Asia, the Pacific, and South America also showed hefty tourist increases. Mexico's inbound traffic was up nearly 20%, the healthiest increase in more than 12 years. Brazil, South Korea, and Taiwan were the fastest-growing inbound markets.

With international airfares discounted for much of the year, outbound travel from the United States rose nearly 5% in 1996. With the U.S. dollar strong against several European currencies, Europe was again the top destination. European Travel Commission figures posted 9 million U.S. arrivals. Scotland was the hot spot in Great Britain. Italy, Greece, Turkey, and Portugal posted large gains. Tourism to Eastern Europe continued to grow at a slower pace.

Bookings were strong for Japan, Southeast Asia, and the Pacific. Hong Kong and China tourism was down slightly due to high hotel and air costs, but Australia saw U.S. visitor numbers pass the 300,000 mark. New cruises on the Amazon, Chilean Patagonia, Costa Rica, Belize, and the Alaskan wilderness intrigued intrepid U.S. travelers.

U.S. Domestic. U.S. domestic travel grew in 1996, with more than 1 billion person-trips of more than 100 mi (160 km) away from home. Florida, California, and Hawaii continued atop the domestic vacation-site list; Washington state and Tennessee were newcomers. Pleasure travelers took five or six short trips, usually with their families, in 1996. They spent an average of 8.5 nights away from home, up from 7.9 nights in 1995. The average cost per trip was $1,076. Visits to national parks and forests were up 2%. Tours were getting shorter and more varied to accommodate multigenerational family travel. Operators looked for destinations where entertainment could be found for a variety of ages. Megaresorts with indoor theme-park attractions were popular.

Thanks primarily to the Summer Olympic Games in Atlanta, foreign arrivals increased 2%, to 44.8 million. The largest percentage of visitors came from Europe, followed closely by Asia and the Middle East. Improved economic conditions in Canada and Mexico, the nation's two largest inbound markets, were reflected in a slight upswing in visitor numbers, with 14.7 million arrivals from Canada and 8 million from Mexico.

Cruising. The supply of cruise berths rose rapidly in 1996 with the debut of seven new ships accommodating a total of 13,400 passengers. Included in the lineup was Carnival Cruise Line's *Destiny*, the largest cruise ship ever built and the first to top the 100,000-ton mark. Although the cruise industry reported an 8.75% increase in North American passenger boardings for the year, cruise revenues and passenger numbers from the United States were flat through the summer. The European market burgeoned, however. Upscale Seabourn Cruise Line was ranked highest in overall quality and client satisfaction among 14 major lines.

BARBARA J. BRAASCH, *Freelance Travel Writer*

TUNISIA

Tunisia's weak political opposition received another blow in 1996 with the separate convictions and imprisonment on spying charges of the two leaders of the main opposition party, the Movement of Social Democrats (MDS).

Politics. MDS leader Mohammed Moada was sentenced in February to 11 years in prison after a court found him guilty of being a Libyan agent. His trial was condemned by Amnesty International, which described it as unfair and said that no convincing evidence had been presented. Moada had been arrested in October 1995 after his party made public a letter he wrote to President Zine El Abidine Ben Ali, criticizing restrictions on political activity in the country and the total control of politics exercised by the ruling Constitutional Democratic Rally.

Moada's deputy, Khemais Chammari, who is also a founder of the Tunisian Human Rights League, was sentenced to five years in prison in July for having disclosed documents relating to Moada's trial to a Belgian lawyer who the prosecution alleged was a Libyan agent. Human-rights organizations again condemned the trial, and Chammari himself said the charges were purely political.

In May the European Parliament issued a resolution criticizing the Tunisian government's harassment of political opponents and calling on the European Union (EU) Commission and Council "to take steps to persuade the authorities to...honor their international human-rights commitments." This prompted an angry reply "deploring" the resolution from the speaker of the Tunisian parliament, Habib Boulares. The two men were freed on humanitarian grounds in late December.

The Economy. In July the World Bank agreed to lend Tunisia $750 million over three years. In return, the government pledged to speed up privatization. By late 1996 the World Bank had started the disbursement of the loan, which would depend on the government selling off during the three years assets worth $500 million from a total of 112 companies slated for privatization. Some of the money was aimed at making Tunisia's industries more competitive as the country proceeded with dismantling trade barriers under the terms of its agreement with the EU. The latter envisioned setting up a Mediterranean-wide free-trade zone in 2010

Foreign Relations. In January, Israel and Tunisia agreed to establish low-level diplomatic missions in each other's capitals; and in April, Israel opened an interests bureau in Tunis and appointed Tunisian-born diplomat Shalom Cohen as its head. Tunisia later set up its own interest bureau in Tel Aviv.

In April, Pope John Paul II visited Tunisia, where he spoke about the need to overcome the "historical misunderstanding" between Muslims and Christians. It was his first visit to North Africa in 11 years.

In November, Tunisia's Foreign Minister Habib Ben Yahia criticized plans by Italy, France, Spain, and Portugal to establish a rapid-military-intervention force for the southern Mediterranean region. He said the force was set up without consulting the countries of the southern Mediterranean and that it was incompatible with Tunisia's aspirations for dialogue and consultation between the two banks of the Mediterranean.

HEBA SALEH, *BBC North Africa Correspondent*

TUNISIA • Information Highlights

Official Name: Republic of Tunisia.
Location: North Africa.
Area: 63,170 sq mi (163 610 km²).
Population (mid-1996 est.): 9,200,000.
Chief Cities (1994 census): Tunis, the capital, 674,100; Sfax, 230,900.
Government: *Head of state,* Zine El Abidine Ben Ali, president (took office Nov. 7, 1987). *Head of government,* Hamed Karoui, prime minister (took office Sept. 27, 1989). *Legislature* (unicameral)—Chamber of Deputies.
Monetary Unit: Dinar (0.962 dinar equals U.S.$1, August 1996).
Gross Domestic Product (1994 est. U.S.$): $37,100,000,000 (purchasing power parity).
Economic Indexes (1995, 1990 = 100): *Consumer Prices,* all items, 132.4; food, 131.9. *Industrial Production,* 105.
Foreign Trade (1995 U.S.$): *Imports,* $7,903,000,000; *exports,* $5,475,000,000.

TURKEY

Both domestically and internationally, the year 1996 was a turbulent one for Turkey.

Domestic Policies. The results of the December 1995 election were indecisive: The Islamist Welfare Party came in first with 21.38% of the vote, Motherland polled 19.65%, True Path took 19.18%, and two social democratic parties received a combined 25.35%. After Welfare Party leader Necmettin Erbakan was unable to convince any of the secular parties to form a coalition, President Suleyman Demirel appointed Mesut Yilmaz, the Motherland leader, to head a government. Yilmaz and the True Path Party agreed in early March to a plan under which Yilmaz and the True Path leader, former Prime Minister Tansu Ciller, would alternate as prime ministers. They proved unable to work together, however, and the government fell in early June.

President Demirel once again called on Erbakan, who this time persuaded True Path to form a coalition, and Turkey had its first Islamist prime minister in the 73-year history of the republic. Ciller was designated deputy prime minister and foreign minister. The new government aroused considerable concern in the United States and Europe, particularly when Erbakan asserted that he would seek to reorient Turkey toward other Islamic nations.

Among the prime minister's actions during his first months in office were dramatic visits to Iran and Libya, and hints that he did not consider Turkey's pending association with the European Union (EU) as important as most other Turkish leaders did, but that he instead envisioned an "Islamic NATO [North Atlantic Treaty Organization]." Political observers expected, however, that Erbakan's powers would be constrained by the strongly secularist and Western-oriented armed forces, and by the fact that although the Welfare

© Shandiz/Sygma

The August 1996 trip of Turkey's new Prime Minister Necmettin Erbakan (right) *to Iran caused consternation in the West. During the tour, he conferred with Ayatollah Ali Hoseini-Khamenei* (left) *and signed a natural-gas agreement.*

Party finished first in the election, Islamist votes still were only one fifth of the total.

International concern about Turkey's violations of human rights in its battle against Kurdish separatists was somewhat quieter in 1996, but a variant of the human-rights topic drew international attention in summer when there was a dramatic nationwide hunger strike by some 2,000 inmates in Turkish prisons protesting their treatment. The strike ended with major government concessions after 69 days and the deaths of several strikers.

Economic Affairs. Inflation continued at about 85%. Although inflation was down from some earlier periods, it still was well above the target of the International Monetary Fund (IMF) of 40%. Despite continued increases in exports, the value of the lira fell to the benchmark point of more than 100,000 to the dollar by late in the year.

Several events gave rise to optimism for the longer run, however. In December 1995, Turkey had been admitted to the European Customs Union, which many saw as a major step for eventual admission to the EU. In August 1996, Turkey signed a 23-year, $23 billion agreement to purchase natural gas from Iran. Although Turkish hopes for resumption of Iraqi oil exports—from which Turkey receives large transit revenues—received a temporary setback in September as a result of Iraq's new clash with the Persian Gulf coalition, the resumption did take place in December. In May the foundation for the Karkamis dam was laid, marking another step in the gigantic Southeast Anatolia Project, which is the basis for major development in that region. Tourism continued to increase.

The Kurdish Problem. The Turkish government's efforts to suppress the rebellion of the Kurdistan Workers Party (PKK) in the southeast continued, with little more success than there had been earlier. The army again made several raids into Iraq in pursuit of Kurdish guerrillas. A new international dimension was added to the problem in the form of heightened Turkish border-security concerns in connection with the Iraqi government's military moves into the internationally protected Kurdish enclaves in that country's northwest, and the fighting there between Iraqi-backed and Iranian-backed Kurdish factions. New worldwide public attention to the general subject of Kurdish autonomy also was seen in Turkey as complicating its own situation. In July, Turkey approved a new extension of the Gulf coalition's Operation Provide Comfort.

Foreign Affairs. Troubles with Greece flared up anew. In winter and spring there were new clashes over the ownership and occupa-

TURKEY • Information Highlights

Official Name: Republic of Turkey.
Location: Southeastern Europe and southwestern Asia.
Area: 301,382 sq mi (780 580 km²).
Population (mid-1996 est.): 63,900,000.
Chief Cities (mid-1993 est.): Ankara, the capital, 2,719,981; Istanbul, 7,331,927; Izmir, 1,920,807.
Government: *Head of state,* Suleyman Demirel, president (took office May 16, 1993). *Head of government,* Necmettin Erbakan, prime minister (took office June 1996). *Legislature*—Grand National Assembly.
Monetary Unit: Lira (107,712.00 liras equal U.S. $1, Dec. 30, 1996).
Gross Domestic Product (1994 est. U.S.$): $305,200,-000,000 (purchasing power parity).
Economic Indexes (1995, 1990 = 100): *Consumer Prices,* all items, 1,872.3; food, 1,938.2. *Industrial Production,* 116.
Foreign Trade (1995 U.S.$): *Imports,* $35,710,000,000; *exports,* $21,600,000,000.

tion of the small Aegean islet known as Kardak to Turkey and as Imia to Greece. In August there also was new violence on Cyprus. During the unrest, in which two Greek Cypriots were killed, protesters attempted to tear down a Turkish flag in the United Nations–patrolled buffer zone. The incidents led to heightened new internationally sponsored efforts to settle the decades-old dispute, but again to little avail.

There continued to be considerable Turkish interest in the Turkic republics of the former Soviet Union. President Demirel visited several of these, and the chiefs of state of almost all of the former republics continued their frequent visits to Ankara. Negotiations for new economic and cultural agreements made considerable progress.

Turkey also signed two agreements with Israel for limited military cooperation, including rights for both countries to use the other's airspace for training exercises.

WALTER F. WEIKER, *Rutgers University*

UGANDA

In May 1996, President Yoweri Museveni won a landslide victory in Uganda's first freely contested elections since independence, but disparities between the north and the rest of the country, as well as ongoing problems of poverty and indebtedness, continued.

The Elections. In an election judged relatively free and fair by international observers, Museveni crushed his two opponents by gaining 72.4% of the vote. His main rival, Paul Ssemogerere, gained 23.7%, and Mohammed Majaya won 2%. Museveni, a Protestant Ankole from southwestern Uganda, handily defeated his principal rival even among the traditional allies of Ssemogerere—namely, Catholics and the Baganda. In parliamentary elections that followed one month later, Museveni's National Resistance movement obtained a clear majority.

Ssemogerere's only stronghold was the north, which has not enjoyed the same level of economic prosperity as the south and has suffered from increasing rebel activity.

Rebel Activity. The northern rebel movements were dominated by the West Nile Bank Front (WNBF) and the Christian fundamentalist Lord's Resistance Army (LRA). Both were thought to be backed by Sudan and Zaire in retaliation for Uganda's alleged support of the Sudan People's Liberation Army, which was fighting an Islamist government in Khartoum, and the Rwandan Patriotic Front, which drove the former government of Rwanda into Zaire in 1994. Museveni had offered amnesty to the ordinary fighters from both groups, but had vowed not to negotiate with either, to crush them on the battlefield, and to impose the force of the law on their leaders.

Taming the rebels had proven very difficult for Uganda's National Resistance Army, which—in spite of consuming nearly 40% of the national budget—was poorly equipped to fight a hit-and-run force of some 1,000 men. While government forces had increased in number from 20,000 to 30,000 in the north, the rebels continued to play upon the poverty of the region and the effective use of terror.

The Economy. The nation's economy posted a growth rate of more than 8% for 1995–96, which was one of the highest in Africa and marked the tenth year of Uganda's current boom. Servicing a foreign debt of more than $3 billion continued to consume more than 30% of export earnings and growing insecurity in the north undoubtedly would siphon funds away from road construction, primary education, and poverty-reduction programs. In spite of growing tax collection, more than 80% of all public investment was funded through external assistance.

In January, Uganda, Kenya, and Tanzania agreed to strengthen their economies by reviving the East African Community (EAC). Subsequently, national banks were permitted to open branches in neighboring countries and individuals were permitted to open accounts using the currency of a neighboring country. In July the currencies were declared convertible.To facilitate travel within the region, the EAC began issuing a travel document that would enable citizens of the three countries to move with limited formalities among the three member states.

WILLIAM CYRUS REED
The American University in Cairo

UGANDA • Information Highlights

Official Name: Republic of Uganda.
Location: Interior of East Africa.
Area: 91,135 sq mi (236 040 km^2).
Population (mid-1996 est.): 22,000,000.
Chief Cities (1991 census): Kampala, the capital, 773,463; Jinja, 60,979; Mbale, 53,634.
Government: *Head of state,* Yoweri Museveni, president (took office Jan. 29, 1986). *Head of government,* Kintu Musoke, prime minister (took office Nov. 18, 1994). *Legislature* (unicameral)—Constituent Assembly.
Monetary Unit: Uganda shilling (1,071.7 shillings equal U.S.$1, August 1996).
Gross Domestic Product (1994 est. U.S.$): $16,200,-000,000 (purchasing power parity).
Economic Index (1995, 1990 = 100): *Consumer Prices,* all items, 243.3; food, 212.6.
Foreign Trade (1995 U.S.$): *Imports,* $1,056,000,000; *exports,* $461,000,000.

UNITED NATIONS

The 1996 session of the United Nations (UN) was held under the umbrella of two important events: the election of a new secretary-general and the U.S. election campaign. Outgoing UN Secretary-General Boutros Boutros-Ghali described the body's 1996 session as "the year of hard questions and difficult decision, of reexamination of our tenets, of reevaluation of the direction in which we are headed." During the year, UN members searched for ways to transform the organization from an institution guided by Cold War exigencies to one capable of meeting new challenges—ethnic rivalries and small wars, famine and environmental issues, and a new attempt by the organization to help bring justice to countries ravished by apartheid, genocide, and dictatorships. But before the UN could heal the world's wounds, it needed to be given the means to do so. Without the financial resources to carry out its functions, the organization was unable to operate efficiently.

Peacekeeping remained one of the UN's main tasks. As of Dec. 1, 1996, the UN was overseeing 16 peacekeeping operations—with 25,919 military and police personnel serving abroad—at an annual cost of about $1.4 billion. The UN did have some success in bringing peace to such nations as Afghanistan, Angola, and Guatemala. But the news was not all good, with renewed fighting in Somalia.

General Assembly. Malaysia's Razali Ismail was chosen president of the 51st session of the General Assembly. Among the accomplishments of the 51st session was the passage of the Comprehensive Test-Ban Treaty (CTBT) in September. Two weeks later the five declared nuclear powers—Britain, China, France, Russia, and the United States—signed the CTBT. Shortly after signing the treaty, U.S. President Bill Clinton told the General Assembly that the CTBT "points us toward a century in which the roles and risks of nuclear weapons can be even further reduced until ultimately eliminated." The main opponent to the treaty was India, which argued that the declared nuclear powers must eliminate their nuclear arsenals before asking others not to acquire such weaponry. In addition, Indonesian Foreign Minister Ali Alatas argued that the treaty would permit nuclear-weapon states to test under simulated circumstances in labs. By November, 136 governments had signed the treaty, but only Fiji had ratified it.

The General Assembly voted to promote the establishment of an International Criminal Court, which would have the mandate to punish those guilty of genocide and crimes against humanity. Italy offered to host a conference in 1998 to sanction its birth.

Secretary-General. UN Secretary-General Kofi Annan of Ghana became the seventh individual to hold that post. On Jan. 1, 1997, he succeeded Egypt's Boutros-Ghali, who was elected in 1991. Traditionally, most secretaries-general are given two five-year terms and most regions expect the post to rotate. Nonetheless, Boutros-Ghali was denied a second term. The United States, charging that he had failed to reform the UN, said that as long as he held the office, Congress would continue to hold back funds that it owed the organization. In June 1996, Washington let it be known that it would veto Boutros-Ghali's attempts at a second term. Defiantly, he refused to back out of the race. In November, when the Security Council took its first straw poll, Boutros-Ghali won the support of 14 of 15 members. But the United States used its veto to block his victory. With the deadline approaching, Security Council members realized that U.S. officials would stand by their threat. On December 13, not wanting to lose their chance at a second term, the African members of the council selected Annan, 58, a veteran UN insider who was serving as undersecretary-general for peacekeeping, as their candidate. After the Security Council recommended Annan's candidacy, the General Assembly passed a resolution on December 17 electing him secretary-general for five years.

The United States, after voting for Annan, welcomed his election and promised to work with him. For his part, the new secretary-general pledged that, within the first six months of his tenure, he would indicate where the UN should be headed in the future and what kind of reforms it would need in order to get there. On the issue of peacekeeping, Annan stressed that the UN had learned that a clear mandate was necessary before the sending of forces to an area.

Guatemala. The presence of UN Secretary-General Boutros-Ghali at the December signing of an agreement that ended 36 years of civil war indicated the important role the UN had played in bringing the Guatemalan government and guerrilla leaders of the Guatemalan National Revolutionary Union together during six years of negotiations. Both Guatemalan President Alvaro Arzú and rebel leaders praised the role of chief UN mediator Jean Arnault in keeping talks on track. In 1997, UN peacekeepers were slated to be sent to Guatemala to monitor the disarming of the rebels and to verify the implementation of the peace accords.

Haiti. At the beginning of December, the UN Security Council extended the UN's role in Haiti until May 31, 1997, but while a two-month extension could be applied, it appeared possible that the UN would not continue to keep troops in Haiti after that time. In fact, in December, when it came time to extend the UN presence in Haiti, both Russia and China threatened vetoes if the council did not consider cutting off the force. Both countries argued that the situation in Haiti was not a threat to international peace and security. However, the United States, Canada, and other nations argued that the situation in Haiti was far from stable. UN Secretary-General Boutros-Ghali, in a December report on democracy and human rights in Haiti, said that while the situation has improved, it "nonetheless remains fragile." The report pointed out violations by state agents of the right to life and listed glaring violations of legal and constitutional procedures. At the end of the year, the UN had roughly 1,300 military personnel in Haiti.

Angola. There was new hope that peace would come to Angola. The government of President José Eduardo dos Santos and Jonas Savimbi's National Union for the Total Independence of Angola (UNITA), with the help of the UN, began negotiations aimed primarily at building a coalition government and uniting the two armies. The UN force in Angola represented the organization's largest peacekeeping operation. But it had the difficult task of overseeing the demobilization of armies, monitoring the cease-fire, disarming troops, and verifying areas vacated by UNITA. In December financial pressures forced Secretary-General Boutros-Ghali to call for the withdrawal of four military-support and infantry units before the end of the year, and, following that, the withdrawal of all UN forces from Angola. At the end of 1996, the UN had roughly 6,600 military personnel of all ranks in Angola. Boutros-Ghali said that the UN would concentrate on political, police, and human-rights monitoring and vital humanitarian activities in the future.

Afghanistan. The UN had been trying to bring peace to the Afghani people since 1979, when the Soviet Union took over the country. In February 1989 the UN monitored the Soviet withdrawal from Afghanistan, and when Afghani rebel forces fought among themselves, it continued to work toward a peaceful solution. By October 1996 one of the factions, Taliban—an extreme Islamic fundamentalist group—controlled the capital and two thirds of the country, although fighting with anti-Taliban factions still continued in some regions. The UN threatened to withdraw all aid from Afghanistan as a result of Taliban's refusal to permit women to be educated or to work. Boutros-Ghali informed Taliban that the UN Charter insists on equality of the sexes and that no restrictions should be placed on the eligibility of men and women to participate in any capacity and under conditions of equality in its organs.

Iraq. Since the invasion of Kuwait in 1990, Iraq had been under severe Security Council sanctions that prevented it from selling oil or doing any business with the rest of the world. The sanctions were meant to prevent Iraq from rebuilding its weaponry industry and threatening its neighbors. But after years of sanctions, many in the international community insisted that something be done to help the suffering Iraqi people, while keeping the sanctions in place. The Security Council came up with the idea of letting Iraq sell $2 billion worth of oil over a six-month period, and then using the proceeds to purchase food and medicine for the Iraqi people. In November, Iraq agreed to meet UN terms; in December the nation began selling oil for the first time since 1990.

Finances. The UN remained under the threat of bankruptcy. To survive, the world organization borrowed from its peacekeeping funds in order to pay other debts. The crisis was due to the fact that many nations, principally the United States, had failed to pay their assessed dues to the organization. In order to impose reforms, the UN implemented a no-growth budget, reduced its staff, cut back on meetings, restricted travel by staff members, and began streamlining the organization.

Each year the the U.S. debt was less than $1 billion and that UN financial crisis grows more serious. As of Dec. 31, 1996, governments owed the organization $2.2 billion. Of that amount, $1.6 billion was owed for peacekeeping and $500 million was owed to the regular UN budget. UN officials asserted that the United States alone owed $1.3 billion. U.S. officials argued that it would not pay unless the UN put through severe reforms. After his election, Annan was asked what he would do to convince the United States to pay its debt. He said that he expected to work with the Clinton administration—and, through it, the U.S. Congress—to get the nation to pay. It was not in the interest of the United States not to pay its dues, he said. Many in Congress were still hesitant about paying the UN, asserting that they wanted to see more reforms.

RUTH PEARSON, *"Business Week"*

ORGANIZATION OF THE UNITED NATIONS

THE SECRETARIAT *Secretary-General:* Kofi Annan (until Dec. 31, 2001)

THE GENERAL ASSEMBLY (1996) *President*: Razali Ismail (Malaysia)

The 185 member nations were as follows:

Afghanistan
Albania
Algeria
Andorra
Angola
Antigua and Barbuda
Argentina
Armenia
Australia
Austria
Azerbaijan
Bahamas
Bahrain
Bangladesh
Barbados
Belarus
Belgium
Belize
Benin
Bhutan
Bolivia
Bosnia and Herzegovina
Botswana
Brazil
Brunei Darussalam
Bulgaria
Burkina Faso
Burundi
Cambodia
Cameroon
Canada
Cape Verde
Central African Republic
Chad
Chile
China, People's Republic of
Colombia
Comoros
Congo
Costa Rica
Croatia
Cuba
Cyprus
Czech Republic
Denmark
Djibouti
Dominica
Dominican Republic
Ecuador
Egypt
El Salvador
Equatorial Guinea
Eritrea
Estonia
Ethiopia
Fiji
Finland
France
Gabon
Gambia
Georgia
Germany
Ghana
Greece
Grenada
Guatemala
Guinea
Guinea-Bissau
Guyana
Haiti
Honduras
Hungary
Iceland
India
Indonesia
Iran
Iraq
Ireland
Israel
Italy
Ivory Coast
Jamaica
Japan
Jordan
Kazakhstan
Kenya
Korea, Democratic People's Republic of
Korea, Republic of
Kuwait
Kyrgyzstan
Laos
Latvia
Lebanon
Lesotho
Liberia
Libya
Liechtenstein
Lithuania
Luxembourg
Madagascar
Malawi
Malaysia
Maldives
Mali
Malta
Marshall Islands
Mauritania
Mauritius
Mexico
Micronesia
Moldova
Monaco
Mongolia
Morocco
Mozambique
Myanmar
Namibia
Nepal
Netherlands
New Zealand
Nicaragua
Niger
Nigeria
Norway
Oman
Pakistan
Palau
Panama
Papua New Guinea
Paraguay
Peru
Philippines
Poland
Portugal
Qatar
Romania
Russia
Rwanda
Saint Kitts and Nevis
Saint Lucia
Saint Vincent and The Grenadines
Samoa
San Marino
São Tomé and Príncipe
Saudi Arabia
Senegal
Seychelles
Sierra Leone
Singapore
Slovak Republic
Slovenia
Solomon Islands
Somalia
South Africa
Spain
Sri Lanka
Sudan
Suriname
Swaziland
Sweden
Syria
Tajikistan
Tanzania
Thailand
The Former Yugoslav Republic of Macedonia
Togo
Trinidad and Tobago
Tunisia
Turkey
Turkmenistan
Uganda
Ukraine
United Arab Emirates
United Kingdom
United States
Uruguay
Uzbekistan
Vanuatu
Venezuela
Vietnam
Yemen
Yugoslavia
Zaire
Zambia
Zimbabwe

COMMITTEES

General. Composed of 28 members as follows: The General Assembly president; the 21 General Assembly vice-presidents (heads of delegations or their deputies of Andorra, Angola, Bahamas, Burundi, China, Cyprus, France, Ghana, Honduras, Latvia, Libya, Niger, Pakistan, Paraguay, Philippines, Russian Federation, Sudan, Turkey, United Arab Emirates, United Kingdom, and United States); and the chairmen of the main committees below, which are composed of all 185 member countries.

First (Disarmament and International Security): Alyaksandr Sychou (Belarus)

Second (Economic and Financial): Arjan Hamburger (Netherlands)

Third (Social, Humanitarian and Cultural): Patricia Espinosa (Mexico)

Fourth (Special Political and Decolonization): Alounkeo Kittikhoun (Laos)

Fifth (Administrative and Budgetary): Ngoni Francis Sengwe (Zimbabwe)

Sixth (Legal): Ramon Escovar-Salom (Venezuela)

THE ECONOMIC AND SOCIAL COUNCIL

President: Jean-Marie Kacou Gervais (Ivory Coast)
Membership ends on December 31 of the year noted.

Argentina (1998)
Australia (1997)
Bangladesh (1998)
Belarus (1997)
Brazil (1997)
Canada (1998)
Cape Verde (1999)
Central African Republic (1998)
Chile (1999)
China (1998)
Colombia (1997)
Congo (1997)
Cuba (1999)
Czech Republic (1998)
Djibouti (1999)
El Salvador (1999)
Finland (1998)
France (1999)
Gabon (1998)
Gambia (1999)
Germany (1999)
Guyana (1998)
Iceland (1999)
India (1997)
Ivory Coast (1997)
Jamaica (1997)
Japan (1999)
Jordan (1998)
Latvia (1999)
Lebanon (1998)
Luxembourg (1997)
Malaysia (1997)
Mexico (1999)
Mozambique (1999)
Netherlands (1997)
Nicaragua (1998)
Philippines (1997)
Poland (1997)
Romania (1998)
Russia (1998)
South Africa (1997)
South Korea (1999)
Spain (1999)
Sri Lanka (1999)
Sudan (1997)
Sweden (1998)
Thailand (1997)
Togo (1998)
Tunisia (1998)
Turkey (1999)
Uganda (1997)
United Kingdom (1998)
United States (1997)
Zambia (1999)

THE SECURITY COUNCIL

Membership ends on December 31 of the year noted; asterisks indicate permanent membership.

Chile (1997)
China*
Costa Rica (1998)
Egypt (1997)
France*
Guinea-Bissau (1997)
Japan (1998)
Kenya (1998)
Korea, Republic of (1997)
Poland (1997)
Portugal (1998)
Russia*
Sweden (1998)
United Kingdom*
United States*

THE TRUSTEESHIP COUNCIL

Composed of the five permanent members of the Security Council: China, France, Russia, United Kingdom, United States. The Council amended its rules of procedure in 1994 to drop the obligation to meet annually and agreed to meet as occasion required.

THE INTERNATIONAL COURT OF JUSTICE

President: Mohammed Bedjaoui (Algeria, 2006)
Vice-President: Stephen M. Schwebel (United States, 2006)
Membership ends on February 5 of the year noted.

Carl-August Fleischhauer (Germany, 2003)
Gilbert Guillaume (France, 2000)
Géza Herczegh (Hungary, 2003)
Rosalyn Higgins (United Kingdom, 2000)
Pieter H. Kooijmans (Netherlands, 2006)
Abdul G. Koroma (Sierra Leone, 2003)
Shigeru Oda (Japan, 2003)
Gonzalo Parra-Aranguren (Venezuela, 2000)
Raymond Ranjeva (Madagascar, 2000)
José Francisco Rezek (Brazil, 2006)
Shi Jiuyong (China, 2003)
Vladen S. Vereshchetin (Russia, 2006)
Christopher G. Weeramantry (Sri Lanka, 2000)

INTERGOVERNMENTAL AGENCIES

Food and Agricultural Organization (FAO); International Atomic Energy Agency (IAEA); International Bank for Reconstruction and Development (World Bank); International Civil Aviation Organization (ICAO); International Fund for Agricultural Development (IFAD); International Labor Organization (ILO); International Maritime Organization (IMO); International Monetary Fund (IMF); International Telecommunication Union (ITU); United Nations Educational, Scientific and Cultural Organization (UNESCO); United Nations Industrial Development Organization (UNIDO); Universal Postal Union (UPU); World Health Organization (WHO); World Intellectual Property Organization (WIPO); World Meteorological Organization (WMO); World Trade Organization (WTO).

United States

For the United States and its people, 1996 was the year of ambivalence. Throughout the year the attitudes of the nation's citizenry and the actions of its leaders seemed shaped by a crosscurrent of often-contradictory hopes and anxieties.

Cynicism about politics and government—a hallmark of the post-Vietnam, post-Watergate era—showed no sign of lessening. Yet Americans also were determined not to surrender the benefits that government had brought them. This attitude was epitomized by an anecdote, possibly apocryphal, but much repeated on Capitol Hill, about a constituent who—in the midst of the seemingly endless debate over the federal budget—admonished his congressman: "Don't let the government take away my Medicare."

The economic outlook was equally blurred. Statistical indicators argued that the recovery from the recession of the early 1990s continued apace. But critics charged the fruits of prosperity were distributed unevenly, with the lion's share going to wealthy individuals and giant corporations, while middle-class workers struggled against wage stagnation and were haunted by the fear of downsizing. Indeed, polls showed that roughly half or more of Americans, while recognizing some economic improvement, still felt the country was on the wrong track.

Inevitably this muddled mood carried over into the presidential-election campaign—where the reelection of President Bill Clinton seemed to represent, on one hand, an endorsement of the status quo, but on the other hand, presumably reflected support for Clinton's hazy pledge to "build a bridge to the 21st century." But whatever the limitations of the election campaign in defining the fundamental choices before the country, it clearly was an inevitable outgrowth of the anomalies that marked the year. (*See* THE 1996 U.S. ELECTION, page 24.)

In terms of foreign policy, peace in the Middle East and Bosnia, issues of trade, and the fear of terrorism were prime concerns.

Domestic Affairs

"The era of big government is over," President Clinton declared in what was the most memorable statement of his State of the Union address on January 23. No sooner had Clinton uttered this phrase than in the next breath he qualified it. "But we cannot go back to the time when our citizens were left to fend

© Cynthia Johnson/Gamma-Liaison

President Bill Clinton and First Lady Hillary Rodham Clinton were joined by Vice-President Al Gore and his wife, Tipper, as they returned to the White House following election-night celebrations. The Clinton-Gore ticket just had been reelected for four more years.

for themselves," he said. "Instead we must go forward as one America, one nation working together to meet the challenges we face together." This broad credo left the president plenty of room to maneuver, and during the course of the year, his actions often seemed to swing from one side to another on the issue of what role government should play. But much of the time he was willing to give government more leeway and more of the benefit of the doubt than his Republican opposition.

The Presidency. The first important milestone in this ideological journey came on January 6, when President Clinton signed a stopgap funding measure that authorized the federal government to resume full operations, concluding the longest shutdown in its history—a 21-day hiatus during which 280,000 federal workers had been furloughed and another 480,000 considered to be essential had worked without being paid on schedule. The shutdown was a product of the bitter battle over the federal budget in 1995, which came to symbolize the conflict between the commitment of the new Republican majorities on Capitol Hill to the goal of drastically reducing the role of government and the Democratic president's insistence on holding the line on some social programs, notably Medicare, that he regarded as essential.

While the final agreement on the 1996 fiscal-year budget, which the president signed on April 26, represented a compromise that included significant spending cuts sought by the Republicans, the president gained major concessions from the Republicans on issues such as environmental regulation. The GOP also suffered because the public held it mostly responsible for the prolonged government shutdown. "The political victory belongs to the president," the *Washington Post* declared. Few, even among the ranks of Republican leaders, disputed that verdict.

UNITED STATES • Information Highlights

Official Name: United States of America.
Location: Central North America.
Area: 3,618,768 sq mi (9 372 610 km²).
Population (mid-1996 est.): 265,200,000.
Chief Cities (July 1, 1994 est.): Washington, DC, the capital, 567,094; New York, 7,333,253; Los Angeles, 3,448,613; Chicago, 2,731,743; Houston, 1,702,086; Philadelphia, 1,524,249; San Diego, 1,151,977.
Government: *Head of state and government,* Bill Clinton, president (took office Jan. 20, 1993). *Legislature*—Congress: Senate and House of Representatives.
Monetary Unit: Dollar.
Gross Domestic Product (1994): $6,738,400,000,000 (purchasing power parity).
Economic Indexes (1995, 1990 = 100): *Consumer Prices,* all items, 116.6; food, 112.7. *Industrial Production,* 115.
Foreign Trade (1995): *Imports,* $771,272,000,000; *exports,* $584,743,000,000.

In another demonstration of his philosophical differences with the Republican Congress, Clinton on January 9 vetoed a welfare-reform measure that purportedly would have saved $58 billion in seven years and called for an end to the federal guarantee of cash assistance to the poor. Clinton contended that the legislation did not do enough to help welfare beneficiaries find work that would take them off the welfare rolls, and that it would cause severe hardships for poor children. But later in the year, the president ultimately signed welfare-reform legislation similar to the measure he vetoed in that it, too, shifted much of the responsibility for welfare from the federal government to the states through a series of block grants. But the president said compromises agreed to by the Republican Congress had removed some of his objections. And while Clinton acknowledged that the new law had "serious flaws"—notably the elimination of benefits for legal immigrants—the president claimed it was "the best chance we will have in a long, long time" to redeem his 1992 campaign promise to "end welfare as we know it." As for the defects, Clinton pledged, if reelected, to work to correct them in his second term.

In an additional act that seemed to draw a distinction between himself and the Republicans, this time on the functioning of the country's market economy, the president on May 2 vetoed legislation that would have set limits on the awarding of punitive damages in product-liability lawsuits. Supporters of the measure contended that without such restrictions, the threat of lawsuits and substantial awards to plaintiffs would discourage companies from marketing new products. But Clinton said: "The bill tilts against American families and would deprive them of the ability to recover fully when they are injured by a defective product."

On another issue with political implications, the president on June 12 condemned a recent wave of fires at predominantly black southern churches in which arson was suspected. He asked Americans to say "we are not going back, we are not slipping back to those dark days" prior to the civil-rights movement and the gains it won in battling discrimination. Some civil-rights leaders blamed the fires on racial tensions in Dixie. But Deval L. Patrick, assistant attorney general for civil rights, told a congressional committee that there was no evidence that the incidents were part of a national conspiracy. And Republican leaders, like GOP National Chairman Haley Barbour—who denounced the president's speech as "transparent, shameless politics"—claimed that the president's rhetoric was intended mainly to rally the support on election day of blacks and of white voters sympathetic to the civil-rights cause.

Meanwhile the president made several appointments to fill vacancies in his administration, naming U.S. Trade Representative Mickey Kantor to head the Department of Commerce, replacing Ron Brown, who was killed in an April plane crash while on a trade mission to Croatia. The president also picked Franklin D. Raines, who had been vice-chairman of the Federal National Mortgage Association (Fannie Mae), to replace Alice M. Rivlin as director of the Office of Management and Budget. Clinton had selected Rivlin to become vice-chairman of the Federal Reserve Board.

© Mike Theiler/Reuters/Archive Photos

Trent Lott (R-MS) (left)*—who succeeded Bob Dole as Senate majority leader in June—and House Speaker Newt Gingrich led Congress as it passed major bills late in the 1996 session.*

Scandals. Various allegations of past misconduct clouded the year for President Clinton, for First Lady Hillary Rodham Clinton, and for one of Clinton's most prominent political opponents, Republican House Speaker Newt Gingrich of Georgia. Most of the charges against the Clintons were linked to the so-called Whitewater affair, having to do with the failed investment the couple had made in a resort-land-development scheme when the president still was governor of Arkansas.

Clinton himself once described his Whitewater venture as "a simple, straightforward thing," on which he lost money. Yet evidence that emerged during his presidency suggested it was part of a tangled system of financial juggling and speculation operated by James McDougal, a Little Rock real-estate developer and the Clintons' financial partner in Whitewater. McDougal also had headed the Madison Guaranty Savings and Loan, which eventually collapsed at a cost of $50 million to taxpayers. And investigators taking note of the shifting of Madison funds among McDougal's various enterprises sought to determine whether Clinton personally or his gubernatorial campaigns had benefited from these transactions.

Although no firm evidence of wrongdoing by the Clintons had been unearthed by congressional investigations in 1995, new interest in the case was stirred when the White House on January 5 belatedly released records to congressional probers and to Kenneth Starr, the chief independent counsel investigating Whitewater, providing details on legal work Hillary Clinton had performed as a private attorney for the Madison Guaranty Savings and Loan. Republicans in Congress claimed that the records showed the first lady had done more work for the thrift institution than she had indicated previously. At any rate, at Starr's behest, on January 26 she testified before a federal grand jury investigating Whitewater, proceedings that were closed to the public. This was the first time in history that a first lady had testified under oath before a grand jury.

The president himself also was called to testify in the affair by attorneys representing James McDougal, his former wife Susan, and Arkansas Gov. Jim Guy Tucker. The defense lawyers wanted Clinton to rebut charges made by a former Arkansas municipal judge, David Hale, that Clinton had pressured him to make a fraudulent loan to Susan McDougal, allegations that Clinton had denied publicly. The president's role as a defense witness added to the embarrassment of the White House when, on May 28, the McDougals and Tucker were convicted by a federal jury on charges of fraud and conspiracy.

The White House gained a measure of relief on August 1, when two Arkansas bankers were acquitted on four of 11 felony counts in an another Whitewater-related fraud and conspiracy trial in which Clinton also provided testimony for the defense. The jury deadlocked on the other charges.

Meanwhile new allegations about issues apart from Whitewater arose to put the president and his supporters on the defensive. On June 5 the White House revealed that it improperly had obtained from the Federal Bureau of Investigation (FBI) confidential files on more than 300 persons, including a number of prominent Republicans. Republicans called this action an abuse of authority. Independent counsel Starr launched an investigation into the matter, as did committees of the House and Senate. The probers were unable to establish the White House's motive for getting the files, but on the other hand, the White House had difficulty providing a legitimate reason for its actions. Meanwhile a federal appeals court expanded Starr's jurisdiction in the case to determine whether former White House counsel Bernard W. Nussbaum had lied to a House committee about the case.

Gingrich's problems stemmed from a previously launched inquiry into charges that he improperly had received gifts and campaign contributions from GOPAC, the political-action committee he once headed. On December 21 the panel of two Republicans and two Democrats announced that it had found that Gingrich had brought discredit to the House by using tax-exempt money for political purposes and by providing the committee with "inaccurate, incomplete, and unreliable information" about the role of the political-action committee in a college course he once taught. The speaker then admitted that he had brought down on the House "a controversy which would weaken the faith people have in their government." Although Gingrich went on to win reelection as speaker in early January 1997, the full House Committee on Standards of Official Conduct still was to release its report on the case.

Terrorism. One year after the tragic bombing in Oklahoma City, two traumatic events in midsummer—the July 18 crash of a TWA airliner that claimed 230 lives and a bomb blast at the Atlanta Olympics on July 27, which killed one person and injured more than 100—jarred Americans into a renewed sense of the threat of terrorism.

Both cases proved tough to crack. Though witnesses to the plane crash into the Atlantic Ocean off Long Island, NY, said they saw two midair explosions, and officials believed that a bomb was the most likely cause, hard evidence was difficult to find. Investigators were frustrated when traces of explosives they had viewed as a clue turned out apparently to be the residue of safety tests that had been conducted on the aircraft. As for the Olympic blast, though the FBI inquiry at first focused on Richard Jewell, 33, a security guard who worked at Olympic Centennial Park, where the pipe bomb exploded, no compelling evidence was found to link him to the crime. On October 26 the Justice Department formally notified Jewell that he was no longer a suspect, noting that he had endured "highly unusual and intense publicity." That left investigators without any prime suspect.

Despite these uncertainties, President Clinton on September 9 proposed to Congress a set of antiterrorism and aviation-security measures that would cost $1.1 billion, including the installation of 54 new high-technology bomb-detection systems in U.S. airports and the creation of a profiling system that would rank plane passengers as security risks. And the FBI announced that it would reassign at least 500 of its agents to its counterterrorism force. (*See* TERRORISM.)

Congress. The second session of the 104th Congress, which started off in January gridlocked by a divisive partisan battle, concluded in October in a spate of compromise and productivity. This contrast reflected the schism between the first and second sessions of the 104th Congress. Under its new Republican leadership, the 104th came to Washington in 1995 infused with ideological zeal and driven by sweeping ambition. Speaker Gingrich rejected all talk of compromise as he pledged to overturn the results of 60 years of rarely broken Democratic hegemony on Capitol Hill.

But the impasse over the budget that started in the fall of 1995 and lasted into the new year took much of the revolutionary wind out of the GOP's legislative sails. Chastened by the negative reaction of the public, which largely accepted the Democratic contention that the GOP's goals and tactics were extremist, and concerned about their own reelection chances, the Republicans set about trying to do business with the Democratic minorities in the House and Senate and with the Democratic incumbent in the White House. As a result the Republican-controlled Congress left its largely conservative mark on broad sectors of the nation's social and economic structure, restricting New Deal–era programs to give the states more control over welfare and the free market more influence over agriculture. It also imposed new curbs on unlawful immigration, modestly expanded health-insurance coverage, and even adjusted the constitutional balance of power by arming the chief executive with the line-item veto on spending measures (*see* SIDEBAR, page 565).

In most cases these changes were not as profound as Gingrich and his cohorts initially sought, and the Republican leaders adjusted their rhetoric accordingly, discarding the revolutionary battle cries of their much heralded Contract with America in favor of more prosaic language. In a session-ending speech, Speaker Gingrich told Americans: "You asked for real change in 1994. We kept our word. We used common sense." And while

Democrats sought to minimize many of the GOP-backed accomplishments, most analysts concluded that the 104th's second-session output was likely to prove durable if only because many of these measures had received strong Democratic backing. Some of its most important accomplishments were:

• *Welfare.* The federal guarantee of cash assistance to all eligible low-income mothers and children was ended. The states were given broad authority to run their own programs, along with block grants to offset the costs. Recipients were required to work within two years of receiving benefits and generally were limited to five years on the rolls. The law left it to the states to decide whether to deny benefits to children born to welfare mothers.

• *Immigration.* Border enforcement was stiffened, deportation procedures were streamlined, and income requirements for sponsors of legal immigrants were set. A controversial provision that would have allowed states to bar children who are illegal immigrants from public schools was scrapped.

• *Health Insurance.* The portability of health insurance to workers who have lost their jobs was guaranteed and insurance companies were restricted from excluding preexisting conditions from coverage. A pilot program for individuals with high-deductible insurance plans was established to set up tax-deductible medical savings accounts to be used solely to pay for medical expenses.

• *Minimum Wage.* For the first time since 1991, the nation's hourly minimum wage was increased—from \$4.25 to \$4.75 on Oct. 1, 1996, and to \$5.15 on Sept. 1, 1997. The legislation also provided more than \$21 billion in tax relief to small businesses through the year 2006.

• *Environment.* Local governments were granted more flexibility in monitoring water quality. Federal aid to water suppliers was expanded, and the regulation of pesticides, particularly those potentially threatening to children, was tightened.

• *Farm Policy.* Depression-era policies of paying growers of certain crops when market prices fell were replaced with a payment system that generally would decline over seven years. The requirement that land be idle for farmers to receive payment was eliminated.

• *Telecommunication.* Regulatory barriers were removed and local telephone, long-distance service, and cable television were opened to new competition. Television manufacturers also were required to equip new sets with devices, called V-chips, to allow parents to block out violent programs.

• *Same-Sex Marriages.* Federal marriage benefits were denied to homosexual partners who married and states were allowed to ignore such unions even if they were sanctioned by other states.

Transition. President Clinton's reelection victory on November 5 produced a flood of resignations in the upper echelons of his administration. Besides his own chief of staff, Leon E. Panetta, cabinet departures included Secretary of State Warren M. Christopher, Defense Secretary William J. Perry, Energy Secretary Hazel R. O'Leary, Labor Secretary Robert B. Reich, and Commerce Secretary Mickey Kantor. Clinton quickly selected Erskine B. Bowles, a North Carolina businessman, who had been deputy chief of staff until leaving to go back to the private sector, to replace Panetta. But the other vacancies were not filled until December.

On December 5, President Clinton named UN Ambassador to the United Nations Madeleine A. Albright as his new secretary of state. Once confirmed by the Senate, she would be the first woman to hold the post. He

Line-Item Veto

The U.S. executive branch gained important new powers on April 9, 1996, when President Bill Clinton signed into law a bill that would authorize the functional equivalent of a line-item veto. (A true line-item veto would require a constitutional amendment.) Support from congressional Republicans allowed Clinton to gain authorities that his predecessors had sought without success.

The law, which was slated to take effect on Jan. 1, 1997, would allow the president to reject specific items in appropriations bills, new entitlement programs, and special-interest tax breaks without vetoing the entire bill. Provisions in the law would protect many items—including Medicare and other existing entitlement programs, as well as tax breaks affecting more than 100 people—from the veto pen. Congress also would have the power to reject some or all of a president's rescissions by passing a bill to overturn them. A constitutional challenge was expected after the president used the measure for the first time. Critics argued that it shifted too much authority to the president.

also announced the appointments of William S. Cohen, a Republican from Maine who had decided against seeking reelection to the U.S. Senate, as secretary of defense, and Anthony Lake as director of the Central Intelligence Agency. Samuel Berger was designated to replace Lake as head of the National Security Council. Approximately one week later, Clinton picked William M. Daley, the son of the late mayor of Chicago and the brother of the city's current mayor, as secretary of commerce; U.S. Rep. Bill Richardson (D-NM) to take over at the UN; Gene Sperling, a presidential economic adviser, as the new head of the National Economic Council; and Acting U.S. Trade Representative Charlene Barshefsky to assume the post full time.

Just prior to Christmas, the president completed the process of filling his cabinet vacancies. Alexis M. Herman, a White House staff assistant; Andrew M. Cuomo, an assistant secretary of the Department of Housing and Urban Development (HUD) and son of the former New York governor; and Secretary of Transportation Federico F. Peña would take over as secretaries of labor, HUD, and energy, respectively. Federal Highway Administrator Rodney E. Slater was selected to succeed Peña at the transportation department. The president also named Janet Yellen, a member of the Federal Reserve Board, to be chairman of the Council of Economic Advisers.

ROBERT SHOGAN
Washington Bureau, "Los Angeles Times"

© R. Ellis/Sygma

Erskine B. Bowles, a 51-year-old investment banker, was scheduled to return to the White House, succeeding Leon Panetta as chief of staff in President Clinton's second term.

The Economy

Inflation was a word in the news all year long. It was a concept that claimed believers in all walks of life, a fear, a forecast that seemed at times to be inevitable. However, inflation and its threats and dangers, including rising interest rates, never materialized in the United States in 1996.

Still, its presence, if not in prices, was real, and throughout the year the investment community and the media—and eventually the public overall—awaited the monthly economic numbers, convinced that the slightest indication of rising prices would compel the Federal Reserve to raise short-term interest rates and bring the third-longest post–World War II recovery to an end.

Publications and television and radio commentators reported economic statistics and events in a way associated more with ball games and pennant races, aware that most adult Americans had a vital interest in financial markets through pension or mutual funds, or through direct ownership of stocks and bonds.

The recovery, modest though it was, persisted. Stocks rose; mortgage rates fell; interest rates held steady, or even fell—the 30-year Treasury bond averaged 6.8% for the year; prices stabilized—the Consumer Price Index edged up only to 3% from 2.8% in 1995; unemployment dropped as low as 5.1% before rising slightly later in the year; industrial capacity and business plans remained strong; confidence measurements stayed high; and consumers continued to build credit balances. Academics and practical business economists alike were puzzled. Alan Greenspan, the Federal Reserve chairman, expressed his wonderment in December, remarking that perhaps Americans were "irrationally exuberant" about their investments, whose fortunes depended on the economy's strength, which lay on a foundation weakened by debt.

In spite of the excitement, Greenspan and other professionals were aware that the economic growth rate hardly had reached runaway speed. DRI/McGraw-Hill economists termed it "the tortoise economy," pointing out that growth was only half that at the equivalent stages of the country's two longest economic expansions in the 1960s and 1980s. Growth in the first 22 quarters of recovery measured 25.3% in the 1960s and 36.7% in the 1980s. In the 1990s, it was 14.6%. Nevertheless, they and others concluded that in view of various factors—slow labor-force growth, lagging productivity increases, and budget deficits—the economy was doing as well as it could. Many disagreed; former Treasury economists Gary and Aldona Robbins of the Institute for Policy Innovation, a Dallas-based think tank, referred to the "dumbing down of economic growth." A growth rate unacceptable in the 1960s, they declared, was being praised as exceptional in the 1990s.

The Consumer. The enigmas were most obvious in the consumer area. The University of Michigan and the American Society for Quality Control reported a two-year decline in how pleased people were with goods and services. In a study for the conservative Heritage Foundation, Mark Wilson, a former Labor Department economist, argued that while income finally was rising again, it still had not reached the 1989 record of $42,049. Studies for the Competitive Policy Council found that the number of two-income households was at the highest level ever, but that families overall were not doing much better. Fordham University researchers reported that their index of social well-being fell to its lowest in nearly 25 years. And time after time, reminders came from government and academic sources that despite a shrinkage in the number of people in poverty, the gap between rich and poor had widened. Still, measurements of consumer confidence remained high.

Where was all the money coming from? Economists pointed out that while disposable personal income in November rose almost 3% over 1995 levels, spending exceeded income; the personal savings rate dragged at about 4%—half the level of two decades before. Rather than relying on income to explain consumer confidence, analysts called attention to the confidence-building "wealth effect," since $2 trillion had been added to stock prices in less than four months through November. Henry Kaufman, the interest-rate guru of the 1980s, observed that the public's financial net worth had risen by $5.5 trillion since March 1991.

Such additions to assets, though considered unstable by many critics, made borrowing much more possible, and Americans took full advantage of the situation. Home-mortgage borrowing rose $230 billion in one year, and the home-to-value ratio reached 64%. Credit cards proliferated, and so did the sums borrowed on them. The total of consumer-installment debt, including car leases and home-equity loans, approached an unprecedented 30% of disposable income. Credit-card delinquencies rose to more than 3.5%; mortgage delinquencies were well over 4%; and personal bankruptcies headed toward a new record of more than 1 million for the year. Americans had assets aplenty, but they were illiquid, and spenders needed to borrow against those assets. As the year wore on, more and more people reached mandatory or self-imposed limits, and the pace of credit extensions slowed.

Government Concerns and Indicators. While popular interest centered on consumer affairs, more basic issues occupied government officials and long-term economic thinkers: budget deficits, the imbalance of trade payments, business investment and the level of profits, lagging productivity growth, the need to finance increasingly costly Social Security and Medicare programs, and the transition to an economy in which defense played a less conspicuous role. The news was mostly good, but some of it aroused concern.

Perhaps the best news of all from a congressional viewpoint was the decline in the budget deficit—an issue that had captured the attention and support of both liberals and conservatives. Every politician, it seemed, was for paring government spending. It was one of the rare areas of agreement.

Hopes were realized. The deficit for the 1996 budget year declined to $107.3 billion, 35% lower than in 1995 and 63% below the all-time high of $290 billion in 1992. While President Bill Clinton sought credit for the decline—"the first time a president has reduced the deficit in all four years of a term in the 20th century"—critics were loathe to give it to him. "This low deficit has been achieved by the last two presidents and the last three Congresses," said Robert Reischauer, former head of the Congressional Budget Office (CBO). Worries persisted; the CBO projected a deficit of $212 billion in 2002, the year the president vowed to achieve a balanced budget. Particularly worrisome was a $4.2 billion decline in the Medicare trust fund that pays hospital bills; without changes, the trustees warned, the program would be bankrupt by 2001. Social Security officials sounded equally ominous; unless changes were made, they said, the aging baby boomers, born after World War II, would deplete the fund two or three decades later. Among suggestions to solve long-term problems, a federal advisory panel considered investing some Social Security funds in securities, but it remained split at year's end on how to do it.

A more basic response to these and other funding problems, some said, was a resumption of economic growth to the 3%-plus levels that had prevailed through much of the postwar period. Countering that argument was the fear, shared by the Federal Reserve, that growth of that sort under existing conditions was impossible without inviting inflation.

One of the largest drags on the economy was a deficit of another sort. Americans continued to import more goods and services than they exported—at an annual rate of $114 billion late in the year. Higher oil prices were a major contributor to the imbalance, but an equally troubling factor was emerging in U.S.-China trade. The imbalance with that nation in September alone rose to $4.7 billion, exceeding even the trade deficit with Japan. The administration pressured the Chinese to lift what it said were barriers to U.S. goods, but these efforts generally were frustrated. As the year ended, the trend line indicated China soon might replace Japan as the most difficult trade partner. Meanwhile, the large size of deficits forced economists to lower estimates of U.S. gross domestic product (GDP).

Though still sluggish, growth speeded up as spring neared, beginning yearlong speculation about whether or not the Federal Reserve would raise interest rates. Those worries reached a crescendo when the Commerce Department reported a second-quarter growth rate of 4.7%, and they persisted even as the economy slowly cooled through the rest of the year. Estimates indicated growth for the year of 2.4%, producing a total domestic product of $7.57 trillion in current dollars. Measured in constant (1992) dollars, the GDP rose to $6.9 trillion from $6.74 trillion in 1995.

Changes in Styles. The breakdown revealed some remarkable changes in lifestyles. Light-vehicle sales totaled slightly more than 15 million units for the year, compared with 14.8 million in 1995. But it was the composition of sales that told of change. Car sales dropped from the year before, while light trucks became increasingly popular. In November, for the first time ever, the sales rate for light trucks—6.9 million annualized— exceeded that for cars—6.8 million. Equally notable was an astounding 39% rise in sales of computing and office equipment as companies spent heavily to link computers, thus integrating the information flow between divisions and employees. The Conference Board said the percentage of families with home computers had climbed to 40%, compared with 22% six years earlier.

Such evidence and more described continuing rapid changes in business and personal styles. One of the biggest "changes" was, in fact, not one at all, but merely a new perspective of old events that inevitably would alter Americans' view of their economy. A panel headed by former White House economic adviser Michael Boskin of Stanford University concluded in December that the Consumer Price Index overstated inflation by 1.1 percentage points a year. A more accurate index, panel members stated, would produce $691 billion in deficit savings over a decade.

The potential consequences of such a change would be huge and pervasive, embracing almost all aspects of macroeconomics and microeconomics. The savings would come from the trimming effects of lower inflation readings on Social Security and other government pensions received by 60 million Americans, and by rising tax payments. The latter would be achieved by altering the adjustments that kept taxpayers from being ratcheted into higher tax brackets. Since many labor-union contracts included cost-of-living clauses, non-government workers also would be affected. In dollars, the immediate loss to Social Security recipients would be $96 a year in the first year. By one estimate, a family of four using the standard deduction with $60,000 in taxable income would pay $150 more in taxes in the first year.

The political impact, especially from the retiree segment, would be greater. In fact, some economists long had advocated a review of other economic statistics, contending that the compound effect of annual small errors distorted understanding of the economic condition. To correct these errors, they said, would be to explain the puzzling contradictions of the 1996 economy.

JOHN CUNNIFF
Business News Analyst, The Associated Press

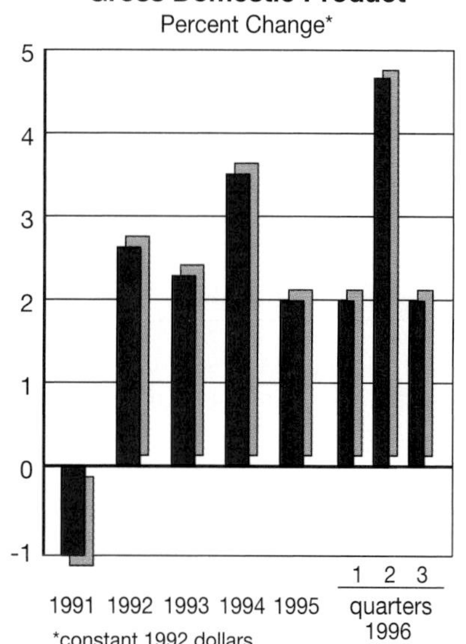

© W. McNamee/Sygma

On Dec. 5, 1996, President Bill Clinton announced the new national-security team for his second term—(left to right) *Anthony Lake, director of the Central Intelligence Agency; Madeleine Albright, secretary of state; Vice-President Al Gore; William Cohen, secretary of defense; and Samuel Berger, head of the National Security Council. Rep. Bill Richardson later was named ambassador to the UN.*

Foreign Affairs

Barring some intense crisis, U.S. foreign policy seldom dominates public debate during election years. In 1996 the few foreign issues that found their way into the presidential campaign tended to follow the formula of concern about trade, dictators such as Saddam Hussein, the fragility of peace agreements in Bosnia and the Middle East, and military preparedness.

Republican challenger Robert Dole lamented that the presidential debates lacked sufficient focus on foreign policy and accused the Bill Clinton administration of not having one. On a campaign swing to Detroit, President Clinton touted his plan for the eastward expansion of the North Atlantic Treaty Organization (NATO) by the end of the century, while Dole accused him of dragging his feet. And the Dole camp accused the White House of accepting dubious financial contributions from Indonesian and other Asian interest groups. The president, claiming that Dole also had accepted foreign money, advocated a ban on such contributions.

Meanwhile, policy toward such major powers as Russia, China, and Japan—along with such global challenges as population, social, and environmental policy—largely were ignored in the campaign. The United Nations (UN)—and particularly Secretary-General Boutros Boutros-Ghali—came in for criticism from both parties, but especially from the Republicans, who implied that U.S. sovereignty had been sacrificed to the world organization. That charge was rejected hotly by the president. Indeed, Clinton, reversing his advocacy of multilateral diplomacy, showed a tendency to act alone in foreign policy, and vetoed Boutros-Ghali's reelection when it came before the Security Council.

Much of the discussion during the year concerned foreign-policy matters with domestic implications. This was particularly apparent with the issues of immigration, drug enforcement, and terrorism. Immigration was tied to the domestic budgetary debate; most categories of legal immigrants were excluded from welfare benefits, and border enforcement and deportation of criminal aliens were boosted, but denial of schooling to children of illegal aliens was averted.

One of the most contentious issues was the effort to enforce the economic embargo on Cuba, a policy with obvious relevance to Florida politics. Reacting to Havana's downing of two Cuban expatriate aircraft, the administration spoke of implementing the Helms-Burton Act, allowing suits against foreign companies doing business with Cuba. Similar action was promised against Iran and Libya. Several U.S. allies, including Canada and the European Union (EU), challenged the legality of this and vowed to bring a case before the World Trade Organization (WTO). Citing progress in allied talks, the president delayed implementation of Helms-Burton.

While Congress resisted administration proposals for domestic terrorism legislation, Attorney General Janet Reno attended the Ministerial Meeting on Terrorism in Paris in July, which set standards for bomb detection and laid plans for an international treaty to outlaw terrorist bombing. The administration also pushed for antidrug agreements on training and extradition, and crop eradication and substitution in Latin America. It also denied an entry visa to Colombia's President Ernesto Samper.

Arms Control. Some of the year's major achievements were in the area of arms control. A comprehensive nuclear-test-ban agreement was reached, after negotiations had been moved to the UN General Assembly to circumvent India's opposition to such a ban. India insisted that the major powers set a timetable for eliminating their own nuclear arsenals, and Washington was unable to devise a compromise satisfactory to New Delhi to assure that the treaty would come into force legally. Congress also was slow to ratify the Chemical Weapons and Nuclear Safety Conventions, and in July the Senate killed a resolution to establish a code of conduct for arms exports. Earlier, the White House decided to waive its own ban on delivery of $368 million of military hardware to Pakistan.

The administration also ran into domestic opposition to a plan to store spent weapons-grade nuclear-fuel rods from foreign reactors in Idaho. Nevertheless, in August the Senate voted to restore full funding of the Korean Peninsula Energy Development Organization (KEDO), an agreement whereby the United States, Japan, and South Korea propose to avert nuclear developments in North Korea. In May, North Korea had agreed to joint searches for remains of Americans killed in the Korean War, and in December it apologized for sending commandos to South Korea.

Republican opposition and uncertainties of Senate ratification also held up several other treaties, including the 1995 nuclear-nonproliferation-agreement renewal, the Law of the Sea agreement, and the treaty on children's rights. President Clinton announced his backing of a global treaty that would ban most forms of land mines, but Washington did not impose a unilateral moratorium on the mines' production or use.

Relations with Major Powers. Relations with Russia, bolstered by a Clinton visit to Moscow in April, hinged on the summer presidential elections there. President Boris Yeltsin was returned to office, but his severe health problems during the summer and fall spelled uncertainty for U.S. policy planners. Washington's assurances to Russian nationalists about the nonthreatening nature of NATO's expansion seemed only partly successful, even as diplomats began to discuss updating the 1990 Conventional Armed Forces in Europe Treaty.

U.S.-Chinese problems appeared to ease somewhat in 1996, as the two sides struggled toward agreements to end piracy of copyrights and to devise joint approaches to protecting the environment. In early December, just weeks after China sentenced a former pro-democracy student leader to 11 years in prison, Chinese Defense Minister Gen. Chi Haotian led a military delegation to Washington, DC, for two weeks of talks with President Clinton and Defense Secretary William J. Perry. Among the topics discussed were human-rights issues, Beijing's supplying of nuclear-capable military equipment to Pakistan and Iran, and tensions on the Korean Peninsula. Taiwan and Hong Kong also were part of the agenda, with China agreeing that U.S. warships could continue to visit Hong Kong after the Chinese takeover in July 1997. Earlier, Clinton and Chinese President Jiang Zemin agreed to an exchange of visits in 1997 and 1998.

Rather than stressing economic concerns, U.S.-Japanese negotiations throughout the year—including a springtime Clinton–Ryutaro Hashimoto Tokyo summit—revolved around the question of basing arrangements for U.S. forces on Okinawa and elsewhere, in light of popular opposition to the troops. The Liberal Democratic Party's (LDP) reelection, together with a yearlong plunge in the value of the yen, promised recurrent trade disputes but a basically continued security cooperation between the two countries.

Regional Concerns. President Clinton attended the Asia-Pacific Economic Cooperation (APEC) summit in November, concluding a year of regional-security and economic consultations. In July, Secretary of State Warren Christopher's discussions at the Association of Southeast Asian Nations (ASEAN) Regional Forum in Jakarta, Indonesia, included U.S. concerns about human rights in Myanmar (Burma); administration critics, however, accused Washington of being too soft on Indonesia's human-rights situation in East Timor. The United States also pushed for trade liberalization, especially in financial services and telecommunications, at December's first ministerial meeting of the WTO.

An election victory for Israel's Likud coalition in May spelled severe difficulties for the Palestinian peace process. Following renewed violence and delayed Israeli withdrawal from the West Bank town of Hebron, Israeli Prime Minister Benjamin Netanyahu and Palestinian leader Yasir Arafat visited Washington for urgent talks with President Clinton. A pledge of at least resumption of bilateral negotiations resulted. Worsening Israeli relations with its Syrian, Jordanian, and Egyptian neighbors also caused U.S. concern. A U.S.-mediated agreement on Hebron seemed near as the year ended.

Elsewhere in the Middle East, President Clinton seized the occasion of Baghdad's late-summer troop movements into northern Iraq (to aid one Kurdish faction against another) to renew cruise-missile bombing of Iraq's military facilities and to extend the "no fly" zone in the south. Some viewed this as an election move, but the administration's prior failure to broker a cease-fire between the two Kurdish factions opened the door for Saddam Hussein's renewed influence. Late in the year the Kurds tentatively agreed to the renewed cease-fire.

With the bombing of U.S. military barracks in Dhahran, Saudi Arabia, in June, terrorism continued as a major administration concern. By November the Saudis claimed to have apprehended one of the bombers, with connections to both Iran and Syria, but the United States did not confirm these findings immediately. Despite considerable speculation, no apparent foreign connections emerged from the crash of TWA flight 800 off the coast of New York or from a bomb explosion at the Summer Olympic Games in Atlanta.

Tensions involving U.S. allies and interests mounted elsewhere in the Mediterranean and North Africa. Summer clashes on Cyprus raised awareness—even as Clinton hosted the Cypriot president and spoke of a peace initiative—that the status of the divided island remained unresolved. Turkey's new government encountered tensions and embarrassment in its overtures to Islamic states, particularly Libya. In the spring, Defense Secretary Perry warned Libya against completion of an underground chemical-weapons plant. U.S. proposals for a UN arms and commercial-flight embargo on Sudan fell short, though milder sanctions were imposed, seeking the extradition of terrorists accused of plotting against Egypt's President Hosni Mubarak.

Africa drew significant administration attention in 1996. U.S. forces had to rescue Americans caught in Liberia's civil war in April. In early fall, Secretary of State Christopher visited the continent for extended discussion, and proposed to help establish and equip a 10,000-member multinational continental peacekeeping force to intervene and quell crises such as those looming in Burundi, Rwanda, and Zaire. He met questioning and opposition from African leaders such as South Africa's Nelson Mandela and from the French, who resented Washington's intrusion in what has been a French sphere of influence.

The acute refugee crisis in Zaire and Rwanda garnered the headlines in November, and Washington hurriedly consulted with its allies in trying to devise a humanitarian-relief operation, finally agreeing in principle to send troops to join a Canadian-led force. Concern eased somewhat with a massive return of Hutu to Rwanda, but uncertainties remained about the necessity for military commitments and about the splintering of Zaire, which was under attack by various opponents, including Tutsi rebels with ties to Rwanda.

The Dayton Accords for Bosnia held tenuously, but remained frayed. National elections were flawed, but returned a three-way combination of ethnic leaders to power in what was supposed to be a joint presidency. Progress on training and equipping the Bosnian army was delayed by U.S. insistence that a government official with arms connections to Iran be dismissed; evidence mounted that heavy arms got through to Bosnia through Croatia, and alarming new fighting erupted between Serb and Bosnian forces in November, along with civilian attacks on U.S. soldiers. Despite technical commitment to a March 1997 date for removal of U.S. forces, the Clinton administration announced that the mission would be extended.

Policy Challenges. During the year, meetings on global issues of the environment and human and economic development resulted mainly in the maintenance of existing policies. The administration supported binding but rather liberal targets for the reduction of greenhouse gases. Trade pressures were brought to bear on Guatemala and Pakistan for commitments to enforce labor standards for children and adults. The United States and Japan deferred offers of additional food aid to famine-ridden North Korea, while agreement was reached with Vietnam on the orderly processing of refugees seeking U.S. asylum.

It was a difficult year for both the Pentagon and the Central Intelligence Agency (CIA). Accusations of a cover-up of possible nerve-gas effects on U.S. service personnel in the 1991 Persian Gulf war gained substance. Press reports that the CIA was involved heavily during the 1980s with leaders of the Central American drug trade, which funneled crack cocaine to U.S. cities, were denied strongly. In November the agency conflicted with the Federal Bureau of Investigation (FBI) over the arrest of a former Soviet agent, and an agency training official was charged with passing information to Russia.

FREDERIC S. PEARSON
Wayne State University

URUGUAY

During 1996 officials in Uruguay made efforts to change the political process, improve competitiveness, and lower inflation. Regional integration with other South American nations also gained momentum.

Government and Politics. An electorate opposed to market reforms gave a 23% approval rating to a reformist coalition of President Julio Sanguinetti—the leader of the centrist Colorado Party—and his rightist National (Blanco) Party predecessor, Luis Alberto Lacalle, in May. Although the two parties had commanded more than 60% of the popular vote in 1994, efforts in Congress at reducing the public sector and assuring the continued dominance of their declining parties—erstwhile bitter rivals—were rejected by the leftist Broad Front, which was hoping to win national elections in 1999. The left-wing coalition, already dominant in Montevideo, was confronted with an internal crisis in February when its founding leader, former Gen. Liber Seregni Mosquera, 79, stepped down after 25 years, apparently exhausted by factional bickering. An advocate of a multiparty system, Seregni was accused by dissidents of presidential aspirations in the 1999 contest. The charismatic Tabaré Vásquez, the former mayor of Montevideo, was campaigning openly for the Broad Front endorsement.

The armed forces responded to three books released in September treating military rule and its excesses between 1973 and 1985. Far from apologizing for their abuses, those in uniform justified them, indicating that they would act again if minorities attempted to "undermine democracy."

Economy. Economic recovery remained elusive. Gross domestic product (GDP) was expected to grow very slightly in 1996, following a decline of 2.5% the previous year. At $277 million in May, the foreign-trade deficit was $43 million higher than a year earlier. With the foreign debt at a record $4.8 billion, or 30% of GDP, borrowing continued; $284 million was obtained from the Inter-American Development Bank (IDB) for an ongoing reform of the social-security system. The IDB also approved a $153 million loan in September for sewerage and drainage projects in Montevideo and other urban areas. Unemployment remained above 12%, in part because of continuing staff reductions by the government. Up to 8,000 public employees were expected to leave in 1996, amounting to a savings of $43 million.

Some positive signs emerged, however. Inflation dropped below an annualized rate of 25% in June. Russia's largest auto manufacturer, Avtovaz, planned future production of its Lada model in Uruguay for export to members of Mercosur, the Southern Cone common market. New projects were announced, including a $102 million dredging project in the Río de la Plata. Two major contracts for bridges connecting Uruguay and Argentina were signed in May. The first was a 27-mi (43-km) bridge across the Río de la Plata at a cost approaching $1 billion. Another would cross the Uruguay River at Salto. Construction began in November on a pipeline to supply natural gas to Argentina and Uruguay.

Foreign Affairs. The process of regional integration gained momentum when President Sanguinetti traveled to Madrid on behalf of Mercosur. On Dec. 14, 1995, he was one of many officials to sign a cooperation agreement with the European Union (EU). Under the pact's terms, free trade between the two trading blocs would begin in 2001. Exports by Mercosur members to the EU in 1994 had amounted to nearly $24 billion. Following two years of negotiations, the gradual entry of Chile into Mercosur was approved by Sanguinetti and heads of state from remaining Mercosur partners on June 25. During an official visit to Chile in August, Uruguay's chief executive underscored access to Pacific ports and Asian markets gained by Mercosur through Chile's adhesion to the heretofore Atlantic-oriented pact.

LARRY L. PIPPIN, *University of the Pacific*

URUGUAY • Information Highlights

Official Name: Oriental Republic of Uruguay.
Location: Southeastern coast of South America.
Area: 68,039 sq mi (176 220 km²).
Population (mid-1996 est.): 3,200,000.
Chief City (1985 census): Montevideo, the capital, 1,251,647.
Government: *Head of state and government,* Julio Maria Sanguinetti, president (took office March 1995). *Legislature*—General Assembly: Chamber of Senators and Chamber of Representatives.
Monetary Unit: New peso (8.70 new pesos equal U.S.$1, financial rate, Dec. 31, 1996).
Gross Domestic Product (1994 est. U.S.$): $23,000,000,000 (purchasing power parity).
Economic Index (Montevideo, 1995; 1990 = 100): *Consumer Prices,* all items, 1,079.5; food, 893.9.
Foreign Trade (1995 U.S.$): *Imports,* $2,867,000,000; *exports,* $2,117,000,000.

VENEZUELA

The continuing drama of economic crisis and recovery dominated events in Venezuela during 1996. Mounting domestic and international pressure persuaded President Rafael

Caldera Rodríguez to back the kind of economic shock program that he long had opposed. By October the reform program was producing positive results.

The previous year ended with rebuffs to the president's party, National Convergence, and his coalition partner, the Movement Toward Socialism (MAS), whose candidates won few gubernatorial elections in December. Negotiations with the International Monetary Fund (IMF) continued without result during the first quarter as the government postponed decisive action to correct the huge budget deficit or halt rapidly accelerating inflation. Business leaders and organized labor complained loudly about the incoherence of the government's economic program. Unions representing 700,000 public employees protested a large bonus decreed by the president because it was only temporary and applied only to workers in the private sector. In March, 180,000 teachers walked out of their classrooms, shutting down public schools for more than six weeks. During that time, Finance Minister Luis Raúl Matos Azócar survived a censure motion introduced by the opposition, but support for his economic plan was evaporating. The MAS even threatened to withdraw from the governing coalition unless one of its leaders was named to a responsible cabinet post. Underscoring its waning loyalty to Caldera, the MAS also formed a legislative alliance with the Social Christian Party (COPEI) and the radical Causa R Party—the two sponsors of the censure motion—to pass judicial and electoral reforms that the president opposed.

In late March, Caldera appointed Teodoro Petkoff, a prominent MAS leader, as minister of coordination and planning, and gave him authority to design a new economic program. In a complete turnabout from his past as a communist guerrilla leader, Petkoff proposed an orthodox shock program that was endorsed speedily by the IMF. On April 15, Caldera announced that price and exchange controls would be dismantled, gasoline prices would increase nearly sixfold, the sales tax would increase from 12.5% to 16.5%, and interest rates would be allowed to float. To cushion the shock, he simultaneously increased transportation subsidies and selective food, housing, and family subsidies, and granted public employees (excepting himself and his ministers) a 70% raise. Isolated student protests greeted the announcement, but there were no disturbances on the scale of the rioting in response to the shock program of February 1989.

As Petkoff warned, the economy got worse before it got better. Inflation soared for months after the announcement, peaking at an annualized rate of 115.2% in September. Inflation began declining in the following months, although it remained at the highest rate in Latin America. By late October foreign investors considered Venezuela one of the most attractive investment opportunities in Latin America.

Much of the new investment was attracted by the government's decision, announced in January, to grant contracts to foreign oil-exploration companies for the first time in 20 years. Thirteen companies based in the United States, Japan, Great Britain, France, Germany, and Argentina won contracts that were expected to expand Venezuela's oil reserves by 10% and double its oil production by 2005. Most Venezuelan leaders agreed on the wisdom of opening up the petroleum sector to foreign investment.

Amnesty International and Americas Watch issued reports strongly criticizing the lack of due process, extrajudicial killings by police, judicial corruption and inefficiency, and prison overcrowding in Venezuela. The issue gained further attention in October, when national guardsmen were accused of burning some 25 prisoners alive in a crowded cell because of unpaid drug debts.

Another concern was the future of former President Carlos Andrés Pérez, who had been impeached in 1993. In May the Supreme Court found him guilty of misuse of funds and sentenced him to 28 months in prison. Because Pérez already had served a long house arrest, he was able to complete his sentence in September and to begin campaigning for election to the Senate.

MICHAEL COPPEDGE
University of Notre Dame

VENEZUELA • Information Highlights

Official Name: Republic of Venezuela.
Location: Northern coast of South America.
Area: 352,143 sq mi (912 050 km²).
Population (mid-1996 est.): 22,300,000.
Chief Cities (June 30, 1990 est.): Caracas, the capital (incl. suburbs), 3,435,795; Maracaibo, 1,400,643; Valencia, 1,274,354.
Government: *Head of state and government,* Rafael Caldera Rodríguez, president (inaugurated Feb. 2, 1994). *Legislature*—Congress of the Republic: Senate and Chamber of Deputies.
Monetary Unit: Bolívar (475.0075 bolívares equal U.S.$1, official rate, Dec. 31, 1996).
Gross Domestic Product (1994 est. U.S.$): $178,300,000,000 (purchasing power parity).
Economic Index (Caracas, 1995; 1990 = 100): *Consumer Prices,* all items, 609.4; food, 585.3.
Foreign Trade (1995 U.S.$): *Imports,* $12,273,000,000; *exports,* $22,714,000,000

VIETNAM

After a decade of rapid economic change and some loosening of political controls, Vietnam's Communist leaders slowed the pace of reform in 1996.

Politics. Do Muoi, the 79-year-old secretary-general, was reappointed by the Eighth Party Congress, which met in Hanoi from June 28 to July 1. The charismatic former housepainter met with reporters during the congress and told them he wanted to see reform continue, but then he told the congress members, "If you run too fast...you fall over."

The congress also reappointed President Le Duc Anh (age 75) and Prime Minister Vo Van Kiet (73)—probably because the congress could not resolve disputes over who should succeed them—but Le Duc Anh became seriously ill at the end of the year and was not expected to survive. If one member of the leadership trio was replaced, the others were likely to be as well, because they represented a delicate balance between the Communist Party's central bureaucracies (Do Muoi), the military (Le Duc Anh), and the reformers (Vo Van Kiet).

The party congress injected some new blood into the leadership by enlarging the Politburo and the Central Committee. Almost half of the members of each body were new. The Central Committee was also younger and better educated than in the past. Truong Tan Sang (47), the new party secretary for Ho Chi Minh City, and Le Xuan Tung (60), the new secretary for Hanoi, were both aides of the founder of the reform movement in the 1980s. They seemed to have embraced reforms aimed at improving economic growth in the nation's cities.

The congress created a Standing Committee of the Politburo, consisting of the three top leaders plus Gen. Le Kha Phieu and Nguyen Tan Dung, the lowest-ranking Politburo member. In an unusual display of dissent, many delegates applauded when one spoke out against giving the Standing Committee the power to make policy.

Despite a slight relaxation of controls on the media and religious groups, several party members, including Nguyen Xuan Tu, were arrested prior to the congress for advocating democratic reform. In one of Tu's recent essays, entitled "Farewell to Ideology," he argued that Marxism-Leninism no longer served any purpose and was damaging the country's economic prospects. He also offended the Communist Party by calling for political reform in a radio broadcast to Vietnamese living in California.

The party waged a vigorous campaign against such social evils as crime, pornography, and prostitution, which it linked to "foreign" influences. Analysts have noted that the country also suffered from growing corruption on the part of low-paid party cadres. Adam Schwarz, the U.S. correspondent for the *Far Eastern Economic Review*, wrote an article on the difficulty of doing business in Vietnam without paying off officials, and in October the government refused to extend his visa.

Economy. Vietnam's economy continued to expand briskly in 1996, with gross domestic product (GDP) growing by 8%–9%, as it had for the previous three years. But one very worrying indicator was the record-high deficit in the current account, which measures trade in goods and services. The annual shortfall was nearly $3.5 billion by October. Nevertheless, aid donors meeting in Vietnam in December pledged $2.4 billion in new aid, the largest amount ever, while emphasizing the need to continue to reform the economy.

The budget deficit was only about 1.5% of GDP, and the inflation rate was about half the previous year's rate of 13.5%. Rice prices also declined, while rice production and rice exports rose compared to 1995. Per-capita annual income reached the level of $300, although this still left Vietnam one of the world's poorest countries.

Foreign Affairs. Vietnam and China continued to claim the oil-rich Spratly Islands, and in April they leased overlapping sites in the Spratlys to foreign firms to prospect for oil. In search of allies in this dispute, Vietnam in 1995 joined the Association of Southeast Asian Nations (ASEAN). Two other members of ASEAN—the Philippines and Malaysia—also have interests in the Spratlys. Vietnam endorsed an Indonesian proposal for

VIETNAM • Information Highlights

Official Name: Socialist Republic of Vietnam.
Location: Southeast Asia.
Area: 127,243 sq mi (329 560 km²).
Population (mid-1996 est.): 76,600,000.
Chief Cities (April 1, 1989 census): Hanoi, the capital, 3,056,146; Ho Chi Minh City, 3,924,435; Haiphong, 1,447,523.
Government: *Head of state,* Le Duc Anh, president (took office Sept. 23, 1992. *Head of government,* Vo Van Kiet, prime minister (took office Aug. 9, 1991). *Legislature*—National Assembly.
Monetary Unit: New dong (11,000 new dongs equal U.S.$1, October 1994).
Gross Domestic Product (1994 est. U.S.$): $83,500,000,000 (purchasing power parity).
Foreign Trade (1994 U.S.$): *Imports,* $5,000,000,000; *exports,* $3,600,000,000

multilateral development of the Spratlys in order to block China from seizing the island chain.

After removing the main barriers to normal diplomatic and commercial relations in 1995, the United States and Vietnam were slow to complete the process of normalization in 1996, perhaps partly because it was a U.S. election year. The appointment of U.S. Rep. Douglas (Pete) Peterson as ambassador to Vietnam was delayed while lawyers debated whether he was barred constitutionally from holding a position he helped create, but his approval was considered likely in 1997. Peterson had been a prisoner in Vietnam for six and one half years.

Lacking a formal trade agreement with Vietnam, the United States delayed granting it "most favored nation" trade status, and U.S. investors were unable to obtain Export-Import Bank credits, which put them at a competitive disadvantage. But the U.S. Congress approved compensation for 281 Vietnamese former agents of the U.S. military and intelligence services. And reportedly the United States and Vietnam were not far from an agreement on how to deal with the last of the "boat people" who fled Vietnam after 1975 and still wanted to go to the United States.

PETER A. POOLE
Author, "Eight Presidents and Indochina"

WASHINGTON, DC

The District of Columbia continued to struggle over its financial problems in 1996 as a financial control board worked to bring the U.S. capital out of debt.

The five-member independent control board was created by Congress in 1995 in response to the district's dire financial situation. It worked to cut spending by the district's government agencies and shrink the payroll in an effort to cut the city's $54 million deficit. The district must balance its budget for four years in a row before the board relinquishes control. While the board struggled to halt the city's decline, some politicians believed more-drastic action was necessary. "The District of Columbia government is a mess," was how House Speaker Newt Gingrich (R-GA) summed up the situation.

Persistent Problems. The U.S. capital continued to have enormous problems. The independent board issued a scathing report in November giving the city's public-school system "an absolute F." It alleged the city's school board and its superintendent wasted hundreds of millions of taxpayer dollars and cheated schoolchildren out of a proper education. The report blamed Superintendent Franklin Smith and other administrators for spending heavily on their own office operations while there were textbook shortages in the schools. The system continued to be plagued by declining student test scores, a high dropout rate, and crumbling buildings. In November the board fired Smith, hired a replacement, and set up an advisory panel to oversee the failing system.

Meanwhile other problems plagued the district. Unemployment rose to 8.7% and the city lost more than 14,000 jobs in 1996. The district's federal workforce shrank by nearly 10,000 jobs. City services remained in dire need of a cash infusion. The city morgue required $800,000 in repairs. On any given day, 30% of Washington's police vehicles were in the shop for repairs; on occasion police officers had to dig into their own pockets to fix the vehicles. The city was plagued by elevated levels of bacteria in its water supply.

Possible Solutions. Speaker Gingrich and other lawmakers, including Congressional Delegate Eleanor Holmes Norton, proposed cutting taxes for every resident in the district as a way of stimulating the economy. The cuts would put a 15% ceiling on federal taxes paid by each city resident in a move to keep the middle class in the city while the federal government deals with the financial crisis.

Several other tax-cut plans were proposed, including a commuter tax on suburban residents who work in the district. Another plan involved increasing the federal government's annual payment to the city to replace the taxes the district does not receive on more than a quarter of city land that is federal property and, thus, tax-exempt. Mayor Marion S. Barry, Jr., reelected to a fourth term of office in 1994 after serving six months in prison on a misdemeanor drug charge, introduced a plan to streamline the city's government. A White House task force was set up to help city agencies improve services.

Washington also was plagued by a low credit rating; its bonds were rated as "junk," and it could not borrow long-term funds in the credit markets. But in one sign of improvement, Wall Street offered to help the city raise $220 million in short-term notes—the first time in nearly two years that investors had been willing to lend money to the city.

In its first annual report, the control board said it had made substantial progress cutting 7,500 jobs from the city's payroll and shrinking the size of the deficit. It put in place an inspector general to investigate illegal or questionable activities and to make sure money was being spent properly.

Crime. In a sign of the capital's persistent crime problem, Supreme Court Justice Ruth Bader Ginsburg's purse was snatched as she walked from the Kennedy Center to her home at the Watergate apartment complex.

JUDI HASSON, *"USA Today"*

WOMEN

By a huge margin, women backed U.S. President Bill Clinton in his bid for reelection in November 1996. Clinton benefited from the largest gender gap in the nation's political history. Polls showed women preferred Clinton over rival GOP candidate Robert Dole by a 17% margin. Although several women resigned from the Clinton administration following the election, the president named perhaps an equal number of women to serve in various posts in his second term. If confirmed, Madeleine Albright would be the first woman secretary of state.

Elections. Clinton set out to win the women's vote by tailoring his message to them. He signed a law requiring insurance companies to pay for longer hospital maternity stays and provided more funds for breast-cancer research—both issues that primarily affect women. He campaigned on a record that included support of the V-chip, which screens out objectionable television programming; the assault-weapon ban; the Violence against Women Act, which is designed to prevent domestic violence and other crimes against women; and the Family and Medical Leave Act, which gives men and women time off from their jobs to care for a newborn or a sick relative. On crime, he talked about victims' rights as well as putting more police on the streets and building more prisons. On welfare, he stressed the importance of helping people get jobs.

The election year saw the emergence of the so-called "soccer moms," the suburban working mothers whose votes were undecided. Dole failed to win their support. His strategy of opposing affirmative action and attacking Clinton even may have triggered a backlash among women, according to pollsters.

For the first time, the wives of both major-party presidential candidates were women with careers and accomplishments of their own—and each had a law degree from an Ivy League law school. Elizabeth Dole (*see* BIOGRAPHY) hoped to become the first first lady to hold a job outside the White House. With her husband's defeat, she returned to her $200,000-per-year job as president of the American Red Cross. First Lady Hillary Rodham Clinton (*see* BIOGRAPHY), whose financial dealings while she was an Arkansas lawyer were under investigation, kept a low profile during the political season. But she received a big welcome when she addressed the Democratic National Convention and stated that, in her husband's second term, she would continue to work on issues that affect children.

Women made modest gains in Congress and in gubernatorial races. The House of Representatives of the 105th Congress would include 51 women—a record number. Thirty-nine incumbent women members—including Rep. Susan Molinari (R-NY), who gained national attention when she delivered the keynote address at the Republican National Convention in San Diego—would return to the House. Six women members retired and three incumbent women were defeated.

In the Senate, the number of women held steady at nine despite the retirement of Sen. Nancy Kassebaum (R-KS) and the departure of Sen. Sheila Frahm (R-KS), who was defeated in a primary after being appointed to fill the Senate seat left vacant when Dole resigned to run for president.

The two newly elected women senators were Susan Collins (R-ME) and Mary Landrieu (D-LA). Both women won open seats. With the election of Collins, who joined Sen. Olympia Snowe (R) in representing Maine, the state became the second one to have two women in the Senate. The other was California, which was represented by Sens. Dianne Feinstein (D) and Barbara Boxer (D).

In New Hampshire, Jeanne Shaheen (D) was elected governor; she and New Jersey's Gov. Christine Whitman (R) were the only two women holding governors' offices.

Military. Two all-male state-supported U.S. military colleges—Virginia Military Institute (VMI) in Lexington, VA, and The Citadel in Charleston, SC—lost court battles to keep women out. The Citadel opened its doors to four young women in August; two of them withdrew in January 1997, alleging they had been harassed and hazed. VMI was expected to admit women in 1997.

In November scandal erupted at the Aberdeen Ordnance Center near Baltimore, MD, following charges that drill sergeants coerced female recruits to have sex with them. The army announced it had filed criminal sex charges against two drill sergeants and a cap-

© Ed Bailey/AP/Wide World Photos

Carolyn McCarthy (left) *was elected to the U.S. House of Representatives from New York's 4th District in November 1996. A lifelong Republican, the 52-year-old nurse had switched to the Democratic Party after the incumbent congressman—her election-day opponent—had voted against gun control. McCarthy's husband was killed and her son was injured by a gunman aboard a Long Island Railroad commuter train in 1993.*

tain and was interviewing all women who trained at the facility in the previous two years. The army set up a hot line in the wake of the disclosures and received thousands of calls that included complaints about other installations.

Law. Affirmative action continued to be a divisive issue nationwide. In California, voters approved Proposition 209, which prohibits the state from favoring members of one sex or racial group over another in hiring for state jobs. The results were being challenged in court by civil-rights groups that contended the proposition was unconstitutional.

In Virginia a lesbian mother ended her three-year legal battle for custody of her 5-year-old son. She felt she could not overcome prejudice in the courts. In a case that attracted national attention, Sharon Bottoms had fought her mother, Kay, for custody of the child. State courts ruled that Bottoms was an unfit mother.

The Workplace. Women's share of the total labor force continued to rise, according to the Labor Department. Women accounted for 46% of the total U.S. labor force. Nearly six out of every ten women age 16 or over were working. Women also made great strides as entrepreneurs. According to the Labor Department, women owned more than 6.4 million of all U.S. businesses, employed more than 13 million workers, and generated $1.6 trillion in business revenue.

However, a study by Catalyst, a New York–based nonprofit group that tracks women in the workplace, said that—among top corporate hierarchies—only one of ten executives was a woman. The study reported that 105 of the top 500 U.S. companies had no women officers in their ranks.

A report by the National Foundation for Business Owners found that women business owners were finding it easier than in the past to get credit from banks. The foundation contended that women were less likely to be denied financing because of their sex. In its annual survey of Americans and their money, a *Money* magazine poll found that women worry more about finances and have a gloomier economic outlook than do men. And a survey by the Women's Research and Education Institute showed that women were half as likely as men to receive an employer-provided pension.

International. Overseas, women experienced setbacks. Pakistan's Prime Minister Benazir Bhutto was ousted from office and put under house arrest on charges of corruption and abuse of power. She maintained her innocence and vowed to fight the charges.

In Afghanistan, forces of the Taliban, an extremist Islamic faction, took over the capital of Kabul and began a relentless campaign against women. They banned women from going to work and girls from going to school. There were reports that the militia beat women who were not dressed properly.

Women continued to make strides in elected offices in other countries. The Scandinavian countries continued to have the highest percentage of women legislators, with Sweden topping the list at 40%. Norway's Prime Minister Gro Harlem Brundtland resigned.

JUDI HASSON, *"USA Today"*

YUGOSLAVIA. *See* pages 96–101.

ZAIRE

During 1996 the economic woes of Zaire, potentially one of Africa's wealthiest states, remained the most pressing problem of the nation's fractured government.

Economy and Politics. The near collapse of the road and river infrastructure, combined with corruption at all levels and the lack of central-government leadership, led to failure to capitalize on Zaire's vast mineral wealth. The state had been near bankruptcy for more than a decade; its foreign debt in 1996 exceeded $10 billion. Failure to comply with International Monetary Fund (IMF) standards cut off the flow of international aid. President Mobutu Sese Seko's refusal to relinquish power as urged by the United States and European countries resulted in sharp curtailment of investment. Inflation was in double-digit figures, and urban unemployment remained astronomical.

Tension between Mobutu and his opponents in the High Council of the Republic–Transitional Parliament (HCR-TP) prevented any major improvements in the lives of its citizens. The failure of a strong opposition to Mobutu was due partially to the lack of a significant number of educated people (the nation has only four universities) and to the lack of a free press. The country's 12 newspapers were controlled tightly by Mobutu.

Major changes in political control were likely to come with the implementation of the draft constitution, adopted in May and to be approved by referendum before February 1997. The new constitution would create a federal system with a presidential/parliamentary central government. Elections for the president and legislature were projected for mid-1997. An electoral commission was formed and $400 million was approved for the election. Disagreement between Prime Minister Kengo wa Dondo and opposition parties in the HCR-TP, particularly the Union for Democracy and Social Progress (UDPS) led by Etienne Tshisekedi, allowed Mobutu to continue to dominate the government. This was not changed significantly by Tshisekedi's dismissal as leader of the opposition coalition in July.

In December, President Mobutu returned to Kinshasa after recuperating from prostate-cancer surgery in France. On the day after his return, he named Lt. Gen. Mahele Bakungo Lieko as chief of staff of the military, succeeding Gen. Eluki Monga, who was suspended in November after stating publicly that Zaire's army was demoralized and ill-equipped.

Refugees and Foreign Affairs. Zaire's problems were complicated by the presence of hundreds of thousands of refugees from Rwanda and Burundi in United Nations (UN) camps in the northeast. The camps were centers of crime, poverty, starvation, disease, and corruption, and were blamed for serious environmental damage to the region. In mid-November, however, some 500,000 refugees—most of the ethnic Hutu—began a mass exodus back to Rwanda. The exodus had been sparked by recent military victories by Zairian Tutsi rebels over Hutu militants in the area. The refugees' voluntary return came just as UN members were preparing a substantial relief mission to aid and repatriate the refugees.

The return of Rwandan refugees to their country was Zaire's foreign-policy priority. The ongoing civil war in Burundi led Zaire to cooperate with other East African states in a boycott of trade to that state. Mobutu paid a state visit to France in April. However, the U.S. government refused in May to grant him an entry visa to attend a conference.

Aircraft Disaster. The nation's worst air disaster in years occurred in February, when an overloaded cargo plane went down directly into the largest fruit market in Kinshasa, killing 350 persons.

HARRY A. GAILEY
San Jose State University

ZAIRE • Information Highlights

Official Name: Republic of Zaire.
Location: Central equatorial Africa.
Area: 905,564 sq mi (2 345 410 km²).
Population (mid-1996 est.): 46,500,000.
Chief City (1987 est.): Kinshasa, the capital, 2,500,000.
Government: *Head of state,* Mobutu Sese Seko, president (took office 1965). *Head of government,* Leon Kengo wa Dondo, prime minister (appointed August 1994). *Legislature* (unicameral)—parliament.
Monetary Unit: New zaire (23,903.0 new zaires equal U.S.$1, February 1996).
Gross Domestic Product (1994 est. U.S.$): $18,800,000,000 (purchasing power parity).
Foreign Trade (1994 U.S.$): *Imports,* $382,000,000; *exports,* $419,000,000.

ZIMBABWE

Zimbabwe held a controversial presidential election in 1996 as the country remained plagued by economic uncertainty and by strikes that adversely affected such important areas as health-care delivery.

Presidential Election. Robert Mugabe was elected to his third term as president in

March. The election was in many ways an embarrassment for Mugabe. Two leading opposition candidates—Rev. Ndabaningi Sithole of the Zimbabwe African National Union–Sithole (ZANU-S) and Bishop Muzorewa of the United Parties—dropped out of the election, claiming that it was rigged against them. Only 31% of the electorate voted in the election. While Mugabe received 93% of the votes cast, the turnout was the lowest ever recorded in a national election. The nation's government-controlled television and radio stations and daily newspapers made campaigning very difficult for the opposition. The country's only major independent newspaper, *The Financial Gazette*, was pressured into dismissing its editor and its main political columnist. The ruling ZANU–Patriotic Front (PF) had access to state funding in the campaign, while opponents had to finance their own campaigns. In addition, Sithole was accused of plotting the assassination of Mugabe and campaigned while on bail. Sithole maintained that the Central Intelligence Organization (CIO) had framed him.

The Economy. In July the country's 1996–97 national budget was presented in Parliament by new Minister of Finance Herbert Murerwa. He promised to curb government spending, which had been responsible for a budget deficit running at 10% of gross domestic product (GDP). The prime lending rate in the country reached 40% and unemployment was said to be as high as 45%. Murerwa estimated that Zimbabwe's budget deficit for 1996–97 would be more than Z$68 billion (about U.S.$7 billion—roughly 8.5% of GDP. The minister acknowledged that the budget deficit was the major threat to Zimbabwe's economy and that the country suffered from huge losses by inefficient and uneconomic parastatals. The government expected to raise close to Z$1 billion (about U.S.$105 million) from the sale of government assets.

In May the International Monetary Fund (IMF) canceled a Z$1 billion disbursement for Zimbabwe's economic-reform program because the government had not reduced budget deficits and continued to finance parastatals that were running at a loss. In response, the government began to implement some austerity measures. With the completion of the first five years of economic structural adjustment, the government was to begin a new round of discussions with the IMF for a new three-year agreement. On a more positive level, good rains ameliorated drought conditions, tobacco prices rose, and inflation was relatively stable.

ZIMBABWE • Information Highlights

Official Name: Republic of Zimbabwe.
Location: Southern Africa.
Area: 150,803 sq mi (390 580 km^2).
Population (mid-1996 est.): 11,500,000.
Chief Cities (1983 est.): Harare (formerly Salisbury), the capital, 681,000; Bulawayo, 429,000; Chitungwiza, 202,000.
Government: *Head of state and government,* Robert Mugabe, executive president (sworn in Dec. 31, 1987). *Legislature* (unicameral)—Parliament.
Monetary Unit: Zimbabwe dollar (9.961 Z dollars equal U.S.$1, July 1996).
Gross Domestic Product (1994 est. U.S.$): $17,400,000,000.
Economic Indexes (1995, 1990 = 100): *Consumer Prices,* all items, 335.1; food, 388.1. *Industrial Production,* 89.
Foreign Trade (1994 U.S.$): *Imports,* $2,241,000,000; *exports,* $1,882,000,000.

Striking Workers. In August the government dismissed thousands of public-service workers—including nurses, doctors, magistrates, customs officials, morticians, and firefighters—who had gone on a strike for increased wages. The weeklong strike, which was a rare challenge to President Mugabe, was based on the claim by the Zimbabwe Public Service Association that wages had not kept up with the inflation rate. The workers were demanding more than the 6% raise offered by the government, especially since cabinet ministers and members of Parliament had awarded themselves a 130% raise. Even though President Mugabe seemed out of touch with the workers and their demands, at the end of August the government offered an increase of 20% backdated to July.

Nurses went on strike in October, demanding increased allowances for night duties and the introduction of a risk allowance. Later in the month they were joined by doctors. The government responded by dismissing nearly 2,000 nurses and 300 junior doctors, causing a major health-care crisis. The government seemed confident that it could replace the doctors and nurses with foreigners. However, while the Zimbabwean strikers were receiving invitations to work in South Africa and adjacent countries, there was no interest from foreigners for the vacant positions. The strike ended in December.

Book Fair. In July the Zimbabwe International Book Fair became the center of acrimonious national debate for the second year in a row. The Supreme Court declared null and void a government order prohibiting gays and lesbians from exhibiting at the fair. The court ruled that the board of censors did not have the power to ban such groups from exhibiting at the fair.

See also AFRICA.

PATRICK O'MEARA, *Indiana University*

ZOOS AND ZOOLOGY

Sophisticated technology was being put to good use at a number of U.S. zoos during 1996. At Zoo Atlanta (GA), for example, computers have been enlisted to give visitors insight into the experiences of a gorilla. Larry F. Hodges and computer-science colleagues at Georgia Institute of Technology designed a virtual-reality system that re-creates the terrain of the zoo's gorilla habitat and combines it with gorilla vocalizations, physical reactions, and movements. Visitors are outfitted with a headset and goggles, which allow them to play the role of a juvenile gorilla and enter the three-dimensional domain of Willie B., Zoo Atlanta's 439-lb (199-kg) dominant male.

Advanced technology also is being used to improve the reproductive odds of endangered wild animals. For the first time, a cheetah cub was born successfully as a result of artificial insemination, at Rio Grande Zoological Park in Albuquerque, NM. Cheetahs historically have bred poorly in captivity. In an effort to introduce new genes into the captive North American population and reduce the need to remove cheetahs from the wild, the Cheetah Conservation Fund and the Namibian ministry of the environment invited North American experts to Namibia to examine cheetahs in the wild and collect viable sperm from males.

In a similar vein, the world's first test-tube western lowland gorilla was born at the Cincinnati (OH) Zoo and Botanical Garden. Fertility experts collected 12 eggs from Rosie, the zoo's female gorilla. The eggs were fertilized in vitro with sperm that had been collected from a male at the Henry Doorly Zoo in Omaha, NE. Three of the embryos were transferred back into Rosie and five were cryopreserved for possible use in the future.

Exhibits. On its 100th anniversary, the Denver (CO) Zoo opened Primate Panorama, which spans more than 7 acres (2.8 ha) and displays a wide variety of primates, from tiny tamarins to huge gorillas. Large habitats allow social groups of apes to live together, and Primates of the Night re-creates the nocturnal world of owl monkeys and douroucoulis.

In June the San Diego (CA) Zoo's polar bears made a big splash at the Polar Bear Plunge. A jagged coastline of exposed rocks runs along the shore of a deep bay, where the white bears can swim and sunbathe. A glass wall allows visitors to watch the animals' activities both in and out of the water. The display also includes arctic foxes, reindeer, diving ducks, Eurasian goldfinches, and snowy owls.

The National Zoological Park in Washington, DC, takes the visitor experience to a new level, as orangutans traverse about 400 ft (122 m) overhead from their residence to the

An 8-year-old female gorilla named Binti Jua (shown at right with her offspring) *became an international celebrity in August 1996 after she rescued an unconscious toddler who had fallen into her cage at the Brookfield (IL) Zoo.*

In June 1996 the San Diego Zoo unveiled a new polar-bear environment, complete with expansive swimming and sunbathing areas for the animals. Later that summer, the zoo suffered a major setback with the death of Castor, the exhibit's popular adult male.

Think Tank, an innovative concept in zoo display. In the Think Tank, visitors can watch scientists probe the learning abilities of orangutans, chimpanzees, and other animals. Special displays reveal the differences between learned behavior, demonstrated with interactive games and events, and the innate behavior of such creatures as colonial leaf-cutter ants, which go about their fungus tending and harvesting with machinelike regularity. (*See* page 92.)

In the first phase of a sweeping $57 million project, Monterey (CA) Bay Aquarium opened its Outer Bay galleries, featuring life in open ocean waters. The 1-million-gal (3.8-million-l) indoor ocean exhibit features an acrylic window through which visitors can watch soupfin sharks, giant ocean sunfish, barracuda, and the first permanent North American exhibit of yellowfin tuna. In addition, the aquarium added a marine-mammal learning center and displays that explain marine conservation and the changing ocean environment.

In December 1995 the Philadelphia (PA) Zoological Garden suffered a devastating fire in its primate house that killed 23 animals. Plans were under way to rebuild the display. And the Stanley Park Zoo in Vancouver, BC, emptied its animal habitats for good. The closing was spurred by a 1993 referendum in which the city's electorate had voted to relocate the animals and close the zoo.

The Copenhagen Zoo in Denmark added an unusual exhibit to its primate collection: *Homo sapiens*. For three weeks beginning in August 1996, a Danish couple lived in a clear acrylic enclosure located between the baboon and lemur exhibits. Zoo officials said that the display would help visitors confront their primate origins.

Zoology. After much speculation and testing, scientists in Florida concluded that a toxin from algae blooms—the so-called red tide—had caused a record number of manatee deaths in that state. At least 300 of the gentle marine mammals were found dead in Florida's coastal waters in 1996. Scientists feared that the losses could affect the breeding season. Only about 2,500 West Indian manatees remained in Florida waters.

Two nests of Kemp's ridley sea turtle eggs discovered on Padre Island National Seashore in Texas fueled optimism about the fate of this critically endangered reptile. The nests are the first documented successes of a program started in 1978 to persuade female turtles born in Mexico to make Texas their preferred nesting site. Biologists collected turtle eggs from Rancho Nuevo, Mexico, and carried them to Padre Island, where they were incubated. After the turtles were hatched, they were raised in captivity and then released. Scientists hoped that this process would imprint the female turtles to return to Texas as adults to lay their eggs.

A notebook computer helped field scientists identify bats in Belize. Bruce and Carolyn Miller from the Wildlife Conservation Society cruised old logging roads with a sonic "bat detector," recording the calls of echolocating bats. Using a computer in which the vocalizations of known species of bats are stored digitally, the Millers discovered that some species, such as the shaggy-haired bat, are not as rare as previously believed.

DEBORAH A. BEHLER
"Wildlife Conservation" magazine

Statistical and Tabular Data

Nations of the World [1]

A Profile and Synopsis of Major 1996 Developments

Andorra, S.W. Europe

Population: 64,000 **Capital:** Andorra la Vella
Area: 174 sq mi (450 km²)
Government: Marc Forne Molne, head of government

Angola, W. Africa

Population: 11,500,000 **Capital:** Luanda
Area: 481,351 sq mi (1 246 700 km²)
Government: José Eduardo dos Santos, president; Fernando José da Franca Dias van Dunem, prime minister

The November 1994 peace accord between President José Eduardo dos Santos' ruling Popular Movement for the Liberation of Angola (MPLA) and Jonas Savimbi's rebel National Union for the Total Alliance of Angola (UNITA) made little progress in 1996. By year's end, UNITA still had failed to demobilize all of its troops, and talks between UNITA and the government on constitutional changes—a prerequisite for forming a government of national unity that included UNITA—were at a standstill. Some 6,600 members of the UN peacekeeping mission remained in the country. The government also faced a separatist rebellion in the enclave of Cabinda.

Antigua and Barbuda, Caribbean

Population: 100,000 **Capital:** St. John's
Area: 170 sq mi (440 km²)
Government: James B. Carlisle, governor-general; Lester Bird, prime minister

In early April, in an effort to increase revenues, the government announced a 10% tax on all earnings above $450 by foreigners living in Antigua and Barbuda.

Bahamas, Caribbean

Population: 300,000 **Capital:** Nassau
Area: 5,382 sq mi (13 940 km²)
Government: Orville Turnquest, governor-general; Hubert A. Ingraham, prime minister

On July 9, Hurricane Bertha caused moderate damage in the Bahamas.

Bahrain, W. Asia

Population: 600,000 **Capital:** Manama
Area: 239 sq mi (620 km²)
Government: Isa bin Salman Al Khalifa, emir; Khalifa bin Salman Al Khalifa, prime minister

Riots and demonstrations by Shiite Muslims who opposed Bahrain's Sunni Muslim government—and who demanded political reforms and improved social conditions—continued to rock the nation in 1996. Following antigovernment protests in April 1995, the ruling emir, Sheikh Isa bin Salman Al Khalifa, had met with opposition leaders in an attempt to restore calm, but these talks ended inconclusively. In January 1996 further Shiite protests brought about a government crackdown, which was stepped up after one opposition group—the Islamic Front for the Liberation of Bahrain—exploded a bomb at a hotel in the capital city of Manama. By February more than 600 dissidents had been arrested. The situation worsened in March after a dissident accused of killing a police officer was ex cuted. And in June, the government arrested 44 people, accusing them of plotting to overthrow the regime and establish a Shiite government similar to the one in Iran. The government accused Iran of backing the plot.

Barbados, Caribbean

Population: 300,000 **Capital:** Bridgetown
Area: 166 sq mi (430 km²)
Government: Sir Clifford Husbands, governor-general; Owen Arthur, prime minister

Benin, W. Africa

Population: 5,600,000 **Capital:** Porto Novo
Area: 43,483 sq mi (112 620 km²)
Government: Mathieu Kérékou, president; Adrien Houngbedji, prime minister

In the March 18 presidential election, Mathieu Kérékou, Benin's former Marxist military ruler, won 52.5% of the vote to defeat incumbent President Nicephore Soglo. Kérékou promised to retain the free-market policies that had been initiated by Soglo. (See also AFRICA—Democracy in Africa.)

Bhutan, S. Asia

Population: 800,000 **Capital:** Thimphu
Area: 18,147 sq mi (47 000 km²)
Government: Jigme Singye Wangchuck, king

On September 10 at the United Nations General Assembly, Bhutan joined its powerful neighbor India, as well as Libya, in voting against the Comprehensive Test-Ban Treaty. The treaty was approved by a vote of 158–3, with five abstentions.

Botswana, S. Africa

Population: 1,500,000 **Capital:** Gaborone
Area: 231,803 sq mi (600 370 km²)
Government: Ketumile Masire, president

The government announced plans to increase the size of the Botswana Defense Force from 7,000 to 10,000. It also purchased fighter-bombers and tanks from Canada, Germany, the Netherlands, and the United Kingdom. Botswana's dispute with Namibia over the sovereignty of Sedudo (Kasikili) Island in the Chobe River was submitted to the International Court of Justice for resolution.

Brunei Darussalam, S.E. Asia

Population: 300,000 **Capital:** Bandar Seri Begawan
Area: 2,288 sq mi (5 770 km²)
Government: Hassanal Bolkiah, sultan and prime minister

At the 29th ministerial meeting of the Association of Southeast Asian Nations (ASEAN) in Jakarta, Indonesia, Brunei and the other nations with disputing claims over the oil-rich Spratly Islands in the South China Sea (China, Vietnam, Malaysia, and the Philippines) endorsed tentative steps toward resolving their differences with a view to possible joint development in some areas.

[1] *Independent nations not covered in pages 96–581.*

Burkina Faso, W. Africa

Population: 10,600,000 **Capital:** Ouagadougou
Area: 105,869 sq mi (274 200 km²)
Government: Blaise Compaoré, president; Kadre Désiré Ouedraogo, prime minister

In February, ten opposition parties announced that they would merge with President Blaise Compaoré's Organization for Popular Democracy/Labor Movement to form the Congress for Democracy and Progress—a move that would give the president the support of 87 of the 107 deputies in the parliament.

Burundi, E. Africa

Population: 5,900,000 **Capital:** Bujumbura
Area: 10,745 sq mi (27 830 km²)
Government: Pierre Buyoya, president; Pascal-Firmin Ndimira, prime minister

Burundi's army, dominated by the minority Tutsi ethnic group, seized power on July 25. It ousted Hutu President Sylvestre Ntibantunganya, dissolved the parliament, and outlawed political parties and demonstrations. The UN Security Council condemned the coup, and the Organization of African Unity (OAU) imposed economic sanctions on Burundi. Maj. Pierre Buyoya, a moderate Tutsi who was named president by the coup leaders, pledged in October that he would reopen parliament and move the country toward democracy. (See also AFRICA—Turmoil in Burundi and Rwanda.)

Cameroon, Cen. Africa

Population: 13,600,000 **Capital:** Yaoundé
Area: 183,568 sq mi (475 440 km²)
Government: Paul Biya, president; Peter Mafany Musonge, prime minister

During the first half of the year, Cameroonian forces clashed with Nigerian soldiers over the contested Bekassi Peninsula, which lies between the two countries on the oil-rich Gulf of Guinea. Earlier, the two nations had placed the issue of sovereignty over the peninsula before the International Court of Justice.

Cape Verde, W. Africa

Population: 400,000 **Capital:** Praia
Area: 1,556 sq mi (4 030 km²)
Government: Antonio Mascarenhas Monteiro, president; Carlos Wahnon Veiga, prime minister

In February, two months after his ruling Movement for Democracy Party (MPD) won at least 50 out of 72 seats in Cape Verde's parliament, President Antonio Mascarenhas Monteiro was reelected to a second five-year term. He ran unopposed.

Central African Republic, Cen. Africa

Population: 3,300,000 **Capital:** Bangui
Area: 240,533 sq mi (622 980 km²)
Government: Ange Patasse, president; Jean-Paul Ngoupande, prime minister

In April, May, and again in November, soldiers mutinied in the capital city of Bangui. On the first two occasions, French troops stationed in the country joined local government forces to put down the mutiny. The insurrectionists, who initially demanded only that they receive back pay, escalated their demands to include the resignation of President Ange Patasse. When French troops used helicopter gunships to rout the mutineers, anti-French demonstrators took to the streets of Bangui demanding their removal. At year's end, four African heads of state were acting as mediators in an effort to resolve the situation. Jean-Bedel Bokassa, who had ruled the Central African Republic ruthlessly from 1965 to 1979 as "president for life" and "emperor," died in Bangui of a heart attack.

Chad, Cen. Africa

Population: 6,500,000 **Capital:** Ndjamena
Area: 495,753 sq mi (1 284 000 km²)
Government: Idriss Déby, president; Djimasta Koibla, prime minister

On July 3, in the first democratic presidential election since Chad became independent of France in 1960, incumbent President Idriss Déby was reelected with 69% of the vote. (See also AFRICA—Democracy in Africa.)

Comoros, E. Africa

Population: 500,000 **Capital:** Moroni
Area: 838 sq mi (2 170 km²)
Government: Mohamed Taki Abdoulkarim, president; Tadjidine Ben Said Massoundi, prime minister

In the March 16 presidential election, Mohamed Taki Abdoulkarim, leader of the National Union for Democracy (UNDC), was elected with 61.2% of the vote. He defeated Abbas Djoussouf, leader of the Forum for National Recovery (FRN). French mercenary Bob Denard, who had launched an unsuccessful coup in 1995, was released from prison in July 1996. (See also AFRICA—Democracy in Africa.)

Congo, Cen. Africa

Population: 2,500,000 **Capital:** Brazzaville
Area: 132,046 sq mi (342 000 km²)
Government: Pascal Lissouba, president; David Charles Ganao, prime minister

In May, in accord with a 1995 agreement between the government and opposition parties, former President Denis Sassou Nguesso, leader of the opposition United Democratic Forces, announced that his private militia would be integrated into the nation's armed forces. In July, however, the government announced that Nguesso's militia had occupied the town of Mossaka, north of the capital city of Brazzaville. In August, Prime Minister Jacques Joachim Yhombi-Opango resigned and was replaced by David Charles Ganao.

Djibouti, E. Africa

Population: 600,000 **Capital:** Djibouti
Area: 8,494 sq mi (22 000 km²)
Government: Hassan Gouled Aptidon, president; Barkat Gourad Hamadou, prime minister

In March the Front for the Restoration of Unity and Democracy (FRUD), the former Afar rebel group, was recognized as a legal political party. In April, Eritrean troops entered Djibouti and clashed with Djiboutian troops.

Dominica, Caribbean

Population: 100,000 **Capital:** Roseau
Area: 290 sq mi (750 km²)
Government: Crispin Anselm Sorhaindo, president; Edison James, prime minister

In May, Prime Minister Edison James, who also was serving as Dominica's foreign minister, and Cuba's Foreign Minister Roberto Robaina signed a protocol establishing diplomatic relations.

Dominican Republic, Caribbean

Population: 8,100,000 **Capital:** Santo Domingo
Area: 18,815 sq mi (48 730 km²)
Government: Leonel Fernandez Reyna, president

The Dominican Republic began pursuing a policy of improved relations with its neighbors. Accordingly, President Leonel Fernandez Reyna of the Dominican Republic conferred with Haiti's President René Préval in Miami, FL, in December. Protection of their borders, immigration, and commerce reportedly were the topics discussed. The two presidents also agreed to meet again in 1997 to sign a treaty cementing improved relations. In November the Dominican Republic announced that it would open an embassy in Jamaica.

Equatorial Guinea, Cen. Africa

Population: 400,000 **Capital:** Malabo
Area: 10,830 sq mi (28 050 km²)
Government: Teodoro Obiang Nguema Mbasogo, president; Serafin Seriche Dougan, prime minister

President Teodoro Obiang Nguema Mbasogo was reelected on February 25. Three of the four opposition candidates earlier had withdrawn from the race. (See also AFRICA—Democracy in Africa.)

Eritrea, E. Africa

Population: 3,600,000 **Capital:** Asmara
Area: 46,841 sq mi (121 320 km²)
Government: Issaias Afeworke, president

Eritrea's dispute with Yemen over three disputed islands in the Red Sea—Greater Hanish, Lesser Hanish, and Zuqur—moved toward a resolution in May when the two countries signed a French-brokered agreement to bring their dispute to international arbitration. In August, Eritrea agreed to withdraw its troops from Lesser Hanish.

Fiji, Oceania

Population: 800,000 **Capital:** Suva
Area: 7,054 sq mi (18 270 km²)
Government: Kamisese Mara, president; Sitiveni Rabuka, prime minister

Some 500 Fijian soldiers stationed at a United Nations camp housing Lebanese refugees in southern Lebanon escaped injury when the Israeli army launched an artillery attack in retaliation for rocket attacks against northern Israel by Hezbollah guerrillas.

Gabon, Cen. Africa

Population: 1,200,000 **Capital:** Libreville
Area: 103,348 sq mi (267 670 km²)
Government: El Hadj Omar Bongo, president; Paulin Obame, prime minister

In February the World Health Organization (WHO) reported that 13 people had died from the Ebola virus after eating a chimpanzee at a feast in a small village in northeastern Gabon.

Gambia, W. Africa

Population: 1,200,000 **Capital:** Banjul
Area: 4,363 sq mi (11 300 km²)
Government: Yahya Jammeh, head of state

*In an August 8 referendum, Gambian voters approved a draft constitution that would permit a return to civilian rule. In the September 26 presidential election, Yahya Jammeh was returned to power. (*See also AFRICA—Democracy in Africa.*)*

Ghana, W. Africa

Population: 18,000,000 **Capital:** Accra
Area: 92,100 sq mi (238 540 km²)
Government: Jerry Rawlings, president

*Tourism earned Ghana some $248 million in 1996, as nearly 300,000 visitors—mainly from the United States, Britain, Germany, and the Netherlands—visited the African nation. President Jerry Rawlings was reelected on December 7 (*see AFRICA—Democracy in Africa*).*

Grenada, Caribbean

Population: 100,000 **Capital:** St. George's
Area: 131 sq mi (340 km²)
Government: Reginald Palmer, governor-general; Keith Mitchell, prime minister

Guinea, W. Africa

Population: 7,400,000 **Capital:** Conakry
Area: 94,927 sq mi (245 860 km²)
Government: Lansana Conté, president; Sidya Touré, prime minister

Twenty people were killed and hundreds wounded in early February when soldiers in the capital city of Conakry mutinied.

Guinea-Bissau, W. Africa

Population: 1,100,000 **Capital:**Bissau
Area: 13,946 sq mi (36 120 km²)
Government: João Bernardo Vieira, president; Manuel da Costa Saturnino, prime minister

An outbreak of cholera struck Bissau, the capital of Guinea-Bissau, in October.

Guyana, N.E. South America

Population: 700,000 **Capital:** Georgetown
Area: 83,000 sq mi (214 970 km²)
Government: Cheddi Jagan, president; Sam Hinds, prime minister

In April the International Monetary Fund (IMF) approved a loan to Guyana of $26 million.

Ivory Coast, W. Africa

Population: 13,900,000 **Capital:** Yamoussoukro
Area: 124,502 sq mi (322 460 km²)
Government: Henri Konan Bédié, president; Daniel Kablan Duncan, prime minister

By 1996, some 350,000 Liberian refugees fleeing the civil war in their country had made their way into Ivory Coast. In May, however, Ivory Coast officials refused entry to an additional 4,000 refugees who were aboard a boat off the nation's southwest coast.

Jamaica, Caribbean

Population: 2,600,000 **Capital:** Kingston
Area: 4,243 sq mi (10 990 km²)
Government: Sir Howard Cooke, governor-general; P J. Patterson, prime minister

Jamaican athletes excelled at the Summer Olympic Games in Atlanta, GA, winning six medals—one gold, three silver, and two bronze.

Kiribati, Oceania

Population: 74,000 **Capital:** Tarawa
Area: 277 sq mi (717 km²)
Government: Teburoro Tito, president

Kiribati President Teburoro Tito made an eight-day visit to China in September, during which he met with China's President Jiang Zemin. At the conclusion of the visit, the Kiribati chief executive traveled to Hong Kong.

Kuwait, W. Asia

Population: 1,800,000 **Capital:** Kuwait
Area: 6,800 sq mi (17 820 km²)
Government: Jabir al-Ahmad al-Sabah, emir; Saad al-Abdallah al-Sabah, prime minister

In September, after Iraq fired a missile at U.S. planes patrolling the "no-fly" zone over northern Iraq, Kuwait allowed the United States to send F-117 stealth fighters to Kuwait—a move that brought condemnation from Iraq. In October, Kuwait held its second parliamentary election since U.S.-led forces freed the nation from Iraqi occupation in 1991. Pro-government forces gained two seats at the expense of Muslim fundamentalists, who retained 17 seats in the 50-member parliament. While Kuwait has the only elected parliament in the Persian Gulf region, its powers remain strictly limited by Emir Jabir al-Ahmad al-Sabah.

Lesotho, S. Africa

Population: 2,100,000 **Capital:** Maseru
Area: 11,718 sq mi (30 350 km²)
Government: Letsie III, king; Ntsu Mokhehle, prime minister

King Moshoeshoe II died in a car accident on January 15 near the capital city of Maseru. His son, Crown Prince Letsie David Mohato, assumed the throne as King Letsie III on February 7.

Liberia, W. Africa

Population: 2,900,000 **Capital:** Monrovia
Area: 43,000 sq mi (111 370 km²)
Government: Ruth Perry, chair of the State Council

Despite the signing of an August 1995 peace agreement to end the civil war in Liberia, fighting erupted once again in April 1996. Hundreds of Americans and other foreign nationals were evacuated. A cease-fire eventually was effected between the warring factions, and by the end of May they largely had withdrawn from the center of

Monrovia, the capital. The fighting was primarily between the forces of Charles Taylor and Alhaji Kromah and those of D. Roosevelt Johnson. Beginning in May, representatives of the Economic Community of West African States (ECOWAS) met in Accra, Ghana, in an effort to end the fighting. At the end of July, the rival factions agreed to begin disarming their troops, and in early September, Ruth Perry—a former Liberian senator—was named head of state. The ECOWAS-sponsored peace plan also called for elections to be held in May 1997 and for the ECOWAS peacekeeping force to be increased from 8,500 to 18,000.

Liechtenstein, Cen. Europe

Population: 30,000 **Capital:** Vaduz
Area: 62 sq mi (160 km²)
Government: Hans Adam II, prince; Mario Frick, prime minister

Luxembourg, W. Europe

Population: 400,000 **Capital:** Luxembourg
Area: 998 sq mi (2 586 km²)
Government: Jean, grand duke; Jean-Claude Juncker, premier

In April, Cie. Luxembourgeoise de Télédiffusion and Bertelsmann AG of Germany announced merger plans. The new company would be the world's third-largest media group, after Time Warner and the Walt Disney Company.

Madagascar, E. Africa

Population: 15,200,000 **Capital:** Antananarivo
Area: 226,656 sq mi (587 040 km²)
Government: Didier Ratsiraka, president

Following the announcement that the High Constitutional Court had upheld an August vote by the Parliament to impeach him for contravening the constitution, President Albert Zafy resigned. The December presidential election pitted Zafy against former military ruler Didier Ratsiraka, who won by a narrow margin.

Malawi, E. Africa

Population: 9,500,000 **Capital:** Lilongwe
Area: 45,745 sq mi (118 480 km²)
Government: Bakili Muluzi, president

The coalition government of President Bakili Muluzi's ruling United Democratic Front (UDF) and the Alliance for Democracy (Aford)—forged in August 1995—collapsed in June, leaving the UDF four seats short of a majority in parliament. Former President Hastings Kamuzu Banda, who in 1995 had been accused of being involved in the deaths of a lawyer and three government ministers, was acquitted by Malawi's High Court.

Maldives, S. Asia

Population: 300,000 **Capital:**Malé
Area: 116 sq mi (300 km²)
Government: Maumoon Abdul Gayoom, president

The Maldives adopted a 1996–97 fiscal-year budget estimated at $167.3 million.

Mali, W. Africa

Population: 9,100,000 **Capital:** Bamako
Area: 478,764 sq mi (1 240 000 km²)
Government: Alpha Oumar Konare, president; Ibrahim Boubacar Keita, prime minister

The six-year-long Tuareg rebellion in northern Mali, which killed more than 50,000 people, ended in January when the rebels laid down their arms.

Malta, S. Europe

Population: 400,000 **Capital:** Valletta
Area: 124 sq mi (320 km²)
Government: Ugo Mifsud Bonnici, president; Alfred Sant, prime minister

In October 27 elections, the socialist Labor Party upset Prime Minister Eddie Fenech Adami's ruling Nationalist Party, winning 50.7% of the vote and a one-seat majority in the parliament. Nationalist Party leader Alfred Sant became prime minister. After taking office, Sant ended Malta's membership in the North Atlantic Treaty Organization (NATO) Partnership for Peace program. And while he did not withdraw Malta's application for membership in the European Union (EU), he did call for the renegotiation of Malta's relationship with that organization.

Marshall Islands, Pacific Ocean

Population: 54,000 **Capital:** Majuro
Area: 70 sq mi (181 km²)
Government: Kunio Lemari, acting president

Amata Kabua, the president of the Marshall Islands since 1979, died on December 19 while undergoing medical treatment in Honolulu, HI. The 68-year-old Kabua had been reelected to a fifth term in 1995. Kunio Lemari, minister of transport and communications, was named acting president.

Mauritania, W. Africa

Population: 2,300,000 **Capital:** Nouakchott
Area: 397,954 sq mi (1 030 700 km²)
Government: Maaouya Ould Sid Ahmed Taya, president; Cheikh Afia Ould Mohamed Khouna, prime minister

Mauritius, E. Africa

Population: 1,100,000 **Capital:** Port Louis
Area: 718 sq mi (1 860 km²)
Government: Cassam Uteem, president; Navin Ramgoolam, prime minister

Micronesia, Federated States of, Oceania

Population: 100,000 **Capital:** Kolonia
Area: 271 sq mi (702 km²)
Government: Bailey Olter, president

Monaco, S. Europe

Population: 28,000 **Capital:** Monaco-Ville
Area: 0.7 sq mi (1.9 km²)
Government: Rainier III, prince; Jacques Dupont, minister of state

Princess Stephanie, the daughter of Prince Rainier III of Monaco, was divorced from her husband, Daniel Ducruet, on October 4, after a marriage of 14 months.

Mongolia, N. Asia

Population: 2,400,000 **Capital:** Ulan Bator
Area: 604,247 sq mi (1 565 000 km²)
Government: Punsalmaagiyn Ochirbat, president; Mendsaihan Enhsaihan, prime minister

In a surprise landslide victory, the Democratic Union Coalition (DUC) defeated the ruling Mongolian People's Revolutionary Party (MPRP)—the nation's former Communist party—in June 30 parliamentary elections. The DUC parties won 50 seats in the 76-seat legislature, while the MPRP won 25, down from 70 in the previous parliament. The Mongolian Traditional Conservative Party won one seat. With inflation and poverty on the rise, the election campaign had dealt primarily with economic issues. Prior to the election, northern Mongolia was devastated by fires that burned 23 million acres (9.3 million ha) of forest and grazing lands.

Mozambique, E. Africa

Population: 16,500,000 **Capital:** Maputo
Area: 308,641 sq mi (799 380 km²)
Government: Joaquim Chissano, president; Pascoal Mocumbi, prime minister

Mozambican armed forces joined with those of Zimbabwe in an effort to rout Zimbabwean dissidents operating out of western Mozambique.

Namibia, S.W. Africa

Population: 1,600,000 **Capital:** Windhoek
Area: 318,259 sq mi (824 290 km²)
Government: Sam Nujoma, president; Hage Geingob, prime minister

Namibia signed a military-cooperation agreement with Russia in May. The pact calls for Russia to train Namibian officers and to supply the Namibia Defense Force with military equipment. Botswana's dispute with Namibia over the sovereignty of Kasikili (Sedudo) Island in the Chobe River was submitted to the International Court of Justice for resolution.

Nauru, Oceania

Population: 10,000 **Capital:** Nauru
Area: 8 sq mi (20.7 km²)
Government: Kennan Adeang, president

Nepal, S. Asia

Population: 22,100,000 **Capital:** Katmandu
Area: 54,363 sq mi (140 800 km²)
Government: Birendra Bir Bikram Shah Dev, king; Sher Bahadur Deuba, prime minister

A 4-year-old boy from Seattle, Washington—who in 1993 had been enthroned as the next head of a Buddhist monastery near the capital city of Katmandu—arrived in Nepal in January for ten years of religious training. Tibetan Buddhists believe that the boy, Sonam Wangdu Lama, is the reincarnation of a high lama who died in 1987.

Niger, W. Africa

Population: 9,500,000 **Capital:** Niamey
Area: 489,189 sq mi (1 267 000 km²)
Government: Ibrahim Baré Maïnassara, president

Mahamane Ousmane, Niger's first-ever democratically elected president, was ousted by a military coup in January. Col. Ibrahim Baré Maïnassara took control of the government, and in July—in what observers labeled a fraudulent election—he was elected president. The new government banned all opposition parties.

Oman, W. Asia

Population: 2,300,000 **Capital:** Muscat
Area: 82,031 sq mi (212 460 km²)
Government: Qaboos bin Said Al Said, sultan

In April, Oman signed an agreement with Russia and Kazakhstan to build a 900-mi (1 400-km) oil-and-gas pipeline from Kazakhstan's Tengiz oil field on the Caspian Sea to a new Russian port on the Black Sea.

Palau, N. Pacific Ocean

Population: 20,000 **Capital:** Koror
Area: 177 sq mi (850 km²)
Government: Kuniwo Nakamura, president

Papua New Guinea, Oceania

Population: 4,300,000 **Capital:** Port Moresby
Area: 178,259 sq mi (461 690 km²)
Government: Wiwa Korowi, governor-general; Julius Chan, prime minister

In June the government launched a seemingly unsuccessful military offensive in an attempt to end an eight-year-long separatist rebellion on the island of Bougainville.

Qatar, W. Asia

Population: 700,000 **Capital:** Doha
Area: 4,247 sq mi (11 000 km²)
Government: Hamad bin Khalifa Al Thani, emir; Abdallah bin Khalifa Al Thani, prime minister

Emir Hamad bin Khalifa Al Thani, who in June 1995 had ousted his father, Khalifa bin Hamad Al Thani, and assumed the reins of power in Qatar, moved in 1996 to retrieve several billion dollars that the former ruler had in bank accounts in France and Switzerland.

Rwanda, E. Africa

Population: 6,900,000 **Capital:** Kigali
Area: 10,169 sq mi (26 337 km²)
Government: Pasteur Bizimungu, president; Pierre Celestin Rwigema, prime minister

In mid-November, some 500,000 Hutu who had spent more than two years in refugee camps in eastern Zaire returned to Rwanda. Tens of thousands more returned to Rwanda from Tanzania. But perhaps 150,000 others, including Hutu militants and their supporters, moved deeper into Zaire. The militants remained loyal to the Hutu-dominated government of Rwanda that had been ousted by Tutsi in 1994. Many Hutu who returned to Rwanda found that their farms had been taken over by Tutsi. A United Nations (UN) plan to send a 10,000-strong multinational force to help the refugees—to be led by Canada and to include some U.S. forces—was rejected by the Tutsi-dominated Rwandan government in late November. (See also AFRICA—Turmoil in Burundi and Rwanda.)

Saint Kitts and Nevis, Caribbean

Population: 40,000 **Capital:** Basseterre
Area: 139 sq mi (360 km²)
Government: Clement Athelston Arrindell, governor-general; Denzil Douglas, prime minister

In July, Saint Kitts and Nevis suffered moderate damage from Hurricane Bertha.

Saint Lucia, Caribbean

Population: 100,000 **Capital:** Castries
Area: 239 sq mi (620 km²)
Government: George Mallet, governor-general; Vaughn Lewis, prime minister

In April it was announced that Vaughn Lewis had become prime minister and head of the ruling United Workers' Party, following the resignation of Prime Minister John Compton.

Saint Vincent and the Grenadines, Caribbean

Population: 100,000 **Capital:** Kingstown
Area: 131 sq mi (340 km²)
Government: David Jack, governor-general; James F. Mitchell, prime minister

San Marino, S. Europe

Population: 30,000 **Capital:** San Marino
Area: 23 sq mi (60 km²)
Government: Giancarlo Venturini and Maurizio Rattini, captains regent

São Tomé and Príncipe, W. Africa

Population: 100,000 **Capital:** São Tomé
Area: 371 sq mi (960 km²)
Government: Miguel Trovoada, president; Raul Braganca, prime minister

On July 21, President Miguel Trovoada was reelected to a second five-year term with 52.2% of the popular vote. His opponent, former President Manuel Pinto da Costa, garnered 47.8% of the vote.

Senegal, W. Africa

Population: 8,500,000 **Capital:** Dakar
Area: 75,749 sq mi (196 190 km²)
Government: Abdou Diouf, president; Habib Thiam, prime minister

Despite appeals from President Abdou Diouf, separatists in the Casamance region of Senegal refused to take part in peace negotiations.

Seychelles, E. Africa

Population: 100,000 **Capital:** Victoria
Area: 176 sq mi (455 km²)
Government: France Albert René, president

Sierra Leone, W. Africa

Population: 4,600,000 **Capital:** Freetown
Area: 27,699 sq mi (71 740 km²)
Government: Ahmad Tejan Kabbah, president

In January army officers overthrew Capt. Valentine Strasser, the leader of the nation's military government, and replaced him with Gen. Julius Maada Bio, who pledged to hold scheduled multiparty elections and called on the rebel Revolutionary United Front (RUF) to join the government in peace talks. In the March 15 presidential election, Ahmad Tejan Kabbah of the Sierra Leone People's Party emerged the victor with 59.5% of the vote, and on March 29 the military government handed over power to him. Less than a month later, the new government announced that a cease-fire agreement had been reached with RUF, and by the end of the year a peace agreement—brokered by Ivory Coast—was signed, ending five years of civil war.

Solomon Islands, Oceania

Population: 400,000 **Capital:** Honiara
Area: 10,985 sq mi (28 450 km²)
Government: Sir Moses Pitakaka, governor-general; Solomon Mamaloni, prime minister

Suriname, S. America

Population: 400,000 **Capital:** Paramaribo
Area: 63,039 sq mi (163 270 km²)
Government: Jules Wijdenbosch, president

See CARIBBEAN.

Swaziland, S. Africa

Population: 1,000,000 **Capital:** Mbabane
Area: 6,703 sq mi (17 360 km²)
Government: Mswati III, king; Barnabas Sibusiso Dlamini, prime minister

Following nationwide strikes and pro-democracy demonstrations early in the year, King Mswati III announced the formation of a constitutional commission to organize political reform.

Togo, W. Africa

Population: 4,600,000 **Capital:** Lomé
Area: 21,927 sq mi (56 790 km²)
Government: Gnassingbé Eyadéma, president; Klutse Kwassi, prime minister

In August 4 elections, President Gnassingbé Eyadéma's Togolese People's Rally (RPT) won three additional parliamentary seats, giving it and its allies 40 seats in the 81-seat National Assembly.

Tonga, Oceania

Population: 97,000 **Capital:** Nuku'alofa
Area: 289 sq mi (748 km²)
Government: Taufa'ahau Tupou IV, king; Baron Vaea, prime minister

Members of Tonga's pro-democracy movement won at least six of the nine seats reserved for commoners in Tonga's 30-seat legislature, but control of the island nation remained firmly in the hands of the king and his 11-member Privy Council.

Trinidad and Tobago, Caribbean

Population: 1,300,000 **Capital:** Port-of-Spain
Area: 1,981 sq mi (5 130 km²)
Government: Noor Hassanali, president; Basdeo Panday, prime minister

On March 3, Trinidad and Tobago hosted U.S. Secretary of State Warren Christopher, who signed a new U.S.–Trinidad and Tobago extradition treaty and symbolically turned over four high-speed boats to be used by the government in the fight against drug trafficking. (See also CARIBBEAN.)

Tuvalu, Oceania

Population: 12,000 **Capital:** Funafuti
Area: 10 sq mi (26 km²)
Government: Manuella Tulaga, governor-general; Kamuta Latasi, prime minister

United Arab Emirates, W. Asia

Population: 1,900,000 **Capital:** Abu Dhabi
Area: 32,278 sq mi (83 600 km²)
Government: Zayid bin Sultan Al Nuhayyan, president; Maktum bin Rashid Al Maktum, prime minister

The March 27 Dubai Desert Classic—the richest horse race in the world, with $4 million in prize money—was won by the U.S. horse Cigar, which took home $2.4 million.

Vanuatu, Oceania

Population: 200,000 **Capital:** Port-Vila
Area: 5,699 sq mi (14 760 km²)
Government: Jean-Marie Leye, president; Serge Vohor, prime minister

Vatican City, S. Europe

Population: 1,000 **Capital:** Vatican City
Area: 0.17 sq mi (0.438 km²)
Government: John Paul II, pope

Western Samoa, Oceania

Population: 200,000 **Capital:** Apia
Area: 1,104 sq mi (2 860 km²)
Government: Malietoa Tanumafili II, head of state; Tofilau Eti Alesana, prime minister

In April general elections, government supporters won a two-thirds majority in the Western Samoa legislature. Tofilau Eti Alesana, leader of the Human Rights Protection Party (HRPP), later was reelected prime minister by the legislature.

Yemen, W. Asia

Population: 14,700,000 **Capital:** San'a
Area: 205,356 sq mi (531 870 km²)
Government: Ali Abdullah Saleh, president; Abd al-Aziz al-Ghani, prime minister

Yemen's dispute with Eritrea over three disputed islands in the Red Sea—Greater Hanish, Lesser Hanish, and Zuqur—moved toward a resolution in May when the two countries signed a French-brokered agreement to bring their dispute to international arbitration. In August, in an effort to further the arbitration process, Eritrea agreed to withdraw its troops from Lesser Hanish.

Zambia, E. Africa

Population: 9,200,000 **Capital:** Lusaka
Area: 290,583 sq mi (752 610 km²)
Government: Frederick Chiluba, president

In November 18 general elections, which were boycotted by former President Kenneth Kaunda's United National Independence Party (UNIP) and other opposition parties, President Frederick Chiluba won 69.5% of the presidential vote and his ruling Movement for Multiparty Democracy (MMD) won 131 seats in the 150-seat parliament. Observers said that the elections "cannot be said to have been free and fair." (See also AFRICA—Democracy in Africa.)

THE UNITED STATES GOVERNMENT

Executive Branch

(selected listing as of January 1997)

President: William J. (Bill) Clinton

Vice-President: Albert Gore, Jr.

Executive Office of the President

The White House

Chief of Staff to the President: Erskine Bowles
Senior Policy Adviser to the President: Rahm Emanuel
Assistant to the President and Deputy Chief of Staff: Sylvia Mathews
Assistant to the President and Deputy Chief of Staff: John Podesta
Assistant to the President and Director for Intergovernmental Affairs: Marcia Hale
Assistant to the President for Legislative Affairs: John Hilley
Assistant to the President for Communications: Donald Baer
Assistant to the President and Senior Adviser: Bruce R. Lindsey
Assistant to the President for Domestic Policy: Bruce Reed
Assistant to the President for Economic Policy: Gene Sperling
Assistant to the President for National Security Affairs: Samuel Berger
Assistant to the President for International Economic Affairs: Dan Tarullo
Counselor to the President: Douglas D. Sosnik
Deputy Assistant to the President and Press Secretary: Michael D. McCurry
Senior Adviser for Policy Development: Ira Magaziner
Office of Management and Budget, Director: Franklin D. Raines
Council of Economic Advisers, Chairman: Janet Yellen*
Office of the United States Trade Representative, United States Trade Representative: Charlene Barshefsky*
Office of Science and Technology Policy, Assistant to the President for Science and Technology and Director: John H. Gibbons
Office of National Drug Control Policy, Director: Barry R. McCaffrey
Office of Administration, Special Assistant to the President for Management and Director: Franklin Reeder

The Cabinet

Secretary of Agriculture: Dan Glickman
Secretary of Commerce: William M. Daley*
Secretary of Defense: William S. Cohen*
  Joint Chiefs of Staff, Chairman: John Shalikashvili
Secretary of Education: Richard W. Riley
Secretary of Energy: Federico F. Peña*
Secretary of Health and Human Services: Donna E. Shalala
  Surgeon General: Audrey F. Manley, acting
  Commissioner of Food and Drugs: vacant
Secretary of Housing and Urban Development: Andrew M. Cuomo*
Secretary of Interior: Bruce Babbitt
Department of Justice, Attorney General: Janet Reno
  Federal Bureau of Investigation, Director: Louis Freeh
Secretary of Labor: Alexis M. Herman*
Secretary of State: Madeleine K. Albright*
  United Nations Representative: William Richardson*
Secretary of Transportation: Rodney E. Slater*
Secretary of the Treasury: Robert E. Rubin
  Internal Revenue Service, Commissioner: Margaret M. Richardson
Secretary of Veterans Affairs: Jesse Brown

Independent Agencies (selected listing)

Central Intelligence Agency, Director: Anthony Lake*
Consumer Product Safety Commission, Chairman: Ann Brown
Environmental Protection Agency, Administrator: Carol M. Browner
Equal Employment Opportunity Commission, Chairman: Reginald Earl Jones
Export-Import Bank of the United States, President and Chairman: Martin A. Kamarck
Farm Credit Administration, Chairman: Marsha Pyle Martin
Federal Communications Commission, Chairman: Reed E. Hunt
Federal Deposit Insurance Corporation, Chairman: Ricki T. Helfer
Federal Election Commission, Chairman: Lee Ann Elliott
Federal Emergency Management Agency, Director: James Lee Witt
Federal Labor Relations Authority, Chairman: Phyllis N. Segal
Federal Maritime Commission, Chairman: Harold J. Creel, Jr.
Federal Mediation and Conciliation Service, Director: John Calhoun Wells
Federal Reserve System, Chairman: Alan Greenspan
Federal Trade Commission, Chairman: Robert Pitofsky
General Services Administrator: David J. Barran (acting)
National Aeronautics and Space Administration, Administrator: Daniel S. Goldin
National Foundation on the Arts and Humanities
  National Endowment for the Arts, Chairman: Jane Alexander
  National Endowment for the Humanities, Chairman: Sheldon Hackney
National Labor Relations Board, Chairman: William B. Gould IV
National Science Foundation, Director: Neal F. Lane
National Transportation Safety Board, Chairman: James E. Hall
Nuclear Regulatory Commission, Chairman: Shirley A. Jackson
Office of Government Ethics, Director: Stephen D. Potts
Office of Personnel Management, Director: James B. King
Peace Corps, Director: Mark Gearan
Postal Rate Commission, Chairman: Edward J. Gleiman
Securities and Exchange Commission, Chairman: Arthur Levitt
Selective Service System, Director: Gil Coronado
Small Business Administrator: Philip Lader
Social Security Administration, Commissioner: Shirley Sears Chater
Tennessee Valley Authority, Chairman: Craven Crowell
U.S. Arms Control and Disarmament Agency, Director: John D. Holum
U.S. Commission on Civil Rights, Chairman: Mary Francis Berry
U.S. Information Agency, Director: Joseph D. Duffey
U.S. International Development Cooperation Agency, Director: J. Brian Atwood
U.S. International Trade Commission, Chairman: Marcia E. Miller
U.S. Postal Service, Postmaster General: Marvin Runyon

The Supreme Court

William H. Rehnquist, chief justice
John Paul Stevens
Sandra Day O'Connor
Antonin Scalia
Anthony M. Kennedy
David H. Souter
Clarence Thomas
Ruth Bader-Ginsburg
Stephen G. Breyer

*Nominated but not confirmed

The 105th CONGRESS
First Session

SENATE MEMBERSHIP

(As of January 1997: 55 Republicans, 45 Democrats.) Letters after names refer to party affiliation—D for Democrat, R for Republican, I for Independent. Single asterisk (*) denotes term expiring in January 1999; double asterisk (**), term expiring in January 2001; triple asterisk (***), term expiring in January 2003. [1]Elected in special election Jan. 30, 1996.

Alabama
R. C. Shelby, R*
J.B. Sessions, III, R***

Alaska
T. Stevens, R***
F. H. Murkowski, R*

Arizona
J. McCain, R*
J. Kyl, R**

Arkansas
D. Bumpers, D*
T. Hutchinson, R***

California
D. Feinstein, D**
B. Boxer, D*

Colorado
B. N. Campbell, R*
W. Allard, R***

Connecticut
C. J. Dodd, D*
J. I. Lieberman, D**

Delaware
W. V. Roth, Jr., R**
J. R. Biden, Jr., D***

Florida
B. Graham, D*
C. Mack, R**

Georgia
P. Coverdell, R*
M. Cleland, D***

Hawaii
D. K. Inouye, D*
D. K. Akaka, D**

Idaho
L. E. Craig, R***
D. Kempthorne, R*

Illinois
C. Moseley Braun, D*
R. J. Durbin, D***

Indiana
R. G. Lugar, R**
D. Coats, R*

Iowa
C. E. Grassley, R*
T. Harkin, D***

Kansas
S. Brownback, R*
P. Roberts, R***

Kentucky
W. H. Ford, D*
M. McConnell, R***

Louisiana
J. B. Breaux, D*
M. Landrieu, D***

Maine
O. J. Snowe, R**
S. Collins, R***

Maryland
P. S. Sarbanes, D**
B. A. Mikulski, D*

Massachusetts
E. M. Kennedy, D**
J. F. Kerry, D***

Michigan
C. Levin, D***
S. Abraham, R**

Minnesota
P. Wellstone, D***
R. Grams, R**

Mississippi
T. Cochran, R***
T. Lott, R**

Missouri
C. S. Bond, R*
J. Ashcroft, R**

Montana
M. Baucus, D***
C. Burns, R**

Nebraska
J. R. Kerrey, D**
C. Hagel, R***

Nevada
H. Reid, D*
R. H. Bryan, D**

New Hampshire
R. C. Smith, R***
J. Gregg, R*

New Jersey
F. R. Lautenberg, D**
R. G. Torricelli, D***

New Mexico
P. V. Domenici, R***
J. Bingaman, D**

New York
D. P. Moynihan, D**
A. M. D'Amato, R*

North Carolina
J. Helms, R***
L. Faircloth, R*

North Dakota
K. Conrad, D**
B. L. Dorgan, D*

Ohio
J. H. Glenn, Jr., D*
M. DeWine, R**

Oklahoma
D. Nickles, R*
J. M. Inhofe, R***

Oregon
R. Wyden, D*[1]
G. Smith, R***

Pennsylvania
A. Specter, R*
R. Santorum, R**

Rhode Island
J. H. Chafee, R**
J. Reed, D***

South Carolina
S. Thurmond, R***
E. F. Hollings, D*

South Dakota
T. A. Daschle, D*
T. Johnson, D***

Tennessee
F. Thompson, R***
B. Frist, R**

Texas
P. Gramm, R***
K. B. Hutchison, R**

Utah
O. G. Hatch, R**
R. F. Bennett, R*

Vermont
P. J. Leahy, D*
J. M. Jeffords, R**

Virginia
J. W. Warner, R***
C. S. Robb, D**

Washington
S. Gorton, R**
P. Murray, D*

West Virginia
R. C. Byrd, D**
J. D. Rockefeller IV, D***

Wisconsin
H. Kohl, D**
R. D. Feingold, D*

Wyoming
C. Thomas, R**
M. Enzi, R***

HOUSE MEMBERSHIP

*(As of January 1997, 227 Republicans, 207 Democrats, 1 Independent.) "At-L." in place of congressional district number means "representative at large." *Indicates elected Nov. 5, 1996; all others were reelected in 1996. [1]Appointed to Clinton cabinet.*

Alabama
1. S. Callahan, R
2. T. Everett, R
3. B. Riley, R*
4. R. Aderholt, R*
5. B. Cramer, D
6. S. Bachus, R
7. E. F. Hilliard, D

Alaska
AT-L. D. Young, R

Arizona
1. M. Salmon, R
2. E. Pastor, D
3. B. Stump, R
4. J. Shadegg, R
5. J. Kolbe, R
6. J. D. Hayworth, R

Arkansas
1. M. Berry, D*
2. V. F. Snyder, D*
3. A. Hutchinson, R*
4. J. Dickey, R

California
1. F. Riggs, R
2. W.W. Herger, R
3. V. Fazio, D
4. J. Doolittle, R
5. R. T. Matsui, D
6. L. Woolsey, D
7. G. Miller, D
8. N. Pelosi, D
9. R. V. Dellums, D
10. E. Tauscher, D*
11. R. W. Pombo, R
12. T. Lantos, D
13. F. P. Stark, D
14. A. G. Eshoo, D
15. T. Campbell, R
16. Z. Lofgren, D
17. S. Farr, D
18. G. Condit, D
19. G. Radanovich, R
20. C. Dooley, D
21. B. Thomas, R
22. W. H. Capps, D*
23. E. Gallegly, R
24. B. Sherman, D*
25. H. P. McKeon, R
26. H. L. Berman, D
27. J. E. Rogan, R*
28. D. Dreier, R
29. H. A. Waxman, D
30. X. Becerra, D
31. M. G. Martinez, Jr., D
32. J. C. Dixon, D
33. L. Roybal-Allard, D
34. E. E. Torres, D
35. M. Waters, D
36. J. Harman, D
37. J. Millender-McDonald, D*
38. S. Horn, R
39. E. Royce, R
40. J. Lewis, R
41. J. Kim, R
42. G. E. Brown, Jr., D
43. K. Calvert, R
44. S. Bono, R
45. D. Rohrabacher, R
46. L. Sanchez, D*
47. C. C. Cox, R
48. R. Packard, R
49. B. P. Bilbray, R
50. B. Filner, D
51. R. Cunningham, R
52. D. Hunter, R

Colorado
1. D. DeGette, D*
2. D. Skaggs, D
3. S. McInnis, R
4. R. W. Schaffer, R*
5. J. Hefley, R
6. D. Schaefer, R

Connecticut
1. B. B. Kennelly, D
2. S. Gejdenson, D
3. R. DeLauro, D
4. C. Shays, R
5. J. H. Maloney, D*
6. N. L. Johnson, R

Delaware
At-L . M. N. Castle, R

Florida
1. J. Scarborough, R
2. A. Boyd, Jr., D*
3. C. Brown, D
4. T. Fowler, R
5. K. Thurman, D
6. C. Stearns, R
7. J. L. Mica, R
8. B. McCollum, R
9. M. Bilirakis, R
10. C. W. Young, R
11. J. Davis, D*
12. C. T. Canady, R
13. D. Miller, R
14. P. J. Goss, R
15. D. Weldon, R
16. M. Foley, R
17. C. Meek, D
18. I. Ros-Lehtinen, R
19. R. Wexler, D*
20. P. Deutsch, D
21. L. Diaz-Balart, R
22. E. C. Shaw, Jr., R
23. A. L. Hastings, D

Georgia
1. J. Kingston, R
2. S. Bishop, D
3. M. Collins, R
4. C. McKinney, D
5. J. Lewis, D
6. N. Gingrich, R
7. B. Barr, R
8. S. Chambliss, R
9. N. Deal, R
10. C. Norwood, R
11. J. Linder, R

Hawaii
1. N. Abercrombie, D
2. P. T. Mink, D

Idaho
1. H. Chenoweth, R
2. M. D. Crapo, R

Illinois
1. B. Rush, D
2. J. Jackson, Jr., D
3. W. O. Lipinski, D
4. L. V. Gutierrez, D
5. R. R. Blagojevich, D*
6. H. J. Hyde, R
7. D. K. Davis, D*
8. P. M. Crane, R
9. S. R. Yates, D
10. J. E. Porter, R
11. G. C. Weller, R
12. J. F. Costello, D
13. H. W. Fawell, R
14. J. D. Hastert, R
15. T.W. Ewing, R
16. D. Manzullo, R
17. L. Evans, D
18. R. LaHood, R
19. G. Poshard, D
20. J. M. Shimkus, R*

Indiana
1. P. J. Visclosky, D
2. D. M. McIntosh, R
3. T. Roemer, D
4. M. E. Souder, R
5. S. Buyer, R
6. D. Burton, R
7. E. Pease, R*
8. J. Hostettler, R
9. L. H. Hamilton, D
10. J. Carson, D*

Iowa
1. J. A. Leach, R
2. J. Nussle, R
3. L. L. Boswell, D*
4. G. Ganske, R
5. T. Latham, R

Kansas
1. J. Moran, R*
2. J. Ryun, R*
3. V. Snowbarger, R*
4. T. Tiahrt, R

Kentucky
1. E. Whitfield, R
2. R. Lewis, R
3. A. Northup, R*
4. J. Bunning, R
5. H. Rogers, R
6. S. Baesler, D

Louisiana
1. R. Livingston, R
2. W. J. Jefferson, D
3. W. J. Tauzin, R
4. J. McCrery, R*
5. J. Cooksey, R*
6. R. H. Baker, R
7. C. John, D

Maine
1. T. Allen, D*
2. J. Baldacci, D

Maryland
1. W. T. Gilchrest, R
2. R. L. Ehrlich, Jr., R
3. B. L. Cardin, D
4. A. R. Wynn, D
5. S. H. Hoyer, D
6. R. G. Bartlett, R
7. E. E. Cummings, D
8. C. A. Morella, R

Massachusetts
1. J. Olver, D
2. R. E. Neal, D
3. J. McGovern, D*
4. B. Frank, D
5. M. T. Meehan, D
6. J. F. Tierney, D*
7. E. J. Markey, D
8. J. P. Kennedy II, D
9. J. J. Moakley, D
10. W. D. Delahunt, D*

Michigan
1. B. Stupak, D
2. P. Hoekstra, R
3. V. J. Ehlers, R
4. D. Camp, R
5. J. Barcia, D
6. F. S. Upton, R
7. N. Smith, R
8. D. A. Stabenow, D*
9. D. E. Kildee, D
10. D. E. Bonior, D
11. J. Knollenberg, R
12. S. M. Levin, D
13. L. Rivers, D
14. J. Conyers, Jr., D
15. C. C. Kilpatrick, D*
16. J. D. Dingell, D

Minnesota
1. G. Gutknecht, R
2. D. Minge, D
3. J. Ramstad, R
4. B. F. Vento, D
5. M. O. Sabo, D
6. W. P. Luther, D
7. C. C. Peterson, D
8. J. L. Oberstar, D

Mississippi
1. R. Wicker, R
2. B. Thompson, D
3. C. W. Pickering, Jr., R*
4. M. Parker, R
5. G. Taylor, D

Missouri
1. W. Clay, D
2. J. M. Talent, R
3. R. A. Gephardt, D
4. I. Skelton, D
5. K. McCarthy, D
6. P. Danner, D
7. R. Blunt, R*
8. J. Emerson, R*
9. K. Hulshof, R*

Montana
At-L. R. Hill, R*

Nebraska
1. D. Bereuter, R
2. J. Christensen, R
3. B. Barrett, R

Nevada
1. J. Ensign, R
2. J. Gibbons, R*

New Hampshire
1. J. E. Sununu, R*
2. C. Bass, R

New Jersey
1. R. E. Andrews, D
2. F. LoBiondo, R
3. H. J. Saxton, R
4. C. H. Smith, R
5. M. Roukema, R
6. F. Pallone, Jr., D
7. B. Franks, R
8. W. J. Pascrell, Jr., D*
9. S. R. Rothman, D
10. D. M. Payne, D
11. R. Frelinghuysen, R
12. M. Pappas, R*
13. R. Menendez, D

New Mexico
1. S. Schiff, R
2. J. Skeen, R
3. B. Richardson, D[1]

New York
1. M. P. Forbes, R
2. R. A. Lazio, R
3. P. T. King, R
4. C. McCarthy, D*
5. G. L. Ackerman, D
6. F. H. Flake, D
7. T. J. Manton, D
8. J. Nadler, D
9. C. E. Schumer, D
10. E. Towns, D
11. M. R. Owens, D
12. N. M. Velazquez, D
13. S. Molinari, R
14. C. B. Maloney, D
15. C. B. Rangel, D
16. J. E. Serrano, D
17. E. L. Engel, D
18. N. M. Lowey, D
19. S. Kelly, R
20. B. A. Gilman, R
21. M. R. McNulty, D
22. G. B. H. Solomon, R
23. S. L. Boehlert, R
24. J. M. McHugh, R
25. J. T. Walsh, R
26. M. D. Hinchey, D
27. B. Paxon, R
28. L. M. Slaughter, D
29. J. J. LaFalce, D
30. J. Quinn, R
31. A. Houghton, R

North Carolina
1. E. Clayton, D
2. B. R. Etheridge, D*
3. W. B. Jones, Jr., R
4. D. E. Price, D*
5. R. M. Burr, R
6. H. Coble, R
7. M. McIntyre, D*
8. W. G. Hefner, D
9. S. Myrick, R
10. C. Ballenger, R
11. C. H. Taylor, R
12. M. Watt, D

North Dakota
At-L. E. Pomeroy, D

Ohio
1. S. Chabot, R
2. R. Portman, R
3. T. P. Hall, D
4. M. G. Oxley, R
5. P. E. Gillmor, R
6. T. Strickland, D*
7. D. L. Hobson, R
8. J. A. Boehner, R
9. M. Kaptur, D
10. D. Kucinich, D*
11. L. Stokes, D
12. J. R. Kasich, R
13. S. Brown, D
14. T. C. Sawyer, D
15. D. Pryce, R
16. R. Regula, R
17. J. A. Traficant, Jr., D
18. B. Ney, R
19. S. C. LaTourette, R

Oklahoma
1. S. Largent, R
2. T. Coburn, R
3. W. Watkins, R*
4. J. C. Watts, R
5. E. J. Istook, R
6. F. D. Lucas, R

Oregon
1. E. Furse, D
2. R. F. Smith, R*
3. E. Blumenauer, D
4. P. A. DeFazio, D
5. D. Hooley, D*

Pennsylvania
1. T. M. Foglietta, D
2. C. Fattah, D
3. R. A. Borski, D
4. R. Klink, D
5. J. E. Peterson, R*
6. T. Holden, D
7. C. Weldon, R
8. J. Greenwood, R
9. B. Shuster, R
10. J. M. McDade, R
11. P. E. Kanjorski, D
12. J. P. Murtha, D
13. J. D. Fox, R
14. W. J. Coyne, D
15. P. McHale, D
16. J. R. Pitts, R*
17. G. Gekas, R
18. M. Doyle, D
19. W. F. Goodling, R
20. F. R. Mascara, D
21. P. English, R

Rhode Island
1. P. J. Kennedy, D
2. R. A. Weygand, D*

South Carolina
1. M. Sanford, R
2. F. D. Spence, R
3. L. Graham, R
4. B. Inglis, R
5. J. M. Spratt, Jr., D
6. J. E. Clyburn, D

South Dakota
At-L. J. Thune, R*

Tennessee
1. W. Jenkins, R*
2. J. J. Duncan, Jr., R
3. Z. Wamp, R
4. V. Hilleary, R
5. B. Clement, D
6. B. Gordon, D
7. E. Bryant, R
8. J. S. Tanner, D
9. H. E. Ford, Jr., D*

Texas
1. M. Sandlin, D*
2. J. Turner, D*
3. S. Johnson, R
4. R. M. Hall, D
5. P. Sessions, R*
6. J. Barton, R
7. B. Archer, R
8. K. Brady, R*
9. N. Lampson, D*
10. L. Doggett, D
11. C. Edwards, D
12. K. Granger, R*
13. W. M. Thornberry, R
14. R. Paul, R*
15. R. Hinojosa, D*
16. S. Reyes, D*
17. C. W. Stenholm, D
18. S. Jackson-Lee, D
19. L. Combest, R
20. H. B. Gonzalez, D
21. L. S. Smith, R
22. T. DeLay, R
23. H. Bonilla, R
24. M. Frost, D
25. K. Bentsen, D
26. D. Armey, R
27. S. P. Ortiz, D
28. F. Tejeda, D
29. G. Green, D
30. E. B. Johnson, D

Utah
1. J. V. Hansen, R
2. M. Cook, R*
3. C. Cannon, R*

Vermont
At-L. B. Sanders, I

Virginia
1. H. H. Bateman, R
2. O. B. Pickett, D
3. R. C. Scott, D
4. N. Sisisky, D
5. V. H. Goode, Jr., D*
6. R. W. Goodlatte, R
7. T. J. Bliley, Jr., R
8. J. P. Moran, D
9. R. Boucher, D
10. F. R. Wolf, R
11. T. M. Davis III, R

Washington
1. R. White, R
2. J. Metcalf, R
3. L. Smith, R
4. D. Hastings, R
5. G. Nethercutt, R
6. N. D. Dicks, D
7. J. McDermott, D
8. J. Dunn, R
9. A. Smith, D*

West Virginia
1. A. B. Mollohan, D
2. R. E. Wise, Jr., D
3. N. J. Rahall II, D

Wisconsin
1. M. W. Neumann, R
2. S. Klug, R
3. R. Kind, D*
4. G. D. Kleczka, D
5. T. M. Barrett, D
6. T. E. Petri, R
7. D. R. Obey, D
8. J. Johnson, D*
9. F. J. Sensenbrenner, Jr., R

Wyoming
At-L. B. Cubin, R

AMERICAN SAMOA
Delegate, E. F. H. Faleomavaega, D

DISTRICT OF COLUMBIA
Delegate, Eleanor Holmes Norton, D

GUAM
Delegate, R. Underwood, D

PUERTO RICO
Resident Commissioner Carlos Romero-Bardeló, D

VIRGIN ISLANDS
Delegate, Donna M. Christian-Green, I

Contributors

ADRIAN, CHARLES R., Professor of Political Science, University of California, Riverside; Author, *A History of City Government: The Emergence of the Metropolis 1920–1945*; Coauthor, *State and Local Politics, A History of American City Government: The Formation of Traditions, 1775–1870, Governing Urban America*: ***Los Angeles***

ANDERSON, JACK, Poet and Dance Writer, *The New York Times*; Author, *Choreography Observed, The American Dance Festival*: ***Dance***

ARNOLD, ANTHONY, Author, *Afghanistan: The Soviet Invasion in Perspective, Afghanistan's Two-Party Communism: Parcham and Khalq, The Fateful Pebble: Afghanistan's Role in the Fall of the Soviet Empire*: ***Afghanistan***

ATTNER, PAUL, Senior Writer, *The Sporting News*: ***Sports****—Basketball, The NBA Draft, Football, Olympic Games*

BATRA, PREM P., Professor of Biochemistry, Wright State University: ***Biochemistry***

BEAUCHAMP, LANE, Freelance Writer: ***States, U.S.****—(in part)*

BECK, KAY, Department of Communications, Georgia State University: ***Atlanta: An Olympic City***

BEHLER, DEBORAH A., Executive Editor, *Wildlife Conservation* magazine: ***Zoos and Zoology***

BEST, JOHN, Chief, *Canada World News*, Ottawa: ***Canada****—New Brunswick, Prince Edward Island, Quebec*

BONN, ROBERT L., John Jay College of Criminal Justice, City University of New York: ***Prisons***

BOWER, BRUCE, Behavioral Sciences Editor, *Science News*: ***Anthropology; Archaeology; Medicine and Health****—Mental Health*

BOWERS, FAYE, *The Christian Science Monitor*: ***Transportation****—The Safety Issue*

BRAASCH, BARBARA, Freelance Travel Writer, Palo Alto, CA: ***Travel***

BROCKMAN, AGGIE, Freelance Writer, Yellowknife: ***Canada****—Northwest Territories*

BUGAJSKI, JANUSZ, Director of East European Studies, Center for Strategic and International Studies, Washington, DC; Author, *Ethnic Politics in Eastern Europe: A Guide to Nationality Policies, Organizations and Parties*: ***The Former Yugoslav States; Albania; Bulgaria; Hungary; Romania***

BURKS, ARDATH W., Professor Emeritus, Asian Studies, Rutgers University; Author, *Third Order of the Rising Sun*: ***Biography****—Ryutaro Hashimoto;* ***Japan***

BUSH, GRAHAM W. A., Associate Professor of Political Studies, University of Auckland; Author, *Governing Big Cities, Advance in Order: The Auckland City Council 1971–89*: ***New Zealand***

CHAMETZKY, PETER, Department of Art and Art History, Adelphi University: ***Art***

CHAYES, SARAH, The Christian Science Monitor Radio, Paris: ***France; Obituaries****—François Mitterrand*

COLLINS, BUD, Sports Columnist, *The Boston Globe*; Author, *My Life With The Pros*: ***Sports****—Tennis*

CONRADT, DAVID P., Professor of Political Science, East Carolina University; Author, *The German Polity, West European Politics*: ***Germany***

COOPER, ILENE, Children's Book Editor, *Booklist Magazine*: ***Literature****—Children's*

COOPER, MARY H., Staff Writer, *CQ Researcher*; Author, *The Business of Drugs*: ***Abortion; Energy; Ethnic Groups****—Native Americans Today;* ***Law****—Same-Sex Marriage*

COOPER, MARY LOU, Program and Public Relations Manager for Western Office, Council of State Governments: ***States, U.S.****—(in part)*

COPPEDGE, MICHAEL, Helen Kellogg Institute for International Study, University of Notre Dame: ***Ecuador; Peru; Venezuela***

CRONK, DOUGLAS R., Open Learning Agency; Author, *Canadian Viewpoint: An Anthology of Canadian Writing*; Editor, *Wacousta, Or The Prophesy, A Tale of the Canadas*: ***Canada****—The Arts;* ***Literature****—Canadian*

CUNNIFF, JOHN, Business News Analyst, The Associated Press; Author, *How to Stretch Your Dollar*: ***Business and Corporate Affairs; Business and Corporate Affairs****—The Tobacco Industry;* ***Industrial Production; United States****—The Economy*

CURRIER, CHET, Financial Writer, The Associated Press; Author, *The Investor's Encyclopedia, The 15-Minute Investor*; Coauthor, *No-Cost/Low-Cost Investing*: ***Stocks and Bonds; Stocks and Bonds****—The Dow Jones Index Turns 100*

CURTIS, L. PERRY, Professor of History, Brown University: ***Ireland***

DAVID, LEONARD, Director, Space Data Resources and Information: ***Space Exploration***

DECKER, ANDREW, Contributing Editor, *ARTnews* magazine: ***Art****—The Art Market*

DE GREGORIO, GEORGE, Sports Department, *The New York Times*; Author, *Joe DiMaggio, An Informal Biography*: ***Sports****—Boxing, Swimming, Track and Field*

DELZELL, CHARLES F., Professor of History Emeritus and Adjunct Professor, Vanderbilt University; Author, *Italy in the Twentieth Century, Mediterranean Fascism, Mussolini's Enemies*: ***Italy; Italy****—Romano Prodi*

DENNIS, LARRY, Editor, *Senior Golfer* magazine: ***Biography****—Tiger Woods;* ***Sports****—Golf*

DUFF, ERNEST A., Professor of Politics, Randolph-Macon Woman's College; Author, *Agrarian Reform in Colombia, Violence and Repression in Latin America, Leader and Party in Latin America*: ***Colombia***

DUSHKIN, LELAH, Associate Professor of Sociology, Kansas State University: ***Sri Lanka***

EADINGTON, WILLIAM R., Director, Institute for the Study of Gambling and Commercial Gaming; Professor of Economics, University of Nevada, Reno; Author, *Gambling Behavior and Problem Gambling*: ***Gambling***

ENSTAD, ROBERT, Writer, *Chicago Tribune*: ***Chicago***

FALLESEN, LEIF BECK, Editor in Chief, *Boersen*, Copenhagen: ***Denmark; Finland; Norway; Sweden***

FIERO, ROBERT C., Technical Services Specialist, Grolier Interactive: ***Communication Technology***

FRANCIS, DAVID R., Economy Page Editor, *The Christian Science Monitor*: ***International Trade and Finance***

FREEMAN, ALLAN, Environmental Reporter, *Congressional Quarterly*: ***Environment***

GAILEY, HARRY A., Professor of History, San Jose State University; Author, *History of the Gambia, History of Africa, Road to Aba*: ***Nigeria; Zaire***

GOLDSTEIN, HARRY, *Civil Engineering*: ***Engineering, Civil***

GOODMAN, DONALD, Associate Professor of Sociology, John Jay College of Criminal Justice, City University of New York: ***Prisons***

GORDON, MAYNARD M., Detroit Bureau Chief, *Ward's Dealer Business* magazine; Author, *The Iacocca Management Technique*: ***Automobiles; Automobiles***—*The Centennial of Automobile Mass Production*

GRAYSON, GEORGE W., Class of 1938 Professor of Government, College of William and Mary; Author, *The Politics of Mexican Oil, The United States and Mexico: Patterns of Influence, Oil and Mexican Foreign Policy*: ***Brazil; Mexico; Portugal; Spain Spain***—*José María Aznar*

GROSSMAN, LAWRENCE, Director of Publications, The American Jewish Committee: ***Religion***—*Judaism*

GROTH, ALEXANDER J., Professor Emeritus of Political Science, University of California, Davis; Author, *People's Poland, Contemporary Politics: Europe, Comparative Resource Allocation, Public Policy Across Nations*: ***Poland***

HASSON, JUDI, Congressional Reporter, *USA Today*: ***Washington, DC; Women***

HAYDEN, ROBERT, Associate Professor of Anthropology, University of Pittsburgh: ***Law***—*International*

HELMREICH, JONATHAN E., Professor of History, Allegheny College; Author, *Belgium and Europe: A Study in Small Power Diplomacy, Gathering Rare Ores: The Diplomacy of Uranium Acquisition, 1943–54*; Coauthor, *Rebirth: A History of Europe Since World War II*: ***Belgium; Netherlands***

HELMREICH, PAUL C., Professor of History, Wheaton College; Author, *Wheaton College: The Seminary Years, 1834–1912, From Paris to Sèvres: The Partition of the Ottoman Empire at the Peace Conference of 1919–1920*; Coauthor, *Rebirth: A History of Europe Since World War II*: ***Switzerland***

HOPKO, THE REV. THOMAS, Assistant Professor, St. Vladimir's Orthodox Theological Seminary: ***Religion***—*Orthodox Eastern*

HOYT, CHARLES K., Senior Editor, *Architectural Record*; Author, *More Places for People, Building for Commerce and Industry*: ***Architecture***

HUFFMAN, GEORGE J., Science Systems and Applications: ***Meteorology***

HULBERT, DAN, *Atlanta Journal & Constitution*: ***Television and Radio; Theater; Theater***—*The Finances of Broadway*

HUSTED, THOMAS, Assistant Professor, Department of Economics, The American University: ***Taxation; Taxation***—*The Flat Tax*

JACKSON, PAUL CONRAD, Editor, *The Calgary Sun*; Columnist, *Saskatoon Star-Phoenix*; Author, *Battleground: The Social Assault on Grant Devine's Canadian Dream*: ***Canada***—*Alberta*

JACOBY, BRUCE, Freelance Writer: ***Biography***—*Christiane Amanpour, Bob Costas, Shannon Lucid;* ***Sports***—*Beach Volleyball—A New Olympic Sport;* ***States, U.S.***—*(in part)*

JASUTA, JILL, Managing Editor, *The Catholic Review*: ***Religion***—*Roman Catholicism*

JENNERMANN, DONALD L., Director, University Honors Program, Indiana State University; Author, *Born of a Cretan Spring, Literature for Living*: ***Literature***—*English*

JOHNSON, LONNIE, Austrian Academic Exchange Service; Author, *Introducing Austria*: ***Austria***

KARNES, THOMAS L., Professor of History Emeritus, Arizona State University; Author, *Latin American Policy of the United States, Failure of Union: Central America 1824–1960*: ***Central America***

KENNICOTT, PHILIP, Music Critic, *St. Louis Post-Dispatch*: ***Music***—*Classical*

KESSLER, ANN, American Bankers Association: ***Banking and Finance***

KIM, HAN-KYO, University of Cincinnati; Author, *Korea and the Politics of Imperialism 1876–1910, Studies on Korea: A Scholar's Guide*: ***Korea***

KING, PETER J., Professor of History, Carleton University, Ottawa; Author, *Utilitarian Jurisprudence in America*: ***Canada***—*Ontario*

KINNEAR, MICHAEL, Professor of History, University of Manitoba; Author, *The Fall of Lloyd George, The British Voter*: ***Canada***—*Manitoba*

KIRBY, DAVID, Professor of English, Florida State University: ***Literature***—*American;* ***Literature***—*The Poetry Revival*

LAI, DAVID CHUENYAN, Professor of Geography, University of Victoria, British Columbia; Author, *The Forbidden City Within Victoria: Myth, Symbol and Streetscape of Canada's Earliest Chinatown*: ***Hong Kong: A Time of Dramatic Change***

LAWRENCE, ROBERT M., Professor of Political Science, Colorado State University; Author, *The Strategic Defense Initiative*: ***Military Affairs; Military Affairs***—*Land Mines*

LEEPSON, MARC, Freelance Writer: ***Drugs and Alcohol; Social Welfare***

LEVINE, JOHN R. Freelance Writer, Lecturer, Consultant on Computers; Author, *Internet for Dummies*: ***The World of the Internet; What Is the Internet?; How the World Wide Web Works***

LEVINE, LOUIS, Professor, Department of Biology, City College of New York; Author, *Biology of the Gene, Biology for a Modern Society*: ***Biotechnology; Genetics; Microbiology***

LEWIS, ANNE C., Education Policy Writer: ***Education; Education***—*Charter Schools;* ***Education***—*College Costs: Always Up*

LOBRON, BARBARA, Editor, Photographer, Writer: ***Photography***

LOESCHER, GIL, Professor of International Relations, University of Notre Dame; Author, *Refugees and International Relations, The Global Refugee Crisis: A Reference Handbook, Beyond Charity: International Cooperation and the Global Refugee Crisis*: ***Refugees and Immigration***

MacLEOD, ALEXANDER, British Isles Correspondent, *The Christian Science Monitor*, London: ***Great Britain***

MADDOX, TOM, Writing Coordinator, Evergreen State College: ***The Science Fiction Invasion; The History of Science Fiction***

MANDESE, JOE, Senior Vice-President, Editorial Director, *The Myers Report*: ***Advertising***

MARCOPOULOS, GEORGE J., Professor of History, Tufts University: ***Cyprus; Greece***

MATHESON, JIM, Sportswriter, *Edmonton Journal*: ***Sports***—*Ice Hockey*

MAYERCHAK, PATRICK M., Professor of Political Science, Virginia Military Institute; Author, *Scholar's Guide to Southeast Asia*; Coauthor, *Linkage or Bondage: US-ASEAN Economic Relations*: ***Malaysia; Singapore***

McCORQUODALE, SUSAN, Professor of Political Science, Memorial University of Newfoundland: ***Canada***—*Newfoundland*

McGEE, GLENN, Assistant Professor, University of Pennsylvania School of Medicine; Author, *The Perfect Baby*: ***Medicine and Health***—*Medical Ethics*

MICHIE, ARUNA NAYYAR, Associate Professor of Political Science, Kansas State University: ***Bangladesh; Biography***—*H.D. Deve Gowda;* ***India***

MILLER, RANDALL M., Department of History, St. Joseph's University; Author, *Shades of the Sunbelt: Essays on Ethnicity, Race and the Urban South*: ***Ethnic Groups, U.S.***

MILWARD, JOHN, Freelance Writer and Critic: ***Music***—*Popular and Jazz;* ***Obituaries***—*Ella Fitzgerald*

MITCHELL, GARY, Professor of Physics, North Carolina State University: ***Physics***

MORRIS, BERNADINE, Fashion Journalist; Author, *The Fashion Makers, American Fashion, Valentino, Scaasi*: ***Fashion***

MORTIMER, ROBERT A., Professor, Department of Political Science, Haverford College; Author, *The Third World Coalition in International Politics;* Coauthor, *Politics and Society in Contemporary Africa*: ***Algeria***

MORTON, DESMOND, Director, McGill Institute for the Study of Canada; Author, *Working People: An Illustrated History of the Canadian Labour Movement, A Military History of Canada, Bloody Victory: Canadians and the D-Day Campaign, 1944:* ***Canada***

OBER, JOYCE, Physical Scientist, U.S. Geological Survey, U.S. Department of the Interior: ***Mining***

OCHSENWALD, WILLIAM, Professor of History, Virginia Polytechnic Institute and State University; Author, *The Middle East: A History, The Hijaz Railroad, Religion, Society and the State in Arabia*: ***Saudi Arabia***

O'MEARA, PATRICK Dean of International Programs, Indiana University; Coeditor, *Africa, International Politics in Southern Africa, Southern Africa, The Continuing Crisis*: ***Africa; Africa***—*Democracy in Africa, Turmoil in Burundi and Rwanda;* ***South Africa; Zimbabwe***

PAPER, HEATHER J., Freelance Interior Design Writer: ***Interior Design***

PASCOE, ELAINE, Freelance Writer; Author, *South Africa: Troubled Land, Neighbors at Odds: U.S. Policy in Latin America, Freedom of Expression: The Right to Speak Out in America*: ***Medicine and Health***—*Attention Deficit Disorder;* ***Stamps and Stamp Collecting***

PEARSON, FREDERIC S., Director, Center for Peace and Conflict Studies, Wayne State University, Detroit; Coauthor, *International Relations: The Global Condition, Fuel on the Fire? Effects of Armament During Warfare*: ***United States***—*Foreign Affairs*

PEARSON, RUTH, United Nations Correspondent, *Business Week*: ***United Nations***

PEIRIS, SARATH, Journalist, *The Star Phoenix*: ***Canada***—*Saskatchewan*

PENDICK, DANIEL, Contributing Editor, *Earth Magazine*: ***Geology***

PERETZ, DON, Professor Emeritus of Political Science, State University of New York at Binghamton; Author, *The West Bank—History, Politics, Society and Economy, Government and Politics of Israel, The Middle East Today*: ***Biography***—*Benjamin Netanyahu;* ***Egypt; Israel***

PERKINS, KENNETH J., Professor of History, University of South Carolina: ***Libya; Religion***—*Islam*

PERRY, DAVID K., Associate Professor, Department of Journalism, The University of Alabama: ***Publishing; Publishing***—*A Milestone for "The New York Times"*

PIPPIN, LARRY L., Professor of Political Science, University of the Pacific; Author, *The Remón Era*: ***Argentina; Paraguay; Uruguay***

POLLNER, FRAN, Managing Editor, *The NIH Catalyst*: ***The Ongoing War Against Cancer***

POOLE, PETER A., Author, *The Vietnamese in Thailand, Eight Presidents and Indochina*; Coauthor, *American Diplomacy*: ***Vietnam***

PRESTEGARD, RENÉE, Edmonds Community College Library, Lynwood, WA: ***Libraries***

REBACK, MARILYN A, American Numismatic Association: ***Coins and Coin Collecting***

REED, WILLIAM CYRUS, Director of African Studies, The American University in Cairo, Egypt: ***Kenya; Tanzania; Uganda***

RICHTER, LINDA K., Professor of Political Science, Kansas State University; Author, *Land Reform and Tourism Development, Policy-Making in the Philippines, The Politics of Tourism in Asia*: ***Myanmar; Philippines***

RICHTER, WILLIAM L., Associate Provost for International Programs, Kansas State University: ***Pakistan***

RIGGAN, WILLIAM, Associate Editor, *World Literature Today*, University of Oklahoma; Author, *Pícaros, Madmen, Naïfs, and Clowns, Comparative Literature and Literary Theory*: ***Literature***—*World*

ROBERTS, SAM, *The New York Times*: ***New York City***

ROBINSON, LEIF J., Editor, *Sky & Telescope*; Author, *Outdoor Optics*: ***Astronomy; Astronomy***—*Great Comet Hyakutake*

ROSS, DAVID A., Senior Scientist, Woods Hole Oceanographic Institution; Author, *Introduction to Oceanography:* ***Oceanography***

ROVNER, JULIE, Health-Policy Writer: ***Medicine and Health***—*Health Care*

RUBIN, JIM, Supreme Court Correspondent, The Associated Press: ***Crime; Law***

RUFF, NORMAN J., Assistant Professor, Department of Political Science, University of Victoria, B.C.; Coauthor, *The Reins of Power: Governing British Columbia*: ***Canada***—*British Columbia*

SALEH, HEBA, BBC North Africa Correspondent: ***Morocco; Tunisia***

SAWATSKY, DON, Freelance Writer/Broadcaster; Author, *Ghost Town Trails of the Yukon*: ***Canada***—*Yukon*

SCHLOSSBERG, DAN, Baseball Writer; Author, *The Baseball IQ Challenge, The Baseball Catalog, The Baseball Book of Why, Cooperstown: Baseball's Hall of Fame Players*: ***Biography***—*Eddie Murray;* ***Sports***—*Baseball*

SCHROEDER, RICHARD, Freelance Writer, Specialist on the Caribbean and Latin America: ***Bolivia; Caribbean; Chile; Dominican Republic; Haiti; Latin America***

SCHWAB, PETER, Professor of Political Science, Purchase College, State University of New York; Author, *Ethiopia: Politics, Economics, and Society, Human Rights: Cultural and Ideological Perspectives*: ***Ethiopia; Somalia***

SCHWARZ, CHRISTOPHER, Freelance Journalist: ***States, U.S.***—*(in part)*

SEIDERS, DAVID F., Chief Economist and Senior Staff Vice-President, National Association of Home Builders, Washington, DC: ***Housing***

SENSER, ROBERT A., Freelance Writer: ***Human Rights; Labor***—*The Reemergence of Sweatshops*

SETH, R. P., Professor Emeritus, Department of Economics, Mount Saint Vincent University, Halifax: ***Canada***—*The Economy;* ***Canada***—*Nova Scotia*

SEYBOLD, PAUL G., Professor, Department of Chemistry, Wright State University: ***Chemistry***

SHAPIRO, WILLIAM E., Freelance Writer and Editor, New York City: ***Obituaries***—*Edmund S. Muskie, Ronald H. Brown;* ***The Commonwealth of Independent States; Nations of the World***

SHARLET, ROBERT, Professor of Political Science, Union College; Author, *Soviet Constitutional Crisis*: ***Russia as an Emerging Democracy: Five Years After the Fall of the USSR; Baltic Republics; Russia and the Commonwealth of Independent States***

SHOGAN, ROBERT, National Political Correspondent, Washington Bureau, *The Los Angeles Times*; Author, *A Question of Judgment, Promises to Keep*: ***The 1996 U.S. Elections: A Vote for the Status Quo; The Rise of Political Consultants; Biography***—*Bill Clinton, Robert Dole, Al Gore, Jack Kemp, Trent Lott;* ***United States***—*Domestic Affairs*

SIMON, JEFFREY D., Freelance Writer; Author, *The Terrorist Trap*: ***Terrorism***

SIMON, SHELDON W., Professor of Political Science, Arizona State University–Tempe; Author, *The Future of Asian-Pacific Security Collaboration*: ***Asia***

SNODSMITH, RALPH L., Ornamental Horticulturist; Author, *Ralph Snodsmith's Tips from the Garden Hotline*: ***Gardening and Horticulture***

SPENCE, MIKE, Olympic Reporter, *Colorado Springs Gazette Telegraph*: ***The Olympic Games: 1896–1996***

SPYCHALSKI, JOHN C., Chairman, Department of Business Logistics, College of Business Administration, The Pennsylvania State University: ***Transportation***

STARR, JOHN BRYAN, Managing Director, Annenberg Institute for School Reform, Brown University; Author, *Continuing the Revolution: The Political Thought of Mao*; Editor, *The Future of U.S.-China Relations*: ***China; Taiwan; Taiwan***—*Lee Teng-hui*

STEIN, LANA, Associate Professor of Political Science, University of Missouri-St. Louis; Author, *Holding Bureaucrats Accountable: Politicians and Professionals in St. Louis*: ***Cities and Urban Affairs***

STIEBER, JACK, Professor Emeritus, School of Labor and Industrial Relations, Michigan State University; Author, *U.S. Industrial Relations: The Next Twenty Years, Governing the UAW, Public Employee Unionism*: ***Labor***

STUART, ELAINE, Managing Editor, State Government News: ***States, U.S.***—*(in part)*

SUTTON, STAN, Sportswriter, *The Courier-Journal*, Louisville, KY: ***Sports***—*Auto Racing, Horse Racing*

TESAR, JENNY, Science and Medicine Writer; Author, *Introduction to Animals, Parents as Teachers*: ***Six Major Cancers; Computers; Medicine and Health***—*Overview, "Physical Activity and Health," The Drug-Approval Process;* ***Obituaries***—*Roger Tory Peterson, Carl Sagan*

TURNER, ARTHUR CAMPBELL, Professor of Political Science, University of California, Riverside; Coauthor, *Ideology and Power in the Middle East*: ***Iran; Iraq; Jordan; Lebanon; Middle East; Syria***

TURNER, DARRELL J. Religion Writer, *The Journal Gazette*, Fort Wayne, IN; Former Associate Editor, Religious News Service, New York, NY: ***Religion***—*Overview, Far Eastern, Protestantism*

VAN ZANDT, CHRISTINE, U.S. Government Analyst on East Asian Affairs, Washington, DC: ***Cambodia; Laos***

VAUGHAN, KRISTI, Freelance Writer: ***Biography***—*Hilary Rodham Clinton, Elizabeth Dole, Tommy Hilfiger;* ***Family; Literature***—*Overview;* ***Television and Radio***—*Rosie O'Donnell*

VOLL, JOHN O., Professor of History, University of New Hampshire; Author, *Islam: Continuity and Change in the Modern World*; Coauthor, *Sudan: Unity and Diversity in a Multicultural Society*; Editor, *Sudan: State and Society in Crisis*: ***Sudan***

VOLSKY, GEORGE, Center for Advanced International Studies, University of Miami: ***Cuba***

WEATHERBEE, DONALD E., Department of Government, University of South Carolina: ***Indonesia; Thailand***

WEIKER, WALTER F., Professor of Political Science, Rutgers University: ***Turkey***

WEINBERG, MATTHEW, University of Pennsylvania: ***Medicine and Health***—*Medical Ethics*

WILLIS, F. ROY, Professor of History, University of California, Davis; Author, *France, Germany and the New Europe, 1945–1968, Italy Chooses Europe, The French Paradox*: ***Europe***

WINCHESTER, N. BRIAN, Office of International Programs and Former Director, African Studies Program, Indiana University: ***Africa; Africa***—*Democracy in Africa, Turmoil in Burundi and Rwanda;* ***South Africa***

WISNER, ROBERT N., Professor, Iowa State University; Coeditor, *Marketing for Farmers;* Author, *World Food Trade and U.S. Agriculture*: ***Agriculture; Food; Food***—*Fat-Free Foods, Meat Inspection*

WOLCHIK, SHARON LEE, Director of the Russian and East European Studies Program and Professor of Political Science, George Washington University; Author, *The Social Legacy of Communism, Czechoslovakia in Transition: Politics, Economics and Society*: ***Czech Republic; Slovakia***

WOLF, WILLIAM, New York University; Author, *The Marx Brothers, Landmark Films, The Cinema and Our Century*: ***Motion Pictures; Obituaries***—*Gene Kelly, George Burns*

YATES, ANNA, Freelance Writer and Translator; Author, *Leifur Eiriksson and Vinland the Good*: ***Iceland***

YOUNGER, R. M., Journalist and Author; Author, *Australia and the Australians, Australia! Australia! A Bicentennial Record*: ***Australia Biography***—*John Howard*

ZELENAK, MEL J., Department of Family/Consumer Economics,University of Missouri-Columbia: ***Consumer Affairs; Retailing***

Acknowledgments

We also wish to thank the following for their services: color separations and electronic file output, Gamma One, Inc.; text stock printed on Champion's 60# Courtland Matte; dust jacket and covers printed by Mid-City Lithographers; cover materials provided by Ecological Fibers, Inc.; and printing and binding by R.R. Donnelley & Sons, Co.

Index

Main article headings appear in this index as bold-faced capitals; subjects within articles appear as lower-case entries. Bold-faced page numbers indicate the location of the article about the subject. Both the general references and the subentries should be consulted for maximum usefulness of this index. Illustrations are indexed herein. Cross references are to the entries in this index.

A

I

J

N

O

P

Q

R

T

U